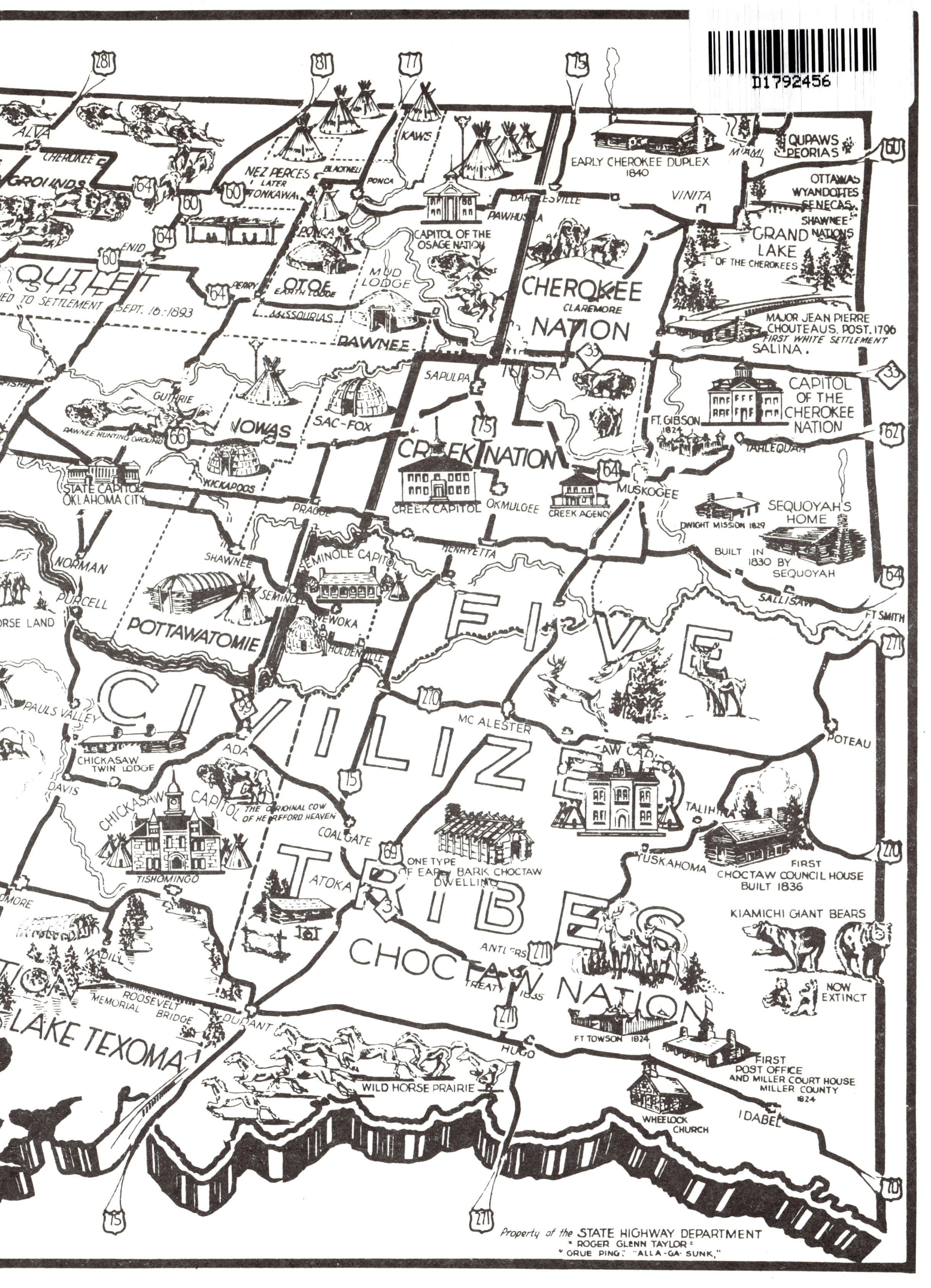

History of NOBLE COUNTY Oklahoma

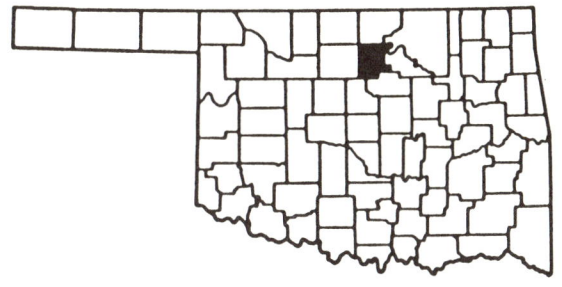

compiled and edited by

The Noble County Genealogy Society

Type Traditional
457 W. Gray
Norman, OK 73069

Type Traditional
457 W. Gray
Norman, OK 73069

Additional copies of "History of Noble County, Oklahoma" may be purchased for $59.00 plus postage and handling of $4.50 (Oklahoma residents please add $3.54 sales tax) from The Noble County Genealogical Society, 601 12th Street, Perry, OK 73077 or Type Traditional, 457 W. Gray, Norman, OK 73069.

First Edition, May, 1987

Copyright © 1987　　　　　　　　　　Noble County Genealogy Society

All rights reserved, including rights of reproduction and use in any form or by any means, including the making of copies by any photo process, or by any electronic or mechanical device, printed or written or oral, or recording for sound or visual reproduction or for use in any knowledge or retrieval system or device, unless permission in writing is obtained from the copyright proprietor. The materials were compiled and produced using available information. The Noble County Genealogy Society and the Publisher regrets they cannot assume liability for errors or omissions.

Printed in the United States of America
by McNaughton & Gunn, Inc.
Saline, Michigan 48176

ISBN 0-941195-01-5

CONTENTS

Chapter 1
INDIAN TERRITORY 1
Early History of Noble County, Cattle Trails Across Oklahoma, Indians in Noble County, Ponca Indians, Otoe-Missouria Indians, A.T. & S.F. Railroad, Indian Allotments in Noble County, Lawmen and Outlaws.

Chapter 2
OPENING THE CHEROKEE STRIP 17
Boomers and Sooners, Opening of the Outlet, Registration Booths, The "Run" of September 16, 1893, Birth of Perry, Congressional Investigation.

Chapter 3
COUNTY ACTIVITIES 26
Sports, Politics, 101 Ranch, Early Oil Fields, County Agents, Homemaker's Groups, Garden Clubs, Rural Life.

Chapter 4
TOWNSHIPS OF NOBLE COUNTY 42
Auburn, Autry, Black Bear, Buffalo, Bunch Creek, Carson, East Bressie, Glenrose, Lowe, Missouri, Noble, Oakdale, Otoe, Red Rock, Rock, Santa Fe, Walnut, Warren Valley, Watkins, West Bressie, White Rock.

Chapter 5
COMMUNITIES PAST AND PRESENT 87
Perry, Perry Churches, Stagecoach Theatre, Perry Lion Club, Ladies Tuesday Afternoon Club, Perry Brush and Pallette Club, Poor Boys Club, Cherokee Strip Museum and Henry S. Johnston Library, Billings, Billings Churches, Morrison, Morrison Churches, Marland, Sumner, Lucien, Ford, Lela.

Chapter 6
BUSINESSES 113
The Charles Machine Works, Inc., Citizen State Bank, Exchange Bank, Sooner Power Plant.

Chapter 7
FAMILIES 119

Appendix A
HOMESTEADERS 414

INDEX 421

Dedication

The Noble County History Book Committee consisted of Mildred Highfill, Dorothy and Charles Durkee, Alta Marie Frick, Glenda Grange, Joe Highfill, Darlene Rhodes, and Jewel Humphries. Their family histories can be found in this book. Each one of the above contributed their time, talent and miles on their personal cars in putting this book together. The committee would like to thank the staff of the Perry Daily Journal for help and support during the time of the preparation for publication. Without the publicity this work could hardly have been accomplished. Also, thanks go to the people who spent time and effort in researching and writing their family histories and to all the people who voiced encouragement and faith in the worth of preserving our history.

From the following sources material was extracted for the general history section:

    Perry Daily Journal
    Billings News
    Morrison Transcript
    History of Noble County — Ernie Jones (1923)
    Oklahoma State & People — Thorburn and Wright (1927)
    101 Ranch — Collings and English
    The Oto — William Whitman
    The Otoes and Missourias — B. B. Chapman
    The Black Dog Trail — Tillie K. Newman
    Oklahoma History Textbooks — Dale
    Atlas of Noble County, Oklahoma (1912)
    U.S. Congressional Record — 1893
    Town and Place Locations Oklahoma Department of Highways (1975)
    Oklahombres — Nix
    West of Hell's Fringe — Glen Shirley
    Autobiography of Charles Colcord
    Morrison, Oklahoma — Gladys Swearingen
    Songs of Oklahoma — Daisy Lemon Coldiron (1935)

    Photographs were received from the Montana Historical Society and Oklahoma Historical Society and the Cherokee Strip Museum, Perry.

Every effort was made to eliminate errors in the text. However, we realize it is impossible to create a perfect anything in this world. If you find errors we hope you will notify one of the committee so, in case, there is ever a Volume II we can make a correction.

In the process of preparing this book we had to change publishers. If, by chance, any stories got lost in the process these too can be included in the next book when enough interest is generated to publish another volume.

Chapter 1
INDIAN TERRITORY

Early History of Noble County

Noble County is located in the north-central part of Oklahoma, with Kay County on the north; Garfield County on the west; Logan and Payne Counties on the south; Pawnee County on the east. The first census (1900) gave the population as 14,015; the 1980 census gave the population as 11,298. Rock and Walnut Townships were a part of Payne County in the 1900 census. Perry is the largest city and the county seat. The land is drained by Red Rock and Black Bear Creeks which have flooded since the history began. Wild horses once ranged on Black Bear Creek.

Fossils found in Noble County indicate that it was at one time a part of an inland marshy sea, but for thousands of years, before the white man came, it had been an almost treeless plain with lush grass. Plains Indians used the region as a hunting ground yet no evidence has been found to show any permanent Indian settlement existed here.

Probably the first white people in Noble County were the French. Evidence of a French town or trading post named Camp Ferdinandina, believed established about 1700, has been found north of Noble County on the Arkansas River. Early maps of western North America, made by cartographers in England and Scotland gave Ferdinandina near the mouth of a small stream on the west side of the Arkansas River a few miles south of the present north boundary of Oklahoma. The name is found on British maps as late as 1870-72. Historical researchers had searched for years for the site but it was not found until around 1920, when Joseph B. Thoburn of the Oklahoma Historical Society visited the site, twenty miles north of Ponca City and determined the ruins found there to be Ferdinandina. At that time, there was still convincing evidence that the French fur traders who estalished Ferdinandina had an immense stockade, built of high upright posts and with ample earthworks thrown up as a protection from the various Indian tribes. The trench, excavated in throwing up the earthworks, shows the stockade to have been fully 250 feet in diameter. This trench was still intact, marking the outline of the post.

According to Mr. Thoburn, the trading post, where deals were made with the red men, was located within the stockade. The stockade also housed the fur traders and the soldiers. In the 1920s, the location of a large Indian village could be seen, surrounding the old stockade. There was evidence of sixty houses: 40 Wichita houses and 20 Pawnee houses. The Wichitas built their earthen houses on the surface and when they caved in, the mounds remained; the Pawnees excavated before throwing up their earthen dwellings and when these caved in, the depressions were left. Not far from this Indian village is the old shop site of the Indians where they wintered and manufactured the various crude tools that they used, made chiefly from flint. This site had been selected by the Indians because of a rock bluff, forty feet in height that runs parallel with the river for almost three quarters of a mile. It shields the site from the winter winds. It was quite evident to Mr. Thoburn that after establishing Ferdinandina post, the French made a deal with the Pawnee and Wichita Indians to kill buffalo, the squaws preparing the hides. Legend has it, that the French traders with the aid of the Indians, rounded up the buffalo herds until they would get near the edge of this rock cliff; then by frightening the animals, causing a stampede, many of the buffalo would be pushed over the cliff by those in the rear of the herd. These would be killed by the fall or would be so badly wounded that they could be finished easily by the Indians. It was then the squaws' work began — skinning the buffalo, the hides of which, tanned into robes, were desired so greatly by the French.

These Frenchmen, transporting merchandise up and down the Arkansas River on barges and canoes would touch the northeastern boundary of Noble County. It is entirely believable that these men would have explored what is now Noble County in search of the buffalo herds, but no papers or diaries of any of these men have been uncovered to date, as far as is known.

Ferdinandina was located in the western half of the Mississippi Valley that was called Louisiana. It was claimed first by Spain, and then by France. France returned it to Spain in 1763 to repay that country for aid given to the French in the Seven Years War. Spain ruled it for nearly forty years but there is no evidence that Spain continued the fort at Ferdinandina. In 1800, Louisiana was returned to France but the fort was not re-established. In 1803, President Thomas Jefferson bought Louisiana from Napoleon, the ruler of France.

One of the first things President Jefferson wished to do was to send out explorers to visit the remote parts of this vast new possession and to report what they found. The men chose to head the first party were Captain Meriwether Lewis and William Clark, who crossed the northern part. The party sent to explore the southern portion was led by a young soldier, Captain Zebulon Montgomery Pike. He took with him as his second-in-command, Lt. James B. Wilkinson. Pike for whom Pike's Peak was named, and Wilkinson set out in July 1806. They followed first the Missouri River and then the Osage. They left their boats and pushed on west across the plains of Kansas. Near the most nothern point of the great bend of the Arkansas River, Wilkinson became ill; hence it was decided that he should take five men and return home while Pike continued on to the mountains. On October 28, 1806, Wilkinson and his men made two boats, one of buffalo skins stretched over a framework of poles, the other made by hollowing out a large log. The water was so shallow, however, that at the end of the first day, they left the boats and proceeded on foot. A winter storm raged, delaying further progress for two days. Pressed by cold and hunger, the expedition went forward for a week, arriving in a region of game where there were "herd of buffalo, elk, goat (antelope) and deer." Lt. Wilkinson asserting that "if I saw one, I saw more than 9,000 buffaloes during the day's march." Within a few days, timber was found along the river, large enough for "splitting out" new canoes. After delaying for ten days to construct the craft, the men again set out on their voyage down the river, only to meet with the distressing accident of upsetting one of the boats and losing nearly all of their provisions and ammunition.

During the last week in November, 1806, they drifted down the Arkansas

Ferdinandina: First White Settlement

(Sketch by L. P. Thompson, 1956, in The Daily Oklahoman)

An artist's conception of how Ferdinandina looked in the early 1700's, with the stockade trading post in the midst of the Indian village.

River, amidst large sheets of ice, through what is now the northern part of Oklahoma. Though ill much of the time, Wilkinson kept careful notes of each day's journey. White traders and trappers had of course, been in what is now Noble County before the time of Wilkinson, but he was the first American official to visit this region and to write a report of what he saw.

The Osage Indians claimed this part of Oklahoma and relinquished their title to the land north of the South Canadian River in 1825. There was once an Indian trail, called Black Dog Trail for Osage Chief Black Dog I, that crossed what is now northern Oklahoma and southern Kansas. Black Dog was seven foot tall in his deer-skin moccasins and weighed three hundred pounds. Due to a childhood injury he was blind in his left eye. The Osages lived near where Baxter Springs, Kansas is now located, but they made many trips to the western part of what is now Kansas and Oklahoma in pursuit of the buffalo and to gather salt from the salt plains. One spring in the early 1800s, Chief Black Dog decided to make a trail using the labor of the squaws, old men and the young ones too young to hunt. It was a wide trail, wide enough for thirty horsemen to ride abreast if need be. One branch of this trail came down Salt Fork River and a branch of this trail went down the north bank of the Red Rock Creek which was called "Pawnee-no-washie-cow-how-shing-gah" which in English would mean Poor Pawnee Creek. The Osages once found a lost Pawnee on this creek who was almost starved to death when they found him. They killed and scalped him.

From the time of the Louisiana Purchase, lands that are now Oklahoma

BLACK DOG, OSAGE, 1834
(From Painting by Catlin)

were considered as a home for the tribes of Indians living in the southeastern United States. These tribes, the Cherokees, Choctaws, Chickasaws, Creeks and Seminoles, were called the Five Civilized Tribes. In 1818, a treaty with the Cherokee Indian tribe gave them, along with land for their nation in what is now northeastern Oklahoma, an outlet to the plains to hunt buffalo, "for as long as grass grows and water runs." The land was known as the Cherokee Outlet. To reach this land the Cherokees came over the Trail of Tears in 1838.

John C. McCoy, son of Rev. Isaac McCoy, noted Baptist missionary, surveyed the boundaries of the outlet in 1837. This strip of land was about fifty-seven miles wide and extended from the Cherokee home land to the hundredth meridian, which was then the western boundary of the United States. This did not include the Panhandle of Oklahoma which became known as Cimmarron Territory and "No Man's Land."

In the summer of 1843, Captain Nathan Boone, youngest son of Daniel Boone, made an expedition northwest from Fort Gibson into what is now central Kansas. This expedition, consisting of a troop of 1st United States Dragoons, crossed what is now Tulsa, Osage, Pawnee, Noble, Kay and Grant counties.

The Cherokees did not depend on the buffalo but farmed and ranched, so the Cherokee Outlet lay idle until after the Civil War.

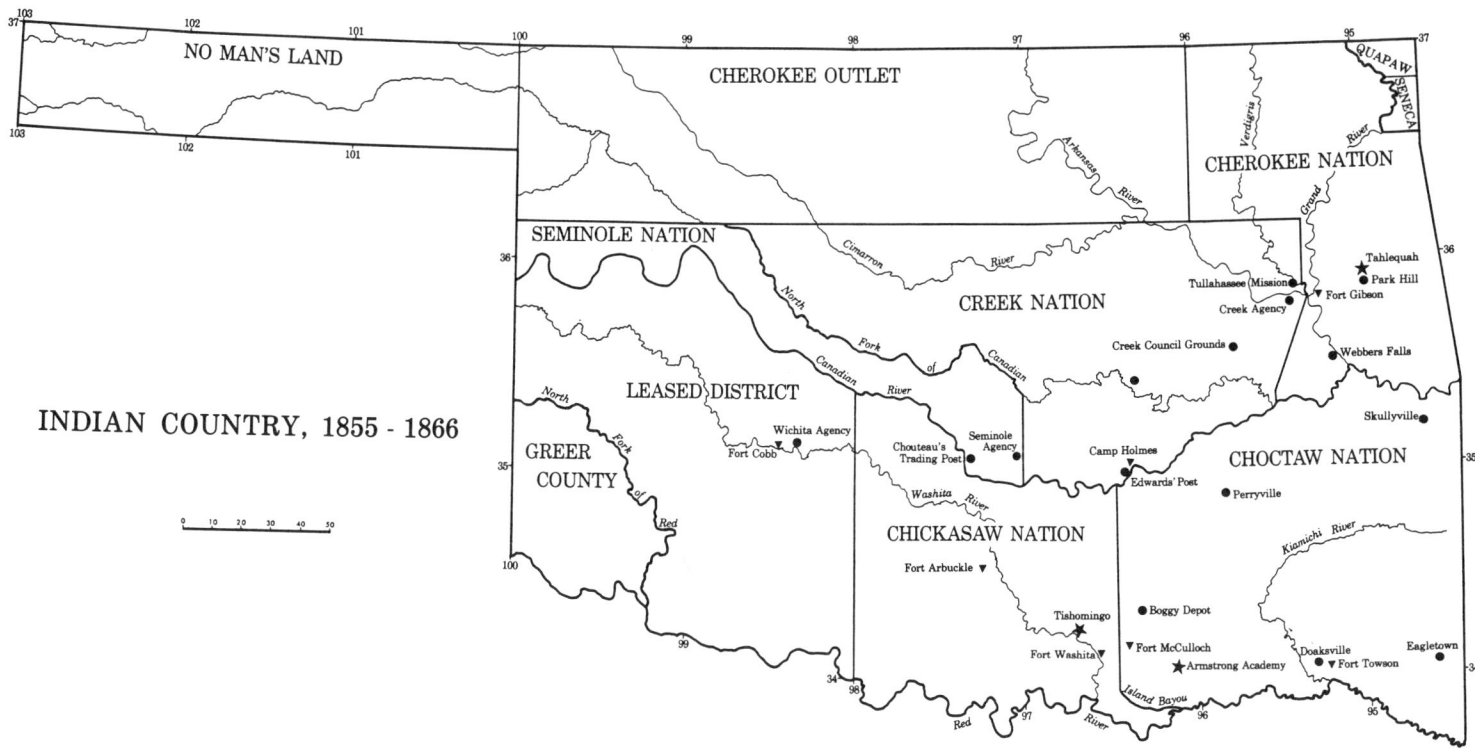

No battle of the Civil War was fought in Noble County but the war's effect was felt here. Slaves were owned in all the Five Civilized Tribes, however the tribal members were divided among themselves over the slavery question. At the beginning of the war, all of the troops of the United States had been withdrawn from the forts in Indian Territory, consequently the Indians were left without any soldiers to protect them. The new government of the Confederacy was eager to win the friendship and help of these five little nations in the west. The Confederacy felt that the Indian nations could protect Texas from a Union attack by way of Kansas and might also furnish many soldiers for service with the South. After many conferences, the tribes one by one joined the South. The Cherokees were the last to join and many in the tribe were not in favor of this. About ten thousand five hundred of the seventeen thousand Cherokees remained loyal to the Union. Of that number two thousand two hundred volunteered as soldiers in the Federal army and made a creditable record for themselves in defense of the nation's flag.

Nevertheless, the United States government made new treaties with the Indians because they had taken up arms against the United States. The new treaty of 1866, provided for purchase of that land in the western part of Oklahoma not being occupied by the Five Civilized Tribes, by friendly tribes and by railroads for right-of-ways across Indian lands. This included the Cherokee Outlet.

The government surveyed the Outlet in 1866. The north and south line from which this survey was made, known as the Indian Meridian, is not a true meridian but is two townships west of the 97th meridian. All of Oklahoma, except the panhandle is measured from this line. At this time, it was found there was a mistake in McCoy's survey and a strip of land, about two and a half miles wide was actually in Kansas. This land was ceded by the Cherokee council to the United States for $1.25 per acre and became a part of the state of Kansas. That strip of land, two and one half miles wide by two hundred miles long was the real Cherokee Strip although the entire Outlet is often so called.

Cattle Trails Across Oklahoma

Within fifteen years after the war between the States, the eager desire to engage in ranching had become almost a craze. United States senators, judges, bankers and many other leading men invested in cattle raising. Literally thousands of men from the East came to the western prairies to start new ranches or to work as cowboys. Young men of wealth who had just finished college, of whom Theodore Roosevelt is an outstanding example, came west to give their personal attention to the business. The news of great profits to be made in cattle raising spread to Europe. Much British money was invested in the business and many came to America to engage in ranching. By 1880, most of the Great Plains area was covered with cattle. Texas remained the chief breeding ground. Nearly all of these cattle were driven across Indian Territory on the way to the ranges in the northern plains.

Traces of the Yellow Bull Trail, a branch of the West Shawnee Trail, can still be seen in northern Noble County.

Ranching on the Indian lands was of course, contrary to law. Yet as the drovers (cattle drivers) moved their herds slowly northward they had to pasture the animals on the grass along the trail. After a number of herds had passed, the grass along the trail was cropped so close that later drovers would sometimes turn aside and drive their cattle several miles off the trail in order to find better pasturage. These men would often linger for several days or even weeks to rest and fatten their animals before proceeding farther north. When the Indian agent visited them to urge that they move on, they would promise to do so, but after he was gone they would still remain and

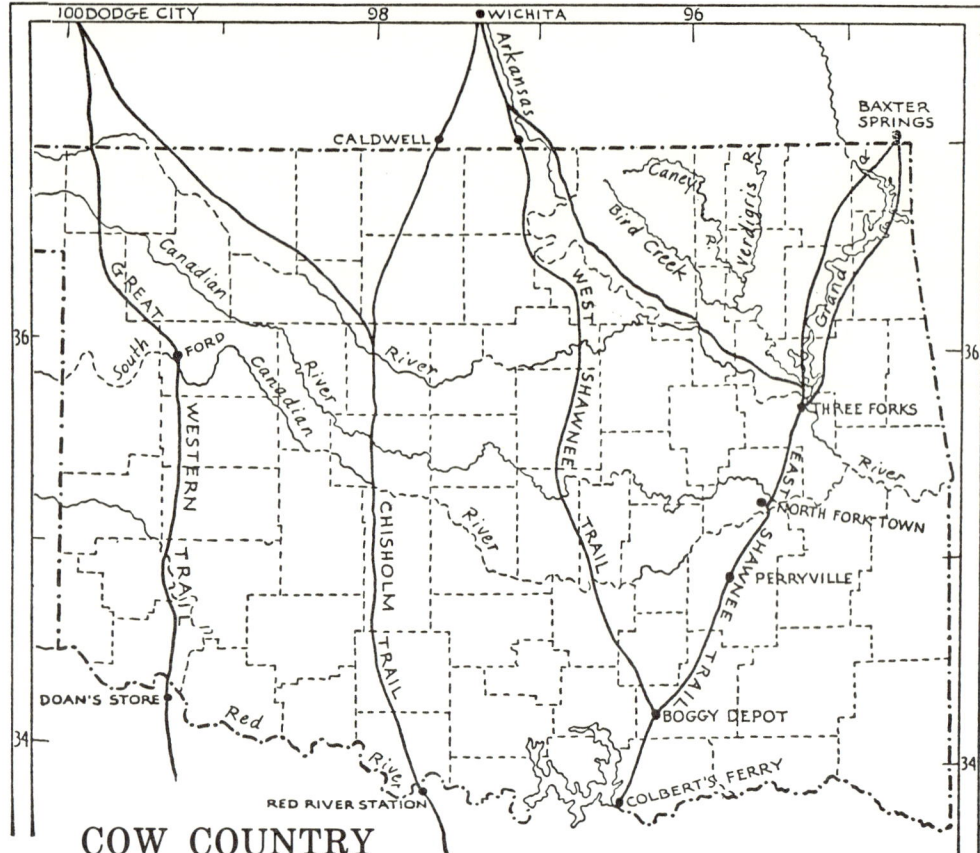

COW COUNTRY

repeated warnings were required to induce them to continue their drive. Also, as good range became scarce elsewhere, many of these men began to wish that they might be permitted to establish ranches on these rich pasture lands and keep cattle there permanently.

As the buffaloes began to vanish before the guns of the white hunters, the Indians were often hungry and asked their agent for food. Since the food they wanted was largely meat, the United States government began to make contracts with cattlemen to supply the Indians with beef. These men were called "beef-contractors" and were the only white men who had legal right to graze cattle on Indian land.

Ranchmen of southern Kansas began to pasture their herds on the Cherokee Outlet. Some animals merely strayed across the line but herds were driven in by their owners and held there for weeks or months. This region was so far from the Cherokee country proper that the Indians knew little of the use that was being made of the property by ranchmen.

In 1879, officials of the Cherokee government decided to collect a grazing tax from the men who pastured cattle on the Outlet lands. The first years they realized very little but in 1880, a sizable sum was collected, in 1881, over twenty thousand dollars and in 1882, forty thousand. The charge was forty cents a year for grown cattle and twenty-five cents for cattle less than two years old. Each ranchman, who paid the tax, was given a grazier's license. This tax money was turned over to the treasurer of the Cherokee Nation and used for schools and expenses of the government.

The Cherokees soon found that they could not secure payment for all the cattle grazing on Outlet lands. Some men whose cattle had been there for months claimed that they had only strayed across the line. Others said that they were on the trail going north and had stopped only a few days, although they often lingered all summer. Ranchmen living along the border would sometimes drive cattle into the Cherokee Outlet to avoid payment of property taxes on them in Kansas and then drive them back to Kansas to escape paying a grazing tax in the Outlet. All this made it hard for the honest ranchmen who were willing to pay for grazing. Accordingly, early in 1883, these ranchmen met at Caldwell, Kansas and formed the Cherokee Strip Live Stock Association (C.S.L.S.A.). It was chartered under the laws of Kansas for the purpose of growing, breeding and improved livestock, but its real purpose was to attempt to secure from the Cherokee Government a lease of the entire Outlet.

They did finally secure a lease of the Outlet for five years beginning October 1, 1883. For the grazing privileges, the Cherokees were to receive one hundred thousand dollars a year. This great association, through this lease and another one made when the first expired, controlled the Outlet for 10 years. The lands were fenced, but wide strips were left open along the trails for the use of herds moving north. Each member paid about two cents an acre for his range.

The cowboys who rode the range in the Outlet before it was opened to white settlement met years later and formed the Cherokee Strip Cow Punchers Association (C.S.C.P.A.). They held their annual meeting on Cowboy Hill, a 10 acre plot of land set aside for this purpose by the 101 Ranch. Cowboy Hill is located on Highway 156 just over the line from Marland in Kay County.

The following poem, composed by Cowboy John Livingston, was read at one of the reunions:

An Undying Preference

I would rather be a cowboy
  As we lived it years ago,
Than any other thing on earth
  Of which I've heard or know;
That frontier mode of living,
  Was so differed from the rest.
That in every cowboy's memory,
  It's indelibly impressed.

We had real independence
  In so many different ways
Was why we loved the prairie,
  In those early cowboy days.
We'd escaped the late depression
  And prosperity enjoyed.
Had they left the west a prairie
  With us cowboys all employed.

Destroy one's occupation,
  Which in life he had imbibed,
And that fellow's dire condition
  Is not easily described;
And the hearts of all old cowboys
  With joy would fairly throb
Had he the opportunity
  Of getting back his job.

When farmers took our prairies
  Our jobs diversified,
And many old time cowboys
  Have bowed their heads and cried;
But true to what he worshipped,
  The "range" he still salutes
And when he can afford it
  He is wearing cowboy boots.

We had some keen society,
  Old timers will recall.
You had to know your onions,
  Or you got no job at all;
For we'd men like Oscar Brewster
  As our headquarters cooks
And riders such as Billy Fox
  The Eastons and Van Hooks.

It's true some acted ugly
  Which fact is not so strange
When you think how wild and wooly
  One got while on the plains.
And when we'd ship those dogies
  Imagine, if you can.
How we could keep from yelling
  Like a thoroughbred Cheyenne!

Some cowboys went in business
  And are doing well today
While others have to hustle
  To find a place to stay.

Ranch house outside of Perry.

A few broke in the movies
   But many on the tramp
Are longing for the comfort
   They had in cowboy camp.

When farmers took our prairies
   You've noticed what occurs.
Where once grew choicest pasture
   Grows weeds and cockleburs.
And where a Texas rancher
   Raised a thousand sheep or goats
When farmed, won't pay the taxes
   And the interest mortgage notes.

In painting cowboy paradise
   The facts I state explains
Why we loved to be a cowboy
   And live upon the plains.
No females there to dictate
   Suggesting "this" or "that"
And every cowboy was at home
   When he took off his hat.

And when we hold reunion
   In September, Labor Day,
We are always glad to get there
   And we hate to come away.

For we notice thinning numbers
   Bind us closer year by year
But there's one that's no far distant
   When there'll only be two here!

And when they go we forfeit
   Our deed to Cowboy Hill
When editors with eulogies
   Will columns try to fill;
You could write our cowboy history
   In these few words and say:
"No better fellows ever lived
   Than the C.S.C.P.A."

Through the ages, as the currents
   Of the dear Old Salt Fork will,
Continue washing gutters
   In the side of Cowboy Hill
If their ripples were a language
   And translated, it would say:
"Old cowboys held reunions here
   Till the last two passed away."

Imagine, we had standing
   On Cowboy Hill today
The last surviving member
   Of the C.S.C.P.A.
Oh, what a glorious picture
   If all cowboys that he knew
Could come and gather round him
   And take a one last view!

Is it really any wonder
   We've a preference like this?
If you never were a cowboy
   You don't know what you miss,
This country may be Eden, yet
   And to me it will be, when
They seed it down to blue-stem grass
   And make it "range" again.

Indians in Noble County

Six tribes of Plains Indians purchased land in the Cherokee Strip — the Osage, Kaws, Pawnees, Nez Perce, Poncas and the Otoe-Missourias. The Nez Perce under Chief Joseph were unhappy here and escaped back to their home in the Rocky Mountains. Eventually, they were allowed to stay there. The Tonkawa tribe was then assigned the land where the Nez Perce had been. Two of these tribes, the Poncas and the Otoe-Missourias, had land in what is now Noble County.

The Poncas and Otoe-Missouria Indians share many traits in common with the tribes of the Plains and central woodlands, while maintaining a culture that is peculiarly their own. They lived in village groups which were divided into clans. These clans were divided into sub-clans and then into families. The clans were conceived to be a blood-grouping. Each clan had its own hereditary chief and warrior class and its priests who were in charge of clan rituals, each clan had its commoners and its poor. Cutting across this clan grouping were the secret societies, benevolent societies and dance societies, which were essentially controlled by families.

Among many of the Plains Indians, seven is a sacred number and the number of clans reflect this. If you ask an Otoe or Ponca, they will tell you there are seven clans, seven chiefs and seven pipes. There seems to be more than seven clans especially among the Otoe-Missouria which may have been caused by each tribe keeping the clans of their tribes when they confederated.

Theoretically, there was an hereditary chief over the whole tribe and it was said he came from the leading sub-clan of the Bear clan, again theoretically each clan, except Elk clan, had its hereditary chief. It is assumed that several such hereditary chiefs would be resident in any village, and that they represented the supreme authority. William Whitman in **The Oto**, published in 1926, says, "The last hereditary chief died beyond the memory of any living Otoe and the installation of chiefs named by the whites has blurred the old pattern."

The Poncas still clung to the old custom of naming persons in connection with some peculiar incident of their lives. Thus on the reservation were Mary Buffalo Head, Horse Chief Eagle, Mary Iron Thunder, Alford No Ear, Weak Bone, Sits-On-Hill, White Deer, Eugene Big Goose, Mean Bear, Wolf Robe, Short Tail, Hiding Woman, Red Elk, Girl Bear Head, Big Turkey, Long Pumpkin, White Buffalo, Running After Arrow, Willie Cries for War, Little Dance, White Eagle, Peter Knows the Country, Little-Man Stand Up and Thomas on-Two-Lean-Bear's-Ear.

No Indian wore a beard, for as soon as a hirsute growth appeared, he pulled out the hairs with tweezers. Some of the older men deprived themselves of their eyebrows in this way. They wore two long braids of hair which decended from the crown and were plaited with bright

THE MOST KNOWN INDIAN IN AMERICA. YOU LOVED, HANDLED, PATTED AND HUGGED HIM. **CHIEF IRON TAIL THE INDIAN ON THE NICKLE** FOR OVER 30 YEARS WAS ON THE PAWNEE BILL AND BUFFALO BILL'S COMBINED WILD WEST SHOWS, 1900 TO 1910 1910 TO 1921 ON MILLER BRO'S 101 RANCH REAL WILD WEST SHOWS. IN 1912 HE WAS CHOSEN FOR HIS PROFILE, FIRST APPEARING ON THE 1913 NICKLE WITH THE BUFFALO "CHALLENGE" HE WAS WITH WILL ROGERS, TOM MIX, BUCK JONES, HARRY CAREY ON THE RANCH SHOW *WILL ROGERS SAID HE WAS THE FINEST LOOKING SPECIMAN OF AN INDIAN IN THE WORLD*

ribbons. The hair was pulled out until the braids were the size of a finger and resembled a rawhide lariat.

The dance was the dominant feature of the Plains Indian's life. He was born, baptized, married and died with the dance and tom-toms marking the events. The dance expressed joy, and it was the symbol of grief and bereavement. It was the expression of great exploits and the commitment of routine duties as well as deep religious rituals.

The Indian's wail in honor of the death or burial of one they loved was incomparable with anything of the kind in white man's civilization. The wailing song with its wistful, appealing intonations climbed to heights of tremendous emotion. No shrill notes were heard in the wailing song. The songs had their sources deep in the throats of the mourners. The thread of the wail was kept intact with the pulsating throb of the tom-toms.

They retained their old time customs and ceremonies. The men remained strangers to work and refused to be introduced. They insisted upon the wife performing all labor — whether there was one wife or three. The squaws carried the baggage, built the fires, erected the tipis, saddled the horses and were experts at making beadwork. The beadwork made by an Otoe squaw was especially prized among other tribes. The men made drums, bow and arrows, they would sit for hours carving out some seemingly weird design without looking up or saying a word.

The tribes brought to western Oklahoma were placed under the control of officers of the United States called Indian Agents. These agents were mainly retired military men who had been given these appointments for their work in the service, usually with no knowledge of Indian culture. Each officer had charge of an agency. The Ponca Agency had four reservations: Ponca, Otoe-Missouria, Pawnee and Tonkawa. The agent, as an official of the government of the United States, looked after the

Otoe squaw making bread on Otoe Reservation.

Indian Summer in Oklahoma
(The Give Away Feast)
by Daisy Lemon Coldiron

The Spring rains are over
The sun grows warm on the hills,
The snows are gone from the hollows
And the little winds are calling
The little winds are softly calling
The little winds are calling,
Calling the Red Man home.

Poncas, Osages, Otoes, Kaw-
See, they are building lodges
With long poles overhead,
Covered with leafy bunches
And open to every breeze.
In front of the tepee the jerked beef hangs
Toska-ta-nu-ka, drying in the sun,
Toska-ta-nu-ka, the jerked beef.
Drying in the sun,
When the sun-fire has burned low
And twilight is creeping
Over the Nesctunga Valley,
The medicine man come healing the sick
Mumbling incantations.

He makes medicine for the young men
Who make war no more.
They sit cross-legged on the ground
And beat the tame tom-tom
The squaws dance the squaw dance

Hitching along in shoulder to shoulder circle.
Chanting the ancient burden
Of a plaintive racial song.
And the little winds are calling,
The winds are softly calling
The little winds are calling
Calling the Red Men home.

Soon the Cheyennes will go home
Laden with many presents
From the give-away-feast of their Kinsmen
Horses, blankets and calico.
The Poncas, Osages, Otoes, Kaws,
They go back to the fishing pole, the campfire
And the lazy shadows creeping
The jerked beef hangs by the tepee
Taska-ta-nu-ka drying in the sun
Taska-ta-nu-ka the jerked beef
Drying in the sun.

welfare of the Indians placed under his care, tried to keep them on the reservation, urged them to send their children to school, and fed and cared for the old and helpless. Also, he regulated the grazing of cattle on the reservation, prevented the trespassing of white persons, and sought to teach the Indians farming and the ways of the white man.

The agents complained bitterly of their troubles with these Indians, declaring that most of them were savage, dirty and lazy, with no desire to learn the arts of civilization. The agents built frame houses and furnished milch cows and work horses to the Indian families. The Indians soon moved out of the houses and back into their tipis because the tipis were easier to heat. They ate the milch cows and rode the horses to visit neighbors or run races. They used the building to house the horses. The agents were trying to make white farmers out of the red warriors without much success.

Round house at agency.

Ponca Indians

The Poncas were a small tribe numbering slightly more than 700 people. They were closely related to the adjacent Omaha tribe and inhabited a reservation in the southeast corner of Dakota Territory. In drawing up the Sioux treaty in 1868, the Indian Bureau had ceded to the Sioux, 46,000 acres that the Treaty of March 1865 had granted to the Poncas. Since the Treaty of 1868 was still in force in 1877, and the Sioux demanded possession of the area, the Interior Department claimed it had no alternative but to remove the Poncas. At first, the Poncas refused even to discuss the matter, but when pressed for a decision by Indian Bureau officials, one of the Ponca head men, a fifty-eight year old chief named Standing Bear, assumed the role of spokesman for the tribe. "We do not wish to sell our land" he told the officials, "and we think no man has the right to take it from us. Here we will live, and here we will die."

Finally, the officials persuaded Standing Bear and nine other leading men of the tribe to accompany them to Indian Territory and inspect the lands set aside for them. But when the Poncas saw the designated area they insisted that the land was not as good as their Dakota land. Standing Bear told the Indian Bureau representatives that they would not agree to removal. When the officials refused to provide them transportation for the return journey, the delegation decided to walk back to their Dakota reservation. After fifty grueling days on starvation rations, they reached the Otoe Agency in southern Nebraska. There, the sympathetic agent gave them horses and provisions. At the Omaha reservation, a missionary convinced Standing Bear that he must take his case directly to the Great Father, President Rutherford Hayes. On his way home, Standing Bear made a stop at Sioux City, Iowa, gave his story to the Sioux City Journal and sent a telegram to President Hayes, explaining why he opposed the removal to Indian Territory.

The next morning, the officials placed Standing Bear under arrest for refusal to obey government orders and took him before a military tribunal in Yankton, South Dakota. However, after hearing his testimony, the commanding officer released him and sent a telegram to Washington, D.C., asking the Ponca removal to be abandoned. But the Indian Bureau officials were not to be so easily dissuaded. They called another council with the Poncas and announced that the Indian Commissioner would not revise the government's concentration plan. Therefore, there was no choice. The tribe must move to Indian Territory.

Meanwhile, the tribe had split over the issue. Finally, of the 717 tribesmen, 170 agreed to begin the trek south. After a miserable journey of 59 days in stormy, cold weather, the contingent finally reached its new reservation. According to Indian Inspector Kemble, the Poncas seemed "exceedingly well pleased with their new home."

Meanwhile, the Indian Bureau had ordered the army to remove the remainder of the tribe at once. They were asked if they "would go peaceably or by force." Realizing the futility of further resistance, they sullenly agreed. A succession of disasters marred the 65 day trip of the second party. This march also was hampered by heavy rain storms, mud and high water, but in addition, many became seriously ill. To compound the misery, a tornado struck the camp in southern Nebraska and caused one death, several serious injuries and considerable damage to wagons and supplies. As the journey continued, death from illness began to multiply. By July 2, after 47 days on the road, nine Indians had been buried along the way.

These later arrivals were far from satisfied with their new reservation. They had inadequate housing and suffered from the oppressive heat and an epidemic of malaria — a disease new to this northern tribe. In desperation, Standing Bear asked permission to visit the President in Washington, and in the fall of 1877, he and several Ponca head men met with President Hayes. They asked to be allowed either to return to their reservation in Dakota or to join their kinsmen, the Omahas in Nebraska. The President said they could do neither because removing any Indians from Indian Territory was both unwise and impossible. Such a move would be directly contrary to the government's policy of concentration. However, the disappointed delegates were told they could select a permanent home in a more desirable location. Meanwhile, influenced by the Ponca case, Indian Commissioner Hoyt concluded that a modification of the original concentration plan was necessary. He reported on November 1, 1877, that a revised policy would still embrace a steady concentration of the smaller bands on the large reservations but there would be a "discontinuance of the removal of the northern Indians to the Indian Territory."

Unfortunately, the commissioner's decision did not take effect in time to prevent the removal of the Ponca tribe. Meanwhile, the Poncas were becoming increasingly unhappy. Malarial fever and chills caused severe suffering and so many deaths that by the end of the first year a census of the tribe showed a decrease from 684 to 639. These figures presented an alarming contrast with the total of 717 that had left the Dakota reservation the previous year. Late in December 1878, Standing Bear saw his last son die from malaria. He then made up his mind to defy the government and return to his old home. He placed the body of his child in an old wagon and with thirty other Poncas began the long trip north to Dakota. By early spring, the party managed to reach the Omaha reservation in Nebraska, where the Omahas welcomed them.

However, the government had no intention of permitting such a brazen flouting of its authority. In May, General George Crooke was ordered to arrest the runaway Poncas and escort them back to Indian Territory. In due time, the Ponca chiefs were arraigned before General Crooke. All wore citizen's clothes, except Standing Bear, who was attired in the full dress of a Ponca chief, a red and blue blanket, a beaded belt and a necklace of bear claws. To the assembled officers, he said: "I want to go back to my old place north. I want to save myself and my tribe. My brothers, it seems to me as if I stood in front of a great prairie fire, I would take my babies and run to save their lives, or as if I stood on the bank of an over-flowing river, I would take my people and fly to higher ground — If a white man had land, and someone would swindle him, that man would try to get it back, and you would not blame him. Look on me. Take pity on me, and help me to save the lives of the women and children. My brothers, a power which I cannot resist, crowds me down to the ground. I need help."

By this time, newspaper accounts of the tribulations of Standing Bear and his fellow tribesmen were attracting national attention. The Poncas received widespread support of their refusal to return to Indian Territory. With the counsel of several prominent Omaha, Nebraska, lawyers, Standing Bear brought suit before Judge Elmer Dundy of the United States District Court for a writ of habeas corpus. On May 19, 1879, Judge Dundy ruled that an Indian was a person within the meaning of the habeas corpus act and thus was entitled to sue a writ of habeas corpus in the Federal courts.

After this victory, which has been hailed as the day the judge ruled Indians were human, Standing Bear and his band went home to Nebraska and buried his son with his tribal ancestors on the

Ponca Indian singers and tomtom beaters at Col. Joe Millers funeral. (L to R): White Deer, Ed Lightening, John DeLodge, Horse Chief Eagle, Charles Primeaux, Geo. King, John Bull, Jesse Waters, Crazy Bear, Albert Primeaux, Jim Williams - all co-chiefs.
(Courtesy Oklahoma Historical Society)

Niobrara River. Thus fulfilling the promise he had made to his dying son. Standing Bear died here in September, 1908.

While the Poncas were near Newtonia, Missouri, George W. Miller and his young son, Joe, became acquainted with Chief White Eagle. Joe played with the Ponca children and learned their language. Later, when George and his son were driving cattle across some of the land the government was offering the Poncas, he saw some he thought they might like. He knew White Eagle was about to turn down this offer without seeing the land. In spite of the danger in crossing the unfriendly Osage lands, he sent Joe back to the Poncas where he met with White Eagle and other headmen, probably the first white boy ever to sit in their council. Speaking in their language, he convinced them to return with him to view the land. As a result of this, the Poncas moved their reservation on the Arkansas River in the Cherokee Strip. It was through this friendship, continued down the years, that enabled Joe Miller to lease the vast pasture lands from the Poncas. This saved him from having to sell his cattle when the Strip was opened. Most of the other cattle on the Strip had to be sold for lack of pasture, causing a glut on the market and lower prices. This helped enable Joe, his brothers, George and Zack to build the 101 Ranch.

Most of the Poncas lived in what is now Kay County but a large part of their pasture lands (hunting grounds) were in Noble County, covering three townships.

Otoe-Missouria Indians

The Otoe-Missouria are a small group of Chiwere speaking people who have been classified as Southern Sioux. It is believed they originated in the Great Lakes region, west of Lake Michigan. Their beadwork reflects the influence of the woodland Indians, with leaves and flowers, while the Ponca beadwork is more geometrical in design.

They may have been one tribe with the Iowa and Winnebago. Migrating south in search of buffalo, the Winnebago, separated from the others, stayed in Green Bay, Wisconsin. As they came south of the Mississippi River, the Iowa stayed at the junction of the Mississippi and Iowa Rivers, while the rest of the tribe moved south and west to the Missouri River. It was here at the mouth of the Grand River, the French traders called them Missouria Indians. They called themselves Neutache (those that arrived at the mouth).

Here at the mouth of the Grand River, the tribe split after a quarrel over a Chief's daughter who had been seduced by one of the young men of the tribe. This young couple and his family left the rest of the tribe and were known as the Otoe. The Otoe continued up the Missouri River, to the land, now in southeastern Nebraska. Nebraska is an Otoe word meaning flat water.

In 1833, Henry L. Ellsworth, a member of the Stokes Commission visited the Otoe village on the Platte River to make a treaty. He was accompained by John T. Irving, who gave this description: "We found nearly the whole tribe assembled, and seated in circles in the large lodge of the Iotan Chief. At the far end of the building, was the Iotan, and by his side, were stationed these two worthies — The Big Kaw and the Thief. Next then, were the stern forms of the older warriors and braves. There was something solemn in the unyielding features of these war worn veterans. They sat motionless as stone-moving not a single muscle of their dusky contenances. They had thrown aside their usual careless deportment, and all were prepared to listen, with intense interest to the terms of the treaty. This was observable, not only in the principal braves, but throughout the whole assembly. Even the lowest man assumed an air of dignity befitting the occasion.

The lodge was excessively crowded. One ring was formed beyond another, one dark head rose behind another, until the dim, dusky outlines of the more distant were lost in the shadow and their glistening eyes could be seen. The passage which led to the air was completely crowded with women and children, and half a dozen curious faces were peering down through the round hole in the roof."

Before the disintegration of the old culture, the Otoe did not live together as a tribe, but they formed villages which were essentially voluntary groupings of families. A village might be made up of from forty to seventy mud lodges. According the Otoe legends these lodges were made of birch bark before the Otoes came to the plains, where they adopted the plains Indians mud lodges. They were circular in form about forty feet in diameter with a projecting part at the entrance of ten or twelve feet in length, in the form of a porch. The porch was an inclined plane to the level of the floor, about two and a half or three feet below the level of the ground. Around the sides of the lodge was placed from fifteen to eighteen posts, forked at the top and about seven feet high from the floor. In the center, a circular space was dug to the depth of two feet, four strong posts were placed in the form of a square about twelve feet asunder and at equal distances from this space. These posts were about twenty feet high and cross pieces were laid on the tops. The rafters were laid from the forked tops of the outsides posts over these crosspieces and reached nearly to the center, where a small hole was left for the smoke to escape. Across the rafters, small pieces of timber were laid over the sticks and a covering of sods and lastly earth. The fire was made in the middle of the central space, round the edges they sat and beds were fixed betwixt the outer posts. The door was placed at the immediate entrance of the lodge. It was made of buffalo skin, stretched in a frame of wood and was suspended from the top. On entering, it swung forward and when let go, fell to its former position.

In these villages of mud lodges, which were set up along the rivers, the people lived the greater part of the year. The men hunted along the neighboring streams, the women hoed and planted and cared for their gardens in the river bottoms. When game grew scarce or the villages became dirty or the pressure of neighboring tribes compelled them to move, the Otoe would gather together their possessions and packing them on their backs moved to a new site where the hearth fires would be relit and the old life begun all over again.

Nellie Shadlow and child.

In creek bottoms, in places that had been used for years, they planted corn, beans and melons. The ground was worked by the women using big hoes. The women put the corn in rain water, soaked it a night or two, and after it had swelled up, put it in the ground. Children were forbidden to meddle with the seed corn, which was thought to be sacred. They planted the seed of pumpkins, squash, and corn of all colors in this way. They raised three kinds of pumpkins: squash, big pumpkins and little pumpkins. They would take the pumpkins, build a fire and roll the pumpkins over the coals. They would let the pumpkin skins burn a little, then pick them out of the fire, scrape the top off, and put them away on long poles. When the pumpkins were soft, they were pulled down, braided and flattened and put in the sun. When they got hard the pumpkins would keep a long time. They cut squash, dried the meat and took the hard shell off.

Twice a year, during the spring and fall, were the buffalo hunts. Each family had its own skin tipi. The family consisted of a man, his wife and unmarried children. To this group might be added a married daughter and son-in-law or some unattended close blood realtive.

By 1833, the Missouria who had suffered severe losses from sickness and in their wars with the Omaha, Ponca, Sioux, Osage, Kansas and Pawnee Loups, had joined the Otoe.

As game became scarce due to the immigration of white settlers, the Otoe-Missouria were often hungry. They began to make treaties with the United States government, each time losing some of their land.

The white settlers began to crowd them and in April of 1872, a delegation of tribal headmen left Gage County, Nebraska and made a visit to Indian Territory with the purpose of selecting land for a home for their people.

The tribe split into two groups, the Coyotes or "Wild Party" who wanted to establish a place where they could hold to the old ways and traditions and the Quakers, who wanted to wait and see what the United States government intended. They were so called because they followed the Indian Agent who was a Quaker.

Early in the autumn of 1874, about one-fifth of the Otoe-Missourias, without permission, left the reservation to visit southern tribes and find a place where they could procure game and other subsistence. They were looking for a place where they could live as their ancestors had before them.

They were captured by the military, the leaders confined for a time at Fort Hays, and the others sent home. The military named the leaders: "three principal men of the Otoes and five others." They were Medicine Horse, chief; Little Pipe, sub-chief; Giaka, sub-chief; Tingabusta or George; Kashingua or Robert; Dunsquna; Hahe-tupe; and Wa-ne-ques-qua.

In November of 1874, a vote was taken in the Otoe council on the question of removal. The "Wild Party" carried the day by a small margin, 229 persons voted to remove, 213 voted to remain on the reservation and 17 were absent.

The tribe met in council and, seeing the handwriting on the wall, asked the government to settle the matter, stating that they were agreeable to moving to the land they had heard of to the south where they could live like Indians.

Congress, by an act of March 3, 1881, provided for the sale of the last portion of the Otoe-Missouri lands in the Big Blue River and provided means by which the tribe could finance their removal to Indian Territory. Henceforth, it was a vital question in the tribe as to what lands in Indian Territory they should occupy. A delegation was sent to Indian Territory to select a future home. They rejected the lands near the Sac and Fox because they were too far from a market and also the lands that had been selected earlier because they did not want to be "set up as a fence between other tribes and whites in

Kansas." Instead, they selected land on Red Rock Creek, just south of the Poncas and west of the Pawnees, embracing 129,113 acres.

On October 5, 1881, the Otoe-Missourias in Nebraska and Kansas set out for the new reservation and arrived there, October 23. On November 19, 1884, the tribe reimbursed the United States government for the lands of their reservation in Indian Territory at the rate of 47.49 cents an acre or a sum of $61,315.85. Their lands in Nebraska and Kansas were appraised at from $2.50 to $12.00 an acre, the average about $6.00 an acre.

The government decided to sell these lands in Kansas and Nebraska to the highest bidder. A group of men banded together to control the public sale and defeat its purpose, prevent the land from being sold to the highest bidder and secure the sale to the members of the combination at a lower price. The bids for the land went to highly inflated figures, the people believing the government would adjust the prices to the appraised value.

For nearly two decades, land debts were a part of the Nebraska and Kansas politics, while the settlers protested their ability to pay. The settlers were getting the full benefit of the land without even paying taxes. What monies from the lands that was collected were put in trust for the tribal members at 5% interest. Each year the Indians received a share of the interest, on sale of the land, grazing rights, oil leases or any other revenue from tribal lands.

They needed these monies because the land in Oklahoma was so different from what they had in the old homeland. Instead of garden spots that had been tilled for centuries, they found red clay and black gumbo, packed hard from countless hooves of buffalo in ages past. There were no trees suitable to make the lodges they had lived in for generations. Even the skins of the tipis had to be replaced with canvas furnished by the white man.

Numerous bills were introduced in the United States Congress to settle these claims but each time they were defeated. November 20, 1899, Inspector James McLaughlin arrived at the Ponca Agency and met with fifty of the eighty-eight adult male members of the Otoes. The tribe voiced complete opposition to adjusting for three days but the next day, McLaughlin held an informal council and secured signatures on an agreement whereas the Otoes would take a lesser sum for their land. For decades signers claimed that McLaughlin obtained signatures by going to hut and field and inducing adult individuals to sign an agreement under pretense that it was a paper that would secure payment to them of over $70 each.

The agreement was not made or ratified in open council, the recognized legal agency by which consent was required. This questionable agreement was the subject of many bills in the United States Congress, but it was not until December 1, 1952, that it was resolved and the Commission of Indian Affairs awarded the Otoes the sum of $1,156,034.35 for this and other lands that were not sold at the going prices.

Funeral rites may be used to illustrate one of the tribal customs that is fading out as the Otoes travel the white man's road. From antiquity came the practice of a feast and of giving presents at a funeral, an expression of love for a departed friend. This is called the Give-Away Feast.

In order to show that life is more dear than all material things, the family distributed gifts among those present. Sometimes this was an elaborate affair, including horses, blankets and scores of other things. Some gifts were things the deceased had owned.

At the grave, a song, beautiful in sound and thought, conveyed by prayer to Wah-Kon-Tan, a message that the deceased was on his way to a brighter land.

Interred with the deceased were items that had been greatly admired by him in his lifetime. These might include blankets, dishes and instruments of wide variety. If the deceased had a horse that had been highly prized by him, it might be killed and buried near the grave in order that he might have the horse in the spirit world. Pow-wows also featured the give-away feast.

A.T. & S.F. Railroad

In 1887, the Atchison, Topeka and Santa Fe railroad completed the branch line from Arkansas City to Purcell, Oklahoma, completing the line to Gainesville, Texas through Noble County. Work began late in the summer of 1886. One thousand teams and practically twice that amount of men were employed on the work between Arkansas City and the Canadian River. The track was laid to Ponca station by the middle of December. The track layers reached the vicinity of the present site of Perry by the end of the year, and it reached the Canadian River early in April. Some delay was necessary there while the bridge was being completed.

John Gillespie cooked for part of the crew building the railroad and camped near the Perry townsite. It was then called Mendota. All shipments of material were labeled "Mendota" Railroad station. Later, the name was changed to Wharton. Here, the railroad company built an immense coal chute and water station, one mile south of the present site of Perry because of the springs of water found on Cow Creek at this point which could supply water for the steam engines of the trains.

In 1888, there were a few telegraph offices on the line such as the one at Wharton. Freight could be sent to these places if fully prepaid and put off at the risk of the owners, but there were no regularly authorized agents to handle it. After the opening of the Unassigned Lands, there was a freight trail from Wharton to Stillwater.

Emery E. Westervelt was appointed telegraph agent sometime in 1891, living south of the Wharton Depot in a "cottage" owned by the railroad. Mr.

Wharton (Perry) 1892 - men unidentified.

Westervelt said, "The only people there in 1891, were the man who pumped water for the railroad tank and Andy Banks, the man who shoveled coal in the coal chute and one or two fellows who loafed around there. Andy Banks was quite a character. He used a very large shovel and unloaded two or three cars of coal daily for which he received 10 cents a ton. The contractor, who contracted to handle the coal finally agreed to handle the coal for a lower price and cut Andy's rate to 7 cents a ton and Andy quit. It took two men to do the work he had been doing and after two or three months Andy went to work again at 7 cents. He would make about $100.00 a month at 7 cents so you can see he had broad shoulders and could shovel coal all day in a cloud of coal dust."

The trains stopped only to take on coal and water. Passengers were discouraged from leaving the trains. Few wanted to do this as there was a widespread fear of the Indians. The span of railroad track through Indian Territory was nicknamed, "The longest tunnel in the world."

Wharton - September 30, 1893.
(from Cherokee Stirp Museum - Perry)

Indian Allotments in Noble County

Make another treaty with the great white father,
Smoke the peace pipe and depart,
Give, give, give, ignorant children,
Sign away your lands to your flattering brothers,
Soon you will have no land to sell
(for thirty cents an acre)
Soon you will wish you could make a treaty
Daisy Lemon Coldiron

People going across Indian lands on the train cast envious eyes at the rich lands apparently going to waste. Many people felt it was unfair for a group of "back east" cowmen to have control of the vast grazing lands that could be used for families to establish homes. Much pressure was being put on Congress in Washington, and it seemed only a matter of time before the Cherokees would be forced to sell.

It was felt the land of the other tribes in the strip would be divided into allotments to the individual Indians and the rest of the land opened to white settlement. With the memory of what happened to their lands in Nebraska and Kansas fresh in their minds, the Otoe-Missourias were determined that this would not happen again. As one Indian man said, "Fool me once - shame on you. Fool me twice - shame on me."

On March 17, 1891, the government appointed a women, Helen Pi-o-to-po-wa-ka Clarke to be a special agent to make allotments on the reservations under the supervision of the Ponca agency: Oakland (Tonkawa), Pawnee, Ponca and the Otoe-Missouria.

Helen P. Clarke was the only woman who served in Oklahoma Territory as a special alloting agent. Her father, Malcolm Clarke, was one of the best known frontiersmen in the region of Montana. He had two wives. His first wife, Coth-co-co-mia, was the mother of Helen P. Clarke. Coth-co-co-mia was the daughter of a Blackfoot chief, a descendant of a line of warriors, and according to most statements, she was a full blood. Miss Clarke wrote: "The older children had been sent to the states for school privileges, and we scarcely knew our father." However, she loved and admired him, and was at home with him when he was killed and her brother wounded by the Blackfeet in an uprising on August 17, 1869.

Miss Clarke had served as superintendent of school at Lewis and Clark County, Montana, 1882-88. Her appointment, October 3, 1890, as a special alloting agent concerned lands in Kansas belonging to the Prairie Band of Pottawatomies and to the Kickapoo Indians. She was about forty-three years old. Miss Clarke was twenty-three in the 1870 census. If her age as given in the census is correct, she omitted seven years when she mentioned her age to commissioner, W. A. Jones on April 15, 1899. Her commission specified a compensation of eight dollars per day and actual and necessary traveling expenses, exclusive of subsistence. Her appointment should continue during the pleasure of the President for the time being.

On May 19, 1891, she began making allotments on the Oakland (Tonkawa) reservation and completed the work of allotment there on June 30. The next day she began work as an alloting agent on the Otoe-Missouria reservation. She went there on the advise of agent D.J.M. Wood, "notwithstanding, the Otoes were much more pronounced in their opposition to allotments than the Pawnees or Poncas."

The Otoes soon told her to leave the reservation. She ignored their request, and proceeded to survey the lands. They threatened to kill the one who took his allotment first, and then commenced to remove the stones which had been set to establish the lines. Agent Wood ended such resistence under threat of punishment.

On August 4, 1891, Miss Clarke said, "There would be no trouble in alloting the lands to the Otoe tribe, if it were not for the pernicious influence of three men. These three men are William Faw-Faw, James Whitewater and George Arkeketah.

Miss Clarke felt if she could finish the work with the Otoes, the allotment to the Pawnees and the Poncas would be an easy matter, as "The Otoes had the reputation of being the most stubborn of the four tribes of the Ponca Agency, and had always managed to have their way with the Indian agents."

After two or three weeks of work it looked, according to Miss Clarke as if the works would succeed, "when along came officials pretty high in the Department to tell the Indians that a woman had no business at this work, which the Indians construed to mean that she has no legal right to do this work."

Some of the Indians agreed to take their allotments if they could have 160 acres instead of the 80 the law allowed. Some, when Miss Clarke assigned them land, would trade with another Indian and the work would have to be done over, only to have the land change hands again.

Scarcely any progress was made in 1892 in the work of allotment on the Otoe reservation. On November 22, Special Agent James G. Hatchitt was assigned to duty at the Ponca agency to assist in making allotments on reservation there. At the Otoe subagency, he was informed that "those who had been alloted say they made no selections and do not know their land."

Miss Clarke considered the Indians as "children", urged that they "be not crowded too fast," and said she was content to work "From early morn to dewy eve" and desired to keep all things ready so that whenever an Indian showed an inclination to take an allotment she could immediately "clinch the nail on the head."

On the other hand, Hatchitt had little patience with the Poncas and Otoes and felt that "nothing but an exhibition of power will do good," and observed that if Chief White Horse and Chief Arkeketa and James Whitewater be imprisoned for obstructing allotments, they would come to their senses and make their selection." Hatchitt was recalled from the field on September 14, 1893.

The Tonkawa and Pawnee lands were opened with those of the Cherokee Outlet. These tribes had agreed that each Indian should take an allotment and that the rest of the land should be sold to the United States. At the time of the opening, the Indians of the Ponca and the Otoe-Missouria reservations had not agreed to take their allotments and their reservations were intact.

Miss Clarke wrote: "I am working among a people whose very soul abominates anything tending toward civilization ultimately." It seemed to Miss Clarke that some of the Otoes would have to be assigned lands since there was little likelihood of their selecting them. Many of the Otoes remained firm, believing that if they took allotments, they would be compelled to sell the surplus land, and they were anxious to keep it all.

On August 31, 1894, Miss Clarke was directed to notify the Otoes that unless they made selection within thirty days, assignment would be made to them, as provided in the General Allotment Act.

Helen P. Clarke

Her work was completed December 31, by which time all Otoes had received allotments, being 362 in number. There had been reserved for agency school, mission and cemetery purposes 720 acres, leaving a surplus of 81,860.17 acres.

Regardless of allotments, the Otoes were not disposed to part with any of their lands. An insertion in the Indian appropriation act of March 2, 1895, authorized the Secretary of the Interior to negotiate with them for the purchase of a sufficient quantity of surplus lands to allot to about forty-five Iowas in Kansas and Nebraska. On March 22, a protest, over the names of the principal chiefs of the Otoes, was addressed to the President requesting that no consideration be given to any petition for the allotment, or for an agreement for the sale of the reservation. On October 5, Inspector Paul F. Faison held a council with the tribe, but they unanimously voted against the sale of any of their lands for the purposes of making allotments to the Iowas.

Soon after the Office of Indian Affairs recommended approval of the schedule of allotments, a delegation of Otoes

Helen P. Clarke near wagon - lady by tree was cook - Indian men unidentified.

went to Washington to explain that the tribe were "all in one line," "all in one row" in their opposition to taking allotments. The delegation consisted of Par-thapinga, William Faw-Faw, Clem Jones, White Mule, Albert Green, James Whitewater, James Cleghorn, and Mitchell Deroin.

At a conference with the Commissioner of Indian Affairs on April 25, 1895, Clem Jones introduced Mitchell Deroin in these words: "The allotment is the most important thing to talk about, and we have chosen a man who will tell you about it."

Deroin spoke as follows: "We are here in regard to our land. We ask you to ask the Secretary not to sign any papers issuing patents until the next Congress. That the land we are living on was bought for the Otoe tribe with their own money. The land in Kansas and Nebraska was sold and before that time the Otoes had a great tract of land, but the chiefs made a treaty with the Government and they kept a piece about as big as a hog-pen; outside of that land the rest went to the Government and so when the government sold this land for us they took some of the money and bought some of the land where we are living now, and we expect to live on that land as long as the earth is under the heavens, and as long as there is an Otoe under the heaven.

Now if I take allotments in severalty and cut it up, letting each person have a piece of land, how would I find my home in twenty-five years? I cannot live up in the air, nor in the water; if I go into the water I sink, if I go into the air I fall. We know what happened yesterday but not what will happen in front of us. We say if we take allotments in 25 years we get our patent, and after we get our patent we have a right to do anything with the land.

It is this way. When the Indians get a patent they must pay taxes, and lots of white people who have land when they cannot pay taxes must mortgage their land to pay taxes. If you cannot pay taxes on first, you go and borrow again, and finally all the land goes, and then the man is out of a home. Then he runs about and tries to find a home but he has no money to get a home.

It is not right for my people to take allotments. We can live like white men without cutting up our land. Look at us; you can see me with pants and coat on, but we are Indians all the same. Why cannot we work like a white man and hold our land as it is? We would rather be naked and have our toes sticking out than to take allotments and to have that land go out of our hand at some future time. But if we hold the land in common and till the ground, we will have a home as long as the world is under the heaven."

Deroin was 34 years old. When Deroin had finished, William Faw-Faw said; "We have appointed this man to talk for us and whatever he has said my tribe has said."

The Otoes continued their opposition to the allotments and in October, 1898, a delegation consisting of Albert Green, William Faw-Faw and James Whitewater, called on Governor Cassius M. Barnes and asked him to write to the President that they were unalterably opposed to the division of their lands, in spite of the representations of Helen P. Clarke or any other person to the contrary.

On April 25, 1899, Miss Clarke was ordered, upon completion of her work on the Otoe reservation to proceed to her home in Montana. Thus ended her work as an alloting agent. Miss Clarke's

Interior Helen P. Clarke's tent on reservation 1892.

later years were spent at Glacier Park in Northern Montana. She was a devout Catholic, never married, died March 7, 1923, and was buried at the foot of the Rockies near where she had lived.

On January 1, 1904, the Otoe sub-agency was segregated from the Ponca agency. An act of April 21, 1904, authorized the Secretary of the Interior in accordance with the General Allotment Act, to cause 640 acres of Otoe land to be reserved for common use of the tribe and 720 acres reserved for administration, church, and school and other public purposes and the remained unalloted and unreserved lands were to be allotted in such a manner as to give all the members of the tribe as near as practicable an equal quantity of land in acres. The reservation was divided among 514 Otoes, each one received about 290 acres. No surplus lands on the reservation were sold to the federal government and no white settlers took homestead on lands of the reservation.

At the same time the lands of the Poncas were divided in the same manner. Shortly afterwards, the Osage allotments were made and the Osage nation became Osage County. Thus ended the Indian reservations in Oklahoma.

Lawmen and Outlaws

From the time of removal of the civilized tribes into Oklahoma, a serious problem of law enforcement became evident. The Indians policed and tried their own people but their courts had no jurisdiction over U.S. Citizens. Since no Federal Court had jurisidction in Indian Territory this situation created a haven of refuge for criminals from surrounding states.

In 1834, Congress passed a law extending control of the U.S. Courts in Arkansas over U.S. citizens in Indian Territory. In 1844, headquarters for these courts were established in Van Buren and later at Fort Smith. These two courts had jurisdiction over all U.S. citizens in Indian Territory and over Indians who committed crimes against U.S. citizens. In 1875, Judge Isaac C. Parker was appointed the judge at Fort Smith. In 1883, U.S. courts were established in Wichita, Kansas and Paris, Texas. This provided the people of Oklahoma with more convenient courts, making it easier for lawmen to bring in their prisoners. But the law enforcement situation was still unwieldy.

To sign a complaint against a criminal, the accuser had to go to the court, up to a hundred miles away. This was both expensive and time-consuming since travel was entirely by horse power. Also, the criminal had ample time to disappear before an officer could come in after him.

The courts made every effort within their power to bring order in the territory. The Fort Smith court sent a force of 200 federal marshalls into the roadless wilderness to search out criminals and bring them back for trial. Indians were often employed to track them down. The officers either rode a horse or traveled in the wagons that they took along to bring their prisoners back. Often they would be weeks or even months tracking down their men. This meant that for long periods of time desperate criminals were under their care in a country swarming with the equally ruthless friends of the prisoners. Although men were hired to drive these prison wagons while the deputies rode behind with a ready winchester and the prisoners were shackled to wagon wheels at night, many lawmen were killed while bringing in their men.

Indian inhabitants of the territory tried to remain out of the conflict between the white out-laws and peace officers. When they did give information it was dependable.

It was easy for a wanted man to hide out in Oklahoma and Indian Territories. There was a dense tree coverage over much of the old, well-known "Cross Timber" region. The "Cross Timbers" was a strip of land from 15 to 30 miles wide extending from Kansas into Texas through east central Oklahoma. It was believed that this strip of land was so covered with scrub oak called Black Jacks, briar vines and native cedars that it was necessary to cut a road before wagons could go through. Although there were places where the "Cross Timbers" region was almost impassable, it was not a wall as was first believed. It did give the outlaws hideouts in box canyons where the brush gave good coverage. These regular hideouts swung a giant circle through the area. Beginning on the Red River in the Chickasaw Nation, it extended north and east through the land of the Seminoles, across Pawnee and Ponca country, south into the Glass Mountains, downward through Custer County, across the Wichita Mountains and back into the Chickasaw Nation.

Marshal William Tilghman.
(Courtesy Oklahoma Historical Society)

During the years in which law officers and outlaws struggled for mastery in Oklahoma, many lawmen whose names were already famous throughout the west came to the aid of the courts. Men who had helped to tame other frontier communities just as rough and tough as Oklahoma. These included such men as William Tilghman, Chris Madsen, Heck Thomas and Bud Ledbetter, who made names for themselves as U.S. Deputy Marshalls. A small army of U.S. Deputies operated under these chief deputies. These deputies were not paid a flat salary. They received around six cents a mile while on official business. 50¢ for each paper served, $2.00 for each arrest made and $1.00 a day expense money while after a criminal. Since they had to present vouchers for this last payment, they often failed to collect since they operated in a country where many of the inhabitants could neither read nor write. They were sometimes able to collect the rewards offered by express companies.

The Dalton gang was the first big organized group of outlaws to make a reputation in Oklahoma. The Dalton brothers — Bob, Gratton, Emmett and Bill — were cousins of the Younger brothers who were members of the Jesse James gang in Missouri. With Bob Dalton as the leader, these brothers and their followers robbed trains and banks for eighteen months before they were almost wiped out at a double bank robbery at Coffeyville, Kansas, May 9, 1891. Well known members of the gang were: Bitter Creek Newcomb, Charlie Pierce, Bill Powers, Dick Broadwell, William McElhanie and Bill Doolin.

When the Dalton gang was destroyed one of the survivors, Bill Doolin, immediately formed his own more vicious gang. Bill Dalton, Pierce and Newcomb, old Dalton men, became followers of this new outlaw leader. Little Dick West, Bill Raidler, Red Buck Waightman, Dan Clifton or "Dynamite Dick", as he was known, Jack Blake, known as "Tulsa Jack", Al Yantis and Dougherty alias Tom Jones alias "Arkansas Tom" were added to the gang as time passed.

These outlaws found it easy to evade the lawmen. Either from sympathy or through a justifiable fear of reprisal many settlers refused to help the law by giving information. Some not only refused to talk, they actively gave aid to the criminals by warning them when marshalls rode into the area and by providing supplies. Some of these semi-members of the gangs were women.

Among the women outlaws were Annie McDougal, known as "Cattle Annie" and Jennie Stevens, known as "Little Britches". These girls acted as informers for the outlaw gangs and, at times, took part in cattle rustling operations. They were finally arrested and sent to a reformatory back east.

"Rose of Cimmarron" most controversial figure aong the women outlaws, was the girl friend of Bitter Creek Newcomb. She is reported to have run through a hail of bullets to take a gun to Bitter Creek during the battle between officers of the law and outlaws at Ingalls in Payne County.

Flora Quick, alias Tom King, was a member of a farm family in Missouri but after her first taste of frontier life, she took to the outlaw trail with zest. She was best known as a horse thief although she dabbled in other criminal activities. Tom King's only known photograph shows her to have been an attractive woman. The picture was made after she had married and was living in the northwest.

E. D. Nix in **Oklahombres**, says "Red Rock, Oklahoma, was a little Indian trading station built upon the rolling red clay prairies in the Cherokee Strip, and so isolated that even today the state highways do not touch it and the Santa Fe trains hoot disdainfully as they whiz by. The depot was situated about a mile from town, and it was here the bandits could work quickly without fear of interference by the officers of the little community. At nine o'clock on the night of June 1, 1892, the Dalton gang rode into a deep washout near the railroad and near the Red Rock station. Leaving their horses concealed here, they waited in the shadows for the arrival of the southbound Santa Fe passenger train. As the small wood-burning engine labored into the station and came to a stop, a blanketed Indian with a squaw and two papooses alighted. The telegraph operator ran to the engine to give the engineer his orders, when Black Faced Charlie Bryant and Dick Broadwell dashed past him and leaped into the cab of the locomotive. An armed guard sat on a pile of wood on the tender eating a sandwich. The surprise attack so demoralized him that he gave a hysterical jerk at his gun, causing sticks of wood to roll beneath him and he sprawled across the coupling into the cab of the engine at the feet of the two bandits who quickly disarmed him. The express messenger and his guard had just been congratulating themselves that there were no shipments to be put off the train at Red Rock, and they went on placidly with a game of checkers. When the command came for them to reach for the sky, the checkerboard fell from their trembling knees and the checkers rolled all about the car. They were looking into the guns of Bill Doolin and Gratton Dalton. Back in the passenger coaches, Bob and Emmett Dalton and Bill Powers were herding the frightened passengers out onto the station platform. With the express messenger and his guard disarmed and bound Grat and Doolin looked about for the large safe that was supposed to contain several thousand dollars in currency. There was a slip somewhere, for they found only a small box-like safe that contained only two or three hundred dollars.

While Bob, Emmett and Powers were forcing the passengers to give up their valuables, Black Faced Charlie left Broadwell in the engine to hold his prisoners there while he ran back to assist the others. In passing the station window, he saw the frightened face of the operator in the dim lamplight as his nervous hands trembled on the telegraph keys. Assuming that the operator was sending news of the robbery, Bryant sent a bullet crashing through the window, and with a moan the slender boy inside slumped from his chair. The telegraph instruments clicked frantically for him to complete his message. Within fifteen minutes the terrified passengers were herded back into the cars and the train was on its way. The disappointed bandits slunk away with but a part of the booty they had hoped for."

While the details of planning the opening of the Cherokee Strip were being wound up, Bill Doolin and his gang, during the month of August, rode wildly into the little town of Wharton (later named Perry) a few minutes before the arrival of a Santa Fe southbound night train. By this time, they were so well organized and they had developed so perfect a routine for the handling of crews and passengers during a train robbery that within fifteen minutes they were riding off toward the Osage Hills with several hundreds of dollars in money, a considerable lot of registered mail and with the money and valuables of the surprised passengers. Their haul in cash from the express car would have been much greater had they chosen to rob one of the day trains, for by this time, the express company was making its larger shipments during the daylight and under heavy guard. Following the robbery the gang flew quickly to its cave in the Creek Nation.

With settlers coming into Oklahoma in droves with each new land opening, the demand for law and order became urgent. The outlaws desperately wanted this last refuge so they openly challenged the power of the law. Open conflict resulted. In 1894, word came from Washington to put an end to the reign of terror, Chris Madsen, Bill Tilghman and Heck Thomas were given the assignment of overseeing the needed cleanup. Bill Doolin was killed by Heck Thomas in 1896, and that broke the back of his gang.

A few years later, a relative of Bill Dalton and family lived for a time in Walnut township which is now in Noble County. On November 1, 1905, Amelia F. Dalton, purchased the southwest ¼ of section 30 from Frederike Volz (widow) for $1725.00. On March 13, 1909, Amelia and husband, Bill Dalton, sold his farm to James D. Shepard for $2300.00.

Although they kept much to themselves, there were times they hired labor from the neighbors as well as purchasing supplies such as fresh fruit, that they needed.

Chapter 2
OPENING THE CHEROKEE STRIP

Boomers and Sooners

People who boomed the opening of Indian lands in Oklahoma to settlement, or who tried to occupy it in defiance of the law, were called "Boomers". The work of the Boomers did much to attract attention to the Oklahoma lands and to advertise their beauty and fertility. In 1880, the Boomers secured a new leader, David L. Payne, who led a number of groups into the territory only to be removed by the U.S. soldiers.

They finally succeeded in 1889, in opening the "Unassigned Lands" in the heart of Oklahoma. These lands had not been assigned to any Indian tribe, hence the name. They were also called "Old Oklahoma" and "Oklahoma Lands." March 23, 1889, President Benjamin Harrison issued a proclamation that these lands should be opened to settlement under the homestead laws of the United States. The land was surveyed into 160 acre tracts. Under the Homestead Law, the first person entering upon such a tract had the first right or claim to it. At noon, April 22, the great crowd camped along the border dashed across, each person striving to be the first on a homestead. This came to be known as a "run" or a "race." In Old Oklahoma, two towns Stillwater and Orlando, sprang up close to the border of what is now Noble county. These provided jumping off places when the Strip was opened.

At the time of filing the claim, the claimant must swear he was qualified under the law and that he had not been on the land within the 30 days before the day and hour set by the President. Those who entered the land before this time were called "Sooners" and if caught, were subject to arrest and trial for perjury, which is punishable by a long term in prison.

Land Openings or the five runs: 1. Old Oklahoma (Unassigned Lands) April 22, 1889; 2. Sac and Fox, Iowa and Shawnee-Potawatomi lands, September 23, 1891; 3. Cheyenne-Arapahoe, April 19, 1892; 4. Cherokee Outlet, September 16, 1893; 5. Kickapoo country, May 1895. The Kiowa-Commanche-Apache Reservation was opened by lottery.

The settlers of Oklahoma Lands lived for more than a year without any government except such as they formed for themselves. U.S. Marshalls and soldiers helped to keep order and to enforce the laws of the United States. The people of the towns quickly organized local governments based only upon the common consent of the citizens.

On May 2, 1890, an act of Congress called the Organic Act was approved by the President. This act provided that the Oklahoma Lands and the Panhandle should be joined to make the Territory of Oklahoma. All other lands west of the country of the Five Civilized Tribes, except the Cherokee Outlet should become a part of this territory as soon as they were opened to settlement. An exception was made of the Outlet since it still belonged to the Cherokee nation. When opened to settlement later, however, it was joined to the Oklahoma Territory by a special act.

Opening of the Outlet

Ever since the opening of the Oklahoma Lands in 1889, officials of the United States had been trying to induce the Cherokees to give up their claim to the Outlet so that it might be opened to white settlement. The last lease of the Cherokee Strip Live Stock Association was for two hundred thousand dollars a year which gave the Cherokee people a good income from the Outlet, therefore they were unwilling to sell it at the price of one dollar and twenty-five cents an acre, which was what the United States offered them. Besides a group of cattlemen offered to buy the entire area at three dollars an acre but the Cherokees could not sell the Outlet without the consent of the United States and permission to sell was refused.

The Cherokee Commission, set up by the government to deal with the Cherokees, and other officials of the United States said that the title held by these Indians to the Outlet was probably not good because they had never used the land. The officials also asserted that the cattlemen had no right to occupy these lands, that their presence there and the money they paid to the Cherokees made these Indians refuse to accept the offer of the United States. Accordingly, in February 1890, the President issued a proclamation ordering all the ranchmen to remove their herds from the Outlet by October first. Also a bill was introduced in Congress to allow the government to take the lands and seeing that the bill was certain to pass, the Cherokees agreed to bargain. They finally sold the entire Outlet to the United States for about one dollar and forty cents an acre.

March 3, 1893, Congress enacted the necessary legislation for the opening of the Cherokee Outlet to homesteaders. As the lands of the Outlet had cost the government a little more than $1.40 an acre, it was sought to have approximately that amount paid by the settlers. The eastern part of the Strip was judged to be the best land so from the eastern boundary to a line two miles west of the west boundary of Noble county, the land was to cost settlers $2.50 an acre or, including fees, $516 for 160 acres. The middle section extending from two miles west of Noble county's west line to two miles east of Woods county's east line was to cost settlers $1.50 per acre which with the other fees would make 160 acres cost $317. The far west farms were to cost $1.00 per acre and with fees were to cost $228 for 160 acres.

Four land offices were provided for by the President, at Perry, Enid, Alva, and Woodward. The law provided the division of the Outlet into counties so Secretary of the Interior, Hoke Smith created seven counties designated as K, L, M, N, O, P, and Q, renamed at a later date Kay, Grant, Woods, Woodward, Garfield, Noble and Pawnee. The government surveyed the land and marked cornerstones were buried at each corner of the quarter section. Three hundred and twenty acres were reserved in each county seats, also a plot of four acres for court house and in land office counties, one extra acre for the land office. The Chilocco Indian school land, The Osage, Kaw, Otoe-Missouria and Ponca lands, Fort Supply Military reservation and saline lands were withheld from homestead entry. Section 16 and 36 of each township were set apart for the benefit of public schools. Sections 13 and 33 in each township were set apart for college and normal schools or public buildings. Two rods were reserved on each side of every section for highways thus fixing a road four rods wide on every section line.

It was a time of utter confusion and conflicting instructions as shown in an item from the Perry Daily Times date September 16, 1893: "A stone with six marks on its edges marks the corner of a township. These corners are six miles apart each way, and the line of five corner stones, north and south and east-west between them are marked only on two sides. The north and south line are marked only on the north and south edges of the stone, one mark on the north for every mile the corner is from the township corner on the north and as many marks on the south side as it is to the south township corner."

"In the same manner the east and west line are marked on their edges, indicating distance east and west to the corner of the township. In the interior of each township there are twenty-five section corners and a large number of quarter section corners. The latter are all marked 1-4, the marks facing the west on the north and south lines and on the east and west lines, the north. The section corners extend in five lines east and west and it is west from the east line of the township, and on its south side one mark for each mile it is from the south line. Thus, if a corner stone has three marks on the east side and two on the south by refering to a township plat you will find that the section southwest of it is 27, the one northwest 21, etc. or if there are four marks on the east and one on the south side of the stone, the section is 16, the one to the northeast is 9 and so on. By practicing picking out different sections on the plat in that way you will soon be able to tell the numbers."

Maps of the Cherokee Strip, which showed the lands to be homesteaded were available to the settlers, but it took someone familiar with land markings to be able to understand the section and township lines. The settlers had to study the above information in between the times they were getting themselves and their horses in shape for the "run".

A most perplexing question was whether intending settlers could make the run from the east side of the lands to be opened. The Act of March 3, 1893, provided that the Secretary of the Interior should prescribe rules and regulations regarding the opening. The proclamation of August 19, placed no inhibition on intending settlers from making the run from any Indian reservation nor did it state the 100 foot strip did not lie along the eastern side of the lands to be opened, but on August 14, Silas W. Lemoreux, Commissioner of the General Land Office said that no entry would permitted from the Osage or Creek counties. On August 28, Secretary Hoke Smith said in answer of a letter of inquiry, "They will not be permitted to do so" meaning entering from the Osage or Ponca reservations, and on August 30, Acting Secretary John M. Reyno said "that settlers would not be permitted to enter the Strip from any Indian Reservations." These conflicting orders caused several legal fights over the lands. At a later date the courts upheld the rights of the people who made the run from the eastern edge of the Strip.

Registration Booths

A strip of land one hundred feet wide just inside the line was opened as a zone where people might camp. An effort was made to avoid the evils of earlier openings and check the Sooners by having every person who expected to make the run register. Nine registration booths were set up in the zone: #1 north of Stillwater; #2 north of Orlando; #3 north of Hennessey; #4 south of Goodwin and a mile north of Higgins, Texas; #5 Kiowa, Kansas; #6 south of Cameron, Kansas; #7 near Caldwell, Kansas; #8 near Hunnewell, Kansas; #9 south of Arkansas City, Kansas.

On Monday, September 11, the nine booths, five on the northern border of the Outlet, and four on the southern border, were opened to persons wishing to register. Forty-five clerks were detailed from the General Land Office to take charge of the booths. The booths were kept open to the public from seven am to six pm each business day.

On September 14, at Booth #2 north of Orlando, certificate No. 14,892 was issued. Sometime during that day Booth #9 south of Arkansas City issued Certificate No. 12,370. The next day certificate No. 10,892 was issued at Booth #1 north of Stillwater.

Here were issued: 1. Homestead entry form designated A. 2. Soldiers

Orlando, September 15, 1893 — Boomers.

Cherokee Strip 1893

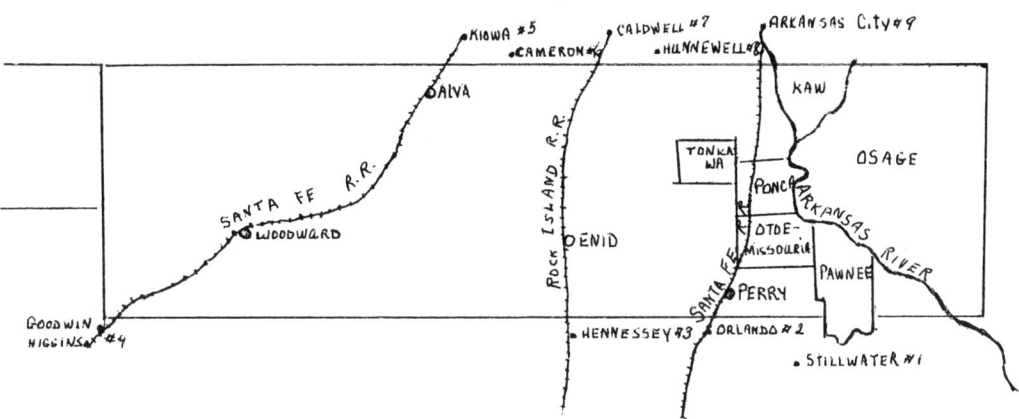

Registration booths were set up on the cattle trails leading into the Strip or on the railroads. The land office towns were located on the railroads near springs of water.

declaratory statement designated B. 3. Soldiers declaratory statement as agent designated C. Town lot entry form designated D. When these forms were filled out settlers were issued certificate E for A, B, and C entry forms, F for entry form D. A settler could get both homestead and town lot certificates.

The plan to discourage Sooners did not work but did cause needless suffering. The lines were still blocks long with people waiting to register at 12:00, the hour set for the run. So it was decided on the spot that it was not necessary to register.

One disgusted would be settler who departed, as many did, wrote in rhyme a letter to Hoke Smith, Secretary of Interior:

"O Hokey Smith enclosed herewith
Please find my compliments
I went to the Strip, but never a nip
Had I in recompence
I stood in line 3 days and nights
I never slept or drank
Believing I'd secure my rights
And give to you my thanks
O Hokey Smith ... O Pokey Smith,
I'll sure get even yet,
I'll load my gun, We'll have some fun
Be sure you don't forget"

Another unknown poet left the following:

A Tenderfoot's Lament

Jest haul up a stool and chuck down yer grip.
You see I'm fresh back from the Cherokee Strip.
Hain't flyin' so high as I did when I went.
I'm all busted up. There here life in a tent.
Is cracked up too far - Its no palace car.
Say, wuz you ever down to Orlando
That town near the Strip called Orlando?

Twuz September 16th o'th year '93-
Ketch onto the date and listen me
It makes me smile yet to think o'that ride;
All creation wuz there and several beside
A whalin' big band, All red hot for land.
The land that you see from Orlando-
That sweet scented town of Orlando.

It looked pretty much like a big county fair
For all kinds of things wuz a'goin' on there-
Faro and shell games right out on the grass.
With water a sellin'n at five cents a glass.
Just betwixt you and me. There was nothing much free
But scrappin' an' the air at Orlando-
That free-for-all town of Orlando.

Fer five scorchin' days we stood in ranks
Fer five weary nights we slept on the banks
Of a dried up creek near "Booth number 2"
Each waitin' his turn and gee! How it blew.
Wuz it hot? You'v hern tell
How the same is in _____ well
That climate wuz wuss at Orlando
It's the south side of H____L at Orlando.

The fellers what run fer to get'em a claim.
They faired purty much, I recon, the same;
The grass wuz all burned, and the creeks wuz all dry.
An' Old Boreas, he got on a terrible high,
An' the way folks lit out Wuz more like a rout
Than you'ever see in Orlando
In ten thousand years at Orlando.

Hoke Smith's Booths "Orlando" Cherokee Outlet, 1893.
(Courtesy Oklahoma Historical Society)

The "Run" of September 16, 1893

The President's message published August 19, fixed the date for the opening of the Cherokee Strip for Saturday, September 16, 1893, at 12 o'clock noon central standard time.

Some of the settlers were planning to enter by train, others purchased horses for riding. Many had thoroughbreds, others had bronchos from Wyoming, some had cow ponies familiar with the plains. There were covered wagons, spring wagons, buggies, buckboards, carts, even surreys were on hand. Some had fixed up hind wheels of wagons by inserting poles in the place of coupling poles for tongues and then had fastened on ordinary wagon spring seats. One such outfit drawn by a set of mules made a very successful run. Some would-be settlers even tried bicycles. According to one writer two bicycles were connected by a bar so as to operated on the railroad track but this ingenious contrivance was ruled out.

All sorts of reports were circulated to the waiting settlers. One was that everyone must walk, one that no trains would be allowed to enter. Another that trains could run only 5 miles an hour, another report was that lumber wagons

First train leaving the line north of Orlando for Perry Sept 16, 1893.

(Courtesy Oklahoma Historical Society)

must have white horses driven by red headed girls.

In an order of September 11, Secretary Hoke Smith directed that no railroad train be permitted to enter the Outlet during the six hours before the time of opening. For three hours after said time of opening trains should be allowed to enter the Outlet only under the following regulations: 1. They must be for general use and not leased or chartered to any favored passenger or passengers. 2. The trains should be stationed at the edge of the lands to be opened at least thirty minutes before the hour of opening. 3. No one should enter a train as a passenger unless he held a certificate from one of the booths. 4. The trains might start upon lands of the Outlet any time after the hour of the opening. 5. Trains must stop at every station, and at intermediate points not more than five miles apart. 6. The trains should be limited to fifteen miles per hour. 7. The regular local rates of passenger charges should not be exceeded. 8. No one should be allowed to board the trains after they entered the Outlet.

The morning of the run there were 10 trains of 10 box cars each at Arkanas City; 39 cars with a huge Mallet engine at Hennessey; 42 cars with 3 engines at Orlando. Perry, the county seat of County "P" and the principle townsite on the main line of the Santa Fe was the goal of thousands of settlers. It was predicted that Perry would probably be the metropolis of Oklahoma which was probably the reason that Perry was thoroughly Soonered.

At regular intervals along the line, army troops' commanders were located. Each was attended by a trumpeter. At the signal of twelve o'clock from the commander the trumpeter was to blow the note of advance. Soldiers along the line were to fire their rifles as signals to go.

At 12:00 noon September 16, 1893, the plain of Perry was as vacant as on the morning of creation, it was an area of no inhabitants. Then over the dry and dusty region a gun shot rang out — thousands and thousands of people sprang into action, they moved in frantic disorder, yet within a short time they settled into comparative quiet. They came, all classes and kinds, from all directions, afoot, horse-back, on lumber wagons, carriages and railroads. There were honest men and thieves, bankers and paupers, adventureres, who wanted homes.

The Opening
By Daisy Lemon Coldiron

Morning

September 16, 1893,
   O day of promise, O day of Destiny!

Dawn! the past is behind you.
The Cherokee Strip is before you.
This! is the day of the Run!

Along a far-flung border line
The smoke of a thousand camp fires greets the dawn.
Smell of bacon and coffee sizzling over cow chip fires;
Horses eating oats from feed boxes nailed to the rear of the wagons;
A rooster sticks his head through the slats of a chicken coop
And crows a welcome to the sun.
A woman climbs down from a prairie schooner
And children tumble out after her,
Rubbing the sleep from their eyes
To meet the dreams in the eyes of their mother.
The dawn fire glows on the eastern horizon, a smoldering crimson flame,
Then bursts into bloom like a great golden calla . . .
And the long, slow lines move steadily on.
Prairie schooners, covered wagons, surreys, buggies,
Two wheeled carts, jiggling in and out of the line.
(Wagon umbrellas over the drivers) leaving their dust behind.
From the bank of the meandering Chicaskia
I see you breaking camp and moving on . . .

On the line.

On banks of Cow Creek September 16, 1893. L-R: James Stumpff, Elmer Rice, Theodore Stumpff, Col. Rice, unkown, Mrs. Rice, Mrs. Perry, Ladd Stumpff, Mr. Bennett, Bill Stumpff, little girl unknown.

And soldiers of peace from the Cimarron bottoms,
Each seeking your place in the sun.
A tense, suppressed excitement,
A tightening of saddle girths,
Stout hands inspecting stout harness,
Strapping on canteens, loading the water casks.
Laughing, jibing, sweating,
Faces streaked with dust and brine,
Pouring over maps of the "new country,"
U.S. soldiers riding the line.

Noon

Now the sun is in his zenith!
The trooper in front raises his hand!
A pistol shot rings out, sings out —
Ho for the Promised Land!

Simultaneously other shots ring out
Along a far-flung, embattled line,
And before the smoke has cleared away
Hell breaks loose on the border.
A mad stampede of cursing man,
Snorting beast, careening carriage!
Lashing! Panting, Yelling!
Horsemen silently leaning forward
With heads bent low upon their horses' necks,
Nerves tense-drawn, every muscle fiber in action!
Parched and swollen tongues!
Sun-baked, scorching prairies!
Deep-rutted cattle trails with disappearing horsemen
Leaving behind a saffron fog of choking, blinding dust!
. . . Dry creek beds, prairie dog towns . . .
Jack rabbits bobbing up and down
Through the wiry, blue stem grass . . .
A Coyote looks back once over his shoulder
And lopes off to the hills in the distance.

Oh the long scattered line comes rushing on
Pell mell, panting in the sun . . .
Leaping gulches! Rushing on ! on ! on !
As if the mouth of hell had spewed them forth
And all the grinning imps of Satan were prodding them on!

Night

Beyond the dying rim of the world,
The sun sinks at last to a well-earned rest
And healing wings of the night come fanning
The slumber of a new-born State in the West.
On the cooling breast of the billowing prairies
Settler lie down to sleep and dream
Of an empire founded on toil and struggle,
Faith and Hope and the rainbow gleam.

Birth of Perry

It was thought that Perry would be located at the stops on the railroad at Wharton or four miles north at Arnett, but land here was claimed by some Cherokee Indians. A rider was attached to the bill that opened the Cherokee Strip, designed to protect a few Cherokee families who had improved land in the extreme eastern edge of the Strip. These families, not to exceed 70, would be allowed to claim the land they had improved. A group representing a family of Cherokees, mainly minor children, took advantage of this rider to claim land around the depots of the railroads. When the Townsite Commission, appointed by the U.S. Government, found these claims, they moved the site for the land office town a mile north. Unfortunately, this put a portion of the townsite in Cow Creek. Perry was named for one of these commissioners, J. A. Perry.

Maps of Perry supposedly from the U.S. Land Office, were handed out to the settlers. These maps showed "Block A" which could be settled and "Block B" which was government property. This was confusing as the government had put down two water wells — one in "Block A", the other in "Block B". The post office, which was little more than a shack, was placed between the two wells in "Block A". While the soldiers sent by the government were in "Block B", the instruction to the man building the land office, was to put it near the depot, so the land office was not on either block but by the railroad tracks. Soldiers stationed at Perry kept settlers off "Block B" until friends of the "right" people could claim it, then the soldiers cleared the settlers from "Block A" the real property of the government. James Malone, register in the land office was indicted for taking bribes in connection with the land office, but charges were dropped when he resigned and left town.

To further confuse the issue, no agency was appointed to file the claims for town lots. The original townsite comprised 320 acres, legal description: NE 22 and NW 23 21N 1W I.M. This platted land, exclusive of reservation for city parks and school reserves, made 635 residential lots of fifty by one

"Hell's Half Acre Perry O.T. '93." — (Courtesy Oklahoma Historical Society)

hundred forty feet. The settlers spread over the original townsite, and to care for the immense throng of future residents, five additions were settled and platted. They are known as Northeast, North, Northwest, West and South Perry. The streets were numbered on November 16, 1893.

Ernie W. Jones, lawyer, newspaperman and Judge, described the first hours of Perry thus: "The first persons arriving from the south line, about twelve miles, were surprised to find the townsite covered with settlers. Evidently the over anxious, or overly smart, lot seekers, had started before noon or had lain in the bed of Cow Creek near the new City until noon and then within fifteen or twenty minutes had their lots staked for ownership. It was a seething mass of humanity from a half mile south of Government Acre, now the Court House Park, the center of the City, to more than a half mile north and west. Morning came and the new City was in full bloom. Thousands of tents had been erected, wooden buildings started in construction with the multitude moving like an army of ants, everybody on the rustle making preparations for their new home. Every kind, style, manner of store was in operation. The tramp of the thousands of feet of humanity and horses had rendered the air unbearable almost to the degree of suffocation from the dust created. For the next three weeks one could not see for a distance of twenty feet ahead in the Government Acre. The black sand covered everything. Men went to the creek to wash their clothes and hang them out to dry, finding a friend to guard his lot while he was away doing his laundry work. Each lot had from one to a dozen claimants. Fighting and turmoil began. The sheriff and his score of deputies were kept busy. A dozen Deputy U.S. Marshals were assisting. The county officials took up their quarters in tents and hastily constructed shacks. Water was scarce while beer sold at one dollar a bottle the first day. Ham and eggs with crackers were the regulation meal the first few days. Signs of "Restaurant", "Coffee like your Mother made", greeted the eye at every turn. It was necessary to line up for everything you went after, from saloon, postoffice, restaurants and even to the stores for a change of socks or a clean shirt. With a few weeks of this going on, if somebody gave a yell "line up" one instinctively hastened to get close behind the first person he saw in front. It had come to line up or be shut out."

More confusion was caused by doubt about the land around the land office. This block, called Hell's Half Acre, was bounded on the north by "D" street, on the west by the ally running through the block north and south, on the east by the Santa Fe tracks and the south by "C" street. This attracted not only the land attorneys and agents but, according to E. W. Jones in his "Early Day History of Perry, OK" "Also came the saloons, gambling houses and dance halls. Tents were packed and jammed taking every inch of available space. The homesteader lined up, awaiting his turn to gain entrance to the land office, slept in the narrow passage ways between tents for a month until the land office was moved to the Court House square. "Hell's Half Acre" not for a minute belied its name. No night passed but that the discharge of fire arms was promiscuous. Every person sleeping in a tent layed a little closer to the ground as the bullets traveled overhead and but one death was reported, that of a poor fellow found lying in a tent with the bullet hole entering the corner of the right eye and passing through the head.

The Buck Horn Saloon, doing business from the first hour after the opening in a large tent near the Land Office on the acre amassed a fortune in the first few days. Under the management of Joe and Ted Hill it came afterwards to be known as the Honk a Tonk Saloon, dance hall and gambling house combined in a frame structure that succeeded the tent.

Riot reigned supreme day and night. Each saloon on the acre as well as over the city for that matter had its music, the fiddle and piano being the limit in orchestration and the latest popular airs of the day were on tap at all times, sung better or worse dependent on the condition of the singer from an alcholic standpoint. "After the Strip is Opened" a very appropriate parody on "After the Ball," was a reigning favorite. It was sold on the street for the small sum of ten cents, and one singer in the Blue Bell made $23.00 by singing that many

Post Office in Government Acre (Courthouse Park).
(from Cherokee Strip Museum - Perry)

verses or one verse that many times to a disappointed homeseeker who ran against a sooner on his contested farm and was trying to drown his sorrows.

> After the Strip is opened, After the run is made,
> After your horse is buried, After your debts are paid,
> Many a sucker is kicking, many have lost their grip,
> Many a man will wish he had died coming to the Strip.

With the removal of the land office, the lawyers departed, saloons went out of business, buildings were moved off, Hell's Half Acre was short lived.

Government Acre or Courthouse Park is a five acre tract of ground that was reserved in the center of the business section of the city when the townsite was laid out by Uncle Sam. For a month, until driven off by the soldiers, businessmen conducted various businesses on the four sides facing the streets. From November 1, 1893, for a year the square remained windswept and dusty, this expanse broken only by the small frame post office building and the land office which had been moved from Hell's Half Acre and placed on the west side of the square just north of where the Library is now located. The post office had been moved from the southwest corner to the northwest corner.

In the spring of 1895, the ground was plowed and sowed to alfalfa to keep down the suffocating cloud of dust and sand. The alfalfa was cut and fed to the horses of the fire department.

In 1896, Will T. Little, newspaperman and homesteader in Black Bear township obtained permission from the commissioners to plant the square to elm trees. After plowing up the alfalfa the ground was thoroughly disced and harrowed and 8,600 seedling Wisconsin white elm sprouts were placed in furrows east and west. These little sprouts were from six to eight inches in length and apparently every one took root. From this crop, one or two years later, Mr. Little sold enough trees to repay the county for all the expenses of stock and planting. Also trees were transplanted to a second city park of three acres and to two school reserves of three acres each.

Government Acre
(from Cherokee Strip Museum - Perry)

The west acre of the courthouse park was reserved by the Federal Government. The south half of this acre was deeded to the City of Perry for a library building. Andrew Carnegie donated $10,000 for the building and the citizens of Perry voted a one mill tax levy. The library has served the county since 1909.

The county officials of "P" county were housed in rooms upstairs and down around the square. A courthouse became a necessity with no funds from taxation for construction. T. M. Richardson and Sons, lumberman of Perry, came to the rescue and constructed a two story frame building 70 x 100 feet, on the east side of the square. This frame building did noble service for nearly twenty years. The present structure was constructed in 1916.

The first post office building was replaced by a stone building. It was constructed with money from subscriptions of merchants on the north and west side of the square and was leased to the U.S. government for $1.00 a year.

Rev. Simon P. Myers, Presbyterian, called his flock together and held services on Sunday, the day after the run. Several of the other churches held services the following Sunday.

The first schools were subscription schools, where each pupil paid by the month to attend school. In 1894, the three story native stone schoolhouse had been built in time for the fall term.

Before the year's end in 1893, a telephone line was constructed from the southeast corner of the square in Perry to Wharton, a mile south. Trains did not stop at Perry but did at Wharton. This created a problem with freight that had to be hauled over roads fording Cow Creek. To make matters worse there was no way to know if the freight had arrived except by making a trip to Wharton. Passengers also had to detrain there with no way to communicate their presence. This telephone line was soon extended to Pawnee and Stillwater because of a lack of train service to these towns. This line was further extended and in 1919 became the Southwestern Bell Telephone Company.

Congressional Investigation

In the 53rd Congress, 1st session, House resolution no. 27 of the United States House of Representatives dated September 28, 1893 requested the Secretary of War to report to the House what part the Army of the United States had in the opening of the Cherokee Strip, September 16, 1893 and whether any outrages were committed by the troops upon any civilians entering said Strip. The following was extracted from the report by the Secretary of War to the House on November 2, 1893.

"First District, south, Wharton, Capt. John B. Johnson, commanding Troop B, Third Cavalry, was sent out in June with instructions to clear the strip of intruders and cattle, and remained on this duty until the operation in connection with the opening of the Strip. He says as far as he knows, his district was clear of "Sooners" at time of opening. No force was required here to hold the people back before the proper time to start, but at about three minutes before 12 o'clock someone fired a shot, which was the prescribed signal to start, the line broke and Capt. Johnson seeing the impossibility of checking the people, and to make it fair to all, gave the signal to go. There was no conflict here, and the immense crowds were managed without riot or bloodshed, and order was maintained throughout. The conduct of corporals Jacob Tolin and August Arnold is highly commended.

Perry Land-Office Capt. B. H. Rogers, commanding Company G Thirteenth Infantry had charge of affairs here. Twenty-four "Sooners" were arrested on the morning of the opening. The town was opened in a very orderly manner and there were no disturbance that required the interference of the command. No soldiers were placed outside of the land office to run the line, that duty being performed by deputy United States Marshals.

The following was abstracted from testimony given under oath. All gave the soldiers a clean bill of health.

Camp U. S. Troops, Perry, Oklahoma, October 4, 1893, Capt. Benjamin H. Rogers, 13th Infantry states as following: "I arrived here with my company on the 14th of September. The grass was mostly all burned then. It was extremely dry weather and the supposition was then that it was done by sparks from the locomotives. A well-believed rumor was in circulation that it was done by people who were to ship forage into the country to sell and who had sent agents in at night to do the work. I had no drunkenness amongst my men during the opening, and did not until they were paid some two weeks later. Twenty-four "sooners" were arrested by me on the morning of the opening, they being hidden in the several ravines running through the town site of Perry. They were held until the rush was over and then released.

The town was opened in a very orderly manner. There were no general disturbance that required the interference of troops. One man, a supposed murderer, was arrested by me and held all night until it was found the man he assulted was not in as precarious a condition as first supposed, when he was released after ascertaining his name, address, etc. which information was turned over to the chief deputy United States marshal on duty at Perry. The names of the twenty-four "sooners" arrested were turned into the land office, with the time and place of arrest noted.

My orders when I came here were from the commanding officer at Fort Sill, Oklahoma. They were to proceed to Perry, Oklahoma and to camp there; to cooperate with the civil authorities to preserve peace; to protect the United States land office and United States post office, and all government property when necessary. General instructions covering all the points in the President's proclamation were received by me from Lt. Col. D. Parker, 13th Inf. commanding troops in the Strip, on the 19th of September — three days after the opening. They had been sent in ample time, but blocked up in the mail somewhere. In the absence of these special instructions, I used my own judgment regarding the part the troops were to take at the opening.

I did not place any men outside of the land office to run the line; and that duty was performed by deputy United States marshals. I visited the land office frequently to see that order was preserved, and on no visit did I see anything but an orderly crowd. I kept my men well in hand in case of disturbance. That has been done up to the present day; all men being required to remain in camp during the open hours at the land office unless special permission is given to be absent."

Perry, Oklahoma, October 5, 1893 — J. C. Scruggs, sheriff of P county (county seat, Perry) stated under oath as follows: "I came here on Saturday, the 16th of September, from the line — starting at 12 o'clock about 9 miles from Perry. I entered on duty as sheriff immediately after arrival here, Capt. Roberts turned over to me a man he had in arrest for knocking a man on the head who was thought to be murdered. Prairie fires were burning in every direction; I crossed three fires on my run. I do not think the soldiers had anything to do with starting the fires. I started half a mile west of Orlando to make the run. Capt. Johnson's men were there. A false start was made to the west of me about one and a half minutes before the time. The soldier got out of the way, as it was useless to try to stop the crowd. No shots were fired there at all.

Perry, Oklahoma, October 5, 1893 Harry Colton, farmer of Logan county, Oklahoma states under oath as follows: I have been here since about September 12, 1893, was here under orders of the Departments — Prairie fires were general, burning in every direction. Saw many between here and Arkansas City night September 14, when returning to Perry. Am satisfied they, or many of them originated from railroad engines — wind blowing — county dry. Fires were burning where there were no troops.

Perry, Oklahoma, October 5, 1893, Dick T. Morgan, lawyer of Perry, Oklahoma, stated under oath as follows: "I came here on September 16, on second train. Have been here since, except Sundays. I was at the booth on the line near Arkansas City two different days, as I recall, during registration; also, on two different days at booths near Orlando, south of here."

W. S. Morris of Perry, Oklahoma, fully corroborates, under oath, statements of others as to the good conduct of the troops.

Perry, Oklahoma, October 5, 1893, Emery E. Westervelt, railroad agent at Wharton, being duly sworn, states as follows: "I have been agent at Wharton over a year; was here at the opening and prior and since. Capt. J. B. Johnson

Land Office in "Hell's Half Acre"
(from Cherokee Strip Museum - Perry)

came here about the 1st of September with about 60 men. They arrested a saloon-keeper from Oklahoma City, dressed in old soldier's clothes. He was not a soldier; they held him here until after the opening. Capt. Rogers came here about two days before the opening and Capt. Johnson left soon after his arrival. On the day of the opening there were any number of sooners here — several hundred. There were twenty-five or fifty men who were on the town site by some kind of permission before the opening and immediately after 12 o'clock many of them went right onto lots. By 12:20 all of the center of Perry was taken — hundreds of men in here then. The nearest line to run from was from 8½ to 9 miles south. I was here about 12:10 and so far as I saw, the troops did nothing to prevent the sooners taking lots. No sooners came here until noon; they were all around in the brush waiting for the crowd to commence to come in. There was no cavalry here, only infantry, and it was impossible for dismounted soldiers to keep such a large number of sooners out of the country around the town site. There were the usual prairie fires burning at this time of year. Know nothing as to origin of fires."

Perry, Oklahoma, October 5, 1893, J. E. Malone, register land office at Perry, Oklahoma stated under oath as follows: "I have been on duty here since the night of September 15, and have seen the troops daily. They have proffered their assistance to the officials in my department whenever requested."

Perry, Oklahoma, October 5, 1893, J. H. King, receiver land office at Perry, Oklahoma stated under oath as follows: "I have been here on duty since the 14 of September about noon and the troops have performed their duties fully. I saw them go out and come back, hunting for sooners and so did the chief clerk of the land office, Davis."

To whom it may concern: This is to certify that I was upon the Perry townsite in Oklahoma Territory, before and after the opening of the Cherokee Strip (in the capacity of boarding boss) sworn to 7th of October, 1893.

Perry, Oklahoma, October 5, 1893, Mr. C. P. Drace, postmaster at Perry, Oklahoma, stated under oath as follows: "I have been here since about the 8th of September, 1893, as postmaster. Have heard no complaints about the troops whatever, neither as to bribery, drunkenness, nor misconduct.

(note by Capt. Lee — Parties in Perry say that the postmaster, Drace, immediately after opening 12 o'clock at Perry, was seen dragging a tent from his office; and his brother held down a good lot immediately after 12 o'clock.)

Camp of United States Troops Perry, Oklahoma, October 9, 1893, Capt. Benjamin H. Rogers, 13th Inf., states as follows: "I arrived at Wharton, Oklahoma, on the morning of Thursday, the 14th of September with my company G, 13th Inf., and went into camp on the railroad right-of-way. On that day, I visited Perry townsite, a mile distant, to pick out a camping ground, and found no one on the townsite but the postmaster, who pointed out block B, which had the Government well bored in the center, and said he thought that it was reserved as a public park. I returned to camp and that afternoon was visited by a Mr. Mora, who stated that he was in the employ of the Government and had been sent to Perry to survey the townsite. He showed me a map which had B block marked as a public park reserve, and which he stated was in accordance with his survey. On the morning I moved my company and camped them as marked in ink on map (herewith). My left line of tents were in a 50 foot alley and my right line on the rear of the lots on south side of block B. Officer's tents were mostly in Seventh street. The lots on block B run north and south, therefore my occupation of the block presented no obstacle to the people who wished to take their chances on staking out lots there. The next day, at about half past 12, the rush commenced, and the first intimation I had that B block was not a reserve was about a quarter of 1 o'clock, when I saw Mr. Mora himself show a person where to place his stakes on that block. I, in the meantime, had advised several people that they were wasting time by staking out lots in that block, as it had been reserved as a public park I instructed my men to do the same thing and ex-Governor Swineford, special agent in charge, who was standing by my tent advised them the same.

"I immediately accosted Mr. Mora and asked him what he meant by advising people to locate on that square, and he gave me some evasive answer. Shortly after I again saw him locate another person on block B, and I again asked him what he meant, and he then told me that block B was not reserved as a park but was open to settlement, and he pulled a blue map out of his pocket which he said was the latest map from Washington, and which placed the public park reserve at the other end of the town, east of Cow Creek. I asked him how long the map had been in Perry, and he replied, "a day or so" but he had no time to notify me. From that time I and my men notified everyone interested that the block was open to settlement.

"I understand that the first map made out at Wichita and sent to Washington was not approved in so far as having the park reserve adjoining the courthouse square as it would injure the city to have so much open space in one place, but the corrected map was, according to Mora himself, there in ample time for me to have been notified and to have moved my company over to the Government Acre. But I charge that Mr. Mora, for reasons best known to himself, kept the map in his own possession until his scheme was carried out. My reasons for camping on the supposed park reserve instead of on the courthouse square were that the government well had been sunk on the park reserve and as it comprised the only water fit to drink in that section of the town I knew I would have to guard it and wished to camp close to it for that purpose."

The Engineer. (Running the line with a transit on the Plains.)

Chapter 3
COUNTY ACTIVITIES

Sports

Ernie Jones in his "Early Day History of Perry, Oklahoma" reported "A baseball game was played on the square the first Fourth of July between the Perry team and the Ponca Indians, the red skins being badly defeated."

"In the summer of 1894, Perry fans enjoyed some good contests on the diamond at the fairgrounds on the Russell claim adjoining town on the south side of Cow Creek and west of state highway 86. The team was known as the 'Famous' named after the store owned by Lobsitz and McCreedie who furnished the uniforms gratis. The team was as follows: McIntire, catcher; Billie Wayne and Kid Bevis, pitchers; Billy McCoy, 1st base; John McClintic, shortstop; Homer Bostick and O.H. Bevis, third base; Butch Meyers, Frank Adams and Hank Bevis, outfielders."

Baseball was very popular in the early 1900s and every town and village seemed to have at least one ball team complete with uniforms supplied by local businessmen. Even the boys had teams as shown in this picture taken in Billings, Oklahoma about 1905. The uniforms were supplied by Cooper and Beaty who had a general merchandise store in Billings. Baseball was a favorite sport of the Indians. In the photograph of the Red Rock team several of the players are Otoe Indians.

Perry sometimes calls itself "The Wrestling Capital of the World." One

Early day Red Rock Baseball Team. (Front Row L to R): Charles Arkeketa, C. L. Atherton, Ernie (Judge) Jones, Ted Borash, W. E. (Judge) Rice. (Standing L to R): Barney Woolverton, D. R. (Doc) Swaney, Walt Babb, Horton Homoratha.

of the pioneers of wrestling in Noble County was Frank Briscoe. He was born and raised on his father's homestead north of Perry. Following grade school at the Nelson rural school and high school at Perry, he attended Oklahoma A & M (OSU) where he wrestled on the college team. After serving in the Infantry during World War I, he returned to Perry in 1922.

There was no wrestling program here at that time, in fact there were only five teams in the whole state. He got the programs started in the Perry High School. The first state champion that he produced was Jap Wood, brother of Mrs. Ted Newton, who won at 125 pounds. The first olympic champion that he coached was Jack VanBebber who came along in 1932 (see Jack VanBebber).

John Divine, for whom John Divine Hall at Perry High School is named, coached several wrestlers to fame, the most famous, probably, is Dan Hodge. Dan won everyone of his 46 bouts for the University of Oklahoma, 36 of them by falls. Three times a National Collegiate Champion of 177 pounds, he twice was voted the outstanding wrestler of the NCAA tournament. Twice he was an olympic wrestler, placing fifth in 1952 at Helsiki, Finland, before his college career started and winning the silver medal in the 1956 Games at Melbourne, Australia. After his collegiate wrestling career, Dan Hodge won National Amateur and National Golden Glove Championship in Boxing becoming the first athlete in

Boys baseball team — Billings, Oklahoma 1905.

more than 50 years to win national championship in both sports.

At one time in the mid 1950s, all but one of the first string wrestlers on the University of Oklahoma wrestling team were natives of Perry. The other was from the east coast and was quickly adopted by Perry.

In the 1960s Dan Hodge began a career as a Professional wrestler and appeared on National television. He won the title of Junior Heavyweight champion. During the 1970s and 1980s the Perry High School wrestling team won a record of 12 consecutive Class 2A state championships.

Jack VanBebber and Dan Hodge were inducted into the National Wrestling Hall of Fame in Stillwater, Oklahoma on September 11, 1976. They were among the 14 original members inducted.

Politics

By proclaimation of the Governor, the first city election in Perry was held October 21, 1893. Conventions were held and many tickets placed in the field. Booths were erected around the square to give the orators the opportunity to air the merits of the different candidates. John Brogan, who conducted a grocery, was the Democratic nominee for mayor and defeated E.B. Mentz, prominent in legal circles, leader of the Republican ticket. Volney Hoggatt, lawyer; G. W. Doughty, a one armed pension attorney and old soldier, Green B. Raum, Jr. who conducted his campaign in the saloons of the city also ran for mayor.

At this election George Farrar was elected treasurer over John Kirby and Arnold Miller. Duff Tillery easily defeated H.G. Stewart, H.M. Garn and A.D. Taylor for the city attorneyship. Lon Whorton was elected city clerk over E.B. Guthrey, J.D. Gilbert, and H.A. Daughtery. For Police Judge A. Jacobs defeated J.R. Campbell and W.B. Taylor. George S. Livingston was elected assessor over Joe Lynch and J.M. Couch, a son of Captain Couch, the historic boomer. For council men of the first ward S.E. McMichael, John Banks, W.H. Vonderheiden, C.A. Weidemen and J.T. Hill were the candidates, the last two named being elected. Both were prominent saloon men. In the second ward J.C. Dulaney and Howard Friend were elected over Sol Arkush, Mike Lynch, C.B. Taylor and Tom Morris. In the third ward Lawrence Drake and Henry Flock defeated the field composed of J.E. Burlingame, S.E. Richardson, C.L. Parke and H.C. Wallerstedt. For the fourth ward J.P. McKinnis and W.T. Cutler were successful while J.S. Ammerman, R.T. Conover, W.J. Hoyt and Daniel Ainsworth also ran.

The first body of law makers for the new city met October 28, 1893, on the upper floor of the Hill Brothers saloon and gambling house. The gambling tables were brought into legitimate use while the hired help took a welcome rest for the night. The first ordinance adopted was defining the corporate limits of the city. Mayor Brogan appointed William Tilghman chief of Police and John Thornhill "Fatty Hopkins" and Heck Thomas, policemen.

From Autobiography of Charles Francis Colcord: "My most interesting experience in active political work was in 1896. On the farm adjoining mine on the east was Charles D. Shrader, a big fine looking fellow from Nebraska who had been a lawyer and was one of the leading men in the "Populist" party. The Democrats and Populists were in fusion at that time, trying to best Dennis T. Flynn for delegate to congress. The Democrats had promised to support a Populist and Shrader, who was one of the leading Populists of the territory, was the logical man. I was out of the territory when the convention was held. When I got home Shrader came over to my house and told me how Dennis Flynn's friends had manipulated the convention and nominated a preacher by the name of J.Y. Callahan, who was believed to have no chance of election. A few days later at the Guthrie fair I met Joe Severns, a Deputy U.S. Marshal and a Democrat. He was one of the fellows who, Shrader told me, had helped make Callahan the Populist nominee for Flynn. So when I shook hands with Joe I chided him about beating my friend Shrader and told him I was going to take this preacher and beat Flynn. "You can't do it," he said, "I will do it." I said "and I'll bet you $500 that I can." Then a Guthrie doctor wanted $500 more which I covered. In a little while I got another bet of $500 making $1,500 in all. Bill Grimes, ex-U.S. Marshall and friend of Flynn bet "the preacher will lose the territory and the county he lives in and won't even carry his own township."

When I went back to Perry we Democrats there held a conference and decided to invite Callahan to open his campaign at Perry with a big barbeque. When the time came a week or ten days later we killed several head of cattle, several fine, fat muttons and some fat shoats. Crops had been short, so a good meal went mighty well with the Cherokee Strip settlers. We had an immense crowd. When we had everybody ready for the barbecue, Bob Galbreath and I walked over to the hotel to inquire about Callahan. While we were standing there he drove up in an old buckboard. He was unshaven, had a black Prince Albert coat covered with dust from the road and had on a dollar wool hat. He was about the toughest looking hombre I ever saw. At that moment it looked to me like my bets were worth about fifteen cents. I whispered

Street Scene.

to Galbreath to take charge of him, get him shaved and cleaned up. When the crowd began to arrive and fill up the public square, I began to feel genuinely nervous. Finally the preacher got up and began talking in his old sing-song way and I knew my bets were all gone. But when he warmed up it wasn't long until he had the whole crowd standing and yelling. He was a wonderful talker and had Dennis Flynn beaten a mile. I loaned him some money for his campaign and he went to Pawnee and all over the eastern part of the Territory and got fine results. Callahan was elected by a majority of over eleven hundred votes.

During that same campaign in the fall of 1896, the county candidates asked me to take charge of their campaign and handled it just as I used to handle a cow outfit. I borrowed a big show tent from Joe and Ted Hill, the one in which they had sold iced beer the afternoon of the opening of Perry, and I made every candidate bring along his roll of bedding.

With two grub wagons loaded with plenty of "sow-bosom" and beans and other good things to eat, we started out. I located a camp in the center of a township and started each candidate up a section line with instructions for him to visit every farmer and his family on that line and invite them all to come over and take supper with us, have a good time and hear some good speeches and music. We repeated this program in every township in the country. We certainly had good speakers, Henry Johnston, Sam Harris, Joe King,

Mrs. Henry S. Johnston - January, 1927.

Tom Doyle, Jim Diggs and others, as well as the candidates, would come out and make talks. This novel campaign was a great success and we elected a full Democratic ticket in Noble County. Judge Ethan Allen, Thomas Bryan, and W.M. Bowles were among the county officers we elected."

Politics in Oklahoma has always followed a rocky road. There was a rumor circulated when Henry S. Johnston was brought up on charges that if Oklahoma impeached another governor, she would revert back to a territory (see Henry S. Johnston). At the election of Manuel Herrick, Oklahoma was represented by a Noble County representative few people were proud of. However, Noble County has contributed two Oklahoma governors including the first Republican elected to that office (see Henry Bellmon). Two representatives to U.S. Congress (see Dick T. Morgan and Manuel Herrick), and a U.S. Senator, Henry Bellmon.

Noble County's reputation for being serious about politics caused an amusing incident during Henry Bellmons' campaign for office of Senator. Four Democratic ladies invaded Billings, hometown of Henry Bellmon. Their colorful bus attracted the attention of a group of patients from the Billings Nursing Home, taking a morning stroll. Nearly all these patients are grown-ups who formerly were in the Enid State School for the mentally retarded. Residents of the Billings area greet them on their strolls and find them friendly, cheerful people. The Democratic women saw the canes some of these people carried and reported an angry mob of "about 50 people armed with shovels, sticks and stones, chased them out of town. One of the Okahoma City newspapers printed the story across the top of page one. The Midwest City and UPI story said it was presumed that most of the residents of Billings were Republicans, since it is Bellmon's hometown. (Records show there were about 75 Republicans in the Billings precinct compared to about 225 Democrats.)

101 Ranch

Col. George W. Miller was one of the hundred cattlemen who leased the Cherokee Outlet under the Cherokee Stip Cattleman Association. His brand was 101 on the left hip of all livestock he owned. He built a half dugout on the Salt Fork of the Arkansas River in 1879. Col. Miller, a Confederate veteran had moved westward from Kentucky via Baxter Springs, Kansas, to Oklahoma's Cherokee Strip. When the government ordered all the cattlemen to tear down their fences and move off the Cherokee Strip, Miller and his sons, Joe, Zack and George L., rented the hunting grounds of the Ponca Indian tribe. In the spring of 1895, 2,000 acres of pasture land were plowed and put into feed crops for winter feed although their lease was for their grazing purposes only. The original sod house served as their headquarters

101 Ranch White House 1923.
(Courtesy Oklahoma Historical Society).

until 1903, when the first three-story frame was built. This house burned to the ground six years later and was replaced by the even grander 17 room frame named "The White House." This massive home had porticoes on two sides and a porte cochere. Col. George W. Miller died in 1903, but his sons carried on and by 1905, the Millers had 15,000 acres under cultivation in corn, wheat, Kaffir corn, alfalfa, cane millet and various other feed crops. Melons were raised in large quantities and special attention was given to the selection of farm seeds. At that time, the Millers "white wonder" corn became famous the world over.

With their large herd of buffalo, cattle by the thousands and stallions of all breeds, from Arabian to Thoroughbreds, the prominence of the 101 Ranch as a diversified livestock breeding enterprise was well known.

On June 11, 1905, the Miller brothers presented an outdoor show. It is believed to have been the biggest show of its kind ever presented at that time in the United States, drawing an estimated 75,000 persons to the area. It was entertainment given for members and friends of the National Editorial Association. The show, was presented in a mammoth arena just west of the town of Bliss (now Marland).

For the show, the Santa Fe railroad laid a side track out of Ponca City to Bliss. Trains were run in from all directions and stopped at the Bliss substation. Members of the national Editorial Association from every state in the union were present, traveling in sleeping cars where they stayed at night since there were no other accommodations in the community. The show began shortly after two o'clock when the procession, nearly a mile in length and escorted by the Miller Brothers, came in the east entrance. In the lead was the cavalry band, behind which came the famous old Indian war chief, Geronimo, hero of a hundred battles with the whites. He bowed and smiled and enjoyed immensely the attention he attracted. The procession was followed by bronco busting, Indian ball, cattle roping and the Indian dance and powwow. The performances of Miss Lucille Mulhall and her trained horse attracted the most attention. At the closing of the day a wagon train was attacked by the Indians on a hill south of the amphitheater and the spectators were given a chance to see what an Indian raid meant to the pioneers. In the gathering dusk, the burning wagons with howling Indians riding fiercely about them, caused a feeling of awe to settle over the entire assembly and there was hardly a person present that didn't feel the blood tingle in his veins at the portrayal. From 1904, down

101 Ranch, Indians appearing in the show.
(Courtesy Oklahoma Historical Soceity).

through the following years, the Miller brothers continued holding the annual round-up at the ranch. A rodeo arena was constructed at the headquarters with a seating capacity of ten thousand.

In addition to the rodeos, they had many industries due to their diversified farming operation. The meat packing industry was perhaps the major one on the ranch. It had a capacity daily of a hundred hogs and fifty cattle. In the 1920s, the meat products were sold and delivered by refrigerated trucks within a radius of one hundred miles of the ranch. Soon after the establishment of the packing plant, the Millers built a tannery for the hides and as the price of the cured hides dropped, built a harness and saddle shop which also made buffalo and cattle robes, rugs and fur and leather coats, fancy pocketbooks, etc.

A modern dairy barn and creamery were built to house the five hundred registered Holstein cows and to take care of the dairy products. In connection with the dairy there was a modern ice cream plant.

Several oil wells produced sufficient oil for the Millers to have an oil refinery of their own at the ranch headquarters. This refinery made a hundred barrels of gasoline daily. The gasoline was sold at the ranch filling station. Large quantities of kerosene and fuel oil sufficient to supply ranch needs were made from the crude oil produced on the ranch.

The 101 Ranch operated a large general store, which was the mercantile center for northern Oklahoma for a number of years. The 101 Ranch cafe developed from the old "ranch chuck house" into a restaurant modern in every respect. Every article of food with the exception of olives, sugar and coffee were produced right on the ranch. In the same way the "bunk house" became a modern hotel.

A modern laundry was operated by the Miller brothers. It was equipped with modern machinery and did all the laundry work of the ranch, including that for its employees. In addition it served the needs of the surrounding country.

A special building was erected and equipped for the cider and canning industry. Approximately two hundred barrels of cider were manufactured each fall. Several thousand pounds of apple butter and jelly were manufactured annually. On each original jar of apple butter was the following guarantee: "This apple butter is guaranteed to keep all winter, if you can keep the children away from it."

The ranch had its own machine, blacksmith, woodwork, and repair shops. Two blacksmiths were kept busy shoeing horses and repairing farm machinery. In addition to the ranch work, the shop served the needs of the farmers of the surrounding country. There was a complete ice plant with a capacity of ten tons daily maintained on the ranch. The plant provided ice for the ranch and its employees as well as the farmers of the community.

Perhaps one of the most interesting industries was the novelty factory. All kinds of Indian rugs, beaded belts and clothing, drums, bows and arrows, silver jewelry, etc. were manufactured in this factory by Indians employed by the Miller brothers. In addition, a large assortment of souvenir leather goods such as cowboy belts, boy's chaps and vests were made and sold along with the Indian articles.

The 101 Ranch lands contained approximately 172 sections. They embraced an approximate total of 110,000 acres that sprawled like patchwork over the Oklahoma plains in Kay, Noble, Osage and Pawnee counties. Necessarily, several sets of improvements were maintained, so that the employees could be near their work. The Bar L headquarters was such a place. The improvements consisted of a large ranch house for the foreman, barns and corrals, silos, blacksmith shop, and several bunk houses for the cowboys. At this place the cowboys lived throughout the year caring for the livestock and repairing fences of the ranges.

On this vast domain there were located three towns: Marland, Red Rock and White Eagle, and three hundred miles of fences, costing $50,000 enclosed its tremendous confines. For twenty-two miles US Highway 77 crossed these lands and was paralleled most of the way with the Santa Fe railroad which had a station at Marland, located three and one half miles south of the "White House". Large warehouses and shipping pens, accommodating more than two thousand cattle at one time, were located at Marland, the shipping center and the telephone in the central business office at the headquarters connected with every foreman on the ranch, over thirty-five miles of private wire, and long distance service was used. Mail was delivered from Marland to and fro by mounted carriers detailed at all times for this purpose.

The guest book "who's who" included Presidents: Theodore Roosevelt and Warren G. Harding; Vice President, Charles Curtis; boxers, Jack Dempsey, Gene Tunney, Jess Willard and Jack Johnson, author, Mary Roberts Rinehart visisted the ranch to add atmosphere to her book, "Lost Ecstacy." Sidney Smith drew Andy Gump on the "White House" walls. Nancy Astor, General John J. Pershing, newspaper tycoon, William Randolph Hearst, Bacon Rind, Osage chief; all visited the ranch house.

Adm. Richard Byrd rode an elephant. Bandmaster, John Phillip Sousa was inducted into the Ponca Indian tribe. William Jennings Bryan

Parade and Show Wagons 101 Ranch - 1923.
(Courtesy Oklahoma Historical Society)

shook hands with Tony, the ranch's pet bear. (Tony drank soda pop by the case. He died of a kidney ailment, blamed on too much soda pop.) Will Rogers sang cowboys songs all night long with Mrs. Pawnee Bill at the piano.

Spectacular sights greeted presidents and celebrities at the gate of the ranch's majestic white house: flocks of ostriches, zebras, camels, wild boars, tigers and anteaters. Sometimes they saw performers rehearsing, mounted cossacks, dancing mules, clowns, charioteers and stagecoach "hold-ups" and Indian "attacks."

The 101 Ranch continued the spirit of the west through its Wild West shows and Miller Bros. Circus that toured the United States and Europe, as well as through entertainment on the ranch, round-ups and rodeos. Hard-riding cowboys became show performers as trick ropers, riders and shooters, bronco busters and bull riders. Will Rogers started his career with the Wild West show, doing his trick rope act. One day he had to stretch his act because the group following him didn't show up. In order to cover the fact he was repeating his act, he started talking. This was such a hit that soon he was doing more talking than rope twirling. He eventually discontinued the rope tricks. The Millers were among the first to produce moving pictures and some movies were filmed on the ranch. The "thundering herds" of buffalo, which no longer existed at the time of movie cameras, were recreated by the herd of buffalo on the ranch which was driven in a circle around the camera. The same was done with the herd of longhorns to depict the herds that had made the cattle drives. Tom Mix spent several years on the ranch and made his first movie there. Other cowboy stars were Ken Maynard, Buck Jones and Hoot Gibson. One of the best known cowboys performers was Bill Pickett, Choctaw-Negro, who invented bulldogging.

Hundreds of persons, about 3,000 at one time, were employed at the ranch. Nearly everything they needed was on the ranch. Besides these things already listed, the ranch had schools, its own newspaper, magazine and script (money).

The Millers gave the world another

Three threshing outfits in one field - 101 Ranch.
(Courtesy Oklahoma Historical Society)

sport, the terrapin derby. It became an annual Labor Day event with 114 terrapins in the first and 2,373 two years later. All the entry money went to the winners. Santa Fe ran excursion trains to the events such as terrapin derbies and round ups. In 1923, twenty trains took 50,000 people to the 30th Anniversary of the Cherokee Strip to see the Wild West show presented by 1,000 Indians and 500 cowboys.

The empire which had flourished in all its ventures started fading after the stock market crash of 1929. Three major causes of its downfall were death, debt and depression according to Ellsworth Collings and Alma Miller English, only daughter of George W. Miller, in their book **The 101 Ranch.**

The 1927 death of Joe Miller, overcome by carbon monoxide, actually started the downfall. His imagination as a showman and vision as a ranchman had been major factors in the success. George Lee, the financier who kept the ranch on an even keel died in a car accident on an icy road in 1929. Zack, the cowman and horsetrader, was left with the enormous task of operating the ranch.

Zack was forced to sell the Wild West show in 1931. Most of the livestock and equipment were sold and then the land. He tried desperately to save the "White House" with an auction of its rosewood furniture, valuable paintings, antiques and Indian relics. He fought bitterly to save it but the big home was cleaned out "to the last fruit jar."

Zack left for Texas in 1937 and died in Waco in 1952. He is buried on Cowboy Hill overlooking the once vast empire. The federal government acquired the land for resettlement with 8,000 acres subdivided, leased and eventually purchased by the settlers. In 1943, the grand old house was sold and razed by the purchasers who hauled away the lumber. The assets of the ranch were liquidated in 1943.

Early Oil Fields

The North American Indians were using oil as medicine, as a constituent of paint and in religious ceremonies long before Columbus. The white people used the oil for medicine and it was sold as "Indian oil" and "Snake oil" but some oil had been refined into "coal oil" or kerosene to burn in lamps. The beeswax and tallow candles, and the lard-oil, sperm-oil and whale-oil lamps were unsatisfactory and fuel supplies were limited. Kerosene was still the main purpose of oil exploration even in early Oklahoma as one oil company was the I.T.I.O., the initials standing for Indian Territory Illuminating Oil Company. The coming of the automobile with its demands for gasoline and oil made even exploration in Noble county attractive.

In 1902, the businessmen of Perry financed a drilling outfit and began operations a mile south of the city. The hole was abandoned at close to 1,200 feet on account of caving trouble, the drill still being in the red beds or red shale. Then a location was made east of the city just north of the Grace Hill cemetery. Mother earth was punctured here to the extent of about 1,100 feet and the hole again "blowed up" by reason of drilling difficulties and financial disability. Thus ended the operations of the Perry Oil and Gas Co.

The red beds posed real problems for the early oil drillers. These beds are a succession of red shale and sand from the surface and extend deeper than they could drill at that time. From the center of this mass of red beds below the Cimarron River, the individual beds change color to the east, north and west, the red beds and accompanying sandstones give place to light colored shales and limestones.

In December of 1908, E.W. Marland, a Pennsylvania oil operator visited the 101 Ranch. The Ponca area attracted his attention and he secured a lease from the Miller Brothers and started a well in February of 1909. This well was abandoned and the second, completed in the spring of 1910, was a gas well. Marland and his associates continued operations until 1917, when their ninth well marked the discovery of the Ponca City pool. It was the Willie Cry number 1 in section 8 township 25 north range 2 east (Kay county) with an initial production of 130 barrels of oil at a depth of 1,500 feet. An item of interest from the Billings News of December 2, 1927: "Ponca City, November 29. Announcement of the death of "Buck"Essary somewhere in South America has been received by the Miller brothers of the 101 Ranch, for whom Essary, an oil well drilling contractor drilled a wildcat test just north of the old town of Bliss, about ten years ago. Essary, a former minister, had a varied career, ending with his becoming an oil drilling contractor. He had been working in the northern Oklahoma area when the Miller brothers contracted with him to drill the deep test at Marland, on acreage which they owned. When at a depth of between 500 and 600 feet, Essary had the misfortune to lose a bit in the hole and all effort to regain it proved futile. Finally in desperation, Essary informed George L. Miller that he was going down into the hole and find out what was wrong. "You'll do nothing of the kind" Miller declared. "Well, I sure am." responded Essary, "and if you don't want to see me do it, you'd better get away from here pretty quick." "I'm gone" announced Miller, "but I want you to remember that I forbade you going into that hole, and really prefer very much that you should not go."

Miller left the location and Essary, catching a chicken, lowered the fowl into the hole to a dept of something over 500 feet to ascertain if there was any gas. When the chicken was pulled back alive, Essary got ready for his descent, and before he quit he had made five separate trips downward over 500 feet, his last one being successful. Essary tied a rope around his body and had his men lower him into the hole. The first trip downward was just something of an exploration trip to see what was wrong and learn if anything could be done. On each succeeding trip he took some instrument with him, hoping to be able to dislodge the fastened bit so it could be raised. The first four trips availed him nothing. "Essary came up mad one time." says Will A. Brooks of the ranch in relating the experiences. Brooks was present at the test all the time Essary was making his round trips into the hole. "We had certain signals whereby we raised and lowered Essary in the hole. For some reason the signals were mixed up and instead of raising Essary the boys lowered him and he found himself underneath the fastened bit and looking up at it, he ascertained evidently all at once just what a predicament he was in and how near death really was. But he was not conquered by any means and then made the fifth trip down. This time he took a small crowbar with him and with this he did dislodge the bit. After he was brought up from the hole, his driller and tool dresser got the bit out. He finished the hole without any further trouble, although eventualy it was a duster."

Mr. Essary made his residence in Billings for over a year and Lew Robinson, an old resident and driller was one of the boys that lowered Mr. Essary into the Marland test. Mr. Essary was the contractor on the Chas. Brinker test six miles east of Billings during the early oil boom. (end of quote).

In 1907, two brothers named Cunningham, put down a hole near Morrison on the Tyre farm in section 7 of Autry township to a depth of 2,850 feet. 13 sands were found in this well and all filled with water except at 2,477 feet where a 6 million cubic feet gas flow was struck, the well finally drowned out with the strike of sand at 2,850 feet while drilling a five-inch hole making further casing off of the water impossible.

Just after the Tyre well started a hole was begun in section 36 of Rock township, southeast of Perry 10 miles by A. VonTackey of Pittsburg and Stillwater Associates. This hole was drilled to a depth of 2,100 and raised much excitement at times with showing of gas and oil found at different depths. After nearly a year of troublesome drilling, the well was abandoned though the promoters still insisted that oil was to be found at this location if the depth could be reached.

At this time the geologist or "rock hound" was unknown in local oil circles. Locations were made regardless of anti-clines, syn-cline, structures or formations. "Wildcatters", men who drilled for oil in new fields, often used "doodlebugs", men who witched for oil with a forked stick or played a hunch as to where to drill. One man related that he tied a can to a dog's tail and where the can fell off was where he drilled his well. In the latter part of January 1916, the geologist came to Noble county, but it took several years and a few successes in finding oil before either the "rock hound" or his young assistant, the "pebble pup" was respected.

In the spring of 1915, Dr. G.P. Sutherland and his partner Dr. Gist of Amarillo, Texas, became interested in copper and lead prospecting southeast of Perry. They had no original intention of getting into the oil business but along in July after fruitless prospecting for their favorite metals, they secured a block of leases in Walnut township. A light rotary rig was installed, the first used in northern Oklahoma. The rotary was a success at the beginning but at a depth of about 1,400 feet the machinery proved too light and trouble began. The hard limestone stratas were encountered along about a thousand feet and alternated with blue shale and two or three shallow oil sands. At 700 feet a substantial showing of oil was had. The drilling was intermittent and development was deferred until a company took over with a standard rig.

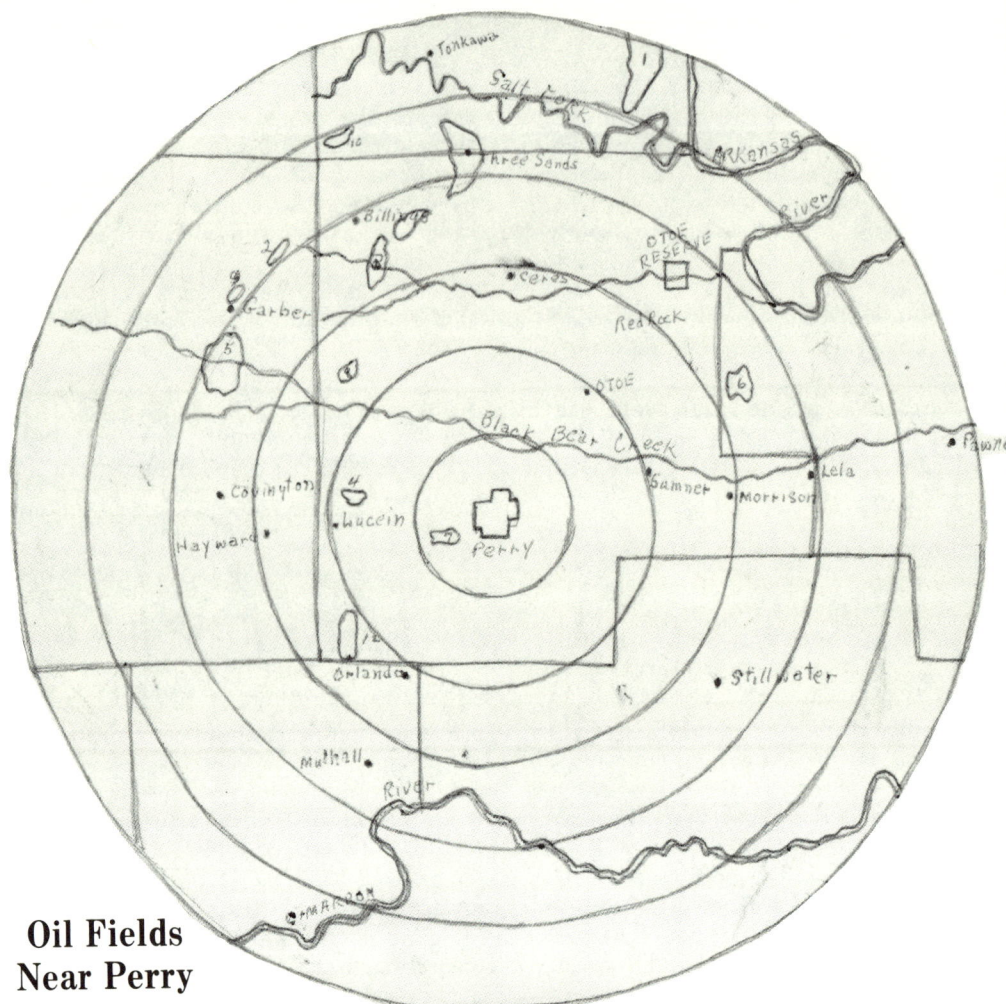

Oil Fields Near Perry

1. Ponca City
2. Barnes
3. Billings
4. Bu-V-Bar
5. Garber
6. Morrison or Watchorn
7. Perry
8. Polo
9. Sarah Whipple
10. Thomas
11. Tonkawa or Three Sands
12. Lucein

In the fall of 1915, Robert Watchorn and associates started drilling on section 33 Township 23 north Range 3 east, just over the county line in Pawnee county. Morrison is the nearest town to this, the Watchorn field, and was headquarters for oil field supplies.

Here the red beds and real difficult drilling was passed at about 1,600 feet with limestone at 2,060. At this depth a gas flow of 35,000,000 cubic feet was struck. Another well was drilled a half mile south of this well by Watchorn resulting in another big gasser. The Altafer well, a half mile west of Watchorn number 1, was drilled to 3,890 feet and a flow receded and the well made but about twenty barrels daily at 4,010 feet which was not considered sufficient flow for such a deep undertaking.

In February, 1917, the Mid-Co Petroleum Co. completed the discovery well of the Billings pool in section 22 of White Rock township. This production in this well was 250 barrels of oil per day from sand at a depth of 2,121 to 2,136 feet. In June, 1919, the initial well was deepened to 2,334 feet at which depth it produced 150 barrels of oil per day. The Billings pool proper covered a small area, about one section square, the adjoining extensions of north and east Billings increased the length of the pool four miles.

The first well completed as a producer in the Polo pool was drilled by the Prairie Oil and Gas Co. in section 17 of Oakdale township with an initial production of 25 barrels of oil per day from sand at a depth of 2,074 feet in 1920.

In the latter part of 1922, a wildcat well was drilled on the Munn brothers structure southwest of Perry. The Twin State Oil Co. completed the discovery well in section 29 of Watkins township which had an initial production of 6 million cubic feet of gas at a depth of 1,500 feet. Later, the Perry Service Co. drilled a second well in section 28 for 2 million cubic feet of gas in the 1,500 feet pay sand. The wells in this field furnished the gas supply for the city of Perry for many years.

The discovery of the Thomas pool was completed by the Marland Oil Co. in May, 1924, as a 250 barrel oil well. It was drilled to a depth of 2,055 feet, where a productive sand, since called the Thomas sand, was found; however, the major portion of the oil in this pool came from the Wilcox sand. The name, Wilcox, was given to this sand from a well completed in the Glen Pool near Tulsa by H.F. Wilcox on April 29, 1914. It is below the Mississippi line and is of the ordovician age. Most of the oil in Oklahoma has been found in the Wilcox sand. The age of the surface rocks in Noble county is either Permian or Pennsylvania formations.

There'll never be days again like they had in Three Sands when oil fever seized the minds of men along the Noble county - Kay county line. Men talked millions, spent millions, made millions, turned down millions and otherwise dwelt in a heady but tough boom town.

It all started in June, 1921, when Lew Wentz struck oil on his Sam McKee lease near what was to become one of the state's most spectacular boomtowns and went on to recover 9.5 million barrels of oil from the 160 acre tract.

Three Sands appeared overnight, and by 1923, had reached a population of 6,000. The post office came on May 4, 1923. In its most illustrious moment, Three Sands never appeared to be anymore than a shanty town. A newspaperman, visiting the town made this classic remark: "Three Sands isn't a town — it's a crowd."

More than 500 wooden, 84-foot California Standard derricks dotted the Three Sands skyline in an area four miles long and two miles wide. The derricks were so thick because a well was needed for each depth or "sand". Fourteen levels, four of these major oil sands, were found in this field. In many places, legs of three different derricks rested on one corner base.

Three Sands was known as the "Billion Dollar Spot" in the early 1920s. In two years from the date of its discovery, the pool produced 60 million barrels of high grade crude which tested 43 B. Sales for the period brought over $250 million. In 1923 alone, the field produced 33 million barrels of crude oil. During its peak, production ran an average of more than 100,000 barrels of crude daily. Sam McKee, who sold none of his royalty, at one time was drawing $140,000 a month. In April, 1924, Tom B. Slick, known as the greatest wildcatter of them all drilled 4,000 feet into the Wilcox sand.

Three Sands "never shut down." Men worked 8 hour tours (pronounced towers) after which they would unwind for 8 hours, mostly in the saloons, then would sleep 8 hours and back to work. With a third of the workers on each tour, the town was lively the whole 24 hours.

Then by 1930, the boom was over. The post office with its sagging roof, held down by guy wires lingered on, long after the boom had passed but finally closed in 1957. Only a few wells are left, pumping sluggishly, some on reclaimed land that is sowed to wheat, and some on ravaged land, land that fell victim to salt water, oil and disregard.

From a wheat field, to a boom town, to a ghost town in ten years is the story of Three Sands, today marked only by a dot on the Oklahoma state highway map.

County Agents

S. E. Laird came to Perry from New Salem, Illinois, September 1, 1899. Following is an account of his first impressions of Perry. "On arriving in Perry, we purchased a claim from a Mr. Gilliand one mile north on what is now highway 77."

"Lining the street were 17 saloons and around the square teams were hitched to all kinds of vehicles. The streets were deep with dust which was blowing into the business houses and covering merchandise."

"Perry during those days was a busy place. Freight was transferred to all the surrounding towns and long strings of wagons could be seen daily, winding their way to and from Perry."

"On September 16, 1910, a spectacular flower parade was put on and a good agriculture exhibit displayed. This was the first year that I had taken part in the celebration to any great extent having a farm product float in this procession. This gave the celebration committee the idea of entering an agriculture exhibit in the state fair at Oklahoma City. Consequently, I was asked to donate and place the exhibit with the assistance of J. H. Nelson and Mrs. Laird. We selected the very best products from our county exhibit and were awarded fourth premium in Oklahoma City. In 1911, Mr. Nelson and I made another exhibit at the state fair and were able to win first prize. It was at the State Fair this year I was appointed as County Agent hired by the government to begin work on February 2, 1912. It being a new project, it was hard to get the work started as the farmers did not understand what it was all about."

Noble County agriculture exhibit at Oklahoma State Fair - 1913.

"In 1912 and 1913 county agriculture exhibits were made at the state fair, which was a part of the county agent's duties. Our 1913 exhibit was shipped directly from the state fair to the National Dry Farming Congress at Tulsa and won a prize there. It was then brought to Perry and placed in the real estate office of W. H. Kirchner, who was chairman of the Celebration committee."

S. E. Laird, first county agent in Noble county continued until the spring of 1922 being transferred to Kay county and later to Garfield County.

The Passing of the County Farm Agents
Mrs. Jessie McCafferty
Home Demonstration Agent

An Agent for eleven years
Worked hard and shed bitter tears,
Agricultural work to advance
And give the big boys a chance;
Now he has an amusement park
And is giving the boys a lark.
Now this is not a fake.
The name of the place is Laird's Lake.
Then came E.E. Horton who seemed
 true blue.
He came in nineteen twenty-two.
In just a year, ill health came
In a sanitarium he still remains.
A third Agent then was tried
And with Agricultural problems vied.

S. E. Laird with his "cotton picker". It allowed three men to harvest as much cotton, in the same period of time, as it had taken nine men earlier.

B.B. Braly was his name.
Alas, now he's in the oil game.
A fourth Agent now comes on
With no hair on top his dome,
He worked so hard trying to find out

What the work was all about;
At last he saw some things to do
Financing fairs to see them through,
Boys clubs, dairy work, prairie dogs
 and such,
Handing out information in a bunch;
He knows all the county roads.
Knows the solid, knows the clubs,
Knows enough now a good agent to be,
Ready to do work for thee,
Sadly now I must relate,
Another county acts as bait,
To lure this expeirenced man
They offer him so much more mon.
R.C. Guthrie is the name
Of the great man of fame.
Goodbye old - hello new
County Agent we welcome you.

Lake Laird 1930s. The slide in front of the bath house on left. At right is the toboggan slide (electrically operated), behind is the concession and dance pavilion which was also used as a meeting place for large groups.

Homemakers' Groups

The forerunners of the present Homemakers Groups were called "tomatoe clubs." The Home Demonstration Agents would go to the home of a member and give a demonstration on canning tomatoes. Tomatoes were important in the diet of the early settlers as they added vitamin C and could be used in many ways to vary the foods served. A group of ladies gathered for the demonstration. They picked the tomatoes, scalded and peeled them, washed the canning jars and canned all the tomatoes that were ready. The pressure cookers, used to can the tomatoes, could and did explode sometimes. The heat was hard to regulate with the coal or wood-burning stoves.

Even after the clubs were expanded to include other demonstrations, it is hard to trace their histories as they would disband during the summer work season and then reorganize in the fall, sometimes changing the name of the club in the process.

Mrs. E. M. Whitney was the first Home Demonstration Agent. Her husband had a drug store on the square. In 1918 and 1919 Mrs. George (Ada) Sims was the next. She served as County Superintendant of Schools for Noble County as well as teaching in Noble County for four years. Later she moved to California. Mrs. Elizabeth Richardson Ritthaler was next.

Mrs. Jessie S. McCafferty came to Noble county from Jefferson county, Kansas on January 1, 1922 to begin duties as Home Demonstration Agent.

Mrs. Jessie S. McCafferty.

She organized the clubs the first year she was here, the first two clubs,

Homemakers' Groups / 35

Chicken Calling Demonstration — men are county Agents and specialists from Stillwater extension at Oklahoma A&M (OSU).

Sewing School - January 29, 1930 in Home Demonstration agent's room in court house. (on back of photo): Snow was 4 ft. deep outside. Mrs. McCafferty second from left.

Marland Club and the Merry-Go-Round dropped out, but the Black Bear, Hunter and Oak Grove have survived.

On January 24, 1922 a chicken culling demonstration was held at the home of Mrs. John M. Steichen by Mrs. McCafferty, assisted by Ott Edson, extension specialist of Stillwater Poultry Department. Twenty persons were present including Mr. E. E. Horton, county agent. Plans were made to organize a community club. On February 21, 1922, the women gathered at the home of Mrs. J. H. Clark. A club was organized with twelve charter members: Mrs. John M. Steichen was elected president; Mrs. J. H. Clark, vice-president; and Mrs. Charles Thrash, secretary. Other members were Mrs. Wilbur Wallerstedt, Miss Illa Wallerstedt, Mrs. Ben Undernear, Mrs. W. Milligan, Miss Mary Hejtmanek, Miss Susan Steichen, Mrs. Henry Hicks, Mrs. Anna Hayne, Mrs. John Clark, and Miss Creta Clark. Mrs. McCafferty gave a demonstration on making a fireless cooker. The club was named the Community Welfare Club. On October 21, at a meeting with Miss Susan Steichen the name was changed to Black Bear Club.

When the Oak Grove Home Demonstration club met November 1, 1939, minutes of the Oak Grove Benefit Club of October 13, 1922 were read. This club was organized at Mrs. R. Notley's west of Morrison, with twenty members. The club became a demonstration club a few weeks later at a meeting in the home of Mrs. Jack Crane. Three charter members still belonged to the club in 1939. They were Mrs. J.D.E. Owen, Mrs. Jack Crane and Mrs. S. Fitchett.

The meeting in 1939 was shortened because of Mrs. James' son being brought home painfully injured. Members present were Mesdames S. Fitchett, John Highfill, Bill James, J.D.E. Owen, Gottfried Schmaltz, John Sloan, Charles Van Arsdell, Adolph Masat, Jack Crane, George Wills and Minnie Frank.

Mrs. McCafferty was agent for twelve years during which time "Patiently she worked with us through the toddling stage until, as she said, we were able to work alone," Black Bear Club. To the 414 club members she was "Just like grandmother." She seldom came to the 4-H club meeting without a treat for the children, such as a sample of soap, baking powder or cook book. One time she gave each one a sea shell she had collected on a trip to California.

When Mrs. McCafferty took sick suddenly and died in 1934, it was a shock to the county-wide groups. A memorial was held and each club read a paper or sang a song in her memory. One long poem from the Ceres Club contained these lines:

When August meeting time had come,
We gathered in the Mornhinweg home.
We noticed as we gathered there
A new face in Mrs. McCafferty's chair
Upon inquiry our hearts with sorrow did fill
For we learned our leader was seriously ill

Willing Workers Club. When they cooked in the club meetings they were required to wear white dresses and white caps.

So with saddened hearts we planned to send
Cards and flowers to our dear friend
But greater yet was our sorrow, indeed
When we learned that she was too ill to read.
And ere the morning sun did arise
She had gone to join the great club in the skies.

Mrs. McCafferty was followed by Miss Myra Moore, Mrs. Grace Hampton, Mrs. Gladys Umwake and Miss Betty Qualls.

Over the years many clubs came and went but Hunter club south of Perry is another one that has lasted since 1922. The Happy Home Club was organized in 1924. A club called the Willing Workers south and east of Perry disbanded in 1926 some of the members started a new club called the Ladies of 76 because they were in school district #76. Most of the clubs were named for the school, community or town where the members lived but some were named for other reasons. One is called Wimodausis, short for wives, mothers, daughters or sisters, their relationship to the breadwinner.

Garden Clubs

The Columbine Unit of Perry Garden Clubs was organized April 10, 1929 in the home of Mrs. H. C. Nicholson. Charter members were Mrs. John Mildfelt, Mrs. Bush Bowman, Miss Bell Hosteller, Mrs. Leo Lobsitz, Mrs. W. B. Ringler, Mrs. Fred Lindeman, Mrs. G. A. Ley, Mrs. H. G. Donley, Mrs. E. R. Martin and Mrs. George Clark. Mrs. Nicholson was elected first president of the group and Mrs. Ringler, vice-president. One of the first projects was giving free petunia seeds to residents all over Perry.

On June 10, 1930, the next spring after they were organized, the club sponsored a flower show which was attended by 613 guests. They also sponsored a yard contest for adults and a garden contest for children under the age of 14 which had 30 entrants.

In a paper by Mrs. H. G. Donley is found: "We had real nice flower shows. I remember one on the south side of the square, one on the north side, another on the west side and one on the northwest corner in the Masonic building. At that show we had a small art exhibit of paintings in connection with it and it was there that my mother, Mrs. S. E. (Maybelle) Laird and myself with the aid of my father, S. E. Laird made a yard scene on a table. My father cut blocks of Bermuda grass from our yard, to use for the lawn on the table. We borrowed a pretty card board house (replica of a large house, used by one of the lumber yards for a window display), which we used in a back corner, having a small electric light in it and a small lattice fence at the rear in the back yard. It also had a rock garden and pool, using a mirror for the pool, with little trees, shrubs and flowers.

Our club had so many enjoyable times. We would go around to view different flower gardens and we had such large nice family picnics, some at Perry Lake Park (CCC), Lions west park, Lake Laird north of town where a new addition is now being developed called Quail Creek Addition, in the backyard of Mrs. Fred (Carrie) Lindeman and also Mrs. Ray (Elsie) Cruts' backyard and in the basement of the Presbyterian Church one rainy night."

On guest day each year the Garden Club ladies would dress for their afternoon teas: "On May 16, 1937 in the backyard flower garden of Mrs. H. C. Nicholson, Mrs. Lonzo Grant and Mrs. Everett Nelson, wearing ankle length gowns of pastel organdie and picture hats, officiated at the punch bowls which had been placed on either end of the long refreshment table. The table had been placed at the south end of the shaded yard, near a rose-filled bird bath. A crystal bowl of dark red rose buds centered the table and was flanked with miniature May poles composed of tall green tapers with cellophane streamers in rainbow colors. The grass was of parsley." - *The Perry Daily Journal.*

When Mrs. Charles Forney was president of the North Central District, the Columbine Club organized units for Garden Clubs at Shidler, Kingfisher, Tonkawa, Red Rock, Covington, Blackwell, Newkirk, Pawnee and Lucien as well as four units in Perry: The Petunia, The Marigold and two black units, one for ladies and one for boys to help them landscape and care for the grounds at the Blaine school.

The Petunia Unit was organized January 11, 1937 with Mrs. Everett Frueh as the first president. Charter members were Mrs. W. W. Carson, Mrs. G. E. Doyle, Mrs. R. J. Huston, Mrs. Harry Hartman, Mrs. Milt Devore, Mrs. Ivan Kennedy, Mrs. Forrest Currell, Mrs. Louise Nicewander, Mrs. W. S. Wilson, Mrs. L. O. Render, Mrs. Emil Voigt, Mrs. Veril Brorsen, Mrs. Ralph A. Hackinson, Mrs. W. B. Cavitt and Mrs. Henry Grant.

The Marigold Unit was organized January 1, 1938 with Mrs. Merle Allen as president. Mrs. Marion Watson, vice-president, Mrs. W. F. Redding, secretary and Mrs. George Dolezal, treasurer. Other charter members were Mrs. Dick Eby, Mrs. Joe Dolezal, Mrs. Pete Cordes, Mrs. A. L. Smith, Mrs. Tom Wetzel, Mrs. Wilbur Mouser, Mrs. Bill Lynch, Mrs. Melvin Bereihan, Mrs. W. A. Box, Mrs. A. W. Tucker, Mrs. Luther Dotts, and Mrs. Jake Casparis.

The Perry Garden Club Council was organized in 1939. Some of the projects of the Garden clubs are planters and entry markers on the roads leading into Perry. A marker was placed in the courthouse park honoring Mr. Will T. Little who was instrumental in getting the elm trees planted in the parks. Pin oaks were planted around the marker. The road to Grace Hill cemetery was improved from an unsightly and unkept county road into a landscaped road leading into the cemetery. Other projects have been done through the years to keep Perry beautiful.

At Red Rock the Zinnia Garden Club was organized April 14, 1938 at the home of Mrs. Ray Purvis with eight members. Mrs. Arthur Veach was elected president, Mrs. Anis Sullins, vice-president, Mrs. Lewis Evans, secretary and Mrs. Clint Atherton, treasurer.

The Mum Garden Club of Billings was organized on march of 1968 by the Petunia Unit of Perry. Charter members were Mrs. Gladys Baker, Mrs. Glen Combrink, Mrs. Oscar Combrink, Mrs. Charles Durkee, Mrs. Ronald Horn, Mrs. Fred Kingery, Mrs. Perry Mason, Mrs. Rex Mattiesen, Mrs. Herman Schultz and Mrs. Charles Young.

Sweetpea Garden club of Lucien had the following charter members: Mrs. Lester McNeal, Mrs. Alfred Hamm, Mrs. Miles Maxwell, Mrs. Grimes, Mrs. Otto West, Mrs. Clara Rupp, Mrs. Harold Staats, Mrs. Ott Clark, Mrs. James Coffelt, and Mrs. Loys Hise.

Highway Department — Division Four

Noble county's first paved road project was let in 1924 for a stretch of highway from the city limits of Perry to a point ten miles north. This was a part of highway 77 and when completed linked Oklahoma City with Wichita, Kansas.

In 1930, higway 64 was paved from Perry to Bill's Corner, leaving a stretch of ten miles unpaved from Lela to Bill's Corner. When highway 64 was completed it connected east and west Oklahoma.

The road from Bill's Corner to Stillwater was paved in 1933, but it was not until 1949 that pavement extended north from Bill's corner to Ponca City. At this time it was highway 40 but is now highway 177.

In the early days of the Oklahoma Highway Department, the north central counties of Oklahoma were under the jurisdiction of Division Seven, Enid. In 1930, the department was reorganized into six divisions and Division Four headquarters was established at Perry. It included Blaine, Canadian, Garfield, Grant, Kay, Kingfisher, Lincoln, Logan, Noble, Oklahoma and a portion of Osage, Pawnee, and Payne counties.

The Highway Department completed a building at 301 South 8th Street in 1933. Before that a temporary office was maintained in the First National Bank Building. In the next ten years many improvements were made, a paint shop, blacksmith shop, large warehouse shed as well as black top streets on the grounds. The Perry Police Department now occupies the building.

Under the supervision of W. E. Johnston, Perry Highway department division gardener, a drive called Buena Vista Drive was landscaped. It was part of the highway leading into Perry and covered a mile starting at the Catholic cemetery and coming on into Perry. It was made up of six parks: Lacy Park, named for C.D. Lacy, Huston Park, named for R.J. Huston, Garden of the Gods, Garden of Eden, Sunken Gardens and Santa Fe Park. Some of the shrubs planted at that time still remain in 1986.

H.E. Bailey, for whom the Bailey turnpike in Oklahoma City was named, was Noble County's member of the State Highway commission when honored in 1939 by a banquet when 300 attended.

In 1947, Roger Glenn Taylor, long time Perry resident, was employed by the State Highway Department making pictorial maps of the states historic spots. These maps were on the cover of the "detour" maps issued by the Department every three months. It was important for the traveler to know which roads were being repaired because the detours were almost impossible and with the maps he could plan a new route.

Land was purchased in 1977 for a new headquarters, west of the first building in the southeast quarter of section 20 in Watkins township. The new headquarters is located adjacent and to the north of state highway 164 approximately one-half mile east of Interstate 35. Old timers often told that Indians camped near the big spring on the west side of this place. Sometimes they did their butchering there and hung up their meat to dry on temporary fences, which they put up for the purpose. This was before the opening in 1893. This land was homesteaded by Hiram L. Boyes which he held until his death February 21, 1934, when it was inherited by his wife and his sister's children. At the time of the building of the new headquarters the land was owned by Ed Malzahn.

In October 1978, Division Four moved into the new buildings which consisted of the main building, a two story building 60' x 168' with an auditorium on the second floor, a shop building 150' x 192' and the Engineering building 24' x 200'. Other large buildings are on the east and west for housing equipment.

Division four is responsible for construction and maintenance on highways in eleven counties in central Oklahoma: Canadian, Creek, Garfield, Grant, Kay, Kingfisher, Lincoln, Logan, Noble, Oklahoma and Payne.

Land Office in Perry, Oklahoma Territory, October 12, 1893. Second from left in the front row of men is William Tighlman. Next to Tighlman is Charlie Colcord and on the far right in the front row is Heck Thomas - all U.S. Deputy Marshalls.

Chapter 4
TOWNSHIPS OF NOBLE COUNTY

Legal Land Descriptions

When Oklahoma was being surveyed prior to opening to white settlers, the government divided the area into counties which were given letters of the alphabet. As soon as possible the settlers selected a name for their county — thus "P" county became Noble county by popular vote. Some people voted for this because they had come from Noble county, Ohio, and others chose the name for John M. Noble, secretary of the Interior under President Harrison. On the four corner section where Noble, Garfield, Grant and Kay counties met ws a store and post office named Polk for the original letters given these counties.

Prior to 1785, land was laid out by "metes and bounds", a system which depended on natural or manmade landmarks. This was very unsatisfactory as rivers could change course or a grove of oak trees could be cut for lumber. Smith's pasture could become Jones' potatoe patch, etc. The rectangular system was adopted for Public Domain land, that is land that originally belonged to the government. This system divided the land into squares, the boundaries being north and south or east and west.

Oklahoma was laid out using the rectangular system based upon the establishment of a principal meridian and a base line. The principal meridian runs a true north and south direction; the base line runs east and west at a right angle to the meridian. The point where these lines cross is referred to as initial point or starting point. The geographic location of a meridian and base line is not fixed by law, therefore the 34 principal meridians in the U.S. were located to meet the convenience of the government surveyors.

Land in Oklahoma is located with respect to two principal meridians; the Indian Meridian which runs from the Red River to the Kansas line through the central part of the state, and the Cimarron Meridian which runs the width of the Panhandle at its extreme western end. The base line to the Indian Meridian runs east and west from border to border across the southern part of the state. The base line to the Cimarron Meridian runs the length of the Panhandle along the southern border. All legal descriptions in Oklahoma therefore, will end with the notation Cimarron Meridian (C.M.) or Indian Meridian (I.M.).

After the principal meridian and base line are laid out, the surveyor comes back to the point of beginning and lays out lines north and south every six miles on either side of the meridian. He then lays out lines parallel to the base lines six miles apart east and west of the base. The lines surveyed result in a grid. Each square in the grid is a congressional township and is not to be confused with a named Civil township. The township marked "A" is referred to as Township 2 North Range 4 East because it lies in the second row of townships north of the base line and in the fourth column of townships east of the principal meridian. Township "B" is referred to as Township 2 South Range 3 West for the ame reasons.

Once the township and range lines are laid out, each of the squares is further divided in 36 sections. Numbering always begins with 1 in the upper right hand corner of the township to number 36.

When the section lines are designated the half mile points are located so as to divide the section in four quarters. These quarters may be further divided if desired.

A section theoretically contains 640 acres and, of course, a quarter section has one fourth of 640 or 160 acres. However, because of the curvature of the earth and thus convergence of the range lines some sections are not exactly 640 acres. Sometimes surveying errors result in a discrepancy. One sometimes finds discrepancies in size when the survey of public lands join Indian lands. For example in Payne county, land was originally surveyed up to the southern border of the Cherokee Outlet. Then when the Outlet was surveyed, the newly laid out section along this border were odd sized. Correction lots are found along the south border of Noble county (Walnut, Rock and Lowe townships).

However, the normal expectation is that all sections will be full sections except those on the north and west sides of a township. Surveyors generally were instructed to confirm any size deficiencies in the townships to section 1 thru 6 and 7, 18, 19, 30 and 31. Even in these sections, shortages were to be confined to the outer borders of the section. These fraction 40 acre tracts are called "lots" or "government lots". The above information was taken from OSU Extension bulletin No. 9407.

Township Life in Noble County

"P" County was generally believed to include the Otoe-Missouria and the Ponca Indian reservations and all the land laying south of these reservations and west of the Pawnee reservation in the Cherokee Strip. At the opening of the Strip, a group of Stillwater businessmen were able to annex four townships in the Cherokee Strip to Payne county. There was a county seat war between Stillwater and Payne Center, and as the county seats were to be located as near the center of the county as possible, Stillwater needed the extra land to the north.

When the Indian reservations were abolished in 1904, and the lands became a part of the counties where they were located, the Ponca reservation was divided between Kay and Noble counties, likewise the Otoe-Missouria lands were divided between Payne and Noble.

James N. Miller, editor of the Morrison Sun, placed the following editorial with map on the front page of the November 4, 1904, issue of the paper.

At the coming of statehood, two townships, Walnut and Rock were placed in Noble county through the efforts of Henry S. Johnston, who served with the Oklahoma Constitutional Convention. Thus, in 1907, the boundaries of Noble county were established as they are today. In the beginning seven townships were named, each one containing two of the 14 townships that were outside of the Indian reservations. As these township officials had the job of establishing the roads along the section lines and maintaining them, it soon became apparent each township needed its own crew. A poll tax was levied to take care of the roads. The poll tax gave the men the right to vote. Each resident had to work four days by himself or 1 day with his team. Those unable or unwilling to work could pay their poll tax with money. Many settlers donated extra work so they could have road to town. As soon as possible, the townships were divided into four school districts. The first schools were often held in a home. Sometimes a bachelor would consent to the school being held in his shack when he was away all day. This arrangement worked out fairly well as the children could study without being disturbed by the household noises and the bachelor came home to a warm house.

Schoolhouses were soon built using donated lumber and sometimes donated materials. At first the schoolhouses were located as near the center of the school-age population as possible. Usually an acre of land was donated by one of the homesteaders, hopefully, located so no child would have to walk more than a mile and a half to school.

The schoolhouses were also used for Sunday school and "preaching" on Sunday until churches could be built. Most of these buildings also served as community meetings called "Literaries" and socials.

*A "Pound Party" meant that the evening meal and chores were hurried through so each member of the church or Sunday school, dressed in his best and with a pound of something edible under his arm, would stop at the minister's house to leave his pound to "help out" the fare of the minister and his family. Everyone was served cake and ice cream by the ladies of the church. The minister always seemed to enjoy being "pounded".

Square dancing was held in the homes. If the house was small, the furniture was moved out for the occasion. Music was usually a fiddle and organ played by members of the party and the "calling" was done by one of the adept members of the crowd.

Everybody belonged to and attended the Literary Society meetings at the local school where refreshments were not served except on regular social meetings. There were musical numbers and recitations, the members taking turns in providing the entertainment. The recitations were readings or poetry, sometimes written for the occasion. Debates made up a large part of these programs. Such subjects as "Which is more interesting — farm life or city life?" and "Which is more dangerous, fire or water?" were

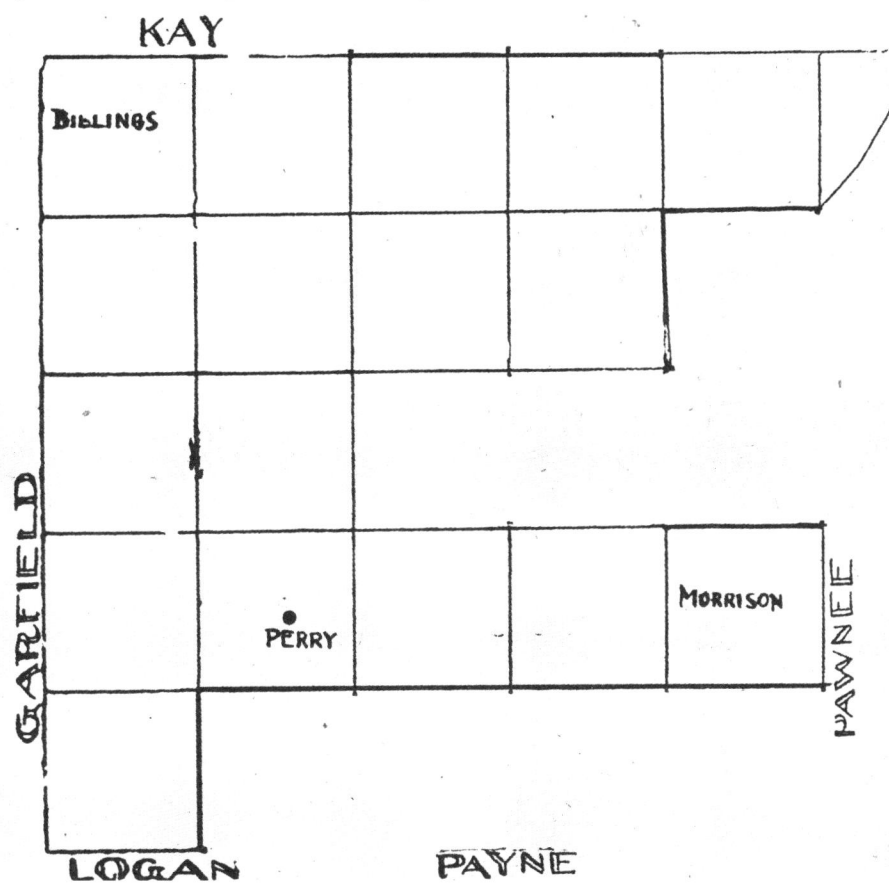

THE map above shows Noble county as it exists today, leaving out the two townships of the Otoe reservation which lie north of Auburn and Noble. These two townships do not now belong to any county, as they are not described in the bill that attached the other townships of the reservation. As they are contiguous to both Pawnee and Noble, they can be attached to either according as congress chooses.

We do not publish this map for the purpose of asking any one to vote against Mr. McGuire because of the injury he has inflicted on our county, but to show just what has been done. We are no more interested in this matter than any other taxpayer in Noble county. Our taxes have been made higher, our county has been placed in ridiculous shape, and the town of Morrison will always suffer in a business way because of this taking away of our territory, but we can stand it if the rest can. The people of four townships now go to Pawnee and Newkirk instead of to Perry to transact their county business and do part of their trading. We can stand it if Perry can.

A vote for Mr. McGuire next Tuesday will virtually approve his action, and encourage his taking the other two townships, and perhaps even more of the reservation. Go ahead! Noble county has been a fat goose for the surrounding counties to pluck. It has lost one wing and most of the tail feathers, and hasn't enough down left for a sofa pillow.

hotly and hilariously debated.

Birthdays, weddings or a new neighbor moving in were all good excuses for a party. Thus, without the benefits of radio and television, the settlers created their own entertainment.

But most of the time it was hard work on the farm. The women cared for the children, milked the cows, fed the chickens, gathered the eggs and did the laundry on a wash board in water they carried from the well or spring.

In the kitchen was a wood stove for cooking. Besides the oven on one side, opposite the fire box was a reservoir which was filled with water and kept hot by the heat from the stove. There was a work table and a wash stand. A towel roller above the wash stand held towels with the ends sewed together so one could pull down a clean dry part.

Women also tended the garden. Along the fence so as not to be distrubed by the fall plowing and the spring planting were winter onions, asparagus, and rheubarb which they usually called "pie plant" as it was used mostly for pies.

Wild plums and currents were plentiful and were made into jams and jellies. Wild blackberries were gathered for pies and jams and were canned for winter use. In the fall, the wild grapes were gathered for jelly. These were so tart they were sometimes mixed with apple juice before making into jelly. Wild black walnuts and the native pecans were gathered and stored in the cellars. The walnuts were dumped near the wood pile until they were dry enough to shed their heavy outer shell and could be cracked on a stump of wood with a heavy hammer. Mulberry trees also grew wild and were loaded with berries. These were so sweet that vinegar or lemon juice would be added before they were baked into pies. Persimmon groves also gew in some parts of the county and these were eaten raw usually.

Hogs were butchered and the hams and bacon were smoked so they would keep. The sausage was ground, fried down and put into earthen jars, then covered with lard. These were placed in a cool place where the lard would set and perserve the sausage. When the lard was rendered the skins were left and were eaten for a snack as potato chips are eaten today.

When lard became old or had absorbed flavors that made it unusable for cooking, it was made into laundry soap.

The men worked long hard hours in the fields, cared for the horses, watered and fed the cows and hogs, repaired the farm machinery and cut wood. Truly it was "Man works from sun to sun but woman's work is never done."

The settlers had oyster suppers, shingle suppers (where the food was served on brand new shingles, no paper plates in those days) ice cream socials, and box suppers, in order to finish the building and make it comfortable for classes that were to follow.

Rural Life

Noble County can be divded into several different regions. The southern tier of townships had some timber that could be used for lumber. Also there were places where grew scrub oak called "black Jack oak" good for firewood but little else. The sod was not good for sod houses but many people lived in dugouts, however, most of the houses were built of lumber. Claim shacks often had a rope or cable over the house to keep the roof from being blown off in a strong wind. Farm land was in small patches planted to corn, oats, and cotton. In the northeast was the Indian lands used mostly for pasture, although the land along the Arkansas River raised corn and hay. In the northwest part of the county the land is flatter with larger fields ideal for wheat. The sod here was good for making sod houses.

To make a "soddy" the sun baked prairie sod, complete with its grass and weeds, was plowed into low furrows and allowed to dry. Then the sod was cut into pieces, each about two feet long, 12 inches wide and six inches thick. These blocks were stacked like a brick wall to form walls of the house. The end walls were built to a point which formed the center of the roof. On the point, a ridgepole was placed and branches covered with sod were used to form a sharply slanting roof. The roof had to slant at a proper angle to prevent the sod from being washed away during a hard rain and also to prevent leaking on the roof of the soddy. In the spring it was not unusual to see grass and flowers growing on the roof of the soddy.

The floor was hard-packed earth which could be swept and even mopped. The windows, door frames and even the door were often made from packing crates in which the family belongings traveled to Oklahoma.

The sod house was warm in winter and cool in summer. It was soon made "homey" with family possessions. Pegs were driven into the white-washed walls. Clothing and cooking utensils were hung on the pegs. A gun rack was placed above the door. But the sod house needed repairs everytime it rained. The dirt from the roof sifted down in dry weather. Spiders, mice and snakes soon moved in, so the sod house was soon a thing of the past as frame and rock or brick houses replaced them.

Effort was made before 1900 to improve livestock. Blooded cattle, horses, hogs and chickens were purchased and brought to Noble County. Also improved seed for crops were tried. It was unknown what crops would do best here, so records were kept on different varieties. The winter wheat that had been developed in Kansas did well. The railroad was extended into northwest Noble County to move the wheat. In

(Left to Right): Will, Samuel, Rachel, Pearl, Jesse, Benton (all standing) and George (on horseback) Harlow. Taken ca 1889.

Wheat harvest in early 1900s.

1911, corn was piled on the ground at Morrison and Bliss/Marland because of a shortage of railroad cars. Alfalfa yielded in the valleys and was shipped out by rail.

Perry was once called the Caster Bean Market of the world. Thousands of acres of these plants were cultivated and threshed in Noble county. The plant yielded beans which produced castor oil. It grows about five feet in height and has a smaller bean than that which was grown as shrubbery.

In order to thresh castor beans, huge rings were built on top of the ground, similar to circus rings. The caster bean pods were placed herein and occassionally stirred while the heat of the sun caused the pods to burst thus threshing them. The caster bean is very poisonous. The horses used around them had to be muzzled and the men working with them began to be sick so the industry began to die.

Cotton was raised in the southern part of the country for a cash crop until the boll weavils destroyed the crop and infected the fields so cotton could not be raised. Cotton gins were built in the first years after the run. Perry had three gins at one time. Morrison, Sumner, Gansel and Lucien all had cotton gins with many bales of cotton shipped on the railroad. There were 3100 square and 650 round bales of cotton baled in Noble county in 1906.

Another crop in the early years was fruit. Apples were raised in the Arkansas Valley in the Ponca reservation. Several peach orchards were located near Perry with at least two canneries here. Orlando Walkling southeast of Perry was one of the shippers. In 1906, T.P. Watts and J.W. Smith 4 miles northeast of Perry put up 1,500 cans of peaches, beans and tomatoes. Fruit growing is not as profitable today due perhaps to the lowering of the water table by water consumption over the years. The main agricultural products of Noble county today are cattle, wheat, alfalfa, barley with some corn, milo, oats and soybeans.

Nearly every family raised a large garden, with cellars being filled with the surplus for winter use. Milk cows, hogs, and chickens were raised for family use with any left over sold in the neighboring store.

Sometimes a baseball diamond, tennis court and/or a croquet court was scraped off in the field on a flat place. Large groups of young people in the area gathered at a farm pond to skate. After a good rain a favorite activity was wading in round pools with sandy bottoms in the pastures. The wading pools had been buffalo wallows for many years and grass had not grown back to cover them.

Haybarn on A. I. Acers homestead about 1897.

Farm hands enjoy a game of croquet around 1895.

Plowing near Billings about 1915. Copied from glass negative.

Chapter 4
TOWNSHIPS OF NOBLE COUNTY

John Frank home. Middle section was the Day Post Office in southeast Noble County.

Bill's corner — Sadie Turner by gasoline pump.

Wheat field near Billings about 1915. Copied from glass negative.

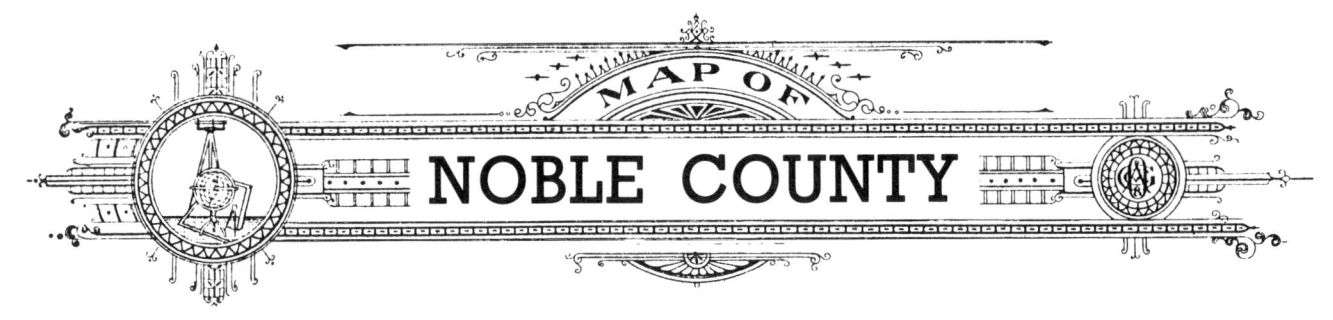

MAP OF NOBLE COUNTY

	2 WEST	1 WEST	1 EAST	2 EAST	3 EAST	4 EAST
24 N	BUNCH CREEK	GLENROSE	BUFFALO	WEST BRESSIE	EAST BRESSIE	
23 N	WHITE ROCK	RED ROCK	CARSON	OTOE		
22 N	OAKDALE	BLACK BEAR	SANTA FE	MISSOURI		
21 N	WARREN VALLEY	WATKINS	NOBLE	AUBURN	AUTRY	
20 N	LOWE	ROCK	WALNUT			

INDIAN MERIDIAN

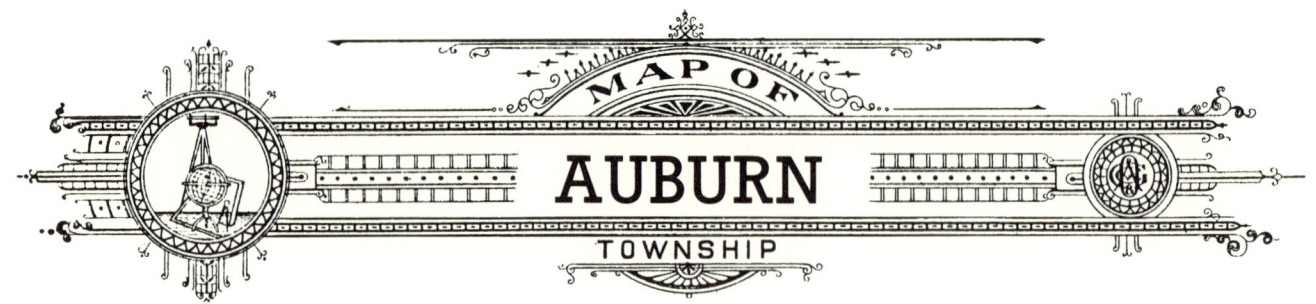

MAP OF AUBURN TOWNSHIP

Township 21 North, Range 2 East of the Indian Meridian

Auburn Township

Auburn township was a part of Autry township when first formed in January, 1894, by the county commissioners. Auburn was separated from Autry on December 1, 1896. Sumner in the northwest section was the only village to survive the coming of free delivery of mail service. Sumner was named for Henry T. Sumner, a Perry business leader.

Near the southwest part of Auburn township in section 36 of Noble Township was a post office called Richburg. The postoffice was also a store and moved several times before it was moved to the Steve Diebold farm. It was there used for a schoolhouse for Negro children after segregation. It was called Oak Grove #2 (district #41). The White Oak Grove school (district #41) was in Noble township.

In the southeastern part of Auburn township was a little settlement called Day which served for a time as a halfway house on the stage line. It was named for William R. Day, secretary of state under President McKinley. Day had a post office from April 10, 1899, until November 15, 1905. Day was located on the east side of the road from where the O.G. & E. substation is today. The store was operated by the Vandeventer boys. The store changed hands many times.

The story was told of the lady who rushed up to the stage coach driver at Perry and demanded to go to Day. He told her to hop in as he was leaving right then. It was not until they arrived in Morrison did she realize they were not going to Day but "today". She had to catch the next stage back to Perry and start over. Many people called Day -"Daytown", to avoid this confusion.

In about 1922, Bill Turner, whose father, George Turner, had a homestead in section 21, opened a filling station and grocery store at what is now the intersection of Highways 64 and 177. It was the intersection of dirt roads connecting Ponca City and Stillwater north and south and the east-west road connecting Perry and Pawnee. This corner is still called Bill's Corner for him.

In the fall of 1894, a group of farmers organized a school in the center of the northwest district (northeast quarter of section 8). William B. Poole, a stock buyer, donated an acre from his claim adjacent to the present site of Sumner on March 9, 1901 (district #43). Others in the district raised money and built the native lumber schoolhouse. C. H. Lacy was the first teacher. This school was called Poole but was soon moved to Sumner.

Between Sumner and Morrison the foundations for the Oak Grove school (district #46) were laid early. While they were still living in the claim house, the older Mitchell children attended school regularly for one year, 1895, with Mrs. Gertrude Altice, the sister of A. O. Hall, the teacher and his housekeeper. The school was held in one of the rooms of the house Hall had built on the extreme northeast side of the Mitchell claim, after filing a contest four days after the race. The teacher worked hard for her $27.00 a month. In the Hall house, also, Frank Milligan taught one term.

It was not long before school officials wanted to buy an acre in the center of the district. Instead, W. N. Mitchell donated land from the southeast corner of his claim to be used for school, church, literaries and singing school. The latter conducted by a Mr. Brewer from Long Branch. The first term classes were held in the hall of what was to become the first Oak Grove school. Frank Whinery, later one of the principals of the Morrison school, was the first teacher. Oak Grove was annexed to Morrison and Sumner on July 7, 1947.

Soon after the Oak Grove schoolhouse was built, W.N. Mitchell, with several neighbors, including Dave Linden, J.D.E. Owens and Billy Budworth, built an arbor on the grounds for Sunday School and church. He also, heading the list with his donation of ten dollars, carried the solicit papers among the settlers to start the Sunday school - buying books and literature. J.N. Thompson, known as Broomcorn Thompson throughout the county as he grew the raw materials for brooms he manufactured for sale, and his good wife, were also main spokes in this effort, helping the Sunday school keep going long after the arbor had fallen down. The arbor was made of logs and covered with boards and brush, with roughly hewn seats and a little organ on a small rostrum covered with canvas which fluttered and flapped in the wind.

The first school in district #44 was held in a one room house on the Wood's farm in 1895. It was named Spring Hill, later changed to Pleasant Valley and finally nicknamed "Windy Center". Three gentlemen in the community were known for their tall tales and it was "windy" when they got together. Ben Coats was their first teacher. There were 50 pupils in a small one room schoolhouse. Wood was used for heating the room and water was carried in pails from a nearby well. Benches were made from native lumber. Few children had paper. Arithmetic problems were worked on slates. Windy Center was annexed to Sumner on April 2, 1943.

Shiloh was the name of the school in the southeast (district #45) of Auburn township. Joe Zemp donated an acre of his land for the school. The schoolhouse was moved to Morrison where it serves as the kindergarten room. The district became D-14 and was annexed to Morrison in 1956.

The Pleasant Valley cemetery received its name from the Pleasant Valley Christian church which held its first services in the Pleasant Valley schoolhouse. John Volmer, a member of the church, donated three acres of land for the cemetery on April 9, 1898. When the town of Sumner was platted on the new east-west railroad line, a town lot was offered to the churches of the community and this church was moved to Sumner.

J. N. Thompson's Broom Factory.

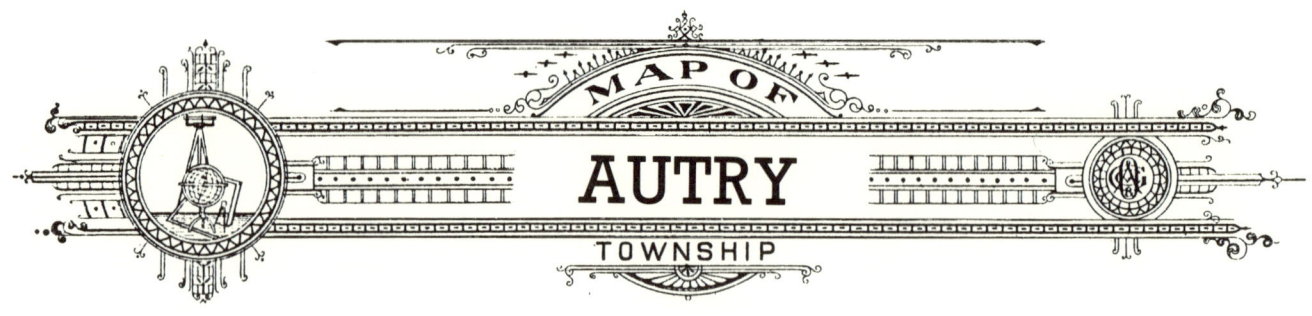

MAP OF AUTRY TOWNSHIP

Township 21 North, Range 3 East of the Indian Meridian

Autry Township

An attempt was made in 1890, to establish a town near the present day Morrison. A rumor circulated that the Cherokee Strip had been opened by President Harrison. A number of hopefuls rushed in from adjoining lands and staked claims. Among them was J. E. Slater, later a leading Stillwater businessman and vice-president of the Morrison State Bank. Believing the land location with only a slight slope to the north a favorable one, he laid out a town naming it Dolliver, after an Iowan who was a congressman at the time. It wasn't long, however, before the U.S. Soldiers marched in, removing all the intruders from the territory. In 1893, Slater was unable to make the race and permanently abandoned the idea. His claim was the one on which Harley Elwood filed in the legal opening. Within a few years it had again become a townsite.

Previous to this, however, a man by the name of Autry had established a store in 1893, located a short distance southwest of the present school building. It consisted of a general store and post office operated by Mr. Autry. The Perry to Pawnee stage delivered the mail.

Within a year, James H. Morrison, who had staked a claim nearby, purchased Autry's holdings and continued running the business with the addition of a hotel. Morrison gave 40 acres of his claim for a townsite and unincorporated Autry became Morrison with six blocks, a park, and a school reserve being laid out. The engineer's plan was filed in August, 1894.

Schools started in Autry township in 1894, when Minnie Norris, a fifteen-year-old daughter of early settlers taught a subscription school in a tent on their school lease (ne ¼ of section 16), directly south of the Dollarhide claim. Rural people, as well as a number from Morrison attended even when the ground was snow covered. Some paid their fees in milk or other food, some in cash at fifty cents a pupil per month. Some of the people were: Belle and John Heatherington; Mattie, John and Joe Emick; Goldie, Gertie, and Jerome Hiatt; George and Louis Jelinek; Emma, and Anna Adams, Cynthia, Lilly, Mary, and Harley Hull; Johnny Montgomery; Herb Monhollon and Claude Kent.

The first school in Morrison was Mrs. Meriam Hull's, conducted in the old Methodist church and in 1895-96, Daisy Crawford taught in a building on the main street of Old town for $20 a month. In the fall of 1897, Mr. Husselton taught in the lower room of Col. Morrison's story and a half store building on the east side of the street, just south of the present school site. In 1899, the first real school building in the district was a one-room school located on the Abe Kents' claim, near the town limits.

In 1903, school started in the new two-story four room building in the north part of town on land platted from Col. Morrison's farm with 110 pupils which had increased to 150 by January. The old one-room building was sold for $250.00 to Amos Nichols who in the fall moved it north to his blacksmith shop about two blocks south of the new school, to use for his wagon repair shop.

South of Morrison in sw ¼ of section 28 on the J. W. Prather farm was the Jefferson school (district #48). The land was deeded on October 1, 1903. On the L.J. Bates farm (ne ¼ section 26) was the White Hall school (district #49). The land was deeded by William and Lydia Bates on March 13, 1907. North of Morrison on the Norris claim (sw ¼ section 4) was the Prairie Center school (district #47). The land was deeded by Zachery T. Ashby on February 15, 1899.

On the C. M. McClellan farm in s½ ne¼ of section 11 was the Lela school (district #50).

The old Lela school (district #50) started with a three month term in 1894, in a small frame building topped with a belfry and bell. Pupils sat on cottonwood slabs sawed by a local mill. George State taught a three months subscription school at $3.00 a pupil per month.

From Gladys Sweringen's unpublished manuscript: "When the railroad was being built in 1903, one of the work camps was near the school. By this time, single seats had replaced the double ones, but with the extra pupils the doubling-up process followed with the newcomer's children nearly crowding out the settler's offspring. It wasn't just that there were too many of them, but that no one could be much interested in the three R's with crawling creatures, head and body lice, pestering them and the itch adding victims day by day. Mothers rubbed salty bacon grease on their children's scalps with a scrubbing intensity, used fine combs, and suds after suds washing their head, hoping to exterminate the vermin before they could multiply. Many of the pupils remembered the unusual singing of the Negros as they worked on the railroad grade not far away. They had established camp in a grove east of Black Bear on the W. A. Sayer claim.

Disagreements in districts were sometimes brought before the school board or for citizen's trial. One such was the W. A. Sayer and Charley Bradley dispute; the former a board member, the latter the teacher. Bradley was recognized as a good teacher, jockey and horseman and champion checker player. To him, nothing seemed more worthwhile than a winner. He practically lived for May Queen and Old Frog Legs, his racers. Sayer was a prominent farmer, a breeder of fine horses, a deacon in the Methodist church and a man who observed Sunday so rigidly that he would not mail a letter unless it could reach its destination without being on route on the Lord's Day. He strongly disapproved of Bradley's dancing and horse racing. He had warned without appreciable effect.

But when Bradley raced Old Frog Legs in Pawnee on the Fourth of July, 1904, at the close of his third school term, and his horse fell, breaking his leg and collarbone, so that he had to be killed, the dispute was brought to a climax. Though Bradley was heart-sick, Sayer was fuming! He, with the aid of the Berrys, renters on one of his farms, brought Bradley to a citizen's trial, trying to gain support to have his contract cancelled.

Opposing sides lined up parallel, facing each other in the main street of Morrison. Pastor Williams, the spokesman, stated the case. Ben Jones, also a board member and an enthusiast of horse racing, supported Bradley as did D.L. Dever. After many pros and cons with Sayer presenting his reasons for Bradley's dismissal, preacher Williams spoke: 'Well', he said, much to the delight of the majority, 'even I dance, but I dance religiously.' Whatever that means. But it was enough to turn the decision almost completely in Bradley's favor. Now he could continue teaching with more united support. Only the Berrys transferred their daughter to another district. However, Bradley did not apply for renewal of his contract."

The Lela district was annexed to Morrison and the original building was sold to the owner of the former Laten Hall claim, moved there and used as a hay barn.

The Morrison cemetery is located on the northwest quarter of section 21 in Autry township. The five acres of land were sold to the Morrison Cemetery Association by Irwin Houck for $50.00 on June 28, 1897.

The Lela cemetery is located on the southeast quarter of section 2 in Autry township. The 1½ acres of land were deeded to the Lela Cemetery Association by John and Lydia Ashlock for $62.50 on April 23, 1917, although it had been used as a burial plot since before 1900.

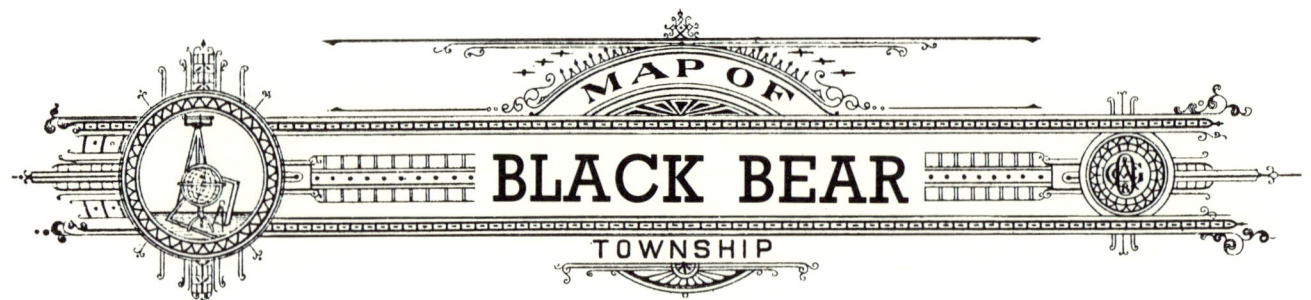

MAP OF BLACK BEAR TOWNSHIP

Township 22 North, Range 1 West of the Indian Meridian

E Dolezol	DM Johnson	RL Thompson	HH Willbarger	HJ Schmutzer	F Swartz	D Casey	FA Palmer	E Moore	F Hynek	JW Minor	AG Keith
	A Vavra										
	6		5		4		3		2		1
W McMullen	JJ Lovenburg	P Gengler	JR Darmer	ED Thompson	A Eret	JKO Young	NH Jones	FF Jones	CH Jones	JL Minor	M Cook
J Datel	J Sokol	W Wilson / H McLinnas	NE Taylor	J Newton	A Nemec	CM Beale	JP Brokaw	DD Rothgeb	AE Warren	CS Thompson	J Cizek
	7		8		9		10		11		12
RW Morgan	FR Novak	B Kasl / JR Silver	F Blecha	CC Humphrey	EJ Stroud	AL Nemec	F Prokop	JH Hynek	MP Field	CS Minor	ME Bowman
TC Everett	GG Romine	WN Carter	S Baker			TJ George	CL Holcomb	C Seton	NP Henriksen		
	18		17		16		15		14		13
JE Holmes	CP Risdon	ML Barnes	JJ Kasl			MJ Lester	R Monnett	EJ Waltermire	CL Arnold		
J Skalenda	LA Minor	GA Barnes	JR Hock	S Smith	GA Smith	C Lausen	V Prucha	JB Queen	P McCarthy	V Palecek	F Sykora
	19		20		21		22		23		24
FH Hostetter	SL Pease	M Dykes	ME Hubbard	EJ Coyle	HS Davidson	L Barnes	TW Grant	CE Gravin	A Thompson	A Hausam	T Kostecka
PL Kirchner	WT Little	WM Kirkley	LW Fairbanks	TM Kerns	IJ Quinton	AF Willcozen	NN Monnett	AJ Jodlicka	TH Moore Jr	A Civish	W Prochazka
	30		29		28		27		26		25
BL Swarens	R Rasmussen	J Routh	H Kirkley	WW Pattison	W Chisam / S Jacob	SE Firestone	WH Brown	WH Kirchner	C Rendta	J Kostecka	JL Canatser
CI Pomeroy	J Janousek	GH Mouser	JW Howard			WA Parker	CH Parker	CS Maupin	WJ Taylor		
	31		32		33		34		35		36
WC Harrah	AC Nicewander	A Chrz	H Harrison			AI Acres	OM Kenton	H Briscoe	A Briscoe		

Black Bear Township

Black Bear Township was named for the Black Bear Creek which flows from west to east across the southern part of the township. Oakdale was a part of this township when it was formed in 1894.

Many Bohemians settled in this township. The Bohemian National Cemetery is located in the southeast quarter of section 10 on land that was owned by Frank Prokop. It was deeded on January 10, 1899. Mr. Prokop couldn't sign his name so the deed is marked with an "X". Many of the tombstones have inscriptions in their native language.

In 1906, the community organized the Bohemian Club. At once they purchased land from V. Pruca in the northeast corner of Section 22 and built a club house costing $1200. This club house, called the Bohemian Hall, has been a landmark in the community and brings back fond memories of the polkas danced there over the years.

Three miles west of the Bohemian Cemetery is the Mt. Carmel Cemetery for those settlers who were not Bohemian. It is in the northwest quarter of section 17 homesteaded by William M. Carter. The cemetery was deeded by Barbara Blecha on May 3, 1900.

Just before World War II the United States government purchased land for an auxilliary landing field in section 14 and 15 for military planes to practice take-offs and landings and for emergency landings. Three runways were built each 5,200 feet long. In 1946, the airport was turned to the City of Perry — which has benefited from agricultural leases. Oil was discovered in the 1960s

Al Acres Thrashing Team.

which also benefitted the City of Perry.

In the northwest district of Black Bear township was the Fairview School, District #30, on land homesteaded by John Newton. It was annexed to 4-D school on June 23, 1947. In the northeast district was Sunny Slope, District #29, on land homesteaded by Charles H. Jones in the southeast quarter of section 2. It was annexed to Perry and Red Rock on June 23, 1947. In the southwest district was the 4-D school, district #31, named for the four men who had a cowboy camp in the area before the Strip opened. It was on land homesteaded by Mary E. Hubbartt, formerly Mary E. Rorobow in the southeast quarter of section 20. It became Dependent school district number 13 and later annexed to Oakdale center.

On land homesteaded by Thomas H. Moore, Jr. was the Rose Hill school district #32. It was annexed to Perry July 16, 1947. The school house was donated to the City of Perry to be placed in a museum if and when such a museum came into being. The school house was moved to the airport grounds where it stayed for several years on a temporary foundation. It was moved to the Cherokee Strip Museum grounds in the summer of 1970. Much planning went into moving the building to the site as it was placed in a bend of the stream that runs through the grounds, the site being across the stream from the road. It was brought in from the northeast over privately owned land through the pasture.

The school building was restored by the Oklahoma Parks Department. The bell tower was rebuilt, a new roof had to be added and new plaster. Care was taken to restore it to its original appearance. The piano, teacher's desk and some of the students desks were returned to the school after it was restored. Also the library with most of the books have been donated by the patrons of the school district. It has been an education and source of enjoyment to visitors to the museum since it was placed there.

Iron wheeled tractors on farm of A. I. Acres.

MAP OF BUFFALO TOWNSHIP

Township 24 North, Range 1 East of the Indian Meridian

Buffalo Township

Buffalo township was a part of the Ponca Indian reservation. This was the hunting grounds of the tribe and most of it was leased to the Miller Brothers' 101 Ranch. The map on the facing page was made in 1912. Section 13, 16, 33, and 36 in the Indian Reservations were not set aside for schools and public buildings as were the other townships. A boarding school was built for the Ponca Indian children.

In the northeast corner of section 5 was the Birdsnest school named for the creek of the same name. It was a brick building with a little two-room teacherage near by. Moody Parks was one of the early teachers. Part of this district was annexed to Marland and part to Kay county on October 1, 1929.

Buffalo school, sometimes called Buffalo Center was located on the southwest ¼ of section 16 on the W. L. Collier place. It was annexed to Marland, March 2, 1921.

The town known as Bliss for 26 years was changed to Marland in 1924 as a result of the influence of W. A. Brooks, who was mayor at that time. Brooks, a cousin of the Miller Brothers of the 101 Ranch was personally acquainted with E. W. Marland who was going places in the oil business and Brooks conceived the idea that Marland would help foster projects in the town if it were named for him. Such was not the case, however. The town has been able to stand on its own feet, but the population has dwindled to the 200 mark. During the Three Sands oil boom days and the Miller brothers activities the population reached 1,000. Bliss was named for Cornelius N. Bliss, secretary of the Interior.

In 1898, Fred Balduff of Ponca City leased a five acre tract of land from the federal government for building purposes and that same year built a lumber yard. P. C. Viering and R. J. Ray also of Ponca City built and operated a general merchandise store arriving at Bliss the same time as Balduff. Until that time a box car flag station, a stock pen and scales along the Santa Fe tracks was all that made up Bliss. The scales were used by Nathan and Neal Williams to weigh wheat bought and loaded by the scoop method to cars for shipment. In 1900, two grain elevators were built and in 1904, the first school was held in the scale-weigh house. Mike Monahan, the Santa Fe section foreman was elected to the school board and served for more than 35 years. H. L. Derry served for more than 30 years. In 1900, Fred Balduff opened a general store which he operated many years. H. L. Derry and Fred Grund of Girrard, Kansas purchased the general store from Viering and Ray in 1903, which Derry ran for nearly 37 years.

"Trail Dust" an eight reel motion picture by William Hines and the old Cherokee Strip scenes were enacted in 20 reels by the Patton Production Company of Los Angeles in pastures north of the town of Marland.

A bend of the Salt Fork of the Arkansas River leaves a horseshoe section of land in Noble County with no access to the rest of the county.

The land along the Arkansas River produces some of the best agriculture products in Noble County.

On March 28, 1911, J. E. McKenney, agent for the Atchison, Topeka and Santa Fe Railway reported that 771 cars or 30 trains of 25 cars, had been shipped from Bliss in one season. He also said, "at the close of the season's business there were 192,000 bushels of ear corn on the right of way or adjacent thereto awaiting shipment, making this station, at 1,000 bushels to the car 192 cars short."

There were 278 carloads of livestock holding 6,990 head of cattle, 1680 head of hogs and 240 horses and mules. Also shipped were 194 carloads of wheat at 58,200 bushels; 284 cars of corn, 284,000 bushels; 24 cars of hay, 240 tons and 18 carloads of watermelons, 249 tons.

Also raised in the region was oats, rye and potatoes as well as fruit such as apples, peaches, pears, etc.

In this region natural gas has been found at a depth of 900 feet. In 1911, one of the largest gas veins in the world at that time had a daily production of 30,000,000 cubic feet.

Bliss (Marland) in the Ponca Reservation.

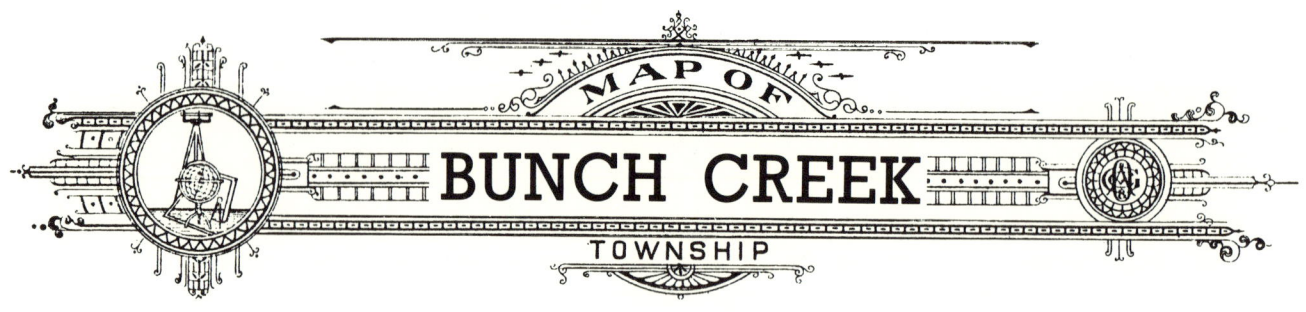

Township 24 North, Range 2 West of the Indian Meridian

Bunch Creek Township

Named for the creek that drains most of the township, Bunch Creek Township was a part of White Rock Township when Noble County was first divided into townships. Bunch Creek was created July 21, 1896.

Happy Star school (district #3) was located in the southeast part of the township, northeast corner of section 26. The land was deeded by George P. and Sadie Murray on November 11, 1902. It was annexed to Glenrose (district #23) on June 30, 1947. Mt. Victory (district #53) was located in the northwest of the township, southwest corner of section 4. Fairview (district #2) was located in the northeast of the township, southwest corner of section 1. It was started early and served as a church as well as a school. The school district was annexed to Glenrose on June 19, 1947. The land was deeded to the Freedom Baptist church of Harperville, Noble County, Oklahoma, by Zimri W. Hoge and his wife Nannie on December 17, 1898. The church services were union (no special denomination). A group of French people who had migrated to Illinois from Canada and later to Kansas around Moundridge and Hesston, came down to this area, some of them settling in Glenrose township. They were nearly all Baptist but at one time had been of another faith. They organized as a church in Kansas and called themselves the Freedom Baptist church. Not many, if any of them, actually made the run but in a year or two families of the new settlement began coming to the new country and bought farms. When the church people outgrew the school houses, these Freedom Baptists decided to build a church. All the men in the neighborhood pitched in to do the work, even those who didn't attend church helped. W. M. Hoover was the carpenter directing the building operation. A small general store was run by Adam Wolfe, who furnished the hardware, and a new stove for the church. The lumber was hauled by the settlers who were hauling wheat to market. After the wheat was unloaded, the wagons were brought back loaded with lumber for the new church. Dedication services were held in 1898. There were no other churches for miles and for the first few years, the membership of the Freedom Baptist was larger than the First Baptist church in Ponca City at that time. Some of the early French families, who were connected with the Baptist church were: the Phil Chartrands, the C. Wards, the Denzil Belairs, the Frank and Henry Mannys, the Murrays, Fred and George, the Steve Lamberts, the Napoleon Carifells, the Amos Fravels and the Will Curbys and others. A post office, Harperville, was near the church from May 3, 1894 to October 31, 1900.

Pleasant Hurst conducted a school during the spring months of 1894, at his home, three quarters of a mile north of the present site of Billings. He had been a teacher and agreed to teach a day for each day of "sod busting" by his neighbors on his farm. For an additional month he received twenty-five dollars.

A new school house was built in the fall of 1894, and was called Pleasant Valley (district #4), with H. H. Murdock as teacher. It was located on the southwest corner of J. C. Noonan's claim. The school house was blown down by a storm and the school was moved to the new town of Billings.

Almost immediately following the opening a man named Dick White who had a claim just north of Red Rock Creek about four miles south of the present townsite of Billings and one mile east applied for and received permission to establish a post office on his land. A small townsite was laid out and named White Rock (in White Rock township).

The community became so rich in the production of live stock, wheat and other farm products that the Rock Island railroad running through Enid, built a spur to haul these products to market.

A group of men saw the importance of a townsite on the right of way. Harry Thompson, Rock Island railroad townsite agent, gave Billings its name for his wife, whose maiden name was Mary Ann Billings. The town was laid out and invitations for a "Grand Opening" were sent far and wide. There was a huge barbecue on opening day, October 23, 1899, and a sale of town lots to hundreds of prospective purchasers who attended. Most of the people in White Rock moved their homes and businesses, building and all, to the new town. White Rock's newspaper, "Red Rock Valley News" was moved to Billings and renamed "The Billings News". The editor, W. W. McCullough, was also Post Master at White Rock, applied for the post office at Billings before being released at White Rock.

Another business that was moved was J. G. Back's general merchandise store. Large stone buildings were built in the first few years. The first one was the Old Coney Island Saloon building erected by Heim Brewery interest during the first year of Billings existence.

When school district #4 was moved to Billings it became Billings school, first with two rooms upstairs and down of rock, then another wing was added in 1911. A high school was built in 1921.

Billings — July 4, 1901.

54 / History of Noble County

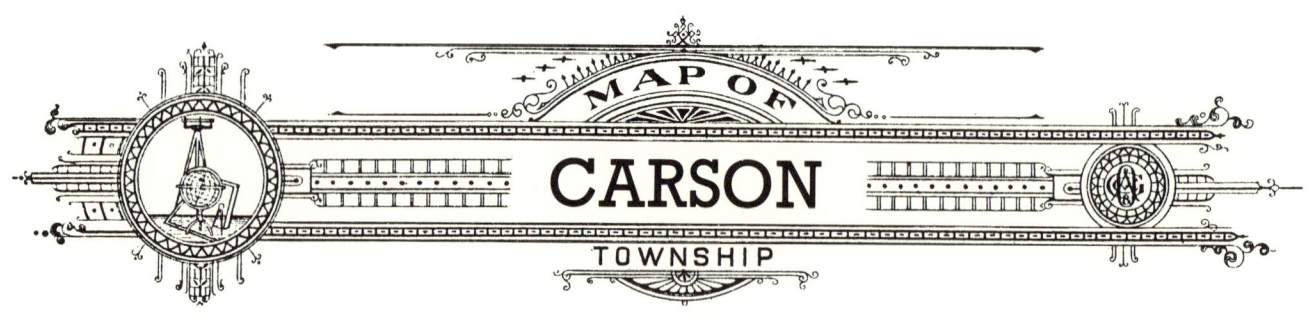

MAP OF CARSON TOWNSHIP

Township 23 North, Range 1 East of the Indian Meridian

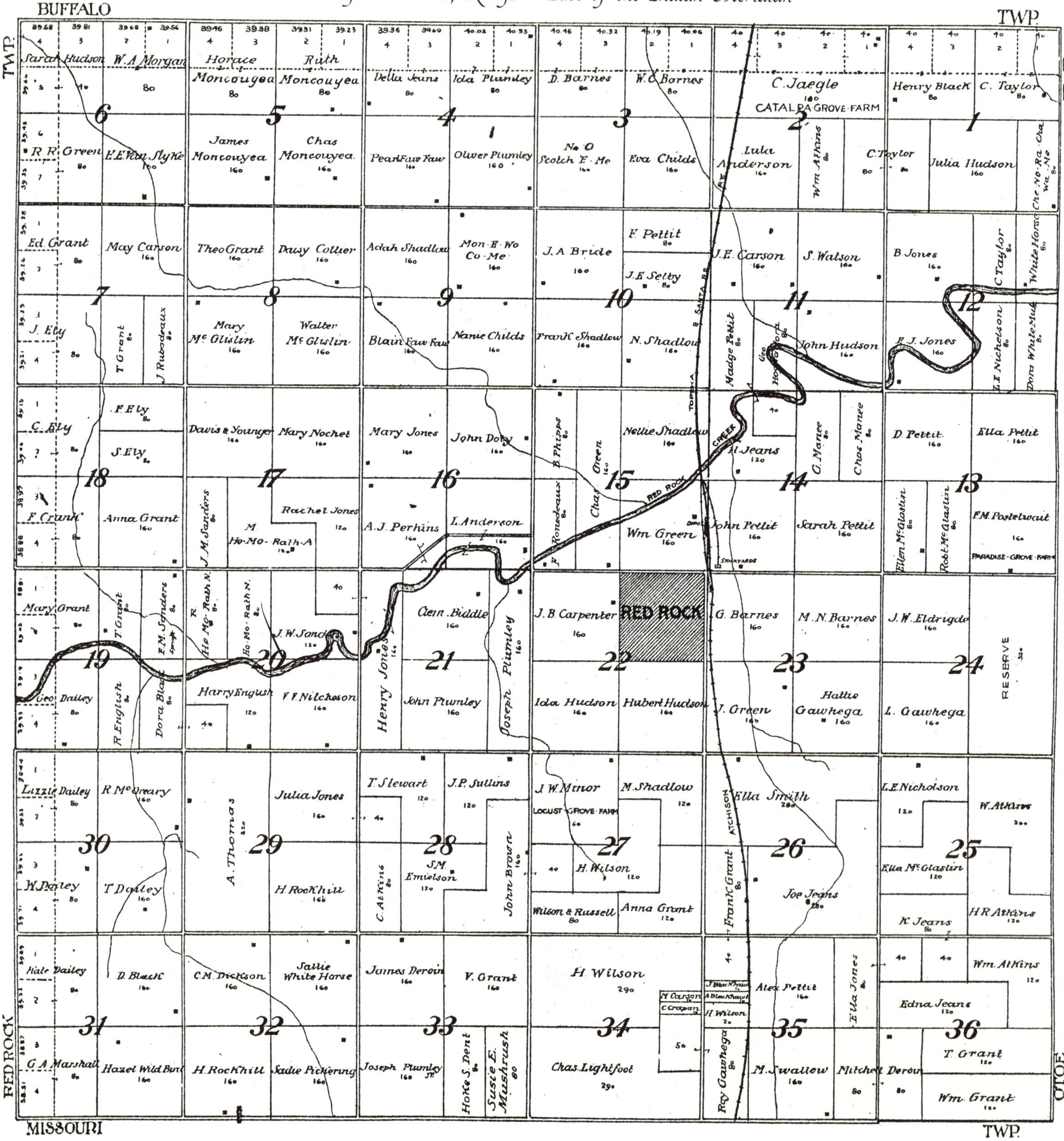

Carson Township

Carson township was a part of the Otoe reservation. This township was a part of the Otoe hunting grounds and much of it was leased to the white man who used it for cattle pasture.

On July 20, 1903, the town of Red Rock as it now stands, was opened. The name is a continuation of a former post office which was located six miles south in Santa Fe township. Several of the buildings were moved to the new site which comprised 160 acres, all the land available at that time. Joe Plumley owned the land which he platted into lots and sold for business and residential lots. The first building to be erected was a bank building constructed of brick by George Sevey. "A metropolitan Livery Company and Bus line" was run by Zack Miller. A newspaper "Red Rock Opinion" was housed above Bob Grey's merchandise store. The dipping vat in Red Rock was located directly south of where the Farmers Cooperative elevator now stands. Here many carloads of cattle were dipped for Texas fever ticks since the railroad was the dividing line for infected cattle for many years.

In 1917, Red Rock had a population of 500. It had a bank, two drug stores, four grocery and general merchandise stores, two grain elevators, two hardware stores, one hotel, one cafe and a lumber yard.

At present, Red Rock school district is one of the richest schools in northern Oklahoma due to oil on the Otoe land.

Red Rock's first water works.

In 1967, Victor Coldiron recalled the following incident which happened on the Otoe Indian Reservation about 1915. "Most of you people don't know what carbide lights are. In the early days of the automobile all cars used a method of illumination called carbide lighting which consisted of a tank about six inches in diameter and possible 18 inches high that was mounted on the running board of the automobile and was connected to the headlights with a little brass tubing that ran to a sort of Y shaped burner and the light was caused by pouring water into the top of the tank of carbide which was a white powder and this water mixed with the carbide caused carbide gas to form and it flowed through the copper tubing into the lights and then you lifted the door of the light and lit a match and ignited the gas and that gave you a real white brilliant light. One day my father and I went out to make a call on the Otoe Indian Reservation where he was the Indian Reservation doctor and due to some unexpected circumstances we were delayed in getting away from the agency which was 8 to 12 miles from town, until late afternoon. Dark was falling before we traveled half way back to town so we drove to a little creek not far ahead in hopes we could get some water from the creek to pour into the carbide gas so we could see since there was no regular highway that traveled this area and it was important that you have lights in order to travel across country. But unfortunately the creek had gone dry, being a dry summer, and there was no water in it. We were more or less stranded until my father conceived the brilliant idea of obtaining some liquid for this carbide from the only available source. He stood me on the running board and lifted the lid off the carbide gas tank and told me to perform my duties into the carbide gas which I promptly did. I, being a small boy was not quite sufficient to generate enough power so my father contributed a little larger portion so that we clamped the lid on the tank, lit a match and lo and behold we had a very good light which carried us to town safely.

George W. Daily and his son, Truman, 1899.

Map of East Bressie Township

Township 24 North, Range 3 & 4 East of the Indian Meridian

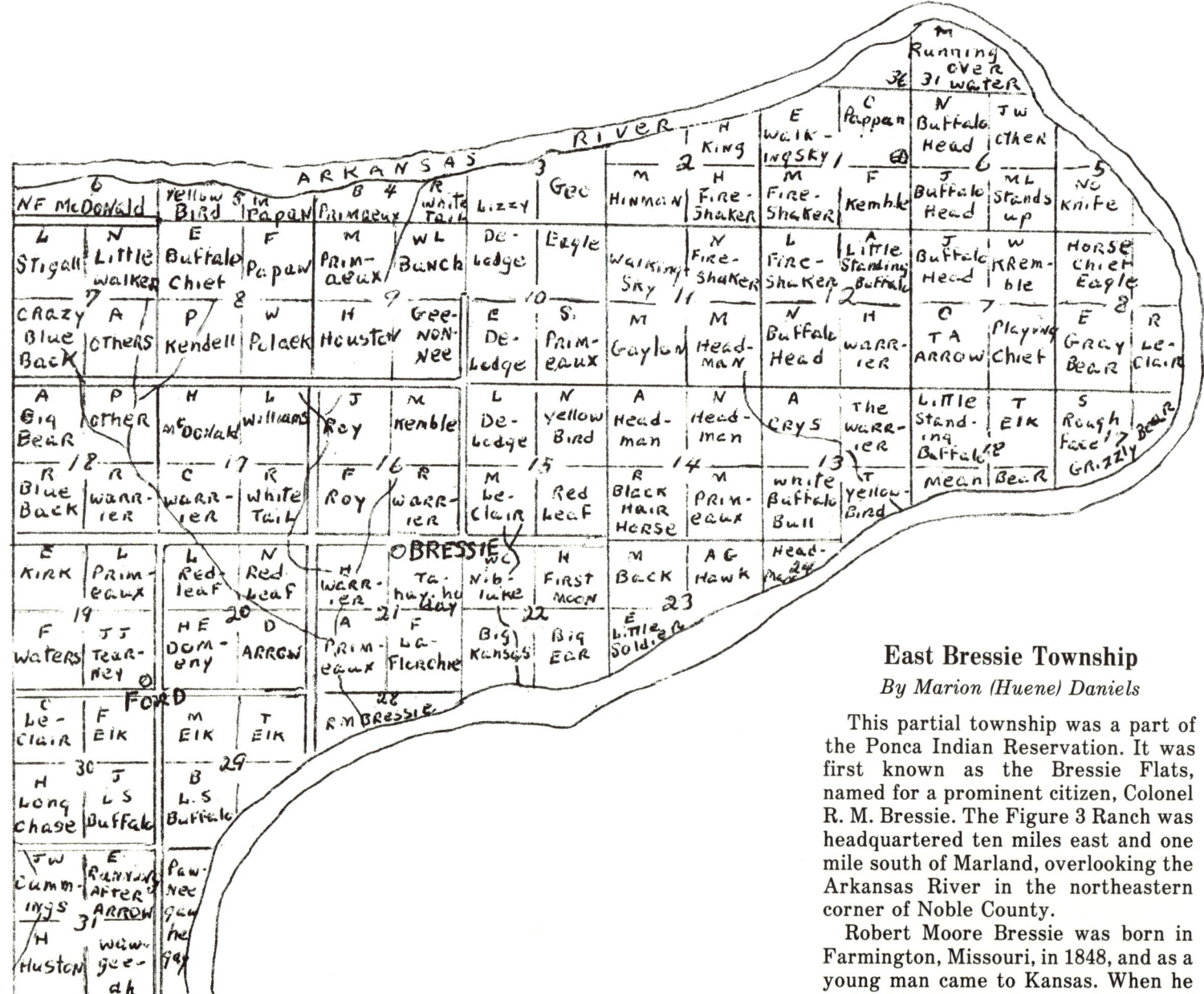

East Bressie Township
By Marion (Huene) Daniels

This partial township was a part of the Ponca Indian Reservation. It was first known as the Bressie Flats, named for a prominent citizen, Colonel R. M. Bressie. The Figure 3 Ranch was headquartered ten miles east and one mile south of Marland, overlooking the Arkansas River in the northeastern corner of Noble County.

Robert Moore Bressie was born in Farmington, Missouri, in 1848, and as a young man came to Kansas. When he arrived in Kansas, he was broke and asked for a carpenter job. The carpenter asked, if he could shingle, he replied that he could. He started nailing shingles as he had nailed clap board in Missouri, in a few minutes he found that wasn't the way to shingle.

He became a buffalo hunter and was recognized as an excellent marksman. It is told that in hunting buffalo it was necessary to shoot so fast the guns became hot. Water had to be kept as they had to put the guns in water to cool them for reloading. He was so effective in marksmanship that it was necessary to hire a man to load his guns, while he felled the buffalo. His system was to shoot the first one then the others would mill around in circles, and in this manner he shot as many as fifty buffalo out of a herd.

On a buffalo hunt in 1874, he came as far south as the horse shoe bend of the Arkansas River in Oklahoma. He noted the fertile soil and the beautiful valley and from that day, he planned to establish a ranch there. In 1896, twenty two years later, he succeeded in leasing this land from the Ponca Indians, paying fifty cents an acre for the farm land and seven cents an acre for the prairie land.

The following year 1897, at the age of 49, he came from Big Springs, Texas, with his wife and two small children, Clarence and Frances. He started with over 100 head of range horses, but some were lost in quick sand in the rivers he crossed. He arrived at his ranch with about 100 head.

The following year he brought cattle from Texas and hired men to break out the land, paying them $1.00 an acre, using horses for money.

By 1899, headquarters was a small village of dugouts, tents and soddies, housing nearly twenty families. John Andrews, was foreman over the 22,400 acre Figure 3 Ranch, which extended from the Bar-L Ranch west to what is now highway 177 bounded on the north by the Arkansas and Saltfork River and the south by the Otoe Reservation line.

1900, found headquarters no longer a village. Most of the people had moved to lands on the ranch which had been broken out, leaving only seven or eight men who were employed throughout the year at headquarters, which now consisted of a four-room house, living room, Mr. Bressie's office and combined dining room and kitchen, and a bedroom. There were about 2,000 cattle all branded with the Figure 3.

The hog ranch was one mile north and one-half mile east of the headquarters where an average of 100 brood sows were kept. Here the pigs were fattened for market. They drove the hogs to the railroad station at Bliss (now Marland), sometimes as many as 1,000 head in a herd. It was the habit of the Indians to follow the herds and butcher the hogs that fell from exhaustion. In 1906, the average production was eight pigs to a litter.

Over this period of years, Mr. Bressie bought much inherited Indian land, commonly called "Dead Indian land." The ranch had increased its activity to the point that its owner thought it necessary to install a private telephone line from White Eagle Indian Agency to headquarters, fifteen miles distance. The ranch built the line using native posts.

The Bressie Post Office was established in 1904. Mrs. R. M. (Emma) Bressie was the post-mistress. The post office was served by a star route carrier, at first two or three times weekly, later daily. The first mail carrier was Henry James.

Mr. Bressie was very active in political affairs, many historical characters of territorial days were entertained at the Figure 3 Ranch, and one occasion he hired a special train for Bird McGuire (territorial Congressman) to campaign throughout Oklahoma Territory.

Mr. Bressie was progressive in all national, territorial and community interests. In 1904, he gave the Bressie Community one acre of land on which to build a school house and later one acre for a public cemetery. His strong feeling for people less fortunate than he, was displayed each Christmas by presenting the Salvation Army at Ponca City with a butchered beef, with instructions to his men to leave this message only, "From Santa Claus."

The first school was held in a dugout. This was a room dug out in a bank with logs about four feet above the ground with a shingled roof, located one-half mile west of the Ranch headquarters. Miss Alice Hall was the teacher.

A meeting was held at the blacksmith shop at the ranch in 1903, plans were drawn up to build a school house. In 1904, a building 25 by 26 feet was built by Brasher and Demsey. Lumber was hauled from White Eagle Agency and it was necessary to ford the Salt Fork River. A young man named Daniels taught the first term in the new school house. Sometimes over 100 children were enrolled during corn shucking season. Some children came a distance of seven miles. One boy forded the river on horseback.

The greater portion of Mr. Bressie's land was farmed by Share-croppers, corn, wheat and feed crop, mainly cane and millet. By 1904, his share-croppers had obtained leases in their own names and began praying on Mr. Bessie. In his generosity to help his fellowman, a great many of his acres were lost to individuals.

The year 1905, was a bumper corn crop, the corn produced 65 to 85 bushels per acre and lease competition began cutting more and more acres from the Figure 3 Ranch. Also in 1904, Mr. Bressie had suffered heavy financial losses due to the purchase of northern cattle, which were not acclimated to the region.

These events marked the downward financial trend of the Figure 3 Ranch, that completely collapsed in 1915.

More members were added to the Bressie family, following Clarence and Frances (Mrs. Chris Anderson) then Rachel (Mrs. Rowe Abbott of Billings, Oklahoma), R. M. Bressie Jr., who died at the age of twelve, with a kidney disorder, Nellie born 1908, and Roymane 1912. Clarence went to work for the Government and was sent to Panama, Mr. Bressie left the Ranch in 1915, to find other enterprises. Mrs. Bressie, with Nellie and Roymane moved to Perry.

Reasons for naming it the Figure 3, remain unknown today. The area of the Figure 3 Ranch is one of the most fertile farm land in Oklahoma. The Bressie School is gone. The cemetery with early residents graves (John and Nancy T. Beck, Nellie O. Beck, Infant of J. W. and Annie Brasier, A. Huene, Ann Huene, Mamie Huene, Ellen E. Kirk, and Joseph Kirk), remains as a memorial to Robert Moore Bressie as well as the name Bressie Township and Bressie Community.

Bressie school (district #63) overflowed with students in 1909. For the next three years, classes were held in Ford Hall for children of the area. At that time Ford was an active community. It began to diminish in 1916, and the store closed in 1926.

In 1912, Rein school (district #70) and Tearney school (district #71) were established in the northwest and southwest areas. In 1930, a small Bar L school (district #63) was built to accomodate children living in the northeastern part of Bressie community. The school was located on pasture land owned by Charlie Thompson. Rein school, a wooden structure was torn down and replaced with a native stone building in 1939.

About 1948, the three school districts were consolidated. Bressie and Tearney school buildings were sold, children were bused to Rein school until 1961, when the school was annexed to Marland. Rein school is now used as a community center, but the Bressie and Bar L schools have been torn down.

The Ford school was moved a mile west and named Tearney about 1927. Part of the district was annexed to Bressie. Tearney was annexed to Rein school (district #70) on June 23, 1947.

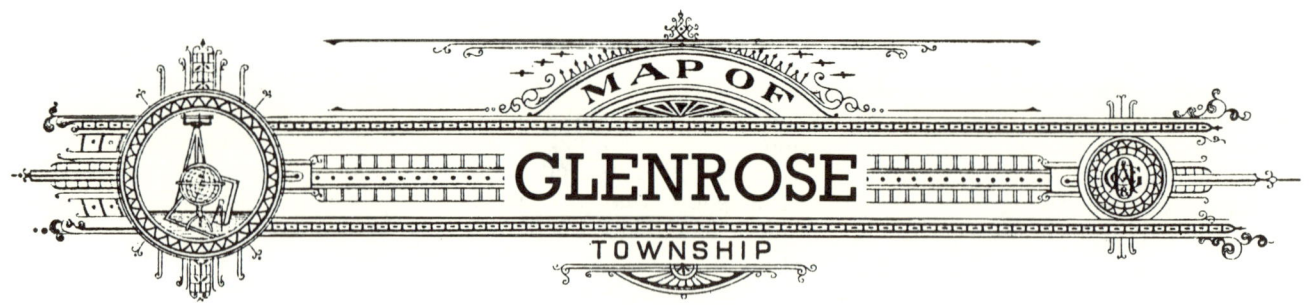

MAP OF GLENROSE TOWNSHIP

Township 24 North, Range 1 West of the Indian Meridian

E Gasaway	OC Billups	J Turner	HC Brookhart	CM Brookhart	JD Frederick	A Ruzek	F Justra	L Shawver	GW Cook	CA Southworth	P Sipe
J Logan	FH Jones	J Writt	J Southard	R Kirk	WH Wintermute	GA Hays	R Ruzek	A Vanek	J Moore	JA Campbell	LJ Regnier
		6	5		4		3		2		1
FF McGowan	JE Writt	WR Welch	MA Saper	ME Pearcy	WA West	JD Sumner	DE Evans	DH Rence	RL Moore	F Beeks	HHJ Johnson
TA Frailey	J Sauer	H Manny	F Manny	BB Pearcy	FA Freiday	EB Phelps	A Hubka	GG Hays	WF McCutchen	FP Folk	WP Wallace
		7	8		9		10		11		12
WC Corley	WT Frailey	WE Huff	FG Wieland			ER Wells	E Plumb	R Eastman	P Long		
F Sokol	BP Rosecrans	PB Holeman	F Murry			SW Wyckoff	J Morris	LD Eastman	GH Graber		
	18	17		16		15		14		13	
D Blair	M Barrett / W Barrett	W Carter	RF Kirkpatrick	WR Emmons	EB Chapman	CD Talbott	J Folk	JW Siler	GB Siler	AD Siler	J Kopecky
OT Chubb	GH Seymour	PW O'Neill	T Pettit	JM Burch	R Osborne	CP Norman	GW Kite	MI Folk		MJ Collier	WL Collier
	19	20		21		22		23		24	
W Pettit	WH Murray	FM Case	HA Reed	J Jones	FS Chambers	G Blubaugh	EB Kite	A Baggs	JA Norman	JN Yates	TH Collier
AR Carpenter	SR Buck	S Fountain	GD Bellmon	H Garrett	LM Cobb	MA Robb	WN Osborn	J Stanek	J Novacek	WH White	EC Wyckoff
	30	29		28		27		26		25	
FJ Wilkins	JD Mayhew	S Lusk	AJ Reed			FM Birks	FB Wilkins	J Stransky	AA Pilkington		
WD Carpenter	SW Postelwait	WC Hook	JR Owens			J Ranes	DC Cannon	W Stransky	TF Pilkington		
	31	32		33		34		35		36	

Glenrose Township

Three Sands Oil Field

Glenrose township was created July 22, 1896. Since January 1894, it had been a part of Red Rock township. In the vicinity of Three Sands was a post office called Burton which operated from February 6, 1894, until May 15, 1900. A small community sprang up here with the Grandview Baptist church and a small cemetery. All that remains are some tombstones and the foundation of the church. Just north of the church was the IXL school (district #21), in section 2. The land was deeded by Zacra T. Miller on March 25, 1901. The school was annexed to Kay County September 16, 1941.

In section 4 was the Hope school, (district #22). The land was deeded by William H. and Lola Kirk on September 13, 1905. Part of the district was annexed to Kay County on September 29, 1942, the rest was annexed to district #23, Glenrose on June 19, 1947.

In section 24 was the Elm Grove school (district #24), the land was deeded by Thomas H. Collier. In section 28 was the Glenrose school (district #23). The land was deeded by Jay and Louisa N. Jones on July 9, 1910. The district became D-9 and was later annexed to Billings, Red Rock, Marland and Tonkawa on June 19, 1947. The school is still standing.

Floral Ridge cemetery was organized in 1895. John R. Owens and Henry A. Read each donated an acre of land. When a small son of Mr. and Mrs. Jack Reed died, Jay Jones, a neighbor, made a small coffin and covered it with black material. The boy was buried on the H. A. Read farm. After that, several settlers were buried there and so a small cemetery began.

On one particular night thieves who had stolen a team and harness from another community came through and hitched the team to a surrey, that belonged to Jack Reed. They had gone only about a mile further when the wheels began coming off. It seemed that Reed had a habit of removing the nuts from the wheels when the surrey wasn't in use — just in case. Jack Reed had staked his claim near what was then White Rock (in White Rock township). He relinquished it that same fall and bought a claim from a man called Al Smith for $25. The first couple of years, crops failed and a neighbor, William Pettit, to save every grain of wheat possible, made a bag attached to his mowing machine similar to grass catchers on lawn mowers today that would catch the wheat heads. They were then run through the thresher. This saved much more of the grain than if it was bound and shocked in the usual way. Pettit, then loaned his machine to the neighbors.

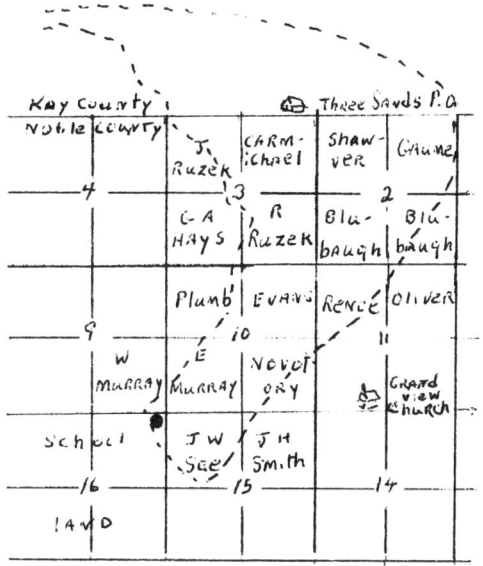

● DISCOVERY WELL

Land owners of oil rights in the Three Sands oil field.

Frank G. Wieland made the run on horseback and staked a claim two miles north of the Glenrose school as a young single man. It took him two years to break out 110 acres of ground for farming. He had no bedstead in his shack so he boarded off one corner of the room and filled it with straw to sleep on.

On June 30, 1921, oil was discovered in the ne¼ of section 16, which was school land. The off-set well to the east flowed naturally 3,000 barrels a day. This developed into one of the best known oil fields in history — the Tonkawa field or "3 Sands."

Owners of royalty became rich overnight. Many others benefitted in various ways — for example, muddy roads were a very big problem with so much heavy materials needed for the drilling wells that farmers with teams were kept busy pulling cars and trucks out of the black gumbo. Any man who could swing a hammer could find a job building houses, or board sidewalks, one such sidewalk extended for three miles north and south from the Three Sands post office. Many men were employed building the wooden derricks and rebuilding them when they burned. During every electrical storm many of these caught fire and between storms any kind of sparks would send fire racing up the oil soaked wood.

A temporary low-water toll bridge was built over the Salt Fork River directly north of Three Sands. It was made of 2" lumber of suitable widths to form two L-shaped tracks for car wheels to follow. Support for the bridge which was only about two feet above the water, was made by driving lengths of two inch planking into the river sand at close intervals with proper cross bracing. The L-shaped tracks were nailed to this sub-structure. It was always one way traffic managed by a flagman at each end of the three or four hundred yard length of the bridge and the fare was 35 cents per car.

The major oil producing companies usually built groups of company houses conveniently located on their leases for employees. These were called "Camps" and the houses were often "shotgun" houses, the three or four rooms all in a line.

Comar Oil Company's main camp and headquarters were located near the discovery well. They erected a large cafeteria for company employees and a gymnasium there for the community meetings and entertainment. The cost of the gymnasium was $60,000 and it seated 2,500 people.

A big red barn on the southeast corner of section 9 was used by a big liquor operator for dispensing his ware which could be had from a case to a carload. One half mile east of Three Sands was a place operated by an illicit liquor dispenser by the name of Springtown Frank, who sold twelve ounce bottles of near beer over the counter, spiked with an ounce or so of alcohol from under the counter. It went for 50 cents per sale and they said a few bottles made you feel as though you had sails.

For the many people who lived in the Three Sands Field 12 schools supplied the needs for the children's education but the center of this activity was the Three Sands Grade and High School which at the time as the largest school of its kind in the state. It was located about half a mile north of the Three Sands Post Office.

The Prairie View cemetery was located just north of the Noble-Kay county line in section 34. At the height of the boom a drilling contractor, named Charlie Knox, from Enid acquired a lease from the cemetery board to drill a well on the cemetery grounds. He was getting ready to move his drilling rig in when he was confronted by the people of the neighborhood with their attorney who disputed his right to drill a well in their burial grounds. There was much arguing and lots of words exchanged, but after the facts were sifted, Mr. Knox laid down his arms, or better said, his drilling rig. The cemetery plot had been deeded by the original land owner to the cemetery association for burial purposes only and any different use of the ground caused it to revert to the original land owner.

MAP OF LOWE TOWNSHIP

Township 20 North, Range 2 West of the Indian Meridian

F Noonan	GW Guthrie	T Chadwell	JL McKeown	Baltimore / GA Smith	JL Allen	CM Hamblin	FM Cooley	M Sisk	JP Stanford	ET Bailey	WL Albin / EL Albin
C Mayer	W Cox	WW Strode	J Lippincott	JM Huntzinger	D Mills	RC Johnson	JG Kirk	SA Harman	LN Ditto	GM Moutray	S Staig
MR Pratt	WS Snodgrass	AJ Donahey	M Snyder / ANTRUM	A Hoffsommer	CL Sampson	FW Pratt	MA Mosely	HV Pratt	EL Donahoe	JG Montray	GA Minugh
J Naureth	EE Pfrimmer	A Snyder	O Axhelm	JN Cox	JR Whitemore	RM Johnson	JB Beadles	ET Rice	RS Palmer	DM Haines	LB Jones
G Pratz	E Moelling	M Wolff	R Hay			JH Johnson	LA Stumpff	R Snyder	SM Hines		
C Koseba	L Miller	M Weid	P Sult			M Jerome	AA Rotterman	JT Brier	MC Shelton		
EA Dorland	J Moelling	PS Rocker	J Mauthe / C Webb	J Bolay	DM Spreng	GW Evans	L Wustenhofer	H Tubbs	AR Ketch	GA Anthis / PF Dunn	N Vanbebber
C Urban	MF Farr		WJ Webber	W Weber	M Steinner	A Bolzinger	G Wolff	FS Foot	JL Adcock	AW Ketch	P Smith
F Mayer	GJ Pheiffer	SS Tate	SW Young	JH Long	F Mugler	A Starkey	J Simkins	G Harleman	LF Huff	GJ Ketch	A Schnurr
W Braunling	H Linden	DD Smith	F Henn	WS Kolb	E Fredericks	AE James	H Schafer	RL Morton	GW Fowler	HH Isenburg	WF Young
FD Dowell	E Ellison / T Elson	GR Cowan	W Henn			EG Sharp	A Wagner	FH Neiman	E Johnson		
					AL Shoemaker	AE Hitsman					

LOGAN COUNTY

Lowe Township

Lowe township was formed in January of 1894, at that time Warren Valley township was included in Lowe township. Harmony school (district #17) was located in the northeast ¼ of section 8 on the Snyder farm. It was annexed to Orlando, Perry and Hayward. Located east and south was the Antrim post office with James H. Lippincott as post master. Antrim was discontinued in 1904 and mail sent to Lucien. Antrim got its name from County Antrim, Ulster, Ireland.

In the southeast ¼ of section 2 the Lawn View school (district #18) was erected in 1898. Prior to that time, school was held in a small one-room building, one half mile west and a quarter south of the new location. It was first called Fairview but the name was changed in 1915, because so many schools in Noble county had the name of Fairview. The Lawnview church was located west of the school on the corner. The church and parsonage were built in 1900. The parsonage was built first so ladies from surrounding farms could use it for cooking for workers while they built the church soon after. A farmer, Elmer Rice, was the carpenter and other farmers helped. Lumber was hauled from Orlando.

Soon after the church was built the Modern Woodmen held their meetings in the basement, which was also used for Sunday School classes, ice cream socials and get-togethers of various kinds.

Mrs. Pete Rolling recalled "We used to have big Sunday school conventions and folks for miles around attended. On Decoration day we gathered at the church with flowers, then the children and young people marched to the Lawn View cemetery, one half mile north, to decorate the graves."

The Lawn View school was destroyed in 1912 by a tornado but was rebuilt to accomodate the 52 pupils in the district. In February 1929, the school caught fire from the stove and burned to the ground. The term of school was completed in the Lawn View church. A new school was built that summer. It was annexed to White School (district #15) and Hunter school district (#78).

The church building was sold in 1937 and torn down. Other buildings in the area had been gone for many years prior to that time.

The Oak Point school (district #20) was located in the southeast ¼ of section 20. It was annexed to Orlando, April 17, 1935. In the northeast ¼ of section 26 was the Union school (district #19) on land homesteaded by Gabriel Harleman. Part of this district was annexed to Noble county and part to Logan county.

In the southwest ¼ of section 30, Mahlon H. Parks gave land to build the German Southern M.E. church while in the southeast ¼ of section 27, Henry Schafer deeded ½ acre of land for the Mt. Zion cemetery.

A correction line extends across the southern line of this township, making a jog in the southern boundary of Noble county. This corrected a mistake in the surveying when the Unassigned Lands were opened for settlement in 1889. This correction line extended through Rock and Walnut township but these townships were in Payne County, the line was corrected so there is no uneven line although some of the farms are odd-shaped.

Like the other schools throughout the country, the school here held box and pie suppers, etc. to raise money for the upkeep and improvement of the school buildings. The girls and ladies spent hours decorating the boxes and preparing the "goodies" to pack inside. Great pains were taken to keep the owner's name secret as this added to the fun. After the auction was over the young (or old) man who bought the box ate with the young (or old) lady who had brought it, which could cause a lot of disappointment to a young man who had saved his pennies in hopes of eating with his best girl only to end up with the "old maid" of the community. Likewise a girl who had spent time and effort on her box might eat with a young man she did not like. Another way to separate the young man from his money was the contest for the "Prettiest Girl." At a penny a vote this usually went to the girl whose boy friend had the most money. The prize for this was a box of candy. The prize for the winner of "the man with the dirtiest feet" was a bar of laundry soap. The "sourest man" got a dill pickle and the "most hen-pecked husband" got a rolling pin which all added to the fun of the evening.

History of Noble County

MAP OF MISSOURI TOWNSHIP

Township 22 North, Range 2 East of the Indian Meridian

Missouri Township

Missouri township was named for the Otoe-Missouria Indian tribe. This part of the reservation was hunting grounds and leased to the white man for pasture.

Few people lived on these reservation lands and only two schools were located in this township. Liberty school (district #68) was in the southeast corner of section 4. In the northeast corner of section 31 was another school. Among the children attending here in 1912 were the Van Meeter, Tillman, Jensen, Gawhega, Jackson, Biddle, Dupee, Taylor, Clifton, Daily, LaDue, Plumbley and Marshall families.

Two Otoe-Missouria Indian cemeteries are located in the southeast corner of the township. The Clifton family burial grounds is located in section 31. With about 20 graves with few stones, it is on allotted lands of Josephine (Clifton) Taylor.

In southeast ¼ of section 32, located in a pasture on allotted lands of Augusta Tillman is the Tillman family cemetery. Buried here is Augustus LaDue who was caretaker of the toll bridge over Red Rock Creek. His wife is buried in an Indian cemetery in Otoe township.

The following letters were found when the Swiler Brothers Store in Stillwater was being cleaned out. They were published in the Payne County News March 25, 1932. They show the language barrier that put the Indians at such a disadvantage. The payments Mr. Faw Faw refers to are the moneys from interest payments on money for the land sold in Nebraska. The agent controlled the Indians by withholding their money.

Red Rock Otoe Agency
Indian Territory
October 10, 1890

Swiler Bros.
Dear Friend:

I will write you a few lines to let you know how we are doing here. The news we have here only $10,000 for payment sometime this month. But I have very doubt not paid you what Otoe owes you, but we will tried best to talk with tribe to paid you debts if we can. Agent Wood says going give them checks, not cash, so cannot tell you what to do, but we send messanger to Washington. The answer yet come back. Everybody complaint about. May we bring checks down there to you if we can. But myself and white mate both of us paid you all we can. When you received this you better drop a few lines let us know as soon as can, but we want to know if you are going to give beef to tribe. I was very sorry some white man or Indian they stole both work horses. I found them both this afternoon. Somebody tied up inside bushes. I am alright now. This is all I can say yours truly,
William Faw Faw, James Whitewater.

Feb 23, 1896

Dear Sirs:

We are very good friends to each other and I should like to talk with you but I couldn't talk English very much; So I let this man write for me. Otoes owed you some money, but it wont be long while to pay their debts. They get $15,000 sometimes in this quarter. If you send me all the Otoes name and what they owed you, I should try to get every cent for you or else I let Agent get it for me. We got a store here, but the Trader says everything too high. That is reason I want you to trust me. That is the only way I could get something cheap. I never hear of you for long while, I should like to know how you is getting along. I am well and hope these few lines might reach you all well. I am going over there to get them Otoes names. So I'll do all I can for you to get some money for you. This is all.

Your Friend,
William Faw Faw

Otoe Agency, I.T.
June 1890

To Swiler Bros:

Red Eagle want your trust him three dollars. He said he pay you every time he owe you. So he think he could pay as soon as possible. Faw Faw says he will see this man he pay you.
Yours in haste, your true friend,
William Faw Faw

Red Rock, I.T.
April 25, 1890

We are going over there on Sun. but agent wont let us go. That is reason we didn't come. Agent said he ain't going to give us our payment, that is if we go over to dance. Payment is coming very close. Commissioner of Indian Affairs heard that we are going over there to dance, so he went to agent and told him not to go but I can't go with Agent permission. Agent says he let you fellows know that we ain't going come up there. I don't know whether he did or not. We should get our money we are going down there no matter what Ageny says. We are all well. I am in Red Rock today. This is all.
Your friend,
William Faw Faw

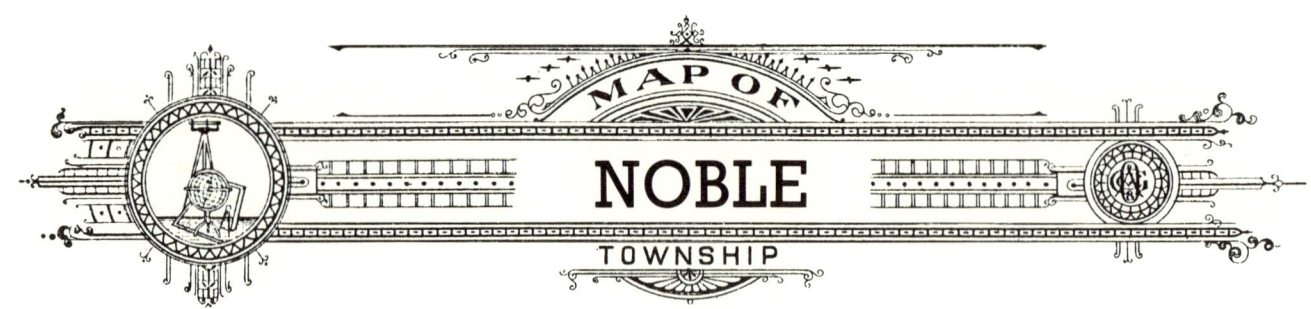

MAP OF NOBLE TOWNSHIP

Township 21 North, Range 1 East of the Indian Meridian

H Viets	TL Bowden / J Campbell	KRAI / J Hendrick / M Rowland	WH Baker	S Crain	JH Sarles	Osborn / Osborn	J Nemecek	J Masek	BT Steadman	FM Allen / E Arnett	CW Browing
L Wilbur		L Newcomb	J McGrath	A Hargrove	WH Malcolm	J Soulek	W Neel	TL Lancaster	LJ Sullivan	CA Clifton / EL Renfro	AS Pickering
A Henderick / T Ramey	M Henderick / L Henderick / MT Dempsey	DA Hurley	EH Lumbert	M Lambert	JC Evans	RW Clark	J Horn	WA Flower	Omelia / Omelia	WT Dalton	JM Brennan
JF Broome / CF Singleton	JF Piatt	TH Williams / JF Ireland	JL Butterfield	F Sommars	HM McKay	JJ Metz	R Davis	DV Hall	K Brubaker	HG Lattin	JH Swope
GW Willis	HC Nicholson	TP Ewart	A Eisfeldt			TD Field	RE Reed	G Friedekind	J Cejka		
ES Rice / AL Kramer	E Enfield	HA Williams	J Stahl			J Ritthaler	C Benke	LJ Rounsavell	J Straub		
Coldwell / AL Strickland	O Stevens	RH Durkee	JT Jacobs	JA Douglass	WA Cleland	FS Bowlby	EC Sneed	D Layman / JS Boyle	WM Triggs	P Fetter	WT Webster
JC Wood	A Koelzer	JC Mathis	W Ewart	W Rupp	GD Diller	WA Warner	JF Keeler	ME Hansen	O Waikling	R Allen	AN Hemstreet
CH Christner	EJ Finlayson	WF Brasch	JJ Douglass	J Sylvester	CC Rathburn	JW Dotts	J Piterka	JR Lawing	HC Linville	IA Moore	JF Ellis
IB Carpenter	H Koelzer	JJ Gorath	H Latimer / A Lennox	W Brown	ML Swanson	E Ewy	J Siama	L Ritthaler	JW Tobin	E Stickel	M Mark
TH Soward	H Barkley	GA Widiger	Barrett / SC Barrett			SM Keele	WG Bommer	J Ziesch	P Johnson / S Ziesch		
S Aigner	W Manzilla	J Herrick	T Russell			T Moore	M Stiver	ME Wilkinson	WG Albertin		

Noble Township

There seems to be several reasons given for the naming of Noble Township. The most widely accepted, bases the name from Noble county, Oklahoma. It was a part of Watkins township when first formed in January, 1894. It was separated from Watkins township April 21, 1896.

Three miles northeast of Perry in section 7 of Noble township, a townsite, called Liberty, was developed in 1893, by E. P. McCade, prominent Territorial black, formerly auditor of the state of Kansas, as a Negro town. Not withstanding extensive efforts, especially by the African Methodist church to secure settlers, the project did not survive. Near the townsite, the Santa Fe had established a switch and loading point known as Arnettville. Later the name for the stop was changed to McMahon, named for J. E. McMahon, Santa Fe official.

In the southeast ¼ of section 8, a one-room school was built called Willow Creek (district #39). The land for the school was donated by John L. Butterfield on February 21, 1901.

In the northeast ¼ of section 11 was the Independence school (district #42). The land was sold to the school district for $35 by J. C. Nielsen, a bachelor, on September 6, 1907. Independence became a part of Sumner on June 2, 1920.

In the northeast ¼ of section 29 was the Pioneer school (district #40). Pioneer was annexed to Perry on June 24, 1947.

In the southwest ¼ of section 25 was the Oak Grove school (district #41). Several black families had children attending this school. When segregated schools were made mandatory by the first amendment of the Oklahoma Constitution, a black school was held in the old Richburg store a mile and a half east of the white school. It was called Oak Grove #2 (district #41).

On May 2, 1902, Jan Cejka deeded to the Bohemian Catholic cemetery, ground for a cemetery in the northeast ¼ of section 14. The names on the tombstones are: Mary Cejka, Lesh family: John, Frank and John, sons of J. T. and K. Lesh, Sylvia Osborn, Joseph Soulek, and Vaglev Korp Zemrel. The cemetery was apparently abandoned in the 1920s for burials.

A Mennonite church was located on the southwest corner of section 27 on the Edward Ewy homestead, the cemetery was a mile south in Walnut township. Rev. Henry Koller, one of the early ministers is buried in this cemetery.

Many Lutherans came to the area from Kansas. Worship services were held in homes until churches were established. Zion Lutheran congregation, now located five miles east of Perry on highway 64 and associated with the Lutheran church in America, began as a preaching poast and was

John A. Thompson.

visited by circuit-riding pastors on the Missouri Synod. On February 22, 1897, Ludwig Ritthaler donated land to the Lutheran church. The land was used for a church and a cemetery. The cemetery was first used in May, 1897. In April, 1897, the Zion Lutheran congregation was formally organized. The date is indefinite as to when the building was erected on the present site of the Zion Lutheran cemetery. Most of this congregation were Germans coming to America from Germany/Prussia or Russia. A number of the group settled in Kansas where they established homes. At the opening of the Strip, a group of these Lutherans formed a wagon train to travel to Oklahoma and many of them staked claims. They were joined by others who had other cultures, languages and religious backgrounds. Eventually, there wre differences of opinion on various issues, which finally led to a split in the congregation. The cemetery is located in the southwest ¼ of section 26.

In the year 1901, approximately 14 of the 24 members decided to leave the Missouri Synod and joined the German Nebraska Synod of the General Synod. The 10 members remaining with the Missouri Synod organized the Emmanuel Lutheran church at Richburg. They worshipped in the Mennonite church for a period of time prior to erecting a building on the site of the Richburg cemetery (southwest ¼ of section 34). The oldest tombstone in the cemetery is dated 1912. This land was deeded to the congregation by Carl F. Mielke, who is buried in the cemetery. The dedication service for the church was on April 21, 1907. The Emmanuel congregation of Richburg merged with the Christ Lutheran congregation in Perry in 1929.

Willow Creek school children.

Township 22 North, Range 2 West of the Indian Meridian

Oakdale Township

Oakdale Township was a part of Black Bear Township when first formed in January 1894. Oakdale was separated from Black Bear on December 3, 1896. It was named for Anderson Dale and John Oakley.

At one time, there were six grade schools in this township: Antelope (district #9) in section 6; North Valley (district #57) in section 10; Central in section 1; West Lawn (district #21) in section 19; Polo (district #58) in section 22; and Happy Hill in section 26. Happy Hill was also called Hughes because it was on the homestead taken by Ben Hughes in the run. Antelope and North Valley became Antelope Valley.

Polo, on the southeast corner of section 21 and southwest corner of section 22, was comprised of a church, school and grocery store for many years. The post office was established on January 31, 1894, and was discontinued September 15, 1904 and the records turned over to the Perry post office. All that is left is the cemetery which is located a mile north of where Polo once stood.

Polo Christian Church   Audrey Carter

In the run of 1893, claims were staked all around the area 7 miles west and 5 miles north of Perry. A water pump stood in the center of the intersection, providing water for the businesses that popped up here and there.

Andrew (Polo) Anderson, having staked a claim on the southwest corner of the intersection, opened a blacksmith shop. It is from him that Polo got its name. Mr. Vandevender opened a General Store across the road to the north from the blacksmith shop.

It is not known how long the Vandevenders operated the store, but they sold to A. B. Nichol, another pioneer of the Land Run, having staked a claim 3½ miles north of Polo. Mr. Nichol operated the store until his death in 1918. After Mr. Nichol's death George Merriman, his son-in-law, was in charge of it until it closed.

A school was built on the northeast corner of the intersection and was to be used as a place of worship as well as education for area children.

On April 4, 1903, while C. F. Trimble was ministering there, the group voted to build a church and was to be Christian-Disciples of Christ. Bob Hannah, who had staked a claim on that corner, donated part of his land for the church building. Building was started in March, 1904, and was finished June 20, 1904, at the cost of $1,257. Brother White, from Perry, delivered the Dedication Sermon July 10, 1904. It was named Polo Christian Church.

On July 14, 1905, the congregation voted to hire Brother Ed Kirtly as minister for one year. He was required to deliver two sermons each Sunday and would be paid $2.50 each sermon.

Besides the regular Sunday services and youth meetings, the church served as a meeting place for family reunions, box-suppers, funerals, and special programs. One special program being at Christmas when "The Birth of Christ" was presented by the youth of the church, followed by the usual visit from Santa.

Easter would usually start with a sunrise breakfast service out in the hills of pasture land west of the church.

Memorial Day was another special time when families would travel a great distance to attend the Special Memorial services, followed by a basket dinner and fellowship. Later, we would go to the Polo cemetery which is located 1 mile north and ¼ mile west of the church. Church services were discontinued in 1964, after serving the community for 60 years.

Antelope Valley Church   Gladys Schnaitman

The Antelope Valley Church of the Brethern is located nine miles south of Billings in northwest Noble County, on a two acre plot.

Though busily engaged in making shelters, breaking sod, and planting their crops, the settlers felt the need for fellowship and worship. The Antelope Valley Church of the brethern was organized in 1901 and known as the Bear Creek Church, later changed to Antelope Valley. The "Old Timer", — before 1900, say that the Antelope roamed the valley — hence the name Antelope Valley was put on the first school house and later on the church.

The first two years meetings were held in homes and school houses — one was called "Lone Star", later the Antelope Valley school building was built and meetings were held there. Rev. W. G. Cook came to Antelope Valley in August of 1905. Other early ministers were J. D. Fisher, E. J. Smith, and W. B. Sell. Some of the first families were the George Pfrimmer, Calvin Young, J. D. Fisher, the Stines, the Choates, Underwoods, Schnaitman and Peebler.

The first church building was built in 1914. It had Gothic windows, acteylene lights, opera chairs, a large wood-burning stove for heating and ceiling fans were used during the summer months. In 1943, the church was remodeled and the vestibule added. A six room parsonage with full basement also was constructed at that time. The Rev. K. O. Thralls served as pastor during the remodeling period.

The church burned to the ground May 23, 1946, and services were conducted in the basement of the parsonage until a new building was constructed. The new building was dedicated August 22, 1948.

Since it is near the county line, a number of the members come from Garber as well as Billings, Perry and the local area.

Several ministers have served the Antelope Valley Church as well as a number of student ministers from Phillips University. There is a membership of about 55.

It is a community church of several denominations, but is sponsored by the church of the Brethern. Some of the members are great-great-grandchildren of the early members, such as the George Pfrimmers, the W. G. Cook and the John Jake Schnaithman families. The present minister is the Rev. John Holderread.

Antelope Valley Church.

MAP OF OTOE TOWNSHIP

Township 23 North, Range 2 East of the Indian Meridian

Otoe Township

Otoe township, a part of the Otoe Indian Reservation, was known as the south part of Otoe in 1912. The north part of Otoe is now East and West Bressie, which belonged to the Ponca Indian tribe.

The Otoes moved to the reservation in Indian Territory in October, 1881, and the Otoe Boarding school was in session the following May and June. It was on a section of land, crossed diagonally by Red Rock Creek. In 1882, excellent progress was made. The boys performed daily labor in the cultivation of the school farm and garden and the girls were taught sewing and housework. In 1884, five acres were cultivated by the school. There were three teachers, an enrollment of 54 pupils and capacity for 70. Agent John W. Scott found the children bright and teachable, but found it exceedingly difficult to induce the parents to send their children to school. By 1886, special pains were taken by confine the children to the English language alone. The school was a frame building consisting of three sections joined together.

When the first allotment schedule was approved in December, 1899, the Otoe Boarding School had been in operation a quarter of a century. It was a place for youth to live as well as to learn. Orphans found refuge there and small children from many homes learned the white man's language and some of his ways of life. Reluctance of parents to send children to school emanated in part from close family association. The child at school learned to wash and be clean, to dress, eat in the white man's fashion, drink milk, brush his teeth and care for property. He learned to work, and this in a tribal background where a man who worked was derided as a squaw.

The Indian had a distinct individuality, he was not simply a white man with red skin. He tended to cling to the ways of his ancestors, thought they were better than those of the whites, and sometimes he resented efforts of the government to "educate" him and his children.

In the allotment of the reservation, the Otoes remained in common a tract of 720 acres for administrative, church, school and other public purposes. In 1901, the school had a capacity of 75 pupils and an average daily attendance of 92. Each student was allotted a plot of ground to plant and cultivate. The school farm produced 700 bushels of oats, 1,000 bushels of corn and 65 tons of hay.

On September 10, 1902, fire destroyed the Otoe school building. At a council on November 20, the Otoes requested Congress to provide for the expenture of $30,000 from tribal funds to rebuild in good substantila manner the school, dormitory, laundry and other necessary building and to complete the waterworks and sewer system. For two years, the Otoes had no school of their own, but many of the children attended the Chilocco Indian school which had been in operation since January 15, 1884. A brick building was erected and school began in the new building on September 19, 1904 with 54 pupils. The school had capacity for 75 children which it soon attained, steam heat, acetylene gas lights and a ring and tub bath system. On the site were 22 structures such as: dormitory, office and commissary, agency barn and physician's residence all two-storied. Other buildings were the acetylene gas house, coal house, school barns, cattle sheds, ice house, council house, guard house, cottages and shops.

Superintendent Horace W. Newman told of the boardwalk, painted buildings and fences, and of the walnut grove in Kentucky blue grass.

On May 3, 1907, fire destroyed the Agency office and school commissary, but the rest of the buildings were saved.

The settlement of whites on the reservation and the establishment of district schools raised the problem of the attendance of Indian children living on trust lands. A limited number from the better homes were accepted at the schools. There remained a need for the Otoe for the Otoe Boarding School because some full bloods were shy, and sometimes they came from homes where white ideas of cleanliness did not prevail, and they were soon made to feel in one way or another that they were not wanted at the public school.

There were four district schools within the line of the Otoe Reservation and to these, Indian children were admitted on payment of tuition. It was a fixed practice for children to attend a non-reservation school at age 14.

In section 2 in the southeast corner was the Dailey school. In the southwest corner of section 4 was the Evans-Dale school and in section 28 was the Long Branch all district #64. The Otoe cemetery is located in the southeast part of section 20. The Cleghorn family cemetery is located in the northeast part of section 12.

The Otoe school was closed June 30, 1919 and the Otoe children mainly attended the boarding schools at Pawnee and Chilocco and the public school at Red Rock.

The schoolhouse, known as the Community Building, had a card value of $12,250. Nearing was a garage, cottage and water tower which raised the total valuation to $18,838. On July 1, 1955, the tribal council requested that the property be released to the tribe unconditionally, and this was done.

On this historic site the Otoes have gathered from time to time and in the basement of the old school building they counciled on common problems. Among these were assistance to youth including education, relief to the poor, loans to the worthy, and not least was the successful effort to gain a day in court where a financial accounting ws had for tribal lands acquired by the federal government. For years the site was but a ghost of its former self, but Otoes who associate with it the charm of youth had no wish to sell it or to have it alloted. In the words of Mitchell Deroin, they would retain it in tribal control "As long as there is an Otoe under the heaven." The building was restored and rededicated in 1960.

Otoe Boarding School - built in 1904.

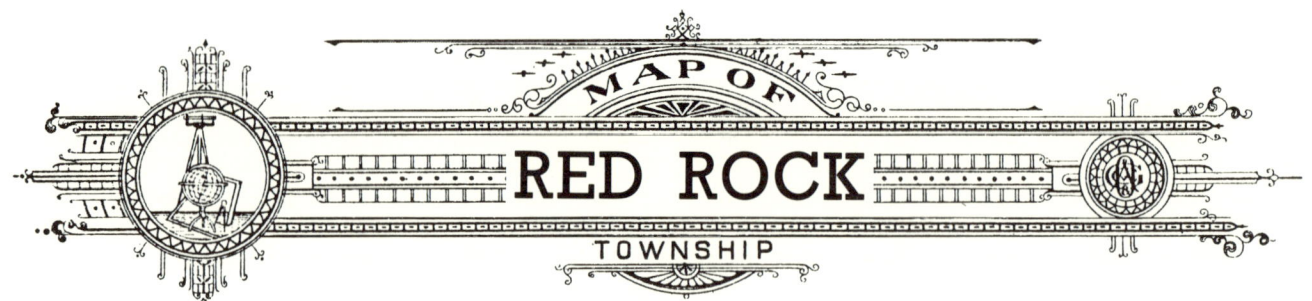

Township 23 North, Range 1 West of the Indian Meridian

Red Rock Township

Red Rock Township was named for Red Rock Creek which runs through the township from west to east. It was included in Glenrose township when first formed in January of 1894.

Four schools were located here, the Banner school (district #26) in the southeast corner of section 5. In the southwest corner of section 1 was located the Longview school (district #25). Pleasant Valley (district #27) was located in the southeast corner of section 20 and Bowden school (district #28) was located in the southwest corner of section 24, both served the south part of the township.

A post office called Bowdenton was in the southeast ¼ of section 23. It was a post office from July 21, 1894 to August 4, 1897, and was named for R. A. Bowden, first post master.

In the northeast corner of section 15, McKinney post office was established on December 12, 1893, named for George R. McKinney, first postmaster. The name was changed to Ceres on February 6, 1897. It was named for the Roman Goddess of Harvest.

A local newspaper in 1902 gives this account of Ceres: Ceres is located on the northeast corner of Byron Covey's farm, a part of which has been surveyed and platted for a town site. It is located on the main public north and south thoroughfare from Blackwell to Perry. It has two telephone systems: The Arkansas Valley and the long distant phones of Missouri and Kansas company. It has two churches, the Baptist and the Christian denominations, an MWA lodge of 40 members with plans for erecting a two story building.

Some of the businesses mentioned were B. Covey and son merchandise, Byron and Erwin Covey both secured fine claims. The business is conducted by Erwin assisted by brother Ed; Haley and Sullins, merchandise; Frank Haley and Walter Sullins, succeeded E. E. VanSlyke and do business in his building, the first erected here, long before the town was contemplated. Mr. VanSlyke is still the postmaster with his office in the rear of the building; J. M. Schnore, Restaurant and Livery stable, opened about a year ago. He is assisted by his wife; J. W. Wilson Blacksmith shop, one of the old landmarks of the town. His shop was the second erected here three years ago. He does everything in the line of blacksmith and wagon work; A. J. Atchison's Meat Market and Feed Yard, opened in September. He reports he sometimes has to kill three beaves per week to supply the demand. He also has a good farm near Ceres; Dr. O. E. Lovelady came to Oklahoma from Illinois about 32 years ago and came to Ceres in November; B. Covey, real estate, formerly one of the county commissioners of this county is owner of the townsite; R. J. Stackhouse occupies a large, nicely furnished residence on the corner of his farm adjoining Ceres; Bud Silver, barber, opens twice a week and L. E. Nichols, resient contractor, is now putting up the Woodman Hall."

The mailman brought mail from Red Rock each day at about 2 p.m. and a large gathering of people were usually on hand to get their mail.

Ceres did not have good well water, as most people had cisterns, and as it did not have a school or railroad, the people began to leave and the bank and some businesses later moved to Red Rock.

Frank Sanders, a leading citizen of Ceres, had at one time a Ford Automobile and tractor agency, a Bull Tractor agency and later a Case tractor agency at Ceres.

As wheat became the main crop, people would get together to haul wheat to the railroad at Red Rock. Wheat was hauled from as far away as Billings in caravans of 10 to 20 wagons so they could help each other ford Red Rock Creek near present day Red Rock.

In 1921, a tornado blew away the building of the Ceres Christian church. A new building was built on a new lot along the highway.

Ceres Baptist Church — Helen Ratliff

The story of the Ceres Baptist Church is truly one of the demonstrations of God's love and power. On Sunday March 4, 1899, seven members of the Ceres community met at the Bowden schoolhouse, three miles southeast of Ceres, and organized the Salem Baptist Church. Rev. James E. Eldridge was called as the first pastor. The charter members were: Charles J. Greer and his wife; Frank D. Greer and his wife, Juliette; John S. Greer and his wife, Julia; and Minnie Minor. Articles of Faith found in Pendleton's Church Manual were adopted. Brother Charles Greer was elected church clerk.

After organization other candidates for baptism were Mr. and Mrs. Rolandus A. Bowden, Henry Rogers, James Minor, Alma Dunham, Edward Brock, Fred Bowden, Laura Dunham, James W. Minor, Sam Dunham, Susie Rogers, Estina Dilliplain, Katie Orr, P. R. Dunham, Mr. and Mrs. Carrol Ratliff, Isaac Hoskins, Mr. and Mrs. W. C. Dilliplain. Others joined by promise of letter were P. R. Washabaugh, Mr. and Mrs. Will Crow, Rev. James A. Eldridge and wife.

First Sunday School officers were James W. Minor, Superintendent; Juliet Greer, assistant Superintendent; Laura Dunham, Secretary; James W. Minor, teacher for Bible Class; Charles Greer, teacher for Intermediate Class; Juliett Greer, teacher for Primary Class. Frist Deacon was Henry Rogers.

July 22, 1899, the church sent letter of Petition to Perry Association asking for admittance. On motion Church agreed to take the Lords Supper every quarter.

For the first two years the church continued to meet in Bowden schoolhouse, then a postoffice was opened in the new town of Ceres. March 23, 1901, the church raised funds to construct a building at Ceres, and changed the name from "Salem" to "First Baptist Church of Ceres." The church was built on the Carrol Ratliff farm. Brother Ratliff was elected janitor and to receive $1.00 per month for his services.

A parsonage was built in 1902, for the sum of $325.00. Brother Rogers was hired to paint the parsonage, two coats at $13.00, he donated $3.00 of said amount.

The church grew and was filled to capacity. The original church structure still stands, although the original east entrance was changed to the west side, an entry was constructed and two class rooms built. Later, a new wing was added on the south, and the auditorium redecorated as it is now.

On the 50th, 60th and 75th anniversary of the church organization, special services were held, with many former members and friends returning for a "Homecoming Day". March 4, 1985 the 86th anniversary of the church, Mr. and Mrs. Earl Ratliff hosted a supper for the church members in their home.

First Baptist Church of Ceres isn't so lively today, however it still maintains worship services each Sunday morning. Only one Sunday school class with fifteen members, some with failing health not able to attend regularly. One day the doors will probably close with only pleasant memories for some of us.

Ceres Baptist Church, 13 miles north of Perry on U.S. 77.

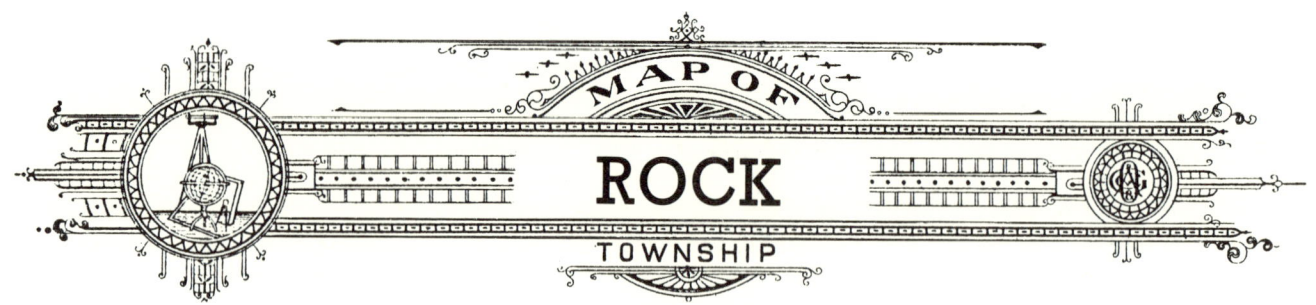

Map of Rock Township

Township 20 North, Range 1 West of the Indian Meridian

Rock Township

Rock township was in Payne county from September 16, 1893 until statehood in 1907. The legal records can be found in the Noble county courthouse but the 1900 census was in Payne county. Rocks can be found on the surface of the land, some flat enough to be used in making walks as well as building walls for sheds and barns.

In section 18 on the Santa Fe railway was the Asp station. The townsite was established about 1902 and was named for Henry E. Asp, prominent Oklahoma City attorney. In section 15, a post office named Donnelly existed from May 2, 1900 to April 30, 1901. It was named for Frank Donnelly, first postmaster.

The Hunter school (district #78) in the northwest corner of section 8 was named for Alex Hunter, a leader in organizing the school. Martin E. Augustine donated an acre of land for the school. The schoolhouse burned in 1970 from an unknown cause.

Pike's Peak school (district #79) was so called because it sat on a knoll. It was located in the northern section line of section 11 on land homesteaded by E. Berger.

Vernon school (district #77) was located near Little Stillwater Creek on the southwest quarter of section 20. Several black families lived here and at statehood separate but equal schools had to be provided so another school house was added called the Star school to accomodate these children. It was located in a half mile east and a half mile north on land homesteaded by Charley Pohlman. William Haynes donated an acre of land for the school. Both schools were district #77. A small cemetery for black people is located in the southeast ¼ of section 29. Few of the stones can be read but funeral records show that several of the black family named Green are buried here or in a corner of the Fairview cemetery.

The Fairview school (district #76) was located on the John Swendig farm in the northeast quarter of section 26. John Swendig donated an acre and a half for the school. This school was one of the last rural schools to close and the building was used for a community center for several years. It still stands and belongs to the man who owns the farm.

A half mile west of the Fairview school is the Fairview cemetery. It was sometimes called the Crockett cemetery because Daniel J. Crockett donated land from his homestead for the cemetery.

The Pleasant Grove Baptist church was located in the northeast quarter of section 30 on an acre of land donated by Joseph McGuire. It was later moved to the southeast quarter of section 29 on an acre of land donated by Charles F. Rogers. The Little Zion Presbyterian church of the U.S.A. was located in the northeast quarter of section 29.

Part of Perry Lake, source of Perry's water supply lies in section 6 of Rock township.

Flavio Calori homesteaded the southwest quarter of section 21. Mr. Calori was from Italy. He built a dam to hold the water from a spring that is still running water (1986). He irrigated a piece of land for a truck garden and sold fresh vegetables to stores and restaurants in Perry. He built an underground storage for his produce. The roof that covered the structure is gone but the underground part is still in good condition. It is hewn of solid rock. Six steps lead to the lower level of construction which is six feet deep, 20 feet long and 12 feet wide and hewn of natural sand rock. On the west wall is an arched doorway leading into another section. The construction boasted shelves chiseled into the rock and in the back room a bench maybe large enough for a half mattress, which leads one to belive it may have been used for a storm cave. In the east wall was a storage area approximately four feet long, three feet high and three feet in depth. The arches in the structure are well made and show the same degree of arch. A portion of the spring flowed through the structure to keep the temperature and moisture right for the vegetables. There is a well nearby, hewn out of the rock that tapped this same underground source of water.

Storage caves of Flavio Calori where he stored his produce. He used dynamite to help dig the cave.

74 / History of Noble County

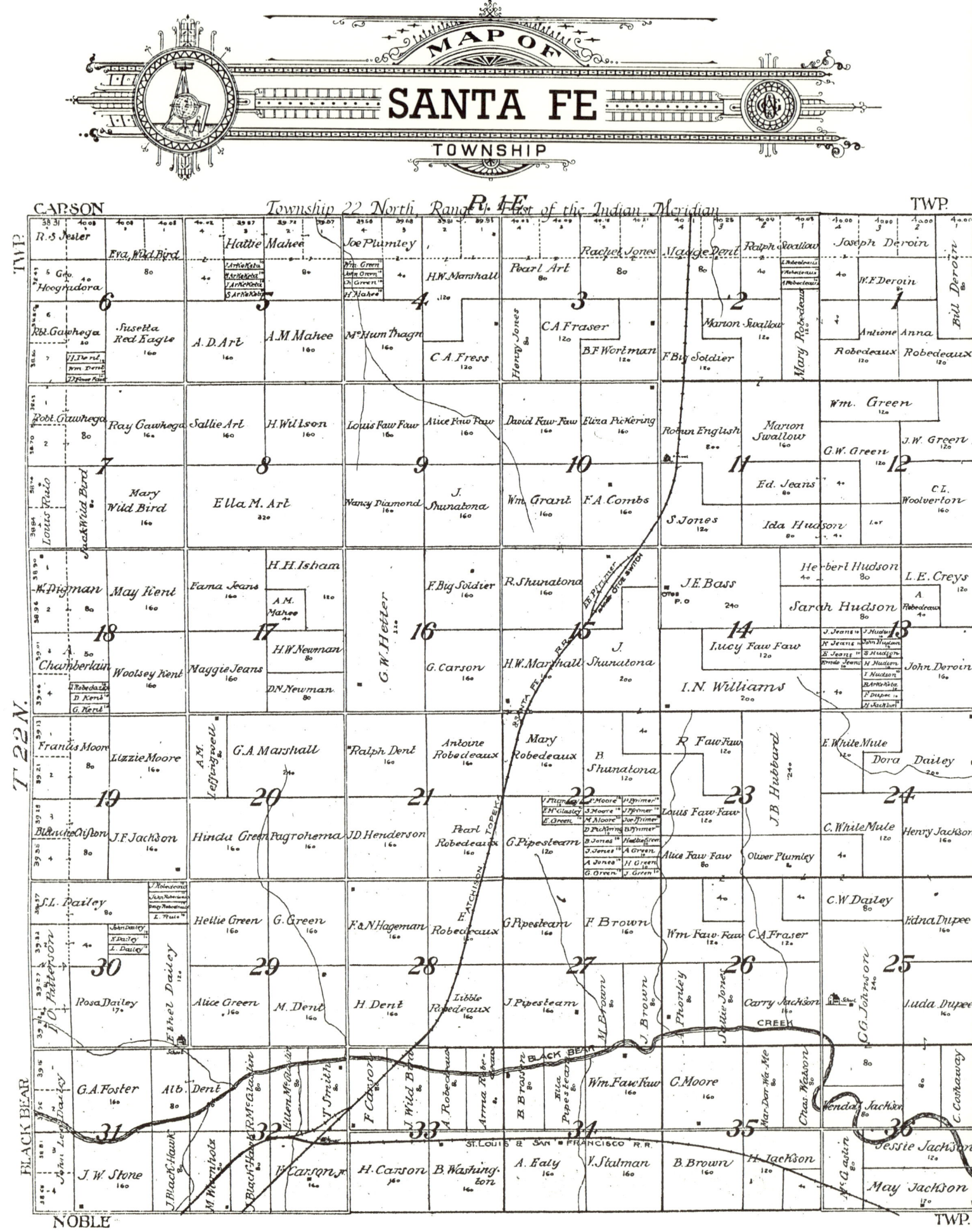

Santa Fe Township

Santa Fe township was named for the Atchison, Topeka and Santa Fe railway that crosses the township from southwest to northeast. The map on the opposite page was made in 1912.

A post office called Redrock was established November 8, 1881 and the name changed to Otoe May 3, 1892. A railroad switch was established here for shipping cattle from the cattle ranches in the Cherokee Strip before the opening to white settlement. Large sums of money were shipped to this station. This included the money received from cattle sent north, also the Indian allotment monies and salary and expenses of the agents. As there were no banks this cash money was sent by train. If the bandits could catch a shipment coming in, they could make a good haul by robbing the trains.

Zip Wyatt and his brother, Bill, held up the telegraph operator at the Redrock station some four years before the opening of the Strip. Zip Wyatt was the son of John F. Wyatt, a volunteer union soldier in the 85th Indiana Regiment during the Civil War. At the opening of Old Oklahoma, the family settled on a claim on the Cimarron River on what came to be known as "Cowboy Flat." The boy whose real name was Nelson Wyatt was frequently engaged in brawls and gradually went from bad to worse. Chris Madsen, who was a peace officer on the frontier at that time, said Zip Wyatt was the most ruthless of killers. Surrounded by officers of the law, he was fatally wounded and died in the Garfield county jail in Enid, Oklahoma in September 1894 at the age of 31 years, leaving behind a trail of banditry, train robberies and murder.

There was no land to build a town here as the land was owned by the Otoe Indians. Later a town was established six miles north in Carson township and was called Red Rock.

Drace in section 33, on the railroad, was first known locally as Black Bear. Drace operated as a post office from April 17, 1894 to October 14, 1905. It was named for James A. Drace, prominent Perry resident.

After the opening, white people leased lands from the Indians and some of these lived on Indian lands. Three rural schools were established in this township. In section 11 on the western line near the center of the section line was a school called Lilly (district #67). In later years, this schoolhouse was moved to Red Rock and made into a home for teachers. In section 29, near the southeast corner was the Dotts school (district #1). This school was moved later one mile north and one mile east and renamed Highland. Rosenwald (district #36) was in the southwest corner of section 25.

The Holdup at Redrock 1889
By Daisy Lemon Coldiron

The lamps in the Trading Post were out
  And the north star winked alone,
When Zip and Bill came a-riding up
  From Cowboy Flat on the Cimarron.

There in a bend of the Red Rock Creek
  Squatted the little railroad station,
The only town for many a mile
  In the Otoe Reservation.

The night was dark and the settlement still
  But the telegraph keys clicked on
When Zip and Bill rode up to the Door
  From Cowboy Flat on the Cimarron.

"Stick 'em up, pardner, and that damn quick!
  Now kindly turn over the mon!"
The operator turned from his keys to look
  In the face of Zip Wyatt's gun.

He stood up quick, both hands in the air,
  While Bill went after the mon.
But Zip's thumb slipped and the poor man slumped
  With a bullet from Zip Wyatt's gun.

The bandits fled and the dying man
  Across the table where he lay,
Clicked out the story of the hold up
  While his life's blood ebbed away.

When the south bound train roared in from Bliss
  The conductor found him there.
Holding the key in his lifeless hand
  Zip was an outlaw for many a year.

Left to Right, Sitting: Mitchell Deroin, James Arkeketah; Standing: Richard W. Shunatona, John Pipestem. The "chief flag" is held by Pipestem.

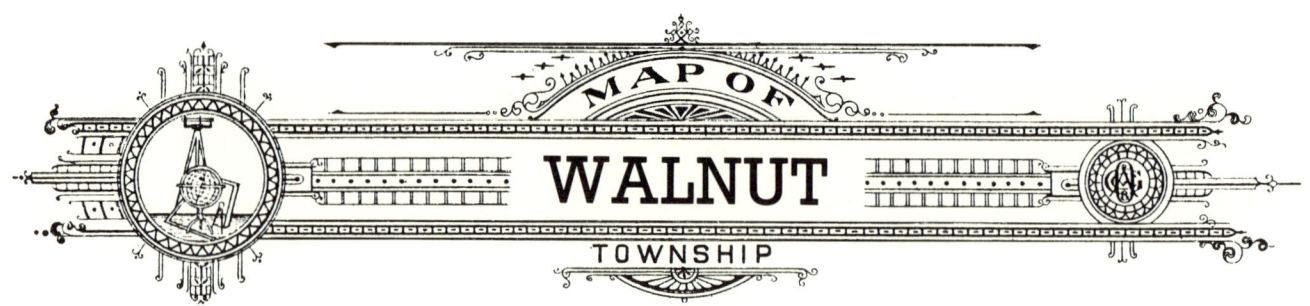

MAP OF WALNUT TOWNSHIP

Township 20 North, Range 1 East of the Indian Meridian

Walnut Township

This township is in the watershed of Stillwater Creek and one of the few townships in Noble county that had walnut timber for lumber, hence the name. It was in Payne county from September 16, 1893 until statehood. The land records were transferred to Noble county but the 1900 census is listed in Payne county.

A small general store, in the southeast quarter of section 30, operated by Reinhart Swart, was called Swartville for several years. A town called Ironton, was platted on the southwest corner of section 33. It was hoped that a post office and stage stop could be established here and take the business from the village of Yates a few miles south. This took the stage road up a very steep red clay hill, where even the mules could not pull the stages and loaded wagons up the hill, when it was muddy, so the stage drivers refused to change their route. Across the section line in the southeast corner of section 32 is the Shelton cemetery named for J. P. Shelton, homesteader.

In the northeast quarter of section 8 was the Lone Elm school (district #80). It was discontinued in 1957. In the southeast corner of section 3 was the Lone Elm Free Methodist Church. In the northeast corner of Peter Ewy's homestead (northwest quarter of section 4) is the Mennonite cemetery, the church was a mile north in Noble township. In the southeast quarter of section 2 was the Barrett school (district #81), named for Edwin Barrett, homesteader. Barrett district was annexed to Lone Elm (district #80) and Oak Hill (district #74) on June 15, 1947. This schoolhouse was purchased by Theodore Hughes and modeled into a home.

In the northeast quarter of section 26 was the Oak Hill school (district #74). When separate schools for black

New Hope — District 75 School House. Perry P. Key was the teacher in 1936.

students were required by Oklahoma law the Dunbar school was built one half mile north of Oak Hill school on the homestead of Robert Johnson in the southeast quarter of section 23. A small black cemetery is located on the northeast corner of section 22 on land homesteaded by Isaac Steadman.

New Hope school (district #75) was located in the northwest quarter of Betsy Allen's homestead that she had taken in the run (northeast quarter of section 29). Part of the New Hope district is now under Lake Carl Blackwell and the rest annexed to Fairview (district #76) on June 15, 1947.

The New Hope school (district #75) was organized in the spring of 1894 and the school board elected: Garret Zimmerman director, James K. Thurman, clerk, and T. J. Coate treasurer. These, with the help of neighbors, built a neat log house at small expense, completed and ready for the school term, beginning that fall. The first term of school was taught by Mr. J. C. Burton who later sold his farm to Walter J. Coate who "proved up" and homesteaded it. Sunday school had been held in J. H. Moore's home and through the heat of summer it was held in a shady grove on the farm of Rev. J. L. Dawson. When the schoolhouse was built it was held in the new building. T. L. Springs, called Grandpa Springs, was the Sunday School Superintendent.

They gave us the name of New Hope
Ever suggestive of a better day
When we might flourish and prosper
And be guided by God's Holy way.
     Mrs. W. J. Coate

In 1925, Mrs. Coate writes how the school board reached the Model School score for the New Hope school. "We purchased an Ocean Wave for the playground, and a new modern oil stove and how the children do enjoy the hot noon lunch. Cement walks were built from the school building to the well and all outbuildings, a new barn was erected, a new hanging light globe, sanitary drinking fountain, and a school clock were bought for the school room, and the library was replenished with a good supply of good books. An extra half acre of ground was added to the original acre of school ground, and lastly cloak rooms were built and painted and all out buildings were painted in time for the Model School Inspector. All this was accomplished at a cost of about $630.00.

The two years prior to this school term, we had repaired the school building and it had received a new roof, new floor, new blackboard, new windows and paint inside and out. The pupils of this school sold enough lead pencils to buy a volleyball and we had pie suppers to raise the money for nice new gas lamps and window shades." The board, at this time, announced they would let contract for an arch cave 8 x 20 feet. Members of the school board were A. Busse, director, Mrs. W. J. Coate, clerk and A. M. Elgin, member. This school was remodeled into a home and is being occupied by the Shelton brothers, Ray and Dick.

Part of the southern part of Walnut township was covered by the waters of Lake Carl Blackwell. Lake McMurtry covers the southcentral part of this township. These lakes furnish water for the city of Stillwater.

Cherokee Strip Fruit Farm - Thomas J. Coate, owner.

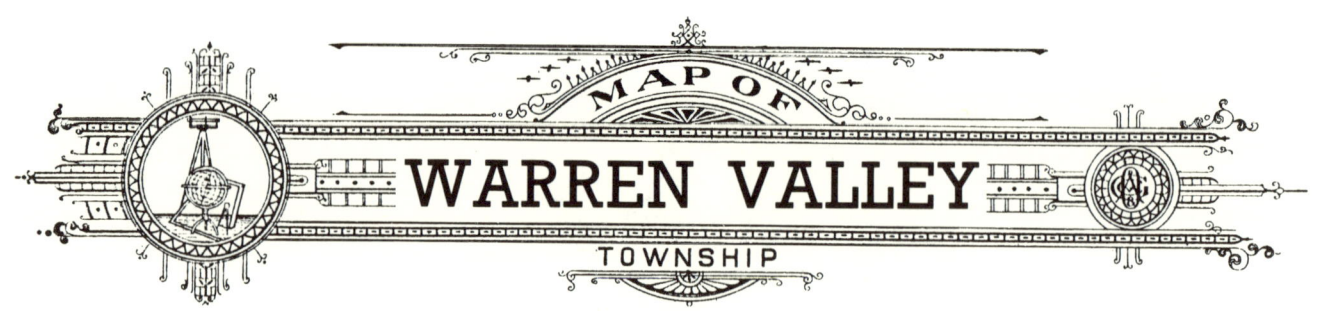

Map of Warren Valley Township

Township 21 North, Range 2 West of the Indian Meridian

E A Cox	H Kindt	A Doyle	N W Bales	Wm Curtis	W J Burke	A R Friend	H C Hoover	T A Kiser	L C Rosa		
E A Colvert	L Mossler	J Corbett	E Burke	L A Burke	G T Godsey	Wm Moore	H J Dayton	A E Dayton	C E Tobin	C S Huffington	
6		*5*		*4*		*3*		*2*		*1*	
H C Barnes	J Beatty	M A Keating	C A Johnson	R Burke / A D Snelser	W T Cady	J E Cockrum	N A Howe	W L Kinnaman	G W Warner	J S Bryan	F M VanBebber
G W Mills	J F Troub	B Mosier	J M Dowell	R Dowell	S S Glotfelty	W Painter	E Ballard	J Tobin	W Ford	F M Beitman	R M Ely
7		*8*		*9*		*10*		*11*		*12*	
A Mills	W E Johnston	C H Rice	W McGuire			W A Maloch	F Ballard	E W Goodwill	P B Woffinger		
L Myers / C M Haynes	I Shields	F Macy	W Markwell			N L Sams	E Ballard	A L Davis	J D Patterson		
18		*17*		*16*		*15*		*14*		*13*	
C Myers	J W Smith	G W Clark	C B Scrivner	E Kunz	J Dorsey	J Young	A Weeder	J Neuerburg	A M Craig	J Grimes	M Bechtel
J W Richart	B J Dennis	C F Sattler	D McGuire	F Neuerburg	J P Martin	A Ableidinger	L Pugh	W H Zink	H J Groetken	G E White	Compton / H Price
19		*20*		*21*		*22*		*23*		*24*	
Lucien	J Rist	J K Mateer	J L Lewis	A Gaston	J W Patterson	G W Cooper / D Miller	W S Graham	M R Heisinger	A Flusche	F J Carrier	E Haley
E Rupp	F Stahl	Wm Schuler	J Lichti	E M Driskill	A Wolleson	J Dunlap	J E McKee	C M Belwood	T Compton	J M Hughes	L D Nieswander
30		*29*		*28*		*27*		*26*		*25*	
G Lord	J T Gillespie	N A Barker	C F Swank			S Guthrie	E Pugh	J A Madden	W M Jenkins		
H McNeal	W Guthrie	R L Tiger	J Amson			J Whittaker	J C Highsmith	J M Powell	H A Smith		
31		*32*		*33*		*34*		*35*		*36*	

Warren Valley Township

Warren Valley township was named for Warren Creek that drains the township. It is not known how the creek received that name. This township was a part of Lowe township when it was first formed in January 1894.

In the northwest corner of section 29 on the homestead of John K. Mateer a post office called Mateer was started soon after the strip opened. The mail was delivered to this post office by star route and the carrier was Cal Hamblin. The Rock Spring school was located just northeast and it was thought a town would be located here. A family by the name of Emerson built a store here and their son was the first doctor. The Frisco railroad was being built about now which was then called the Arkansas Valley and Western. They decided to build their depot where the town of Lucien is now.

The steel was laid on the railroad through Lucien in the fall of 1903 and the town was called Woolsey. The first bank in Lucien was called the Bank of Woolsey. When the post office department put in a post office they found there was another Woolsey in Oklahoma so the name was changed to Lucien, for Lucien Emerson.

Mrs. Rosie McNeal, whose father, Jasper Anson, homesteaded the southeast quarter of section 32 — three miles southeast of Lucien recalls, "Bill Primrose owned the 160 acres on which Lucien was located. I think Edd Moelling's store was the first in Lucien. Primrose built a hotel and there were four grocery stores in Lucien at one time. They were operated by Mrs. Hugh Meyers, Dr. Emmerson, Jim McKee and Moelling. The town also had two blacksmith shops, a drug store operated by Elmer Rice and two churches, a Methodist and a Christian. The Christian was later sold to George Guthrie who made it a residence. George Dennis was pastor of the Lucien Christian church.

"There was a cotton gin that later burned down, a pool hall and saloon operated by "Peg Leg" Martin, two physicians, Dr. Emerson and Dr. Gaines, a post office, barber shop and livery stable where it cost 10 cents to stable a horse." Mrs. McNeal remembers when each Lucien business had a hitching post out front.

"There was a Frisco depot in Lucien and freight trains regularly came through the town. There was no passenger train, but for 15¢ each, people could ride the freight train caboose to Perry and return to Lucien later that day. The train left Lucien at 9 a.m. and people could catch a train back to Lucien at 3 p.m."

Adoris Anson, Mrs. McNeal's brother, was the town barber and her mother, Mrs. Jasper Anson ran a hotel. "I remember once in 1910 when it snowed so much the trains couldn't run and men were hired to shovel snow off the tracks. It was hard to cook enough food for the workers."

"Jim Dennis owned the hardware store and a real estate office. The building later was converted to a hospital operated by Dr. Gaines. There was also a school, a telephone office and a shoe repair shop."

Mrs. McNeal remembers, "Mary Hamblin used two old mules to deliver the mail. Later, Kent Kirkhart took over the mail route and Mrs. Kirkhart operated the post office.

One cemetery is located in Warren Valley township called the McGuire cemetery. It was deeded to the Board of Directors of Lowe township by Oswell McGuire on June 8, 1895. It is 18 rods square and there is no charge for lots, the county commissioners still keep this cemetery.

Several rural schools were located in this township. The Rock Spring school was moved to Lucien (district #16). In the southeast corner of section 6 was the Twin Mound school (district #13). It was named for two small hills to the west. When it was no longer in use for a school, Raymond Curtis bought the building and used it for a granary. The district was annexed to Lone Star and Hayward on June 15, 1947.

The Lone Star school (district #59), was located in the southwest corner of section 3. Lone Star became D-15 annexed to Perry on September 7, 1955. The first Whipple school (district #14), located in the northeast corner of section 11, was very small with benches for seats. The benches were replaced with seats with desks. A box supper supplied money for the bell. When the school was discontinued, the building was remodeled into a community building. Whipple was annexed to Lone Star (district #59) and White (district #15) on June 29, 1947.

The Cooper school (district #60) was located in the northwest corner of section 27. Cooper was part annexed to White (district #15) on December 4, 1929, the rest was annexed to White on June 27, 1947.

The White school (district #15) held school until 1968. The building and land was sold to Larry Jarrett who remodeled it into a three-level home on the 1¼ acre lot.

In March of 1925, the Bu-Vi-Bar oil completed the discovery well of the pool in section 15 township 21 north, range 2 west, east of Lucien. The name of the pool was derived from the names of the three men who composed the company: J. Garfield Buel (Bu), Mr. Vincent (Vi) and Bob Bartlett (Bar). The well produced 130 barrels of oil at 1,902 feet. The discovery well was on the Nathan Sams homestead and was named for Mary Louise Sams.

80 / History of Noble County

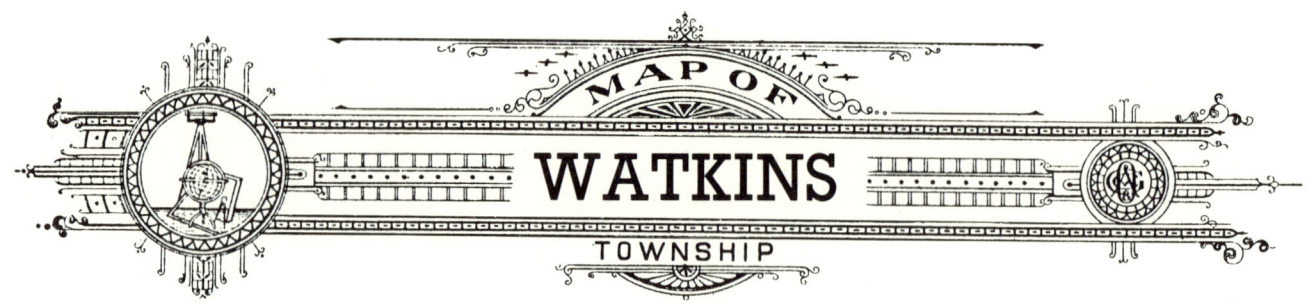

Township 21 North, Range 1 West of the Indian Meridian

Watkins Township

Watkins township was one of the seven townships first formed in 1894. What is now Noble township was included in this township at that time. As the Perry land office was located in Watkins township it was the center of the activity in the land rush.

There were five rural schools located in Watkins township. In the northeast corner of section 11 was the Pleasant Hill school #33. It was sometimes called the Nelson school. It was annexed to Perry, July 2, 1948. The Wing Spring school #37 was located in the northeast corner of section 35. On March 16, 1932, the district was divided, part going to Pioneer school #40 and the rest to Pike's Peak #79. Freemont school #34 was in the southeast corner of section 4. It was annexed to Perry July 16, 1947; on the north line of section 20 was the Watkins school #35. It was annexed to Perry July 16, 1947. The Hempling school #38 was in the southwest corner of section 28. It was annexed to Hunter school #78 on June 23, 1947.

A race track was built in the first years just south of Perry. It was located south of Cow Creek and west of what is now state highway 86. Dr. S. A. Moore had a stable of race horses here. The first county fairs were held in the buildings and the National Guard held manuevers in the open space. A bridge over Cow Creek, west of the present bridge connected the town with the track and many people walked to the races.

On the east edge of Perry was a pond of water where the cowboys had built a dam to hold water for the cattle on the drives north. After the opening a man by the name of Wills built boat docks and bath house here for the people of Perry.

It was called Wills Lake and covered twelve acres, while the grounds covered about twenty acres. The lake was stocked with bass, crappie and perch. A dancing pavilion, shoot-the-shoots and boat houses with nice skiffs were features of the resort. All that remains is the pond located north of the Grace Hill cemetery. Another spot of interest for the young people was "Shale Hill" a cliff on the southeast side of Perry that could be climbed and a view of the town seen from the top.

Springs along Cow Creek were believed able to furnish water for a city the size of Perry. Several dams were built over the years but they either washed away or filled with silt as they were shallow, the water flowing over the entire dam. Then Lake Perry southwest of Perry in section 31 was built and now furnishes water for the City of Perry. In 1940, it was stocked with bass, bram and crappie.

The Civilian Conservation Corps (CCC) constructed the lake and built the shelter house and picnic facilities, which are still in use, in the Perry Lake Park southeast of Perry. In the later 1930s and early 1940s the CCC camps housed hundreds of young men who

Dr. L. O. Render's houseboat, a familiar sight on Lake Perry, for many years.

found a livelihood, however meager, when there were no jobs. The city council renamed the park but the name never caught on and it is still known as the CCC park, even by those who may have forgotten what the initials stood for.

Franklin Roosevelt created the corps shortly after he became president for young men 17 to 23½ years old. In short order 275,000 were enrolled in the camps and by the time the progam ended in 1942, more than three million had been a part of the CCC. The enrollees were paid the magnificent sum of $30 a month but they were required to send $25 of that amount back home. When World War II was a reality, the demand for manpower in the armed forces ended the need for finding something for young people to do.

May 1, 1934, the CCC Lake boat dock was started, officially known as State Lake Park number 10. 15 months later the CCC crew moved out. A bathhouse had been built and a raft anchored in the lake for swimming. Hundred of tons of sand, hauled to the site, provided an artificial beach. No lifeguard was on duty and after a girl drowned, no swimming was allowed. Mother nature reclaimed the sand and only the foundation of the bath house is left. This beach was located just north of the main shelter which still stands. The lasting benefit of the CCC is visible today and many people remember how the programs gave them an opportunity to find a place to live and three square meals a day while they performed valuable service for their country. Perry has enjoyed the scenic park in this community for nearly 50 years, something lasting that came out of the chaos in the depression and drought.

Beach at CCC Lake (L to R): Hugh Ed St. Clair, Norma Lee Crocket. Girl buried in sand not identified.

82 / History of Noble County

Township 24 North, Range 2 East of the Indian Meridian

West Bressie Township

For many years this township was called "North Part of Otoe" by the government, although it was a part of the Ponca Reservation. Most of the Ponca Indians lived on the part of their reservation that was in Kay county. The only school in this township was the Ponca Boarding school located on the school reserve located in east ½ of northeast ¼ of section 4 and the west ½ of northwest ¼ of section 3.

White Eagle was chief when the Poncas moved from Nebraska to northeastern Oklahoma in the vicinity where Miami now stands. The Poncas did not like that location and were then moved to their present home just south of Ponca City. White Eagle served as chief for approximately fifty years and just prior to his death resigned in favor of Horse Chief Eagle, his son.

The Poncas were still practicing polygamy during a considerable portion of his lifetime and he had seven wives, several of them at the same time. They included Mary Elk, Ne-glee-dah-ee, Gambling, Carry-Water, Amelia Primeaux, Julia Primeaux and Victoria DeLodge. He was the father of fifteen children including Horse Chief Eagle, Mrs. Emily Crazy Bear, Mrs. Ethel Red Leaf, Mrs. Romona Rough Face and Mrs. Elaine Waters.

During the lifetime of White Eagle, he led the Poncas in their last war with the Sioux and was the last war chieftain of the Ponca tribe. This was just prior to the tribe being moved from Nebraska to Northeastern Oklahoma in 1877.

In the autumn of 1883, White Eagle was in Birmingham in company with fifty to a hundred of his people, who were an exhibit at the Alabama State Fair. The Indians had been taken there by Colonel Joe Miller of the 101 Ranch at the solicitation of officers of the fair who believed the Indians would be a great attraction.

Colonel Miller related, "It was while we were giving our exhibitions on the fair grounds that the invitation came to White Eagle to speak at the First Baptist church. White Eagle was the tribal chief and, as such, was the one who preached to his own people in regard to their centuries-old religious beliefs. It was in this way that I was accustomed to introduce White Eagle to the crowds on the Alabama State Fair Grounds. I have seen lots of crowds, but I have never seen anything to equal that which assembled to hear White Eagle preach. It was necessary for the police of Birmingham to attend in squads to handle the crowd, thousands of which could not even get inside the church. White Eagle was equal to the occasion in every respect. He attired himself in the full regalia of his office, with flowing blanket and long head feathers, and wearing his beaded moccasins. Drawing his blanket around him and holding it in place with his left hand, the chief spoke slowly and deliberately, using his right arm frequently for gestures. He would talk a while, and I would interpret.

"White Eagle explained the religious belief of the red man to some extent. He told them that the Indians had but one church whereas the white people, even down in Oklahoma, have many churches, one on every corner and each declaring his own way, the only true way, whereas the others face eternal hell fire. White Eagle said the Indians do not belive in hell, that people have their hell on earth, that when an Indian does wrong it makes his heart hurt and he is sorely troubled, sometimes for a long time, and in this way he experiences his hell. That God is good and that all people, the Indian believe, eventually reach heaven — the Happy Hunting Ground of the red men."

White Eagle died on February 3, 1914, at the age of 78 years. A few years later the Miller brothers rededicated to Chief White Eagle a "signal mound" similar to the one used by the Indians in the old days. The mounds consisted of pillars of stone placed on hills about fifteen miles apart by which the Indians were guided. About ten miles south of the White House of the ranch on highway 77 in Kay County, one of the pillars was erected and a white eagle carved in stone was placed on the top of the shaft in tribute to the chief.

It was for him that the Santa Fe named the little railway stop at Whiteeagle near the Ponca reservation headquarters. Originally this stop was called Ponca, when the line was built through from Arkansas City, but when Ponca City was formed and called "New Ponca", the Santa Fe changed to the chief's name to save confusion.

Near the bend of the Salt Fork of the Arkansas River on the north border of West Bressie Township is a little "Cowboy" cemetery where Bill Picket, famed Negro Cowboy of the 101 Ranch is buried.

Chief White Eagle of the Poncas from Cherokee Strip Museum - Perry.

Map of White Rock Township

Township 23 North, Range 2 West of the Indian Meridian

White Rock Township

White Rock township also included what is now Bunch Creek township when it was first formed in January of 1894. It was named for Richard M. White who homesteaded land. The following is condensed from a paper written by Loid Armstrong: "The Main subject of this article will be about a school in a small town located in the northern part of Noble County in 1894. It was called White Rock. The first county superintendent of schools was R. R. Talley who was appointed and served three months. An election was held and G. W. Crosby was the first elected county superintendent. The first duties were to divide the county into school districts and to give them names and numbers. White Rock came up with its school district name and was numbered 61 in 1894. The first thing the school districts were supposed to do was make some kind of accommodations to hold school, such as the little sod school house. White Rock was a town of around 250 and all seemed to want to do their share.

Most of the lumber was hauled from Red Rock and by the fall of 1894 a school house was completed and furnished with benches and some seats. A blackboard was painted on the wall. The school house was used for school and church services and all other activities of the community. It was a kind of social place.

The first teacher at White Rock was W. M. McCollough at a salary of $18 a month. Length of term was four months and the number of pupils 29. The second teacher, during 1895-96, was Mrs. Ruby Goff at a salary of $20 a month, term four months, number of pupils 33."

On May 24, 1905, at 8 p.m. a tornado hit White Rock and the school house was scattered in four directions. School was held in a tent in 1905-06. In the spring and summer of 1905 a new school was built and furnished. White Rock town and school was located in the northern corner of section 2. On the south section line of section 1 was the Indinola school and in the southeast corner of section 6 was the Elkhorn school district 5.

In the northeast corner of section 9 on the banks of the Red Rock Creek was the school called Frog Holler. It was moved across the creek and named Red Rock Valley school. In 1934, Red Rock Valley, Indinola and White Rock districts merged and a new building was built. It went into use September 14, 1934 and was named Valley Center, district 55.

In the south part of White Rock township in the southeast corner of section 19 was a Compton school (district #18).

A school in the southwest corner of section 22 was named Highview (district #56) but was called Chicken Coop. The first school house was a donated building that had housed chickens and still had chicken mites when school first started. Later it was known as Mid-Co during the oil boom days. Echo school (district #7) was in the southeast corner of section 23.

During the early oil boom a post office was established near the Mid-Co school to accomodate the oil field workers. Charles Durkee gives this account: "After the number 1 Hoover Oil well came in a gusher in the early teens to start the Billings oil boom, hundreds of people came to work there. It was called the Mid-Co camp named for the principal oil company, the Mid-Co. Most of the camp was located on the northwest corner of section 27, now owned by Charles Durkee. Located there was a large warehouse and supply yard, a machine shop, two large bunkhouses and a boarding house. Also the office building, a repair garage and several housed for the gang bosses and superintendent. It differed from other oilfield camps as it had its own water and sewer system plus an electric system.

The Nickels general store was moved from Polo, 6 miles south, to the northeast corner of section 28, known as the Falke farm. It was a two-story building with a garage on the west end, run by Mr. Nickles' son-in-law, George Merriman. The store also served as a post office called Wouldbe from March 3, 1920 until October 15, 1921. There was another store and filling station, built by a Mr. Wilson, on the southwest corner of section 22 just east of Highview school, with a barber shop on the east ran by Roe Abbott.

On the southeast corner of section 21 were houses running ¼ mile east and ¼ mile north. An eighth of a mile north was an open air theator plus two dance halls, one later converted to a second school for the 5th through 8th grades.

When the wells were all drilled and construction stopped and the single men either married or moved away the post office was no longer needed as the rural mail route from Billings could handle the mail.

The old superintendent's house still stands on the corner, all that is left of a town people thought "Wouldbe" but because of depletion of oil "couldn't be".

1918 Washburn lease. This 160 acres had 16 wells, each one a producer, number 9 is still producing. Concrete foundation of pump houses is still there in 1986.

September 16 Celebration

Fleming and Farmer entry in parade about 1905.

Woodruff entry in Parade about 1911. Men not identified. Ladies (L to R): Miss Nell Stone, Mrs. Fred Gum, Mrs. B. J. Woodruff and Mrs. Russell G. Lowe.

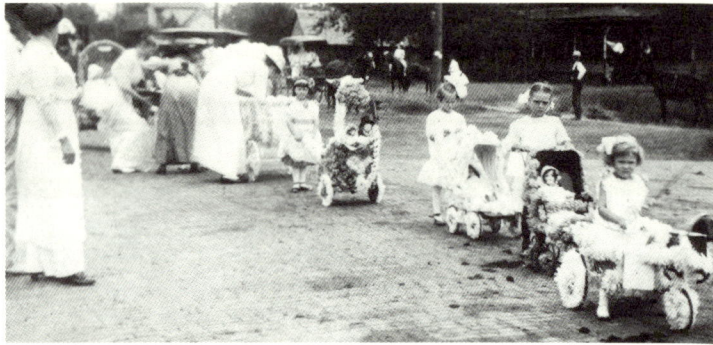

Decorated doll buggies in the 16th parade about 1915 - Looking northeast from corner of 7th and Fir Streets. (Fourth from Right): Kathryn Laird McQuiston.

Parade entry about 1911 - Decorated with crepe paper flowers. Horses hoofs were painted silver or gold.

A feature of parade for 31 years. Frank and Mable Eby on bicycle built for two about 1947.

Parade float early 1920s. (L to R): Mrs. C. T. Bobbitt, Miss Nell Stone, Mrs. Charles Hirschman, Miss Anna Jelly, unidentified.

Entry by Suffragettes in parade about 1920.

Kentucky Fried Chicken float - First place winner in 1986 parade.

Chapter 5
COMMUNITIES PAST AND PRESENT

Perry

The government square in Perry was dry and dusty with old buffalo wallows in the eastern half. These had to be filled in before the courthouse could be built. The northwest corner was much higher than the southeast and as the streets were not leveled, this caused the business buildings to have foundations much higher on one side so the floors would be level. The sidewalks were built level with each building with steps either up or down between businesses.

When Street Commissioner Buck cut the streets down to grade, some of the buildings were left four or five feet above the street level. Boardwalks were constructed leaving a drop of some feet from the sidewalk to the street. This was convenient for wagons backing up to take a load of hardware or groceries, as well as for horseback riders to step off for an easy mount. With the erection of permanent buildings evacuation was necessary to bring the buildings to the common grade around the square. Cement sidewalks replaced the board ones. In 1910, Perry began paving the streets with bricks. Hitchracks were a necessity for the farmer folk and the wooded structures of the first year were removed and stone blocks with chain attachments were put up. With the retirement of "Old Dobbin" and the coming of the automobile, these blocks and chains were thrown into the discard.

At this time no Santa Fe trains were stopping in Perry. Wharton, a mile south and the depot and trains went through Perry at high speed. An ordinance limiting the speed to four miles an hour through the city limits remedied the matter and in the spring of 1894 the depot was moved up to Perry and later a half block north to its present location.

A bridge across Cow Creek on east C street was built in the first year after the run. This served the people to the east as far as Pawnee. Perry was the nearest railroad to these people. In January 1894, Grace Hill cemetery was platted on forty acres of the Hart homestead. Prior to this the school land section adjoining Perry on the west had been used for cemetery purposes. The graves were moved to the new cemetery.

July 20, 1895, the Howe Pump and Engine Company of Kentucky completed the waterworks and electrical systems.

The original townsite comprised 320 acres located in ne¼ of section 22 and nw¼ of section 21 of Watkins township. This platted, exclusive of reservations for city parks and school reserves made 634 residence lots of fifty by one hundred forty feet. The settlers spread over the original townsite and to care for the immense throng of future residents five additions were proved up and platted and known as northeast, north, northwest, west and south Perry. The original town was enclosed in the space bounded now on the south by "A" street, on the east by First street, on the west by Ninth street and on the north by "F". The five additions added to the town 2,145 residence lots and all were absorbed in the year after the opening. They were incorporated into the city limits in 1894.

Ernie Jones in his "Early Day History of Perry, Oklahoma" tells about the townsite additions: "The quarter section upon which North Perry is located was claimed the first day by Henry Linn, he having tried to establish proof of his prior settlement and occupancy against thousands who were upon the land staking and claiming lots within an hour after the opening. A contest of course resulted between Linn and the settlers, the same being instituted in the local land office. The case was fought to the departments at Washington with the result of the settlers winning after three or four years of expensive litigation. After losing his contest Linn drifted on farther west and when last heard of was exploiting a gold dredging scheme in the

East side of square about 1905. Big Horn Market owned by A. I. Acers was named for pair of long horns on display. Opera House is tallest building. The bank building on far corner is only one existing today.

rivers of Idaho.

Northwest Perry was homesteaded by "Billy" McCoy, one of the clerks in the local land office. His contest was short lived however, the claimants getting rid of him in a few months. Billy was a Milwaukee product and after the boom days of the town subsided he went back to take his old place on the police force which he had resigned to come to Perry.

John Malone, brother of the register of the land office, was the contestee of northeast Perry. The settlers defeated him in his fight, which was shortly followed by his becoming insane. He was taken to Jacksonville, Illinois and committed to the asylum, which then took care of our insane where later he died.

The contest over West Perry was a battle royal. Henry Bowie, filed his homestead entry on the quarter section and against him were a thousand town lot claimants. Bowie had come here from Texas. He was a direct descendant of the illustrious defender of the Alamo. The contest for West Perry continued for several years but Bowie lost and like Henry Linn, down and out, winded his way back to his old home in Texas.

South Perry was the battlefield where various and sundry characters made their mark in early history. Charles E. (Doc) Reed a veterinarian and practical horseman, Charles (Buffalo) Jones a pioneer and plainsman, later game warden of the Yellowstone park, a friend of President Roosevelt and breeder of the catalo, a cross of the domestic cow and the buffalo; John McClintie, "Jack" Combs, soldier of fortune, all were contestants for the homestead right while against them were arrayed hundreds of settlers seeking town lot titles. This was the last of the townsite additions to be adjudicated and resulted in Doc Reed winning against all claimants, the first time in history of land openings of a homesteader winning against settlers. Reed obtained a deed for the land and later transferred it to Judge Thomas H. Doyle. The tract consisted of eighty acres. The east forty was platted and became South Perry addition. After the Doyle purchase he platted the west forty acres and it became the Doyle addition. Reed was a reckless fellow of not too pleasant disposition when sober, which was with him periodically and he had few friends at the finish of his local career, realizing comparatively nothing after having his claim to the land recognized. The story of the "run" made by himself and "Buffalo" Jones, as recited in the record of the land office, would make several chapters of the spectacular history of Perry. Their relays, change of horses and break neck speed, demonical riding and driving coming from Orlando over the rough country makes a story of dime novel interest.

Depot after it was moved to Perry townsite. This building burned a few years later.

On November 3, 1893, the Townsite Board of Perry opened its office. People with town lots could not file. Up to this time they had to hold their lots by staying on them. This board, appointed by Hoke Smith, then Secretary of the Interior, created to hear contests, determine title and issue deeds for lots in the new city was made up of Amos B. Fitts, Timothy McGrath and Fred Bailey. The first name good Democrats and the last a Kansas Populist. McGrath, president of the board came from Illinois, where he returned after a two year term on the board. Bailey held his job until the change of Federal Administration came and he returned to his old home in Kansas. Fitts was appointed from Georgia and was the disbursing agent of the board. He served about six months and retired to take up his profession as a journalist assuming the editorial chair of the Perry Democrat and doing work for eastern publications. In the latter field he made a most wonderful reputation. His versatility earned for him the envious title of the "Perry Liar." This came about principally from a story of a sand storm, sent out to the Associated press that startled the whole world. People all over the United States and abroad who had friends within a hundred miles of Perry, wrote, wired, and cabled to learn the fate of the dear ones in the awful halocaust where the burning sand was reported to have smothered live stock, drifted over fences, covered small buildings and caused the death of thousands of people. Amos emphatically denied the authorship of the story, being at that time a pillar of one of the local churches."

In 1903, Porter Addition was added to the original city on the north. This contributed 15 blocks and 528 lots to the townsite area.

The streets of the city running east and west were named from A to L consecutively. In 1928, a change was made giving them names with the original initial such as Fir for F.

Perry Newspapers

Bert Green came with the Perry Times, a daily and weekly. The issue of September 16, 1893, was printed in Guthrie and brought to Perry for distribution during the afternoon. Jack Gaiser was foreman of the times and Jack Humphrey, editor. Green sold the Times to V. C. Welch after a few years and the Enterprise-Times was conducted by Welch until absorbed by the Perry Republican. Welch and Ed Perry had come down from Alma, Kansas and installed the Weekly Enterprise. Mark Abel was their printer foreman.

Tom Stumbaugh and Bob Galbreath had the Perry Democrat, a daily, on the streets a few days after the opening. Bert Jones was the star reporter. The Democrat passed on to numerous publishers, with Charley Merrill and Amos Fitts the "pall bearers" at the final laying away of the corpse.

Other sheets came and went. Colby and Olds had their Perry Populist; Sidney Sapp had his Perry Independent; the Perry Rustler and McKinney Teller by the veteran Frank Prouty; The Oklahoma Herald started and ended with Edgar Watkins as publisher; The Perry Eagle was an orphan and Bee Guthrey kept alive populist propaganda for one campaign with his Populist Independent. Lon Wharton came over from Chandler the first day with his Perry Sentinel, later the Noble County Sentinel. The outfit consisted of a Washington hand press and the conventional shirt tail full of type. Newspaper life with Lon was one continued round of pleasure. He thrived on argument. He fought the grafters, was blacklisted and abused, burned out, started anew and in fact had one _ell of a time until growing old the game lost its glamour, he sold out to R. E. Bagby and retired to live in California until his death in 1930.

When Judge A. H. Boles was made register of the land office in 1889, he staked his son Arthur who was a printer and Jim Casey to the Perry Republican. This paper was run as a daily and weekly for many years, after Casey purchased young Bole's interest. Following with different ownerships the Republican was finally absorbed with the Sentinel by the now published Perry Daily Journal.

Opera House

The first Opera house in Perry was the Perry Opera House located on the south side of Delaware Street in the 500 block, operated by J. C. Delaney. This building burned in 1902. The Grand Opera House was built in 1901 and on May 30 that year it was first opened to public gathering for a Memorial Day service. The building was erected by J. B. Tate and John Pressler. Pressler was associated with the business only a few months. J. C. Delaney became associated with J. B. Tate in 1902.

The immortal Will Rogers once presented his famous rope act in the Grand Opera House for a tidy sum of $5.00. The building was converted into a motion picture theater in 1913. Live acts were presented in the building, along with the showing of films. The first talking pictures in Perry were shown in the famous Strip landmark. The first "talkie" had only the sound of voices. During the three-reel, 30 minute thriller, six men worked behind the screen to provide the sound effects. Admission for these first sound movies was 5 cents for children and a dime for adults. "Tiger Lilly" was one of the first talkies shown here.

Among the movie stars who appeared on the screen were Charlie Chaplin, Mary Pickford and Douglas Fairbanks, Sr. "Perils of Pauline" was an early serial shown in the movie house. Many other famous pictures and performers in person appeared in the opera house. It was these attractions that made this Perry building famous in the Cherokee Strip and set it up as a landmark in Perry.

The Annex moving picture theater was built on the first floor of the opera house building in 1918. The Annex operated until 1942, when closed by John B. Terry. This business was operated by the Tate family from 1918 until 1941. The opera house was on the second floor of the building until 1933. From 1913 until 1933, both live shows and moving pictures were shown on the second floor of the opera house. The building had a stage 50 by 36 feet. There was a mass of scenery and equipment. Many famous traveling show companies played in the building because of Perry's central location. Perry was an ideal stopover place with excellent rail connections. The famous John Philip Sousa directed the Sousa band in person at the opera house. The famous Polly circus

Opera House - the addition on top of building held the backdrops for stage.

once appeared there with a live elephant, five horses and a troop of shetland ponies on the stage. Buster Keaton appeared here with his parents.

Early one morning in June of 1960, the northeast corner of the sandrock wall collapsed. The building had not been used for theatrical purposes since the early 1940s but had been converted into apartments. Because of the danger of more walls collapsing, the building was torn down.

Perry Schools

At the city election October 31, 1893, a school board was elected: A. J. Garvin and W. M. Bowles 1st ward; Dr. O. W. Long and R. E. Bagby 2nd ward; T. J. Taylor, Sr. and J. A. Cruickshank 3rd ward; W. H. Dwyer and Dr. W. J. Gillett 4th ward. The first schools after organization were greatly handicapped for want of room and supplies, only frame shacks about town being available and far from inviting as to convenience and equipment. A local paper at that time said, "The committee on renting of buildings for school purposes reported the following buildings and prices per month, which was accepted: Boyde building on F street between 5th and 6th at $10 per month; Neilsen building on sixth at $10 per month; church building on C at $12 per month. During the summer of 1895 bonds were issued in the sum of $20,260.00 for the construction of a high school building and two ward buildings. The Blaine School in South Perry served the Black children for many years. The Holmes building in East Perry was destroyed by fire in November 1897. The corner stone of the high school building on the School Reserve on 9th street between E and F streets was laid October 16, 1894 with ostentatious ceremonies, under the auspices of Perry Masonic Lodge number 15. Henry S. Johnston gave the address. A $30,000.00 building was built in northwest Perry in 1911. In 1925, the three story native stone

Interior of Opera House.

building was replaced by a building on the same site and in 1928, a gymnasium and auditorium was built. These were torn down in the mid 1960s and replaced by the present buildings.

Perry has celebrated the opening of the Strip every year except for two years during WW I and II. A parade is held which features decorated floats which started with wagons and buggies covered with crepe-paper flowers. In the early parades even the harness for the horses was often ordered so it would match the color scheme of the flowers, dresses and umbrellas carried by the ladies. This celebration comes at the end of the county fair which has been held for many years.

Downtown Perry (1920s-1930s)
Johnnie L. Tilman

I was brought up, and went through school in Perry and this is how the various businesses were in sequence during that time. Sixth Street south from Fir Street — east side of the street, the Cain Hotel with a small restaurant and drive-in, the Springfield Hotel, owner "Shorty" Springfield, Ford Motor Agency, owner a man named Krisher. From Elm Street south on Sixth, Long-Bell Lumber Company, Sheets Plumbing Company, Taliferro grocery, cafe owned and operated by "Speck" and Stella Roads, Chevrolet car agency. On the east side of the square from Delaware were Foster's Drug, owned and operated by Ralph Foster, Sr. the other pharmacist on duty was Wilbur Trumbla, the Roxy Theatre, owned and operated by Charley Wolleson, his younger brother was "Bud", Mrs. Charley Wolleson took tickets at the box office, Kraemer's shoes and clothing, owned and operated by Mr. and Mrs. Ott Edson, Shaw's Beauty Parlour, owned and operated by Mr. Bert and Ethel Shaw, Sponholz Barber Shop, the Palace Cafe, owned and operated by Billy Rickert. It also served as the Bus Station. The Annex Theatre, owned and operated by Mr. and Mrs. Henry Tate. Mrs. Tate sold tickets. Crowder's Grocery and Meat Market, owned and operated by the Crowder family. Wiehe's Bakery, Ben Wiehe, the kids went there to buy penny candy. The arcade pool Hall and beer tavern, the First National Bank, Schwarz Poultry and Produce just east of the bank. From Cedar Street south on Sixth were: Malzahn's Machine Shop and Treeman and Munger Mill and Feeds. On the south side of the square were: Ringler's Harness and Saddle Store, Dolezal's Abstract Co., Henry Dolezal, barber shop, owned and operated by two brothers-in-law, Charlie Longacre and Ira Stanley. Hair-

West side of square about 1920.

cuts were 25¢ each, shoeshine 10¢. Marcy's Cafe, owned and operated by Guy and Lila Marcy, Lobsitz hardware, Dotts and Monroe Hardware, owned and operated by the elder Mr. Monroe and later on by his son-in-law "Tiny" Lang. Nelson's Pharmacy, Ned Foster worked there as a pharmacist for many years. Also the town's photographer, Barney Enright, had his studio in the back of the drug store. Safeway Grocery, The Famous Department Store, owned and operated by three brothers, Morris, Rudolph and George Gottlieb. Former Governor Henry S. Johnston maintained his office above the Famous for many years, after his return to Perry from the Capitol. Farmer's Exchange was a grocery and feed store operated by Johnny Lau. Trumbla's Barber Shop, the two barbers were the elder Trumbla and his son. Pete's Beer Tavern, owned and operated by Pete Eby. It had a juke box and a small dance floor in the back, a favorite of the high school crowd. Then was Lindeman's Grocery, Farmer's and Merchants Bank and Galloway's Grocery and Market.

On Seventh Street south from Delaware on the east side of the street were: Diamond Ice Co. the ice company of the town, with lockers for frozen food storage, and a butcher to cut and prepare meat for the lockers, Mr. Sam Dunham. The owner and operator of the plant was Clarence Page. On Seventh Street south from Delaware on the west side were: Alvin Cockrum's Conoco station, a monument company, the Perry Steam Laundry, the Cozy Rooms, hotel and also the towns only brothel, and Schwarz Oil Co. On Seventh Street north, west side of the square were: Christoph and Newton Furniture store, also served as a mortuary, and sold

"Old Central" School located at 9th and Fir.

caskets, the Toggery, ready to wear and millinery, owned and operated by Mrs. Doggett and Mrs. Owen (the widow of a pioneer doctor), Kretch's Grocery, owned and operated by Fred and Mrs. Kretch. Mr. Kretch was the mayor of Perry for twenty-two years consecutively. The Brownie Drug Store was owned and operated by Charles "Brownie" Watson. The most popular soda fountain was located here. The High School students made it a hangout. Next was the Goodyear tire company, and later Forney's Ice Cream store, the Hamous and Hopper Drug Store, owned and operated by Merrill Hamous and Jim Hopper. Hamous was a druggist at Brownie Drug for many years before that.

From Delaware north on the west side of the street were: Davis Furniture Store, upstairs over that was the telephone office and a dentist's office, by the name of Dr. Croak, Hendren's Grocery, owned and operated by the elder Hendren and son, Glen, Sherman's Ice Cream Parlor, Betty Ann Bakery, Oklahoma Natural Gas Office, believe it was supervised by a man named Pancoast, Huffman Grocery, owned and operated by Mr. Charles Huffman, Kennedy's Roller-Skating rink, owned and operated by Ivan Kennedy, Eby's Dry Cleaners, owned and operated by "Pee-Wee" Eby, Wollson's Garage, owned and operated by Tom Wolleson.

On the north side of the square was: A. C. Lamb's Jewelry, M & W Grocery store, Elmer Davis Shoe Repair, Beers Drug Store, Power's Abstract Co., Exchange Bank, operated by Joe McClellan and Ora Hall, Hill Dry Goods, later Zorba's Dry Goods, owned and operated by Tony Zorba, J. C. Penney Co. managed by Mr. King Montgomery, Sr. upstairs were the offices of the two Drs. Driver, and also Judge Ledbettor, Mossman's barber shop, the elder Mossman and his son were the barbers, the Kumback cafe, owned and operated by Eddie Parker, this was a favorite spot to eat, the owner never failed to say "Thank you and Come Back", hence the name of the cafe, Kerr's hardware, a dry cleaners and tailor shop, the Elite Cafe, McCoy's Grocery, Joe's Smokehouse, pool hall and beer, owned and operated by Joe Appleman and "Bush" Bowman for years and years. Behind Joe's Smokehouse was Walking's Grocery and Meat Market, owned and operated by Orlando Walking.

Fire Department, Cedar Street about 1910. Identity of firemen unknown.
(from Cherokee Strip Museum - Perry)

Perry Fire Department
Lois M. Moore

Shortly after the opening of the Cherokee Strip to settlement, the town of Perry was a rapidly growing "tent city".

The early day water supply was a problem not only as a household necessity, but as a fire fighting commodity. The flimsy buildings that lined the streets burned like dry grass. The city council required two barrels of water at each residence. The "bucket brigade" (people standing in a line passing buckets of water) was then the only fire fighting method.

In 1907, during the administration of Judge H. A. Smith, R. E. Delaney was appointed fire chief. He served four years. Tom Brandon was chief as of February 1912. At that time, the department was located on 7th Street and had besides the chief, an assistant chief, two paid firemen and eight call firemen. The city had 40 hydrants covering a 160 block radius.

In 1916, E. G. Cooper was chief with Arthur Hendren, assistant chief. By 1917, the fire department was equipped with an auto fire truck with chemical attachments displacing the horse-drawn equipment in use for over 20 years. It carried about 2,000 feet of hose, sufficient to reach to any building in the city limits.

Leonard Winters was appointed chief to succeed Cooper and Loyd Berger was named chief October 15, 1953, to succeed Winters. During the administration of Chief Burger, the department was able to hire more paid firefighters. Also under Chief Berger

Parade float about 1910. E. J. Coyle standing by horse.

the fire department took over the ambulance service in January, 1967.

In July, 1967, Chief Berger and June Voss were to be married. Shortly before the ceremony was to take place, a major fire developed at the elementary school. Chief Berger left the blaze long enough to go to the church for the 8 p.m. ceremony, after which he returned to the scene of the fire.

When Loyd Berger retired September 1, 1973, the assistant chief, Bill Hodge, was promoted to chief with Tom Moore named assistant chief. Hodge retired April 28, 1979. Jack Shaw was named chief in May, 1979, and resigned the post in January of 1981 at which time Tom Moore was appointed.

The fire department at the present time has one fire chief, one assistant chief, one captain, three lieutenants, one sergeant, five full time firefighters and 10 volunteer firefighters. The department is equipped with three pumpers and two rural trucks.

The Rural Association was formed in 1950 by the Farmers and Ranchers in Noble County. They furnished the rural trucks and the City of Perry houses and mans the trucks.

The Perry fire department also operates the Emergency Medical Services for Noble County. All members of the department are E.M.T. trained or in the process of being trained.

The department headquarters, which has been remodeled and enlarged, is presently located at 732 Delaware Street. It has been at this location since 1923.

First Baptist Church

By Betty L. Ripley

The first Baptist meeting was held October 8, 1893 in Banks and Wade's furniture store on 6th street between "C" and "D" Street. Two Baptist ministers were present, a Reverend J. M. Berry of Stillwater, Oklahoma Territory and Reverend T. R. Bozeman of Texas, and each gave a short discourse. At the close, a meeting of all Baptist present was called for the purpose of arranging future meetings. On the next evening, at the same location, a business meeting was held, deciding to hold services twice on Sundays, and on Wednesday evening.

On October 15, 1893, a number of Baptist met after preaching and decided to organize a church as soon as possible after a sufficient number of letters of faith could be procured. On the following Wednesday night's business meeting, moderated by Reverend Berry, various officers were elected. John E. Shanafelt was elected the first clerk, and a motion was made ordering the clerk to "spread" these minutes upon the church records.

On Sunday, December 17, 1893, Reverend S. J. Dyke, Missionary for Oklahoma Territory, preached to his fellow Baptists in the District Court Building at 6th and "D" Streets. After a strong sermon, he proceeded to organize the church. The church was named "The First Baptist Church of Perry, Oklahoma Territory." Ten charter members signed the new church roll, presenting letters of faith. The above was taken from the first minutes of the church.

January 14, 1894, it was decided to build the church on lots #19 and #20 in Block 44 at the corner of 7th and "F" Streets in the city of North Perry, paying the price of $225.00 as agreed. (In the minute records, each time a dollar figure is quoted, the dollar sign is printed back of the figure rather than before, thus: 225.00$).

The new Baptist Church was dedicated on Sunday September 2, 1894. Reverend N. B. Rarrdon of Omaha, Nebraska preached the sermon. Missionary S. J. Dyke gave a short history of the fund raising starting with $500.00 donated by the Baptist Home Mission Board to the Perry church, to start their building. Included also was the donation of $1,000.00, by a preacher's daughter of New York. Along with the money would be given an organ and a bell. The bell was hung in the belfry, the organ graced the new church sanctuary and the money was used to help build the church. On dedication Sunday there was noted that the church debt still owed on the church was $261.00. The amount of $249.00 was received that day, but at the evening service, the rest was given, with one dollar to spare, being a total of $13.00. The congregation was dismissed with the doxology, "Praise God from whom all blessings flow."

The new church activities began that very week for on Tuesday, Wednesday and Thursday the first Cherokee Strip Baptist Convention was held in the new church. Some of the items recorded in the planning minutes for the convention were appointment of committees for the decoration of the church appropriately. The new song books had arrived and the Ladies Aid Society was instructed to sew new covers for the books so they would wear well and stay clean. Country brethren were appointed to bring posts suitable for hitching posts and were to arrange them conveniently around the church. The treasurer was to pay M. A. Hunt for feeding visiting delegates. The clerk was to see that the bills were procured at the livery stable for entertaining the teams of visiting delegates. Twelve churches were represented at

First Baptist Church 1896 — 7th and "F" Streets.

the organizing of the Perry Baptist Association.

On June 29, 1910 an all day meeting was held and a roll call of members showed fifty-one members out of 112 answered roll call. On June 23, 1926, a new building was begun, starting with the basement. January 5, 1927, the regular business meeting was held in the new basement. A complete new church was ready for worship in November, 1927. The Women's Missionary Union gave the church a grand piano, debt free in 1930. Dr. Andrew Potter, executive secretary of the Oklahoma Baptist Convention delivered the sermon at the dedication of the new church and the 50th anniversary. Former pastor's wives cut the huge birthday cake at the lunch hour. Gov. Robert S. Kerr gave the dedicatory address.

In November, 1961, a new educational building was added. In 1974, a summer assembly two-story cabin was completed at Falls Creek near Davis, Oklahoma. On April 24, 1981 a dedication was held for the new auditorium, the building is a two story L shaped with a kitchen and nursery on the lower level. By using part of the old church that was connected to the new, a space was set aside as the "Memory Room". Enclosed in it are objects used in the original church. The first pulpit, the pastor's chair, table, and silver pitcher used for the Lord's Supper, the first pulpit bible and the original rolltop organ. Other objects of a later date are also enclosed.

The church has grown from the small beginning of ten charter members on the roll to a total of 1271 in July 1986. The first full time pastor was called April 11, 1894 and to this date twenty nine pastors have served the church for various amounts of time to lead the congregation to greater service for the Lord.

St. Rose of Lima Catholic Church

A few weeks after the mad stampede of the opening of the Cherokee Strip, a young priest who had just arrived from Belgium and who was little familiar with the English language and not at all with western ways, visited Perry. He was Reverend A. Borremans, assistant to Father Felix de Grasse of Guthrie. Among the first Catholics to great him were Mr. and Mrs. Conrad J. Lindeman, Mr. and Mrs. John E. Coyle and James A. Donegan. Father Borremans also became acquainted with many others and resolved to return in the near future to celebrate mass for them in a suitable place.

The first mass was said in a room at the rear of Lindeman's grocery store on 7th and D Streets. It was in that same room that Father Borremans performed a double wedding ceremony, marrying James Kennedy to Elizabeth Hess and Japtha Sturgeon to Catherine Hess on October 31, 1893.

Masses were irregular and in different places, but in a few months after the opening Father Borremans succeeded in organizing the 90 Catholic families into a station, that is, a Catholic congregation without a church. The question of acquiring property on which to erect a church buiding was uppermost in the minds of the congregation. It was the subject of conversation and deliberation after the Sunday Mass had been celebrated on a table in a store, on a teacher's desk in a school, or on a square piano in a residence.

John E. Coyle offered his residence-barn as a temporary place for mass to be celebrated regularly, and in January 1894, Coyle deeded the lot with the barn and two adjoining lots to the church. The foundation of the church building was laid at the end of February and the church was completed at the beginning of August 1894.

Volunteers from the congregation worked in crews for several days at a time to complete work on the building. Among the workers was Patrick Burns, father of Mrs. Rosa Sanders, who was still a member of the congregation at the 80th anniversary in 1975. She recalled that her father would take the wagon into town and stay in a tent while working on the church building. Until that time, Mass was said at various farm houses in the area including the Burns, with a dresser used for the altar and the congregation seated in the living room.

On August 26, 1894, St. Rose of Lima Church was dedicated by Bishop Theophile Meerschaert, Vicar Apostolic of the Indian Territory. Just 11 months after the founding of the town and for the sum of $1,211, the Catholics of Perry had a suitable place to worship. Father deGrasse gave the honor of naming the new church to the newly formed Altar Society headed by Mrs. Rose Doyle, Mrs. Rose Lindeman, Miss Anna Coyle and Mrs. Nora Mockley. They chose the name of the first cannonized saint of America, St. Rose of Lima, Peru. Two other ladies of the Altar Society were named Rose: Rose McCormick, and Rose Abledinger.

On January 1, 1895, Father Willebroard Voogden, pastor of Ponca City, took over the St. Rose mission as resident pastor where he remained for 35 years. Father Wilbur, as he was called, was born in Oud-Gastel in the province of North Brabant, Holland in 1857. He became a member of the Benedictine Order (O.S.B.) and was elevated to the priesthood in the Cathedral of Mechlin on February 21,

Father Willebrord Voogden in front of church under construction. The school is in background.

1880. Four years later his religious superiors sent him to Eastern Bengal in British India. In 1880, when the Benedictine fathers relinquished the direction of that mission he returned to Belgium for a short time. In 1889, he became a missionary in the Indian Territory, serving in Ardmore, Oklahoma City, Edmond, Muskogee and Pawhuska before coming to Perry in 1895.

St. Joseph's Academy opened its doors in September, 1900 after years of hopeful planning by Father Wilbur. It was a frame building measuring 64 by 40 feet with four classrooms on the south side, a private chapel on the second floor and living quarters for the Sisters on the north side. The work was started and ended within two months. On September 8, St. Joseph's Academy opened with about 175 pupils, Catholic and non-Catholic. Teaching in the new school were the Sisters of Divine Providence of San Antonio, Texas. Besides the regular courses and studies, St. Joseph's offered a complete course of vocal and in-

Father Wilbur inside church under construction - 1925.

strumental music. It was said that most of the prominent musicians of Perry in the three musical bands in Perry during the 30s received their musical training at St. Joseph's. In 1935, the high school was closed because of decreased enrollment, and in 1968, the grade school was closed. A church hall was built on the grade school building to create a meeting place for church and social functions in Perry.

In March of 1896, a six room house was purchased, moved onto the church lots and remodeled for the priest's residence. In November, 1898, land for Mt. Carmel (St. Rose of Lima) cemetery was purchased from Frank Lugent for the sum of $200. Richard Quinton was the first to be buried there and on December 2, Martin Delany was the second.

In order to complete the church building, Father Wilbur and the parishioners decided to construct a steeple and subscribe for a bell of 700 pounds. The tower was completed and the bell installed in February 1900.

The need for a new, larger church building was felt by the parishioners as well as by the pastor. Plans were discussed for several years and in 1922, the work was begun in earnest. In October, 1923, Bishop Merschaert dedicated the new St. Rose Lima Church, one of his last pontifical functions.

In February, 1931, Father Wilbur resigned his pastorate because of ill health to become chaplain of St. Joseph's Orphanage in Oklahoma City. After six years of service there, he died in January, 1937. Several priests have followed Father Wilbur to the present Father Ward Pankratz.

Christ Lutheran Church

By Dorothy Bowers and Marge Martin

A few scattered Lutherans lived in Perry and the surrounding area from the time of the opening of the Cherokee Strip for settlement in 1893. Worship services were conducted in homes until churches were established. Various missionaries and traveling pastors held services at Orlando, Orlando Townsite, Marena, Perry, Stillwater, Pawnee and Morrison.

On December 9, 1900, a group of Lutheran families met for the first of a series of services in Perry with Reverend Julius Huchthausen in charge. This led to the organization of Christ Lutheran Church on November 10, 1901. Charter members were Wm. Brasch, H. Viets, Hans Stoltenberg, Fred Oestereich, Edward Pollman, F. H. Piel, John Gorath, John Ritthaler, Albert Oestereich, Herman Heldt, and Ernest Stoltenberg. Other families figuring in the early history of the congregation were F. Just, A. Hermann, Hy. Just, P. F. Lau, Gottfried Heldt, Friederich Wilde, Gustav Pietrusky, and Christ Voss. The congregation's first house of worship was erected on the northeast corner of Seventh and Maple Streets and was dedicated in April, 1905. Rev. Huchthausen designed and constructed the altar and pulpit. This church building served the Lutherans in Perry for 45 years, even though it was damaged by a tornado in 1917 and was struck by lightning in 1920 and 1943.

Christ Lutheran School was opened immediately after the first worship service. Pastor Huchthausen was the instructor. He rented a hall and installed an old second-hand stove. He walked to the lumber yard, purchased the necessary boards, and carried them home on his shoulder. Twelve children came on the first day and were asked to bring two dollars each for their new "desks."

First building of Christ Lutheran Church.

In 1905, a parsonage was purchased. It was a small house and three lots on the corner of Sixth and L. Streets.

Reverend Walter Cook was the next pastor. Ready cash was not plentiful and by 1985 standards life was rather primitive. The minutes of Christ Lutheran, dated October 14, 1906, states thus: "Since the congregation needs heat during the winter, it was decided that each member should serve by turns as a fireman during the services. In 1907, the congregation became affiliated with and has continued to be a part of what is now called the Lutheran Church - Missouri Synod.

Between 1905 and 1908, the first choir was formed with Guy Pietrusky as choir director. The accompanist was Mrs. Wm. (Flora) Voss, who served as a church organist for many years. Her father, Dr. Lambertus Kuntz, became official organist in 1908 and also led the choir. Dr. Kuntz played the organ on the Sunday before his death, which occurred on June 25, 1933. Mr. Louis Meyer also was elected as parish organist in 1908.

In 1907, the Ladies Aid began. Mrs. Lambertus Kuntz was the first president.

Rev. A. W. Oetting was pastor from 1908-1913. During this time a white frame school building was erected on

Maple Street east of the church for a total cost of about $400.00.

The fifth pastor was Reverent W. E. Klaus, during whose time English services were introduced on Sunday afternoons to supplement the usual German services in the mornings.

Rev. A. Merkel served as pastor from 1917-1919. A frame parsonage was built on lots north of the church. On January 10, 1919, Rev. Merkel died of influenza during the famous flu epidemic.

Reverend Edward Hauer was installed on June 15, 1919, and worked faithfully without interruptions for 23½ years. After 1934, Christ Lutheran became independent of a financial subsidy from the district. However, financial hardships continued. Years later, Rev. and Mrs. Hauer revealed how concerned they were on one occasion during the depression. They honestly didn't know how they would have meat for the next meal. Trusting in the Lord, they were happy to see how He provided for them. Mrs. Hauer saw a rabbit hopping in their cellar. She exclaimed, "Papa, here is meat for our dinner!"

In 1920, the school was reopened. It had been closed since January 1, 1917. Rev. Hauer was the teacher until 1923. He was followed by Miss Gertrude Brauer, who taught from 1923-1925. In 1925, Miss Martha Maehr came; she taught here until 1945. In 1930, her brother, Martin Maehr, was added to the staff. Miss Maehr taught grades 1-4, and Mrs. Maehr taught grades 5-8. Mr. Maehr left in 1944.

In 1920, the Sunday School was begun. The first superintendent was Herman Voigt. The first youth group was organized in 1921. It affiliated with the International Walther League. Rev. Edward Hauer was the first president. In the 1980s the name was changed to Luthern Youth Fellowship.

The Aid Association for Lutherans, Branch #1476, was organized in Perry in November, 1926, with 13 members plus four juvenile members. Herman Voigt was the first president of this organization also. The Men's Club was organized in 1934.

The English language became more generally used and by January of 1943 German was discontinued entirely in the worship services. Until the middle of the 1920s the minutes of the congregational meetings were written in German; thereafter, in English.

In 1929, Immanuel Lutheran Church of Richburg merged with Christ Lutheran. Immanuel had dedicated its church building in April, 1907, five miles east and two and one-half miles south of Perry. Next to the church they put a cemetery, which became the property of Christ Lutheran in 1929. Although the church building no longer remains, Christ Lutheran congregation continues to maintain the cemetery. Many improvements have been made in recent years. Members of Immanuel fondly remember the brass band which played for services. At one time the band had ten members.

Reverend A. J. Brase became pastor in 1943 and served here until 1952. The Ruth Guild, a women's service organization, was formed in 1943 with Mrs. Charles Francis as president. The first Vacation Bible School was held in 1947. In the fall of 1947, the Ladies Aid and Ruth Guild dissolved and the Women's Missionary League of Christ Lutheran church was formed. The new group is part of the International Lutheran Women's Missionary League.

On February 5, 1950, a new church building was dedicated. Faced with Silverdale Limestone, it was located across the street west of the old frame church, which was converted to a parish hall. In May, 1952, a refugee family sponsored by Christ Lutheran arrived in Perry. The Paul Rode family from Poland lived here for five years.

Reverend Charles Keturakat served the congregation from 1952 to 1958. The congregation discontinued the seventh and eighth grades in the school and added a kindergarten. In 1955, a new brick parsonage was erected on the site of the old frame house north of the parish hall. In 1957, the parish hall was torn down and a new school erected on that site.

Rev. V. P. Schulz served from 1958-1960. Stewardship and missions were emphasized.

Reverend Edwin F. Lange served here from 1960-1969. A Junior Youth group was started in 1961 for grades 7 and 8. The first sponsors were Mr. and Mrs. Stephen Shiever and Mr. and Mrs. Robert McDaniel. The first president was Patty Ewy. An Altar Guild was formed in 1965. Mrs. F. L. Scheibe was directoress.

In 1961, St. Paul's Lutheran Church at Orlando disbanded and most of the members joined Christ Lutheran. St. Paul's had been organized in 1904 under the leadership of Pastor R. J. Reininga. The Charter members were Henry Gieschen, Henry Gerken, Conrad Mueller, and Carl Brase. Pastor Julius Huchthausen from Perry also served Orlando in 1905; and Pastor Walter Cook, from 1905-1908. Pastor P. B. Fritsche was installed in 1909. The Church had its own school. In 1914 and 1915 then Henkes, Karchers, Dittelmiers, Seeligers, and others from another small Lutheran congregation in Marena transferred to Orlando. In 1923, a new 1,000 pound bell was purchased. The bell came to Perry in 1961 and is set in concrete next to the Christ Lutheran church building.

Reverend Walter Wehmeier served from 1969 to 1984. In 1973, women were allowed to be voting members of the congregation. Pre-kindergarten classes were added to the school in 1973. In 1980-1981 the congregation sponsored the Nen Samoeun family, refugees from Cambodia.

Reverend Myron C. Maltz assumed his duties here in September, 1984. That same year an addition to the church was dedicated; this is used for offices and meeting rooms.

Fred Gorath, still a member of Christ Lutheran, was the first to be baptized after the organization of the congregation. The first to be confirmed was Mrs. Emilie Walter. Emma Viets and Emil Hermann constituted the first confirmation class. Albert Oestereich and Auguste Voss were the first to be married. The first death was that of Flora Helena Malzahn, age 12 days, on July 6, 1906.

Church of Christ

By Clarence M. Koch, Jr.

In the year 1932, three families and one widow, started the Congregation of the Perry, Oklahoma, Church of Christ. This group first met in the home of Charles P. and Etta Smith, but after a few months, when the group began to swell in numbers, arrangements were made to meet on Sunday at the Seventh Day Adventist Church building located at the Southeast corner of 7th and Grove Streets in Perry. The church met here until late in 1938.

The church had a steady growth in the 1930s and the members could foresee the necessity of owning their own place of worship. A building fund was started, and in the year, 1938, the decision was made that the time had arrived to move, and on the 20th day of August, 1938, the church acquired title to the lot and existing church building located at the northwest corner of 7th and Grove Streets in Perry. This church was originally acquired and occupied by the Episcopal Church at the turn of the 20th century, but was abandoned in later years. Before the church could occupy the building for services considerable refurbishing was done, and by the end of 1938 the work was finished and the members of the church started meeting there for all worship services.

In March 1951, the decision was reached to build a new building to accomodate the expanding congregation, and a new building fund was started. In 1952, a location was purchased for the building at the southeast corner of 7th and Jackson Streets in Perry, and actual construction was started in February, 1953, and completed the same year. The first regular services in the new building began the latter part of 1954. The dedication services were held Sunday, January 9th, 1955. About 300 were expected for this service, but more than 500 crowded into the building and others were never able to get inside.

The old church building, was sold on December 21, 1955 to the Episcopal Church of Perry. In the early 1970s an annex was added to the present church building to accommodate the further growth of the congregation. This annex was built to provide additional class rooms and an all-purpose room.

The first full-time minister was J. W. Channel, who was followed by Joe Hunter, George Bonds, Daniel Haile, R. J. Stevens, Jeff Stafford, Forrest Magness, Kent Ellis, Gerald Stewart, Terry Edmondson and David Burdue. Jeff Stafford served as minister of the church for eight years, from 1950 to 1958, and it was during this time the main church building was constructed. Gerald Stewart served as the minister for thirteen years, from 1964 to 1977. During this time the church experienced a rapid growth in numbers, and the construction of the church annex was completed. The present minister, Michael Watters, began serving as minister to the church in 1983 and is continuing a good work.

Perry Methodist Church

In 1893, Thomas Wolcott was sent to Perry by the Missouri Conference to do Missionary work in Perry. He arrived here the day of the run, September 16, 1893. He then met with three South Methodists who joined in organizing the First Methodist Church in Perry on October 14, 1893.

A lot was purchased at 10th and Elm Streets for $165.00. Methodist women served a benefit supper making a profit of $165.75 and paid for the lot. A building was finally erected and dedicated on the lot October 7, 1894. On December 8, 1893, the women of the church were organized as the Susannah Wesley Society. The first achievement of the women was the purchasing of a bell for $195.00 and the bell now stands in a bell tower at 7th and Elm Streets. The bell has served for some 93 years. The church had a membership of 114. The most terrible blizzard of the season was on the day the chapel was dedicated.

In 1901 a lot at 7th and Elm was purchased for a new church.

In 1918, W. H. Beers was transferred from the New England Conference to Perry. He filled in as elementary school principal. Mrs. Beers organized Camp Fire work in Perry.

After 28 years in the frame structure at 7th and Elm the official board agreed that a new church was necessary. A building committee, composed of Charles Christoph, J. W. Yoce, D. O. W. Boyer, H. L. Boyce, George Sims, John Mugler and Everett Nelson, was established. The cost of the new church was estimated at $50,000. The beautiful structure was dedicated June 8, 1930. The ceremony continued for a week with former pastors preaching each night.

In 1941, the corporate name of our church was changed from the "First Methodist Episcoapal Church" of Perry, Oklahoma to the "First Methodist Church" of Perry, Oklahoma.

Land was purchased just north of the church for $1,000 for the building of the Lucy Minor Boyce parsonage. The old wooden parsonage had been partly destroyed by fire, so the Beck family was the first to occupy the new residence. The parsonage was dedicated by Rev. Don H. LaGrone, November 2, 1941.

In February of 1940 the Women's society entertained the church women of Perry at the twentieth anniversary of their "Washington Tea." They also had a Thanksgiving Tea each year.

After leaving Perry in 1950, after 3 years here, Reverend Jack S. Wilkes was minister at Crown Heights Methodist Church in Oklahoma City and on March 6, 1958, he became president of Oklahoma City University where he was installed by Bishop Angie Smith. He was also elected Mayor of Oklahoma City during his presidency.

Howard Bush served from 1950 until 1953. He presented the need for a Youth Building and as the lot adjacent to the church was available it was purchased. The building committee was: O. J. Moore, Everette Morrow, Raymond Frailey, John Mugler, Art Coffee, George Spradberry, and Frank Eby. The building was completed in 1953. It consisted of a large auditorium, parlor, and a modern well furnished kitchen. In April 1955, the building was converted into a two story structure with class rooms on the 2nd floor.

R. C. Veirs, Jr. served in 1960-1963. His great interest was in aviation. A short time after leaving Perry he lost his life while piloting a plane.

Dr. Kermitt Hollingworth (1976-1977) had a wonderful memory of Bible verses, especially the Psalms,

First Presbyterian Church of Perry

By Irene Treeman

On September 17, 1893, the dust was only beginning to clear from the air over the prairies. The sounds of yesterday — the firing of the starting gun, the shouts of the horsemen, the rumble of wagon wheels — all were quiet. A small remnant of pioneers was listening as the voice of God spoke to them "out of the whirlwind". They met for worship on the Sabbath.

A copy of the "minutes" of the first meeting reads as follows (note unique spelling) Minutes of Session-First Service: "The First Presbytereans, who came into Peery and vicinity, at or after the opening of the Cherokee Strip, which was on the 16th day of September, in the year of our Lord, 1893, met for worship on the first Sunday, after the opening of said "Strip".

The next Public Service, was also held by the Rev. Simeon Peter Myers, who was sent by Presbytery to take charge of the work at Perry, Oklahoma Territory. The first regular service was held on Sunday, October first in J. O. Young's grocery store. Services were held here for several weeks until on October 22, 1893, nineteen Presbyterians gathered together for the purpose of organizing a Presbyterian church. These charter members were M. S. Stahl, Joseph O. Young, Morris C. Latta, George H. Todd, Charles L. Wenner, W. V. Raymond, Anna C. Stanly, Willis B. Stanly, Minnie M. Stanly, Arsula Myers, Maggie S. Todd, Maggie M. Coyle, Bernar S. A. Brook, Jennie Bethan, Earl S. Myers, Carrie M. Graham, Fred A. Caster, Fannie Young, Alford E. Robinson, A. Stahl and Ella Duncan. When Mrs. Ronald Felt of Virginia, Illinois, visited here in 1953, she told an interesting bit of early church history. She said that the first time her family attended church services in the J. O. Young grocery store, that it was communion Sunday. The elements of communion were passed in tin cups and tin pie plates. Her mother, a native of Maine, wrote to a cousin in Haverill, Massachusettes about this pioneer service. That cousin and friends in his church, sent to the new little church in Oklahoma Territory, its first real communion set; two tall cups appropriately decorated and plates for the bread. When a new communion set was purchased, the first one was given to the Bethel Presbyterian church near the southeast edge of Noble County and were returned to the church in Perry in later years. Mrs. Felt (Florence Bullen) had united with the church the day of its dedication December 24, 1894. By October of 1893, a tent known as the Presbyterian Tabernacle was located where the Fellowship Hall now stands. The seats on the first Sunday were boards resting on kegs, but soon these boards were made into benches.

As early as December 28, 1893, "The Ladies Aid Society" was organized. The first president was Mrs. Stone, whose husband was mayor of Perry — The first social affair was an apron bazaar, the proceeds of which were used to put a board floor in the tent where church services were held. The tent was blown away in a storm in the spring of 1894. The congregation moved to a building in the 400 block on the west side of the street just north of the square, until the first wooden church was built. On December 24, 1894, a large one room frame building was dedicated on the site where the present church now stands. The dedication services were preceded by a week of social evenings, during which a fair was held. One feature of this fair was the auctioning of a photograph of the wife of Presdient Grover Cleveland which she had graciously autographed and sent on request. This brought quite a sum of money for the treasury.

The little wooden church was to serve adequately for 25 years. The last Sunday in the church was October 17, 1920, and the next day, workmen began to tear down the old building. At this time the congregation held services in the District Court Room of the Noble County Court House. The corner stone of the above building was laid January 30, 1921. This corner stone became quite famous when it was televised at the time of Governor-elect Henry Bellmon's inauguration, January 14, 1962. At his request, he took communion in this church, before going to Oklahoma City to take the oath of office.

On October 25, 1953, at the 60th anniversary of the church a large crowd heard Mrs. E. J. (Maggie) Coyle talk on the early days of the church. She was the only charter member left. Her daughter, Mrs. J. J. (Pearl Coyle) Vivian has been a member for 80 years, having joined in 1906.

In 1955, a six room manse was built at 1404 Kaw Street. In 1960, the Morgan Memorial Building and Fellowship Hall was built in honor of Mr. John M. Morgan and Miss Jennie Morgan, early members of the church.

The last service in the sanctuary of the stucco church was held July 22, 1973. On June 14, 1974, the new church was dedicated. A new manse was built in 1985 at 1911 Lakeview.

Sixteen ministers have served the church in the 93 years from the first, Rev. Simon Peter Myers, to Rev. Jim Dunkin, the present minister. Rev. David Thomas served the longest from 1919 until 1946. Many of the present worshippers are decendants of the early members.

Presbyterian Church at 8th and Elm, 1921-1973.

Mt. Olive AME Church

The Mt. Olive African Methodist Episcopal Church was found in Perry in 1902 at a location in the northwest corner of Ninth and Holly Streets. The church as founded under the leadership of A. W. Washington who pastored the church until 1906.

In 1909, a decision was made to move the church to its present location at 520 Grove Street. The cost of moving the church building was paid by Ben Steinson. In 1912, Reverend Louis began serving the church as pastor, a position he held approximately three years. Mt. Olive then was without a pastor for nearly two years. During this time, stewards of the church were in charge of services.

In 1922, Reverend W. A. Davis began serving the church, a position he held one year. Several other ministers followed, including Reverend R. C. Jenkins, who served nine years and later returned to serve another six years.

A number of well-known residents have been active in the church including Clem T. Talliaferro, Joe Reed, William M. Johnson, Mrs. Gillie Banks, Henrietta Mayfield, Anthony Bourland and Blanch Bourland.

In 1942, a remodeling program was begun at the church, under direction of Reverend Ellison. Under direction of Reverend Tolbert, new siding was added in 1947.

Reverend R. C. Jenkins was in charge of beginning the construction of the present church building. Reverend Nancy Newton has been pastor for six years.

Zion Lutheran Church - Perry, Oklahoma

By Darlene Roads

As homes took shape and seeds of crops were planted following the opening of the Cherokee Outlet, September 16, 1893, settlers were also nourishing their seeds of faith. They met in homes for fellowship and worship services until 1897, when Zion Lutheran congregation was officially organized. On February 22, 1897, Ludwig Ritthaler and his family donated two acres of land in the southwest corner of his homestead for a church building and cemetery. Volunteer labor by church members was used to build the church which took about a year.

The first ministers were supply pastors of the Missouri Synod and were shared with other struggling congregations in the area; therefore formal services were not held every Sunday. Many of the older members recall having to meet the train in Perry on Saturday evening to pick up Sunday's minister and provide his "board and bed".

Between 1901 and 1905, a split occurred in the congregation and those who remained at Zion left the Missouri Synod and joined the German Nebraska Synod which has evolved into the Lutheran Church in America. From that time until 1960, Zion and her sister congregation in Stillwater, Salem, shared their ministers.

Rev. J. Hediger served Zion for thirteen years, the longest pastorate in the history of the congregation. During his tenure, the original church building was destroyed by a tornado and a second erected in 1917. He organized the first Sunday School for children.

The entrance of the second building was on the south and there was a small balcony along the south end which was used for Sunday School classes. Pews were arranged on each side of a center aisle. A large wood stove heated those within three feet of it and everyone else froze. Traditionally German, the men sat on one side of the church and the women and children on the other. Services were conducted in German but as English became more common, German faded and disappeared completely in the 1950s.

The church had no kitchen or eating facilities, but the congregation still observed special feasting days. Following Sunday worship services, the big double front doors were removed and placed on top of the pews. Food was brought in from vehicles and placed on the doors and — the table was set! The church steps, blankets on the ground, backs of wagons and car running boards served as seating.

Rev. William Krauleidis was the first of three ministers to marry into the congregation. He married Sophia Bamberger. The others were Rev. Herbert Pett who married Emily Ziesch and Rev. James Little who married Sandra Musick. Rev. Krauleidis, his wife and a son, William Lee Jr., were en route to Zion for a funeral when they were all killed in a tragic car accident. They are buried in Zion cemetery. Another son, Pfc. Walter Krauleidis, was killed April, 1945, during World War II.

One of the early ministers, possibly Pastor Pett, had a camera with a delay action. To many families, the camera itself was a rarity, but the delay action was really a novelty. On one special occasion, he wanted to take a picture of the entire congregation, including himself! What a thrill the younger children (and adults, too?) had in watching him set up the camera, press the button and run like mad to get to his appointed place in the set-up before the camera snapped the photo. As I recall, he had to take several pictures because most of the group were to busy watching him to look at the camera and smile.

Another of the early ministers was either near-sighted or did not want to wear out the brakes on his car. Each Sunday, the congregation patiently awaited his arrival. Finally, a distinct "bump" was heard and felt at the side of the church. The pastor had arrived! He stopped his car each Sunday by bumping into the side of the church — sometimes none too gently.

Pastor Edward J. Amend arrived to serve Zion and Salem in 1945 and Zion began to look to a more modern facility in a more accessible location. Mr. and Mrs. A. A. Kemnitz donated two acres of their farmland, five miles east of Perry on Highway 64, to the church. One year later, the old church building which had served for over 25 years, was razed and the lumber was moved to the new location. Again, volunteer labor was used for construction. Pastor Amend designed the church in every detail and supervised its construction. The land has now been deeded solely to the church.

After the church was moved to the highway location, there were many break-ins and thefts. Dishes, silverware, coffee pots, lawn mowers, fans and many small items have been taken. At one time, the thieves even moved the Altar to see if anything had been hidden behind it. One of the most recent thefts included a piano bench and the chancel chairs which the pastor and organist used during Sunday morning worship services.

Zion Lutheran Church / 99

Old Zion Lutheran Church and congregation.

In the late 1950's, Zion began making plans to call their own minister. Pastor A. J. Duis, who served from 1953 to 1960, assisted in making preparations, but elected to stay at Salem. Rev. David Gieschen came in 1960 as Zion's first own minister.

At times when Zion was without a minister or the minister was away, laymen of the congregation served as "preachers". Lillie Brokop gave her first sermonette only a short time after she was confirmed in the 1930's. Carl Smith took his turn in the pulpit and his brother, John, also filled the pulpit many times. Many members expressed the thought that John would have made a very good minister; however, his thought was that it took many talents to make a minister and he didn't have enough of the others.

In January, 1973, Rev. Richard Pearson arrived at Zion just out of seminary, with a new bride and fresh ideas. He instituted family communion services, Good Friday Tenebrae services and introduced monthly children's service into Sunday worship.

A building program which was born during Rev. Pearson's five years at Zion has been completed during the tenure of Rev. Charles Ledin. The earlier idea was improved upon and the final plan nearly doubled the size of the ground floor adding a modern kitchen, fellowship hall and chapel extension, ramps and a covered entrance.

Zion is the oldest organized Lutheran congregation of the Lutheran Church in America in Oklahoma and has been recognized as such at various state-wide meetings. Zion church is proud of her heritage and traditions and though times change and the church, too, must change, she steadfastly remains true to her basis for existence and to the God of her creation.

Stagecoach Community Theatre

By Marjorey Martin

The Stagecoach Community Theatre began March 18, 1975, when a group of 26 people met and decided to present the play "Oklahoma".

From the Perry Daily Journal June 7, 1975: "A power blackout called a halt to the first performance of 'Oklahoma' in the school auditorium Friday night, less than an hour after the show started. The cast and crew stood valiantly by, ready to resume the show when the power was restored. After a 45 minute wait they gave up and went home. The show came to an abrupt stop about 9 pm when the storm interrupted power and blacked out the auditorium. Steve Daniels went to the stage when the storm sirens sounded and announced that a tornado alert was in effect, and asked those in the audience to remain in their seats and to remain calm. He said the building is regarded as a storm shelter area and the absence of glass added to the safety factor. Shortly thereafter the power failed. Few left. Most of the crowd remained and were entertained by impromptu performances by musicians and local comedians, lighted mostly by flashlights."

From March 1975 to June 1986, 33 plays have been produced. All of the musicals have been performed at the Perry High School auditorium which seats about 1,000. Many dramas also were performed there. "And No Birds Sing" was put on in the parish hall of St. Mark's Episcopal Church in Perry.

First play "Oklahoma" June 6, 1975 (L to R): Gene Kirby (chorus), Gerald Payne (Ali Hakim), John McLemore (Curly), Peggy Rymer (Laurie), Mike Ennis (chorus), Harold Long (Ike Skidmore), Bruce Self (chorus).

"A Pair of Lunatics" was part of the entertainment for the Cherokee Strip Art Show at the Women's Building at the Noble County Fairgrounds. "Maker of Dreams" was the entry in the Oklahoma Community Theater festival. Previously, act three of "Plaza Suite" was entered in the 1977 festival in Ardmore. "Dust of the Road" was presented in two Perry churches, the United Methodist and First Presbyterian, as Christmas gifts to the community from Stagecoach. "Barefoot in the Park" was the first attempt at dinner theater and was followed by several more.

"The Night of January 16th" is a comedy-drama and portrays a murder trial. The director, Jim Garvey, arranged for the production of this play to be in the District Courtroom of the Noble County Courthouse. Members of the audience became the spectators who always came to a juicy trial. The jury was chosen from the audience.

Rehearsals have been held in various places through the years: the cold armory, church halls, a dusty upper room over a downtown business and a cozy basement room. Storage for wardrobe, properties and "portable" dinner theater stage has been a problem over the years. In December of 1985, a building at 517 Cedar Street was purchased. It formerly housed an automotive repair business and is divided into three large rooms. The building is used for storage, rehearsals, meetings and workshops.

Perry Lions Club

Temporary organization of the Perry Lions Club was effected January 8, 1926, in a meeting at Carnegie public library. Approximately 30 men attended and more than 20 of them signed the charter roll. Five more Perryans joined the charter ranks of the club at the charter meeting held January 14, 1926 at the library. The first club officers included W. F. Boone, president; Dr. O. W. Boyer, first vice-president; Ross Johnson, second vice-president; Dr. B. A. Owen, third vice-president and district representative; Paul Harding, secretary-treasurer; Bill Fry, Jr. Lion tamer; Carl Voris, tail twister; Reverend J. A. Nagle, chaplain; and Ed Coyle, H. L. Johnson, George Doyle, Jr. and Charles Collins, members of the board of directors.

Other charter members included: Walter A. Bittman, George W. Clark, Ralph E. Foster, Rudolph Gottlieb, Joe E. Howard, Henry L. Johnson, Henry S. Johnston, Ivan L. Kennedy, A. C. Lamb, W. A. Maloch, W. J. McCuiston, Charles Monroe, Walter S. Powers, W. J. Reckert, W. H. Sheets, L. F. Sowers and Leonard O. Winters.

Since the organization of the club, the Perry Lions have been well known for community service projects. The club supports and maintains Lions West Park in Perry, supports the Perry Pee-Wee baseball program, the Perry Meals-on-Wheels program, an annual Christmas project in which baskets are provided for the needy and gifts presented to residents of the Perry Nursing Home and Green Valley Convalescent Center. Each spring, the Lions Club sponsors an Easter egg hunt with cash prizes and candy for young Perryans. Also in the spring, the club annually hosts an athletic track meet for boys and girls below the high school level. In addition, Lions present awards for outstanding high school athletes.

During the fall, a service day is

Parade float in 16th celebration. The lion is now in the Perry Lions Park.

organized in which a day is set aside for Lion members to take part in work to aid the Perry Community. Winter activities sponsored by the Lions include sponsorship of refreshments and fellowship for students following athletic events and serving of hot chocolate after the annual Christmas sing by Blue Bird and Camp Fire groups.

Each year the Lions Club provides transportation and seating for residents of both Perry Nursing Homes during the Cherokee Strip parade. The club also helps support the Noble County livestock fair and sale, athletic funds, the annual Cherokee Strip celebration and the Noble County free fair.

The Perry Lions club was instrumental in the establishment of the Lions Eye Bank in Oklahoma in 1957, and regularly makes contributions to the Oklahoma Eye Bank and the Dean A. McGee Eye foundation at Oklahoma City. The club purchases eye glasses for local residents who cannot afford them. The local club also contributes $5 per member per year in support of the IOA Boys Ranch near Perkins.

In 1943, the Perry Lion's Club

Lion's Club Trio 1943 (L to R): Doris Rodolph, Director, Margaret Plumer, Lila Lee Davis and Betty Lee Moore.

adopted a Girls Trio: Margaret Plumer, Lila Lee Davis and Betty Moore directed by Doris Rodolph. This group represented Perry at Amateur programs at the State Lion's Club Convention in Oklahoma City in 1943, where they placed first and in Tulsa in 1944, where they placed second. The trio, Doris Rodolph, Lion's president, Dale Ream and wife, June, and several delegates made the trip to Tulsa by bus, standing all the way. Gasoline was rationed and if a trip was not necessary, you took the train or the bus.

Ladies Tuesday Afternoon Club

By Irene Treeman

The Ladies Tuesday Afternoon Club was organized on December 4, 1894 in the home of Mrs. J. H. Bullen, now 707 Grove street. Thirteen charter members were present and Mrs. L. A. Hudson, wife of an early-day lawyer, was the first president. The records of the club from that early-day are intact. The club is proud that in this way, they can verify their 80 years (1974) of continuous active history. The early records are filled with word pictures of pioneer women, their homes and interests: October 10, 1899 "In spite of the dust storm that was raging, twelve members were present," and April, 1899 "On account of approching storm, the meeting hastily and informally disbanded without having the rest of the papers." Sometimes, however, they weakened and recorded "Rains have been heavy, walking was bad, so the meeting was postponed."

They didn't even have sidewalks then, let alone street crossings. And so it is surprising that they waited until April 20, 1908, to appoint a committee to carry a petition to the city council to see what could be done about better crossings and sidewalks.

Those early-day club women spoke in no uncertain terms of many varieties. In 1898, they limited their business meeting to 20 minutes and ended with this cryptic note: A motion prevailed for each member to mind her own business during the business meeting. In other words, each is to be allowed to state her business "without interruption or interference."

Subjects on their programs were such that we can understand that they wanted no long business sessions to keep them from such spicy discussion and debate as — for instance; March 1, 1899, "The Power of Harem." January 30, 1900, "Is Polite Society Really Polite?" and "Have Women a Sense of Humor?" March 3, 1900, "Shall We Educate Our Boys as Well as Our Girls to be Homemakers?"

Their main idea was the betterment of their town and community , so in January 1903, when the Women's Christian Temperance Union opened a reading room, the LTAC gave its support in books, magazines, furnishings and funds. Their reading room was the beginning of the present-day library. Because they thought that the pioneer community needed cultural entertainments, they helped to bring lyceums and chautauqua courses. They sold tickets and even got together and purchased the entire gallery of the Opera House in 1914 so the high school and eighth grade students could get in free.

They wrote letters to congressmen and state legislators about homes for junior criminals, child labor laws, compulsory education, suffrage, library maintenance, peace-even in the far-off 1900 the secretary's minutes say: "An anti-polygamy petition was circulated at the club meeting."

In August 1898, the club made bandages and gowns for soldiers in the Spanish-American War. Through the First and Second World Wars the LTAC contributed time, money and strength.

Book showers for the schools' libraries were thought up during dry seasons and free flower seeds for the

Meeting of LTAC and guests about 1900. The building in background was the home of Dr. F. C. Seids at 10th and Delaware.

children of the town, when it rained.

Floor pads were provided for the school gymnasium and medals furnished for county track meetings. LTAC even put a shoulder to the wheel in 1915 and helped to organize a patron's club-now PTA.

One of the highlights was the financial aid it gave to the building of the American Legion hut, and to the fingerprinting project sponsored by LTAC in which 787 persons were fingerprinted in Noble County.

Outstanding among club activities of recent years has been the participation in Perry's annual September 16th celebration of the opening of the Cherokee Strip. The club has had displays of antique jewelry, early-day clothing, pioneer kitchen equipment, old photographs and antiques furniture, besides entering decorated floats in the parades.

In 1968, the Cherokee Strip museum was completed with the help from many of the LTAC members, who were members of the Noble County Historical Society.

LTAC trough the years has lived up to her motto selected by those pioneers in 1894 — Mutual Good Will and Mutual Benefit.

Perry Brush and Pallette Club

In the early 1950s, under the leadership of Ethel L. Johnston, wife of former governor, Henry S. Johnston, the Perry Brush and Palette Club was formed. The instructor was Jacques Hans Gallrein, noted artist of the southwest. Gallrein was born in Magdeburg, Germany on June 29, 1888, where at the age of fourteen he studied art at the Kounstgwerbe and Handwerker Schule, a technical art school. At an early age he was influenced by Franz Van Stuck for color and correct drawing and by Arnold Boecklin for allegorical and misty compositions. His father taught him the importance of ecology, which influenced his choice of subject matter towards the out-of-doors. At eighteen, he was admitted to the Royal Academy of Art in Munich, where he studied under the artist-lecturer Wilheim Trubner.

On arrival in New York City in 1908, he was employed by the Fisher Art Studio, where he was advised to go westward to paint the wonders of the west. In the early spring of 1911, he arrived in southern Oklahoma where he came to know personally the Governor of the Chickasaw Nation, Douglas Johnson and two state governors, Henry S. Johnston and William H. "Alfalfa Bill" Murray.

His influence was felt by the little group of artist in Perry where he taught for several years. It continues to be felt as it influences artist in Noble County through some of his pupils who became teachers. Once a week, on Thursdays, he came to Perry, spending the entire day with the group. Much of the time they used the club studio on Seventh Street across from the Post Office, over a piece goods and mens wear store. The studio was open all week and members put in many happy hours there, alone or in small groups. On the spur of the moment, they would sometimes pack their field equipment and "brown bag it" to the banks of the Cimmarron River or the hospitality of a state park, to paint from nature on the spot. The Perry Brush and Palette Club evolved into the Noble County Art Association. Among the many awards Mr. Gallrein received was from the 34th session of the Oklahoma Legislature declaring June 29, 1974 "Jacques Hans Gallrein Day" in Oklahoma. This was followed by the Governor's Proclamation designating the same honor. In 1975, he received a citation from the Legislature for the endowment of the oil painting, of the state tree: "Red Bud" which hangs in the speaker's room at the Oklahoma State Capitol.

In celebration of the Oklahoma Diamond Jubilee, he received a second citation for this painting. The most current honor is a certificate awarded by the Diamond Jubilee Committee to Mr. Gallrien and his assistant, Lucille Ritthaler Graham, for their artistic portrayal displaying of paintings depicting the Oklahoma environment. He has been interviewed on WKY-TV and OETA television in Oklahoma City and featured in *Oklahoma Today* magazine and numerous other publications. He has had art exhibits in Platt National Park, Sulphur, Oklahoma; First National Bank at Stillwater and the Oklahoma Historical Society building in Oklahoma City. He has paintings at the University Museum at Stillwater; Ponca City Art Center, Marland Mansion at Ponca City, Oklahoma Historical Society building in Oklahoma City and the Oklahoma State Capitol.

Mr. Gallrein, up until his death at the age of 97, maintained his residence in the Studio Gallery where many of his paintings are kept and where he continued to critic in weekly art classes. The Studio gallery at 724 S. McDonald, Stillwater, Oklahoma, is in the home of Lucille Ritthaler Graham, Artist Assistant, teacher, and Custodian for the Gallrein Collection of Art. Mrs. Graham, noted artist in her own right, cared for Mr. Gallrein and conducts tours by appointment. The standard of art set by Mr. Gallrein is reflected in the outstanding art exhibits at the Noble County Fair each year.

Perry Brush and Palette Club 1956 (Front Row) (L to R): Mrs. H. C. (LeOla) Donley, Mrs. W. H. (Avis) Leatherock, Mrs. L. E. (Girtha) Plumer, Mrs. C. B. (Jennie) Forney and Charles Forney. (Back Row): Mrs. Ted (Mary) Swart, Mrs. Jim (Pearl) Berger, Mrs. Fred (Allien) Kruse, Mrs. D. T. (Minnie) Sherrard, Jacques Hans Gallrein, Loren Snodgrass and Mrs. Henry S. (Ethel L.) Johnston.

Poor Boys Club

By O. B. Campbell

It was in 1931, that the Poor Boys Club was organized in Perry for it was in the heart of the depression and young men were seeking fun and civic service opportunities at the least cost.

That was the way Paul Cress and O. B. Campbell viewed the situation that year. Cress was county attorney. Campbell was managing editor of the *Perry Daily Journal.*

So they worked out details for the organization which was described as a "blend between a Junior Chamber of Commerce, a college fraternity, a standard civic club and a fraternal body or lodge."

The full name was the Broke and Bankrupt Order of Poor Boys. A ritual was used in the initiation that required the new member to carry an armload of bricks around the room, dipicting the burdens of the average young man. These were painted and lettered with such words as "mortgages", "notes", "bills", "rent", and the like. As he circled the room he would stop at the stations of the Chief Mortgator, Chief Bankrupt and Chief Deadbeat, and be relieved of his "load".

Eddie Parker catered the weekly luncheon in the basement of the library. The charge was 25 cents.

To be a member, one had to have been born in 1900 or later. He could not smoke cigars or cigarettes at a meeting but the smoking of a cob pipe was acceptable. There were no dues or assessments.

When Campbell went to Medford in 1932, he organized a club there. Both clubs were active in civic projects for years. They also held conventions together.

The club at Perry disbanded about 1940.

Cherokee Strip Museum and Henry S. Johnston Library

By Mrs. Charles F. Malzahn

Prior to 1964, through the untiring efforts of Mrs. Henry S. Johnston and Robert Taylor, as well as other interested citizens, many artifacts were collected and stored in various places, mainly in the basement of the Perry Carnegie library.

In December, 1964, application was made for a charter. A constitution and by-laws were written by the historical organization. With Governor Henry Bellmon in office, Senator Don Ferrell and Ruth Patterson our state representative, the legislature appropriated $35,000 with which to construct a building. Ettamae Reed was a member of the board of affairs and with their approval, we immediately proceeded to set the wheels in motion. With part of the money of a gift of $8,000 from the Perry Industrial Foundation we hired an architect, Frank Davies of Enid. Also other contributions, memorials and memberships dues were forthcoming and with this community cooperation we felt that the center would become a reality.

The first step was to obtain a location. A building committee was appointed which consisted of David Matthews as legal advisor, Arthur Kerr to represent the Morrison and eastern Noble County area, Gordon Hayton for Billings and the northwestern part of the county, John Pat Carpenter for the Red Rock, Marland and Northeastern Noble County, Bill Elliott for the City of Perry, Milo Watson for publicity director and Glenn Yahn of Perry to represent the citizens at large.

Through this committee as well as a general survey conducted by the *Perry Daily Journal,* 10 possible locations were considered. When Robert Donahue, son of Mr. and Mrs. H. C. Donahue came forward with a gift of five acres of ground, one and one fourth miles west of Perry, on the four lane highway, the committee could not turn a deaf ear to such a generous contributor.

With the location, $35,000 in state money, an architect and Edwin Malzahn as chairman of the Oklahoma Development Commission and Parks Department, who supervised the construction, we had come a long way in seeing this project became a reality.

The ground breaking ceremony was celebrated on March 5, 1967, with Governor Henry Bellmon turning the first dirt with a team of horses and a sod plow. Lawrence Seeliger was employed by the state as building supervisor and on July 24, 1968, the building was officially opened to the public. Everything was moved from the library and storage places in time for the celebration on September 16, 1968.

Alice Mae Svelan was appointed as curator with Mildred Highfill her assistant. Under the articulate cataloging and management of Alice Mae, 712 items have been entered and are on display.

In 1970, four picnic tables were built along with a bridge across the creek. In 1971, the Rose Hill School house was moved to the grounds and completely restored. A tepee contributed by the George Kihega family and Bryon Neal was erected on the grounds. Since the opening date starting with September 16, 1968, we have had 30,175 visitors of whom 10,329 were from out of state. Every state is represented as well as several foreign countries. We must have something of interest to attract an average of 28 people per day.

This winter we hope to have a storage building for tools and etc. Next we will ask for an outside shed so that the farm implements and tools that have been given can be displayed. Before long we also hope to have an addition to the original building. This museum was established to preserve the life history of our forefathers and it belongs to every family in Noble County. (Written in September 1971.)

Billings

By Mildred Highfill

The town of Billings was founded in November 1899. It has been moved from White Rock located southeast of the present town in White Rock township. When the Rock Island railroad extended their line out this far from Enid, the town was moved and re-named Billings in honor of Mrs. Harry Thompson whose maiden name was Mary Ann Billings. Harry Thompson was with the railroad. The land for the northeast part was purchased from Mrs. Millie Weaver, the southeast from the Kettenring farm, the northwest from James L. Young and the southwest from Mrs. Kate Wilson.

The town grew rapidly, and soon there were 24 business places counting restaurants, blacksmith shops and the like. Much of the rock used for building purposes in the early days here was quarried from the William P. Lemmon farm south of town. William W. McCullough published a newspaper in White Rock which he called the Red Rock Valley News. He was also the postmaster. He moved his business to the new town and renamed his newspaper the Billings News. Later, Loren C. "Brownie" Brown bought the equipment and machinery and continued to publish the paper until 1928 when he sold out to A. M. Miller who published the Billings News for many years.

The Citizen Bank was established in 1899, by Roy Kinnerman, Tom Miller and Nick Ellis. In 1918, the name was changed to the First National and on November 12, 1931, the name was again changed and has been known since as the First State Bank. The Billings State bank was organized at about the same time as the Citizens bank and was located at the east end of Main Street. It was later known as the Billings National Bank.

Charles Christoph of Perry opened the first furniture store in Billings. Oscar W. Long worked for him and later bought the stock and was the funeral director for many years. Roy Robbins owned the first drug store. Dr. Thomas F. Renfrow owned a livery barn. Alex Younger and Ernie Davis opened the first livery barn and later became horse and mule buyers, doing the largest business of any buyers in the state. John English was one of the first dry goods merchants. Anton Cades, who had come here from Russia, bought the stock and fixtures and continued the store for several years. He called his store "The Bee Hive". Other stores of the early days were those of Henry and Seymour Graves, Quince Cooper, Swartz and Beatty, W. R. Johnston, R. E. Drum Variety store, George Faragher, Prentice grocery, C. A. Saylers clothing company and others.

A. R. Garrett was an early day hardware merchant, Larren A. "Add" Brown was a pioneer blacksmith. The Weaver blacksmith shop was one of the first. Jacob Lowe put in a drug store. Dr. Renfrow, who moved here with the town, built a number of stone houses. The first hotel was opened by a Mr. Brafford who came here from White Rock. It was the Rock Island Hotel. The Oakland Hotel was built by a Mr. Parks in 1900. In the early days B. M. Athey operated a lumber yard.

At the fourth of July celebration in 1901, high winds kept the speakers from being heard, the hot air balloon could not be inflated until late in the evening so the parachute jump could not be made but the editor of The Billings News declared the moon rise a success.

The Billings telephone exchange was installed in 1903 by Plez Bain. Mr. Carter bought in and later Roy Henry and Carter bought Bain's interest. Henry continued in the company several years and built most of the country lines. After several other owners it was sold to the Southwestern Associated Telephone Company.

In 1903, a disastrous fire of unknown origin started in the business block on the north side in one of the stores and burned every building between the two banks, except one, the building where O. W. Long furniture store was later located. Some of the stores to burn were H. C. Graves and Disney and Quince Cooper stores and the Cal Swingle residence.

The first school was held in the building on the corner of the James C. Noonan farm at the northeast edge of Billings. By 1901, a school house was built on the townsite just west of where the high school building now stands. It was a tall stone building with two rooms and a hall. At first only two years of high school was given, later three years and then a four year course was offered. In 1902, the present high school was built. May 21, 1926, the original school building which was then used as a grade school was condemned as unsafe. It was torn down and a new grade building erected. This served until 1974 when a new elementary building was ready for the fall term.

Mr. and Mrs. Lou Lowe operated the picture show here for a number of years and later a drug store.

The first municipal band was organized at White Rock by John White and moved with the town. Those playing in the band were: L. A. Brown, cornet; Walter Brown, drum; Newt Brookhart, cornet; Walter Harrison, piccolo; Sam Brafford, alto horn; Fred Bowers, tenor; Lee Lane, baritonet; Dick White, bass horn; John Huddleston, solo alto horn; Loren Williams, alto horn; Reed Carpenter, snare drum; John White E flat cornet; Eli Cox, tenor horn; and Bert Garnett, cornet. The band continued to play for several years after which they disbanded. Later, L. A. Brown organized a band. Among the players were the four Caskey brothers, Albert, Joe, Will and Glenn. The Caskey brothers formed a

Rock Island R. R. Engine.

Street in Billings - 1905.

quartet and were noted singers, touring several states with a chautauqua.

In May 1924, L. A. Brown organized the first school band here. He was band director in the school for a number of years. In 1936 and 1937 the school band was re-organized with Ashley Alexander as band instructor. This band consisted of about 35 pieces.

The city water works were completed and the water tower built in 1914. In the year 1915, oil was struck on the Hoover farm and midco field flourished for a time. The oil boom lasted several years, during which time the population of Billings was 1,200. In 1945 the population was about 700.

Electric power lines were put in from Enid in 1912, in the summer of 1926 natural gas was piped in. In the spring of 1926 the sewer system was put in. On March 31, 1926, Billings was isolated for nearly a week because of a heavy snowfall. Men were hired to shovel snow off the highways. On October 22, 1926 the Green Construction Company was awarded the contract to pave the highway from the Garfield county line to Perry via Billings. Billing's streets were also paved.

May 26, 1926, the railroad was completed from Billings to Ponca City and a celebration was held in Billings where the golden spike was driven. The railroad put on a motor car which carried passengers and mail for several years.

The Billings churches were organized early. Mrs. Zillah Holmes who came to Oklahoma with her husband, John L. Holmes at the opening of the Strip, helped to organize the First Christian Church here. Meetings were held first in the school house on the Noonan farm. Reverend Shives of Cherryvale, Kansas, held the first services of meetings under an arbor.

Reverend Tom Crumley was the first pastor of the Methodist Church here, Reverend J. A. Davis, the second and Reverend R. L. Grant the third. The Grants came here in 1902 and at that time there were two saloons in town. The Methodist parsonage was built for Reverend and Mrs. Grant, two rooms were moved over from White Rock and two more rooms built on. October 12, 1941, Reverend and Mrs. Grant closed a unique pastorate. Coming here as bride and groom they filled this, their first charge three years 1902-1905. Returning in 1937 they filled this, their last charge, four years ending where they began thirty nine years before. In Biblical symbolism the number seven signifies completeness. Reverend Grant completed his ministry with his seventh year at Billings. In his farewell service he sang with five members of the choir he had directed earlier: Mrs. Eva Lemmon, Misses Osce and Mabel Kettenring, Miss Oral Williams, and Mr. Leland Kettenring.

The South Methodist Church with Reverend Savage as minister, was located where the Catholic church now stands. There were so few members they sold the building to the Catholic Church people.

The Presbyterian Church was built in 1903. Prior to that the members, numbering about 60, held meetings at the Pete McKeown farm and at the John Young farm. The first minister of this church was Reverend Calvin Paden. This church was transferred to the Perry Presbyterian Church.

The Baptist Church was also organized before they had a building. Reverend W. L. Dunaway was the first pastor. The building was built in 1903.

Billings Catholic Church
By Dorothy Hines Mercing

Catholic Church services were first held in homes by missionary priests, who stayed over night in early-day pioneer's homes, after the opening of the Cherokee Strip before the town of Billings was established in 1899. One of the homes where Mass was held was the Mike Conway's home, south of Billings. As membership grew, services were held in the lodge located on the south side of Main Street which was built in 1900. The present church building was purchased on December 29, 1905, from the South Methodist Episcopal Church whose trustees were Alex McCluskey, O. W. Long and J. Savage. Another lot next to the church was purchased on November 21, 1906, from George Disney. Later a plot of ground was given by the Klufa family for the cemetery.

Some of the early families were the Mike Conway, William Menihan, Walter Walsh, Dan Hines, John Reilly, Dick Moore, Thomas Garrett, Dan Calnan, Dennis O'Donnell, Christopher Odenwald and Alois Partsch. In the next few years more Catholic families moved into the area. From 1950 until 1970 many families moved out of the area.

Remodeling was started in March 1967 and services were held in the American Legion Hall. Extensive remodeling produced a brand new look for the Sacred Heart Catholic Church. The building was completely done over on both exterior and interior. It bears little resemblance to the white clapboard building formerly used by the parishioners. Open house was held for

Catholic Church - the first building.

Catholic Church in Billings - 1986.

the public on May 21, 1967. Pastor was Rev. B. Havlik, Tonkawa.

May 30, 1967, a meeting was held to set up a perpetual care fund for the Catholic cemetery. Elected for Trustees were Frank Hickl, Jr., Ed Brinker and Robert Walsh with Dorothy Hines Mercing as secretary-treasurer.

In 1938, Dean Shaubroek, Enid, had as his assistant, Rev. Edward Voegele. Rev. Edward Voegele organized a young people's group who held meetings in the homes. In 1940, the house east of the parish was purchased and used for vacation religious classes, social meetings and Altar Society meetings. The Billings Catholic Church has not had a resident priest consider a mission. Priests have been assigned over the years coming from Enid, Ponca City, Marshall and Tonkawa.

Bell of Catholic Church.

Morrison

By Mildred Highfill

Morrison in Autry township was established as a community in the first days after the opening of the Cherokee Strip, although it was called Autry. A man by the name of Autry opened a general store and post office on the stage route from Perry to Pawnee. L. A. Fry in 1948, recalled that he ran the early day hack, as it was called, from April 1902 until December 1903, when he sold the stagecoach to Jim Wilbarger and Tom Kelly of Perry. Fry who was aided in his venture by his brother O. M. Fry and a brother-in-law, J. S. Akers began his run at Perry about 9 in the morning and would end at Pawnee six hours later. His route would take him through Sumner, Lela and Morrison. Another hack made the same trip in the opposite direction. The Star route stage carried passengers and mail. Charges without baggage was $1.50 but with a trunk the rate was $2.00. A driver made $175 a year carrying the mail but most of his salary came from express and passenger.

Fry said they rented barns for stations. John L. McGehee owned the station at Perry, Ralph Teel at Morrison and Les Davis the one at Pawnee. The hack was drawn by 14 range horses which had to be broken in. There were many disadvantages on the run, such as drunks, Osage cowboys, storms and floods. If a storm would come, it would take a full day to make the entire route. If people had mail boxes, the mail was put in them, but otherwise it was all taken to a station. The only bank located along the route was at Morrison, Fry recalled.

Tom Hull was another of the stage drivers. The town of Autry was located about where the present school is located. James H. Morrison bought out Autry's holdings and platted land for a town which became the town of Morrison, August of 1894.

When the railroad was built through Morrison in 1903, the town was moved south to the railroad tracks and the business houses were built of rock.

Rollo P. Arterburn, known officially as Shorty, was the owner of the first automobile in Morrison — the one-cylinder model that sounded like a Big Bertha when the engine would exhaust. He owned the car as early as 1909.

In 1912, Morrison had three medical doctors: Cavitt, Kelly and Stewart and a veterinarian G. S. Gray; three barbers; R. P. Arterburn, S. W. Wyatt, Oliver DeLaute; two blacksmiths: Archie Fawcett and Amos Nichols; three hardware stores: A. C. Watson, M. H. Whaley and A. C. Newell who was also an undertaker; three general stores, I. S. Boyer, Jim Simmons and Dawson Brothers; Cunningham and Lehew had a grocery store, Wilson Brothers, a meat market, D. O. Woodside, Produce; J. W. Prather Sr., ran a hotel and G. W. Griffith a restaurant, L. H. Kreigh a shoe shop, John Dubois, a pool hall; Guy Coffman, a drug store; John Robinson sold coal; Tom Hull had a Livery barn, Swearingen and Greenleaf a stock barn, Morrison had two banks: Morrison State Bank and Citizens Bank, two cotton gins and a coal loading station. There were Mason, Odd Fellow and Woodman organizations and a brass band conducted by N.

Third Street, Morrison, Oklahoma - 1913. The windmill in background was there until June, 1945.

Coyle Cotton Gin - Morrison about 1905.

S. Brookhart.

In 1912, F. G. Logan took over the Morrison Transcript. Several newspapers had been printed here: the Morrison Sun and the Morrison New Era the longest run. The job presses were run by foot pedals. The newspaper press was run by attaching a handle to the balance wheel. Several times the editor alone would run the newspaper press. He would feed in a paper, grab the handle on the wheel and turn out the paper and continue the procedure until the entire edition was run.

The first picture show in Morrison was in the summer of 1912. E. M. Reid obtained a moving picture machine and opened a show in a building known as the L.D.S. Hall which was later destroyed by fire. There was no electric light system at that time and a carbide light was used. An airdome west of the old theatre building was used in good weather during the summer.

A phonograph played fitting music to emphasize the pictures. The selection "Souvenir" was always held in readiness to be played when tragedy lurked or the villain was about to be hanged.

A short time later Mr. Reid purchased the store building that had been used by Gil Carter for a feed store and converted the building into a theater with a silver screen for moving pictures, also a stage for road shows. He then installed an electric lighting system. Newt Roads was chief engineer and whenever the belt on the dynamo slipped or the engine would miss a spark, Newt could be seen hitting around the corner on high to the engine room which was at the alley. Reid opened the New Electric Theatre on Saturday, October 11, 1913. He owned and conducted this theater for a number of years. A different time he leased the building and the name was changed. It was the Grand for awhile, then the Palace. Mr. Reid sold the building in 1932. Among those who ran the show for a time were John and Guy Folger, John McCurry and a man named Conner. There was a show, two sometimes three nights per week.

Before 1935, Morrison had several roller skating rinks at various times.

Morrison was the closest town to the Watchhorn gas producing field, one of the largest in the state. Morrison was filled with oil workers. Houses and rooms were in demand, business in all lines was good. Strange as it may seem the town of Morrison did not install gas despite the fact that the gas field was only nine miles from town and a pipe line passed almost through the town.

The accredited high school in Morrison was established in 1920. Allen Fitchett when elected to his first term as county superintendent, was the youngest man ever elected to that office in the state. He had attended Morrison schools.

Morrison Baptist Church
By Chester Speer

The Morrison Baptist Church was organized on February 18, 1899, with the following members: J. F. Colvin, Elizabeth Colvin, D. L. Dever, Carrie

Morrison school built in 1903 to replace the one-room school.

Dever, T. E. Donaldson, Mattie Donaldson, Amanda C. Edmonson, G. W. Griffeth, Mrs. G. W. Griffeth, Ida Lane, S. M. Lewis, Mary Lauderdale, J. F. Wilkerson, and Mrs. J. F. Wilkerson. Samuel Lane was received by relation in March of that year.

The following became members of the church in January 1901: Cleveland Hall, Ethel Hall, Gracie Dever, and Will Griffeth. Those joining the church in November 1901 were Grace Colvin, Lillie Colvin, Rosie Colvin, Florence Dever, W. B. Lane, Gracie Lauderdale, and Marcus Lauderdale. Ora Hall joined the church June 21, 1903.

T. E. Donaldson became the first pastor in March 1899. He was followed by J. W. Rankin in August 1900, S. R. Williams in October 1902, E. F. Curle in October 1904, J. E. Rector in October 1906, M. B. Hurt in October 1909, Brother Barrett on October 23, 1915, Brother Austin and Brother Bowels in 1916.

The first deacons were George Griffeth and D. L. Dever in March, 1899. J. F. Wilkerson was elected clerk in March 1899, followed by S. M. Lewis in December 1899, Carrie Dever in March 1900, and D. L. Dever in July 1901.

One of the staunch supporters of the church for many years was Pearl (Prather) Notley. She continued to teach a bible class there at times when the church was without a pastor. She acted as the church treasurer until her later years when her health failed. Pastor M. B. Hurt was the one who baptized Pearl and later performed her marriage ceremony.

On June 15, 1902, Brother _____ was found guilty of drunkenness and could not be brought to repentance. By a unanimous vote, the hand of church fellowship was withdrawn from him.

The Baptist Church had met in the Congregational Church Building until September 20, 1903, when the present church building was dedicated. The cost of the building was approximately $600.00. A mortgage on this building was paid off in 1915.

On October 17, 1903, the church voted to fight the establishment of a saloon in Morrison.

On April 18, 1908, the church voted to request Brother S. W. Wyatt to remove his business to some other place than the pool hall.

The church held a 75th Anniversary Celebration on February 16, 1974 at which time an historical marker was unveiled showing the names of the original members. This marker was hand painted by Louis Faw Faw, Jr. who was the song leader of the church at that time. Thomas Lazenby was the pastor.

The Morrison Baptist Church was featured in a film made by the Oklahoma Department of Transportation in about 1980. The film was entitled "Keep the Good Things" and was used to promote the construction of better roads in the State of Oklahoma. The film shows the church bell ringing and the congregation in worship service. It also shows the members leaving the church to attend a picnic at Lagunitas, which is the home of Chester and Evelyn Speer.

The National Park Service has listed the Morrison Baptist Church in the National Register of Historic Places as of September 28, 1984. The current pastor of the Morrison Baptist Church is Kelly Chronister.

Morrison United Methodist Church
By Alta Marie Frick

The Morrison United Methodist Church of today had as diverse and interesting history as most of the Noble County residents. In 1895, a group of residents met to organize a church. The community was small and several denominations were represented, but they did agree that they would build a church governed by the congregation. Therefore, they agreed to call it the Congregational Church.

On April 18, 1895, James H. Morrison and Rosella Morrison deeded Lots 13 and 14, Block 4 of the original town of Morrison to the Trustees of the Congregational Church. Services were held in a tent until the church was completed. Details of the first six years of existence are very sketchy and the name of ministers who served the church during that period seems lost forever, although it is known that the building served as both church and school, and that the first teacher (1895-96) was Mrs. Merian Hull, and the second (1896-97) was Miss Becky Harris, who later married Merill Abbott.

Morrison Methodist Church - 1950. This church burned in 1956.

The true history of the Methodist Church begins on April 5, 1901, when the Trustees of the First Congregational Church deeded to the Trustees of the Methodist Episcopal Church, South, Lots 13 and 14, Block 4, Original Town of Morrison. Those M. E. trustees were Dr. W. C. Whittenberg, John Thompson, David Crockett, and J. T. Perryman. Charter members of the church were Dr. and Mrs. W. C. Whittenberg, Mr. and Mrs. A. C. Newell, Mr. and Mrs. John Thompson, Mr. and Mrs. J. T. Perryman, Mr. and Mrs. David Crockett, Mr. and Mrs. Davis Sanders, Mr. and Mrs. J.D.E. Owen, and Dr. and Mrs. Cavitt.

On April 6, 1903, the Arkansas Valley Townsite Company deeded Lots 11 and 12, Block 4, to the Methodist Episcopal Church, South. Trustees at that time were John Thompson, David Sanders, R. E. Bagby, J. T. Perryman and I. Monhollon. There have been 57 pastors from H. J. Browen (1901) to the present pastor, Bob McCoy.

During the 1930s members dug a basement for class rooms and a kitchen. The walls were native stone. All materials and labor were donated by the members.

Also during the 1930s important events were taking place within the main body of the church. In 1939, three main branches of Methodism came together at the Methodist church thus healing the schism dating from 1844, the result of differing philosophies. Much later all branches joined

Morrison Baptist Church 1984. L to R: Louis Faw Faw, Jr., Chet Speer, Nolan Tanner, Tom Lazenby (Pastor).

together to become the United Methodist Church.

In 1942, the Church was remodeled and painted, a belfry was added, and floors and furniture were refinished. During WW II there were 35 names on the Honor Roll Service Flag.

In 1952, chimes were donated. But in 1956 all the donations and labor so lovingly donated were destroyed by lightening.

Smashed but not defeated, the Church voted to rebuild. The round of solicitations and donations began again. The parsonage was used for Sunday School and church services while the new church was built. Like the mythical Phoenix a new and more beautiful church rose from its ashes. On April 15, 1958 (Easter Sunday) first services were held in the new church but it wasn't until April 15, 1964 that all debts were paid and the church was officially dedicated.

Morrison Methodist Church built in 1957.

Marland
By Mildred Highfill

Marland was formerly the town of Bliss. The name was changed in 1922 for oilman E. W. Marland of Ponca City. He was later governor of Oklahoma.

Bliss was in the center of the Ponca Indian reservation. Because the land in this section of Noble County was owned by the Indians who were not allowed to sell their land unless permission was granted by the United States government it was not possible to develope a town along the railroad of any size. The 101 Ranch had bought some land that was offered for sale. This land had been allotted to minor children and the land was sold so the money could be used for their benefit.

The Miller Brothers, Joe, George and Zack, developed Bliss to accommodate their ranching operations in this area. On the opening day of Bliss the public bought over 800 lots in the original townsite. It was east of town where the famous "wild west" show was held in 1907. Before this the eastern visitors were taken to the little settlement in the middle of the Indian reservation, with the Indians making an appearance for the benefit of "big city" bigwigs, so they could see a part of the Old West. The railroad built a spur into the town as it was a mile from the town to the railroad to accommodate the 1000 visitors to this special event.

When land became available near the railroad, Bliss was moved to a more convenient location. Lots again were sold and land was set aside for churches and a school. The 101 Ranch developed the stockyards and grain elevator. A telephone exchange, general store and a special warehouse for their seed corn.

The Carson Hotel was located also in Bliss, W. Clark sold hardware, implements and buggies. H. L. Derry had a general store, L. Stockdale ran a livery, feed and sale barn which also houses a camp house, Hess Brothers too had a livery, feed and sale barn. There was also a lumber yard. The land along Arkansas also raised fruit and farm products which were shipped from Bliss.

The newspaper "The Bliss Banner" in June, 1909, boasted that an everyday occurence in Bliss were 19 double team wagons and 5 buggies hitched up in one block on Main Street.

Marland
United Methodist-Christian Church
By Nell Lewis

The Marland Methodist Church had its humble beginnings in the town of Bliss which was located about one mile southeast of the now town of Marland. Since the church and town are so interwoven, it will be necessary to write of the town in order to understand the movement and changes in the church.

Mrs. Mollie A. Miller of the famed 101 Ranch donated the NE ¼ section 24, Township 24 North, Range 1 East of the Indian Meridian on March 31, 1906, for the location and formation of the town of Bliss. The town was laid out with 49 blocks and all the streets were named. A small school was built and one of the first teachers was Miss Lettie Taylor, who later married Edgar Cruts. She and her family, the Charles E. Taylors, with a few other families started a non-denominational religious organization in March, 1907, which later became the Methodist Episcopal Church.

The first meeting place was in the school building, but this wasn't satisfactory, so the Masons let them use their place which was the second floor of a building on Main Street. The first floor housed the Rynearson Drug Store. Later, the Methodist Conference sponsored and helped this organization to become the Methodist Church. Seminary students from Winfield, Kansas, or Guthrie, Oklahoma, would board the train to Bliss to give morning and evening sermons. As there were several passenger trains each day, they had no difficulty getting back and forth.

On November 17, 1910, Mrs. Mollie Miller donated lots 8 and 9 in block 22 in Bliss to the Methodist Episcopal Church for the purpose of locating a church building. Then on April 26, 1911, she donated two more lots, 13 and 14 in Block 34 for a parsonage. Soon a church and a small parsonage were built on these lots, and now the church had a real home.

The Santa Fe Depot was located about one mile from Bliss and as passengers embarked, they had to hire a hack or walk one mile to Bliss. Drummers or salesmen, as well as other passengers, didn't particularly care for that walk. Eight cowboys in their silk

Marland in 1920s.

shirts, boots, and spurs, and ten gallon hats would meet the passenger trains to advertise the 101 Ranch.

As the depot seemed to be the nucleus, the Founding Fathers decided the town should be moved closer to it. So on March 15, 1917, Zack Miller, son of Mrs. Mollie Miller, gave land near the depot so the town could be moved. Naturally, the town was now called New Bliss. The job of moving the buildings began and the Rynearson Drug store was moved to Main Street and the Methodists again held their meetings in the Masonic Lodge upstairs.

A school was soon built on the site of the present school building. In a few years, the Buffalo School located three miles west decided to annex, so their building was moved in behind the other one. Soon after, the Methodists began to hold their services in the building from the Buffalo School District.

On November 22, 1919, Zack Miller deeded to the Methodist Episcopal Church Lots 10, 11, 12, in Block 12 of New Bliss for a church location. He also deeded Lots 1, 2, and 3 in Block 18 for a parsonage.

With the help of the 101 Ranch to the north, the Three Sands Oil boom to the west, and the Santa Fe on the east, New Bliss became a thriving bustling town with its hotels, cafes, bank, and varied businesses. The Founding Fathers came up with another bright idea, so on April 3, 1922, papers were filed to incorporate the town and change its name to Marland. The Fathers were hoping E. W. Marland of Ponca City, oilman and later Governor of Oklahoma, would in some way assist his namesake.

The people of Marland decided they needed a new brick school building since the high school classes were added. The new building was completed in 1924, and consisted of two floors with the elementary classes on the first floor and high school on the second floor. It also had a combination gym and auditorium.

The school did not need their old buildings, so the Methodist bought one half of the main building and moved it to Lots 10, 11 and 12 in Block 12 which became their church building until 1965. A house was moved in on their other lots which became their parsonage. For a second time they had a real home of their own.

The 101 Ranch became bankrupt in the Thirties and the Three Sands oil field played out, so without their support, the town of Marland also began its decline. Of course, this created small memberships and financial difficulties in the churches. In August, 1965, the Methodist Church and the Disciples of Christ Church, after several meetings and discussions formed the Marland United Methodist Christian Church which was the first in Oklahoma. The student ministers come from Phillips University and are usually Methodist or Christian. The congregation decided to use the better building which was the Christian Church. The Methodists didn't want to see their church building vacant and deteriorating, so it was sold to Mr. John McAlister for a small sum and he agreed to tear it down and clean the lots. The parsonage was sold to the school in 1969, and that money was used to help carpet the sanctuary of their new church. On August 25, 1985, the Marland United Methodist-Christian Church celebrated its 20th Anniversary with joy and thanksgiving for the successful combination.

Sumner

By Mildred Highfill

Sumner was originally a mile and a half south from where the school house is now located. The first post office was in the store of Alexander Youree. Mr. Youree let a family camp on his land for awhile. When they did not move on, he ordered them to leave. The man told Mr. Youree that he should leave because they needed the land more than he did. When he disagreed they shot him. His body was taken to Perry in a spring wagon but no charges were pressed against the people who shot him. Mr. Youree's heirs got the land so the people had to move on anyway.

J. E. Dawson and Edith ran the post office for many years. Neva Rupp was the last person to serve as postmaster and was there when it closed in July, 1957.

When the railway was built in 1903, the town was moved to the present site. A townsite promoter, Wolf, platted the town and called it Robertal but the citizens did not like this name and petitioned for the name Sumner.

At one time Sumner had two blacksmiths, one thirteen-room hotel, one stockyard, two lumber yards, two banks, two grocery stores, two churches — Christian and Baptist — one cotton gin, two grain elevators, one feed lot, one garage, a post office and a school.

The school at Sumner was the first consolidated school in Noble County and one of the first in the state. The Tilman school, Nielson school (Rosenwald) district #36, and the Poole school district #43 were consolidated.

There was a great need for a high school at Sumner in the early 1900s. High school students at that time had to go to Morrison or Perry. Some rode the train to Perry at the start of the week, staying there for school during the week and coming home on week-ends.

The new building was supposed to be finished in the fall of 1920 but it wasn't. The first half of that year, school was held in the Christian Church and in a store building in Sumner. When the students and teachers finally moved in, they had new Aladdin lamps and wood or coal stoves for heating. They took their lunches, usually in a syrup bucket. Water was carried from a well down in the northeast corner of the school yard. There were two brand-new four-holed outhouses that were cold as the North Pole in the winter and hot as the equator in the summer. Much later furnaces were installed in the north end of the basement.

Before the gym was built, a cistern was here. Water was collected from the roof with a system of gutters. The water went through a filter made of sand, charcoal, and lime. Water was hauled at the beginning of the term to fill up the cistern so they would have water to start out with, water was carried from the cistern to a 30 gallon water container in the school building.

Children were transported to school in "school trucks." They were Ford Speedwagons. They were long trucks with a top and wire screen for windows. During bad weather, canvass shades on the outside were lowered.

The gym for the Sumner school was built by the W.P.A. in 1938. It was lighted by the new rural electric system that had just been put through. Sumner school was filled to capacity many times in the early days. Then, like so many small towns, Sumner's population started declining. The high school finally had to close its doors in 1964, where there were not enough students to attend. But the grade school lasts and is even increasing in students. Sumner grades range from kindergarten to eighth. There were 58 students in 1982. It is the only dependent school left in Noble County.

Lucien
By Mildred Highfill

At the opening of the Strip, John K. Mateer put in a little store and applied for a post office on his farm in Warren Valley, just east of the O.G. & E. station east of Lucien and another post office was located east of this station on the north side of the road near the creek. The mail was delivered to this post office by star route and the carrier was Cal Hamblin. The Rock Spring school was located on the corner northeast of the O.G. & E. station and it was thought the town would be located here. A family by the name of Emmerson built a store here and their son was the first doctor. The Arkansas Valley and Western railroad (later Frisco) was being built about now but they decided to build their depot where the town of Lucien is now.

The steel was laid on the railroad through Lucien in the fall of 1903 and the town was called Woolsey. The first bank in Lucien was called the Bank of Woolsey. When the post office department put in a post office they found there as another Woolsey in Oklahoma so the name was changed to Lucien. The name came from Lucien Emmerson, mother of Dr. Emmerson.

Louis E. Plumer lived on a farm near Lucien and attended Rock Spring school. In 1975 he recalled "When the railroad was being built my father and I worked for a contractor building a fill on our farm. We each had a team hitched to a slip. There was a man to fill the slip but I had to dump it." Jim Dennis owned the hardware store and a real estate office. The building later was converted to a hospital operated by Doctor Gaines. There was also a school, a telephone office and a shoe repair shop. Shell Petroleum company had a gasoline plant in Lucien in 1934.

Ford
By Helen Ratliff

Ford, Oklahoma, was located eight miles east, one mile south of Bliss, now Marland, Oklahoma. According to George Shirk's book, *Oklahoma Towns*, Ford, Oklahoma got its name from nearby fords across the Arkansas River. Both the east and south fords were just a mile and a half away.

But native Bressians claim the town was named for a man, Ford Marks, who established the first mercantile business around the time the postoffice was officially instituted on July 6, 1905.

Lucius Moore, a brother-in-law of Rod Marks, was the first postmaster. One building housed the post office, general store and living quarters in the back. Groceries, hardware, shoes, dry goods and even jewelry supplied the needs of all of what today is called the Bressie community as well as the Big Bend country of Osage County.

Big Bend community members whose mailing address was also Ford, Oklahoma built a ferry so they could cross the Arkansas River from the east to get their mail and supplies when the river was to high to ford.

The building to the north of the general store was the blacksmith shop, operated by the Watrous brothers. Across the road the large meeting hall, built by the Modern Woodmen, was never used by the lodge, because they learned that lodge meetings could only be held in an upstairs hall that provided privacy. But others, not under such compulsions, attended Saturday night dances, church on Sunday and even community sponsored lyceum shows that made their way to the Ford hall.

Ford, a lively center, was different from many old towns of the west, because it did not have a hotel or a saloon, even before Oklahoma became a dry state in 1907.

Corn was hauled by team and wagon to Ford where it was dumped in huge piles to be run through two corn shellers, one operated by Ora Beck and the other by Luther Crabtree. The shelled corn was hauled to Bliss, now Marland, for shipment on the railroad.

During those early years, Ford was a tent city. Many of the families moved in to shuck corn and stayed until it was shelled and marketed. The children overflowed the Bressie school, so had to be held at Ford Hall. When the Watrous family moved to the growing city of Bliss, the blacksmith shop was operated by Housh who had several sons to assist him.

After Ford Marks moved to Red Rock, the store was operated by Mr. and Mrs. Claude Gotchel and later by Mr. and Mrs. Elmer Domeny. After Elmer's untimely death of diabetes, Mary his widow was assisted by her brother and his wife, Mr. and Mrs. Lester Hess. Mr. and Mrs. Dewey Tidwell were the next proprietors and the last proprietors were Mr. and Mrs. Lloyd Dunn.

Cars came to the community in 1914. The Ford post office was closed when the rural route from Bliss was started

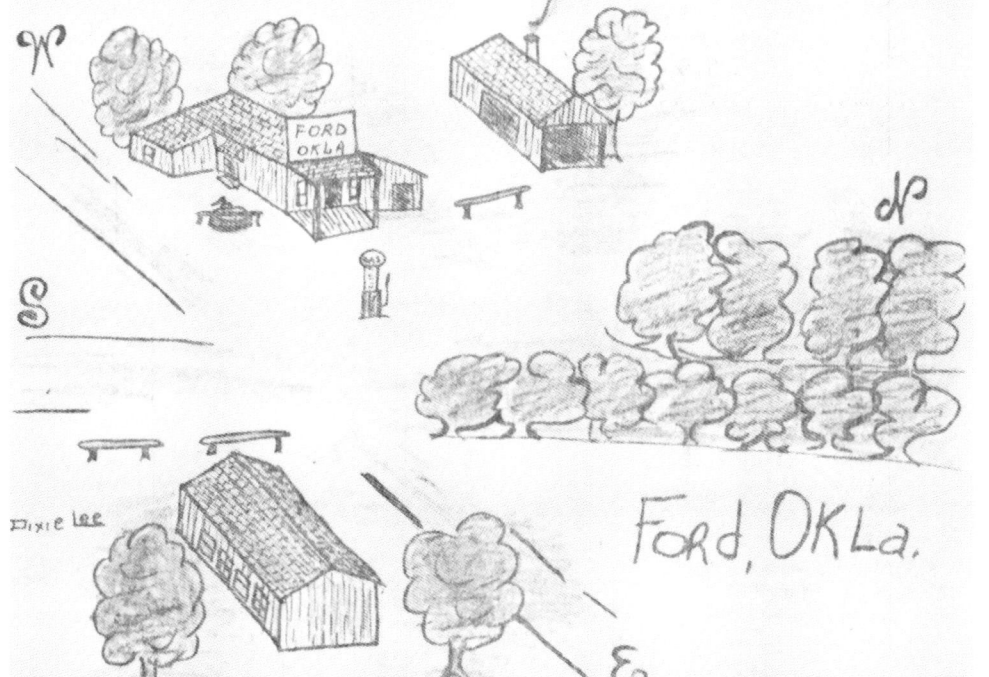

Ford, Oklahoma as visualized by Mrs. Charles (Dixie) Lee.

in 1916. With the addition of a filling station and garage, Ford still did business as usual. But when the highway, now 177, was opened and a bridge built across the Salt Fork River in 1921, business started to fall off and the store was closed in 1926.

Few people in Bressie today can even visualize the activity and bustle of Ford, where neighbors met and swapped stories. When business slowed for the night there was usually a card game going, poker or pitch, if anyone wanted to join in, they had a supper of cheese and crackers with Bevo, prohibition beer, and stayed sometimes until the wee hours in the morning.

Lela

By Pauline Nichols

Lela was first located a mile west and a half mile south of the present site. When the railroad was put through the location was changed to be closer to the railway. Stock-pens and loading chutes were built here so cattle could be shipped out. Little is known about Old Lela except for the school house and the cemetery. After the school house was no longer used for school, Clark Fields used it to store hay.

The old historical swinging bridge was located on the Black Bear Creek just south of the school house. It was destroyed by a wheat truck in 1986. The bridge was fun for young people to swing on when they had weiner roasts and outings in the big pecan grove nearby.

After Lela was moved it was located on the junction of Highway 108 to Glencoe and State Highway 64. A small community grew up around the post office and grocery store.

On January 1, 1905, the name of the post office was changed to Valerie but on March 31 of the same year the patrons petitioned to Washington and the post office department changed the name back to Lela. Lela was named for Lela McClellan, daughter of Charles McClellan, early-day rancher.

The grocery store in the photograph on the far right also housed the post office run by Mr. Fugerson. The road by this building runs north and south and is the road to Glencoe. The Fugersons lived back of this store with an artiesian well nearby. The little white building in the background was the first filling station. Mr. Fugerson built another north of this store which burned a short time later.

David Beard built a rock building for a feed store. After it was no longer used as a feed store the building was used for "Play parties" by the young people. These were similar to square dances except the players sang the instructions for the dance. Couples held hands and skipped around in a circle side by side. Lyrics for one of these "games" was Miller Boy: "Happy is the miller boy who lives by the mill. The mill turns around with a free good will. Hand on the hopper and the other on the sack. Ladies step forward and the gents fall back." Young people, whose parents objected to dances, were allowed to go to "play parties." Barn dances were held across the road on the Charles Akers place.

The rock building and the big round elevator are still standing. The old post office and grocery store building was used by Ray Nichols in 1963 as a home and as a produce market.

The last store building in Lela was built in later years across the road from this filling station by Art Mullenex. As the community built up on the opposite side of the highway, it put part of Lela in Pawnee County and part in Noble County.

The filling station in the photograph had "Delco" lights. Electricity was stored in large glass batteries. It was produced by a generator powered by a small engine which made a pop-pop noise as it built up the pressure much to the amusement of the children.

Not much is left now except two small houses and the Arhberg elevator to mark the spot where Lela once stood. Lela shares the fate of several "ghost towns" in Noble County.

Filling Station at Lela 1925. (L to R): Oakley Porter, Mr. Haley, Mr. Bishop, Bob Johnson, Martin Collins, unknown.

Chapter 6
BUSINESSES

Top: H. G. (Dock) Donley in his pressing shop, north side of the square - Perry about 1912. Middle: Coyle Cotton gin, "C" Street and 5th - August 8, 1903. Bottom: Interior of the Famous store - women's side.

The Charles Machine Works, Inc.

Perry is the headquarters for The Charles Machine Works, Inc., manufacturers of Ditch Witch underground construction equipment. Ditch Witch equipment is used around the world to install telephone lines, cable TV, and electrical lines, as well as other types of underground systems. The machines to do these jobs are invented, tested, refined, built, and shipped from the Perry factory.

Carl Malzahn began the basis for the business in a Perry blacksmith shop in 1902. His son, Charlie, carried on the family business during the 1930s and 1940s by repairing farm machinery and oil field drilling equipment. The name of the company changed from The Malzahn Brothers Blacksmith Shop to Charlie's Machine Shop and began manufacturing portable drilling rigs in 1940.

Ed Malzahn, president of The Charles Machine Works, Inc., began working for his father, Charlie, after graduating from Oklahoma State University with an engineering degree. His first job was repairing oil field equipment. But he pursued engineering projects at night on the kitchen table and invented an oil rig safety escape device now called "Geronimo." One day in the late 1940s he watched a large trencher used for digging water mains set idle while a crew used picks and shovels to dig service lines to houses. He conceived the idea for a small trencher to do this hand labor. His invention was refined several times before becoming the first Ditch Witch trencher. Soon, trenchers became the primary business of The Charles Machine Works, Inc.

The name Ditch Witch was chosen because it described the equipment that trenched "somewhat magically." But the invention almost became known as "Ed's Ditcher." Through the process of elimination, "Ditch Witch" evolved, along with the company logo of a witch riding a shovel across an orange crescent moon. Now the Ditch Witch logo is recognized around the world as the symbol of the best in underground construction machinery.

The company is the third largest employer in north-central Oklahoma, with about 750 employees. The physical plant and offices have grown considerably since moving to its present location west of Perry in 1959. Twenty acres are under roof and used for manufacturing. In addition to the plant and offices, there is a separate engineering facility where design teams invent and build new machines while striving to improve the current product line.

Although a large, innovative corporation today, the pioneering spirit that began in a small blacksmith shop nearly ninety years ago keeps on working,

The seven-horse power Ditch Witch pedestrian trencher.

designing and building practical machines to make work easier and more rewarding. The current product line ranges from a seven-horsepower pedestrian trencher (about the size of a roto-tiller) to a large, 100-horsepower production trencher (the size of a large farm tractor). But trenchers are not the only machines built by The Charles Machine Works, Inc. Ditch Witch pioneered the use of vibratory plows, machines that put lines underground without digging a trench, and earth saws for trenching through asphalt, concrete, and solid rock. Ditch Witch also manufactures an innovative backhoe/loader.

Perry and The Charles Machine Works, Inc., enjoy a warm relationship. All employees are encouraged to do civic work, and the company contributes generously to projects for the enjoyment of the Perry community. But the approach is low-key, reflecting Ed Malzahn's philosophy that what is good for Perry is ultimately good for the company. With that philosophy and quality workers who embody the pioneering spirit of the settlers of the Cherokee Outlet, Ditch Witch products should continue to lead the industry for years to come.

The 100 horse-power Ditch Witch production trencher.

Citizen State Bank - Morrison

In 1902 there were three banks in Morrison, Oklahoma. They were the Bank of Morrison, Morrison State Bank and The Citizens Bank.

The Morrison State Bank

The original Directors meeting of The Morrison State Bank was held in August 1902 and on August 29, 1902, Paul F. Cooper, Territory of Oklahoma Bank Commissioner issued a certificate of authority for the bank to open.

The original stockholders were J. F. Heathrington, F. D. Hall, M. L. Lauderdale, Morrison; J. E. Sater, M. L. Walker, Stillwater; J. D. E. Owen, Sumner; and J. Walter Dunn, Knox, Indiana. The First President of the Morrison State Bank was J. E. Heathrington, Vice-President was J. E. Sater, and the Cashier was F. D. Hall.

Bank of Morrison

In August 1902 the Bank of Morrison was formed. The directors were J. P. Woolsey, W. L. James, R. E. Bagby, Allen Daniels, W. B. Webb, F. S. Gum, and J. T. Perryman. J. P. Woolsey was named President, W. L. James, Vice-President and R. E. Bagby, Cashier.

The Citizens Bank

Little is known about the Citizens Bank due to a lack of records.

There were many changes in Directors during the next five to seven years. It is believed that in 1905 (exact date unavailable) the Bank of Morrison and the Morrison State Bank became one Bank. At this time Directors were J. P. Woolsey, W. L. James, Fred Schroeder, W. W. Woolsey, S. F. Swineford, M. L. Walker, S. D. Woolsey and Frank James. The name remained Morrison State Bank.

On February 18, 1920 a reorganization meeting was held and the assets of the Citizens Bank was transferred to the Citizens State Bank. The stockholders were as follows: A. Cunningham, John A. Hansen, J. L. Liggett, Russell I. Testerman, S. A. Testerman, Fred Schroeder and John Frank. A. Cunningham became President at the bank. Fred Schroeder and John Frank were elected as Vice-President's and J. L. Liggett became Cashier. Russell J. Testerman was elected secretary to the Board.

In 1928 A. Cunningham died and the vacancy of President was not filled until September 7, 1928 when E. F. Blake, Frank Blake and S. G. Blake purchased controlling interest in the bank. E. F. Blake was named President. The Blake's maintained ownership from May 1928 to March 1946.

In March 1946 the Blake's sold their interest to Wylie B. Reed, Ettamae B. Reed and Clarence McGinty. The Directors were Fred Schroeder, W. B. Frank, Wylie B. Reed, Ettamae B. Reed, and Clarence McGinty.

In 1961 Dwight G. Rymer and Mary J. Rymer purchased controlling interest of the Citizens State Bank of Morrison. In 1967 a new Bank Building, Citizens Room and Post Office were built and now house the Citizens State Bank. The bank has grown many times over and at present maintains over 29 million dollars in assets. The present officers are Dwight G. Rymer, President and Chairman, Rick McSwain, Executive Vice-President, Dan Barrick, Vice-President, Ruby Veit, Cashier, Peggy Wreyford, Ass't Cashier. The Directors are Dwight G. Rymer, Mary J. Rymer, Peggy Wreyford, Lenel Keefer, Donald Rymer, Kevin Rymer, Martin R. Diehm, James Wasson, F. G. Armstrong and Rick McSwain.

State Bank Morrison - This building was used after the banks merged to become Citizen State Bank.

Citizens Bank - Morrison. This bank no longer stands - Fred G. Logan published his newspaper here later.

Exchange Bank

By George Hall

The founders of the Exchange Bank of Perry, Oklahoma were Fred G. Moore, President and Harry A. McCandless, Secretary; the bank began with capital of $5,000.00 and the first day of operation ended February 20, 1896 with total deposits of $1,008.79. Mr. Moore's previous education was through the Naval Academy at Annapolis, Maryland and at Princeton College. Mr. McCandless was a very distinguished person.

Moore and McCandless were brother-in-laws as Mrs. Moore was Mr. McCandless's sister; her name was Anna. She was born February 29, 1867 and died January 4, 1937. Mr. Moore was born October 25, 1866 and died June 8, 1936. Harry A. McCandless was born December 8, 1860 and died July 28, 1923, his wife's name was Florence D. McCandless, she was born September 7, 1875 and died March 1, 1967. All are buried at Grace Hill Cemetery in Perry, Oklahoma.

The bank's first location was at the southwest corner of 7th and Delaware streets in a wooden building. Before the bank was established the building had been occupied by "Jake Leon's Kentucky Liquor House". One of the bank's first customers was a saintly woman who came to the bank door and with lowered head asked for fifteen cents worth of whiskey.

When she looked up and saw the cashier of the bank, Harry McCandless, whom she knew, she explained, "my goodness, what are you doing here? I was getting this for a sick friend."

As the community grew and business increased the small working force at the bank was kept busy. All monetary transactions through the bank were kept in longhand in what was called a Boston Ledger. For each customer, there was a column for the old balance, a space for deposits, a column for checks, and another for the new balance. Loans were made on real estate, and personal property, mostly consisting of livestock. Sometimes a second mortgage would be taken on real estate if personal property was not enough to cover the loan. Nearly all farms in the area were covered by first mortgage loans.

In 1900 the bank's location was moved to the north side of the downtown square. Also, this was the year oil was discovered in Noble county which helped deposits grow to $150,000.00 in 1912. This was followed by less than average rainfall for two years, a slower economy and slightly lower deposits when war was declared in Europe in August, 1914.

At this time the price of wheat was .88 cents per bushel, but because of the wheat shortage in Europe, the price soared to $2.26 per bushel by the end of the year. Despite another drought in 1916-1917 the community prospered because high prices received for farm prices offset the shortage.

The '20s marked a period of prosperity for Perry. The business district was enlarged and many new homes were erected. In the fall of 1925, the Exchange Bank began remodeling. These operations were so extensive that it practically amounted to the erection of a new building.

By January, 1929 Fred Moore retired and Joe McClellan, who had lived in Perry for years and was active in oil development became President and O. R. Hall continued as Cashier. Hall had first joined the organization in 1909; he was a native of Noble County, having been born inside Cherokee Strip Territory before the run. In October, 1917 Hall resigned from the Exchange Bank to work for The Producers State Bank in Tulsa; here he remained except for service in the army during World War I.

In December, 1921 he left The Producers State Bank to accept employment with The First National Bank in Bristow, Oklahoma where he remained until December, 1924 when he resigned to become Cashier of the Exchange Bank.

The '30s ushered in a period of economic depression in our community, as well as in the nation. In 1933 the price of oil reached a low of .40 cents per barrel at which time Governor Bill Murray, by executive order, declared that oil could not be purchased for less than $1.00 per barrel. Cattle prices became so low that on occasions would not bring enough to cover the cost of taking them to market.

Wheat prices dropped to a low of .25 cents per bushel during these trying times. The problem in this area was intensified, however, because throughout the decade there was another drought. The dry conditions affected not only the crops, but the roads as well. Thick dust accumulated on the heavily traveled dirt roads; however, little could be done in maintaining them satisfactorily as long as the dry weather continued.

Although there was a depression throughout the beginning of the '30s, its depths were reached in 1931 when deposits at the Exchange Bank were at a low of $323,000 as compared with $428,000 just two years before. As a result of the failure of a large number of banks in 1932-33, all banks in the U.S. were temporarily closed by a

Original location of the Exchange Bank in 1896.

Exchange Bank's location from 1900 to 1963.

Presidential Proclamation on March 4, 1933.

Prior to 1935 there were fifteen banks in Noble County of which four were banks in Perry that failed. From 1893 through 1935 the Exchange Bank was the only bank in the county that did not fail or that was not required to re-organize under a new bank charter. The Exchange Bank was among the sound banks and was allowed to reopen in two weeks.

In the early days the people used banks for convenience and not especially to safeguard their money. This lack of confidence was due to inadequate federal backing. The Federal Deposit Insurance Corporation, organized under the Banking Act of 1933, eliminated the fear of bank failures by insuring the deposits. Also, President Roosevelt upon his inauguration immediately enacted the New Deal directed toward the relief of the destitute, economic recovery, and permanent social reform. The community benefited as money from the New Deal poured into the economy.

In December of 1933 Joseph McClellan retired and Y. V. Willett, a native of Perry who had been directing a bank at Goltry, Oklahoma bought stock in the Exchange Bank and was elected President and Hall was an equal owner and Cashier. At this time the deposits were $340,000. Deposits continued to increase until Willett's death in 1941, at which time deposits totaled $667,000.

Upon Willett's death, O. R. Hall became Chairman of the Board and President. During Hall's administration the bank expanded its facilities in 1950 to a major remodeling and expansion to a partial second floor. Then again in 1963 the bank vacated the old bank building to a new building and a different location on the northeast corner of the square, where it now stands.

Even though Hall had given up the Presidency to Kenneth K. Coldiron on January 14, 1964, Hall continued to be quite active in the bank to his death, March 3, 1970. He had spent a total of 61 years in banking.

On August 11, 1970 Kenneth K. Coldiron, who had been an officer since employed by the bank in 1947 and President since 1964, became Chairman of the Board. He had retired as a full-time employee April 7, 1980 but continued on as Chairman of the Board until February 9, 1982. He continues now to serve as a valuable member of the Board of Directors.

George W. Hall, son of O. R. Hall, joined the bank in 1950. He became Chief Executive Officer January 9, 1968 and continues to serve in that office to the present. He succeeded Coldiron in 1970 as President. On February 9, 1982 Hall accepted the position as Chairman of the Board and Robert F. McDaniel, a native who had been with the bank 28 years became President, which offices they now hold.

In December, 1980, the bank completed another major expansion which allows additional expansions to the basement, as well as a partial second floor. Keeping up with banking, an automatic teller machine was installed in 1984 at Perry Plaza, which provides for a branch location when needed.

As of March 31, 1985 the Exchange Bank had total assets of $60,642,298.81 with capital and undivided profits of $6,481,413.76 making a strong capital ratio of 10.69%. Today the Exchange Bank is one of only 30 banks in the state of Oklahoma that has been in existence for 89 years or longer.

Left is Fred G. Moore, President and right is O. R. Hall, Sr., Cashier. This picture was taken around 1924-1925.

Sooner Power Plant

By Dave Raybern

Oklahoma Gas and Electric Company, an investor-owned electric utility, decided in the early 1970s that Noble County would be an ideal location for a new power plant.

In 1975, property negotiations were completed and construction began the following year on Sooner Power Plant.

The construction included a large reservoir to provide cooling water for the plant. From the start, OG&E planned to make the facility available for recreation and as a haven for wildlife.

A 5,800-foot earthen dam was built, requiring 2,400,000 cubic yards of earth fill. Some of the water for the reservoir comes from natural runoff and some is pumped from the Arkansas River.

As the reservoir now stands, the water at the dam is 90 feet deep, and average depth is 28 feet. The reservoir covers approximately 5,400 acres and contains 149,000 acre feet of water when full.

Prime contractor for the construction of the plant was Brown and Root Construction Company. At the peak of the construction work, 1,200 workers were involved.

In keeping with OG&E's plan to diversify the fuel mix, Sooner was planned as a coal-fired generating station. The coal, contracted for the life of the plant, comes from Black Thunder near Gillette, Wyoming. The Wyoming coal was chosen because of its low-sulphur content, which allowed OG&E to build the plant without expensive scrubbers and still comply with all environmental protection regulations.

The first unit, Sooner One, was completed in 1979. Coal for the unit began arriving in March of that year to provide a stockpile of fuel.

About the time the first unit came on line, construction was completed on the two public recreation facilities, located on the south shore of the reservoir. Swimming, boating, fishing and picnic facilities are available for the public.

In 1980, Sooner Two was completed. Both the generating units have a 515,000 kilowatt capacity. There is room for additional units at Sooner.

Wildlife has played an important part of OG&E's development of Sooner Power Plant. During construction of the reservoir, worn-out heavy equipment tires and cable-anchored brush piles were strategically placed to provide habitats for fish. Once the reservoir filled, the state wildlife department stocked it with several species of game fish, including black, Florida and hybrid bass and catfish.

In 1982, there were 246 giant Canada geese released on plant property to develop a nesting colony. Both migratory and resident wildlife abound at Sooner.

In addition to 28 varieties of fish found in the reservoir, no less than 30 species of mammals, over 70 types of birds, 20 varieties of reptiles and 10 species of amphibians have been observed.

A sailboat cruises past Sooner Power Plant. Since the reservoir was completed and opened to the public, it has been increasingly popular for boating, fishing, swimming and picnicking

Chapter 7
FAMILIES

Allen I. Acers
By Helen L. Morrison

Allen Irving Acers, was the son of Annie Austin Acers. She was born in 1835, and died June 2, 1912, at the home of her son, northwest of Perry and was buried in Grace Hill Cemetery, the service being held at the Baptist Church. She died from general breaking of health incident to old age. A.I. Acer's father was William Acers born 1820, and died in 1904 and was buried at Grace Hill Cemetery.

Allen Irving Acers was born November 10, 1859, at Manchester, Iowa, and married Sudy Nix, July 1, 1888, in Mt. Vernon, Texas. A.I. Acers was one of the persons racing north of Orlando at high noon, Saturday, September 16, 1893, into Noble County for a choice section of land in the Cherokee Strip Territory for the purpose of raising grain and cattle. Records on file at Noble County Court House for Homestead Application shows final receipt received from A.I. Acers the sum of four dollars being in full, for balance of payment required by law for the entry of the southwest ½ section 34 township 22 north range 1 west Indian Meridian containing 160 acres.

A.I. Acers brought along to Perry, his wife, daughter, Addie Alta, born April 26, 1887, and Allen Acers born October 26, 1890. The family arrived here the 16th from Oklahoma City, with friends Mr. J.H. Scott and wife Catherine and their two children. Acers was a cowboy and butcher by trade. Acers opened the Big Horn Meat Market located at 6th and Cedar on the east side of the square in Perry. He moved into the Jack Kabrick Building located at the corner lot, now the Corner Drug Store of Ralph Foster a present two story concrete building. Acers previously had run a foot race winning a pair of mounted long horns, so came about the name of Acers Meat Market. The horns are now owned by his great-grandson, Michael D. Keyser of Dallas, Texas.

A daughter, Lottie Ardella, was born October 10, 1894, in Noble County, Perry, Oklahoma. Another son, McKinley, born March 4, 1897, died of pneumonia December 5, 1901 and was buried at Grace Hill in the Acers lot.

The Acers family chose a location on the homestead to build a small, wood frame, two-story house with an open bucket well in front of the house. A cellar was located by the east side of the house, and a cattle and hay barn was built with a basement in the side of the hill. A piece of land south of the house was always called the orchard piece where fruit trees were plentiful, grape vines grew up and down the creek and lots of wild plums and wild flowers grew in the pasture. A fire destroyed all building about the year 1932.

A.I. Acers and family moved to Don Luis, Arizona in the year of 1905, where he engaged in the wholesale butcher trade. They went there for the health and treatment of son Allen but he died at the home of the family on January 21, 1908. Acers disposed of his property to return to Oklahoma. Allen Acers was buried in Acers lot at Grace Hill Cemetery.

A.I. Acers and Sudy moved to Muskogee where they owned property which consisted of five houses and a grocery store located on North Fifth Street. December 5, 1919, Acers was shot down in his store by a bandit with a 38 Revolver who attempted to rob him. Mrs. Addie Bruce, the grocer's daughter and eye witness of the killing was at no time in danger of being charged with the murder. Words of the bandit prior to the shooting said "Put up your hands." also: "You do not know me; I am a stranger in town." In making his escape from the store after the shooting, the "Highwayman" was able to retreat with out making an imprint either of hand or foot, without having a sample of his clothing, without dropping any article that would tend to identify or lead to his indentification. Chief McAfee of Muskogee received a note which purported to come from the slayer. The letter read: "Chief McAfee: 'Why don't you came and get me? I'm in Muskogee and I'm not going to leave. Old Man Acers compelled me to shoot him or be shot myself or arrested.' The Highwayman, A Gentleman Bandit." Chief McAfee said that a man called the police station and then the Muskogee Daily Phoenix over the telephone in an effort to learn whether the grocer had died. The caller refused to give his name and was denied information. It was believed the caller was the one who sent the note. Efforts to photograph fingerprints from the message were fruitless. The note was delivered in a plain envelope that bore no return address. A reward of $1,000 was posted but no trace of the robber was ever found. The body of the grocer was sent to Perry, Oklahoma, his old home for burial in Grace Hill Cemetery.

A. I. Acers family about 1902. (L to R): Addie Alta, Allen, Sudy, Allen I., and Lottie Ardella.

Acers farm home about 1897.

Mrs. Sudy Acers of Muskogee made her home with her daughter, Mrs. George Keyser, north of Perry in the year of 1941. Mrs. Acers died November 15, 1942. Services were held at the Newton Funeral home. Rev. James V. Gray, pastor of the First Baptist Church, was in charge of services. Burial was in Grace Hill Cemetery in the Acers lot. She was a member of the First Baptist Church.

Addie married Earl Bruce and were the parents of two sons named Earl Allen, who was connected with the US Secret Service in the Hawaiian Islands in the 1940s and who died suddenly of a heart attack in California. William Irving lives with his wife, Mae, at Oxnard, California, where he is with the Civilian Component of the United States Coast Guard Auxiliary Department of Transportation. He is in Public Affairs and contacts Marine Dealers in the Oxnard and Ventura area. Addie died of cancer in California March 7, 1938. Services were held at the Newton Funeral Home. Burial was in Grace Hill. She was a member of the Baptist Church and Order of the Eastern Star.

A. I. Acers and his horse.

Francis M. Allen
By Violet Allen Folger

Francis Marion Allen was born March 4, 1853, at Clinton, Iowa, the son of Zephaniah K. Allen and his wife, Margaret McCullough. Z. K. died November 22, 1899, age 99 years and is buried in Mount Vernon, Washington.

Francis was a dedicated Democrat. He did not have much formal education but was an avid reader and could talk with great knowledge on most any subject. He married Caroline Trout, April 7, 1881. Caroline was born December 20, 1856, near Kitchener, Ontario, Canada, the daughter of Catherine and Samuel Trout. Catherine was born in Canada, August 16, 1830. Samuel, on August 10, 1823, was born in the US. There were fifteen children in the family including three pairs of twins, Caroline was herself a twin, her twin sister's name being Angeline. They were called Carrie and Angie. Their nationality was Dutch. Francis was postmaster at Grainville, Iowa from January 1881 to March 1882.

Between 1882 and 1889, Caroline gave birth to five children at Stockton, Kansas: Lona Bell - October 28, 1882; Angeline Marion - December 8, 1884; her third pregnancy produced twins. Jessie Elizabeth and LeRoy Stanley on April 19, 1887; Toney Francis was born May 4, 1889. For a short time the family lived in Missouri, where Francis worked in the coal mines. This was where their youngest child, Mable, was born on April 26, 1893. At one time, Francis worked for the railroad in Kansas. He helped to build the line to Canon City, Colorado.

On March 9, 1893, Francis M. and Caroline sold their land near Stockton, Kansas for $500. On September 16, 1893, Francis Allen lined up on the Kansas border and made the run into the Cherokee Strip, where he succeeded in staking a claim on 160 acres of fairly good land with a creek running through it (Noble township). After he had filed on his claim, he bought lumber and built a small house before going back to Kansas for his family.

By the time he returned to Kansas, it was fall and cold weather could be expected any time. He started south with his wife and six small children in a covered wagon when near South Haven, Kansas, it began to snow so hard they could not go on. They stopped at a farmhouse and asked permission to camp there until the storm was over. The family invited them to sleep in the house. Francis had an accordion which he played and they sang, turning a disaster into an almost party-like affair. When the weather cleared and they could go on their way, he gave the accordion to their hosts as a token of appreciation. The weather turned much warmer as they neared Perry. The children got out and walked along beside the wagon for exercise. Jessie fell and the wagon ran over her arm and broke it. They went to Perry and found a doctor to set it. By then it was late so they decided to camp for the night at a location near Perry. Roy found a ten dollar bill in the grass near their campsite which he excitedly showed his father. Francis, knowing what ten

Caroline and Francis Allen on their homestead about 1918.

dollars would mean to them before a crop could be raised, gave him a nickle for it and everyone was happy.

The next morning they started out on the final ten miles of their journey looking forward to sleeping in their own house that night. As they went up the hill three quarters of a mile from their farm, Francis said, "As soon as we get to the top of the hill you can see your new home." But when they got to the top of the hill there was no house in sight. Someone had torn it down and stolen the lumber. There was only one thing to do; cut timber and make a log and sod house for the present time.

That first winter, Francis hunted squirrels and rabbits for food. Rabbit and dumplings were their main meal. Sometimes a wagon load of wood was cut and taken to Perry to sell for $1.00 a load. Francis dug a fruit cellar and rocked up the sides with such skill that in 1976, the rock walls stood as firm as when he placed them there. In due time, this cellar was filled with jars of fruit, bushels of potatoes, onions and five and ten gallon earthen jars filled with pickles, saurkraut and green beans. The only was to keep green beans at that time was to pickle them.

Francis was finally able to build a permanent home, a two story white house on the hill near the cellar and well. On the ground floor was one bedroom, living room, dining room, and kitchen. Upstairs was a big bedroom for the four girls and a smaller one for the two boys.

Francis Allen died February 16, 1920, after an illness of only three days. Carolyn died December 27, 1928 from a heart attack. They are buried in the Pleasant Valley cemetery at Sumner.

William Akers
By Pauline (Akers) Nichols

My father, William Akers, was born July 14, 1886 in Indiana, died September 3, 1954 and is buried in the Union Cemetery at Glencoe, Oklahoma. He was the son of Elizabeth (Lane) and Charles Edgar Akers. I was told my

(L to R): Pauline, Aaron Kirkendall (baby); Charlie, and Jerri - 1981.

great grandfather or my great-great-grandfather Akers came to America from Ireland. He was ship-wrecked on the way with his two brothers who were never heard from again.

My mother, L.C.O.C. Collins, she later changed the initials to Elsie Ocie, was born August 14, 1886 in Shell City, Missouri. She was the daughter of Virginia (Cummings) and Martin Louis Collins. My great grandfather Henry Collins fought in the Civil War. My great grandmother applied for a pension from the government because great grandfather had died from effects of war injuries. She told them "her coal bucket was empty."

I remember seeing my grandmother's high-heeled and pointed-toed shoes which buttoned up high on her leg. I remember my Uncle Henry Collin's wife, Mae, smoking a corn cob pipe. My Aunt Maud, mother's sister had to be married in a cornfield at Lela across the road in Pawnee County because they had bought their license in Pawnee County.

I remember my Aunt Lou, daddy's sister telling me, when she was over 90 years old, about swimming in the Black Bear Creek with my mother and her brothers and sisters. She said it seemed like a hundred years ago, then her bright eyes lit up with laughter and she said "I guess it was almost a hundred years ago."

It was rumored that a close neighbor of ours, kept horses in the early days with which to supply outlaws. This was near the old Lela school where we went to grade school. I remember a favorite teacher here, Rubin Poteet, who would play with us each noon hour on the creek such games as Cowboys and Indians and Tarzan. This was near the old historical swinging bridge that was destroyed in 1986.

We had a half-Indian cousin, Mickey (Max) Akers and I remember many trips to Pow-wows and the Pawnee Indian Trading Post that had a mud adobe, thatched roofed sod house. My twin brother, Paul, tells about riding in Pawnee Bill's luxurious long touring car and we remember seeing Indian Joe riding a horse on the streets of Pawnee. He was a cowhand of Pawnee Bills and Buffalo Bills Famous Wild West Circus which we had the privilege of attending at the old 101 Ranch near Ponca City. We also attended medicine shows and was a dancing family.

Howard Anthis

By Callie Anthis DeVilbiss

Howard Judson Anthis (December 5, 1878-September 29, 1940) on September 24, 1905, married Hattie May Pritchett (September 10, 1884-July 18, 1972). The new bride was taken to the Anthis homestead north of Orlando, where they lived with Grandma Anthis. They became parents of six daughters.

Howard farmed, and also dragged country roads for the county. For quite a spell he was clerk on the school board for #19 Country School. In those days, the schoolhouse was the center of all community activities. Christmas programs were special.

As the years passed, the family grew. Etta Elizabeth Ann arrived November 22, 1906. Those days, all generations lived together. Grandmothers were built in babysitters. Then in turn they were taken care of as needed. In the fall of 1907, Grandma broke her hip and was cared for at home. On April 22, 1908, Iva Levina was born. Grandma was then able to rock the new baby. She lived on until February 2, 1910.

Three other daughters came to join the family. In the fall of 1921, the Howard Anthis family moved to a rented farm 5 miles southeast of Mulhall. Now the children could walk to Grandma's house. These five years were filled with work and activities as the family grew. The last daughter, Ina Marie was born April 22, 1924.

Etta finished highschool at Mulhall, took a job at Guthrie. Iva went into nurse training at Enid. At the end of 1926, they moved 5 miles northwest of Mulhall, then in late summer, back to the Anthis homestead north of Orlando. #19 school had now been consolidated into Orlando. That meant high school without paying, as had been done at Mulhall. Callie Mae was now ready for high school. The country was in depression years and every penny counted. It was free high school or none at all.

Howard went down with Parkinson's disease, Hattie's faith held firm. She and the daughters farmed the 40 acres, raised large gardens and canned winter supplies. They had a flock of chickens, and milked cows to keep things going. Everyone was struggling

Howard Anthis and Hattie Pritchett wedding - September 24, 1905.

against the depression which broke over the country in the fall of 1929.

In August of 1940 the Anthis family gathered on the old homestead for a Reunion. Then September 29, 1940, Howard passed away. A few months later, Hattie and Ina moved to Portland Oregon where Iva and family and Elsie and family made their home. She spent 12 years there then moved to Guthrie, Oklahoma, where she finished her days, July 18, 1972. The parents were buried at Rose Lawn Cemetery, Mulhall.

Etta (Anthis) Rinehart (November 22, 1906-September 9, 1974) on February 8, 1927 married James Hubberd Rinehart (July 11, 1907-November 24, 1982) of Guthrie. Both became school teachers and Etta served two terms as County Superintendent of Schools at Guthrie. Both were buried at Guthrie cemetery. They had two sons: James Howard Rinehart died at age 9 months; and Edgar Allen Rinehart (born October 16, 1930).

Iva (Anthis) Werner (April 22, 1908-October 28, 1983) was married at Enid November 19, 1932 to Noble Theo Werner born at Hurley, Missouri (April 15, 1906-February 5, 1978). Both died at Spokane Washington and were buried at cemetery west of Spokane. They were the parents of five children: Jewel Dean Herbranson, Mary Ann Lyons, Rose Marie Borchers, Sharon Lee Nicholson, and Noble Jr.

Callie (Anthis) DeVilbiss born November 3, 1913, was married July 24, 1932 to Wiley Wayne DeVilbiss born March 20, 1910. They are the parents of Glen, Gene and Jerry.

Dorothy (Anthis) Foote born September 19, 1918, was married April 30, 1938, at Morrison, Oklahoma to Wilber Foote born April 2, 1915. Their first home was northeast of Orlando. They had one daughter Anna Mae Foote married Buddy Lafferty.

Elsie (Anthis) McKeown born

November 9, 1920 moved to Oregon and married John (Jack) McKeown (January 7, 1914-March 5, 1982). They are the parents of one daughter, Barbara Kathleen (McKeown) Jones.

Ina (Anthis) Hodge was born April 22, 1924. She married Paul W. Hodge, March 9, 1946 at Hyattsville, Maryland. Paul was born April 21, 1921. He works for Oil Co. They had six children each born in a different place. Paul Jr. born January 1, 1947 at Ashtabula, Ohio, Sherry Marie, July 26, 1948 at Portland, Oregon, Sandra Kay, November 19, 1950 at Seymour, India, Shiela Ann, May 8, 1954 at Lancaster, Ohio; David Dewey, April 1, 1959 at Chambersburg, Pennsylvania, Patrick Michael, August 6, 1962 at Roswell, New Mexico. These families are now in west Texas and New Orleans, Louisiana.

Madison Anthis
By Callie Anthis DeVilbiss

Madison Anthis was born in Wabash County, Illinois, October 13, 1829. Immigration records show his original kin came from Freinshein, Germany in Rhine Valley. They also prove the name is spelled, Antes, or Athis or Antis. Madison Anthis was a descendent (great-grandson) of George Anthis Sr. who came into the Northwest Territory, north of the Ohio River sometime during the late 1790s. He and wife Margaret were traced over several states and 32 years before they finally settled in Knox County, Indiana as well as in Wabash County, Illinois, just across the Wabash River. Anthis was the name established by this group. Any Anthis in America can trace back to George Antis Sr. Madison Anthis' siblings were: John Jr., Alfred, Clark, Martha, Perry, Polly, William and Sally. The parents were John Anthis Sr. and Mrs. Sarah (Johnson) Philpot, widow of Lt. John Philpot killed in War of 1812, their young child, Margaret, was raised with the Anthis siblings. She married Robert Leek. The grandpa of Anthis siblings was George Antis Jr. After a long journey, Madison Anthis died in Noble County, Oklahoma February 24, 1901.

Georgeann (Jenner) Anthis was born in the states, in Richland County, Illinois, May 10, 1834 and died in Noble County, Oklahoma February 2, 1910. She had an English background. Father, George Jenner came from London, England. He was the brother of the famous Dr. Edward Jenner. Her mother was Mary (Starwinner) Jenner of west Pennsylvania. She had a few drops of Indian blood in her veins: not enough for a headright. It was from a small Narragansett Tribe now almost

Madison and Georgeann (Jenner) Anthis about 1893.

extinct. As of 1986, there is a group of about 4,000 left in Rhode Island. George and Mary had two children: Georgeann and her brother, Edward Jenner, named after the famous uncle.

Madison Anthis and Georgeann (Jenner) Anthis, married October 4, 1852 in Richland County, at Olney, Illinois. Madison was a carpenter and a preacher. His first sermon was November 1952 at Maroia, Illinois. They were parents of 14 children, 13 born at Marioia, youngest of family, Howard Judson Anthis was born at Olney, Illinois. Five children died young. When Howard was one year old, they moved west into Kansas near Maple City. Daughter Ina died, age 14, and was buried at Maple City in an unmarked grave. The family later moved into Arkansas City. Funeral home records there show Arthur Anthis died May 3, 1902, buried at Maple City, probably a close relative.

Madison Anthis and Georgeann (Jenner) Anthis came into Oklahoma after 1889, they lived southeast of Mulhall on son Leo's place. The six married children proceeded the parents, took land April 22, 1889, in old Oklahoma. Madison took land 3 miles north of Orlando when the Cherokee Outlet opened up September 16, 1893. Madison had helped start Christian Church at Mulhall, also Antioch, southeast of Mulhall. Then he and three sons built and helped start Orlando Christian church. Madison and Leo did carpenter work, Cyrus and Howard hauled material and quarried rock for foundations. Rock was taken from Ray Ryerson farm northeast of Orlando in Noble County. The original sanctuary still in use with the north side as it was.

Madison and Georgeann Anthis had the following children: Charles Henry Anthis (July 3, 1853-February 7, 1935) married Mary Elizabeth Bowman, of Cassville, Missouri, who died February 1921. They had 9 children: Bessie, Freddie, Rollin, Leo, Lulu, Charles L., George, Edyth and Hubert. Charles moved to Cushing, Oklahoma, he and Elizabeth are buried there.

Columbus Anthis was born in Illinois July 1855, died young - no date.

Madison (Mat) Cameron Anthis Jr. (June 25, 1856-October 9, 1925) married Mary Patten of Winfield, Kansas. They lived for a time in Adair County, Oklahoma and moved to St. Louis, Missouri and had four children: Art, Burt, Laura and Clara. The marriage dissolved. He married Cattie Robins (1867-1932) in Oklahoma. Mat and Cattie lived at Cushing, Oklahoma. They are buried there at Fairlane cemetery.

May Owen (Anthis) Hamil (October 12, 1858-April 20, 1932) married Allison Hamil at Dexter, Kansas, January 9, 1881: They took land northwest of Kingfisher, Oklahoma. They had 11 children, only 3 lived to adulthood: Morgan Lee, Robert Elmore, and Earl. They are buried in the family cemetery Hennessey, Oklahoma. Younger generations have settled around Tulsa, Oklahoma.

Leo James Anthis (September 23, 1860-February 28, 1942) married Amanda Blakesley (April 26, 1868-April 5, 1940) at Arkansas City, Kansas, January 1, 1889. They had five children: Georgia (Anthis) Ireton; Nellie (Anthis) Richardson; Ruth (Anthis) Arnold; Ralph Anthis, wife Lucille Hunter; Leo James Anthis Jr. wife Laurine Irwin. Leo Sr. was a preacher and carpenter.

Sarah V. (Anthis) Millaway (June 6, 1862-December 20, 1906) married William Millaway; they had four children.

Harriet Jan Anthis (April 5, 1864-September 10, 1864); Ina F. Anthis (July 18, 1865-1879); Oscar N. Anthis (December 16, 1867-October 21, 1868); unnamed infant, died at birth 1869; Edgar Austin Anthis (June 16, 1870-September 22, 1871).

Cyrus Herman Anthis (September 10, 1872-May 5, 1927) married Clara Hawkins in Oklahoma, lived on east ½ of Madison Anthis homestead deeded him February 2, 1903. Later moved to Billings, Oklahoma. Buried there in Union cemetery. They had two children: Herman Anthis (September 20, 1902-1965) and Mamie Ethel Maryester Anthis (born April 20, 1905). She married Raymond King.

Georgia Ann (Anthis) Bishoff (July 6, 1875-November 12, 1941) married Louis Fredrick Bishoff (March 27, 1860-June 15, 1934). He was from Edina, Missouri, buried there. They had five children: Blanch Bee Bishoff (April 26, 1897-May 15, 1912); Louis J. Bishoff (April 8, 1899-January 16, 1963); Thelma Henrietta Bishoff (May 22, 1902-May 3, 1903); Julius Henry Bishoff (November 13, 1907-July 30, 1963); and Fredrick (Freddie) Earl Bishoff (September 13, 1912-after 1969). Georgia later married C. L. Killpatrick and is buried in Cushing, Oklahoma.

Howard Judson Anthis (December 5,

1878-September 29, 1940) married Hattie May Pritchett (September 10, 1884-July 18, 1972). They were the parents of 6 daughters: Etta (Anthis) Rinehart; Iva (Anthis) Werner; Callie (Anthis) DeVilbiss; Dorothy (Anthis) Foote; Elsie (Anthis) McKeown; Ina (Anthis) Hodge.

Madison Anthis and Georgeann (Jenner) Anthis homestead in Oklahoma was west ½ northwest ¼ of section 24, 20N 2W in Noble County. Madison was still preaching at Orlando Christian church, February 17, 1901. He had walked in as usual, got caught in cold rain on way home; He died one week later, February 24, 1901 of pneumonia. He and wife Georgeann are buried at Roselawn cemetery, Mulhall, Oklahoma. Part of the above story came from book by June B. Barekman.

Max Baetz
By Joan Miller

Max William Baetz Sr. was born February 3, 1866, at Ueckermuende, Tommern, the son of Otto Baetz (May 30, 1821-April 6, 1908) born in Spandau, Prussia and Lena Langhoff Baetz (February 8, 1831-September 2, 1897) born at Wolgert, Pomnurn. Marie Pauline (Fritsche) Baetz was born January 5, 1867, at Taucha, Saxony. They came to America in 1890 and never had an opportunity to return to Germany, their homeland. On April 21, 1890, they were united in marriage at Chicago, Illinois.

Max Baetz was well educated. He had several brothers and no sisters. He was familiar with the English language before coming to America. Information is vague concerning Max's reason for coming to the United States. He was in service and had received an absence for some reason. He continued to report from America until after his father's death.

Marie was from a family of 14 children and her parents raised another boy in addition to their own large family. She was not as well educated as her husband, but was determined to learn. She studied with their children when they started to school.

Both Max and Marie found employment in Chicago. Max was artistically inclined and painted stencils for wallpaper borders. He also painted designs for wallpaper patterns. In addition to this work, he served as a signal man for a railroad company. Marie worked in a shirt factory. She became skillful in ironing shirts and even in later years took pride in ironing.

Their first son, Otto William Max, was born March 23, 1892, in Chicago. Three daughters were born in Laclede, Missouri. They include Lena Martha, born March 17, 1894; Gertrude Anna, June 16, 1896; and Emme Ethel, September 8, 1898. They moved to Fairview, Oklahoma, about 1900. Three children were born at Fairview, Oklahoma. They were Martha Helen, February 8, 1901; Marie Elizabeth, April 15, 1903; and Max William, September 13, 1905. Nena Hazel was born December 11, 1907, at Ringwood, Oklahoma.

Mr. and Mrs. Max Baetz in front of their home at 901 Wakefield Road.

Although the Baetz family did not come to Fairview, Oklahoma, until about 1900, they experienced many of the circumstances that were common to the homesteaders. They made the trip from Missouri to Oklahoma in a covered wagon. Lena was only six years old but can remember that her mother was burned while preparing the evening meal. They had stopped travelling in order to eat and spend the night. The usual campfire was built so that Mrs. Baetz could cook for the family. A brisk breeze blew her long skirt into the flames. Mr. Baetz immediately wrapped a blanket around her and rolled her on the ground to smother the blaze. Medical supplies in the wagon were used for treatment of the burns. Emma recalls her parents telling of the generosity of people they met enroute to Oklahoma. Many gave them vegetables and syrup. The family lived in a house which was partially covered with sod at Fairview. The kitchen was underground and had a dirt floor. Instead of the usual rocked arch covered with dirt, the ceiling of the cave was wood flooring. This was for the remainder of the house which was above the ground. When a big rain washed away part of the sod covering; the house had to be reinforced.

Max and Marie had no farming experience but made the most of the situation. Broom corn was their principal crop and the children remember helping with the work. Emma said her mother really was a good cook and could make something out of nothing. For example, when they had no nuts to put into a coffee cake, she boiled peach and prune seeds, then cracked them open and took the hearts from inside and used them for nuts. Flour was purchased in 48 pound sacks. The sacks were made into clothing items. Mrs. Baetz took deep red colored wild berries and boiled them to make dye for the sacks. This made the fabric brown colored. Marie was an excellent seamstress.

Neighbors were always ready to help

Max Baetz family in 1934. Back Row (L to R): Henry Grundeman, Don Lumbers, Roy Cowell, Max Baetz, Jr., Otto Thiele, Charles Schaeffer, William (Bill) Piel. Next Row: Martha Grundeman, Emma Lumbers, Lena Cowell, Meta Baetz, Nena Thiele, Gertrude Schaeffer, Marie Piel. Next Row: Doris Baetz, Manila Baetz, Ethel Delores Cowell, Otto Baetz, Myrtle Baetz, Opal Baetz, Joe Lumbers. Front Row: Paul Thiele, Bill Piel, Mrs. Max Baetz, Sr. (holding Rose Marie Piel), Max Baetz, Sr. (holding Ronald Baetz), Otto Cowell, Charles Baetz, Betty Jean Schaeffer and Dorothy Grundeman.

each other. Mrs. Baetz helped as midwife for neighbors and they reciprocated when her babies were born. Young people also assembled for entertainment, sometimes for a ballgame, or maybe a barn dance in someone's hayloft. Dances also were held in homes.

In 1912, the Baetz family moved from Ringwood to a farm five miles west of Perry. The resided on many farms in the country before settling on a small acreage, which they purchased. They remained there until their later years, at which time they moved into Perry near two daughters. Mrs. Baetz lived 11 years longer than her husband, who died August 4, 1944. She died June 9, 1955.

Fred Balduff
By Mildred Highfill

Fred Balduff lived in Pueblo, Colorado, when he decided to come to Oklahoma and in 1893, came to Arkansas City, Kansas. "Upon arriving there I found the town crammed with people. It was so dusty, I felt that I did not want to open my mouth or eyes. So I said to a friend 'Let's go to Orlando. Maybe there will not be so many people.' We went to Orlando by train and registered there. It took two days to register as hundreds were in line. When the "run" took place I watched, not wanting farm land. My friend and I took the fourth train to Perry, finding people as thick as flies there, too. We located on the present site of the cemetery. After getting our claims, one of my neighbors on an adjoining lot asked. " Will you watch my lot while I go to town to get someting to eat?" I consented and he started off toward town, which was easy to locate because there was even more activity and dust in that direction. When he returned he agreed to watch my lot while I went for some food. I never went back! In town I had seen a man with a sign on a piece of muslin selling a lot and I gave him fifty dollars for the property. The lot turned out to be an alley and I had been cheated out of my fifty dollars."

He took a flat car to Orlando determined to go back to Colorado when a letter came from his family saying they were ready to leave for Oklahoma. He went to Ponca City, bought a lot, and started building a frame building. The family arrived and lived in two tents until the building was finished. They lived in the upstairs and started a bakery on the ground floor.

In 1898, he sold the bakery and came to Bliss to put in a lumber yard on a five acre lease. There was only one person at Bliss, Nathan Williams, a wheat buyer with his business set up in the scale office. A store was started with Balduff, P.C. Viering and R.T. Ray. They sold much coal for the thrashing machines.

In 1907, the town was moved over on the hill, one mile southeast of Bliss, where George Miller had bought land, laid it into lots and induced the people to move there. This location was too far from the railroad and later the town was moved back to the present site where he again laid out lots.

Fred was born in February 1857, in Germany. His parents also were natives of Germany. His wife, Ella, was born in August 1861. Her parents too, were natives of Germany. They had two children: William (b-February 1886), and Emma (b-October 1887).

Abraham L. Banta
By Dorothy Tipps

Abraham Lincoln Banta was born at Clinton, Missouri, January 1, 1865, the son of John O. Banta and Margaret Dorothy Chalmers. When he was 13, he went to Wichita, Kansas. In 1879, he went to work for the "Open A" Ranch which was located at the mouth of Pond Creek where Lamont is now located. While here he helped drive several large herds of cattle from Texas to Wichita and later to Hunnewell, Kansas, to where the railroad was built in 1881. In 1881, he went to work for the "Box E" Ranch near where Ponca City is now located. It was during that year the first pastures were fenced in the Cherokee Strip. During the year, 1885, he was employed by the "Flying V" Ranch which was located between the north and south Canadian rivers near the present site of Watonga. During the spring of 1886, he hauled buffalo bones from the Territory between the Cimmaron and the Kansas line into Caldwell, where he received $11 a ton for them. In the spring of 1889, he went to work for Smith and Tuttle on the head of Black Bear, the distance around their pasture measured 67 miles.

He made the run into Old Oklahoma on April 22, 1889, and located a claim on Skelton Creek, southwest of Marshall. He gave this claim to his mother and retained his job on the ranch where they handled 7,000 head of cattle each year,

(L to R): Frank Taggart, Mary Banta, Tom Taggart and A. L. Banta about 1895.

many herds of cattle from Texas were driven to the ranch in the spring, held until fall and shipped to market. All the branding was done on the open range. When the cattlemen were ordered out of the Strip in 1891, Abe went to the Osage country where he worked on a ranch until September 16, 1893, when the Strip was opened.

In 1892, Banta was located near the station of Whiteagle, just south of Ponca City. That was a year of great drought throughout this section. It was especially bad down in Texas, cattle were dying down there by the thousands and many of the remainder were being shipped out. They would come to Whiteagle by the thousands and then be unloaded to be sent to the ranges in the Osage and surrounding section, so weak were the cattle from lack of food that many would die on the train. Disposing of the dead cattle became a big problem. Col. George W. Miller had the contract with the Santa Fe to skin the cattle. A huge sand pit was shallowed out in the hills just east of the station and efforts were made to cover the carcasses, but the number were too great. Finally they were just hauled out of sight and dumped. Banta estimated that some 40,000 dead cattle were unloaded at the Whiteagle stockyards during that summer. The smell and the flies, "Well," he said, "folks can get used to a lot of things when they have to."

He registered at Hunnewell, Kansas; lined up on the south line of Kansas, three miles east of Hunnewell and made the race for a homestead where he staked a claim south of Billings. Abe Banta was one of the organizers of the Cherokee Strip Cow Punchers Association and its first president.

He married Mary Francis Taggart, the widow of William A. Taggart on December 3, 1895. She was born Mary Francis Fortner November 8, 1864, at Fort Scott, Kansas. She had three children by her first marriage, a daughter who died in infancy, a son, Thomas Allen Taggart who died July 24, 1904, and William Francis Taggart. She came to Oklahoma about 1894 with her two small boys. Abe and Mary had one daughter, Dorothy Banta Cole. They moved to Brownsville, Texas in 1921, where he became a prosperous fruit farmer. Mary Banta died October 22, 1937, in Brownsville, Texas. Abe died June 30, 1949. They are buried in the family plot in the Union cemetery at Billings, Oklahoma.

Abe's mother, Dorothy Chalmers, was born Margaret Dorothy Chalmers in Boonville, Missouri, December 21, 1840. After Abe's father, John died in 1869, she married T. G. Wright. She died December 13, 1909 and is buried in the Union Cemetery at Billings.

Almeda Bartow

By Mina Bartow

Almeda Bisbing was born November 23, 1866 in Johnstown, Pennsylvania, the daughter of Thomas Bisbing and Rosanna Ling. Rosanna's parents were Katherine and Daniel Ling. Almeda was called "Bee" since she was so small. Bee had come down from Frankfort, Kansas, with her sister and Seth Barrett, her brother-in-law, who was herding sheep down into the fresh grazing land. Almeda had made the run into Pottawatomie county and staked a claim, but not having any money to prove up on it, a claim jumper took it away from her. She had written her father in Kansas, asking for money. He turned her down saying that if she chose to live with all the outlaws she could depend on them for her money.

She then went to Mulhall where she worked in a cafe. It was in the cafe she met her future husband, Charles Thomas Bartow. Charles made the run into the Cherokee Outlet and staked a claim at section 10 township 20 north range 1 west (Rock township).

After Charles had everything on the claim ready, he went into Mulhall and brought Bee out to see if it was okay. She thought it was a mansion! It was all hers! So they walked across the prairie to Pastor S.P. Meyer's house and got married, went back home and started cutting potatoes to plant!

She would scrub the kaffer corn out on the washboard to brown in the oven for coffee, to grind and make flour and to soak and cook for cereal. Money was scarce then, but they traded some kaffer corn for an old hen and some little chickens. Soon they had eggs. They got another horse and a wagon. They were doing fine. They thought they were rich. Later, three children were born on the claim. Lester Charles, Cecil Thomas and a girl named Sylvia who lived for only five years. While they were struggling, Bee sent several bushels of kaffer corn, some eggs and some butter with Charles into town. While he parked the wagon to find out where the best bargain was someone took all of the food. Charles returned home tired and penniless.

As soon as the children were of school age, it was necessary to move into town. Charles got some lots just west of what was afterward Birch street and Seventh (Block 42) in Perry. Two more children were born there. On December 24, 1905, Mina Almeda was born. On February 5, 1907, Byron Barnibus was born. Byron was married to Mary McKinney and to them was born the only grandchildren of the Charles Bartow family. There were three girls: Arlean, Iva, and Opal. All married and moved away.

Charles Thomas Bartow and Almeda (Bisbing) Bartow about 1930.

We were all raised and schooled from block 42 and all have died in Perry except for Mina Almeda who is writing this narrative and I am 80 years old. We all became members of the Methodist church when it was on the corner of seventh and Birch, when it first opened. We were taught to be honest. We were honest with all people and helped anyone we could. My mother was a godly woman, a perfect helpmate and was cherished and loved dearly by her children and all who came to our house. She said on her death bed, "I've had a good life". She died February 23, 1945 in Perry and is buried in Grace Hill cemetery. We were all glad to have been a part of this new country and we hope it is richer because of people like the Bartows.

Charles T. Bartow

By Mina Bartow

Charles Thomas Bartow was born October 11, 1864, in Altoona, Pennsylvania, to Barney Bartholome Bartow and Martha Ann Witters. Barney Bartholome was born March 13, 1835, out on the Atlantic Ocean. He was the son of Elizabeth Hughs and Jonathan Bartow. Martha Ann was the daughter of Sophia Glass and Samuel Witters. She was born in Cambria county, Pennsylvania on September 18, 1838. Both Martha Ann and Barney served in the Civil War. She was a nurse and attended the battlefield wounded. He served in Co H 208 Pennsylvania Infantry. Both are deceased and buried in the Fairview cemetery south of Perry, Oklahoma. Charles Thomas Bartow came west with his parents to White Hall, Illinois. Then in 1870, the family moved, by covered wagon, west to Gibbons, Nebraska. Settling there, Martha and Barney raised their ten children.

Charles was a young man when news of the government opening new land to the south reached him. He mounted his saddle pony and went in search of a life for himself. He got a job on the Santa Fe railroad just south of Guthrie. One day while watching the fire wagon make a run, he noticed a girl watching, too. Charles said to himself, "that is my wife!"

The railroad came north to the town of Mulhall. There were millions of people everywhere and they were all hungry and thirsty. Being only one cafe in the town, Charles went in to eat and who does he see there but the girl he had seen in Guthrie! So Charles decides that if he was going to get the girl, now was the time. But there were so many people and she had no time to chat. As she went back to the kitchen to wash up her dishes, he followed her and said, "Bee, (he had heard this was her nickname) I'm going to make that run into the Strip and if I get me a claim, will you marry me?" And Bee said, "I sure will!" So Charles made the run and got a claim at secton 10 township 20 North range 1 West (Rock township).

Charles on claiming his land, started to prove up on his claim. He dug a cave and used it for shelter for himself while he worked. Then he dug a well, striking a vein of wonderful water and a bountiful supply. Then he broke out a plot of ground for a garden for food and planted a patch of kaffer corn. Next he built his house, a 12x16 slab board room with lath nailed up and down the cracks to keep out the dust and wind. The floor was flag rock layed close together. There were no windows, only one door. There was a coal stove with an oven. When Charles had everything ready, he

Back Row: Charles T. Bartow and Almeda (Bisbing) Bartow. Front Row: Lester Charles, Sylvia and Cecil Thomas - about 1903.

Byron Barnibus Bartow and Mina Almeda Bartow - about 1912.

went into Mulhall and brought Bee out to see if it was okay. She thought it was a mansion! It was all hers! So they walked across the prairie to Pastor S.P. Meyer's house and got married, went back home and started cutting potatoes to plant!

Soon Charles and Almeda Bisbing (Bee) Bartow became parents. Three children were born on the claim. Lester Charles, Cecil Thomas and a girl named Sylvia who lived for only five years.

While they were on the claim a tornado was coming one night. Charles was fearful of the danger and he quickly got his wife and children into the cave. The next morning he looked around for his pants. He couldn't find them and finally went to the house and got another pair. He told "Bee" he was worried since all his money was in them. Later, he found his pants twisted on a wire. All of his money was still in the pocket (23 cents).

As soon as the children were of school age, it was necessary to move into town. Charles got some lots just west on what was afterwards Birch street and Seventh (Block 42) in Perry. Two more children were born there. On December 24, 1905, Mina Almeda was born. On February 5, 1907, Byron Barnibus was born. Charles worked some more on the railroad and he rolled and made cigars for a man named Masters on the south side of the square. Charles went to work buying and shipping grain for the Red Star Elevator Company, owned by different operators, H. L. Boyce, Thomas Munger and Ralph Treeman, being some I remember. Charles terminated 35 years employment there in 1927. He lost all he had worked so hard to make in the crash of 1929. And the stress of that loss I believe caused him to contract cancer of the stomach. He died on April 11, 1937, and is buried in Grace Hill cemetery in Perry.

No one was ever turned away from Charles Bartow's door, hungry, as far as we could provide. Charles ruled his household and was respected and loved by all who knew him.

Carrie Bay-Swelander
By Ruby Saxbee

My mother, Carrie Bay Swelander was born in Kansas on March 17, 1883. She was the fifth child of Joseph Bay (born 1845) and Mary Francis Bay (born 1857), who had thirteen children, Sara Jane, Dora Etta, Christina, William Arnel, Carrie, Mary Artie, Joseph Leonard, Florence Francis, Clarence Gilbert, Charles Harrison, Frank Orville, Floyd Raymond and Pluma Elsa.

The family moved to Oklahoma in 1893. Carrie attended West Long Branch School located across the road south of the homestead. She went to work as a cook at an Indian School in Stillwater in 1903 or 1904.

My father, John Roy Swelander was born in Minnesota on March 3, 1880. He was traveling with horse and van selling coffee door to door for Milburn Wholesale Company when he met Carrie Bay. They were married in Stillwater on March 29, 1905. They moved to Minot, North Dakota where their first son, Wesley, was born December 31, 1905. Eight more children were to follow: Mary, John, Clifford, Raymond, Ruby, Eugene, Maurice and the youngest Irene, was born April, 1922. John Jr. passed away in 1960, Eugene in 1976, and Clifford in 1977.

The Swelander family moved to Grassy Lake, Alberta, Canada in 1908, where Dad started a homestead and settled the family in a sod house. Dad became a Canadian citizen in 1911.

The homestead was sold and in 1912, the family travelled to Perry, Oklahoma to visit Mother's family and to Great Falls, Montana to visit Dad's family. It was the last visit they would make to see their families.

After returning to Canada in 1913, the family settled in Rumsey, Alberta, one hundred miles northeast of Calgary. The family lived in a tent until a two story framed house was built.

The family moved to Big River, Saskatchewan for three years before settling in Flin Flon, Manitoba, where Dad ran a grocery store.

In 1936, the family moved to Kelowna, B.C. where they built up a fruit farm. Then in 1942, they moved to Abbotsford, B.C. (forty miles from Vancouver). They lived there until their deaths. Dad passed away January 17, 1967, and Mother February 1, 1969.

Mother told us about an incident in Kansas in 1888, when her sister and brother both died of dysentery the same day. Her father also had dysentery and was saved by an Indian visitor who mixed up a herbal tea that cured his illness.

My niece, Lorene Severn and I visited Perry, Oklahoma in June 1985. We visisted cousins, Eugene and

Swelander Family - 1925. Back Row (L to R): Wesley, Clifford, Mary, John Jr., Walter (Mary's husband), John Sr. Middle Row (L to R): Maurice, Eugene, Ruby, Carrie, Raymond. In Front: Irene.

Evelyn Bay. It was very interesting to see the land Grandfather Joseph Bay got in the run where he homesteaded. The Perry Museum was very interesting. We attended the Wigwam Dedication.

Joseph Bay
By Gene F. Bay and Glenn Bay

One of the old settlers who made the run in the Cherokee Strip left several descendants who still live in Noble County. Joseph Bay was born in Indiana, February 15, 1845. He passed away December 10, 1922. When small, he moved to Illinois and later to Sedan, Kansas. He married Mary Francis Trexler. She passed away January 28, 1934.

During their early married life they farmed in Sedan, Kansas. One of their experiences was when they received word a renegade of Indians was coming. They got on their horses to get away. Mary was heavy with their first child. The baby was born along a creek bank under a clift. They later went back to their home and found it had been ransacked.

Joseph came to Old Oklahoma and brought his daughter, Christina, with him in the spring of 1893. He rented a farm three miles west and one north of Stillwater on which he put in a crop. Christina, thirteen years old, did the cooking and housework for her father. He went back to Kansas and brought his family and possessions before the run.

On the trip back to Oklahoma, one night while they were camping out their dog woke them. They heard someone trying to steal their horses. Bay took his 38 Winchester and shot above their heads and scared the thieves away.

Joseph homesteaded his claim on Section 6 in Eden Township in Payne County. The homestead was eleven miles northwest of Stillwater. When he staked his claim, a Sooner came from the creek and told him this claim had already been staked. Bay told him his stake was not in the right place and his horse wasn't lathered like he had made the run. He told him that he would race him again for it. The Sooner refused and said he would contest him for it. Rather than have trouble, Bay agreed to give him a horse.

Joseph started building his home getting lumber from a saw mill set up on East Long Branch Creek, about three miles east, finishing it in the spring. They lived in the West Long Branch School District. The school was across the road south of the homestead. Joseph farmed and raised cattle, hogs and mules. They planted a large orchard of apples, peaches and apricots. They also had a sorghum mill and cider press.

In about 1907, he bought the farm across the road west from a man named Harrington for $3,500. He built a large two story home where they lived until he died. Mary Francis had a farm sale after which she and son, Frank, moved to Three Sands, where he worked in the oil fields for about three years. They moved back to the farm where she lived until her death.

To this marriage thirteen children were born: Sara Jane, Dora Etta, Christina, William Elmer, Carrie, Mary Artie, Florence Francis, Clarence Gilbert, Charles Harrison, Frank Orville, Floyd Raymond, Pluma Elsa.

Sara Jane, born in Kansas, January 17, 1876 and died 1876.

Dora Etta, born in Kansas, March 31, 1877, died May 14, 1898. She was married to Steve Diebold. They had one daughter, who died in 1898.

Christina, born in Kansas, January 12, 1879, died April, 1966. She was married to Tom Lewis and had one daughter, Luella. They lived in Cushing. She later moved to Perry and was married to Earl Ewing.

William Elmer, born in Kansas, January 22, 1881, died 1964. He was married to Francine Cowen. They lived in Oilton and worked in the oil fields and later farmed. They had eight children: Floyd, Mable, Cecil, Willis, Hershal, Vern and Verl (twins), and Bob. He retired in Westville, Oklahoma.

Carrie, born in Kansas, March 17, 1883, died February 1, 1969. She married John Swelander. She lived in Abbotsford B.C., Canada. She had nine children. Wesley, Mary, John Clifford, Raymond, Ruby, Eugene, Maurice, and Irene. The family travelled to Oklahoma in 1912, which was the last visit to see her family.

Mary Artie, born in Kansas, May 9, 1887, died August 6, 1888.

Florene Francis, born in Kansas, July 31, 1888, died 1965. She was married to Floyd Jones of Perry. They lived in California and had one son, Vern.

Clarence Gilbert, born in Kansas, November 12, 1890, died November 1966. He was married to Iva M. Biggs. He farmed in Noble and Payne Counties, later moved to Perry and carpentered. They had two sons, who reside in the Perry vicinity. Gene F. is married to the former Evelyn Lampe. They have three children, Phyllis Bonfy, Betty Hildebrand and Wayne, nine grandchildren and three great-grandchildren. Gene was a farmer and stockman, served as County Commissioner fourteen years, 1959-1973.

Glenn is married to the former Dollie Dufek. They have three children. Glenda Bartlett, Pattis Strothman and Bobbe Keddington and five grandchildren. Glenn spent four years in World War II with the 45th Division in the European Campaign. He worked at the Ford garage from 1946-1960. He is now a farmer and stockman.

Charles Harrison, born in Kansas, 1893, died 1974. He was married and lived in Odessa, Texas. He worked in the oil fields.

Frank Orville, born in Oklahoma, in 1898, died February 12, 1972. He was married to the former Alice Jirous. He also farmed and worked in the oil fields

Homestead 1894 (L to R): Joseph, Mary Francis, Christine, Carrie, Dora, Florence, Clarence, Charlie and William.

in Odessa, Texas.

Floyd Raymond Bay, born October 15, 1900, in Oklahoma, died July 16, 1961. He married Faye Goodwell. They were farmers and raised seven children. Five of them live around the Perry vicinity. They are Floyd Jr., Raymond, Glenn LaVerne, Charlotte, Donald Lee, Wanda and Karen.

Floyd Jr., is married to the former Pauline Cromwell. They have one daughter, Saundra Kukuk and two grandchildren. He was a farmer and now works at Ditch Witch.

Raymond, married to the former Lila Thompson, they have one daughter, Delilah Denney and two grandchildren. He served in World War II in the Navy. He is employed by the Oklahoma Department of Transportation.

Glenn LaVerne, served in World War II in the Navy. He is married to the former Beverly Vinson and has four children, Allen, Larry, Carolyn Clark and Vernon and twelve grandchildren. He farmed, did custom combining, worked in oil fields and now owns a business in Perry.

Charlotte, married to Arthur C. Rupp, has four children, John, Marvin, Barbara and Bonita Beier and four grandchildren. They farm and did custom combining.

Donald Lee, called for training during the Korean War is married to the former Wynema Stout. They have four children, Ronnie, Cheryl Mack, Donna Galoway and Shelby and four grandchildren. They farm and raise stock.

Wanda, married to John Rink, has two children, Gary and Dale. They farm and raise stock.

Karen, married to Donald Keith, who works for Ditch Witch, has two children, Melinda and Aaron.

Pluma Elsa Bay, the youngest of Joseph and Mary Francis, born in Oklahoma, February 10, 1903, was married to Clarence Settle of Stillwater, Oklahoma. They lived in Modesto, California and had two sons, Jack and Bob. She passed away November, 1978.

Nicholas J. Beach
By Kathy Bradford

Nicholas J. Beach was born at La Grange, Indiana, December 23, 1854. He remained at the place of his birth until young manhood, when he moved to El Dorado, Kansas. Here he was married to Miss Gertrude Pierce December 8, 1880. Gertrude Pierce was born in Bushnell, Illinois, October 27, 1861, the daughter of Martin Monroe Pierce and Lydia Ann Joshlin. When she was nine years old, her parents moved to Butler Co., Kansas, where her father took a homestead. The family remained here until the death of her parents. Mr. and Mrs. Beach resided for five years after

Beach homestead about 1900. Clarence Pierce on horse. Man, woman and child on left are unidentified. Belle, Gertrude Pierce Beach and N.J. Beach holding team of horses.

their marriage on a farm near El Dorado. They moved into the city and lived there until the opening of the Cherokee Strip.

"Nick" Beach homesteaded land in Bunch Creek township near the settlement of White Rock. The lived on his homestead the rest of their lives. They belonged to the Methodist church.

Their three daughters were: Myrtle May Beach (January 17, 1882 - March 24, 1965). She is buried in the Union cemetery, Billings, Oklahoma. She was married four times. Her first husband was Ray Jackson, who is buried in the Union cemetery. They had two children, Ray and Roy Jackson. Her second husband was John Kappas, her third husband was John Betz. On September 16, 1920, she married Charles Dewitt Jones. They had two children: Juanita and N. J. Jones.

Goldie May Beach was the second daughter (d-October 5, 1965 in California). She married Edward Hoff December 25, 1904. He was born February 1881 in Lawrenceville, Indiana, the son of Mary and Valentine Hoff. Their children were Emery and Otis.

Belle Beach (b-February 9, 1893 in El Dorado, KS) married Roy Phillips Sr., who was born July 5, 1892 in Iowa.

Gertrude died July 1, 1927 and is buried in Union cemetery in Billings. Nick married Mrs. Colorinda Manning of Oklahoma City in February 1930. He died November 5, 1931 on his farm and is buried in Union cemetery beside his first wife.

William G. Bean
By Luther E. Bean

William G. Bean was born in June, 1862 in Ohio. In 1884, he came from Fairfield, Illinois to Dodge City, Kansas. He went to work for Rettig and Johns of Moline, Kanas, feeding the longhorns using a team of oxen because the cattle were so wild. His wages were $15 a month and room and board. On November 4, 1885, he married Hannah M. Hussleton at her father's home near Moline, Kansas. She was born in June 1862, in Illinios. Her parents had come to Kansas in 1883, which was why Will had come to Kansas because they were "keeping company" back in Fairfield, Illinois.

Early in the spring of 1891, Will, his father, his brothers-in-law, Will and Ed Husselton; a friend, Tom Mills, and two or three others came down into Old Oklahoma. They decided to open a hardware and implement store in Perkins. They returned to Kansas and purchased a store of hardware stock and moved it to Perkins. Their first stop was the Ponca Indian Agency where they spent the night. A son of the Chief had died and it was the mourning period so they didn't sleep much that night as the wails of the mourners kept them awake. The next day, they crossed Cow Creek near where Perry is now located. A boy of sixteen who was riding on one of the loads of hardware was thrown off. He fell under the wagon and the hind wheel ran over his left leg, breaking it. They had to set the boy's leg as the nearest doctor was at Stillwater, two days away. When they got to Stillwater the doctor said it was a good job.

When the Cherokee Strip was opened to Settlement, Will decided to give up the store and make the run, so "Uncle" Tom Mills took charge of the hardware store at Perkins. Will couldn't find a horse to buy so he decided to break and condition an iron grey broncho named "Snap". She was already halter broke and gentle so it was not a hard task to break her to ride. Every evening after work, Will would mount her and go for a ride and by the first of September he was galloping for several miles. It was decided that Mrs. Bean and a neighbor, Mrs. Riley Inscho would set up a tent at registration Booth No. 1 north of Stillwater, and serve food to the people in line to register. The tent, 12' x 14', did not have a roof. Across the front were placed two boards off which the customers ate. The tent was used to cook in and the family lived in it. A 2½ gallon iron pot was filled with navy beans over a camp fire. Bread, beans and coffee was served. Pies made from dried fruit were baked when the oven was not full of bread. Salt pork was cooked in the beans and an attempt was made to place a small portion of this in each serving. There was sugar for the coffee but no milk or cream. A pint of coffee, a cup of beans and two slices of bread sold for 25¢ or 35¢.

Mr. Bean and Mr. Inscho did not have to stand in line when the men found out they were with the cook tent but their places were held for them if they would cut wood and help with the food. The lines were so long that trips had to be made every day to Perkins or Stillwater for supplies. They had a hand washing machine and had to wash every morning. One day the soldiers checked the tent and found about half of it was over the line, which was strickly forbidden. The sergeant gave Mrs. Bean 15 minutes to get it off the line. As the men were gone, she could not comply but some men stepped out of line, went to the creek, cut some green poles about 6 feet long and with the help of four big men the hot stove filled with pies was carried back across the line. Then the tent and all supplies were moved. Each man who helped received a nice piece of pie when they cooled.

Will Bean made the run and obtained a farm (se ½ section 29 in Watkins township), part of it good bottom land on Cow Creek. One portion was a rocky ledge but he soon found he had a good spring of water there but Snap, his horse, was exhausted and never completely recovered. Will camped the first night near a coyote den and they serenaded him all night. The next day, Mrs. Bean and their two sons, Luther E. (born March 1887) and Edwin M. (born December, 1890), arrived in Perry about 11 o'clock with beans and bread, Mrs. Bean had cooked the day before. She soon had a fire to heat the beans and sold all she had very shortly except that she saved for Will and Riley, who soon found them. The dust was so bad that the kettle of beans was kept covered except for the few seconds it took to dip out the cup full of beans.

Riley Inscho found he had staked a quarter of school land so gave it up. The two families ran a restaurant in Perry the first winter. The Inschos left the next spring and went thirty miles east to the Flatiron country where he had been able to file on a claim.

The Beans moved to their claim which had been staked in the meantime by a young man. After Will filed the young man filed a contest. Will built a small shack near the spring and lived there to hold his claim while the family ran the restaurant in Perry. Will would come to Perry on Saturday night and take his family back to the claim on Sunday to do their washing at the spring because water had to be purchased in Perry. One Saturday night someone stole the shack by placing wheels under it and hauling it away. It was never found but a better house was built on the site. When the contest came the contestant failed to show so lost by default.

The first year, not many crops were raised because of draught, however, they did have some hay and put up hay on the shares. They opened a feed store in Perry to sell the hay. Small potatoes, some not much larger than a marble, had been saved from those bought for the restaurant. Will turned the sod with the sod buster while his wife dropped the little potatoe seed in the furrows every other round and they would be covered by the next furrow. The plants came up between the sods and the potatotes formed between the sod and subsoil. They would turn up the sod with a hoe and there would be a cluster of spuds. They yielded well, too, so there was quite a few to sell as they didn't keep well. The coyotes were bad to catch the chickens and turkeys so they built a sod chicken house. Before this the chickens were kept at night in a big box which had been used on the "line" to cut the bread served the customers waiting to register.

Asthma bothered Mrs. Bean and her doctor, Dr. S.A. Moore, advised that she go west to the mountains. In the spring of 1901, they sold the farm and headed for Colorado. She improved the first day out and lived to be 76 years old.

Abner C. Beck
By Abner C. Beck

Abner, son of John Robert Beck and Nancy P. Beck born April 22, 1900, near Era, Texas. In the spring of 1902, my parents came to Oklahoma by way of covered wagon, they ferryed the Red River, but forded all other rivers on their way to a farm eight miles south of Billings, Oklahoma. They lived there for four years, and then moved to a farm eight miles east of Bliss, Oklahoma which is now called Marland, Oklahoma, and was in the Ponca Indian Reservation, their house was a two roomed boxed house. I had 6 sisters and 3 brothers. My sisters were Nellie, Hazel, Virga, Lucy, Martha, and Lillie. My brothers were Ora, John and Burnis.

We were a very poor family. I was the seventh child. My older sisters worked and my oldest brother was married, so it left me to help do all kinds of field work, which at that time, was walking equipment. You walked behind a plow, while it was pulled by horses. I plowed with a walking plow, walking lister, and all other walking tools, at the age of eight years old. At the age of 13, I did hard labor work. At the age of 16, I ran a 25 horse on the draw bar, steam engine, and we threshed around 35 days each year. I ran them several years after, when threshing time came.

We went to bed around 11 o'clock and got up at three o'clock and had to have the steam up by the time the sun came up, that was the time we began or started threshing. We got only about four hours of sleep. I walked a lot of the time two miles to get to breakfast, at the Cook Shack, where we all ate at mealtimes, it had to be near a good well of water.

In the early days we had no roads on section lines just trails across the country, and no bridges. We forded the rivers and creeks, then when the township opened, roads were put on the section line, and we put in bridges, there was no money to put the dirt fills up to them, so the farmers donated their work to put the fills in, so people could get on the bridges.

I helped put the dirt fills on the first bridge over the Salt Fork River on Highway 177. I worked many days, with four head of horses, and no pay.

As I said, "we were a very poor family, when I was nine and ten years old, I had no shoes to wear, winter nor summer. I worked days upon days on public roads in the Bressie Community, without pay." At the age of 19, I attended the Sweeney Auto and Tractor School in Kansas City, Missouri, and became one of the best mechanics at that time.

In 1923, I met Pearl Pfrimmer. Her parents were George and Ella Pfrimmer. They homesteaded nine miles south of Billings, Oklahoma. They made the Cherokee Strip run in 1893. On the 24th of February in 1924, Pearl and I were married in Perry, Oklahoma, by the Christian Church minister, G. Frank Sanders. We made our first home nine miles south of Billings. We were engaged in farming. I became interested in the affairs of the community. I helped my neighbors and was soon put on the school board. I went out and collected money to put a good fence around the Polo Cemetery. Mr. Cole and I went to Perry and bought the wire and posts to build the fence. I hauled the post and wire out to the cemetery and helped build the fence.

Our first child was born at our home south of Billings, Oklahoma on August 10, 1926. Her name is Gwenneth Ruth. We lived just four years south of Billings, then we moved to a farm eight miles east of Marland, Oklahoma.

Soon after we came to the Bressie community, I was elected to serve on the school board, as chairman. I served 14 years in this capacity. Then I became interested with children. I helped the 4-H boys and girls for over 20 years.

Our second child was born, Bruce Leon Beck on July 4, 1930. Our third child was born October 4, 1934, Jerolynn Lee was her name, Dwight Bentley was born July 14, 1937, and Sandra Lee was born June 14, 1940.

I was in the draft of World War I, and was called to duty. I was also in the draft of World War II. Then soon after the United States entered the War, I was asked by the government of the United States to do some top secret work for the government without pay, so I accepted, and did the secret work during the war. If I ever told anyone, during my lifetime what I did, the penalty would be life in prison or death.

I became involved in church early in my life, and served on the Church Board where I served 40 years. I taught the elderly Sunday School class for over 35 years. I was an active church worker. In 1966, the Methodist Church put out a book: "Who's Who in the Christian Movement," and my name and my family's names are in this book. We also put two boys and a girl through college. I could never have done all of these things had it not been for my wife, Pearl. She was with me all the way.

February 24, 1984, we were married 60 years. We can remember many things that came into being. I remember when there was no motorcycles, no automobiles, no airplanes, no paved roads, no television, no radios, man on the moon or in outer space, walking in space, the Atomic Bomb, Nuclear bombs, and many other things that have come into being during my lifetime.

Pearl and I had five children, but we lost Jerolynn Lee quite young in her life, with acute leukemia. Gwenneth Ruth married John Thompson, in 1942. John passed away in 1985. They have two children, Gary and Sharon. Gary married Kay Rinehart, they have three children. Bruce Leon, our second child, married Darla Bennett, they have no children. Sharon married Alan Smith and they have no children. Dwight Bentley, married Helen Ludwig, they have three boys, Dwight II, David, and Douglas, Sandra Lee married Dr. Fred Reynolds, they have two girls, Ann and Susan.

Pearl and I have worked hard all of our lives. Pearl helped me with all kinds of farm work, and field work, and I helped her with house work, and we both raised the children.

I have lived in the Bressie Community 74 years in Noble County, 83 years at the end of 1985. I have lived on this home place 69 years to date, as this is the home place of my parents. Our farm home is modern in every way, and we intend to live here the rest of our lives. I still do all kinds of farm work at the age of 85 years. Baled most of the alfalfa hay, which is around 15,000 bales each year. We have seven grandchildren and six great-grandchildren. My ancestors on my father's side came to America in the early seventeenth century.

Fred W. Beers
By Fred G. Beers

When Fred William Beers came to Perry in 1895, the prairie community was barely two years old but was fast shedding the tent city look that followed the Cherokee Strip run of 1893. Unpaved streets, wooden sidewalks and kerosene street lights were part of the landscape, but the civilizing influences of churches, schools and diverse businesses were preparing the hardy pioneers for the 20th century.

Beers was a pharmacist. He had worked for E. E. Howendobler in a Wichita drug store, and when Howendobler made the decision to gamble on the future in Perry, he brought his young employee with him. By 1903, Beers had opened his own drug store here. Eventually it became known as the City Drug Store, and it was something of a local institution for nearly 40 years.

Beers was a native of Galeburg, Illinois, the son of William C. and Harriet Beers. His father was a railroad conductor on the Burlington line between Chicago and Quincy, Illinois. William Beers later farmed around Golden City and Cathage, Missouri.

Fred Beers attended Lewis Academy in Wichita and graduated from the Era School of Pharmacy there.

His first drug store in Perry was on the west side of the square, where the Masonic Temple later was built. A spectacular fire destroyed the wooded building housing his store in 1908, but before the embers had cooled Beers had boarded a train for Kansas City, Missouri to buy stock and fixtures for a new location on the north side of the square.

On October 18, 1911, Beers married Ivy Isabel Bucklin, one of the town's fair young belles. The officiating minister was Rev. S. H. Parvin of the First Presbyterian church.

The brides parents were Mr. and Mrs. Alfred E. Bucklin. They arrived here on February 2, 1902, from Mexico, Missouri, to open a combination chili parlor and notions store on the north side of the square. The Bucklins' secret chili recipe — now long since lost — kept the adult customers coming back for more, but school children found the store a treasure house of knick knacks, plus the necessary pencils, pads and slates for homework.

Bucklin had been in business in Mexico before coming to Perry, and also had tried his luck in Rogers, Arkansas. His two daughters, Ivy and Essie, were born in Mexico. Bucklin died in 1923, during a business trip to Texas. His wife, the former Margaret Nummy, moved to Chandler in 1926, when Essie became a court stenograher in Lincoln county. They returned to Perry in 1956, and both died here. Essie had been a secretary in the law office of P. W. Cress, a prominent Perry attorney, before moving to Chandler.

Fred and Ivy Beers had three children: Jeanice Margaret, born February 19, 1917; Gloria Mae, born February 11, 1922; and Fred Gordon, born August 19, 1924. Jeanice married Sydney L. Wade in 1934. They had two children: Sydney Jean Flynn, now living in Madrid, Spain; and Leigh Frederick, serving in the Army in Little Rock, Arkansas. Jeanice died in 1982.

Gloria married Raymond Miries in 1946, and they had a daughter, Karen Sue, born in 1947, and now living in Alaska. Gloria died in 1964.

Fred G. Beers married the former Laura Belle Thomas of Oklahoma City in 1954, and they have two daughters: Kathleen Faye and Susan Gail. Kathleen, now manager of corporate development for Hallmark Card Co. in Kansas City, Missouri, married Ron Lindsey in 1983. Susan, state coordinator for the U.S. Department of Agriculture's computer service for the Agricultural Stabilization and Conservation Service, married John Bieberdorf, member of another pioneer Noble County family, in 1980. They live in Stillwater, but Bieberdorf is employed as an engineer by the Charles Machine Works, Inc., in Perry. Kathy's husband, Ron, is employed by a printing broker

City Drug Store — Ivy (Bucklin) and Fred W. Beers proprietors.

firm in Kansas City.

Laura Beers is a retired medical technologist at Perry Memorial Hospital. She came here from Oklahoma City, where her mother, Mrs. Atra Thomas, still resides.

Fred W. Beers was a civic and church leader as well as a progressive businessman until his death on May 13, 1931. The depression's grip on the U.S. was growing tighter at that time, but the responsibility of operating the drug store was thrust upon Ivy, his widow, along with the task of rearing three children. For nine years she was assisted in the business by a nephew, also named Fred W. (for his uncle), but in 1940, the store was closed. (The nephew, Fred W. Beers, is now retired and lives in West Palm Beach, Florida, with his wife, Jayne.) Ivy died in 1967.

Fred G. Beers, the surviving member of the family, and his wife continue to make their home in Perry. He is Graphic Communications manager of the Charles Machine Works, Inc.

Alvina Karcher Beier

By Eddetta Beier Grant

An early immigrant to Noble County was my grandmother, Alvina Karcher Beier. She was the firstborn of Jacob F. and Anna Marie Karcher on February 22, 1899, in Wolhynien, Ukraine, Russia.

Jacob Karcher was born November 10, 1853, and died June 9, 1935. Anna Marie Karcher was born January 1, 1865, and died September 17, 1944. Both had previously been married and widowed with children from those marriages. Jacob had four children from his first marriage: Adam Karcher; Frederika Karcher Wilde; Karlein Karcher Hamann; and Wilhelm Karcher. Anna had three children from her first marriage: Mikeal Rutschinski; Otilia Rutschinski Muller; and Bertha Rutschinski Pansegrau. Jacob and Anna Karcher had five daughters from their marriage: Alvina Karcher Beier; Adolpina Karcher Klingbeil; Albertina Karcher Krieger; Elsie Karcher Thiele; and Hertha Karcher Rudat.

Because of the social persecutions of the time, Alvina's family decided to seek their freedom in America. On July 16, 1906, the Jacob Karcher family arrived at the port of Galveston, Texas, aboard the S.S. Hanover. I assume because they already had family living there, the family settled on a farm in the Orlando/Marena area of Oklahoma. The small community of Marena was located west of Stillwater, Oklahoma. Only some old buildings remain today. Marena was the focal point for many Germans from Russia immigrating to America.

On May 2, 1919, Alvina was married to Emil Beier in Orlando, Oklahoma. They lived and farmed on various places in Noble County until they purchased their own farm on August 6, 1946, located four miles east, two miles north and a quarter mile west of Perry,

Front Row (L to R): Jacob F. Karcher, his wife Anna Marie, and daughter Hertha. Back Row: Elsie, Adolpina, Alvina, and Albertina.

Oklahoma, described as the NE¼-8-21N-1E.

Alvina and Emil had ten children: Leona Anna who married Arlie A. Musick; Rudolph Lawrence who married Dorsie D. Thompson; Lorene Catherine who married Harold E. Loveless; Lillian Marie who married Roy E. Jones; Edward Jacob (my father) who married Cleva Jo Howard; Marjorie Edna who died in infancy; Emil Rinehart who married Lena Bell Knight; Arnold Harry who married Eunice Fields; Marlene Evelyn who married Karl Oltmanns; and Carol Kay who married John H. Fuxa.

Alvin became a citizen of the United States on May 9, 1956, and received her Certificate of Naturalization.

My grandmother died this past Spring on March 21, 1985. She as a hard working farm wife and homemaker. I can still remember her baking loaves of bread; making homemade sauerkraut; or putting cucumber down to make dill pickles. I know all of her 24 grandchildren would agree she made the best dill pickles around.

Food was important to Alvina; perhaps because it was so scarce during her early life. Whenever you went to visit her, she always made sure you had something to eat or drink. This usually meant coffee, tea, homemade bread with jelly, or the best was her homemade coffee cake with so much cream that when you lifted a piece out of the dish, the cream left was thick in the bottom of the dish. In fact, you would hurt grandma's feelings if you refused to eat or drink something.

Alvina Karcher Beier came to Oklahoma as a young child with her family seeking freedom from many forms of oppression. I know I'm certainly glad and thankful these poor immigrants had the courage to seek a better life in America.

Edward Beier

By Eddetta Beier Grant

In his search for freedom and escape from oppression, Edward Beier, his wife, Marie, and their seven children set sail for America from Bremen, Germany, aboard the S.S. Breslau. What their journey was like, no one will ever know. They arrived at Baltimore, Maryland, on July 25, 1908. From here they boarded a train for Oklahoma Territory. It is hard to imagine such a family traveling across America. They did not speak English and nearly starved before reaching Oklahoma. Their destination was Morrison, Oklahoma Territory, but they failed to get off the train. When they realized their mistake, they walked the five miles back into town and were met by Edward's sister, Gustene (Justina) Just and her family. Edward and his family then picked cotton to help pay back their passage money to the Justs.

Edward Beier was born March 28, 1868, in Germany, to Fred and Anna Beier. Two sisters and one brother also traveled to America and settled in the Morrison/Perry area, namely: Gustene (Justina) who was born May 25, 1864, and died December 6, 1921; Ludwig who was born January 21, 1874, and died November 1, 1916; and Mary Beier was born February 28, 1876, and died November 8, 1942. Gustene (Justina) was married to Ferdinand Just and they had two daughters, Emilie Just Walters and Elvina Just Scott. Ludwig was married to Abertina and they had two daughters, Olga Beier Schiever and Pauline Beier Stieferman. Mary Beier was married in 1908, to Frank Tolsdorf and they had five children, Lydia Tolsdorf Pricer, Gustav, Ludwig, Edward and Albert.

Marie Schuette and Edward Beier were married on December 18, 1891, in Russia. They had eleven children, namely: Lydia who married William S. Voise; Albert who married Minnie D. Adler; Emil who married Alvina Karcher; August who married Bertha Tuetken; Emilia (Millie) who married Rudolph Rupp; Alwin (Winnie) who married Henry Voise; Julius, who married Alice Johannes; Alexander; Emma who married Arthur Rupp; and Bertha who married Harry Frank. One child, Benjamin, had died as a child in the old country.

In 1920, Edward achieved his dream and purchased 80 acres of his own land

Ludwig Beier Family: Albertina and Ludwig seated with infant, Pauline and daughter Olga standing.

situated at the S½ NW¼ of section 1-21N-1E. The farm was located seven miles east and two and a half miles north of Perry, Oklahoma.

In 1954, Edward and Marie retired and moved to Perry, where they resided at 618 Fir Avenue until their deaths; Edward died on August 18, 1964, and Marie died on December 17, 1966. At the time of his death, Edward had over

Edward Beier Family. Front Row: Alexander, Edward (seated), Julius, Bertha, Marie (seated), Lydia (seated) and Emma. Back Row: Alwine (Winnie), Emilia (Millie), Emil, Albert and August.

Ferdinand Just Family: Ferdinand, Gustene (Justina) and daughters Emilie and Elvina.

104 living descendants.

Edward was a farmer and had received very little education. He learned to speak a very broken English which even his great-grandchildren found hard to understand. As far as I can determine, he came from a long line of farmers that went back many generations and which continues to this day. One of his grandsons and namesake, Edward Jacob Beier, my father, continues the farming tradition of his ancestors and has passed in on to his sons, Robert Lee and David Edward. Hopefully they will pass this tradition on to their children. My great-grandfather was a strong and stubborn individual. He left behind very few wordly riches, but left instead a priceless legacy — the gift of freedom.

George D. Bellmon
By Henry Bellmon

George Delbert Bellmon came to Oklahoma from Sedan, Kansas, a few months after the run. At the time he was 19 years old and too young to qualify to stake a claim. He paid a homesteader $700.00 "to relinquish" his claim on the southeast ½ of section 29 in Glenrose township. He lived with his wife in a dug-out on that claim for the next four years during which time they proved up their rights to the claim and were issued a patent or title to the land.

Meanwhile the neighbor to the south who had built a new frame home decided to leave Oklahoma and Bellmon purchased his land, northeast ¼ of section 32 in Glenrose township for $4000.00. He moved his wife and children to this home. Later, he added to the home and raised two families there.

George Bellmon was born June 1874 in Pittsburg, Kansas. In 1894, he married Annetta Jane (Nettie) Hays. Nettie was born May 1, 1872 at Centralia, Illinois and the following year her parents moved to Chatauqua County, Kansas where she spent her childhood days. She received her education at Sedan, Kansas.

The 1900 Census shows George's household to contain wife and two daughters, Alta Elnora born October 1895 and Cora Elvira born September 1897 and his mother-in-law, Alvira Hays who was born January, 1834 in Illinois.

Besides Alta Elnora (Blakey) and Cora Elvira (Regnier) seven more children were born to George and Nettie: Winfred Lavina (Bloom) born October 1899; Leo Emmerson born February 16, 1901; Lillie Ester (Fisher); Lida Jane (Gilchrist); Weldon Delbert; Adaline Annetta (Eveland); and Auretta May (Denton). Nettie Bellmon died November 10, 1918 and is buried in the Prairie View Cemetery north of their home.

After his first wife died George married Edith Eleanor Caskey. She was born at Clarinda, Iowa March 6, 1883. The Caskeys had moved from Iowa to Oklahoma in 1907. Edith was trained as a school teacher and taught in the rural schools of Noble and Garfield Counties for 16 years before she met the recently widowed George Bellmon. They were married on August 18, 1920.

She was first a member of the Presbyterian Church but was transferred to the Methodist where she served as Superintendent of the Billings Methodist Sunday School 25 years. During WWII she again returned to teaching.

To this union was born four sons: Henry Louis, first Republican governor of Oklahoma; Irwin Caskey born January 14, 1923 was killed by lightning July 22, 1940; Sheldon George and Randall Yingling.

Edith Bellmon died June 7, 1945 and is buried in the Union Cemetery, Billings beside her son, Irwin C.

Henry Bellmon
By Henry Bellmon

Henry Louis Bellmon was born on a farm near Tonkawa September 3, 1921. He is the son of Edith Caskey and George D. Bellmon. He attended the Glenrose rural school and graduated from the Billings High School in 1938. He graduated from Oklahoma Agricultural and Mechanical College (now Oklahoma State University) in 1942 with a degree in Agriculture.

During World War II, Bellmon joined the United States Marines and served over three years with a tank battery participating in four Pacific battles, including Iwo Jima. He received the Legion of Merit and Silver Star in recognition of his military service.

He returned to his farm after the war and began his political career at age 25. In 1946, Bellmon was elected to the Oklahoma House of Representatives. In 1962, he was elected the first Republican governor of Oklahoma. In November, 1968, Bellmon was elected to the United States Senate, a position to which he was re-elected in 1974.

Copy of Patent filed in courthouse, Perry, Oklahoma.

Bellmon family in 1968 (L to R): Henry, Pat, Gail, Ann and Shirley.

He chose not to seek re-election in the 1980 election. He retired from the Senate in 1981 and returned to his farm. However, Bellmon's retirement from political service was short. He was co-founder and served as national co-chairman of the committee for a Responsible Federal Government. In 1983, he was appointed director of the Oklahoma Department of Human Services.

In 1985, Bellmon was appointed receiver for the financially troubled National Cowboy Hall of Fame in Oklahoma City, Oklahoma. He also joined the RAM group, working to assist financially troubled farmers in avoiding foreclosures.

In recent years he served as professor/lecturer at Oklahoma City University, Central State University, the University of Oklahoma and Oklahoma State University. He also served as a commentator for an Oklahoma City television station. He raises wheat and cattle and enjoys hunting and fishing.

Henry married Shirley Osborn in January of 1947. Shirley is the daughter of Laurine Ponton and Ray Osborn. Both of Shirley's grandfathers, Louis Ponton and Sidney "Bert" Osborn, were early settlers in the strip.

In 1967, Shirley started a dress making business in the basement of her home, a demand for her special design dresses climbed rapidly and the "Shir-Lee" fashions, (made by hand) was moved to a business building in Billings. Each dress bears a distinctive appliqued design. First of the designs worked out by Mrs. Bellmon was the scissortail flycatcher, Oklahoma's state bird.

Shirley, who had always made most of her own clothes, as well as her daughters', has since added five other designs; cotton, wheat and mistletoe plants, an oil well and a quail.

Henry and Shirley are the parents of three daughters: Pat (Lewis/Copeland), Gail (Wynne) and Ann (McFerron) and the grandparents of three boys.

On November 4, 1986, Henry was elected to his second term as Governor of Oklahoma.

Leo E. Bellmon
By Edna Bellmon

Leo Emerson Bellmon was born February 16, 1901 to George Delbert and Annetta Jane (Nellie) Bellmon. He was born seven miles east of Billings, Oklahoma on the family farm which they bought two or three years after the Cherokee Strip Run. They moved here from Sedan, Kansas. Leo lived here with his parents until he married Edna Pauline Back in September 1921.

Leo attended school through the eighth grade at Glenrose School east of Billings. He then attended Tonkawa Prepatory School, now Northern Oklahoma College. After one year he attended Hill's Business College in Oklahoma City, Oklahoma.

Leo married Edna Pauline Back September 28, 1921 at the home of Edna's parents, Joseph and Annie Back. Edna was born June 17, 1901 at the farm two and one-half miles south of Billings. The legal description of the farm is NE¼-6-23N-2W. Edna's father and mother brought the family from Guthrie, Oklahoma in 1894, one year after Joe made the run to claim land in the Cherokee Strip Opening.

Edna attended school at Elkhorn School District (5) one-half mile south of the home. She graduated from the eighth grade and attended four years of high school at Billings graduating in 1920. That summer Edna attended Edmond Teacher College now called Central State University. Edna taught one year at Antelope Valley School located nine miles south of Billings.

Following the marriage Leo and Edna moved to Tonkawa, where Leo worked in Sheehan Clothing Store for a year. Farming was his love though so he and Edna moved to a farm southeast of Tonkawa that belonged to his father. Several years later they moved to a farm nine miles north of Billings, Oklahoma on the Salt Fork River. August 1930 they moved to Edna's parents' homestead two and one-fourth miles south of Billings. They continued to live there. Leo farmed and worked for Phillips Petroleum Company pumping wells mostly in the Billings-Midco area. They moved to Ponca City in September 1960.

Leo retired from Phillips Petroleum Co. in 1963, when he was 62 years old. After retiring, Leo worked at the First Christian Church in Ponca City, Oklahoma.

At the age of 65 Leo retired. He died at the age of 71 in 1972 following failing health due to Parkinson's Disease. He is buried in the IOOF Cemetery at Ponca City. Edna remains in the home in Ponca City.

Leo's mother died in November, 1918, but he was blessed with a loving father and eight brothers and sisters: Alta Elnora Bellmon Blakey and Cora Elvira Bellmon Regnier, both born in Kansas. Winifred Lovina Bellmon Bloom also born in Kansas. The rest of the family including Leo were born in the farm home and delivered by Doctor Thomas Refrow. They are Lillie Ester Bellmon Fisher, Lydia Jane Bellmon Gilchriest, Weldon Delbert Bellmon, Adeline Annetta Bellmon Eveland, and Auretta May Bellmon Denton.

Leo's father remarried later to Edith Caskey. To this union were born Leo's four half-brothers: Henry Louis, Irvin Caskey, Sheldon George and Randall Yingling.

Edna Bellmon's brothers and sisters were: Joseph W. Back Jr.; Estella Back Dupy, Alma Back Derr, Edgar David Back all born in Boonville, Missouri. Hattie (Harriett) Back Dupy was born in Guthrie, Oklahoma Territory.

Leo and Edna were the parents of three children: Charlotte Ann born November 30, 1922 on the farm southeast of Tonkawa; Hugh Emerson was born August 5, 1924 on the farm nine miles north of Billings, Oklahoma. Anita Jayne was born April 21, 1942 at Enid while the family lived at the homestead south of Billings.

Babora Altman Koller with children by 1st husband: Joseph, Emma, Jennie, Otto, Libbie and Emil.

Barbara Benes
By Alice Benes

Barbara Altman was born in Czechoslovakia January 6, 1870, the daughter of Jan and Anna Altman. Her mother died and her father married a woman with a family. Barbara came to the United States at the age of nine years with her brother, Charles Altman who was two years older. They made their home with an aunt and uncle at Wilber, Nebraska where she grew to womanhood. She married Simon Koller on June 6, 1889. To this union were born six children, all born in Plainview, Nebraska. They were Joseph (b-March 19, 1890); Emma (Chadek) born March 9, 1893; Jennie (1982-May 3, 1911); Otto (1895-June 9, 1917); Libbie born November 11, 1896 died August 2, 1902; and Emil born May 7, 1898. Simon Koller died June 2, 1899.

On May 16, 1902 Barbara married John Benes at Osmond, Nebraska. To this union was born two sons, Edward born July 12, 1903 and Louis born December 16, 1904. In 1906, the family moved to Oklahoma locating near Morrison. Barbara and her second husband divorced. He moved to Illinois and she helped with the farm. The older children got jobs. The girls, Emma and Jennie worked as housekeepers, when Jennie died in Tulsa unexpectedly of an apparent heart attack. Emma worked in Oklahoma City in a home and then for the Jackson Cookie Company. Libbie helped at home because in early childhood she had what they thought was polio and she was left crippled and wore a brace on one leg the rest of her life.

Joe and Otto worked on farms in Nebraska. Otto wrote to Libbie that he was getting $40 a month and had bought a horse and buggy on May 27, 1917. He accidently fell on his gun and died June 9, 1917.

Ed finished 8th grade and worked on the farm and finished paying for the place northeast of Morrison; where he and his wife Alice Kelley raised six children. Louis worked in the oil fields for Kerr-McGee company in Israel. He married Nellie Anderson. They had no children.

Barbara could speak some English and could read and write. She loved to cook. She was a Catholic from an early age. She attended monthly meetings of the Lodge (ZCBJ) or Western Bohemian Fraternal Association of Morrison of which she was a charter member.

In 1937, she moved to Pawnee where she died March 18, 1948. She is buried in the Morrison cemetery.

Babora Altman, age 9, and brother Charles when they left for America - 1879.

Family History / 135

Charles Benke
By Mary H. Sommars

The enclosed material is from information prepared by Emma Benke Albers before her death in 1975. Charles and Caroline Benke and family came to Noble County in 1896 after living in Kansas for several years.

Charles Benke, my father, was born March 3, 1845, in Bennisch, Austria. Caroline Neugebauer, my mother, was born April 19, 1851, in Bennisch, Austria, also. They were united in marriage there on October 2, 1871. Charles Benke served four years in the Austrian Army (German) and was discharged December 31, 1878, at age of thirty-three years.

Seeking freedom from military oppression, in 1881, Father, Mother and four children, Julius, Charles, Anna, and Theresa came to America. One son, Joseph, died and is buried in Austria. A trying voyage with two climbing boys and two little girls, they all lived to reach America with only what they could pack in a wooden chest. This chest has remained in the family all these years.

Father reached Topeka, Kansas, where he got work in the Santa Fe railroad shops. They and another family lived in one house. To help out Mother took in washings. Pay was 10¢ an hour. The boys became shoe shine boys. It was a time to work or starve. They worked. They lived near public school. Boys would be boys, threw mud on clean clothes — had to wash them over.

It came election time. Santa Fe shops had an interest in the outcome of the election. They helped my Father and other foreigners to become naturalized citizens of the United States.

Santa Fe would throw discards into the river. That is where Father would retrieve old metal wheelbarrows and pieces of railroad iron. It served as an anvil. The wheelbarrow was used to transport small loads. The wheelbarrow was important to me, Emma, because that was where I first learned the

Caroline and Charles Benke - October 2, 1921 - on their Golden Wedding Day.

English language taught by my sister, Helena, two and one-half years older than I, as we sat in the old wheelbarrow.

Father was a farmer at heart, so after seven years of shop work he moved his family to Westphalia, Kansas, where he farmed. Times were hard and prices low.

Cherokee Strip land opening in Oklahoma came in 1893, the year I was born. Three years later, Father bought a claim right to 160 acres of land 5½ miles east of Perry for little more than $500. This was all the money he had. The house on the land had two rooms and a lean-to. It turned little wind and water.

Father, Charlie and Theresa came overland with two wagons and all our worldy goods, including chest. Theresa, 17, drove a horse hitched to a light buggy. Got possession of land right away; others were just waiting to contest his claim right to homestead because his wife would not live on a farm and "make a home" as is required when you file on land. Mother, Lucy, Helena and I (Emma) came by rail a week later to join others on the land. Our family made it the best we could with long days of hard work. In Kansas, our home had been 1½ miles from a small town, so the drive to the farm 5½ miles from Perry seemed endless to a little girl three years old in 1896, near Christmas time. Am sure Christmas was a lean one that year and also later years too. Am certain we had coffeecake (Kuchen) with apples in it.

At first we had no cow. Father bought a red cow at a sale. Feed scarce, not much milk. We used every drop. Rare occasions Mother bought eggs at 4¢ a dozen, when she had 4¢. Few people had machinery, one time a neighbor borrowed a corn planter. He gave Father 25¢ when he returned the planter. That bought three yards of cloth to make a shirt for Father which he desperately needed. Charity was needed on all sides. Once friends lost a child and home by fire, a family of three in need. Mother gave the little girl the only dress I had to wear to church. I hunted for the dress but it could not be found.

Not all children stayed in Perry. Julius was handicapped and could do little farmwork. He went to Cleveland, Ohio and learned the cigar maker's trade; eventually, he established a business in Norman, Oklahoma, where he did well, until a sudden illness, pneumonia, caused his death in 1923. Theresa married John Stahl, a Kansas man, who had bought a claim right near Theresa's family home at Perry. They were married but a few short years when she died in childbirth of twins, December 1901. Mother and twins were buried in one grave in St. Rose of Lima cemetery. Anna never lived in Oklahoma. Married a Kansas man, Frank Stahl, and made her home in Westphalia, Kansas. Charlie became a farmer and got a quarter of land in Big Pasture opening near Lawton. Before he left, he married Allie Brand and they went overland to make their home. Their three children were born and grew up there.

Benke Sisters
By Mary H. Sommars

The following is information on the younger Charles Benke daughters, Lucy, Emma, and Helena.

Lucy Benke married Alfred Hise in St. Rose of Lima Catholic Church January 20, 1931 by Father Willebrord. Hise was employed by the Santa Fe railroad as section foreman. They lived in different areas of Oklahoma. They had no children. Upon his retirement, they moved to 406 Holly in Perry. He died January 28, 1957, at Santa Fe hospital in Topeka, Kansas, after a long illness. Lucy lived in Perry until her death on September 23, 1966, at age 80. Both are buried in Perry.

Emma Benke married Joe Albers, whose family had moved to Noble County in 1901, from Paxico, Kansas where Joe was born. Joe's family settled on a farm south of Perry. Emma and Joe were married on September 2, 1930, by Father Willebrord at St. Rose of Lima in Perry. They settled on the Benke homestead 5½ miles east of Perry. Joe was a farmer who was very interested and active in county political affairs. Emma, before her marriage, taught schools in Noble County, also in Norfolk, Marland, and Sumner, Oklahoma. They lived on the Benke homestead until their retirement in 1964, moving to 406 Holly in Perry. Joe Albers died September 26, 1972. Emma died December 7, 1975, at Chanute, Kansas, where she had moved to be near her sister, Helena, and relatives, after her husband's death. Both are buried in St. Rose of Lima Catholic cemetery. They had no children.

Helena Benke married Albert Joseph Sommars, May 18, 1920, in Perry. A. J. had served in WW I, with the 90th Division, 357th Infantry in France and Germany, returning to the US in 1919.

Albert Joseph Sommars was the son of Frederick and Mary Madgeline Ripperger Sommars. Frederick Sommars was the son of George Jacob Sommars and Julia Ann Weiss. He was born October 22, 1845, in Alsace-Lorraine near Landau, Bavaria. He came to America via ship from Le Havre, France, at age seven in 1832, with his parents. Frederick married Mary Madgeline Ripperger on May 30, 1870, at Bauer, Iowa. She was born in Franklin county, Indiana, May 30, 1852, the daughter of

(L to R): Emma Benke Albers, Helena Sommars, Lucy Benke Hise.

Michael Anthony Ripperger and Agnes Stephens. The Frederick Sommars family lived in Iowa for several years where Anna, John, Julia, Agnes, and Nick were born. They moved to Stanton, Texas in 1883, where Clara, Albert Joseph, Paul and Clarence (who died in infancy) were born. The family came to Noble County, Oklahoma, around 1900, and settled on a farm east and north of Perry. Mary Madgeline Ripperger Sommars died in 1904, and Frederick Sommars died in 1922.

Albert Joseph and Helena Benke Sommars moved to Kansas after their marriage. They returned to live near the family home in Perry in August, 1921, with the infant daughter, Mary H. On October 2, 1921, Helena's parents, Charles and Caroline Benke celebrated their Golden Wedding Anniversary at the family home with all their children present. Caroline Benke died March 24, 1926, at age 75 and Charles Benke died October 9, 1929, at age 84. Both are buried at St. Rose of Lima cemetery in Perry.

Two sons, Charles and Louis, were born to Helena and Albert Sommars, in Perry. In 1937, the A. J. Sommars family moved to Chanute, Kansas. A. J. died July 30, 1965, at age 79, and Helena (Lena) Sommars died March 28, 1980, at age 89.

Joseph Bolay
By Gertrude Bolay

Joseph Bolay was born January 17, 1861 in Willmadigen by Reutlingen, Wurtemburg, Germany. His father was a tinsmith by trade. His mother was born Wilhelmine Mock. She died in 1910 in Germany. At the age of nineteen, Joseph came to America and located at Atchison, Kansas. Two years later he went to California but returned to Kansas in 1885 and moved to a farm near Farmington, Kansas. On March 24, 1886, he married Anna C. Haber in Kansas.

Anna C. Haber was born February 10, 1868, in Farmington Kansas. She was

Joseph and Anna Bolay on their 50th wedding anniversary, March 24, 1936.

the daughter of Christ and Caroline Haber family. There were nine children in the Haber: Charles, John, Otto, Lena, Rosetta, Albert, Herman, Ernest, and Anna. The Habers were originally from Germany. They lived on a farm near Atchison, Kansas.

Herman Bolay, son of Joseph, told about his father's trip to America. Joseph and a cousin stowed away on a ship bound for America. He was nineteen years old. They were discovered the third day out at sea, and had to work out their passage. They landed at San Francisco. Joseph went to Sacramento, where his sister, Maria Gruhler lived. He later went to Atchison, Kansas where his cousin had gone, as he had relatives there. It was in Atchison where he met Anna Haber. They married and lived on a farm for four years before coming to Oklahoma. Joseph received his citizenship papers on June 10, 1884.

Joseph and Anna came to Oklahoma in 1891. They lived on the Hartmann place near Orlando. He staked a claim and proved up on it.

Anna and Lillie (a baby of 7 months) followed behind the men in the run. Anna drove a team and wagon filled with tools and supplies. The prairie had been burned off and they were all black. Anna walked four miles the next day to some friends. Two men on horseback offered her a ride, but she said she'd walk. They took Lillie to Mrs. Plumer and she did not want to take her. They assured her that Anna was coming and Mrs. Plumer after looking at Lillie's clothes (which she had made) accepted her.

The family lived in a dugout until 1902 when their house was finished. Joseph Bolay farmed, did blacksmith work, custom threshing, and worked as a road boss on the county roads. He was tax assessor of his township for 12 years. He was a member of the Board of Directors of the First National Bank. He retired and moved to Enid in 1927. He died June 28, 1954 at the age of 93 and is buried in the Zion cemetery, Orlando, Oklahoma.

Joseph always held the small ones on his lap. He had a key wind watch which he let them hold and listen to it tick. He played his harmonica for them to put them to sleep. He had a white mustache and all the little ones pulled it. He said it did not hurt as long as he didn't pull back. He was a wise and kind man. He had a roly-poly build like Santa Claus. He had the most delightful whistle you ever heard. It made you feel good just to hear him. He always whistled while he worked. He said it helped him to concentrate on his job.

Although Anna Bolay was very busy with her own family she always had time to help a sick neighbor. Their home was always open to folks in need. The visiting pastors were always sent to stay at the Bolays.

Anna delivered many babies in the early days in the Cherokee Strip. She said there must have been a hundred, and she wished she had written down the names. Many of them were folks just passing through the new territory. She seldom received any pay as few folks had any money. She said she always made them promise to get a doctor if she thought it would be necessary. Doctors were scarce and folks had no money for them.

Joseph and Anna Bolay were the parents of ten children: Herman, Charles, George, Lillie, John Walter (who died in infancy), Sam, Dennis, Clarence, Albert and Christina.

Anna died in 1948 in Enid, Oklahoma, after an illness of several years. She is buried in the Zion cemetery, at Orlando, Oklahoma.

Edward S. Bowles
By Marjorie Bowles

The following article was written for the Bowles family's descendants. Let no one interpret any part of this record as boastful. For each individual member of this family has a deep and abiding faith in God; each considers all good in their lives to be gifts from HIM, and each is convinced that in the Final Day, worldly accomplishments — wealth, position, power, prestige — will count for nothing, but that all will be judged according to their relationships to God, and how they have treated their fellow human beings.

Edward Shrader Bowles and Marjorie Belle Laird, from the beginning, had much in common: Both were born and raised in Perry, both born of parents who were pioneers of this area; both attended public schools and were graduated here; both were Presbyterians, and both Democrats. All of their children were also born in Perry and all but the last received their schooling here.

Edward Shrader Bowles was born January 14, 1902; the handsome son of the prominent pioneer lawyer, Judge William McMullen Bowles (1868-1944) and Clara Margaret Shrader (1872-1958), and the paternal grandson of Dr. Edward Bowles MD and Molly Patton; and the maternal grandson of Charles Duncan Shrader and Ellen Celeste Young. He received a Law degree from CU, but did not inherit his father's enthusiasm for the practice of law. He was appointed postmaster of the Perry Post Office in 1934, and served for a number of years; then, on his request, was transferred to a rural mail route, which he carried until he retired in 1967, after which he moved to Stillwater, Oklahoma.

He was a violinist, and performed in concert with Prof. Leopold Radgowsky's community symphony orchestra for several years. He had a mellow baritone voice, and sang in the First Presbyterian Church choir in Perry for many years. He was an avid reader, and his favorite past time was listening to classical music. He was a gracious gentleman, and was never known to spurn another human being. He lived the principles of Christianity, yet professed his personal faith in Christ only six days before his sudden death on May 9, 1986. He is buried in Grace Hill Cemetery, Perry.

On September 17, 1934, he married Marjorie Laird, daughter of Samuel Elmer Laird (1867-1944) and May Bell Shinn (1871-1952), paternal granddaughter of J. McGinley Laird and Jane Walker McKinney; and the maternal granddaughter of John B. Shinn and Charlotte Fielding. Marjorie was born March 10, 1911. She moved to Stillwater in 1959 so their children could attend the university there. She was, for several years, a technician in Biochemistry and graduated from OSU in 1970, after which she was employed as a Social Worker in Tulsa until her retirement.

She is an observer and learner of life; and has an interest in all living things. She likes to draw; and cooking is her favorite part of housework. Her constant love and concern for her family is exceeded only by her spiritual faith. She and her husband celebrated their 50th Wedding Anniversary in 1984. They are the parents of six children — three sons and three daughters — all growing in the "Faith of their Fathers."

James Edward Bowles was born September 2, 1937. He has a degree in Aeronautical Engineering from OSU, and is an engineer with the Northrop

Bowles Family 1984 (L to R): Janis Elaine, Jean Frances, Elizabeth Ann, Joseph Samuel, John Charles, James Edward. (Seated): Edward S. and Marjorie Bowles.

Corp. of Hawthorne, California — dividing his time between that and being a pilot with Trans World Airlines. He was also a pilot in the Viet Nam War.

Jim has a rich baritone voice, and was a member of the high school Men's Quartet, and was in demand as a soloist for church services and other functions. He is multi-talented, resourceful, organized and creative. He has been involved with several religious denominations in California, and is a student of the Bible. He lives in Palos Verdes Estates, California with his wife, Penny Arthelia Overholt (1939). They have two children, James E. Bowles II (1964) and Malinda Elizabeth Bowles (1969).

John Charles Bowles was born June 6, 1941. He was an expert drummer in the highschool band. He has an Accounting degree from OSU. During the time he was employed at Arthur Young Co. in Tulsa and at Exxon Co. in Houston by day, he was attending university classes at night to become a CPA, and to earn a Law degree from the University of Houston. He is blessed with a virtually photographic memory. He was Tax Counsel for Exxon in N.Y. City, and is now Senior Tax Counsel for the R.J. Reynolds Co. in Winston-Salem, North Carolina. He is married to Judith Margaret King (1942).

His honesty and integrity are above question; and he has the enviable ability to see humor in almost any situation.

He is family-oriented, and his greatest pride is in his four daughters: Cheryl Lynn Bowles (1968); Tracey Elizabeth Bowles (1970); Carrie Margaret Bowles (1974); and Leigh Ann Bowles (1979).

Joseph Samuel Bowles was born September 19, 1943. He completed his senior year of highschool in Stillwater. After receiving a Master of Business Administration degree at OSU, he was employed by Phillips Petroleum Co. at Bartlesville, and later by Hardee's at their home offices in Rocky Mount, North Carolina, where he was Assistant to the president. He now owns two Chicken Kitchen restaurants in North Carolina.

He has a keen business instinct, and a discriminating sense of piroritites. He is a sensitive, caring person, and is concerned for his fellow man. His wife is Daphine Buist Riley (1935). They are both members of the Calvary Baptist Church in Rocky Mount. They have one son, Jospeh Samuel Bowles II (1976).

Elizabeth (Jane) Anne Bowles was born November 28, 1944. After she received her Associate degree in Secretarial Science from OSU, she moved to Tulsa where she has been employed by the National Bank of Tulsa, the Public Service Co. as an Executive Secretary and the Cities Service Oil Co. before transferring to its sister company, The Permian Corp. where she is still employed.

Ann is quiet, gentle, feminine and loving; and like so many wives of today, has two simultaneous careers — as a dedicated home-maker and an efficient, conscientious employee. At her father's death she rededicated herself to her high Christian principles. She is married to Philip Dean Henry (1933), and has one daughter by a former marriage, Lauri Ann Pryor (1966).

Jean Frances Bowles was born September 28, 1948. She attended OSU, then transferred to Tulsa College, where she received her course work for Nurse's training; and completed her training at St. John's Hospital; passed the State Board examination, and is now a Registered Nurse. She has been employed by Hillcrest Hospital, Tulsa, Stillwater Medical Center, and the OSU Health Clinic, Stillwater. She is currently with the Perry Memorial Hospital, Perry, and the Home Health Service it provides.

Jean is a sensitive, sincere, mature Believer, and considers the relieving of suffering a Christian privilege. She and Roger Duan David (1948) are the parents of a daughter, Natalie Jean (Jenny) David.

Janice Elaine (Jan) Bowles was born November 14, 1952, and attended schools in Stillwater, Oklahoma. Jan is much like her father's side of the family. And she has never lost the qualities of enthusiasm and excitement. In spite of the fact that caring for her family's needs and efficiently running her household is time-consuming and confining, she takes time to work for her church. She is married to Charles David Hempfling (1948), who is the son of Charles David Hempfling, Sr. and Phyllis Keller; and grandson of the Neuerberg family who were early settlers of Perry.

Jan and David have three children: Charles David Hempfling II (1973); Elizabeth Jean Hempfling (1976); and Joseph Edward Hempfling (1977). Elizabeth was stricken with juvenile diabetes when she was four, and in caring for her, Jan has become an expert in the study and care of diabetes.

William M. Bowles
By Mary Maughan

Judge William McMullen Bowles brought wide recognition to Perry and became a vital part of its heritage through his broad range of legislative, legal and community activities. As a pioneer lawyer, he was a dominant force in Noble county and the State of Oklahoma for over fifty years.

William McMullen Bowles was born in Lane's Prairie, Missouri, November 7, 1868, the son of Dr. Edward Bates Bowles and Mary Patton Bowles. He died on March 18, 1944, in his Perry law office. As an expression of admiration

Judge William McMullen Bowles.

Clara Shrader Bowles.

and respect, local business county, and government offices were closed for his funeral services.

Following his early education in Missouri and Indiana, William Bowles taught school for four years, studied law and was admitted to the bar in 1892. At the opening of the Cherokee Strip in 1893, this young lawyer made the Run, arriving in Perry on the tender of a southbound train from Missouri. He started his law practice on the day of the opening, launching a career that led to the Bench and the edge of the Governor's chair.

During the fifty-one years that Judge Bowles resided in Perry, he took an active part in civic, community and political affairs. He served several terms as president or member of the Perry Board of Education. He was appointed the first City Attorney and later Noble County Attorney. In 1903-05, he was a member of the Territorial Legislature. Always an ardent Democrat, the Judge was frequently a delegate to National Conventions and became a candidate for Governor of Oklahoma. He was appointed District Judge, serving Noble, Kay, and Grant counties shortly after Statehood on November 18, 1907, and served continuously until January 11, 1920, when he retired to private practice in Perry.

William McMullen Bowles and Clara Margaret Shrader were married in Perry, December 21, 1898. Clara Shrader was born December 8, 1873, in Lancaster, Wisconson. She moved to Noble county in 1895, with her parents, Mr. and Mrs. C. D. Shrader. For a time, she worked with Mrs. H. C. Nicholson in her Perry millinery shop. During her long residence in Perry, Mrs. Bowles was active in the PTA, the Progress Club, P.E.O., and Pioneer Bridge Club, and the Presbyterian Church. Clara M. Bowles died November 12, 1959, in Tulsa, Oklahoma, where she had moved to live with her daughters, Ellen and Clara.

Judge and Mrs. Bowles and their family resided at 1003 E Street (now Elm St.), later moving to 801 Holly Street.

Four children were born to William and Clara Bowles: Mrs. Ellen Henriksen, Tulsa, Oklahoma; Edward S. Bowles, Stillwater, Oklahoma; Mrs. Claire Pellow, Arvada, Colorado; and Mrs. David C. (Mary) Maughan, Wayzata, Minnesota.

Clarence Eugene Branson
By Mildred Highfill

Clarence Eugene Branson was born April 19, 1867 in Lawrence, Kansas. He came to Oklahoma at the opening of the Cherokee Strip where he homesteaded the northwest quarter of section 23 in Autry township. He batched on his claim and one day went to town for supplies. When he returned, he carried a hundred pound sack of flour into the dark house on his shoulder. Someone was hiding in the house with an axe which he brought down on Gene's shoulder. The sack of flour saved his life but he had an extensive bruise. No one ever found out who the person was or why he attacked Gene Branson.

Gene married Bessie Emick February 22, 1896. Bessie was born April 25, 1876 in Nicholas County, West Virginia. She moved west with her parents, William P. and Lucy Catherine Emick, finally settling in what is now Noble County. When she lived on the homestead her father had claimed, she worked in Morrison for $1.00 a week at the store run by the Morrison family. As her family needed supplies more than cash, this was how she was paid.

After they were married he was the jailor for the Perry jail and Bessie cooked for the prisoners. Later they moved to a farm east of Morrison and one mile east of her parents farm. Gene became a farmer and rancher with cattle as well as row crops. They had two children Clarence and Ettamae.

Gene was an ardent supporter of the Republican Party and at the time of his death, July 16, 1931, was state party committeeman. From the early days of the settlement, to his death he manifested a great interest in politics. He was active in every campaign, and had served as chairman of the county central committee. He was with Vice-President Curtis when, as a candidate, he came to Oklahoma. Bessie died in 1962. They are buried in Highland Cemetery in Pawnee, Oklahoma.

Clarence F., son of Gene and Bessie Branson was born in December 1896. He married Nellie Capstick and they had one daughter, Mary Evelyn Branson who married Glen Loewen.

Ettamae, daughter of Gene and Bessie Branson, was born December 23, 1905. She married first Wiley Reed and second Jim Neal. She had no children. She was the first woman to serve as secretary, treasurer and managing officer of the Stillwater National Farm Loan Association, was a

Richard M. Nixon and Ettamae Reed at the Republican National Convention in Chicago.

cashier and president of the Citizen State Bank of Morrison, chairman of the Noble County Heart Association, was a state committeewoman from Noble County Republican Party and was serving with the Payne County Republican Party at the time of her death. She was a member of both the National Association of Bank Women and the National Bank Auditors and Comptrollers. She was a member of the American Legion Post 343. She had served as treasurer of the United Methodist Church of Morrison and had served as district secretary of the Federated Women of 1940. She held the distinction of being the first woman appointed to the Board of Affairs during the administration of Governor Henry Bellmon.

Ettamae, the last member of this family, died October 23, 1980 and was buried in the Highland Cemetery of Pawnee where her parents are buried.

Jens Breinholt
By Mrs. Thelma Holmes

Jens Breinholt was born in Marso, Denmark in 1865, and came to America in 1890, with his brother, Paul, who made the run to the Cherokee Strip with him. The two arrived at Caldwell, Kansas from Colorado a short time before the Race and had to sign with the government to show that they were naturalized citizens and were twenty one years of age. He said they made the run in about three hours and staked their claims two miles west and four north of Billings, Oklahoma. Brother Paul's claim was across the road to the west of Jen's. Jens said, "The government had cleared a wide strip for all of us to race over, so the going was pretty easy — all we had to do was to find an empty strip of land, plant a stake and then get ready to run off anybody who wanted that same place."

The next winter a pretty eighteen year old school teacher, Anna Prather, whose father had staked a claim five and one half miles north of Billings, came to the Strip. She was from Virginia. She organized the first school in the area, teaching eighteen frontier youngsters. Breinholt met the young teacher at one of the Friday night Literary Society meetings and in 1898, they were married. To this union were born three daughters: Maren (Mrs. Harry Tull); Gladys (Mrs. Mark Dierlam) and Thelma (Mrs. Quincy Holmes). Anna was very active in community activities as well as keeping her well run home. She was also so helpful to a little four year old neighbor, Clara Danford who lived just north of the Breinholts. Clara's mother had passed away in 1900, leaving three little boys and Clara. Anna taught her so much about homemaking and was so kind to her.

Jens and Anna Breinholt.

The Breinholt brothers owned and operated their custom threshing machine seperator, steam engine, cookshack, etc. — besides their wheat and stock-farm.

The Breinholts made their first trip to Galveston, Texas, in 1919 and liked it so well that they wanted to go back to a coastal town since they had been born on the coast of Denmark. They started shrimp fishing and built their own business which prospered over the years.

Jens was confirmed in the Lutheran Church and lived an upright life, being an example of all that was good in life. Jens and Anna were laid to rest in the Riverview cemetery northeast of Billings, Oklahoma.

Daniel D. Brengle
By Marcia W. Dunn

Daniel David Brengle, M.D., was born October 19, 1866, in Winchester, Illinois, and first came to Perry in January, 1895, from Bluffs, Illinois. After six months he moved back to Bluffs for four years, returning to Perry in 1899, to join his brother Dr. Will, who had made the run into Perry in 1893.

The father of Dr. Dan and Dr. Will was Dr. Daniel David Brengle, a native of Germany. He came to America and settled in Winchester, Illinois, where he practiced medicine for sixty years and was still alive in 1901, at the age of eighty-three years. The mother, formerly Mirinda Vivian Muir, was born in Kentucky and died in Illinois. She became the mother of four sons and two daughters. All the sons were physicians. Dr. Dan was a graduate of the College of Physicians and Surgeons in Chicago, Illinois. It was the first class to be granted diplomas from the University of Illinois.

In 1891, Dr. Dan married Blanche Ebey in Winchester, Illinois. She, too, was born in Winchester. Their children: Quine (b-Dec. 1891), Winifred (b-June 1895) and Dan. During their married life Blanche assisted Dr. Dan in his office. She was the official bookkeeper and also arranged his appointments.

In 1951, Doctor Dan closed his general practice after sixty years. He was famous for his nightly walks which usually covered about three miles each time.

"I practiced eight years in Bluffs and fifty-three in Perry," he said.

When Dr. Dan first came to Perry, he registered, as was required by law, to practice his profession. The record was duly recorded in Guthrie, then the state capitol. He was the 454th doctor to register in Oklahoma Territory. However, a fire destroyed most of the records at the state capitol, Dr. Dan's being among the ones that were lost. A few months after he resumed practice on his return to Perry, in 1899, he received notice from the state to show reason why he should not be prosecuted for practicing medicine without a license. It seems some enterprising rival had looked up his registration in Perry in the Noble County records and not finding the record there failed to look in the "P" County record where Dr. Dan was duly and lawfully registered, so reported him to the state who had lost his record in the fire. The "P" county record was immediately and readily accepted at the capitol and the incident closed.

The Brengle's first home in 1895 was a four family house on the north side of the square. In 1899, they lived on F street in the block between 7th and 8th streets. They lived on 7th street in three different houses. The last one was 822 7th.

When they returned to Perry the se-

Dan and Blanche Brengle.

cond time, Dr. Dan came ahead to select a house. He purchased a new, shiny nickel-plated cook stove and put it in place. It was a new house, and as bed bugs were plentiful especially in new lumber, Dr. Dan decided to fumigate. He got a lot of sulphur, set it on fire and left the house closed for four days — Alas! The shiny nickel of the new stove resembled rust, but he did get nearly a quart of bed bugs.

Dr. Dan was the kind of physician who inspired his patients with confidence. He kept abreast of all the latest developments in medicine. However, medicine alone, did not absorb all of his interest. During Dr. Dan's years in Perry, sports were a number one hobby. The Perry High School football team and the Perry Merchant semi-pro baseballers rarely played a home game without the doctor in attendance. Everyone in town knew he was a great admirer of the New York Yankees, so it was no surprise when he received a letter addressed only to "The Best Yankee Fan in Perry".

William B. Brengle
By Mildred Highfill

William Burgess Brengle, MD son of Dr. D.D. Brengle and brother of Dr. Dan, was born in Winchester, Scott Co., Ill, January 7, 1853, where he received his education, graduating from the high school in 1870. He later studied in the University of Columbus, MO, then entered the Rush Medical College at Chicago and graduated in 1879.

His first practice was in Winchester, Ill., he later located in Wellington, KS, where he practiced until 1886. He praticed medicine in Los Angeles, Seattle; WA, and San Francisco. In 1892, in Cripple Creek, he combined medicine and mining and opened a drug store.

In September of 1893, he made the run and located in Perry. For the first three years he operated a drug store, but this he sold in order to devote his entire time to his profession. His first wife was Ella Rockhold. They had two sons: Harry Ferguson Brengle and Dr. Dean Rockhold Brengle.

October 9, 1893, in Albion, NE, Dr. Will married Grace Liddle. She was born in Galesburg, IL on November 30, 1873. Her father was born in England. Her father and mother died before she was six years old and she was raised by a sister, Mrs. Wallace (Mary) Ladd. Dr. Will and Grace had one child: Vivian (b-September 1894).

Vivian remembered: "Raising white horses was one of my father's greatest interest. My mother was a good horsewoman. Her riding horse was Cricket. With Nell, they were the team she drove.

Among the vehicles we owned was a Victoria, a low four-wheeled carriage with a clash top, designed for two passengers with a raised seat in front for the driver; a surrey with "fringe on top"; one buggy called a stanhope, with a high seat; and for a time a brouham, a light closed carriage with seats inside for two or four."

"We had a faithful Negro man, John English, who was my father's driver until my father died in 1911. He took care of the barn and the several horses, cleaning, feeding and saddling them or hitching them to the wagon when needed."

"The circus came to town often and my father was Ringling Bros. doctor while they were in Perry, attending many of the circus people in their illnesses and accidents."

"Shortly before his death, my father sold Cricket and Nell and Nell's colt, Twilight to Ringling Bros. Circus. Cricket and Nell were trained for the statuary act and Twilight was sold to Hagenback circus where she did a solo act as a trick performer."

From the Noble County Sentinel, December 23, 1897: "Dr. Brengle has all modern appliances for use in medicine and surgery. His offices and apartments are the largest and most commodious in the city, occupying the entire second floor on the New York Hardware building. There is a large reception room beautifully furnished, a laboratory, operating room and private hospital for the use of patients."

Dr. F.C. Seids tells this about Dr. Will in his "memoirs", "Dr. W.B. Brengle, who had been treating nasal conditions and in many cases affecting a cure, was seized with the notion of a catarrh wagon. There was such a demand that people came from surrounding communities to have him treat nasal troubles. He conceived the idea that the quickest way to a fortune would be to put the equipment on a mobile arrangement and carry it to the people far and wide. From Ringling Bros. circus he acquired white ponies, which he used sometimes as a team, sometimes tandem and sometimes he used six ponies. John English, in appropriate dress was his hustler. The Catarrh Wagon was painted white. Dr. Brengle sported a plug hat and Prince Albert coat and, in winter, a long fur coat. Angus Miller, a most spectacular dresser, was spieler for the set up. They traveled over northern Oklahoma and made a fine and attractive picture on the landscape, as well as relieving many patients of their ailments."

Grace Brengle, wife of Dr. Will, was an Episcopalian and attended Brownwell Hall in Omaha, NE. She was one of a small group who started St. Mark's Episcopal church in Perry. She helped in Dr. Will's office and became interested in the study of the eyes. She took a correspondence course in optometry, concluding with attendance at two schools — one in Kansas City, the other in Omaha. She practiced her profession in Perry until her death September 23, 1923. She is buried in Grace Hill cemetery, Perry beside her husband, who died May 18, 1911.

Dr. Will Brengle's office: Dr. Will is standing behind a patient, John English is in front.

James Brier
By Marjorie Brier Cramer

James Elba Brier was born in Chillicothe, Missouri, December, 1883, to John Thomas Brier and Jennie Carnahan Brier. John Thomas McBrier was brought to this country from Northern Ireland when a baby. He married Jennie Carnahan in Coshocton, Ohio, and when their first daughter, Alma was two years old, they came to Missouri, in a covered wagon. Jennie Carnahan was born in Coshocton on March 21, 1842, and died February 5, 1888.

They had four daughters and one son: Alma Elizabeth (Mrs. James Shipp) born in Ohio; Agnes (Mrs. John Adcock) born in Missouri; Belle (Mrs. Virgil Botts) born in Missouri, Maggie (Mrs. Charles Goff) born in Missouri; and James Elba Brier born in Missouri.

James' mother died when he was four years old and his sisters raised him. When he was 15 years old, his father along with Agnes moved to the Orlando Community. Leaving the married daughters in Missouri. They bought a farm four miles northwest of Orlando, Oklahoma. James Brier married a neighbor girl, Edith Stumpff in 1905, at Orlando.

Agnes Brier married John L. Adcock in 1910, in Perry. John homesteaded three miles north of Orlando on Strip Opening day. That is where they made their home until 1930. They moved into Orlando. Later, their house burned to the ground. All they had left was a picture of my grandmother and a little chair. But they built a new home on the same spot. Both were members of the Christian Church in Orlando. They never had any children. Agnes passed away in 1941 and John in 1955. They are buried in Lawnview Cemetery.

James and Edith Brier had two daughters born on the Stumpff farm: Marjorie, born in 1907; and Maxine in 1909. When the girls were small they moved to Enid and then on to Oklahoma City where Mr. Brier was a conductor on a street car. A few years later, they moved to Memphis, Tennessee, where Mr. Brier worked for Wells Fargo. The next move was to Ft. Smith, Arkansas and then on to Marianna, Arkansas, where Mr. Brier was express agent for Wells Fargo. In 1923, they moved to Perry, Oklahoma, where Mr. Brier was associated with The Daily Oklahoman and drove to Three Sands Oil Field with the papers every day. He distributed the Daily Oklahoman and Tulsa World many years in Perry. He also had the Mistletoe Express for a few years. Edith Brier opened a hat shop and later had dress shops in Perry.

Marjorie and Maxine started to High School together and graduated together in 1926. They both sang in the Glee Club and girls quartet. They were charter members of the Rainbow Girls Masonic Order and Charter members of the Campfire girls. Also they helped to organize the Red Hots Perry High pep squad.

Back Row (L to R): Edith Stumpff Brier, Mary Ida Stumpff. Front Row: Maxine Brier, Christine Epperson Maxwell, Marjorie Brier - September 16, 1910. Photographer - A. A. Hughes Perry.

Marjorie married Gerald Sanford Cramer whose parents had moved to Perry in 1916, when Gerald was 10. His father, Samuel Wesley Cramer, was born in Wilkes-Barre, Pennsylvania, October 24, 1866, and married Minnie M. Campbell at Kingman, Kansas, in 1884. He was a blacksmith by trade and Mrs. Cramer a piano teacher. They had 10 children. Gerald, next to the youngest, was born in Ames, Oklahoma, July 15, 1906. Mr. Samuel Cramer passed away in December, 1940. Mrs. Minnie Cramer died in 1958. They are buried in Grace Hill Cemetery. Gerald died in 1958, nine months after his mother died, he also is buried in Grace Hill Cemetery.

Gerald Cramer and Marjorie had three children: Virginia St. Pierre of Tulsa, Gerry Cramer of Houston, and Sally Russell of Ardmore.

Gerald Cramer had a Body and Fender Shop in Perry until 1942. Then the family moved to Tulsa where he went to work for McDonald Douglass. Virginia was 16 when they made the move. She started to Will Rogers High School and was a junior. The next year, 1944, she graduated. Gerry was 12, when they moved and he also graduated from Will Rogers. Sally the youngest went to Sequoyah grade school and to Will Rogers where she graduated in 1957.

Virginia had two daughters: Mrs. James Hager (Phyllis) and Mrs. Christopher Phillips (Suzanne). Phyllis has one son. They live in Tulsa.

Gerry has two daughters and one son. The oldest daughter lives in Tulsa and she has three sons. Her name is (Caren) Mrs. Anthony Conwell. Her three sons are Jeffrey, Tracy, and Brian.

Cinda Lee (Mrs. Charles Dutton) lives in Chattanooga, Tennessee, and she has two sons. Taylor and Colby.

Terry Cramer lives in Claremore, Oklahoma, he has a son, Trenton and a daughter, Tara Danielle.

Maxine Brier Douglas went to college after graduating High School. Two years at Edmond and two years at Stillwater. She got her degree and taught Art in the schools. She was teaching in Okmulgee, when she met and married Paul Douglas of Okmulgee. She taught for six years. They had two sons, Tate and Jim. Both boys served in the navy. Tate went to college in Boulder, after serving in the navy. The family moved to Ft. Morgan, Colorado and Paul died there in 1958, and is buried in the Okmulgee Cemetery. Tate was killed the next year in 1959, in an automobile accident. He also is buried in Okmulgee.

Maxine moved back to Oklahoma and James went to OSU to college, where he got his degree. Maxine worked for seven years in Enid, Oklahoma for a newspaper. She moved to Stillwater in 1971, to be near Jim and had been there only a few months when she took Viral Pneumonia and died in the Stillwater hospital, August, 1971. She is buried in Okmulgee Cemetery.

James Bier Douglas got his degree at OSU and then worked for several Television Stations. One in Ada, Oklahoma and then on the Kennewick, Wasington to a TV station. He met and married Debra Hickey who was raised in Kennewick. They have two daughters, Jennifer Ann, and Laura Brier. Jim is now in the real estate business.

After Marjorie Cramer's husband passed away she lived with Sally, her youngest daughter in Tulsa, from 1958 until 1970. They moved to an addition two miles east of Broken Arrow. They moved to Ardmore in 1973. Marjorie came to Perry to live with her aging parents. She still resides in Perry and is a member of the First Christian Church, the Builders Class and the Hulda Circle of the CWF.

Doris Ann Bronner
By Doris (Petermann) Bronner

Doris Ann (Petermann) Bronner was born June 22, 1930 in Noble County, Oklahoma. After graduating from Shiloh School and Morrison High School, she went to Perry and worked at the Jack Smith five and ten cent store and Mrs. C. B. Forney's Ice Cream Parlor. She was married to Paul David (Pete) Bronner from Sunray, Texas on November 23, 1949 in Clovis, New Mexico. Pete served in the Navy on board the ship *USS Montague* until June of 1950 when he was discharged.

He went to work for Charles Malzahn as a field welder. When the company began making the Ditch Witch trenching machines, Pete helped build the new office and shop which has been added onto several times. Pete worked for Ditch Witch thirty-four years and eight months until his death February 14, 1985.

Paul and Doris had six children, five girls and one boy. Connie Ann was born March 10, 1951 in Guthrie, Oklahoma hospital. She attended kindergarten through sixth grade at the Lutheran School in Perry and Junior and Senior High School at Perry. She married Terry Chenoweth of Tulsa on January 31, 1970 at the Lutheran Church where she was a member. They live at Mannford, Oklahoma and have two children: Steven Todd born May 4, 1971 while his father was serving in the army in the Vietnam War. Kathryn Elizabeth was born July 24, 1977. Terry is a machinist and works in Tulsa, Oklahoma. Connie is working on a degree in elementary education at Oklahoma State University.

Deborah Faye was born July 14, 1953 at Perry Memorial Hospital. She attended the Lutheran School in Perry and graduated from Perry High School. She worked for Frank Ley Insurance until she married May 26, 1972. She married Daniel Pike of Eunice, New Mexico. He is vice-president of Engineering of Prime Cable. They live in Austin, Texas. They have one daughter, Miranda Rebecca born September 21, 1984. Daniel is working on his Doctorate. Deborah attended St. Edwards University. She works part time in accounting and computer work for CATV Design Associates.

Pamela Sue was born January 8, 1957 at Perry Memorial Hospital. She attended the Lutheran School and graduated from the Perry High School. She worked for Ditch Witch one summer and Swan Rubber Company before getting married on November 23, 1977 to John Everett Lovell of Glencoe, Oklahoma. They live on a farm eight miles east of Stillwater, Oklahoma where he farms for his parents. Pamela works for Moore Business Forms in Stillwater. They have two boys: Nathan John born August 30, 1979 and Mathew Everett born May 22, 1982.

Paula Jean was born June 13, 1960 at Perry Hospital. She attended the Lutheran School and Perry Junior High. After receiving her GED, Paula attended Sapulpa Vo-tech enrolled in a medical careers course. She attended Sand Springs Beauty College. Paula married Joel Smith November 9, 1984. She has two children from a previous marriage: Heather Gail born June 29, 1976 and Russell David born February 6, 1979. Joel is employed by Union School System near Tulsa, Oklahoma. Paula is employed at Mannford, Oklahoma as a cosmetologist.

Barbara Lynn was born at Perry Hospital on January 15, 1967. She attended the Lutheran School and graduated from Perry High School. She is employed locally.

Brian Eugene was born at Perry Hospital February 1, 1974. He attended the Lutheran School in Perry and is currently enrolled in the Junior High in Perry.

Napoleon B. Bryant
By Laura Pitts

This is the story of the family of Napoleon Bonapart Bryant and Martha Alice (McPheeters) Bryant, who were married in Hutchinson, Kansas, on May 11, 1889. My father was born July 4, 1849, near Madison, Missouri. His parents were Henry Bryant and Evelyn (Stevens) Bryant. My mother was born October 24, 1869, in Canton, Missouri. Her father was Charles Wesley McPheeters; her mother, Susan P. Moffit. Napoleon and Martha were living in Hutchinson, Kansas, when their first son, Elmer W., was born on June 16, 1890.

My father staked a claim in the run of 1892, 5 miles southwest of Kingfisher. As soon as he had built a large one-room house, he brought mother and Elmer to live on the claim and prove up and received their title to it. Another son, Charles Ora, was born October 16, 1892. He died on April 11, 1893. Henry Lynn was born January 17, 1894. Three years later, I, Laura, the first of 6 girls was born on January 26, 1897. Then Susan arrived on March 29, 1899. She was followed by Ruble on February 24, 1901.

Dad then had the opportunity to sell our farm and buy a half section in Reno county, Kansas, near my mother's people. So we moved with covered wagons, taking furniture, cattle, horses, a sow, chickens, and everything with us. We camped out at night and cooked on a campfire.

When we arrived at our new home, we had a large two-story, 4-bedroom house, a large barn, big chicken house, and windmill and pump house. No more drawing water up by the bucket out of a dug well. Also we were only a little more than a mile from a country store, doctor, church and school. About a year after we arrived in Kansas, a baby boy was born on July 3, 1903. He only lived a short while, dying that day. He is buried in the Lerado cemetery. My sister, Alpha, arrived August 3, 1904, followed by Amy Jo on October 10, 1906. Two years later, my brother, N. B. Jr. (Bud), arrived on November 24, 1908. Four years later, on January 1, 1912, the last child, Jessie Lee, was born. My mother, having born 5 sons and 6 daughters. Three of the boys lived to be adults, and all six girls made it.

N. B. and Alice Bryant and two daughters taken in 1907. (L to R): Alpha Nellie and Amy Jo.

My father was a brick-layer and stone-mason by trade and worked away from home much of the time. He also owned and ran a general store in Lerado for several years. In 1914, he sold the store and farms and bought 2 farms southwest of Billings — by that time Elmer was married and Lynn was planning on marriage — so in 1914, we again loaded up the covered wagons and moved lock, stock and barrel to near Billings. That fall, three of we girls enrolled in high school. We had to furnish our own transportation, so we drove in with a gray horse and a buggy. It was only about 3¾ miles.

Dad and mother lived on the home place until his death at the age of 86, on April 9, 1936. Mother stayed on the farm alone for several years then bought a house and moved into Billings, where she lived until her health failed her. She too, died at the age of 86, on March 16, 1956. She was 20 years younger than Dad. They are both buried in the Union cemetery at Billings, Oklahoma.

I remember Mother telling of the hard times they had when they first were on the claim down by Kingfisher. The Indian Reservation was not far from them. The Indians usually rode in groups going to town and many times they would leave the trail and ride in and ride around and around her house until she would come to the door. Then one would try to get her to say how many ponies he would have to give her for the white-headed (blonde) papoose. When she would tell them the girls were not for trade, they would ride away. But in a few days, here they were circling the house again and trying to see if she had changed her mind.

Elmer was the first to die. He died at 75 years of age on December 4, 1965. Elsie, his wife, had passed away September 27, 1957. He was survived by 3 children: Leo, who died May 7, 1966, and Twila Shoemake who died August 10, 1972, and Mrs. Carol Curby of Billings.

Jessie Lee died November 10, 1983, at Tonkawa. She was survived by her second husband, Leonard Hembree, three sons, Tommy, Jerry, and Keith Hannah. One son preceded her in death Don Hannah, who died January 22, 1976. Her first husband, A. J. Hannah, died many years ago.

Susan was never married but lived to be 85 before she died in Enid, on January 3, 1985. She was survived by four sisters, Laura Pitts and Ruble Lemmon of Perry, Alpha McWilliams, Tonkawa, and Amy Thorpe of Garber; two brothers, Lynn Bryant, Ponca City; and N. B. Jr. of Tulsa. Six girls and 3 boys grew to be adults, all excepting Susan, married and raised families. We have a family reunion the second Sunday in October, and usually have at least 75 there.

As I write this, it is just as I remember things in my 88th year on earth. I recall my mother telling when they were first on the claim down by Kingfisher, my father had a horse he rode to stake his claim but he had no plow. Their neighbor had a horse and a plow. My father let the neighbor use his horse if he would plow and plant for both of them. Dad would walk five miles into Kingfisher, where he worked from daylight until dusk for a dollar a day as a stone-mason. He then shared the dollar with the man who was doing the plowing and planting.

We were a large family, but if we were underpriviledged, we never knew it. I never recall being hungry nor having to do without clothing. We were a happy fun-loving bunch and most of us graduated from high school. Only one of the girls, Alpha, went to college.

Lula May Bush
By Frances Bush Lynn

Lula May Howard was born near Fountain Run, Kentucky June 4, 1885. Her parents were Mary Angline (Frances) and Thomas Hart Howard. Her grandfather was John Howard who came across the mountains to Kentucky and settled on the river where there was much large timber. He cleared the land, built his family a house and many tenant houses for his workers. He built the Howard school house and paid a teacher to come teach all the children. Lula's grandfather Francis married her grandmother when the grandmother was 14 years

Bryant family reunion about 1950 at Laura Pitts' home in Perry, OK. Bottom row (L to R): Lynn Bryant, Elmer Bryant, Alice Bryant, N. B. Jr. "Bud" Bryant. Top row (L to R): Laura Pitts, Susan Bryant, Jessie Lee Hannah, Amy Thorpe, Ruble Lemmon, Alpha McWilliams.

old, at which time her parents gave her a slave.

He fought in the Civil War and always said he would kill the man who killed him. He did. After the war, in a little country store, a man pulled a gun and shot him. He pulled a knife as he fell and ripped the man's stomach open.

Lula May was the middle child of nine who lived to be grown (2 brothers died in infancy). Her father built a family home near his father's house and the family grew up there. When she was a young woman, her father moved to

Lula May Bush on her 93rd birthday with her son Rev. Howard Bush and daughter Frances (Robinson).

Scottsville, Kentucky where he bought a store and lived for several years before moving to Bethpage, Tennessee. While they lived in Scottsville she was a telephone operator. She wanted to be a nurse but her parents didn't think it was proper for she might have to take care of a man.

In September 1909 she married Henry Bishop Bush. They lived with the family near Bowling Green, Kentucky until the last of December when they came to Oklahoma settling four miles south of Tulsa. Two sons were born there Henry Burton and Edward (Ed). They moved back to Tennessee in 1914 because of Lula's failing health. Francis Neal was born there in 1916. In 1917 they moved to Warren County, Kentucky near Bowling Green. Lula May was born there and died at the age of 2. They moved to Simpson County in December 1919, nine miles east of Franklin, Kentucky. James Howard and Lena Jewel were born here. They moved back to Tulsa in the fall of 1931. They moved to Morrison, Oklahoma May 1, 1954 where their daughter Frances and son-in-law Ray Robinson could help her care for her husband ill from hardening of the arteries. He died May 29, 1954 and was buried in Collinsville.

After putting her house in order and visiting her son at Santa Fe, New Mexico where he was pastor of the First Methodist Church she returned to Morrison where she lived the rest of her life. She joined the Methodist Church and the W.S.C.S. She made lots of new friends such as Mrs. Rudolph Harting and Mrs. Masheter with whom she talked on the phone everyday. When they died, it was hard for her to adjust. Fern (Hull) Hurt returned to her home next door and they became very good friends. She was president of W.S.C.S. when she was 80 years old and they ordered candy to sell to raise funds. She would take 3 or 4 boxes and go over town to sell them. First to the business where everyone in the store would buy. Then she went door to door. She not only sold all the candy but she met everyone in town. People said "How can you resist a little 80 year old lady carrying candy?"

The neighbor children called her "Grandma Bush" so it was easy for the children at church, who she had to hug every Sunday, to do the same. She never missed Sunday School or Church Services. The church gave her a plaque for always being there. Her grandchildren said they were going to be like grandma and always go to church.

In March 1979 she had a stroke and went into a coma. She recovered but her memory was so affected that it was not possible to care for her at home. The family has felt she willed herself to life until her two youngest granddaughters had their babies in June. Mary (Robinson) Christensen had a baby girl on her birthday and was named Elizabeth. Patricia (Sanders) Haskill's baby was born June 29 and is called Sarah. After she received this news it just seemed she lost her will to live. She died July 13.

John M. Carpenter
By Sam Carpenter

John Martin Carpenter was born October 29, 1842 in Garrard County, Kentucky, between Crab Orchard and Paint Lick. At the start of Civil War, he joined the 7th Regiment of the Kentucky cavalry as a sergeant and was with General Sherman on his famous March to the Sea. He also took part in the battle of Lookout Mountain, Gettysburg and Chacellorsville. Upon his return home, Carpenter discovered many of his neighbors had been fighting for the Confederate Army, so the fighting continued.

John M. married H. Fannie Reid in Garrard County, Kentucky where they had lived for several years. Fannie was born February 2, 1841 in Kentucky.

Across the road to the north from Carpenter's home stood the cabin of the slave who was depicted in the book, *Uncle Tom's Cabin* and the residence of the negro slave's owner. The owner of Uncle Tom shot Carpenter through the shoulder. Firing back, Carpenter shot the slave owner in one of his eyes. Because he was surrounded by Confederates, Carpenter decided it was time to leave.

John and his brother, Will, also a Union soldier, headed west and made it to Kansas where they farmed and ranched a few miles west of El Dorado.

In one of the Civil War battles, the regiment to which the Carpenter brothers were assigned captured a Confederate general, John Hunt Morgan. Morgan and the Carpenters had been friends in Kentucky before the war.

General Morgan gave his 14 inch knife with an ivory handle decorated with gold plate and encased in a solid silver sheath, to the Carpenter brothers for safekeeping. Morgan died and the knife was taken to Kansas when the Carpenter brothers traveled west.

The knife, kept in the Carpenter family for over 100 years, was presented in 1980 to the Oklahoma Historcial Society and now is displayed in the Confederate Room of the Oklahoma Historical building in Oklahoma City.

When Harriet Beecher Stowe wrote the novel, *Uncle Tom's Cabin*, she stayed in a residence two houses from Betty Carpenter's home in Crab Orchard, Kentucky.

Across the road west from the Carpenter plantation house, a two-story log structure, was the colonial home of the Walker family, orginator of the Walker hunting hound. The Walker family home still stands.

After locating near El Dorado, John and Will Carpenter surveyed Winfield and Wichita, Kansas. They hauled lumber for the first frame house in Wichita. John did some hunting, freighting the game to the railroad and at one time worked on the Santa Fe south into the "Strip."

When the Cherokee Strip opened for settlement, John M.'s son, Sam Carpenter, made the run for land and located two miles west of Ceres, Oklahoma. All of Sam Carpenter's brothers settled in Oklahoma. The Carpenters established a hardware store in Red Rock, Oklahoma and farmed in the vicinity of Red Rock.

John M. sold his land in Kansas and moved to Florida where he lived for 17 years. Later he bought a house in Red Rock where he died, June 18, 1928. Funeral services were held in the High School auditorium, after which the body was taken to El Dorado, Kansas to be buried beside his wife and four daughters.

Carpenter Brothers
By Sam Carpenter

James Butler Carpenter was born July 28, 1868 in Green County, Illinois, the son of H. Fannie (Reid) and John Martin Carpenter. His parents had lived in Illinois for three years before moving to Eldorado, Kansas where he grew to manhood.

James Butler (Jim) made the run and settled on a farm five miles west of Ceres, Oklahoma where he began to break sod and plant his crops. On July 28, 1898, he married a young French girl by the name of Cora Blair. Cora was born in March, 1878 in Kansas. Both of her parents were born in Indiana. They had one daughter, Mildred Fannie born November 26, 1904 in Red Rock.

When the townsite of Red Rock was opened, Jim and Cora left the farm and moved to town engaging in the Hardware business. He built a store building and then built a house. In April, 1902, his brother, Dick, came to Red Rock and lived with them until his marriage. Dick bought a half interest in the business.

In 1913, Jim sold his half interest in the store to a younger brother, Logan, then bought the farm adjoining the townsite on the west, where he resided and farmed until his death. The original house was small but Jim eventually enlarged it, over several years, to a nice bungalow.

Besides farming, Jim served as assistant mail carrier out of Red Rock to the west for several years. When the Baptist Church was built in town, Jim and Cora became early members where Jim served as deacon for 15 years and a member of 29 years.

Jim died July 14, 1917 and is buried in the cemetery at Ceres. Cora and daughter, Mildred moved to Ponca City to make their home when Cora married E. Crocker. After his death, she moved to Sedgwick, Kansas to live near her daughter. Cora died April 3, 1971 in the Perry Nursing home and was buried in the Ceres Cemetery.

Andrew Reid Carpenter was born February 8, 1871 at El Dorado, Kansas, the fourth child and second son of John M. and Fannie Carpenter.

When the Cherokee Strip was opened, Reid made the run with his brother, Jim. They camped at the border the night before where hundreds of others camped. Reid filed on a claim west of Ceres where he built a house and began breaking sod to plant crops.

As soon as farm life was established, Reid returned to El Dorado in 1895 and on January 16, married his sweetheart that he had left behind, teaching school near there. He returned to Oklahoma with his new bride, the former Eva V Hess, to set up housekeeping and raise a family.

Two of their girls were born on the farm near Billings. Reid then sold the farm and moved into town where he ran a grocery store. Around 1902, he returned to El Dorado, then later moved to Harrisonville, Missouri, where he died October 9, 1940 and Eva, December 31, 1950 and are buried in the Orient Cemetery east of Harrisonville. Their children are: Irene M. — May 1, 1896; Helen M. — January 4, 1901; and Leo M. — December 11, 1904.

Samuel Davis Carpenter was born April 13, 1873 at El Dorado, Kansas the fifth child of John M. and Fannie Carpenter. He came to Oklahoma from Kansas in 1893 in the run but was a little too young to stake a claim so in 1894 he bought 80 acres three miles west of Ceres, Oklahoma.

On April 10, 1895, he was married to Lura May Jones, daughter of William W. and Alice M. Jones, in their home near Perry, Oklahoma on the Black Bear Creek. Lura May was born near South Bend, Indiana in May 1876 but moved to Kansas when she was three years old. She grew to womanhood in Kansas about two miles from the Carpenter homestead. Their first son, Chester Ray, age 6 months died August 6, 1898. In October 1899, a tiny daughter, Vera Blanche, was born weighing three pounds. She was laid in a shoe box wrapped in cotton and hot water bottles.

In 1900, Sam bought 160 acres four miles west of Red Rock, along the Red Rock Creek. Here they raised a family of five children. Besides the two mentioned their other children were: Esther Lucy, born May 30, 1904; Mahala Juanita born August 12, 1907; Samuel David born December 27, 1912; and James Butler born October 18, 1918.

Sam died February 22, 1954 at Red Rock. Lura May died July 17, 1931. They are buried in the Ceres Cemetery.

William D. Carpenter was born October 3, 1875 at El Dorado, Kansas, the sixth child of John M. and Fannie Carpenter. Will made the run along with his brothers, then later bought a farm and lived in a log cabin four miles east and two south of Billings, Oklahoma. In 1898, he married Ida Fannin, who had moved with her parents from Dyersburg, Tennessee, settling 12 miles north of Perry. Two sons, John and Floyd, were born in the home near Billings. Will later built a comfortable home on the land.

In 1907, Will, with his family and youngest brother, Ollie, moved to Kiefer, Oklahoma and worked several teams in the oil field there. In 1910, they all went to Florida where his father, John M. bought land, the boys helping him to clear it and set out a large orange and grapefruit orchard. Then in 1913, Will and family returned to Oklahoma buying a farm south of Broken Arrow, Oklahoma. Ida died August 15, 1930 and Will April 13, 1938. They are buried in Tulsa Memorial Park Cemetery.

Arthur B. Carrier
By Melvern S. Rupp

Arthur Benjamin Carrier was born March 18, 1896, to Frank and Sarah Paulina Smith Carrier in Perry, Oklahoma. The farm located five miles west of Perry, homesteaded by Arthur's father in the Cherokee Strip Run of September 16, 1893, was the only home Arthur knew during his years as a youth.

Arthur was drafted into the army in World War I and received basic training at San Antonio, Texas. He was sent overseas where he served in the infantry on the front lines in France. He was awarded the Purple Heart for injuries received two hours after the Armistice was signed, but before word of the signing was received in the battlefields.

Less than a year later on December 20, 1919, Arthur married Ethel Margaret Golliver. Ethel was born July 15, 1898, at LaRosa, Illinois. At the age of nine she came to Oklahoma with her parents.

Arthur and Ethel established residence on the section east of Arthur's parents and farming became their lifelong career. Ethel taught school for a short time. They lived at that location until after Arthur's mother died September 7, 1926. Soon after that, in 1927, they moved into the house on the homestead to live with Arthur's father. They lived with Frank until his death August 22, 1935.

Sometime after Frank's death, Arthur and Ethel purchased the shares of the farm owned by his sisters, Myrtle Baetz and Alta McCormick and his brother, Ernest. Arthur retired from farming in 1961, but they continued to live on the farm until after their farm equipment and cattle auction in July, 1964. They moved to Perry in August, 1964 where they lived until their deaths, Ethel's on March 11, 1970 and Arthur's on April 15, 1980.

Arthur and Ethel were active in community affairs. Ethel was active in church activities, women's clubs, Americn Legion and DAV Auxiliaries. They both did weekly volunteer work at the Veterans Hospital in Oklahome City, for a short while after Arthur's retirement and their move to Perry.

Arthur was a member of the White School Board and an Elder of the First Christian Church in Perry for many years. He was an active member of the Ellis-Jirous post of the American Legion in Perry and the Disabled American Veterans.

Arthur and Ethel had two sons, Arthur Burl, born October 22, 1931 and

Ethel and Arthur Carrier - west side of house on the homestead farm.

Cleo Wayne, born August 29, 1933. Burl and Wayne both served in the Army during the Korean Conflict. Burl married Rena Rupp from near Perry, Wayne married Roberta Fox from Hugoton, Kansas.

Burl and Wayne now own the farm, homesteaded by Frank Carrier, their grandfather, and then owned by their parents, Arthur and Ethel. Burl lives in Stillwater, Oklahoma and Wayne lives in Yukon, Oklahoma.

Arthur and Ethel have two granddaughters and one grandson by each of their sons, Burl and Wayne. They also have (as of 1986) three great-grandchildren.

Frank J. Carrier
By Mrs. Ed J. (Doris) Brown

Frank James Carrier was born June 20, 1871 in Cameron Mills, New York to Mariva Jane (Talbot) and George Carrier. In the 1900 Census of Noble County, Oklahoma in the city of Perry, George Carrier is listed as born in May of 1846 in England and both parents were born in England. His occupation was shoemaker and he came to America in 1860. His wife, Mariva, was born in January 1853 in New York, her father in New Hampshire and her mother in New York. There were two children in the household: George born in September 1881 in New York and Bessie born January 1888 in Kansas. At the opening of the Cherokee Strip he made the run on horseback, and staked a farm five miles west of Perry

First frame house on homestead about 1900. The man in background is unknown. (L to R): Ernest, Frank James, and Sarah Paulina Carrier.

the northwest ¼ of section 24 in Warren Valley township. This farm is still in the family. On April 23, 1894, he married Sarah Pauline Smith. She was born January 25, 1873 at Mt. Sterling, Ohio, the daughter of Margaret McCafferty and Isaac M. Smith. As an early teenager she moved to Kansas with her parents and in 1890 moved to Oklahoma.

Frank and Sarah lived in a sod house on the farm he had staked, later building a small home. In later years a nice home was built at the same location and they lived there until their deaths. Frank supplemented his farm income with a threshing crew during the summers months. In the winter months the family lived in a small house in east Perry, while he worked in the cotton gin. Frank and Sarah Pauline were members of the First Christian Church of Perry.

Frank loved to use his pocket knife. The grandchildren loved to watch him whittle on wood and also watch as he sat in front of the fire paring apples without ever breaking the skin. Sarah Paulina's cellar was always filled with canned fruit and vegetables, which was a delight to her grandchildren.

Born to Frank James and Sarah Paulina Carrier were Arthur Benjamin Carrier, Myrtle Manila Carrier Baetz; Alta E. Carrier McCormick and Ernest E. Carrier.

Sarah Paulina died September 7, 1926 following surgery and is buried in Grace Hill cemetery. Upon her death their oldest son Arthur B. Carrier and his wife, the former Ethel Golliver, moved into the home with Frank James Carrier. He died on August 22, 1935 of apoplexy and is buried beside his wife in Grace Hill cemetery, Perry.

Arthur and Ethel Carrier continued to make their home there until their retirement when they moved to town.

The homestead is still owned by the sons of Arthur and Ethel Carrier; Burl Carrier and family of Stillwater, Oklahoma and Wayne Carrier and family of Yukon, Oklahoma. The living children of Frank and Sarah Paulina Carrier are Ernest E. Carrier of Florida, and Mrs. Otto (Myrtle) Baetz, who resides in Perry. Two daughters of Myrtle Baetz still live in Perry with their husbands. They are Mrs. Charles (Manila) Francis and Mrs. Edward (Doris) Brown.

Rebecca Schaffer Cartwright

By Dorothy Durkee

Rebecca Caroline Schaffer was born January 8, 1861, in Walnut Township, Polk County, Iowa. Her mother was Margaret Jane Wilson born December 21, 1825 in Brooks County, West Virginia to Mary Duke and William Wilson. Her father was Richard Schaffer born July 3, 1824. Margaret Jane and Richard married February 27, 1845 in Ohio and moved by oxen and covered wagon from Athens County Ohio to Polk County Iowa with six children, three more including Rebecca were born there.

I met Rebecca in 1937, she was an energetic 76. Based on our relationship and things told me I would describe her as a five foot red head, even after it was white, educated, opinionated, intelligent, independent, shrewd in business, talented seamstress, skilled cook, and maybe generous to a fault. She opened her home to people who needed a place to live. She had what she called "old people" living in her home that she cared for after I knew her.

Her first marriage, September 1, 1880, was to Henry Cartwright. He was born January 20, 1845, in Newmarket, Ontario, Canada to Dorothea Consort and Henry Cartwright, Sr. He was seven when his family moved to Keokuk, Iowa. Five years later they moved to the Des Moines area.

Henry Senior must have appreciated the care given him by Rebecca, as he gave her a full child's share in his estate.

Their first child, Gertie Blanch was born April 22, 1885, on the same Polk County farm where her mother was born. Next came George, March 22, 1888 and then Dorothy in 1897.

The Cartwright and Veitz families rented a box car for the move to Oklahoma. George and Eldon Veitz rode in the box car, probably illegally. The rest rode coach.

They settled first in White Rock Township, where Gertie met and married George Day Durkee March 15, 1903. We know little about this time, just that Henry and Rebecca moved to Perry before February 15, 1904, as Willard S. Durkee was born to Gertie in their home.

We know also that Henry had served as a janitor of the Perry Methodist Church for two years at the time of his death March 18, 1906.

George Cartwright finished 4th grade in Iowa and didn't go back to school in Oklahoma. He worked on the farm, then started work for a telephone company. He installed the last switchboard that was in Billings. He was on the organization of Southwestern Bell and was a General Manager at the time of his death May 20, 1940.

Margaret Jane Schaffer joined her daughter in Perry in 1906. She bought a ⅓ interest in Lot 12 Block 62 NW Perry for $210. She sold it to Rebecca for a profit, but Rebecca sold it for a larger profit. Margaret also bought the SE ¼ of Section 19 23N 1E for $4,500. Margaret Jane died in Perry, June 2, 1909. Her will was probated in Noble County, the farm was in it and Rebecca served as administrator.

"Mrs. R.C. Cartwrights" was the name of Rebecca's Perry Cafe. Her ad in the 1910 Perry Business Directory read "Best Short Orders" and "Chili" in the city. We were told that her chili recipe brought her more money than her cafe when she sold it.

We wonder why, and are amused that her son-in-law, George Durkee, applied for and bought the marriage license when Frank Wilkins and Lina (Frank's name for her) married December 21, 1911.

Frank's wife, Ceola, had died Oc-

Rebecca (Schaffer-Cartwright) and Frank Wilkins.

tober 29, 1901, leaving five children. The oldest 15 years old, Iva; the youngest 2 year old Kate. So each contributed a 13 year old girl to the family.

They farmed and lived north of Perry, "Lina", who loved growing things joined Frank in the outdoor work.

Dorothy married Robert Wright February 27, 1913, with her mother's permission. They were divorced and she married Claud Pease. They had two daughters, Gladys and Geneva.

Frank and Lina were prosperous and started taking a trip every year. Driving a Model T loaded with a tent and camping equipment. She told me about the pants, boots and other clothes she wore, which were not considered appropriate apparel for a lady in that day.

They even drove a Model T up Pikes Peak. On the way down, the brakes went out. He said, "Lina, hold on I'm going to head her into the mountain." He did, and neither were hurt but the car was demolished. It didn't stop their love of mountains or camping. Through the years they traveled extensively.

Wanting conveniences such as electricity, gas and running water, they bought the house at 517 Fir St. in Perry. Frank died in 1931 and was buried at Ceres Cemetery by his first wife.

Rebecca was a victim of the beliefs and laws of that time. Everything belongs to the man. When they married they were about equal financially, but by the time he died, everything was in his name. His will gave her the use of and income from their property during her lifetime, with everything to go to his children upon her death.

She continued to live at 517 Fir in the large two story house, set on several lots. A large garden was usually planted, there were grape vines, fruit trees, berry plants, and flowers, especially rose bushes and climbing roses.

She rented out the upstairs as apartments or rooms. Sometimes offering room and board. At times, Frank's daughter, Ora and Gertie were also there. Always busy, they sewed, pieced quilts, tied comforts, braided rugs, knitted and crocheted in their spare time.

Rebecca remained active in the Methodist Church, walking to and from as long as she was able. She never learned to drive so shopping, paying bills, etc. were done on foot. A taxi was for lazy people or a luxury to be indulged in when ill.

She died at home August 9, 1944, and is buried at Grace Hill by Henry on a lot with her son, George, and granddaughter, Thelma Durkee. At the time of her death, she had only eighteen grandchildren, but now there are great grandchildren by the dozen.

Florian W. Cermak
By Joe Cermak

Florian W. Cermak was born in April or May 1862, near Prague, Czeckoslovakia where the family farmed and raised geese. As a young boy he herded the geese in the country side. Everyone lived in villages and went back and forth to the country. Most of the homes were more than one story high. On the ground level the horses, cattle and geese were housed and the family lived up above.

All young men were required to serve several years in the army. While he was in the army, he and a buddy decided they didn't like the army so they made plans to come to America. Florian didn't tell his parents but did tell his sister. One night they boarded a ship and set sail for America. Some on board became sea sick during the 30 days the trip took but Florian made it OK.

The ship landed in New York, the two worked at odd jobs. Work was hard to find as neither could speak English only Czeck. They moved on to Chicago where Florian drove a beer wagon. He saw no future in that so he and his buddy separated, the buddy going back to Czechoslovakia and Florian going to Nebraska to work on a farm.

This was about the time of the opening of the Cherokee Strip and he decided to come and see what it was like. He found a 160 acre farm for sale (SE ¼ of Section 25, 23 North, Range 1 East). After buying the farm and one horse he had to trade his watch for a second horse. He made a dugout to live in and planted a crop of corn. He sold the corn to a man in Red Rock who turned hogs into the field. The man had to fence it. Florian had enough wire to fence his whole 160 acre farm. Florian married a neighbor girl Anna Hynek (1870-1954).

Florian and Anna's first home was a one room and to help weigh it down so the winds wouldn't blow it away the walls were filled with rock. As the family came along the house was enlarged to eight rooms, five rooms downstairs and the half story above with three rooms.

They had a windmill installed at the well which was 400 feet from the house. A large tank was placed in one bedroom which was above the kitchen. The water was piped down to the kitchen which gave them running water. When the tank was being filled it had to be watched or it would overflow.

The closest telephone was three miles. There was no electricity until the late 1940s. When the house was wired, the rock between the walls was found. It made it difficult to run the wires in this space.

Florian and Anna had seven children: Adolph born in 1897, Elizabeth 1900-1985; Anna 1902-1970; Wesley 1904 - ; John 1907 - ; Albert 1909-1948; Joe 1910 - . Adolph and Joe were farmers, Elizabeth, Wesley, Anna and John were school teachers. Albert did some farming. He was attending college when he became ill and had to leave. He died in his late 30s in 1948. He is buried in the Bohemian National Cemetery north of Perry beside his father, Florian W. who died in 1952 and his mother Anna who died in 1954.

Frank Chace
By Charles W. Chace

Frank Chace was born at Lockport, Niagra County, New York the 17th March 1873. He was a descendant of William Chace of Roxbury and Yarmouth, Massachusetts, a 1630 emigrant from England. Frank married Clara Ellen Anderson 24th December, 1893 at Larone, Butler County, Kansas. Larone was founded by an uncle of Frank soon after the Civil War.

Frank and Clara moved to Snyder, Oklahoma about 1900 with their three children. Between the years of 1902 and 1915 four more children were born to this family.

Frank was a farmer and did custom threshing throughout Kiowa County, Oklahoma. He had several threshing machines and steam engines during this period of time, including one of the biggest steam engine and threshing machines ever manufactured.

About 1921, Frank moved his family to the Morrison, Oklahoma area. The children born to Frank and Clara were: Leta, who married Henry Viet; Lloyd, who married Olga Kopp; Harold, who married Julia Coffelt; Eugene, who was killed at the Frisco Railroad Crossing, north of their house the 6th of May,

Frank and Clara Chace December 24, 1943 - 50th wedding anniversary.

1922; Virgil, who married Gertie Farr; Leland, who married Hazel L. Akers, granddaughter of two Cherokee Strip Runners and Homesteaders, Martin L. Collins and Charles Akers; Rayford who married Grace Curtis.

The family's threshing equipment and livestock were shipped from Snyder to Morrison by rail. The large steam engine and threshing machine were rarely, if ever, used in Noble County because there were many bridges that would not support the weight of the machines. However, Mr. Chace did have a machine he used in that area, that had two bundle racks, one on each side of the throat, with two men with pitch forks, one on each rack could not choke down, as was sought by many a young man so he could get a rest period while the machine choked down. This was never successful.

In the 1920s and 1930s it was common practice for oil companies to dump salt water and other pollutants into water-ways. Frank was involved in a law suit because Black Bear Creek was polluted and caused livestock deaths. Former Governor Henry S. Johnston was his attorney. It is believed this was a class action suit. Possibly Frank was one of the first environmentalists in the Cherokee Strip area. The outcome of this is probably found in Noble County Court records.

Frank was too young to run in the Cherokee Strip opening. He bought a farm 3 miles east of Morrison from the Hall family. This family raised horses. They had a large house and a barn for horses. The floors of the stalls were made of oak. The mow was used for storing bales and loose hay. This was a favorite place to play for Frank's grandchildren during holidays and family get togethers.

All of Frank and Clara's children are deceased at this time, (1985) except Leland of Morrison, Oklahoma. Many grandchildren, great-grandchildren and great-great-grandchildren of Frank and Clara still live in Noble, Payne and Pawnee county areas.

Calvin William Cheek
By Joe Highfill

Calvin William Cheek was born in 1826 in North Carolina. He married Corneilia Penelope Tinnen on November 27, 1854 in Orange County, North Carolina. She was born in 1826 in North Carolina, the daughter of David and Jane Tinnen. The Cheeks had three children: Bedford, Robina Jane (Moore), and Theopholus.

Mr. Cheek was a Baptist minister and preached in North Carolina, Indiana and Kansas. He also farmed in Kansas. In the 1890's they were living in Arkansas. When Mrs. Cheeks's health failed they moved to Noble county to live with their daughter, Robina Jane Moore in Walnut township. One day a tornado hit the house and almost had a tragic effect. Mrs. Cheek was too ill to move and when the tornado hit, it lifted the kitchen table up and left the table covering Mrs. Cheek. When the debris fell, the table kept it from hitting her and saved her life. Mrs. Cheek died about 1902 and was buried in the Shelton cemetery.

Rev. Cheek stayed on with his daughter. This was not a very pleasant situation for him. He was a Baptist minister in the home of a staunch

Calvin and Cornelia Cheek in the 1880s; photo taken from a tin type.

Presbyterian son-in-law. Rev. Cheek was forbidden to talk about religion since it would cause an arguement. When asked how they remembered their grandfather his granddaughters replied, "very quiet".

Rev. Cheek died on January 6, 1911 in Noble county and was buried beside his wife in the Shelton cemetery. Only two small foot stones with the initials C.W.C. and C.P.C. mark their graves.

Clark B. Chenoweth
By Dorothy Ewy

Clark (Click) Braden Chenoweth Sr. (born February 10, 1885 in South Haven, Kansas, Sumner County, died

Anna (Christensen), Clark Chenoweth and son Star - 1910.

December 24, 1978) married November 26, 1908 in Perry, Oklahoma Anna Elizabeth Christensen (born May 2, 1890 in Lincoln, Nebraska, died October 10, 1946). She was the daughter of Neils Christensen and Libbie May (Hook) Christensen of Perry.

He was a direct descendant of immigrants John and Mary (Calvert) Chenoweth. His great-grandparents James Hackley and Artemecia Catherine (Birkhead) Chenoweth left Nelson County Kentucky to reside in Perry, Illinois, Pike County. Clark's parents Joseph Steven and Anna Marie (Davis) Chenoweth came to Kansas in 1878. They had eleven children Percy, Reu, Bob, Nellie, Minerva, Joe, Asa Luella, Ruth, Clark and Lee.

His mother died when Clark was fifteen months old. He remained with his father. Soon he was to have a grocery, clothing store in South Haven. At the age of eight Clark, made the Cherokee run riding his pony along side of his father's wagon. They staked out land about three miles south of Braman. They later sold the claim and went back to Missouri for a few years. His father married three more times. Clark and his dad, Joseph came to Oklahoma in 1902 and lived and worked with his brother Bob who lived three miles northeast of Perry. This year they were building the Old National Bank, and the railroad northeast of town.

Clark never had much education, he finished the fifth grade McGuffey reader age thirteen in Missouri. He was a very good speller and had a gift of gab!

In 1912, Clark worked for American Bell Telephone in Carmen, Oklahoma, by then he had four children: Star,

L-R: Clark, Anna, Star, Luella (Ewy), (Gregg), Edd P., Dorothy (Ewy), Vira M. (Hejduk) (Horton), Clark B. Jr., Gladys M. (Meier), Libbie (Norton), Mary (Goodwin), Billie Joe - 1945.

Luella, Edd, and Dorothy were born in Carmen. Clark and wife, Anna, lived on many places renting, share croping.

In 1921, the family moved to Fellows, California, Kern County where he worked in the oil fields, he returned to Oklahoma in 1924 and farmed.

During the Depression in 1930 he was foreman on the county roads. He became a master rock mason, he helped build the Perry Armory, Stadium, Elementary school that burned, Perry Plumbing Co. Building and the Church of God in Enid where he was baptized.

When war was declared in 1941, he worked in Norman, Oklahoma building barricks for soldiers, Bert Hejduk was made foreman (Bobbie's husband). He traveled from Lexington, to Sentinel and Alva working, he became a member of the union.

They sold their home in Garber and bought a home at 503 Maple in Perry in 1944. Anna died 1946, Clark lived to be almost 94 and had over a hundred descendants.

Clark and Anna had thirteen children and raised ten: Star Steven (born December 11, 1909 died December 11, 1981 in Perry). He married October 18, 1933 in Pawnee, Mattilene E. Shelton (born March 19, 1914 in Guthrie died September 9, 1984 in San Diego, California). Their children: Starletta, Gayle, Joyce, Norleta, Ila, Star Jr., Ray.

Luella Victoria (born July 28, 1911 in Perry) married first October 18, 1930 in Perry, Harold Ewy December 22, 1908 in Noble County. He died February 16, 1969 in Perry. Children: Betty, Melvin, Ruth, Connie Vickie, Dan. She married second C.O. Gregg (Tiny) of Lucine.

Edd Preston (born September 16, 1913 in Carmen) married December 29, 1936 in Perry to Alta Madia West (December 15, 1918 in Arkansas) Children: Patricia, Nancy Donna and Capt. Edd.

Dorothy Ann (born February 29, 1916 in Carmen, Oklahoma) married September 10, 1932 to Paul Ewy (born April 18, 1911 in Noble County). He died June 10, 1976 in Perry. Children: Peggy, Janet, Jim.

Vira M. (Bobbie) (born July 7, 1918 in Perry) married (first) Bert Hejduk in 1935. They had a daughter, June. Bobbie married the second time in 1948 John Horton. John raised June.

Clark Braden Jr. (born June 11, 1920 in Perry) married first June 23, 1946 to Francis V. Hurt in Fort Worth, Texas. Children: Timothy Terry, Betty. He married the second time November 7, 1973 Janice Pate Rhoades (born May 12, 1947 in Los Angeles, California). Children: Susan (Rhoades) Chenoweth, Manley Clark Chenoweth.

Gladys Mae (born May 3, 1922 in Fellows, Calif.) married February 13, 1945 in Corvallis, Oregon to Paul E. Meier (born March 29, 1920 in Corvallis). Children: Wade, Jill, Barry, Dan.

Libbie Gean (born August 16, 1924 in Perry) married November 7, 1943 in Sapulpa, Oklahoma, Sgt. Hope Norton (born November 23, 1917 in Sand Springs, Oklahoma).

Mary Mildred (born September 1, 1926, Perry) married August 14, 1945 in Tulsa to Shirley James Goodwin (born March 4, 1921 in Vale, Oregon) Children: Shirley (girl), Wiley, Miles, Sally.

Bill Joe (born December 31, 1928 in Perry) married August 27, 1954 in Sharon, Wisconsin, Roberta J. Brandenburg (born October 24, 1932 in Beloit, Wisconsin). Children: Allen Scott.

Dollie Marie was born October 19, 1934 and died four hours later in Noble County.

Neils C. Christensen

By Libbie Gean Norton

Neils Christian Christensen was born January 24, 1854 in Alback Hjorring township, Jylland, Denmark. He was a sailor in Denmark before he came to America in 1885. He was the son of Julianne (Neilson) and Christen Christensen. He married Libbey Mae Hook, August 17, 1889, in Lincoln, Nebraska. She was the daughter of Harriet Elizabeth (Wells) and William Hook. She was born March 30, 1871 in Wheatland, New York. Her brother's story (William Chesterfield Hook) can be found in this book.

Neils and Libby had three children when they moved to White Rock, Oklahoma Territory in 1894. They bought a farm, improved it and farmed until 1909, when they sold out and moved to a farm near Perry.

Neils started a livery stable and blacksmith shop where he also bought and sold scrap iron and hides. This business was located two blocks east of the courthouse square across the tracks from the Santa Fe depot. They later bought a house at 405 Locust street on fourteen lots. On this acreage he had one of the first filling stations. He built a two room cabin; the homeplace and barn are still there today (1985).

The Christensens had five children as follows: Anna Elizabeth, born May 2, 1890 at Lincoln, Nebraska, died October 10, 1946, married November 26, 1908 at Perry, Oklahoma, Clark Braden Chenoweth Sr. Their children: Star, Luella, Edd, Dorothy, Vira (Bobbie) Clark Jr., Gladys, Libbie, Mary, Billie and Dollie.

Christeanne Victoria Christensen was born at Lincoln, Nebraska, March 3, 1892, and died November 5, 1963 at Oklahoma City. She married, first, Roudolph Starkey, March 4, 1910. They had one child, Elsie C. Starkey. She married, second, George Cass, in 1922. Their children are George (Pete), Guy C. and Alice M. Cass.

Neal Robert Christensen was born March 6, 1894 at Lincoln, Nebraska and died June 11, 1958 in Perry, Oklahoma. He married Ida Louise Reschke, February 4, 1920. They have one daughter, Esther.

Roy Gilbert Christensen was born August 26, 1896 at White Rock, Oklahoma and died May 11, 1933 at Sawtell, California. He married Josephine Chamblin, June 13, 1919. Their children were: Wilbur, Ruth, Roy G. Jr., and Hellen J.

Harry Allen Christensen was born March 3, 1899, at White Rock, Oklahoma and died July 30, 1984 at San Bernardino, California. He married Ada Elizabeth Holt. Their children were

Livery Stable and Salvage at 421 Cedar. (L to R): Steve Diebold, Libby Christensen, Gladys (Porter) and Neils Christensen.

Maxine H. Neal, Charles, Mable and Calvin.

Mary Mildred Christensen was born July 25, 1901 at White Rock, Oklahoma. She married Toby Eugne Rogers January 29, 1923. Their children: Robert L. and Clara M.

Alice Buelah Christensen was born July 8, 1904, at White Rock, Oklahoma. She married Edgar W. Tate, September 26, 1926. She lives on the homeplace at Perry. They had one child, Lillie M.

An infant son died before being named. He was buried in Floral Ridge cemetery near White Rock.

Gladys Mae Christensen was born April 26, 1910 at Perry, Oklahoma. She married Otis Porter January 16, 1927. They live at Pawnee, Oklahoma. Their children: Betty, Otis, Harry, Mary, Sherman, Roy, and Gladys.

Neils and Libbie also raised a foster son, Jens Karl (Carl) Rasmussen, who was born March 17, 1887 in Denmark. He died June 25, 1972 at Perry, Oklahoma. In 1909, he worked for the Creamery and later in the blacksmith shop with Neils Christensen. He retired from the railroad and lived on the old homeplace at 405 Locust Street. Carl and Neal R. Christensen served in France during World War I. George Cass served 22 months on foreign soil and Roy G. served in American Theater during World War I.

Neils died February 13, 1936 and Libbie died July 26, 1957, in Perry, Oklahoma. They are buried in Grace Hill cemetery, Perry, Oklahoma.

Libby M. (Hook) and Neils Christensen about 1889.

Charles Christoph
By Mrs. Ted Newton

Charles Christoph was born in New York, May 8, 1860. Both of his parents were born in Germany. He was in Kansas when the Cherokee Strip was to be opened for white settlement. Christoph made the run, riding one of the first trains coming north from Orlando. He first built a 12' x 14' building on the courthouse square facing the east and started a second hand store. After he had made the run he quickly returned to Kansas and took over the contents of a furniture store in payment for a debt. He shipped this furniture to Perry and started a business. A couple of the chairs are still in the family.

When he was required to vacate his position upon notice that he was

Charles Christoph May 8, 1860 - December 10, 1932.

situated on government land, he moved his building and merchandise to a site on "B" street between 6th and 7th streets. At this time he specialized strictly in second hand furniture.

He married Mattie Newton about 1889, a widow with four children: George A. born July 1881, Avis born in July 1882 in Kansas; Frank born February 1884 in Kansas and Fred born December 1885 in Kansas.

In 1894, Christoph employed as his assistant his step-son, George A. Newton. In the meantime, he had made his first advancement, having moved into a 25' x 40' building on 7th street between "B" and "C" streets. His next development came with his changing his location a half block north, just south of where the Conoco Filling Station now stands. He moved to the south side of the square in 1898, at which time his new business really developed. It was here he added undertaking to his flourishing business and it became the Christoph-Newton furniture and undertaking business. Two years later, he established his business in the old Dr. S. A. Moore building where the Masonic building is now located, while they were erecting the building on the south west corner of the square.

In 1900, the south part of this building was finished and on January 18, 1901, they moved into the building complete with elevator. This elevator is believed to be the first one in Perry. The building is still standing, being 50 feet in width, 150 feet in length and is three floors high. Charles Christoph died December 10, 1932 and his wife, Mattie died December 23 in the same year. They are buried in Grace Hill cemetery.

Albert Pierce Clark Sr.
By Elnora Sappington

With America just reaching its 100th birthday, Albert Pierce Clark was born, January 27, 1876, in the snow covered foot hill country of northwestern Missouri, at Union Star, the son of John and Susan Clark. Pierce's father, a former Alabaman, had started home to join the Southern cause when he found that his money had been stolen from his vest pocket. He lost his money and didn't get to go home when the war started. He finally ended up in the Confederacy but never saw battlefield action. Eighteen years after Pierce's birth, his father came to Oklahoma to see a friend. "He was so taken with the country that it took him all of 30 days to sell out in Missouri and move down here." Pierce recalled of his November 1893 move to Oklahoma Territory. The warm weather lured the Clark family away from the cold, bitter winds of northwestern Missouri. They settled on a ranch just over in Payne County on the Old Perkins Road.

Entering the state as a stowaway, Pierce explained his railroad trip to Oklahoma, "Dad had a crippled-up hand but the railroad wouldn't let him bring me along to help with the cattle he was shipping from St. Joseph, Missouri. He needed me to help, but they wouldn't hear of it, so I just hid in the boxcar. I never did feel bad about cheating the railroad on that deal. They should have been able to see that a man with a crippled hand couldn't handle those cattle by himself, and they should have let me ride down with him in the first place."

Pierce Clark married Lela Fox. Their children were Albert Burton and Betty (Evers). Lela died of blood poisoning and fever.

July 3, 1915, at Pawnee he married Sara Myrtle Bazzell. Her parents immigrated from Callie County, Kansas in a covered wagon and bought 80 acres four miles west of Morrison in March 1894. Myrtle was born April 4, 1889. She married at the age of 15, Tom

Clark family - Pierce Clark in chair. 2nd Row (L to R): Betty (Evers), Mildred (Giger), Elnora (Sappington), Marie (VanDeventer), Myrtle. Back Row (L to R): Chester, Albert Pierce Jr., Jack and Albert.

Bazzell. They had two children, Marie (VanDeventer) and Chester Bazzell before Tom was killed while working as a dray man. A dray was a strong, low cart or wagon without sides, which was used in those days to haul goods. He was lifting the tongue of the wagon when the horses moved forward, instead of backward, and drove the tongue into his stomach — pinning him against a pole.

Pierce and Myrtle had four children of their own, making eight children they raised. Their children were Elnora (Sappington), Mildred (Giger), Edgar Jack and Albert Pierce, Jr.

They farmed near Morrison until 1965, when they moved to Stillwater. They moved to Morrison in 1972. They were members of the First United Methodist Church where he was a life member of the official church board. They celebrated their 60th Wedding Anniversary. Myrtle died February 18, 1976, and Pierce, age 102, March 22, 1978. They are buried at the Union cemetery at Glencoe.

Star Steven Chenoweth
By Libbie G. Chenoweth Norton

Star Steven Chenoweth born November 19, 1909, Noble County, Perry, Oklahoma, died December 11, 1981, at Perry, his home on East Holly St. He was the son of Clark Braden, and Ann Elizabeth (Christensen) Chenoweth. Star was the first born of thirteen children, his father age 24, mother 19, when they married at Perry, lived in a small home eight miles east of Perry, Anna's mother cooked whole roast pig with a red apple in his mouth and all the trimmings for the wedding dinner. Star's father met his wife at a dance. He said, "He asked her to marry him the first night" and she said, "Yes!" Those days he courted her with a horse and buggy.

Star attended Noble county schools. Sister Luella V. born July 28, 1911. At the age of three Star's father got work in Carmen, Oklahoma working for American Bell Phone Co. Anna, Star's mother, and baby sister moved to Carmen to live and stayed till two more babys were born, Edd Preston-September 16, 1913, and Dorothy Ann-February 29, 1916. Star's father made him a harness to climb telephone poles with, this made a small boy very happy. I should mention here that Star's grandfather was living with them for about two years. His grandparents were Joseph Steven, Anna Marie (Davis) Chenoweth of South Haven, Kansas. Star returned to Perry at a very young age, he spent much of his time at his grandparents Neils C., Libbie M. (Hook) Christensen, place east of Perry.

In 1921, Star's parents had a big farm auction, packed up the family and went by train to California at Bakersfield in Kern County, where his father found work in the oil boom fields, while there baby Gladys May was born May 3, 1922, Fellows, California. The story is told that Mother became homesick for mother and Oklahoma. So in 1924, the family returned to Oklahoma in a Jeffrey car with snap on windows, 3 seated, running boards and hot weather coming on. The family consisted of nine all in one car, Oklahoma or bust. Star's father's sisters and brother lived in California being Ruth T. (Chenoweth) Teilhet, Ogden; Luella Gladys M. (French) Dunlap, Travers; Mae (French) Baysie, Clapp; Ruth (Avery) Cutten. Also great aunt, Uncle Stephen, Nerve (Davis) Mullins who helped raise Ruth and Luella and Joe at Bakersfield, California.

In 1924, Star and family returned to Oklahoma, the family rented the Nell Stone place east of Perry for two years where sisters Libbie G. was born August 16, 1924, and Mary M. born September 1, 1926. In 1927, Star joined the Home National Guards for one year at Fort Sill, Oklahoma. The next year his folks moved to the Albertine farm east of Perry. In 1929, his parents went bankrupt, so in 1930 parents and nine children, two cars - Jewett, Studebaker and provisions. Star drove one car and his father the other and headed to Idaho to find work, they arrived at Emile Hanes Place, Twin Falls, he gave them jobs picking up potatoes by the sack and apples by the box. This lasted three months and winter coming, they had $150. They all decided to return to Perry. The Studebaker car broke down near Price, Utah somewhere ten miles out of town this rancher let us (family) live in a cabin till we got our car fixed, the farmer killed a goat and let us have it to eat, was real good when you are hungry. The cabin was near the railroad tracks, the kids played there and picked up fools gold we thought we were rich! The family got as far as Las Animas, Colorado when the car broke down again this time we shucked corn, had to pick it up out of the snow. We got to live in the farm house while we were there it was so cold, the turkeys froze on the roost one night so we have frozen turkey next day and this rancher raised honey bees, so he had a lot of empty cans with a little dab of honey in them. Mother warmed the cans and drained out about five gallons of honey, so we had honey and pancakes for a long time. In 1930, we arrived in Perry flat broke on Thanksgiving Day, rented a one room cabin for 75 cents a day for one week. The family went back to farming. Star found work in 1931 driving a truck for John Lau Creamery to Arkansas City twice a week. His brother Edd found work at Earnest, Amelia Wilsons Produce Co. His father found work hauling water for Pipe line at Ponca City and Fairfax, Oklahoma for $5 a day. Bought another Model T Ford.

October 18, 1933, at Pawnee, Oklahoma Star married Mattilene Eulalia Shelton, born March 19, 1914, at Guthrie, Oklahoma making his home in Perry. Mattilene graduated Perry High Schools and was a member of Eastern Star. She was the daughter of Joseph William Shelton born July 27, 1892 died March 26, 1955 and Austa Louis Leek born 1893 died 1981, they resided in Perry and Covington, Oklahoma. Mattilene E., Star's wife died September 13, 1984 at her daughter's home in San Diego, California.

During World War II, in 1942, Star went to work building navy barracks at Lexington, Oklahoma as a carpenter. He lived in Colorado several years and worked in the Slick Rock mines. He drilled water wells in Utah, and resided at Dove Creek Co. he returned to Perry to live and worked seven years for Perry City Municipal water supply lake as caretaker. All of Star and Mattilene's children were born at Perry. Starletta E. born January 30, 1935 died October 17, 1981 in Hutchinson, Kansas; first husband Glen W. Saunders, step-son Carl; second husband Elmer Fenwick. Gayle D. born May 16, 1937 married December 24, 1952, in Iola, Kansas to Floyd L. Stotler, had three children Floyd J. born 1954; Neeley Wayne born 1956; Malinda Gayle born 1960, all born in Iola. The family resides now in Wichita, Kansas. Joyce M. Chenoweth born January 27, 1939 married June 30, 1956 Donald Ray Mitchell born November 25, 1936 they reside in Hooker, Oklahoma. Issue: two children Phillip Lee born November 10, 1957; Dianna Kay born May 31, 1960.

Insert: Austin Chenoweth. Back Row (L to R): Starletta, Gayle, Maralie. Front Row (L to R): Star, Ila, Norleta - 1946.

Star and Mattilene Chenoweth - 1979. Star was named for Halley's comet which lit the sky the day he was born.

L-R: Clark, Anna, Star, Edd, Luella, Dorothy, Vira, Clark Jr., Gladys Chenoweth - 1924. Car is a 12 passenger Jefferys.

Norleta Dee Chenoweth born July 5, 1942 in Perry married first Roy J. Montgomery 1933-72. Issue: Roy D. February 26, 1960 died same day in Cortez, Colorado; Paul A. born February 3, 1961 in Greenriver, Utah, La Reasa Fay born April 3, 1962 in Monticello, Utah.) Norleta married second Clarence L. Watkins, residing San Diego, California, now Alaska in 1985. Ila Vivian Chenoweth born August 6, 1944 married October 29, 1954 Lowell W. Rockwell born in 1936. Issue: Nedetta Fern born Montecello, Utah and Bud Edward born May 4, 1963 in Montecello, Utah. Star Steven Chenoweth Jr. born January 11, 1946, Perry died March 7, 1971 in Telluride, Colorado. He married Vickie Rae Wester, now Mrs. Vern Foust of Clifton, Colorado. They had one son Star Ray Chenoweth born October 24, 1970 in Telluride, Colorado. Star S. Jr. served in Vietnam Specialist 4C. Bravo Co. 16 Inf. Reg. died in car wreck in the Colorado mountains. The youngest son of Star and Mattilene, Corporal Austin Ray Chenoweth, born February 19, 1947 died in action in Vietnam January 15, 1969 US 54403472 173 ABN. His name is on the War Memorial in Washington D.C. He graduated from Dove Creek High School, Colorado.

James W. Chessher

By Thelma Bittman

James Wesley Chessher was an early day Justice of the Peace in Perry. James and Theresa Stufflebean were married and to this union four sons and two daughters were born, Wesley, Tom, Fred, and Ed, Mary and Lenorah.

When Wesley was bringing Theresa to Oklahoma, she died on the train. Wesley covered her face with a handkerchief, till they arrived in Perry. She was buried in the old part of Grace Hill cemetery in May, 1898. She was 50 years and seven months at the time of her death.

James lived at 2nd and F where he had fruit trees and a truck farm, he sold vegetables, cantaloupes, and watermelons, as well as being a Justice of the Peace.

He married Louisa Johnson in early 1900. She was an early day teacher teaching in Whipple, Polo and North Valley schools and in District #35.

The Chesshers moved to Colorado in 1924, and he passed away that year. Mrs. Chessher died in 1926.

Edward Elza Chessher, son of James and Theresa, was born January 9, 1877. He served in the Spanish-American War, and was given an Honorable Discharge. He was in poor health because of his time in service. He was in and out of Walter Reed Hospital many times.

Edward and Delia Morrow were married in Pawnee, Oklahoma Territory, December 19, 1905. He was a cigar maker and had a small factory on the south side of the square. He hired high school boys to split tobacco after school.

The tobacco came in flat bundles and had to be stripped and put on screen racks and were sprayed and let cure. He then made cigars by hand, packed

James Wesley Chessher.

them in boxes, that had to be pressed to close. All this was done by hand.

Edward rode the caboose to Red Rock, Morrison and Lucien to sell his cigars.

A daughter was born to Edward and Delia Chessher, October 11, 1908. Thelma was born in a small house that stood where the old stock barn is now at the Noble County Fairgrounds.

The Chesshers raised cotton and several blacks picked cotton for them. Edward worked in cigar factories in Chandler, Ponca City and Lawton during World War I.

Edward passed away from cancer in Oklahoma City, June 8, 1926. He was buried in Blackwell cemetery.

Mary Chessher Knight was killed on a motorcycle at Newcastle, August 19, 1929. She was buried in Oklahoma City.

Tom and Fred worked on a sheep ranch in Wyoming after Tom came home from World War I. Then he disappeared and was not heard from again.

(L to R): Winnie Chessher Clark (daughter of Wesley), Delia Chessher, Stackhouse Whitmarsh (friend), Anne Chessher (wife of Wesley) and Wesley Chessher. (Back of car): Faye Whitmarsh and Charlie Clark.

Fred moved to California and died in San Jose, California in 1948.

Wesley had a claim north of Perry. Later, it was sold to Virgil Mornheniweg. He then moved to Bramain and Blackwell, where he died November 15, 1936.

Lenorah was married and moved to Missouri, passing away in 1927.

The only members of the third generation living — Ernest Chessher of Blackwell and Merle Chessher of Little Rock, Arkansas, sons of Wesley and Thelma (Chessher) Bittman of Perry, daughter of Edward.

Thomas J. Coate

By Joe Highfill

Thomas Jefferson Coate was born February 20, 1852 in Celina, Ohio. He was a genealogist and traced his family back six generations to Marmaduke Coate. Marmaduke was a secretary to William Penn and came to America from England in 1715. The family settl-

T. J. and Mary Coate at their home 125 Holley Street in Perry.

ed in Burlington, New Jersey. T.J. Coate's direct ancestors were pioneers in the states of New Jersey, South Carolina and Ohio. T.J.'s parents, Isaac and Sarah Catherine Walker Coate were both native to Ohio. T.J. pioneered in Nebraska, Oklahoma and, following the death of his wife, he pioneered in Montana.

Thomas Jefferson Coate married Mary Jeanette Leland August 4, 1872, at Meridian, Nebraska. Mary Leland was born September 9, 1851 in Wisconsin. Her parents, Samuel and Barbara Swingle Leland were both natives of Pennsylvania. Samuel Leland was a lumberman in Michigan and Wisconsin, and farmed in Nebraska. T.J. Coate farmed in Nebraska where his two sons were born: Walter Jefferson (December 1, 1873 in Saltillo), and Marion Francis (October 3, 1876 in Riverton). The Coate family then went to Tennessee where T.J. operated a grist mill with his father, Isaac. It was here that they adopted Anna Belle Huggins and raised her. She came with the family to Oklahoma at the time of the run.

The Coate family were on their way to New Mexico then they heard about the run. T.J. decided to make the run from near Orlando. Walter was too young to take land in the run but served as a witness for his father. T.J. laid claim to 80 acres in Walnut township. To the south his brother-in-law, Stephen D. Courtright, staked 80 acres. T.J. soon set up a fruit farm which he called the Cherokee Strip Fruit Farm. His fruit was sold all over the area and was very popular with many of his neighbors.

An early day neighbor of the Coates was Amelia Dalton, wife of Bill Dalton. On many occasions, one of the Daltons would come to the Coate farm to purchase a chicken or eggs. My great-grandmother, Edna Coate Highfill, remembers being told by her grandfather, T.J., that she was not to worry if Emmett Dalton came to the chicken coop but to help him and get the money and thank him. Edna said she wasn't worried about the Daltons because her grandfather said it would be all right.

Shortly after their arrival in the Cherokee Strip, Mary's mother, Barbara Leland, came to live with them. She died June 13, 1899, and is buried in the Shelton cemetery. Mary Leland Coate was very frail for much of her life so she and T.J. moved to Perry and lived at 125 Holly Street. The house is still standing. It was here that Mary Coate died on June 25, 1918 and is buried in the Shelton cemetery. Following her death, T.J. moved to Montana at the age of 70, where he homesteaded 80 acres.

While in Montana, T.J. Coate was contacted by lawyers trying to "help" descendants claim land that was rented in a 99 years lease. This land was near Philadelphia, where T.J.'s great-grandfather had lived. To recieve a portion of the "estate" T.J. needed to prove his lineage. He did this and his records have been passed down in the family. However he never did receive any inheritance. The lawyers had set up a get-rich scheme, however the lawyers were the only ones who got rich.

As old age and ill health caught up with him, T.J. was forced to leave Montana and he returned to Oklahoma and lived with his son, Walter, in Walnut township in Noble county. He became very frail and needed two canes to get around during his last year. He died March 2, 1937 at the age of 85. He is buried in the Shelton cemetery beside his wife.

Walter J. Coate
By Joe Highfill

Walter Jefferson Coate was born December 1, 1873 at Saltillo, Nebraska. He was the son of Thomas Jefferson Coate and Mary Jeanette Leland. The family then moved to Henryville, Lawrence county, Tennessee, due to Mary Coate's poor health. The family later moved to Columbia, Tennessee to receive better education. Walter was frequently the best in class, best in school as announced by the newspapers. Walter however, lacked a great deal of common sense. It was here in Tennessee that the family operated a grist mill.

The family was going to New Mexico when they heard about the run. T.J. made the run and was able to stake land in Walnut Township. Walter was too young to take a claim and served as a witness for his father.

In the spring of 1895, T.J. bought Walter a homestead relinquishment in Walnut Township. Walter moved to the farm, where he raised corn and hogs. He lived in a small room frame building. In October of 1895, he moved back with his parents. On November 3, 1897, he married Louisa Jane Moore in Stillwater. Louie was born December 17, 1878 in Eureka, Kansas. She was the daughter of John Harvey Moore and Robina Jane Cheek, who were also homesteaders in Walnut Township, Noble county.

Following their marriage, the couple moved to Walter's bachelor farm. Their first child, Edna May, was born August 8, 1900. John Moore built a one room addition on the north of the house shortly afterwards. This area became the kitchen complete with cookstove. Water was brought in from a nearby well. Their son, Herbert Roland, was born February 23, 1902. Shortly after this, John Moore built a one room addition to the west. It was in this room, on August 4, 1913, that Alice Augusta was born.

About 1916, John Moore and T.J. Coate built a two story house by the old house. The old house was taken

Walter and Louie on their homestead prior to 1900.

down with the lumber being used to build chicken coops. Walter was now raising cotton as well as fruit and corn.

The children attended New Hope school. Walter was elected to the school board for a single term; when it was over, Louie took the position and served on the board for many years. Louie also kept herself busy as a Sunday school teacher in the Bethel Church. She had grubbed out land for her garden and helped to keep the machinery in repair. She also loved to cook. Having come from a family of thirteen children she had a lot of experience. She frequently would have her brothers and sisters over and would easily feed a crowd of 25-30 people on any Sunday afternoon. She also canned. Her canning was so good that when some of the club ladies came to her at the time of the fair needing some canned goods, she could go into her basement and pick any jar and get a third place ribbon or better. In her spare time she would write the New Hope news for the newspapers in Stillwater and Perry, her column would appear every week. She would relax in the evening by writing poetry.

Walter loved to travel. He would frequently take Alice and one of her friends on a trip with him. One of his favorite trips was to Turner Falls.

Louie died on March 24, 1937 in Perry, Oklahoma. Walter then sold his land to the government during the time they were buying up land for Lake Carl Blackwell. He moved to Perry and lived at 203 Delaware. In 1961, ill health forced him to go to a rest home. He died January 29, 1965 in Perry, Oklahoma. They are buried in Grace Hill cemetery, Perry.

Charles F. Cockrum
By Dorothy Cockrum

Charles Franklin Cockrum came to Oklahoma at the tender age of eight years, and Mary Maggie Tontz arrived with her parents at the age of two. Their respective parents were James and Rebecca (Davis) Cockrum and Chris John and Maggie Tontz.

Charles Cockrum was born March 16, 1884 in Edina, Missouri. Mary Tontz was born April 21, 1891 in Mexico, Missouri. The parents of Charles and Mary made the Cherokee Strip run in 1893. James and Rebecca Cockrum homesteaded a farm seven miles west and three miles north of Perry in the Warren Valley Township.

The Cockrum family arrived in a covered wagon in 1892 and lived in Mulhall for one year before the run. After the claim was staked, the family lived in a dug out for one year, until the family home was completed. There were seven children born to the James

Charles and Mary Cockrum.

Cockrums and they are: Charlie, Floyd, Grace, Annie and Fannie, Fay Etta and Edwin. The children attended Lone Star School. Mr. Cockrum was a township assessor and farmed for many years and lived to be 86 years old.

Charles Franklin Cockrum and Mary Maggie Tontz were married July 14, 1909 and Mrs. James Cockrum sewed Mary's wedding dress. To this union, twelve children were born. They were: Gilbert, Bernice, Lorren, Barren, Alvin, Maxine, Lenora, Marietta, Milton, George, J.E. and Gracie. The Charles Cockrum children attended Lone Star, Central and W. Lawn schools. The Central school was located on the Cockrum homestead.

Two of the sons, Alvin and Lorren, have been in business in Perry all of their adult lives. Gracie McKee lives in the Lucien community. Charles and Mary Cockrum were members of the First Christian Church.

Gilbert L. Cockrum was born October 3, 1911. He married Wanda Mae Nelson on March 15, 1939. They have one son, Gerald Lee Cockrum.

Bernice Helen Cockrum was born December 2, 1912. She married Jack B. Rice on February 12, 1937. They have one daughter, Mary Margaret Rice.

Larren Tontz Cockrum was born December 3, 1914. He married Lorene Grother on July 7, 1940. Their children are: Karen Sue, Stanley K., and Forrest Craig Cockrum.

Barren Charles Cockrum was born March 6, 1916. He married Juanita Jones on May 13, 1938. Their children are: Patricia Ann Cockrum, Raymond Charles Cockrum (born August 25, 1941), Duane (the Dude) Gary Cockrum and Jeffrey Lynn Cockrum.

Alvin Christian Cockrum was born February 25, 1918. He married Dorothy Mae Chaney on April 26, 1941. Their children are: Ronye Christian Cockrum, Alvin Randall Cockrum, and Candace Diane Cockrum.

Maxine Mary Cockrum was born October 13, 1919. She married Walter Pryor on September 20, 1945. They have one son, Gary Pryor.

Lenora Stella Cockrum was born August 21, 1923. She married Oakley Price on April 15, 1943. Their children are Sheryle Lynn Price and Beverly Jean Price.

Marietta Cockrum was born March 31, 1926. She married Leo Moran on November 6, 1945. Their children are:

(L to R): Gilbert, Barren, George, Alvin, Charles, Lorren, Milt and Jim — Cockrum men about 1943.

Landreth Leo Moran, and Larry Keith Moran.

Lewis Milton Cockrum was born December 18, 1927. He married Josephine Micken on June 17, 1951. Their children are: David Milton Cockrum, Bradley Steven Cockrum and Patty Denice Cockrum.

George Layton Cockrum was born March 31, 1929. He married Marjorie Mae Forshu. Their children are: Brenda Jane Cockrum, Dwight Lee Cockrum, and Sandra Kay Cockrum.

James Edwin Cockrum was born June 17, 1931. He married Laverne Logue on June 4, 1956. Their children are: Lisa Joe Cockrum, Marsha Fay Cockrum, Calvin James Cockrum, Leon Edwin Cockrum and Lynda Jane Cockrum.

Grace Elizabeth Cockrum was born August 4, 1936. She married Clarence McKee. Their children are William Brent McKee, Wirt Douglas McKee, and Marla Renee McKee.

Four of the Cockrums graduated from Perry High School in 1938, Lorren, Barren, Alvin and Maxine.

The Charles F. Cockrums celebrated their 60th wedding anniversary before Charles passed away on August 16, 1969. At Mary's death, December 12, 1973, there were 31 grandchildren, 43 great-grandchildren, several in this area. Charles and Mary are buried in the McGuire cemetery along with Charles' parents James and Rebecca and grandparents, Benjamin and Malinda.

James E. Cockrum
By Mrs. Lavern (Bill) Golliver

James Edwin Cockrum was born November 17, 1857 in Edina, Missouri, the son of Benjamin and Malinda (Bright) Cockrum. James had three sisters: Mary, Rachel Fannie and Bertha.

On September 11, 1881, James married Rebecca Elisabeth, daughter of Charles and Martha Ann (Lewis) Davis. Rebecca had two brothers Charley Henry and George Washington Davis.

James and Rebecca farmed in Missouri. Three children were born there: Charlie, Floyd, and Grace.

In 1892, the Cockrums came to Oklahoma in a covered wagon and stayed at Mulhall about one year waiting for the run, they lived in a dugout. Aunt Grace told of being able to bring her baby kittens on the long journey to Oklahoma. James staked a claim 2½ miles east of Lucien and 3 miles north. There he built a house for his family where they all were raised.

A few years later, L.B. and Emily (Hurlbert) Kennedy and their family came to Oklahoma from Missouri. They came by train and they lived with the Cockrums until they could get a house built on a farm that L.B. had bought. This information was given to me by Mable Kennedy Hise, at the Green Valley Home. Mable said her mother, Emily was a cousin of James.

James's parents, B.F. and Malinda also made their home with James and Rebecca. Malinda died in 1909 and B.F. in 1913. They are buried in McGurie cemetery at Lucien.

James farmed most of his life and he loved to fish. Rebecca died in 1922, Floyd and Edwin continued to live on the farm with their dad. When Edwin and Lizzie married, they lived with James for seven years. James spent time living with all his children. The last few years of his failing health he spent with Grace and Milt Devore in Perry. James died April 14, 1944.

James and Rebecca's children were: Charlie (1884-1969) married Mary Tontz (1891-1973); Floyd (1886-1968) married Inez Smith (1886-1963); Grace (1889-1983) married Milt Devore (1885-1957); Annie (1895-1965) married Leon Golliver (1894-1971); Fannie (1897-1965) married Dean Golliver (1896-1977); Faye Etta (1900-1902); and Edwin (1902-1967) married Lizzie Wells (1907-).

All of James and Rebecca's children went to Lone Star school, which was just north of the family farm. Also a number of grandchildren and great-

Cockrum Girls about 1966 with mom and dad. (L to R): Maxine (Pryor), Charles, Mary, Marietta. Back Row: Grace (McKee), Bernice (Rice) and Lenora (Price).

Back Row (L-R): Grace (DeVore), Charles Franklin, Floyd, Ed, Fannie (Golliver). Front Row: Annie (Golliver), Rebecca and James Cockrum.

grandchildren attended the same school.

There are a number of grandchildren, great-grandchildren and great-great-grandchildren still living in and around Perry.

Guy Coffman
By Wayne Coffman

Guy M. Coffman was born eight miles north of Parsons, Kansas on December 26, 1880. His father, George M. Coffman, was prominent in affairs of Neosho County for over a half century as a school teacher, hardware merchant, banker and farmer. His mother, Addie Ferguson Coffman had a quiet uncomplaining disposition, and considered the duties connected with her home and family greater than all else.

Guy graduated from highschool then attended Kansas University two years where he received his degree in pharmacy. Now the course is twice as long, but they teach you merchandising and other things a druggist did not need in those days. After working in a drug store in Pawnee for six months he bought a drug store in Morrison from a doctor named Whittenburg in 1903. His pharmacy certificate was numbered 136 and had the seal of Oklahoma Territory. It was dated Pawnee, 1903. Now there are over 10,000 certificate in Oklahoma.

The next 55 years were spent as proprietor of the center of social and business activity for the farm community of Morrison.

Mrs. Coffman was the former Grace L. Colvin. She was born in Nevada, Missouri, on July 9, 1881, to Jacob Francis Colvin and Elizabeth Walker Colvin. Her father made the run on the Opening of the Cherokee Strip, September 16, 1893. He staked a claim on a farm, the one on which the main part of the city of Morrison is located. Somebody contested the claim, and he, not having been too zealous to move to this undeveloped country in the first place, took his family and went home to Missouri. Later, he was notified a title to the claim could still be obained as he was a War Between the States veteran, had a "soldiers declaratory", which gave him a reasonable first claim to the land, a homestead. Colvin did not look with too much favor on trying to get that farm but did return to Morrison a year later where he worked as a carpenter and farmer.

Grace had one brother, John Colvin, and three sisters, Sarah Kent, Rose McKinstry, and Della James, who were also pioneers in the Morrison community. Other sisters were Ida Cavin of Afton, Oklahoma, and Molly Chastain of Cortez, Colorado.

Guy and Grace were married in Perry on March 7, 1906. On September 18, 1908, their first son, Gleason was born. The second son, Wayne, was born on March 25, 1914.

Guy M. Coffman family. Gleason (top left), Grace (top right), Wayne (bottom left), Guy (bottom right).

Dr. and Mrs. Coldiron and son, Victor.

Daniel F. Coldiron
By Kenneth Coldiron and Kara Lee Eikleberry

Daniel Frederick Coldiron was born February 1, 1877, in Harlan County, Kentucky, the son of Moses William Coldiron and Jane Harris Farmer. He attended schools in Harlan County, a United Presbyterian school, Geneva College in Beaver Falls, Pennsylvania, and Maryville College Prep school in Maryville, Tennessee. In 1898, he volunteered for the Spanish-American War. After the war, he came to Oklahoma, looking for farm land for his father. The family moved from Kentucky to near Pond Creek, Oklahoma in 1902. In Oklahoma, he attended normal school in preparation to be a teacher and taught one year near Pond Creek.

Daniel F. Coldiron studied medicine in 1901 and 1902 at the University of Oklahoma and continued his studies at the Kansas City Medical College in 1903-1905. After graduation, he married Daisy Emma Lemon, on August 4, 1905, in Pond Creek, Oklahoma.

He practiced medicine in Noble County for 56 years starting in Billings, Oklahoma, then Bliss (Marland), Red Rock, and moved to Perry in 1918, and practiced there the remainder of his career. It was estimated he delivered more than 4,000 babies during his career. A regular office call was 50¢. Recently his son, Kenneth, received a check from a man for $25.00 with a note that stated he had owed this to Dr. Coldiron for about 40 years for delivering one of his children.

When he began practicing medicine he used a buggy pulled by two horses to make house calls. This rig he had to borrow from his father, who was living near Pond Creek. He made his calls nights as well as days. He started practicing medicine in 1906 and bought his first automobile in 1914. It was a Ford Runabout which he bought from Frank Sanders at Ceres, Oklahoma. When people asked about the car he would say "It's a run-about. It runs about 5 miles and stops." Dr. Coldiron served in WW I in 1918, and later served in the Oklahoma National Guard, 45th Division for many years.

In 1956, the County Homemakers

Groups organized a "Dr. Coldiron Day" at the fair grounds in Perry. Many of the children he had delivered were there. Other groups joined the Homemakers in honoring Dr. Coldiron, the Rotary Club, American Legion, Lions Club, and Perry Chamber of Commerce, as well as friends and neighbors. Some 750 people attended the event. He was presented with a TV set and a movie of the occasion.

Dr. and Mrs. Coldiron had three children: Victor, born November 24, 1907, in Billings. Victor attended school in Red Rock and Perry school, Central State University and Oklahoma A & M College. On November 15, 1930, he married Nell Wetzel, whose father, Tom Wetzel, had been sheriff of Noble County. They lived in California, where he worked for Firestone Tire and Rubber Company for 40 years. They had three children: Daisy Ann, Vicki, and Terry. He died February 14, 1980, in California.

Kenneth Kay — (see Kenneth Coldiron).

Kara Lee (born October 2, 1914, in Red Rock, Oklahoma) attended school in Perry and Maryville College, Maryville, Tennessee and Oklahoma State University. She married Robert Eikleberry in 1936. They had four children: Melvyn Robert, Lana Kay, Daniel and Jane. Kara has been very active in Nebraska politics and has done much genealogy work and written several family histories. She retired from the County Division of Public Welfare in 1980, and resides in Lincoln, Nebraska.

Dr. Coldiron died November 26, 1961, at the age of 85 and is buried in Grace Hill Cemetery beside his wife who died November 25, 1946.

Daisy Lemon Coldiron

*By Kenneth Coldiron
and Kara Lee Eikleberry*

Daisy Emma Lemon was born October 8, 1876, in Shady Grove, Kentucky. She was the daughter of Dr. William Blount and Fannie (Word) Lemon. Both parents were of Welch-English descent. She came with her mother and brothers, John Eli (Jack) Lemon and Gustavus Ersasmus (Gus) Lemon, to settle on a claim in Grant county, southwest of Round Pond (now Pond Creek). Her father had died in her early childhood. They had to leave the train at Salt Fork, as there was the usual county seat fight and trains refused to stop at Round Pond. Her brother, Gus, met the train with a wagon and a team of ponies. They forded the Nescatunga River, now called the Salt Fork, at the old Chisholm trail crossing on the site of the old Bull Foot Cattle ranch. Daisy taught school near Pond Creek.

Dr. D. F. Coldiron, Daisy Lemon Coldiron and Victor Coldiron - 1911 near Red Rock, Oklahoma.

She married Dr. Daniel F. Coldiron, August 4, 1905. Her brother, Jack, was twice elected to the Oklahoma Legislature from Grant county.

Daisy Coldiron was active in Oklahoma Public Health and received a Distinguished Service Cross from that agency. She had a column in the Daily Oklahoman for some time on homemaking using the pseudoym "Aunt Sally". She was best known for her poetry which was published in high grade publications many years before she published her books. The books were **Songs of Oklahoma**, a book about the early days in Oklahoma; **Who Touches This**, a collection of ballads, sonnets and lyrics "profoundly philosophical in subject matter and tone." according to Kenneth Kaufman, literary reviewer; **There was a Garden**, a tribute to flowers which grow in Oklahoma and elsewhere; and **Ballads of the Plains**, published posthumously, wider in scope than the other three books as it extends far beyond Oklahoma boundaries. Her Songs of

Daisy Lemon Coldiron - 1904.

Oklahoma, was nominated for a Pulitzer Prize in the historical category. Her book necessarily competed with those of noted historians and, since it was poetry, did not carry the needed weight as history — to win.

Her poems have been published in Harlow's Weekly, Daily Oklahoman, Ozark Life, American Author, Blue Moon, Poer O'Poets, Dallas Journal, and by David C. Cook and the Southern Baptist Board of Sunday School Publications. Also they were read on many radio programs.

Mrs. Irene Treeman wrote the following about Mrs. Coldiron: "I learned to know and appreciate Daisy Lemon Coldiron before I knew her as a poet. In 1912-13, I taught school in Red Rock and the Coldirons lived there. After she moved to Perry and was becoming well known as a poet we often visited each other. Always she was interested in any aspiring young writer, especially a poet, and encouraged them to get something into print.

Mrs. Coldiron was an invalid for many years but her natural beauty became more evident as her indominable spirit rose above her suffering. I feel Daisy Lemon Coldiron produced a poetic, historical record of Oklahoma, particulary of our Cherokee Strip. Often in talks of Early Day Perry, I have been so proud to use the first lines of her stirring poem:

The Opening
September 16, 1893

O day of promise, O day of destiny!
Dawn! the past is behind you.
Day a home must be won!
The Cherokee Strip is before you.
This! is the day of the Run!"

Some of her poems can be found in the general history of this book.

Daisy Lemon Coldiron died November 25, 1946, after being an invalid for 11 years with arthritis. She is buried in Grace Hill Cemetery.

Kenneth K. Coldiron
By Kenneth K. Coldiron

Kenneth K. Coldiron was born in Red Rock, Oklahoma, November 10, 1911. He was the son of Dr. Daniel F. Coldiron and Daisy Lemon Coldiron. He attended the first and second grades at Red Rock School. He had a brother, Victor, and a sister, Kara Lee.

The family then moved to Perry in September of 1918. All of the family furniture was moved on two horse drawn hayracks. The drivers loaded the furniture and left from Red Rock to Perry before daylight. They tied a red lantern on the coupling pole at the rear of the second hayrack. They arrived in Perry after dark at their new home at 922 Fir St. The furniture was not unloaded until the next day so the family was invited to stay the night with the E. R. Martin family who lived next door. They were the first friends the Coldiron family had in Perry and the families have remained good friends all the years since then.

Kenneth completed his grade school, Jr. High school and graduated from Perry High in 1929. During this time, Kenneth worked for Huffman's grocery store and for Eddie Parker in the Kumback Cafe on the north side of the square. He also worked in the summer time for Zack McCubbin's 1-2-3 Cleaners, also on the north side of the square.

In 1930, he started to College at Oklahoma A. & M. in Stillwater. He graduated in the spring of 1935, with a degree in Business Administration. In the summers during his college days he was with the Cap Swift's "Zouaves" on the 101 Wild West Show, headquartered at Bliss, Oklahoma. During these years the show traveled in nearly all the major cities and many of the small cities in the North and East United States. Kenneth was with the show in 1931, when it went broke in Washington, D.C. After many days of legal manuevering between the Government and the show officials, the show was loaded on railroad flat cars and allowed to return to Bliss, Oklahoma. The return trip on the railroad took several days due to the low priority of a defunct Wild West Show. The supply of food played out down to boiled potatoes which were sometimes supplemented with "roasting ears" obtained from corn fields as the train was stopped along the way.

In September, 1935, Kenneth went to work for the Lower Auditing Company, a National Auditing Company headquartered in Cincinatti, Ohio. In this position he traveled and worked in many cities throughout the United States.

After Pearl Harbor, he went into the

Kenneth Coldiron - 1985.

Army in 1942, and went into the United States Airforce when it was formed in 1943. He served in the European Theatre of Operations until 1945, and was being sent to the Island of Luzon in the Phillipines in preparation of the airborne invasion of Japan when the war was ended. He was discharged in 1946.

In 1947, he went to work for the Exchange Bank in Perry, Oklahoma and served as Cashier, Vice President, President and Chairman of the Board. He retired from full time duty in the bank on April 7, 1980, and has served on the Board of Directors until the present time.

In 1942, Kenneth married Maxine Gray. They had two sons, Clark Scott Coldiron, born February 11, 1947, and Daniel Fredrick Coldiron, born September 21, 1949. Maxine died April 24, 1952. Kenneth then married Reba Lee Beard, a sister of Maxine. They had two sons, Reed Lewis Coldiron, born May 19, 1954, and Carl Lee Coldiron, born May 31, 1955. Kenneth and Reba were divorced in 1961. Kenneth married Mary Ellen Dunivan in August of 1962 in Sumner, Oklahoma. Mary Ellen worked in the Exchange Bank 29½ years. They reside at 1008 Delaware St., Perry, Oklahoma. They are members of the First Presbyterian Church in Perry. The have six grandchildren. Clark is married to Beth Speir and they have two children, Nathan and Nicole. Dan is married to Beverly Hughes and their children are, Daniel Fredrick Coldiron III, "Trey" and Abbi Dawn. Reed is married to Ronita Montgomery and they have two sons, Derek James and Brett Allen. Carl Lee Coldiron resides and works in Oklahoma City, Oklahoma.

Cliff Collins
By Florence Denslow

Banajy Clifford Collins was born July 4, 1870. Nothing else is known of his childhood. Cliff started from west of Orlando to make the run of 1893. He rode a horse named Cricket that was very fast and high strung. He rode bareback to lighten the load for the horse. When the shot was fired and the shouting began his horse took off and as they came to a creek he couldn't turn the horse around to go to a crossing. The horse jumped off the high bank into the creek bed. As the horse hit the sand Cliff rolled off and rolled the horse out of the sand. He mounted and rode off. From then on he led the race as no other land competitors ever passed him that day in the run.

Cricket as an honored and esteemed horse after that day. He never had to work except to pull a buggy a few times. When he was on his death bed at the age of 27, and no longer able to get up, Cliff and the family carried water and feed to him and kept him blanketed until he died.

When Cliff saw the land seekers coming from the north he decided it was time to stop and drive his stake. His claim was located on the SE ¼ of Section 7, township 23 N and Range 2W (White Rock township). This is about three and a half miles south of the present town of Billings, Oklahoma.

He arrived about 6:30 in the evening and slept that night under the stars. The next morning he rode to Perry, the county seat of P County, later named Noble County, to file his claim. His homestead patent is #1000 and is dated June 25, 1901.

When Cliff returned from filing (Perry is about 26 miles from his claim) he found someone had jumped his claim. He ran the claim jumper off at the point of a gun. He said he would have killed the man if he had had to do so. Cliff had been cheated out of a claim in the run of 1889 by a claim jumper and he didn't intend to lose another chance to get land.

He made a dugout in the SW corner of the place. It was made of sod brick twenty-four inches square and four inches thick. He built a one-room house several years later nearer to the east central side of the place. He and his wife, the former May Derr, who lived one mile east of his claim, lived in this one room house until they built the home. The new house was made of all new lumber and bought from a discount place. By buying a car load, it was much cheaper than he could buy the lumber from the lumber yard. The discount house cut the lumber and marked and labeled each piece as to where it was to go. So with the one carpenter, who laid out the plan, Cliff with the aid of his father-in-law and brother-in-law built the house. Raymond, the only child of Cliff and Mae, was born on the claim.

During the year of 1917, the family moved to Billings because of May's health. Here Cliff was in the sand hauling business with his son, Raymond. Two years later the family moved to Enid, Oklahoma and built a home at 1310 East Broadway where Raymond still lived. Using horses and a truck they continued in the sand hauling business and opened a concrete block business. Cliff was active in this business until he had a heart attack about 15 years later.

Before the run, Cliff worked as a cowboy around the area of Cement, Oklahoma. While proving up the claim, Cliff worked in the coal mines at Tulsa, on the railroads, and snapped corn in Kansas, and doing anything he could to earn some cash. He was an expert corn snapper.

He told the story of working for 25 cents a day and the ranchers feeling sorry for him and telling him at the end of their first day's work, to take a load of corn to town and buy some clothes. He would always work until he paid them back for the clothes.

His wife told of his walking to Tulsa barefooted to work in the coal mines even after they were married. Several times he even had to swim the Arkansas River when he had to break the ice.

Cliff was an uncle by marriage to me and one of the things I loved to have him do was to play the harmonica and tell stories of his cowboy days. One song he played and sang that was a favorite of mine was called "Little Dog Tray". It was about a puppy that got his tail cut off. I wish I could remember the words to the song but I can't. Another song he liked to sing was about "Two Little Girls". I do not know whether these are the exact titles or not. He also sang cowboy songs. He and his father-in-law, Jake Derr, also played for dances in the area. Jake played the fiddle.

Martin L. Collins

By Pauline Nichols

Martin Louis Collins, was born April 14, 1856. He came to Oklahoma from Kansas. He was the son of Henry Collins, who died of complications from his service in the Civil War at Eldorado, Kansas and was buried there. Martin's mother was Emma Collins, born October 3, 1835, in Atkinson, Ohio. Martin's mother and father were married May 20, 1855, she never remarried and spent her remaining years at Lela, where she died in 1928. She was buried in the Lela Cemetery.

Martin staked a claim ½ mile north of Lela, Oklahoma, just across the Black Bear Creek on the west side. He lived in a dug out first and then built a log cabin. A man tried to settle on the west side of his claim. He had to be driven off at the point of Martin's gun. Not long after that an Indian came to their door to report to them that a white man was at their corn crib, stealing their corn, he told Virginia, who was on the claim alone, (for Martin had returned to his place, east of Stillwater to bring up another load of corn) to get a gun and shoot him.

Martin married Virginia Lillard Cummings, born in Clark County, Missouri on June 24, 1855, when she was around 16 years old.

They later ran a filling station, north of the old Lela grocery and post office store which was on the east side of the road, in Pawnee County and was ran at one time by Mr. Ross and one time by Mr. Furgeson. When the highway (64) was built, he then moved to a station on the west side of the street, and next to the highway, they didn't have electricity, so they had old fashion delco lights, which when the engine was running had a pop-pop sound.

They then bought a 10 acre strip in the southeast part of Lela on the south side of the highway, which joined the Lela school ground on the north. Their little house still stands and also his mother, Emma Collins' two room house to the north of it.

Martin died and was buried in the Lela cemetery. Virginia died March 20, 1927 and also was buried in Lela Cemetery.

They had seven children. Henry Giddon Collins was born January 28, 1878. He died February 18, 1951. He was buried at Lela Cemetery, Lela, Oklahoma. He married Mary Wire. She had one son, Johnie Wire, and he had one son, Billie Joe Wire. Henry and Mary

Collins Family — (Top Row): Rosie, Maud. (2nd Row): Emma, Frank and Henry. (Bottom Row): Martin Jennie and Elsie.

(Mae) did not have any children. She died March 2, 1936 at Pawhuska, Oklahoma, at the age of 55 years. She was buried March 4, 1936, in the Lela Cemetery.

Martin's second child was an infant son who died June 28, 1880.

The third child was a girl, Rosilla Collins Porter, born August 16, 1881. She married James Lonza (Lon) Porter on September 10, 1899. She was 12 years old when her father Martin ran in the opening of the Cherokee Strip. Their children were: Elmer Lewis Porter, Born May 27, 1901. He married May Hughes Porter, December 25, 1922. Okley Orn Porter was born February 17, 1904. He lived at home with his parents and never married. Floyd Edward Porter died at the age of 14. Lola Lovell Porter Burk was born February 11, 1909. She married Cecil Burk on January 4, 1925. Teddy Ray Porter was born June 15, 1921. He married Freda Foch in 1932. Zola Juanita Porter Bay was born January 20, 1924. She married Cecile Bay. Junior Alonzo Porter was born August 14, 1924. He married and lived in Missouri.

Benjamin Frank Collins died February 22, 1969. He was born January 27, 1884. He married Inez Porter Bishop. She had two sons, Dewey and Alfred Bishop. They had seven children: Luther Collins, Ardell Collins, Vineleta Collins Panning, Granville (Bub) Collins, Dale Collins, Ada Collins, and Chester Collins. Chester was killed during World War II.

Emma Collins was born April 2, 1886, at Wichita, Kansas. She married Alva Thomas. They had seven children: Charles Ara Thomas born near Pawnee

July 22, 1903 married Phyllis Mair. Zetta May Thomas was born near Pawnee April 17, 1905. She married Bennie Schneider. Ava Lee Thomas was born in Arlington, Washington. William Thomas died at birth. Biddy Bridget (Peggy) Thomas was born June 14, at Green Court, Alberta, Canada.

OCLC (Ocie Elsie) Collins Akers Coombs was born August 14, 1888, at Shell City, Missouri. She married William Akers and had seven children. Later when alone she married Guy Coombs of Pawnee. Virgia Marie Akers was born March 14, 1907. She married Glenn Burk, they never had children. She died August 12, 1927.

Charley Akers was born August 11, 1907. He married Leta Wagner. Joe Edwin Akers was born May 19, 1911. He married Josie Drawberg. Later, he married Lois. Hazel Laru Akers was born February 27, 1914. She married Leland Chace. Evelyn Geraldine Akers was born February 20, 1917. She married Orville Childress, Lloyd Warner and Rudy Nedbaleck. William Paulieree Akers was born January 31, 1922. His first wife was Ruth, his second was Collene. Elsie Pauline Akers was born January 31, 1922. She married Lloyd Nichols.

Modie Mae (Maud) Collins was born October 20, 1889. She married Aniel Kelly and had three children. Henry T. Kelly was born June 29, 1907. He married the second time to Hazel Kahn. Jack Harry Kelly was born May 30, 1910 and married Mary Dick. Virginia Kelly was born around 1922 and died when around four years old.

Elsie Ocie (Collins) Akers Coombs
By Pauline (Akers) Nichols

Elsie Ocie Collins was born August 14, 1886 in Shell City, Missouri. She married William Akers November 6, 1904 just east of the New Lela school house. William Akers was born July 14, 1886 in Indiana. He died September 3, 1954. They both came with their families from Kansas, when their parents ran for their land in the Cherokee Strip.

William was a hard working man who loved to dance. He was an avid hunter and had many coon dogs. He farmed until a few years after the depression.

Elsie worked with the sick. They had seven children: Virgie Marie was born March 14, 1906. She married Glenn George Burk. They did not have any children. She died August 12, 1927. Charley (August 11, 1907 - March 10, 1985), Edwin (May 19, 1911 - 1977), Hazel (Chase) born February 20, 1917. Geraldine married 1st Childers, 2nd Warner, 3rd Nedbaleck and twins

(L to R) Seated: Pauline, Paulieve, Elsie. Standing: Joe and Hazel Akers about 1978.

William Paulieve (Paul) born January 31, 1922 and Elsie Pauline (Nichols).

Paulieve made his spending money by hunting, so after a hard day of working his mother would go hunting with him at night. He started hunting when he was so young she feared for his life. Paul did without his senior ring so he could buy a coon dog which he came to love. He received from 20 to 75 cents for his animal hides he caught in traps.

I'll never forget how mortified I was when I was in high school and we moved into my grandfather Collin's part-log house north of Lela. The first evening we moved in, Dorothy Richmond, my basketball coach and my friends brought me home. But when we walked in, my mother had papered the kitchen completely with one foot square white pieces. She had used the back side of the wallpaper sample catalog. She had curtains up, a table cloth on the table and a hot supper waiting. How proud and happy I was, instead of ashamed.

At Christmas time each of the girls received dolls with crochet hats and booties. The dresses were decorated with lace and ribbons and the hems were scalloped around the bottom with hand sewn button-hole stitches. She must have stayed up at night after the others were in bed to make these. I remember coming home one cold January birthday evening from school. She had our play table and chairs set up by the wood heater with a hot supper in our play dishes. By Paul's and my plate was a Milky Way candy bar. What a wonderful surprise.

It was very difficult for the mother to watch the twins when they were toddlers. On at least two occasions their dog went to the house and barked until the mother came to see what was wrong. One time Paul fell on a rock hill

(L to R): Elsie and Guy Coombs about 1974.

and lay bleeding, another his supenders caught on a nail and he was left hanging in the barn manger. The good Lord must have been with us. J. D. Turner saved my life when I fell into the dugout artesian well, just east of the Lela store and post office.

I remember the excitement of our first 1,000 hour battery radio. Mother and I picked cotton to buy it.

Paul graduated valedictorian from Morrison High School. He completed two years of college at Norman, Oklahoma. In order not to be outdone by twin brother, I worked very hard and missed being Salutatorian by one-forth point.

After my parent's marriage dissolved, my mother married Guy Combs at Columbus, Kansas on June 26, 1946. We had a very good relationship with his children, Arlie, Forest and Delbert Combs.

Elsie died in 1978 and was laid to rest in the Glencoe Union Cemetery.

John F. Cordell
By Mildred Highfill

The ancestry of John F. Cordell can be traced back to St. John Cordelle of France, the latter-day descendants having dropped the final "e". The paternal great-grandfather came from Loraine, France and settled in Virginia. John Cordell was born in Loudoun Co. VA, September 27, 1838, and there also were born his father, Adam, and his mother, Susan (Slater) Cordell. The former was a farmer and the latter was a daughter of Samuel Slater, a farmer. The Slater family was of German descent, and the great-grandfather was a soldier in the Revolutionary War. There were eleven children in the family of which John Cordell was a member, he being sixth and the one who came to Oklahoma.

The early life of Mr. Cordell was passed on his father's farm in Virginia, and his education acquired at the early subscription schools. His mother died when he was fourteen. He learned the carpenter's trade as well as being a shoemaker. This combination of labor furnished a variety of occupation, for during the summer time he built houses and during the winter he made shoes. In 1859, he moved to Ashland, Ashland Co, Ohio, and followed his trades until the Civil War. April 17, 1861, he volunteered in Company B, Sixteenth Ohio Volunteer Infantry, and during the first three months participated in the battles of Philippi, Laurel Hill, Rich Mountain and Garrick's Ford, and was mustered out August 18, 1861.

He re-enlisted, September 10, 1861, in Battery D, First Ohio Light Artillery as a private. Later, he was promoted to Corporal and chief of cassine. January 5, 1864, he again enlisted for three years at Strawberry Plains, in East Tennessee, and was raised to the rank of gunner. He was mustered out at Cleveland, Ohio, July 15, 1865.

He was at the battle of Shiloh, seige of Corinth, and in Nashville, Murgreesboro, Munfordville, at which place General Wilder surrendered after a four days' engagement. After being paroled and exchanged, he returned to Louisville, and was in the battle of Knoxville. Then followed the battles of Bean's Station, Lenore Station, and the conflict on Strawberry Plains.

He also took part in the battle of Carterville, Lost Mountain, Burnt Hickory, Zera's Church, Blaine's Cross Roads, Little Kenesaw Mountain, Lovejoy Station, Chattahoochee River, Decatur and the siege of Atlanta. Mr. Cordell was twice wounded

After the war, Mr. Cordell went back to Ashland, and was foreman for William Walston, a shoe dealer until 1868 when he located at Pleasant Hill, MO and went into the shoe business for himself. At the same time, he had stores at Butler and Harrisonville, Missouri and was also traveling salesman for Appleton, Noyes and Co. In 1888, he traded out his business for real estate in Cass Co. Missouri, and Sumner Co. Kansas. April 22, 1889, he came to Oklahoma and settled on a claim three miles south of Oklahoma City for a time, and then retired to Missouri to look after his interests there. In September, 1893, he came to Perry.

The first wife of Mr. Cordell was Jane Thomas, a native of Ashland, where she died. She was the mother of two children: William, and Mrs. Mary C. Moore. By his union with Frances Stoneburner, Mr. Cordell had one child: John F. The third Mrs. Cordell was formerly Mary Rozella Boles. She was born in July, 1877 in Missouri, and a daughter of T. J. Boles, a veteran of the Civil War. She had three children: Orville McKinley (b - January 1896), Ernest Dewey (b - January 1898) and Teddy, making six children for Mr. Cordell.

He was a Republican and a delegate to various county and territorial conventions. He served on the school board, was a Mason, a member of the G.A.R. in Perry and the Lutheran church.

At the age of 74, John Cordell died August 29, 1912 from an operation and is buried in Grace Hill cemetery beside his third wife who died August 8, 1904, age 27 years 9 days.

Peter J. Cordes
By Thelma Bittman

Peter Johann Cordes was born July 17, 1884 in Germany. His parents, Deitrich and Maria Cordes and their 3 sons settled in Lincoln township, Iowa County, Iowa. The three boys each had Johann in their name, Johann W., Peter Johann and young Deitrich Johann.

Deitrich farmed in Iowa, where three sons and one daughter were born, Carl, Lewis, Henry and Anna. The family all came to Guthrie, Oklahoma to farm.

Mrs. Cordes raised goats and carded the wool to make warm clothes for her family. She raised a large garden to have their winter food, canning and drying fruit and vegetables. She buried her carrots for winter use. She wasted nothing.

The Cordes were living east of Guthrie when Carl, Lewis, Henry and Deitrich fought in World War I. Later, they found they had fought against their cousins in several battles.

Carl and Lewis worked in Malzahn Blacksmith shop for Charles and Gus Malzahn. The shop was on south 6th street.

Pete was a bartender in Guthrie before he came to Perry in 1910. He was a carpenter in Perry and trained many men to use a hammer and nails. He contracted and built a number of business buildings and houses in town and in the country. He was in charge of the building of the Armory building, a W.P.A. job.

Pete and Delia Chessher married in Guthrie August 12, 1918. During World War II, he was on the Tire and Gas rationing board. He was a member of the Lutheran church. Later, he joined the Masonic lodge, and was a Royal Arch Mason.

Delia had a stroke and died in Cook's Perry Hospital June 29, 1945 and was buried at Grace Hill cemetery.

Pete retired from the building business in 1960, because of ill health. He passed away at the Norman Hospital, February 28th, 1962 and was

Pete Cordes and his horse Dan.

buried in the Grace Hill cemetery by his wife's side.

Arthur Covey
By Wendell Sullins

Arthur Covey was born June 13, 1877, in Leroy, Illinois, the fourth son of Byron and Emmeline Covey. In 1908, he married Mary Dorothea Sale. They were married in London, England. They had two children: Margaret Sale, July 6, 1909, Englewood, New Jersey; and Laird Fortune, April 25, 1917, Weehawken, New Jersey. Dorothea died in May, 1917. In June, 1921, Arthur married Lois Lenore Lenski. They had one child, Stephen John, February 8, 1929, New Rochelle, New York.

Arthur made the run with his father and two brothers, Erwin and Edwin, in 1893. He had been told to stay home. But he stowed away in the wagon. By the time they found him it was too late to take him home. He drove the wagon while his father and brothers rode horses. They told him where to meet them. But he managed to get lost from them. Their claim had been jumped and they had moved on. Arthur kept driving the horse until he heard them calling his name. It was a welcome sight to see his family.

By March of 1894, their new home was completed. They headed for Kansas to bring the rest of the family to this new country.

One day when Arthur was seventeen, he drove into the barnyard with his father's wagon and team. With a dramatic flourish to no one in particular, he announced that he hated farming and would not follow in his father's footsteps.

Vague yearnings had begun to stir within him, planted there perhaps by a mother's frustrated love of the beautiful and a father's constant longing for something better.

With his meager earnings, Arthur began his study of art at Southwestern College in Winfield, Kansas in 1895. He was the only boy in the class and was very fortunate to have an understanding woman teacher, Edith Dunlevy. She befriended him, counseled him and sent him on to continue his study of art at the Art Institute of Chicago.

He studied at the Art Institute of Chicago from 1897-1899. In 1904, he went to the Royal Academy of Munich. From 1905-1908 he studied in London, England. He was an assistant to Frank Brangwyn, a noted mural painter.

In 1914, he painted a mural for the Wichita City Library in Wichita, Kansas. It was the first ever individual commission for a painting. The mural has since been removed from the library and is on display at one of the local banks in Wichita at the corner of Douglas and Topeka.

In the years 1916-1917, he painted an eighteen panel mural, entitled "Romance of the Trade" for Lord & Taylor of New York. In 1919-1920, he painted a four hundred foot frieze for Wm. Filene & Sons of Boston, titled "Ten Centuries of Men's and Womens Costumes".

He has also done a mural for the Kohler Company, Kohler, Wisconsin; murals, stained glass and carvings for the Norton Company, Worchester, Massachusetts; industrial murals in Toledo, Ohio; the ceiling in the Squibb Building in New York; post offices in Bridgeport and Torrington, Connecticut, and Andersonville, South Carolina; the ceiling at the Trinity Lutheran Church, Worchester, Massachusetts; the circular dome and globe at the Land Plane Building at LaGuardia Airport, New York City; the library at the Horace Mann School, Riverdale, New York. He also did the Aztec Indian head, which was a full scale model, and was a portion of the design, over the entrance to the Contemporary Arts Building at the 1939 New York World's Fair.

Arthur's second wife, Lois Lenski, was a noted person in her own right. She wrote and illustrated children's books. She wrote "Strawberry Girl", "Cotton in my Sack", and "Boom Town Boy". She also wrote and illustrated the "Big, Little" series. "Boom Town Boy" is about the life of a small boy growing up in the Three Sands area during the oil boom. She stayed with her in-laws while she wrote the book.

Arthur Covey was my great-uncle on my father's side of the family. Arthur Covey died February 5, 1960 and is buried at Tarpon Springs, Florida.

Byron Covey
By Wendell Sullins

Byron Covey was born December 15, 1843, in Leroy, Illinois. He was a soldier in the Civil War. In 1868, he married Emmeline Edwards. She was born April 25, 1850, and was the daughter of an alderman in Bloomington, Illinois. They had five children: Cornelius Erwin, January 27, 1870; Edwin Fletcher, 1872; Carrie Dicey, 1874; Arthur Sinclair, June 13, 1877; all born in Leroy, Illinois; and Floyd Byron, April 22, 1884, Avalon, Missouri. Carrie was my grandmother. In 1899, she married Arthur Denton Sullins. They had six children: Orville Arthur, April 10, 1900; Ethel Mae, September 24, 1901; Erwin Oscar, October 24, 1905, (my father); Nelva Clare, August 10, 1908; Edwin Leroy, January 25, 1919; Vera Aliene, August 18, 1921. All were born in Red Rock except for Nelva, born in Perry.

Byron Covey and his family lived in El Dorado, Kansas before coming to Oklahoma. They were in the feed business there, plus doing other odd jobs to make ends meet.

In 1892, Byron received a small inheritance from his father's estate. He had heard about the free land south of Kansas. Byron took his son, Erwin, and his brother, John, and went to investigate the land. They decided to make the run.

Young Arthur was told to stay home. But he stowed away in the wagon. They could not very easily make him go home. They let him drive the wagon while his dad and the others rode the horses. They staked one claim and started to dig a hole for a well, when they were run off by claim jumpers.

Byron and his boys pitched a tent on their new homestead that night. They had to file their claim in Perry the next day. Their claim was at the present day site of Ceres.

Byron's new home was not to be like most settlers homes — made out of sod. His was a wooden structure, twenty-four feet square and one and a half stories high. It had four gables with four valleys between, making four bedrooms upstairs, every room with a window. It was the best house in the country.

By March the house was completed and the family moved from El Dorado to Red Rock. Erwin, Emmeline and Floyd drove in the buggy. The team and wagon carried Byron, Carrie, and Edwin. Arthur walked behind, driving the cow twenty-five miles a day. The cow had to be left behind in Blackwell because her hoofs wore out. They traveled 120 miles before reaching their new home.

In the early 1900s, Byron made a bet with his neighbor J. W. Swiker, on the outcome of an election. The loser would push the winner to Perry in a wheelbarrow. Byron lost the bet. He pushed J.W. from Ceres to Perry, thirteen miles. It took them a day and a half. The present highway 77 was only a dirt road then. J.W. thoroughly enjoyed his free ride, waving flags from both hands.

Byron Covey was also a county commissioner for Noble County sometime around statehood. No definite dates are available. He has also been given credit for planting the trees in the courtyard before the court house was built.

Erwin, Edwin and Floyd had a grocery store at one time in Ceres. They gave tokens with the Covey name on them instead of giving money for change. The store was destroyed by fire. No dates are known here, either.

Byron platted the town of Ceres. The Ceres Cemetery is a part of the original Covey Homestead. Several members of the family are buried there.

Emmeline died March 10, 1900. Byron died March 7, 1917 at the Soldiers Home at Sawtell, California. Both are buried at Ceres.

Jasper Newton Cox
By Sue Roberts

Jasper Newton Cox was born September 13, 1850 in Chambersburg, Ohio. This is the first town south of Gallipolis on the river. Jasper was the eldest of ten children. His father, Abraham, died in 1866 when Jasper was sixteen years old. His mother was Elizabeth Waugh.

Jasper married Julia Ann Wooten January 28, 1874 in Gallia County, Ohio. Julia was born October 31, 1852 in Gallipolis, Ohio. Her father was Anderson Wooten and her mother was Eustatia Martindale. Julia's family lived near Jasper's on the river.

Jasper's brother, Albert, was the first to leave home for Kansas and Jasper followed about 1888.

The Indian Territory was soon to be opened for settlement. So Jasper went down to Oklahoma Territory and looked over the land. He spotted 160 acres that he wanted. Jasper went back to the starting line and waited for the race to start for claiming land. As he entered the race by horseback, he was able to outrun most who had their teams hitched to wagons. So he was with the lead groups and with the additional advantage that he knew exactly where to run to. But when he arrived at his land some men, "Sooners" were already camped there! A hot argument took place and Jasper won it when he ordered them off and they left. They could not have been in the race.

The land Jasper claimed was the southwest quarter of Section 9, Lowe Township. His patent number was 2135.

Jasper dug a cave and built one room above it where his family joined him. They lived there until the present home was built. He made a good living from his farm, borrowed money, added improvements and paid off his loans.

It was a sad time for Julia when they

decided to retire and have an auction. She cried to see her loved animals sold off.

They went to San Diego, California for awhile, then returned to Oklahoma. Julia fell and broke her hip and was confined to a wheel chair for the rest of her life. She died September 10, 1928 in Lucien, Oklahoma and is buried in McGuire Cemetery.

Jasper went back to San Diego, California and again returned to Oklahoma. He died April 29, 1931 in Lucien, Oklahoma and is also buried in McGuire Cemetery.

Jasper and Julia had the following children: Minnie E. born November 15, 1874 in Gallia County, Ohio; Melvin Wade born November 8, 1876 in Gallia County, Ohio; Virgil E. born October 8, 1877 in Gallia County, Ohio; Annie L. born August 26, 1880 in Gallia County, Ohio; Lottie Louise born October 27, 1882 in Ohio; Addie C. born June 7, 1885 in Ohio; William Albert born August 21, 1887 in Dayton, Ohio; Flossie Lee born March 20, 1889 in Kansas.

Robert E. Cox
By Robert Cox

Robert Edwin Cox was born January 19, 1921 at Yale, Oklahoma, where he attended grade school, the son of Albert and Nola (Cooper) Cox. On December 10, 1940, at Stillwater he married Nathalee Inman. She was born August 29, 1921 at Ripley, Oklahoma, the daughter of John William and Rose Anna (Kershner) Inman.

After serving in the army three years from 1942-1945 he returned to Oklahoma. He was wounded at Okinawa. In 1946, he bought a farm in Noble county four miles northwest of Glencoe, where they have since lived. They have three daughters: Diana Rose, born March 21, 1946, Debera Ruth born September 29, 1954, and Margaret Ann born April 23, 1958, all in Stillwater, Oklahoma.

When Robert Cox wanted a violin as a youngster he discovered he couldn't afford to purchase a good one, so he figured he could make one himself. He got a pattern off an old fiddle his brother had and fashioned his first violin. However, it did not have the right sound to it. Undaunted, he tried again, but that, too did not turn out right. He didn't have the information on how to produce a good violin and the material was too high for him to buy. But the interest wouldn't go away.

Cox, a retired finish carpenter, realized making an excellent violin depended on getting the right wood, but more importantly, the right measurements and graduations. He finally got the information, using measurements and graduations from the Oklahoma State Univer-

Robert Cox and daughters (L to R): Diana, Debbie and Margaret with their violins.

sity library. He's been making violins ever since, making more than 30 violins, as well as repairing them in his repair shop.

He started making violins in 1944 as a hobby. About 1979, he retired because of health problems and has since devoted his time to violin making and farming.

He did not learn the trade from anyone nor did he play the violin regularly. Most of his tools he used, he designed himself and everything is done by hand. Making a violin is time consuming taking about 125 hours from start to finish. He estimated he had made about 30 violins and sold them to various individuals in Oklahoma, California, Colorado, Texas, Arkansas and Missouri. When he wasn't making violins he was repairing them.

Cox made violins for each of his three daughters, although they didn't play the violin. He made them a little different and fancier than the others he made by using mother of pearl in places on them. He made the three at the same time.

He never took violin lessons and didn't know one musical note from another, learning to play by ear. Nor did he prefer to play for people. It made him nervous and he would rather listen to someone else play. He just enjoyed making violins for others to play.

Edward J. Coyle, Sr.
By Pearl Vivian

Edward John Coyle, Sr. was born in 1861 in Rippen, Wisconsin. Margaret McCosh was born in 1864 in Davenport, Iowa. They were married in 1890. Ed J. Coyle made the "run" to Perry on September 16, 1893, from Guthrie in a small wagon with a few groceries to sell, and staked a lot over on the east "Leo Park" in Perry. This park was later found to be a Government Reservation, so he had to relinquish that, but was fortunate right away finding a man who had staked a 160 acre farm north of Perry, but decided he couldn't stand the hub-bub of this wild country and agreed to sell out his right to Coyle for $40.00 and buy a railroad ticket back to Missouri. Coyle managed to borrow this large amount from one

Edward J. Coyle, Sr. 1861 - 1937.

Edward J. Coyle, Sr. home at 1124 "G" Street in Perry. Taken on November 8, 1896. (L to R): Pearl, Margaret, Edward.

of the new bankers who set up business and got his total claim to this farm for that amount. Of course, he had to go ahead and live there 3 or 4 months every year and make certain small improvements, etc., on it until he had filed the claim (as was done on all the farmland). Mrs. Coyle and a small daughter stayed out on the farm for the required time each year, with Ed coming out on Sundays. This farm is still in the possession of the Coyle family.

The first town residence was a small four room house at 1124 "G" street in Perry, which was on the north edge of Perry.

Later, a larger house was built by Mr. and Mrs. Ed Coyle at 11th and Elm. This house is one of the best kept older houses in Perry.

Coyle's first business venture was a grocery store, located on the southwest corner just off the square.

A good many cotton farmers, both white and black, had come in with the "Opening" and could make a good crop with a minimum of machinery. (Sometimes only a good crooked stick) which made cotton the first crop to be planted in a very large amount and therefore called for a Cotton Gin.

The gins of that day were very primitive, and many times in the first 4 or 5 years there were 3 or 4 active gins running with a total out-put of several thousand bales of cotton a year. About the 2nd or 3rd year, Coyle got in the cotton business and also bought and sold grain together with hogs and cattle on the side. He also established grain elevators and cotton gins in Pawnee and Noble counties at Morrison, Pawnee, Skedee, Marland, Sumner and other points. Several of these were still operating at the time of Ed J. Coyle's death in 1937. He as a charter member of the Lions club as well as a member of the Modern Woodmen of America.

On the day of the opening of the Cherokee Strip, Ed Coyle's father, John Coyle and the women of the family came up from Guthrie on the train and John Coyle staked a lot at the corner of 9th and "C" street (where the Kehres house now stands) and was able to build a make-shift barn on the alley. In this hastily constructed barn, the first Catholic service was held Sunday morning. (I'm sorry I don't know the name of the priest for sure, but think it was Father Willebord, as he was the earliest one I remember).

Mrs. Ed Coyle was one of the original members of the First Presbyterian Church in Perry and attended the first service the day after the Opening (which was held in a tent on the present location). I think the preacher was Rev. Meyers from Guthrie, who later helped in services here often. Mrs. Ed Coyle died in 1959 and was buried beside her husband in Grace Hill cemetery.

Mr. and Mrs. Ed Coyle had three children. Margaret Pearl was born in 1894 in Perry. She married J.J. Vivian of Gilmer, Texas. She lives in Perry. Edward John Coyle, Jr. was born in 1900 in Perry. He married Grace Sparrow of Perry. He died in 1972. Robert John Coyle was born in 1903 in Perry. He married Beulah Unzicker of Enid. She was an instructor of Commerce in Perry High school. Robert died in 1953.

William Penn Craig
By Jane Harnden

Like so many other pioneer families, William Penn Craig and his wife, Emma, settled on a farm close to relatives in Noble County, Oklahoma Territory. Within three miles of their farm southeast of Billings were farms of seven of their brothers and sisters. As their children grew up, the country school and neighborhood activities included 43 first cousins of the Hicks and Craig families.

William Penn Craig was born March 20, 1873 in Higby, Howard county, Missouri. His wife, Emma Hicks was born August 20, 1876 in Capionma, Nemaha county, Kansas and they were married July 4, 1900 at Pawnee in Oklahoma Territory. They first set up housekeeping in Pawnee where Penn was employed by a granite company that made tombstones. Their first two daughters were born there, Leona Mae in 1901 and Bessie Leigh in 1903. Penn then moved his young family to a partial sod dug-out house 11 miles southeast of Billings. Their family grew with the birth of Chester Cecil (1906), Marjorie Julian (1907), Dorothy Loraine (1910), Helen Marie (1913), Homer Wilson (1916), and Madelyn Isabelle (1918).

The first Noble County home provided shelter for the small family but also was a shelter for scorpions and Emma told in later years of having to carefully shake garments each morning before dressing. The family lived on two different farms before buying 160 acres of school land 1½ miles south of Echo school in 1917. Water was provided by a rock lined, dug well 200 yards from the house. A rock outcropping on a nearby family farm provided excellent building material for more permanent housing as rectangles could be cut from the rock and used like oversized bricks. The remains of the old rock kitchen built from this material are still visible on the farm.

Living close to relatives was a plus for the families helped each other with building houses and outbuildings, butchering, child care, and farm labor. Penn supplemented the family income by working as "road boss" in White Rock township handling records as people worked out their poll tax.

The Craig children attended the Echo school through the 8th grade. Leona, the oldest child, boarded with the F.D. Harnden family in Stillwater to attend highschool and then came back to teach at the Echo school. This same pattern of education was to be repeated many times in various forms and after Leona married E.E. Harnden and moved to Stillwater, younger siblings stayed with her to attend highschool. All eight children graduated from high school and five of them taught school at some time. Chester Craig made it a lifelong profession and taught many years in Kay and Noble counties.

Providing for a large family was not easy. Emma made all the clothing for her family with the girls helping sew as soon as they were old enough to hold a needle. A garden was raised to provide vegetables in the summer. Helen remembers picking potato bugs from the plants and putting them in a can with coal oil to kill them. For 100 killed bugs, the children were paid one penny. In the winter months the menu consisted of items made of flour ground from home grown wheat, eggs and milk from the farm, and meat raised and butchered by the family. Items that had to be purchased with cash at Billings 11 miles away or Perry 15 miles away, were very limited. For birthdays, Emma baked a cake but there were no gifts.

Christmas was observed with a cedar tree branch from a neighbor's farm for there were no trees on their 160 acres. The cedar "tree" was decorated with pop corn strings and a few cranberries plus paper chains. Gifts for the children were homemade. A typical Christmas stocking had a few pieces of candy and a fresh orange. Fruit salad was the traditional Christmas treat and it was made of tapioca with a few pieces of orange, banana, plum and nuts.

The family's first car was a 1925 model Ford purchased second hand in 1926. It was a two seated touring car. Before the car was purchased, transportation was in the wagon or buggy pulled by the family's work horses.

Like other pioneer families who had struggled through starting a farm on the prairie, the depression and dust bowl years 1930-1937 were major setbacks. Penn died in 1937, and Emma moved the next year to Stillwater to be near three of her daughters. Leona Harnden, Marjorie Eyler and Helen Ricker. Chester Craig and his wife Alice moved to the old farm house in later years and remodeled it to make their home. Dorothy Forshee lived in Oklahoma City, Bessie Whelan settled in Albuquerque, Homer in Farmington, New Mexico, and Madelyn Brown made her home in Texas. As this is written in July, 1985, the only surviving members of the family are Bessie, Helen and Homer.

The Noble county farm with its close knit family ties provided a rich heritage of memories for the Craig children.

Martin L. Crowder
By Gail Johnson

Around 1910 the Martin L. Crowder family came to the Perry area from Buxton, Iowa. Martin and his wife Rachel Katherine (Katie) Kennedy, daughter of John and Sarah Kennedy had four children, Elsie Mae, January 3, 1888; Gertie, February 18, 1892; Lavinia, September 11, 1893; and Ansel, April 19, 1895. Martin and Katie were married November 18, 1885, in Missouri.

Martin was born in Adair County, Missouri in 1860, on October 11. His parents were William T. and Miranda (Mason) Crowder. Martin's ancestors came from Virginia and Illinois. And while he was on a visit to Springfield, Illinois, he had the honor of sitting on the lounge that Lincoln courted his bride on, received a piece of the table cloth that was used at Lincoln's wedding, and received 2 gavels, made from an apple tree that Rueben Crowder, his great grandfather, had planted. Philip Crowder is the oldest known Crowder of this family.

Dr. A. M. Crowder about 1933.

Martin's daughter, Elsie had married Henry Leonard Johnson prior to their move to Perry, and Elsie and Henry came and established their home in Perry also.

Martin and Henry opened a grocery store called Crowder and Johnson and established the business on the east side of the thriving Perry square. The business was very prosperous and grew steadily until Martin's death in 1931, the 27th of April. Some of the ways that Martin and Henry advertised for the store were the local newspaper and something usual for this day and age they used postcards.

When Martin died Henry continued the running of the grocery store with the help of his sons, and another local man, Orvil Foster. The store finally closed in 1942, after Henry's sons had to serve their country in the military forces.

Martin and Katie's other children married after they had moved to Perry, their marriages are as follows: Gertie C. married Joyce B. Webster, November 18, 1915. To this union two children were born: Armond Burnell, January 17, 1924; Dolmer George, November 22, 1925.

Lavania C. married Walter E. Crowder, October 31, 1915; to this union there were four children born, two dying in infancy, the others as follows: Walter Martin, June 11, 1917; Floreine, November 25, 1919. Lavania married two more times, first to Arthur Crawford, January 19, 1940; secondly to Harry Phenis, June 23, 1944, no issue to either union.

Ansel Martin Crowder married Florence Kraemer, June 16, 1924. To this union one child was born, Betty June, June 1, 1925.

Katie Crowder remarried much later in her life to Fred Carter on February 14, 1942. She died May 13, 1951, in the Perry General Hospital.

Other information about their children is as follows: Gertie lives in a nursing home in Tulsa, Oklahoma. Her husband and one child have since passed on. One child, Armond, is still living possibly in the Tulsa area also.

Lavania out lived all of her husbands and died on June 27, 1977, in Perry, Oklahoma. Martin, her son, died June 14, 1984 in Layton, Utah. Her daughter is still living in Anahiem, California, married to Marvin Mielke, with five children to their union.

Ansel Crowder is still living in Perry, Oklahoma and was a very well known dentist for 50 years, between 1920 and 1970. His wife still lives at their own home and he stays in a nursing home because of health reasons. His daughter Betty June lives in Tulsa with her husband Richard. They had three children to their union.

Ansel followed in his father's steps by becoming a Mason, joining the Perry Lodge in August of 1916. He earned his Master Mason Degree. He became a Life Time member of the lodge during construction of the masonic building that now houses Chris' Pharmacy and other businesses. For many years Crowder was superintendent of this building, and he had his dental practice offices on the second floor of the Masonic Building at the northwest corner of the square.

On Friday, January 17, 1986, Dr. Ansel M. Crowder received his 70 year pin from the Masonic Order in Perry, and the state of Oklahoma. Robert Bazzell presented the pin and said that Crowder was the only Oklahoman to ever receive a 70 year pin and prior to that he was the only Oklahoman to ever receive a 65 year pin and he still holds that single honor.

The Crowder family has been in the Perry area for over 70 years now and they have been a guiding force in the community and in the state.

Good Christian people like the Crowders deserve recognition for their deeds, which Ansel Crowder has by being a recipient of a 70 year masonic pin. Also Martin L. received recognition by having his funeral at midnight with a full masonic order and ceremony and he was decreed a 33rd Degree Mason the highest honor a mason can receive.

For other information on Elsie see Henry L. Johnson story.

All the generations of Crowders

Crowder Family about 1905 — (L to R): Elsie Mae, Katie, Ansel, Gertie, Martin L. and Lavania.

have been given except for Mathew who is the son of Rueben and the father of William T. Crowder. This family of Crowders goes back as far as 1760, with Philip Crowder being born in that year.

This poem was written by Elsie (Crowder) Johnson, in her pamphlet, "Inspirations".

Country Doctor

He calls no hour of day or night his own.
Through heat and cold he goes his rounds alone,
Here, to bring some mortal into being.
There to ease some soul that must be fleeting.
He listens earnestly to tales of grief,
Forgets himself that he may give relief
To bodies suffering, to tortured minds:
in service to all men his pleasure finds.

Rosa LaDue Dailey
By Mildred Highfill

The following information was collected from an interview of Rosa LaDue Dailey dated August 28, 1937 for the W.P.A. I am ¼ Otoe Indian and the daughter of Augustus and Millie (DeRoin) La Due. I was born in Gage county, Nebraska, on January 16, 1872. When I was about 8 years old my parents with several other families came to Indian Territory, locating on Red Rock creek near the Otoe Agency. The trip was made in wagons and on horseback, bringing only necessary things for camping. The company all located together in camps but shortly afterward some thought it would be best to locate on land where gardens could be made.

My parents moved to the southeast and found a place on Black Bear creek. On this place, there was a one room log cabin that had been used by ranchmen, nearby was a good spring of water and we stoppd here and built a fireplace of rock and did our cooking on it, as we did not have a stove.

The team my father had was a small pony team, but he had a plan and we broke some sod and made a garden, also planted some corn.

We had a hard time to get food at first until we could raise some. Mother often parched corn and made coffee of it.

We did a great deal of hunting and fishing and secured most of our living in this way, when we needed supplies we went to Arkansas City (Kansas). It took us several days to make the trip there and back. I went to school at the Otoe Agency at the boarding school called the Mission. This school is not operating now and I later went to the Chilocco school. I do not remember the date when my father was hired by the Government to operate the toll bridge over the Red Rock creek near the Otoe Agency. The Goverment paid father $20.00 a month and he camped at the bridge. Mother kept the family and stayed on the land where we had established our home, later moving to the camp with father.

When the allotments of land were made in 1893, mother and we children received our allotments. In December 1904, I was married and all but three of my children have received allotments. I am now living on the land of one of my daughters, who is dead.

Rosa died in 1956. She married James B. Dailey, December 12, 1894 in the Otoe Indian chapel. She is buried in the Otoe-Missouri cemetery. Millie La Due was born August 26, 1852 and died October 27, 1896. She is buried in a little Indian cemetery in Otoe township (ne 4). Augustus La Due was 60 years old at the time of his death. He is buried in the Tillman cemetery in Missouri township.

James R. Dale
By Mildred Highfill

James R. (Stick) Dale was born July 11, 1870 in Illinois. His father died when James was three years of age and his mother when he was nine. His oldest brother, Neal Dale, took him into his home in Weir City, Kansas. Neal was a coal miner and James found employment as a miner. His job was to handle the mules in drawing the coal cars out to the stock pile. As he developed age and strength he worked into more important jobs and, before he was twenty-one had developed into an expert in the use of dynamite in shot firing in the mines. He held his position in the mines for several years. On November 18, 1888, he married Ada Ollie Hastings at Midway, Kansas. Officiating was Rev. Hendrix of the Latter Day Saints. While off duty from the mines for the purpose of his marriage there was an explosion and mine disaster at Frontenac, Kansas in which 180 miners and all the mules in the mines were killed. Every miner on duty was killed.

James continued his work as a miner until the opening of the Cherokee Strip, when he made the run. He came to the south line of the Strip at a point which is almost due south of what is now Morrison, Oklahoma. He ran through that location and crossed the Black Bear Creek and staked a claim adjoining the Otoe south line and remained there through the fall and winter. In the spring, he returned to Weir City, Kansas for Mrs. Dale and the two children, Grace Bell and James M. After coming to Oklahoma, he became a well digger and drilled many of the water wells in eastern Noble County and western Pawnee County. He was employed at times in intricate work of blasting with dynamite.

He was connected with the sheriff's office for about 20 years. He assisted in the Fells murder case. Isaac W. Fells was a farmer in the Indian Reservation near the Otoe Switch. Henry T. Armstrong and Albert Mitchell murdered him for a team and wagon. Stick Dale helped capture them and was present when Armstrong was hung in the courthouse park. One of his sons, George Dale, was also an officer of the law and was shot and killed by a bandit on January 15, 1915 at Eucha, Oklahoma. Two highjackers entered a cafe where George was being served a meal. George killed one, but he was shot by the other one and lived only three hours.

The children of James and Ada were:

James M., Thomas Everete, Olive Haskell, Charley H., George A. and Grace Bell Dale.

Stick Dale died June 14, 1951 and Ada April 20, 1947. They are buried in the Morrison Cemetery. Services for Stick Dale were held in the Newton Funeral Home at Perry with former Governor Henry S. Johnston officiating.

John R. Darmer
By Clara Darmer Shelton

My Dad, John Robert Darmer, born in Champaign County, Illinois, October 3, 1861, was 9 months old and took his first step the day his father left for the Civil War. His parents were William Cornelius Darmer and Martha Ann Rose. His mother farmed with oxen and didn't recognize her husband when he returned in ill health, rags and without shoes.

Dad was one of the original cowboys riding the Chisholm Trail. Then, August 12, 1891, he married Clara A. Armstrong, for whom I am named. Clara was born January 4, 1866, in Mercer County, Missouri, the daughter of Thomas Jefferson Armstrong and Novey Elizabeth Rose. March 4, 1904, they with their children, Letha, W. T., Glenn, Fern, and Bennett (I completed the family in 1906), came by train from Perry, Iowa to Perry, Oklahoma arriving in a raging blizzard. Their household goods, farm implements and "old Bob", a black Morgan stallion, came with them by freight. The first night was spent in a shed added to the main room of the filled hotel. Later, they learned, several children in the hotel had measles and the Darmer children had not.

Dad brought a farm 8 miles north and 2 miles west of Perry from Mr. Ponds, who had not moved his family of 5 sons, so for a time, our families, totaling 15 persons, shared a 3-room house and the measles!

The first years were very hard. The first crop was destroyed by greenbugs. The next year, Dad had made one round in the wheat field with the binder when with just time to get into the cellar, a hail and wind storm wiped out the wonderful crop, ruining roofs, smashing windows and shredding the tops of cars belonging to a fortunate few. Before moving to Oklahoma, my family had heard how the children in the "sunny south" could go barefoot the year 'round — now they learned the real reason — times were too hard to afford shoes.

A few good years followed and in 1915, Dad and Jim Dolezal built barns. Dad's was a huge red one with J R Darmer in big white letters on the front. He fenced our farm with hand hewn corner posts of native stone that are still in use. Fairview (District #30) was built just a quarter mile from our home and Dad served on the school board for years as well as being a member of IOOF. A trip into Perry for supplies was an all day affair by horse and wagon, leaving early in the morning and returning late at night. After one such trip we arose to find the family cat frantically trying to "cover" the Limburger Cheese Dad had purchased. Dad introduced the first mules into our neighborhood and they were quite a novelty. Mothers cautioned their children not to ride those "funny animals." Each year we had a gathering of neighbors and among the refreshments Dad always served a keg of beer and an entire stalk of bananas. Neighborhood boys had boxing matches and baseball games in the pasture, learning to swim in the still existing pond north of the barn.

It was said by anyone who met Mama, that she had the bluest eyes they had ever seen. She played the organ and sang for community affairs and funerals. At a Crane family funeral, Mr. Nick Steichen Sr. joined Mama in an impromtu duet that was so lovely it was spoken for years. On a beautiful Easter Sunday, April 8, 1917, Mama died of appendicitis while a surgeon and his nurse Dad had summoned from Oklahoma City were preparing the kitchen table for surgery. The funeral was held in our home with Dr. Milliard, Presbyterian minister, conducting the services. Mr. and Mrs. Mugler, Mrs. Poage, and Mr. Yahn provided the music. Friends and neighbors joined us in following the horse-drawn hearse to Mt. Carmel Cemetery where Mama was laid to rest.

Dad owned several farms at one time and lived out his life in Noble County. Glenn contrcted a paralysis and Dad cared for him at home until his death. Bennett lived out-of-state his adult years. Serving in the Navy Submarine Division after WW I, and in the Seabees Division of the Navy during WW II. Letha spent her married years away but returned a widow to spend the rest of her life. Fern became a teacher, teaching in country one-room schools in Noble County but finishing her teaching career in Pawnee, Oklahoma. She now lives in the University Village Retirement Center in Tulsa. W. T. and I chose to live our lives in Noble County. W. T. had one son, Remley, and a daughter, Phyllis. Remley has four sons so the Darmer name continues though not in Noble County. Phyllis has two sons and a daughter. My husband, J. Roy Shelton, and I purchased the family farm in

(L to R): John Darmer, Evelyn Jensen, Clara Darmer Shelton taken about 1918 on the Darmer farm.

1946, and in 1953, a tornado destroyed the barn and machine shed. Our son, Leonard, purchased the family farm where he raised Leslie, J. D. and Karen. He continues to make it his home. Our youngest child, Ralph, also chose to make his home in Noble County. He lives and is raising David, Kristi, Shelby, and Jeffery on a farm south of Perry. Our daughters, Barbara and Verna Lee, married and moved to other cities where Barbara raised Bill, Candi, Bonni and Boyd Sweger. Verna Lee had Marva, Terry, and Beverly Swart.

Florence Denslow
By Florence Denslow

I, Florence Frances Derr Denslow was born to Alma (Back) and Raymond (Ray) Derr on October 10, 1911 on the farm three and one-half miles south of Billings, Oklahoma, and one and one-fourth east. The legal description of the land is NW ¼ section 16 Township 23 North, Range 2 West.

I had one sister, Cora Mae Derr Lawhon. Cora died September 28, 1963.

I attended school at Elkhorn school (district #5) for two years and finished through the seventh grade at Frog Holler school. The name was later changed to Red Rock Valley school. I graduated from the eighth grade and high school at Billings, Oklahoma. I attended Oklahoma Agriculture and Mechanical College for two years. This College is now known as Oklahoma State University.

I began my teaching career with a life elementary certification in the rural school of Noble County. I attended summer school at O.A.M.C. and taught in the winter. I then taught in the rural schools of Garfield county for six years. I got my B.S. degree in 1937, in elementary education. I then taught in the Kremlin school system for one year. I had an opportunity to teach in the school for the Blind in Muskogee. While there I took extension course and correspondence courses so was able to get an M.S. Degree in 1942 with a life certificate in the secondary level of education. I returned to Stillwater to teach for two years in the school in which I had done my practice teaching.

I married Frederick B. Denslow while teaching in Stillwater. He was a Sgt. in the 56th Armd. Inf Bn 12 AD WW II. Frederick was sent to Abeline, Texas, and then overseas.

I started teaching in Enid, Oklahoma in 1945. While teaching in Enid, I took college work at Phillips University and received certification to be a Counselor and to teach Remedial Reading. I taught in Lincoln school, Adams school, and Waller Junior High.

When I retired at age 65, I had taught 45 years. Since retirement I have been a substitute teacher for the Enid school system.

My husband and I bought a home in Enid when he returned from overseas service. He died in 1971 on Memorial Day. I have continued to live in the only home we ever had.

Wiley W. DeVilbiss
By Callie Anthis DeVilbiss

Wiley Wayne DeVilbiss was born March 20, 1910, across the road south of Noble county, northwest of Stillwater on Ebenezer Stotts farmplace. Callie Mae (Anthis) DeVilbiss was born November 3, 1913 in Noble County, north of Orlando on Madison Anthis homestead. Both graduated from Orlando High School. They married July 24, 1932 in First Baptist Church, Pawnee, Oklahoma by pastor Earnest Hitt. Six months were spent in parternal DeVilbiss home. Wiley worked for his dad for team of horses, bought used machinery and moved to Silket farm January 12, 1933. His folks loaned us 3 cows to milk, my folks gave us 24 laying hens. Orlando friends at O.W. Gentrys gave us a shower. These were depression years, it all helped!

People lived from the land, as much as possible. Farmers took wheat to the mill, had white and whole wheat flour ground; gave portion for labor. Women did all the baking at home. Butchering and meat care was done at home, beef canned, pork cured; sugar cane raised and made into sorghum portion given for labor. Popcorn and sorghum taffy were winter favorites, while ice cream, summer fun!

Farm wages were $1.00 per day, wheat between 75 and 50 cents a bushel. We sold eggs at 10 cents a dozen, butter-fat in cream, 14 cents lb. We had no electricity in the country, kerosene for lamps was 10 cents a gallon, gasoline about the same price. Clothes were made at home! Phone lines were maintained by farm people, no private lines, only specified numbers. Five Longs was a general ring for emergencies. We lived at the extreme north edge of Lake Carl Blackwell Area.

These people were given a chance to land north of Marland, Oklahoma which the government bought up after the 101 ranch went broke. We took 140 acres northeast of Marland, on the south side of Salt Fork River. We were now the parents of three sons, Glen, Gene, and Jerald (Jerry). Wiley's parents, Mr. and Mrs. Ray DeVibiss moved east from Lake area summer of 1937.

The evening of January 8, 1938, we settled on our new farm. This could be called, Last Frontier in Oklahoma. Familys came from every direction. Some came soon enough to plant wheat in the fall of 1937, others came in early 1938. Improvements were new, but all fences had to be built. Forty years was given to pay the government for land. A shorter time sufficed; economy improved!

The 101 Ranch school on the north bank of river was abandoned; north of the river went to Ponca City, south side went into Marland. The river became another dividing line when 101 Baptist Mission joined Marland. Electricity came in 1948 which improved country living.

Wiley and Callie DeVilbiss and sons (L-R) Jerry, Gene and Glen-1939

Florence Denslow.

Years passed, we raised our family here. The spring of 1953, Glen DeVilbiss and Gene DeVilbiss graduated from Marland High School. August 12, that year Glen was taken into 2 years compulsory military training. He spent 18 months of that time in Army Repair shop at Belvor, Virginia. Gene missed the service because of a childhool accident. Spring of 1954, Jerry DeVilbiss graduated from Marland High school. He later joined and served eight years in the Air Force; the last four years were spent amid erratic over-sea-trips caused by war-scare! Jerry was a mechanic on planes; men were sent where needed, riding supply planes amid supplies and terrific noise!

Glen Arthur DeVilbiss was born March 21, 1933, lives at Farmington, New Mexico. On March 31, 1957, he married Aloha Fay Reed at Oklahoma City. She was born November 14, 1934 at Sayer, Oklahoma. They are the parents of two sons born at Farminton: Danny Wayne DeVilbiss, October 13, 1958, not married; Wesley Dean DeVilbiss June 17, 1961, married Rhonda Candelaria at Farmington, August 31, 1985. Glen barbers and drills oil wells.

Gene Ivan DeVilbiss was born June 25, 1934, on April 24, 1956, he married Opal Ann Bowlen born January 22, 1938 at Cushing, Oklahoma. They moved to Durango, Colorado, later to Farmington, New Mexico. They are the parents of three children: Ivy Lea DeVilbiss born at Durango, December 14, 1957, married Dan Brooks, one son Tucker; Nicky Gene DeVilbiss was born September 22, 1959 at Durango, married Shannon Mossbury, one son, Shane; Ricky Ray DeVilbiss born October 5, 1960 at Farmington, married Kristi Kaps. Gene barbers in Glen's Shop.

Jerry Dean DeVilbiss was born January 25, 1956, he married Eleanor Kay Rheam at Ponca City, Oklahoma. She was born December 27, 1939. They are the parents of four: Jerry Jr. baby boy DeVilbiss prematurely born and died March 7, 1957; Dennis Edward DeVilbiss born March 19, 1958, at Oklahoma City, not married; Scott Allen DeVilbiss born at Chandler, Arkansas May 11, 1960, married Deborah Sandoval at Santa Fe, New Mexico, August 11, 1984. They live at Mace, Arkansas; Denay DeVilbiss born at Clovis, New Mexico, August 29, 1963 not married. Jerry Dean DeVilbiss died February 10, 1971. He is buried at Grace Hill cemetery, Perry, Oklahoma. These three children carry the name, Petty, from step-dad, Wayne Petty.

Edson DeVilbiss
By Callie Anthis DeVilbiss

The DeVilbiss name is French. Four DeVilbiss brothers immigrated to the United States. The oldest known ancestor is great-grandfather William DeVilbiss. William was born November 15, 1811 and married twice, first Ruth Carpenter September 11, 1831. She died in February 1832. His second wife was Julie Cornell who died in February 1865. William had five children: Lewis, Cyrus, Edson, Frank and Emma. These families were in Missouri. This is where Edson was probably born.

Edson (Ed) DeVilbiss was born February 21, 1856. He married Rosetta Horn, March 18, 1878. Some years later this couple moved to Altamont, Kansas. They were parents of one daughter and six sons.

From Indian-Pioneer History Foreman Collection in Oklahoma Historical Society in Oklahoma City -Interview with Rosetta (Horn) DeVilbiss August 17, 1937: "I was born in Knox County, Ohio, September 11, 1861 and when nine years old my parents moved from Ohio to Missouri, coming by train as far west as Jefferson City, that being the end of that railroad, then by covered wagon to near Carthage, Missouri, later moving to Kansas. My father was David Horn born in Knox County, Ohio, my mother Judith Ann Reecer born in Williamsport, Pennsylvania. In the late fall of 1894, my husand and I and our family moved to what is now Noble County, locating on a farm in Walnut township. In securing this farm we traded a forty acre tract of land in Kansas for the rights of the man who had staked this claim, thereby we proved up on this land and became one of the pioneers of Noble County. On our trip to this country we came by covered wagon, bringing three teams and wagons and I drove one team during the trip.

The farm we secured was not very good farm land, and we were told by others who had already settled here that we would starve to death on that land. Our first home was a one-room box bouse 14' x 16' in which we lived two years, then we built a story and a half house of five rooms; for this house the lumber was hauled from Perry. This was a difficult task for the roads were very rough with deep ravines and creeks to cross.

Our first crops were Kaffir corn, oats and cotton. The oats we mowed and used for feed. The second year we raised some broom corn along with other crops. We made a thresher to seed the broom corn, this was done by putting nails in a circle form and turning it by hand. In this manner we could seed the broom corn after which we tied it in bundles and stored it until we could get it made into brooms. My husband sent to Kansas City for coloring and handles, then made the straw into brooms which we traded to merchants at Perry for food supplies and enough cash for the handles and coloring. Together with our farming and the continuance of the broom corn made into brooms we proved up on our land and later bought land from the party that told us we would starve to death. Since my husband's death I reside in Perry with one of my sons. I have raised five sons and one daughter. My third son is now Deputy Sheriff of Noble County. Their children were: Bertha (1879-1956) married Ray Sachs; Walter (1881-1957) married Grace Wells; marriage dissolved and he married Marie Winger; Earnest died at age two buried in Missouri; Clarence Raymond (Ray) (1887-1968) married Nora May Stotts;

The five sons of Edson and Rosetta DeVilbiss (Left to Right): Walter, Ray, Chester. Back Row (Left to Right): Melvin, Vern - about 1914.

Chester Orville (Pete) (1891-1983) married Juanita Long. Juanita deceased and Pete married Bernice Long; Melvin Dewey (1898-1919) died of Typhoid fever; Vernice Pierre (Vern) (1903-1957) married Ruth Hetherington, marriage dissolved and Vern married Beulah Knight.

After the death of David Horn in Kansas, Judith came to live with her daughter, Rosetta. She died here September 21, 1914 and was buried in the Shelton Cemetery in Noble County.

Edson died July 17, 1936 and Rosetta died August 2, 1948. They are buried in the Grace Hill cemetery, Perry, Oklahoma. Nearby is the grave of their son Vern and his wife, Loran.

Ray DeVilbiss
By Callie Anthis DeVilbiss

Clarence Raymond (Ray) DeVilbiss (December 12, 1887-July 11, 1968) was born in Monett, Missouri, in Neosho county. Sometime after that, his parents Edson DeVilbiss and Rosetta (Horn) DeVilbiss moved to Altamont, Kansas, in Labette county. This move was made before the next child was born. Chester Orville (Pete) DeVilbiss was born there December 10, 1891, and Melvin Dewey DeVilbiss was born there May 8, 1898. Later the family moved again.

Ray DeVilbiss was a 12 year old lad when his parents left Altamont, Kansas, and came down into Oklahoma to live. Edson DeVilbiss had been down in Oklahoma and bought a quarter section of land southeast of Perry, Oklahoma. It was the northeast ¼ of section 31 20N 1E in Noble county. They settled on the farm, coming there in 1900. Ray and his brothers enjoyed this trip coming from Kansas. Of course, the traveling was done by wagon, and they were able to play on the way and still keep up. By preference, they walked most of the way, we were told.

One of the first crops planted in Oklahoma was broomcorn. Ray told of how they worked with a hand turned (homemade) thrasher that took the grain off heads. Edson DeVilbiss farmed, but it could be said that he raised the family by making and selling brooms. Grandchildren remember the hand-thrasher at Grandpa's place which was still there after he died.

The DeVilbiss children went to New Hope school. There they mingled with the Abraham (A.B.) Stotts family children. Years passed as the young folks grew to adulthood. In time, Ray DeVilbiss courted Nora May Stotts. They were married "twice" February 22, 1909. Ray bought a marriage license at Stillwater in Payne county and they went up to old man Fillmore's place to be married. Before the day was over Ray and Nora May were informed that they were not properly married. Thus the ceremony was repeated and marriage legal. Mr. Fillmore, David's dad who performed wedding ceremonies, lived across the line in Noble county.

The new bride, Nora May (Stotts) DeVilbiss was born in Sumner county, Kansas, March 9, 1889, came with her parents, Abraham (A.B.) Stotts and Mahala Lucretie (Powers) Stotts into Oklahoma in 1893. Later, as a small child, because of illness and hard-times in the family, she was taken back to Cottonwood Falls, Kansas, to live with Uncle Ebenezer Stotts. A few years later Ebenezer and wife, Sarrah, moved to Stillwater, Oklahoma, and Nora May went back to join her family. Soon after this Ebenezer bought land northwest of Stillwater, Oklahoma, but never lived there. It was on this farm where Ray DeVilbiss and Nora May first lived. They were the parents of four children.

Wiley Wayne DeVilbiss was born in Payne county, March 20, 1910. He married Callie Mae Anthis, born in Noble county, November 3, 1913. They had three sons, Glen, Gene, and Jerry. (See Wiley DeVilbiss story.)

Leslie Raymond DeVilbiss was born in Noble county, June 30, 1913. He married Betty Branham July 30, 1950. They had four children: Barbara Gayle DeVilbiss (June 17, 1951-February 21, 1981) buried at Grace Hill, Perry; Leslie Allen DeVilbiss born July 22, 1952; Paul Mark DeVilbiss born December 28, 1955; Raleigh Leon DeVilbiss born October 19, 1957. This marriage dissolved about 1968. He married Thelma Dawson June 26, 1971. These families live in or around Perry, Oklahoma.

Ralph Paul DeVilbiss was born in Payne County, June 12, 1916. He moved to Oregon and married Maxine Peabody June 13, 1952. Their three children were born near Jefferson, Oregon: Larry Wayne DeVilbiss March 15, 1944; Ray Allen DeVilbiss December 11, 1945; Susan Dianne (DeVilbiss) Herr November 21, 1947. They moved to a farm near Palmer, Arkansas, when children were small, and did mission work at Lazy Mt. Children's Home. In 1963, they adopted two small lads from Korea; Brian Rye and Billy Park. Ralph died in 1978.

Velma Faye DeVilbiss was born in Payne county May 27, 1918. She married Gerald Bilyeu September 11, 1938. They had one son, Danny Philip Bilyeu, who died at birth November 15, 1939. They live west of Stillwater.

Ray and May DeVilbiss rented farm land for several years. Wiley was born

Last homeplace of Ray and Nora May DeVilbiss. Now under the waters of Lake McMurtry.

Ray DeVilbiss family in their new 1918 Chevrolet. L-R: Velma, Nora May, Wiley, Ray, Leslie and Ralph - 1919.

Nora May and Ray DeVilbiss - 1959.

on Eb Stotts place, Leslie was born on Sherrard place, Ralph was born on Swanson place. They then bought Emmons Homestead where Velma was born. Years later this place was taken for Lake Carl Blackwell. They bought and moved east to George Hoggett place in Noble county 1937. They were there till it was taken for Lake McMurtry. The dam is on the south end of this 80-acre home place. Ray died 1968, May died in 1973, both are buried at Grace Hill cemetery in Perry.

Martin Diehm
By Erma Stockton Diehm

Martin Diehm was born July 11, 1898, in Norman, Oklahoma Territory, the son of John and Elizabeth Diehm, who had come over from Germany. Martin was working in Texas, and had come home on vacation. His brother, John, who lived in my community broke his leg. It was harvest time and he needed help. So Martin came up just to help him for two weeks. We met at a party and after a while, we fell in love and he never did go back to Texas.

In 1922, he put out a wheat crop and we decided to get married after he harvested the wheat. The wheat was a complete failure, but Martin said he wouldn't let a little thing like that keep us apart. We were married in Perry, July 25, 1923. We had rented a farm, but had no money so everything we bought was borrowed from his brother, John.

We went in debt $400.00 for a new Fordson tractor. We bought an old Ford car for $50.00. Not much but it would run. The top was down and when we raised it, it was full of holes. Martin ordered some material and made a new top. He bought side curtains and we had a fairly warm car.

Brother John gave us 2 dozen hens, my dad a calf, and we bought a cow. All the furniture was second-hand but our bed and a kitchen cabinet. The first year we were able to pay John off what we owed him.

Just before our first daughter was born, Martin was cutting off a bolt — it flew off and put his left eye out. He sav-

The Diehm family about 1938. (L to R): Martin, Martin Ray, Erma, Anna Mae, Bonnie Lou, Lois.

ed the ball but never could see anything out of that eye. It wasn't long before he bought another tractor and rented more land.

Bonnie Lou was born July 26, 1925, and Lois Elaine, February 13, 1927. We lived on that farm for 9 years. It overflowed a lot. We couldn't get to the barn from the house without hip boots. We put the hogs in the grainery, and left the cows in the stantions. Water got in the barn. We kept people at our house who were caught in the flood.

The next year we moved on another place upland. This was a hard year during the depression. We had lots of hogs but no way to feed them. One day a man came to our house and said he had a stack of fodder hay he would sell for $15.00, but we did not have $15.00. Then Martin happened to think we had a $15.00 gold piece, his dad had given us for a wedding present. With this, Martin could thresh his wheat and get grain to feed his hogs and straw for the cows. And you know, things began looking up as soon as we parted with the gold piece.

We went into the cattle business with Richard Schultz, a banker with a place east of Red Rock. We rented his land and did all the work with the cattle and got half of the calf crop. This place had a bigger house. Martin Ray was born here, December 11, 1929, and Anna Mae, October 28, 1936.

During WW II, we had sugar stamps and meat stamps. Gas was rationed with stamps. We couldn't get tires, so we jacked our car up on stumps and drove the truck. Since Martin was a big farmer he could get tires for the truck. We had our own hens and meat, and faired pretty good.

Martin always said he would build me a home someday. So we sold out and bought a farm of our own. And true to his word, he built me a lovely rock 4-bedroom house. He went everywhere and got rock. It is so pretty.

We thought we would live there forever, but Martin's health failed and we thought if we could get off the farm, he would get better. We moved into Perry, then in 1964, to Arizona. In 1968, we decided to come to Oklahoma on vacation. Martin had pneumonia and died August 28, 1968, and is buried in Grace Hill cemetery. I went back to Arizona, sold my house, and came back here to live.

Bonnie Lou married Jim Frazier and lives in Laconna, Washington. They have three daughters Diana (Christenson) Terry, and Karen (Bergen).

Lois married George Elmore and lives in Richardson, Texas. They adopted a boy, David, and a girl, Margaret (Enright).

Martin Ray married Shirley Ann Gemmell. They had a boy, David and a girl, Kim (Gililand). His second wife is Clara Mae Elliott. They live on the home place.

Anna Mae married Eldon Briftol. They had a boy, Bryan and a girl,

Sherlyn. Her second husband is Whity Luuttila. They live in Springfield, Illinois.

I thank God, he was so good to me. Gave me a wonderful man, 4 great kids, 9 grandchildren and 2 great-grandchildren.

Henry Ellis Domeny
By Helen Ratliff

Henry Ellis Domeny, born July 22, 1855, in Harrison township, Vinton County, Ohio, the youngest son of John Domeny, Sr. and his wife Alzira Stevens Domeny. Henry Ellis Domeny and Joyce Elizabeth Dixon were married February 1878, in Vinton County, Ohio by the Rev. Charles H. McCormick. Joyce Elizabeth Dixon was born April 15, 1858, near Raye, Ohio, the daughter of Joel Dixon and Rosanna Murry Dixon.

Farmers in Vinton County cleared the timber from the crest of the steep hills, creating farms. Henry Ellis Domeny owned one of these "hill top" farms. Four of the Domeny children were born in Ohio: Mary Florence, 1878; William Elmer, 1880; Eliza Homer, 1883; Rose Zella, 1885. In the spring of 1885, Domeny sold his "Hill Farm", reserved the house, barn, hoglot, and pasture till November, 1885. He went to Kansas, left his family on the farm. Locating in Morton County, Kansas, two and one half miles east of Richfield, only there was no Richfield there then. In October, 1885, Mrs. Domeny had a sale and came to Kansas. (Brave lady did all this with four small children, one a month-old baby.) Domeny met his family at Ft. Dodge. A man with a team met them at Faken. They went 60 miles south and a little west, where Domeny had a good half dugout on the claim. Harry Owens Domeny was born December 1, 1887, Pearley F. Domeny was born May 18, 1889.

In September, 1889, the Domeny family started east, locating at Winfield, Kansas. Mabella Opal Domeny was born July 4, 1892. The Cherokee Strip was opened for settlement on September 16, 1893. Domeny lost his horse in the race and got no claim. Domeny bought a claim two miles west of Tonkawa, Oklahoma, moving on it in March of 1894. Hazel Mae Domeny was born there February 20, 1897. In February, 1904, Domeny bought a farm eight miles east and one south of Bliss (now Marland), Oklahoma, moving on it in 1905.

Henry Ellis Domeny and his wife Joyce were married sixty two years and endured many hardships. Joyce died at their home on April 25, 1940, age 82. Henry Ellis joined her ten years later on January 10, 1950, at age 94.

Henry Ellis and Joyce Domeny's fifth

Henry Ellis Domeny home built 1905 - 8 miles east, 1 south of Marland, OK.

child, Harry Owens Domeny, remained in the Red Rock-Marland area from 1905 until his death March 10, 1962. Harry Owens Domeny married Bessie May Fowler, daughter of John Edwin Fowler and Sarah Elizabeth Shingleton Fowler on March 10, 1909, at the Otoe Mission, Noble County near Red Rock, Oklahoma. To this union was born five children: Beulah Opal, February 3, 1910; Elmer Leroy, June 16, 1913; Earl Evert, April 11, 1915; Helen Josephine, May 16, 1918; all born on the Domeny farm, the area known in George Shirk's book **Oklahoma Towns**, as Ford, Oklahoma. Ford, a lively center, had a post office, mercantile store, general store, blacksmith shop and Ford Hall, where community activities, Saturday night dances and Sunday church services were held. About 1926, Ford, Oklahoma was past history. However, Ford is on my birth certificate dated 1918, and I am proud to have Ford, Oklahoma as my birth place.

Harry and Bessie moved in 1919 to Red Rock. The fifth child, Edith Mae was born January 12, 1920. Harry farmed in this area until 1942, moving back to the place he left in 1919. In 1943, Harry and Bessie moved to the home of the elder Henry Ellis Domeny to care for him until his death in 1950,

The Domeny farm is still in the Domeny family. Living in one of the farm houses since early 1940s is Earl Evert Domeny and his wife, Dorothy. Earl, a grandson of Henry Ellis Domeny, still maintains the Domeny land.

Helen Josephine Domeny Ratliff, a granddaughter of Henry Ellis Domeny, had always lived in the Marland-Red Rock area, her history will be in the Earl Ratliff history.

William T. Downey
By Lucille Downey Frank

William Thomas Downey was born January 9, 1877, in Brown County, Kansas. He was the son of James William Downey and Mahala Jett Downey. He married Myrtle Almina Johnston, the daughter of J. K. Johnston and Mary Sumilla Sugg Johnston. She was born October 8, 1879. They were married June 19, 1896.

When they were first married they lived in a dugout in Payne County, southwest of Stillwater, probably about ten or more miles. Times were hard those days and they ate a lot of eggs and gravy.

William Downey bought the relinquishment from the man who staked the claim. The man didn't want to prove up on the land himself so Bill proved up on the land, I was told. The farm was the northwest ¼ of section 28, 21N-3E. They came to this place in the early 1900' and lived there many years. The east eighty is still in the Downey name, a son, Garrett, owns it now and they live there. The west eighty of this 160 is no longer farmed for crops but is used for grazing cattle.

My parents built a 14 ft. by 25 ft. house up in the pasture on the east 80 and later moved it to the present location, turning it the opposite way that it set up in the pasture. The south 2 rooms of the present house is what they moved to this location. They built onto the house in 1904, 2 more rooms on the north side with an upstairs over these 2 rooms. They also had a porch on the eastside of the south two rooms. The house has since been remodeled and built on to.

They had eight children. They were: John Henry Downey born April 28, 1897, in Payne County. He married Odessa Laughlin, June 28, 1923. She died September 6, 1935. He died June 25, 1973.

Roy Edward Downey was born June 29, 1898, in Payne County. He married Vera Ittner on December 25, 1919.

A son was born January 13, 1901, in Payne County. He died January 27, 1901 and is buried in the Mount Vernon Cemetery near where they lived at the time. It is a very small cemetery.

Garrett Andrew Downey was born May 24, 1904, near Morrison on the home place. He married Izora Masheter, February 11, 1928.

Ruby Ehloe Downey was born May 11, 1908, near Morrison. She married Ray Earnest Boulton on May 21, 1927.

Lucille Beatrice Downey was born March 29, 1914, near Morrison. She married Eugene Frank, April 22, 1936. Eugene Frank died January 15, 1985.

Mary Mahala Downey was born March 24, 1916, near Morrison. She

William Downey family L-R Front Row: Mary, Lucille, William and Myrtle. Back Row: Garrett, John, Ruby and Roy.

married Darius Melvin Pendley September 20, 1939.

Jimmy Joe Downey was born May 1, 1920, near Morrison. He died May 31, 1921. He is buried in the Morrison Cemetery.

The Downey children went to the Jefferson School. William Downey was a farmer and raised a variety of crops, hogs, cattle and some horses. My brother Garrett told me one bad year, when it rained so much, they made a boat to go under the big binder wheel so it wouldn't slip in the mud so much. They used six horses on the binder. There were two horses in front and Garrett rode one of the front horses and guided them. He said one year they snapped cotton and put it upstairs. In the winter, when the chores were done, they would sit by the fire and pull the cotton out of the bolls, and put the bolls in the stove and burned them for heat.

They always raised a lot of garden and put up a lot of food for winter. Some was canned and some dried.

My father belonged to the Odd Fellow Lodge and the Modern Woodmen. He was on the Jefferson School Board for many years. He also was on the Auty Township Board. The men had to work on the roads to work out their poll taxes. They could hire someone to work in their place I am told. There was a road boss there to oversee the work.

He bought his first car in 1924. It was a 1924 Ford Touring Car. They moved to 202 East A Avenue in Morrison in 1930. This house had a little interesting history. I heard Dr. Whittenburg and another doctor had a hospital in this house for awhile.

Myrtle Downey died January 6, 1942, at Waynettee, Oklahoma. William Downey died January 8, 1942, at his home in Morrison. They are buried in the Morrison Cemetery.

Thomas H. Doyle
By Mildred Highfill

Judge Thomas Henchion Doyle was born near Uxbridge, Massachusetts, December 21, 1862. He was the son of John and Johanna (Henchion) Doyle, both of whom emigrated from Ireland.

Judge Doyle's mother, Johanna, died in Massachusetts. There were five children and Judge Doyle being the eldest spent the first seventeen years of his life in and about the Massachusetts county of Worcester, graduating from Whitin's Academy at Northbridge, Massachusetts.

His father, John Doyle, about that time concluded to move west and located in Osage County, Kansas. Young Doyle attended the University of Kansas for some time. In order to give his family better support in the trying years of drouth and famine in Kansas, he entered the employment of Fort Scott and Gulf railroad and was a trainman for two years. He became a student of law under Judge Benson in Ottawa, Kansas and was admitted to the bar in that county in 1893. In a little while, he had accumulated enough money to start a banking interest and moved to Garnett, Kansas, where he remained until 1893, when he came to Perry, and established the law firm that was known as Doyle and Barrett.

In Kansas City, the marriage of Mr. Doyle to Miss Rose O'Neil was solemnized in 1893. She was born in May, 1864, in New York state. Her parents were also natives of Ireland. She graduated in the Emporia, Kansas State Normal, and then engaged to educational work in Kansas City. They had one daughter, Marguerite (b - May, 1894, in Oklahoma), who married J. Frank Martin.

While in Perry, Mr. Doyle was active in platting the new additions that had been added because of the unplanned numbers of people who settled in Perry. He lived at the northwest corner of 9th and F streets. He bought the land south of Perry from the man who homesteaded it and part of it became known as the Doyle addition.

He resided in Perry until he was appointed to the Supreme Court of Oklahoma. Judge T.H. Doyle, who served continously as a Justice of the Court of Criminal Appeals, from its establishment in May, 1908, to January 1929, not only served longer than any other judge of the Appellate Courts of Oklahoma, but also gained nation-wide distinction because of the soundness and fairness of the opinions which he handed down. His rulings have also been accorded international recognition in the courts of some of the other English-speaking countries.

John E. Dronberger
By Lawrence Dronberger

John Ezra Dronberger was born at Rootstown, Ohio to Thomas and Julia Ann (Shaw) Dronberger who had moved from Houstontown, Pennsylvania. Early in his life, his parents moved to Deschler, Ohio-Henry County. Due to abundant rainfall, a flat terrain and poor soil drainage, the area was known as the "Black Swamp." John's father was a farmer. As he grew up, John became proficient in the use of the crosscut saw and the broad axe. He also learned to do carpenter work. He used the axe and saw to make railroad ties for which he received nine cents each. He could make as many as ten in a day. The country was being settled and workers were needed. John worked in the area and at the age of seventeen, he built a house on the family farm. In later years, John said, "It was the incessant mud that caused him to leave Ohio."

Records show that in 1880, John went to Breckinridge, Colorado. There he worked as a carpenter at the gold mines, building mine shaft houses, and making and installing shoring in the mine shafts. When he accumulated enough money for a grubstake, he prospected for gold. He built a log cabin southeast of Breckinridge to live in. He staked several claims on mine sites, but did not find 'pay dirt'. He worked intermittently for others until in December of 1887, when he returned to Ohio, Again he did carpenter work in the area and built a barn for his father. His diary shows that on May 2, 1888, he took the train from Deschler to Chicago and from there to Wamegeo, Kansas, to visit his brother, Hiram. During his visit, he helped build stairs and did other work on the house. From there he went to Nebraska to visit his brother, Andrew, and back to Colorado. This time he constructed a barn near Golden for Jonas Wannamaker and around the mines near Leadville. He returned to Kansas in December, 1888.

His diary shows that he left Manhattan, Kansas, on April 10, 1889, on his way to Indian Territory. He recorded the various places that he camped and places where he ate lunch on the way south. "We crossed Skeleton Creek on April 20 and camped at Old Soldiers Camp near Hennessy. We broke camp at noon on the 21th and moved up to the line to await the bugle. At twelve o'clock standard time on April 22, the grand rush began. About seven hundred wagons and buggies and at least one hundred horsemen went a hellin. We went on south and camped at Kingfisher at 8 pm. On the 23rd, Mr. Goff went up and filed his declaration. We continued to go south and camped at Old Soldiers Camp between El Reno and Yukon, near the future town of Frisco." Note:(Civil War Veterans had been given priority and were allowed to file claims on Lots before the run.) Their settlement was called Veterans City and later named Frisco. Dronberger did not find suitable land that was unclaimed and did not stake a claim. He remained at Frisco doing carpenter work. It was at Frisco that he met Maria Jane (Dolsen) Howe, a descendant of a pioneer family in Chatham, Ontario, Canada, who was to become his future wife. The diary shows that "June 15, 1889 commenced work for Major Howard at Minco. Worked 33½ days at $2.50 per day. Payment full $78.75."

Family legend has John and Maria Jane and her son, Preston Howe, in Leadville, Colorado in 1891. From there they moved to Wichita Falls, Texas, where their oldest son, Dickson Dolsen, was born in December, 1891. John supported his family by again doing carpenter work. In 1893, they returned to the Frisco area. John bought a cow pony which he named 'Old Boy'. He planned to run for land when the Cherokee Outlet was opened. He trained the horse to travel long distances and to run. He traveled north on the Honeywell Trail, which extended from Honeywell, Kansas to Texas. It crossed Noble County three miles east of what is now the Garfield-Noble county line. He was conditioning his horse and scouting the area to locate the best land. The creek bottoms were best. "They were covered with blue stem grass as tall as my shoulders while on horseback." He selected Red Rock Creek bottom as his target.

On September 16, 1893, he assembled with many others at Orlando. At high noon when the signal was given he rode north of the Honeywell Trail, on 'Old Boy' heading for Red Rock. When he crossed Dean Creek, about three miles south of Red Rock, he noticed that his horse was limping. He stopped to ex-

Dronberger Home constructed in 1894, as it looks in 1986.

amine the horse and discovered bleeding at the hair line above a front hoof. He would not sacrifice his horse by going further. He turned east along the creek until he found a corner stone, which had been placed there by the government surveyors. The stone was easily visible because the entire area had been burned the day before. From that point he went NE arrroximately 45° until he could see all four corners of what is now NW¼ of section 26-23N-2W in Noble County. He used his spade to make a pile of dirt on which he placed a flattened stick bearing his name, the time and the date. It had been one hour and fifteen minutes from the time he left Orlando. When his horse was rested they went on to Red Rock Creek to find water for the horse. Later, in the evening, he scanned the horizon and discovered a man on the southwest corner of his claim. He went over and told the man what time he had staked the claim. The man went on north. John slept on the ground beside his horse that night. The next day he went to Perry and filed a claim to the land that was to become his home for the rest of his life. He also located a friend who had carried some of his belongings in his wagon.

Early in 1894, John started to prove

John E. and Marie J. Dronberger 1927.

up on his land. He and Maria Jane and the two boys were camped in a tent on Dean Creek while John built a house. The one room story and a half house was almost completed in April when it started to rain during the night. The creek started to rise and the family had to wade water to get out of the creek and move into the house. The ensuing years were spent breaking sod, planting crops, digging a well and meeting the requirements to receive title to the land. John paid his 'prove up fee' of $14.20 on September 29, 1903. He received the Patent to the land February 12, 1904.

Settling virgin territory was a rigorous life. Every quarter section was occupied. Some of the settlers did not have the same stamina, skill or financial resources to succeed. Just getting enough food was a problem. One near neighbor was so lacking in food that they peeled their seed potatoes, ate the potatoes and planted the peelings. They soon moved away. All work had to be done by hand. Neighbors helped neighbors. They had no income unless they had learned a trade before settling and could find work. Money was scarce and bartering was done.

John did carpenter work to earn money. A house he built south of Billings is still occupied. He also built the original part of the house which is now the home of Charles and Dorothy Durkee five miles south and two miles and one half east of Billings. He built other houses in the area including two on F Street in Perry. He had a two wheeled cart, pulled by "Old Boy", which he used to go to and from work and carry his tools. The tool box was suspended beneath the cart. During the years he planted an orchard, planted trees along the creek for future fence posts, built a barn and a chicken house. His chicken house was lathed and plastered as was that essential of all farmsteads, the out house. As the years passed, John added on to his house which eventually contained seven rooms, a bath and a pantry room. John and Maria had four more children, namely: Blanche Mina, Otis Jay, Tildred Wendell and Lawrence, who was born April 18, 1907. All four were born before Oklahoma became a state. John had become a farmer and did very little carpenter work.

Dronberger kept ledgers. In 1901, he was selling eggs at 8¢ per dozen and wheat at 55¢ a bushel. He sold wheat to Donahue in Perry and later at Billings. He also sold eggs and bought groceries at country stores at White Rock, Compton, Polo and at Rodney Durkee's which was one half mile from home. Some of his neighbors that he sold eggs to were the Jerry, Jason and Dan Deals, the Art and Sherm Kearnes, John Dupy, Dan McCoy, Miles Yost, and George Fry.

The ledger was bought at the New Book Store; J.E. Shanafelt, Prop. Perry, Oklahoma. Other entries show; detailed expenses for a roundtrip train trip to Ohio, Detroit, Michigan, and Chatham, Ontario, Canada, in 1903, the purchase of a buggy for $37.50 in 1903; the purchase of the NE¼ SE¼ section 26-23N-2W in 1905 and a Maxwell car in 1916. Before they bought the car, they had made various train trips but in December, 1916, they drove to Wamego, Onaga and Topeka, Kansas, to visit relatives.

Early day social activities were infrequent. They held ice cream socials in warm weather and oyster suppers in winter. These events included the entire family down to the youngest baby. Occasionally barn dances were held. A neighbor, John Fruits, fiddle player, often furnished the music. The school house was the center of community activities with school programs and church services being held there.

John and Maria continued to live on and farm the farm after the children were grown and gone and on their own. They enjoyed the fruits of their years of labor. Many changes had taken place, neighbors had moved away or died, new people had moved in and some had lost their homes as a result of the depression of the 1930s.

John had lived through the Civil War, Spanish-American War, World War I and the start of World War II. He expressed a desire to live to see the end of World War II. He died at home, March 6, 1942, survived by his wife, all of his children, eight grandchildren and one great-grandson. He and Maria are buried in Polo cemetery, south of Billings.

The farm is now owned and occupied by his youngest son, Lawrence and his wife, Berniece.

Rufus N. Dunagan

By Rufus N. Dunagan II

Rufus and Grace Dunagan moved to Red Rock, Noble County, Oklahoma on or about November 2, 1908. Rufus Newton Dunagan was born December 20, 1867, near Waldron, Missouri and moved as a small boy to Mayetta, Kansas. His parents were Elizabeth Louisa (Malott) and Daniel Duncan Dunagan. Daniel's grandfather, who was also Daniel, came from Ireland in the late 1700s and fought in the American Revolution in the 6th Regiment of Virginia.

Rufus and Mattie Grace Cox were married January 3, 1899 in Topeka, Kansas. Grace was born June 19, 1881 in Mattoon, Iffinois. She was the great-niece of Wade Hampton, the famous confederate general and governor of South Carolina in 1876, although she

Rufus N. Dunagan general store red Rock

was not a Southerner herself, having been born in Illinois and raised in Kansas. Two children were born to Rufus and Grace in Topeka: Elizabeth, who died as an infant, and Glen Rufus.

In the summer of 1901, he moved by "team and wagon" to Shawnee, Oklahoma where his father and half brother were farming. Before moving to Oklahoma, Rufus had worked in a packing plant, operated a butcher shop in Holton, Kansas and worked in a creamery in Mayetta, Kansas.

Rufus was not enamoured of farming and wanted his own business. He was friends with the William Colemans from Red Rock and through them heard of a grocery store for sale. This was where his previous experience had trained him. So he and Mattie bought the small grocery store from J.W. (Buck) Eldridge and moved their sons, Glen and Everett to Red Rock. Everett Daniel having been born in Shawnee. The housewives of that time baked biscuits for breakfast because it was easy and fast. Bread was sourdough bread baked at home during the day, and was served at dinner and supper. Rufus was the first in Red Rock to ship in fresh yeast bread. Red Rock was on the railroad line and Rufus contracted with a bakery in Oklahoma City to ship the bread up several mornings a week by 7:00 am. Grace did not often bake bread after this luxury was inaugurated.

The Dugan grocery store sold all the typical food items of the day. Pickles were available in a big barrel, vinegar, lard, crackers, coffee, sugar were all in the bulk, and candy in big glass jars. The store also was stocked with shirts, socks and Round House brand overalls which were made in Shawnee, Oklahoma (and still are today). The Dunagans had both white and Indian customers. Most of the purchases were on credit-the farmers paying when the crops were harvested and the Indians when the government allotment checks were received.

Grace and Rufus increased their family in Red Rock. A son R.N. Jr. and a daughter, Gladys were born there R.N. Jr. operated a gas service station and bulk gasoline/kerosene distribution service there before WW II and served as mayor of Red Rock in the 1940s. Red Rock had its own telephone switchboard for many years and Gladys Dunagan worked for a time as the local telephone operator. The Dunagans also purchased a farm of 360 acres east of Red Rock which is still in the family today. The Rufus Dunagans attended the First Christian Church in Red Rock.

Their children were: Elizabeth (June 11, 1900-September 22, 1900); Glen Rufus (July 21, 1901-August 2, 1919, in a farm pond diving accident); Everett Daniel (November 4, 1903) married Kittie A. Whitaker, Roy Newton (October 12, 1905-January 3, 1906); infant)September 30, 1906); R.N. Jr. (November 7, 1910-) married Alma Antonia Zavodny; Gladys Marie (December 14, 1912-) married 1st Donald Francis Patterson, 2nd Marvin Leander McClung.

Rufus died May 5, 1956 and Grace, August 6, 1974. They are buried in the Red Rock cemetery.

Basil Dundas, Sr.

By Ellen Mae Gower

The family known as Dundas originated over 800 years ago in Scotland. One of the oldest Title of Land Grants in Scotland was bestowed to Helias de Dundas in 1086 by the King of Scotland. The Grant of Land is on display in the Archives in Scotland. There were many generations of Dun-

Dude and his horse Dixie, during World War I.

dases, many of whom served their country and king well, among them barristers, doctors, generals, etc. After the union with England, one Henry Dundas, First Viscount Melville, was named Lord Advocate for all of Scotland and served in this capacity, representing the whole of Scotland in British Parliament, for over 30 years. Sir Henry built his home, a castle, just south of Edinburgh, Scotland. It is now a hotel and still contains all the family treasures and antiques which belonged to Sir Henry Dundas. Sir Henry was nicknamed King Henry IX and King Harry by those who both admired and cared for him as well as those with whom he did not see eye to eye. He had the dubious honor of being the last man of nobility to be tried for impeachment in British history. He was cleared of all charges however, having tired of public life, he retired to his estate and lived out the rest of his life in peace.

During the "Clearances" after the union with England, many of the Dundases were exiled to Ulster in Northern Ireland as slaves to wealthy English landlords and were used as slaves on the "plantations" where the English were trying to "plant" their beliefs on the people of Ulster. Many of these landlords became very attached to their people and became aware that many of them were very learned and educated. They eventually gave their people large plots of land and released them from any bondage. The Dundases of that time became quite well-to-do and sent for some of their relatives in Scotland to join them in this land of opportunity. They stayed in Ireland (Ulster) for approximately 200 years when the potato famine became so bad. At that time, about 1822, the Dundases, at least many of them, emigrated to Canada where lands were being opened for homesteading. John Dundass and Mary Carr with their 13 children travelled by boat from Ulster to Upper Canada (now Ontario). They eventually settled in Ontario around the location of London, Ontario. John's eldest son, James Dundas, left Canada with his family of about seven children and settled in Kane county, Ill. He received his Naturalization Paper in 1856 with his eldest son, Wesley, as Registrar.

From Kane county, Ill, James and his large family of 13 children moved to Auburn County, Neb. where they lived for some time. Wesley and his brother, Henry John (who preferred to be called John Henry), bought some land through their town with the agreement that the railroad would run within one mile of their property and paved the way for the building of the railroad in that area. H.J. started his own newspaper and was editor for many years. He was a representative for his state for a time serving as a Senator.

The family gradually married and moved away, some of them going to Agra, Kansas, where many of them are now buried. Albert Galveston Dundas was born in Agra, and died in Lebam, WA. He had one son, Basil Rudolph Dundas, who he never saw. He left the home before "Dude" was born. Basil was called "Dude" since his mother would dress him up in fancy clothes and people would say "Look at the Dude". Dude and his maternal grandfather, H.D. Glenn, lived together with Dude's mother, Ellen May, until Dude lost his mother in Puebleo, Colorado. At that time, Dude and his Grandpa Glenn travelled in a covered wagon following the building of the railroad from Pueblo, Colorado, through Kansas and in to Oklahoma. They decided to settle in Red Rock, OK in order for Dude to get some formal education. Dude was about 9 years old at that time. They lived in Red Rock, OK until Dude went into the Army. Dude called his army horse Dixie. He was discharged in 1919 and returned to Noble county. He was a lineman and went to work for the telephone company where he met and married Martha Catherine Moore, July 28, 1921. Martha was born August 5, 1897, the daughter of John Harvey Moore and Robina Jane Cheek in Noble county. She was a telephone operator when she met Dude. Dude was a lineman for the telephone company in Red Rock until 1928, when the family moved to Perry. Later, they moved to Enid, where Dude worked for OG&E after having taken a correspondence course in Electricity. He helped build some of the first electric lines in that part of Oklahoma. The family moved to Medford, Oklahoma about 1933 where Dude was Representative for OG&E, taking care of several small towns around Medford. Most of the seven children grew up around Medford (Charles, Basil Jr., Grace, Ellen Mae, John Daniel, Katherine, and Robert). Dude suffered a heart attack in 1946, just before his 50th birthday. The older children had grown up leaving only Dude, Martha, Katherine and Bob at home. Dude died March 28, 1951 in Enid.

Thomas J. Dunivan
By LaWanda Dunivan

Thomas J. Dunivan, born in Waterlou, Iowa in 1872, was one of twelve children born to Irish parents, Patrick Dunivan of County Cork and Mary Bridget Toben of Waterford County, Ireland.

Thomas J. Dunivan (Tom) had just lost his wife while residing in the vicinity of Iola, Kansas. He and his children, Clarence, Maud, Hazel, and John started south to Oklahoma leaving behind the baby, Florence, with an aunt on her mother's side. She was later to be returned when she got old enough that Tom could manage to take care of her; but she was moved to Pennsylvania and raised there. Florence's son, Jim Reno, still visists in Oklahoma as often as possible. Tom moved his family this long distance by team and wagon to (Bliss) later to be Marland, Oklahoma; and then about 1912, migrated to Red Rock where he lived and ran a grocery and meat market on the south side of Main Street. Here he married Rosie Jones who passed away a short time later.

After Rosie's death, Tom and his family moved south of Perry on a farm, but later returned up north not too far from Red Rock where he had relations. A later move for Tom was to settle on a farm on Black Bear northeast of Morrison. It was here in 1925, that he married Grace Lauderdale Lee, who had one son, Robert Lee.

Tom and Grace lost their first-born twin boys in 1927 and later had Tom Dunivan Jr. A short time later, they built a home one and one-half miles east of here which was land left to Grace by her father, M. L. Lauderdale, who had received it in the run of the Cherokee Strip opening. Tom Dunivan Jr. was six months old by the time the house was finished. It wasn't long until most of the family had married — Hazel to James (Curly) Donovan, Maud to Earl Ralston, John to Gertrude Speer, and Clarence died in the service in World War I.

Robert Lee grew up and joined the services in World War II and now resides in California. Tom Jr., when reached the age of 17, joined the US Army. Upon returning from the service, Tom Jr. and LaWanda Chace were married in 1948 in Idaho while Tom was following construction work. With Morrison being their home, they returned in 1953 to stay. At this time, Tom and LaWanda had two children, Cheryl and John. Tom went into the LP gas business for himself. In 1958, another daughter, Debra, was born. Tom's family was complete and the business ventured into a 25 year span. Tom Sr. passed away in 1963 at the age of 91 and Grace passed away in 1969 at the age of 82. At this time in 1986, Tom Jr. is at home on the farm that has been in his family since the opening of the Cherokee Strip.

George C. Durbin
By Gail Johnson

The George Cleveland Durbin family came to the Perry area in 1935. They came from Henryetta, Oklahoma, where George worked for the Sun Oil Co. out of Pennsylvania. He continued to work for them until his retirement in 1957.

George's family originated in Maryland in the 1700s with Samuel Durbin. His son was unknown at this time of writing and his grandson is known to be Christopher. Christopher had a son named Thomas born in 1784, then James is his son born 1818. James had a son named George born in 1845 in Mt. Pleasant Township, Green County Pennsylvania. George and Clarinda and a son named George C., born September 9, 1892 in Pennsylvania.

George C. married Ida Christina Loyd, daughter of William and Elnora Loyd of Arkansas April 19, 1919. She was only 13 years old at the time, being born May 27, 1905, in Pope County, Arkansas. On the marriage license she states her age as 19 which allowed for the marriage to take place without parental consent.

Children born to this union are as follows: Dorthy Elnora (Johnson) July 4, 1920; Fern Christina (Swart) July 15, 1922; Agatha Grace (Queen) June 26, 1924; Georgia Mae (Mauney) July 23, 1926; Mary Lue (Rupp) April 14, 1929; Patricia Ann (Faw Faw) February 13, 1941. Only Patricia was born in Perry, at the Durbin home, 829 Jackson street.

The Durbins lived in many different homes during their 50 years in Perry. Some of the homes were on Delaware, Tenth Street, Grove (twice), eighth street, and finally 823- 7th street was the last house that they lived in for many years.

George became a Christian just before his death on December 10, 1969. He is buried in Grace Hill cemetery in Perry, Oklahoma.

Durbin Family, Summer of 1962. (L to R) Back row: Georgia Mae (Mauney), Mary Lue (Rupp), Patricia Ann (Faw Faw). Middle row: Dorothy Elnora (Johnson), Fern Christina (Swart), Agatha Grace (Queen). Front row: Ida Christina and George Cleveland Durbin.

George C. was a man who loved to play cards, all types of cards. He taught his girls and they taught their families to play. There were many family gatherings where the entertainment consisted only of playing game after game of Pitch, Rummy, and Poker.

Ida Christina was a member of the Christian Church in Perry. She was also a member of the Royal Neighbors for over 50 years, receiving her 50 year pin while living in Perry. She was presented her pin on August 14, 1979, by her daughter, Dorthy Johnson. Ida enjoyed doing many things for her grandchildren of which there were 20 in all. She also had 21 great grandchildren. She cared for her grandchildren like they were her own children and loved them each the same.

The family of Durbin girls had many enjoyable times in the Perry area. They played a big part in the school of Perry and were members of various groups.

Dorthy Elnora (Durbin) Johnson married Jesse Gail, March 27, 1945, Perry, Oklahoma. Children to this union are as follows: Jerry Gene, December 12, 1946; Gail Ann, June 12, 1949; Larry David, April 16, 1951; each of them born in Stillwater. These children grew up in Perry and attended O.S.U. in Stillwater.

Fern Christina (Durbin) Swart married Verdis Owen, May 5, 1937. Children from this union are as follows: Lyle, July 10, 1938; Owen Durbin, March 9, 1958, Germany. Lyle lived with his grandparents for many years while his father was in the service in many parts of the world. Owen was born in Germany during one of his father's tours of duty.

Agatha Grace (Durbin) Queen married Hugh Quentin August 15, 1943, Perry, Oklahoma. Hugh was under age and had to have parental consent to be married before he left for military service. Children to this union are as follows: Linda Ann (Bolinger), November 12, 1946; Mary Christina (Harvell), January 1, 1950; Steven Hugh, November 20, 1954. These children have lived most of their lives in the Tulsa area where their parents established their home.

Georgia Mae married Charles Clifton Mauney, September 22, 1949. Children to this union are as follows: George William, July 5, 1950; Charles Richard (Dickie), September 14, 1953; June Ellen, November 10, 1962; Chris David, August 8, 1964. The first two children were born in Perry, Dickie at the Mauney home. The last two in North Carolina which has been the Mauney place of residence for many years.

Mary Lue married A.H. (Sonny) Rupp, May 12, 1950, Perry, Oklahoma. Children of this union are as follows: Rebecca Ann (Kreig), June 11, 1952; Teresa Lynn (Snyder), August 15, 1954; Randolph Keith, November 6, 1958; Russell Wayne, September 9, 1962. These children were all born in and around the Perry area. Russell was also born on his grandfather George's birthday, 70 years to the day.

Patricia Ann married Billy Don Faw Faw, July 21, 1959, in Perry. The children to this union are as follows: Mark Todd, February 27, 1960; Tamara Dawn (Cramer), December 24, 1961; Michael Don, January 3, 1965; William Victor (Willie), April 23, 1969. These children are all born in the Perry area.

The family of Durbin has been in the Perry area for over fifty years and some of the descendants of George and Ida are still maintaining their residency in the same area. Dorothy Johnson is well known as the flower lady at the local T.G. & Y store. Mary Lue and her husband are farmers in the Noble County area. Fern has returned from many years of residing in California to make her home in Noble County. Patricia works for the social security office in Stillwater. Agatha and her late husband have lived in Perry as well as Tulsa and are avid antique buffs.

George Burton Durkee
By Mary E. Durkee

George Burton Durkee was born June 29, 1918 on the farm 8 miles south and 2¼ miles east of Billings, Oklahoma, the son of Gertrude (Cartwright) and George Day Durkee. He married Mary Ellen Holt on February 5, 1938 at Shawnee, Oklahoma. Mary was born March 24, 1921 at Newton, Kansas. She lived in Kansas City, Kansas and Kansas City, Missouri, before moving to Billings, Okahoma with her parents in

1930. Her parents were Nellie Clara (Halsey) and Mayberry Holt. Her father was a veteran of World War I, having served in France. Her parents were active in the Christian Church and the American Legion.

George Burton worked in the oilfield as well as being a farmer. He also operated a garage with his brother, Charles. He raised shorthorn and white face cattle. He lived in Oklahoma all his life except for two years spent in Grimes, Iowa to live with his mother after she divorced Mr. Durkee. He bought a farm 7 miles south and 2¼ miles east of Billings, Oklahoma, and was living there at the time of his death. He died March 11, 1983 at the hospital in Enid from a heart attack.

The children of George Burton and Mary Ellen were: Burton Duane, Marily Sue, Loren Bruce, Karen Jean and Mary Jane.

Burton Duane was born November 28, 1938 at Tonkawa, Oklahoma. He married Cecelia Romero. They have three children: Donna Kay, Joseph Duane and Carol Ann. Duane is a farmer and pumper in the oil field. They live in Perry, Oklahoma. They belong to the Catholic church.

Marilyn Sue was born March 3, 1940 at Lucien, Oklahoma. She married Fred Waltermire. Fred is a teacher and assistant coach in Perry High School and also farms. Marilyn Sue works as secretary to Ford Motor Company. They have three children: James Bruce (J.B.) is a cadet in the Air Force Academy in Colorado; Julie Ann is attending Oklahoma State University in Stillwater, Oklahoma and Scott Wade is attending Perry High School. They are members of the Presbyterian church.

Loren Bruce was born November 14, 1941 in Lucien, Oklahoma. He married Karen LaRue Spencer. They live on their farm one mile north and three-fourth miles east of Billings, Oklahoma. Bruce also is manager of Field Operations for Ultramar Oil and Gas Limited. They have two children: Sandi Gale attending school at Weatherford, Oklahoma and Bryan Wayne attending Billings High School. They are members of the Billings Christian Church.

Karen Jean was born June 14, 1944, at Enid, Oklahoma. She married Richard George Culp, a farmer. They live on their place three miles west and two miles north of Billings, Oklahoma. They are members of the Billings Christian Church. They are parents of three children, Jeffery George Culp attending Oklahoma State University in Stillwater; Todd Lewis attending Billings High School and Lori Elaine attending grade school in Billings. They live in Houston, Texas where he works for Doner Norriseral Corporation. Mary Jane works as a secretary in Cypress Fairbank school. They have two children: Brad William, and Barry Douglas. They are members of the Christian Church.

After the death of her husband, Mary Durkee lives on the homeplace. She is a member of the American Legion Auxillary, the Mum's Garden Club and is a volunteer for a Super Reader for children in the Billings school.

Charles Durkee
By Dorothy Durkee

Charles Henry Durkee, born September 10, 1912, was the middle child in a family of nine children born to George Day and Gertie Blanch (Cartwright) Durkee. He was born on the farm his father homesteaded (sw¼ of section 27 23N-2W). The only move he has made in his lifetime was to the nw¼ of section of 27 23N-2W in 1936 and bought in 1944 from O.B. Berry at his own price of $3,000.

When Charles was four years old a wild cat oil well came in a mile north of their farm, changing the life of his family and to act as an influence on him for the rest of his life.

The oil boom brought a large number of families of various types from many places. A small town sprang up, a grocery store, barber shop, boarding house, cafe, and even a movie, which was a real treat for a farm child. The family started a milk delivery route, and dad Durkee teamed.

Some of the children got jobs as soon as they were old enough. Charles got his first job at age 13, helping survey a new gasoline line to Billings.

All the children attended Highview (Midco) School just a mile north of home. One spring morning during his first year in school he became so interested in picking daisies that he forgot about time. No one was in sight when he got to school. Timidly with his hands behind him he ventured on in. The teacher angrily asked, "Charlie, where have you been and why are you late?" Innocently he held out the flowers to her. It was a false assumption but she said, "Oh how sweet of you picking those flowers for me." He was smart enough to say "yes". Apparently the teacher thought he was a really good boy, as others got blamed for his pranks. One of which was throwing some shells in with the paper he put in the wood burning stove.

He put in his first wheat crop in 1932 with horses. He was living alone on the home place, his parents divorced, his mother took the three youngest and went to Iowa. George, having been injured riding bare back, had gone to Oklahoma City for surgery, then on to California to visit his half sister, Edith.

His first tractor was a Fordson bought in 1933 for $50. His first car was a 1927 T touring car, bought in 1929 for $125. Then in 1933, a Model A roadster for $135, next a 1934 Ford roadster bought in 1935 for $282 and the model A.

He was driving it when he started dating Dorothy Dott Rhea in the fall of 1936. She was born October 10, 1921 in Billings, to John Elmer and Gladys Mae (Austin) Rhea. She had moved

Charles and Dorothy Durkee - May 3, 1937

with her family to Ponca City. Living next door to a Nehi bottling plant was great fun as the men were generous with the pop. She started school in the South Ponca field. It was called a Progressive School and may have been as they furnished everything, even the pencils and taught Phonics in 1927. It was on to Blackwell and then back to Billings.

It must have been a boring year in Billings considering the excitement stirred up by the elopement to Fairview by Charles and Dorothy the 3rd of May 1937. The chivarie crowd was so large as to be frightening. Even if they had cut the candy bars into confetti size they couldn't have served everyone. Dorothy just worked her way quietly through them into a wheat field. Charles mingled with the crowd in the dark. He was following a group searching the barn when a girl yelled, "I hope I haven't stepped in what I think I did." She had. Occasionally, he set off some dynamite, that made for silence before the screaming resumed.

Couples paired off and then were excitely yelling, "We found them!" only to discover they were finding each other. They gave up and came back the next week, but their enthusiasm was dimmed by finding Charles with the mumps.

At the time they married, Burton and Richard had come back from Iowa and were living with Charles. In August they made room for the boys' father, George, who stayed until November. Burton married Mary Ellen Holt, February 3, 1938 and all thought they were happy.

The happiness was shattered May 18, 1938, when their son, Leroy Earl was born dead. Mary and Burton rented a farm and moved that fall.

Phillips Petroleum Co. had struck oil in the Wilcox in 1935, so again, there was work in the oil field to supplement the farm income. The added income was a big help to all of them. They had a $650 note on the cattle and George's old machinery. Charles had made a deal with Mr. Overstreet, a Ponca City banker, to take over his dad's note for half the amount his dad owed. Then said he had no money. The banker asked if he had feed, he did. Mr. Overstreet smiled and said, "I like your nerve, it's a deal." Charles and Burton divided the cattle when Burton and Mary moved. The machinery became the basis of the Durkee Brothers partnership which continued and prospered until Burton's death in 1983.

It was a great day for them when their son, Gary Rhea was born March 15, 1940, then came Diana Day, March 26, 1952 and Thelma Denise January 11, 1955. The years went by fast, lots of work and lots of pleasure. The four wheel wheat trailers gave way to at least four trucks. The first combines were pulled by a tractor which Dorothy drove, followed by the several self propelled of today. The old Fordson was followed by John Deers that got bigger and better. Fertilizers and better equipment made for larger yields from more acres as the farm business grew.

As oilfield work became more scarce Durkee Brothers Garage was born and grew to be a big business offering more work than could be done. About 1952, they started pumping oil wells and over the years the wells to pump increased, making less time for the garage. In 1949, they got their first TV and with a one wheel trailer took their first long trip, going to California and on to Canada. They took many great trips with the children, were in all the states west of the Mississippi, many times in some of them. They covered many states in the south and east too.

Gary married Suzanne Elizabeth White June 2, 1962. The 3 week family vacation to the Seattle Worlds Fair was their honeymoon. The family has been afilliated with the Billings Methodist Church for many years, serving and participating in many activities.

Charles served for seven years on the Highview School Board and Dorothy served ten years on the Billings School Board. She also served on NODA's Health Planning Council, over the years on the State PTA board, Noble County Republican Central Committee, State Conservation Auxiliary and has been a member and officer in several social organizations.

Following the precedent set by George Durkee, Dorothy took Farm Census in 1959, Federal Census in 1960 and Crew leader for the 1970 Census.

The year is 1986 and nearing fifty years of marriage and both are in fairly good health. The old farm house is a large modern home. Their youngest daughter, Staci Dawn, was born September 10, 1976, and keeps them involved with school, sports, 4H and music. Duane Durkee took his fathers place in the Durkee Bros. business.

George Durkee
By Charles Durkee

George Day Durkee, twenty days past twenty-one and $40 in his pocket rode a mule into the Cherokee Strip September 16, 1893. Events in his early life had proven him a survivor with courage needed to leave city life for a barren homestead.

He was born August 26, 1872 in Chicago, Illinois, the 4th child of Samuel Crampton Durkee, born May 13, 1837, at Oswego, New York and Amanda Day, born May 28, 1849, at

George and Gertie Durkee about 1910.

Port Washington, Wisconsin, daughter of Oscar Day and Abigail Royce. Sam, a Civil War veteran was employed in the Round House of the Iron Mt. Railroad, and transferred to Little Rock, Arkansas about 1879. George's fond memories of taking lunch to his dad were marred by the time he was crossing the trestle over the Arkansas River and a train was overtaking him. By the whistle of the train and screams of the men he knew he had to jump. Luckily he had cleared the deep water and received only a mouth full of sand and bramble scratches.

As he reached his teens his parents divorced. Amanda married James Serby and taking George and his sisters, Clara, and Florence, moved to Mt. Home, Arkansas, in 1885. He got a summer job carrying the mail horseback between Mt. Home and West Plains, Missouri. Fate smiled on him again in that he and his horse survived being swept down the flooding White River.

While still in school he started setting type for the Baxter Co. News. One night as he left work he got between two angry drunks. One threw a scale weight missing his target and hitting George in the head. The town doctor, a war veteran, enlisted the aid of the blacksmith, and a silver dollar was pounded out to fit the skull hole.

He left the paper to join his uncle Rodney Durkee in Texas to plan for the land rush. They started from Orlando and staked claims east of Perry. He had neither the money nor desire for a fight, so lost out to a claim jumper. He then got a job hauling hay and feed from Pawnee. In November he heard about an abandoned claim, the southwest ¼ of section 27 Twp. 23N Range 2W, which he filed on and homesteaded.

His uncle Rodney loaned him a horse, a covered wagon and a walking plow. He camped out that winter plowing small fields for spring planting. He made a dugout 12' x 14' by 4' deep and from plowed sod walled it up another 3½ feet, covering the top with 1'x12' roofing boards. He moved in before the winter of 1894. During 1895, a 14'18' building bought in Perry was hauled to the farm, the beginning of the house to which rooms would be added later.

Durkee brothers (L to R): Paul, Richard, Burton, Charles, Willard.

During the first years lack of machinery dictated the cash crops be corn, Kaffir corn, cotton, castor beans, oats, and native grass. George gathered up bones which he hauled to Guthrie to sell. Arriving home from a trip late one moonlit night he looked in a window and could see a man laying on his cotton he had stored on the floor in the house. Getting up his nerve he went in calling out, getting no answer, thought could he be dead? As he nudged the body with his toe he realized he was the victim of a joke. Someone had stuffed a shirt and trousers with cotton. Amanda and his half sisters Anne and Edith lived with him from 1899 until 1902.

March 15, 1903, he married Gertie Cartwright in Perry, Oklahoma. Gertie was born April 22, 1885, in Iowa to Henry Cartwright and Rebecca Schaffer. To this marriage was born Willard Samuel, February 15, 1904, Welthy Mable, March 21, 1906, Margaret Elsie, March 30, 1908, Thelma Gertrude, October 4, 1909, Charles Henry, September 10, 1912, Mildred Irene, May 12, 1914, George Burton, June 29, 1918, Richard Eldon, January 15, 1922, and Paul Edward, October 13, 1923.

George raised outstanding mules and horses in addition to the usual cattle, chicken, hogs and small grains. Some of the mules and horses were sold to the US Army at the beginning of WW I and he was very active selling bonds. He took census by horseback or buggy in 1910 and by Model T in 1930.

Discovery of the Hoover well in 1916, brought many people to the area and the family started delivering milk, cream, butter and eggs. George did teaming, Willard drove truck, Welthy worked for awhile in the boarding house, and even Charles soon drew a check for working.

Thelma was one of three girls killed in an amonia explosion at the Midco Gasoline Plant October 10, 1926. Margaret married Clarence Kukuk and lives in Perry. Burton married Mary Holt; he died February 11, 1983. Charles still lives in the county. Willard died June 13, 1971. Welthy married Marion Pursiful who worked for Sinclair, retiring to Perry. Their health failing they now live in an Oklahoma City retirement village.

Mildred married Gerald Osborn and lived the last 25 years of her life in New Orleans, Louisiana, dying July 19, 1963. The Mildred Osborne Elementary School in New Orleans honors her contributions to education.

Richard was a jet mechanic at Tinker Field. He served as an Air Force MSgt. in England during WW II. He married Faye Sullivan, and had been retired from Tinker a short time at his death, February 11, 1982.

Paul married Bonnie Sue Creel. After serving 35 years in the Air Force he retired. They live in Florala, Alabama.

George retired in 1933. He and Gertie lived the last years of their lives in Perry. Gertie died June 12, 1946; George died September 12, 1951. Both were members of the Perry Methodist Church and are buried in Grace Hill Cemetery.

Rodney Horace Durkee

By Charles Durkee

The pioneer spirit, love of adventure, the desire for land or just itchy feet, I wonder if even he knew why he wanted to make the run in 1893.

Rodney Horace Durkee was born January 7, 1842, the fourth son of Welthy Ann (Crampton) and Horace Durkee, probably at Franklin, Vermont. He was preceded by Samuel, born May 13, 1837, Stephen Kize 1839, and Charles born in 1840.

No record has been found on what happened to Welthy. Horace married Adeline Sheperd and the first of their seven children was born in 1846. They raised the boys and named one of their girls Welthy, which seems more believable if the boys' mother had died.

The name was carried on when Rodney insisted his nephew, George, Sam's son, name his first daughter Welthy Ann Crampton. They agreed just to the Welthy part.

Rodney, Samuel and Charles went to Pentwater, Michigan about 1860. They got jobs on a sailing ship on the Great Lakes. Charles died at Pentwater in 1861 and Samuel enlisted in Illinois in April of 1861. Rodney remained on the Lakes. Fearless to the point of stupidity, he tried to stop a knife fight between two sailors. One of them almost ran him through with a dagger. Whiskey was poured in the wound. A doctor was brought to the ship. He said, "There is nothing I can do, he will be dead by morning." Rodney's reaction, "I'll outlive the S.O.B!" Thus started a lifetime hatred of doctors. He was considered unfit for service.

He was a Captain when Samuel returned from the army and bought a ship called a Trader. They transported cargo from various ports on the lakes, primarily Lake Michigan.

They married sisters, daughters of Abigail Royce and Oscar Day. Elizabeth and Rodney married November 22, 1866. Amanda and Samuel married November 26, 1866. Living in Pentwater, the brothers sailed the lakes until a winter storm in November of 1869 or 1870 caused the lake to freeze. Their ship was broken up by the ice three miles from shore. All hands made it to shore lucky to be alive.

The families were living in Chicago by December of 1870. Rodney helped in the clean up of the Chicago fire. They used dishes for years salvaged from the fire. The straw they were packed in burning left its patterns.

Rodney and Libby had no children but upon the death of Libby's sister, Harriet, took Burton Joseph and Harriet Day Pollard to raise. Burton took the name Durkee. Rodney and Libby also raised Harriet's son, Ralph Minor.

We are not sure when Rodney bought the ranch at McKinney, Texas, where he was living at the time he decided to make the run. Sam's son, George, joined him there in preparation for the run.

Amanda and her daughters, Florence Durkee, Anna, and Edith Serby, came from Arkansas to Guthrie joining Libby and the children in Guthrie until after the run when they came on to Perry.

The men started from three miles east and 1 north of Orlando. Rodney rode a horse. He staked a claim three miles east of Perry. The kids and Libby were put on the farm in a covered wagon and tent on the other side of his farm. He thought nothing about the questions they ask until the next day. There was a lot of excited talk about three wild Indians, probably drunk who had roped a tent and drug it off, turned loose a horse and created a great commotion. The last he heard of his claim jumper, he was headed south trying to catch up with his horse.

Rodney sold his claim and bought the SE¼ of section 27-23N-2W. Again he started a grocery store and the Pee Dee post office was moved there. He also bought from the farmers for resale. It was a hang out for boys who he enchanted with his tales of ships and cities.

Rod McCoy said he picked up walnuts and traded them to Captain Durkee for candy. He said his family started calling him "Rod" instead of Roe, his name. The nickname stuck, and most people think his name is Rod.

"Captain", as he was fondly known as, sold this farm to be eligible for the Sac-Fox drawing. He didn't get a farm.

He and Libby then moved to Tonkawa. He built a shoe shop and hired cobblers who made and repaired shoes.

He had walked with a cane for several years when in his seventies, he decided walking with a cane wasn't for him. He threw them away and started exercising. Never again to use a cane and living to age 92. He died November 30, 1934.

Libby had gone to Tulsa in 1918 to care for Amanda who was dying of cancer. She fell on the ice and broke a hip. She died as a result. Rodney and Libby are buried at Rose Hill cemetery in Tulsa.

Willard Durkee
By Charles Durkee

Willard Samuel Durkee was born February 15, 1904, at his Grandpa and Grandma Cartwright's home in Perry. His parents, George Durkee and Gertie Cartwright, decided it was too risky for their first baby to be born on the farm with no phone and eight miles to ride a horse for a doctor.

Willard attended school at Highview District #56, better known as "chicken coop." Built in 1894, it was bought for $75 from a farmer who lived in it and then used it for chickens from 1895 until it became the school. It was used until the new school was built in 1914. Willard told me of a game the kids played. When a mite or louse would get on their slates, they would draw chalk circles around them to see if they would cross it, and found it an amusing pastime. He attended Billings High School walking one and a quarter miles to ride with the Dunbar girls. The girls drove their dad's (Tom Dunbar) Oakland and often they broke the monotony by racing the Wheeling brothers in their dad's Case.

In 1922, Willard started work for Midco Oil Co. teaming. The next year he started driving one of their two White trucks which was one of the largest trucks in the oilfield at that time, having a Tulsa winch and trailer and gin poles. They had roadster cloth tops and no battery but magnetoes and carbide lights. Their rear tires were two to three times as large as their front tires. There were no duals. Mud chains were a necessity and heavy iron stakes were always carried. The stakes were driven in the ground so you could winch yourself through the mud holes. Nearly all roads were just dirt.

Willard's salary at this time was $135.00 per month. He worked six days a week, seven if a well was drilling. There was no such thing as overtime.

In the spring of 1929, he quit truck driving to be a tool dresser for the same company. A tool dresser is now called a roughneck. In those days drilling was done by the use of an eccentric which pulled a cable up and then dropped it to literally pound a hole in the ground. A bit was attached to a heavy iron shaft which fastened to the cable of the eccentric. The bit was kept sharp by heating it in a forge and pounding it out with a sledge hammer. Hence a tool dresser. He also kept the boiler fired to supply the steam for the power needed to drill. The hole was kept full of water and when it got thick with pounded up rock the drilling tool was pulled out and set aside. A bailer was lowered into the hole to bring out the mud. They would then run fresh water into the hole and start over.

Willard married a neighbor girl, Cecil Muriel Gould July 16, 1929. She was born July 27, 1909, to Luther Gould and Emma Hentges. They bought a Texaco service station in

Willard Durkee and 1923 white truck.

Perry and ran it until the next year. He got a job with Sinclair Oil Company as pumper, sold the station and moved to the Oklahoma City field which was booming.

Retiring after twenty plus years with Sinclair, he enrolled at Oklahoma University in Electrical Engineering. His next job was with the government and led to him being on the Electrical Staff at the SAC Air Force base in Clinton, Oklahoma. He retired in 1971.

The family home was in Norman from the time he left the oil company until his death. Cecil was employed at Tinker Field for many years. Her work was very secretive during the war; afterwards we found out she had been working on "Nordan Bombsights."

To this marriage were born two sons: Willard Eugene, April 12, 1930, and William Donald, February 6, 1936. Both graduated from OU; Gene in petroleum engineering and Bill in chemical engineering. Gene is involved in the exploratory side of the petroleum field. Bill went on to get a law degree and is a member of a firm of lawyers in Houston, Texas.

Willard died June 13, 1971, and Cecil died March 19, 1979. Both are buried at Grace Hill cemetery.

George W. Eby
By Frank Eby

George W. Eby was born and reared at Little York, Ohio near Dayton. His parents were both Dunkard ministers. In 1890, George left Ohio to seek his fortune in the "West." He stopped at Kansas City, where he worked in a machine shop. While there he boarded in the W.S. Hutchison home. The Hutchisons had come to Kansas City from Barre Run, Pennsylvania. Among their children was a daughter, Ermina

Frank Eby and Hazel Eby Kennedy, the oldest and youngest of George and Mina's nine children.

Hutchison. "Mina" worked in a dressmaking shop in Kansas City and must have been a good cook as well, since the fastest way to a man's heart is through his stomach, for in a short while after George came to board with the Hutchisons he and Mina were married.

By 1893, George and Mina moved to a farm near Wellsville, Kansas, where their first three children were born — Hazel Elizabeth, William Hutchison, and Cecil Wenger. Then George bought a quarter section of land near Caldwell, Kansas, where the family lived for about seven years. While there five more children were born — twins, Florence Faith and Helen Hope, Harold Ephraim "Hal", George Alney "Dick", and Homer Perry "Pete".

Schooner wagons came through the Caldwell area and the families often camped overnight near the Eby home. Many of the travelers were on their way to Oklahoma where Indian land called the Cherokee Strip had been opened for settlement, hoping to claim some of the free land. The excitement of this movement toward Oklahoma Territory intrigued George and he made a trip to Perry to check out the situation. He liked the bustling frontier city in the Cherokee Strip so he returned to Caldwell, sold the farm, stock and all, and returned to Perry, where he bought a hardware store. Very soon his family joined him in Perry. The youngest Eby, Frank Winsor, was born in Perry, Oklahoma Territory. By Frank's first birthday Oklahoma had become the forty-sixth state of the United States of America.

The store, "Eby Hardware Store" did well for a number of years. George had a tin shop in connection and also sold harness and a line of spring wagons and buggies including a carriage with fringe on the top, called a Phaeton, which was popular at that time.

By the time Hazel, the eldest child, was sixteen years old, she had become an accomplished musician and had an opportunity to attend to Conservatory of Music in Kansas City. Along with her studies, Hazel played at night for silent picture shows in Kansas City. In a few years Hazel returned to Perry to help her mother with the large family since at this time George was a traveling salesman and Mina was supplementing the family income by keeping boarders.

By now Perry had its first picture show, the Wonderland Theater. It was located on the corner of Sixth and D Streets. Hazel got the glamorous job of playing for the silent pictures and it was here that she met Ivan Kennedy, an accomplished violinist who was attending Oklahoma A & M College in Stillwater. She and Ivan were married and after spending a few years on a music circuit, returned to Perry to rear their family.

George's life on earth ended May 8, 1925, at the age of fifty-seven. All of the Eby children worked as soon as they were old enough. The twins, Faith and Hope, were very stylish young ladies and often participated in fashion shows put on by local department stores. At an early age Faith went to work at "Everybody's Store". She married Herbert Johnson who with his brother, Charlie, owned and operated a very large ranch near Sumner. Hope worked in the County Treasurer's office, met and married John Wolfe who became an attorney for Continental Oil Company in Ponca City.

Like their father, the Eby sons were self-employed. "Billy" had a picture enlarging and framing business in Oklahoma City. Cecil a tire shop and Mistletoe Express Agency in Garber, Oklahoma. Hal was an expert brick mason. He built several lovely brick homes in Perry as well as the two story buff brick building on the north side of the square. Originally it was the Elite Hotel. Dick owned and operated the Eby Buick Garage in Perry for many years. Pete owned and operated a restaurant in Perry and later went into the photography business both in Perry and Wewoka, Oklahoma. Frank owned and operated Eby's Cleaners in Perry for about forty years.

As long as Mina lived the family got together every Thanksgiving in some family home. Always there was much music, fun and food on these occassions. Mina passed away January 22, 1946, at the age of 84.

As adults all nine of the Eby children made their homes in Oklahoma. Hazel, the eldest, wrote, "We grew up in the West, proud of our heritage, glad to live in the great state of Oklahoma where we can still see the harvest come in, see the oil industry progress and visit with our friends of many years."

J.W. (Buck) Eldridge
By Mildred Highfill

J.W. (Buck) Eldridge operated a saloon, The Yaller Dorg, from 1903 until 1907 in Red Rock, Oklahoma. His first saloon, no more than a shanty with a canvas top, was thrown up in a single afternoon. The shack was soon replaced by a brick structure and the saloon became celebrated in song, poetry and stories.

Eldridge credited a conversation with Zack Miller for naming the saloon. Miller asked him the day after his place of business was opened what he intended to call it. "I believe I'll name it after that old yaller dorg that came in last night. I think that'll bring me luck." "And it did," he said twenty-five years later "I took care of that old dog for a couple of years, but he finally wandered off."

The opening night of the "Yaller Dorg" was all that could have been expected for such a welcome event in such a dry territory as the middle of Otoe reservation. Of course, it was illegal to sell liquor to the Indians and as far as it is known Eldridge did not break this law. On the opening night, Zack Miller "rode down" with a delegation of 75 of the 101 Ranch cowboys and "others came, too."

As Eldridge recalled it: "The celebration got going pretty good when the boys got out their firearms. I'll never forget what happened. They riddled the roof of my shack and I decided right then and there that there would be no more gun play in my saloon and there never was."

The day after the opening "the boys" came back for another "shooting spree" but Eldridge backed them into a corner and laid down the law: "If there's any shootin' around here, I'll do it myself." Eldridge told his customers and he backed up his demand with a deputy sheriff's commission and a handy pistol.

Among the customers of the "Yaller Dorg" between 1903 and statehood in 1907, Eldridge numbered the great and near-great who visited the 101 Ranch from all corners of the globe. Henry Starr when he was not "on the dodge" and Tom Mix, a cowboy on a nearby ranch were among his customers. Hundreds of visitors from the east got a glimpse of a "western" saloon at the

Yaller Dorg as guests of the 101 Ranch. There were so many requests for souvenirs of the place that Eldridge had some cards printed bearing a picture of a bedraggled yellow dog. The reverse side carried a touching "Yaller Dorg" poem written by Ernest Jones.

Joseph William Eldridge was born near Maltoon, Illinois, November 2, 1875. He came to Oklahoma Territory in 1899, with his widowed mother, Mary Elizabeth Bilbrey Eldridge and his brothers, Jesse, Leslie and Grover. His father was John Calvin Eldridge, a Confederate soldier with the Tennessee Seventh Calvary. The family moved to Red Rock from Orlando Oklahoma Territory early in 1900.

J.W. (Buck) married Ella M. Reed, an 89er of Orlando, on April 22, 1906 and established a home in Red Rock. In 1903, Buck opened a saloon in the middle of the Otoe reservation. After statehood came and prohibition closed the Yaller Dorg Saloon, Buck turned his full attention to ranching and farming. He and his partner, Bob Hughes leased land from the Otoe-Missouria Indians and ran cattle on the spread. The headquarters for the ranch was a tent.

He was a partner with Zack Miller of the 101 Ranch in building the first dipping vat for cattle in Noble county. Then in partnership with Lee L. Russell of Fort Worth, Texas, he contracted to bring whole trainloads of long-horn cattle from Texas and old Mexico to fatten on the leased lands. A large barn was built and a corral put up for breaking the many horses they used on the ranch. In the summers a large number of cowboys worked long hard hours riding bucking horses, mending fences, branding cattle and dehorning them, riding herd, and preparing for the annual roundup. The cowboys slept in bunkhouses near the barn but they ate in a special arbor at the ranch house.

The ranch house was a crude one-room shanty for the kitchen, a tent-like bedroom, and a large fenced-in arbor covered with a tin roof. This was the domain of an old Negro ex-slave, who prepared the meals for the cowboys and the family. Old Walker Johnson could cook a feast in no time on that wood-burning iron cookstove.

The Eldridge family moved to Perry in 1915, but continued to go to the ranch until the operations were closed-out after World War I. Grandmother Eldridge and her youngest son, Grover lived in Red Rock. The family of J.W. and Ella M. Eldridge included five children all born in Noble county: Irene Eldridge Mitchell, 1907; Joe Eldridge, 1910; Dorothy Eldridge Dodson, 1912-1952; Maxine Eldridge Oliver, 1915; and June Eldridge Gloeckler, 1919.

The family moved to Guthrie in 1924 and resided there until their deaths in 1967 and 1968. A beaded tobacco pouch is in the Cherokee Strip Museum that was given to Buck Eldridge as a token of the chief of the Otoe-Missouria tribe. At the birth of Irene, the Indians gave cradle gifts; a pair of beaded moccasins, a beaded purse and Indian blankets. The baby moccasins and small purse are also in the museum.

Monroe and Nora Nellie Elgin about 1916.

Monroe Elgin
By Margaret E. Smith

Armadum Monroe Elgin was born in Cantervill, Iowa, April 23, 1871, the oldest of five children born to James Simpson Elgin and Ellen Kiser Elgin. His father was Scotch-Irish and his mother, Pennsylvania-Dutch. He graduated from Centerville High School, having played cornet in its illustrious marching band. Then began the Elgin trek across country to discover a new home. They farmed near Anton, Kansas from 1894-96, but were continually riding horseback to the "Indian Territory" to hunt, fish and seek a better place to live. This came about when Monroe found a homesteader living west of Perry, who would trade his claim for a team of horses and wagons. So, in the spring of 1896, the Elgin clan piled all their worldly goods into a wagon and started their journey to the "Indian Territory". The farm was in the Whipple community, across the road from Uncle Tom Kiser, brother of Ellen Kiser Elgin.

However, the climate did not agree with their youngest child, Ella Elgin, who developed severe arthritis. The doctors prescribed a higher, drier climate; so Grandmother Elgin took her small daughter and headed, by train, for Clairshome, Alberta, Canada, where she established a boarding house. In the meantime, Monroe had married Clara Adams and traded the first claim for a quarter section (nw 19 20N 1E), which adjoined his wife's homestead on the west. One of the Elgin boys had died after coming to Perry and the other two had followed their mother to Canada to seek homesteads there. By 1915, Monroe and Clara had divorced and Monroe decided to visit his mother, sister and brothers in Canada.

While in Canada, Monroe met and married Nora Nellie Crowe Milner, a widow with three young sons. They were married at Clairshome on April 3, 1916. Nora Nellie Elgin was born in Hull, Yorkshire, England on November 16, 1881. She was reared by her maternal grandparents who were "landed gentry" and was educated in private schools, taking her final exams for her "Certificate of Perceptorate" from Cambridge. Being a highly independent person, she eloped with one of the farm workers (a person who groomed the horses) and was immediately disowned by her irate grandparents. Following the birth of three sons, one of which died of spinal meningitis at age three, Nellie and her husband, Henry Milner decided to emmigrate to Canada, having received glowing tales of success from her two brothers Frank and Charles Crowe, who had already moved there. So, with two small sons, John and Leonard, and all their wordly goods, they sailed for Canada in 1911. Henry acquired work on the Canadian Pacific Railroad and on November 11, 1912 another son, Ronald, was born. When Ronald was 6 months old, Henry was run over by a train and killed. With her three small sons, Nellie moved to Barons, Alberta, Canada to live on a wheat farm with her bachelor brother, Frank. Here it was that Monroe and Nellie met and married. They homesteaded near Rosemead, not far from Travers and settled down to farm. Two children were born while they lived in Canada: Francis Lee (January 17, 1917) and Margaret Ellen (October 30, 1918). Due to Monroe's health problems, the family decided to return to the Oklahoma homestead near Perry in the fall of 1919. Here three more children were born (one dying at birth), Warren Patrick (March 17, 1921) and Aley Nellie (June 26, 1926). Thus was established Nellie's contention that she was Cosmopolitan Mother, having given birth to three children in England, three in Canada and three children in the US.

Throughout the hardships of the

pioneer times and the depression and dust of the "dirty thirties", Nellie gave unstintingly of her talents and love to her family and community. She was one of the "shakers and movers" who organized the Willing Workers of Oklahoma Extension Club' the 4-H Club and the Union Sunday School that met in the New Hope school house each Sunday for many years. She helped organize community plays, and was noted for her interesting and entertaining "readings". She also became the local "Florence Nightengale" by assisting Dr. Coldiron with the delivery of babies in the neighborhood and helping set broken limbs, tend the sick and just be a good neighbor.

There being no school buses from Perry, Lee and Margaret rode horseback 6 miles each way to catch a bus into Orlando to attend highschool. So their mother led the fight to acquire school busses from Perry.

Monroe, while continuing to operate the farm at Perry, traveled back and forth to Canada to put in wheat crops and to later harvest it. He purchased a new 1925 Model T Ford and took the whole family to Canada for a visit in 1927.

Following their teens, the three older boys returned to Canada to live and remain Canadian citizens; Lee and Margaret graduated from Oklahoma A&M College; Aley still resides on the homestead and Patrick served four years in the armed services during WW II. Monroe Elgin died July 16, 1946 and Nora Nellie Elgin died January 10, 1967. Both are buried in the Grace Hill cemetery at Perry, Oklahoma.

William P. Emick
By Katherine (Emick) Frank

The Emick family arrived about 1880 from Nicholas County, West Virginia, at Kansas City, Missouri, where William Emick may have changed the spelling of the last name from Amick to Emick. They then moved to Concordia, Kansas and still later they moved to Guthrie, Oklahoma. William made the run into the Cherokee Strip and staked a claim. Under Homestead Certificate 5741 he was granted the land at the northwest quarter of section 22 in Autry Township.

For reasons unknown contact was lost with the family remaining in West Virginia. The family is of German decent. The Civil War was a disturbing factor within the family, as some fought for the south and some for the north.

William P. Emick (b-November 3, 1849 - died August 19, 1902) was a stone mason and a builder as was his father before him. He was born in Nicholas County, Virginia that later became West Virginia. October 20, 1874, he married Lucy Catherine Emick (no known relation). Lucy (born May 17, 1885 - died November 20, 1924) was born in Nicholas County in what is now West Virginia, near Charleston. At the age of 15 she became a member of the Methodist church. Nine children were born to this union, three girls and six boys, all are now deceased.

William was a man of small stature, gentle and kind. He observed and appreciated nature. He liked to draw and read and enjoyed people. In Concordia, Kansas some of the business buildings's corner stones still bear his name as builder. He chose his Oklahoma claim for three reasons, one - the spring in the southeast corner that provided water, second - the rock formation for the stone to build a house and third - the land lay high so there was a nice view and there was timber.

He and his sons cut the timber as needed. They hauled it by team and wagon to Perry where they sold it for $1.50 a wagon load. Some they turned into lumber at the saw mill and hauled it home to build the barn and other buildings.

They camped by the spring. Indians still came across the land to use the spring to water their horses as they had always done. At first Lucy was afraid for her children but the Indians were friendly and through sign language, she traded with them chickens, grain and cornmeal for other meat, plants, etc.

From the rock quarry William shaped stones and built a rock house on the northwest corner of the land. There were four rooms plus a frame kitchen. He also built a rock smoke house where meat could be cured. This building still stands.

He worked in Morrison helping build the stone buildings on Main street. The old citizen bank building which is still standing is the last he worked on. He died August 19, 1902. After his death Lucy received the patent to the land as the widow of William P. Emick. Lucy later married Leland P. Roberts, no children were born to this union. Lucy died November 20, 1924. Leland Roberts died in 1942. They are all buried in the Morrison cemetery.

The children of Lucy and William Emick were: Bessie (born April 25, 1976) (see Eugene Branson); Arthur born July 8, 1877 died about 1890 at Guthrie, Oklahoma; Mattie Ann born February 8, 1878; David Emick born April 2, 1881 left home and returned to Kansas City, Missouri. Contact with this family was not close. He married and had two daughters with the last name of Hill. He died in the 1960s and is buried in Phoenix, Arizona; John born October 6, 1883 left home at an early age moving to Montana and later South Dakota to a small town called Timberlake. He was nicknamed "Curly" because of his black curly hair. He never married and was in ranching. He came to Oklahoma for a family reunion at his sister's home (Bessie Branson) and died suddenly from a heart attack. He is buried in the Morrison cemetery; Joseph born June 22, 1885 married Dovie C. James, October 19, 1915 at Pawnee, Oklahoma. They moved to Portland, Oregon where Joe worked as a pipe fitter in the ship yards during WWI. In 1921, they lived in the Garber-Covington area in Oklahoma. Joe worked for Sinclair Oil Company as a driller and tool dresser. Their only child, Katherine Arlene was born there March 27, 1923 (see Willie H. Frank). Joe followed the oil fields to Seminole and Hobbs, New Mexico. In early 1930s they returned to Morrison to live on the Emick farm. After his daughter married he went to San Francisco to work in the ship yards during WW II. Joe retired in 1950 and was living with his sister, Bessie Branson at the time of his death February 2, 1952. He is buried in the Fairlawn cemetery at Stillwater, Oklahoma. George born March 20, 1889 married Gretchen Ulmstead and helped his mother by farming the Emick farm. Later he moved his family to Covington, Oklahoma where he worked as a welder for an oil company. He had three children: Hazel who married Harold Bebee; Nellie who married Harold's brother, Robert Bebee and Richard. When George retired he moved to the Emick farm and tore down the rock house built by his father and added two small rooms to the kitchen. He sold the farm and moved to Garber, Oklahoma where he died August 29, 1966 and is buried at Garber.

Edith born April 20, 1893 married Ray Testerman. They had three children: Bob, John and Clara Mae. The Testerman family moved to Exeter, California.

The last child of William and Lucy Emick was a little boy. He was stillborn and is buried in the Morrison cemetery.

Edward U. Engler
By Alta (Engler) Proctor

My father, Edward U. Engler was born in Elmore, Wisconsin. His family were Swiss farmers. He had taken a barbering course and was ready to start in business. The man who owned the building he rented gave him back his rent money and said that since he, the landlord, owned the saloon next door he wanted to rent the building to a man who would patronize his place of

Cooper and Beaty store in Billings. (L to R): Mr. Cooper and Mr. Beaty, next two unidentified, the ladies identified as Eva and Jennie.

business and since my father didn't drink he was returning the rent money.

So my father packed away his equipment in about 1900, and told his parents he was leaving for Oklahoma. I imagine he probably hitch-hiked and bummed rides on the railroad. He said the first town he went to was Garber. It was then about 5 months old. He looked at several surrounding towns and decided he would locate in Billings. So until he could send for his equipment he started business with a kitchen chair, his razor, shaving mug and scissors.

He said he had his A.R.D. commission and his USID commission transferred to Oklahoma. I have no idea just what those were except that one was a secret U.S. Government agency. He said that in Billings he worked under a George A. Disney.

With my father was his brother Arnold Engler. His sister, Louisa Hangartner and her husband lived on a farm between Garber and Billings. They had three daughters Lynda (Pyland), Estelle (Husband) and Amy (Davis).

Also in Billings was my mother's sister, Elizabeth Cooper and her husband Quince Cooper. Uncle Quince had a drygoods and grocery store in partnership with Mr. Beaty.

Although Uncle Quince and Aunt Lizzie had no children, Uncle Quince really enjoyed them. He sponsored boy's baseball teams in Billings. He came to Billings in 1900.

My mother was Jessa (Lydick) Engler from Mooresville, Missouri. She was a sister of Mrs. Quince Cooper. She met my father when she was visiting her sister in Billings. In 1927, Uncle Quince sold the store and moved to Rogers, Arkansas where he died.

In 1902, my father bought, jointly with his brother, Arnold and sister Louisa Hangartner a farm in Kay County (SW ¼ of Section 26, Township 25 North, Range 2 West). About 1916, he bought two farms in Noble County NW ¼ of Section 11 in Oakdale Township and N ½ of the SW ¼ of Section 7 in Red Rock Township.

In 1906, my father moved to New Mexico and later to Hutchinson, Kansas. Then in 1941 he and mother moved back to the Kay County farm and rebuilt the house.

On August 25, 1945, my father died at the Kay County farm. My mother, Jessa Engler moved into Billings. In December 1967, she moved to Hutchinson, Kansas. She died March 29, 1971

John Ewy
By Dorothy A. Ewy

John Ewy, ancestry-German, was born November 1, 1867, at Galezien, Austria, left his home land to Austry to Hamburge, Germany. There he boarded the steamship Cimbria, April 8, 1883, and with his brother, Peter, Henry Rupp, Dan Rupp, and on April 24, 1883 landed in New York. They also carried a stowaway, Pete Rupp, in a sack. He was so small no one noticed. Then they boarded a train for Halstead, Kansas, where John worked at many jobs, farming, carpentry, and painting. Seven years later, he married his cousin, Susie Brubacher, born October 9, 1871, Lamberg, Austria. She was the daughter of Philip and Kathrine (Rupp) Brubacher. Kathrine died in 1919. John, Susie and Kathrine are all buried in the Ewy cemetery four miles east of Perry 3 mile south and ¼ mile east in Noble County. John Ewy was the son of Peter Ewy (born 1841) and Katherine Brubacher (born 1835). John and Susie took a train from Halstead, Kansas to El Reno, Oklahoma to get married. They saw Oklahoma, then said, "Some day we will come to Oklahoma to live," but it took a few years of hard work and five children, before they left Kansas to come to seven miles east of Perry and two miles south. They brought three children along. They had already lost two sons.

In Perry, they had eight more children and lost three girls. They raised eight children, built two homes (lost one in a fire). Their first home in Oklahoma was a dug out close to a spring, son Dan, was born there, 1898.

They were members of the Mennonite Church, sometimes they never had a church, so they met in homes and John was the preacher and song leader. After a few years not enough members for that, but John played his organ, sang and read his bible every Sunday morning (no working on Sunday). Their children respected them, never had any problems, he told them their chores to do and that was it. On February 19, 1940, John suffered a stroke and passed away, February 20, 1940, he had a hard but, a joyful life.

Susie was a wonderful woman, she made lots of quilts, sewed them with beautiful stitches and quilted them. She made garden, put up pickles, sourkraut, green beans by the barrel and meat smoked to a most delicious flavor or fried it down and put it in five gallon cans of lard, sausage balls covered with lard. She could fix a meal for a king (never thought about going to the grocery store when company came, she had it all) baked bread, coffee cake, butter, cream and eggs. John couldn't eat beef, they always had pork raised and butchered their own hogs, made all kinds of sausage liverwurst and head cheese. They used the intestines and stomach for casings, it was a job and art to clean those intestines, but they were good eating.

Susie suffered a stroke October 1940 and was left with one side paralyzed, she was in a wheelchair for four years. Then she had another stroke, she was put to her bed at this time for two years, she was as helpless as a baby. At the time of her death, she lived with her son, Paul Ewy and his wife, Dorothy, at 503 Maple Street, their home. They took care of her until her death, December 7, 1946.

The issue of John and Susie Brubaker (also spelled Burbacher) Ewy were Emma Ewy, born July 23, 1891, Moundridge, Kansas died October 8, 1967. She married Henry Ritthaler, born 1884, died 1955. They had six children: John, Margaret, Vernon, Lucille, Paul and Frank.

Matilda Ewy born October 15, 1892,

Home of John and Susie Ewy about 1900.

John and Susie (Brubacher) Ewy - 1939.

at Moundridge, Kansas, died June 1957. She married 1912, August Busse. He died June 11, 1958. They had four children: unnamed baby, Mildred, Lucille, and Eugene.

Henry Ewy died in infancy in Moundridge, Kansas.

Clara Ewy born June 24, 1895 in Moundridge, Kansas. She died March 5, 1979. She married William Krug, he died 1951. They had seven children: Harold, Elmer, Dorothy, Monetta, Melvin, Marvin, and Fern.

Walter Ewy died in infancy in Moundridge, Kansas.

Dan Ewy was born November 15, 1898 in Perry and died July 19, 1956. He married Mollie Krug.

Three girls were born and died in Noble County: Elizabeth (1900-1901), Olga (1903-1904) and Katie (1905-1907).

Mary Ewy was born November 29, 1906 in Perry. She married Horace Richards and died in 1957.

Harold Ewy was born December 22, 1908 and died February 19, 1969. He married October 18, 1930, Luella V. Chenoweth (born July 28, 1911). They had six children: Betty L. (Ewy) James, Ruth Ann baby died, Melvin Clark Ewy, Bonnie Ewy baby died, Vickie (Ewy) Maine, and Dan Paul Ewy.

Paul Ewy was born April 18, 1911 in Perry and died June 10, 1976. He married September 10, 1932, Dorothy A. Chenoweth (born February 29, 1916). They have three children: Peggy (Ewy) Devine, Janet S. (Ewy), and Jimmy Harold Ewy.

Edna Ewy was born July 29, 1914 in Perry. She married July 29, 1933 to Glenwood Groom. They have seven children: Ethel, Barbara, Tom, Susie, Norma, Leonard, and Duane.

Paul Ewy

By Dorothy Chenoweth Ewy

I was born in Carmen, Alfalfa County, Oklahoma on leap year, February 29, 1916. I'm the daughter of Anna E. (Christensen) and Clark Braden Chenoweth. In 1921 when I was five years old my parents sold out and went to California on a train. I had at that time three brothers and two sisters, Star, Edd, Clark Jr., Luella and Vira. I started to school in California and also got a new sister, Gladys, in 1922. We were in California three years when Dad got tired of the oilfield so we came back home to Oklahoma. We lived on a farm three miles northeast of Perry for two years. I got two more sisters, Libbie in 1924 and Mary in 1926. We attended Pleasant Hill school, then we moved to near Sumner where I attended the 5th and 6th grade. We moved to one and a half miles northeast of Perry and went back to Pleasant Hill school. In 1928 we moved to seven miles east and three south of Perry and went to the Oak Grove school. I failed the eighth grade and got another brother, Billie Joe in 1928. There were ten of us now. Dad said "He raised his own ball team" - he played with us and soon we were going all over the country, playing ball every Sunday. There was a colored team, mainly from the Doyle Tillman family and we had some great games. We also went swimming in the pond and rode horses.

In winter we went to neighbor's houses, danced and ate popcorn. This is where I met Paul Ewy. Paul played the violin and his brother Harold played the guitar. Everyone played the Jazz Horn. There were the Ewy, Ritthaler, Ziesch, Galloway and Chenoweth kids. In 1929 we moved a mile north and one mile east so we were still in the same school. I didn't want to go back to school since I failed so at 13, I went to work for Mrs. A. Watkins who had had a stroke. I decided to go back to school and in three months I passed, graduating from the eighth grade.

That summer Dad went bankrupt so we sold out and went to Idaho in 1930 in two cars, a Jewett and a Studebaker and nine kids. My oldest sister Luella stayed in Perry and on October 18, 1930 she married Harold Ewy.

In Idaho we went to work picking apples and potatoes for an old friend of Dads, Emile Hansen. With winter coming on they decided to return to Perry. On September 10, 1932 Paul Ewy and I were married. After a working honeymoon to Colorado, we came back to Perry and moved in with his parents, John and Susie Ewy. On October 19, 1934 our first daughter, Peggy Ann was born. February 20, 1940 John Ewy passed away and that fall Susie had a stroke. She never walked again but got around in a wheelchair. May 1, 1941 our second daughter, Janet Sue was born. A year later Susie had another stroke that put her to bed. She had to be tend-

Ewy Family - 1948. Back Row (L to R): Paul, Peggy (Divine), Dorothy. Front: Jimmy H. and Janet (Mack).

ed like a baby. On February 12, 1945 our son was born so we stayed on. The farm wasn't paying off and Paul had to work for the county to pay bills. My mother passed away October 10, 1946 and a month later my father wanted to sell their home at 503 Maple Street in Perry. Paul and I bought it and moved to town. Two weeks later, December 7, 1946 Paul's mother passed away.

In August of 1947 Paul and my brother Bill Chenoweth bought a Service Station together and Bill moved in with us. The station was a half block east of our house. In 1951 Brother Bill was drafted into the Navy. I helped Paul run the station for ten years, then we sold out and ran a new Gulf Station on the south edge of Perry for five years.

Peggy married Melvin (Curt) Divine on September 3, 1952. They have three children: Judy, Sandra and Tony. Sandra married William Belk and have a son, Brandon. Tony married Jana K. Rodda. Peggy and Curt have a flower shop in Pendleton, Oregon.

Janet Sue married Ronnie Mack April 3, 1958. They have two sons Bruce and Bryan. Bruce married Arleen Knopfel and they have a daughter Stacy Dawn. Bryan married Sheryl Taylor. Janet works for Elwell Auto Supply and Ronnie has been with Charles Machine ship for twenty-seven years.

Jimmy Harold married Marilyn Shirman, July 27, 1968. They have twin sons, Jimmy and Timmy. Harold spent four years in the Navy. He works for Charles Machine Shop. His wife is a fourth grade teacher in Perry.

On June 10, 1976 my husband died in his sleep. I'm proud of my family. I will be 70 my next birthday. I keep up my yard and home as much as I can. I have traveled by car, pickup camper, bus, airplane, train and covered wagon but Perry is my home. I have a rock collection I picked up all over the United States. I don't leave much history, but maybe some of my family will.

Peter Ewy
By Patty Ewy Bible

"Free, only want to be free, We huddle close and hang on to that dream... They're coming to America, Never looking back again." This is a part of a song written by the popular modern singer named Neil Diamond, but it could have been written in 1882, about the immigrants who docked in New York harbor that June.

Aboard that ship, the Cimbria, were my great-great grandfather Peter Ewy, his wife Katharine, and their sons, Johnn, Heinrich, Gustav, Eduard, Rudolf, and Peter (born 1865). Their daughter Lizzie had arrived in the states a few months earlier.

The cost for that one-way trip from the port of departure at Hamburg to New York harbor (and on to Halstead, Kansas by train) was $88. Peter and Katharine had arranged to work for a preacher in Kansas for $9 per month for 9 months to pay for their fares.

The Ewy children would one day relay to their children their memories of that long voyage — of the family's life possessions crammed into one big trunk, and of the smell of that cheese (rotten cheese) aboard the Cimbria.

After setting foot on American soil, Peter and his family traveled by rail to Halstead and later settled there and in the surrounding communities of Hanston and Moundridge.

His oldest son, Peter (my great-grandfather), was about 17 years old when he left his homeland of Austria to come to America. He and Maria Brubacher (born 1868) were married in Moundridge on February 18, 1886, and they lived in Hanston, and then Moundridge. In 1887, their first son, John Peter was born, and their first daughter, Katherine arrived in 1889. Then my grandfather, Rudolph was born October 17, 1890, in Moundridge. Their second daughter, Matilda Sophie, did not survive infancy, a not too uncommon fate in those days.

Peter and Mary had another journey yet to make — to the great state of Oklahoma. They had heard many rumors about "free land" to be found there. So, after living a year in Orlando, Oklahoma, Peter and Mary joined thousands of others hoping to stake a claim at the opening of the Cherokee Strip in 1893. They did stake a claim on land they found about six miles east of Perry in a community later to be called Walnut Township.

Peter Ewy family. Seated (L to R): John, Peter with son Peter, Mary with Mary Margaret, and Katherine. Standing (L to R): Ed, Gus, Clara, Rudolph, Susan, Henry, and Elizabeth. Photo taken February 12, 1917.

Although they now had firm roots on American soil — their OWN land — Peter and Mary and their children kept many of the "old" ways. The remained Mennonites, and had a large family, naming many of their children after their own brothers and sisters (which also made it confusing for some of their descendants!).

Peter was a mason by trade as well as a prominent farmer in Walnut Township, and was well respected in the community. His family increased by leaps and bounds — their children born in Oklahoma are as follows: Gus, 1895; Susan Matilda (Bowers), 1897; Clara Mae (Voise), 1899; Henry, 1902; Edward, 1904; Elizabeth (Davidson), 1907; Peter, 1909; and in 1911, Mary Margaret (Hasenfratz).

It was not easy to feed and clothe 11 children in the early 1900s, but Peter and Mary brought with them attributes more valuable than money or possessions: the spirit of their ancestors — courage, stamina, pride in one's work, and faith in the future.

My great-grandfather Peter died at the early age of 52 in 1918. His final resting place is the Ewy cemetery located near his homesite east of Perry. The "Ewy cemetery" is located on land Peter Ewy got in the run. Mary died thirty years later in 1948. Many of their children, grandchildren, great- and great-great-grandchildren, live in or near Perry to this day. The entire list of descendants now stands at several hundred — my grandfather and grandmother alone have over 50 descendants.

Although my grandfather Rudolph died almost 25 years ago (1961), I remember him well. He had many of the same qualities that brought his ancestors to America and sustained them in this land: a warm, loving nature, a strong sense of "family", intense courage and stamina, and faith in the future.

The Ewy descendants carry on this tradition with a special gratitude for the sacrifices their ancestors endured in order to call America their homeland, for the country of our origin is now part of Poland and under Russian control.

John R. Fairchild
By Mildred Fairchild Fisher

John Roush Fairchild was born November 1, 1836 in Delaware County, Ohio, the son of Catherine (Roush) and George Anson Fairchild. He married Emily Hickey July 31, 1867 in Edgar County, Illinois. Emily was born May 13, 1840 in Edgar County, Illinois the daughter of Margaret (Smith) and Henry Hickey. Six children were born to them all in Edgar County: Thomas Elza born July 31, 1868; George Samuel born April 20, 1870; Margaret May born May 18, 1872; James Albert Leroy born January 15, 1875; Lois Emily born April 3, 1877 and John Emery born February 27, 1879.

John R. finished the 9th grade in

school and after serving in the Civil War from December 18, 1863 to December 1865 he became a teacher. Emily died January 19, 1892 of pneumonia. Having lost his wife and a son, John R. wanted a change and he decided to make the run into the Cherokee Strip.

The following are excerpts from his auto-biography: I made the race and got a claim, not just what I wanted, for I wanted bottom land, but did not get it for, as I have told you, the best of these claims were "soonered" but I would not now exchange my farm for some of the bottom claims that I coveted.

Some had been permitted to monopolize whole blocks while others were restricted to a single lot as pleased the townsite court and U.S. Marshalls, at least this seemed to be the case in Perry, the county seat for Noble County, where I was employed for a time as court stenographer.

Having made my filing, I built a shack first, then a dugout, then a two-room house and an arched cave walled with rock and cement. I had about one hundred acres broken, a two-wire fence around the whole, four wires on top of the sides, a pasture of forty acres, fenced with with a three-wire fence, a granery 8 x 16 feet, a bank stable walled with rock without cement and covered with prairie grass, this with a chicken house and garden enclosed with woven wire constituted my improvements. I had apples, pears, peaches, plums, apricots - also about one hundred grape vines, trellised and a blackberry patch." - end of excerpts.

John R. Fairchild had been a teacher in Illinois and after coming to the Strip, he helped organize a school and helped build a school house, then taught the school. My mother, whose parents homesteaded across the road from him but in Garfield County, went to school to him. Later, when he quit as a teacher, his son, John Emery Fairchild, who came out later from Illinois taught and my mother and her brothers and a sister went to school to him. In 1926, I went to Antelope Valley and taught the school making three generations of Fairchilds who taught there. The Fairchild land was one mile west of the Antelope Valley school and a little south. My mother lived one mile west and across the road, putting her in Garfield County.

My parents John Emery Fairchild and Nora Spencer were married in Perry, Oklahoma Territory October 22, 1901 and lived with John R. for a year before moving to Kiowa County and later to Dewey County.

In the late twenties and early thirties Thomas Elza and his family lived in the house. His son, Bennie, of Tonkawa still owns part of the land.

I, Mildred Fairchild Fisher taught also at Polo and Otoe schools in Noble County.

George L. Faragher
By Florence Denslow

George Lincoln Faragher was born October 22, 1867 at Dodgerville, Wisconsin. The ancestors of Mr. Faragher were natives of the Isle of Man, a small island midway between Ireland and England, who came to America and settled in the north central states in pioneer days. George grew to manhood in the city of his birth and was married to Anna Peterson, April 13, 1899. They lived here until 1901 when they established a home in Billings. He erected a two story business building. In 1903, they returned to Wisconsin for the summer due to Mrs. Faragher's poor health. She died on August 6, 1903 at the home of her parents. The doctors pronounced it a case of ptomaine poisoning, probably from eating some canned goods on the trip.

George lived at Dodgerville for three years and on October 1, 1906, he married Catherine (Kate) Davis. Kate was born January 6, 1876 on a farm near Dodgerville, Wisconsin. They came to Billings after their marriage and established a home.

They were the parents of four children. Catherine was born January 23, 1908 at Billings. She married Otis Alvin Bilderback April 2, 1930. They had two children: LaDonna Jean (Strahan) and Charles Alvin. George Stanley Faragher was born June 10, 1909. He died April 18, 1951. He was a bachelor and a merchant. Anna May Faragher was born April 8, 1912 at Billings, Oklahoma. She married Fred Wilkins, a farmer at Pond Creek, on November 26, 1933. They adopted a son, Harold (Hess) Wilkins. Judson Davis Faragher was born August 17, 1915 at Billings, Oklahoma. He married Juanita Henson in Enid, December 4, 1939. He died May 4, 1983 and is buried in Enid, Oklahoma. They had two children: David Lee Faragher born in Enid, Oklahoma January 2, 1941 and died in Enid December 20, 1947. He is buried in the Billings Cemetery. Gary Lynn Faragher was born August 16, 1943 in Enid, Oklahoma. He married Myra Lewis of Alva, Oklahoma, they have two sons.

When George returned to Billings in 1906, he was almost continuously in the mercantile business, selling the first business house on the north side of main street and buying a business house on the south, which was under the management of his brother, John, during his long sickness of heart trouble which took his life on June 18, 1926.

Kate and her children moved to Enid June 1, 1928 where she lived until her death October 22, 1933. George and Kate are buried in the Union cemetery at Billings, Oklahoma.

Benjamin R. Fillmore
By Mr. and Mrs. Julius V. Holsinger

Benjamin R. Fillmore was born October 12, 1834 at Bayside, Westmorland County, New Brunswick, Canada, along the waters of Baie Verte - close to Port Elgin. He was the son of Agreen and Sarah Jane Reed Fillmore. He was married May 3, 1854 to Ann Cathrine Brodie in New Brunswick, Canada. She was born July 22, 1838 in New Brunswick.

Benjamin was a farmer most of his life and a Baptist minister.

The family consisted of five children, born in New Brunswick. In 1869, they came by a schooner from Port Lawrence, Nova Scotia, just south of Sackville, New Brunswick, west through the Cumberland Basin, then through Chignecto Bay and Bay of Fundy. They stopped at St. John Harbour to unload and take on freight, then continued on southwest on the Atlantic Ocean to Boston, Massachusetts.

From here they traveled overland by train or covered wagon to Nigara Falls, New York, where they visited Millard Fillmore, President of the United States (1850-1853). Then Ben and family traveled by water and land to Chicago, Illinois and then to near Rockford, Illinois where a brother, John Edward Fillmore and family lived. John came over the same route in 1867. In 1870, Benjamin came to Kansas, near Osage City, where he had another brother, Cyrus. Cyrus came to the United States in the early 1850s. He married in Wiconsin in 1853.

Benjamin Fillmore lived on a farm seven miles northwest of what is now Reading, Kansas. Later his brother, John came from near Rockford, Illinois and Ben and John and their families lived in the same two story house, near their brother, Cyrus. Then a year or two later, Ben and John moved to Butler country, near Beaumont, Kansas. Ben owned about one half section of land at one time, about 7 miles northwest of Beaumont.

In January of 1892, Benjamin and John and their families moved to near Langston, Oklahoma. Ben worked for Benjamin Dobson here for about one year.

On September 16, 1893, Ben made the run into the Strip and homesteaded land in Walnut Township (sw section 35).

Ben R. Fillmore died at Stillwater, Oklahoma, December 28, 1913. His wife lived with a daughter until her death,

March 7, 1917. Both are buried in Shelton cemetery near their farm. They had eleven children: Charles E., Arthur, Anna M., Ada L., Raglan A., Rebecca, David H., William R., Bertha, Mary E., and Alvuis E.

Delbert Foltz
By Mary Lou Foltz

Delbert and Mary Lou Foltz came to Noble county from Enid when he was named ranger for the county by the Oklahoma Department of Wildlife Conservation in 1969.

Mr. Foltz was born at Nash, Oklahoma, the son of Sam and Tina Foltz. He grew up in the area of Hillsdale and Goltry and attended school both places. He enlisted in the Navy in 1945, served in the Seabees, then returned to graduate from Goltry High School in 1947. He also attended Northwestern State Teachers College in Alva. Mrs. Foltz was born and raised in Helena. Her parents were John and Edith Liebrand. She graduated from Helena High School and attended Phillips University in Enid.

Following their marriage in 1948, the Foltz's made their home in Enid where he was employed by Union Equity Cooperative Exchange. They built their own home just north of Enid, and their children attended the North Enid School. They were active members of the Willow Road Christian Church. Mary Lou served two terms on the North Enid Board of Education, the first woman in Garfield county to serve in such a capacity.

While in the North Enid community, Delbert coached both little league football and baseball. Their daughter, Betsy, had the distinction of being the only girl out of 25,000 participants to take part in the Police Athletic League, a summer baseball program. An avid sports fan, Delbert played both baseball and fast pitch softball until he moved to Noble county.

In 1961, Mary Lou returned to Phillips University as a second semester senior, completing the work for her bachelor's degree the following spring. She began teaching fifth and sixth grades in Carrier and commenced work on a master's program at the same time. She received a M D degree in 1968.

In 1969, after having worked for Union Equity for twenty years, Delbert took the ranger's exam and was hired by the Wildlife Department. He was assigned to Noble county in March of 1970. Delbert was named to be a hunter safety instructor very soon after becoming a ranger. The students he has certified, number in the thousands. In 1973, he was selected to represent the department, along with

Delbert and Mary Lou Foltz

personnel from the Oklahoma Tourism Department, at the Canadian National Exhibition in Toronto, Canada. In 1978, he was named Oklahome State Game Ranger of the Year. He has been named an honorary member of both the county and the state 4H clubs. He was named Friend of Extension in 1986.

After teaching four years at Carrier and North Enid, Mary Lou began teaching fifth grade at Billings. She remained in that capacity until 1977, when she was made principal of the grade school. In 1985, she and Delbert were made honorary members of the Billings FFA Chapter.

The Foltz's live nine miles south of Billings in the Antelope Valley community. Mary Lou's hobbies include gardening, reading, and watercolor painting. They both enjoy hunting, fishing, spectator sports, and raising Angus cattle. They have three children, Suzy (Mrs. Michael Crouch), Betsy (Mrs. Bill Honeyman), and David. There are five grandchildren, Cory, Jaci, and Jennie Honeyman, Justin and Sarah Crouch, all of whom live with their parents in Waukomis. David, who followed in his dad's footsteps and became a game ranger, lives in Garber.

John Pearl Foreman
By Valinda Sullins

John Pearl Foreman was born at Winterset, Iowa, southwest of Des Moines, July 28, 1869. In that wooded area of Iowa, he became an experienced timber cutter.

One evening, after visiting a young lady, Pearl was going home through the woods, which were four miles across with a gate at each end. When he was still 7 or 8 miles from home, he heard a scratching sound on a tree, and the bay mare he was riding began to run. Pearl said, "Whoa there Queenie, let's go back and see what that was," but the mare lunged and wouldn't go back. Fortunately, the gate at the far end of the woods was open and the mare ran home as fast as she could and was white with foam when they got there. Pearl heard a couple weeks later of a man killing a cougar twenty-five miles away with a hide nine foot long. The cougar was laying on the man's haystack and the man killed him with a pitchfork. Pearl traveled the distance to see it. Another time a pack of coyotes followed him through the snow for four or five miles.

Pearl would drive cattle across the Big North River to graze and when he would bring them home, he would wait until the last cow went into the river, then he would grab her tail and let her bring him across.

One of Pearls uncles was an engineer on a train and Pearl decided he would go to a school to learn to also become a train engineer. But before the time came for him to attend school, there was a train wreck in which his uncle was killed. Therefore, Pearl did not go to the train engineer school. John Pearl Foreman and Violet Amelia Young were married June 8, 1892 in Winterset, Iowa. She was born November 8, 1871.

Pearl came to Noble County with his father and two brothers on horses in 1897 to farm. They each bought 40 acres from the man who owned the 160 acres of the SW ¼ of Section 21-23N-1W, located 2 miles south and 1¼ miles west of Ceres, Oklahoma on the north side of the road, or 11 miles north and 1½ miles west of Perry.

Later, Pearl brought his wife and two daughters, Millie and Sylvia, to Noble County in a covered wagon pulled by a white horse named Charley and a bay Morgan horse named Morg. The trip from Winterset to the farm southwest of Ceres took 21 days. Coming across the Kansas prairie they saw a great number of buffalo. Violet brought a lot of boiled eggs with them from Iowa to eat on the way to Oklahoma because they would keep fairly well on the trip.

As his father and brothers wanted to go back to Iowa, Pearl bought 40 acres from each one of them until he had the full 160 acres, which he farmed with horses. Several years after coming from Iowa, Pearl drove a wagon pulled by a young mare and the horse, Morg, that had come from Iowa and was now pretty old, to Red Rock to get a load of coal. By the time they had started home it had begun to rain and the travel in the mud became slow and the young mare became worn out and could no longer help pull the load by the time they got to Bowden School. They were about five miles from Red Rock and still had nearly three miles to travel to get home. Pearl hitched the stay chain behind Morg onto the double tree so that the mare no longer had to pull and

Violet and Pearl Foreman in Redwood Forest.

the old horse, Morg, pulled the load of coal the rest of the way home in the mud mostly by himself with the mare possibly helping out at times.

Pearl served on the Pleasant Valley school board and on the Red Rock township board. He died November 25, 1952, and Violet died January 4, 1948.

Pearl and Violet were the parents of 12 children: Olliver Ellsworth, (April 10, 1893 - October 1893); Millie Viola (Kearns) (July 27, 1894); Sylvia May (Paris) (November 3, 1895 - December 5, 1978); Johnnie Pearl, Jr. (February 14, 1898 - 1899); Annie Lee (May 12, 1900 -May 31, 1900); Charley Curtis (July 4, 1901 - July 5, 1984); Bertha Ann (Roesler) (December 4, 1903 - July 9, 1978); Gladys (June 24, 1905 -November 24, 1905); Roy Ernest (March 14, 1907); Lillian Irene (Sullins) (September 20, 1911); Clarence Orville (October 29, 1912); and Carrie Elizabeth (Nemec) (December 4, 1913).

Millie married Albert Kearns and were parents of: Thelma (Johnson), Velma Alice (Craighead), Doris (Yeary), and Raymond. Sylvia married John Paris. Charley married Irene Tabor and were parents of an adopted daughter, Marion. Bertha married Herbert Roesler and were parents of Marvin and Gordon. Roy married Elsie Hayne, November 24, 1925, and are parents of: Marie Kathleen (Cooper), Clara Nadine (Megenity), Norma Jean (Sullins), and Donna Mae (Hopper). Irene married Erwin Sullins and were parents of: Robert, Wilma Faye (Condit), Richard, Vera Mae (Bolay), and Wendell. Clarence married Marjorie Brorsen and were parents of Johnny and Harlow. Carrie married Edd Nemec, Jr. and were parents of: Rhonda (Humphries), and Mike.

George A. Foster
By Mildred Highfill

George Alford Foster was born May 8, 1856, in Morning Sun, Preble county, Ohio and was the oldest son in a family of nine children. His father, Samuel C. and mother, Hannah Ann Sayer were born in Camden, New Jersey, The town of Fosterville, west of Camden was named for the family. The father settled in Ohio about 1840, and engaged in his trade as wagon maker. During the Civil War, he served in the 93rd Ohio Regiment and was honorably discharged for disability which later caused his death.

After finishing the courses offered in the public schools, Mr. Foster studied for a time at Morning Sun Academy. In 1881, he left the east and went to Brekenridge, Colorado, for eighteen months, then to Philipsburg, Montana, for two years as overseer in the Granite Mountain mines. In the fall of 1884, he came to Lincoln county, Kansas, about six miles from Lincoln Center, near the junction of the Elkhorn and Sabine rivers and settled on a farm he purchased.

Here, he met and married Sarah Rebecca Deppen, September 30, 1889. She was born August 21, 1868, in Reading, Pennsylvania, the daughter of F.Z. Deppen, a farmer of Lincoln county, Kansas. He had enlisted in the Fifty-fifth Pennsylvania Regiment, when he was sixteen, and had reached the rank of Captain.

When the Strip was opened, Mr. Foster sold his Kansas farm and came to Oklahoma. At the firing of the gun, he started out on his Arabian horse staking a claim in section 18, Red Rock township. Mrs. Foster stayed in Kansas until Mr. Foster got established in building a home. Two of their children, Ralph E. and Faye F., were born in Lincoln, Kansas, and born later in Oklahoma were Mabel E., "Baby" Foster and George A. Jr.

He was elected Sheriff of Noble county in 1899, and served two terms, then became a deputy United States Marshall until statehood. He continued farming, expanding acreage and raising Hereford cattle as well as other interest. One was bringing the Frisco Railroad through Perry by a large cash donation. He became stockholder and was President of the First National Bank in Perry for a number of years. In 1921, he became under-sheriff of Noble county serving until his death at the age of seventy-two in 1928. From 1895 to 1900 he used a bicycle to make most of his official trips, thinking nothing of riding seventy-five miles in a day.

One of the interesting events of Mr. Foster's life was his capture of "Bert" Welty, a partner of "Ben" Craven, one of the most notorious outlaws of the west. In 1901, these men attempted to rob a store at Red Rock and in the fight which ensued, Welty was wounded by

George A. Foster (1856 - 1928).

Cravens who mistook him for one of the pursuers. Welty found refuge in a farm nearby, and was discovered by Sheriff Foster.

Mr. Foster's solving of what was known as the "19003" mystery was the result of his independent efforts. The body of a young man was found in Woods county who evidently had been killed some three months before. The first useful clue was a newspaper notice that a Mr. Wright was advertising for his son, Rolla, who had left home with a team to work in the harvest fields, some months before. The team was easily identified but had not been sold by Rolla Wright, so Mr. Foster proceeded to hunt for a man know only as "Shorty" and a man known as McPherson, who had been with Mr. Wright. McPherson, when located was able to exonerate himself from any share in the crime and stated the other lived in the Kickapoo country, under his real name. After a discouraging search, he was found and arrested. In the course of a seemingly casual conversation, Mr. Foster asked his prisoner if he could write and receiving the reply of yes, Mr. Foster asked him to write the date, August 3, 1903. This was done but was written August 3, 19003 which appeared on a cancelled check found in Rolla Wright's pocket. When brought to trial the prisoner pleaded guilty and was sentenced to life imprisonment.

George A. Foster died October 26, 1928 and is buried in Grace Hill cemetery, Perry, Oklahoma. His wife died March 6, 1960 and is buried beside him, as is the baby that died December 26, 1898, age 8 days.

Jospeh P. Foucart
By Millie Highfill

Joseph P. Foucart, architect for the above building, was a resident of Guthrie. He was born in Arlon, Belgium, the son of John Pierre and Katherine (Mater) Foucart. He came from a prominent Frence family, whose ancestry was traced by the records back

The First National Bank Building designed by Joseph P. Foucart.

to the year 1560, showing it to be an old patrician family of Curgies, near Valenciennes. John Pierre Foucart was born in Carignau, Ardennes, France, and was a farmer by occupation. Moving to Belgium, he died there in 1890, age 70 years. He married Katherine Mater, who was born in Becherich, Belgium. Her father, Francois Joseph Mater, was born there in 1799, and was of French descent. Mr. Foucart died in 1898, at the age of seventy years, leaving five children of whom Joseph was the oldest.

Born November 14, 1848, in Arlon, Belgium, Joseph P. Foucart received his early education at his native place. After completing his classical studies in the Royal Atheneum, at Arlon, he took a thorough course in a civil engineering and architectural school of Ghent, from which he graduated in 1865. For four years he was assistant engineer for a railroad in Belgium, and in 1869, went to the mines at Longwy, France, as mining and civil engineer. He served in the Franco-Prussian War in the Tenth Regiment of Artillery, Fifth Battery, of the French Army. At the battle of Sedan, he was taken prisoner, but made his escape and returned to Longwy. He was there a non-commissioned officer of the fortress until its surrender, January 23, 1871, when he was again taken prisoner. Three days later, he made his escape to Belgium, where he remained until March 1871. After the treaty of peace was signed he rejoined his regiment and was honorably discharged.

In 1872, Mr. Foucart superintended the building of the castle of Mr. Roussile, at Castle of Viere, Belgium, which was constructed at a cost of $400,000 and required two years' time. In 1875, he entered the service of Mr. Govaerts, the private architect of the King of Belgium, and superintended the erection and arranging of the winter garden of the King at Lacken. He then superintended the building of the Grand Central hotel of Brussels, and in 1877-1878, the courthouse of Charteroi, Belgium, at a cost of $328,000. In 1879, he superintended the erection of Pouhon at Spa, a watering place of Belgium, the cost of which was $80,000. In 1880, he went to Paris as chief draughtsman for drawing the details and finishings of the new city hall of Paris, which cost $16,000,000. Later, he engaged in business for himself as architect and superintendent of building until 1888, when he came to America. After three months in Texas, he went to Kansas City, where he remained until the opening of Oklahoma, settling in Guthrie in June, 1889.

Among the many buildings erected by him are the following: Alva Normal School; Library Building; Agricultural and Mechanical college at Stillwater; public school at Pawnee; the dormitory to the college at Kingfisher; Victor Block, Lyon Block, Royal Hotel and the State Capitol building. He had his office in the Victor block, on the corner of Harrison and First streets.

Mr. Foucart was married in France to Henrietta Jacques, who was born and died there. Two children were born to them: Pierre Julian and Mrs. Marie Julia Toye. Mr. Foucart was again married in Paris in 1885 to Mary Philomene, nee Coen, widow of John Charles Jacquart. During his residence in France, Mr. Foucart was made a Mason. He was also a member of the Odd Fellows, Knights of Pythias, Unifor Rank, and the Order of Elks. He was a staunch Republican.

After the coming of statehood in 1907, Mr. Foucart left Guthrie and it is not known where he lived out the remainder of his life. Even his own relatives do not know where he is buried.

Christ Frank

By Dorothy Vasek and Rosie Crane

Christ Frank made the Cherokee Strip run of September 16, 1893. His horse played out so he stopped and staked his claim. His claim was three miles south of Sumner, Oklahoma. This land is still in the family. Their daughter, Kathryn James, and husband bought the farm after the death of her parents and is now owned by her son Fredrick James.

Christ James was born June 26, 1871 in Germany, the son of Maggie (Migler) and John Frank. He and his five brothers came to America and settled in Seward, Nebraska. When he heard of the land run, he came to Oklahoma to stake a claim. His brothers, Fred, Christ, Dave, and Charlie came to Oklahoma, but Bill married in Nebraska and stayed there near Seward.

In 1897, Christ married Wilhelmina (Minnie) Spahr. Christ's brother, John, married Minnie's sister Hanna Spahr. Minnie was born March 22, 1877 also in Germany and at the age of sixteen she came to America with her parents and settled at Galveston, Texas for a time before coming to Oklahoma.

Christ and Minnie had eight children: Flora who married John Ricker; Sophia married Louis Vasek and had two sons, Louis A. and Theodore J. Her husband died in 1944 and she later married J.D.E. Owen; Kathryn married Clarence James and had three sons, Fredrick, Leonard and Collins; Rosa married Gerald Caine, Carl married Pauline Reynolds and had one son Carl Reynolds (C.R.); Eugene married Lucille Downey; Christ married Helen James; Fredrick (Fritz) married Carmelita Nichols and had one daughter, Rosalee.

In 1919, Christ and Minnie purchased more property two miles west of Morrison and this is where the family was raised. Christ bought his first car and one day was taking the children for a ride. There was a car accident on Mule Creek and Christ was badly hurt. He died a week later on December 10, 1920. Minnie died August 14, 1940. They are buried in the Pleasant Valley cemetery near Sumner, Oklahoma.

A few years after Christ's death Minnie had a bigger house built. Fredrick (Fritz) purchased the place after his mother's death. The house has been remodeled and is still being used. This farm is school land and is now leased from the state of Oklahoma with all the buildings owned by Fritz. Fritz is still farming the land.

Frank Family 1973. Back Row (L to R): Fredrick (Fritz), Christ, Carl and Eugene. Front Row (L to R): Rosa (Caine), Kathryn (James), Sophia (Vasek) (Owen), and Flora (Rieker).

Eugene Frank
By Lucille Frank

Eugene Frank's parents were Christ Frank and Wilhelmina Spahr Frank. Christ came from Germany to Nebraska and Wilhelmina came from Germany to Texas. They met at his brother's and her sister's home (John and Hanna Frank's home). Eugene's parents were married in December, 1897.

Eugene Frank was born November 7, 1899, on the farm his father homestead a mile south of Pete's Corner. He drove horses and worked in the field when he was young. One time a team of four horses ran away when they were in the field, as horses did sometimes.

One of his sisters told me when he was young his parents brought him a watch and he wanted to see what made it tick. He opened it up and before he was through investigating the main spring came out and he couldn't get it back together again. He felt very bad about it but nothing could be done about it then.

His parents moved to a farm about two miles west of Morrison in 1919. His father was in a car wreck and died December 10, 1920. His mother was left with 8 children. Eugene helped raise his younger sisters and brothers. They said he was good to them. His mother died August 14, 1940.

He went to Kansas City, Kansas to Sweeney Mechanic School for awhile and learned to do mechanic work so he was able to do a lot of his mechanic work when he farmed.

He married Lucille Downey, whose parents were William Thomas Downey and Myrtle Almina Johnston Downey. Lucille was born March 29, 1914, southeast of Morrison. Eugene and Lucille were married in Morrison at the Downey home, April 22, 1936. They didn't go on a trip for their honeymoon so down through the years he would take her somewhere for the day and tell her "We are going on our honeymoon today." He took her on a lot of trips like this of course it was a happy day for both of them. They lived in Morrision when they were first married. In a little over one and a half years, they moved to a School Land which they bought. It was about a mile west and three-fourths mile north of Morrison. They moved into a little frame house there in November, 1937. There was no electricity there. They used kerosene lamps and a kerosene cook stove. They also had a gasoline iron to iron their clothes with. The REA put in electricity. It was a happy day when the electricity was turned on for the first time. They had a lot of happy times but of course there were hard times too.

Lucille and Eugene Frank.

They raised most of the vegetables they ate and they raised chickens for meat and sold eggs to the Stillwater Hatchery a long time.

He was a farmer. He raised wheat, oats, alfalfa hay and maize. He also raised cattle. He had a threshing machine and a hay baler and he did custom work with these for some of the neighbors. It took a lot of men to thresh the wheat and oats. The wheat and oats were cut with a binder and made into bundles which the binder tied with binder twine. The bundles were shocked and left to dry for a time before they were threshed. These bundles were hauled on bundle wagons pulled by horses to the threshing machine. It was pitched into the threshing machine and it threshed the grain out, which was hauled with grain wagons pulled by horses. Eugene was so glad when people got tractors for the poor horses to have to work so hard and they would get sore shoulders from the collars they had to wear. They got sore shoulders when they had to pull too hard and too long.

He farmed with tractors for many years. They lived on the farm until December, 1975, when they moved to 105 East A Avenue in Morrison.

They were both members of the Methodist Church in Morrison. He belonged for over fifty years to the church. He was Sunday School Superintendent for many years. He taught the adult Bible Sunday School Class for a long time. He did whatever he could to help the church. One pastor's wife said something nice about something he had done for the church and he told her he was doing it for the Lord. This was always his thought about things he did for the church. One pastor, Rev. Rex Bowen, called him Mr. Methodist. Rev. Bowen said, "A lot of people will go a mile with you." He said Eugene went the second mile with him when he was pastor of the church.

Eugene died January 15, 1985, at Stillwater and is buried in the Sumner cemetery. Lucille Frank also worked in the Church, taught the Junior Sunday School Class for years.

John Frank
By John Frank

John Frank was born in Wuertenberg Germany August 11, 1867. His father was also John, born in Wuertenburg, Germany in 1837, and died near Morrison in 1902. His mother was Maggie Migler who was born 1838 in Germany and died near Morrison in 1901. John had five brothers and one sister who died in infancy. His brothers were Fred, Chris, Bill, Dave and Charles. In 1886, John and his brother, Fred came to America and lived in Seward County, Nebraska.

On September 16, 1892 John married Johannah (Hanna) Spahr. In 1894, they came to Oklahoma in a covered wagon. They purchased the south half of the northwest quarter of section 26 in Autry Township southwest of Morrison, Oklahoma. He later purchased the north half from Joe Seeligar.

His parents came later to Oklahoma. His brothers: Fred, Chris, Dave, and Charlie came to Oklahoma but Bill married in Nebraska and continued to live near Seward. Fred and Chris also settl-

John Frank and wife, Hanna (in car). (L to R): Maggie, Bertha, Mary, Charlie, Anna, Herman, Lillie, John, Harry, Katie and Bill - in front of home - 1920.

ed southwest of Morrison and Charlie settled near Mt. View, Oklahoma.

John and Hanna had twelve children: Charlie, Maggie, Katie, Bill, Mary, Bertha, Anna, Lillie, John, Herman, Harry and Edith.

John's brother Fred married Flora Emick and had three sons: Fred, Henry and George. His brother Chris married Minnie Spahr and they had eight children: Gene, Flora, Carl, Sophie, Katherine, Chris and Fred. His brother, Bill, had four children: Edgar, Jess, Willard and Eunice. His brother Dave lived at Oklahoma City and had no children. His brother Charlie married Lillie Grubbs and had six children: Carl, Earl and Edna - (twins), Harley, Beulah and Ethel.

Later John purchased land near his farm from Fred Hilburg. He also purchased 320 acres east of the home place.

The Day, Oklahoma post office and general store was on the southwest corner of the home place. The building was moved and is now a part of the home. Mrs. Hanna Frank deeded each of the children 40 acres and kept the 240 acres of the homeplace until she died.

Herman and his wife, Ruth, purchased the home place from the estate and Ruth still lives there. There are many descendants of John and Hanna still living around Morrison, Perry and Stillwater not far from the old home.

Willie Wendel Herbert Frank
By Katherine (Emick) Frank

Willie (Bill) Wendel Herbert Frank was born 7 December 1920, Karlsruhe, Germany. He came to the United States October, 1927 and lived with his parents Elizabeth and Charley Frank on a farm southwest of Morrison. He attended Shiloh country school and Morrison High School.

At the Salem Lutheran Church, Stillwater, Oklahoma, he married Katherine Emick, daughter of Joseph and Dovie Emick. They made their home on the Emick farm, east of Morrison. Their only child a son, Roland Herbert Frank was born July 25, 1942. In October 1942 Bill entered the army and served with the 222 Searchlight Battalion in New Guinea and the Philippines in the southwest Pacific. At the end of World War II, he returned to his family and purchased a farm near Glencoe, Oklahoma. After about a year of civilian life he decided to return to the U.S. Air Force and make a career of it. He and his family were stationed in Florida, Georgia, Alaska, California, Germany, France, Africa, South Carolina, Oklahoma and New Mexico. Bill retired from the Air Force in 1967.

Willie (Bill) H. Frank, Katherine (Emick) Frank and Roland H. Frank - January 25, 1944.

Katherine Emick Frank was born 27 March 1923 at Garber, Oklahoma, the only child of Joseph and Dovie James Emick. She attended schools at Maude, Oklahoma, Hobbs, New Mexico and Morrison, Oklahoma. After marriage to Bill Frank, they lived on the Emick farm, southeast of Morrison.

The farm always was a special place although I never knew my grandparents - he died in 1902 - she died when I was 20 months old. I always felt close to them on the farm. My grandmother especially - maybe it was because I was named for her and really wished I had known her. Everyone always spoke of her with much affection, she must have been a dear lady. I'm glad I spent much of my childhood on that farm. The freedom to wander alone over all of it - take a book - go off to read and dream. I liked going to the spring and looking for Indian arrowheads, to climb to the high pasture south of the house my grandfather had built from the stone quarry near the spring. From the high pasture you could see for miles around. That place had been used by Indians to protect themselves. The buffalo also gathered there and there was huge buffalo wallows still there, where they had rolled in the dust. It was easy to visualize what it must have been like before the white man came, to see it as God had created it, in its natural state. I always felt good that my grandfather, who was a builder, loved nature and was a bit of a dreamer had been the first to own this piece of land, since it had been created by God, a rather awesome thought, but I had great respect and love for that special land.

I'm glad I lived there during my childhood, also that for a short while it was home to my husband and son.

After World War II and Bill had returned to the air force we traveled extensively. I worked as a secretary and later was able to continue my education at Sacramento Jr. College, receiving my degree and becoming a registered nurse in 1957. I worked at this profession until I retired in 1980.

At times Bill lived with his aged parents at Morrison. We owned a home in Sacramento, California.

Our son, Roland H. Frank lives in Sacramento, California. He was married to Kathleen Kenney April 11, 1965. They have three children: William Herbert Frank (24 May 1968), Timothy Mark Frank (11 June 1971), and Lara Anne Frank (25 April 1976).

Roland was in the Air Force for four years and has worked at the Royal Oakes Post Office in Sacramento, California since leaving the military service.

W. E. Franklin
By Linda Ratliff

William Elmer Franklin, son of James Madison Franklin and Lucy Howe Franklin, was born in Cleburne, Texas, January 26, 1885.

Ida Elnora Lee, daughter of William Franklin Lee and Susan Cowan Lee, was born in Albany, Kentucky, February 11, 1893.

They were married at the Bethel Methodist Church in Shawnee, Oklahoma, on October 25, 1913. The children of this marriage are: Elwood Paul, born August 25, 1914, at Shawnee; Pauline Mary, born February 13, 1916, at Olney, Texas; Wayne Elmer, born December 20, 1920, at Shawnee; Wanda Marie, born June 12, 1924, at Earlsboro; and Norma Lee, born April 21, 1930, at El Reno.

When Elmer was five years old his mother died and his father remarried. He married Sarah Howe, a cousin to his first wife. Elmer and his step mother didn't have a good relationship. He left home about the time he was twelve years old to live with his older sister, Molly, for a period of time. As a young man he worked as a cowboy in Texas before coming to Oklahoma.

While in Oklahoma he met and married Ida Lee and it was while they lived at Shawnee that their first child, Elwood, was born. When he was a baby, they moved to Texas, where the next child, Pauline, was born while they lived at Olney, Texas. When Pauline was six months old, they moved back to Oklahoma.

When thinking back to these difficult times, Elmer would recount this story from time to time. He was helping build a pond. As they worked it started to rain, but they continued working trying to finish the job before they quit. He got a bad chill and it developed into pneumonia. He tells of feeling so sick he wanted to die, but remembered he had let his insurance expire to save some money. The thought came to mind that

William Elmer and Ida Elnora Lee Franklin, wedding day October 25, 1913.

Ida could never raise those two babies by herself. He determined he had to get well, and he did!

The three younger children were born while they lived in central Oklahoma. Wayne at Shawnee, Wanda at Earlsboro, and Norma at El Reno.

The family moved to the Red Rock area in 1932, where they continued to farm. Their first home in Noble County was eleven miles north of Perry just south of the Red Rock Creek.

Ida became active in home demonstration club work and was known to her granddaughters for having a special gift of turning used feed sacks into dresses for them. She also enjoyed raising chickens and exhibited them at the Noble County Fair.

They lived on a farm one and a half miles south east of Red Rock when she died in July 1951, after a short bout with cancer.

Elmer had to learn to take care of household chores after her death. His speciality was a stew that he slow cooked in a large pan while he was in the field.

On June 30, 1960, he married Mable Wilson. She was known to everyone in the community as "Granny." They lived on a farm she owned located five miles east of Red Rock until her death in May 1971.

Elmer continued to live alone for several years, but would spend most of the winter months visiting with his children to avoid the cold Oklahoma winters. Elwood made his home in Morrisville, Pennsylvania, Wayne in San Pedro, California, Wanda (Mrs. Stanley VanTuyl), settled in Burns, Kansas, Norma Lee (Mrs. Gordon Brant), lived in Sunnyvale, California, until her death in 1976, and Pauline (Mrs. Orphie Love), at Ponca City.

About three years before his death he made his permanent home with Nona and Cecil Cales, his granddaughter and her husband, who live east of Ponca City in Osage County. His funeral was held May 17, 1980, at the Methodist-Christian Church in Marland where he had been a faithful member since 1939. He was buried in the Red Rock Cemetery beside his first wife, Ida.

Frederick-Cook

By Gloria Frederick Cook

Gloria Ann (Frederick) Cook was born on the homestead, in the same house were my father Clarence had been born 22 years earlier. My grandfather, Fred Frederick claimed this homestead in the Cherokee Strip opening, September 16, 1893.

Around the time I was born, Grandpa Frederick's first oil well was drilled just west and a little north of the house. An oil well drilled in the Misner sand came in in 1934, in almost the same exact spot where he had placed his stake 41 years previously. It was an exciting time for all. He was blessed with some oil wells and used what he got to help others whenever he could. That's one of the many wonderful traits Grandpa had and the one that I hope can be said about me someday.

I attended school all 12 years at Orlando, seeing many changes as I came through the years. One of the memories of my early school days was the fact that we could walk across the street to a little gasoline station/hamburger place that was run by Mr. and Mrs. Meyer. You could buy a hamburger, soda pop and candy bar for 25 cents — Can you believe that? Our school at that time consisted of the brick classroom building that is still there and a little two room school house that had been moved in from one of the country school locations. Later, around 1945, another country school was moved in and turned into our first lunch room. Mrs. Reed and Mrs. Farber were the cooks. We were starting to

Grandpa Fred Frederick and Gloria Ann in front of one of Fred's oil wells.

Sitting: Bob and Gloria Cook. Standing (L to R): R. Todd, Judy, Eddie, and Patty Cook.

come up in the world. Around 1954 the new gym was built, and now the old cafeteria is gone and a new modern one is standing in its place. Also, a science building and Vo-Ag building has been added.

I still live on the five acres received from my father in 1971, to build our new house on. It is built right in front of the old one. In fact, the original rooms of the old house are still standing and I hope to some day restore it to its original look.

I take great pride in my family tree and Noble County History. I have worked on my family tree and am interested in someday finishing it; but to go further on my Grandma and Grandpa Frederick's history, I need to go back to the records in Germany as they each came to the United States at an early age.

I married Robert E. (Bob) Cook, March 27, 1954 after a whirlwind courtship. I was working at Continental Oil Company in Ponca City, when Bob came home from three years in the military service, 28 months overseas, 19 in Japan and 9 in Korea. We met on a blind date and that was it. We were married in the Evangelical United Brethern Church in Orlando, now the United Methodist Church, by Rev. Pauli, with Janice Bolay (Ferda) and Charles Ross as attendants. The church had come down from the Zion Evangelical church that was started in the yard of my Great-Grandparents, Henry and Katherine Dierolf, in 1890.

Our first daughter, Judy Gayle Cook (Miller), was born in Dallas, Texas in 1957; and in April, 1959, our oldest son, Edwin Clarence Cook, was born in Perry. When Eddie was a month old we moved back to the "Ole' Homestead" and have been there since. Eddie has not gone far from the homestead. He lives across the road on the 80 acres his great-grandfather bought. It was an original "School Land". Our youngest son, Robert Todd, was born in 1968 and has lived all his life on the land that his great-grandfather homesteaded. Our youngest daughter came to live with us in October 1978. She never had the privilege of knowing her Grandfather.

As most families now have to have supplemental jobs, it is necessary for us to look to the cities for jobs to live on. However, Bob does custom swathing and baling to supplement his other job. I also work outside the home. Eddie is following his grandfather's footsteps in his love for cattle and has quite a nice herd started.

Our daughter Judy married Dale W. Miller and they have two boys: Dale Wayne Jr. and Matthew Brian.

We are all proud to be a part of the Frederick Family History, Noble County History, and especially Americans.

Clarence Frederick
By Gloria Frederick-Cook

Clarence W. Frederick was born June 24, 1912, on the farm homesteaded by his father, that was claimed on September 16, 1893. He grew up and received his schooling on this homestead, attending a little country school through the first eight grades and then attending Orlando High School. When starting school, Clarence and his brothers and sisters did not speak much English; but in the country school this was no problem as their teachers usually were German speaking, as was most of the community. Miss Susie Kolb was one of the teachers I heard him speak of many times. The Kolb family lived on the adjoining farm to the west.

He married Lula Mae Webb, January 29, 1934. They lived on the homestead until 1951, when he moved across the road to the School Land, 80 acres bought from the state by Fred

Barnyard with cattle and horses. Building to right of picture was very first house turned into grainery. Photo refinished by Robert O. Lovvorn.

Frederick around 1931, and rented out the farm land of the homestead quarter. To this union was born two daughters, Gloria Ann and Judy Gayle. Judy Gayle was stillborn. Gloria still lives on the "Ole Homestead" with her family. Clarence and Lu moved to Perry, Oklahoma, December, 1952.

Clarence bought the "Ole Homestead from Fred after he and Lula Mae were married. When that was paid off, he then bought the quarter that Fred had bought from John Viets in 1932.

The second house built on the place is where Clarence and family lived. They closed in the porch and remodeled a little here and there. Clarence farmed the land as well as working the oil field with horses, maintaining the lease roads and other tasks to keep an oil lease up in top shape. There were many times when Clarence would not see me in the daylight hours for weeks at a time, as some jobs took him a great distance from home. With all the oil boom in the area, called the Lucien Field, there was a lease house on the school land, belonging to Sinclair Oil Company and one on the Viets Place belonging to Standlin Oil Company.

When the government set up the farm programs telling the farmers how much wheat they could plant, Clarence turned his land all back to pasture planting all the fields with grass. He never gave up his cattle and loved to walk around them for hours if you didn't hurry him a little once in while.

Clarence was interested in sports and played baseball with an Orlando Alumni team for many years. The baseball field was usually someone's pasture. He also coached an alumni basketball team sponsored by Phillips "66", when Ray Warren had the Phillips "66" dealership for the Perry area. Also, he would help transport college basketball teams from Perry Depot to Stillwater for games before they started flying or using university owned buses.

Clarence and Lulu Mae had a ready made family almost from the day they were married. Lulu Mae's mother had died previous to their marriage and her dad died a couple of years after they married. Therefore, they took in the two youngest brothers and youngest sister of Lu's. Their home, as well as that of Fred and Lizzie Frederick was open to all of the brothers and sisters. Gloria was never made to feel like an only child, as all of Lu's brothers and sisters seemed like hers. Clarence treated them all as his own and in his last day's on this earth asked for them when he was to have very serious surgery. Everyone of them came to be with Lu and Gloria during this period of time in the hospital. Their love for him was as evident as his love for them. My father passed to his reward March 9, 1978. He is greatly missed.

Fred Frederick
By Gloria Frederick Cook

Cherokee Strip pioneer, Fred Frederick, born Friedrich Friedrich, November 17, 1870, in Nitzehausen, Germany, one of six children, 4 sisters and one brother. The brother died in infancy and was a twin to his oldest sister, Maria, who remained in Germany. Fred came to the United States as a very young man and settled at Clay Center, Kansas, in the time between 1884 and 1888.

House where Clarence and Gloria were both born. Photo refinished by Robert O. Lovvorn.

Lizzie and Fred Frederick - standing in front of original house. Photo copied by Robert O. Lovvorn.

The run was off with a pistol shot at high noon September 16, 1893, one mile north of Orlando.

Fred Frederick rode a black and white pony to stake his claim to the 160 acres in section 28, township 20 North, range 2 West, two miles north and 2 west of Orlando. His stake was in the middle of the NE 40 acres.

Mr. Frederick stayed all night of this September 16, 1893, on the premises of his claim. He was a 23 year old bachelor.

He married Eliza Dierolf on January 13, 1897. Eliza (Dierolf) Frederick was born January 12, 1879, in Gelbingen, Germany, near Swabish Hall. She came to the United States with her parents, Henry Dierolf and Katherine (Hildenbrand) Dierolf and was working in Orlando as a waitress at the time of the Cherokee Strip opening. Nine children were born to them. Their first three children, John, born September 20, 1897, died October 2, 1897; Kathryn M. born February 22, 1899, died April 7, 1978; Rose born February 9, 1901, died January 15, 1902; were born in this first home. They then built another one room structure, with an attic bedroom, in which, Henry J. born November 28, 1902; died December 4, 1983; Elizabeth F. born April 11, 1905, died January 7, 1973; Alma E. born September 2, 1907 died January 5, 1970; were born. They later added to that room, four more rooms, in which, Marie F. born February 15, 1910; Clarence W. born June 24, 1912, died March 9, 1978; Elmer F. born February 16, 1916, died November 10, 1930 were born.

Kathryn M. married Ramee R. Johnson, November 27, 1919 and lived and farmed till her death, on a farm three (3) miles north of Kathryn's home and on Ramee's parents' farm, and Ramee still lives there at age 86. They reared four (4) boys: Ramee Elmer who is deceased, Ralph M. lives at 1019 Grove Street, Perry, Wayne F. lives at Stillwater, and Gerald Lee, who lives in Casper, Wyoming.

Henry J. married Catherine L. Ferguson, September 6, 1927. They lived all their life in Raymond, Washington. Catherine died April 1, 1976. They reared three (3) boys: Henry E. of Florida, Richard M. (Dick), Raymond, Washington, and Gary C., Ellensburg, Washington.

Elizabeth F. married Walter Anderson December 2, 1936. They farmed on a farm NW of Covington until retirement at which time they moved to Sunnybrook Lane, Enid, Oklahoma.

Alma E. married Joe Andrew, December 24, 1928. They reared Jackie of Guthrie; Marlene of Champaign, Illinois, and JoAnn LeGrande of Guthrie.

Marie F. married Edwin F. Dowell, October 27, 1952. They lived all their married life until Edwin's passing April 1, 1982 at Pritchett, Colorado. Marie has since moved to Perry, Oklahoma.

Clarence W. married Lula Mae Webb, January 29, 1934. They reared one (1) daughter, Gloria Ann, who still makes her home on the "ole homestead".

Grandpa had many stories to tell of the Run for land in the Cherokee Strip. One I remember most was the one where he stayed to watch the claims for himself and Uncle Fred Mugler, while Uncle Fred went into Perry to register their claims. You dare not leave the claims unattended because someone would "jump" your claim.

Grandpa Frederick owned this land until he retired and moved to Orlando in 1943. He lived on the homestead 15 days less than 50 years. He then sold it to Clarence and Lula Mae (Webb) Frederick.

Fred and Eliza celebrated their 50th wedding anniversary January 13, 1947.

Grandpa and Grandma Frederick leave a great heritage in this land which will continue through the ages.

John Eugene Frick
By Alta Marie Frick

John Henry Frick, Sr. was born near Liberty, Missouri, in 1887, to Sarah and James Frick. In 1889, James and his family moved near Oklahoma City. They later moved to a farm near Stillwater and lived there until their deaths.

Laura Tabor, daughter of Alice Mertin and Charley Tabor, married John Frick, Sr., in 1916. He farmed in Pawnee, Payne and Noble counties. In 1947, they moved from Liberty District in Noble County to the Morrison area and lived there until their deaths. Laura passed away in 1949, and John passed away in 1959. They are both buried at the Fairlawn Cemetery in Stillwater, Oklahoma, near his parents and her father.

John Sr. and Laura had a daughter, Pauline Ware, and a son, John Jr. who later changed his name to John Eugene. He was born July 17, 1921, in the Olive Hill Community, Pawnee County. He moved with his parents to Payne County, near Stillwater, during his first year of school, and received his education there. He graduated from Eureka High School at Glencoe. During his senior year of high school he commuted fifty miles a day to graduate with his class. He went on to receive a bachelor's degree from Oklahoma Agriculture and Mechanical College (later named Oklahoma State University). Two and a half of his college years he again commuted, this time, 55 miles each day.

November 14, 1942, John Jr. married Alta Marie Gilchirst at the Methodist Church in Stillwater, Oklahoma by Joe Bawers. They lived in Stillwater until John finished college and then moved to the Liberty District of Noble County. They then lived briefly in Ponca City before moving to the Lela community in 1948.

On knees in front row: Ramee Elmer and Ralph M. Johnson. Secnd Row Left to Right: Ramee R. Johnson, Henry J. Frederick, Fred Frederick, Lizzie Frederick holding Henry Eugene Frederick, and Kathryn (Frederick) Johnson holding Wayne F. Johnson. Back Row Left to Right as faces show: Elmer Frederick, Elizabeth Frederick (Anderson), Alma (Frederick) Andrews, Mrs. H. J. (Catherine) Frederick, Joe Andrews, Marie Frederick Dowell and Clarence Frederick.

(L to R): Patsy (Newman), Alta Marie, John Frick Jr. and Sherry (Sayre), July, 1946.

When John was 35 years old, he returned to school and acquired a teacher's certificate. He then taught science and shop for three years in the Morrison School System. He has been a farmer, dariyman, mechanic and rancher over the years. He is a past member of the Board of Directors of the Federal Land Bank of Stillwater, and the Board of Directors of the Vinita Northeastern Production Credit Association.

One of John's hobbies is building soils and pastures. He has received awards in conservation in Pawnee and Payne Counties.

In 1963, the Frick family was named Farm Family of the Month by the Tulsa Tribune Newspaper. In 1955, Alta won recognition for yard improvement from her Extension District and was named Farm Woman of the year in Pawnee County be her Homemaker's Group.

Alta Marie was born July 10, 1921, near Glencoe, Oklahoma, to Mary Dunsmore Lyne and James Franklin Gilchrist. She attended the Eureka School for twelve years. She went on to attend Oklahoma A. & M. College for three years. She was a member of Homemaker (Extention) Clubs in both Noble and Pawnee Counties for 25 years. During this time she was the President of the Liberty Club in Noble County. She also held all the offices in the Home Circle Club and several of the offices in the County Council in Pawnee County. She is the only woman ever to have served on the Morrison School Board, which she did for two years.

John and Alta Marie have been active members of the Morrison United Methodist Church since 1955.

They have two daughters, Sherry Ann and Patsy Kay. Sherry, of Perry, was born December 27, 1946, and married John Charles Sayre (who later became a physician) in 1966. They divorced in 1984. Their children (Laura Anne, born September 23, 1970, in Nuremburg, Germany, and John David, born January 19, 1974, in Edmond, Oklahoma) are prize winning Scottish dancers and have competed in five states at various Highland Games. They entertain frequently and are sometimes accompanied by their father on his bagpipes.

Patsy, of Dover, Oklahoma, was born October 23, 1948, and is married to Robert Allen Newman, C.P.A. The Newman's have three sons: Robert Allen II, born June 23, 1966; Michael Craig, born August 5, 1969; Timothy Joe, born July 19, 1971.

Robert is an engineering major at the South Dakota School of Mines and Technology. Tim has won honors with his wrestling. Mike, being 6'5", excells in basketball and baseball.

Patsy earned a Clothing, Textiles and Merchandising Degree at Oklahoma State University. Since graduating, she has sold real estate and mobile homes and taught clothing courses on the college level.

Sherry has a degree in Psychology from Oklahoma State University. She has spent the majority of her time during the last 18 years as a homemaker. But during that time she also found time to do volunteer work for the Perry Memorial Auxillary, the Perry Elementary School and the Perry Arts and Humanities Council. She was a member of the Ladies Tuesday Afternoon Club, a state officer in the Clan MacDonald and an avid supporter of the Scottish Club of Tulsa. She has been a member of the Unitarian Church Choir of Stillwater for nine years.

Burdette Garvie

By Marilyn (Garvie) Kerr

As all of us know, sometimes one small event can alter the course of our lives. Burdette Garvie was born April 12, 1916, in Woodward County. He was the oldest of three children. His parents were Isaac and Blanche (Benefield) Garvie. He had two sisters: Fayanna (Garvie) Winters and Ruth (Garvie) Holloway. Burdette and Aylene (Cross) Garvie, the daughter of Mervin Cross and Eva (Renshaw) Cross, grew up and married in Woodward County.

In 1946, Burdette and Aylene took their two young sons, H. B. born May 9, 1937, and Larry, born July 26, 1941, on an overnight trip to Sedan, Kansas. They had seen a grass lease advertised in a paper and they went there to see about it. When they arrived in Sedan, they found out that the grass had already been leased so they started back home.

On their way back from Sedan, they decided to stop in Perry and get something to eat. When they got to Perry, they noticed that Larry had lost a shoe somewhere between Sedan and Perry.

Burdette Garvie working cattle in October, 1984.

Burdette decided that they should buy Larry some shoes so Aylene took Larry to Krammer's store (then located on the east side of the Perry square). While Aylene took Larry to Krammer's store, Burdette walked over to the courthouse park and began visiting with some men on a park bench. One of the men was Ralph Swallow, an early Noble County resident. He told Burdette about two sections of grass that could be rented with an option to buy it when the Dee Donaho estate was settled.

The Garvie family decided to spend the night in Perry and look at the grass the next morning. The next morning they looked at the grass and rented it. After renting the grass they decided to move to Noble County.

When they moved to Noble County, they lived in Perry for a year (1946-1947). Then they moved to a farm south of Red Rock where they lived until 1956. While they lived near Red Rock, Burdettya and Marilyn were born. Burdettya was born November 4, 1948, and Marilyn was born February 20, 1950. In 1956 Burdette and Aylene built a house a mile east and a mile north of Sumner. Aylene still lives in this home.

H. B. graduated from Red Rock and married Barbara McClure. They have three daughters: Teresa, Alecia and Dana. H. B. and Barbara live in the Sumner community and H. B. farms.

Larry graduated from Sumner and Oklahoma State University. He married Sharon Pauley and they live in the Sumner community with their two children: Shawn and Larri Jo. Larry also farms.

Burdettya graduated from Morrison and Oklahoma State University. She married John Aaron Linn from Red Rock and they live on a farm in the Red Rock community with their two children: JoDawn and Dee Jay.

Marilyn graduated from Morrison and Oklahoma State University. She

Burdette Garvie going to work on his tractor in 1966.

married David Kerr and they live on a farm south of Morrison with their two children: David Jr. and Joanna. Marilyn teaches at Morrison High School.

Burdette Garvie loved the land and took great pride in raising his crops and cattle. Even towards the end of his life when farming was becoming a non-profit business, he still had hope. He once said, "I love farming; I never wanted to do anything else."

Even with all of his land and material possessions, his most cherished asset was his family. He was a loving husband, father, and grandfather who was always around for his family to "lean on".

Burdette Garvie died of a heart attack on January 23, 1985, in the Stillwater Medical Center. He is buried in Grace Hill Cemetery overlooking Perry, a place filled with many friends and many fond memories. Thirty-nine years earlier, Perry had only been a place to stop and eat.

Harry Gengler
By Gertrude Gengler

Harry Gengler was born March 12, 1895, to Peter and Julia Faber Gengler, near Merril, Iowa, a small town 6 miles south of LeMars, Plymouth County. His parents had immigrated from Luxemburg to the U.S. They farmed in Iowa, for 5 years and, because land was cheap, decided to buy a farm and moved to Perry, Oklahoma Territory. They bought 160 acres 8 miles north and 2½ miles west of Perry. Harry received his schooling in Fairview District #30 but often had to miss the first and last part of the school term, to help plant and harvest crops. He said he never remembered being there for final exams after the 5th grade.

They worked hard and prospered. At the time of his parents' death, they had accumulated 720 acres of land. In those days, most children shared in the work but owned nothing of their own. Harry lived at home until we married - except for a period when he entered the U.S. Army in 1918, and served until 1919.

Gertrude Koelzer was born to Henry and Jane Schneider Koelzer, December 7, 1898, at St. Benedict, a little village 4½ miles northwest of Seneca, Nemaha County, Kansas. I was three months old when we came to Oklahoma, and bought a farm southeast of Perry. Hard times caused us to trade the farm for the Perry Custom Mill and we moved into Perry, where we all attended St. Joseph's Academy. We moved to Senaca, Missouri, in 1914, and to Seneca, Kansas, in 1916. My mother died at 45 on August 20, 1917, of a kidney ailment and pneumonia, leaving 9 children, the youngest 3 and the oldest 22. I was 18 and had one sister, Marie, 5. I kept house for 10 of us and grandfather, who lived on his farm, with us. It was no small job cooking, sewing, etc. for 11 of us. I baked 6 loaves of bread 6 days a week plus lots of cornbread and much plain cooking. Harry Gengler and I were married at Seneca, Kansas, August 9, 1927, - he was 32 and I was 28. We took a five-week wedding trip to the west coast and back in our little "Star" coupe, with complete camping outfit.

Then, back to Oklahoma, and we moved to the farm his parents had lived on when they came to Oklahoma. Soon we had Maxine, Robert, William and Dorothy and all was well. We worked hard, raised crops, cattle, pigs, chickens and sheep. The depression was a time of stress, no one had money, but Harry was a good manager. We milked and sold cream and eggs about enough to pay for our groceries. Of course, we had our own meat, milk, eggs, and raised and canned vegetables, so we had plenty to eat. I made all their clothes - many made-overs and from printed feed sacks.

During the dust bowl times, we had a very bad drouth and heat, especially in 1936, and '37. The prepared field for alfalfa blew so bad so could scarcely see the barn from 120 feet away.

In the fall of 1935, Harry and his brother, Leo, bought the McCormick Deering Agency. With no crop in 1936, and not much in 1937, it was a losing venture and they sold out to Carpenters of Red Rock. We had a hired man work for us for over 2 years for 50¢ a day and board and room - but we could scarcely afford that. In 1932, wheat was 28¢ a bushel, oats 6¢, cattle 5¢ a lb. and pigs 20¢ to 25¢ each, eggs 5¢ to 7¢ a dozen. It was hard to exist.

We bought the farm in 1940, to settle the estate and Albert bought the southeast quarter of section 11-21N-1W. He died in 1943, but had sold us this place. We sold the north farm by auction in 1943, probably one of the first farms in Noble County to sell this way. (It burned down at night from unknown causes on April 17, 1985).

I have copies of the original patents to the land that Peter Gengler and Henry Koelzer bought from people who had made the run and sold out later. Some are hand-written and signed by Presidents William McKinley and Theodore Roosevelt.

As of this writing, May, 1985, five Koelzer sons and two daughters are living, ranging in age from 71 to 86. I am the oldest. Harry Gengler died September 20, 1971, of a long series of strokes, he was 76. Our eldest daughter, Maxine, married Paul Wheelock, both are deceased. They had 3 sons and 1 daughter. Robert married Vickie Zers and they have 3 sons. William married Virginia Turvey, they have 3 daughters and 1 son. Dorothy married Bruce Lehmkuhl and they have 3 sons. I am still on the farm.

Seated: Gertrude and Harry Gengler. (L to R): Maxine (Wheelock), Robert, William and Dorothy (Lehmkuhl).

Peter and Julia (Faber) Gengler family; (Standing Left to Right): Lucille, Albert, Mary, Harry, Pauline, and Josephine. Seated; Agnes, Peter, Julia and Leo.

Peter Gengler
Gertrude Gengler

Peter Gengler was born July 27, 1863, in Buschdorf, Luxemberg, the son of Peter Gengler and Anna Mehr. He immigrated from Buschdorf, Luxemberg to LeMars, Iowa about 1889. He had first landed in South Dakota and stayed for a short time. He deliberately spent his last dollar, before he started working on a farm, so he could truthfully say that he started out in the United States without a cent. He started working for an English speaking family, so he could learn to speak English quicker. He married Julia Faber, April 3, 1894, in LeMars, Iowa. She was born February 28, 1866, in Pratz, Luxemberg, the daughter of Peter Faber and Marianna Johanna Pusch. She immigrated to LeMars, Iowa with her brother, when she was about 23 years old. She worked in homes for several years and met Peter Gengler. They did not know each other in Luxemberg. They lived on a farm west of Merril, Iowa, about six miles south of LeMars. Peter and Marianna Faber came over to live with them. Both died there within a few years.

In February, 1899, Peter and Julia Gengler and their three children: Harry, 4; Mary, 3; and Pauline, 2; moved to Perry, Oklahoma. Peter came on the freight train to look after his livestock machinery and household goods, and Julia had brought a girl along to help her manage their three children.

Peter Gengler bought 160 acres of land, eight miles north and two and a half miles west of Perry, (sw ¼ 5 22N 1W) on December 26, 1900. On March 5, 1900, he also bought the nw ¼ of the same section from Robert L. Thompson, a widower. They had an Iowa man, Andy Sutmeyer, build them a nice five room home with cellar underneath and two rooms upstairs. The family stayed in a hotel in Perry while the barn was built, as quickly as possible. As soon as it was built, they enclosed two rooms in the southeast corner of the barn, where they lived while the house was being built. Being February, I am sure there were many cold days and nights. But it seemed so much better than they had in Luxemburg. They often talked of how poor the people were in Luxemburg, with very little land and a scarcity of food, and they considered the American people very wasteful of land and everything.

When Peter Gengler came to the United States he had all his belongings in a fair-sized homemade trunk. It was about 42" long by about 20" square with a rounded top with leather handles and a hasp for locking it. Julia also brought a much smaller truck 24" square with handles to carry it and a hasp lock. They brought all their belongings in these trunks. They were told to bring only what they could carry. What courage it took to leave family and their homeland

The first home of Peter and Julia Gengler in Noble County.

with such few belongings.

Peter and Julia's family consisted of three boys and five girls: Harry, Mary (Wagner), and Pauline (O'Grady) were born in LeMars, Iowa; Albert, Josephine (Freymann), Lucille (Dennard), Leo, and Agnes (Jones) were born after they reached Oklahoma. They had 18 grandchildren.

Peter and Julia Gengler were highly respected in the community, they were successful, industrious and hardworking people. Peter Gengler had sandy hair and mustache, blue eyes, was about 5'10" in height, sturdy built and very strong and rugged. Julia had dark brown hair, that greyed young, big blue eyes and was 5'3" tall.

Peter Gengler developed stomach cancer and died February 9, 1924. Julia Gengler died August 26, 1937 of a liver ailment. They are buried in the family plot in the Catholic cemetery at Perry. At the time of his death, they had accumulated 720 acres of land and had built two new homes.

At this time, (May 1985), only Pauline O'Grady, Lucille Dennard and Agnes Jones are living of the Gengler children. The first home burned completely in the night April 17, 1985 from an unknown cause.

Thomas Jefferson Gilbert
By Marjory Gilbert LeMaster

On June 2, 1846, Thomas Jefferson Gilbert (Thos. J.) was born in Crawford County, Missouri, to Nathan (Virginia, 1804), a farmer, and Elizabeth (Stafford) Gilbert (Crawford, County Missouri, 1807). Nathan and Elizabeth were married December 14, 1825, in St. Francis County in Missouri.

In 1850, their son, Thos. J. Gilbert, at five years of age, was one of eight children (Lucinda, 16; Martha, 14; Sarah, 10; Richard J., 8; E.-female, 7; William, 3; Rebecca, 1).

Very little is known about the early life of Thos. J. On March 13, 1864, at the age of 17, he joined the Missouri Cavalry of the Union Army in St. Louis, Missouri, and was honorably discharged July 1, 1865. In 1869, he married Pamilie Stevens at Charles City, Iowa. Pamilie died in Cedarvale, Kansas, February 17, 1872. In 1876, when he was 30 years old he came to Oklahoma, where he was the first man to take a lease in the Otoe Reservation.

On August 19, 1877, Thos. J. married Anna J. Thompson (March 23, 1849, Morgan County, Indiana), at Emporia, Kansas, the daughter of Thomas A. and Eliza (Stratton) Thompson. They made their home at Kaw Agency, Indian Territory, where Thos. J was an agent for the Kaw Indians. While living at the Kaw Agency, he and Anna had two children — Anna Grace, (July 27, 1878), who married Frank Fuller in San Francisco (June 29, 1907); and Thomas Thompson (Tom) born February 28, 1880. Anna, the mother of the two children, died at the time of Tom's birth; and Thos. J., her husband married Lydia E. Thompson (June 18, 1859, Morgan County, Indiana — Anna's younger sister) at Emporia, Kansas, March 1, 1881 — one year and one day after Anna's death. They, too, made their home in Kaw Agency, Indian Ter-

Thomas Jefferson Gilbert in Arkansas City, Kansas about 1900.

Lydia E. Gilbert in Emporia, Kansas prior to her marriage in 1881.

ritory, where their first child, Robert B. Gilbert, was born January 4, 1883. Robert married Ada B. Cranford September 23, 1904 in St. Louis, Missouri. Robert worked with an oil firm in Oklahoma and later he worked for the railroad for many years.

Thos. J. was truly a pioneer who dreamed no small dreams. Legend tells us that he walked into Oklahoma in 1876 and in 1883 he leased over 52,000 acres of Indian land (Kansas and Kaw tribes) for 4¢ an acre for grazing purposes. He was a farmer and rancher and most of his operation took place in Noble and Kay Counties.

Sometime between January, 1883, and February, 1885, Thos. J. and Lydia moved their three children from Kaw Agency to Arkansas City, Kansas, where they resided until the early 1900s. While they were living in Arkansas City, two more children arrived — Eva E. (February 16, 1885) who married Frank Cottingham in Red Rock, Oklahoma, June 20, 1906. Frank and Eva spent a number of years in Oklahoma where Frank worked with an oil firm. Later, they were to move to Arkansas City, then Winfield, Kansas, where he was with an abstract firm. Ruth J. (April 24, 1887), the youngest of the five children, taught school in Red Rock, Oklahoma, in 1906 and 1907. Later she taught in Perry, Oklahoma, where she met and married R. Charles Edwards, principal of the Perry schools, June 1, 1910. They spent many years in Eldorado, Kansas, where he was a principal of schools. After he retired from the field of education, they moved to Winfield, Kansas, where Charles spent his retirement years as a residential building contractor.

Thos. J's grandchildren remember hearing the story that their grandfather was shaving one morning in late June when his children rushed into the house to tell him that the wheat field was on fire. They were truly astonished when he continued shaving — he later commented that there was nothing he could do about it. This may explain why Thos. J.'s grandchildren saw their own father, Tom Gilbert, stand in his stocking feet on frozen ground on a cold night in March and coolly watch his garage, car, and stored material burn.

Tom, son of Thos. J., purchased 240 acres in Pawnee County in 1910, from an Otoe and Missouria Indian family, who had received their patent from the US Government in October, 1909. Tom farmed and ranched, while "batching", from 1910, until he and Frances V. McMeekin were married in Perry, Oklahoma March 1, 1914. Tom told his children that as a young man he took cattle to Arkansas City to sell for his father. After the sale, he went to the bank to get the money which he placed inside his boot, walked out of the bank, mounted his horse and started home. At the Arkansas River, a man with a mask and gun stepped out of the shadows, removed the money from Tom's boot, took his horse and left him to get home as best he could — by "shank's mare".

Tom and Frances did not live in Noble County, but their land was in the southwest corner of Pawnee County just across the Noble County line; and since Frances was a Perry girl, they undoubtedly spent many happy hours with friends and relatives in Perry.

Thomas Jefferson Gilbert died in Red Rock, Oklahoma, October 30, 1914, just five weeks before his grandson and namesake was born to Tom and Frances Gilbert in Perry, Oklahoma. His wife, Lydia, died in Kansas City, Missouri, January 8, 1919. Both Thos. J. and Lydia were buried in Red Rock, Oklahoma.

Thomas Thompson Gilbert
By Marjory Gilbert LeMaster

Naturally not in the beginning, but as far back as we know, ancestors of Thomas Thompson Gilbert, better known as Tom Gilbert, came from Ohio and North Carolina to Indiana to Kansas to Oklahoma; and from Virginia to Missouri to Kansas to Oklahoma. On February 28, 1880, Tom arrived at the home of his parents in Kaw Agency, Indian Territory, where his father, Thomas Jefferson Gilbert, was an Indian agent. Tom was the second of two children born to his father and Anna Thompson Gilbert. His mother died when he was born and he and his sister, Grace, were nurtured in the home of Anna's parents and sisters in Emporia, Kansas. So it would not be unusual that their father, when visiting his children, should fall in love with and marry one of Anna's younger sisters, Lydia Thompson, on March 1, 1881 — exactly one year and a day after the death of Anna.

Tom, whose life began in Indian Territory later to be known as the State of Oklahoma, moved with his family (a brother had been added in 1883) to Arkansas City, Kansas, where he was educated. His children remember that there was in their home a fifth grade reader in which he had listed his brothers and sisters, their births and the notation, "All still alive!" which tells us that many of the families he knew had possibly lost a child and the fact that they were all (5 of them) still alive was very unusual. And all of them were to attain adulthood, marry and rear families.

We do not know how much education Tom had, but when he and his brother Robert were boys, they were sent to a military school in Fort Worth, Texas.

Frances McMeekin Gilbert near Black Bear Creek near Morrison, Oklahoma.

Thomas Thompson Gilbert (Tom) on Black Bear Creek bridge - Morrison, Oklahoma.

This may not have been an extended experience. Tom's children were told that he and Bob "ran off" and returned to their home, but there are pictures of them in their uniforms.

As a young man Tom helped on his father's ranch and farm in Noble and Kay counties. He also at one time worked with the 101 Ranch. In 1910, he purchased approximately 240 acres of land from the Carsons, an Indian family who received their patent in 1909. He farmed, ranched and "batched" until he married Frances V. McMeekin, a telephone operator, in Perry, Oklahoma March 1, 1914, when he stopped "batching", but his story was that he taught Frances how to cook biscuits, bread, etc. The property in the southwest corner of Pawnee County was to be the "home place" for the Gilbert couple while they reared four children, increased their acreage, and did their part in building Oklahoma for the future.

One evening they had been to visit neighbors in their buggy when, as they were returning home, the horse became frightened as they crossed a creek bed. Tom jumped out to calm the horse, and Frances, thinking she was as agile as her husband, jumped from the buggy into the rocks and broke her ankle — six weeks before their first child, Thomas Jefferson "Jack" was born on December 9, 1914.

The young Gilbert couple was instrumental in the organization of a Sunday School and Church and also in the building of a church in Watchorn, an oil boom town four miles northeast of their home. Frances and Mrs. Isaac McClurg worked together tirelessly (with others) to keep the Sunday School operating for the many children of oil field workers, farmers, and ranchers in a community of approximately 60 square miles. Sunday School was first held in the Diamond school building and later moved to the new building in Watchorn. Tom was the clerk of the school board for many years and during his tenure a second school was added in Watchorn to serve the children of that area. In the years before and during this time of providing an education and religious training for the young people of School District 37, and a good portion of the west side of Pawnee County and extending into Noble County, three more children arrived in the Gilbert household: Marjory M., September 15, 1916; Olive Ruth, October 19, 1918; and Richard M. "Dick", September 13, 1920. All of the children were graduated from Pawnee High School and three of them attended Oklahoma State University.

The years passed swiftly as they do for all of us and they were to bring joys as well as sorrows, but Tom and Frances, grateful for all of the gifts that a loving God provides, weathered the loss of many material things including their home to a fire in 1938 — two earlier fires had taken a car, garage, and stored material and the second home for the men who worked there while a new home was being built — fluctuating cattle markets; drouth and depression years taking their toll; but as Mr. W. E. Rice wrote of Tom at his death on October 1, 1951, "Tom Gilbert was an individualist in all the term implies. He was one on the diminishing list of old time Oklahoma cowmen. From the privations and hardships of that precarious business, he never flinched. Many times, using an expression of William Allen White, his 'hopes like clouds were blown away before the winds of circumstances.' Finally his persistence, never failing, was rewarded in a handsome way. In a very real sense, the life and work of Tom Gilbert can be said to be an almost cross section of the forces which make America great."

George Gipe

By James Gipe

George and Matilda Gipe came to Oklahoma from Ohio in 1900 and bought some land in section 25 of Rock township. The family consisted of six children: Ollie I. Gipe born in February, 1886 and was married at one time to George Adams, whose family lived near by. She died in Montana in 1976. Romney H. Gipe was born October 6, 1890, died October 10, 1950. Robert J. Gipe was born September 8, 1890, and died September 6, 1965. Curt B. Gipe was born in February 1893, and died April 15, 1945. George W. Gipe was born in 1895 and died December, 1968. Howard W. Gipe was born September 21, 1899 and died in the end of March 1979.

Romney H. Gipe married Anna Marie

Romney and Bob Gipe holding two of their fighting chickens, on homestead near Perry about 1900.

Harrington in Stillwater, OK, April 17, 1912. She was the eldest daughter of Steve and Mary Harrington, born in a cave on her parents' farm on February 2, 1893 and died April 24, 1963. The Harringtons owned 160 acres in section 1 of township 19 north range 1 east in Payne County, Oklahoma.

When Romney was living near Perry, some of the neighbors had fighting chickens and Romney got the fighting chicken bug and raised and fought fighting chickens until the time of his death in 1950.

During his life in Noble Co. Romney worked for some relatives of the outlaw Dalton brothers, who lived near the Gipe homestead.

George and Matilda moved to Chester, MT, in 1913. Romney and Anna moved to Montana in 1917, with their son, James, who was born on September 13, 1915.

Ulysses G. Goe

By Marie Goe

Ulysses Grant Goe was born December 6, 1868 at Knoxville, Ray Co., MO, and died November 24, 1933 at Hayward, OK. He was the son of John Crawford Goe and Narcissus Evaline Campbell. On February 21, 1893, at Cowgill, MO, Ulysses married Sara Etta Michael (November 3, 1873-September 9, 1946) the daughter of John Newton and Ruth (Moad) Michael. Ulysses and Sara went to a home in Mattewsou, OK, immediately after their marriage. On September 16, 1893, Ulysses staked a claim in the Cherokee Strip 14 miles west of Perry just over the line in Garfield county. Sara Etta and baby son, Walter, lived on the claim for two years while Ulysses taught school in Mattewsou, OK. After coming to their

Ulysses Grant Goe, great-grandson of Daniel Boone.

homestead, Ulysses farmed and taught school three years, riding five miles on horseback morning and evening.

From about 1904 until his death he owned the Bank of Hayward, OK in addition to farming his homestead. He also owned a bank in Lucien in the 1920's. Everytime he got money ahead he bought more farm land. At his death, he willed 760 acres of land to his widow and children. He also left a house and lot in Perry, OK, that he had bought for a town house but never lived there.

Sara Etta gave piano lessons as a young girl. After the death of her husband, she lived with her son, Frank Goe. Ulysses and Sara Etta are buried at Hayward, OK, in the cemetery that had been his land before he gave it to the township (Wood Township).

Their children are: Walter Boyd-b. April 11, 1894; John Wesley-b. August 20, 1896; Edith Ruth-b. December 13, 1898; Frank Michael-b. January 14, 1904; Mary Evaline-b. March 18, 1906; Myrtle Mae-b. September 20, 1908; and Bonnie Fay-b. November 22, 1910.

The father of Ulysses Goe, John Crawford Goe (February 22, 1840 - Ray Co. MO — March 16, 1919 at Hayward, OK) was the son of Noble and Jane (Smith) Goe. On February 16, 1868 in Ray Co. MO, he married Narcissus Evaline Campbell (March 5, 1837 - Richmond, MO — March 16, 1919 - Hayward, OK). She was the daughter of Jeremiah and Elizabeth (Vanderpool) Campbell. John Crawford Goe served in the Civil War as a Private in Co A 3 Reg Missouri.

John G. Goe and wife came to Oklahoma and spent his last years with his son, Ulysses. He had in his possession, a trunk that he said belonged to his great-grandfather, Daniel Boone. This trunk is in the Cherokee Strip Museum at Perry.

John C. Goe's father was Noble Goe (b. Ky — d. before April 5, 1847 in Ray Co. MO). Noble married Jane Smith on November 5, 1817. She was born February 7, 1801 and died February 27, 1862. Noble's father was Phillip Goe (b-March 24, 1767 d-March 1805). He married Rebecca Boone (b-May 26, 1768 in NC d-July 14, 1805). She was the daughter of Daniel and Rebecca (Bryan) Boone.

Frank Goe, son of our subject, married Marie Elizabeth Rupp, November 28, 1928 at Lucien, OK. Marie was born July 30, 1907 at Lucien, OK, the daughter of Jacob and Louise (Just) Rupp. Frank was killed November 1971, in rural Noble Co. OK, while serving as a substitute rural mail carrier. Frank attended school at Hayward and two years at A & M college. He worked as an oil driller, substitute rural mail carrier, farmer-rancher, and bank teller. Marie attended grade school in Lucien and Perry High School. They adopted two children: Elroy Cordell Goe (b-July 11, 1933) and Alice Marie Goe (b-May 22, 1940).

Theodore C. Goley
By Gladys Sherman

Theodore Claudius Goley was born at Noblesville, Indiana, December 8, 1869, the son of John and Hannah Goley. The Goley family originally came from North Carolina. When T. C. was quite small, his parents moved from Indiana to Douglas, Kansas. It was at Douglas, he met his future wife, Ida Elizabeth Renfro, who was born February 11, 1873, in East St. Louis, Missouri, the daughter of John Seth Renfro and Marinda Narcissus Chase Renfro. John Renfro was a Civil War veteran. The Chase family can be traced back to the Revolutionary War.

T. C. Goley took part in the Cherokee Strip opening and established his claim September 16, 1893, one mile east of Perry, first plowing a furrow around his claim and then building a dugout. He had started from a point a short distance east of Orlando and arrived on his claim in a wagon drawn by a team of mules. He made the race in a wagon because of a leg injury. Clarence Young, a brother-in-law, filed on a claim just across the road south.

On November 1, 1898, he was married to Ida Elizabeth Renfro in Douglas, Kansas. The marriage was written up in the local paper as follows: "Goley-Renfro-Married: Tuesday, November 1, 1898, at the residence of the bride's father, J.S. Renfro, four and one-half miles southwest of Douglas, Rev. J. Albert Hayden, officiating, Theodore C. Goley and Ida E. Renfro. It was a quiet affair, only a few most intimate friends invited. The bride was attired in a handsome royal purple and olive green novelty goods with cream silk organdy over waist and smilax and white blossoms. The groom looked his best in a conventional dark suit. After the ceremony, the guests were invited to partake of refreshments. The table was loaded with every delicacy the season offered. They left Rock, Kansas, on the six o'clock train for Perry, Oklahoma, where the groom possessed a fine farm where they will reside."

It was a two-room house, T.C. brought his bride to from Kansas. They lived there until 1941, when they retired and moved into Perry.

While on the farm they raised eight children. They first added two rooms to the house, then four bedrooms and a

50th Wedding Anniversary T. C. and Ida (seated). Girls (L to R): Thelma, Gladys, Fern and Agnes. Boys (L to R): Leonard, Harold, Ralph and Wilbur.

Goley homestead. (Left to Right): T.C., Ida, Gladys, Agnes, Ralph John Goley and Alfred Goley.

second story to accommodate the eight children. All eight children attended Perry grade and high school. They sometimes walked, sometimes by buggy or by horseback. Often the children would go by B.J. Woodruff's Grocery and Mercantile Store after school and waited for their father to pick them up. Six of the eight children attended Oklahoma State University (then Oklahoma A & M) located in Stillwater. The children are: Gladys May (Sherman), Agnes Mildred (Springer), Ralph Theodore, Harold John, Fern Elizabeth (Ingersol), Wilbur Renfro, Leonard Andrew, and Thelma Miranda (Morgan). Leonard was the only child who served in the military, as he served in the army in World War II.

Mr. Goley served on the school board and in other community activities. The family was very active in the Presbyterian Church. Mr. Goley worked closely with the Extension Department in Noble County, planting wheat, oats, corn, cotton and prairie hay. He and the boys did all of the farming with horses and mules. He also had a herd of registered Holstein cows. The children belonged to the 4-H Club, showing cows, calves, hogs and grain at the Noble County Fair. They won trips to the State Fair at Oklahoma City and to the International Fair at Chicago, Illinois.

T. C. Goley passed away in 1950, and Ida passed away in 1965. All of the children are still living except Leonard, who passed away in 1984.

George L. Golliver
By Mrs. Lavern Golliver

George L. Golliver was born February 28, 1858, near Murry, Wells county, Indiana. He was the son of James M. and Mary E. Golliver. George was left an orphan at an early age. His brothers and sisters were James, Lida, Mary, Sarah Catheran, Rachel, Ida Bell and Martha Ellen. George spent his boyhood days in Indiana. At the age of twenty, he went to Washburn, Illinois.

On September 13, 1883, he and Margaret Whitten were married. Margaret's parents, Thomas Whitten and Margaret Stephens were married in

George and Margaret - Thanksgiving Day 1941

Scotland in 1850. They migrated to the United States in 1849. They settled in Belle Plain Township in Illinois, where the Whitten home was established.

George was a blacksmith by trade, after marrying Margaret he went into the general mercantile business until coming to Oklahoma in 1907. George and Margaret bought a farm northwest of Perry, and there they raised their five children. James, the oldest son, died at the age of nine while they were in Illinois. In Oklahoma, George went back to the blacksmith trade, and farming. He and his sons ran a threshing machine and steam engine business.

All five of the Golliver children, and later ten grandchildren and two great-grandchildren attended the Lone Star school which was on the southwest corner of the Golliver farm.

George had a severe stroke while living on the farm, he recovered from that and was able to walk and drive a car. As time went on George became deaf.

George and Margaret moved to Perry in the 1920s, where they lived at 720 Maple Street until their deaths. George died in 1950, and Margaret in 1953.

Their children were: Harry (1888-1958) married Mary Smeltzer (1893-1984); George Leo (1894-1971) married Anna Cockrum (1895-1965); W.A. (Dean) (1896-1977) married Fannie Cockrum (1897-1965); Ethel (1898-1970) married Arthur Carrier (1896-1980); and Edna (1900-1973) married James Hentges (1899-1968).

Several of the grandsons and families still farm in Noble county. Leland, son of Harry LaVerne (Bill) son of Leo, Jim, son of Dean, and Gene Hentges, son of Edna. These original family members and their marriages into other pioneer families of Oklahoma gave a rich heritage to all the generations of yesterday, today and for the tomorrows to come

Dale Grange
By Glenda Grange

Dale Gene Grange was born June 9, 1950 in Eugene, Oregon. Dale's family moved a lot during his childhood years. His father, Donald Grange, born November 8, 1922 in South Dakota, served in the Air Force, Coast Guard and Navy for a total of twenty years. Donald married Maudie Imagene Price September 12, 1948 in Claremore, Oklahoma. Maudie (Jean) was born January 23, 1929 in Rush Springs, Oklahoma. Dale has a younger sister and brother. Donna Jo was born January 17, 1957 in Dallas, Texas. Dean Robert was born April 6, 1960 in Olathe, Kansas. Dale's father retired from the service and settled around Choctaw, Oklahoma. Dale graduated from Choctaw High School in 1968.

Dale married Glenda Ann Landress February 12, 1975, in Fort Smith, Arkansas. Glenda was born October 28, 1952, in Norman, Oklahoma. Her father Hoyt D. Landress born February 14, 1925, in Lexington, Oklahoma has driven a truck for Safeway Stores for over twenty years. Her mother is Gearldine Mae Biggs born February 14, 1928, in Tuttle, Oklahoma. They were married January 19, 1946, in Norman, Oklahoma, and were divorced in March of 1980. Glenda has one older brother, Kenneth Lynn born September 5, 1947, in Norman, Oklahoma Glenda grew up in Del City, Oklahoma. Her family moved to Choctaw, Oklahoma during the 1960's and she graduated from Choctaw High School in 1971.

Dale and Glenda lived in Midwest City, Oklahoma, for about three months after they were married. It was while they were living here that Dale got a job with Dresser Atlas in Odessa, Texas. Dresser Atlas is a oilfield wireline service company. They provide open hole electric logs, perforating and other cased wireline services. They moved to Odessa, Texas, during the summer of 1975. Dale started as a operator on a truck with Dresser Atlas.

In June of 1977, Dale was sent to Houston, Texas to attend a Dresser

Gollivers - 1942. Back Row (L to R): Ethel, Leo, Harry, Dean, Edna. (Front): George and Margaret.

Top: Danny, Middle: Dale, Glenda and Shaun, Bottom: Jerri Ann.

school. Dale and Glenda were expecting their first child when Dale left for Houston. Dale came home from school on September 16. Their son Danny Gene was born September 18, 1977, in Midland, Texas. Dale became a completion engineer after attending this school.

After living in Texas for four years, they decided to move back to Oklahoma and asked for a transfer. Dale and Glenda were sent to Perry in October of 1979. They were expecting their second child at this time. In February of 1980, Dale was told that by May 15 he would be in Houston, Texas to attend another Dresser Atlas school. It seemed everytime a baby was expected, Dale was sent to a Dresser school. On April 30, 1980 their second son Shaun Robert was born. Two weeks after Shaun was born, the whole family went with Dale to Houston. After attending this school Dale became a logging engineer.

Dale and Glenda moved out by Orlando, Oklahoma in 1981. While living there they had a daughter. Jerri Ann, born February 21, 1982. This time Dale wasn't sent to school, but he was asked to transfer to Elk City. He turned the transfer down. Shortly after Jerri was born, Dresser Atlas promoted Dale to District Engineer and they moved back to Perry.

In January of 1986, the oilfield work was getting bad. Dresser had to cut back on employees in the Perry shop. Dale had worked for Dresser Atlas for ten and a half years.

Dale went to work for Kentucky Fried Chicken in March. He was a manager trainee for six weeks. At the end of his six weeks training, he was made an assistant manager at the Kentucky Fried Chicken store in Guthrie, Oklahoma.

Robert Grant
By Myron Grant

In the spring of 1889, Robert Grant and his young wife, Phoebe, left their families and friends in Axtel, Kansas, Seneca County. Loaded all their household goods and provisions in a covered wagon and started the long journey to the new land of Oklahoma Territory.

Their son, William, or Willie, as he was called, was about four years old at the time. Their daughter, Anna Lulu, was a little over one year old and another daughter was born on the farm in Oklahoma, May Grant Maze. They had horses hitched to the wagon and three cows tied to the back end of the wagon. There was a crate of chickens, about 20 of them on one side of the wagon and on the other side their plow, hoe and garden rake.

When they camped for the night they would tie the chickens' legs together so they couldn't get away. They would pick and scratch until dark and then they untied their legs and put them back until the next evening. Phoebe said that they never lost even one of them. Their dog, Rover, trotted along and when he got tired Robert would take him up in the wagon and let him ride with Willie.

Across Kansas the traveling was fairy good until they got to the south border where the road was just a trail. Robert had to do all the driving. There were no bridges at creeks or small streams. Phoebe had to do a lot of walking. She walked behind the cows to keep them moving. She walked all the way across the strip in this fashion. It took them two weeks, always stopping on Sunday for rest and worship. Also traveling with them were Robert's two sisters and their husbands, Mr. Doc Gallant and Mr. Detilier, and their children. The families went to Edmond, Oakhoma Territory and settled on school land until the Strip opened September 16, 1893.

Josephine (Herbert) Grant - 1908.

William Grant - 1908.

They came to Orlando and waited. They ran northwest and all succeeded in getting a claim. The next morning Robert noticed at daybreak someone had jumped his claim after dark. So he put the saddle on his horse and rode off. He said there was plenty of land and he was not going to spill blood over it.

In the year 1894, Robert heard about a man wanting to sell his claim south of Perry, so he came from Edmond and bought the man's relinquishment. He paid $200 for it. There were 160 acres with a shack as living quarters. They built a dugout in a nearby draw and used it and the shack as their living quarters, during the time it took them to build a three room house. More rooms were added later when their daughters were born. The final papers were not completed until July 1904.

Teddy Roosevelt, our President at the time, signed and sealed the patent. Robert Grant died in February 1913. Phoebe and their children had the farm until 1951, when they sold it. The farm has been sold several times since 1951, and all the buildings have been torn down. It was a good home for many years.

The Grant's home was in the Fairview School District #76, where Willie and his sisters went to school. Josephine Grant has a picture of the scholars and teachers taken in 1904. In these days of so called, energy shortage it is interesting to note that Pheobe Grant often told how they had to burn cow chips for fuel.

The children of Robert and Pheobe Grant were: William Henry Grant born March 6, 1888; Anna Lulu Grant Campbell, and Anna May or May as we knew her married Walter Maze.

Joseph Herbert came to Oklahoma by way of train or railroad, in March, 1907. His children were: Jennie Herbert Cross (born September 11, 1886, at Atchison, Kansas, died in 1927 or 1928), Josephine Herbert Grant (born February 13, 1888, at Philadelphia, Pennsylvania), Margie Herbert Baustert (born November 30, 1893, at Huron, Kansas), Myra Herbert Schoonover (born March 11, 1895, at Huron, Kansas, died in the 1970s).

Willie Grant and Josephine Herbert became friends at church and later fell in love. However, the courtship became somewhat complicated after one year when the Herbert family moved to the Polo community.

Robert complained to Willie because the horse that Willie drove would be worn out for the week's work after the trip to Polo and back. But since Josephine and Willie seemed to get along fine, the Herbert family did not object to the marriage. But when Willie asked his father to sign his marriage license, Robert just told Willie to wait until he became 21, which was another nine months. So Willie and Josephine made a plan. They would catch the morning train and go to Enid, buy their license and get married and return on the afternoon train and keep it a secret until Willie was 21. But the Lord or the weather became involved and the train was delayed on the return trip. When Willie and Josephine arrived in Perry from Enid, both sets of parents were there to meet them. Josphine ran to her mama and said, "Mama, I want to go home with you." Her mother was just a little angry; so she told Josephine, "You're not my little girl any more, so you better go home with Willie."

The Grant family accepted Josephine as part of the family. Willie and Josephine raised 12 children: Kenneth Herbert Grant born Wednesday, April 21, 1909, at Perry, Oklahoma; Ivan Keith Grant born Friday, August 12, 1910, at Perry, Oklahoma; Katherine Phoebe Grant Dormire born Friday, April 19, 1912, at Perry, Oklahoma; Roberta Margaret Grant Whitlow born Friday, November 27, 1914, at Hanover, Kansas; Wilda Enid Grant Coleman born Tuesday, March 7, 1916, at Hanover, Kansas and died March 7, 1980; Jennie Mae Grant Moore born January 28, 1918, at Newton, Kansas; Myron William Grant born Friday, November 21, 1919, at Newton, Kansas; Murry Almeth Grant born Sunday, September 3, 1922, at Perry, Oklahoma; Raymond Phillip Grant born Friday August 22, 1924, at Newton, Kansas; Lorene Elmira Grant Hardy born Friday, October 1, 1926, at Orlando, Oklahoma; Paul George Grant born November 12, 1928, at Perry, Oklahoma, died December 14, 1932; and Joan Pauline Grant Kistler born November 21, 1930, at Perry, Oklahoma.

Laton J. Hall family. Front Row (L to R): Charles R., Layton J., Delcie Hall (Herber), Mary Elizabeth and Alma Hall (King). Back Row (L to R): Ethel Hall (Shellady) Cleveland and Ora R.

Laton J. Hall
By George W. Hall

The Hall family can be found in many places in Utah, California, New Mexico, Arizona and Oklahoma. What was their source? What led this family of investors, bankers, lawyers and community leaders?

Samuel William Hall's father, Nathan Hall, was a Scotchman, his mother was Elizabeth Dowell (Pennsylvania Dutch). Both Samuel William Hall and Elizabeth Dowell were born in Albermarle County, Virginia, and later lived in Taylorville, Virginia and Troy, Missouri (Lincoln County, Missouri).

Samuel Hall was a farmer. He and his wife had twelve children. Laton Jackson Hall was the youngest. Laton Jackson Hall was born in Joplin, Missouri, on January 4, 1841, and died January 15, 1928. Laton Jackson Hall married Mary Elizabeth Little (born June 15, 1866, and died February 2, 1928) February 1, 1885, at Fayeteville, Arkansas.

Laton Jackson Hall and Mary Elizabeth Hall homesteaded a farm which was acquired with the opening of the Cherokee Strip in 1893. They remained on this bottom land farm located close to Black Bear Creek between Lela and Morrison until the time of their deaths. Both are buried in Grace Hill cemetery at Perry, Oklahoma. They had eight children: Cleveland Hall (1886-1975), Ethel Shellady (1888-1946), O.R. Hall (1891-1970), Delcie Herber (1897-1971), Alma King (1902-1944), Arley Hall (October 14, 1900-December 7, 1900), Charles R. Hall (1894-1971), and Virgil Lee Hall (1908-1954).

Laton Jackson was a Civil War veteran who fought at the Battle of Pea Ridge in Northwestern Arkansas, then came on west after the conflict.

Several years prior to 1893, Hall had already settled his home and family inside Cherokee Strip Territory. Immediately prior to the Cherokee Stip Land Run, he moved his family from inside the Cherokee Strip Territory to an area one mile east of Stillwater, and prepared to come in from the south. His small family remained behind.

Hall knew the land and had already chosen the quarter section he wanted. A man by the name of Bennett also had chosen that particular tract and a spirited race was inevitable. Hall rode a Morgan horse while Bennett was mounted on a Thoroughbred. Both knew they could not be beat in the race, but each feared the other.

While the Thoroughbred could outrun the Morgan on open country, it lost on the rough land. And the final destination was about even as far as smooth and rough country went, and when the objective was sighted the race was still undecided. In a final effort over a stretch of smooth ground, the Thoroughbred inched ahead enough to put his forefeet on the land desired, and Hall came in second, but there was no second price in this contest.

The disappointed and defeated rider moved on and took the 160 acres north of the one Bennett secured and decided to make the best of it. He stayed the required time and proved up on his land and was a help in trying to solve one of the many crimes to the area. A contest followed between Bennett and a man by the name of Cook, which went into the Courts. Court litigation over who had the valid claim to the land resulted. Hall met Bennett's bond knowing he had true claim to the land.

Hall moved his family onto the claim. One night while he and Ora, his son, were doing chores they heard gun fire coming from the Bennett claim. Mr. Bennett was seen no more. Mr. Hall knew that nobody had outrun him and that Mr. Bennett was first on the land. Since Mr. Hall was responsible for the land on behalf of Mr. Bennett, he joined the search party that was organized among the neighbors to find Mr. Bennett. The party discovered a mound of freshly turned earth that looked suspiciously like a new grave. They proceeded to examine the mound more closely when a man on a horse, believed to be Cook, rode up and stopped abruptly when he saw the men examining the mound of new earth. Then he turned and left the scene as fast as his horse would go. His behaviour convinced the men examining the mound that they would find the body of Bennett, which they did, and that this suspicious visitor was the murderer. However, the murderer could not be apprehended or punished. Such incidents were not infrequent in the Cherokee Strip during those difficult times.

Ora R. Hall

By George W. Hall

The parents of both Ora R. Hall and Tillie Ringler made the run into the Cherokee Strip at the opening of 1893. Barney Ringler operated a Taxidermist and Shoemaker shop on the west side of Perry square. Matilda Victoria Ringler was born in Las Vegas, New Mexico, March 4, 1889. Matilda was a long time telephone operator in the Perry Exchange and also served as the chief operator.

Ora R. Hall's parents were Mary Elizabeth and L. J. Hall, who homesteaded in the Cherokee Strip land run. O.R. Hall was born January 27, 1891, in a dugout on old Lela Townsite, Noble County, Oklahoma, two years, seven months, twenty days before the opening of the Cherokee Strip. Old Indians say that he is the first white child born in the Cherokee Strip.

Tillie Hall around 1919.

The Halls were married on June 22, 1919, at the home of the bride's parents, Mr. and Mrs. Barney Ringler, at the corner of Fifth Street and Fir Avenue.

The Halls had five children: Ora R. Hall, Jr. and his wife, Ione, live in Ogden, Utah. They have five children, Mrs. Betty Fry, Ogden, Utah; Mrs. Mary Ann McFall, Ogden, Utah; Lawrence Jackson Hall, Austin, Texas; Patricia Hall Wechel, Raton, New Mexico; and George Elliott Hall of Ogden, Utah. Betty's children Allen Deacon Fry, Alton Danner Fry and Alec Daron Fry. Mary Ann's children are Kata McFall and Clay McFall. Patricia has four children: Geoffrey, Bryan, and twins Tabitha and Elizabeth. George Elliott Hall is married to Pam. They have three children: Stacy, Bill and Melanie.

Mrs. Robert (Willa June) Morgan lives in Gilroy, California. Robert and June Morgan have two children: Marilyn Morgan Towery of Gilroy, California; and Robert Hall Morgan of San Jose, California. Marilyn and Jim Towery have two children: Mark Towery, who attends West Point, and Terry Adamson, a sophomore at Gilroy High School. Bob and Susan Morgan have five children: Robert Scott, Ryan William, Cory Benjamin, Nathan Thomas, and Kathryn Linn Morgan.

Mr. and Mrs. Hoover (Betty Ruth) Wright live in Santa Fe, New Mexico. The Wrights have three children: Dan Harley, Richard Charles and William Henry. Dan and Tricia have a son, Scott, in Santa Fe. Bill and Cindy live in Waldon, Colorado, and have two daughters, Christie and Amy.

George and Juana Hall live in Perry, Oklahoma. They have three children: Charles Richard, Patti Vee, and Zack Nelson.

Barney Jackson Hall was born July 14, 1928 and died January 5, 1929.

O.R. Hall was prominent in civic affairs in the community. He was a past president of the Perry Chamber of Commerce, the Perry Rotary Club and the Perry Gold & Country Club, where he served several terms.

He was a member of the American Legion, the Masonic Lodge, the Odd Fellows Lodge, and the First Baptist Church.

O.R. Hall served in the banking business all his business life. O.R. Hall, as President of the Exchange Bank, gathered a dependable and loyal staff which contributed to the bank's success and earned much good will. His motto for the bank was "Safety, Service and Security". Two of his favorite expressions were: "A soft answer turneth away wrath; but grievous words stir up anger" and "Never let anyone think better of you than you think of yourself."

His wife, Tillie, who was a part of the beginning of Perry, contributed immeasurably to the successful and exemplary life of her husband. She was a member of the First Baptist Church, Perry Study Club, Perry Garden Club and Eastern Star.

A friend wrote in memory for Tillie in 1969: "I thought I would write this down so you all could see how much Tillie meant to folks like me in Church, at home, and every place. Tillie always had a friendly smile shining from her face. I have never known a single soul over which Tillie didn't have complete control. She loved everyone and she didn't mind showing it. One look at her face and you just seemed to know it."

Mr. and Mrs. Ora Hall celebrated

Ora R. Hall around 1919.

Ora R. Hall in 1962.

Tillie Hall in 1962.

their Golden Wedding Anniversary Sunday, June 22, 1969, at their home, 823 Eighth Street. Friends and family members were present to honor them on their anniversary.

Mrs. Tillie Hall died July 3, 1969, following a long illness. Mr. Ora R. Hall died March 3, 1970.

Robert Lee Halsey
By Mary E. Durkee

Robert Lee Halsey was born May 31, 1867 at Piney Creek, North Carolina, the son of Polly (Dixon) and John Reed Halsey. John had fought with Robert E. Lee during the Civil War and named his son after the southern general.

There were three Halsey brothers who came from England, outside of London, about 30 miles from Hartford to the United States. One settled in New York, one in New Jersey and John Reed Halsey settled in Mouth of Wilson, Virginia. There are many Halseys still living there and in Piney Creek, North Carolina but don't claim to be related as some were Republicans and others Democrats.

Robert married Clara Ellen Senter October 3, 1886 at Mouth of Wilson, Virginia. She was born January 12, 1863 at Mouth of Wilson, Virginia, the daughter of Rosemond (Pug) and Calvin Senter. They had two children born at Mouth of Wilson, Virginia: Mamie Cedella (Willey) born August 8, 1887 and Calvin Orla born April 7, 1889. In 1890, they were farming in Conway Springs, Kansas. Here was born Andrew Clyde April 3, 1891; Roy Addison February 19, 1894; Maude Alice (Carothers) born March 3, 1897. Then they moved to Crestfield, Kansas where the last four children were born: Rose Virginia (Martin/LaBelle) born July 2, 1899; Nellie Clara (Holt) July 19, 1901; Ruth Edna (Holt) January 25, 1903 and Roberta Elaine (Ross/Green/Higgins) born March 5, 1906.

Robert came to the Cherokee Strip from Crestfield, Kansas and staked a claim near the old 101 Ranch. Ill health forced him back to Kansas.

They moved to Billings, Oklahoma in 1919 and owned and operated the Billings Produce and Ice company.

They helped build the Church of Christ and Clara Ellen preached until her death. She had firey red hair and personality to go with it. She played the pump organ and was accompained by guitars and banjos at the church. Their music was ahead of the time, it had quite a beat. She had attended Oak Hill Academy at Oak Hill, Virginia. She taught school for four years. Her home place was still standing until 1975 when it was sold to the Appalachian Power and Light company to build a dam. She liked to make quilts and enjoyed quilting them. Besides raising her nine children, she raised three grandchildren, Gordon Willey (1906-1928), Mildred Willey (Crocker) born May 3, 1909 and Jeanne Ross (Williams) born November 20, 1922.

Clara Ellen died January 17, 1941 at their home in Billings, Oklahoma of pneumonia. Robert died April 14, 1952 of cancer at the home of his daughter Nellie Holt in Billings. They are buried in the Billings Union cemetery.

Samuel T. Harlow
By Gertrude Hartung Lockett

Samuel Thomas Harlow was born October 11, 1831, in Fountain County, Indiana, the son of Jeremiah and Elizabeth (Work) Harlow. Little is known of his life before he came west, but we know he enlisted in the army in 1861, and served for three years during the Civil War. He was married first to Anna Carey, who died at about age 25, leaving four children. A son, Quincy, had died in infancy.

Elizabeth Rachel Boydston was born

Seated: Samuel T. and Rachel E. Boydston Harlow. Standing (L to R): George Harlow, Benton Harlow, Pearl Harlow and Jesse Harlow about 1888.

September 22, 1846, at Rockport, Missouri, the daughter of William Pruitt and Mary E. (Warren) Boydston. Rachel married David C. Hull, a school teacher, June 11, 1865, at St. Joseph, Missouri. They had three daughters when Hull left their home to find work. He never was heard from again. Rachel needed help supporting her family, and it is probable that she turned to her sister, Mary Ernest "Molly" (Boydston) Carey, for help. Molly was married to Jacob "Jake" Carey, a relative of Anna. It is likely that Samuel heard of Rachel's situation through their mutual relatives. He hired her as his live-in housekeeper, to help care for his motherless children, and to make a home for her three at the same time. The Harlow children were: Martha, Lewis Johnson "Jonce", Dora, and Minnie. The Hull girls were Martha, Victoria, and Ella. Both Martha's died young, in Missouri.

Sam and Rachel fell in love, and were married March 6, 1877, at Osceola, Missouri. Together they had six children, born near Appleton City, Missouri: George Thomas, who lived and died in Noble County, Benton, who lived and died at Binger, Oklahoma. Asneeta who died in infancy, Etta Pearl, who married John Hartung and lived and died in Noble County, William Franklin "Will", who lived and died at Tescott, Kansas.

The older children were grown and on their own in 1893, when news reached the Harlow's of the opening of the Cherokee Strip to settlers. Sam and Rachel decided to brave the hardships and try to stake a claim in Indian Territory. The trip was very difficult. They traveled in two covered wagons, followed by the boys, riding horses, and a cow which was led. They lived off the land as they traveled, killing game for meat, and gathering berries, etc. along the way. After they made camp each day, Rachel did the cooking for

Robert Lee Halsey and Clara Ellen (Senter) Halsey.

the evening meal and whatever was to be eaten later, before they made camp again. Whatever they did not need then, was cooked or dried to preserve it, and eaten later.

The details of Sam's experiences in the land run are lost, but he did get a claim, consisting of lots 1 and 2 and the east ½ of the NW ¼ of section 7, township 23N R 2W, of Indian Meridian, totalling 153.4 acres. This is southwest of the present site of Billings, Oklahoma.

Samuel Harlow was a veterinarian and farmer. He and his family raised and gathered plants and herbs to dry to make the medicines used for the family, as well as for the animals Mr. Harlow treated. Alcohol also was heavily used in the treatment of animals. Sam did minor surgery when necessary and would even build a sling to keep a horse off an injured leg while it healed. Some ailing animals were brought to the Harlow home, but others, too sick to travel, were treated on their owner's farm, because Sam would make "barn calls" any time of day or night. This occupation made Samuel T. Harlow a highly respected citizen of Noble County.

Quoting from his obituary, "Samuel T. Harlow died at his home three miles southwest of Billings, February 4, 1911, in the 76 year of his age. Although a long time feeble, the result of army exposure, he was in his usual health until Tuesday when he came down with pneumonia." Samuel was buried at Union Cemetery, at Billings, Oklahoma. There is a GAR marker on his grave.

After Sam died, Rachel married William Hoisington. She died August 17, 1926, at age 80, at Perry, Oklahoma, and is buried at Union Cemetery, Billings, Oklahoma.

Claude Hartung
By Gertrude Hartung Lockett

Claude Vernon Hartung, son of John and Pearl (Harlow) Hartung, was born March 7, 1914, on the Hartung farm southeast of Morrison, Oklahoma. On April 26, 1935, Claude married Sadie Faye Wolf, daughter of Adam and Pearl Wolf of Morrison, Oklahoma. They had: Lois Faye Sanders Sharpton, October 31, 1941, Rita Mae Cordes Ashley, January 4, 1947, and Vernon Adam Hartung, March 15, 1957.

Through the eighth grade, he attended Jefferson rural school, where he was active in the 4-H Club. After he graduated from Morrison High School, in the spring of 1932, he attended Northwest State Teachers College, at Alva; Oklahoma A&M College, at Stillwater; and in 1946, received his Bachelor of Science degree in Educa-

Claude Hartung in 1944.

tion, from Central State College at Edmond, Oklahoma. His Masters of Science degree in Education and Administration, was received from Oklahoma A&M College in 1952. Later, from Wichita State University, he earned certification to teach Special Education.

Claude taught ten terms in the rural schools of Pawnee and Noble Counties before leaving for the US Navy. He served on the battleship, West Virginia, and participated in all the major battles in the Pacific theatre during World War II. The West Virginia was anchored in Tokyo Harbor, when the peace terms were signed, September 2, 1945, ending World War II.

Claude was Principal of the Elementary School at Lone Wolf, Oklahoma, for four years; at Billings, Oklahoma for three years; and at Newkirk, Oklahoma for one year. In October, 1954, he began working as an industrial engineer for the Boeing Airplane Co., at Wichita, Kansas. He worked there for fifteen years, after which he did subsitute teaching in the Wichita schools for one year. After that, he became Special Education Teacher in the Derby, Kansas schools, and held this position until he retired in 1979.

Sadie passed away May 28, 1979, following a long illness. Claude lives in Mulvane, Kansas, and is a substitute teacher in the schools of Derby, Kansas. Claude farms a large garden each year, with occasional help from his children and grandchildren. When it is time for harvesting, it is not unusual for the whole family to gather and take part in the harvesting and preserving of the crop for winter food for all. His hobbies include: stamp collecting, crafts and gardening.

Claude had four grandchildren: Donna Faye Sanders, daughter of Lois Faye Hartung and the late Donald Sanders. Her two sons, Ricky and Donald, are Claude's only great-grandchildren.

Sandra Ilene, Christopher Scott and Robert Michael Cordes, are children of Rita Mae Hartung and Gary Cordes. Claude also has two step-grandchildren.

Lois Faye and her husband, James Sharpton, received their Doctorate degrees, July 26, 1985, from Oklahoma State University. They live at Stillwater, Oklahoma, where Lois is a full-time professor at Oklahoma State University, and James works for the Oklahoma State Department of Vocational Education, at Stillwater.

Rita Mae Ashley is working toward an associate degree at Wichita State University, and is employed as a bookkeeper for Pizza Hut, at their corporate offices in Wichita, Kansas. She and her husband, Jerry, and the three children live at Wichita, Kansas.

Vernon Adam Hartung graduated from Wichita State University in 1979, with a Bachelors Degree in Business. He graduated in 1982, from Harvard University, having earned the degree of Masters of Business Administration (MBA). He is working in the executive branch of Pizza Hut, at their corporate offices in Wichita, Kansas.

Clarence O. Hartung
By Gertrude (Hartung) Lockett

Clarence Oliver Hartung, youngest child of John and Pearl (Harlow) Hartung, was born April 11, 1921, on the Hartung farm, southeast of Morrison, Oklahoma.

While he was completing the first eight grades at Jefferson rural school in Noble County, he worked on the family farm with his father. They were diversified farmers, and raised cattle and hogs to sell, in addition to their crops. Later, Clarence also did part-time farm work for neighbors. For several years, he worked as a part-time farmhand for Bruce miller and Clark Field.

In Wellington, Kansas, February 1, 1946, he married Marie Sappington. They lived with his parents on the family farm until it was sold in August, 1946, and the two couples moved to 722 Birth Street, in Perry, Oklahoma.

Clarence enlisted in the army, October 6, 1946, and went by train from Oklahoma City, to Stoneman, California, where he was processed for overseas duty. He served in the 8th Army and was located at Camp Polk, Louisiana, until November 21, 1946, after which his troop was sent to Japan. Because of his height and weight, Clarence was selected to serve in the Military Police. He was sent to the 727th M.P. unit at Nakana, a surburb of Tokoyo, where he served for 13 months. It was his duty to patrol the Mimatsu and Eden clubs, and the

Clarence Hartung about 1946.

Tokyo beer halls, every other night.

During his time off-duty, he was able to travel to many parts of Japan and saw most of the Island of Honchu. Upon his return to the states, following his discharge, he worked as a mechanic and studied welding with the financial help of the G.I. bill. He became known as one of the best welders in Noble County. In 1954, he took a part-time job as a mechanic for Howard Stengle, in Morrison, and worked there for thirty years.

Clarence and Marie Hartung had four children: Jimmy Ray, (April 3, 1949), Lucky Lane (October 29, 1950), Mary Ellen (May 28, 1952), and Pearlie Lee (January 5, 1954). Mary married Bill Saunders. They had: Ella Mae, (January 3, 1971), Beccky Ann (July 26, 1973), Tina Louise, (December 18, 1975), Julie Ann, (July 25, 1979), and Billy Earl II, (April 26, 1982). Pearl married William Frick. They had: Cheryl Ann (December 2, 1973), and William Laurence (May 15, 1980).

Mary and Pearlie are members of the White Hall Home Demonstration Club, of which their grandmother, Pearl Hartung, was a charter member. Clarence, Jimmy and Lucky are members of the "Steam Engine Association", and are very active at the "Steam Engine Show" which is held each May in Pawnee, Oklahoma.

Gladys Hartung-Hostutler

By Gertrude Hartung Lockett

Gladys Silvia Hartung was born February 13, 1906, on a farm near Oxford, Sumner County, Kansas, the first child of John Adam and Etta Pearl (Harlow) Hartung. In 1908, the family moved to Oklahoma and settled near Billings. When Gladys was seven years old, they moved to a farm near Morrison, Oklahoma, where the family stayed until they moved to Perry, Oklahoma in 1945.

Gladys finished eight grades at Jefferson rural school, where she belonged to the Busy Bee 4-H Club for four years. She attended one year at Morrison High School; spent one year at home and then spent six months visiting with relatives in Oxford, Kansas.

Six months after she met Bertie Hostutler, a WW I veteran, Gladys and Bert were married June 13, 1926, at Perry, Oklahoma. They set up housekeeping on his farm, six miles northwest of Pawnee, Oklahoma, on Black Bear Creek. Here they lived throughout their 54½ years of marriage, and here their four sons and their daughter grew up. On their farm, the Hostutlers always had a large truck garden, raised cattle and feed crops. They were members of the Pawnee County Farmers Union organization, and are shareholder in the Farmers Cooperative, at Morrison. Their home was among the first in the area to have a telephone line, which they shared with eleven other families.

Bert was born January 24, 1894, at Delhi, Kansas, to Mr. and Mrs. Moore. He was adopted at an early age by Dennis and Alice Hostutler and, in 1900, moved with them to Oklahoma Territory, in a covered wagon. Bert died January 17, 1981, at his home of a heart attack.

Gladys and Bert Hostutler had five children: John Dennis "J.D.", (August 18, 1927), living in Texas, Alice June (June 14, 1930), living in Arizona, Ralph Vernon (March 16, 1933) living in Texas, Sidney Ray, (December 3, 1937), living near the home farm, Gene Autry (July 14, 1949), living in Nebraska.

The children all went to the Olive Hill rural school, until it closed, after which they attended Pawnee public schools. J.D. served in the US Navy during WW II, and Ralph was in Korea with the US Army, during that conflict.

Gladys and Bert also had eleven grandchildren (two are deceased), four great-grandchildren, and eight step grandchildren, and five step great-grandchildren: J.D. had children, Jay, Dennis, Cynthia Kay, Michael, (1958-1976) and Suzanne Denise Hostutler and grandchildren, Jonathan Davis and Charity Michelle Hostutler, and James Michael and Laura Lee Johnson. June and Kenneth Kelly had Tom, who married Mary Beth Swasnon; Kennth; and Deanna June Kelly. Ralph married Mrs. Kathy Dubose, whose son, Clifford Dubose married Geannie, who has a daughter, Jennifer, Cliff and Geannie have a son, Branden Dubose. Sidney

Seated (L to R): Sidney Hostutler, Gene Hostutler. 2nd Row (L to R): Bert Hostutler, Ralph Hostutler (standing), Gladys Hartung Hostutler. 3rd Row (L to R): J.D. Hostutler, Alice June Hostutler.

has stepchildren, Carl, Jay and Nathan Furrh, Maudie Shafer and Ellie Carte. Gene Autry has stepchildren, Larry and Tammy Massey and children, Gene Edward, Donald Lee, Sara Lynn and Mary Sylvia (born and died April 23, 1973) Hostutler.

The first three Hostutler children named above were adopted by other families. The name changes are: Gene Edward to John Longan; Donald Lee to Paul Quick, and Sara Lynn to Sara Lynn Feken.

Gladys is a charter member of the Farmerette Club, in which she has been active for many years. She continues to live on the home place, where she does excellent hand-quilting for others. She is active in the Senior Citizens organization and meets with them weekly for dinner, quilting and visiting.

Gertrude Hartung-Lockett

By Gertrude Hartung Lockett

Gertrude Mae Hartung was born, April 15, 1910, on a farm known as the "Blakley Place", southwest of Billings, Oklahoma, the second child of John Adams and Etta Pearl (Harlow) Hartung, who had come to Billings, in 1908, from Oxford, Kansas.

In 1912, the family bought a farm three miles southeast of Morrison, Noble County, Oklahoma. Through the 8th grade, Gertrude attended the Jefferson rural school, where she belonged to the Busy Bee 4-H Club of which she was president for four years. In 1928, the Jefferson and Shiloh Clubs were combined to form the Shiloh Willing Workers, and Gertrude was elected president of the new club. She later served as president of the Noble County 4-H Club Federation, and the Sumner District 4-H Club Federation. She was Distict Captain at Stillwater

Gertrude Hartung Norman - 1953.

Farm Congress, and at the Oklahoma State Fair.

She graduated from Morrison High School, in 1929, and with the help of the $160, Bankers 4-H Club Scholarship, which she'd won in 1928, she attended Oklahoma A & M College at Stillwater in 1929 and 1930. After one year, she qualified as a teacher, and taught in the Central and Lone Elm Districts, in Noble County. While in Stillwater, Oklahoma, attending a 4-H function, during her junior year at Morrison High, Gertrude met Ernest Norman, of Eagle City, Oklahoma, youngest son of George and Rose (Leonard) Norman. They were married April 22, 1932, at Perry, Oklahoma.

They attended college at Alva, Oklahoma, for a time after their marriage, and then taught one term in Blaine County, Oklahoma, sharing a two-room, rural school. After that Gertrude "retired" to have a family. They had four daughters and one son, all of whom were born in Blaine County: Rozetta Mae, October 25, 1933, M. L., a son, who lived only six days, December 25, 1934, Margaret Lenore, February 7, 1936, and twin daughters, Carolyn Sue and Marilyn Lou, August 17, 1938. The marriage was dissolved January 9, 1950.

From 1936, they owned and operated a shoe repair shop in Canton, Oklahoma. In August, 1944, the family moved to Perry, Oklahoma, where they bought a shoe repair shop downtown, and purchased a home at the corner of 6th and Ivanhoe streets.

In 1948, Gertrude resumed teaching in the rural schools of Noble County, where she taught a total of 11 years. Through correspondence courses and summer school, she earned the degree of Bachelor of Science in Education from Oklahoma A & M College, in 1949, while continuing to teach. In 1955, she received a degree of Masters of Science in Education from Oklahoma A & M College, also while continuing to teach. For 16 years she taught 5th and 6th grades in the Perry school system, which is a total of 27 years of teaching in Oklahoma.

Gertrude served as president of Perry Business and Professional Women's Club, 1958; director of District #9, of Oklahoma Business and Professional Women's Club, 1967; president of Perry's Parent Teacher Associaton, and president of Noble County Artists Association, which she helped to organize, and of which she is a charter member. She is also a long time member of the American Association of University women.

In 1971, Gertrude retired from teaching and married J.D. Lockett, of Houston, Texas, who died in 1979. Gertrude still lives in Houston, and does substitute teaching in the nearby Pasadena, Texas schools, as well as volunteer work at the Shrine Hospital for Crippled Children. In Houston, she is a member of Order of Eastern Star, and Ladies of the Oriental Shrine. Her hobbies are: oil painting, cactus and succulents culture, macrame and crochet.

Her seven grandchildren are: John and David, sons of Rozetta and Dean Beasley, Tulsa, Oklahoma; Susan and Elizabeth, daughters of Margaret and Dick Froebel, Houston, Texas; Mark Wasemiller, son of Marilyn Wasemiller, Dearborn, Michigan; and Jerry Wasemiller of Bartlesville, Oklahoma. Her great-grandchildren are: David Brent, son of David and Jill Beasley, Oklahoma City. Jarad and Layla Mattingly, son and daughter of Teresa, wife of John Beasley, Tulsa.

Seated (L to R): Rozetta Norman Beasley, Gertrude Hartung Norman, Carolyn Norman Davenport. Standing (L to R): Margaret Norman Froebel, Marilyn Norman Wasemiller in 1968.

John A. Hartung
By Gertrude N. Lockett

John Adam Hartung was born February 25, 1883, Oxford, Kansas, youngest child of Lorenz and Katherina Haselwander Hartung. Etta Pearl Harlow as born April 9, 1885, Appleton City, Missouri, daughter of Samuel and Rachel Boydston Harlow.

Following their marriage, June 25, 1905, at Enid, Oklahoma, they lived with John's parents, near Oxford, Kansas, until the bought a farm south of Belle Plains, Kansas. Thier first child, Gladys Sylvia, was born here, February 13, 1906. The young couple worked very hard, but could not make the farm pay, so they had to take a small equity, and let the mortgage be foreclosed. They moved to Oklahoma, in 1908, settling southwest of Billings, on what was known as "The Blakley Place". Another daughter, Gertrude Mae, was born on this farm April 15, 1910.

In 1911, Pearl's father died and she received $1100 as her share of his estate. The young couple took this money and made a down payment on a farm three miles southeast of Morrison, Oklahoma.

In February, 1912, the small family moved from Billings to Morrison in two wagons. Pearl, with her two daughters alongside, drove one of the wagons and John drove the other. Pearl's brothers, Jesse and Will Harlow, helped with the moving on horseback, driving the cattle ahead of them. They had to ford the Black Bear Creek near Morrison, as there was no bridge. At one point, a snow storm blew in, and the temperature dropped so low, that the travelers suffered from frostbite. They made the move all in one long day, arriving well after dark. There was nothing in the house yet, so they unloaded the stove, built a fire, and

Etta Pearl Harlow Hartung circa 1904.

John and Pearl Harlow Hartung in June, 1955, at their golden wedding anniversary.

bedded down for the first night in their new home.

Claude Vernon was born in this two-room house, March 7, 1914. John and Pearl later added two more rooms and a porch to the house, and Clarence Oliver was born here April 11, 1921. The barn, blacksmith shop, chicken houses, etc. were all built by John.

Pearl was a charter member of the White Hall Women's Home Demonstration Club and held all elected offices. Through their clubwork, the Hartung women learned how to can the vegetables from their garden for winter use. They made their own laundry soap, and Pearl made most of the clothes worn by the family. They butchered and cured their own pork and beef and, for many years, sold meat to Boyer's Grocery Store, in Morrison. They also sold eggs and cream, for the cash needed to buy necessities such as sugar, flour and coffee. John was an active member of Farmer's Union, the Anti-thief Association of Morrison, and a shareholder in the Farmer's Cooperative there.

The Hartung farm consisted of 160 acres, where they raised cattle and hogs for market, as well as food for the animals and the family. When they had paid for the home place, John and Pearl purchased 80 acres, undivided interest, in the 160 acre farm which adjoined theirs on the south. This 80 acres was sold in 1956 or 1957. They rented the other 80 acres, and farmed it until John retired.

In 1924, the Hartung family received a $10.00 per acre oil lease on their farm. In April, 1925, John spent most of this windfall to pay for three major operations he had to have. After the hopsital was paid, there was just enough left of the oil money to buy a Model T Ford, which he did.

In 1945, they sold this farm and moved into Perry, Oklahoma. They bought a two-story, retirement home at 722 Birch Street, where John read and tended his large garden and Pearl had time for her crochet. John died June 19, 1958. He was the first person in Noble County to donate his corneas, through the Oklahoma Lion's Club Eye Bank, for transplantation.

Pearl remained in her home for several more years, until she entered the Green Valley Nursing home, in Perry, where she died May 14, 1977. Pearl and John are both buried at Grace Hill Cemetery, Perry, Oklahoma.

R. G. Hay
By Violet L. Hay King

Reinhold Gottfried Hay was born November 1, 1871, in Steinheim A Der Murr, Wurtemburg, Germany. He was the oldest son of Gottfried David Hay (1827-1913) and Matilda Gall Hay (1841-1914). Word had gotten to Germany that land was being opened for settlement in America under the Homestead Act approved by Congress in 1862. The new land held many promises and high hopes for the farmers in Germany.

In 1881, the Gottfried David Hay family, four daughters (Sophie, Minnie, Nannie, and Friedricka) and four sons, (Reinhold, Jacob, Gottleib, and Ernest) left their home land of Germany and came to America. It took 17 days to cross the ocean. They landed in New York City then went to Kansas by train. It was a long hard trip and by the time they reached their destination their money was nearly depleted.

They settled on a farm near Winkler, Kansas. They applied for a Homestead and the land was granted to Mr. Hay, October 11, 1885, by the US Government and signed by President Grover Cleveland. In 1881, soon after arriving in Kansas their youngest son, Otto, was born.

The older daughters and Reinhold did not go to school after arriving in Kansas, but worked for neighbors at any odd jobs they could find to help out the family budget. Needless to say their wages were very meager. Self-education was very important to the family, and numerous "How To" books were found in R.G.'s belongings.

The Cherokee Strip in Oklahoma Territory was opened September 16, 1893. R.G. came to Oklahoma soon after that and purchased a claim 12 miles southwest of Perry. In 1894, he planted wheat, built fences, dug a water well, and built a one room house. A note written in 1947, by R.G. said, "In 1894, we plowed up the prairie and sowed wheat, 1895, was a very dry year. Wheat made 2½ B. to the acre. In 1896

R.G. and Mrs. Hay taken at their home in Perry, about 1935.

Plumer sowed the wheat for half, as I was sick that fall, the wheat made 13 B. In 1897 the wheat made 28 B. and we got 80¢ a bushel for the wheat. From then on we had money until this day, and Thanks be to God for that blessing." The farm was granted to him in 1903 by the US Government, and signed by then President Theodore Roosevelt.

In 1896, R.G. went back to Green, Kansas, and married Elizabeth Lizzie Hofmann, born April 11, 1875. She was the daughter of David and Barbara Ehrmann Hofman who were both born in Germany and came to America in 1874. Mr. Hofmann was a lay minister and helped to establish a German Methodist Church known as Ebenezer Methodist Episcopal Church of Green, Kansas, which is still in use today.

Soon after R.G. and Elizabeth Hay were married they moved to the farm in Oklahoma. They were the only ones from both the Hay or Hofmann families who moved to Oklahoma. Most of the people thought that only wild Indians and outlaws lived in Oklahoma. It must have taken a lot of courage and determination to move that far from all family and friends. Neighbors were all important to them. They helped each other in times of illness, births, deaths, or any task they could not handle alone.

All eleven Hay children were born on that farm. Edith Lydia, September 7, 1896, David Hofmann, June 23, 1898, Edna was born in 1900 and died March 4, 1904. Amelia Sophie, August 16, 1902, Reinhold Fred (Jack) July 19, 1904, the twins Ellsworth Henry and Elsie, May 2, 1906, Elsie only lived two months and then passed away July 11, 1906, Violet Lucille, February 20, 1908, John Arthur, September 23, 1910, Evelyn Mabel, November 14, 1912, she passed away September 27, 1922, and the youngest Carl Wilhelm, July 15, 1916.

The Hay children attended school thru the 8th grade at Harmony School. It was a typical one room country school with one teacher for all eight grades. It also served as a community center for all social, political, and church meetings. The Hay children all continued their education beyond the eighth grade; which was not too customary in those days.

In 1933, after most of the children were grown, the Hays rented their farms out, bought a home in Perry and moved there to retire. Mrs. Hay passed away June 3, 1939, and was buried in Zion Methodist Church cemetery west of Orlando. This was the church where they were active members most of their married lives and where all of their children were baptized.

In 1948, after living alone for nine years, R.G. married a widow, Avis Dozier Lewis. They lived in Perry for 18 years before Mr. Hay died on August 16, 1966. He was buried in Zion Cemetery beside his first wife. Avis Dozier Lewis Hay died September 16, 1975.

Henry Hayne
By Valinda Sullins

Henry Hayne, born July 8, 1879, came to the United States with his parents from Czechoslovakia in 1886, and settled in Diller, Nebraska. His father, Antonin, was born July 7, 1836 and died September 28, 1911. Henry's mother, Antonia, was born August 3, 1840 and died February 16, 1906.

Henry's brother, Anton M. Hayne (1872-1959) probably came to the United States at the same time, in 1886. Anton M. and Anna M. Hayne (1878-1957) were the parents of George (May 24, 1899-May 17, 1982), Jim, Jerome, and Nellie Ann. Henry and Anton had a sister, Agnes, and a stepsister.

Henry came to Noble County in 1895. In 1904, Henry married Jennie Shultz in Perry, Oklahoma. She was born in Brainard, Nebraska, March 2, 1886. She was the daughter of Anton and Antonia Shultz, who lived on their farm 11 miles north, 2 miles west, and ½ mile north of Perry. Anton Shultz was born January 18, 1847, and died February 2, 1918. Antonia Shultz was born June 4, 1858 and died February 28, 1941. Jennie had six sisters and five brothers.

In Nebraska, when he was young, Henry had a job taking care of 1000 head of cattle for a man. Later, in Noble county, Oklahoma, Henry and Jennie farmed on the land his father had owned 6 miles north and 4 miles west of Perry. His father remained on the farm with them until his death in 1911. Henry owned a threshing machine and threshed wheat for many farmers in the county. One year he had the

Jennie and Henry Hayne 1930s

threshing machine sent by rail to Idaho and by the time it got there it was nearly off the train.

In 1916, Henry and his family moved into Perry. When Donaldson and Yahn Lumber Company first opened, June 1, 1919, in Perry, Henry was their first customer.

Among his various other occupations, Henry was a taxicab driver. From 1926 until 1935, Henry operated the Hayne Motor Company, a REO auto dealership, in Perry. Later, Henry was a night watchman at the Perry airport when it was being built. After that, he worked for the Highway Department.

Henry and Jennie were the parents of four children: Cyril, born June 19, 1905; Elsie Mae, born May 12, 1907; Oscar Henry, born July 18, 1909; and Agnes Elanore (August 24, 1911-March 3, 1928).

Cyril married Margaret Sisk, July 16, 1935. He operated the Cyril Hayne Garage in Perry from 1946 until his death, January 30, 1986.

Elsie and Roy Ernest Foreman were married November 24, 1925. They lived 10 miles north of Perry and 1 mile west, before moving near Worland, Wyoming in August 1929 to farm there for five years. Some of the products they raised while in Wyoming were Great Northern beans, sugar beets, and potatoes. In 1934, they returned to the farm north of Perry for a few months, then moved to farm land located 1 mile north and 1½ miles west of Red Rock, where in the year of 1986 they are still farming wheat and raising Charolasis cattle.

Roy and Elsie Foreman are the parents of four daughters: Marie Kathleen, Clara Nadine, Norma Jean and Donna Mae. Marie married Charles "Chuck" Cooper and are the parents of Charles Roy, Craig Lee and Cheryl Marie (Sharp). Clara married J.A. Megenity and are the parents of Karen Ruth (Root) and James Dale. Jean married Darrell Sullins and are the parents of Daniel Ernest (February 10, 1956 -August 29, 1985, Mark Wayne and Valinda Jean. Donna married Charles Hopper and are the parents of Jennifer Mae.

Oscar Hayne married Viola Lampe who was born in 1912 and died in 1961. Oscar farmed northwest of Perry until his death in 1959. Oscar and Viola were the parents of Doris and Robert. Doris married Robert McDaniel and are the parents of Brad, Barry and Brenda. Robert Hayne married Janet Redman.

Jennie Hayne died January 13, 1956, at the age of 69. Henry died September 10, 1972 in Perry at the age of 93. At the time of his death, Henry still owned a 1930 Reo, which he had bought when he operated the Hayne Motor Company.

Gordon Hayton
By Jannis Culver

William Gordon Hayton, son of English parents, William and Mary Ann Hayton, was born in Billings, Oklahoma, May 17, 1906, the same year his parents came to Billings to make their home and operate the Pearson & Hayton grain elevator. Gordon attended the Billings schools and the University of Oklahoma.

On January 9, 1927, he and Viola Minnie Whitlow, daughter of Washington and Viola (Enyart) Whitlow, were married. To this union two children were born, a son, Billy Gordon, January 5, 1928, and a daughter, Jannis Viola, February 4, 1930.

Gordon became associated with his father, William, (Will) in the grain business at this time, and the firm's

Viola and Gordon Hayton 1949 at Celebration of Billings, Oklahoma 50th Anniversary.

Hayton Elevator, Billings, Oklahoma about 1955.

name was changed to Wm. Hayton & Son. There were many changes in the grain business during Gordon's lifetime; from 40 bushel, horse-drawn wagons to 60 bushel pick-ups, followed by 300 bushel trucks. In the 1940's, advanced technology in agriculture brought the introduction of dry fertilizer to the industry for increased crop yields, then, liquid and pellet fertilizers. Through these years, as production increased, storage and equipment were expanded. Further expansion, during the 1950's, was needed for the government surplus wheat program. By 1959, a large flat storage elevator of 600,000 bushel capacity was built and another 400,000 bushel elevator in 1961. The elevator complex, now, consisted of five local elevators, feed mill, fertilizer storage, feed storage, and a cleaning mill; in addition, to the Alcorn elevator northeast of Billings. The firm's total capacity was 1,200,000 bushels.

Since Billings is located in the northwestern corner of Noble county, it is included in a four county area of Oklahoma, known for the highest wheat production in Oklahoma. For many years the Rock Island Railroad was the only means of grain transportation from Billings to Enid terminal elevators and mills. This railroad, at one time recognized the Hayton elevators for shipping more wheat by Rock Island than any other grain elevator in Oklahoma. Since no railroad, now, serves, Billings, semi-trailer trucks transport the grain to ports and terminals.

In 1945, after the death of his father, Gordon became sole owner of the business and continued as such until his death in 1967. Gordon adopted the slogan, "Your friendly grain dealer" a saying he put into practice in his business through the years.

Being active in the support and growth of the community, as well as, the grain industry, Gordon served four years as president of the Oklahoma Grain and Feed Association, and was recognized in that organization's Hall of Fame, as one of Oklahoma's outstanding independent grain dealers. He served as a member of the Billings School Board for 14 years, was an active member and elder of the Christian Church, was Past Master of the Billings Masonic Lodge, and a 32nd Degree Mason. Gordon served as a bank director of the Billings First State Bank and the First National Bank of Perry, Oklahoma. He was a member of the Board of Regents for Northern Oklahoma College at Tonkawa, Oklahoma, at the time Dr. Edwin Vineyard was named president of Northern Oklahoma College. Gordon remained active in his business and community affairs until his sudden dedath of a heart attack, March 20, 1967.

Gordon's wife, Viola, was born July 17, 1907, in Minco, Oklahoma. She was a graduate of Billings High School, actively involved in community affairs, Billings Eastern Star, Billings Research Federated Club, and various offices of the Billings Christian Church, where she served as a Sunday School teacher many years. Following her husband's death, Viola moved to Stillwater, where she purchased a home, and served as a fraternity and sorority housemother on the University Campus until ill-health forced her retirement, and later, her death October 15, 1983.

At the time of her death, Viola had five grandchildren and ten great-grandchildren. The Hayton's daughter, Jannis (Hayton) Culver resides north of Pawhuska, Oklahoma; while their son, Billy Gordon, resides in Billings, where he manages the elevator firm, originally established as, Pearson & Hayton Grain in 1905. The firm was incorporated in 1969 and later, purchased by W. B. Johnston Grain of Enid in 1983. New improved facilities, with a storage capacity of 2,000,000 bushels, is now located on Highway 15 in north Billings.

William Hayton
By Jannis Culver

William Hayton born August 7, 1869, in Lakethewaite Farm, Firbank, West Moreland County, England came to the United States from Crake Hall, New Hutton, England. His diary, dated Saturday, June 15, 1895, records his departure from Liverpool, England to the United States at the age of 26 years. The night before sailing, he walked down to the docks, where he watched the unloading of corn and wheat, knowing that the ship carried about 4,000 tons. This observation is worthy of mention, in view of the fact, that grains, such as corn and wheat, became such a vital part of his life in the United States. The journey to the States took six days, before the 770 passengers aboard arrived on Friday, June 21, 1895. Nearing New York, in an evening fog, William Hayton described the scene as, "A splendid sight! All the electric lights are lighted, and it is a picture never to be forgotten for miles up either side of the coast. It is norththing else, but a mass of lights, all colours."

He went by train from New York to Chicago. In Chicago, he purchased a ticket for seventeen dollars to Pierson, Iowa, in Woodbury county. There he joined his half-brother, John C. Pearson, who had a meat market business, having come to the United States two years earlier in 1893. Sometime later, William (Will), as he was called, became quite ill with typhoid fever, and following a very slow recovery, the brothers decided to search out the prospects of a different occupation. They sold the meat market and by June 1, 1897, the were operating a grain elevator in Pierson. This business went well for them, and two years later, in 1899, Will left Pierson, Iowa to buy an elevator in Anthon, Iowa. Will found the grain business very challenging.

After six years in the United States, Will decided to return to England for a

William Hayton.

William Hayton's home Billings, Oklahoma about 1912. William, Gordon and Mary Ann Hayton.

visit. His passage to Chicago was paid in exchange for taking livestock to market in Chicago. A livestock commission company in Chicago had hired him to manage their consignment of cattle by railroad to St. Johns, New Brunswick, Canada, where the cattle would be shipped to Liverpool, England. He was very glad when the cattle were delivered safe and sound. While Will was visitng England in 1901, he and Mary Ann Pearson were married. She was born August 23, 1872, in Benton, Wisconsin; however, her family had moved from the United States to England when Mary Ann was quite young. Will and Mary Ann left England and arrived back in Anthon, Iowa in time for the buying of grain in August, 1901.

In 1905, it became necessary for the brothers to begin looking for grain businesses in other states, because Iowa had a large agricultural movement underway, which was buying up smaller businesses and increasing the competition. In the fall of 1905, they sold the elevator in Anthon, Iowa, and having already surveyed prospects in Oklahoma, the brothers came to Oklahoma and established businesses in Marshall, Hunter, and Billings. By 1906, John was settled in Marshall in Logan county, and Will and wife were in Billings, Noble county. Eventually, the Hunter elevator was sold, but the Billings elevator continued to operate under the partnership name of Pearson & Hayton until 1918, when Will Hayton became the sole owner of the Billings grain establishment. The firm, also, operated a cotton gin as early as 1907, and sold coal, flour, chicken feed, livestock feeds, and all types of seeds, in addition to garden seeds and baby chickens in the spring. Coal was a very important item for fuel in the homes. It was scooped from box cars to coal bins for storage until it was purchased by the customer. Then it was scooped into wagons for delivery. Flour was sold in 50 and 100 pound sacks. There was a potbellied stove with benches and chairs for the customers to rally around to spin their tales of yarn. Two sons were born to William and Mary Ann Hayton, William Gordon, born May 17, 1906, and another son who died in infancy in 1911, and is buried in the Billings Union cemetery.

In 1927, their son, William Gordon, at the age of twenty-one, became associated with his father in the business, and the firm's name was changed to Wm. Hayton and Son.

Will Hayton was a member of the Oklahoma Grain and Feed Association for forty years. He served as Noble County Commissioner two terms. Both he and Mary Ann were members of the Methodist Church. Will was a 32nd Degree Mason and a member of the Billings Masonic Lodge. Mary Ann belonged to the Billings Eastern Star.

William (Will) Hayton died at Enid, August 12, 1945, of a cerebral hemorrhage at the age of 76 years. Mary Ann Hayton died at Billings, May 30, 1953, at the age of eighty-one years. Both are buried in the Billings Union cemetery, Noble County.

Mary Ann Hayton.

Samuel Arthur Hayward
By Verda Hayward Hay

My father, Samuel Arthur Hayward was born June 7, 1870, in Adair County, Missouri. He grew to manhood on a farm near Kirksville, Missouri, helping his father. He came to Oklahoma Territory, bringing his riding horse by Santa Fe train from Kirksville to Orlando, to take part in the opening of the Cherokee Strip Land Run, and staked a calim about thirteen miles west and south of Perry. While proving his claim, he, also, started his first business venture, a general store, not far from his homestead at a place called Goff. U.S. mail came to Goff, but locally, Goff was known as Ladysmith. All supplies and building materials had to be hauled by wagons from Perry.

When the Frisco railroad came through, it missed Goff, so father and Henry Corall bought land bordering the railroad and laid out a townsite. Goff moved there and father had a store that handled everything from groceries to dress material, drugs, and hardware. The store, also, contained the U.S. Postoffice for a time. Overhead was the IOOF Lodge Hall, of which he was a member. He also built the first house there, and later, a cotton gin. The town's name was changed to Hayward in his honor, as a townsite developer. Hayward became a thriving country town, but like so many in Oklahoma, it has, now, almost become a so-called ghost town with only a few homes and the Methodist Church which has services each Sunday. The Frisco freight trains still roll through, but they don't have to stop at the Hayward Lake for water, as the old steam engines did in the past. Samuel Arthur Hayward and Roxie May Owen were married in Perry, August 15, 1903. She was the youngest daughter of William G. Owen and Sarah Ellen (Michael) Owen.

Roxie's family had moved to Hayward in 1902; however, her parents

Arthur Marion, Samuel Alton and Verda Ellen Hayward taken in 1909 at Perry.

Samuel Arthur and Roxie May Hayward in 1903 (wedding picture) taken in Perry.

and nine children had come from Montana in several covered wagons to Old Oklahoma Territory in 1889, purchasing a claim near Oklahoma City. On the claim was a stone quarry, which yielded good revenue, since building material was in great demand for the fast growing Oklahoma City, nearby. During the Civil War, Roxie's father served in the Union Army, Company H, Fourty-fourth Missouri Infantry.

Samuel Arthur and Roxie May became the parents of four children, Virgie May, born 1904, died in infancy, Verda Ellen born 1905, Arthur Marion born 1907, and Samuel Alton born 1909. Samuel Arthur, well on his way with a promising business career as an Oklahoma pioneer, suddenly died from a cerebral hemorrhage at the early age of 38 in 1909. After her husband's death, Roxie May and children moved to Perry in 1911, and from Perry to the Lucien area in 1913, where Verda Ellen, Arthur Marion, and Samuel Alton attended the two-room Lucien school and grew to adulthood.

Our mother, Roxie May, died in 1927. Both parents are buried in the Hayward Cemetery. Father was from a large family in Missouri, but he was the only one to come to Oklahoma, and as a result, our branch of the family is known as "The Oklahoma Haywards". Verda Ellen lives in Billings, Oklahoma, Arthur Marion, Kingston, Oklahoma; Samuel Alton, South Fork, Colorado.

Thomas J. Hendrick
By Roy W. Hendrick

Laura and Tom, to me "Mother" and "Dad", were born within 40 miles of each other near Shelbyville, Illinois. Laura Malinda Fairman was born in October of 1865, and Thomas Jefferson Hendrick in April of 1861. In their early childhood both their families moved to seperate localities in southwestern Missouri, within 40 miles of each other but they never met until later. In the 1893 run after being driven off the first site which they chose, they took up adjoining sites. At least that was the romantic tale I told for many years. They finally married in 1897 and I was born Roy Wesley Hendrick in November, 1899. They sold out the claim in 1901 and we moved to a farm near Schell City, Missouri, not far from their childhood area where some of the family still lived.

In the spring of 1985, I returned to Perry for the first time, finding the story was not exactly correct. Dad didn't homestead and they were not driven off their claims. Dad worked on the railroad and was in the Strip before the opening, therefore was not eligible for homestead land. In the run of 1889, my mother's sister, Epha and her husband, Charles Chennault had taken a claim between Kingfisher and Okarchee lured by "free land." Mother had visited them and caught the fever. With the aid of her brother-in-law she took part in the 1893 run. She homesteaded NE¼ of section 34 in Watkins Township. Her sister and brother-in-law also helped her build the first house. Shortly after repeated crop failures they sold out and went to Iola, Kansas, nearer the rest of the Fairman family, leaving Laura alone. Laura was a seamstress and, like many other women of the time, she would go to the home of a family, especially those with many children, and do the needed sewing. In exchange, she would sometimes receive cash but more often the men of the family would do the required cultivation and physical development of her claim.

As a young man, Dad had left his folks near Lamar, Missouri, to work on railroad construction in Oklahoma. He was also a volunteer worker with the Quaker missionary, Jeremiah Hubbard, at an Indian Mission. In 1896, he was a section hand quartered at Perry, Oklahoma. He, as well as my mother, had been raised in staunch Methodist homes. Both responded when it was announced soon after the opening that a Methodist group was being organized. My middle name (Wesley) was the result of Methodist influence. My mother hoped I would be a minister but she was disappointed.

The section house was less than a mile across the open country to where Laura had built her house. Soon Tom was helping her on the claim.

The land my mother homestead was on a hill overlooking Perry. It is a nice building spot but water was a problem, then as it is today. There is not much farm land which was necessary to make a living after the run. It is now part of the Frailey cattle range with a large metal stock barn and corrals. There is also a tall radio mast.

After leaving the homestead in Perry we were on a farm near Schell City until 1903, when we moved to El Dorado Springs. Here my only brother was born in 1904, but only lived a few days. In 1906, my only sister, Mary Lo Vetra was born. In 1921, when we lived at Palo Alto, California, she died from a perforated appendix.

I, now 85 years old, am the only surviving member of this family. Mother died at the age of 78 and my father at 4 months over a century of life.

I attended the University at Boulder, Colorado for two years. I entered the

Hayward Store, owner Samuel Arthur Hayward at center with hand on post, others unknown - taken in 1905.

Hayward Cotton Gin, owner Samuel Arthur Hayward at far right, others unknown - taken in 1905.

Stanford University in Palo Alto and received a B.A. in 1923. Then I went to UC Berkeley for a masters. I met student Viola Gockley and we were married in January, 1924. I was then teaching high school at Fresno. I retired in 1959, after a total of 40 years. I had taught in Claremont, Long Beach, Lynwood, Los Angeles and Huntington Park in California. Most of these were part of the Los Angeles System.

My wife died in December, 1977 after 54 years of wonderful married life. I have one daughter, two sons, ten grandchildren, and three great-grandchildren.

Joseph Herbert
By Virginia Graves

In 1893, Joseph Herbert came to Perry, Oklahoma to run in the Cherokee Strip Run. Some friends got him drunk and he didn't make the run. His wife, Kate Herbert, was so angry that she walked four miles to Purcell, Kansas and bought some black satin to make a dress... I guess women haven't changed over the years.

Joseph Herbert returned to the Perry, Oklahoma area again in 1906, traveling with his daughters, Josephine and Margie, in a covered wagon. They left Emporia, Kansas and traveled for about twelve days to Oklahoma. In Newkirk, Oklahoma, Joseph said to the girls, Josephine and Margie, "There's something that you've never seen before." It was a team of oxen moving a building.

Next Joseph, Josephine and Margie passed through Ponca City, Oklahoma. At that time, it was mostly saloon after saloon. Then they passed through the 101 Ranch. Joseph was in a hurry to get through the ranch because he had heard rumors that some of the cowhands had killed some people, but Josephine and Margie were excited about crossing the ranch because there were buffaloes there.

After Joseph and the girls arrived in Perry, they stayed with his sister, Annie White. Joseph only stayed about ten days and then he returned to Kansas, taking Margie with him. Josephine stayed on with Aunt Annie White.

Joseph finally sold some young horses and got enough money together to bring the rest of the family to Perry. They put their furnishings on a freight car and they rode the train to Perry.

After they got to Perry, they settled south of Perry at a place called Yates which was at that time a stage coach stop. One evening while living in Yates, Josephine was getting ready to go to a party in the neighborhood when Joseph heard a knock on the door. He went to the door and there was a young man standing there. He introduced himself as William Grant, who lived about three miles west of them. William wanted to know if Josephine might like to go to the party, so Joseph called Jody, (that's what Joseph called his daughter) downstairs and William asked her if she wanted to go to the party with him. Jody said yes and after that evening they dated for awhile and fell in love. In June of 1907, Bill and Josephine ran away to Enid, Oklahoma where they were married in the home of Reverend Wagner. They returned to Perry where they established a home and eventually had twelve children. (See the William Grant story).

One of the children, Paul Grant, died at the age of four, of pneumonia. Four of the boys served in the armed forces during World War II. All returned safely except for Myron Grant who was injured on Okinawa. One of the girls, Lorene, worked where they gave out ration stamps during the war.

Bill had many jobs over the years working to support his family. He sold fruit on the railroad, worked in the oilfields hauling timbers, and as a flour packer in the mill at Perry and also at Newton, Kansas. In later years he was also a farmer.

They moved many times between Kansas and Oklahoma. In the early part of 1920, Bill and Josephine headed for Oklahoma again with their family. They were traveling in a covered wagon and had stopped on the side of the road to camp. One of the girls, Katherine, who was nine at the time, heard a coyote howl for the first time. It was an eerie sound and one she never forgot.

Josephine cooked very little on a campfire during the family's travels. They mostly ate cold meats and homemade bread and apple butter.

Katherine, the oldest girl in the Grant family, was born April 19, 1912 about eight miles south of Perry. She went to work for a family named Fallis, in the 1930s when she was seventeen. Mr. Fallis was the banker in Perry and she did the cooking and housecleaning and helped take care of Mr. Fallis' grandson.

One day, Katherine was walking around the Perry square with her friend, Elizabeth Baumgartner, when they met Elizabeth's uncle, George Dormire. Elizabeth introduced Katherine and George and they visited for awhile. Then George asked Katherine if he could take her home. George took her home in his Ford Model A Roadster.

George Dormire's family lived on a farm six miles east and two and one half miles north of Perry. George was born in Mulhall, Oklahoma on June 23, 1906. When he was four they moved to some Indian land close to Perry and in 1918, they bought the farm north of Perry for $16,000. This land is still owned by George's brother, Louis Dormire.

Mrs. Kate Herbert, driving the horse her husband drove from Huron, Kansas to run into the Strip. With Mrs. Herbert is her daughter Jennie Vollmer and Jennie's children Roy and May (Clark) - 1910.

Katherine (Grant) and George Dormire and daughter Virginia.

George and Katherine dated for nine months and then they got married in Perry by the Presbyterian minister, Reverend David Thomas on August 31, 1931.

They lived with George's family for three months and then moved to a farm west of Morrison called the Hemmie Place. They lived there a year and then they moved to another farm three miles west and three miles north of Morrison, owned by a man named Casteel. They lived and worked this farm during one of the nation's hardest times, the big depression. Most of the people around the area still call it the "Dirty Thirties."

George and Katherine ate a lot of beans and potatoes during this time of Depression. Most of the food they had, they had raised, but one Saturday they went to Morrison and bought a pound of hamburger for about 12½ cents a pound and a big pickle for a nickel. They used Bakers bread for the buns and an onion from their garden. This hamburger meat was the first meat they had bought since they got married, and it was their first hamburger.

On October 20, 1935, their first and only child, Virginia, was born. Dr. Coldiron from Perry was the attending doctor, and Mrs. Sargent from a neighboring farm helped.

Virginia grew up on the farm in Morrison that Katherine and George bought from Mr. Casteel when Virginia was about five years old. Virginia attended Morrison Grade School and Morrison High School. When she was eighteen she moved to Oklahoma City to go to school and to work.

George Dormire died December 19, 1979. Katherine still lives on the farm in Morrison at this time. (1986)

Manuel Herrick
By Millie Highfill

Manuel Herrick was born in September 1875, in Ohio. Manuel's mother, Belinda, would not ride in the wagon seat with her son, believing she was unworthy of such honor. She believed he was Jesus Christ come to earth again. Manuel let his hair and beard grow long and would come to Perry, barefoot. In the hot afternoons he would lay down in the shade of the elms in Government Park and snore. He was the butt of many practical jokes.

Every session of court, Manuel seemed to have at least one suit against his neighbors. When he was not engaged in this, he was running for public office — sometimes as a Democrat and sometimes as a Republican and many times as an Independent.

Manuel filed for the U.S. House of Representatives from Perry. His only opponent was the incumbent, Congressman Dick T. Morgan. Morgan died after the closing of the filing period and before the primary, thus Manuel won the seat during the Harding landside.

Herrick was 43 years old at the time of the election and had lived on a farm six miles southeast of Perry in Noble township, since the opening of the strip, when his father, John, settled on a quarter section of land there. He was unmarried and had lived on the farm alone since the death of his parents several years earlier. He had no close friends.

In his farewell address to the Perry Chamber of Commerce, February 21, 1921, before going to Washington, Herrick compared himself to a beautiful fairy with golden wand who was doomed through life to bring happiness to everyone except himself. After his talk, he picked up his trunk, put it on his back and walked to the Santa Fe Depot, where he boarded a train for Washington, DC. Soon he wrote an official of the Chamber of Commerce that he could have been Speaker of the House if he had gotten there six weeks earlier to line up the votes.

Newspapers from coast to coast featured Manuel wherever news was scarce: San Francisco Chronicle — "From the franking seeds to his constituents, Congressman Herrick, it appears has found time to write batches of tender letters to young women of Washington famed for good looks. He did not sign these billetdoux but, perhaps from force of habit, he absentmindedly franked them, too." Oklahoma newspapers were no kinder, Lawton News: "It becomes more and more apparent that had Manuel Herrick started for Washington by the way of Norman and had stopped when he reached that Oklahoma town, he would have rendered the state and himself an inestimable service. There's an institution at Norman that fairly yawns for Manuel — and it's not the state university either. There is a growing feeling that rather than trying to fit the sockless Oklahoma representative into a niche in congressional halls, he should be backed into a stall in a booby hatch."

The first bill he dropped into the hopper was one that would make it unlawful for anyone except a congressman to conduct a beauty contest. Impatient with the slow process of the law, he decided to conduct a beauty contest on his own. The letters he wrote to the Washington beauties were of such language that they could not be printed in the newspapers. His landlady, whose daughter received one of these letters, chased him down the streets of Washington hitting him over the head with a broom. Incidently, the grand prize of the Beauty Contest was his own pure undefiled self.

After his one term in office, Herrick made news frequently. His being accused of operating a whiskey still in Maryland before the repeal of National Prohibition hit the front pages of Washington and the nation.

In line with his eccentricites, Herrick was seeking gold in Northern California when he was found frozen to death in a snowstorm. In February 1952, a dispatch from Quincy, California said the former congressman who was nearly blind and an old age pensioner had disappeared January 12, of that year. He was buried in California.

The native stone house still stands on the homestead, southeast of Perry, that Manuel's father took in the run (sw 32 in Noble township). When Manuel's mother Belinda, died December 9, 1911, the husband and son expected her to be returned to life in three days. They carried her body upstairs until a court order removed it to the funeral home. She was buried December 16, 1911, near the back door of the home.

John Herrick was born in August 1832 in Ohio. His father was originally from Switzerland, his mother from Pennsylvania. Belinda Herrick was born in January 1841 in Ohio. Her father was native to Virginia while her mother was a native of Pennsylvania.

Charles N. Hetherington
By Vadella (Hetherington) Carroll

Charles Newton Hetherington was born March 1, 1858 in Hendersonville, Illinois. His parents, George Newton and Miss McGraw were Scotch-Irish and came to America in the early 1820's. They settled in Illinois where they had four children: Nancy (Harrison); Charles Newton; Ella (Rust) and Minnie (Donaldson). They moved to northern Missouri when Charles was a young man.

Charles Newton Hetherington and Eliza Jane Robbins were married at Salina, Missouri on September 1, 1878. Eliza Jane was born in Salina, Missouri August 13, 1858. Her family lived in Mercer County, Missouri all their lives. Her father fought in the Militia during the Civil War. Her grandmother on her mother's side, whose name was Collins, was a first cousin to John Quincy Adams, the 6th President of the United States. Eliza Jane's mother was Susan (Collins) Robbins (May 1, 1833 - December 26, 1866). Her father was Wesley Robbins (December 28, 1828 - March 6, 1904).

Charles and Eliza had ten children: William Emmi born January 19, 1880 at Cainsville, Missouri; Bert Evert born

July 18, 1881 at Saline, Missouri; Jesse Murl born September 11, 1883 at Saline, Missouri; Mary Belle born May 18, 1885 at Longpine, Nebraska; John Homer born April 7, 1887 at Longpine, Nebraska; Effie Florence born October 2, 1889 at Stillwater, Oklahoma; the last four were born at Morrison, Oklahoma; Sarah Pearl born April 22, 1894; David Creed born September 24, 1896; Vadella Molene born November 13, 1898 and Maud Cecil born November 25, 1901.

The family moved from Longpine, Nebraska in the spring of 1889 at the opening of Old Oklahoma and settled in Stillwater, which became a tent town overnight. Effie was the second child born in that town, Charles made their living by hauling lumber by team and wagon from Guthrie, Oklahoma Territory to build the homes and store buildings in Stillwater.

Charles studied the map printed before the opening of the Cherokee Strip and picked out the claim he was to stake if possible. The day before the race, they loaded everything they owned in a big wagon. When the race started at a point just north of Stillwater, Charles rode, bareback, a little brown mare named Dolly, for 18 miles and placed his stake on the claim he had chosen. Eliza left at the gunshot that opened the run with six small children in the wagon with their belongings. There were no roads to follow and she had never been over the route before. Just about sundown Charles saw her come over a rise about one half mile south of where he had placed his claim stake.

They built a dugout in the second bank of Black Bear Creek and lived there several years where they battled "sooners" and crooked law officers.

Charles had a saw mill moved on his place in 1897. They cut the trees, sawed the lumber and built the big house in the fall of 1898. The front bedroom was the only room completely finished when Vadella was born November 1, 1898. The ten children all grew up and the parents both died in that house. In 1903 Charles purchased a quarter section of pasture land on the south side of the homestead. When each child was married, the boys were given a team of horses, harness and new wagon, the girls a choice milk cow.

Murl who had polio when he was three years old was an invalid until he was twenty one. The family took him to Colorado in 1904. They traveled in two big covered wagons. He improved and lived to be 72.

Charles N. Hetherington died November 27, 1926 and Eliza Jane February 23, 1931. They are buried in the cemetery at Morrison, Oklahoma.

Benjamin F. Hicks
By Mildred Highfill

Benjamin Franklin Hicks and Ruth Ann (Barnes) Hicks came from Sebetha, Kansas to Oklahoma in a running start in the matter of populating the land. They had 11 children, two of whom were married, when they settled in Orlando, Oklahoma in the spring of 1891. Two years later with five of their children, they made the run into the Cherokee Outlet in a spring wagon. Four members of the family staked a claim and one member paid a Sooner $25 for a claim. The sixth member of the family did not take up a claim until 1895 when he traded a team of mules for 100 acres of land. Later a school lease was added to the family possessions.

Three of these farms joined one another; one was just across the road and the other three claims were only three miles away. Benjamin staked the northeast quarter of section 35 in White Rock Township, Edwin's claim was the northeast quarter of section 30 also in White Rock, Howard's claim was the northwest quarter of section 31 of White Rock, Lillie staked the northwest quarter of section 35 of White Rock Township. Millard's claim was the northeast quarter of section 2 in Oakdale township. These were located about fifteen miles north of Perry.

Benjamin Franklin Hicks was born February 16, 1831 in Ohio. Both of his parents were born in Virginia. He was a Civil War Veteran having served as a corporal in Company D of the 8 Kansas Infantry. He married Ruth Ann Barnes July 4, 1858. Ruth was born April 12, 1839 in Ohio. Her father was born in Maryland and her mother in New York.

Their children were all born in Kansas. They were: Millard Filmore born March 20, 1859, Edwin Sanley born February 12, 1861, Howard Franklin born December 28, 1865, Lillian Mae (Kerns), born October 8, 1867, Ida Gay (Mitchell) born August 31, 1869, Mary Lavina (Kerns) born April 10, 1871, Annie Laurie born December 1, 1872, Betty born September 7, 1875, Emma Louella (Craig) born August 20, 1876, William J. born December 28, 1877, Edith Ruth (Christopher) born October 4, 1879, Leona (Kindt) born February 20, 1883 and Carrie (Freeland) born June 24, 1884.

Ruth Ann Hicks died May 8, 1904 and is buried in the Mount Carmel Cemetery northwest of Perry, Oklahoma near the old homestead. Benjamin went to Colorado on a pleasure trip and stopped at the Soldiers Home in Lavenworth, Kansas where he died December 20, 1905 after a brief illness. His body was returned to Noble County and buried beside his wife.

John and Mollie Highfill at their wedding April 20, 1897.

John Highfill
By Mildred Highfill

John Henry Highfill was born July 25, 1859 in Corydon, Indiana, the son of Adam Clark Highfill and Mary Elizabeth DeMoss. John's grandfather, Henry F. Highfill "came out of the Kentucky hills" to settle in what is now Corydon, Indiana. His marriage to Mary Smith was one of the first on record in Harrison county. Her father, Edward Smith, was born in England and was sent as a soldier in the British Army to fight in the Revolutionary War. He went AWOL and joined the Colonial Army and never returned to England.

At the death of John's father, his mother inherited the estate but at her death, most of the estate went to her son by a former marriage. John, his brother, Tom, and sister, Mary, left Indiana and moved to Kiowa, Kansas. They were here when they heard about the land openings in Oklahoma. They decided Tom would make the run into Old Oklahoma and John would stay in Kansas to settle up their affairs. Tom homesteaded land north of Stillwater, Oklahoma, where Camp Redlands is now located. He lived in a dugout, alone, as he never married. Tom set up a blacksmith shop and his place became a stage shop where horses were changed. There was a drought and a depression and Tom had run out of provisions. He went hunting with a neighbor and all they found to shoot was an old crow. They tried to cook it but the longer they cooked it, the tougher it got.

Meanwhile, John had left Kansas to join his brother. He had two wagons, two teams of horses, his riding horse and a cow. When he came to a stream of water with steep banks, he would hitch both teams to one wagon and move it across, then return for the other. He had polio when he was two years old which left his right arm nearly useless. He missed the turn off at Wharton and continued on to Orlando, which lengthened his trip by several miles. It was getting dark when he got close to where he thought, Tom was located. He came to a farm house and was told he would have to cross a creek however, the farmer went ahead of him with a lantern as John was anxious to get to his destination.

When he arrived at Tom's he was greeted with the question "Do you have anything to eat?" Tom and the neighbor and the neighbor's wife had not been able to get to sleep because they were hungry. Although it was midnight, they built a fire and cooked some of the cured pork John had brought with him and made bread and gravy from the flour.

Although there were many things John could not do with only one arm, it was surprising what he could do. He drew water from the well to water his horse by stepping on the well rope while he moved his good hand up the rope.

John bought a farm just north of Tom's. He married Mary Margaret Conarro on April 20, 1897. Mary was called Molly. She was born December 27, 1870, in Lincoln, Nebraska, the daughter of William Conarro and Martha Ann Douglas. Her father homesteaded land on the line between what is now Noble county and Payne county, near the farm John purchased.

John donated land for the Bethel Presbyterian church where all the people in the community worshiped. Many heated discussions were held in the church house as the "hard-shell" Baptists, and the "dyed-in-the-wool" Presbyterians worshiped together, along with Methodist and Christians.

When Lake Carl Blackwell was built in the 1930s the farmers were forced to sell their land to the government. John had the timber sawed into lumber and stove wood when he saw that he would have to sell. The government moved the lumber and wood to the new home they bought in Auburn township in Noble county. Although this land was near Black Bear Creek, it did not have timber, but John had enough lumber to build sheds and barns he needed and also fuel for his stoves for several years.

The children of John and Molly Highfill were: Russell Conarro Highfill b-August 8, 1898; Herbert William b-December 8, 1903; Thomas John b-May 9, 1912. They took and raised a neighbor girl, Mae Oyster, when she and her two brothers were left orphans.

Herbert was killed July 11, 1923. He was working in the harvest field when a summer storm came up. He picked up several bundles of wheat with his pitchfork and held them over his head for an umbrella. Lightening struck the pitchfork, killing him and the horses and set the wagon on fire.

John lived on his farm in Noble County until his death, October 8, 1942. Molly continued to live on the farm with her son, Tom, until she entered a resthome in Perry due to ill health. She died March 13, 1959. John, his wife and son, Herbert, are buried in the Fairlawn cemetery in Stillwater, Oklahoma.

Lowell C. Highfill

By Mildred Highfill

Lowell Clark Highfill was born February 17, 1920, on a farm nine miles northwest of Stillwater, Oklahoma, on land homesteaded by a great uncle, Thomas Highfill. Lowell was the son of Russell Highfill and Edna Coate Highfill. He attended the first year of school in a rural school near by. The next year, his parents moved to Perry, where he graduated from high school in 1939. He worked during his high school years in the wheat harvest, on a pipeline in the oil field and in the Perry Greenhouse.

He was a member of the National Guard, serving as a station wagon driver in Battery C 158 Field Artillery, 45th Division. He attended one semester at Oklahoma A & M (now OSU). The National Guard was mobilized in 1940 and he was sent to Fort Sill, Oklahoma. When the unit was sent to Camp Barkley, Texas near Abilene, he married Mildred Sarah Hensley, February 27, 1941, at Wellington, Kansas. Millie was born November 29, 1918, at Terlton, Oklahoma, the daughter of Marion Stuart Hensley and Lilly Cleo George Hensley.

When their son, Kenneth Deverl, was born on December 15, 1941, Battery C adopted him as their mascot and gave the proud father a pink and blue baby shower.

Lowell went to Fort Devens, Massachusetts, where he obtained a discharge in order to enlist in the Air Force. He received his wings and temporary rank as Second Lieutenant on March 20, 1943, in Houston, Texas.

He was sent to the brand new school at Frederick, Oklahoma, where he trained student pilots in AT-17s. James Lee was born January 19, 1944, in the Army hospital at Altus Air Force Base, Altus, Oklahoma, as there were no facilities for servicemen's dependents at the Frederick Base.

Early in 1944, Lowell went to Midland Air Field at Midland, Texas, a school for Bomberdeers, where he flew planes used in this training.

He was sent to Forth Worth to train in B-24s and then to Lincoln, Nebraska, to pick up his crew. Before this was accomplished the B-29s replaced the B-24s and he was transferred to Barksdale Field, Shrevesport, Louisiana. Training with this crew on a B-29 was nearly completed when the war ended.

After being honorably discharged, Lowell, with his wife and two small sons, hooked the housetrailer he owned to the back of his 1939 Ford and went 25 miles before the back springs of the car collapsed. A piece of angle iron welded to the frame solved the problem but the car always rode like a lumber wagon. They came back to Noble county and settled on a farm northwest of Morrison. Kathleen Mae was born July 7, 1949, in Stillwater hospital.

Lowell, along with his farming, also baled hay, delivered mail, combined wheat - he took his combines one year to Idaho on the harvest run, and as a

Lowell, Kenneth and Millie Highfill - 1942.

Lowell standing on the wing of a training plane at Fort Worth.

"rough-neck", he worked on a drilling rig in the oil field.

He also worked as a flight instructor at Oklahoma State University for 5 years. In 1960, the family moved to 901 Fir Street, Perry, Oklahoma. They bought and completely remodeled this home.

Six months prior to moving to Perry, Lowell started to work for Charles Machine Works as a District Representative on the sales force. Lowell and Millie were members of the First Presbyterian church at Perry.

Lowell died August 4, 1968, in Perry, from cancer and is buried at Grace Hill cemetery. Following his death, an award, called the Lowell Highfill award, was set up and is given each year by Charles Machine Works to the outstanding Ditch Witch Salesman in the United States.

Russell C. Highfill
By Joe Highfill

Russell Conarro Highfill was born on his father's homestead August 8, 1898, the son of Mary Margaret (Conarro) and John Henry Highfill. He was raised on this farm and attended the Cherokee rural school. He married Edna May Coate July 6, 1918 at Newkirk, Oklahoma. Edna was also of pioneer stock as her father and both grandfathers homesteaded in Walnut Township. Edna was born August 8, 1900 the daughter of Louisa Jane (Moore) and Walter Jefferson Coate.

Russell and Edna lived on the farm until 1922, when they moved to Perry, where Russell worked for the railroad unloading boxcars. He was soon transferred to Arkansas City. They lived here about two years and moved back to the farm northwest of Stillwater in 1925. His uncle, Thomas Fremont Highfill had homesteaded this farm located in Old Oklahoma. After a year, they moved to Perry where Russell worked for a grain elevator loading and unloading grain with a scoop shovel. He also hauled pipe and equipment for the oilfields. For over 30 years he worked at the gas company that supplied the city of Perry with natural gas. He worked for this company when it changed from Apache Gas Co. to the Northern Oklahoma Gas Co. and then to Oklahoma Natural Gas Co. He worked as a maintance man, adjusting the regulators on the lines supplying the city. The natural gas came from wells southwest of town. He also set meters at the homes and businesses and kept them regulated. He inspected stoves for people as well as reading meters each month. He loved to play pitch and to fish. Among the many things he did for others was repairing stoves for people who were unable to have them repaired. He would repair porch steps and banisters for the elderly. He retired in 1965.

He made a big garden every year. He started planting gardens when he was 11 and retired from this hobby the year before his death.

Edna was an active member in the War Mothers where she served in most of the local offices also as State President, State Chaplain and as National Chaplain. She helped organize the Otoe Indian, the only all Indian chapter of the War Mothers. She is a member of the First Baptist church of Perry. For many years she was a member of the Degree of Honor lodge where she kept the books for the insurance. While Russell raised his garden Edna and Russell together canned the produce from the garden. In later years they used a deep freeze.

They had three children who lived in Perry: Donald Harland (born February 1, 1919) married first to Betty Hubbell, 2nd to Leona Bass, Lowell Clark (born February 17, 1920) married Mildred Hensley, died August 4, 1968, (see Lowell Highfill); Ione Marie (born August 19, 1927) married Jasper McNeal, died September 19, 1963

Don enlisted in the army and made a career in the military. After his retirement he went to Silverton, Colorado where he served as sheriff for several years. As the high altitude bothered him he moved back to Perry where he worked for Smith Trucking Company hauling rigs and equipment for the oil companies. He was employed here until his death of cancer October 29, 1984. He had no children but adopted his first wife's boy and girl and raised them as his own.

Russell died April 23, 1986, at the hospital in Pawnee, Oklahoma and was buried in Grace Hill cemetery in Perry beside his daughter, Ione. Edna is in a rest home suffering from Alzheimers Disease.

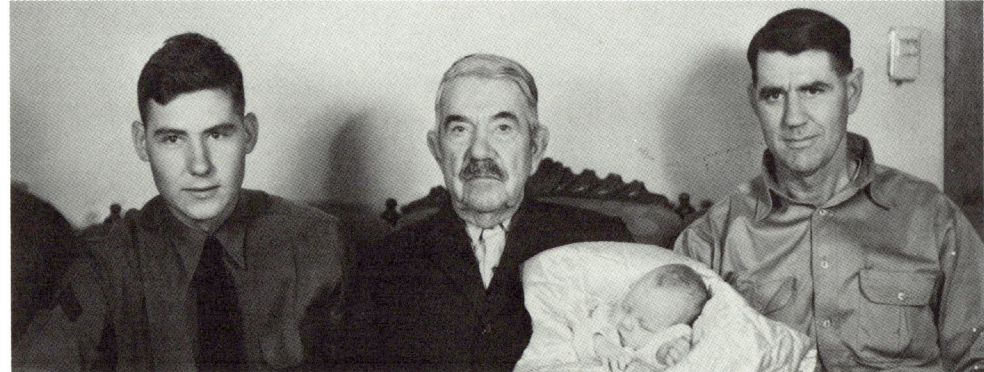

Four Generation Highfills - 1942. (L-R): Lowell, John, Russell and baby Kenneth Highfill

Four Generation Highfills - 1962. Lowell, Russell, Kenneth and baby Joe Highfill

Hines homestead before remodeling.

Hines homestead after remodeling.

Dan Hines
By Dorothy (Hines) Mercing

Daniel Patrick Hines was born June 10, 1857 in the village of Cnoshohocken, Pennsylvania. He was the son of Mary (Herken) and Patrick Hines. The family later moved to St. Joseph, Missouri. On November 23, 1892, he married Mary Frances (Molly) Hart in Hiawatha, Kansas. Mary was born in Homer, Canada, the daughter of Micheal and Mary Hart.

After their marriage, Dan and Molly went to Casion, Oklahoma to spend time with relatives to wait the opening of the Cherokee Strip. He made the run for land on September 16, 1893 and settled on a claim three miles west of what became the townsite of Whiterock. The first Christmas day of Dan and Mary, was in a sod house with dinner guests of two single men, Miles Whitaker and Bert Lemons, who had staked claims south of Billings. Dinner consisted of rabbit, biscuits and gravy. Then in 1900, they moved into the new town of Billings which was one and one half miles north of the homestead.

Dan was a farmer, carpenter and cement worker. He built culverts for roads and storm cellars at rural schools. He dug water wells for Indians around Red Rock. The Hines family had three boys and six girls, all born on the family homestead.

Mike E. was born October 30, 1894, and died December 3, 1970. He married Florence (Shorter) Rieger in 1947. Florence was born February 8, 1907 and died January 24, 1985. They are buried in Riverview cemetery, Tonkawa, Oklahoma.

William C. (Bill) was born January 1, 1897. He married Goldie McCart, December 28, 1927. Bill died in February 1985 and is buried in the Catholic cemetery, Billings, by the side of son, William Eugene (Billy). Billy was born June 22, 1937 and died October 16, 1950. Other children: Gary and Rachel L.

Winifred C. was born November 29, 1899 and died March 1, 1942. Winifred (Winnie) married Tim O'Grady September 3, 1919 at Enid, Oklahoma. Their children: Robert, Kenneth, M. Winifred, Kathleen, Jeanelle, Shirley, Barbara and Colleen. Winnie and Tim are buried in the Catholic cemetery, Billings beside son, Kenneth, age 10 months.

M. Carlen was born January 7, 1902. She married Harry Ingmire January 23, 1929 at Enid, Oklahoma. Their children are: Dannie, Wilbur, Dolores and Mildred. Harry died April 2, 1975 and was buried in Union cemetery, Billings.

Helen C. was born March 20, 1904 and died July 26, 1934. She was buried in the Catholic cemetery, Billings.

Daniel J. was born January 5, 1907. He married Marcella Peter October 16, 1929 at the Catholic church in Billings. Marcella was born July 16, 1910. Their children: Dan, Patrick (Pat) and Betty. Daniel J. died July 10, 1961 was was buried in St. Joseph's Cemetery at Hays, Kansas.

Dorothy was born February 23, 1912. She married Adron V. Mercing April 23, 1945, at Wichita, Kansas. Adron was born September 30, 1906. Their children: Adron Lee, Alexia Ruth and Mary Alice. Dorothy graduated from St. Joseph Academy, Perry Oklahoma in 1930.

Agnes was born May 20, 1914. She married Elzie Dunn July 28, 1938 at Enid, Oklahoma. Eliza was born March 16, 1907. He died Demember 15, 1983 and was buried at the Catholic cemetery at Billings. Their children: Allen and Beverly.

Kathryn was born September 22, 1917. She married C.J. "Joe" Biederman July 28, 1945 at Georgetown, South Carolina. Joe was born Januaury 23, 1917. Their children: Kenny J., Larry and Cleo Kay.

Dorothy and her husband, Adron Mercing moved to Billings, Oklahoma in August of 1952. Their children attended Billings school where Adron Lee graduated in 1964, Alexia Ruth in 1966 and Mary Alice in 1967.

Karl F. Hirschman
By Lucile W. (Hirschman) Plumer

In the spring of 1869, Karl Frederick George Hirschman took the big step of migrating to America where he joined a German settlement in Benton County Missouri. Added to the lure of rich farm land in a new country was his wish to escape compulsory military service which awaited him at age 21. Born 20 June 1849, at Ludwigsburg, Wurrtemberg, Germany, he was fast approaching that time. Trained as a "schuster" (cobbler/shoemaker) he had saved money for his passage, and by toil and thrift was able in a few years to begin farming on his own, marry, and start a family.

He and Katharine Marie Eckhoff, born 6 April 1858, to Herman George Eckhoff and Mariah Miller Eckhoff, were married 17 October 1877. After the birth of Mary Wilhelmina (10 June 1880) and Herman Frederick (24 November 1881), they moved to Pettis County, Missouri, near Green Ridge, where they purchased land and made their home. Here eight more children were born: Charles Peter (23 December 1883-19 December 1950 at Halstead, KS), Henry Louis V. (14 February 1885-30 May 1908 at Perry, OK), William Dick (23 October 1887-2 November 1981 at Pettis County, MO), Otto Jacob (1 May 1889-8 November 1951 at Perry, OK), Katherine Louisa (18 August 1890-1 January 1938 at Perry, OK), Bertha Margaret (28 February 1892-16 May 1953 at Elmhurst, IL), Lawrence Hugo (15 June 1894-15 February 1959 at Enid, OK), Emma Hannah (29 September 1897-19 July 1967 at Enid, OK).

Once again tales of cheap land and virgin soil, in Oklahoma Territory, were heard and the urge to move was strong. A number of German families had already settled near Richburg, a post office on a stage route about eleven miles southeast of Perry. It was in this vicinity in November, 1902, that Karl investigated and bought 160 acre (SW¼-26 Noble Township) from Ludwig Ritthaler who had homesteaded it. March 1903, found the family on the way. The older sons rode with livestock, machinery, and furniture in a railroad box-car, and the rest of the family came in coach cars.

They had left a large, two-story house in Misouri, so the small building with "loft" space must have been a discouraging sight. However, it was placed near a never-failing spring in the northeast part of the farm, and water was a premium. In times of drought neighbors were allowed to get water from it. As the living quarters were entirely inadequate for the large and growing family, plans were set in motion to build a house on a high place nearer the road. It was difficult to find water there, but by "witching" a vein was located that would supply household water and a well was drilled. There was always plenty of water at the spring for the livestock.

The older children soon set out to make their own way. Mary did house-

Hirschman family c. 1905. Seated: Lawrence, Mary, Herman, Katharine (mother), Karl (father), Emma. Standing: Bertha (Bertie), Charles, Otto, Henry, Katherine (Katie).

work for a family in Perry a couple of years, and then married Charley (Carl) Lovekamp in 1905. He owned the IXL Livery Stable, later turned into a garage, and they lived nearby. She died at this home. They had two sons, William, who died in infancy, and Charles Fred.

Herman and Otto hired out whenever possible and saved money to set up farming on their own. In 1906, Herman married Karolena Bamberger and soon bought a farm where he spent the rest of his life. Of their five children, Clarence, the oldest, remained a bachelor and lived with his mother on the farm until her death. The other children were Edna Margaret (Passow), Leopold Otto, Esther Helen (Hodge), and Robert Herman. Leo and Bob died in 1977.

Charles worked as a clerk in Woodruff's Department Store in Perry, and later owned his own men's wear shop. He and Niona Ellis were married in 1915, and established a home in Perry. Two sons, Herbert and Duanie, were born to them. Later they lived in Tulsa, until his death.

Henry was employed by Will Fry of the Palace Meat Market, Perry, and lived in the Fry home. He was killed 30 May 1908, while attempting to rope an animal for slaughter.

In 1912, Otto married Effie Lillian Brewer. Her father, Eli Brewer, owned a farm and blacksmith shop at Richburg. Otto farmed a few years until he trained for auctioneering, then they left the farm and lived in Perry. He was a tall man with a strong voice, desirable assets in his chosen vocation. He enjoyed the work and became a popular auctioneer. They had one daughter, Lo Rene Kathryn (Jensen).

As the older members of the family left home, the younger ones carried on the farm work. In addition to field work, they raised a garden, chickens, hogs, and milked cows to supplement the income. When peaches were ready for picking, there was a great demand for pickers and packers in Orlando Walkling's orchards and packing shed. Every available person in the neighborhood pitched in to help, and the income was most welcome.

In 1910, typhoid fever took the mother, Katharine, and left the family desolate. But the four at home continued to carry on until Bertha married Martin Voise, 20 October 1914. He was farming and they had six children, one dying in infancy. The others: Leona Katherine (McMillin), Helen Marie (Shinglman), Martin William, Gladys Mae, and Berton Vernon. This family moved to Chicago in 1925. There Martin was employed by Western & Southern Life Ins. Co.

Two years later, 20 December 1916, Katie married Charley Bamberger and they also were farmers, but had no children. Before this time, Mary had taken Emma into her home to finish her schooling in Perry. She later attended Business school and did office work in Perry and Enid until her retirement.

By 1917, the country was at war and the following year, Lawrence was drafted. That was the final break-up of the family and farm. The father went to live with Mary where he died 23 May 1919. Lawrence returned from the army and started farming. On 17 May 1922, he and Lucile Warner were married. In 1945, they left the farm which they had bought from the Hirschman heirs, and she returned to teaching.

Snapshot of Hirschman home built c. 1904.

They had two daughters, Evely Fae (Hill) and Laural Lucile (Zavodny). By 1951, they had bought a home in Perry. He was employed by the State Highway Department and she continued to teach.

The family were faithful members of the Zion Lutheran Church which was located on the southwest two acres of their farm. A new church has since been built on Highway 64, five miles east of Perry. The cemetery remains. The pastor was a frequent Sunday guest in their home and lusty discussions between him and father Hirschman were common.

By 1985, there were 12 grandchildren, 31 great-grandchildren, and a number of "gr-gr-grands" scattered throughout the country, involved in various occupations, carrying on the family tradition of thrift and industry, a dependable, substantial, "salt of the earth" type of citizens.

Stan Hodges
By Stan Hodges

Stan Hodges came to Perry in 1977, as a construction worker for the city of Perry. After completing a degree from Oklahoma State University, Stan moved to Perry to go to work for Charles Machine Works, in 1981. Stanley Hodges is descended from the Hodges of Virginia, Tennessee and Oklahoma.

The earliest ancestor known was Thomas Hodges, of Cumberland County Virginia. The descent is as follows: Thomas I, the father of Thomas II, the father of Thomas III, all of these being in Cumberland or Halifax County Virginia. Thomas II married Susanna Bomar, and had a son named Fleming Hodges.

Fleming Hodges married Elizabeth Powell, Fleming and Elizabeth were the last generation to live in Virginia. Their son Edward married Mary Polly Haley and they removed to Claiborne County Tennessee. Edward and Mary had a son named Robert Fielding Hodges born in Claiborne County Tennessee. Fielding Hodges married Penny Shelton. Their children are as follows, Elizabeth, Edward, Fleming, Letta, Robert Fielding, Sarah Susan. Their son Robert Fielding Jr. married Margaret Elizabeth Greenlee, the daughter of James and Sarah (Callison) Greenlee. The children of Robert Fielding Hodges and his wife Elizabeth Greenlee are as follows: Sarah Jane, Mary Alice, Malissia Louise, Bluford Samuel, Joseph Sennitt. Lones, Berdie Ester, Verlin Etheridge, Effie Frances, Garnet Raymond Hodges. Robert Fielding moved his family to Texas and then to Oklahoma in the year 1913, to the Broken Arrow area. Their son Raymond Hodges took over the farm in

Raymond and Grace Hodge about 1940s.

Robert's old age. Raymond married Grace Marie Frogge. The daughter of Perry Lawson Frogge and Viola Faye (Williams) Frogge. The children of Grace and Raymond Hodges are as follows: Alma June, Horace Thomas, Marice Samuel, Bobby Ray, Raymond and Grace Hodges lived on that same farm for over fifty years. Their son Horace Thomas Hodges married Elizabeth Joyce Simpkins on January 30, 1954. Elizabeth was the daughter of Charles Edward Simpkins and Lula Belle (Atkins) Simpkins, of Catoosa, Oklahoma. The children of Horace and Betty Hodges are as follows: Stan Hodges born June 12, 1957 in Waxahachie Texas. Rickey Thomas Hodges born June 30, 1962 in Tulsa, Oklahoma. This lists almost three hundred years of Hodges descendants.

John Lemon Holmes
By Mrs. Walter Dunn

John Lemon Holmes was born in Savannah, Illinois, March 4, 1857 to John Quincy Holmes and Barbara Bazzell Holmes. When John L. was four years old his father enlisted in the Union Army where he served three years. After the war, the family lived on the home farm where John and his three sisters, Emily, Mary and Isadore grew to adulthood. John graduated from the academy at Bloomington, Illinois and then taught school for five years. He was married September 12, 1883 to Zillah Ellen Smith whom he met while attending the academy. Zillah taught school for nine years before their marriage. The young couple established a home on a farm, which they bought, near Vermont, Illinois.

On June 29, 1885, Laura Irene Holmes was born; January 21, 1887, Bertha Holmes and on October 3, 1889, Fred Smith Holmes; Max Gilbert Holmes was born in February 1891.

News of the rich land of the Cherokee Strip soon to be opened reached the land-loving farmers of the mid-west. Among those who sold their homes and moved to Kansas was the John Holmes family. Selling their farm in Illinois, they shipped their farm equipment and household goods to a small farm near South Haven, Kansas; where Emily Holmes Blue (Mrs. McDonald Blue) lived on a farm. John Quincy Holmes accompanied his son and family to Kansas and established a home in South Haven. John Quincy married Mrs. Catherine Adamson in 1891.

During the summer of 1893, John Holmes trained a riding horse in preparation for the run. A friend, Bert Kinney, began training his cow pony. Bert was a cowboy who worked for the Cherokee Strip Livestock Association. They would ride down into the Strip on Sunday afternoons and pick the land, planning the location of improvements.

On September 16, 1893, John Holmes and Bert Kinney lined up with the other homeseekers, a half mile east of Hunnewell, Kansas. Zillah with her four small children, John Q. Holmes and Mrs. Bert Kinney waited in the spring wagons behind the line of people. John and Bert rode directly to the land they had picked. Both men staked their claims and dug small excavations to show their intent to improve the land. As John was preparing his evening meal over his campfire an armed man rode up, ordering him off the land, claiming to have staked it first. As John was not armed he was in no position to argue and rode over to Bert Kinney's claim to spend the night. The next day he returned to Kansas.

In about two weeks, John received word of two claims for sale one mile north of the present town of Billings. He rode down with his nephew, Charles Lalicker and bought the claims for a nominal sum.

About midnight October 24, 1893, John brought his family in his wagons to the claim. He dug back into a hillside for a small dugout and there the family stayed the winter of 1893-94. John built a 14' x 16' house with a kitchen and dining lean-to on the west side of the larger room. In 1901, they added a two story addition to the front of the original building. On September 24, 1896, John Quincy was born and on December 3, 1898, Mary Maine Holmes was born. They were charter members of the First Christian Church of Billings.

Every August, the Cheyennes and Arapahoes near Lawton visited the Poncas near Ponca City, coming by the farm in wagons. John would give them water and extra vegetables so it became the custom for them to stop on their way home.

Irene Holmes attended Phillips University in Enid, and Alva teacher's college. In 1911, she married Charles Owens, formerly of Indiana. Their children: Fred Charles Owens (b-1912); David Owens (b-1914); Virginia Lee Owens (b-1918); Dorotha Elaine Owens

Mr. and Mrs. John L. Holmes, Irene, Bertha, Fred and Max.

(b-1922) and Charles Owens (b-1924).

Bertha Holmes, never married, taught school in Noble county and in the Riverside Indian School in Anadarko for three years. In 1914, she went into government work in Washington, D.C. She graduated from the Washington college of Law and was admitted to the Virginia bar. She continued in government work as an income tax specialist until her retirement in 1950. She died October 24, 1957. She is buried in the Union cemetery in Billings.

Fred Holmes after graduating in 1907 from Billings High school attended business college at Phillips in Enid. He worked for the Foster Lumber company. He was married August 13, 1913, to Ethleen Peacock. Their children: Doris, Lolabelle and Fred Allison Holmes. Fred died January 25, 1923.

Max Holmes after graduating from Billings High, taught several years in Noble and Seminole counties. He worked for the Foster Lumber company. In 1925, he married Mabel Mounts in Golden, Colorado. The couple had one child, Ruthmary (b-1926).

John Quincy Holmes graduated in 1916 from Billings High school, spent a year in the Army in 1917-1918. On May 16, 1920, he married Thelma Breinholt and went into the grocery business in Billings. In the 1940's he went to work for Champlin Oil company. Their children: Annabel, Ellen, Linda and Robert. He died July 14, 1975 and is buried in the Union cemetery in Billings.

Mary Holmes graduated from Billings and attended Oklahoma University. She taught school six years in Noble and Grant counties. In 1919, she married Joseph F. Danford. Their children: Max, Joseph Jr., Don and Michael H. Danford. Joseph Danford worked for the Continental Oil Company in Texas where Mary continued her education at Leias University. In 1952, they moved to Wichita, Kansas where Joseph worked for Boeing company until he retired in 1962. Mary taught school until she retired in 1964. Her graduate work was at Wichita State University and Phillips University.

John Holmes sold his farm north of Billings in 1918, and built a home in Billings. He died September 23, 1924. Zillah maintained the home in Billings until 1932, then made her home with her children. She died December 21, 1956 at the age of near ninety nine years old. They are buried in the Union cemetery in Billings.

Zellah E. Holmes
By Mrs. Walter Dunn

Zellah Ellen Holmes (1858-1956) was born near Lawrence, Kansas. It was shortly after the Quantril Raid in 1863 that her family moved to Illinois where she taught school until her marriage to John L. Holmes (1857-1924) in 1883. Hearing of "Free Land" in Oklahoma, they came to Hunnewell, Kansas where she with her four small children, Irene, Bertha, Fred and Max, watched the Race from the family wagon stationed near the old cattle stockade at Hunnewell, Kansas. That evening, they, with Mrs. Bert Kinney, a neighbor with whose husband Mr. Holmes had made the race, drove down into the Strip to spend the night on claims which they hoped their husbands had obtained near the old Lone Tree, a famous landmark known to all cowboys. It turned out that Mr. Kinney had been successful. Mr. Holmes had no such luck. At the moment of his arrival at the claim of his choice, a man, obviously a Sooner, armed with a rifle, came up from a draw leading a cool horse, which had clearly not made the Run, and ordered Mr. Holmes to move on. So that night was spent on the Kinney claim.

Mr. Holmes started to look for another claim and soon located and purchased one in what is now Noble County, then "P" County, one mile north of the present town of Billings. The seller demanded and received as part payment for his claim, a young brood mare which Mr. Holmes had counted on to help stock his farm as well as to take part in the farm work.

At midnight, on October 24, 1893, Mr. and Mrs. Holme with their children arrived at their new home, having come by covered wagon by the way of an old trail which crossed the claim. In a few days, neighbors and friends from Kansas brought in supplies and material for building a one room house. Mrs. Holmes cooked for her family and builders over an open fire, served meals out-of-doors and slept in a tiny dug-out which Mr. Holmes had made in a hillside. An up-ended table served as a door.

With Mr. Holmes gone frequently to Kansas for supplies, Mrs. Holmes stayed on the claim, caring for the home and children, feeding the hogs and chickens, and in the evenings teaching the children their lessons.

From October 1893, to March 1894, Mrs. Holmes was the only woman for miles around and saw only two women, Miss Kate Nelson and Mrs. James Young. These were overnight visitors having no houses on their claims. Others began to come in March 1894 and build their homes, some of them sod houses. Wells were also dug. The water up to this time had been hauled in barrels from a branch creek a mile away.

Groceries and other necessities were obtained at a little general store owned and operated by George Meece at a junction of the four counties, P O L K, now Noble, Garfield, Grant, and Kay counties. The post office took its name from the four letters which named the cornering counties.

Soon the settlers organized a community Sunday School which in summer was held in an arbor of poles and tree branches brought up from Red Rock Creek and erected on the southwest corner of the James Noonan claim. Wagon seats and planks laid across nail kegs served as seats. In the winter, the school was held in various homes. Until public school could be established, the parents of school age children arranged with Pleasant Hurst to conduct a three month term of school, the fathers paying the tuition of their children by breaking sod on Mr. Hurst's claim. The first one-room school was built on Noonan's claim. A literary society was organized. The programs consisted of music, recitations and debates. Mrs. Holmes was often one of the debators.

In the first school house, Mr. and Mrs. Holmes, Mr. and Mrs. J.A.D. Nelson, Charles M. Sheldon and others organized a Christian Church which upon the coming of the town of Billings, became the First Christian Church of Billings.

Very little of the Settler's life was of a social nature. Mrs. Holmes often helped in the fields and with other women of the neighborhood, cooked for harvest hands and threshing crews. In the first six years after the opening of the Strip, Mrs. Holmes gave birth to two more children: Mary (Mrs. Joe Danford), who made Elementary teaching a career in the Billings area and is now retired, living in California; and Quincy, who owned and operated the Billings Grain and Supply for several years. Mrs. Holmes' attending physician was Dr. S. F. Brafford of Billings, a true Pioneer doctor, who for years made calls on horseback. Mr. and Mrs. Holmes sold their claim and moved to Billings in 1917. Both were laid to rest in the Billings Cemetery.

House built by William C. Hook on claim near Whiterock. (L to R): Wallace Carifell, Mr. and Mrs. Carifell (friends of family) - 1923.

William C. Hook
By Libbie G. Chenoweth Norton

William Checksfield Hook was born November 14, 1866, in Gerbutt, New York, and died March 7, 1960, at Colorado Springs, Colorado at the age of 93. Both his grandparents, (Hook and Checksfield) were born in Tenderkin, Kent county, England. They crossed the Atlantic Ocean in a small sail boat, a stormy trip which took seven weeks. They had eight children: Edward, George, William, Harriett, Nellie, Anna, Frankie and Minnie. Of these children, William, father of our subject was born May 7, 1847, and resided at Garbutt, New York. On February 18, 1866 at Rochester, New York, he was married to Harriet Elizabeth (Wells) Roberts, a widow of Moses E. Roberts of Wheatland, New York. Harriet was born April 2, 1827, the daughter of Myra A. (Goodhue) and Moses Wells. She died February 18, 1899 at Whiterock, Noble County, Oklahoma. She was buried in the Floral Ridge cemetery. Harriet had five children by her first husband: Emily E. (Blair); Edwin Jay; Sidney Allen, who is buried beside his mother; John Goodhue; and Warn. Harriet was twenty years older than her husband, William Hook. She had two more children by Hook: William C. and Libby May who married Neil C. Christensen (see Neil C. Christensen story).

In 1899, William Hook the 1st came to Nebraska to find a farm. He rented a house, and then sent for his wife and children. William C. was thirteen and his sister Libby was eight. They came by train with all their belongings. Harriet was a member of the Presbyterian church of Garbutt and joined other churches. She was a constant reader of the Bible. She always fed anyone coming to her door in need.

In 1890, William Hook left his wife and two children and returned to Fairport, New York where he lived to be 95. This left William C. to care for his mother.

William C. Hook about 1890.

William C. served as road overseer 1891 to 1892 until he moved to Rome, Kansas, where his uncle Jake lived at the time. He rented a farm three miles from the state line. W.C. Hook returned to Nebraska where he traded a team of horses for a team of mules. With his brother-in-law, N.C. Christensen, he returned to Kansas and his rented farm. They brought with them a wagon loaded with farming tools and a light wagon with bows and a canvas top to bunk in. They also brought horse feed, grub for themselves, six head of horses and the span of mules. They planted the crops and boarded up the house to make it warmer. They told of making a trip down into the Cherokee Strip to go fishing in the Chicaskia River. The flies were so bad, the horses they had tied to some trees broke loose and ran away, leaving them to walk twenty miles. They hitched another team up the next day and went back to the river to recover their wagon, guns and other stuff they had hid in the bushes. A neighbor found the team and returned them.

W.C. Hook brought his mother to Kansas in 1892, then the next year on September 16, he made the run into the Cherokee Strip. He stayed in line at the registration booth north of the Chillacco Indian School in the boiling hot sun for four days before he could get his certificate. While they were in line, John Lenons boys kept them supplied with provisions. Water was selling at $3.00 a barrel at Honeywell, Kansas, the nearest town.

The vehicle Will C. Hook used to make the run was the front wheels of a wagon minus the front bolster with a stiff tongue added. An artillery box was bolted on to hold grub, gun, axe and horse feed. Blankets were roped to the top of the box, making a seat to ride on. Four men could ride on this seat, three with their faces to the horses and one with his back to the others. The horses he drove had a trotting record of ten miles an hour.

William C. Hook staked a claim that joined Indian allotments, 24 miles from Kansas, but when he arrived in Perry, he was told his claim was already taken by someone else. Some men were stuck in the mud in Cow Creek and when he pulled them out, they told him about a claim next to theirs, that no one had filed on. They said, "They would show him where it was for $25.00," so it came to be his claim. It was the southwest quarter of section 32 in Glenrose township. He worked a few days in Perry and took some lumber out to his claim. First he built a barn 12' x 24' then a grainery 8' x 12'. The grainery he used to cook and sleep in until he finished his home. He built a two story house and added a kitchen on later. All the lumber was hauled from the saw mill on Red Rock Creek.

The house, built of cottonwood and some ash trees, was finished in the fall of 1894. In 1896, the battons were torn off the main house and weather board siding of cypress lumber was put on. His mother was with him and also his half brother, Sidney Roberts came for a time to live with them.

Will Hook married Minnie F. Chambers, May 3, 1898. She had come to visit her sister, Mrs. Carrie Stewart, who lived on a claim across the road.

In 1899, his mother died at home, the same year their first child, Nellie May was born. In 1900, they moved to Hamilton, Kansas. They later returned to Eureka, Kansas and in 1906, they moved to San Luis Valley, California, going to Colorado Springs in 1921. They have eight children: Nellie May, born May 17, 1899 at Whiterock, Oklahoma. She married Roland L. Cochrane; Zelma Elizabeth, born August 4, 1900 at Eureka, Kansas. She married Ernie R. Smith; Leonard, born January 10, 1902 in Greenwood County, Kansas, died July 1902; William Phillip, born January 25, 1904, Eureka, Kansas; Cyrena M., born September 17, 1906 in Monte Vista, Colorado, married Buford Irion; Clifford C., born January 29, 1910 died in 1972, married Virginia Welker; Minnie Florence born September 14, 1914 in Monte Vesta, Colorado married 1st E.J. Connor, one son Thomas Patrick. She married 2nd Edward Pell and had one son, Duane Greg.

Will and Minnie celebrated their sixty-fourth anniversary of their marriage in 1962.

Oliver H. Hovey

By Mildred Highfill

Oliver H. Hovey was born in New York in 1859. Both of his parents were also born in New York. According to the census for Noble County he was divorced.

O. H. Hovey and his Oldsmobile - 1906.

In 1937, the editor of the Morrison Transcript ran this article. "O. H. Hovey, master printer of Perry, is a musician of exceptional ability. At the dedicatory ceremonies of the Davis and Sons Funeral Home in Perry, a short time ago, Mr. Hovey rendered several selections on the pipe organ. As an organist he has held positions in some of the large churches in the United States. Patriarchal in appearance, with long white beard, he presents an imposing appearance as the classics respond to his touch and flow forth in a harmony that would please the most critical of the master composers. He is adept with wind and reed instruments, and was among the first - if not the first to introduce the saxophone in Perry.

Mr. Hovey is over four score years old, yet continues to successfully conduct his printing business. Mr. Hovey will occasionally issue a free lance paper that seethes with striking force. He is a photographer and in his younger years he was a locomotive engineer and he left a record that during his railroad service he was in no accident that caused anyone to be injured."

Mr. Hovey owned land south of the present fire station. This land was covered with bushes, flower beds and fish ponds. Also he had wild animals in cages in this park. It was a fascinating and sometimes frightening place for youngsters who would walk through so as to catch a glimpse of a coyote or a rattlesnake.

Mr. Hovey died in the Perry General Hospital where he had been for a year and a half following severe burns received when his home burned in November of 1938. Among his survivors was a daughter Nellie M. Hovey of Los Angles, California. He is buried in Grace Hill Cemetery.

The automobile traffic was inaugurated in Perry where Oliver H. Hovey drove into town in the spring of 1906. His "car" was a one cylinder Oldsmobile, bicycle tires inflated by hand pump, no inner tubes. He was able to make about 18 miles an hour at

Fish ponds and flowers on O. H. Hovey's lots in Perry. Young ladies unidentified.

top speed. He put on some wonderful exhibitions around the square and was stopped often by Chief Boright for engaging in dangerous and reckless driving.

In 1907 Fred Beers, the druggist, brought in the next car, being the first Ford in Noble County. Dr. Keeler also had a one cylinder gas wagon. Col. John Cordell was about next on the list with a big family car that was able to weakly grunt its way around the square and with a little man power assistance get back home.

In the first automobile race staged during the 16th celebration in 1907, no one having a car to compete with Beers (Hovey's being out of commission) a dare-devil driver from Oklahoma City was imported. Fred and the visitor started around the square at the crack of a gun. A speed of possible eight miles an hour was attained, but neither finished the lap. Fred skidded around a corner against the hitch rack after negotiating half the distance and the dare-devil quit exhausted, coming west up the hill on the north side. For the effort however the purse of twenty dollars was divided and the race called a draw. - E. W. Jones.

Ena May Howard
By Eddetta Beier Grant

My grandmother, Ena May Humphrey Howard, was one of many early day school teachers in Noble County. She was born Ena May Humphrey on June 22, 1904, to Carria and Cleveland Humphrey.

Ena May attended grades 1-8 at Fairview District No. 30 and graduated from Perry High School in 1923. She then attended summer school at what was then Oklahoma A & M College at Stillwater, Oklahoma, receiving her teaching certificate in 1923.

Lilly School District No. 67 was the first school at which Grandma taught, for approximately $90.00 a month, during the years 1923-1924. While teaching there in 1924, an entire freight train loaded with longhorn cattle arrived at the Otoe Switch from Texas (the Otoe switch was an area approximately six (6) miles south of Red Rock, Oklahoma, where there were large holding pens, weighing scale and chute set up for access to the Santa Fe railroad). The cattle were so starved for water that the cowboys couldn't hold them in the pens. These longhorns were scattered along the roads and broke fences to get into pastures, any place where they could find water. All the children had to be transported to and from school for nearly a week before the cattle were all rounded up.

The weather wasn't too cooperative that year either. A blizzard hit which lasted for two days. The roads were blocked and none of the Lilly students could get to the school. During that same winter, there was a teacher's meeting held in Oklahoma City. The only way to catch the train, which stopped at the Otoe switch, was by horseback. So, Grandma rode a horse to meet the train with her suitcase tied on to the back of the saddle. The snowdrifts were belly deep on the horse as she made her way to the train.

From 1924 until 1941, Grandma took a break from teaching. She was married to Dewey Lee Howard on January 4, 1926, and they had one daughter, Cleva Jo.

After raising her daughter and being a farmer's wife, she returned to teaching in 1941 at the Long Branch school where she taught for one year. The last years of teaching were in 1942-43 at Willow Creek school. One program which started while Grandma taught there, was hot lunches for the students.

The weather was always a challenge to the rural schools. On the 28th day of March in either 1942 or 1943, another one of those late Spring blizzards hit Noble County. The snow drifts covered fence posts and none of the roads were visible. For over a week both students and teacher had to cut through pastures in order to attend school. Grandma quit teaching when the rural school was closed around 1946, earning, at retirement, the astronomical sum of $100.00 per month.

Most of the rural schools were built similar to the one on display at the Cherokee Strip museum. A teacher had eight grades and taught such topics as reading, writing, arithmetic, penmanship, geography, history, language, spelling, etc.

All eight grades were in one large room with a recitation bench at the front of the room. Each grade when called went to the bench and recited their lesson before the class.

Education was a difficult task for

Ena May (Humphrey) Howard - 1922.

both teachers and students in the early history of our county. We owe a great deal of thanks to all those early teachers who put up with all the many hardships which accompanied the rural schools and tried to help provide an education to the early settlers.

Joseph W. Howard
By Eddetta Beier Grant

Like many other pioneers, J.W. Howard was drawn to the last great land run. He was born Joseph Washington Howard on February 22, 1859, in Rushville, Missouri, to W.N. and Mary Howard. The family owned a farm on the Missouri river.

Sometime close to September 16, 1893, J.W. took the train from St. Joseph, Missouri, to Orlando, Oklahoma Territory. He then made the run from the Orlando site on horseback and staked a claim northwest of Perry on the NE ¼ of section 32-22N-1W. His claim was only four miles from the claim staked by my great-great-grandfather, C.C. Humphrey. He later sold the farm in 1910, to Andrew Hess and purchased a farm two miles east, one mile north and one-half mile east of Perry, described as the SE ¼ of section 7-21N-1E.

On February 8, 1895, J.W. Howard and Lena Ottie Conard were married in Perry, Oklahoma. They had six children, namely: (1) Joseph William; (2) my grandfather, Dewey Lee; (3) Wayne Bruce; (4) Robert Benton; (5) Mary Jeanetta and (6) Dora Maude. Joseph and Dewey were both born in Rushville, Missouri; Dewey Lee being born on February 15, 1898.

Around 1921, J.W. retired and purchased a home in Perry located at 604 Sixth Street. J.W. would often walk out to his farm by way of the railroad tracks. On August 30, 1922, while taking such a walk to the farm, he was hit and killed instantly by a south bound Santa Fe passenger train. Because he

Dewey Lee and Joseph William Howard around 1903.

was very hard of hearing, he did not hear the train approaching. His hat and stains of blood were found on the pilot of the train when it reached town. The engineer said he had not seen anyone on the track. His wife, Lena Ottie, died December 25, 1955.

On January 4, 1926, my grandparents, Dewey Lee Howard and Ena May Humphrey, were married at Enid, Oklahoma. They had one daughter born on September 1, 1927, Cleva Jo. She was married on September 29, 1946, to Edward Jacob Beier.

During the summer of 1940, Dewey and his family took over the farming of the family farm. They later purchased the farm on November 9, 1954. My grandfather continued to live on the farm until his death on April 25, 1969. He had turned the farming operation over to his grandsons, Robert Lee and David Edward Beier, prior to his death.

Grandson, Robert Lee Beier, his wife, Terry, and their two children, Lee Dewey (named for his great-grandfather) and Carrie Leann, presently live on the family homestead. Lee and Carrie are the fifth generation to have lived on the farm. J.W. Howard had a sense of pride of the land that is shared even today with his small number of descendants.

Charles Huene
By Mrs. L.B. Daniels

January of 1905, reports of the big corn raised in Bressie in 1904, prompted Charlie Huene to buy 80 acres, located one mile north of the Bressie post office, headquarters for the Figure 3 Ranch, where he, with his wife, Mamie, and two-year-old son, Maynard, built a new two-room house.

Having resided there less than four months, Charlie, on returning from town with a neighbor, saw his wife running about their house in flames; the two-year old son running after his mother. Charlie tried to smother the flames with his overcoat, but too late, she died from inhalation. She had caught fire from burning the trash she had raked together cleaning the yard, and to save her baby son, had to keep running. Mamie was laid to rest, the third grave in the newly established Bressie Cemetery. The tombstone gives her dates as October 17, 1883-March 17, 1906.

Leo, Charlie's 21-year-old brother, after spending his vacation in Bressie, stepped off the train in Kipton, Ohio, to be told of the tragedy. He took the next train back to Bressie — stayed to look after the farm, turned to Ohio for medical attention, as Charlie's hands were badly burned trying to save his wife.

Charlie and Maynard returned and the Huene brothers became well known with their small boy. Maynard thrived, on canned milk fortified with sugar, sleeping in a horse blanket atop a load of corn before daylight on frosty mornings — as they boys hauled corn, with four horse hitch, from the Osage, fording the Arkansas River to Bliss, Oklahoma, the nearest railroad station. Or sometimes supplies from Whiteagle, or Ponca City, fording the Salt Fork River. The good neighbor women's sympathies went out to the two bachelors, and small boy affording many invites to dinners and offers to keep Maynard, but Maynard, use to open range and no fears, seldom received a second invitation.

April 1907 — The retired parents, constant worry about the three boys' welfare, left their 14-room home in Kipton, Ohio, Adolph, 81, and Ann, 71, years of age, moved to Oklahoma in the two-room house. They immediately started construction of a bigger house, requiring help for Ann to cook for carpenters, corn huskers and the boys besides caring for four-year-old Maynard.

The young girl, Hazel Beck, who worked at the Bressie Post Office and Figure 3 Ranch headquarters, whom the boys admired for her capabilities and had sampled her cooking as well as observed her expert horsemanship — and seen her ride a spirited horse in a dead run or sometimes pitching, was just the help their mother needed.

Hazel and the senior Huenes slept in the two-room house, while the men and Maynard slept in a 10 by 14 foot granary until the addition to the house was completed. By that time, Leo and Hazel had new plans and were married August 27, 1907.

August 1, 1908, the senior Huene's longed to return to their Ohio home, as Adolph decided that the virgin soil of Oklahoma would not stand up to being farmed and would all wash away. Charlie and Maynard returned with the parents to Ohio.

After a few months, Charlie, a new bride, May and Maynard returned to Oklahoma and leased 80 acres on the west side of the same section and built a new two-room house. After a few years, Charlie's new wife also became homesick for Ohio, so Charlie, May, Maynard and a new baby daughter, Mildred, returned to Ohio.

In 1911, the Leo Huenes, with their two small children, rented their farm and also returned to Ohio to help care for the senior Huenes. After three years, Leo persuaded his parents to return to Bressie with him, where Adolph and Ann lived out their lives. Adolph died in 1916 and Ann died February 25, 1922. They are buried in the Bressie Cemetery.

After the Leo Huene children, Burt and Marion, were grown, another daughter, Jo Ann was born, who became the first woman elected to a district judgeship in Oklahoma. Leo and Hazel lived on their beloved Bressie farm until his death in 1964. An accident took Jo Ann's life in 1967. Marion, now Mrs. L.B. Daniels, resides on an adjoining farm in Bressie and Burt resides on a farm near Newkirk.

Suprisingly — Maynard Huene, the hearty boy survived — today a retired school principal in Elyria, Ohio. Mildred (Mrs. Paul Whitney) also lives in Elyria, Ohio.

Clinton S. Huffington
By Wilbur Huffington

Clinton Smith Huffington was born September 12, 1843, in Calloway Co., MO, the son of Joshua B. and Elizabeth (Ransom) Huffington. His mother was from Virginia. His father died when Clinton was about ten years old and his uncle, George B. Ransom, raised him.

Joshua B. Huffington was the son of Joshua Huffington, the son of William Huffington, Sr. In the War of 1812, Joshua Huffington was a private in Captain Morgan's company, the 49th regiment which was largely recruited from Cecil and Kent counties, Maryland.

William Huffington, Sr. born in 1738, died in 1819, was a seaman, lumberman, painter, and merchant. In the Virginia Gazette in 1767, he was mentioned as Captain of the sailing vessel "Peggy". His lumber mill was located in Sussex Co. Delaware, 10 to 12 miles up the Nanticoke river from the plantation of his father, John, Jr. Some of the best virgin timber in the eastern part of the country lay along that stream.

The Revolutionary War spelled misfortune for many businessmen of the Colonies, especially in Delaware and Maryland, but William, Sr. like his brother Johnathan, Sr. survived with Jonathan operating the plantation he inherited from his father, and William doing business at his own plantation, lumber mill, grist mill and store. According to family history, William, Sr. was a spy in the war.

John Huffington Sr. great-great-great grandfather of our subject, was an English sea captain, who came to the American colonies in 1700 and was the first of the Huffingtons in this country. Born in England about the year 1680, he became a man of considerable means at an early age. Family history says that in his early 20's he was a merchant on the high seas with seven sailing vessels under English registry. His first wife died and he lost the greater part of his wealth at the same time. He went security on a note for a friend who defaulted. Not long after he married Mary Carlisle. Leaving his children by his first wife, supposedly with relatives in England, he came to the Colonies and settled on a tobacco farm in Virginia.

Clinton S. Huffington served in the Civil War. He enlisted May 10, 1863, in Company K 9th Missouri Cavalry and was discharged July 13, 1865, at Benton Barracks, MO. His discharge papers describe him as 5' 10" tall, with dark complexion, grey eyes, dark hair and his occupation as farmer.

On October 29, 1871, at Eaton, MO, he was married to Nannie Deigal. She was born in May 1854 in Missouri. Her parents were natives of Germany. Their children are: Edwin Joshua (b-September 16, 1872 and was accidentally killed when working in the railroad yards at St. Joe, MO. January 22, 1890); Francis Marion (b-June 30, 1874 d-December, 1963); James Rosco (b-March 6, 1876 d-); Elizabeth B. (Ray) (b-July 21, 1878); Annie Dorcas (b-September 16, 1880 d-July 19, 1929); Nellie A. (Brown) (b-January 1, 1883 d-1948); George Vernon (b-September 22, 1888 d-December 2, 1934) and Wilbur Clinton (b-July 12, 1899).

They made the run into the Strip and homesteaded four miles west and two miles north of Perry (sw quarter of section 1 in Warren Valley township) Patent number 2597. The original patent in is the museum at Perry.

Clinton S. died October 2, 1931, at the age of 88 and his wife died in 1947 at the age of 92 years. They are buried in the Grace Hill cemetery with daughters, Bessie, Ona and Nellie.

Editor's Note: Wilbur Huffington died August 18, 1985.

Carl M. Humphrey
By Jewel Humphrey

Carl Monroe Humphrey was born April 29, 1908, on the farm which his grandfather, Christopher Columbus Humphrey, had homesteaded at the opening of the Cherokee Strip. He was the son of Cleveland Humphrey and

Carl and Jewel Humphrey - 1937.

Carrie Carter Humphrey. He has one sister, Ena May Howard. He attended Fair View rural school and graduated from Perry High School in 1925.

On May 22, 1937, he married Jewel Scoles of Hope, Arkansas, and Tonkawa, Oklahoma. They lived on a farm north of Perry (the old Prusa place) until 1940, when they bought a farm west of Morrison on the juncture of Black Bear Creek and Spring Creek. After the harsh, treeless prairie of his youth, the Black Bear farm looked like a green paradise to him. Years of back-breaking toil and heart breaking flood years never killed his love of the farm.

They had three sons, Theodore Carl, July 29, 1938; Christopher Carter, October 30, 1939; and Michael Houston, December 25, 1945.

Diversified farming and good conservationist practices saved the family during those first lean years. With the help of his growing sons, Carl grew corn, oats, barley, sorghum grains, soy beans, alfalfa, as well as wheat; he raised milking Shorthorn cattle and sold cream to Gold Spot Dairy of Enid; he raised pigs, chickens, and sometimes turkeys; he butchered and cured his own meats. In addition to a large garden, he set out an orchard: apples, peaches, cherries, pears, apricots, strawberries, and blackberries. So although there was little money, the family always ate well. Carl loved to brag to guests, "Everything on the table, we grew."

Floods, which came at any season, compounded his work, since the land had to be prepared and planted afresh after each flood. Other farmers had the same problems. So, under Carl's chairmanship, they banded together into what ultimately became the Black Bear Conservancy District of Garfield, Noble and Pawnee Counties. As the retention structures were built, the floods lessened in severity and duration.

Carl's forte was a good mind, coupled with the ability to reason with people, after listening to and judging all sides of a situation. Never impulsive, his patience and leadership ability were best shown by his seven years (5 as president on the Morrison Board of Education (1949-1956). Those were turbulent years when Morrison first began showing pangs of rebirth and progress. One of his proudest triumphs was the new school building, the first of many so that today Morrison has a school plant, the pride of all citizens.

Carl was instrumental in bringing better telephone service in to the community. He served on the Noble County Free Fair Board. He taught an adult class in the Morrison Methodist Church.

Although not a college graduate, Carl always championed education. He never urged any of his sons to become farmers. He was very proud of their academic success. Both Ted and Chris are Ph.D.'s (Doctor of Philosophy). Mike has his Bachelor of Arts degree and enough hours for a Masters but chose not to complete it. Carl loved his daughters-in-law. They were the daughters he never had. They are all different, yet have one thing in common; they all have at least one college degree. Ted married Linda Tufts, and they have two children: Merritt and Carter, who are presently in college. The four younger ones - Chris's two, and Mike's two, will undoubtedly be lured by the desire for more knowledge, wherever that may lead them. Chris married Carole Suggs, and they have two children: Brian and Caroline.

Carl had his lighter moments, too. He was an excellent dancer and had a remarkable card sense, particularly games invovling skill, such as bridge and poker. Later in life, he enjoyed bowling. Throughout his life, he read widely and well, being partial to history.

In 1977, he suffered a severe heart attack. On the advice of his physician, he sold his cattle and machinery, rented the farm land but continued to live on the farm. But he no longer felt useful and productive. He died June 16, 1980, and was buried at Mt. Carmel Cemetery within sight of the old homestead, place of his birth.

Such men as Carl Humphrey, quiet, unassuming, embued with a powerful work ethic and a strong sense of right and wrong, with civic and community pride, are often lost sight of in the pages of history; yet he and people like him are the heart and backbone of our country, the strength of our nation.

Christopher C. Humphrey
By Eddetta Beier Grant

Family legend has it that the first Humphrey of our particular line was the younger son of a titled family in England. Due to the laws of that time, the younger son would inherit very little of the family estate. My particular

Humphrey family in early 1900s. Front Row: Mary Postelwait, Lucinda, C.C., and Ella Silver. Back Row: Sam Postelwait, Cleveland Humphrey, Carria Carter Humphrey and Jake Silver.

ancestor decided to take his wife and seek their fortune in the American colonies. Little is known about the family until 1843, and the birth of C.C. Humhrey.

Christopher Columbus Humphrey was born on a farm in Iowa, on November 12, 1843, to David W. and Nancy Humphrey. He was married to Lucinda M. Godown on November 22, 1863. Approximately eleven years after their marriage, they moved to Cairo, Pratt County, Kansas. They continued to live there for four years.

In 1891, the family moved to Oklahoma while they waited for the opening of the Cherokee Strip. After the land run in 1983, Christopher C. secured a claim seven miles north and two miles west of Perry described as the SW ¼ of section 9-22N-1W, where he lived until his death on February 28, 1926. His wife, Lucinda, died of approplexy on March 2, 1917. Both were buried at Mt. Carmel cemetery north of Perry, Oklahoma. The first home on this claim was a sod house.

Six children were born to Christopher and Lucinda, namely: Effier, Walker, Cleveland, Ella, Belle, and Mary. Three of their children preceded them in death, and only three lived through adulthood: Ella Humphrey Silver, Mary Humphrey Postelwait, and Cleveland Humphrey, who was born May 9, 1884, in Van Buren county, Iowa.

On July 4, 1903, Cleveland was married to Carria Ollie Carter. She was born on January 21, 1883, in Campbell, Dallas County, Iowa, the daughter of Elijah Thomas Carter and Dicie Anna Fees Carter. Carria had traveled to Oklahoma Territory after the opening of the Strip to work as a maid or housekeeper for Bertha and Frank Daniels of Billings, Oklahoma.

In time, Cleveland took over the operation of the family farm. Two children were born to the marriage of Cleveland and Carria, namely: Ena May born June 22, 1904, and Carl Monroe born April 29, 1908. Cleveland continued to live on the family homestead until his death on September 1, 1945. After his death, his widow, Carria, sold the farm and bought a house at 623 Eighth Street, Perry, Oklahoma. She died August 1, 1972, and was also buried at Mr. Carmel cemetery.

My grandparents, Ena May Humphrey and Dewey Lee Howard were married on January 4, 1926, at Enid, Oklahoma and they had one daughter, Cleva Jo Howard.

View of homestead staked by C. C. Humphrey.

Cleveland Humphrey family in 1908. Ena May, Cleveland, Carria, and Carl Monroe held by Cleveland.

Carl Monroe Humphrey married Jewel Scoles on May 23, 1937, at Newkirk. They had three sons: Theodore Carl, Christopher Carter and Michael Houston. Carl Monroe died on June 16, 1980, and he, too, was buried at Mt. Carmel cemetery.

Christopher C. Humphrey helped achieve the quest for a brighter future in the new land. He also had a great love of fox hunts. Whenever he heard the hounds, he would leave whatever he was doing and join in the hunt, even if he was in the middle of plowing the field. His love of the land continues to this day among his descendants.

Jewel S. Humphrey
By Jewel Humphrey

I was born in Hope, Arkansas, August 18, 1917. My parents were James Summerfield Scoles and Martha (Houston) Scoles. My parents were divorced while I was a baby, so I never knew my father nor his family by a first wife. My own brothers and sisters (really half-brothers and half-sisters by my mother's first husband) were family to me and I have always loved them dearly.

I lived in Hope until I was graduated with honors in 1934. After a brief sojourn in Camden, Arkansas, I went to Tonkawa, Oklahoma, my eldest brother's home, in time to enroll in the spring semester (1936) at Northern Oklahoma Junior College (NOJC) as it was known then. I loved it there, although the work was easy after my rigorous high school training.

After only one semester, my brother was transferred to Great Bend, Kansas. Undaunted, I knew I must stay in Tonkawa, so I applied for and received an NYA (National Youth Administration) grant. Grading English themes and tests for two English teachers, I really earned my $20 a month. Somehow, I lived (existed?) on that princely sum. These were still Depression years and most of the students were hard up for money like me.

That fall I met Carl Humphrey, introduced by two good friends. We "clicked" right away. By February, 1937, we were engaged and were married May 22, 1937, as soon as the semester was over. Marriage was not an easy choice for me to make, since I must give up forever, I thought, my first love — my dream of college and a journalistic career.

Those first few years as a farmer's wife were not easy, but a bride's trials and tribulations, tragic then, funny now, belong to another story. Suffice to say that with a wise and understanding mother-in-law's aid and support, and much help from the Extension Service and the Home Demonstration Clubs, I

Carl and Jewel Humphrey, home after OSU commencement ceremony when Jewel received her Bachelor's degree. The white ribbon signifies election into Phi Kappa Phi, national honor society of Land Grant Colleges. It is the only decoration allowed worn with cap and gown.

became a fairly good facsimile of a farmer's wife.

We had three sons, Theodore, Christopher, and Michael, all bright, beautiful boys. We were always very proud of their accomplishments in school, in 4-H, in FFA, and in later life.

I had a simple creed: If you belong to an organization, then believe in it and work for it. I was not a "joiner".

I worked hard for the Morrison Methodist Church, teaching Sunday School classes, singing in the choir, acting as Children's Superintendent, organizing Christmas programs, helping in Bible schools. I worked hard for the WSCS (Women's Society of Christian Service): serving in various offices, leading study groups, working in food booths, helping to serve dinners and banquets to raise money for the church.

In the Oak Grove Home Demonstration Club, I served in various capacities, including being president, and later serving as president of the County Council. I was a 4-H sponsor and a member of the Noble County Choral Club. I particularly remember directing two plays which the Oak Grove Club presented to the Morrison community. As president of the County Council, a special memory was an appreciation Day, honoring Dr. D. F. Coldiron, a pioneer physician.

When my two oldest sons were in college, I suddenly decided I would return to college, after more than 20 years. There were no programs then to aid the older women in college. We made it, or not, strictly on our own merits. In my way, and time, I was a pioneer too.

My first semester I had a GPA of 3.5. I could do it! and I enjoyed every minute. Giving up my youthful desire to be a journalist, I took the educational courses required for a high school teacher. However, at the instigation of some of my college faculty friends who believed I belonged in college, I applied for and received a teaching assistantship in English and remained at OSU for over twenty years.

Those were happy years; I had the best of two worlds, commuting to OSU, I still had my home, husband, children; as student, teacher, academic advisor to English majors, I had meaningful work I enjoyed doing. Every day was a challenge and a joy.

I took early retirement in May, 1980, to be with my ill husband. However, he died in June, 1980. But I have no regrets about retiring. The University, the College, and the Department have all grown and it is not now the happy "family" it once was. It was the proper time to retire.

Sometimes, some Morrison "friends" have said, "Jewel, you were lucky." Perhaps; but might it not be that we make our own luck?

Charles A. Hunter
By Madge Hunter

Charles Arthur Hunter came to Billings in 1899, at the same time the community of White Rock was being located at that spot. He was born June 2, 1875 in Novelty, Missouri. His parents were Henry Jackson and Lavinda Hunter. They were natives of Illinois and Ohio. Charles (Ted) Hunter came to Billings via Enid with a friend who was a plasterer. They then walked from Enid to Billings. The two men did most of the plastering of the new town.

On September 15, 1904, he married Lena Elizabeth Sahland. Lena was born September 3, 1882, in Coatsburg, Illinois. Her family moved to Le Roy, Kansas. She then moved to Lamont, Oklahoma in 1900, where she was a typesetter. She came to Billings in February 1904.

Ted worked on a threshing crew and set up a saloon, at that time there were five saloons operating in Billings. When prohibition came with statehood, Ted opened a billard parlor which he operated for over 30 years. Following his retirement from the billard parlor he went to work for his sister-in-law in Yale, Oklahoma in Mable Dale hospital.

He was a member of the Knights of Pythias Lodge, Royal Neighbors. He was a member of the Christian Church.

Lena worked for Bill Francis Grocery Porter-Williams Dry Goods Store. When she first arrived she worked for Rose Henthorne in her milinary shop.

They had two children: Madge Bernadine (September 29, 1906) and Arthur Jackson (January 5, 1908). When Madge was eight months old the family moved into a house which Ted had built. Madge still lives in this house. The children attended school in Billings where both graduated from High School, Madge in 1924, Arthur in 1926.

In September 1954, Ted and Lena celebrated their 50th Wedding Anniversary. About 150 people attended the celebration. Ted died June 23, 1955 in the Hamill Osteopathic hospital in Fairfax, Oklahoma. Lena died in January 1979. They are buried in Union cemetery at Billings.

John Wilson Ivers
By Sophia Dahlberg

John Wilson Ivers, born August 13, 1881 in Lincoln, Nebraska, met John and Emma's daughter, Florence Mary Marshall in Perry, Oklahoma, where his father had been in the restaurant business. John's father was Leslie Ivers, born in July of 1855 in Indiana. His mother, Etta was born in November of 1856 in Iowa. John's brothers and sisters were Charles (November 1876), Jessie (February 1879), Chester (November 1884), Bessie (February 1886) and Grover (November 1888).

John Ivers and Florence Mary were married in Tulsa County, Tulsa, Oklahoma June 1, 1904. They moved back to Perry and John Ivers served as Fire Chief for two years. They moved to Ponca City in 1934. Their first child, Lorraine Catherine (Mary) Ivers was born in Perry, Oklahoma, September 10, 1905. She was born at home and delivered by Doctor Brengle. She married an Osage Indian, Hayes Little Bear, born December 19, 1882 (twenty years her senior) and they had two children, Hayesene Rose Little Bear, born April 14, 1926 in Tulsa, Oklahoma and Sophia Florence Little Bear, born September 4, 1928.

Elgin Wilson Ivers was born in Perry, Oklahoma July 26, 1907, the son

Florence Mary Marshall (Mrs. John Wilson Ivers) about 1900.

of John and Mary Ivers. Anthony Marshall Ivers was born October 10, 1911 in Oklahoma City and Nadine Catherine Ivers was born July 6, 1918 in Oklahoma City, Johnnie Leslie Ivers was born February 13, 1923 in Pawhuska, Oklahoma and Paul Hayes was born January 20, 1928 in Tulsa, Oklahoma.

Nadine Catherine Ivers married Ray E. Cox. They had four children, Raydean (Duncan), Cecil Edward Cox, Cathy (Grammer) and Nina (Eccles).

Anthony Marshall Ivers and his wife Alice had one son, Mike Ivers. Johnnie Leslie Ivers married Joy Marie Marak and they had seven children: Mary Leslie, Tony, Chris, Ricky, Gregg, Phil and Keven Ivers. Paul Hayes Ivers and his wife, Mary, had one son, Brett Ivers.

Betty L. James
By Betty (Ewy) James

Betty Lou Ewy was born September 17, 1931 in Noble County, the daughter of Luella Victoria (Chenoweth) and Harold Ewy. She attended Oak Grove rural school until the eighth grade, then Sumner for the 9th and 10th and finishing at Perry High School. She married Lenard Frank James April 6, 1951 at Perry, Oklahoma. Lenard was born February 12, 1931 in Noble County, the son of Kathrine Eva (Frank) and Clarence Franklin James. Lenard worked for the Oklahoma Department of Transportation as well as farming. Before her marriage Betty worked as a milk hand for John Frick and in the Monte Jones drug store in Perry. She is now Postmaster for the city of Morrison, Oklahoma.

Betty and Lenard had three children: Galen Ray, Dennis Delane and Donna Sue. Both were active in 4-H and FFA in Morrison, taking part in the livestock shows, the show animals and trophies and the Sloppy Joes. Lenard served on the Noble County Free Fair Board. He also was Little League baseball coach and the family attended the ball games.

They also had a foster child, Tammy Lou Massa, in their home for eight years. She changed all their lives. She was brought up in town and the living on a farm was a little tame for her.

Galen James married Nancy Fields and they are the parents of Joshua and Jeremy James.

Dennis James married Teri Garvie. Donna James married Kevin Jones. They are the parents of Levi and Mikila Jones.

Lenard and Betty seperated. On October 11, 1986 Betty married Billy Ray Price at the Morrison Methodist Church. The ceremony was followed by an informal wedding reception and dance at LeJunction, Bill's Corner, Highway 64 and 177 intersection.

Henry L. James
By Helen (James) Frank

Henry L. James was born in May 1836 in Philadelphia, Pennsylvania and died at Morrison, Oklahoma November 2, 1909. He was married in 1860 to Zerelda A. Edwards. She was born March 8, 1844 in Indiana and died February 2, 1904 in Morrison, Oklahoma. Both are buried in the Morrison cemetery. The federal census for 1900 shows Henry's parents both born in England and Zerelda's both born in Indiana.

A granddaughter, Dovie Johnson, said in 1977, that "they lived down south, came to Platte County, Missouri, then went to Kansas during the Civil War, returned to Platte County to raise their family, went to Stillwater, Oklahoma in 1893."

Henry and Zerelda made the "run" on September 16, 1893 and staked their claim on 160 acres, the northwest quarter of section 18 in Autry township near Morrison on the Black Bear Creek. They had five children, George H., Sidney Allen, Jessie M., Emma and Carrie.

George II. James (1861-1913) married Sarah L. Sales (1863-1935) and had ten children: Nannie (Curd); Leora married True Arnold; Minor; Willison; Ida married James Hoggatt; Clarence married Katherine Frank; Henry; George Ernie married Audry Gregory; Rhoda married Cecil Nichols; Bessie married Raymond Nichols. George and Sarah are buried in the Morrison cemetery.

Sidney Allen James was born March 20, 1863 in Platte County, Missouri. He married Elizabeth Short in Platte County in 1882. Their children were Mattie E. married James M. Boyston; Jessie Nola married first Julius Shiever, second ___ O'Donnell; Alta Mae married Archie A. Harding; Maud died at age 18 years in Morrison, Oklahoma; Dovie Cecila married first Joseph Emick second Isaac Johnson; Clyde Allen married Ivy Mae French.

Jessie M. James was born April 16, 1870 in Platte County, Missouri. He married Della P. Colvin in 1898. Their children were Louis V. who married Sylvia Wolff; Harry F. married Aileen McClure; Arthur L. married Gibble; Anna E. married Virgil Dover; Doris L. married Roy L. Tate; Helen L. married Christ Frank. Jessie died January 27, 1942. Della died April 5, 1948. They are buried in the Morrison cemetery.

Emma James was born at Edgerton, Missouri. She married Ezra Harmer. They lived on a farm near Glencoe. They had four children: Earie, Mary Ann, Vera and Joe. Emma later married Tom Beathers.

Carrie James was born in 1873 in Platte County Missouri. She married Chauncey Donart. They had one child Wilherta (Edgington). The Donarts at one time ran a hotel in Morrison, Oklahoma before they moved to Glencoe, Oklahoma.

My father, Jessie M. James was with his parents in the run and later bought the 160 acres from his father, Henry and raised his family, here. He was teased about his name being Jesse James. He always said that he held the horses while the other boys robbed banks. He would have made a good stand-up comedian. The men in Morrison, who had grown up with him, would see him coming down the street and would get some story started as they knew Jess, as they called him, would carry it on.

Richard James Jelinek
By Goldie Jelinek

Richard James Jelinek was born February 12, 1923 northeast of Morrison, Oklahoma. The oldest child of Louis and Lola (Swearingen) Jelinek. He went to the Prairie Center Grade School and attended Morrison High School. He was employed at the Farmers Union Feed Store when he was drafted into the Air Force in 1942. He served 3 years as a Glider Mechanic. 1½ years was served in Europe.

Goldie Mae Paulsen was born southeast of Hennessey, Oklahoma May 21, 1926. The oldest child of Bill and Ethel (Chartier) Paulsen. She moved to Morrison with her parents in 1938 at the age of 12. She attended school at Prairie Center and graduated from Morrison High School in 1944 and went to work at Southwestern Bell Telephone Co. in Ponca City.

Richard returned from the service December 7, 1945 and they were married December 30, in the United Methodist Church in Morrison. They are still member of the church. Richard went to work at the Continental Oil Co.

Goldie and Richard Jelinek.

in Ponca City, where they made their home.

Their first daughter, Gail Louise, was born March 31, 1947. She was injured at birth. She never walked or talked and was cared for like a baby till death on February 5, 1954.

The Jelineks bought 80 A. of land 3 miles north of Morrison in 1949 and moved back to Morrison. They farmed, raised cattle, raised most of their food, had chickens and sold eggs to the Stillwater Hatchery in Stillwater, Oklahoma. Richard was the substitute mail carrier for Morrison Post Office. They later bought more land around them.

Their second daughter, Linda Darlene, was born April 24, 1955. She went to school and graduated from Morrison High School in 1973. She worked for Southwestern Bell Telephone Co. in Stillwater till the office closed in 1975.

Goldie went back to work for the telephone company in 1956. She worked as a telephone operator in Perry, Stillwater, back to Ponca City and Tulsa after each office closed. Richard kept things going on the farm.

After open heart surgery in 1975, Richard quit farming and just raised cattle. He baled hay for feed and fed cattle cubes.

Linda married Philip Marlow in 1975. They own a business, Marlow Excavating, and live south of Bills Corner. They have two children, Philip Scott, born in 1975 and Angela Lynn, born in 1979.

The Jelineks have semi-retired. Goldie retired from Southwestern Bell in 1982. They have lived a happy rewarding life, a very rich one, just not money wise. They love to travel and own a travel trailer. They collect rocks and have a rock wall across one wall in their den. They especially enjoy Linda, Phil and the two grandchildren.

Mansfield Jerome

By Willa Mae Kanehl

Our grandfather, Mansfield Jerome, was born July 24, 1863, in Linn county, Missouri. Not too much is known about his youth, he had three brothers and two sisters and was the youngest son of Orrin Jerome Sr. At the age of 20, he married Cazar Hannon on February 15, 1883, and three sons were born to this union, Walter, Charles Frederick (my father), and Samuel Roscoe. Cazar passed away at a very early age leaving Mansfield with three sons to manage. He then married Ida Mae Trumbo and two more sons were born before they left Missouri, Orrin and Oscar.

We suppose at the age of 30, with a new family to raise he wanted to try

Mansfield Jerome Family. Seated: Mansfield and his wife, Ida, holding Bertha. Standing (L to R): Lee, Walter, Charles, Orin, Sam, Oscar and Frank.

his luck with farming in another area so he came to Oklahoma Territory to make the Cherokee Strip Run September 16, 1893. He went to Perkins, Oklahoma to borrow a buckskin horse named "Tag" from his sister Adalade's husband. Mr. Malloy had ridden this horse a short time before to homestead a quarter of land in the Sac and Fox Territory near Perkins. Grandfather wanted a surefooted mount and "Tag" proved himself to be just that when they made the run. As soon as he had filed a claim on the SW 15-20N-2W at the Land Office in Perry, (Noble county), he started building a one-room frame house and a sod barn. The barn may have come first, since the only horsepower available travelled on four hooves, as did the dairy, and represented major investments. The house, at 14 x 20 seems a little cramped by today's standards, but it served its purpose. With his buildings ready for winter, Grandfather returned to Missouri for the family's possessions.

In March of 1894, he sent for his family to come to Orlando by train. Normally, he and his mule went to Orlando every week to get supplies and mail. Orlando, just before the run, had been a metropolis of three saloons, two grocery stores, a bank along with a hardware store, jail, lumber yard and a drug store. So he could get anything he needed at a distance of about six miles.

First home on the Jerome claim (S½ - 8 - 20N - 2W).

It is said that the mule, having a mind of its own, visited every homestead between his place and Orlando, whether grandfather wanted to or not.

The one week that he missed his excursion to Orlando was the very week his family arrived by train. Since Grandmother had no idea how to find the homestead, and no transportation, she went to the livery stable for help. There she hired a surry with a canopy driven by one Jim Reed, who was familiar with the country. At that time, the roads had been surveyed and staked, but not graded, and strangers sometimes incurred the wrath of a settler by unknowingly driving across his homestead.

Mansfield and Ida Mae settled down to make their homestead a home. Two more sons, Frank and Lee, and a daughter, Bertha, were added to their family before statehood. The livestock they raised for the market they drove to the railroad at Orlando for shipment to Kansas City, Wichita, or Oklahoma City.

A preacher, one Reverend Sewel, appeared soon after the settlers and, with their help, hauled rock to build the Lawnview Congregational Church (an early day interdenominational church).

Mansfield and Ida Mae later expanded their farming operation and moved to the S½ 8-20N-2W and built a large barn (100 by 105) which he later rented to Huston & Elliott Contractors. Huston & Elliott were early day dirt contractors in the Lucien Oil Field using horses and mules for power.

Grandfather passed away May 21, 1920, and Grandmother in 1947.

Walter farmed and lived in Missouri. Charles, Samuel, Oscar and Lee all farmed and lived around Perry and Orlando. Orin was a security officer and lived in Stillwater. Frank was nicknamed "Pinky", he worked in the oilfields and lived all over Oklahoma. Bertha Jerome Farr lived in Nebraska.

Barn on the Jerome claim (S¹₂ - 8 - 20N - 2W).

Think all early day land owners had about the same philosophy, "hold on to your land, they do not make anymore".

We hold a Jerome reunion every two years trying to keep alive our knowledge of our ancestors, pass it on to the younger part of the family and teach us to be humble from our early heritage.

Henry L. Johnson
By Gail Johnson

The Henry Leonard Johnson family moved to Oklahoma from Iowa in the early part of 1909, where their first child was born in Ponca City and by 1910 they had moved to Perry.

Henry's parents, Louis Johnson (Swedish name possibly John Bengston), and Johanna Matilda Svenson both came to the United States from Sweden. Hannah, as Johanna was called, came before 1876 to Iowa with her parents, and Louis came before 1877. They were married August 23, 1877 in the Swedish Lutheran church in Ottumwa, Iowa. There were two other siblings born to Louis and Hannah but they both died young. They are as follows: Oscar Algatt, August 16, 1883; Gustaf Harrie Cleophas, September 25, 1885, their deaths are Oscar December 30, 1886; and Gustaf, July 22, 1886. Henry was born August 22, 1887, and he married Elsie Mae Crowder on January 16, 1908 in Buxton, Iowa. This town does not exist at the time of this writing. Louis died in 1921 in Iowa, Hannah in 1901 in Iowa.

When Henry and his family moved to Perry they established a grocery store with Henry's Father-in-law, Martin L. Crowder on the east side of the Perry square. It was a prosperous business and continued to do well even after Mr. Crowder's death in 1931. Henry and his sons maintained the store, until they were called into service of the military forces. At that time Henry closed the store, about 1942; what type of work, if any, that Henry did, until 1945, is unknown. In 1945, when his son, Leo, returned to Perry and his family, from the service, they jointly opened the Perry Cafe and Bus station on the southeast corner of the square. They both ran the station and cafe until 1953, when Henry retired and Leo became the Perry Postmaster.

Henry and Elsie lived at 722 Grove in Perry most of their lives and truly enjoyed collecting beautiful things. They had a very large collection of salt and pepper shakers totalling about 1000 pairs or more at one time. They were very religious people and were members of the First Christian Church.

One thing that stands out about Elsie is that she loved the color of purple, all shades of purple. She had many dresses and a large collection of jewelry that had the various shades of purple in them. One thing that Elsie did accomplish was to have a booklet published with poetry in it that she wrote, also some of Grace Noll Crowell's work. Henry was a very calm and reserved individual who loved his family very much, but also ruled with a very strong hand in many matters. He was a man who believed in the power of the dollar and gave one of his granddaughters a silver dollar on her birthday for the last three years of his life.

Elsie Mae died on October 15, 1958 and Henry died on May 8, 1960. The children born to this union are as follows; Opal E. (Korn) February 5, 1909, in Ponca City; Leo Deverne January 1, 1911, Perry; Merle Gordon, April 28, 1913; Jesse Gail, August 10, 1915; Clyde Henry, March 28, 1921. All except Opal were born in Perry.

Opal E. married John W. Korn, June 6, 1937; to this union there were two children born: Jo Elaine (Royse) July 26, 1939 and Jean Ellen (Fent) September 3, 1941. Opal died September 15, 1966 in Edmond, Oklahoma. John Korn died May 6, 1985 in Edmond, Oklahoma.

Leo Devern married Hortense Irene Bullock in Caldwell, Texas, on June 6, 1934. There were three sons born to this union as follows: Charles Leonard, October 21, 1938; Ray Alan October 12, 1940; and Robert Gail (Robbie) December 7, 1943.

Leo and his family opened a fruit market on the southeast corner of the square which served Perry until Leo had to serve his country in 1943. He served his time in the service and on his return to Perry, he and his father Henry opened the Perry Cafe and Bus Station on the southeast corner of the square which ran until 1953 as I stated before. Then Leo became Perry's Postmaster for 23 years until his retirement in 1976. Leo died October 10, 1985 in Enid, Oklahoma. Hortense died December 16, 1984 in Enid, Oklahoma.

Merle Gordon married Doris Webb, Stillwater, Oklahoma December 24, 1936 in Perry. Nothing else is known about this member of the family. He died in September, 1980 in Dallas, Texas.

Jesse Gail married Dorthy E. Durbin in Perry, on March 27, 1945. There were three children born to this union:

Johnson Family 1913 (L to R): Elsie, Leo, Opal, Henry, Merle in Elsie's lap.

Jerry Gene, December 12, 1946; Gail Ann, June 12, 1949 and Larry David, April 16, 1951.

Jesse worked for Fraileys Inc. for 25 years as the office manager. He maintained his home at 710 13th Street, with three children to care for and raise. He served longer over seas than any other service man of Noble County in WW II. He died January 25, 1974, Perry, Oklahoma.

Clyde Henry married Nadine McKeever June 16, 1943, Perry. Three children were born to this union: Nancy Clydine, November 6, 1947; Henry Kevin, December 9, 1950; and Virginia Mae, June 10, 1955.

Clyde Henry and his family have lived in Sharon, Kansas for many years and continue to do so, with some of the family living in other parts of the state of Kansas. He has been a farmer for these years, working with his father-in-law.

The Johnson name can be remembered for the service it rendered through the selling of food products, food service, and bus service. Plus the thoughtful and courteous service given by the postal service during Leo's time as postmaster.

Plus Jesse's name was known for his work with the Frailey Corp. and his wife, Dorthy was known during the late 1970s and early 1980s as the flower lady at the T.G.&Y. store in Perry.

Hortense and Leo were also known for their generous giving of their home and time for international students from O.S.Y. They also supported the Y.M.C.A. consistently.

Both Leo and Jesse were very involved with Boy Scouts and all functions pertaining there to, serving as leaders and as christian guides.

When Louis came to the U.S. it was under unusual circumstances. All of the story is not really known. But when he got to the U.S. he did change his name from John Bengston (His Swedish name, the spelling unknown) to Louis Johnson a name that a great deal of people had in the Iowa area. We can only guess that he did this in the late 1870s.

Robert C. Johnson
By Bertha Kemnitz

Robert Curtis Johnson was born January 10, 1872, in Gallipolis, Ohio, one of eight children of Susan and William Johnson. The family moved to Bigelow, Marshall county, Kansas, then on to Oklahoma in 1889, when Old Oklahoma was opened for settlement. They homesteaded a farm seven miles west of Orlando.

Robert helped with the farming and taking care of livestock, and all the chores that have to be done on a farm. He worked for the neighbors whenever help was needed, such as clearing land, chopping wood, fencing, putting up new buildings or working in the field.

When the Cherokee Strip was opened for settlement, Robert and two of his brothers, Richard and Hutch, decided to make the run. On September 16, 1893, Robert was on the starting line north of Orlando, in a cart, driving "Old Lucey." He hoped to get a farm five miles north and two west of Orlando. Another man claimed the same land, and the dispute was settled by Robert paying him $10. His two brothers had homesteaded one mile further south, so they were happy to be in the same neighborhood.

He rode horseback ten miles to Perry to file his claim with the Federal Land Office, then returned and started building a one room clapboard house. He cleared some land, chopped wood for the winter, and exchanged work with the neighbors.

As soon as the house was finished, he, his wife, Isabelle and her widowed mother moved in. Isabelle was born in Maysville, Missouri, December 14, 1871, the daughter of Jay Hockenberry and his wife, Elizabeth. They moved by covered wagon to South Haven, Kansas, then to Oklahoma in 1889, where he staked a homestead west of Orlando. Isabelle also made the run but was disqualified on account of her age. Her father, a disabled Civil War Veteran, died a few years later. Isabelle and her mother farmed the land until she married and they moved to the homestead in the Cherokee Strip.

Original house on Johnson homestead (L to R): Robert, Lev, Isabelle and Jennie about 1898.

They brought household goods, a few cows and chickens and Isabelle's riding pony with them. By living frugally, they made it through the winter, and by spring had plowed and prepared some land for planting spring crops and a vegetable garden. Their tools consisted mainly of an axe, saw, hammer, shovel, walking plow and a hoe.

The land was fertile, consisting mostly of level prairie with a few creeks and wooded areas, suitable for farming, especially small grain crops, and had good grass for livestock.

Providing a good supply of water for household and livestock was often a problem, but after a short time water wells and cisterns supplied the household, and ponds and creeks made water available for livestock. Candles and oil lamps furnished light for the homes, and a wood and coal stove was used for both heating and cooking.

The Johnson family was close knit, all working together and sharing success or failure. Although the children carried their share of the work, they also enjoyed a happy life. There was hunting, fishing, horseback riding, swimming, skating, sleigh riding, games of all kinds and a great deal of "make believe" and "play like".

The money received for cream, butter, and eggs was used to buy needed groceries, such as sugar, flour, salt, coffee, etc. If there was any money left over, it was used to buy material for clothing. Isabelle was a good seamstress and made most of the clothes for the family members. Most of the underclothes and many other items were made from the "Pride of Perry" flour sacks.

Robert and Isabelle saw many changes take place during their lifetimes. They got their first telephone in 1912, their first car, an Oakland, in 1917, a Ford tractor in 1919, and electricity in their farm home in 1948. They retired from farming before combines were available, so still harvested with a binder and threshing machine.

They retired in 1920, sold their livestock and machinery at public auction, bought a house in Perry and moved to town. After three years, they moved back to the farm but did not farm the land.

Robert passed away September 19, 1929. Isabelle continued to live on the

The Robert and Isabelle Johnson family — First Row (L to R): Clyde, Sue, Betty. Second Row (L to R): Manila, Robert, Isabelle, Elizabeth Hockenberry, Bertha. Back Row (L to R): Jennie, Lev.

farm for awhile, then rented it to their son, Clyde. She then made her home with a daughter, Betty Kirkhart, who lived nearby, but spent some time with each of her other children. She passed away December 30, 1958. Robert and Isabelle were parents of eight children: Mrs. Jennie (M.E.) Frueh, Lev C. Johnson, Mrs. Manila (William) Adams, Mrs. Bertha (George) Kemnitz, Clyde R. Johnson, Mrs. Sue (H.C.) Kasl, Mrs. Betty (Dale) Kirkhart, and Mrs. Alma (Harry) Edgar.

Ethel L. Johnston
By Mildred Highfill

Ethel L. Littleton, wife of Henry S. Johnston, was born May 24, 1890 at Beloit, KS, the daughter of McKendree and Ema (Strandberg) Littleton. Both of her parents were college graduates and school teachers. She attended schools at Mankato, KS; San Jose, CA; Colonial Beach, VA; Thompson Business College and art classes at Corcoran Art Gallery, Washington, DC.

She was secretary to Senator Stephen B. Elkins of West Virginia at the age of 17. When the San Francisco earthquake occurred, her parents moved to California and on the advice from her father, she came to Oklahoma as a "chance in a lifetime" to be in on the organization of a new state. She hired as a secretary in the state senate, met Henry S. and quoted Mrs. Johnston: "Here I am".

She was very active in Perry as well as many state organizations. Some of her activities include: the American Red Cross where she served more than 20 years as well as being the first Noble county chairman. She was a state and local officer of the Order of Eastern Star for 35 years. She was Grand secretary for 25 years full time.

She was president of many Perry organizations. These included the Perry Progress Club, the Parent-Teacher Association, Band Mothers, P.E.O. and the Carnegie Library. In 1918, she was the first president of the Camp Fire Girls and Guardian of three groups. She was the first mother Advisor in Perry and was a charter member and first president of the Noble County Historical Society.

Her hobbies were nature study and physical culture which included a daily five mile walk. She also painted in oils and was quite talented. She lived in the modest house which was the home of herself and Governor Johnston for a number of years. Her last years she lived with her daughter, Nell, where she died in 1977. She is buried in Grace Hill cemetery.

Henry S. Johnston
By Mildred Highfill

Henry Simpson Johnston, 7th governor of Oklahoma, was born December 30, 1867, in Evansville, Indiana, in the same house as his father, Matthew Simpson Johnston. Matthew was born February 13, 1843. Matthew was married to Jennie M. Lodge. Jennie was born September 2, 1848 in New Albany, Indiana, the youngest of ten children. Her parents were natives of England and Newfoundland. In the spring of 1869, Matthew, Jennie and Henry moved to a claim 9 miles west of Erie, Kansas. Here, Amy was born July 10, 1870. It was here, too, that Henry herded sheep. On January 5, 1876, William Walter Johnston was born in Erie, Kansas where Matthew had a grocery business. In his ledger, Matthew records his father as being, Arthur Mc-Johnston, while he and his siblings are Johnstons. Jennie died May 10, 1901 in Erie. Matthew died December 22, 1905 in Erie.

Ethel L. Johnston in her campfire leader's dress.

Henry S. Johnston during his governorship.

Henry was educated in the common schools of Neosho Co. Kansas. He attended Baker's University and Methodist College at Balwin, Kansas. A diary kept by him when he was seventeen shows his patriotism and his admiration for the leaders of his country. He studied law in the office of C. A. Cox and J. A. Stratton, Erie, Kansas and John A. Deweese, Denver, Colorado. He was admitted to the bar in 1891 in Denver. When his brother, Will, had typhoid fever, he quit his practice to come home to Kansas and nurse him back to health.

He came to Perry, Oklahoma, shortly after the opening of the Cherokee Strip, hung out his shingle as an attorney and lived the rest of his life here except for the two years spent in the Goveror's Mansion.

Henry S. Johnston, Democrat, was elected to the Territorial Legislature in 1897-98. He was County Attorney for Noble county 1901-1904. He was a member of the Constitutional Convention for the state of Oklahoma in 1906. When a member of the first State Senate of Oklahoma from Payne and Noble counties he presided as President Pro Tempore. At the National Democratic Convention in Baltimore, Maryland in 1912, he nominated Woodrow Wilson for President of the U. S.

In the fall of 1926, he was elected Governor of Oklahoma and was the first governor to live in the Governor's Mansion.

He had made many political enemies and impeachment proceedings were brought against him on ten counts. All but one were dropped, and he was impeached January 21, 1929, for general incompetency in office. Three years later, he was elected state senator from Noble county and served for a term of four years. He was much in demand as a speaker on various and sun-

Governors mansion taken from Oklahoma State Capitol steps in 1925. The mansion is no longer visible from this point due to development in the area.

dry occasions. He was a good friend of the Otoe-Missouria Indians.

On June 20, 1909, in Guthrie, Oklahoma, he married Ethel L. Littleton of Washington, D.C. They adopted and raised four children: Nell, Mrs. Joe Burba; Reva, Mrs. A.L. Thurman; Gertrude, Mrs. M.M. Walton; and Robin.

Henry S. Johnston served the Knights of Pythias of Oklahoma as their First Grand Chancellor of the state after statehood. For six years he served the masonic bodies of Oklahoma as Grand Orator of the lodge and again as Grand Mastor for 1924-1925. He died January 7, 1965 at the age of 97, still spry and mentally alert. He was cremated January 12, 1965, and his ashes buried in Grace Hill cemetery, Perry, Oklahoma.

A portion of U.S. Highway 77 was designated in May 1965 as the Henry S. Johnston Memorial Highway. This segment of the highway is between the intersection of U.S. 77 and Interstate 35, east to the intersection of 15th and Terry Avenue in Perry, a distance of 1.5 miles. A bronze plaque had been mounted on a concrete base and placed on this road. His first office furniture and personal library is in the Henry S. Johnston Library and Cherokee Strip Museum at Perry, Oklahoma.

Ernest W. Jones
By Mildred Highfill

Ernest W. was the only one of the six children of Homer C. Jones to come to Oklahoma. He was born in April 1870 in Ohio according to the 1900 census for Noble County, Oklahoma Territory. Ernest W. Jones came to Perry at the opening and hung out his shingle as a lawyer, as the junior partner of Jones, Scothorn and Jones.

In addition to the practice of law, he served for 10 years as editor and publisher of the *Perry Republican*, one of the first newspapers in Perry. He served the country nine and a half years as county judge being elected in 1923, 1925 and 1935.

Judge Jones was an authority on the history of Perry and Noble County. In 1923, he wrote a small book on the history of Perry. Following is an excerpt from this book:

"And so thirty-eight years ago next September 16, was a benign, propitious, fateful, auspicious, eventful but at any rate a wonderful day. "Perfectly Satisfactory" as the wise lady said when she viewed the marvelous Grand Canyon of Colorado. This was our birthday, with stage setting of a dust ridden townsite and barren prairies, marked by cow paths and trails of Indians and traders, a crude network of our pioneer highway system. An occassional dugout of the cowman, the deserted corral, an acre here and there once cultivated by the nomadic tenant, Indian or squaw man, the only visible signs of half civilization. The prairie dog and she wolf, sole promoter of townsite population and disturbed only in their daily routine by lumbering herds driven northward, feeding as they slowly traveled or by the invasion of the Indian hunting party in the fall roundup of game for the winter sustenance.

The rank blue stem nods sleepily to the southern breeze and the raucous crow above croaks felicitations and good bye as he passes swift winged across the strip of solitude to his feeding ground of the corn fields in civilized Kansas.

Then at noon of that September day, dry and dusty, came the pistol shot and then transformation. To us that experienced the event, the wildest of wild people in all history in action. Thousands upon thousands of the masses crazed in excitement, moved in frantic disorder yet within the hour came the reserve. Within the afternoon, unbelievable and miraculous, came order and repose the recoupment of senses, and from the mob, leaderless at noon, before sunset developed leaders. Out of the confusion arose government.

Barren prairies became homesteads, then farms. The prairie dog and she wolf scampered ahead to evade the encroachment of man, the builder and maker of country homes, of towns and cities.

Roads and highways brought to the ideal of smoothness for the speed lover in his gas propelled modern vehicle displaced the cowpath and punchers lonesome trail. The blooded white face and Shorthorn outlawed the long horned ranger and the pedigreed Percheron contentedly munches his alfalfa where the rantankerous cow pony, picketed by his sleeping master, to sound the alarm of rustlers or of coming storms, was the pride and financial market basis of the pioneer judges of horseflesh.

Those days when Perry was a city of tents and canvas are but of memory. But nature has dealt kindly with the survivors and their posterity and this day we should rejoice. The "Sooner" has been displaced by the "Substantial Citizen" and the "How you come in" is obsolete. We are all one people and of that class that can forgive and forget, of the biggest, warmest hearts ever created in mankind and peculiar to our own grandest country on God's footstool.

May our progress continue without contention, bitterness and strife. Let concerted effort, void of harshness, enmity or jealous motive be our slogan and to work in unison and harmony that our next step in history making may reflect upon us with the same satisfaction and glory as the past has upon those pioneers who withstood the hardships, poverty and disappointments to bring Noble County to the marvelous development that we now enjoy."

On April 23, 1938, Judge E. W. Jones fell and suffered a broken hip. He was going up the steps in the Masonic building when the accident occured. Judge Jones was 69 years old and had never married. He died in August of 1938 and his obituary says the Methodist Church in Perry was filled to overflowing when his funeral was held at 5 o'clock. Following services at the church, a band directed by Dr. W. C. Marshall and containing many members who played in the National Guard Band for several years with Judge Jones, led a funeral procession around the square. Taps was sounded at Grace Hill cemetery where the burial rites were conducted.

Homer C. Jones
By Mildred Highfill

Homer Clark Jones served as one of the Senators from the eighth District of Ohio. He was born in McArthur of what was then Athens county but was later Vinton county in 1834. He was raised on a farm and attended the common schools and the Ohio University.

Before he completed the collegiate course, he was elected Surveyor of his county in 1858, in which capacity he served until 1861, meanwhile pursuing the study of law under the jurist, Hon. John P. Plyley. Admitted to practice in the spring of 1861, he was appointed Clerk of Court, for the Territory of Nevada, but when the Civil War broke out he entered the volunteer service as 2nd Lieutenant of Company B, 18th Ohio, which he helped to recruit. In the spring of 1862, he was detached to serve in the signal corps, and was assigned to the staff of General Thomas J. Wood. Afterwards, he was Aid-de-Camp to Major General Negley. Just before the battle of Stone River, he was ordered to report to General George H. Thomas, with whom he remained until that of-

Mrs. Homer C. Jones (on left) with unidentified friend.

Pleasant A. Jones Family.

ficer took command of the army of the Cumberland. He then went back to the line, at his own request, and immediately after the battle of Mission Ridge, took command of his company as Captain.

After the war, he resumed the law in McArthur and in 1868 was elected to the Senate from the 8th District but his election was successfully contested in the next election but in 1870 he again was elected to a seat in the Senate.

The following is a quote from the Biographical Notices of State Officers and members of the Fifty-Ninth General Assembly of Ohio published in 1871. "As a speaker, he is ready, witty, and at times truly eloquent. His tribute to General Thomas is perhaps his best oration, and received flattering acknowledgments not only from his fellow-Senators, but from General Wood and other distinguished soldiers who knew that great Captain. His ability to advocate a cause clearly shown during the struggle over the Soldier's orphans home, and on a parlimentary battle made his inimitable "Cardiff Giant Speech" (Someone has written 8 hours here in pencil).

He is described in this publication thus: "Mr. Jones is 5 feet and 10 inches in height; rather slight, but exceedingly well proportioned and athletic, has dark complexion and Roman features."

Homer C. Jones came to Perry at the opening of the strip with his wife, Louisiana and his son, Ernest W. Louisiana was born in September 1840 in Ohio. The G.A.R. (Union Veterans of the Civil War) was named for Homer Clark Jones. Homer C. Jones died April 22, 1894 in Perry and was buried in the Grace Hill cemetery. Louisiana F. Jones lived with her son, Ernest until her death in 1927.

Pleasant A. Jones

By Wilma (Jones) Maxwell

Pleasant Armstead Jones was born December 23, 1841, in the state of Tennessee. He was the son of Armstead Jones who was born October 31, 1808 in Virginia. (his mother's name, date of birth and death unknown). After Armstead's wife passed away, he came to live with P.A. and family on their farm southwest of Morrison and he resided there until his death on February 27, 1901. He was buried in the Morrison cemetery.

While still a young man, P.A. moved with his parents from Tennessee to Stevenson, Alabama where he lived until the beginning of the Civil War. He enlisted in the Confederate Army and served four and one half years in the Army. It was told, he served in Arkansas and fought in the Pea Ridge Battle.

On December 27, 1866, P.A. married Hannah Marie Copenhaver (born June 5, 1844 in Missouri). The couple were married near Osceola, St. Clair County, Missouri. While they lived in Missouri, the following children were born: Thomas A. (Tom) Jones, born September 14, 1867-died July 10, 1931 in Illinois: Martha Catherine Jones (Osborne) born October 27, 1868-died September 10, 1947-buried in Wichita, Kansas; Andrew Jackson (Jack) Jones born April 25, 1871-died October 2, 1947 buried in Morrison cemetery; George Allen Jones born June 15, 1874-died February 15, 1958 buried in the Sumner cemetery; Nancy Elzora (Ella) Jones (Williams) born December 10, 1875-died February 4, 1949-buried in Wichita, Kansas; William Clemons (Will) Jones- born July 30, 1878-died November 30, 1957-buried in Sumner cemetery.

In 1880, P.A. moved his family from Misouri to Douglas, Kansas. While living in Kansas the following children were born: James Gilbert Jones-born February 11, 1881-died April 23, 1966 in Arkansas; Charles Clifford Jones-born December 31, 1883-died March 2, 1947-buried in Sumner cemetery; Pleasant P. Jones born May 27, 1886-died March 23, 1974-buried in Wichita, Kansas; Sarah Myrtle Jones (Bazzel) (Clark)-born April 29, 1889-died February 18, 1976-buried in Glencoe cemetery. One daughter born to P.A. and Hannah died in infancy.

In 1893, the famiy came by covered wagon to Oklahoma settling on an eighty acre farm southwest of Morrison where they lived until their death. Both P.A. and Hannah became members of the Christian Church in their early life.

The family would gather on Sundays for a dinner at P.A. and Hannah's home. With 9 boys, they frequently got into political discussions. Some would take opposing views regardless of what they really felt. However, most of the time spent at Granddad and Grandma's house was a very pleasant time.

P.A. died December 31, 1920 and Hannah died January 7, 1933. They both are buried in the Morrison cemetery.

Christian Just

By Melvern S. Rupp

Christian Just made the Cherokee Strip Run of September 16, 1893. His son-in-law, Karl Haak, his future son-in-law Jacob Rupp, and Daniel Rupp, brother of Jacob, made the run with him. Christian and Karl staked claims northeast of Morrison in Noble county.

Christian Just was born February 23, 1844, near Schmoroffless, Poland. The Russian Czar encouraged settlement in Russia by offering good concessions to settlers, so Christian migrated to Russia. The next Czar withdrew the concessions and made conditions difficult for the immigrants.

Christian had a wife and children at the time he was drafted into the Russian army to serve seven years. While in the army he learned several languages which aided him while traveling to America. Not allowed to communicate with his family during his army service, after he was discharged he arrived home to learn that his entire family had starved to death.

Christian and Wilhelmina lived in the dug-out until 1910 when Whilhelmina died. Soon after her death, Christian built a three-room frame house where he continued to live until his death in 1926.

Amelia was the only child who did not marry a local citizen. She married a man in Wichita, Kansas. They had one child. When he was three years old, the child, Fred, was put on a train to Perry with a tag tied to his coat with identification and instructions. There Christian met him and raised him as a son rather than a grandson.

Marie and Karl Haak lived near Morrison. Luise married Jacob Rupp and lived near Lucien. Fredrick married Philipina Keehn and lived near Morrison. Emma married Steven Shiever and lived near Morrison.

Although there were only five children there were thirty-one grandchildren of Christian and Wilhelmina. Most have remained in or near Noble County.

He then married Wilhelmina Herman who had imigrated to Russia from Germany. She was born September 2, 1853. Wilhelmina was well educated and at the time of their marriage, she was a purchasing agent for the Russian government. From this union five children were born; Marie, Amelia, Luise, Fredrick and Emma.

Less than one and a half years before the Run, Christian arrived in Kansas with his family from Russia. They migrated from near Kiev, Ukraine. Due to restrictions on emigration the family left Russia by traveling at night and hiding by day. While on the ship as they were coming to America, they were convinced by a man who called himself a company trustee to care for their money. When they were ready to leave the ship neither the man nor their money could be found. They were pennyless when they reached Halstead, Kansas. Marie, the oldest child, was 18 and Emma, the youngest child, was 11 when they arrived in Kansas. Marie was already married to Karl Haak and had a newborn baby when they accompanied Christian to America. They first settled in Halstead, Kansas.

After staking their homestead claims, Christian and Karl went to Perry to file their claims. They remained in line there for two days and nights to file. At the office, Karl learned someone else had already filed for his claim, but Christian got his claim.

Since Karl Haak failed to get his claim, Karl and Marie lived with Christian and Wilhelmina. Christian Just and Karl built a sod house on Christian's farm, retured to Kansas and brought their families to the farm. The sod house soon collapsed in a rainy period. The men quickly built a dug-out where they lived for several years. The next three children of Karl and Marie were born in the dug-out home.

Joseph Z. Keaton
By Mildred Highfill

Joseph Z. Keaton was born near Terre Haute, Indiana, October 9, 1836. When he was 19 years of age, he went with his father to California, where he remained seven years. During his stay on the coast the Civil War broke out and he enlisted in the California Battalion, serving his country faithfully as a Union soldier, was honorably discharged in the autumn of 1865. After the war, he returned to Indiana and was married to Lydia Shirly on June 21, 1886. They had two sons and two daughters: Joseph, Rosa (Jones), Birdie K. (Brafford) and Jessie Bert Keaton.

Shortly after he returned to Indiana, he was engaged in milling and became expert in this occupation. After more than 25 years in the milling business he came to Oklahoma in 1893. On March 14, 1894, he filed a soldier's declaratory statement and obtained the land W.E. Merry had staked in the run. Mr. Merry had signed a contract to teach school in Missouri so he hurried back to his work without proving up on his claim. This farm was the southwest ¼ of section 7 in Watkins township. After the Keatons moved to Perry they lived in the first house east of the Seventh Day Adventist Church. At that time it was the South Methodist Church.

Joe, the oldest son, was about 18 when he came to Perry. Ernie Jones, in his "Early Day History of Perry, Oklahoma," gives this account. "On the government square the first show that came to town spread its spacious tents. It was the Cutler Comedy Company, a family of musicians and performers who had turned out from Edmond. Joe Keaton broke in on the company and his acting was so bad that Cutler fired him without notice, being next to the fact that all the applause Joe got for his bum work came from a bunch of rounders who had been brought in by Joe as boosters. Joe afterward got even with Cutler by marrying his daughter, Myra, from this union was born three children, the eldest being Buster, the famous film comedian."

Joe never lost his ambition and when his first son, Buster, was about 4 years old, he had a very good vaudeville act and came back to Perry to show people he was not so bad. Buster, who had been "born in a trunk" in Kansas while his parents traveled doing their act, always considered his grandparents' house as his home. Joe finally got on the Orpheum Circuit, where the act was considered very good. Then when the Child Labor Law was passed they went to Europe until little Buster could work in the united States, then they came back to Perry and gave an entertainment at the old opera house and it was very good. This time there was another with them, Little Jingle, another son and he had a little stunt of his own and nearly stole the show.

Joseph Z. Keaton died in Perry July 20, 1909, and is buried in Grace Hill cemetery in Perry. His wife's death and place of burial is not known.

When Buster Keaton became famous, his father, Joe, joined him in Hollywood where the father acted as supporting characters in the comedies. Bert Keaton, Joe's brother, married Mame Hurley whose father, David A. Hurley, had homesteaded east of Perry. He joined the rest of the Keatons in California.

The city council of Perry declared May 7, 1957, as Buster Keaton Day when the premiere of "The Buster Keaton Story,' Paramount's film of the life of Buster Keaton, was held in Perry.

Hattie Gang Keele
By Vangie Keele Clendenin

Hattie Fern Gang Keele, born August 6, 1894, is well, alert and active in her family, friends, and church activities. She has excellent recall from early day names and places; she is a first descendant from her father, Fred Gang, who made the run, September 16, 1893. I am her daughter, writing this as she relates it to me in her home in Edmond, Oklahoma, while she looks at old, cherished photographs and names the faces and places. Hattie Gang attended Hughes School and County Normal Institute in Perry. One summer she stayed with L.C. Rosa family, remembers well, daughter Zoma Rosa Tate. And another summer with M.B. Schultz family, and remembers daughters, Edna Schultz Daniels and Ethel Schultz Foster. Hattie taught at Hughes School 1912-1913 and still has her Teacher's Contract signed by: F. Feken, Director; W.W. Cowell, Clerk; Arthur Hoppe, Treasurer. Then taught at the White school September to November 1913, and lived with Mr. and Mrs. George White, they had no children, until she was married to Jesse Keele, November 16, 1913. They had met at his sister's home, Nan and Ben Hughes, who lived across the road and about ½ mile south of the Gang home. Jesse Keele was a Telegraph Operator for Santa Fe Railroad.

Hattie's Grandfather Gang came to America from Germany with his parents when a small boy. He was married in 1830, to her grandmother, who also, had come to America from Germany. To this union, one daughter,

Hattie Fern Gang Keele - 1913.

Mollie, and three boys were born. Her father was the youngest, Fred Walter, born March 2, 1859, near Columbus, Ohio. At the age of 21, he went to Goshen, Indiana, and went to work for Jacob Berkey. There he met her mother, Sarah L. Berkey, who was the youngest child of nine of the Jacob Berkeys. Sarah was born September 16, 1860. The Berkeys had come from Germany. Jacob Berkey was a minister of the Dunkard Church. Fred W. Gang and Sarah L. Berkey were married in 1880, at Goshen, Indiana. Fred called her, "Sade". They moved the same year with her parents to Sherman, Texas, where Jacob Berkey was an evangelist minister. He rode horseback to visit a sick church member, the river was high from recent rains and he drowned. In a few months, they moved back to Indiana. Two years later, 1883, Fred and Sarah moved to Peabody, Kansas, where Fred Gang had a Confectionary Store for about ten years. In 1893, they moved to Guthrie, Oklahoma, to await the opening of the Cherokee Strip. Fred Gang made the run with three other families who came with them from Peabody, Kansas. Fred Gang's reason for Homesteading was he had four sons and thought it a "Golden Opportunity" for them. Fred Gang and his three friends from Peabody, Kansas, came and selected a section of land eight miles northwest of Perry so they could all be together. Each chose their 160 acres: Fred Gang-Northeast; Carl Stovall-Northwest; Murry-Southwest; Harry Shoop-Southwest. Their close friendship helped them all survive those first years. The first year was a drought and a complete crop failure with one exception, a baby girl was born, Hattie Fern Gang. Fred Gang rode a Bay Mare named "Pet" in the run. Fred and sons and neighbors dug a dugout and built a sod house (part below the ground and part above) near the Black Bear Creek. It was all one room, but Sarah sewed cloths together and made partitions for the kitchen, parents' bedroom and children's room. The family lived in the sod house about 13 years until a more modern, comfortable house was built of lumber. The house was well constructed, it is still standing and sound structure. Sarah lived on the homestead until her death, February 1, 1932. Fred moved to his daughter, Docia's, home in Tonkawa, and died November 16, 1938. The following are Fred and Sarah Gang's children.

Ira B. born, May 19, 1881-died October 20, 1960-married Effie Shay, February 24, 1907. Children: Pern Gang, living in Stillwater, Oklahoma; Carlos Gang, living in Pasadena, California; Bob Gang living in California; Tottie, died age 2; Baby girl died, age, a few days. Ira B. and family lived on a farm south of his parents homestead.

Otto B. Gang, born September 19, 1886, died 1923. He married Marie Sommerhouser of Wichita, Kansas, October, 1913. No children. Otto was killed by telegraph poles rolling on him at Cushing, Oklahoma. The initial "B" in sons names stands for Berkey.

Fred W. Gang Jr. born July 27, 1888-died June 3, 1913. He was electrocuted by a live wire during a terrific storm in Pocatello, Idaho.

Orval B. Gang born March 27, 1890-died September 16, 1952-wife, Stella. One son, Fred, born August 26, 1914, now living in Cleveland, Ohio.

Clara born 1892-died age 3 years, buried in new cemetery, fire burned records.

Hattie Fern Gang born August 6, 1894, now living in Edmond, Oklahoma. Married Jesse Keele, November 16, 1913. Four children: Lorraine Fern

The Gang sisters - 1904. (L to R): Docia (Fry) and Hattie (Keele).

Jesse and Hattie Keele wedding picture - November 16, 1913.

(Mrs. John Shiflet) born August 27, 1914, living in Stillwater, Oklahoma, formerly on S/S Ranch, Red Rock, Oklahoma for 50 years. Vangie Marie (Mrs. John Clendenin) born January 1, 1916, living in Kansas City area; James Merrill (Jim) born January 24, 1921, living in Sydney, Australia and Freesport, Bahamas; William Lee (Bill) Keele born May 30, 1924, living in Edmond, Oklahoma. Jesse Keele died November 5, 1972. His parents, the Sam Keele family, made the run and homesteaded east of Perry.

Docia May Gang born December 13, 1896-died February 23, 1976. Married Carl Fry and lived in Tonkawa until her death. There were no children.

A fourth daughter, Mary, was born and lived 4 months, buried at Polo Cemetery. Fred and Sarah Gang and sons, Ira, Otto and Fred are buried at Polo Cemetery.

Sam Keele

By Vangie Keele Clendenin

Three brothers, Bill, Jim and Sam Keele, lived close to Knoxville, Tennessee at small places named, Bull's Gap and Morristown. Their ancestors had come from England. There is a Keele Village with Keele Post Office and Keele University. Bill, the oldest brother, stayed in Tennessee and is buried in the family cemetery plot at Bull's Gap, with the other family members of past generations. J.J. (Jim) came to Oklahoma for the opening of the Cherokee Strip, lost out on his claim and went to the Creek nation, later settled in Okemah, Oklahoma. He was postmaster in Okemah for many years, never married. He was buried in the Okemah cemetery. Samuel Maston (Sam) Keele was born August 23, 1849, in Bull's Gap, Tennessee. He met Mollie (Mary) Lady. Her parents were:

Keele homestead 1897. (L to R): Jesse, Sam, Walter, Uhler, Middie and Mary.

Father-Henderson Lady born May 13, 1818; Mother-Elizabeth Lady born November 6, 1821. Henderson and Elisabeth Lady were married April 5, 1837. They died in 1884; buried in the family cemetery; Bull's Gap. Samuel Maton (Sam) Keele and Mollie (Mary) Lady were married October 27, 1867. They had ten children.

Walter Keele was born September 16, 1870 and died May 2, 1934. He never married.

Nancy Elisabeth Keele was born September 26, 1871 and died April 1, 1959. She married Ben Hughes. They had four children: Winifred (Mrs. Cecil Weathers) lives in Stillwater, Oklahoma; Mildred (Mrs. Orville Wells) living in Ft. Worth, Texas, area; Earl Hughes deceased; and Madeline (Mrs. Bill Blackmon) deceased.

Ollie Anes Keele was born March 5, 1873 and died January 28, 1959. She married D.S. Bruner September 28, 1893. They had one daughter, Pauline (Mrs. Hugh Kyle Bowen) deceased.

George Uhler Keele was born July 22, 1875 and died December 13, 1945. He never married.

Dora (Dode) Keele was born October 16, 1877 and died October 23, 1952. She married Frank Huffington. They had one daughter, Marian, died age 15; and one son, Buster, died age 20.

Mary Eddie Keele was born December 12, 1879 and died May 3, 1882.

Jesse Henderson Keele was born October 1, 1882 and died November 5, 1972. He married Hattie Fern Gang on November 16, 1913. Her parents, the Fred Gang Family, had made the Run and homesteaded 8 miles northwest of Perry. They had four children: Lorraine Fern (Mrs. John Shiflet) born August 27, 1914, is now living in Stillwater, Oklahoma, formerly at the S/S Ranch Red Rock, Oklahoma, the past 50 years. Vangie Marie (Mrs. John Clendenin) born January 1, 1916 is living in the Kansas City area. James Merrill (Jim) Keele was born January 24, 1921 is living in Sydney, Australia, and Freeport, Bahamas. William Lee (Bill) Keele was born May 30, 1924 and is living in Edmond, Oklahoma.

Samuel William Keele was born December 6, 1884 and died April 18, 1886.

Middie May (Mitt) Keele was born May 12, 1887 and died in 1972. She married Harland Weathers on May 12, 1887. There were no children.

Charlie Napoleon Keele was born April 30, 1890 and died July 20, 1973. He married Maude Cline, born January 18, 1892, now living in Frederick, Oklahoma. They had three children: son, Laverne, died age 3 years, Lou Ella (Mrs. Joe Curtis) living in Frederick, Oklahoma, and Pat (Mrs. Bill Rogers) living in California.

Sam and Marie Keele brought their family of our sons and three daughters (they left one daughter, Ollie, in Tennessee, she had married Hugh Bruner, a dentist there). Sam rode in the run of 1893 and homesteaded east of Perry. There was a contest over the claim and Sam Keele had to pay money to get his rights settled. His wife, Mary, was in poor health and could not stand the trials and discomforts of early day homesteading, they moved into Perry and she died in 1918. Walt worked in the Frisco Railroad yards in Perry, Goltry, and Enid. He was struck by a car and killed in Enid. Charlie and Jesse went to Telegraphy School in Tyler, Texas and Charlie worked for the Frisco Railroad, retiring in Frederick, Oklahoma, then moved to Perry during retirement years. Jesse was telegraph agent for the Santa Fe Railroad for 42 years. Uhler and Mitt cared for their father, Sam, on the farm five miles east and four miles south of Perry until they moved into Perry. Mary and Sam and sons, Walt, Uhler, Jesse, and Charlie, and daughters, Nancy and Middie are buried in Grace Hill cemetery, Perry, Oklahoma.

Charles Kemnitz
By Bertha Kemnitz

Charley was the son of Carl August and Wilhemenia Kemnitz. The family lived in LaCrosse, Wisconsin, then later moved to a farm in Snyder, Nebraska. They traveled in two covered wagons. They had six sons, George, Charley, John, Louis, August, and Jake and one daughter, Mary.

Charley helped with the farm work at home until here rented land and began farming for himself. He did his own housework as well as the farming until he married Fredericka Iske in 1890.

Fredericka was born in Helsen, Germany, September 12, 1872, one of five children of George and Johanna Iske. She had three brothers, Ludwig, Karl, Heinrich, and one sister, Marie. She came to the U.S. when she was 16 years old, making the trip by herself. It took 3 weeks by ship. Her possessions and enough food for the trip were packed in barrels for her to bring with her.

A cousin, Augusta Iske, a nurse, met her in New York City, then after a few days, she traveled by train to Dodge, Nebraska, where her brother, Karl, lived on a farm. It was here that she met and later married Charley Kemnitz, who was farming near the neighboring town of Snyder.

Word spread about the opportunity

Keele Family - 1896. Back Row (L to R) as their faces appear: Dr. Hugh Bruner, Ollie (Bruner), Walt, Mary, Dode, Sam, Uhler, Nan (Hughes) holding Winifred, Ben Hughes. Front Row: Mitt, Charlie, Pauline Bruner, Jesse.

Mr. and Mrs. Charles Kemnitz and sons on their 50th wedding anniversary. Standing (L to R): August, Charley, Rudolph, George, Hugo, Ernest.

of obtaining a homestead in Indian Territory (later Oklahoma) and when the Cherokee Strip was opened for settlement in 1893, Charley and two of his brothers were on the starting line north of Orlando, in a buggy ready to make the run. However, they hadn't gone far when the buggy upset and his brother, John, broke an arm. By the time they recovered from the accident and found help for their brother, all the land had been claimed. Charley staked some lots in the Perry Townsite, but later gave them up.

They returned to Nebraska, but had liked the looks of the Oklahoma land, so a few years later, when they heard that some of the homesteaders were getting discouraged and selling out cheap, Charley decided to investigate. He purchased 160 acres of land 8 miles sw of Perry, along Cow Creek, and in 1902, the family moved there, shipping their household goods, machinery and livestock by train. At this time the had four sons, Albert August, Charley Frederick, Rudolph Henry, and George Ernest. Two more sons, Hugo Elmer, and Ernest John, were born in Oklahoma. They were welcomed by friendly neighbors and were soon participating in all the community affairs.

Farming in Oklahoma was always a challenge, mostly due to the weather. There were good years whenever sufficient moisture was available, and poor crops during droughts, but by hard work and good management, most of the farmers prospered. Most of the food for the family was grown on the farm. A garden supplied vegetables, cows and chickens produced milk, butter, and eggs, and hogs were butchered in the fall, the meat cured, smoked, and made into summer sausage. All the fat was rendered into lard.

Since there were no girls in the family, the boys had to help with the housework, much to their dislike. They helped with all the farm work, and said when their father told them to do something, they were expected to run, not walk.

Their home was a favorite meeting place for the boys in the neighborhood. They might go fishing, hunting, swimming, or ice skating in the winter, but playing baseball was their favorite recreation. Charley said he had to replace so many broken windows, he was almost ashamed to buy any more glass.

During World War I, their three oldest sons served in the armed forces, one of them served overseas. When a letter from him arrived at the Orlando Post Office on Christmas Day, their rural mail carrier, knowing how anxiously they had been waiting to hear from him, saddled his horse and rode 5 miles through a snow storm, to deliver the letter to them.

After the older boys returned home from the war, they started working in the oil fields, and the younger ones followed as soon as they were old enough.

In 1923, Charley retired from farming, but continued to live on the farm. In 1937, they purchased a house in Perry and moved to town.

Many changes took place during their life time. They went from horse and buggy days through the machine age. They bought modern equipment and appliances as they became available.

It was the custom for all the family members that could, to gather at the home place on Christmas Eve and exchange gifts. One of the fondest memories for the grandchildren was when their grandmother would sing "Silent Night" in German.

In 1938, their youngest son, Ernest John (E.J.), moved on the farm and later purchased it. Charley died in 1946, and Fredericka died in 1948.

Elias M. Kennedy
By Sara Kennedy

My father, Elias Marion Kennedy, was born October 1, 1850, near DePauw, Indiana. Not much is known about his boyhood. He had very little schooling, maybe because it was necessary to help support the family or too distant from the school.

Mr. Kennedy loved his home state of Indiana and mentioned that he had belonged to the Grange, an agricultural group. He spoke of being baptised in a river by the Campbellites, now known as Disciples of Christ. His home was only a few miles north of Kentucky among many French settlers.

He left home at about age 17, with an extra pair of boots and was on his way cross-country to Kansas. He became employed as a ranch over-seer for a well-to-do farmer. While there, he met and married Mattie Ellen Gowty on August 18, 1885.

They established a home in Frankfort, Kansas. On April 13, 1888, their first son, Ivan Lynn, was born. The second son, Walter Earl was born August 10, 1889.

Mr. Kennedy bought a partnership in a livery stable. They furnished wagons, carriages, buggies, and horses to all who needed transportation, such as drummers (traveling salesmen) to call on their customers. News of Oklahoma land being opened for settlement began to spread through Kansas. During a slack season in the business, Mr. Kennedy decided to see for himself what the rumors were all about. He made a scouting trip to Oklahoma and returned saying the land was worthless for farming in his opinion.

Later, mother's parents, Thomas Jefferson and Sarah Catherine Gowty, came to Oklahoma and staked a claim. They persuaded father and mother to move to Oklahoma with their two young sons. They traveled in a covered wagon over almost no roads or bridges. Indians were watching all along the way but never bothered them. Mr. Kennedy found work in Oklahoma City. He was employed by Mr. Wheeler, planting trees in Wheeler Park. Mrs. Kennedy was an excellent seamstress and was kept busy as a dressmaker for the fine ladies. Soon relatives informed Mrs. Kennedy that there was a claim available near Perry.

To purchase the rights, Mr. Kennedy sold out his interest in the Frankford

Laurraine and Sara Kennedy in 1914.

Mr. and Mrs. E. M. Kennedy and sons: Walter (left), Glenn (center), Ivan (right). House on farm (12-20N-1W) Rock township about 1900.

livery stable and moved to a farm in Rock township. At that time it was in Payne county and they expected to educate the boys at Stillwater A. & M. The farm was on the Indian Meridian, which Mr. Kennedy thought would probably be a main highway. The land was changed to Noble county and the Indian Meridian just another country road.

The living was not easy. Along with other pioneers, the family endured the hardships of drouths, crop failures, making do with very little. One thing mother insisted upon was that her organ (a non-essential) be shipped from Kansas. She met with opposition but finally won. She spoke many times about loading the organ on a wagon, to play the hymns for church services in New Hope and Pike's Peak school houses.

On Octoebr 16, 1896, middle child, Glenn Serguis, was born. It became evident that more educational advantages would be needed for the growing sons, so about 1904, the family moved to Perry.

There the fourth child, a girl, Sara Elois was born February 25, 1906. To complete the family a fifth child, a boy, Marion Laurraine was born June 27, 1908.

Mr. Kennedy served a number of years as street commissioner in Perry, having been active on road improvement work when he was on the farm. He was most desirous to hold the land for his children. The childen all had other interests which did not include farming. Many times he said, "This is God's country. Hold on to the land. Money will slip through your fingers, but if you keep the land, it will keep you."

Father passed away April 15, 1940, and mother died August 16, 1957.

Hazel Eby Kennedy
By Perry Dail Journal

Tom Mix - Mary Pickford - Owen Moore - Charlie Chaplin - famous names in the silent picture era brought fond memories to Hazel Kennedy who once

Pen and ink sketch of the Wonderland Theater by Mrs. Hazel Eby Kennedy.

was a pianist at Perry's first movie house. The first "picture show" in Perry was opened in 1909 by Joe Appleman and Bush Bowman in a building on the northeast corner of the city square.

Mrs. Kennedy recalled, "There was no paving near the building. Hitching posts around the courthouse square and the lots now occupied by the Exchange Bank and Foster Corner Drug Store were used for parking of wagons and buggies by moviegoers. The Wonderland Theater was a small frame building which seated about 100 people. Moviegoers sat on wooden benches with backrests to watch the latest silent pictures.

Frank Johnson operated the picture machine in a room upstairs directly above the cashier's cage. The film broke so often that the pianist had to play to keep the crowd entertained until the film was patched.

Ticket takers at the Wonderland Theater were Olis Hamm, a former employee of the Perry Daily Journal, Kenneth Kirchner and Cecil W. Eby. Included in the theater employees was a piano player and sometimes a drummer and singer to perform the "illustrated" songs which came with the color slides.

Hazel Kennedy was the second pianist to play at the Wonderland Theater. The first pianist was Vivian Brengle, daughter of Dr. Will Bringle, who played for the road shows which came to Mr. Tate's Old Opera House on the east side of the square. Singers for the Wonderland Theater were Nell Vanatas Lucas, Harry Jones, Frank John, Dr. Frank C. Hubbard, and Harry DeLashmutt who sang "The Holy City" for the Passion Play Picture.

"Best of all the musicians" said Mrs. Kennedy, "was a young violinist named Ivan Kennedy, who asked if he could bring his violin and assist me with the music."

Kennedy at the time was attending Oklahoma A & M College (OSU) at Stillwater and on Saturday nights played tuba with Dr. W. C. Marshall's band.

Hazel Eby was born February 14, 1893, at Wellsville, Kansas the daughter of George and Ermina Eby. She moved to Perry with her parents in 1905. She attended Perry schools and the Kansas City Conservatory of Music. Besides working in the local theaters, she taught music.

She and Ivan Kennedy were married at Perry on September 12, 1912. Ivan Lynn Kennedy was born April 13, 1888 in Frankfort, Kansas, the son of Mattie Ellen (Gowty) and Elias Marion Kennedy. They had five daughters: Warenne (Harris), June (Jerome), Marjorie (Talbot), Betty (Anderson), Donna (Golliver) and one son, Robert Kennedy.

Hazel Kennedy was a member of the Christian Science church for which she served as pianist, first reader and president of the church board. Later she became a member of the First Presbyterian church and the Silver and Gold circle of United Presbyterian Women. She was a charter member of the Petunia unit of the Perry Garden Club Council. In her later years, Mrs. Kennedy developed an interest in art and had completed a number of paintings.

Jacob S. Kent
By Norma Snell

Jacob Seth Kent was born in Warren County, Indiana, September 25, 1832, to Joseph and Elizabeth Staley Kent. Jacob's mother died in August 16, 1844, and his father remarried Anna Evans Kent. Jacob and his brothers and sisters were raised mostly in northwest Missouri.

Jacob met and married Francis N.

Jacob Seth Kent - Civil War - 1863.

Kent house at Morrison 1901. (L to R) Adults: Charles and Nellie Dollarhide, John and Martha Frame, Charles and Margret Schlehuber, Mike and Laura Canyon, Jacob and Francis Kent, O.T. and Elizabeth Swearingen, Frame boy, George Schlehuber in Charles' arms, Frank Schlehuber, Russell Dollarhide, John Frame, Willis Frame, Gladys Schlehuber, Flossie Swearingen.

Beal on October 19, 1854, in St. Joseph, Missouri. To this union was born 14 children, the last two of which were twins. The children's names are: Emeline L., born August 11, 1855; Joseph, born in 1856; Elizabeth, born December 21, 1857; Ellen, born December 25, 1859; Abraham L., born March 30, 1861; Mary, born March 27, 1863; Laura, born November 21, 1864; Samuel J., born December 30, 1866; Elocia, born September 2, 1868; Lulu, born October 13, 1870; Jake, born March 12, 1872; Perrin, born December 14, 1873; Margaret, born April 25, 1876; and Martha, born April 25, 1876.

Jacob and Francis (Fannie) moved to Doniphan County, Kansas, near Troy, and farmed before the civil war. But as the threat of war got closer Jacob joined the volunteers. As the raids by Cantrell and other renegades got more often Jacob took his family back to Missouri to be closer to the family and larger towns. When the civil war did start he became a Sgt. Co. B, 13 Kansas. He spent most of his time in Arkansas, Missouri. He was in the battle of Prairie Grove and the battle became known because of the large loss of life. He commanded a troop of Indians. In Little Rock, Arkansas, in 1865, he was mustered out and went home to his family.

It is not known why he left Missouri but lock, stock and barrel they did. They headed south in Missouri along the Kansas line. A daughter died in southwest Missouri and was buried there. Moving the cattle on, they stopped just outside of Tulsa, Oklahoma; and from there on to Stillwater.

One of Jacob's daughters was in the land rush as was her father. She did get some land but Jacob felt sorry for a man with six children who didn't get any land, so he made her give her land to him.

Jacob and Fannie lived in a dugout in the side of a creek just east of Morrison. Building their own home as soon as they could.

Fannie helped a lot of people in the area. She was a mid-wife who was kept very busy. It is said that when the Black Bear Creek was flooding Fannie would take her clothing and tie them on her back and swim across the creek just to help someone.

Jacob never wanted any of his girls to marry, but one by one all of them did. It made him very upset. Sometimes he wouldn't speak to the girls for 3 or 4 years.

On June 3, 1896, Margret (Maggie) Jhrusha Kent married Charles Louis Schlehuber (See Charles Schlehuber). Margret was better known as Maggie.

Jacob and Fannie moved to town in 1913. Jacob died April 16, 1916, and Fannie died June 16, 1919. They are buried in Morrison, Oklahoma. Fannie was a member of the Baptist Church of Morrison.

Arthur "Shorty" Kerr
By Patricia Kerr McEachern, Mona Kerr Peters, and James Michael Kerr

Arthur David Kerr was born December 16, 1905, on a farm between Cleveland and Hallett. He was the son of Melville Coke and Lucille (Mahlo) Kerr. His parents had moved to a school land lease so they could farm. They brought with them Coke's team of mules, Tobe and Dorie. In the old log cabin where they lived, four of their children were born: Verlinda (Mrs. Earl Harting), Arthur, Retta, who died at 9 months, and Cecil (Mrs. Everett Staley). Coke and Lucie had a desire to be closer to their families, so they bought a farm located one mile south of the farm his dad, Dave, had homesteaded and just across the road from Lucie's parents. It was on this farm his brother Melville Coke, Jr., was born.

The Kerr children walked half a mile to catch a ride on the horse-drawn school wagon to Eureka School. It was about a five mile trip. Arthur attended Eureka School through his junior year. His senior year he decided to go to Morrison School. He rode a horse named Bones to school every day. In the winter he would turn around and ride backwards to protect himself from the cold north winds. He loved the sport of wrestling and did very well. He was State Runner-Up in wrestling his senior year and graduated from Morrison High School, where he was affectionaly known as "Shorty".

Arthur had a scholarship to wrestle for Oklahoma A & M College the next year, but an accident kept him from doing so. During the haying season, he was unclogging the gears on a stationary baler when the gears caught his gloved hand. He lost three fingers

Mike Kerr and A. D. Kerr.

Old log cabin where Arthur was born near Cleveland, Oklahoma. (L to R): Melville Coke Kerr, Sr., Arthur D. Kerr, Lucie (Mahlo) Kerr, Retta (baby on lap), and Verlinda Kerr.

Arthur and Audene Kerr in front of the Robinson and Kerr Hardware - 1945.

on his right hand and the accident ended his hopes of being a wrestler for Oklahoma A & M.

When Arthur was nineteen, he taught three months at Eureka School. He decided to go to school and get his teaching degree. He earned his bachelor's degree in education and his master's degree in school transportation from Oklahoma A & M College.

Arthur loved to travel and visited all the Continental United States and Canada. He enjoyed visiting with all people. In 1928, he and a friend, Charlie Sigler, loaded Shorty's Model T Ford and set off to see the sights. They worked their way across the United States that summer. The adventure lasted three months; the stories he had to tell of their experiences lasted a lifetime.

Arthur married Audene Kennemer in May, 1929. Her parents, Sam and Ida Kennemer, lived in the vicinity of Eureka and she was a friend of his sister, Cecil. He courted her by mail that summer he traveled in 1928 and throughout the following year until they were married. She was still a student at A&M and he was teaching at Mulhall. He continued to teach at Mulhall and was also Sueprintendent of Mulhall Schools. They lived there until 1941.

While they lived in Mulhall, their two girls were born: Patricia Jayne, November 18, 1934 and Mona Lou, May 30, 1939.

The Kerr family moved to Wellington, Kansas, during World War II where Arthur worked for the Boeing Airplane Company. Their son, James Michael was born in Wellington on December 29, 1944.

After the war, he had saved enough money to go into partnership with Ray Robinson to buy a hardware store from Frank Houser. He moved his family to Morrison, Oklahoma, and began the operation of Robinson and Kerr Hardware. They moved into the house he had dreamed of owning while he was a student at Morrison High School. The Kerr children attended and graduated from Morrison Schools. Audene was ill many of these years and following a lengthy bout with cancer, died February 11, 1958. Since Pat was married and Mona was attending college, Arthur and Mike lived there and batched the next few years.

One of Arthur's students from Mulhall introduced him to Loyce Long from Shawnee. They were married September 8, 1962. Loyce had two young daughters who came to Morrison with her, Zona Faye and Johanna. They attended and graduated from Morrison High School.

Arthur served as mayor of Morrison, school treasurer, served on the Community Building committee, was on the board of directors which organized the Cherokee Strip Historical Museum at Perry, was a lifetime member of the Morrison Lion's Club, a member of the Pawnee Masonic lodge and a 32nd degree Mason and was a member of the Scottish Rite Consistory of Guthrie.

He retired from the hardware business in 1974, but kept the part of the hardware known as the Shiever building, so he could continue to fix things for people as he had done in the past. Shorty's greatest joy was "fixing" things for someone, and the people of Morrison loved him for it.

If you couldn't find Shorty, chances are he could be located on the mowing machine he and his nephew, Harvey Harting, built. He loved keeping "his town" looking neat, and mowing for those people who couldn't.

It was unnsual for Arthur not to show up for coffee every day for this was his time to visit and reminisce with his friends. A brain tumor ended his life on December 20, 1983. He is buried at Sunset Memorial Gardens in Stillwater where Audene Kerr and his parents, Coke Kerr, Sr. and Lucie Kerr are buried.

During his lifetime he was able to see his children marry and enjoy his grandchildren. Zona is married to Derek VonTorne and lives in Morrison. She has two children: Brian and Eli. Johanna is married to Chuck Auteri and is living in Stillwater; Pat married D. L. McEachern and lives in Garber. Their children are Susan K. and Scott Kerr; Mona is married to Duane Peters and they live in Jenks. Tony Kerr and Jennifer K. are their children: Mike and Cheryl (Van Buskirk) Kerr live south of Morrison and are teachers at Morrison School. Their children are John Michael and Angela Dee (Little A. D.).

David F. Kerr

*By Patricia Kerr McEachern,
Mona Kerr Peters,
and James Michael Kerr*

Our dad, A. D. Kerr, told us many times the story of our ancestors. This story started when we asked him who his great-great-grandfather was. It was in the fall of 1982 when we recorded the following: "I don't know who my great-great-grandfather was. My great-grandfather was Elias Kerr, who came from Indiana to Carney, Oklahoma. I don't remember his wife's name. They are buried outside of Carney. If you look, when you go into Carney, there are two rounded markers on the hill. They had four children: David F. (Dave), my grandfather, Sebastian (Sabe), Sparks and

Original homestead of Dave Kerr. (L to R): Daisy (Crawford) Kerr, David F. Kerr, and Melville Coke Kerr, Sr.

David F. Kerr and Daisy (Crawford) Kerr.

Clara. Clara married a man named Jordan and their family settled in Savonsburg, Kansas. Their people are still there.

My grandfather, Dave married Anna Vanhoy. They had one child, Melville Coke (Coke Sr.), who was my dad. Anna died and is buried in Harrison, Arkansas. After she died, Dave and his son, Coke Sr., moved back to Carney and lived with Elias.

When they opened the Cherokee Strip, Elias came with Dave and Sabe, even though he was too old to make the run. They came on horses and Dave brought his team of mules and wagon, to what is now the home place, 3 miles south and ¼ mile west of what is now Morrison. Elias and Sabe stayed there with rifles to discourage any claim jumpers while Dave went on up to the Black Bear Creek to claim some rich bottom land. When Dave got there, it had already been plowed by "Sooners." After they staked the land, Elias returned to Carney. Dave and Sabe stayed and improved the land on the home place. Sabe decided he wanted to return to Carney, so he sold his half of the land to Dave for a team of mules. He agreed to stay and help with the spring planting before he would leave.

During that spring, a thunderstorm came up and Sabe ran out to get the chickens out of the storm and was struck by lightning. Dave and Elias saw him fall and they ran out to get him. They dragged him up on the porch, still conscious and yelling, "Take off my boots." When they did, there were white blisters all around the bottom edge of his feet where the metal tacks had been on the homemade boots. He died a few minutes later. I didn't know where Sabe was buried until I was mowing one day at the Morrison Cemetery and ran across his marker. Daisy (1871-1931) and David F. (1854-1938) are buried there too.

Dave and Coke Sr. lived alone until Dave married Daisy Crawford on June 3, 1898. Daisy and her mother, Sarah, lived on the land they had homesteaded during the run. The place was a mile east of Dave's place. She taught school in Old Oklahoma and several surrounding schools. When Dave and Daisy were married, her mother moved in with them and Coke Sr.

Coke Sr. started courting Lucie Mahlo. He had to cross several creeks to get to the Mahlo place. Lucie's parents were Carl and Henrietta Mahlo. They came to the U.S. from Berlin, Germany, when Lucie was only eight. The Mahlos originally settled in Minnesota, then moved to Arkansas City to be closer to the opening of Oklahoma Territory. They settled on the place across from you, where Theodore, your Grandma Lucie's brother and his wife, Ellen, live now.

Coke Sr. and Lucie Mahlo were married and moved over between Hallett and Cleveland to farm on school lease land (30 miles east of Dave's corner on

(L to R): Carl Mahlo, Melville Coke Kerr, Jr. and David F. Kerr.

the jog line). Besides me, there was Verlinda (Verlie) and Cecil. Retta died at 9 months. She was very sick. I remember watching from the loft where I slept and seeing Mother rocking and holding her.

In 1907, they bought the land you live on now. Coke Jr. was born on this farm. We lived in the house that was there until it burned down. We lived in the chicken house in a partitioned part for a short time. Neighbors from all around came and built the house back.

The other two eighties were for sale the same time this eighty was, but they were afraid to get too much in debt. They ended up buying then in 1913 and paid twice as much. Your grandpa Kerr traded a team of mules and a little to boot for the west eighty.

When we moved over here, Grandpa Dave still lived on the home place north of here. Grandma and Grandpa Mahlo lived across the road. We were around our grandparents a great deal and this is the story they told us."

Over a period of years, Coke Jr. farmed the land that belonged to his father, Coke Sr. and the homestead that belonged to his grandfather, David F. Kerr.

Now Arthur's son, Mike Kerr, farms the land that belonged to his grandfather, Coke Sr. and Coke Jr.'s son, David N. Kerr, Sr. farms the land his great-grandfather, David F. Kerr homesteaded.

Coke Kerr, Jr.
By Jeanie McCray

Melvin Coke Kerr, Jr. was born October 13, 1918, south of Morrison. His parents were M. C. Kerr, Sr. and Lucie Mahlo Kerr. Almost everyone called him Coke thinking it was a nickname. Actually, Coke was the name of a leader in the Methodist Church. Coke, Sr. was named for him.

Coke lived and farmed most of his life on the farm that was homesteaded

L to R: Arthur David Kerr, Verlinda (Kerr) Harting, Melville Coke Kerr, Sr., Lucie (Mahlo) Kerr, Melville Coke Kerr, Jr.

by his grandfather, David F. Kerr. It was located three miles south of Morrison. Part of the original dugout home is still being used (as a cellar) today. The dugout home was built in the side of a hill, then later the rest of the home was built on to it. This is where Coke, Jr. reared his family.

Coke actually grew up a mile south of the homestead. He attended Eureka School and graduated in 1936. As a boy, Coke wold walk or ride his horse to Yost Lake on weekends to caddy at the golf course. Yost was a small resort village and lake three miles south of his home.

He married his high school sweetheart, Muriel Wilma Phillips, on September 12, 1940. Her parents were Emma Alice (Kidder) Phillips and Noah Phillips. Coke and Muriel moved to the homestead place in 1943. They lived there until 1966, when the built a house in Morrison. They had three children: Donna Jo (Homer), born February 8, 1946, David Nolan Kerr, born December 7, 1948, and Melva Jean (McCray), born November 8, 1951. Donna lives in Moore and has two children: Amanda Lynn Homer and Berri Jay Homer. David lives just east of the homestead place on his own farm. He has taken over the family farming which includes the homestead. His children are David Nolan, Jr. and Joanna Sue Kerr. Jeanie lives south of the homestead on land which her father farmed and owned. She has two children: Marla Lee McCray and Mikah Lee McCray.

Coke continued to farm the homestead plus land his parents owned and lived on. He was exempted from the armed services to stay home and farm. In 1954, they bought land on the Black Bear Creek, thinking they had purchased only cultivated land. They soon discovered the place was covered with pecan trees. Coke and Muriel soon learned that this was a cash crop; the same as farming. For many years they picked the pecans themselves and sold them to regular customers.

Coke's love for the land and farming never grew dim. He got up every morning to do what he loved most; feeding the cows, cultivating, and mostly baling hay. He had many regular hay customers who he hauled to during the winter months. He was still hauling hay just a week before falling ill.

Coke was a supporter of local organizations and clubs. He served on the Morrison School board for eight years. He was known and loved for his easygoing personality and tender heart. He died of cancer on May 28, 1986. He is buried at Sunset Memorial Gardens in Stillwater.

Lottie Acers Keyser
By Helen L. Morrison

Lottie Ardella Acers was born October 10, 1894, in Noble County, Oklahoma, on the farm her father staked in the Cherokee Strip Land Run a year earlier. She was the daughter of Allen Irving Acers and Sudy Nix Acers. Lottie enrolled in Perry High School as a Sophomore in the year 1910. She rode her pony four miles to and from school.

In a Perry Newspaper the following Newspaper article appeared entitled "A Country Hay Ride": On Friday night, October 7th, a crowd of young people surprised Kay Foster with a birthday party. After the festivites were over Mr. Acers, who had been waiting with a hay wagon, took the young folks to his home in the country to enjoy another birthday party in honor of his daughter, Lottie, who had reached sixteen. Innocent games and amusements were indulged in to the delight of the people after which a singing contest was given and prizes awarded to the one rendering the best numbers. The winners were Beatrice Doyle, Wanda Johnson, Sylvia Glentzer and Marsh Woodruff.

Refreshments were served consisting of chicken sandwiches, ice cream, cake and watermelon, a country feast that was enjoyed by the town girls and boys with keenest relish. Those present were: Tillie Ringer, Miss Morgan, Mrs. Kryder, Miss Clark, Miss Beaghler, Minnie Boright, Aletha Shoupe, Beatrice Doyle, Sylvia Glentzer, Maude Yoce, Hazel Sparrow, Gertie Crowder, Lavania Crowder, Wanda Johnson, Bessie Freeman, Mable Foster, Murry McCune, Marsh Woodruff, Arthur Kuntz, Homer McDaniels, Ernest Banke, Fred Banke, Cecil Eby, George Keyser, Charlie Smith, Earl Pennco and Roy Hess.

At a late hour the guests departed leaving the hostess a number of nice presents among which was a fine souvenir silver spoon bearing an engraving of the Carnegie library.

George B. Keyser, son of James Perry Keyser and Miss Lottie Acers, daughter of A.I. Acers living four miles north of Perry, were quietly married at the home of the bride, October 26, 1913, with Rev. Armstrong officiating. Only Immediate relatives and a few friends of the families were present.

George and Lottie built a home on J.P. Keyser's homeplace, located northwest of Perry, in the southwest quarter of section 5 township 21 north range 1 west.

Coke, Jr. and Muriel Kerr on 40th wedding anniversary - 1980. Wedding picture in background.

Wedding Day of Lottie Acers and George B. Keyser — October 26, 1913.

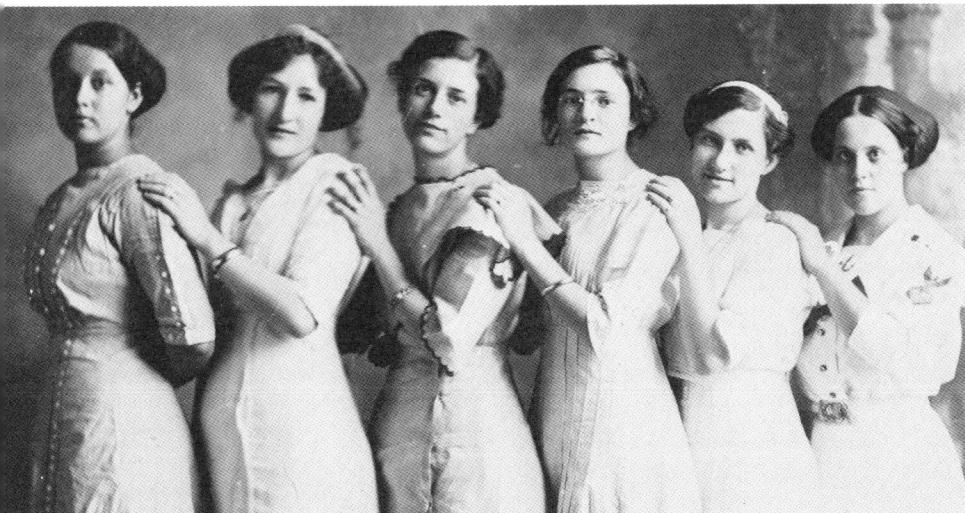

Six young ladies of Perry about 1913. L to R: Minnie Keyser Harrah, Allene Humphrey Dickson, Lottie Acers Keyser, Stella Tontz Haby, Lura Hoover and Effie Dott Keyser.

Keyser Family November 24, 1928 — (L to R): Perry, George, Helen and Lottie.

Perry I. Keyser was born August 29, 1914, with Dr. Daniel F. Coldiron in attendance. Helen Lucile was born July 10, 1925, with Dr. Coldiron also in attendance. They attended Fremont (District #34) Grade School and Perry High School.

George and Lottie lived northwest of town until 1939, at which time they moved north of town and continued raising wheat and cattle. George died at Perry Memorial Hospital August 21, 1966. Funeral was held at Newton Funeral Home with Rev. Clifton McKoy, pastor of the First Methodist Church officiating. Burial was at Grace Hill in the George B. Keyser Lot. He was survived by his wife, a son, Perry I. Keyser, a daughter, Helen L. (Morrison), a sister Minnie Harrah, and four grandchildren. He was preceded in death by his parents, J.P. Keyser and Mary Ann Keyser, and a sister, Effie Viola Keyser. George was a member of the First Methodist Church.

Lottie died at Green Valley Nursing Home April 2, 1969. Services were at Newton Funeral Home, with Rev. Cliffton McKoy, pastor of the First Methodist Church officiating. Lottie was a member of the First Methodist Church and the Black Bear Club. Burial was at Grace Hill Cemetery in the G.B. Keyser lot.

Lottie gave to the Cherokee Strip Museum a rawhide lariat which belonged to her father, A.I. Acers. It is hanging on the wall in the Cowboy Display.

Perry I. Keyser
By Helen Morrison

Perry Irving Keyser was born August 29, 1914, with Dr. Daniel F. Coldiron in attendance. He was the son of George B. Keyser and Lottie Adella Acers Keyser. He was named for his grandfathers Perry Keyser and Irving Acres. Perry attended Fremont District #34 Grade School. He rode Dan, his quarter horse, to and from Perry High School, graduating in the year of 1932. Perry attended and received his Degree from Central State College, Edmond, Oklahoma.

Perry I. received his Master's degree at West Texas State University, Canyon, Texas. Perry I. Keyser and Marguerite E. Dowdy, daughter of Rev. and Mrs. G. S. Dowdy of Stroud, Oklahoma were married August 3, 1940. The ceremony was performed in the parsonage of the Methodist Church in Okeene, Oklahoma, with Rev. George Hutchins, pastor officiating.

Perry and Marguerite had two sons, Perry Irving Jr., born September 11, 1943 at Amarillo, Texas. Perry Jr. graduated from Central State College and is an Elementary and Special Education teacher. Perry Jr., and Peggy Castine, daughter of Mr. and Mrs. Stancil of Kingfisher were married at the bride's home, January 23, 1966. Perry and Peggy are the parents of three children: Suzanne Marie born March 30, 1974 at Blackwell, Oklahoma, Mark Allen born March 21, 1976 at Blackwell, Oklahoma and Kristie Ann, born February 16, 1978 at Dodge City, Kansas.

Michael Duane was born February 14, 1947 at Memphis, Texas. Michael attended Draughns Business School at Oklahoma City and is employed with Southwestern Bell Telephone at Dallas, Texas.

Perry I. Keyser Sr. of Enid, Oklahoma, died November 30, 1981, in an Oklahoma City hospital. The funeral was at Wesley Memorial Chapel of the First United Methodist Church of Enid. Rev. John W. Dowdy officiated. Perry was a member of the First United Methodist Church of Enid and the National Teachers Association. He served with the United States Army Air Corps during World War II.

Keyser Family - May 1960 (L to R): Michael D. Keyser, Marguerite E. Keyser, Perry I. Keyser Sr. and Perry I. Keyser Jr.

Keyser served as band director for 36 years in Oklahoma and Texas. He first became interested in music while taking lessons from Leopold Radgowsky at Perry. He was buried in Grace Hill cemetery.

J. P. Keyser's homeplace (the northwest quarter of section 33 22N-1W) and A. I. Acres homestead (the southwest quarter section of 34 22N-1W) is now owned by Mrs. Marguerite Keyser of Enid, Oklahoma.

George Kihega
By Perry Daily Journal

Mr. and Mrs. George Kihega celebrated their 66th wedding anniversary on July 16, 1977. Mr. Kihega and the former Sarah Hudson, both Otoe-Missourias, were the last couple to be married the Indian way in their tribe. They were married July 16, 1910 in an Indian ceremony and were united in a civil ceremony, July 27, 1910. Mrs. Kihega was 16-years-old at the time of her marriage and Mr. Kihega was only 15. They had never met each other before their wedding day. The Indian way of marriage is for the parents to arrange the wedding. The boy's parents selects a wife and presents gifts to the girl's family as a token of friendship. The girl's family in exchange, agrees to allow their daughter to marry.

Mrs. Kihega's family was given approximately 25 horses and more than 35 broad cloth blankets and shawls, all of which were divided among her parents, aunts and uncles and other members of her family. Mrs. Kihega recalled "The only thing I hated about that was that I had to give up my good cowhorse."

The ceremony was held in the yard of the bride's parents' home. She was attired in Indian clothing and carried one of the shawls given to her family by the groom's family. He was dressed in white man's clothes. The couple held hands as the chiefs of the tribe talked individually with them. Unlike the whiteman's ceremony, there was no preacher or exchange of vows.

Instead, they were told how they must lead their lives, that they must be happy, work hard and have children. The chiefs told them how they should treat people, how to live a good life and that they would live to see their great-grandchildren. They have done just that. One bit of advice Kihega especially remembers was "to never let the fire go out." He says that at the time he didn't understand what the chiefs meant, but now says it means to keep your home safe and to take care of it.

When the couple agreed to try to live their lives as they were told, they were pronounced married in the eyes of the tribe. Following the wedding, a great feast was held in which all members of the tribe and chief Indians from other tribes were present. The meal was prepared by their mothers and spread out on a large tarpaulin. Everyone ate, celebrating the event.

The newlyweds lived with their parents after the wedding until 1914, when they moved to their present residence, four miles west and three miles north of Red Rock. Their farm was located in the northwest corner of the Otoe reservation. The Kihegas have farmed all their lives, raising mostly wheat, but also oats and cattle.

They were both grandchildren of chiefs. She was a granddaughter of Chief white Horse of the Otoe clan and he was a grandson of Chief White Cloud of the Eagle clan. Mr. and Mrs. Kihega were members of the Assembly of God Indian Mission in Red Rock.

They were the parents of seven children: Richard, Lorena (DeRoin), Marion (Stone), Priscilla (Arkeketa), Gene, Ronald, Bob.

James Kirkendall
By Paula Nichols Kirkendall

James (Jim) Ray Kirkendall, Jr. born December 11, 1952 in Tenneck, New Jersey married Paula Kay Nichols of Morrison, Oklahoma. Jim moved to Marland, Oklahoma in 1965. He is the oldest of three children (Jim, Martin, and Thomas) born to James Sr. and Joan Verbeyst Kirkendall. Jim's grandfather, William Elmer Kirkendall, a former ranch hand of the Mullendore Ranch, lived in Marland from 1955 to September 5, 1985, the time of his death.

Jim's fondest memories include the following; playing football in grade school, fishing with his brothers, milking cows by hand for his grandfather, swimming in the river, being a member of the FFA and showing hogs at the county fair, trips to visit grand-

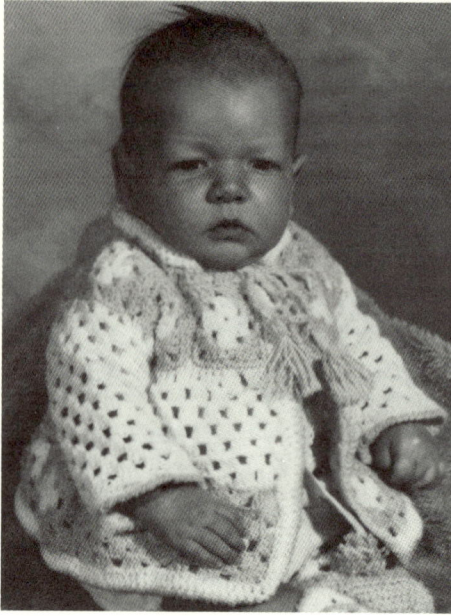

Lloyd Kirkendall

parents, nursing baby calves to be butchered, playing in a band, buying his first pick-up, a 1941 Chevy and his first car a 1952 Chevy, working with motors of any kind, taking a senior class trip to Colorado, plowing fields, the smell of the fresh plowed dirt and fresh bailed hay and walking waist high in snow drifts.

Jim hauled hay, plowed fields and milked cows at two dairies during his high school years. He graduated from Marland High School in 1971 and entered Northern Oklahoma College the following year. There he met Paula to whom he says he fell in love at first sight. They were married 5 months later on August 21, 1972 at Grace Episcopal Church in Ponca City. One month later, Jim entered the army on September 29, 1972.

Paula Kay Nichols born February 26, 1952, in Stillwater, Oklahoma was the second of two children (Charles Lloyd and Paula) born to Lloyd and Elsie Pauline Akers Nichols. She spent most of her growing years on the family farm which her grandfather, William Birdsal Nichols, claimed in the Cherokee Strip Run of 1893. She went to the Morrison School from 1958-70. During those years many days were spent enjoying God's green earth. The Big Ditch, a natural carving of the land a few hundred feet from the house was a favorite playground and cowboys and Indians was a favorite game.

Paula and her brother, Chuck, spent time discovering the wonders of nature: walking barefoot behind the tractor in the fresh plowed ground, running through the ripe wheat fields, jumping into the bins of wheat and sinking knee-deep, picking cotton, watching the pets grow and multiply, picking up pecans, building tunnels through the bails of hay, raising chickens, pigs, rabbits and cows, eating

fresh uncooked peas from the garden, riding bicycles, swinging on ropes in the hay loft from one stack of hay to another, skating on the ice in the winter when the ponds were frozen over and eating fresh baked cookies and cakes.

Paula's most vivid memories of her father are his love for fun and games especially if it included a little round ball (basketball, baseball, softball, volleyball and even bowling). He played softball until he was 51 years old. He coached, he played, and he watched his children and grandchildren play. Pauline once said, "If he had a choice of attending a ballgame or her funeral, he would choose the ballgame." His reply, "Well, it would be a lot more fun."

Paula's mother has a twin brother. Pauline used to tease her twin brother, when they were young, about her being the oldest of the two. She was born 10 minutes ahead of him. Now, he tells her, it is alright if she is the oldest.

Family and relatives were always very important. Almost every Sunday, after attending the Methodist Church, there was a visit to one or both of the grandparent's homes and often a delicious meal. Paula learned to greatly appreciate her parents positive outlook on life, their love of family, and the support they always gave. There was a deep closeness that was easily felt.

Paula was active in 4-H, glee club, pep club, cheerleading and basketball during her school years. Her team went to the state tournament in 1970. One summer she worked, painting outside buildings for some friends and two other summers she worked as a waitress in order to save money for college. The first 2 years of college were spent at Northern Oklahoma College where she met Jim Kirkendall (Red), with whom she fell in love and later married. Her education was later completed at Northwest Oklahoma State College with a Bachelors Degree in Elementary Education.

A month after Jim and Paula were married, Jim was drafted and thus joined the US Army Reserves 95th Division. He left for Basic Training at Ft. Dix, New Jersey. Three months later he moved to Ft. Lee, Virginia for AIT where he was trained as a small arms and supply specialist.

After returning home they moved to Ponca City, then to the country 2 miles from Marland. Jim worked for Evans and Throop Construction until they moved to Alva to let Paula finish her education. There he was employed by the county to grade roads.

In January 1976, they moved back to Ponca City where Jim started to work for Evans and Throop again. A year later he was hired by H.B. Zachry to help with the dirt work for Sooner Lake. From there he was employed by O.G.& E. at the Sooner Plant as a heavy equipment operator in the coal yard. He was later moved up to a Foreman position and the Equipment Operator Supervisor.

Early in 1976, Paula substituted at most of the Ponca City Public Elementary Schools. That fall she was hired as a fourth grade teacher at E.M. Trout Elementary. She worked there until the birth of their first child, James Aaron Kirkendall. He was born on April 10, 1981.

Jim and Paula attend the St. Luke's Church of the Nazarene in Ponca City. Their activities include Bible studies, teaching Sunday School and Bible school, and softball and basketball games.

James Aaron Kirkendall will have memories of going to Sunday School and Bible School, attending a Christian Pre-school and goingto Mini-mites at the YMCA. He enjoys swimming at the neighbors, playing He-Man with his friends, and riding his motorized car and motorcycle. He loves to spend time with his grandparents and he loves fishing with his dad and working on motors. Aaron is now very excited about a new arrival at our house, a baby brother, Lloyd Ashby. He was born December 28, 1985. He is dark complexioned and has dark hair. His first big trip was to Disney World.

Charles T. Kirtley
By Clarence M. Koch Jr.

Charles Thomas (Charley) Kirtley was born November 9, 1887, near Marysville, Missouri, the son of William Harrison and Anna J. (Mahan) Kirtley whose history also appears in this book. At the age of 12 years, Charley and his mother and 2 sisters,

Frances Jane (Jennie) Sokol - High School graduation - 1907, Perry, Oklahoma.

Alice and Nellie came to Noble county in 1900 from Missouri. His father and brother, William M. Kirtley had already staked a claim on a farm in the northwest of 29-22N-2W which is 3½ miles north of Perry on the west side of I-35 in Noble County, during the opening of the Cherokee Strip land run on September 16, 1893.

Charley attended Fourdee school in Noble County until 1905. At that time he entered Perry schools as a Freshman in High School. He was very athletic and played guard for the first

Sheriff's office Noble County courthouse - 1917, Under Sheriff Charles Thomas Kirtley.

Charles T. Kirtley family - 1941. Top Row (Left to Right): Irene, Mabel, Janice, Mary, Alice, Clara. Bottom Row: Bill, Frances Jane (Jennie), Charles, Larkin, Phillip.

PHS football team in 1905. He said he played in the "Good Ole Days" when it was eleven man football, which was very rough and had only a few rules as compared to today. A news item in the Perry Daily Journal in September 1980 featured his picture in the football uniforms they wore then. His two sons, Larkin and Phillip, and Larkin's two sons, Clane and Gary, his grandsons Clarence, Charles and Larry Koch and a great-grandson, Bruce Koch, followed in his footsteps by playing Perry football. Charley was also well known for playing baseball at Perry and Enid and at one time was offered a contract to play for a major league team, which he turned down. He attended Oklahoma Christian College (now Phillips University in Enid, Oklahoma). Studying for the ministry, but took pneumonia and was unable to finish the courses. While living in Enid he married Frances Jan (Jennie) Sokol on June 12, 1910. Jennie was the daughter of Josef and Anna (Vavara) Sokol another pioneer family whose history also appears in this book.

While Charley and Jennie lived in Enid he worked days at a grocery store and nights at the elevators. He built a house in Enid out of cement blocks that he made himself. This house is still standing today and is still being lived in. Charley loved music and poetry, his favorite book was the Bible. He was a member of the Assembly of God church in Perry and was a loyal Democrat.

They moved back to the farm north of Perry and their children stayed during the week with their grandparents, Josef and Anna Sokol so they could attend Perry schools. During the school terms they spent the weekends with their parents on the farm.

In 1942, Charles retired from active farming and moved into the town of Perry. He worked at the Stillwater mill during the war years. In 1915, he was undersheriff serving with Sheriff Tom Wetzel. In 1918, he was elected as Noble County Assessor and served one term.

Grandpa was a pleasure to be around, he loved to talk and never knew a stranger. He was very witty and liked to joke and kid around a lot. He liked to tell stories about the olden days. His favorite pasttime he said was eating, especially cherry pie.

Jennie graduated from Perry High School in the year of Statehood for Oklahoma, 1907. She was born August 15, 1888, in Oxford Junction, Iowa. She took teacher training and taught at Fairview and Sunnyslope schools in Noble County. Pictures have showed her to be a very beautiful young woman, and I remember her as a lovely, industrious grandmother. They were the parents of 10 children: Larkin J., Charles T. Jr., William J., Phillip D., Irene M., Alice E., Mable I., Mary E., Clara R., and Anna Janice. Several of which still live in the Perry, Noble County area.

Larkin J. and Alice E. married sister and brother, Larkin J. married Dorothy Koch and Alice E. married Clarence M. Koch, Sr. children of another pioneer family whose histories also appear in this book under Abraham Koch and Delbert Koch.

I remember Grampa Kirtley telling about when they would drive the Model T cars into town, that they could not go forward up the big hill out by their farm and would have to turn around and back up the hill. This presented a problem to the farmers there and they had to go a long way around so they could get their grains to the elevators in town.

He told me also about being out in the fields plowing when the dust storms would come up and that he would cut the horses loose so they could get back to the barns and he would use whatever he could find to protect himself from the blowing dirt. One time in particular he used a scoop shovel to hide behind to get home. He told me about his "courting days" how he rode on horseback to see his girlfriend Jennie. In those days if you held hands and kissed a girl you "were engaged."

Charles T. died October 26, 1983 and Jennie died June 9, 1974, they are both buried along side their pioneer parents and other relatives at the Mount Carmel cemetery north of Perry, Oklahoma about ½ mile south of the farm that the Sokols got in the land run.

William H. H. Kirtley

By Clarence M. Koch Jr.

William Henry Harrison Kirtley was born June 3, 1842 in Shelby County, Illinois, in or near the town of Shelbyville (possibly born in Summersett, Rockcastle County, Kentucky - just across the state line). He was named after William Henry Harrison the 9th president of the United States. He was the son of Nickolus and Nancy (Lankford) Kirtley and the grandson of Elija and Anna (Bohanan) Kirtley and they were from around Mount Vernon, Kentucky. The Millers of the old 101 Ranch in Oklahoma were neighbors of the Kirtleys in Kentucky.

The Kirtley's are able to trace their ancestry back to Sir Francis Kirtley from Wales, England. He was the first Kirtley immigrant to the US. He was deeded part of the Shendoah Valley of Virginia by the King of England. He also served as a captain in the Revolutionary Army. Nickolus Kirtley died in 1848 at Sommersett, Kentucky after a long bout with malaria.

William was 10 years old when he and his uncle Larkin (Nickolus' brother) and his mother moved from Kentucky to 8 miles east of Savanna, Missouri by wagon train. The grandfather of the DeBord family here in Perry was in that same wagon train. William's uncle and mother bought 1000 acres for 13¢ an acre and while living in Savanna they had negro slaves. While still in Savanna, William's mother, sister, Mary and William's daughter, Nanny died and are buried there on the farm they had bought. Part of this farm is still owned to this day by the Kirtley heirs.

William was married to Anna J. Mahan from Linn, Missouri, from this marriage they had nine children, Hattie, Nanny, William Madison, Edwin Lankford, Barbara A., Mary E., Sarah Alice, Charles Thomas and Nellie M.

William fought in the Civil War on the north side and attained the rank of Corporal. Because of instilled prejudices he jumped into the Cumberland River, swan to the other side to join the Southern Army, another possible reason for his changing sides is that it was reported down the years that he had lost his money racing horses! After the Civil War ended he moved to Colorado with his family and fought the In-

L to R: William H. H. Kirtley, Charles Thomas, Nellie, Alice and Anna J. (Mahan) Kirtley.

Margaret and Constantine O'Roke.

dians at Cripple Creek. While in Denver they were setting around the fireplace one evening and his brother-in-law was stirring the fire and let Hattie touch a hot poker. It made William mad and his picked his family up and moved back to Missouri where he bought 80 acres of land and he worked as a blacksmith.

One son, Will Kirtley, told the story of how a group of horsemen rode into their place one afternoon and asked his father to shoe one of their horses, he was told not to tell anyone of these men because Jesse James had just given his father $10.00 to take care of his horse. This farm was very close to St. Joseph, Missouri (known as St. Joe). St. Joe was where Jesse James was killed. William was working in St. Joe when Abraham Lincoln was killed.

William heard about the land opening in the Oklahoma Territory and he and his son Will bought 2 race horses to ride in the run. They got them in condition and ran the race in the Opening of the Cherokee Strip land run on September 16, 1893. They got a farm and staked their claim on a farm in the northwest of 29-22N-2W, which is 3½ miles north of Perry on the west side of I-35 in Noble County. William and Will guarded their claim from claim jumpers and thieves with their rifles. They worked on their farm and made living arrangements for the rest of the family that did not move here from Missouri until about 1900.

William was an expert with horses and swung a wicked axe. He did not wear glasses and lived to be 93 years old. He knew all types of trees and could name the names of each one of them. One winter on a very cold day William and his grandson (Larkin Kirtley) went out to cut wood and the fence was broken down. William rolled up his pants and waded in the Creek to fix the gap. William told Larkin that if you dip your hand in the cold water, and rub it on your head you wouldn't ever catch a cold — it must not have worked because he kept a "Jug" of cold medicine under his bed and had a "cold" most of the winter!! He was the only man they knew of that could chew and smoke tobacco at the same time. William was an outdoor adventurious man that was not afraid of new beginnings and provided well for his family.

Anna was not afraid of the worst storms, everyone else would go up to the root cellar and they would all try to get her to go and she would stay in the house and read, no matter how close or bad the storms were. She was not afraid to go to the root cellar because she kept her canned goods stored there and went down often for them.

William died January 26, 1935 at the age of 93 and Anna died of a stroke in 1924. They are both buried at Mt. Carmel cemetery, north of Perry, Oklahoma. Their son, Charles Thomas Kirtley married Jennie Sokol, the daughter of Josef and Anna Sokol, another pioneer family whose history also appears in this book.

Abraham Koch
By Clarence M. Koch, Jr.

Abraham Koch was the son of Henry and Lucy (Black) Koch. Lucy was of English descent and Henry was of German descent. Henry and Lucy had four children: Abraham, John, Annie and Emaline. Lucy died and Henry married Mary Hendricks. Henry and Mary had six children: William, Fred, Flora, Carry, Ella and Ida. Ida and her husband, Sam Case, died very young and Henry raised their two children John and Ida. After Mary died Henry married Lillie White and they had no children. Henry Koch was a very good singer.

Abraham was born March 10, 1845, at Wyoming, Pennsylvania and DeEtte O'Roke was born August 8, 1847 in New York State. They were married at Marshalltown, Marshall County, Iowa on October 14, 1867. (A copy of the marriage certificate has been obtained.)

Abraham served his country during the Civil War, he served with Company C 7th Iowa Calvary. He retired from the service to come to the Oklahoma Territory.

Abraham and DeEtte came to Oklahoma in 1891 from Frankfort, Kansas. Harvey Fry who had worked for Abraham in Kansas had staked a claim south of Orlando in a previous run. Mr. Fry's place was Abraham's destination until the Cherokee Strip land run opened. Two of their older daughters and husbands, John and Eva Winter and James and Laura Hotson came from Kansas with them for the run also. Abraham built a sod house for his family and they lived in it while they waited for September 16, 1893 for the land run opening.

On opening day, Abraham didn't get a farm because some "sooner's" jumped his claim. His older son, Delbert staked a claim three miles east of Covington. Abraham moved in with Delbert and later bought a farm south of Hayward, Oklahoma. Some time later, they sold the farm to another son, Harry E. Koch and Abraham and DeEtte moved to Orlando. He was a mail carrier. He was a medium tall man that wore a mustache. They both enjoyed their grandchildren and Abraham liked to bring things to his granddaughter Willa (Koch) Godbey, who was crippled from polio and one day he put an owl in Willa's mailbox and it sure surprised her.

DeEtte's parents were Constintine

Four Generations: Henry Koch - 89 years old; his daughter, Emeline (Klien); Emeline's son, Frank Klien, and Frank's son Kenneth Klien.

Abraham J. and DeEtte (O'Roke) Koch.

and Margaret (Smith) O'Roke and their children were: DeEtte, Jennie, Nettie, Ellen, Addie and Frank. They were from Brown County, Kansas and were highly educated and well fixed financially. They were Irish and both their parents came from Ireland. Constintine never wore glasses and could still see real good when he was 80. He was a good shot and a lot of fun. He was comical and real smart, always saying something funny. His grandchildren never saw a "bitter" old grandpa.

Abraham and DeEtte had nine children: Eva Mae (Koch) Winters, Delbert, Laura Ellen (Koch) Hotson, Clarence Albert, Grace (Koch) Sharp, Franklin Ellsworth, Harry Earl and Allen Guy. Most of them grew up, married and lived in this area, and some of them have histories in this book.

Abraham died October 25, 1918 and DeEtte died April 28, 1912, they are both buried in the Bocox cemetery south and west of Orlando, Oklahoma.

Clarence M. Koch Jr.
By Clarence M. Koch Jr.

Clarence Melvin Koch, Jr. is a descendent of several pioneer families whose history appear in this book including: Josef and Anna Sokol, William Harrison and Anna J. (Mahan) Kirtley, Charles T. and Jennie (Sokol) Kirtley, Abraham and DeEtte Koch and Delbert and Cora Koch.

Clarence was born June 2, 1937, to Clarence M. and Alice (Kirtley) Koch on Grove Street in Perry, Noble County, Oklahoma. He attended Perry schools through his graduation in 1956 except for one year that he attended Hempling country school 2 miles west and 1 mile south of Perry. The school building which is now a barn is on the same corner of Earnest Tappe's farm.

His father was an employee of the City of Perry for many years. They lived at the city lake park southwest of Perry when his dad was caretaker there from 1941-1943. They also lived at the Perry football stadium from 1946-52 while his dad was caretaker there. His dad was later a policeman for the City of Perry.

Clarence worked during his high school days for Forney's ice cream store on the west side of the square. He also worked part time for the parks department of the City of Perry.

February 4, 1957, Clarence left to go to work as a fingerprint clerk for the FBI in Washington, D.C. He left with FBI Agent Jack Bales of Ponca City, Oklahoma by train. In 1958, he bought his first car, a 1955 four door chevy.

Clarence remembers when they lived at the Perry city lake when his brother Larry was born on December 27, 1943, that it was so cold that the goldfish froze solid on the living room table. He likes to tell his children that the snow was waist deep back then. Of course he doesn't tell them that he was only 5 years old at the time.

January 6, 1960 he entered the U.S. Army at Oklahoma City. He took his basic training at Ft. Leonard Wood, Missouri and went by bus to Ft. Devens, Massachusettes and then by train to Ft. Gordon, Georgia. And finally in June 1960 he went by boat to Korea. He was a Spec 4 with the U.S. Army security agency. He was in Korea for 13 months and arrived back in the states by boat to San Francisco, California. He was then stationed at Ft. Mead, Maryland. He was honorably discharged from the Army while serving at the national security agency at Ft. Meade, Maryland, on December 17, 1962.

On January 14, 1963 he was married to Mary I. (Jean) Flanigan at the Church of Christ building in Perry, Oklahoma where he has served as an elder since December of 1980.

In February 1963, they moved to Falls Church, Virginia, where Clarence returned to work for the BI as a cryptanalyst in Washington, D. C. Two of their children were born while the lived there, Carla Dean and Bruce Melvin.

Clarence resigned from the FBI in 1968 and moved his family back to Perry where he worked on a drilling rig for 6 months. They operated a service station at 8th and Fir behind his Grandpa and Grandmother Kirtleys house for a few years. He worked for Ralph Nida in his roofing business before he became a city Policeman in 1970. He became deputy sheriff in Noble county in 1971 and then undersheriff until the end of 1977. He then went to work for the Charles Machine works as a receiving clerk, the position he holds at this time.

Another son Randy William Koch was born on July 15, 1970. He was a kindergarden student in the Perry Schools when he became ill with the flu and contracted Reyes Syndrome and died on March 12, 1976. He is buried in the Grace Hill cemetery in Perry, Oklahoma.

Their daughter, Carla, graduated from Perry High School in 1982 and attended one year at Crowleys Ridge College, Paragrould Arkansas where she met Russel A. Robbins and they were married October 8, 1983 at the Church of Christ building in Perry, Oklahoma. Rusty is from Elizabeth, Arkansas. Bruce graduated from Perry High school in 1985 and attended Central State University at Edmond, Oklahoma.

Clarence has two brothers and two sisters: Charles Delbert and Larry William and Marion Lanette (Koch) Chitwood and Nancy Claire (Koch) Treiner.

Jean was born May 28, 1939 at Success, Arkansas, the daughter of James E. and Lucile (Keelin) Flanigan. She graduated in 1956 from Piggott, Arkansas High School and attended college at Harding University in Searcy, Arkansas. James and Lucile's children are: Joseph F., James H. Lavern, Darrell Lloyd, Viva Dean, Mary Imogene (Jean) and Larry Thomas. Viva Dean is married to Kenneth E. Nida whose family is from the local area. Jean worked at Green Valley nursing home for several years and has worked as bookkeeper at the Farmers Cooperative Exchange for 8 years, she also worked there before her marriage.

Delbert Koch
By Clarence M. Koch Jr.

Delbert Koch was born in LaPort City, Iowa (Blackhawk County) on August 28, 1870. He was the son of Abraham and DeEtte (O'Roke) Koch whose histories also appear in this book.

Delbert and his father came to the Oklahoma territory a few years before the opening of the Cherokee Strip land run in 1893. They made the run and Delbert staked a claim three miles east of Covington, Oklahoma in Garfield County. He later sold his farm and bought a farm across the road west from the farm his father bought near Hayward, Oklahoma.

Delbert married Verlinda Ogden on February 13, 1902, at Perry, Oklahoma and had a daughter, Willa (Billie) (Koch) Godbey. Verlinda died June 6, 1904 and Delbert married her sister, Cora Mae Ogden in 1905 at Fort Scott, Kansas. Delbert and Cora had three children, Viola G. (Koch) McGraw, Dorothy (Koch) Kirtley and Clarence Melvin Koch, Sr. All of whom lived in this local area. Dorothy and Clarence married brother and sister, Larkin and Alice Kirtley whose parents Charles T. and Jennie Kirtley were pioneers and whose histories also appear in this book.

Delbert stayed with his farm until Willa was stricken with polio. He then sold his farm to Howard Cawood, brother-in-law to Harry E. Koch, Delbert's brother. Delbert and Cora moved to Edmond, Oklahoma to be close to Willa's doctor. Willa recovered but was left with a bad limp. She married Lacy Godbey and they lived here in Perry until their deaths except for a short time that they lived in West Virginia.

Delbert was a little short man, very good natured and didn't talk much. He was a hard worker and took good care of his family. He liked horses and knew how to handle them well. Cora was a small woman and walked with one crutch in her later years. She loved to talk and enjoyed visiting and getting mail. She was active in the clubs of the Christian church here in Perry. They bought a house at 906 6th Steet in Perry when they moved back from Edmond and they lived there the rest of their lives. Delbert died on January 15, 1939 in Perry and Cora died April 28, 1972 in Perry. They are both buried in the Bocox cemetery in the Potter community six miles west of Orlando, Oklahoma.

Cora was the daughter of John and Mary (Wilson) Ogden. Mary was born September 2, 1849. Information taken from Cora before her death described Mary as being a very good housekeeper. She died March 10, 1890 when Cora was 9 years old. Mary is buried in a cemetery in Oscalosa, Kansas in the southwest corner and there is a tall slender tombstone marking her grave. Cora had a brother named Tom and his sons now live in Enid, Oklahoma. Cora had two sisters, Verlinda (Linnie) was married to Delbert Koch until her death and Gertrude who was married to Frank Koch, Delbert's brother.

Delbert and Cora's son, Clarence, my dad, has told me these stories. When they lived in the Potter community (west of Orlando, Oklahoma) that the snow in the winter time was deep enough that they could cut across country and not worry about the fence rows, on the way to Perry to buy and sell goods. This story has been told by more than one person, from more than just this family also. He also said that when someone died in the summer time from their community that they would get some blankets and a wagon and drive into Perry to get ice to pack the body with until the funeral. The bodies were kept at home and neighbors, relatives and friends would set up 24 hours a day until the funeral.

When it came time to get the crops in the whole community worked together from one farm to the next until they had their crops in. If a farmer was ill or hurt everyone always pitched in to help. He also told the story that he and his father were working in the field one day and he could hear a train whistle and he told his dad about it, since it was heavily overcast that day and they lived six miles from any railroad his dad got excited — what he really heard was the wind from a tornado forming and they really got excited and turned the horses loose and his dad had them all go to the cellar.

Harry Koch
By Bonnie Koch Roberts

The Kochs had lived in the Potter area until the fall of 1946, when they moved southeast of Perry, and here they spent the remainder of their lives, with their daughter, Ruby caring for them. They were avid gardeners, and Koch, himself enjoyed growing flowers. Sharing what he grew with others was one of the greatest joys of his life.

Harry was born southeast of Home City, Marshall County, Kansas, on August 26, 1885, to Abraham and DeEtte (O'Roke) Koch, the 8th of 9 children. His grandparents were Constatine and Margaret O'Roke, who are buried in Corning, Kansas; and Henry Koch, buried in Zion cemetery, west of Orlando.

He came with his parents to Oklahoma in 1891, at six years of age. His father and brother, Delbert, each drove a covered wagon to Harve Fry's place south of Orlando, where they

65th Wedding Anniversary, May 26, 1974 - Harry and Bertha Koch.

camped until his father could rent some ground, where he built a two room frame house. Here they lived for two years making ready for the "Run". His father failed to get a claim, so they lived with Delbert, on his claim southeast of Covington for two years.

In 1895, his father traded a team and wagon for a farm in the Potter area, south of Hayward, and here Harry lived until 1946, when they moved to Perry. His early schooling was from his mother. In 1895, he started to school at Stanton, which was a 4 month school in a half dugout, near a spring, close to the Ambrose Stanton home. Later, each family signed a note at the lumber yard in Orlando, thus material was obtained to build a frame school, on the corner of the Stanton farm. Church services, literaries, and singings were held here. Harry and his brother, Guy, entertained with singing.

On May 26, 1909, Harry and Bertha Cawood were married at Enid and moved to the old Koch homeplace, which they purchased in 1919, from the heirs. Bertha was born July 16, 1891, near Lamar, Colorado, to W. A. and Maggie (Holt) Cawood, where the family had moved hoping to homestead land. After severe drouths, the family moved in 1894, to the Potter area, where W. A. bought a claim two miles east of Potter. Bertha attended Potter and Blackwell rural schools, and later A. & M. at Stillwater, when Old Central and Morris Hall were the only building on the campus. Her grandparents included: William H. and Nancy McCormack Cawood, and Jefferson and Mary Ann Barnett Holt. Her great-grandparents were John and Lucinda Wells Cawood, and Abraham and Judith McCormack and a great-great-grandfather was Charles Wells.

Their children included: Bonnie Marie born August 7, 1915, graduated from Edmond in 1936, taught in Noble County at Hempfling school from 1936-1940, Lone Star from 1954 to 1958, then 18 years at Marshall, retiring from Covington in 1977. On April 27, 1940 she married Jessie Roberts of Marshall, who passed away on June 2, 1984.

Delbert and Cora Mae Koch.

Melvin Lester was born September 6, 1917, and died at age two from bad water.

Sylvan D. was born July 19, 1920, and is a farmer in the Potter area. He married Alice Caudle on March 22, 1941.

Ruby Maxine was born October 10, 1922, and was married to Don Kirchner of Perry on January 4, 1986, where they made their home.

During their earlier years, Harry and Bertha were both active in the Potter community Church activities. She played the old pump organ, and later the piano, and both sang. Harry served on the Stanton School Board for many years, graded roads with a four horse team, and served as foreman of road work.

The Kochs celebrated their 65th wedding anniversary on May 26, 1974. Eleven months later, she passed away on April 25, 1975. Koch was anxiously awaiting his 99th birthday, when he was taken on January 15, 1984. They were both laid to rest in the Grace Hill Cemetery. They had six grandchildren and 13 great-grandchildren.

Henry Koelzer
By Gertrude Gengler

Henry Koelzer was born March 13, 1868, at St. Benedict, Nemaha county, Kansas, the son of John Peter Koelzer and Margaret Wink. His parents had immigrated from Mittlestrimmig-Koblenz area of Germany. They first settled at Branch, Wisconsin, in the early 1850s. The two oldest children were born there. In 1858, they moved to St. Benedict and were pioneer farmers of that vicinity. At the time they moved there it was open country but soon a small Catholic church was built and a little inland town grew there. Thirteen children were born to them, three died in childhood. The church is about four and a half miles northwest of Seneca, Kansas. Henry was married September 28, 1892, at Seneca, Kansas, to Jane Schneider. She was born June 2, 1872, at Salem, Nebraska, in the southeast corner of the state. Her parents, Matthias Schneider and Elizabeth Birkhaure, with her grandparents immigrated from Cologne, Germany, in 1845, to Wisconsin. They later moved to Salem, Nebraska, then to St. Benedict, Kansas, when she was quite young. Her mother died in 1879, when she was only seven years old. There were six children and the oldest girl was only 13 years old. An aunt came to live with them for a few years. Matthias never married again.

Henry and his family lived at Seneca, Kansas, where he farmed until 1899, when he bought a farm three and one half miles southeast of Perry (SE¼ 30 21N 1E). They brought livestock, farm implements and household goods in a freight car and the family came by passenger train. His family consisted of wife and four children: Elnora, Adolph, Leo, and Gertrude. I was 3 months old. His brother, George Koelzer and wife Anna Huls, came at the same time. After living here a few years, George died of blood poisoning and Anna and her two children moved back to Nemaha county, Kansas.

Seven more children were born to Henry and Jane Koelzer after coming to Oklahoma: Ambrose, Paul, Carl, Edwin, Robert, Marie, and Victor. There was a small house on the claim. Henry farmed and raised cattle but he had a series of bad years. He lost many of his cattle from disease, a mad dog got among them causing more losses, and then a bad drouth. In 1905, he traded his farm for a custom mill owned by Bud (Shorty) Springfield, and moved to Perry, where his children attended the Catholic school. Elnora died April 5, 1904, of measles followed by pneumoia.

Henry operated the mill with one hired man. He made "White Lily" flour, custom made flour, corn meal, ground all kinds of livestock feed, threshed kaffir corn, etc. On March 6, 1909, Leo was killed in the mill. Henry had been having a series of boils and carbuncles and needed some extra help that afternoon so he had Adolph, 14, and Leo, 12½ years old, stay out of school to help him. Leo had a leather belt lacing wrapped around his right hand and was whirling it around in the basement. The leather caught in one of the big fly wheels that ran the mill, jerking his body into it. Before Henry could stop the steam engine, Leo's body was thrown around and around against a rock wall near it. All his clothes but one shoe were torn off. His right arm was torn off above the elbow, the other arm and both legs broken and other injuries. He was conscious and was carried three and a half blocks from the mill on 6th and Fir Street to the family home at 918 Fir Street. A specialist from Wichita, Kansas, was called and he put Leo in a cast but he died before morning.

In 1914, Henry traded the mill for 360 acres of land near Seneca, Missouri, and two years later he sold that farm and moved to a farm at Montrose, Missouri. In the fall of 1916, they moved back to Seneca, Kansas, where they lived on a farm with Jane's father, Matthias Schneider, and farmed his 360 acres. Can you imagine 11 people moving in with him after being alone for years? It was a 6 room house, seven brothers slept in one room. On August 20, 1917, Jane Schneider, wife of Henry Koelzer, died at the age of 45 from a kidney ailment and pneumonia, leaving 9 children ages 3 to 12. In 1925, Henry sold out his farming operation and bought the Seneca Elevator and operated it until he retired in 1929. Henry died October 1, 1937, of a stroke following surgery.

I remember my father having dark brown hair, blue eyes, fair skin and was about 5'10" in height. My mother had auburn hair, blue-grey eyes and a beautiful complextion. She was about 5'4" in height. I was the housekeeper for 10 years, from age 18 to 28, when Harry Gengler and I were married.

Kukuk Brothers
By Jo Kukuk Ehler

John W. Kukuk was born in Chicago, Illinois, March 11, 1860 and his brother, Fredrick Carl William Kukuk was born September 1873 also at Chicago. Their father, Fred Kukuk was born near Berlin, Germany. Family tradition says they are related to the man who made coo-coo clocks. The little bird is saying the name of the manufactur, that is "Kukuk". Their mother, the former Hannah Martin, was born in Chicago, Illinois and died in 1892 in Somonauk, Illinois. Fred and Hannah were the parents of three children: John W., Lena who married Lewis Myers and lived in Iowa and Fred Jr. The two brothers came to Oklahoma and settled in Noble County. John came first.

John began the butcher's trade at the age of 15 years. For six years he successfully conducted a market in Chicago. His first wife was formerly Bertha Burkhart, a native of LaSalle County, Illinois and the mother of two children: Freddie and Emma. On account of his wife's failing health, John went in 1890 to the Chickasaw Nation, but his hopes of recovery were doomed for she died at Pauls Valley. At Chickasaw he engaged in his former occupation until 1893, when he moved to Perry. His second wife was Hattie Hulbert, a native of Lincoln, Illinois. Of this union one child, Alvin, was born.

At first he opened a store on the corner of Eighth and C Streets which he afterwards sold and bought one on the corner of Seventh and D Streets, the northwest corner of the square. He personally attended to all the details of his business, did his own slaughtering and, to accomodate his trade as a buyer and seller of cattle, had a sixty-acre pasturage. At one time he had all the modern appliances for successfully conducting his enterprise. Among other conviences he had a cooler which held at least a dozen beefs.

John was a republican, a member of the Commercial Club of Perry, Independent Order of Odd Fellows, Knights of Phthias, Modern Woodmen of America and the Order of Maccabees.

The younger brother, Frederick C. W. Kukuk married Sarah Anderson in

1896. They had four children: Stella, Ernest, Clarence and Raymond. They moved to Oklahoma and bought a farm seven miles west of Perry (southwest ¼ of section 11 in Warren Valley Township). Raymond was born after they moved to Oklahoma. Sarah died in 1905.

Fred Kukuk married, the second time, Anna Margaret Gerke, in Kurten, Texas on May 10, 1907. They had seven children. Their first child, a daughter, Anna Pauline was born on their first wedding anniversary. Anna married Martin Piel in December 1928. They have two sons — Kenneth and Allen.

In December 1909, the second child, Josephine Marie was born. Jo married Floyd Ehler in 1942.

Walter Edwin, the first son, was born April 27, 1913, married Ethel Warner in 1934. They have a son, James Edwin and a daughter, Judith Karen.

A son, Leslie, was born in 1915 and died two days later. He is buried in the McGuire Cemetery.

Alva Louise, born February 1916, married Alfred Leonard in 1939. They had two sons, Terry and Joe Michael. Alfred died in January 1969. In October 1969, Alva married Raymond Smith.

Carl Fredrick, born in 1919, married Vera Shelton. They have two daughters, Linda and Francis.

Lela Mae was born April 14, 1923, married Hamilton Buffington in November 1942. They have three daughters: Martha, Peggy and Patricia.

Samuel Elmer Laird
By Marjorie Bowles

The Lairds trace their ancestry to Scotland and Northern Ireland. Most were farmers, but among them were also educators, merchants, and a few ministers. Although family records from Ireland are hard to obtain, we know that Samuel Laird, born there in 1776 came to America and settled in Pennsylvania in 1801 was their direct ancestor. His second marriage was to Eizabeth Campbell (1786-1857), and to this union was born Samuel Laird, Jr. (1810-1883) who married Jane Magee (1807-1896). To this couple was born Joseph McGinley Laird (1835-1915), who moved with his parents to Illinois in 1846. Ten years later, at the age of 22, he met and married Jane Walker McKinney (1833-1927), daughter of William McKinney (1786-1868), who was born on the Isle of Man, near Britain, and Nancy McAllister (1794-1856), who was born in Northern Ireland.

In their Illinois community newspaper, this article appeared: "On May 7, 1867, in New Salem, Pike County, Illinois, Jane Walker McKinney, wife of Joseph McGinley Laird, was favored with a young son." This young son is our subject Samuel Elmer Laird. But he was called Elmer, perhaps because his grandfather, Samuel lived in the same community.

Exhibit at State Fair about 1914 - Designed and constructed by Mr. and Mrs. S. E. Laird.

Nature on the farm and in their timberland supplied the lad with his boyhood pleasures, but as he grew, he was expected to do more and more farm chores, until by the age of 14, he was doing a man's work. His former school teacher introduced him to his future bride, May Belle Shinn (1871-1952), and to this union were born six children: LeOla (1890-1971); Carl (1892-1970); Helen (1898-1946); Paul (1901-1959); Kathryn (1909-1970) and Marjorie (1911). In 1899, Laird and his family moved to Oklahoma, and although the new farm was inferior to their Illinois properties, there were unexpected benefits. Mrs. Laird often said that it wasn't until little Helen was allowed to play in the iron-rich soil of Oklahoma, that she finally became a healthy, active child. Laird later gave this account of his first impression of Perry: "Our public square ... impressed me as a expanse of a dense growth of underbrush ... lining the street were 17 saloons ... teams were hitched to all kinds of vehicles ... strings of wagons could be seen daily, winding their way to and from Perry ..." Laird, as before assumed the management of his father's farm. He was a progressive farmer, practicing crop rotation, and selective livestock breeding. He was a largely self-taught engineer, inventor, artist, and musician. One of his inventions was a cotton picking machine. His pen and ink drawings were flawless; and through the years, he would entertain his children and grandchildren with his styllized drawings of birds, making them personal by writing the child's name on a scroll beneath the bird. He played the violin and the piano, and was a gifted storyteller. In the 16th celebration parade of 1910, he entered a float decorated with his farm products. The celebration committee was so impressed, they asked him to enter an agricultural exhibit in the State Fair for the next year. He did and won 4th place. The next year he won 1st place. It was at that fair that he was offered the position of Noble County's first County Agent, which he accepted.

The exhibit was outstanding. It featured a "Goddess of Harvest" standing before an ornated background, surveying before her the boutiful fruits of nature, flanked by a proscenium arch of cascading vines. The entire display was made of natural grains, seeds, fruits and vegetables — all grown in Noble County. The goddess and the background were meticulously created by applying each of the tiny grains of millet, wheat, corn, kaffir, etc. by hand onto the varnished surfaces.

As County Agent, he introduced several innovative programs. He organized Boy's Farm Clubs long before 4-H Clubs were introduced. He organized Corn and Cotton Clubs, then later Kaffircorn, Wheat, Pig, and Calf Clubs. Helped organize Noble County's first Livestock Association, and the first Registered Stock sale held in Perry. And introduced the concept of Farmers Cooperative endeavors, such as quantity buying of seed potatoes, etc. at wholesale prices. And Laird was called by farmers at all hours to attend to their sick animals.

After retiring, he built several homes on Locust Street, and was later a partner in the Boone Drilling Co. and was builder and co-owner of Lake

Laird, Perry's only recreational resort in the early 1930s.

Whatever he did, he did wholeheartedly and enthusiastically. In his later years, he cared for a flock of sheep on the family farm. He was a gentle man who loved his home and was totally devoted to his wife. His favorite times were Sunday evenings, when the whole family gathered in a circle to hear Mrs. Laird, in her soft voice, read from the Bible. He was a man who truly lived according to the Biblical admonition: ". . . to do justly, to love mercy, and to walk humbly with thy God."

In the sad and fateful year of 1944, the three remaining children of McGinley and Jane Laird — Jennie, Elmer, and Grant — all departed this earthly life. Samuel Elmer Laird succumbed to a heart attack, and died in his home on August 25, 1944, and is buried in Grace Hill cemetery, Perry.

Samuel E. Laird Children

By Marjorie Laird Bowles

Samuel Elmer Laird (1867-1944), of Scotch and Irish ancestry, was the son of Joseph McGinley Laird (1836-1915) and Jane Walker McKinney (1833-1927). When he was twenty-two, he married May Belle Shinn (1871-1952), of English and Dutch ancestry, who was the daughter of John Bush Shinn (1830-) and Charles Fielding (1836-1890). At different periods of his life, Laird was a farmer, Noble County's first County Agent; the designer, engineer and builder of Lake Laird and all its facilities for Perry's first recreation park; an oil well contractor, builder of homes, and in his later years, a tender of sheep on the family farm. He was a private, retiring person, gifted in mathematics and given to meditation.

Mrs. Laird, talented in art and management, was a loving, understanding mother, and a devoted, helpful wife. In the early years of their marriage, they lived in New Salem, Illinois, and in 1899, they came to Oklahoma and lived on a farm one mile north of Perry, until 1912 when they moved into town. About 1928, they moved into the new home which Mr. Laird had built for them at 609 Locust St. Their was a close-knit, Bible-reading, church-going family, and during their parent's lifetime, none of their children, after establishing their own homes, ever lived outside the state of Oklahoma.

The Laird's had six children: LeOla May Laird (1890-1971); Shirley Carl Laird (1892-1970); Helen Beatrice Laird (1898-1946); Samuel Paul Laird (1901-1959); Willa Kathryn Laird (1909-1970); and Marjorie Bell Laird (1911).

(Back Row) (L to R): Helen R. Laird, S. Carl Laird, LeOla Laird; (Front Row) (L to R): S. Paul Laird, Samuel E. Laird holding Kathryn Laird, Maybell holding Marjorie B. Laird — 1912.

LeOla devoted her life to her husband and to homemaking. She was a devout Christian, and had a very close relationship with her mother. For most of her life she was in poor health, but seemed to improve as she got older. She loved flowers, and did her own gardening. She was a meticulous housekeeper, and in her later years became interested in art, and worked at it seriously; her numerous oil painting eventually virtually covered the walls of her home. She died of a heart attack at the age of 81. In the early years of her marriage to Horace Greely "Dock" Donley (1885-1967), he owned and operated a pressing shop on the north side of the square. Through the years he was owner of a buick garage, an automobile repair shop, and an insurance agency. He died at the age of 81. The couple had no children.

Carl was married to Gertrude Evelyn Marchbanks (1894-1975), who was the daughter of J. E. Marchbanks and Eva Scovil. Carl was employed for several years at the Beers' City Drug Store, and became a self-taught Registered Pharmacist. Carl was a mature, thoughtful, caring family person. He and his wife were socially active and traveled extensively. He died of a heart attack at the age of 78. The couple had two sons, Carl Laird, Jr (1919) and Donald Elmer Laird (1924).

Helen was married to Charles Day Boone (1893-1972). She was style-conscious, sensitive, and musically talented. Hers was a gentle sense of humor, and she relished the total fulness of life. Her nature was loving and nurturing; and after the sad death of her own infant daughter, she adopted two other daughters. Her husband was a tall, thin, proud, Texas, whose life work was in the oil fields. Their children were Dorothy May Boone (June 1918 -November 1918), Betty Lou Boone (1929) and Rose Ann Boone (1931). Helen died at the age of 48 from complications of hypertension.

Paul was the first of the Laird's offspring to be born in Oklahoma. He was married to Emily Eunice Craig (1902-1963), daughter of Thomas Craig and Sarah Olivia Root. He worked at Foster's Corner Drug Store, and was co-owner of Laird's Drug Store with his brother, Carl; and later was Purchasing Agent for both John Deere Company and the Grand River Dam Authority at Pryor, Oklahoma, where they made their permanent home. He was impulsive, witty, generous, gregarious and fun-loving, yet serious; and was a talented whistler and show card artist. He was active in the church, and was politically active. He died at the age of 58 years from angina pectoris. The couple had four children: Dr. Paul Craig Laird, M. D. (1923); Samuel Lyndal Laird (1925); Dallas Leland Laird (1931) and Dr. Cheryl Laird, Psychologist (1943).

Kathryn was named for her father's late sister, Willa Kathryn, and was married to Keith McQuiston (1906), son of David Clem McQuiston (1869-1941) and Lou Grace Wagner (1874-1959). Kathryn was an outstanding and popular highschool student, and throughout her life remained socially inclined. She was gifted in secretarial skills, and was musically talented; she produced sweet, melodious tones on the pipe organ, and used her talent for the Lord by playing for church services for many years. She was a gentle person, and had many friends. She died at the age of 61 from multiple myeloma. She and Keith had one daughter, Beverly June McQuiston (1932).

Four Generations of Laird Family. Center Front: baby LeOla Laird, her father Samuel Elmer Laird, her grandfather Joseph McGinley Laird, and her great-grandmother Jane Magee Laird - 1891.

Joseph McGinley Laird
By Marjorie Bowles

Joseph McGinley Laird was born in Pennsylvania in the month of December, 1836. His parents were Samuel Laird (1810-1883), landowner and tavern keeper, and Jane Magee (1807-1896). In 1856, he married Jane Walker McKinney (1833-1927). To this union was born Alice A. Laird (1856-1929); Nancy Jane (Jennie) Laird (1858-1944); and Samuel Elmer Laird (1867-1944). It is from his daily journal that we learn much about our subject: he was a faithful church-goer, he belonged to the Literary Society, he had a keen interest in the events of his time, and he was hospitable and friendly. Laird was a successful farmer. Their farmland east of New Salem, Pike County, Illinois, was fertile and productive, but his success was equally due to industry and resourcefulness. He believed in and practiced the Work Ethic. They raised horses, cattle, sheep and hogs; and crops of corn and oats, wheat and buckwheat. And their timberland furnished fuel. They made their own soap, even some of their shoes. Laird was an unwavering Democrat, and had a healthy interest in politics. He was a contemporary of Abraham Lincoln, and fortunately, kept his journal through the war years, and by so doing, has left a priceless heritage in his running account of the Civil War from the perspective of an Illinois farmer. In 1899, he sold all their land holdings, pulled up roots and transplanted his family to Oklahoma and settled on a farm one mile north of Perry, which he had purchased from a man who had staked a claim at the opening of the Cherokee Strip.

I, his granddaughter, made a trip into my ancestors' home territory last year (1985). How beautiful and lush were the rows of tall corn in the fertile Illinois soil! How well-kept the homes in that prosperous agricultural region. I was eager to visit the lovely homestead of my grandfather Laird —

There she stood, staunch and proud and indomitable, with her chimneys rising, alert, from the fireplaces that warmed her spacious rooms. I had daydreamed, since childhood on the early photographs of the place —

But now, the handsome gingerbread trimmings were gone; the formal, functional louvered shutters removed — gone, too, were the cooling, quieting shade trees. In back, though, the little cook-house still stood, like in colonial times, just steps away from the house. I recalled the pictures of the family group — three generations, in the yard, happily relaxing in the shade with friends who had come a-calling, all in their lovely attire; unmistakably depicting gracious living. I stood there pondering, "Why did they ever leave this kind of life? Could a new land possibly offer more than they had right here? Was it the need for a new beginning — or simply the lure of cheap land?" Perhaps I can never know — never be quite sure.

But in an August 1899 issue of the Decatur (Illinois) Guide, there appeared this feature article: "A terrible fever is raging in New Salem which is proving very serious. The doctor's can't give any relief. They say there is nothing in medical books that throws any light on the disease — several have been carried away with it. It is called "Oklahoma fever". Six wagons went last week. This week Emmett Griffith ... McGinley Laird, William Miller and Chauncey Harshamn and others took the train. Six other families are going in the fall." Perhaps this explains it. Caught up in group psychology! Or it could have been simply an inherited tendency to move on to new lands-fresh excitement. McGinley's ancestors must have been imbued with a spirit of adventure for had not his grandfather, Samuel Laird (1776-1845) left his homeland in Northern Ireland, set out for America and settled in Pennsylvania; and his father left Pennsylvania and moved to Illinois?

But in the case of my grandparents, their move to Oklahoma seems to have been unfortunate, materially; for their finances dwindled, and their standard of living lowered. Laird was no longer a young man capable of the strenous labor he was used to in Illinois. His Oklahoma crops had to be urged from the unproductive soil — and the one-and-a-half story house, by comparison, spoke of crude and hurried construction. In 1910, McGinley and his family moved from the farm into a small home in town where he retired. The fine quality furnishings they had brought from Illinois were incongruous with the lowly appearance of the little frame house at 717 Sixth Street. But if they ever regretted their move to Oklahoma, they never said so. McGinley died at the age of 79, and Jane at 94. They are buried side by side in Grace Hill Cemetery in Perry.

Edwin C. Lane
By Harvey Lane

Edwin Carlton Lane (better known as Ed or E. C. Lane was born February 7, 1860 near Springfield, Cass County, Illinois. He married Sarah Tesh February 25, 1886 in Summer County Kansas and lived on a farm near Belle Plaine. Sarah Tesh was born August 18, 1868 near Winston-Salem, North Carolina.

Ed Lane and his brother-in-law, Alex Tesh, hearing that the Cherokee Outlet would soon be opened for settlement, engaged a young half Indian boy, Henry Starr, to guide them across the Strip. Henry Starr later was a brother-in-law of the notorious bandit queen, Belle Starr.

The men looked over the land and then went back to Kansas to await the opening of the strip and to make arrangements for the "run" and preparations for their families during their absence.

Ed and Sarah's children at the time of the opening were Shelby born February 15, 1887, Bessie born May 26, 1888, David born September 27, 1889 and William born January 13, 1893. Also living with the family at this time were two small nieces, Laura and Martha Tesh, Children of Alex Tesh whose wife had died. Also, living with them was Sarah's brother, Rufus Tesh. Later Sarah's father, James Madison Tesh, who had been wounded in the Civil War would make his home with the Lane family.

A few days before the opening, Ed Lane and Alex, along with James Tesh, 22 year old brother of Alex, rode across the Cherokee Outlet down the Chisolm trail. The three men went to the home of Jim and Hennie Martin near Coyle, in Old Oklahoma. Jim Martin was an uncle of Sarah Lane, Alex and Jim Tesh.

Ed Lane and the two Tesh men made the run on horseback, starting near Orlando. Both Ed and Jim Tesh were fortunate. Ed staked a claim to the southeast quarter of section 27 in Walnut township, Jim claimed the southeast quarter of section 28, a half mile west of the Lane claim. Alex was unable to find a claim but was soon able to buy out another homesteader and purchased the northwest quarter of section 27, adjoining the claims of his brother Jim and his brother-in-law Ed Lane.

Stillwater Creek ran across the west side of the Lane homestead. Ed made a dug-out in a high bank above the creek. He began to clear the land and get the ground ready for planting. Ed was able to borrow a mowing machine from John Payne who had settled a few miles south of the Lane claim, and was able to cut enough good grass for winter hay.

As soon as he could leave the claim Ed went back to get his family. It was winter when they started out in the covered wagon that would be, not only their transportation but their home for many months. In addition to the family, their bedding and a few clothes, they had 1,000 pounds of flour, stone jars of lard, crocks of lye soap, cooking utensils and a huge iron kettle, three extra horses, a coop with a few chickens, two cows and a cultivator.

When they arrived in Perry on the day before Christmas, Ed had 35 cents in money. He spent 25 cents for Christmas candy for the children and arrived at their new home with only ten cents in his pocket. At the claim, Shelby and Rufus slept in the dug-out with Ed. Sarah, the two Tesh girls, Bessie and the two youngest boys slept crosswise on feather mattresses in the covered wagon overjet. Harvie, the Lane's fourth son, was born in the covered wagon overjet on August 10, 1895.

The family had planned to build their new home just above the creek bank, but when they dug a well, the water was bad and they had to locate another place. A black man, named Graham, told Ed that he could "witch for water" and could guarantee to strike water within 22 feet of the surface of the ground. Graham did witch for water and did locate an excellent water supply near the east side of the claim. A large log room over a cellar was built where the next two children were born, Marvin on July 3, 1899 and Daisy on February 10, 1901.

Later the larger white frame house was built and became Grandpa and Grandma Lane's house to many grandchildren who always looked forward to happy times there. Here Lillie was born August 3, 1903 and Melvin on July 30, 1908. Melvin died in infancy.

The well located by "witching" was very important to the Lane family. It provided good cold water for drinking, also provided water for cooking, washing clothes, bathing and was the only refrigeration for years. Grandma Lane would hang the cream in the well to cool and then after the cream was churned the butter was hung in the well to keep sweet and good. Muskmellons and watermellons were cooled in the tank by the well.

Ed died November 27, 1942 and Sarah December 16, 1944. They are buried in the Shelton Cemetery close to the homestead.

The Lane farm, so rich in family tradition and so dear to the many Lane descendants who gather every year in a family reunion now belongs to the City of Stillwater, Oklahoma and is under the waters of Lake McMurtry.

Ray J. Laughlin
By Nona Wetzel

Percy Ray Jackson Laughlin was born March 22, 1876 in Kansas, the son of Mary Alameda (Busby) and James Harper Laughlin. Mary Almeda's mother was Molly Ann Norex. She was the daughter of Chief Norex of the Osage tribe. Molly Ann married Dr. James Busby and had two children, Mary Alameda and John. When Mary Alameda was three years old, her mother died and both children were raised by a step-mother. When Mary Alameda was teaching school at 17 in Marshalltown, Iowa, she met and married James Harper Laughlin, from Caddis, Ohio. They lived in Marshalltown for a year or so, then moved by covered wagon to Kansas, with one child. Here they lived with the Indians for awhile where Mary Alameda's father was a doctor for the Osage Indians. James and Mary Alameda had nine children: Lizzie, Odessa, Pearl, Harry, Ray, Iva, Loy, Nora and Sylvia.

Roy's father died when he was young and his mother came to Oklahoma with them. She said that she "was a graduate of Poverty College. I think we must save the patches and patch the patches. They are easier on the nerves than mortgages." Another of her saying was "Some people think economy is a disgrace but it is a character builder. I mean saving, not stingeness. Adam may blame Eve but I do not think many women owe the machine companies or take out mortgages. My idea is to pay as you go or do without." She followed one of her sons to Vermillion, Canada and died there October 18, 1940 at the age of 92, enjoying good health up to the day of her death.

Ray Laughlin came by covered wagon to a farm in east Noble County northwest of Glencoe, Oklahoma in 1893. His wife's name was Lora Laura Penny. She was born December 20, 1877 in Independence, Missouri. Ray traded 23 mules and accepted a $1000 mortgage for the place. To pay off the mortgage he raised corn which he hauled to Stillwater with a pair of mules and a wagon.

Ray and Lora's children were all born near Glencoe, Oklahoma where Odessa was born May 10, 1904; Maynard born January 4, 1910; Nona born February 17, 1912; Mary born June 18, 1914; Edna born August 28, 1920; and Ruth was born March 20, 1923.

Ray had accumulated four quarters of land, 160 acres each. The oldest child was deceased and four of the remaining received a farm, the other inherited the town property and money at his death.

Wesley W. Learned
By Velda Y. Zimmerman

Wesley William Learned, third son of Wilmer and Vivian Hendershot Learned, was born on his grandfather's homestead in Stafford County, near Zenith, Kansas, June 26, 1936. His father had been born, lived and died at the age of 88 on that homestead.

Mrs. Wesley Learned is the former Eileen Fern Zimmerman, daughter of Emil and Velda Young Zimmerman. Her grandfather, Calvin L. Young took a claim in 1893 which is a part of their farm. Her grandfather, Charles B. Zimmerman moved his family to their farm in January of 1910. Eileen lived on the Zimmerman farm until she started to school and on the Young farm since she was married.

Both of Wesley's grandfathers were ministers, Grandfather William Learned a Methodist minister, and Grandfather Charles A. Hendershot a United Brethren minister.

Eileen's grandfathers farmed for a living but her grandfather Calvin L. Young preached anywhere they could not afford a pastor, just for the good he could do.

Wesley and Eileen grew up in the United Presbyterian Church where he had eight years of perfect attendance even when that meant plowing through three miles of snow on foot. They and their family are equally active in the Billings Methodist Church.

Wesley's father grew a thousand kind of iris, which was Eileen's mother's and grandmother's favorite flower, so they met there when the iris bloomed.

Two of Wesley's cousins who grew up on the next farm came to Sterling College, one of them in Eileen's mother's class. The Youngs bought a house in Sterling where they and Velda lived while she was in college, and to which they retired. They also bought a farm nearby, for Eileen's family, but they had to wait until March to get possession so her father planted another wheat crop in Oklahoma, and she lived with her grandparents to go to kindergarten since kindergarten was required in Sterling before first grade. This was a bonus for she became

Back Row (L to R): Laren, Sherilyn, Lewain, Merryl. Front Row: Louella, Wesley, Sandra (Parnell), Alan and Eileen Learned - December 18, 1982.

well acquainted with her grandparents and when she came to high school she was with children she'd been with in kindergarten.

Wesley's mother was a graduate nurse who found him jobs at an early age. He did his work so well he was always welcome back. When he was 12, he farmed a widow's farm for a year. Then his father interested him in cars so he learned mechanics by working with them. Huge trees sheltered wildlife and he often hunted meat for the table. Learning his lessons was never a problem for him. He was slightly built, like his father, but he made up in spirit what he lacked in weight. Eileen was tall enough but had no drive to be athletic. When her father succumbed to cancer her first week in high school, she took over the chores on the farm and the children helped her, milking and caring for livestock. One year a classmate of hers asked to ride to the Fair with us. I had to hurry home to drive the "kid bus" for our rural school and had to drive so fast to be home in time that he was really frightened. The next year I offered to take him as I no longer drove the bus and would not have to hurry. Then I thought of it that too much togetherness can spoil a friendship so I wondered what to do to keep the two from getting "fed up" with each other.

Then I thought of Wesley. Both boys played in the band so they would have something in common. Both would come to Sterling College. I called Wesley's mother and set up a meeting at the Fair grounds. The three spent quite a bit of time together, but the other boy barged ahead while Wesley who is also quick by nature, brought up the rear and did not urge Eileen to hurry.

When Wesley came to college, he helped us on the farm as his brothers and other college boys had when needed. One day Loyalea told me that only one other family in school besides ours did not have a TV, and that since her cow was dry, we could sell her to help buy a TV. They were at school when the man came to haul to cow to the sale so I let him take the wrong cow. When the girls went out to milk, Eileen came in crying — her cow was gone! I would have had no idea what to do but Wesley was there and said, "Let's stop the sale," so he and Ywain and I jumped in the car and drove first to Lyons — no sale there — then to Hutchinson where the sale was over but the cow was in the pen. Wesley found who bought her, called him, told what had happened and the buyer said for us to take her. Wesley found a pickup to borrow and before midnight Eileen's cow was home to be milked. We still turn to Wesley when we get in jams, and he solves them!

He volunteered for two years service so he could farm without interruption, became a paratrooper in Munich, visisted Emil's Swiss cousins twice, came home and he and Ywain farmed, and he and Eileen were married August 13, 1957, and have four sons and a daughter Lewain was born June 30, 1958; Alan February 24, 1960; Laren April 27, 1962; Sherilyn, June 11, 1964; Merryl October 12, 1967; and Lovella, June 5, 1970. Alan married Sandra Parnell, born February 1, 1962, on December 18, 1982. Besides farming, Wesley drove 100 miles round trip daily, to finish his degree and was teaching under contract three days after he finished it and is still teaching 28 miles from home his 15th year.

Eileen also continued her education and took her degree a year ago and subsitutes in classrooms or cafeteria in Billings when called.

Lewain is a Lance Corporal in the Marine active reserve and farms between times, Alan is going for his doctorate in Chemistry, Laren is a senior in architecture in West Virginia, Sherilyn a senior in Austin College, Sherman, Texas after a semester in France and another in Washington, D.C., Merryl a freshman in Sterling College and Lovella a sophomore in high school. Instead of being a "spoiled baby" of the family, Lovella has undertaken the church janitorship and cleans until it shines.

Everyone turns to Wesley for help — his activities would kill him but that he does enjoy every minute of it. His children are very fortunate to have a father who can teach them so many skills. My son was barely nine when his father died but Wesley worked with him like a brother and friend.

Emilie LeBus
By Mildred Highfill

Emilie Anna Tibbs was born September 10, 1860 in Fairfield, Illinois, the daughter of Julia Ann (Wood) and David Perrie Tibbs. Her father was a native of Kentucky born near Bowling Green. He was wounded in the battle of Shiloh in the Civil War, serving with Company I, forty-eight Illinois Infantry and this wound eventually caused his death January 14, 1878. On the paternal side Mrs. LeBus is descended from an honored line of planters and farmers. Her father was a son of Sarah (Covington) and Charles Tibbs and a grandson of Marguerite (Madeira) and John Tibbs. She of the surname Madeira having been a native of Barcelona, Spain. There is in Kentucky a city named Covington, after the family of Mrs. LeBus paternal grandmother. Her mother, Julia Ann (Wood) Tibbs was a native of Fairfield, Illinois born in that city's "Egypt" district, died October 13, 1905. Julia Ann was the daughter of Emily (King) and William Henry Wood, her father having been a son of Lucy (Schackleford) and Otha Wood, both of whom were of Louisville, Kentucky and her mother a daughter of Emily (Crowe- Anglicized French name) and Captain Phillip King. Phillip King lived near the Mississippi River and held the rank of Captain on a river steamboat. Both he and his wife were pioneer settlers of St. Louis, Missouri.

Emilie married first, July 23, 1877, Joseph Obadiah Owen of Owensboro,

Early day WCTU parade led by Emilie LeBus - about 1920.

(Left to Right): Katherine, Frank, Alta and John Lesh.

Kentucky, at Fairfield, Illinois. To this union was born one child, William Owen, March 18, 1881. He married Erma Nelgen of Mt. Carmel, Illinois and they were parents of a child Marguerite Inez born July 17, 1909 at St. Louis, Missouri.

After Mr. Owen's death in Granite City, Illinois, she married John B. LeBus of Flora, Illinois, the ceremony being performed at Louisville, Illinois, October 17, 1913. John B. LeBus was of French extraction, a native of Missouri. He shod horses to "make the run" into the Cherokee Strip and himself filed a claim two miles north of Perry. In this vicinity he remained until his death in 1915.

On September 2, 1916, Mrs. LeBus became librarian at the Carnegie Library in Perry. She spent the next years of her life in improving the library. She died in 1941. John and Emilie are buried in the Grace Hill cemetery.

John Lesh
By Anna Jane Lesh

John Lesh was born 6 October 1850 in Marklin, Bohemia. This is now located in Czechoslovakia. He married Katherina Schevold in 1870 in Marklin. Katherina was born 22 October 1849 in Marklin, Bohemia. To this union 10 children were born, nine of them in Bohemia. John and Katherina came to New York from Hamburg, Germany in 1885. They came to Nebraska where he purchased a sod plow. John brought the plow to Kansas loaded onto his wagon and when the family moved to the Kansas line to make the run into the Cherokee Strip, the plow was tied to the side of their wagon. The Lesh family obtained a homestead in Auburn Township on the southeast quarter of section 19. The plow was used to break out the first land on this farm. When the groundbreaking ceremonies were held for the Cherokee Strip Museum, Henry Bellmon, governor of Oklahoma, used this plow pulled by two mules. The plow is on display in the museum.

Mary, first born child of John and Katherina was born 10 December 1870 in Prague, Bohemia. She died 7 January 1943 at Anadarko, Oklahoma. She married John Ruzicka 16 November 1893 in Yukon, Oklahoma Territory. Both migrated from Bohemia on the same ship. The couple participated in the Kiowa-Commanche-Apache Reservation "Land Lottery" in 1899 and moved to Anadarko in 1900. Mary was able to speak three different languages — English, German and Bohemian. John and Mary were the parents of four sons — John, Henry, Joe and George.

John, the second child of John and Katherina, was born in November 1878 in Marklin, Bohemia. He died 1 November 1901 at Sumner, Oklahoma Territory. He is buried in the little Bohemian Catholic cemetery in Noble Township.

Joseph, the next child of John and Katherina Lesh, was born 15 March 1880 in Bohemia. He died 5 June 1941 at Sumner, Oklahoma and was buried in the Grace Hill cemetery in Perry.

Frank was born in 1884 in Bohemia. He was attending law school in Omaha, Nebraska, when he died unexpectedly. He was brought back to Oklahoma and buried in the Bohemian Catholic cemetery in Noble township.

Alta Katherina was born 13 May 1894 in Sumner, Oklahoma. She was the youngest child of John and Katherina. She married Rudolph Ritthaler (14 December 1889-8 September 1967). Alta and Rudolph were parents of three children: William who married Leta Harlan; Helen, who marred Wayne Knori; and Bertha.

John Lesh died in 1917. Katherina died in 1922. It is believed John and Katherina had another daughter, Anna, who married Henry Bennett as she is mentioned in a card of thanks in 1922 at the time of Katherina's death.

Jack D. Lewellen
By Helen Marie Lewellen

Jack Duane Lewellen was born in Orlando, Oklahoma, January 25, 1922, to E. E. Lewellen and Verna Compton Lewellen. Jack grew up in Orlando and attended school there, playing in the school orchestra and basketball.

Jack, his parents and sister, Norma Jean, moved to Perry, Oklahoma, in 1937, where his father was a rural mail carrier for over 25 years. Jack attended Perry High School where he lettered in Band and Basketball and graduated from Perry High School in 1940. He attended Northern Oklahoma Junior College at Tonkawa and graduated from there in 1942.

On September 11, 1942, Jack volunteered for service in the Army, during World War II, where he served in limited service in the Army Recruiting Stations in Oklahoma City, Chickasha, and Tulsa, also serving in the Induction Stations in Oklahoma City and Tulsa in 1943 and 1944. Jack was transferred to the Prisoner of War

Jack and Helen Marie (Neal) Lewellen - 1943.

Camp for the Germans stationed at Camp Maxey, Paris, Texas in 1944.

Jack was married to Helen Marie Neal in the First Christian Church of Perry, Oklahoma on February 14, 1943, by the Rev. Jack Oliver.

Helen Marie was born August 17, 1922, at Perry, Oklahoma to Nina Thomason Neal and Roy O. Neal. Helen Marie attended all the schools in Perry, Oklahoma, and graduated from Perry High School in 1940. She was employed by Donahue and Mugler as Secretary and Insurance Underwriter at the time of their marriage, where she had been employed for over three years.

While Jack was stationed in Tulsa, Mrs. Lewellen was employed by Robert H. Seigfried Insurance Company as an Insurance Underwriter. During Jack's term of duty at Camp Maxey, Helen Marie was employed by the Red Cross as Secretary in the Station Hospital.

After Jack's discharge from the Army, he was employed by the Famous Department Store here in Perry, which was later changed to Peters Department Store.

On September 15, 1950, Jack began work with the First National Bank serving as teller and bookkeeper. Jack took over the operational bookkeeping of the bank in 1959, and was promoted to Vice-President in charge of Operations in 1972. Jack retired from the bank on June 30, 1985, after almost 35 years of employment there.

Jack and Helen Marie have three children, Sandra Kay (Davison) who was born December 8, 1945, Colin Lewellen, born November 5, 1947, and Kelly Neal Lewellen, born April 6, 1952.

Mrs. Lewellen inherited the farm her grandfather, Charles S. Thomason,

Jack Lewellen family 1954 — Colin, Kelly and Sandra.

claimed in the Cherokee Strip Outlet Run in 1893. Mr. Lewellen inherited in partnership with his sister, Mrs. Norma Jean Lawson, the farm in Logan County that his grandfather, James Compton, claimed in the Oklahoma Land Run of 1889 which is located south of Orlando, Oklahoma.

Jack and Helen Marie are enjoying his retirement by traveling over the United States. Mrs. Lewellen is interested in genealogy and has traced, with the help of several cousins back to her great-great-great grandfather, Jacob Brougher, who first was a wagon maker. Also Jack's grandfather, James Compton was born in or near Selkirk, Scotland. Margaret Compton lived to be 99 years and seven months, one of the cities oldest residents. Among two daughters and four sons she was survived by a sister, Mrs. M. A. Younger of Perthshire, Scotland, many grandchildren and great-grandchildren.

Jack and Helen Marie have 6 grandchildren, Sindy Eileen, born November 9, 1969, Suzanne Marie, born March 27, 1974, Samuel Stinnett Davison, born June 2, 1981, who live in Stillwater; and Carey Ann, born November 9, 1970, Tiffany Dawn, born April 29, 1974, and Jason Duane Lewellen, born November 3, 1978, who live in Perry. Sandra and Sam Davison are the parents of the Davison children. Colin Duane and Marcella (Marcy) Lewellen are the parents of the Lewellen children. God blessed Kelly Neal and Sheila with no children.

Conrad J. Lindeman
By Ruth Queen

Conrad John (born in 1853) and Rose Lindeman (born in 1861) along with their three sons, Isadore, George (1885), and Fred (Dutch) (1890), came to Guthrie to make the September 16, 1893 run into the Cherokee Strip.

Both C. J. and Rose Hempfling Lindeman were Ohio natives who had moved to Westphalia, Kansas to make their home as newlyweds. In Kansas, they ran a boarding house and hotel.

At the Cherokee Strip run, C.J. staked his claim at what is now 712 Delaware Street. He opened a grocery store known as C.J. Lindeman Grocery. In the early days, the grocery store was a gathering place for many organizations. The Catholic services were held in the rear of the grocery store until the first church was built. Father Willebrord Voogden, the first parish priest, also stayed at the Lindeman home periodically. St. Rose of Lima Church was named for Rose Lindeman, and two other old timers, Rose McCormick and Rose Doyle.

Butter, eggs, sausage, vegetables and fruit were bought and sold at the grocery store. Many farmers' grocery bills would be paid only at harvest time — no wheat crop, no money that year for grocery bill. The grocery store was unique in those days. Many families would spend most of Saturday there visiting with friends and doing their weekly trading. The grocery store was managed by C.J. until his death in 1913. He was buried in the Catholic cemetery in Perry.

The eldest son, Isadore, had left Perry as a very young man to enter the business world on the west coast. He spent most of his life in the furniture business in Ranier, Oregon. This left the two younger sons, George and Fred, along with their mother, Rose, to manage the grocery store. George remained single. On November 21, 1916, Fred married Carrie Marie Miller, daughter of E.J. and Ida Miller, another pioneer family. To this union four daughters were born: Mary (1917), Lucile "Sidy" (1919), Ruth (1921), and Philamene (1924).

Rose Lindeman lived a full life with her family and church until her death in 1944. She was buried beside her husband in the Catholic cemetery in Perry, Oklahoma. George's health failed shortly after his mother's death, and he passed away in 1947. He was buried in the Catholic cemetery in Perry, Oklahoma. Many would remember the colorful character George was. His main loves were baseball, circuses, Fred's girls, and playing the clarinet. George played in Dr. W. C. Marshall's "ole time" band that performed in the courthouse park Friday nights.

Fred managed the Lindeman Grocery with little help until his sudden death in 1948. He was buried in the Catholic cemetery, Perry. Carrie Lindeman, with the help of son-in-law, Bob Craft, kept the grocery store open until 1957. She was 66 years old. Her memory of historical events, dates and birthdays amazed Perryans until her death in 1982. She was almost 91 years old and had always done all of her housework and most of her yard work. She was buried in the Catholic cemetery, Perry.

H. A. (Cotton) Linn
By Kathrine Linn

H. A. or Cotton, (as he is called by everyone), was from Verden, Oklahoma. He is the son of Harry and Maybelle Linn. Kathrine, (Katie), was from Orlando, Oklahoma. I am the daughter of John and Elizabeth Pfeiffer. Both of us were from farm families and were very active in 4-H and FFA work. We actually met showing steers at livestock shows. Cotton showed only hereford steers and I showed only Angus cattle. Cotton had the Grand Champion Steer at Oklahoma City Stock Show in March 1939, and again in March 1941. I had the Grand Champion Steer at the Oklahoma State Fair in September 1941.

Cotton attended A & M College, (now O.S.U.) at Stillwater. On January 30, 1944, H. A. and I were married. Cotton worked for my dad, John Pfeiffer, for a few months before he got a job with W. E. Harvey, a hereford breeder from Ada, Oklahoma. He worked there until Harvey's dispersion sale in June of 1946. Our first child, John Aaron, was born at Ada, on March 7, 1945. The cost of the hospital stay was $38.08.

H. A. (Cotton) Linn family in January. Seated (L to R): Ryan Lee Luter, Katherine, H. A. (Cotton), on his lap is Dustin Kyle Luter, JoDawn, Dee Jay. Standing (L to R): Dannie Luter, Patty Jo (Linn) Luter, Burdettya (Garvie) Linn, John Aaron Linn.

Wedding picture of Katherine and H. A. Linn - January 30, 1944.

John Aaron was born just sixteen hours before my birthday.

Cotton's wages were $150.00 a month. We saved half of it each month as we had a big garden, chickens, gathered fruit off trees on the ranch, and had our own milk. Cotton worked seven days a week. After the dispersion sale we moved to Red Rock on a farm owned by my dad.

We then started to farm for ourselves, raising cattle, chickens, a big garden and milking a few cows. Our home was not modern. We had no bathroom, no running water, we cut wood for heat, and we had a coal oil stove for cooking. My Dad gave us an old F-20 International tractor which we used to start farming. We bought a 2-bottom plow for $75.00 and were set. Before our first harvest, we got an old "B" Model truck, a 5-foot Allis combine and a 2-wheel trailer. Each year we tried to add a few more things to work with. Finally we got a black market "LA" Case tractor from a dealer for $3,000.00 and a 4-bottom plow for it. We thought we had really stepped up! Then in 1947, we got a new Chevrolet truck. Each year we bought what machinery we could afford.

Cotton and I both helped my Dad put his hay up and we cared for his cattle which he had here at Red Rock. In dry years, we hauled water for his cattle from Ponca City lots of nights after coming in from the field.

Cotton joined the Red Rock Masonic Lodge in January 1950. I joined the Red Rock Eastern Star in May 1950, in which Cotton had to join later. We are both charter members of Red Rock Eastern Star and are Past Matron and Past Patron. Cotton is also Past Master of Red Rock Masonic Lodge and has been the Secretary of his lodge for nineteen years. He has served as an officer of the Oklahoma Grand Lodge for three years, served as a committee member for five years and a District Deputy for two years.

Cotton and I have always been very active in the Red Rock Christian Church, as well as the lodge, 4-H and FFA work and community activities. Cotton was President of the Noble County Fair Board for nine years. He has also been an Elder and Deacon of his church.

In 1952, we bought our first farm in Noble County. It was just a mile north of where we were living on my Dad's place. We bought more in this area as we could afford it, so as to make our permanent home in Noble County. When we bought our home place in 1959, we needed shed room, so Cotton, John Aaron and I, built our own sheds with some used lumber we purchased from the Marland CO-OP, (out of the old Marland CO-OP elevator that was torn down).

On January 15, 1953, our daughter, Patty Jo, was born at Ponca City Hospital. The hospital bill was $87.70 and the doctor bill was $75.00. This was a special day for Cotton as she was born on his 30th birthday.

When John Aaron was about old enough for 4-H, a neighbor boy, Mickey Ratliff, gave him a Chester White gilt. Then when he had his first litter of pigs, John Aaron gave a gilt to another 4-H boy. John Aaron showed steers he raised and exhibited the Grand and Reserve Grand steer and hogs many times at the Noble County level.

John Aaron purchased forty acres of land with money he made in his 4-H work. As a freshman, he joined FFA. He was the national winner in Livestock Farming in November 1964, and he was named an American Farmer in November 1966. He started to farm with his Dad after graduating from high school and he bought land and machinery of his own as he could afford it.

On August 10, 1969, he married Burdettya Garvie, daughter of Burdette and Aylene Garvie of Morrison. She had just graduated from OSU at Stillwater after being very active in 4-H at Sumner and Morrison. Burdettya taught school at Marland for five years before JoDawn Hope was born on June 25, 1974, at the Pawnee hospital. Burdettya quit teaching to care for her family. Then on February 28, 1979, Dee Jay (D.J.), a son was born. John Aaron and Burdettya and their family are very active at their church, the Marland Methodist-Christian Church. They also stay busy with community, school and 4-H projects as JoDawn is already showing Angus heifers.

Patty Jo worked in the fields when she was old enough. She disced behind the combine and as she has said, "I never had a cab tractor or air-conditioning. I just sat in the dirt and sun." Patty was very active in 4-H. She made all of her own clothes. She sewed, canned, cooked, baked and showed steers, hogs and sheep in her 4-H Club work. She showed the Grand Champion and Reserve Grand Champion lamb and steer at the Noble County Shows at Perry. She raised her own lambs that she showed.

Both John Aaron and Patty graduated from Red Rock High School. Patty went to OSU at Stillwater and graduated in August, 1974. On August 11, 1974 she and Dannie Luter were married. Dannie is the son of Harold and Arvella Luter of Red Rock. Patty taught the third grade at Morridon Elementary School for six years. On July 16, 1980, they had a son, Ryan Lee. He was born at the Stillwater Hospital. Patty quit teaching to be at home with her family. Dannie graduated from OSU and took a job as meat manager at IGA at Stillwater. Then on March 22, 1982, another son, Dustin Kyle was born at Stillwater Hospital. Dannie and Patty are farmers now in the Morrison community and are active in community functions. At this time our whole family is farming and raising cattle in Noble County.

Fred G. Logan
By Awynne Logan Wilkey

Frederick Grant Logan was born May 19, 1890, at Lomax, Henderson county, Illinois. He was an only child. When he was a baby, his father took him away and he didn't see his mother until years later. His father remarried and, by his second marriage, had four girls and a boy. Fred Logan attended law school at Macomb, Illinois, to become a lawyer but financial difficulties forced him to drop out and he went to work as a reporter on a Chicago, Illinois, newpaper. He came to Oklahoma and worked for James Hillman at a printing shop and newspaper at Ralston, Oklahoma. Later, they moved the paper to Salisaw, Oklahoma.

In April, 1912, Fred came to Morrison, Oklahoma as the manager of the Morrison Transcript. On June 9, 1912, at Sallisaw, he married Mabel, daughter of James Hillman. James Hillman had published a newspaper, The Morrison New Era, in Morrison a few years before.

Fred soon bought the paper at Morrison and published it for over 40 years with the help of his wife, who set type "all by hand." Through years that twice brought personal tragedies, they never missed an issue of the weekly newspaper. Morrison patrons paid $1 a

Fred and Mabel Logan.

year (out-of-towners paid $1.50) for the paper.

He was a great admirer of Abraham Lincoln and once published the following in his newspaper:

With Apologies to Lincoln

"One score years ago, there was bought forth upon this continent a new paper, conceived in liberty and dedicated to the proposition that all men are created equal.

We are now engaged in a great moral and physical strife, testing whether that paper or any paper so conceived and so dedicated can long endure. We are met at the threshold of that paper. We have come to try to earn some pork and beans to dedicate to wholesome appetites.

It is altogether fitting and proper that we should do this. But in a larger sense we cannot dedicate — we cannot consecrate — we cannot hallow this enterprise.

The loyal friends and patrons who, through long years of patronage, have dedicated it far above our power to add or detract.

The world will little note nor long remember what we say here, but the world never forgets a friend and loyalty.

It is for us of the paper, rather, to be dedicated here to the unfinished work which the patronage and encouragement of these friends have so far nobly advanced.

It is rather for us to be here dedicated to the cause for which they have given a big round measure of devotion — that we here highly resolve that the confidence of these friends in us shall not be in vain — that the paper shall have a new birth of freedom and that the Transcript of the people, by the people and for the people shall not perish from the earth."

He was a loyal Republican and once ran for representative from the eighth Congressional District of Oklahoma. He was considered a great public speaker.

Fred and Mabel Logan had five children: Embert Lemar born March 29, 1913; Lenora Alice born February 21, 1915; Awynne Mabel born December 8, 1917; Fred Hillman born June 14, 1920, and James Wesley born and died May 19, 1924. Embert Logan is a sign painter by trade and lives in Ponca City, Oklahoma. He did not marry.

Alice Logan died August 7, 1934, following an operation for appendicitis. The next issue of the paper carried the eulogy, "In loving memory of our departed daughter" written by her father. Fred Hillman Logan passed away October 24, 1944. Once again, the father wrote the obituary with the note "You will know friends, why the paper is late this week." He closes with this thought: "We must carry on. With heavy hearts we shall do the best we can. As a printer, our boy would want us to do this. He would want the old paper which he so dearly loved to go out as usual and it is a tribute to him that we carry on."

An excerpt from one column states, "We like a glass of beer and an electric fan on a hot day — and more than one glass if the weather is extremely warm. And it is surprising how few women we think more of than we do our own wife."

Fred Logan died of a stroke November 11, 1952, and is buried in the Morrison cemetery by the side of the three children who preceded him in death. Mabel died June 3, 1983, and is buried in the Morrison cemetery.

Mabel Hillman Logan
By Awynne Logan Wilkey

James and Lenora Hillman moved on a school lease somewhere between Mulhall and Orlando in Old Oklahoma late in the year of 1890, and put up a little cottage made of the barked slabs of timber from a saw mill. At the time of locating here they had a daughter barely 3 years old, and a son, Fred, not quite two. They located here to be near the parents of Lenora, the Jim Chesshers.

The Hillmans were looking for a visit from the stork in the early part of the year, 1891, and had alerted the mother of Lenora, Theresa Chessher and a neighbor, Mrs. Jim Davis, to be present at the event. One beautiful morning on February 24, 1891, Lenora put out a big washing and by afternoon a real storm came. As directed, she hung out a white cloth to let the ladies know they were needed. In due time, a scrawny little crooked footed 6 lb. baby girl arrived. The cabin consisted of one

Mabel Hillman Logan at her daughter's home in Morrison.

large room with a fireplace and a small kitchen. The walls were strips of barked slabs with the cracks on the inside covered by the same. The roof was also of the slabs but it was home while they waited for the Cherokee Strip to open for settlement. By evening, snow had arrived and the bed of the 22 year old mother and the infant, who they named Mary Mabel, was sprinkled with snow. Papa James would carefully lift the colicy infant to a safe position over the coals in the fireplace to warm her crooked little feet.

When the Hillmans wanted to make the run into the strip they learned of the soon opening of the Sac and Fox country to white settlement. Hillman promptly got ready to make the run on a small mule and was successful in filing on a claim nine miles north of Chandler.

True to pioneers, they dismantled the cabin and loaded the young wife and three babies into the wagon and located on the newly acquired farm. They made friends with a young couple by the name of Sanford Dean, whose claim joined theirs. Not long after, Lenora was called to their tent to help deliver the Dean's first child. A town not far from there was later called Agra. The Hillmans and Chesshers had come from Lincoln County, Kansas, so when the men of the newly settled county were searching for a name for their country, Chessher suggested the name Lincoln county which was accepted. Hillman did freighting with his team and wagon from Guthrie to Perry and while away on one of his trips his wife fell into an icy stream while watering the cow which brought on premature birth of a baby son. By this time, Mabel was two years of age.

Hillman who was a carpenter by trade, got itchy feet and decided to leave the claim and move to Kansas, locating in Arkansas City. From Arkansas City, the family moved to Oskaloosa, Kansas, where he farmed a year. The following year, the family moved to a farm 13 miles north of Perry, where they made their home in a sod house.

From here, Hillman moved to a new house on a farm belonging to a merchant by the name of Atkinson, south of Stillwater, in Payne County. On this farm a 9 lb. son, William, was born when Mabel was 5 years old.

Hillman was enticed by his father-in-law to move to an Indian lease 6 miles east of Pawnee, on Camp Creek, where the family spent another year in a log house. Hoping to find a more desirable farm in Arkansas, he started with his family by wagon into the state of Arkansas. Finding nothing there he continued on until he reached Bloomfield, Iowa, where his mother was living with his sister, Mrs. Jasper Sutton. They arrived here in October and spent the winter. It was here at the age of seven, Mabel learned the Lord's Prayer in school.

Hillman's aged mother wished to return to her old farm near Natoma, Kansas, so the following March he loaded his family with his mother and started across the country for Kansas. The mother became ill at Lost Springs, Kansas, and the family had to make a stay of several months there with old acquaintances, the Joe Searings.

Lenora Hillman's mother came from Perry, Oklahoma, to visit her at Lost Springs and became very ill. She was put on the train in care of Mrs. Hillman to return to her home at Perry, but passed away before they reached Newton, Kansas. She was laid to rest, May 30, 1898. This caused Hillman's plans to be changed and he traded his team and wagon for three lots and a small house on the corner of what was called Fifth and I (Ivanhoe) street in Perry.

Hillman had a carpenter shop where he worked until the winter of 1900, when he developed a cough and the daughter, Mabel, underwent a mastoid operation performed in the office of Dr. Dugan. The doctor ordered Mr. Hillman to a higher climate because of his lungs.

Again a trade was made where by the home was traded for a spring team and wagon. Part of the family, Mrs. Hillman, the grandmother, Mabel, and William, visited in the home of Mrs. Hillman's brother, Wesley Chessher at Ceres, Oklahoma, 13 miles north of Perry, while Hillman and the two older children went to Natoma, Kansas, by wagon. They arrived at Natoma, May 15, 1900.

Mr. Hillman and the 11 year old son, Fred, quarried out rock and built a stone house on the homestead of his mother, 3½ miles south of Natoma. It was while the family lived on the farm that Fred and Mable walked the 3½ miles to school to receive their 8th grade education. Mabel then went to school at Fort Hays, Kansas, but had to quit school because her mother needed her as she had a telephone exchange and her mother couldn't run it alone. The aged mother passed on in June of 1908, and the family chartered a car and moved their belongings to Oklahoma, location at Morrison in September of 1908.

The father and older son, then 19, bought the newspaper located there from a Mr. Tucker and named it the Morrison New Era. The Hillmans bought 6 lots north of the Christian Church and erected the house now owned by Mrs. Olga Shiever. On June 9, 1912, Mabel Hillman and Fred Grant Logan were married. A few years had elapsed during which time the Morrison New Era had quit publication.

P.B. Vandament hired Logan to edit a new publication which was published to help elect Bird McGuire to congress. This paper was called the Morrison Transcript. Later, Logan bought Vandament out and published the paper until his passing in 1952. The paper was then sold.

Mabel married Fred Shaw and they lived at Lela and Morrison. He passed away in 1968. She then married Robert Ballinger and he passed away in 1976. They lived in Vinita. Mabel them moved back to Morrison to live with her daughter, Awynne Wilkey. Mabel passed away June 3, 1982, and is buried in the Morrison cemetery.

Oscar W. Long
By Mildred Highfill

Oscar Woodson Long was born in Trigg County, near Hopkinsville, Kentucky, December 11, 1873. He grew to manhood in Kentucky. He lived for two years in Illinois and came to Oklahoma City in 1896. In 1898, he came to Perry where he was associated with the Christoph-Newton furniture store and funeral home. In 1901, a furniture store and funeral home was established in Billings, Oklahoma and he began a 44 year life work, filled with devotion to his family, to his church, to all civic activities and to those who had need of his help. In 1903, he married Catherine Gillen McCluskey at Billings. Cassie, as she was called, was born February 10, 1875 in St. Joseph, Missouri. She was the daughter of James and Mary Gillen McCluskey, a Scotch-Irish couple who had come to this country from Ulster, Ireland. When she was a small girl the family moved to Sumner County, Kansas to live on a farm near Wellington.

There she grew up, attending local schools and later Kansas State Normal at Emporia. Her parents moved to Billings in 1894, and after teaching in Kansas for several years, she joined them there, where she continued teaching, until her marriage.

Both O. W. and Cassie had been members of the Presbyterian Church but joined the Methodist Church in Billings. O. W. was Superintendent of the Sunday School for 18 years. He was a member of the school board for 13 years, a 32nd degree Mason and an Eastern Star.

The Longs had two daughters: Dorothy, and Mrs. Charles O. Guthrie. O. W. Long died December 15, 1945, and was buried in the Union Cemetery at Billings, Oklahoma. In 1952, Cassie moved to Tonkawa to be near her daughter, Dorothy. She died May 26, 1958 and is buried beside her husband in the Union Cemetery, Billings, Oklahoma.

Frank W. Loula
By Lila Loula Pritchett

My grandfather, Frank W. Loula, was born November 9, 1857, near Prague, Bohemia, and came to the United States at the age of seven. He and his parents settled in southern Minnesota. On February 2, 1880, he married Mary Wondra, also born in Bohemia, on October 18, 1860. Her family emigrated when she was six years old.

For a short time, they lived in Montgomery, Minnesota, later moving to Marion, Kansas. To this union eleven children were born: Tillie, Emma, Fred, Mary, Rose, Frank, Elva, Henry, Milton, Ann, and Carolyn. At the time of this writing, Milton Loula and Carolyn Krebbs of Perry, and Ann Speake, of Florida, are still living.

Grandfather Loula heard of the land that was to be given away in the Cherokee Land Rush in Oklahoma Territory and moved his family to Lincolnsville, Kansas, to be nearer the state-line. He bought a running horse and saddle, as well as a team of mules and a wagon, and drove them to Arkansas City, Kansas. From there, he chartered a rail car to transport them to Enid. He rode his horse to Orlando to make the run, staking a claim about four mile southwest of the present site of Billings.

Hauling his lumber and building materials from Enid, he built a home for his family on his new land, moving them to their new home on January 10, 1894. Here they farmed and raised cattle for the next eight years. According to some of Grandfather's correspondence, one year they raised 1,400 bushels of wheat, hauled it to Enid, and sold it for 40¢ a bushel. The cattle were shipped by rail to Kansas City, where they sold for 4¢ a pound.

In 1902, Grandfather Loula sold his farm and moved the family to Lookeba, in Caddo County, where he bought more land. The family continued to farm and raise cattle, with Grandfather also being the first Postmaster of Lookeba.

Another move was made in about 1912, when he purchased two sections of land nine miles northeast of Perry. The family remained on this farm until about 1927, when a new home was built at 1311 Sixth Street in Perry. Grandfather lived in this home until his death February 7, 1937.

Grandmother Loula continued to live in this family home with her daughter, Elva, until her death, November 9, 1943. I remember her as a very loving and caring person who loved to reminisce with me — she speaking in Bohemian and I in English. Although she did not speak English well, nor I Bohemian, we always seemed to be able to understand each other.

My father, Frank R. Loula, was born June 16, 1888, in Minnesota, and made all the moves with his family, helping with the farming and cattle. On January 7, 1913, he married Tillie Nemec, daughter of Albert and Mary Nemec, also emigrants from Bohemia. They moved to Grandfather's farm in Caddo County, later buying a nearby farm for themselves.

In 1916, another farm north and east of Perry was purchased where Father built a house and moved. About two years later, another nearby farm was bought. In 1918, on July 1, I was born at my maternal grandparent's home at 431 Elm Street. I attended rural schools at Highland District, where Father served as a school board member for many years.

In 1940, my father was elected county commissioner from District 3, a post he held for several years. Then in 1947, he and mother bought a home at 609 Ninth Street in Perry. He was elected County Assessor, a position he held until his sudden death from a heart attack on September 12, 1952. His wife, Tillie, was appointed to fill his unexpired term.

Hartsel Love
By Linda Ratliff

Hartsel Love was born at Peel Tree, West Virginia August 12, 1878. He married Eliza Belle Thomas, who was born in Kirksville, Missouri June 9, 1880. They were married on June 4, 1900, at Billings, Oklahoma.

The children born to this marriage that lived to adulthood were: Kenneth Hartsel Love born May 2, 1905, died April 1977; Orville Marcell Love born August 1, 1910, died November 1961; Ophie LeRoy Love born January 28, 1913, died March 25, 1960; and Virginia Belle Love Stout born January 1, 1917. Virginia is married to Roy Stout, who grew up in the Billings area, and they now make their home in Lexington, Missouri.

The Love family made their home in both Oklahoma City and Tulsa where Hartsel worked as a conductor on a street car.

They moved to Red Rock about 1920 making their home in the Ceres community. The children attended Longview, a country school near their home. Their high school years were spent at Red Rock where Kenneth and Virginia both graduated.

Hartsel, Eliza and Ophie are buried in the Union Cemetery at Billings. Orville is buried at Tonkawa and Kenneth is buried in the Red Rock Cemetery. Hartsel died January 10, 1945 and Eliza died May 2, 1954.

Ophie Love
By Linda Ratliff

Ophie LeRoy Love, son of Hartsel and Eliza Thomas Love, was born at Red Rock, January 28, 1913.

Pauline Mary Franklin, daughter of William Elmer Franklin and Ida Elnora Lee, was born at Olney, Texas, February 13, 1916.

For many years, Pauline has used the name Pauline Mary. However, her given name is Mary Pauline. She tells that she heard if your initials stood for something important you would amount to something in life. As a young girl, M.P. only stood for military police so she changed it around to P.M. which she reasoned stood for Prime Minister. The name change has followed her through life.

The couple met a short time after the Franklin family moved to the Red Rock community from El Reno. On July 22, 1933, they were married in Newkirk, Oklahoma. The six children born to this marriage are: Jackie LeRoy, born May 26, 1934; Billy Joe, born January 17, 1936; Nona Lea, born August 29, 1938; Linda Mae, born October 7, 1942; Gary Wayne, born October 1, 1944; and Carl Dan, born June 30, 1948.

Their first home was eleven miles north of Perry south of Red Rock Creek near the Franklin family. The next move was in the fall of 1937, to an Indian lease east of Red Rock near the Otoe Indian Agency. Nona was born there with Hartsel Love doing the midwife chores because the doctor didn't arrive in time.

Linda and Gary were born at Dr. Renfro's Clinic in Billings. By the time Carl was born in 1948, Pauline finally got to have the proper care of the hospital in Ponca City.

In August 1947, the family bought a farm nine miles east of Red Rock just across the Noble County line in Pawnee County.

The four older children graduated from Red Rock High School. In August 1958, the family moved to Ponca City where Gary and Carl finished their education graduating from Ponca City High School.

LeRoy served in the United States Army serving eighteen months in Germany in 1954-1956. He and his wife, Betty (Thompson) Love, make their home in California. They have two children, Elizabeth Ann and Jonathan LeRoy.

Billy Joe enlisted in the United States Air Force in 1955, during his senior year of high school. He completed his high school credits and received his diploma with the class of 1956. His overseas assignment while in the service was spent in Japan. He and his wife, Florence (Speakman) Love, have made their home in Virginia just outside Washington, D.C., for several years and plan to return to Ponca City after retirement. They are the parents of three children, Gayla Sue, Cathy Jo, and Lonnie Joe.

Nona attended Northern Oklahoma Junior College at Tonkawa before her marriage to Cecil Cales, Jr. They make their home on a farm near Ponca City in Osage County. They are the parents of two children, Sherrie Lynn and Steven Wade.

Gary, also, served in the Air Force. He served most of his tour of duty at Ft. Bealle in California. He and his wife, Debbie, make their home in San Antonio, Texas. He has two children. Brian makes his home in Pryor, Oklahoma, and Michalle lives in San Antonio.

Carl graduated from Central State University with a degree in Business Administration. He and his wife, Becky (Johnson) Love, make their home in Hermitage, Tennessee, near Nashville. They are the parents of three children, Shannon Renea, Cindy Michalle, and Chad Michael.

Linda is the only member of her family to remain a resident of Noble County. After high school graduation, she attended business college in Ponca City. She and her husband, Mickey Ratliff, make their home in Red Rock, where she works at the Red Rock Farmers Co-op and Mickey is a farmer-rancher. They are the parents of two children, Kimberly Beth and Michael Jay.

In March 1960, Ophie died after blood clots developed following knee surgery. His funeral was held at the First Christian Church in Ponca City and he is buried in the Union Cemetery near Billings.

Davis Main
By Agnes King

Davis Main, born September 15, 1863, near St. Paul, Minnesota, died March 27, 1940, in Tonkawa, Oklahoma, moved west with his father and mother both of New York. They pioneered several states along the Great Lakes before stopping in Lawrence, Kansas, in 1871. Here they purchased a 160 acre farm. Being a skilled builder with lumber and stone, the father and five sons built a four foot flint rock fence around the farm. They also built two large business buildings of rock in Lawrence. One was on a corner lot and used for a bank.

In 1885, Joseph and family moved to California. Davis remained behind to complete the sale of the farm. He paid the last taxes in 1885.

Davis then began plans for his future in Oklahoma. He worked and earned enough money to buy a new wagon and a good young team of horses. He paid $30.50 for a new set of harness, $35.00 for a new shot gun. This gun is in possession of his grandson, John Robert Main of Billings.

Davis drove his wagon and horses to Guthrie where he spent one winter working. He paid room and board, plus 50 cents a day board for his wagon and team. He herded cattle during the year.

On September 15, 1893, Davis was thirty years old. That day he drove his team and wagon to Orlando and hauled drinking water from a nearby spring, for the settlers before the race. He sold it for 10 cents a tin cup.

As the signal shot was heard September 16, 1893, Davis drove his wagon and team to a claim on Section 6-NE ¼-Red Rock township. The land lays on the west side of Grassy Creek which flowed into the Red Rock Creek.

Here he built a 20 by 12 foot house of lumber, dug and walled a cave and a water well. He exchanged wild plums and sugar for jelly and cow butter. He dug water wells for the Indians in exchange for their large mulberry trees. These were used for corner fence posts.

His first crop of wheat was one acre. He stacked wheat for Mont Howe for the seed. The Banner School (district #26) of Noble County was started in a log cabin on the corner two miles east of his homestead. This became the center of social activities in the community. An organ was purchased by the school. Soon a Miss Cidia Owens, daughter of John and Lydia Owens, helped to provide entertainment with her music. She and Davis became good friends and were married April 20, 1898, in Perry, Oklahoma. To this union four children were born. Harold E., age

Main farm home on the homestead near Billings, Oklahoma.

2 years, died in California, while his parents were visiting the family of Joseph and Mary Main, in 1900.

Homer E. Main, followed his father in farming and lived on the homestead. He had three children, Elsie Lee Klein, of Wichita, Kansas; Alene Bruton of Necedah, Wisconsin; and John Robert Main of Billings, Oklahoma.

Gladys Mary Main graduated with a Bachelor of Science Degree from Oklahoma University in Norman and a Master of Arts Degree from Oklahoma State University, Stillwater. She taught Art in the Perry Schools and the Ponca City High School for 48 years. She never married and died February 24, 1982.

Agnes L. Main graduated from Central State University at Edmond. She taught 30 years, 25 years as an elementary teacher in the Tonkawa School. She and her husband live in the family home there.

Agnes married Rev. William R. King, born in Hart County, Kentucky. He was pastor of the Baptist Church of Newkirk, Oklahoma. Rev. King has pastored several Baptist churches in Kay, Noble, and Garfield Counties. He also was Director of Associational Missions for these three counties which ministered to 40 churches, until he retired after preaching for 50 years. The King's celebrated their 50th wedding anniversary in 1981.

They have three children: Dr. A. Joseph King, an Associate Professor of Conducting and Theory at the Southwestern Baptist Theological Seminary in Fort Worth, Texas. He is married and has two daughters.

Mary Louise Bailey of Thousand Oaks, California. She and her husband have four daughters.

Caroline Ruth Pharr is an Elementary Music Teacher in Jackson, Mississippi. She is the mother of two sons.

Homer E. Main
By Nell Main

Homer Everett Main was born March 12, 1903, in Carney, Oklahoma. He was the son of Davis and Cidia Main. There were four children in the family. One brother, Harold Main, died in infancy and two sisters, Gladys

Homer Main in 1960.

Mary Main, and Agnes Lela Main (King).

Homer spent his childhood on a farm nine miles southeast of Billings (section 6-23N-1W) where his father, Davis Main, homesteaded during the land run of 1893 in the Cherokee Strip area. This land was granted to Davis Main by President Theodore Roosevelt in 1903, and still owned and farmed by the Main family. While living on the farm, Homer attended Banner School. Later, his parents moved to Tonkawa where he attended high school and Northern Oklahoma Preparatory College renamed Northern Oklahoma College.

In 1924, Homer was married to Orabelle Waldrop of Texas. Two daughters were born to this union, Elsie Lee Main (Klein) and Alene Main (Bruton). In 1949, Elsie Lee married Raymond Klein of Dallas, Texas. They had three children, David Melton Klein of Edmond, Oklahoma. Dianne Klein of Wichita, Kansas, and Daniel Klein of Wichita and Germany. Elsie Lee worked for the Internal Revenue Service in Wichita several years.

Alene Main married William O. Bruton of Muldrow, Oklahoma, August 25, 1946. William was in the US Army 1940-1945 serving in Europe and North Africa. He joined the US Air Force 1952-1974, retiring as a Senior Master Sergeant. They had five children: Priscilla Kay Bruton (deceased 1984), Clyde Winston Bruton, Michael Dale Bruton, Paul William Bruton and Mark Robert Bruton. Both Paul and Mark have served in the US Air Force.

In 1930, Homer returned to school. He attended Emporia State Teacher's College in Kansas and later graduated with a BS degree from Central State College Edmond, Oklahoma, majoring in biological science. He taught school one year in Washunga, Oklahoma and later moved back to the farm near Billings. His love for the farm never ceased.

On July 24, 1936, Homer Main and Nell Blankenship of Marion, Illinois, were married in Harrisburg, Illinois. They became friends while both were attending summer school at Edmond, Oklahoma (Central State College).

Nell Blankenship was born March 16, 1908, in Marion, Illinois to Elijah Spencer Blankenship and Cora Edith Chamness (Blankenship). Nell was a BS graduate of Southern Illinois University at Carbondale, Illinois. After teaching seven years in Illinois she and Homer were married and lived on the farm east of Billings. To this marriage was born one son, John Robert Main. During World War II Nell took the Oklahoma History test and received her Oklahoma teaching certificate and started teaching Glenrose school when John was in the first grade. Next year the Glenrose school was transferred into Billings District. Nell taught 29 years in Billings School until retirement in 1970. During this time she was also active in church work, 4-H leadership and Oklahoma Pollette Association.

Homer Main raised wheat and registered Polled Hereford cattle for many years. Homer was involved in many community activities being a deacon, song leader, Sunday School teacher and treasurer of the Billings Baptist Church. He was a 32 degree Mason and member of the Tonkawa Lodge, for 16 years he served as president of the Noble County Farm Bureau and was on the Perry Hospital Board several years during the Baptist Administration.

After Homer's death, October 3, 1974, two years later, 1976, Nell moved to Tonkawa, Oklahoma. She has been active in church work at First Baptist, also in Tonkawa Garden Club, American Association of University Women, Kay County Retired Teachers, and Glenrose Social Club.

John Robert Main still lives on the family farm. John served two years in the US Navy. After returning home he married Linda Lou Angel of Marion, Illinois, June 8, 1963. They both attended school at Northern Oklahoma College and Central State College at Edmond. The next move was to the farm six miles east of Billings, Oklahoma. They also raise wheat and registered Polled Hereford cattle. They now have a craft shop in their home and enjoy the craft work very much. John and Linda have four children. Kevin Main is in the US Marines. Kerri Main will be in college this fall (1985). Kathy Main will be a freshman in Billings High School and Kami Main will be a first grader (1985-86).

John Thomas Marshall and Emma (Crossman) Marshall about 1900.

John Thomas Marshall
By Sophia L. Dahlberg

John Thomas Marshall was born March 8, 1863, in Hamilton, Canada. His parents were from Bohemia and came to America by ship traveling the Atlantic Ocean to the Gulf of St. Lawrence, traveling the St. Lawrence River to Lake Ontario, Canada. The family name was "Maruska". It was later changed to Marshall. John's brother, George, perished in the Jamestown, Pennsylvania flood.

John Thomas Marshall worked for the Atchison, Topeka and Santa Fe Railway System. It was through his work on the railroad as baggage man, that he met and married Emma Crossman at Topeka, Kansas. Emma Catherine Crossman was born April 15, 1866, in Indiana County, Pennsylvania. They were married in Topeka, Kansas September 5, 1888. Her young son, Jess Crossman, born December 9, 1885, was just three years old. He was born in Smithport, Pennsylvania. John and Emma's first child, Florence Mary Marshall was born June 14, 1889 and Nina Alice Marshall was born July 2, 1892, both at Topeka, Kansas.

John and Emma did not participate in the "land rush" as he was not eligible because he was serving as freight agent at Wharton before the opening. Anyone in the Strip thirty days before September 16, 1893 could not make the run. After the opening they lived in Perry at 115 "C" Street. He continued to work for the Santa Fe Railroad.

In April of 1900 their little girl Nina Alice died. Emma died July 29, 1945 and was buried beside her daughter in Grace Hill cemetery at Perry, Oklahoma. John retired as a pensioned freight clerk in 1939. He died April 5, 1947 at the home of his daughter, Mrs. Florence Ivers in Ponca City. He was laid to rest by the side of his wife and daughter.

John Marshall was a 32nd degree mason in Lodge #78. He was an uncle to William C. Marshall, who was a local dentist, and who was also a band master (Marshall's Military Band). When Oklahoma was made a state, "Uncle Doc" played with his band in the opening ceremonies and also after all the speeches were made. He also played with the 101 Ranch shows.

Edwin R. Martin
By Alice Mae Svelan

Edwin Round Martin was born March 15, 1862, at Leavenworth, Kansas, the son of Gilbert Martin. The Gilbert Martins moved from Leavenworth, to Chetopa, Kansas, where they lived for some time, later moving to Denison, Texas. He was a pioneer in the railroad construction boom of the 1880s.

Ed grew to manhood in Denison. He went into the railroad construction business and helped to build many of the railroads in southern Texas and northern Mexico. During these years that were being spent in laying the rails for the "iron horses", the Martins, Ed and his father, went into Old Mexico and operated a silver mine for a number of years. During President Cleveland's administration, they gave up their mining careers and returned to a ranch which was theirs, near San Antonio, Texas.

Ed remained at that ranch until 1893, when he came north and made the run into the Strip. Although he had shipped horses from Texas to Guthrie, he did not ride any of them in the race. Those who claimed to know maintained that the train would get into the strip ahead of the horses, which was true in part. Ed waited for the train at Orlando and when it arrived it was loaded to capacity. He managed to crawl through a window and board the second train to Perry. He staked two lots south of the Frisco depot and it was on these lots that the first primitive water works was established. When he was in Guthrie he noticed some men rigging up water wagons and found they were going to sell water in the Strip. He thought the water business would be profitable and since he had his horses it would not require much investment. He bought three water wagons and had his horses sent to Perry. The first week in Perry he started his water deliveries and received his first water from the railroad but later dug his own wells on his town lots.

Sending out the three water wagons each day he brought in $15 to $20 a piece. Water sold at about 50 cents a barrel at first. When water became more plentiful the price was cheaper but the business lasted about two years.

As the city had no protection from fire, Ed filled the three wagons every night and equipped each with buckets, so they could be rushed to a fire immediately. The Mayor's home was one of the first saved from fire by the wagons. After each fire many of the buckets would be lost and when Ed suggested that the city supply the buckets he found out that they were too poor to buy them.

Later, he opened a feed yard and camping ground on his lots, called the Martin Camp Yard. He provided places for movers to camp and sheds and feed for horses. Still later he shipped stock and farmed for about three years.

Three years later he established the Perry Steam Laundry which he operated for thirty-five years in the same location until his death.

On January 7, 1902, he married Miss Ida Elizabeth Schott in Perry. She was born September 14, 1879, in Newbury, Kansas. They were the parents of four children: Florence (Jehlicka), Ruth, Alice Mae (Svelan), and Edwin J. Martin.

He served on the board of county commissioners, during which he helped direct plans for the present courthouse.

He died January 6, 1940, of a heart attack after shoveling snow during the afternoon. He is buried in the Catholic cemetery at Perry. Ida died April 20, 1960, in Perry. She is buried beside her husband in the Catholic cemetery in Perry.

James Alva Masheter
By Izora (Masheter) Downey

James Alva Masheter was born October 18, 1878 in Sabetha, Nehama County, Kansas, the son of Nancy S. (Wood) and William Banks Masheter. William Banks Masheter was born in Zanesville, Ohio, November 11, 1838. He was a Civil War Veteran, having enlisted in the 36 Ohio regiment. He was a descendant of those who came to America on the Mayflower from England. Nancy (Wood) Masheter was born May 19, 1847 in Salem, Meigs County, Ohio.

James A. Masheter grew to manhood in the place of his birth and on December 27, 1899, he was married to Leslie Gertrude Haskell. She was born November 24, 1881 in Sabetha, Kansas, the daughter of Mary Jane (Allen) and William Ellsworth Haskell.

In 1899, James and his father, William, and family moved to a farm east of Stillwater, Oklahoma. Here were born James and Leslie's first children, Beulah (Freeman) January 21, 1902, Izora (Downey) July 19, 1906 and William James October 27, 1907.

After the birth of William, James and family moved to a farm in Noble County, north of Glencoe, Oklahoma. Here May (Roach) was born April 11, 1909, Mary Ellen (Buntin/Patterson) born January 4, 1912, Emily Ruth (Burch) born April 14, 1914, Charlie John born November 24, 1915 and Doris Elizabeth (Schroeder) October 6, 1922.

When James Alva retired from the farm they moved to Morrison, Oklahoma where they were active in the Methodist church.

James was fond of children and would make a freezer of ice cream which he shared with any children who might be in the street nearby. He would say "It's my birthday. Come in and have some ice cream and cake." Naturally the children of the neighborhood made a point of going by his house if it was ice cream weather.

James Alva Masheter died September 22, 1960 at his home in Morrison, Oklahoma. Leslie Masheter died April 4, 1969, at Oklahoma City, Oklahoma. They are buried at the Fairlawn cemetery at Stillwater, Oklahoma.

Delmar Mason
By Delmar Mason

Delmar Dean Mason was born September 23, 1924 in Billings, Oklahoma, the son of Perry and Emma (Dufek) Mason. Delmar attended grade school at Velly Center rural school. He attended Billings High school. He went to college at Oklahoma A & M and

Foreground (L to R): Gilbert Martin, Ed Martin and Frank Martin.

William Mason and Mary Patterson, natives of Ireland, of Scotch-Irish descent. Born and reared in Tyrone County, Ireland, William and Mary were married in 1779 at Ten Mile Crossing. They came to the United States of America in 1788.

John Hamilton Mason was born December 12, 1837, at Trimble, Ohio, on the farm his family moved to from Greene county, Pennsylvania. He married Margaret Ann Brown (born October 17, 1841 at Sarahville, Ohio) on August 21, 1864 at Sarahville, and they became the parents of four children.

One of these children was John Hamilton Mason, Jr., who always went by the name of John Mason.

John Hamilton Mason was a graduate of Ohio University at Athens, Ohio. He taught school in Ohio until he went to Oklahoma Territory to try for land.

John Hamilton came to Oklahoma for the opening of Old Oklahoma (1889) settling 10 miles west of Edmond where he made his home with Henry Newton (a former pupil taught by John).

He was unsuccessful in getting land so he worked as a carpenter in the rapidly growing young city that later became the state Capitol. Among buildings that he helped construct was the First National Bank, forerunner of the current First National Bank and Trust, one of Oklahoma's largest banks.

He made the run into the Cherokee Strip. He and his son, John, both headed for Red Rock bottoms, but John Hamilton's mule balked when he tried to cross Black Bear Creek. He did not get a good farm and refused to stake a claim on some unclaimed shale pasture land that proved a bonanza to some who came much later as this proved to be an oil pay area.

He made his home with John Mason and served his neighborhood as an arbitor of disputes, surveyed fields, measured and figured hay field yieds giving those less learned the benefit of his education and wisdom. He made his home with John until death on April 3, 1922, at John's home in Perry. His wife died on April 22, 1922, at Sarahville, Ohio.

Perry Mason
By Barbara Mason

Perry Hamilton Mason, the eldest son of John and Elizabeth Orr Mason, was born November 5, 1894 at White Rock. Perry was one of the first four year graduates of Billings High school. He served in France with company F, 47th coast artillery, during World War I.

Upon his return home he worked as a rig builder in the Hoover oilfield near

Barbara, Delmar and Perry Mason taken May 28, 1973, on farm at Billings, Oklahoma.

Billings and as a tool pusher in the Three Sands oilfield. In 1922, he married Emma Dufek and they had one son, Delmar Dean. They divorced in 1927. Perry then moved in with his parents and began farming in partnership.

May 26, 1937, he married Barbara Rosetta Liebrand. Barbara was the daughter of John and Edith Liebrand and was born December 11, 1914, in Alfalfa county, Oklahoma. She was a graduate of Helena high school and Northwestern State Teachers College at Alva. She was teaching at Valley Center rural school when she met and married Perry Mason.

They established their first home in one of the oilfield houses in the Midco field. Evidence of that homesite can still be seen in the spring when the iris they planted still bloom. In the spring of 1939, they started building a home on the NE¼ of section 14 in White Rock township. They made their home there until 1975 when they retired from active farming and moved into Billings.

Living on Red Rock Creek and haveing to contend with the continual threat of flooding gave both Barbara and Perry a reason to be concerned with conservation and more particularly with flood control. They became especially active after having to be evacuated four times from their home in the floods of 1957. Perry served on the committees for conservation and upon his retirement from the board around 1970, Barbara took his place. She was named Noble County Soil Conservation District Director in 1973. She received the Outstanding Service in Conservation Award from the Oklahoma Wildlife Federation in 1970 and received a 10-year service award from the Northern Oklahoma Development Association (NODA) in 1982. She was a member of the Billings Mums garden club and was associated with the state garden club organization.

Both Barbara and Perry were interested in the school and worked for many years with the local FAA while Delmar was in school. Perry managed to "farm" even after his move to town by regular trips to the country to maintain fence rows and by growing a vegetable garden each year. Both were active in the American Legion and Auxiliary, the Union cemetery Association and the Billings Historical Society. Both were members of the United Methodist church of Billings.

*Perry died May 10, 1984, and Barbara November 14, 1984. They are buried in the Union cemetery at Billings.

*Editor's note.

George A. Masters
By Mildred Highfill

George A. Masters was born near Savannah, Ashland County, Ohio, October 14, 1854, and was reared on a farm. When he was less than 9 years of age, his father, Alexander Masters, was killed in the Civil War in the siege of Vicksburg, May 3, 1863.

Alexander Masters was also a native of Ashland County. His father, Nicholas Masters, was born in Somerset, Pennsylvania, in which locality his parents located upon their arrival in the country, their native land being Holland. Nicholas Masters was a pioneer in Ashland County, Ohio, and his son, Alexander, also passed the major portion of his life upon a farm there. Alexander was a member of Company H, Forty-second Ohio Volunteer Infantry.

Alexander's wife, whose maiden name was Jane Beymer, was left with three sons and a daughter. Her father, George Beymer, also being of Holland-Dutch descent, was born in Ohio. She, too, was born in Ohio, and her entire life was spent upon farms in that state.

George's brother, Scott A., came to Perry but John H. and the sister, Mrs. J.W. Wilson stayed in the north.

Until he was twenty-three years of age, George A. Masters lived on the old homestead, where he had shouldered a large share of the responsibilities when quite young. He completed his education in the Savannah Academy, and in 1879, he went to Gallion, Ohio, where he was employed in a pump and well business for some time, later locating in Marengo, Ohio, where he was a hardware merchant until 1887. During the next six years he traveled in the interest of Aultman, Miller & Co., in southeastern Kansas, his home being in Garnett, Kansas. In November, 1893, he came to Perry, and for nearly two years was in the employ of A.C. Hinde. Then resigning, he turned his attention to the grain business. He was one of the first merchants who shipped any amount of grain from this place, and the capacity of the large elevator which he built was usually taxed to the utmost. Mr. Masters was ranked as the most extensive dealer in castor beans and broom corn in this section, and perhaps,

Madalyn and Delmar Mason at Russell, Kansas in 1982.

North Texas Agriculture College at Arlington, Texas. He lived and farmed with Barbara and Perry Mason until World War II when he served overseas with the U.S. Navy.

He joined the navy and was a Radarman 1st Class. He served duty on a LSM 491 landing craft. He served in the Pacific. Delmar received an army discharge ROTC and joined the navy and helped commission the LSM 491 in Houston, Texas. He traveled through the Panama Canal to many stations in the south Pacific. He spent much of his time in the Phillipine Islands. He received his navy discharge in May of 1946, in Oklahoma City, Oklahoma.

Upon his return home he married Joyce Homan August 4, 1946 in Russell, Kansas. They had one son, Nick Mason Neumeyer, born August 2, 1947 in Russell, Kansas. Delmar and Joyce were divorced in 1952.

Delmar married Madalyn Gilman Babb December 31, 1954 at Wichita, Kansas. She had one son, Robert E. Babb, born November 3, 1942 in Hays, Kansas. Delmar and Madalyn had one son, Curt D. Mason born August 4, 1956, in Russell, Kansas.

Delmar owned and operated a Wallgreen Drug store in Russell, Kansas. He also worked for Boeing Airplace in Wichita in contract administration department.

Delmar and Madalyn owned and operated Mason Oil Well Servicing Co. for 18 years in Russell. The last 12 years he had been Asst. General Supt. for Southern States Oil Co.

Ron Babb married Judy Richardson November 17, 1963 at Larned, Kansas. They have twin sons, Kenny and Kevin, and one daughter, Kerri. They live in Hutchison, Kansas.

Nick Mason Neumeyer married Judy Stamm, November 1968, in Denver, Colorado. He has two sons, Scott, and Royce, and lives in Redondo Beach, California.

Curt Mason married Kimberly Kay Hill, January 3, 1976, at Russell, Kansas. He has twin daughters, Staci and Christi. He lives in Hayes, Kansas.

John Mason
By Barbara Mason
(deceased)

John Mason, son of John Hamilton and Margaret Ann Brown Mason was born April 1, 1867, at Sarahville, Ohio. On October 5, 1889, he married Elizabeth Orr at Sarahville, Elizabeth was born December 6, 1868, in Salem Center, Ohio, the daughter of Rev. Perry Orr and Elizabeth Little. Her father, a Civil War Veteran, was a Methodist circuit rider, serving Riversville, Sarahville and other places.

John Mason grew to manhood at Sarahsville, Ohio, where he managed a mine company store and served as postmaster, until he and his family came to "10 Mile Corner" east of Edmond in 1890. They came to Oklahoma because of his father, John Hamilton Mason, who had come to the east of Edmond to live with a former student, Henry Newton. For a time, John rented and farmed a quarter section of land, which later became Jones City. He and Elizabeth had their first child, Hazel, while there. She died as an infant and is buried at Jones City.

John made runs in both the Sac-Fox and Cheyenne-Araphahoe openings but was unsuccessful in getting a claim in either run. Both he and his father registered for the Strip opening at Stillwater and then went to a point 1¼ miles east of Orlando, from which to start the race. Elizabeth, in the meantime, went to a spot south of Perry with the Tom Gorman family of Edmond. They made camp on Cow Creek approximately ½ miles south of the present location of the Cherokee Strip Museum.

Both John and his father made the run on mules. They headed north of their starting place until they reached the crossing on Black Bear Creek. The mule ridden by J. H. balked at the crossing and he lost his chance for a claim. John crossed the Bear and proceeded to follow the Honeywell Trail six miles south of the Red Rock bottom until he reached the bottom. He noted at the time that there was no one in front of him. As he reached the top of the bluff at Red Rock Creek, he glanced over his shoulder and saw John Henry approaching on a race horse. Henry motioned for Mason to go to the left while he took the right in a manner designed to ensure their being on different quarters when they staked their claims. They clocked their time into the run at one hour and twenty-three minute. John Mason claimed the SE¼ of 10-23N-2W.

Three days after the opening, the claims of both Mason and Henry were filed on by Mike and Jack Burke. The former two men protested on grounds of prior settlement and the case went to court. These two cases were among the last of the contests to be settled in Noble county. After losing their case in Perry, Mason and Henry appealed to the Territorial Court in Guthrie and then on to the Department of the Interior. There a decision was handed down awarding each of the four claimants eighty acres of land. While John Mason was on a Santa Fe train headed for the court in Guthrie, a casual conversation with the conductor turned up the evidence which ultimately resulted in the reversal of the last court decision. The conductor inadvertantly inquired about the well-being of his friends, the Burkes, who had traveled his train into the area three days after the run.

The final decision gave the land back to Mason and Henry with the Burkes being given one year in which to vacate the land. The improvements which the Burkes had built, a barn and a house, were sold to Calvin Swingle, who moved them to the SE¼ of 9-23N-2W. It was a great source of pride to John Mason that there was never a mortgage on his homestead as long as it remained in the Mason family. It was sold to Glen Combrink in 1967.

The Masons had eight children, six of whom grew to adulthood. Hazel died as a baby and Juanita (b-July 5, 1911) died when she was about nine. The other six were Perry (b-November 5, 1894), Leedy (b-September 16, 1897), Marguerite (Wilkerson), Pauline (Dotts, Eby) (b-May 7, 1902), Orr, and Reford (b-April 16, 1908).

The Mason home was an 8' x 10' vertical siding house. Later with lumber hauled from Orlando, a two room house was completed . . . just in time for their first son to be born.

John Mason served on the first Grand Jury held in Perry. He, also, along with a neighbor, Frank Wright, served on the committee which selected the name for the county. Both men disputed the idea that the county was named for the then Secretary of the Interior. Mason and Wright both asserted that each of the eighteen men on the committee submitted their choices for a name. Many chose names of counties or towns in their native states. John came from Noble county, Ohio. The name most often suggested was Noble and so became the choice of the committee. John Mason died October 15, 1950, and Elizabeth January 12, 1959. They are buried in the Union cemetery, Billings.

John Hamilton Mason, Sr.
By Barbara Mason
(deceased)

John Hamilton Mason, Sr. was a fourth generation descendant of in the territory. He was called Castor Bean King. He annually handled about sixty thousand bushels of castor beans and besides, dealt in garden, field and flower seeds.

The marriage of Mr. Masters and Miss Hattie E. Hanna took place in Ashland County, Ohio, in September, 1877. She was a native of Crawford County, Ohio, and by her marriage was the mother of five sons, namely: Charles C. (b-October, 1879, in Ohio), Ralph B. (b-November, 1886, in Ohio), Harry S. (b-June, 1889, in Kansas), George Lee (b-October, 1892, in Kansas), and Lloyd (b-January, 1898, in Oklahoma).

He was a Republican and served on the city council representing the fourth ward, and was chairman of the finance committee. He also served as chairman of the board of county commissioners.

His wife died at their home at 634 G. street, and was buried in Grace Hill cemetery. Her stone reads "Hattie Electra Master, May 3, 1856 - May 9, 1911, wife of Geo. A. Masters." There is a child's grave marked: Clara Belle Masters, August 22, 1895 - June 7, 1896. There is no stone for George A. Masters but Newton funeral home records show that he died February 16, 1915, of diabetes gangrene at the age of 60 and was buried in Grace Hill cemetery.

Andrew Matthiesen
By Andrea McCluskey

Andrew Matthiesen, who was born in Denmark, had immigrated to Beloit, Kansas, and was working there in 1893. The chance to acquire land by homesteading gave him a powerful incentive to join the Cherokee Strip Run into Oklahoma.

His experience in the run may be unique in that he came from Beloit with a team of horses pulling a covered wagon loaded with feed for the horses, some groceries for himself and a sod plow. He also brought a riding horse and saddle. Two or three days before the run, he camped at the Kansas-Oklahoma border near Hunnewell, where hundreds of hopeful pioneers were milling around. Andrew was looking for some friends who had asked him to join them and stake their claims in bottom land near the Salt Fork River. He had hesitated to join them because they were known as rough fellows who carried guns, but on the day before the run they were nowhere to be found. It may have been good that he did not find them, because he was later told that during the run some fellows were seen west of Tonkawa where they had camped, dousing their campfires and pouring water on their horses to make it look like the horses had been running.

Matthiesen family about 1930. (Back Row, L to R): John, Paul, Ray, Gertrude. (Front Row, L to R): Gordon, Rex, Andrea, Andrew, Lillian, Beulah.

Andrew lined up at the border with the crowd facing south and was off and running at the starting shot. As he rode across the "Strip" he found every desirable location already occupied. At sundown, when he arrived at Mulhall, he decided to stay overnight. The next day, returning to Kansas where he had left his team and wagon, he came across a man in a white shirt standing alone on the prairie. The fellow was glad to ride double back to civilization. He had spent the night alone, without shelter, and was tired, hungry, and discouraged. His friends had not returned and he thought they had abandoned him. As the two rode double they agreed to exchange the "horse and saddle" for the fellow's right to the claim he had staked. The claim was never contested and became Andrew Matthiesen's homestead (four miles east of Billings, SE ¼ T 24N R 2W, in Noble County) where he lived until his death, January 1962, at the age of 95. His grandson, Robert Matthiesen lives there now so the farm remains in the Matthiesen name.

The first building on the homestead was a sod house constructed of chunks of sod laid flat to form the walls. A wagon sheet was used to cover the structure until a roof could be built of crude rafters covered by Kafir corn stalks. The first trip back to Kansas by the lonely bachelor was memorable. In order to find the way back across the open country a post topped by a pair of buffalo horns was placed near the old cattle trail. On the return trip a snow storm came up and the driver closed the wagon to keep the snow out and the marker was missed. The team of horses followed the cattle trail and stopped at White Rock, one mile west and two miles south of the homestead, near Bunch Creek. The next morning the sun came out revealing a beautiful prairie under its first snowfall.

The first "spring planting" time came with the sod turned but no way to plant. Andrew, with a small bag of kafir corn hanging on his shoulder, a chopping ax to make an opening, a few grains of corn dropped into the slit, and a heavy step with the boot; planted the best crop of kafir raised on that upland.

After four years as a bachelor, Andrew Matthiesen married Annie D. Hansbrough on June 10, 1898. Annie and her mother, who had been living in Missouri, had made the run and homesteaded near Highland (west of Billings in Garfield County). To this union four children were born: Ray Henry, Mary Gertrude, Paul, and John. Soon Annie's claim was exchanged for a quarter one mile south of the homestead. This made it more convenient and brought the farm to a size that was more than one man could handle. In a few years the Tribbey place, a mile east of the home place was purchased. The children remember this time as a busy one with cattle, horses, poultry, gardens, crops and all the products of a self contained farm. Andrew took time from farming to take them to the World's Fair of 1904. Annie became ill and died in 1914, after a four year hospital confinement.

Lillian Elanor Mason, from Braman, had graduated from Tonkawa and become a teacher. She became teacher of Happy Star School (Lost Calf) which was a quarter mile east of the home place. Andrew and Lillian were married in April, 1916. To this union were born four children: Rex Andrew, Gordon Ivan, Beulah Jane, and Sadie Andrea. We became one big happy family so a larger house became a necessity to accomodate us and the ever present visiting ministers and hired men. This house had its own Delco electric system powered by gasoline engines in

Matthiesen home built about 1918.

the basement. It later had the upper porch roofed and the south porch glassed in. The Murray eight was bought because it adjoined the Tribbey quarter and the farm size was complete. Andrew was a forward looking person who was one of the first to purchase gasoline tractors, terrace land, and built his own wagon scale on the farm. When a well was drilled for gas for the city of Billings and found inadequate he piped it to the house and the family enjoyed free gas from their own well. There were many years of busy times interspersed by travel, school literary meets and parties in the big house. The children remember one of their dad's favorite maxims was "Work, work, if it be God's curse, what must his blessing be?" Lillian died in December, 1969.

Andrew was a faithful Christian who was an active member of the Freedom Baptist Church. He attended church regularly and took the family. Each person accepted the Christian faith.

The children grew up and this is what they did: Ray attended Hill's Business College, married Leva Christian, and moved to Tampa, Florida, where he worked for Shell Oil. They lived at various places in Oklahoma, Marshall, Braman, Ardmore and others, finally settling in Oklahoma City. Paul attended OAMC and worked for Southwestern Bell. He married Cecil Harper and lived at Wapanucka, Ardmore, and settled in Enid. John married Radell Jones. He attended OBU and was ordained to the Baptist ministry. He pastored churches in Oklahoma at Morrison, Pawhuska, and Mountain Park, then in Wichita, Kansas. He retired to Enid, Oklahoma. Rex attended N.O.C., served as a bomber pilot in WW II, married Pearl Beck and returned to Billings to operate the Matthiesen farms. He is now retired at Billings. Gordon was only 13 years old when he died. Beulah attended Central State and taught school. She married Lawrence Brown and lived in Billings until she returned to the farm to care for her parents in their later years. She died in 1967. Andrea attended Phillips University and became a school teacher. She married Jack McCluskey and lives near Billings where she teaches and Jack farms.

Lyman B. McClure
By Bob McClure

The McClure brothers, William L. McClure and Lyman Beecher McClure came to Oklahoma from Sparta, Illinois. They were from a family of nine children born to Nancy Jane (McGuire) and Alexander Christopher McClure.

William L. (Bill) was born August 8, 1862 in Sparta, Illinois. He was a young lawyer and teacher in Illinois before coming to Oklahoma to make the Cherokee Strip run. He staked a farm one mile east and a mile and a half south of Morrison, Oklahoma. He taught school and farmed. He never married and lived on the farm that he staked until his death on August 19, 1940. He is buried in the Morrison Cemetery.

Lyman Beecher McClure was born July 28, 1870 at Sparta, Illinois. He came to Oklahoma Territory in the late 1890s. He lived with his brother, Bill, until he married Laura Jane Testerman June 18, 1902 at Stillwater, Oklahoma. She was born September 16, 1881 at Southwest City, Missouri, the daughter of Mary (Shields) and Andrew Jackson Testerman. Lyman taught school and farmed both in Noble County and across the line in Payne County. He enjoyed playing the violin and giving neighbor children violin lessons.

Lyman and Laura were parents of six children, all born in southeast Noble County or north Payne County: Aileen Testerman born July 18, 1903; Robert Jackson born August 26, 1905; Mary Ruth born May 30, 1907; Helen Jane, born August 21, 1914; Louise Lee born November 3, 1916 and Lyman Beecher, Jr. January 19, 1920.

James McCluskey
By Dorothy Long

Mr. and Mrs. James McCluskey came to Noble County in 1898. They established their home on a farm one mile east and two north of Billings, where they lived for the rest of their lives.

Scotch-Irish Presbyterians, they were both born and grew up in the village of Armory, County Antrim in Ulster, Northern Ireland. As he grew up, James had dreamed of migrating to another country, where he could have land of his own. A family story goes that he tossed a sixpence to decide whether to go to America or to New Zealand. The sixpence said America, where his wife, Mary Gillen McCluskey, had relatives.

After their marriage in 1868, they sailed from Londonderry for Canada. Mary was never to see her parents, brothers, or sisters again.

They lived in Brantford, Canada, for some years and then in St. Joseph, Missouri, James working in a variety of jobs. In 1880, they were able to acquire a farm near Wellington, in Sumner County, Kansas. Their family had grown to five sons and three daughters. James was still eager for land and for business opportunities for "the childer", as he called his brood.

Their story is a typical pioneer story. There were good times and bad times, summers of drouth and summers of abundance. As time went on, three of the sons established McCluskey Brothers Hardware in Billings. Two of the daughters became teachers. They all married and had families.

The center of everyone's life was "out home" — the farm. We grandchildren especially enjoyed it, although we all lived in Billings, My mother and her sister-in-laws spent days helping with the wheat harvest, the butchering, the canning, etc. We drove to the farm in a "horse and buggy." With so much work going on, the grandchildren were supposed to "stay out of the way." We roamed in the pasture, played in the barn loft, where they were usually kittens, and when we got big enough, carried cool drinks and sandwiches or cookies to men in the fields. I remember how glad they were to see us coming.

When wheat threshing came, we rode on wheat wagons, bundle wagons. We even climbed on the threshing machine — to be ordered to "be out of the way" and "on your way." At dinner time there might be as many as 20 men gathered around the dining room table. I often had the job of waving a tea towel around the dining room and in the kitchen to drive the flies out the back door. I was often sent too, after the butter crock, which was suspended on a rope into the coolness of the well.

Besides all the housework and cooking, the women also took care of the chickens, made and harvested the garden, milked, took care of the milk and cream and churned. Three times a week they made bread.

Hard as all this work was and in spite of all the ups-and-downs of these early days, the McCluskey family had a lot of the Irish in them and liked to laugh, to sing, to enjoy life.

James McCluskey, stern and strict, was a hard worker. He thought that any farmer worth his salt was in the field by sun-up and worked until dark. In later years his eldest daughter, Mrs. O.W. Long, Billings, would chuckle about what her Dad would have thought about combine farmers having to wait till the dew dried off the wheat before they began cutting. "Heaven

Bless us! It might be 10 o'clock in the morning!"

She would also smile at the sight of fields of contour plowing and remember how her Dad took pride in his corn rows, which were "straight as a string." Times do change.

Mary Gillen McCluskey was a gentle, quiet, kind person, who also had sparkle and a keen sense of humor. Always she was sympathetic to the needs and desires of her family and all other people. She must have liked having her grandchildren around her. She would even give us — between meals — a piece of pie in our hands and we could go outside to eat it.

When she was 50 years old, she considered herself an old women. She made a small black velvet hat, which tied under her chin with black ribbons, and a short black cape. Often she drove to our house in town in her "horse and buggy." My sister and I always rushed out to greet her. "God love you," she would say, then kiss us and give us each a nickel.

She died in 1930, James McCluskey in 1933. Their eight children are also deceased. They were: Henry Carr McCluskey, Blackwell; Cassie Gillen McCluskey (Mrs. O.W. Long) Billings; William Gillen McCluskey, Billings, Alexander McCluskey, Santa Rosa, California; James McCluskey, Billings; John McCluskey, Billings; Rose Ellen McCluskey (Mrs. S.W. Smith), Rio Vista California; and Grace Mildred McCluskey (Mrs. Victor Starr), Culver City, California.

There were 13 McCluskey grandchildren. Five of them are gone: Mary Ola McCluskey, Ruth Long Guthrie, Harry McCluskey, Elzo McCuskey and Dean McCluskey.

The others are Paul McCluskey, Nashville, Tennessee; Dorothy Long, Tonkawa; Wilma McCluskey (Mrs. Ben Matkin), Tulsa; Jean McCluskey (Mrs. Paul Risser), Tulsa; Gilbert McCluskey, Oklahoma City; Gaylon McCluskey, Valley Center, California; Jack McCluskey, Billings; and Collins Smith, Walnut Creek, California. Of his large family Jack is the only member who still lives in Noble County, where, like his grandfather, he farms.

William H. McCormick
By Catherine Gideon

William Henry McCormick and Rose McMillen McCormick, first generation children of Irish immigrants, came to Perry during the Cherokee Strip land settlement in 1893. William McCormick was born September 12, 1858, in Allton, Illinois, son of Thomas McCormick, County Longford, Ireland, and Catherine Moran McCormick, County Antrim, Ireland. At age three his family

Buggies for sale in McCormick Store about 1903.

moved to Farmersville, Illinois, where he attended school and graduated from Jacksonville Business College in 1884. In 1885, he established a business in hardware and general merchandise in Elmo County, Kansas, where he also served as postmaster.

William McCormick married Rose McMillen, daughter of Robert McMillen and Margaret Miller of County Antrim, Ireland, in Chapman, Kansas, on April 25, 1892. They made their home in Elmo until 1893.

On September 16, 1893, William McCormick came to the Cherokee Strip land settlement on the first train from Orlando, Oklahoma. He had previously shipped hardware and general merchandise which was in storage. While checking on his merchandise he was caught by crossfire between two land claimants trying to settle a dispute. He was unharmed, but the incident was indicative of the spirit of the times. At that time, the site which is now the city of Perry was a tent city with numerous saloons. Soon buildings were erected and among them was William McCormick's hardware and general merchandise store.

In 1894, he formed a partnership with an early day mayor of Perry. Later the partnership was dissolved and separate businesses established. McCormick Hardware was located in a two-story building, built from native rock, which is still standing on the south side of the square.

Life was not easy for the pioneers but was exciting and challenging. Water was at a premium with water wells and water from nearby Cow Creek providing the supply. Those hauling water by horsedrawn wagon were in a thriving business. Law and order was a priority. Churches were soon organized along with schools and a social community was established.

For entertainment, the McCormick family purchased season tickets for the Lyceum, a traveling group of performers who presented dramatic and musical programs. All performances were in the Opera House. In the summer the family attended similar shows known as Chautauquas, which were held in tents.

William and Rose were charter members of the St. Rose Catholic church. William was a charter member of the Knights of Columbus, taking an active part in church affairs and serving on early day church boards. Rose was a charter member of the Altar Society and had the honor of being one of the four original Roses of the parish. They bore the name of the patron saint for whom the church was named.

In following years, early in the morning on September 16th, the sounds of horse-drawn wagons could be heard in the streets as local farmers and settlers streamed into the city of Perry to take part in the Cherokee Strip celebration. The Indians were part of the pioneer

William and Rose McCormick - 1893.

McCormick Hardware Store about 1912. (L to R): William McCormick, John Hempfling, Bill McCormick.

celebration, setting up teepees in the courthouse park, dressed in beauiful shawls and blankets, performing their tribal dances.

About 1912, William and Rose moved to a farm southwest of Perry where they made their home. The McCormick family consisted of four sons, Thomas, William, Robert and John, and two daughters, Margaret and Catherine.

Rose McCormick died on November 16, 1933. William passed away on September 29, 1947. They are at rest in St. Rose Cemetery in Perry with children John, Thomas, Robert and Margaret. William is buried in Calvary Cemetery, Kansas City, Missouri. The McCormick name is carried on by two grandsons, William H. McCormick III and Robert H. McCormick, Jr. Catherine, the last surviving member of the McCormick children, lives south of Perry with her husband, A.C. Gideon. They have a son and daughter, William Patrick Gideon, M.D. and Rose Catherine Gideon, M.D.

John McCroskey

By Vernon B. McCroskey

John McCroskey was born in Springview, Nebraska, in 1895, and came to Oklahoma with his parents H.C. and Flora McCroskey, three sisters and one brother in a covered wagon at about five months of age. They settled about three or four miles northeast of Cushing. He grew up in the Cushing, Yale and Quay communities.

Belva Helton was born in Maries county, Missouri, in 1898, and came to Oklahoma with her parents, Robert and Minnie Helton in 1912. Their first residence was near Twin Mounds west of Yale.

John and Belva married, lived on the McCroskey farm, one mile south of Quay or one mile west and two miles north of Yale for a few years. They moved to Noble county in January of 1919 onto the Southeast ¼ of Section 30 21N 3E, a farm that John and Belva's father, R.L. Helton, had purchased in the fall of 1917. They planned to make the twenty-five mile move in one day on snow and ice covered roads. Belva and son, eighteen-month-old Vincent, took the train from Yale to Pawnee, then from Pawnee to Glencoe, planning to ride the wagons from Glencoe to the farm two miles south of Morrison. The sun came out warm about 9:30 a.m., the ice and snow turned to water and the roads became very muddy. Belva spent most of the day in Jake Bunn's store and the night in a hotel. The wagons got to Glencoe the next afternoon. After leaving one wagon and some cattle that became exhausted in the mud, they got to the farm early the second night.

The house was located near three others with the Dennis Christies, Bill McCurrys and Marion Lamberts being close neighbors. They lived on this farm one year. Vernon was born in May and in the summer, John's younger brothers purchased the northwest ¼ of section 29 21N 3E. The next January, John and Belva moved to that farm and Robert and Minnie Helton, who had been living on the Lindin 80, a mile west and one and one-half miles north of Bill's Corner, moved to the Helton 80 as it later became known. They both lived there until their death; Robert in 1946 and Minnie in 1960.

Klein was born in 1921 and named after Klein Riddle, Manager of the Farmers' Trading Association. John served on the Board of Directors of the Farmer's Trading Association for a number of years. John and Belva were members of Morrison Christian Church.

John was elected to the Jefferson School District 48 board about the time Vincent started to school. Some of the teachers were Essie McMillen, Jennie Adams, Gertrude Speer, Verna Dennis, Izora Downey, Leva Lou Tucker and Etta Mae (Branson) Reed.

In the early thirties, John and Belva had a small strawberry patch watered with a windmill pump. It produced during the month of May, furnishing berries for the table and some to sell to neighbors and Morrison town folks. The price was 10¢ per quart, 35¢ a gallon, or 3 gallon for $1.00. The gallons were measured in a one gallon milk crock, heaped up.

The year 1936, was a dry spring and summer. The wheat around Morrison was to short to cut with a binder. John bought one of the first new combines in the community and cut about a thousand acres the first year. Some of the farmers he cut for were Ross Sargent, Duane Speer, Arch Harding, Josh Testerman, Claude Christie, Robert Helton, Harry Hilderbrand, Bert Wilford, Bill Turner, Tom Gibble, C.L. Fuller, Howard Tyre, and Wilton Casparis. The wheat was really poor, yielding 2 to 8 bushel per acre. The best was a 10-acre field that made 11 bushel per acre. The charge was $1.25 per acre for combining that year.

Belva raised chickens and sold hatching eggs to Stillwater Hatcheries including Bigler's, Wilson's and McConkey's.

On September 15, 1942, John moved a house from the "Magnolia Camp" near Quay to the north half of the southwest ¼ section 30 21N 3E. John, Belva and Klein moved there in November.

John bought his first registered Hereford cattle in 1936. About 1950, he decided to change to "Polled Herefords" by crossing with polled Hereford bulls. John sold lots of breeding bulls to neighbors and several club calves to 4-H and FFA members. He had about 35 registered cows at the time of his death in 1978. Belva died in 1984; they are buried in the Lawson cemetery, north of Yale, Oklahoma.

The boys Vincent, Vernon, and Klein went to Jefferson School through the 8th grade and attended Morrison High School.

In 1939, Vincent married Eunice Tate. They have two children: Johnny Lee, and Marilyn Joyce. The same year Vernon married Martha Staley. They had four children: Belva Gean, David Lee, Robert Dale, and Eva Janell, who died of lobar pneumonia when she was four years old. In 1945, Klein married Reba Driesel of the Red Rock area. They had one son, Jerry.

Zack H. McCubbins

By Mildred Highfill

Zack Hilton McCubbins was born in East Tennessee July 5, 1826. His father died when he was a baby and when four years of age, his mother took him to Illinois, the journey being accomplished by horse teams. On a farm adjacent to the city of Paris he spent his boyhood days and received a fair education in the district schools.

At the age of nineteen he began to buy and drive cattle to Chicago where at the time the bunch of cattle brought from down in the state were herded together on the prairies near the town and sold there. After the last animal had been disposed of, the youthful herder would return to his native hearth and collect another lot for the market. In this way, he managed to make two trips a year with considerable profit to himself.

Some time before the Civil War, Mr. McCubbins retired from the cattle business, and, with the money thus accumulated, bought land in Jasper county, Illinois, upon which he built a store and stocked it with the necessities of life in the country. In time the town of Yaleville grew up around this store.

In August, 1862, Mr. McCubbins enlisted in Company E, One Hundred and Twenty-third Illinois Volunteer Infantry, at Mattoon, Illinois, and was commissioned second lieutenant, later being raised to the rank of lieutenant, and eventually to captain. He fought in the Wilderness Brigade, and was wounded with a Spencer rifle. His brigade went to the relief of Andersonville, and was instrumental in securing the capture of Jefferson Davis. He was mustered out in Tennessee in 1865, and returned to his former home in Illinois. At Yaleville he built a larger store and continued in the general merchandise business for nearly fifteen years and was also interested in raising, buying and selling of stock.

His next location was at Bentonville, Arkansas, where he engaged in the nursery business. After four years he took up again the general merchandise business. In 1893, he took up his permanent residence in Perry. Within a couple of weeks he had started the erection of a store on the southwest corner of the square, consisting of two stories and 35x60 feet in dimensions. Here he conducted a grocery business until he retired.

In Jasper county, Illinois, Mr. McCubbins was married to Mary F. Clemmons, a native of Kentucky, but who was reared and educated in Illinois. Their children were: Callie, Mrs. Kraemer, who died in Jasper county, Illinois; Churchill H. who farmed in Noble county, Oklahoma; Avilla V., Mrs. Hayes; Pearlee, who was accidentally killed in Illinois, when seven years of age, by the kick of a horse.

Mr. McCubbins was a member of the Methodist Episcopal Church of which he was a trustee and treasurer. He was a member of the Grand Army of the Republic and the Republican party. In Illinois he was one of the organizers of the Chicago & Puducah Railroad.

Zack H. McCubbins died July 6, 1902, and is buried in Grace Hill cemetery, Perry. Mary F. McCubbins died March 28, 1908, age 75 years 9 months 16 days and is buried beside her husband.

James C. McFarland
By Viola McFarland Wylie

One half mile west of the town of Billings, Oklahoma, can be seen the McFarland homestead. From Crown Point, Indiana, James Calvin McFarland came west hoping to acquire property in the land rush. This McFarland homestead at Billings was acquired and was home for "Jim" and his wife, Nancy McFarland, for twenty-seven years.

Six sons and three daughters were born to Jim and Nancy. Harvey, the first-born, died before any other children arrived. Eight-year-old daughter Vera was killed in a harvest accident in 1913. Names of the seven other children will be listed after details of the run in the Cherokee Strip have been related.

At high noon Saturday, September 16, 1893, Jim McFarland, along with thousands of others in the Oklahoma territory known as the "Strip", stood waiting a gun-shot. The shot was to be fired at Orlando, Oklahoma. Jim knew the claim he wanted. Could he be the first to reach it and set his stake? The noon hour grew nearer. A hush settled over the mob. Then, like the crack of a whip, the shot rang out!

Jim left behind him vehicles compelled to seek trails. He traveled astride a horse and quickly leaped from one horse which began to show exhaustion to another horse he was leading. Two hours passed. Trees were beginning to loom ahead. This was it! There lay the creek. Land nearby was sure to be good bottom land. Jim drove his stake in the ground thanking God for safety and the gift of this new land. Two other family members also won claims of bottom land. The three 160-acre tracts lay close together.

Tomorrow was the Sabbath Day. Yes, the land office in Perry, Oklahoma, would be open. But Jim McFarland, his father-in-law, and brother-in-law would not transact business matters on the Lord's Day. Filing the claims would wait until Monday morning. By Monday morning the three 160-acre tracts were gone. Claims for all three had been filed in Perry on the Sabbath.

There was only one thing to do — go in search of other land not yet claimed. Leaving the fertile, bottom land, Jim traveled north and west about six miles. No trees, no water — but the tracts had not been claimed. Three 160-acre tracts close together were available for Jim and his relatives.

James Calvin McFarland and Nancy McFarland taken at Sterling, Kansas.

Any regrets on the substitute claims? Within five years, Jim's father-in-law's tract had become the town of Billings, and a brisk business ensued selling lots to newcomers. To have a railroad and market nearby was a blessing. Jim and his family were convinced that keeping the Sabbath bought its own reward.

Scarcity of water perpetually faced Jim and Nancy. Well after well was dug. No water even though thirteen wells were tried. So a cistern was Jim's solution to water problems the twenty-seven years Jim and Nancy lived on the Billings homestead. Caves were dug to provide shelter from tornadoes. A lantern, extra matches, some bedding, and an ax always went along when the family huddled together in the cave.

For a railroad right-of-way through Billings, four persons were asked to sell forty acres of land apiece. Jim McFarland gladly donated his forty acres as did three others for joy over the prospect of a railroad. A free round-trip train ride to Chicago was Jim and Nancy's reward for their donation. It was an opportunity for Jim's widowed mother to meet three grandchildren she had never seen. These three were Carrie, William, and A. J. — the three oldest of the McFarland children.

Names of the other seven children born to James and Nancy McFarland are: Carrie (died 1978), William (died 1972), Armour James (died 1962), Luther (died 1982), Wendell (died 1983) Viola living in Hays, Kansas, and Eldo living in Sterling, Kansas.

From 1920 to 1925, the James C. McFarland family lived in the Orlando, Florida, area. Jim greatly missed wheat farming and the cattle and horses of farm life in the plains of the midwest. In 1925, the J. C. McFarland family made another move establishing a home in Sterling, Kansas.

Nancy died in 1934 at age 62. James lived eighty-six years to 1948. Both James and Nancy are buried at Sterling, Kansas. The arrival of ten grandchildren by the early 1930s fulfilled to James and Nancy the promise of Psalm 128:6 - - - "Thou shalt see thou children's children". The Heavenly Father has been good to the McFarland family. They are thankful.

Jane Walker McKinney
By Marjorie Bowles

Jane Walker McKinney's grandfather, George McKinney, was born in Northern Ireland. His wife's name is not recorded. But we know that she died as a result of the birth of their only child, William McKinney (1786-1845), Jane's father, who was born on the Isle of Man, near Britain. William's wife, Jane's mother, was Nancy McAllister (1794-1856). They lived for years in the Glens of Antrim, County Down, Ireland, where William and Nancy were married in 1821. In 1833, they came to America and settled in Ohio; and some time in the early 1840s they moved to Illinois, where they both died.

They are buried in the Maysville Cemetery, Pike County, Illinois. The small community has long disappeared, but the little village of the dead still lies there. Last year I visited their graves.

Their crumbling, marble stones made a sweet and loving picture. For the kindly years had eroded the earth beneath, and had lovingly tilted the two in such a way that each was leaning upon, and was supported by the other. It was impossible not to feel their gentle presence there. William and Nancy had fourteen children, of whom Jane was the seventh. She was born in Ohio in 1833, the very year they had moved there. In 1852, Jane married Joseph McGinley Laird (1835-1915), son of Samuel Laird (1810-1883) and Jane Magee (1807-1896). She was married in a white silk, fringed shawl, still in the family.

Jane and McGinley had six children: Alice A. Laird (1856-1929); Nancy Jane (Jenny) Laird (1858-1944); Orville Laird (1860-1880); Willa Kathryn (Kate) Laird (1861-1884); James Grant Laird (1863-1944); and Samuel Elmer Laird (1867-1944). Orville, as shown died at the age of twenty, and Kate at the age of twenty-three. Surely, the death of a child must be the most tragic loss a parent can suffer. The perpetual silence of their parents spoke more eloquently of the awful depth of their grief, than words ever could.

In 1899 the Lairds — McGinley, Jane, Alice and Jennie — moved to Oklahoma, where they had bought up a claim one mile north of Perry. Their son, Elmer and his family also located there. They later moved into town, where Mr. Laird retired.

(Seated): Joseph M. Laird and wife Jane Walker McKinney; (Standing) (L to R): S. E. Laird, Nancy Jane (Jennie), Alice A. holding Kathryn and J. Grant Laird.

Alice never married, but lived her lifetime with her parents; and with her sister, Jennie, managed their home. Jennie, in mid-life married Slocum Harvey, but returned to the home to be with and help care for her parents when they became ill, and when they died.

To their little nieces, Kathryn and Marjorie, daughter of Elmer and May Laird, who lived nearby, Aunt Alice and Aunt Jennie were saintly. They always took time to give their undivided attention to the children. Both attended the Presbyterian Church faithfully, and belonged to the Royal Neighbors, Rebeccas and the WCTU.

Grant owned and operated a farm in Illinois. He was married to Rose Ella Triplett. Their children were: Merrill, Victor, Vance, Louise and Mary.

Elmer married May Belle Shinn, and moved to Oklahoma at the same time as his parents, in 1899. In 1912, he was appointed the first County Agent of Noble County. He and his wife were parents of LeOla, Carl, Helen, Paul, Kathryn and Marjorie.

In her later years, Jane spent her time sitting in her favorite high-back cane rocking chair, making lovely quilts with infinitely fine stitches. She was quiet, gentle, pensive and dignified. And except for breaking a hip, she enjoyed good health. She had a strong "constitution", and when she became terminally ill at age 94, she lay unconscious for two weeks, the breathing and the beating of the heart, her only signs of life. Then, literally inch by inch, she succumbed, as her strong, unwilling body reluctantly released her spirit. She is buried beside her husband in Grace Hill Cemetery, Perry, Oklahoma.

James W. McMeekin
By Marjory Gilbert LeMaster

On August 15, 1863, a son, James W. McMeekin, was born in Ireland to (James?) and Agnes McMeekin. James and his mother, Agnes, came from Ireland when James was four. This information is subject to question. When a great-granddaughter of James was going to Ireland a few years ago, she tried to learn which part of Ireland had been his birthplace — she wanted to visit her great-grandfather's "Old Stomping Grounds". Lo and behold, she discovered in the 1900 census records that Illinois was listed as his birthplace and his parent's birthplace as Ohio. James' children had always said that Ireland was their father's birthplace and that he came to the United States with his mother when he was four years old. The thought occurs that they came to the United States illegally. The next thought that occurs is — Is it possible that the Department of Immigration will gather up all of his descendants and ship us back to Ireland? When James was about 17 years of age, his mother, Agnes, married John Souter in Iowa.

James McMeekin was in Des Moines, Iowa, in 1886, when he and May Dell Van Trump (August 26, 1864-Ohio) were married on July 2. Four children were born to James and May while they were living in Des Moines — Helen (July, 1888) who died of Pernicious Anemia August 7, 1903; Frances V. (May 6, 1889); Ethel (August, 1891); and Charles (September, 1892) who died of penumonia December 1, 1908. Helen

Top to Bottom: Tom Gilbert, Frances McMeekin, Ethel McMeekin, and Sadie Hendren about 1913 near Perry, Oklahoma.

and Charles were both buried in Grace Hill Cemetery in Perry, Oklahoma.

James came to Oklahoma during the opening of the Cherokee Strip in 1893 and settled in the townsite of Perry. He moved his wife and their four children to Perry soon thereafter. After their arrival in Perry, two other children joined the family — Olive (February 25, 1895) and Wilbur (April 7, 1904).

In 1898, James McMeekin received from the Perry Townsite Trustee the land he had settled on and improved for five years. His work was seasonal as he was a carpenter and during the summers he ran a threshing machine. During one particular summer, when he had managed to complete the season in the "black" as opposed to "red" he crossed a creek and the threshing machine sank in the mud. As far as we know the machine is till there. Within minutes his profit was wiped away.

May, James' wife, was a dressmaker and in this way added to the family income. The illness and death of the two teenagers, Helen and Charles, worked a financial hardship on the family and Frances left school and went to work. She was an industrious person and always set goals for herself — as a child she picked cotton after school and on Saturdays (when she would pick 150#). When she and Thomas T. (Tom) Gilbert were married, Frances was one of Perry's telephone operators. We have no record of what the younger girls did, but we are sure they contributed to the family's livelihood.

Tom Gilbert and Frances were married in the bride's home March 1, 1914 and settled in the southwest corner of Pawnee County on land Tom had bought from the Carson's Otoe Missouri Indians. As the years passed, Tom and Frances were able to acquire more land (his reason for purchasing same, when asked, "It was up against me.") The original purchase of 240 acres was to be the nucleus of their home as long as they lived. Their four children grew to adulthood here — one of whom still lives on the home place. Tom died October 1, 1951, and Frances lived on the ranch until her death April 27, 1972.

Olive McMeekin married a young man of Perry, Michael (Mike) Bernard Howe. In 1910, when Mike was a young man of 19 years he and his parents migrated to Perry, Oklahoma from Chapman, Kansas. On September 27, 1919, he and Olive were married in Oklahoma City, Oklahoma. They moved to Sand Springs, Oklahoma, where Mike worked with Sheffield Steel until he retired. Four children blessed this union.

Ethel McMeekin married Kenneth Dando. They had on child, and they lived a number of years in Beaumont, Texas, where Kenneth worked with Humble Oil Company.

Wilbur McMeekin completed his high school education in Perry, and worked in the Watchorn oil field (Pawnee County); and, as many workers in the oil fields did, he made many moves from "oil boom" to "oil boom". He married a southern Oklahoma young woman, Dolly, fathered three children, and followed the oil boom to Texas. It was while he was working in the oil fields near Corpus Christi, Texas, that he was killed in an accident in the late 1930s or early 1940s.

James McMeekin died April 11, 1932, of pneumonia at his home in Perry. His wife, May Dell, died after lengthy illness, July 13, 1922, in Perry. They were both buried in Grace Hill Cemetery, Perry, Oklahoma.

Joe Merriman

By Audrey Carter

My dad, Joe Merriman, was born March 13, 1893, in Taylor County, Blockton, Iowa. He came to Oklahoma in 1901, with his parents, William and Dora Merriman, and his sisters and brothers. They lived six miles west and seven miles north of Perry.

My mother, Gretta Pennington was born November 26, 1898, at the Pennington farm, just one mile west of the Merriman farm. So, they grew up just one mile apart, both attending North Valley School (district #57) finishing the required eight years of grade school. They attended church at Polo. Mother tells about her being baptized in a spring, in pasture land in the hills west of Polo. It was very cold. Joe and Gretta were married April 4, 1917, at Perry, Oklahoma.

Joe Merriman family - August 11, 1938 as they left the farm. Front Row (L to R): Joe, Gretta, Audrey, and Burnice. Back Row (L to R): Bob and Ed.

They lived at several farms in Noble County for the next six years, spending a short time in Perry where Dad worked at a Service Station. During those six years, four children were born to them. Audrey Blanche was born June 3, 1918; Edwin Harold was born June 9, 1920; Burnice Hazel was born June 12, 1922; Robert Joe was born February 12, 1924.

In 1925, we moved to the Pennington farm, where we remained until 1938. My dad farmed the place, using horses to pull the farm machinery. We also had several cows, providing plenty of milk and butter for the family. Every spring a large vegetable garden was planted and we raised many chickens. The summer months were spent harvesting the crops, canning vegetables and chickens for use during the winter months. Mother baked bread daily as all other farm wives did in that time.

We kids all attended North Valley School for the required eight years of grade school and attended church at Polo. Audrey graduated from Perry High School in 1936. Ed graduated from Billings High School in 1938. Burnice graduated in 1940, and Bob in 1942, both from Classen High School in Oklahoma City.

Times had become quite hard by now, so my Dad decided to give up farming. On July 29, 1938, our household articles, poultry, livestock, and farm

Joe Merriman and Gretta Pennington in Joe's buggy with "Beauty", ready to leave for church in the summer of 1916.

Merriman family 1918. L-R Front Row: Emma, Dora, William and Alice. Back Row: L-R Charley, Mae, George, Hugh, Ross and Joe.

implements were sold at Public auction.

On August 11, 1938, we left the farm life, traveling to the Pacific Northwest to Mount Vernon, Washington, hoping to find a more prosperous living. We were traveling in a 1936 Chevrolet, pulling a four-wheel trailer loaded with our personal things. It was quite an experience traveling over all those mountains. Scary at times, but a great and scenic trip.

In a few weeks my Dad was ready to return to the Plains. The mountains seemed to be closing in around him. He had not found the work he had hoped for, so we returned to Oklahoma City. He worked as a painter and carpenter for several years and at Oklahoma Sash & Door Company. During the war, he worked at Douglas Aircraft and later at Tinker Field, where he was employed when he retired.

After his retirement, he worked as a custodian at a doctor's office and a bank in Midwest City. He was also busy with Masonic work.

Mother was a seamstress and made all of our clothes since babyhood. She also sewed for many friends and neighbors.

They celebrated their Golden Wedding Anniversary in 1967 and the 60th Anniversary in 1977. They lived in Midwest City from 1952 to 1978, where they were when my Dad suffered a stroke and died December 15, 1978. He is buried at Polo Cemetery. Mother lives in Oklahoma City.

William Merriman

By Audrey Carter

William Merriman was born August 22, 1864, in Jones County, near Monticello, Iowa. He was the son of Solomon and Mary Reiger Merriman and the grandson of Jesse Merriman from Scotland and Bessie Wright Merriman from New York State. William had three brothers — Sidney, Carl, and Frank and five sisters — Clara Cobble, Theresa Smelser, Flora Bond, Mary Merriman, and Lilly Miller.

On March 23, 1884, William married Dora Walston, born April 10, 1866, also of Iowa. While living in Taylor County, Blockton, Iowa, ten children were born. They are: Ross, born December 31, 1884, married Gertie Murray on December 21, 1908. Their children are Wesley, Fern (deceased), and Cleo. Ross was a farmer at Woodward, Oklahoma, Osceola, Missouri, and in Noble County in the Polo Community. After retirement, they moved to Perry. Gertie died in 1966, and Ross died in 1967. George, born January 29, 1886, married Edna Nicol on February 14, 1907. Their children are Phillip (deceased), Leta Sharp (deceased), and Valena Jones. George managed the Nicol General Store at Polo and was a farmer. Edna died in 1955, and George died in 1962. Charley, born March 19, 1887, married Orpha White on July 25, 1933. Their only child is Betty Pool. They farmed the Merriman farm until 1944, when they moved to Centralia, Washington, where Charley died in 1970. Mae, born July 11, 1891, married Edgar Stout on February 29, 1908. Their daughters are Clara Schilling and Verna Honeywell (deceased). Edgar and Mae were farmers. Edgar died in 1963, and Mae died in 1975. Joe, born March 13, 1893, married Gretta Pennington on April 4, 1917. Their children are Audrey Carter, Edwin, Burnice Sanderson, and Robert. Joe worked at a Service Station while living in Perry. Moving back to the country, he farmed the Pennington farm for several years. He also worked with the WPA program as Foreman of road maintenance of Oakdale Township. In 1938, he moved the family to Mount Vernon, Washington, but returned to Oklahoma City and Midwest City, where he was living at the time of death in 1978. Twin boys were born December 30, 1894 and died January 18, 1895. Hugh, born September 6, 1896, married Velma Mackey on May 14, 1923. Their children are Margie Blankenship, Maxine Stover, Kenneth, and Gladys (deceased). Hugh served in World War I. He was a farmer while in Oklahoma, moving to Washington State in the 1930s, where he was living at the time of death January 30, 1985 at Seattle. Emma, born December 11, 1898, married Franklin Gallant on May 31, 1921. Their children are Douglas, Thelma Fox, Betty (deceased), Nina Mae Williams, and Faye Gallant. They were farmers and moved to Green Forest, Arkansas in 1930s'. Franklin died in 1973. Alice, born February 23, 1901, married Merrill Wells on August 31, 1924. They were farmers in Oakdale Township. Alice died in 1966, and Merrill died in 1973.

In December of 1900, William and son, George, traveling by train, came to Oklahoma searching for a better place to raise the family. He found a farm for sale in Oakdale Township of Noble County, the NE 1/4 of Section 16. Records show that William M. Crane staked claim to this location in the Run of 1893, and that his claim was canceled in 1895, because of delinquency, so John S. Smelser acquired the land for the $10.00 registration fee. William bought the farm from John Smelser. In the Spring of 1901, the move to Oklahoma was made by train, riding in a boxcar with the livestock and farm machinery. In Oklahoma, their ways of transportation was by horse and buggy or wagon. All of their children attended North Valley School.

William was a corn farmer in Iowa, but in Oklahoma, wheat and oats were the main crops. Hogs, cattle, chickens, and large vegetable gardens provided their food. A cellar was used for food storage and a storm shelter. The only water they had for drinking, household use, and livestock was a salt water well. The taste, being very unpleasant, never improved through the years.

On December 15, 1904, another son, Freddie, was born, but lived only three months. He died March 13, 1905. Dora

William Merriman farm house.

died August 23, 1930, after gallbladder surgery and William died September 22, 1933. They and twenty-five other family members are buried at Polo Cemetery.

Emma Thiele Mielke
By Eleanor M. Kummer

Emma Thiele Mielke spent her hundreth birthday in California, but most of her memories were of early time in Perry. Perry was also a long way from the Russian Ukraine where she was born to her German parents, Reinhold and Katharina Winterle Thiele on February 18, 1884. All she ever mentioned of childhood memories were the snow and wolves, but her parents, by 1893, when she was nine, felt the rising political tensions and injustices made it imperative to come to the New World. So the Reinhold Thiele family of 8 children, plus his mother and father, Johann and Sophia Thiele, left by steamer-freighter from a port on the Black Sea and arrived in New York June 15, 1893.

They traveled by train to Moundridge, Kansas, where a sponsoring Mennonite community and other earlier immigrant relatives were a welcome support group. Life in America, though, was also difficult for different reasons — not enough money and too little food for a large growing family. When there was news of free land in Oklahoma, it seemed the answer to their problems. It is not clear just how or when Reinhold, Emma's father, acquired homestead rights to a farm at Perry, but it was probably part of the land rush of the Cherokee Strip in September, 1893. Life was still far from easy — a large family in a sod house eating just what the land produced. Emma lived and worked on her father's farm for the next 7 years, helping her father with all the heavy farm labor. She learned to speak and write English but that was the extent of her schooling — many times the farm chores took priority over school attendance.

Emma's youth was not carefree and an occassional outing to a square dance was the only break in a life of work and poverty. When she left her childhood, she was suddenly a woman. But what kind of woman? Her formal education was limited but she was conversant in German and English. The Bible was her one source of learning through daily reading. Her faith in Christ and Christian love would stand unshaken all her life. She was proud of her heritage and confident of her own ability. She was adept at anything she tried and had a great poise when with others. She had both beauty and charm.

On November 1, 1900, just four months before Emma's 17th birthday, she married Albert Mielke. He was ten years her senior and he and his family had also migrated from the same community in the Ukraine to this New World.

First, the young couple moved to a farm near Snyder, Oklahoma, and their two children, Agnes and Albert Jr., were born in this location. In 1906, the family returned to Perry to live on a "homestead" farm, 10 miles southeast of Perry.

Now the pioneering efforts started all over again. Emma did all the things a farm wife and Christian woman was expected to do. She had two small children to care for and was pregnant with a third, Richard, who was born in May of 1906. This entire family lived in a 10' x 20' tarpaper board shack. They hauled water, fed the animals, canned vegetables and fruit and farmed the land. Only on Sunday did they take a rest, and always went to church at the little community Lutheran parish followed by gatherings at various homes for food and fellowship. This was their social life for the most part.

In 1917, Albert built a new house for his family and this house remains standing today. It is now owned by Walter Kukuk. The new house made many aspects of life easier and more pleasant but for the next 22 years until 1939, Emma's life was devoted to family and the farm. It meant living a harsh, simple rural existence. There were parish schools for the children with very basic education. There was no TV, few books, magazines and newspapers. Electricity and radio did not come until the early Thirties.

The hard work and trials of farm life took its toll on Albert's health and he died on December 31, 1938, after a year's illness and nursing care by his wife, Emma. He was buried in the Richburg cemetery — on land that had been donated by his family to the church.

Emma was only fifty-four at this time and this was only the end of the second phase of Emma's life. After her husband's death, she went to live in Los Angeles, California with her daughter, Agnes. She did make a few trips back to Perry and finally sold the

Albert and Emma Mielke on November 1, 1900.

family farm in 1944.

Emma died in a California hospital on July 1, 1984 at age 100. It had been her wish for all these years, though, to be buried back in Perry. Her wish was fulfilled when she was brought back to be buried beside her husband in the soil that had been a part of her life for so many years.

Edward J. Miller
By Ruth Queen

Edward John Miller (born in 1860) and oldest son, Victor E., came to Perry early in 1900. E.J.'s wife, Ida E. (born in 1868) and the other children: Carrie Marie (born in 1891) and George McKinley (Mac) (born in 1894), followed by railroad from Adams, Nebraska, later that year. All their belongings were in a boxcar and Mac rode with the family cow in a cattle car.

E.J. Miller was in the grain, coal and cotton business, establishing the first cotton gin this far north and west in the United States. He was well known throughout the Oklahoma Territory as a shrewd businessman and his advice was sought and respected by many cotton and grain investors throughout the country. His wife, Ida, can be remembered for her untiring charitable services towards townspeople. She had a beautiful soprano voice and her singing in German was a great pleasure to her fellow church members. She was a member of St. Rose of Lima Catholic Church and Altar Society. She died in 1922, and was buried in the Catholic cemetery, Perry, Oklahoma.

E.J. married Ida Mae Hitsman in 1923. Some years later, he leased the E.J. Miller Elevator to the Stillwater Milling Company. The cotton gin, and coal company were sold to a pioneer, E.J. Coyle.

Victor J. Miller was the first Buick Car Dealer in Perry. He married Jennie Swank of Nebraska. They had two children, Lorene and Edward. The Victor Miller family later settled in Alhambra, California.

Carrie Marie married Fred William Lindeman, son of Rose Lindeman, on November 21, 1916. To this union four daughters wree born — Mary (1917), Lucile (1919), Ruth (1912), and Philamene (1924).

Mac Miller was in the grain business with his father. He married Lillian Johnson. They had one daughter, Idabelle. Lillian died a young mother in 1925. She was buried in the Catholic cemetery, Perry, Oklahoma. Mac married Gertrude Maxwell in 1928 and they had three children — Mary Katherine (1930) and twins Max and Maxine (1931).

E. J. Miller died in 1939 and was buried beside his first wife, Ida, in the Catholic cemetery, Perry. Ida Mae, his second wife died in 1947, and was buried in Grace Hill cemetery, Perry, Oklahoma.

Mac was in the grain business until 1940, and moved to McAlester, Oklahoma in 1944. In later years Mac and Gertrude retired in Riverside, California. Mac died in 1977 and Gertrude died in 1981. They both were buried in the Catholic cemetery.

Carrie Miller Lindeman lost her husband in 1942. She lived a long and useful life in Perry. She died in 1982. She and Fred were buried in the Catholic cemetery.

J. M. Milligan

Clark C. Milligan

Prior to moving to Oklahoma, the Milligan family of six lived on a farm in Clay County, Kansas, ten miles from Clay Center.

James, the oldest boy, had asthma, a doctor stated that a warmer climate would be more desirable for James.

Mr. Milligan went to Oklahoma to make a survey for a new farm. In the survey he found two 160 acre farms together that were level, close to Billings, and the price was reasonable. He bought the two farms.

His wife, Mrs. Marian Milligan and their four children: Florence, James, Lester, and Clark made the trip from Clay Center to Billings by railroad, together with horses, cows, and implements in March, 1912. Mr. Milligan made the trip later driving two mares that were heavy in foal.

The Milligan children entered the Billings' schools soon after their arrival, and all four graduated from high school there.

The family attended the Covenater (Presbyterian) Church until many members moved to other states, and it was closed.

Mrs. Milligan died of cancer on December 24, 1924. After Clark graduated in May, 1925, the family moved back to Kansas.

Florence attended Sterling College, and Kansas State.

James graduated from Geneva College in Pennsylvania, and Kansas University, with a Masters in Economics. He taught in high school and college. He served in the Air Force in World War II retiring as a major.

Lester operated a 250 acre farm close to Winchester, Kansas and died in 1931.

Clark graduated from Kansas State University, and taught vocational agriculture for 14 years, and served 17 years overseas with the Departments of Army and State.

Florence has six children and lives in Winchester, Kansas. James has one daughter, and lives in Valley Falls, Kansas. Clark lives in Kerrville, Texas.

Mr. Milligan retired to Winchester, Kansas, and died in 1962, at the age of 98.

William Mills

By Bertha (Mills) Passow

This branch of the Mills family of America started from one William Mills in 1742. He and a brother whose name is not known sailed from North Hampton, England in 1742, for America each in seperate vessels. A storm seperated the vessels. William landed in New York and the brother in South America.

The William Mills family who came to Noble County in 1910, was the great-great-grandson of the William Mills who sailed from England. He was born August 17, 1868, in Lapel, Indiana. He married Clara Louise Smith on May 27, 1897; she was born in Brimfield, Illinois, August 16, 1880.

For health reasons they wanted to move to a better climate. So William took the train to Texas and Oklahoma and found the place five miles west and two miles south of Perry for sale. There was a five room house on the place and it was rented out, so he let the renters continue living there for a couple of years. They moved their belongings down on the train and moved into a house a mile north of their farm until they got more rooms built onto their house.

There were five children born in Illinois. Everett Mills was born August 19, 1898, he married Zelma Adkins and they had four children, two sons, George Mills, Charles Ray Mills, and two daughters, Clara Mae (Mills) Stem and Louise (Mills) Bird. Eva Mills was born March 8, 1900, and died in 1911. Mable Mills was born November 23, 1902, she married Charles Kemnitz and they lost a baby boy at birth. Clifford Mills was born June 20, 1906, and died as a baby. Henry Mills was born April 12, 1909, he married Opal Hughes and they had two sons William (Billy Ray) Mills and Richard (Dick) Mills. Bertha Mills was the first child to be born in Oklahoma, on March 22, 1911. She married Clarence Passow and they had two daughters, Charlotte (Passow) Byrd and Neoma (Passow) Petersen. Blanch Mills was born March 19, 1913, she married Perry Bower and they had one son, Billy Tom Bower. Emmett Mills was born September 5, 1920, he married Theresa Voight. All the children went to the White School and William was on the school board.

For entertainment Mom played the accordian, Dad played the Jews harp, and Everett played a harmonica. We had a player piano that we all could play.

We raised almost all of our food. Dad had a smoke house to smoke our meat and we also canned meat. We milked cows and raised hogs and chickens. We had a big garden. Dad would haul wheat or corn to be ground for our baking. The one thing we would have to buy was a load of apples from Guthrie. That would take two days, as it took one day getting there by horses and wagons and picking and loading them, then the next day to get home. We kept them in the cellar and the folks told us to eat the apples with rotten spots. So it seemed we ate rotten apples until they were gone (we did take good apples in our school lunch).

We got our first car which was an Oakland in 1916, it was a touring car which was open like a convertible. It was nice but you had to crank it to start it and it would go about 30 miles an hour. The highway department soon built a paved road in front of our house and we could watch the traffic go past on Highway 77.

Harvest was a big time of the year. Every farmer cut their grain with a binder into bundles which they stacked into tee-pee shaped shocks to cure. Then all the neighbors would work together hauling the bundles by horse and wagon to the thrashing machine in the middle of the field, which left a big pile of straw, called a straw-pile. It took about 12 to 15 men or large boys to make a thrashing crew, as some had to haul the bundles, some ran the thrasher, and some hauled the grain to the grainery and unloaded it. When finished at one farmer's, they moved to the next farmer. The wives cooked for

Hank, William, Everett, Bertha, Blanche, Mable and Clara Mills.

the thrashers, which was a big meal, (that's where they get the expression "looks like you're cooking for the thrashers"). The harvest ended with a big party called a thrashing party, which really was for settling expenses. They usually met at the thrashing machine owner's house and they had homemade ice cream and cake for all the families.

William sold the farm about 1943, and moved to Perry. Clara died in 1947, after a lengthy illness. William built several small houses, he died in 1962. Only two of the children are still living which are Bertha Passow and Blanch Pricer both of Perry. Many of the descendants still live in and around Perry and some have businesses.

Sampson M. Mitchell
By Beatrice Grim

The children and grandchildren of Mr. and Mrs. Sampson Mitchell gathered at the old home place in Morrison, Oklahoma on Sunday April 15, 1951 to celebrate their 62nd wedding anniversary.

Sampson Mitchell was born at Harrisville, West Virginia July 12, 1866, the son of Malinda Ann (Zickefoose) and William Thomas Mitchell. He married Alicia Jane Laird on April 15, 1889 in Harrisville, West Virgina. Alicia was born July 10, 1872 in Harrisville, West Virginia. While in West Virginia they had five children, Jennie May (born May 1890); Ivah V. (born November, 1892) Grace M. (born April 1894); Clarence A. (born May 2, 1895) and Hobart (born in May 1896).

In 1896, they came by train to Arkansas City and then by covered wagon to Noble County. Sam bought a new well-drilling outfit and a team of horses. He drilled water wells in Noble, Pawnee and Payne Counties.

The children born in Oklahoma were Alice, John T., Bertha L., Charles T., Geneva and Beatrice.

May Mitchell married John Homer Hetherington April 15, 1914 in Stillwater. They had four children born in Morrison: Mary Lorraine lived two hours; Hugh Robert (October 25, 1920); Homer Gordon (May 31, 1924) and Dorothy Jane (January 6, 1928).

Ivah married Bill Quick and had three children. Grace married Clyde Sexton. Clarence married Mary Kerns and had five children. Hobart married Zada Trowbridge and had six children. Alice married Fred Pogue and had four children. John married Marion Hastings and had six children. He lived in Pueblo, Colorado. Charles T. (Ted) worked in oil fields in Kansas and never married. Bertha married Cecil Metcalf and had five children. Geneva married Herman Ekhoff and had three children. Beatrice married George Grim and had two children.

Sampson Mitchell died in 1952 and Alicia in 1969. They are buried in the Morrison cemetery.

Edward D. Moelling
By Eldon Moelling

Edward Daniel Moelling was born September 7, 1879 in Clay Center, Kansas. He and other members of his family came to Noble County, Oklahoma in 1896. Ed's father was August Moelling, born June 2, 1854 in Gasconade County, Missouri, the eldest of 9 children. His mother was Minnie Stute, born in the same county as his father, on March 7, 1857. The grandparents of our subject, Ed Moelling, came from Germany. His grandfather, Adolph Moelling, was born in Lippe Detmold, Germany from whence he came to the United States when he was forty years old and still unmarried. After an ocean voyage of seven weeks he landed in New York City, making his way to Gasconade County, Missouri where he began farming. It was there he married Louisa Otto, also a native of Germany, who died in the county of their marriage at the age of thirty-nine. Adolph later moved to Clay County, Kansas in 1878, where he lived until his death May 6, 1887 at the age of seventy-seven.

Adolph Moelling was a Deacon and active member of the Presbyterian Church, to which his wife Louisa also belonged. He was a member of the Republican Party. August Moelling was also a Republican and a Presbyterian.

Ed Moelling began his labor early in life, when at age 9 (1896) he joined others of his family in making the move from Clay County, Kansas to Noble County, Oklahoma, bringing 50 head of cattle. Concerning the three week journey Ed recalled, "We averaged about 10 miles a day...and we planned overnight camps at places on the trail where we could find water for the cattle...We arrived at our half-section of land on Easter Sunday, 1896."

Little is known of Ed's life and activity as a child but he was always proud of the fact that although he went only through grade six, he was very adept at being able to "out-figure anyone else" in arithmetic and certain other practical skills.

In 1907, the Moellings moved five miles north to Lucien, then a very promising town, and opened the Moelling and Moelling General Merchandise Store. Ed recalled that "we sold everything from a needle to a threshing machine." Successful for a number of years, the store closed during the Depression era, victim of hard economic times.

Previous to the establishment of the General Store, Ed and Emma A. Drager were married in the bride's home, five miles south and one mile east of Lucien on Christmas Day, 1904. It was part of a double wedding in which Emma's sister, Lena was married to Hugo Bolzinger, both of whom remained Noble County residents during their life-times.

Ed and Emma spent their life in the Lucien area, children born to them were three daughters, Edna (Passow), Vila, and Lillie and one son, Arthur, who married Lela Conrad. Following the closing of the general store, Ed worked as a carpenter, joining with others in constructing a number of the eary day homes and buildings in the Orlando-Lucien area.

In the early 1930s Ed was joined by his son Art in trucking and hauling merchandise. This came during the oil field development. The business started out with wagon and horses as they hauled 'hand-scooped' sand from the Black Bear Creek, delivering it to lumber yards and oil field sites. They 'graduated' to a Model "T" and "A" Ford truck. In about 1934 they started

L to R: Eldon Moelling, (grandson) and Ed Moelling - 1978.

hauling livestock, transported to Oklahoma City Livestock Exchange. Art purchased livestock at community sales and/or from individual farmer-ranchers, with Ed transporting them to Oklahoma City. Ed performed this service for more than 30 years, and very unwillingly, at age 84, was 'forced' by his family to give it up. He was not involved in a traffic accident in which he was at fault, even though he drove many thousands of miles. His truck was equipped with a special place for crates of eggs where he distributed from office to office to the secretaries and office personnel of the Exchange building in the Stockyards area. His blue bib-overalls, moustached smile, fast walk, sacks or cartons of eggs were all trade-marks for the 'friendly egg man'.

For a number of years, Lucien, like some other small communities, had their own telephone exchange. From about 1925-1955 Ed was the principal overseer and trouble-shooter for the largely rural telephone operation. He purchased supplies, made repairs, mailed the billings to customers, paid the bills, often climbed the poles, drove the roads and walked the pastures in search of the breaks that caused the telephones to 'go on the blink'.

Another task he successfully fulfilled, starting at age 78 (around 1958-1965) was to operate the Grain Elevator in Lucien.

Ed never smoked nor chewed, and boasted proudly that "I never bought a drop of whiskey in my life." Lean and trim from long years of hard outdoor work, he lived to be 99 years, 9 months, and 2 days old, only a few months from the century mark! His moustache, in the fashion of the 1890s was with him from age 18 on and few persons have worn a moustache for more than 80 years, nor lived with more grace and responsibility.

John H. Moore
By Joe Highfill

The following was written on May 8,

John & Robina Moore and their sons. Standing left to right: Henry, William, Calvin Davis, Russell, Archie, John, Sam. Andy is seated.

1929 by Mrs. Robina J. Moore: To begin with, we came to Oklahoma in covered wagons, arriving at our destination, near Orlando, in October, 1892. We had three heavily loaded wagons, my husband's father, W.D. Moore, his wife and daughter, making the trip with us. We rented a farm near Orlando and raised a crop to help keep our stock the coming winter. I, myself, drove one of the teams through from Greenwood county, Kansas, with a two-year-old baby in my arms. My husband drove a herd of horses through, riding one all the way every day. We were two weeks on the road. Our oldest son, William, drove one team for his grandfather. He was a boy, fifteen years old. Mr. Moore's father bought an 80 acre farm near Orlando in Old Oklahoma, and improved it. Here he lived until 1902, dying in April of that year at the age of 83.

September, 1893 came. It was a very hot, dusty fall. I drove over to Orlando to take my husband food, where he stood in line waiting to register. The dust was so thick one could only see a very short distance ahead. Then came the opening day, September 16, 1893. My husband made the race on horseback, starting with the crowd from a point nine miles east of Orlando, on the Old Oklahoma line. It was a great sight, one that I shall never forget. My husband staked a claim and went on to Perry. Here he stood in line several days waiting his turn to file on his claim.

We built a log hut on our claim and moved to it on the 3rd day of November. My husband got some rock and built a kind of fireplace, there being plenty of all kinds of timber on our claim. The Little Stillwater creek ran through it from west to east.

After a few years a sawmill located on our farm and cottonwood, oak and walnut lumber was sawed. We then built a frame structure. The ceiling was made of pine lumber. During the first year, we had 75 cents when we moved into our log hut. My husband borrowed money of a neighbor to buy boards and finish the gable ends of the log house. A neighbor also helped to make clapboards from a good board tree, which covered the roof. We had a dirt floor that first winter. My husband hauled wood and posts to town to buy our groceries.

The first winter on our claim we got two deer for meat. We had hounds we had brought from Kansas and the three older boys and dogs got one when Mr. Moore was working on a house about half a mile away. They went and told him they had killed a deer, he came home and dressed it. We had plenty of good meat for a while. Then after that my husband took his dogs and went down the creek and got another young deer.

My husband, being a carpenter, went on building houses all over the county till spring and summer, then he began breaking out the bottom land for planting crops, hired most of it done, paid for it in horses as we had a great many more than we needed and some other men had none. We just kept working, our older boys finally were old enough so they could help and before long he could go out and work the carpenter trade and make money for the family to live on while I and the boys made the crop. (end of quote)

John Harvey Moore was born January 4, 1851 in Wright county, Missouri, the son of William Davis Moore and Louisa Ann Findley. He married Robina Jane Cheek January 2, 1878 in Eureka, Kansas. Robina was born August 19, 1859, the daughter of Calvin William Cheek and Corneilia Penelope Tinnen. The Moores were very active in the Bethel church in Walnut township. John served as one of the first elders. They raised thirteen children.

The children were in order of birth: Louisa Jane (Coate); William Weaver, Calvin Davis, Samuel Harvey, Mary

John and Robina Moore with their daughters (left to right): Mollie Kepley, Martha Dundas, Lottie Cross, Louisa Coate, and Tillie Edgar. The baby is Lucy Edgar Foster in 1918.

Penelope (Kepley), Corneilia Charlotte (Cross), John Findley, Henry Dyke, Matilda Ann (Edgar), Nathaniel Andrew, Martha Catherine (Dundas), Archie Irvin, and Clarence Russell. The first nine children were born in Eureka, Kansas. The last four were born on the claim in Walnut township.

During the 1920s John and Robina moved to Perry, where John was a bailiff. John died January 2, 1927 in Perry from influenza. Robina died July 7, 1932 in Perry from a stroke and heart failure. They are buried in the Shelton cemetery.

Nathaniel Andrew, (Andy) was killed in an accident while working for the Perry Light Plant on April 25, 1923. He is buried in the Shelton cemetery. He served in the 357th infantry in World War I.

William N. Moore
By W. M. (Nev) Moore (Deceased)

Perry Daily Journal, March 27, 1937

I left Como, Colorado, accompanied by Pat Harding and C. G. Carter and arrived in Pittsburg, Kansas, August 23, 1893. Here we bought our means of transportation to compete in the run into the Cherokee Strip. Mr. Carter bought a team and wagon and I bought a spotted pony, named him Pony Bill. I also bought a buggy. We met Al Harding in Fairland, Indian Territory and from there the four of us drove thru Tulsa, which at that time consisted of a depot and a few small houses. On to Cushing, which was a very small place. Then to Ingalls, a town of three or four buildings. The place was all shot to pieces because a day or two before our arrival there, a band of outlaws had been cornered by Federal Officers and had retaliated with gun fire. We arrived in Stillwater September 11. We camped and awaited the day of the Run. During the time we were in camp two men who owned thoroughbred run-

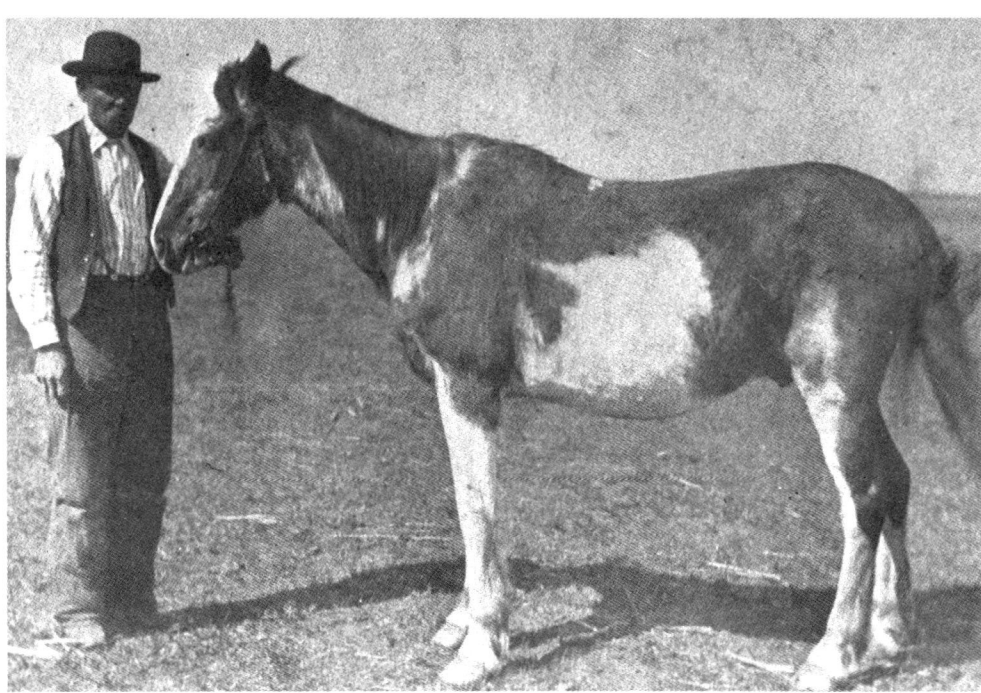

William N. (Nev.) Moore and "Pony Bill".

ning horses, ran them up and down the road many times to keep them in good running condition. We had to wait in line 36 hours to register our right as claimants to be permitted to run.

On the morning of the 16th of September I rode Pony Bill out and got in position. The line was formed about three miles north of Stillwater. As we were going out to line these two fellows on their thoroughbreds passed me and asked, "You think you're going to get there on old Spot?" I answered, "If I don't I'll be crackin' brush close behind." When the shot was fired at 12 o'clock all of us started. When I was about five miles out in the Strip I saw a horse down and a man standing beside it and when I got close enough I saw it was one of the men with his Thoroughbred. As I passed he shouted "You're crackin' bush close behind." I didn't stop to argue with him and on a little farther I saw another horse stumble and fall. Soon I was close enough to see that it was a woman who had fallen off her horse and as I passed she was on her knees driving her stake and shouted to me as I rode by. "I guess I'll stay right here." Just before I reached Long Branch I passed the other fellow standing by his Thoroughbred. The horse was bleeding at the nose. When Pony Bill and I reached Long Branch there was quite a crowd unable to cross as there were but few cow trails. However, Pony Bill was near the trail and he swerved to one side into it and we rode across. There were just a few of us on the north side by this time. Some place, Mr. Carter got lost from us but Al and Pat Harding were riding close to me. We rode north from Long Branch until we saw the Government Corner Stone to the right and we turned toward it.

As we came over the hill from Long Branch we saw a number of men on horses rush out from the creeks and go north. At the Government Stone, Al said, "Which place you want Nev?" I answered. "Since I am on this side I'll take this one." and Al said, "I'll go on north to the next and if no one has staked it, I will take it." I rode Pony Bill about 300 yards out in the prairie and drove my stake, (a lath with my handkerchief tied to it). This was exactly 12:45 p.m. My little spotted Pony Bill and I made the run of nine miles in just 43 minutes. By one o'clock many had managed to cross Long Branch and were congregating at the Government Corner Stone. While we were there a deer ran by but because so many people in all directions those who had guns were afraid to shoot. All of us had a canteen or jug of water and one fellow said to another, "hold my jug let me have your pistol, I'll get him." The transfer was made, later the one who held the jug raised it so all could see and said, "Well this is a H___ of a thing to trade a $16.00 gun for." We never again saw the fellow who borrowed the pistol.

A littler later in the afternoon, Jenkins the fellow who staked the claim west of me, decided to feed his horses. He had a big umbrella folded and lying on top of the feed in the wagon. The wind was blowing, so to keep the umbrella from blowing away when he laid it on the ground, he tied his bottle of water to the handle. But he had no sooner than laid them on the ground when the wind whipped the umbrella open and both skyrocketed out of sight. Mr. Jenkins made the Run in a wagon because a woman by the name of Johnson gave him $10.00 to haul her. She wanted out on the ¼ section now owned by Bill Law. That night each one of us slept where we drove our stake. The next morning a stranger walked up to me and asked, "Where are you claiming?" I answered, "Right here." He answered, "This is mine." I asked him "What time did you come on it?" He answered, "One o'clock. What time did you come?" and I said, "Seventeen minutes is a devilish long time in a race like this, and you've heard just what I said." By this time Mr. Jenkins had walked up and said. "Yes that's right. I saw you over here on this place up when I drove in and this stranger was behind me." Mr. Harding came riding up at that time too and also verified the time I drove my stake on the claim. The stranger asked me to give him eighty acres and both of us farm together but when I refused he left. Mr. Jenkins stayed on his place less than a month, having traded to V. W. Barrows. At present the place is owned by Bill Turner.

On the 17th of September, I rode the claims while Al and Pat Harding went to Stillwater to get a team and plow so that we might break some ground to sow wheat. On the 20th we went to Perry to file. There were so many ahead of us we couldn't possibly file then. Uncle Dick Morgan had a tent in the square and told us if we gave him a nickle and our address he would notify us when our time came for filing. We did this and went to Tulsa where we worked six weeks before hearing from Uncle Dick (later Uncle Dick became Congressman). So the last of October we filed and I went back to Colorado to work during the winter for finances to start improving my claim. Mr. Carter failed to stake a claim so Pat Harding told Mr. Carter to take the one he staked. Pat Harding died soon after.

In March 1894, I returned, borrowed a horse to work with Pony Bill and broke out ten acres, and planted it in kafir corn. After planting kafir I bought native lumber, (cottonwood), from P. T. Perryman, who owned a saw mill on what is now Mrs. Olive Boyer's farm and built my first house, a 10 by 12. The following summer I worked in Tulsa for more finances. In the fall of 1894, when I returned, my 10 acres of kafir yielded about three bushels of grain. So again I borrowed a horse turned the same ground and sowed in wheat. I bought the seed in Stillwater at 25 cents a bushel. The winter of 94 and 95 I went back to work. When I came back in the spring I broke out 30 acres of ground and when I harvested the ten acres I had in wheat I reaped about enough seed to sow the forty acres of broken ground. The winter of 95 and 96 I went away again to work and returned in March of 1896. My forty acres of wheat was good yielding 16 bushels to the acre. Then I stayed on the place and farmed.

The little town of Autry was just a store operated by a man by that name. The mail was carried to Autry by stage coach operating between Perry and Pawnee. In the early days the road ran 6 miles east of Perry, one mile north then east to about ¼ mile north of the store, then south to the store.

In the spring of 1895 I assisted in surveying the north ½ of Auburn Township. This being necessary because of a dispute as to the section lines.

One day during the summer of 1895 I wanted to come to the store in Autry to get my mail and shop so I hitched Pony Bill to the buggy, threw in the spade and started straight east along the section lines. When I came to a little creek or draw I spaded the banks down so Pony Bill could cross with the buggy. I angled across toward the store at about the same place the pavement does today, past where the Telephone office now stands and on to the store which was located just south of the Morrison school house. The next day Al Harding followed my tracks and we were the first ones to open that road to Autry. After awhile, Mr. Autry sold to Mr. Morrison and he conducted the store until his death. In 1902 or 1903, the St. Louis and Santa Fe built the railroad and of course Morrison built their new building nearer the railroad tracks. William Nevit Moore was born July, 1861 in Illinois. His mother, Susan Sutherland was born February 1844 in Ohio.

William W. Moore
By Mildred Highfill

William Weaver Moore was born September 6, 1880, in Eureka, Kansas, the son of John Harvey Moore and Robina Jane Cheek. He came with his parents to Oklahoma a year before the Cherokee Strip "Run". Although he was only twelve years old; he drove a team and a covered wagon on the way to Oklahoma for his grandfather, William Davis Moore.

He came with his parents to Noble county, when his father made the run into the Strip and helped to make a home on the land. They had no money when they came, so Will and his brothers had to do a good part of the work in breaking out and planting the crops. His father was a carpenter and hired out to build houses for the neighbors for money to buy the things the ten children needed.

Will married Anna Bell Coate, a neighbor girl on January 9, 1904 at Perry, Oklahoma. Anna was born Anna Bell Huggins on January 9, 1886, in Columbia, Tennessee. She had been adopted when she was three years old

William W. Moore family about 1916. Back Row: Will and Annie. Front Row (Left to Right): Vern, Chester and Myrna.

by Thomas Jefferson Coate and his wife, Mary Jeanette Leland and came with them to the Strip.

Will and Annie lived in east Perry for many years. They had built a new home when a tornado completely flattened the house. Fortunately no one was injured.

Annie had a garden, kept a milk cow and raised chickens. Will worked at many odd jobs, hauling lumber and rocks, etc. He worked for the City of Perry repairing the streets. When his brother, Andy, returned from World War I, they both were working in the Water and Light Plant for the City of Perry. On April 23, 1923, they were trying to move a heavy generator into the basement. They were below the generator, trying to guide it into place, when the cable broke. Andy was killed and Will injured.

Annie and Will were the parents of four children: Thomas Harvey Moore who was born July 5, 1905. Thomas died October 5, 1916, age five years of typhoid fever; Chester Arthur Moore was born May 14, 1907, and twins Vern Jefferson Moore and Myrna Jeanette Moore (Hoffman) who were born July 8, 1909. All of the children were born in Perry.

Will left his family and went to California where he remarried. He died August 14, 1963, and is buried in California. Annie Moore lived with her daughter, Myrna, until her death January 27, 1965. She is buried in the Grace Hill cemetery, Perry, Oklahoma.

Vern Moore, son of Will, married Martha May Vice, May 22, 1937, at Perry. Martha was born March 25, 1917, at Grove, Oklahoma, the daughter of George Mack Vice and Lena May Fowler. They have lived in Perry, since their marriage.

Myrna Moore married Albert Hoffman November 29, 1938, at Stillwater, Oklahoma. They made their home in Perry until her death on May 18, 1984. She is buried in Grace Hill cemetery by her mother. Al worked in the Chevrolet garage.

Chet Moore, the oldest son to reach manhood, married Velma Elaine Evans December 1, 1928, at Perry, Oklahoma. Velma was born May 20, 1912, at Seymore, Iowa, the daughter of Albert R. Evans and Katie Ann Blair and the step-daughter of Ira Shelton. Chet was a movie projectionist for the Perry Theater. He died January 28, 1959, of a heart attack. He is buried in Grace Hill cemetery.

Chet and Velma's children: Jack Chester Moore b-September 22, 1929; Betty Jean Moore b-May 1 1931, Thomas Ray Moore b-February 4, 1938; and Deanna Faye Moore b-April 26, 1940; all at Perry. Thomas is now the fire chief at Perry.

Dick T. Morgan
By Mildred Highfill

Hon. Dick T. Morgan was born near Terre Haute, Indiana, on December 6, 1854, the son of Valentine and Frances (Thompson) Morgan. His boyhood was spent on a farm. His elementary education was acquired in the "little red schoolhouse" of his district, and in the Prairie Creek high school. In 1872, he entered the Union Christian College at Merom, Indiana, where he graduated in the Centennial year with a Bachelor of Science degree. In 1879, his Alma Mater conferred upon him the degree of master of Science, and in the meantime, he had held the chair of mathematics in the college for one year and had been superintendent of the high school of Hagerstown, Indiana, for two years.

In his leisure hours, Mr. Morgan had pursued legal studies under Colonel Thomas Nelson, of Terre Haute, and Judge I.N. Pierce, and in the autumn of 1870, entered the senior class of Central Law School, of Indianapolis. He carried off the honors of his class, delivering the valedictory and receiving the degree of Bachelor of Law in 1880. His initial practice was in partnership with N. G. Huff, of Terre Haute, with whom he remained until 1886, and during the last two years also was editor of the daily "Courier", a paper of wide circulation. In 1880, he was elected as a representative from Vigo county to the general assembly of Indiana. In 1884, Mr. Morgan was the Republican candidate for state senator, but his entire district, with the state, gave a majority to the Democratic candidates.

In 1887, Mr. Morgan came to the west, and while waiting for Oklahoma's opening to settlement he was engaged in the practice of law in Garden City, Kansas, and was local attorney for the Santa Fe railroad. April 22, 1889, he located in Guthrie, where he was in partnership with Hon. J. L. Pancoast until September, 1893, when they came to Perry, and it was not until 1899, that the firm of Morgan & Pancoast was dissolved by mutual consent.

Mr. Morgan published two books: the first in 1891, *"Morgan's Manual of U.S. Homestead Townsite and Mining Laws"* sold over twenty thousand copies; the second *"Morgan's Digest of Oklahoma Statues and Supreme Court Decisions"* was purchased by the territorial legislature for county and township officers.

In Merom, Indiana on May 30th, 1878, Dick T. Morgan married Miss Ora Heath. She was born near Covington, Indiana, the daughter of Rev. A. R. Heath, and his wife, the former Mary Maxwell. Mr. and Mrs. Morgan had but one child, a son, Porter Heath Morgan, born at Terre Haute, Indiana, October 12, 1880. Dick T. Morgan was chairman of the first convention of the Republican party held in Oklahoma.

When the Cherokee Strip was opened Dick T. Morgan made the run and settled on a lot in Perry. When the First Christian church was organized on September 24, 1893, Dick T. Morgan was Sunday school superintendent. The first service was held in a tent which served as a place of worship until cold weather set in and then the church services were held in Smith's hall and Mr. Morgan's office on West D street.

A condition which was without precedent in the history of primary elections was created in the 8th Congressional District by the unexpected death of Representative Dick T. Morgan, a month before the primary election but after the time limit for the filing of candidacies for nomination having been closed. As a consequence, the nomination went by default to the only other Republican aspirant, Manuel Herrick. The prevalence of a partisan spirit sent him to the halls of Congress to make Oklahoma the laughing stock of the nation.

Helen L. Morrison
By Helen Morrison

Helen Lucile Keyser was born July 10, 1925, the daughter of George B. Keyser and Lottie Acres, with Dr. D. F. Coldiron in attendance. Helen attended Fremont District #34 grade school and Perry High School. After graduating from high school, Helen attended and graduated from Central State College, Edmond, Oklahoma. Helen was an elementary teacher for twenty years in

(Left to Right): John Morrison, John Jr., Kathleen (Brown) and Helen Morrison.

Oklahoma and Kanas and has been a private piano teacher for 35 years.

Vows were held March 27, 1953, in the First Methodist Church at Wichita, Kansas for Helen L. Keyser and John W. Morrison. The groom is the son of Mr. and Mrs. J. H. Morrison of Bixby, Oklahoma.

John and Helen had two children; a daughter, Kathleen Lucile, born April 24, 1954 at Tulsa, Oklahoma. Kathleen attended Haysville, Kansas Elementary School, Junior High and Campus High School. She graduated from Perry High School and attended Northern Oklahoma College at Tonkawa, Oklahoma. Kathleen and Jimmy Charles Brown were married July 3, 1974 in the Church of the Nazarene at Perry, Oklahoma, Rev. John Fechner officiated for the single ring ceremony. Miss Nancy Frazier, of Perry, was bridesmaid, Mr. Perry I. Keyser Jr. Blackwell, was best man. Jimmy C. and Kathleen had a daughter, Patricia Lucile, born December 18, 1975 at Perry Memorial Hospital with Dr. Charles E. Martin in attendance. Patricia has made her home with Grandparents, John and Helen Morrison since July 4, 1977.

John W. Morrison Jr., was born December 6, 1956 at Perry Memorial

(Left to Right): John W. Morrison and Helen (Keyser) Morrison - March 27, 1953.

Hospital with Dr. A. M. Evans in attendance. John Jr. attended Elementary and Junior High at Haysville, Kansas and High School at Perry, Oklahoma. John W. Morrison Jr. and Kathryn Ann Hall, daughter of Mrs. Jean Hall of Perry, Oklahoma were married 1976 in the First Baptist Church, Rev. Hollis Morris officiated for the double-ring ceremony.

John Jr. and Kathryn had two children; a daughter, Katrina Marie, born March 30, 1977 at Perry Memorial Hospital with Dr. C. E. Martin in attendance and Loreeta Jean born January 8, 1981, at Perry Memorial Hospital with Dr. John Sayre in attendance.

Everett C. Mosena
By Betty Mosena

Everett Clark Mosena was born April 12, 1922, in the farm home of his parents. His father was Paul Cecil Mosena, who came to Oklahoma from Kansas, with his parents in 1905. His mother is Mina Jensen, who came to Oklahoma as a teenager from Iowa.

Everett grew up on the farm that his great-grandfather, Patrick Daily, homesteaded during the Cherokee Strip Land run in 1893. Patrick Daily was an immigrant from Ireland. This is the SE quarter of Section 9, Township 21 N, range 2 East, of the Indian Meridian, in Noble county. He was the third child of four children. Helen Elizabeth, born November 17, 1918; Mary Alice, born June 4, 1920 and Robert Cecil, born May 20, 1924.

Everett moved to Perry with the family when he was young and attended Perry elementary school. At age eleven, they moved back to the farm. He and his brother helped his father on the farm. They raised wheat and hogs, and milked cows. Some Saturdays were spent working in the fields and gathering wood to be later sawed for the heating stove. He attended Sumner school and most entertainment had to be made by the kids themselves. They often rode horses on Sunday afternoons. Boys would play marbles. After graduating from Sumner High school in 1941, Everett went on the (NYA) "National Youth Administration School" in Enid for 6 months, and later he was drafted into the Army during World War II. He was inducted at Ft. Lewis, Washington, and took his basic training at Camp Roberts, California. He made PFC and from Camp Roberts was sent to Port of Embarkation in New York and shipped to North Africa. He was assigned to the 105 AAA-AW BN and placed in the Invasion of Sicily. He spent 30 months overseas in Sicily and Italy. The war ending, he was discharged October 6, 1945. Returning home, he drove a truck, contracting to

Everett and Betty Mosena taken June 4, 1950 on their 1st wedding anniversary, in the yard of the family home.

haul whole milk to Swift and Co. in Enid. He trucked milk from the rural areas of Morrison and Sumner.

On June 4, 1949, he married Betty Jean Paulsen of Morrison. Betty was born August 11, 1928, at Hennessey, Oklahoma (Kingfisher co.) to Willselm Paulsen and Ethel Chartier. Her parents were farmers and moved from Hennessey to Morrison in August 1938. Betty attended Prairie Center grade school and graduated from Morrison High school in 1946. She went to work for Southwestern Bell Telephone Co. in Ponca City. After their marriage, Betty resigned and she and Everett built a small house across the yard on the family farm of Everett's parents. They milked dairy cows and sold milk to Gold Spot Dairy, in Enid. Later, they changed and sold cream to the dairy. In September, 1950, Everett got his left hand caught in a corn picker and it had to be amputated just about the wrist. He was fitted with an artificial limb in the spring of 1951.

They had a daughter born May 28, 1951, named Patsy Lee, and a son born May 8, 1953 named Terry Bill. Everett continued to farm the place, raising wheat, corn and alfalfa hay. In 1957, he and Betty bought the farm from his parents, moved into the big house and his parents moved into the small house.

Then a hog house was built and hogs were raised. Those years were pretty lean so Everett went to work for Noble county, driving a sand truck. A few years later, he bought a truck of his own and hauled livestock for the public. During harvest he hauled grain and went north with a harvest crew for two summers. Also he went southwest during the fall maize harvest. In the meantime, Betty went back to work for Southwestern Bell Telephone Co. She commuted to Perry until 1959, and then to Stillwater.

Everett served on the Sumner School Board and was Inspector on the election board for Auburn Township, replacing his father after his death in August, 1963. Another daughter, Donna Kay, was born October 5, 1963. Betty continued to work for the telephone company and Everett was still trucking and farming. They had cattle and a few horses.

In December, 1966, Everett was appointed Postmaster at Morrison, Oklahoma. Their three children attended Sumner grade school and graduated from Morrison High school. Everett and Betty were active in all their children's school activities during their school years.

For entertainment they enjoy camping and fishing, boating and water skiing, card parties and dancing.

Betty retired from Southwestern Bell Telephone Co. February 17, 1982 with 31 years of service. She finds plenty to do living on the farm. She likes horses, traveling and sports. Her hobbies include sewing and quilt making.

Everett retired as Postmaster March 9, 1984, with 20 years of service, counting his army time. He will continue his farming, cattle and horse ranching operations. He and Betty plan to do some traveling.

Paul C. Mosena
By Betty Mosena

Paul Cecil Mosena was born July 5, 1891, at Pesern, (Brown county), Kansas. His father was Treversus Clark Mosena, born in Burlington, Iowa. His mother was Mamie Elizabeth Daily, born in Hamberg, Iowa. They married July 1890, at Rulo, Nebraska.

Their first son, Paul Cecil was born when they lived at Pesern, Kansas. Paul attended school at "Stony Point" in Brown county, Kansas.

In 1905, when illness struck Mamie's father, Patrick Daily, Paul and his parents moved to Oklahoma to live on the farm that Patrick Daily had homesteaded during the "Cherokee Outlet" land run. This is the SE quarter of section 9 township 21 N, range 2 East, of the Indian Meridian, in Noble county. Treversus and Mamie had a second son, Francis Clark, born July 12, 1905.

Paul married Mina Jensen, February 17, 1918. Mina was born in Aarhus, Denmark and came to America with her mother at about age 2 or 3, living with an uncle in Seymour, Iowa. When Mina was a teenager, she came to Oklahoma and lived with her Uncle John Larsen and his wife. The Larsen farm was next to the Mosena farm.

Paul and Mina lived with his parents. They belonged to the First Christian Church at Sumner. Here on the farm were born three of their children: Helen Elizabeth, November 17, 1918;

Mina Mosena and Paul Mosena taken in Missouri on one of their traveling trips in the early 1950's.

Mary Alice, June 4, 1920; and Everett Clark, April 12, 1922.

Paul helped his father farm. They raised wheat, cattle and hogs. Mina helped with all farm chores, raised chickens and a garden.

Paul's brother, Francis, took over helping on the farm after he graduated in the first graduating class of Sumner school. This was in 1924. He also attended college at Oklahoma A & M at Stillwater. He took Engineering and mapped out the terraces on the farm. These were some of the first terraces built in Noble county to stop soil erosion.

Paul and Mina then moved to a place of their own just east of the homestead and later into Sumner. Here their fourth child was born, a son, Robert Cecil, May 20, 1924. Later, they moved to Perry, living on Grove St. and Kaw St. Paul worked for Huffman's Grocery, delivering groceries. Sometime later he worked as a night policeman.

Mamie Mosena died May 5, 1933, so Paul and Mina and their four children moved back to the farm to care for his father, who was losing his eyesight. Francis left for outside work. Paul farmed and Mina became a farm wife again, with chores and a garden. She was a magnificent housekeeper. Everything had to be spotless. She sewed for herself and four children. Treversus died May 30, 1938. He is buried at Sumner cemetery beside Mamie.

Paul and Mina's four children attended some of the grade years at Perry elementary school and the remainder at Sumner. All graduated from Sumner High school.

During World War II both sons, Everett and Robert went to serve their country. Robert was killed June 14, 1944, over "Woleai Island" in the Southwest Pacific.

Paul began doing electrical wiring when electricity became available in the rural area. He helped wire the farm home and several houses in the community.

Paul's brother, Francis was killed November 14, 1947, in an accident aboard a mining dredge boat near Baker, Oregon. He never married, so left no family. His body was shipped back and buried at Sumner cemetery.

After the children married and left home, Mina started work at the Sumner school lunchroom, as one of the cooks.

She and Paul enjoyed playing cards with neighbors and traveled a little. Mina also took up bowling. She bowled on a team in Perry.

Paul leased the "Bill's Corner" Service Station and Cafe. Paul ran the service station and Mina ran the cafe. Mina's good cooking became known to all travelers.

After giving that up, Paul went back to wiring houses for electricity. He also worked on the Election Board, holding the title of Inspector for Auburn Township. Mina worked at "Kumback Lunch" in Perry. They sold the farm to their son, Everett in 1957. They moved into the small house that Everett and his wife had built across the yard.

Paul and Mina again enjoyed traveling and playing cards with friends and neighbors. Paul died August 1, 1963 of a stroke. He is buried at Sumner cemetery. His death upset Mina tremendously, but she continued to work as a waitress and continued her bowling. She also has worked at the "Corner Lunch", "Cherokee Strip Restaurant", "89'ers Restaurant", "Johnson's Cafe" in Morrison and "Pruitt's Sooner Inn."

In the past 20 years Mina has given of herself to all her family, helping them in any way needed. She transferred her church membership to First Christian church at Morrison. She belongs to American Legion Auxiliary (in which she is a Gold Star Member) and the Sumner Homemakers Club. She still enjoys traveling, going places, playing cards, going to ball games, baking and crocheting. Mina is now 85 years old. She has 2 living children, 7 grandchildren, 20 great-grandchildren and 5 great-great-grandchildren. She still drives and goes all she can. She is a joy to all that know her.

George H. Mouser
By Wilbur G. Mouser

George Henry Mouser was born in Lebanon, Kentucky, May 1, 1862. He was one of twelve brothers and sisters. Frederick, his father, raised his family on a farm but his principal occupation was railroad constructing, generally for the Cincinnati and the L. & N. George married Sarah Catherine Caldwell, daughter of James Smith Caldwell, a local plantation owner. George and Kate, as she was called, were descendents of Kentucky pioneers and hoped to make their fortune in the "West". George tried his hand at various occupations. He moved his family, Kate and baby daughter, Violet, from Lebanon to Winchester, Kentucky, a rugged mining town. There he joined the police force and was away from home much of the time. After the birth of a second daughter, May, he moved his family back to Lebanon. With the birth of another daughter, Bertha; George and Kate decided it was time to "Go West."

George left his family in Lebanon and took the train to Kansas where the "run" for the opening of the Cherokee Stirp was to start on September 16, 1893. He made the run on a train starting at the Kansas state line. In later years, George related to his children many interesting stories about that eventful day. One of the stories was about a young woman making the run on horseback. Her horse stumbled and fell. A man riding near her stopped to help her and when he saw the horse had broken its leg he shot it. She immediately jumped on his horse and rode off, leaving him helpless. She was later known as "Little Britches", a notorious outlaw.

George staked a claim on a city lot located catty corner northeast of the present Post Office. Much claim jumping and looting prevailed and being alone he was unable to leave his lot and file a claim. Another man who was also alone had staked a claim and he and George decided between them they could file on one and they gave up George's lot as they thought it the least desireable. Too late they discovered the lot they kept was in the Government square and was the one on which the present Post Office stands.

George joined the police force and by Christmas was able to send for Kate and the little girls. In those days the train stopped at Wharton, south of Perry. The train was never on time and that day it came in early. After a long and tiresome trip, Kate was disappointed not to be met, but she hired the hack to take her to the hotel where she found George busy preparing rooms for them.

Perry was a rugged western town with few frame buildings and many tents. Water was drawn from wells and lights consisted of kerosene lamps. George was eventually able to secure a house for his family. It was during that first summer their baby daughter, Bertha, died. There was no cemetery yet and graves were placed in a field in no particular pattern. Kate tried to keep the baby's grave marked but roving animals and careless riders would

United States Deputy Marshalls in 1895. Standing (L to R): George H. Mouser, Charles Colcord, George Stomer. Sitting (L to R): Ike Steele, Edward Stinnett.

destroy all markers and in time graves became unidentifiable and soon completely lost. It was always a great sorrow to Kate that she could not find her baby's grave. In the fall, Violet and May were taught by a neighbor woman until a frame school was erected on Cow Creek, south of the Frisco tracks. There were a great many children in the new town and all realized a school was a must. It was an integrated school, attended by all races. In 1895, their second summer in Perry another daughter, Florence, was born to them.

George was appointed a Deputy US Marshall in 1895, and worked under E.D. Nix with Bill Tilghman and Heck Thomas in rounding up the notorious outlaws of that time, among them the Dalton Brothers, the Doolan Gang, Jennie Stevens known as "Little Britches" and Anne McDougal called "Cattle Annie". Kate had to accustom herself to the hardships of the pioneer woman and the many inconveniences of being a peace officer's wife. Once George had to bed down his prisoner and his posse comitatus on their kitchen floor, much to the consternation of his little daughters. Another time he was shot by an outlaw but his belt buckle probably saved his life.

In 1897, George took his family to live on a farm six miles northwest of Perry on which he built a two story frame house. His father, a widower, came to live with them and look after the farm while George did his marshalling. In the next few years four more children were born to the Mouser family. First, a long awaited son, Curtis, was born. Then a daughter Catherine, followed by another daughter, Margaret, and last a second son, Wilbur.

In 1907, George moved his family back to Perry at 9th and Kaw Street, the Mouser home until his death in 1945, at which time Kate moved to Tulsa to live with May. After George moved from the farm he went to work for the Lincoln Oil Company selling oil for machinery. He travelled about the country with a buggy and team of horses. He welcomed the advent of the "Tin Lizzie", a more comfortable and faster mode of travelling. He became interested in the prospects of oil in Oklahoma and in 1910, invested in the new industry which proved to be a most fortunate move for him. Most of his drilling activities were centered around Kellyville, Sapulpa, and Drumright. He maintained an office in Tulsa for several years before establishing one in Perry.

The family grew to adulthood in Perry attending the Parochial school which was founded in 1900 by the Sisters of Divine Providence.

Violet married Walter Kehres, a local business man. They built and operated the Elite Hotel and Cafe. Both are deceased. They had three sons, Walter Jr., Robert, and Paul who is deceased.

May married Victor Kinney who operated a ranch in Okmulgee County. He died in 1920. May's second husband was Lonnie Sharp with the Atlantic Oil Co. in Tulsa. They are both deceased. May had no children by either marriage.

Florence married George W. Jenkins of Chicago. They had two children, Sari Joan and Mary Catherine. Florence is a widow and lives in Dallas.

Curtis married Lola Moore, daughter of Dr. and Mrs. S. A. Moore of Perry. They had one daughter, Patricia. Curtis retired from the Continental Oil Co. and they live in New Braunfels, Texas.

Catherine married John F. Melaugh, a Public Accountant from Portland, Maine. He is now deceased. They were the parents of two children: Joanna and John Jr. Catherine lives in Tulsa.

Margaret married John G. Nebergall, who is now retired from the S.H. Kress Co. and they live in Claymont, Delaware. They are the parents of four children, a son, Robert, and three daughters, Mary Ann, Jane, and Sally.

Wilbur married Lillian Mildfelt, daughter of Mr. and Mrs. Peter M. Mildfelt. She is now deceased. Wilbur is the only descendent of George and Kate Mouser still living in Perry. He maintains an office in Perry, having followed in his father's footsteps in the oil industry. Wilbur and Lillian were the parents of two children, Joan and James.

Lewis F. Neal

By Helen Marie Lewellen

Lewis Frederick Neal was born December 28, 1864, in Jennings County, Indiana, near Vernon, Indiana to John W. Neal and Christina Katherine Brougher Neal.

The town of Vernon, Indiana was famous during the Civil War for its "underground railroad". Many went from the south to the north to freedom and hid in dugouts and basements of buildings in this small town.

After the War, Lewis's father, mother, two brothers and six sisters moved to Kansas and farmed around Derby. Lewis became a carpenter, learning to build houses, sheds and leantos.

Rose Ella Ball was born near Rockville, Indiana, January 16, 1869. At an early age, she moved with her parents and brothers and sisters to Kansas, settling near Wichita.

On June 4, 1889, she was married to Lewis Frederick Neal at Derby, Kansas. They later moved to Douglas, Kansas, where four children were born, Roy Otis, Clara Mae (Ricker), Calvin Raymond and Lenora Ann (Gray).

In their growing up years the children attended school in Leon, Kansas. Later they moved to Pauls Valley, Oklahoma, and lived there until 1913, when they moved to Perry on a farm two miles east of Perry. Their home burned down while they lived there. Besides saving a few clothes, the only real piece of furniture and antiquity was a large wall Seth Thomas clock with the date 1860 inside of it. It has the weights inside that have

Neal homestead 1900. L-R: Lewis F., holding Lenora, Clara, Rose, Roy and Raymond.

to be wound up only once every 8 days.

After Mr. Neal built a home for his family in Perry on north 6th Street, they moved to town in 1918. The house is still standing and being used.

Both their sons, Roy and Ray, served in the Army in World War I. Ray was inducted into the Army, April 25, 1918, when he was over 23 years old. He saw service overseas as a private in the Infantry Co. "C" 357th Reg., 90th Div., sailing June 20, 1918, to Liverpool, England and arriving there July 1, 1918. He returned from France and arrived in the USA, June 14, 1919. He was discharged from Camp Pike, Arkansas, June 26, 1919.

Roy, the oldest son, was inducted into the Army July 23, 1918, at Perry, when he was 27 years old. Roy served at Camp Travis, Texas, as a Private in 36th Co. 9th Bn 165th Depot Brigade and was discharged because of the demoblization of the Army at Camp Travis, December 19, 1918.

He came back to Perry and worked as a mechanic in the Tom Wolleson Garage for several years.

Roy married Nina Ellen Thomason November 24, 1921, and he and his father, L. F. Neal, built their new home at 1019 6th St., Perry, and it's still in use. One daughter was born to them, Helen Marie Neal (Lewellen).

A few years later, he started to work for the City of Perry as Mechanical Engineer at the Water and Light Plant, and retired after over 40 years. His wife, Nina, died in 1954. He and Ruth Ball were married in Stratford, Texas, in 1955. They lived in Perry where she was Deputy County Clerk for 34 years. Roy died in 1978, at the age of 88 years. Ruth, his widow, resides here since her retirement in 1977.

Clara Mae, Lewis and Rose's oldest daughter, worked at the Telephone Office and The Famous Department Store. Later, she married Leo Ricker and they moved to Beaumont, Texas. They had three children, Bill, Patty, and Glenn (Pete). Later, they moved back to Perry and then to Oklahoma City, where Clara died in 1968. Her husband had preceded her in death.

Lenora Ann attended Perry schools and graduated here in 1916. She married John F. Gray (Jack) and lived in Tulsa. A daughter was born to them January 28, 1925, Barbara Jean. Lenora died on her own daughter's 2nd birthday, January 28, 1927. Barbara Jean was raised by Rose and L. F. Neal until the Bank Holiday, when they were forced to move in with their son, Roy, and his family, where Barbara Jean attended Perry Schools. She graduated from Perry High School in 1942, and was the first Wrestling Queen in 1941-42.

Ray Neal died May 23, 1939 — just 11 days before their 50th Wedding Anniversary. Rose was a wonderful mother and grandmother; making quilts for each of her children and grandchildren. She was a faithful member of the old-fashioned Methodist Faith and L. F. was the same.

L. F. died Sunday morning, January 14, 1945, ready to go to Sunday school and Church, as he sat in his favorite rocker winding his old pocket-watch.

Frank J. Neuerburg

By Charlotte Palovik
Josephine Timmons and Marguerite Gordon

Frank J. Neuerburg was born December 8, 1863, at St. Lucas, Iowa. He passed away February 18, 1950. He was the son of John N. Neuerburg, Sr. and Anna Marie Meyer. John N. Neuerburg was born April 14, 1826, in Roehl Regb Trier, Germany; the son of Matthew Neuerburg and Elizabeth Maletare. John N. and his sister, Anna Marie, came to America in 1855, on the

Roy and Nina Neal - 1921.

L-R: Barbara Jean (Gray) Colen, Lewis, Rose Neal - 1936.

Frank Neuerburg family in 1922. Front Row, Left to Right: Anna Mae, Frank, Margaret and Lawrence. Back Row: Gertrude, Josephine, William, Leonard, Loretta, Clara, Marguerite and Charlotte.

same boat as Anna Marie Meyer and her three brothers: Bernard, James, and Theodore. They had to take all of their food, bedding, and belongings and were allowed very little space. A terrible storm overtook them and they were on the water for 59 days. The brothers settled in Kansas. John N. Neuerburg and Anna Marie Meyer were married in West Union, Iowa, in June, 1856. Nine children were born to them at St. Lucas, Iowa. They moved to Carroll, Iowa, in 1875, where they both passed away.

Frank J. Neuerburg and Margaret Anne Tobin were married at Carroll, Iowa, September 25, 1894. Margaret was born October 16, 1876, in Carroll, Iowa to John Tobin and Almeda Jane Currier. John Tobin came to the United States, when he was a boy of 8 years, from Ireland. Frank and Margaret had three children born in Auburn, Iowa: Anna Marie (married Chris Schieffer), December 5, 1895 to December 13, 1979; Eugene Lawrence (married Grace Reub) July 18, 1897 to March 26, 1961; and Josphine Evarista (later Mrs. Sherman Timmons) July 3, 1898.

John Tobin came to Oklahoma at the opening along with his two sons, William and Charles, all staked claims in Noble County. A little later, they found a claim for John Neuerburg, Jr. Frank's brother and his wife, Mary Tobin, a sister of Margaret. In 1898, John Tobin found a claim in the SW ¼ of section 21 of Warren Valley Township. Jesse Chaney had staked this claim but became discouraged and wished to leave after building a one-room house with up and down siding and plowing a few acres. They gave $1.00 an acre for this farm.

Frank and Margaret bought this claim and moved to Oklahoma in September of 1898. They rented a box car on a train and Frank rode in it with their team of horses, a cow, a walking plow, furniture, chickens, and feed and hay that was harvested before they left Iowa. Margaret rode a passenger train with the three small children, two of them still in diapers. The trip took two days and two nights.

Frank proved up and obtained a patent to the land. He built on another room to the house and plastered the inside of both rooms. Unfortunately, the weather turned cold and the plaster froze before it cured. This caused it to turn loose and fall off in pieces.

Children born after they came to Oklahoma were: Leonard Matthew (March 26, 1900-) married Louise Secrest; Marguerite Elenore (December 18, 1901-) married Earl Gordon; William Francis (August 8, 1903-December 30, 1960) married Gladys Devine; Gertrude Rose (February 21, 1906-) married Clarence Wheeler; Clara Catherine (April 27, 1907-January 7, 1984) married William Skalenda/Claude Gordon; Loretta Philamene (March 14, 1909-) married Marvin Day/Francis Malone/Melvin Morgan; Charlotte Matilda (March 31, 1911-) married John Palovik; George Bernard (January 3, 1913-June 25, 1913); and Eda Chrysentis (April 15, 1915-August 1, 1915).

The children attended Cooper school until moving, then attended White School No. 15. In 1906, a railroad was built through the place. It was then called the Frisco and now the Great Northern. The railroad workers bought raw milk, eggs, and fresh vegetables from the Neuerburgs.

When harvest was in, there was a shortage of grain storage, so Frank

Neuerberg home built in 1909.

boarded up the windows and doors in one room of what was now the three room house, and stored wheat in it. Ticks were filled with straw and placed on top of the wheat and the children slept on them.

In 1909, Frank sold his claim and purchased 160 acres, three miles east also in Warren Valley Township. The railroad also ran through this farm and a siding was built at the east side of that place. Also, a section foreman's house and several bunk houses for the section workers. This whistle stop was called Gansel. Along the railroad track was a two room house. Frank moved this house up by the section line where the wagon road was. He and the older boys and some hired help built on four large rooms and two porches. While this was being built, Margaret would take a grain wagon of wheat to Lucien, two miles to the west, sell the wheat and buy lumber and take to Frank at the new place, stopping by the old house to check on the children who were in the charge of Josephine, who was eleven. Anna Mae, 14 years old, was at the new place to cook for her father and brothers and carpenters. At times the children would flag down the train and ride to Perry for a fare of 10¢ and would attend St. Joseph's Academy.

Margaret raised chickens, acres for a large vegetable garden, and milked cows to help feed the family. As a true pioneer, she many times took up a gun and hunted rabbits to provide food for her family. Margaret was known as the neighborhood nurse. She attended at serious illnesses, deaths, and several times delivered babies without the help of a doctor. She was always ready to lend a hand when needed.

Later, some grain elevators were built at Gansel. E. J. Miller was the first. Frank managed this one a number of years, until the Farmer's union built one and Frank took over management and ran it until he retired, about 1932. His son, William, took over management. Margaret kept the books for Frank and she with only a fourth grade education and Frank a third grade education, made a good business pair. Margaret also was clerk of White School District for many years and boarded some teachers several different years. She was very active in community affairs and in St. Rose of Lima Catholic Church where the family attended. They moved to Perry in 1930, where they lived until their death. There are 231 living descendents.

Hellen (Pricer) Neuerburg
By Hellen Neuerburg

Hellen May Pricer was born to Emma Gertrude Imel and Columbus

Leo, Hellen and Donald Lee Neuerburg - 1950.

Edwin (Ed) Pricer, February 5, 1905 in Spearville, Ford County, Kansas. It was a very stormy winter - a Kansas blizzard. Her uncle, Charley Pricer, rode horseback through the bitter cold storm to bring the doctor who lived in Dodge City, Kansas. This was several miles from where her parents lived in a railroad section house as her father was a section hand for the Atchison, Topeka and Santa Fe railroad company. The following year her parents moved to Perry, Oklahoma where her sister, Martha, was born September 12, 1906.

Two years later, they lost their mother, Emma, with typhoid fever, September 20, 1908. At Emma's request her mother-in-law, Mrs. Mary D. Pricer took the two little girls and raised them with loving care. Hellen's first trip on a train was to accompany her mother to Dodge City, Kansas where the mother was buried in "Boot Hill" cemetery, October 8, 1908. Ed, the father, made his home with them until 1916.

Hellen attended school in a home just two blocks from her home but the next year Hellen and Martha went to school at Old Central Elementary on west Elm street, a mile and seven blocks from their home. Before Hellen finished her senior year in high school her grandmother became ill and needed her care. From 1925 until 1928 Hellen was employed with the Southwestern Bell Telephone Company.

During the summer months the girls helped their grandfather with his work at Grace Hill cemetery. Most of the graves and lots were mass beds of flowers and had to be hand weeded. Water was hauled in barrels on a sled pulled by a horse to water the small trees that had been planted in rows through the cemetery. They helped with the spraying and would rake the hay after their grandfather did the mowing. The hay was either baled or stacked loose with tie and cover for the stack. Their grandfather was sexton of Grace Hill from 1908 until his death in September 1932.

On April 8, 1928, Hellen married Leo Neuerburg at Blackwell, Oklahoma. Leo was born February 3, 1903. They moved to a farm 6 miles northwest of Perry in the Whipple school district, called the John Tobin place, Leo's grandfather's farm. Their furniture was a 2 burner oil perfection stove with a one burner oven. The cabinets and dressing tables were orange crates, picked up at the grocery stores. They were decorated with paint and pretty home-made curtains. Leo made a one leaf wooden table. The water bucket, dipper and wash pan set on orange crates with curtains to hide the supply shelves. The only new furniture was an iron bed, a chest of drawers and a cotton mattress. A hope chest furnished linens, silver, dishes, pots and pans. At the first harvest, a new Queen Ann dining room set, table, buffet and 6 chairs was purchased because there were 17 men and 2 children to seat for dinner and supper. Alva Kukuk, 10 years old and her brother, 9, hauled drinking water to the men working in the field, using a horse and buggy to carry the jugs covered with wet burlap sacks to keep the water cold. The first harvest Hellen was helped by her sister, Martha, the second year, Josephine Kukuk helped.

The first year of farming they started with one team of horses, a walking plow, 2 milk cows, 12 hens, one rooster, a hoe, rake, a Model T coupe and a wagon. Their first son, Donald Lee, was born February 22, 1930. During the dust bowl days, Leo worked long hours on a dairy ranch at Marland. They moved to Perry in 1932 and lived there 15 years. Their second son, Baby Leo was born in February 1935. He died the same day. Donald attended Whipple school and the Catholic school. He graduated from Perry High School in 1948. He entered the Navy at San Diego, California, January 8, 1951. He married Dorothy Steen July 10, 1954.

Leo farmed and managed the Gansel Elevator for 8 years. He worked at the Farmer's Exchange Grocery store and Mr. Yosts farmers store. In 1954, they moved to Enid and bought a home at 628 North 7th. Leo worked for the Enid Board of Education at Emerson Jr. High School and several other schools.

Leo's health broke in 1957 and he was ill for several years. He recovered and went to work for the new YMCA until October 23, 1968. Hellen was hired as a matron for the schools by the Enid Board of Education and worked until retiring June 30, 1970. She was active in the Enid Friends Extension club holding office of secretary for seven years and president one year. She moved to Perry December 12, 1981 where she joined the Columbine Garden Club. She has been secretary two years, vice-president two years and historian of Perry Council of Garden Clubs for the past two years. She ha six grandchildren, eleven great-grandchildren and one great-great-granddaughter.

George A. Newton
By Mrs. Ted Newton

George Augusta Newton was born July 28, 1881, in Nevada, the son of Dallas and Mattie Newton. His mother was a widow with three children besides George: Avis born in July 1882, Frank born in February, 1884, and Fred born in December, 1885. All were born in Kansas, except George. Mattie married Charles Christoph about 1889. In 1894, George's step-father hired him as an assistant in his second hand store. Two years later, they added undertaking to their business. It became the Christoph-Newton Furniture store and Undertaking.

George married Dorcas Stephens June 4, 1902. Dorcas was born March 28, 1883. Her mother had made the run in a small wagon with a fine team of horses, lent to her by a friend who helped her make the run. Dorcas' father had died of tuberculosis in 1891, and all their money had been spent in a vain effort to restore his health, there had been nothing left to support his widow and their two daughters after he had passed away. They had been living in Kansas City for about a year, when the mother's health, too, had begun to fail and the doctor had advised a warmer climate.

In 1892, she had heard of the land that was soon to be opened in Oklahoma and it seemed to be the answer to her problems. She staked a claim on Red Rock Creek about twenty-five miles from the starting point. Her brother and the girls, Abigail Annette, aged 12, and Dorcas, age 10, were following the runners in a covered wagon with a tent and supplies.

They soon caught up with the mother and spent the night on the claim, however, the next morning they found a man on the claim who said he had arrived before they did. After they lost their claim, the mother moved into Perry, where she supported herself and daughter by working as a nurse.

George and Dorcus had three

George Newton standing alongside the horse drawn hearse, driver is unknown.

children: Charles A. Newton, born March 11, 1903; George Delmar (Ted) Newton born May 1, 1905; and Harry Leon Newton born July 5, 1910.

For years, George Newton served on the school board, two years on the city council, was a member of the Lion's club and the Masonic lodge. He helped establish the Christian Church in Perry. Dorcus died in 1961, and is buried in Oklahoma City.

George later married Nona Daniels who was born July 28, 1880. He died September 18, 1954, and is buried beside his brother, Fred, in Grace Hill cemetery. Nona died July 30, 1978.

Ted Newton
By Mrs. Ted Newton

Ted Newton was born May 1, 1905, at Perry, Oklahoma, the second son of George and Dorcas Stephens Newton. He entered the Newton Funeral Home business in 1923. He became owner-operator in 1946, when his father had to retire because of ill health. He married Elizabeth Wood June 15, 1924, at Ponca City. Elizabeth was born January 15, 1907, at Fairfax, Indian Territory, the daughter of George Wood and Leota Woods.

Ted Newton was a 32nd Degree Mason, served as president of the Perry Rotary Club, as president of the Perry Chamber of Commerce for two terms, as president of the Oklahoma Funeral Directors association and as Mayor of Perry.

He was a member of the Akda Shrine Temple of Tulsa, a Past Patron of the Order of the Eastern Star and member of Perry Masonic lodge no. 78.

He was on the original board of directors of the Perry Memorial Hospital. He worked very hard to get the hospital as he was more aware than most people of the need for a hospital in the Perry community. The only ambulance service for the area was handled by the Funeral homes, and the closest hospital was at Enid. The forty two miles of narrow roads were almost impassable in the winter when the snow drifted over the east-west roads. Many winter nights he made the drive to Enid with a patient, wondering if he would get there in time.

Ted Newton retired from the Newton Funeral Home in 1965 because of ill health and his son, Jack, took over the business. Ted died July 14, 1983, and is buried in Grace Hill cemetery. Elizabeth lives in Perry.

The children of Ted and Elizabeth are Jack Delmar Newton born May 1, 1925 and George William (Bill) Newton, born January 24, 1937.

Jack Newton served 23 months overseas in the Pacific theater during WW II as a pharmacist mate third

Elizabeth Wood and G. D. (Ted) Newton. Taken just before their wedding in Ponca City, Oklahoma - June 15, 1924.

class, his duty aboard the US Detroit. He married Velva Elaine Treadway October 9, 1943, at San Diego, California. Velva was born October 11, 1924, in Perry, Oklahoma, the daughter of Durrell (Dee) Treadway and Koto Mae Kepley.

When Jack returned to Perry, he entered the funeral business with his father, being the fourth generation of the family to serve the Perry community with this service. He retired in 1974.

Jack and Velva have two children: Faith Anne Newton born July 19, 1944 at Enid, Oklahoma and Jack Delmar (J.D.) Newton, Jr. born October 31, 1946 at Perry. Faith Anne married Richard Lemler. Their children are Mark, Dee, and Jackie. J. D. Newton married Diane Start in Sacramento, California. The have a daughter, Kennison Elaine Start-Newton.

Bill Newton was born in Perry, January 24, 1937, in the Newton family home, which had been converted into a hospital. At the age of nine, he moved with his parents into the Newton Funeral Home, around which he helped his father and brother Jack.

Jack and Bill were the third generation to attend schools in Perry, as Grandfather George and Grandmother Dorcas Stephens Newton had attended school in Perry as did their father and mother.

Bill graduated from the University of Oklahoma with a Degree in Law. He married Janie Lou Porter of Jackson, Mississippi June 10, 1960. He moved to Duncan, Oklahoma, after graduation to be Assistant District Attorney. Two children were born in Duncan: Ted, July 6, 1962 and Janet July 1, 1963. They moved to Tulsa, Oklahoma, where he was Assistant District Attorney, later becoming head of the Civil Department of Tulsa County. Son Jon was born in Tulsa December 5, 1967. After leaving the Civil Department, Bill entered private practice in Tulsa.

Lloyd Nichols
By Pauline Nichols

Lloyd Nichols was born September 12, 1920 the son of Lilly Mae (Seltzer) and William Birdsall Nichols. He attended the rural school at Shiloh and at Morrison where he played half back on the football team. He was captain of the team in his senior year.

Lloyd was drafted into the army air force as an airplane mechanic, during World War II. He married Elsie Pauline Akers October 23, 1942 on the farm they now own. Pauline was born January 31, 1922, the daughter of Elsie Ocie (Collins) and William Akers. Pauline attended Morrison school. She was a riviter during the war, riding the bus from Morrison to Ponca City. There was standing room only on the bus because of gas rationing.

When Lloyd returned from service they started out married life with a few cows and a team of horses which his father gave him for not smoking until he was 21. They canned fruits and vegetables storing them in the cellar. Also in the cellar was the sausage in crock jars, they had made, fried down and covered with lard. They raised cows, chickens, turkeys and pigs. They

(L to R): Lloyd, Paula, Chuck and Pauline.

made cottage cheese from the skimmed milk, butter from the cream and had eggs from their chickens. Any surplus was sold to buy other groceries. They made hominey in a big iron kettle using lye.

Lloyd raised wheat, barley, oats, corn and cotton along with feed for his animals. He bound the wheat, barley and oats into bundles and thrashed it with the help of the neighbors. He graded and maintained the roads around Morrison. They have been active in the Morrison Methodist church and the American Legion.

They have two children. Charles Lloyd (Chuck) was born July 4, 1947. He grew up on the farm and attended the Shiloh grade school and the Morrison High School. He belonged to the 4-H and the FFA. He played little league baseball which was coached by his father and he played baseball in high school. During the summer months he hauled hay and saved his money for college. He attended the college at Tonkawa and graduated from Alva college. His marriage to Susan Cowan dissolved in 1982. He has two children: Charles Christopher born July 10, 1972 and David Edward born January 11, 1979. He lives on his father's farm, the same farm his grandfather homesteaded. He teaches school in Glencoe and coaches little league baseball and some basketball.

Paula Kay, daughter of Lloyd and Pauline, was born February 26, 1952. She attended school at Morrison and worked at various jobs during the summer so she could attend college at Tonkawa and Alva. She became a teacher. She married James Ray (Mim) Kirkendall Jr. and they have two children: James Aaron born April 10, 1981 and Lloyd Ashby born December 28, 1986.

Lloyd and Pauline retired from the farm and moved to Morrison where they designed and built a new house. They are still active in the Methodist church and the American Legion. They have both enjoyed bowling for the past twenty years and socializing with their card playing friends.

Raymond Nichols
By Raymond Nichols

I, Raymond H. Nichols, was born near Morrison, Oklahoma, in a dugout on September 3, 1896. The doctor's name was Whittenburg. After that my father, William Birdsal Nichols, built a two-room house, later building more on to it. The other four boys, Russell, Roy, Cecil and Ernest, were born in this house.

My mother, Cora Eva (Hale) took sick with lung trouble so Pop decided to go to a dryer climate. We traveled around in Colorado, Texas and landed at Rosewell New Mexico, but she was getting worse so father put mother and the two youngest boys and myself on the train and we came back to Stroud to our grandfather's Robert Hatten Nichols, to stay until father and the other two boys could bring our teams back. Before father and the boys got back my mother died on January 18, 1907.

Father had rented the home place in Morrison for three years, so we had to stay in Stroud. While we were living in Stroud, there was a large hail storm at Morrison. It didn't leave any windows or roofs on the houses. Mr. Moore, our renter, wrote to Pop and told him how bad it was. I think this was about 1908. Father was planting cotton and didn't go up there till about three weeks after it happened but when he got there Mr. Moore took Pop and they went down on Black Bear and got ice to make ice cream. That was almost thirty days after the hail storm.

On December 14, 1910, Pop got married again to Lilly Seltzer. There were three boys from Pop's last marriage: Birdsal, Milton, and Loyd.

Now this Nichols bunch were baseball crazy. Pop played ball with several good teams. He played first base. At one time we had a Nichols baseball team where he also played first base. He was sixty-five years old and he said he was still going strong.

All of us boys went to school at Shiloh, none went any farther than the eighth grade. One evening when my brother, Russell and I got home from school, Mother told me to put the old horse, that was standing out in front of the house, out in the pasture. I got me a stick and started to make him go. I hit him with the stick and he kicked me in the head just over the right eye. Mother

Raymond and Bessie Nichols - 1921.

Raymond Nichols standing in front of the vault at the Citizen State Bank, Morrison - 1985.

ran into the yard and waved a white rag so my father would see that something was wrong. When the doctor got there and got me cleaned up, he found that my head was busted open. He told my father and mother that I was in very bad shape, but he said, "I will do all I can for the boy." He needed something the size of a nickle but a nickle would corrode so he put a dime in the place where it was busted open. He told them that I would never live to be twenty-one years old but if I live until September 3, I will be eighty-nine years old. My friends and neighbors call me the ten cent nickle.

My step-mother and I didn't get along very good so I left home at the age of sixteen. I went to Ness City, Kansas, to work for a large ranch. I stayed there about a year and a half. I got $17.50 per month and my board.

Then I went to Depew, Oklahoma to visit my Uncle Curt Hale, my mother's brother and that is where I went to the Army. I never got to go across, as some of the boys got the flu and held us up till the armistice was signed.

I married Bessie James at Stillwater, April 12, 1921. Bessie was born at Ederston, Missouri, October 23, 1900. There were five children in this family: Carmlita Eva (February 21, 1922), George William (September 18, 1923), Harry Thomas (September 11, 1925), Wayne Franklin (March 14, 1936) and Linda Mae (January 20, 1944).

My wife died February 20, 1985. If she had lived until April 12, we would have been married for 64 happy years. I saw the town of Morrison build in 1903, when the railroad was to go through and I saw it go down to the bottom and I saw it rebuild. Today we have four good churches and one of the best schools in the county.

William B. Nichols
By Geneva Christie

My grandfather, William Bertsal Nichols or better known to his friends

Back Row (L to R): Lloyd, Milton, Ramond, William Birdsal Sr. Front Row (L to R): Cecile, Roy, William Birdsal Jr.

as W.B. or Bert was born August 26, 1872 in Iowa. When a small boy, the family moved to a farm near Valley Center, Kansas. While living on the farm in Kansas, grandpa said they always raised large gardens and the extra vegetables the children would take to town and peddle from door to door to help with the family expense. Grandpa's dad heard of a new land being opened for white settlement in Indian Territory Oklahoma. The family moved to this land and settled on a farm near Stroud, Oklahoma, in Lincoln County. Not too much is known of grandpa's life here, probably same as any young man in those days.

In 1893, the Cherokee Strip was opened for white settlement. Grandpa, being an industrious man and wanting land of his own, also being 21 years of age, which made him eligible for the run, headed toward Stillwater. On the morning of September 16, 1893, he was on the south line, just north of Stillwater, at noon ready for the 12:00 gun shot to sound and to start his run for a claim. He staked his claim 12 miles east, 1 mile south and ½ mile east of Perry, in Noble County.

After grandpa staked his claim he had five years to prove up on his claim. The first winter he went to Tulsa with his team of horses and worked in the strip coal mines, to have money for this.

On December 14, 1884 he married Cora Eva Hale, in Chandler, Oklahoma. Eva, as she was called, was of Indian blood; probably Cherokee. Five sons were born to W.B. and Eva Nichols, Raymond in September 1896, Russell in September 1898, Ray in January 1901, Cecil in February 1903 and Ernest in November 1905. All were born on the homestead near Morrison.

Eva wasn't well during the last few years before 1906. The boys remember there was a hired lady who came to help with the house work. In early 1906 it was diagnosed that Eva had tuberculosis and needed to go to a dry and warmer climate, which at that time was New Mexico. By the time grandpa had built their home from a dugout to a two room and then four room home and the boys remember a big barn had been built, but grandpa had a farm sale and leased their homestead to a neighbor for three years.

Early in August 1906 the family set out in one covered wagon and one spring wagon on the trail for Roswell, New Mexico. The boys remember that at night when they camped, they would hunt rabbits or other wild game for food. When they arrived in New Mexico they lived in a tent until grandpa got a job from a local farmer, then they moved into a sod house on his farm. The boys that were of school age started school but they had lived there a very short time when grandma got much worse.

One night she had a vision that she was going to die very soon and she wanted to die at home. Next morning she asked grandpa to take her back home. In early December grandpa put grandma on a train with Raymond the oldest to help with Cecil and Ernest. They were to go to Stroud to grandpa's parents. Grandpa was bringing the wagon and Russell and Ray. But on the way they had some bad luck. They ran into a winter storm and when they got to the Cimmaron River it was frozen over. When they started to cross the ice broke thru and it cut the hocks of the horses. When they got to the side they had to camp several days waiting for them to heal. When they arrived home his wife had died, January 10, 1907 being only 30 years of age. Ernest was taken by an Aunt to be raised as Eva had requested. Grandpa rented a farm near Stroud, (as his homestead

Lillie Mae Nichols and William Birdsal Nichols Sr.

contract wasn't up) and put the children in school. In May 1909, Russell became very sick and died within a week of spinal meningitis.

On December 14, 1910 grandpa married Lilly Seltzer, a teacher at the old Baker school. Lilly was born August 25, 1886 in Missouri. A daughter Mable Emma was born to them in December 1911 but died at the age of one month. Shortly after this, they moved back to the homestead and to them were born three sons, Bertsal in December 1913, Milton August 1916, and Lloyd in September 1920. Grandma was a very remarkable person and had to have loved grandpa very much to have married a husband with three sons to raise. Grandma was a very good cook and every meal was a little bit extra special. She raised a big garden and lots of chickens and turkeys.

Grandpa was a very hard worker as was grandma; they were up at the crack of dawn, winter or summer. Grandpa farmed several farms all with horses. He was respected by all his neighbors and friends and known as a man of his word. He served several years on the Shiloh school board and all six boys attended school there.

They were members of the Methodist Church and Grandpa was a registered republican but said, "If we have a republican president we will have hard times."

Recreation for the Nichols family was baseball. All seven boys and grandpa played, usually in a pasture on the Bishop farm, south of Pete's Corner. We also had lots of dinners at the homestead with lots of grandma's cooking.

The homestead is still in the Nichols family, owned by son Lloyd.

Grandpa and Grandma lived on the farm until April 1, 1956 when they moved to Glencoe. Grandpa then passed away on September 14, 1959 at the age of 87.

John W. Oakley
By Mary Louise Allen

First day settler, John Wesley Oakley, was born April 7, 1854, at Toledo, Ohio. His family moved to Kokomo, Indiana, when he was four and this is where he grew up with his sister and four brothers. Nothing else is known of his childhood.

He met Fannie Dora Brown, who was born January 25, 1857, in Howard County, Indiana, and they were married December 31, 1878, at the home of the bride's parents in Sedgwick City, Kansas. Their only child, Fannie Mary, was born July 22, 1889, while they were living in Newton, Kansas.

Mr. Oakley was in the mercantile business and in comfortable circumstances, but like many early settlers,

Fannie Mary Oakley about 1907.

became impoverished in the Kansas boom of the early eighties. In 1892, they moved from Kingman, Kansas, to Oklahoma and after trying his fortune in the mercantile business in Oklahoma City, he made the race into Noble County at the opening of the Cherokee Strip and staked a claim.

Working through the fall and winter he prepared a home and in the early spring of 1894, he brought his family in a covered wagon from Oklahoma City. With them was Bertha Rockwell, an orphan, who at the age of sixteen, had come to live with the Oakleys while they were residing in Murdock, Kansas. She remained a part of the family until her death, August 31, 1953, at the age of 84, at the Oakley homestead.

John and Dora Oakley were active in the life of their community. Sunday School meetings were held at their home and when the need for a place for public worship became keenly felt, they took the lead in building a Baptist church in the southeast corner of the northeast quarter of section 19-22N-2W on the Wm. Hollingworth farm. John Oakley's name "stood good" with W.C. McCune at the Foster lumber yard of Perry for the entire bill of materials, until it was paid. This was one of the first church edifices erected in Noble County.

John Oakley always took an active interest in political and public affairs. He served as a township leader and when old Black Bear township was divided, he was given the honor of naming the new municipal township. He called it "Oakdale" for himself and his neighbor Anderson Dale.

Mr. Oakley was considered to be a good farmer and was proud to have won a bronze medal for an exhibit of his wheat which he entered in the Louisiana Exposition at St. Louis in 1904.

John and Dora's daughter, Fannie, furthered her education by attending the University Preparatory School at Tonkawa, where she especially enjoyed the music courses. She was an accomplished pianist and took great joy in sharing her gift at community affairs. For years she was the pianist for services at the Polo Christian Church.

John Oakley died May 21, 1914, of cancer. Services were held in the Baptist church he helped build, with the Rev. M. M. Munger as pastor.

Dora Oakley stayed on the homestead with her daughter, Fannie, who on January 13, 1915, married Richard N. Allen. Fannie and Richard presented Dora with four grandsons, Wayne, Loyd, Leland, and Dean. Dora died at the farm on February 14, 1930.

Fannie Oakley Allen and her family continued farming the homestead, except for a twelve-year period when Richard Allen was an engineer with the Soil Conservation Service. During this time their sons, Wayne and Loyd took care of the farm.

Retiring and coming home in 1952, Fannie and Richard lived out the rest of their days on the farm. Richard died on August 9, 1960, at the age of 71, and Fannie died the following year on November 27.

To this day the grandchildren, great-grandchildren and great-great-grandchildren are enjoying the beauty of John Oakley's homestead, which he called "Springdale Farm".

Prior A. Overbey
By Opal Daniels

My father, Prior Anderson Overbey, son of Martin and Eliza Overbey was born in Rock Castle, Kentucky on March 24, 1860. His father died in the Civil War and his mother died shortly after his birth. He was raised by Sarah and Ples Fish. He married Malinda Lucinda Coffee December 25, 1882.

My father was a tall man with large hands and feet. He played fiddle music for dances when he was a young man and as he grew older he entertained his family with the old fiddle tunes we loved to hear with his right foot keeping time patting the floor. He was a hard working man, farming for many years to make a living for his family. After he moved his family to Oklahoma, settling near Butler, he farmed for two years. He then moved into town and started a shoe repair shop. He was a very good repairman and made shoes for my mother for many year with turned soles and the finest leather he could buy. His failing eyesight forced his retirement from business and he was blind for twelve years until his death.

My mother, Malinda, was born March 24, 1862 in Rock Castle County, Kentucky, where she grew to womanhood. Mother and Dad had birthdays on the same day which always called for a party or celebration.

Mother's father died when she was young and her mother worked hard to raise the three girls and one boy. When mother and dad were married, mother's wedding dress was made by grandmother of wool. She had raised the sheep, sheared them, carded the wool, spun and wove it into cloth to make the dress. This was the way all their clothes were made.

My mother was a good Christian woman and we were raised in a Christian home where my Dad said grace at every meal. My folks never had much money but we had sufficient supply of love. Mother loved flowers and was a real gardener. She watched the moon to know when to plant. One day my brother, Randall (Pinky) and mother decided to each plant potatoes, mother to plant hers "in the moon" as she called it and Pinky to plant his "in the ground." They had lots of fun about it and Pinky gloated a little when his vines looked so much better than hers but when harvest time came mother had lots more potatoes than Pinky did.

After my mother's death in May 1935, our son, Dennis, was born and when he was three weeks old, my dad moved in with us. He brought his old wooden rocking chair and was a help in rocking Denny to keep him quiet. Dad would sing the same little song to the baby each time "Trot a little horsie up and down the hill. The girls go to meeting and the boys go to mill." Dad always had a can of candy by his chair. He loved lemon drops and white peppermint candy and when Denny got big enough to run around he knew just how to let grandpa know he wanted some candy without making any noise as I didn't want him to have too much sweets. Denny was very unselfish with Dad, wanting to divide any treats with him. Dad lived with us for four years until his death in 1939. My parents are buried in the Union cemetery at Billings, Oklahoma.

Dad and Mother had twelve children: the first two were stillborn, John Elmer, William, Luther, Mary Etta (Henderson), Leona (Mills), two girls who died at two years, named Bennie and Jewell, Jim, Louie Randell, baby, and me, Opal (Daniels).

James D. E. Owen
By Adella Owen Will

My parents were pioneers, as were their ancestors. As the United States developed and people moved westward from settlements in the 17th and 18th centuries, my ancestors too moved westward. My father's people from Pennsylvania to Kentucky to Indiana where my father James Dickerson Ellsworth Owen was born December 11, 1862 in Orange County. They moved to Nebraska then to Kansas and on to Oklahoma in the 1880s. In September 1893, he staked a 160 acre homestead in the Cherokee Strip.

My mother's ancestors came from Northern Europe, Scandinavia, and Germany in the 1600s. They settled in Long Island, then moved to Connecticut, Eastern New York state and Western New York state. From there they moved to Kansas; yet, they returned to Sherman, New York in 1876 for a time. They returned to Kansas in the 1880s to the Verdigris River Valley in Greenwood county to a small settlement of Virgil.

My mother, Jennie Loretta Dean, taught school for two years, 1890-91 and 1891-92, then my parents were married April 7, 1892. They lived at Virgil until October, and then moved to Stillwater, Oklahoma by covered wagon taking two weeks to drive the 200 miles. My father owned property in the small village of Stillwater and they moved into one of his small houses. He worked at various jobs including a sawmill along Stillwater creek and freighting from the railroad station at Wharton on the Santa Fe railroad just south of Perry, Oklahoma. He said he hauled a portion of the roofing for Old Central, the first building on the campus of OSU.

The race of homestead land in the Cherokee Strip (Outlet) occured at noon September 16, 1893. The starting line on the south was two miles north of Stillwater. It was a hot late summer day.

My father rode a mare he had been riding each day to train to endure a long run. He took 43 minutes to ride the eleven or so miles having to cross creeks, hills, and valleys. A Mr. Thompson, a friend, had a horse of race breeding and made the run in 38 minutes staking the adjoining farm and they witnessed for each other. My mother and Mrs. Thompson followed in buckboard and covered wagon, each bringing a young child. Both families camped on their homestead that night. The following day the men filed their claim at the Government Land Office in Perry, the designated county seat for the area. Law required the homesteaders to live five years on the land, making it a home, then was given a "patent" issued by President Theodore Roosevelt. It was a heavy piece of paper having the President's signature and Seal. Thus the homesteader became full legal owners of the land. When two or more staked the same land they could divide the land equally and contest the party holding the lowest claim number, determined by who filed first, usually got all the 160 acres. My father was fortunate having no contestant and a low filing number, so he had no problems.

In February 1894, my parents moved two 8' x 10' buildings from Stillwater, joining them to form a two room house and settled in to live, breaking the sod with a specially designed plow and planted the land to crop that spring.

His claim was the southwest ¼ of section 11 in Auburn Township. He "proved up" in 1900 and in doing so became full owner. He built a permanent farmstead, planted post timber, fruit trees, a vine yard, and ornamental shrubs and shade trees.

They had two children a son and a daughter. Russell Owen is the father of three children: Jeanette, Wayne and Bernita. Adella Owen Will is the mother of four sons: Earl D., Kenneth, William E., and Eldon.

J.D.E. Owen died April 22, 1945 and Jennie died in 1954. They are buried in the Morrison cemetery.

John R. Owens
By Mrs. W. R. (Agnes) King

John Richard Owens b. 1836-Henderson County, Illinois, and Lydia Eckley b. 1836-Richland, Ohio, were married 1860. They made their home on the homestead of his father Sydney Owens in Oquawka, Illinois. Here they reared their family of six children.

In 1880, the Doctor told John Richard he would have to leave the cold, damp weather of the north and go south for his health. He had developed asthma while serving in the Civil War. He traveled, on a cot, by train to Texas. After his health improved he found work and made plans for his family to come for the opening of Oklahoma. They came in the summer of 1889.

There were many family get togethers and tearful farewells with loved ones and friends before leaving. The father of Lydia, Peter Eckley, 83 years old, wanted to go with them but because of his age couldn't. The mother, three sons and three daughters traveled by wagon and team. They stopped in Kansas City for their first rest. The ferry boat carried them across the Mississippi River at St. Louis, Missouri.

In Guthrie they were met by their husband and father. Guthrie was filled

John and Lydia Owens.

with tents, houses and stores since its opening, April 22, 1889. The older children found work in Guthrie. John Richard, his wife, Lydia, and younger children moved to a farm near Hennessey, west of Guthrie.

On September 16, 1893, John Richard Owens, 57 years old, Civil War Veteran, came from Guthrie to Perry by train to stake his homestead. From a map in the land office, he chose SE ¼-32-24N-1W, that was north of Perry. He got two city lots, which he sold immediately for $10.00. Then he hired a man with a horse and buggy to drive him to his land. John returned to Perry to meet his family who were to arrive from Guthrie, by wagon, with one thing in mind, to build a home. Water, grass and wood were plentiful on the farm. It was not long until the big log cabin, with well, cave and barn were ready for the family.

The two younger children Cidia and Milton attended Banner school, two miles south of their farm. A friendship between the Owens family and Davis Main was developed. Davis purchased a new buggy and began dating Cidia. Soon they were married in Perry, Oklahoma, on April 20, 1898.

They began their lives together on the homestead of Davis Main. High courage on the part of Davis and Cidia and their faith in God carried them through their 52 years of marriage. When their three children were ready for higher education, they moved to Tonkawa, Oklahoma. But Davis continued farming. Now the family had two homes. Davis lived to be 78 years of age and died 1940. Cidia died, age of 86 years, in 1962.

On land donated by John Richard Owens and Jack Reed, their neighbor, the Floral Ridge cemetery was organized in 1893. Here John Richard and Lydia Owens, their daughters, Lydia Clark, her son, Ray, Davis and Cidia Main and their daughter, Gladys Mary Main, are buried.

William F. Passow
By Norman Passow

There were five Passow brothers in Germany, four came to America and

Standing (L to R): Albert, Fred, Louis, Clarence, Earl, Irwin, Victor, Norman, James. Front Row: Edward, Pearl, Irene. Seated: Ida.

one stayed behind in what is now East Germany. There is a small town northeast of Berlin named Passow. William F. Passow, a descendant of one of the brothers who came to America, was born in Hobart, Indiana on December 4, 1864. William and his mother went to the Indiana land and homesteaded 320 acres (160 acres apiece) in Ramsey County, North Dakota. He built a sod house using the lumber from his wagon for the roof. After living on the land one year it was his. His mother passed away and he inherited her share. A few years later he built a two story house. He married Ida Ebert and they had eleven boys and two girls, all born on the farm in North Dakota. They are Fred, Albert, Louis, Clarence, Edward, Pearl, Earl, Irvin, Victor, Irene, James, Norman (twins) and a baby boy who died as an infant. They had enough boys that they could have had their own baseball team, and most of them were good at baseball.

About 1919, William talked to some real estate people about buying land in Oklahoma where it was warmer as his health was failing. They sold their land in North Dakota and bought three farms southwest of Perry. In the spring of 1920, when they arrived here they found they couldn't live on the farms as there wasn't a suitable house on them. They moved their things here on the train. They struggled to move into two rented houses. They put up a temporary building for bunks and storage. They fixed up houses on two of the farms for some of the family. Some of the boys took jobs in the oilfields, farms, ranches and etc.

They made plans to build two story house on the corner of 8th and Maple. William died the second year they were here. Ida continued with the plans to build the house. They had two carpenters come from North Dakota to build it. The older boys helped with the manual labor. They sawed all the boards by hand. They brought the horses in from the farms and hauled the lumber and sand and dug the basement.

Ida raised and sold tomato plants and other plants and she had a strawberry patch and she sold strawberries, also chickens and eggs. They had a large garden as they owned the north side of Maple Street between 7th and 8th Streets except for the east 25 feet. Ida was a very hard worker and a strong Lutheran woman giving much of her time and profits to the church, in fact she donated the east 75 feet of her property to the Lutheran church where the Christ Lutheran Church now sets.

Louis was the only son to marry before moving to Oklahoma. He married Anna Anderson from North Dakota and they had four daughters, Beverly (Passow) Orchard, Maxine (Passow) Pricer, Lois (Passow) Mossman, Jeane (Passow) Wiebe, and Bill Passow. They lived on one of the farms.

Albert married Edna Moelling in 1927, and they lived on a farm south of Lucien, they had two daughters, Dorothy (Passow) Vasek and Lila Mae (Passow) Posey.

Pearl married Duel Bodkins in 1927, he was a plasterer. They had three daughters and two sons, Bernice (Bodkins) Hamlin, Ida Bell (Bodkins) Darnell, Gladys (Bodkins) Jackson, Willard Bodkins, and Wayne Bodkins.

Clarence married Bertha Mills in 1933, and they lived on one of the farms southwest of Perry. Her homeplace was just across the road. Clarence's nickname was "Clip", he got this from a play he was in once. They had two daughters, Charlotte (Passow) Byrd and Neoma (Passow) Petersen.

Irvin married Edna Hirschman in 1933, and they lived on a farm. They had one daughter, Virgina (Passow) Hentges and one son, Ralph Passow.

Victor married Leola Smith in 1938, and they lived on a farm. They had one daughter, Joan (Passow) Jackson and one son Richard Passow. They now live in Kansas.

Earl went to College at St. Johns in Winfield, Kansas, and in St. Louis, and became a Lutheran preacher. He married Frieda Schultz in 1940, she was a nurse. They had two daughters, Kristi and Karla. They live in California.

Fred and Edward had a filling station and did hay baling and combining and different jobs. Neither one married.

Irene became a beautician and married Mike Gallagher in 1940, and they had one son, Michael Gallagher.

Norman went into service. After service Norman studied and became a Doctor of Chiropractic still practicing in Perry. He married Wilma Freeze in 1943. They had one son, Mark Passow and one daughter Tana (Passow) Nelson.

James is a contractor in California and married Jeanne Palerma in 1953. They had one daughter Deborah and one son, Keith Passow.

Ida passed away in 1944. All the farms and the big house were sold. Things in Oklahoma were quite different since severe winters were not experienced here, we soon became "Okies" and the experience of Dakota became only memories. The center of social activity and contact became the Lutheran Church. We have a Passow family reunion at the Christ Luthern Church in Perry every year. A large number of the family still live in and around Perry engaged in farming and businesses.

Willselm F. Paulsen

By Betty Mosena and Goldie Jelinek

Willselm Ferdinand Paulsen was born September 7, 1901, at his parents rural home, 12 miles southwest of Hennessey, Oklahoma in Kingfisher county.

His father was Carnelius Paulsen, born in Osterrade, Germany, June 21, 1865. His mother was Auguste Puttenat, born April 19, 1865, in Berstenimea, Germany. They both came to America in 1888, and married at either Logan or Sterling, Colorado. From Colorado, they moved to Nebraska and in 1901, came to Oklahoma and bought the farm home where Willselm was born. Willselm's parents were farmers. They had eight children, five sons and three daughters. Willselm was the sixth child.

After finishing grade school, Bill, as he was known, worked away from home until he married the neighbor

Bill and Ethel Paulsen taken on a trip they made to Colorado in 1953.

girl, Ethel Chartier, March 2, 1925. Ethel Freda Chartier was born August 20, 1906, southwest of Hennessey, Oklahoma also.

Bill and Ethel rented a farm nearby and raised wheat, watermelons and sweet potatoes. They also had milk cows, raised pigs, chickens and turkeys. Bill had a sweet potato cellar that had a wood stove in it to protect the potatoes. Ethel raised canary birds and sent them to market.

Four daughters were born: Goldie Mae, born May 21, 1926; Betty Jean, born August 11, 1928 and twin daughters, Lorrene Nell and Collene Bell, born July 20, 1930.

In the 1930's during the depression years, times were real hard. A fat hog sold for $3.00. Bill and Ethel would peddle watermelons and sweet potatoes in Hennessey to make a few extra dollars. Bill worked on the W.P.A. for a few years.

In August 1938, they moved to Morrison, Oklahoma in Noble county, rented 160 acres from Lewis Schiever, 3 miles north of Morrison. Farming was continued in Noble county. They raised wheat, oats and cotton. They still milked cows, raised hogs and chickens. They planted a big garden and irish potatoes. Ethel would can hundreds of jars of vegetables and fruit. They had their own milk, cream, butter and eggs. We had very little cash money, but always plenty to eat. Our home was heated with wood stoves, and kerosene lamps were used for lighting.

On Saturday afternoon, the family would go to town, which was a big treat. The cream and eggs were sold and groceries bought. Sometimes we would get a dip of ice cream at Coffman's Drug Store.

Ethel still raised canary birds. All laundry was done on a scrub board. She sewed for herself and four girls. Since there were no sons in the family, the daughters helped in the field.

The girls attended Prairie Center grade school. The school house no longer stands as the Cimmaron Turnpike goes thru that corner.

Life on the farm was simple but rewarding. For entertainment there were card parties, and sometimes popcorn or fudge would be made, lots of visiting, helping each other and meals with neighbors, and friends, school activities and Farmers Union Local meetings. Dances were held in the Prairie Center schoolhouse or at some neighbor's home. During the summer all would go fishing and we had the biggest fish frys, and lots and lots of homemade ice cream.

All four daughters graduated from Morrison High school and went to work for Southwestern Bell Telephone Co. in Ponca City. After each married, they all moved back to Noble county: Goldie as Mrs. Richard Jelinek, north of Morrison; Betty as Mrs. Everett Mosena, northwest of Morrison; Lorrene as Mrs. Calvin Pauley, northeast of Morrison; Collene as Mrs. Neils Anderson, on 2nd St. in Perry.

Bill and Ethel moved to several different farms during these years and the last place they lived on was known as the Lou Webb place. In the spring of 1958, Bill, with the help of friends, built a large chicken house. They raised huge flocks of chickens and sold eggs to Stillwater Hatchery. Bill became ill and developed what was first diagnosed as tuberculosis. He entered the Tuberculosis Hospital at Clinton, Oklahoma, May 2, 1960. He spent three months in the hospital. It was there they found he had "histoplasmosis" instead. This is a serious fungous disease resembling Tuberculosis, that affects primarily the lungs of a man. He contacted this from the chickens. His treatment was changed and he was released from the hospital, August 25. The chickens were sold and Bill and Ethel changed their life style. Bill raised cattle and rented out the farm ground. The pecan trees produced a good crop. Bill started driving a Morrison School bus.

Ethel wrote news for the Perry Daily Journal and still raised a moderate garden. They had seven grandchildren that visited them often.

In 1968, the sold the farm to daughter, Lorrene and husband and moved to Morrison. They did a little more traveling, and still visited with friends. Lots of card parties and many a gallon of ice cream were made. They had a very pretty yard of flowers.

On December 17, 1972, Ethel died of a coronary heart attack. Bill, with the help from his daughters, lived alone until January 7, 1976, when he passed away in his sleep. Both are buried in the Morrison cemetery.

Robert Lee Pender
By Glenda Grange

Robert Lee Pender was born March 18, 1861 at Jacksonville, Florida. He was married to Mary Herndon of Covin County, Alabama on March 20, 1880. She was born in August of 1865 in Alabama. They were the parents of three daughters: Bertha born in September of 1885, Bessie born in October of 1887 both in Kansas and Rosa born in July of 1893 in Oklahoma.

They came to Perry at the opening of the Cherokee Strip and obtained a lot on the corner of Seventh and E Streets where he conducted a cab station. Here he had his home, his cab service and his horse lot. This lot is now occupied by the Stillwater Savings and Loan.

Bob Pender died December 25, 1905 of cerosis of the liver and is buried in Grace Hill cemetery at Perry.

From the Perry Republican — "On January 1, 1906, Mrs. Pender engaged in the services of the brilliant young attorney, Henry S. Johnston in a suit against the Santa Fe Railway in charging the death of her husband to the negligence of the road. It seemed that Mrs. Pender was bringing her husband home to Perry from Oklahoma City December 19th on the evening passenger train and, with assistance, had her husband out on the platform of

"Bobs" Bus and Cab Station Seventh and "E" Streets. (L to R): Bob Pender, A. C. Norris and Carl T. Norris. Bus at left and cab on right. Cherokee Strip Museum - Perry)

the train but the conductor did not hold the train in order that the helpless man could be removed to the station platform. Mr. Pender, who was quite sick at the time, was held in a cold depot at Red Rock for five hours until the southbound train could bring him home. He died on Christmas morning."

The Railway employed a high-priced lawyer from "back east" for defense council. H. S. Johnston acted like a country lawyer, unsure of himself, scribling on pieces of paper and asking questions that didn't seem to have much bearing on the case. The lawyer for the railroad relaxed and seemed to think he had the case won. When Henry S. was called to sum up his case, he sifted through the papers on the table and not finding what he was looking for, went forward and won the case. The questions he had asked were very important when put in proper place. One curious on-looker went to the table Henry S. had used and found nothing but scratch paper. Henry S. used this same ploy many times when dealing with "slick big town lawyers."

At the death of Bob Pender, Bill Johnson took over the Bus and Cab station and continued it until the automobile put the "taboo" on the cab business. A service station occupied the lot for many years until the present Stillwater Savings and Loan building was erected.

J. Thomas Pennington
By Audrey Carter

My grandfather, John Thomas Pennington, ws born April 9, 1866, at Terre Haute, Indiana. Like most families of that time trying to find a better place to live and better ways of supporting a family, he journeyed West with his parents, David and Elizabeth, and sisters, Susan, Jane, Minnie, Sadie, and Lillie, to the Cherryvale, Kansas area.

In a few years, he met and married Mary Phillips. On March 22, 1889, Edna was born, but due to complications, Mary died at time of Edna's birth, leaving him with a tiny baby to care for. His sisters helped take care of her until he met and married my grandmother, Maggie Swiger, November 15, 1890. On

Original 2-room Pennington farm house with one addition still existing. The other additions have been removed because of age.

Pennington Family - December 26, 1917. Front: Gilda (Tootsie). 2nd Row (L to R): Harley, Tom, Maggie, Herbert Bagwell. 3rd Row (L to R): Icie Pennington, Edna Henderson, Ethel Bagwell, Gretta Merriman, and Hazel Pennington. 4th Row (L to R): Tom Pennington, Tom Henderson, Hern Bagwell, Denver Pennington, and Joe Merriman.

September 16, 1891, Ethel was born.

After his father, David, died he brought his mother, Elizabeth, and family to Oklahoma, traveling in a covered wagon. It seems they roamed around living in dug-outs on the Cimmarron River, and later on the Canadian River near Oklahoma City.

They had encounters with the Indians, but no serious problems. I was told the Indians left a couple of trunks with my grandmother containing scalps. Before the land rush, my grandfather worked at whatever was available.

Leaving his wife, two daughters and mother in their wagon near Orlando, he rode a sorrel mare, named Fanny, in the Run for free land on September 16, 1893. He staked his first claim on Black Bear Creek, seven miles west and four north of Perry. His mother begged for that location saying, "Tommy, you are much younger than I, let me have this and you go on and find another location." So he did, and found another just three miles farther north, the southeast ¼ of section 9, of Oakdale Township. The house, barn, and elevator that he built still exist.

During the first winter, he built a sod house. Later a two room rock and concrete house was built. The rock was obtained from the Schaeffer place about one and a half miles south of his location. Later a screened-in room was added to the south. Also, a room was added to the west, and the office of his cotton gin was attached for the kitchen. He also dug a cellar which was used as a storm shelter and for food storage, which they obtained from gardens. Meat was salt cured and dried. A cistern was used for household water supply. Coal and wood burning stoves were used for cooking and warming their homes. Kerosene lamps was the lighting system used in those years.

Grandpa was a Blacksmith, and also a farmer. During harvest time, he would tour the country with his big steam engine and threshing machine harvesting the crops. A cook shack was towed behind the machine. My grandmother cooked three meals a day for the crew of eight.

Nine children were born to them at this place: Lizzie, born March 26, 1885, died December, 1899; Icie, born January 29, 1897, lives in Corpus Christi, Texas; Gretta, born November 26, 1898, lives in Oklahoma City; Tom, born April 3, 1901, died January 31, 1985; Denver, born October 10, 1903, died August 8, 1971; Hazel, born January 1, 1906, lives in Oklahoma City; Harley, born January 23, 1909, died December 28, 1980; Gilda (Tootsie) born October 12, 1913, died February 24, 1969; David, born April 25, 1918, lives in Corpus Christie, Texas.

They were a musical family, grandpa played the fiddle while the children sang and played the piano. They were always entertaining.

Grandpa always had plenty of help too, not just from the children, but anyone walking through the country in need, he always gave them a place to sleep and meals in exchange for work.

Grandpa died May 29, 1918, leaving grandmother with seven children to care for, her youngest, David, being only five weeks old. Some of the children had gone away to work and others had married. I never knew my grandpa, as he was buried in Polo Cemetery the day before I was born. Grandmother moved to Oklahoma City, and later to Corpus Christi, Texas. She died August 22, 1962, and is buried at Polo Cemetery.

Joseph Petermann Family (L to R): Joseph and Bertha Petermann, Amelia (Osten), Aurelia (Watson), Ernest and Erwin.

Joseph Petermann
By Doris Bronner

The Joseph Petermann family came to Oklahoma in 1908, and settled on a farm twelve miles east and three south of Perry on the Noble, Payne County line.

Joseph Petermann was born in Mahren, Austria, to Josepha Christ and Johann Petermann, November 2, 1868. He grew up and attended school in Mahren. He was married to Bertha Schimek on July 4, 1896, in Mahren, Austria.

They had a son and a daughter who were born in Austria. They came to America in 1898, and settled in Davenport, Iowa. He worked in a Brewery and thought the farm would be a better place for his wife and children. They had three more children before moving to Oklahoma and the farm. The five children were Godfrey, Amelia, Aurelia, Erwin, and Ernest.

Godfrey was born in 1897, and lived to the age of around two years old when he died of a childhood disease.

Amelia was born on January 26, 1898. She went to Shiloh School. She married Frank Osten and lived on a farm one mile west and one mile south of Morrison, Oklahoma. They had one child, a boy, named Lorey who died at birth. She became ill in December, 1940 and passed away at the age of 42.

Aurelia was born October 26, 1899, she grew up on the farm and attended Shiloh School. As a young woman, she moved back to Burlington, Iowa, and married Earl Watson. They had three girls named June, Roberta and Audrey. Aurelia still lives in Iowa.

Erwin was born June 3, 1901. He grew up on the farm and attended Shiloh School. As a young man and didn't care for farming, he went back to Burlington, Iowa, and got a job with the Burlington Railroad and worked for them until his retirement. Erwin married Grace Stikey in Iowa, April, 1926. They have two children, one boy, Lawrence and one girl, Delores.

Ernest Alfred was born February 6, 1903. After moving to the farm in 1908, he was five years old, each one had chores to do. He also attended Shiloh School. As he got older, and the other children left, he did more of the farming. He helped with the threshing crews and later was put in charge of the threshing machine. He was one of the few farmers that had a hay fork in his barn to put prairie hay in the barn with. Ernest rebuilt the farm house in 1958.

Ernest A. Petermann
By Doris Bronner

Ernest Alfred Petermann was born February 6, 1903, in Iowa, the son of Joseph Petermann and Bertha Schimek Petermann. He moved to a farm near Morrison, Oklahoma with his parents in 1908. He attended school at Shiloh School. He married Kathryn Emma Ritthaler on August 5, 1925, in Perry, Oklahoma. Kathryn was the daughter of a Cherokee Strip Land Rush runner, Jake Ritthaler. They lived on a farm southeast of Perry, Oklahoma.

Ernest and Kathryn bought the Petermann farm in August of 1939. Ernest and Kathryn had six children, five boys and one girl. The first boy was born at her parents' farm and all the others were born on their farm. They were Albert, Alfred, Doris, Walter, William and Harry. They also went to the same Shiloh School their father went to. It was eight grades which they walked to each day. After graduating from the 8th grade they

Walter Petermann - 1959.

rode a bus to attend Morrison High School.

Albert (Bud) Ernest Petermann was born July 13, 1926, on his grandparents' farm. After attending school, he was drafted into the Army (11 FA Batt 24 Inf. Div. Head Q Batry. 8th Army). He took his training at Camp Hood, Texas in the fall of 1944. He served overseas in the south Pacific theater during World War II. He went to College at Okmulgee, Oklahoma after the army. He does electrical and refrigeration work and owns his own business.

Bud was married to Betty Cromwell, June 5, 1954, in Stillwater, Oklahoma. They settled in Perry, Oklahoma at 322 Birch. They had two children a boy and a girl. Ronald Gene was born September 7, 1955, and Cheryl Dean

(L to R): Albert, Alfred, Doris, Kathryn, Harry, Ernest. In front Bill and Walter - 1941.

was born January 22, 1960. Betty has been working with Bell Telephone Company for 31 years.

Alfred Lee (Al) was born December 1, 1927, on the farm. After graduating from school, he joined a highway paving crew, the Brisco Const. Co. He paved highways and streets all over Oklahoma until the company was sold around 1980. He is foreman for his son, David, in his construction business.

Alfred married Helen Alexander on July 19, 1949, in Bartlesville, Oklahoma. They have two boys, David Lee, born October 15, 1957, and Kenneth Eugene, born June 8, 1954. They bought eighty acres southeast of Stillwater and built a house. The boys went to Stillwater and built a house. They were good baseball players while going to school.

Doris Ann was born June 22, 1930. She married Paul (Pete) David Bronner.

Walter John was born August 23, 1932, at the farm. Walter became ill while in the freshman year of High School. After much hard work and many set backs he finally graduated.

Walter was going to College at Okmulgee, Oklahoma, he was taking accounting and he was to graduate in August, 1960. He had joined Medical Research in Oklahoma City and his younger brother, Harry, was taking care of him and helped him to attend College. In June he came very ill and was brought back to Stillwater Hospital where he passed away June 19, 1960.

William (Bill) Gene was born March 30, 1937, at the farm. Bill went to OSU at Stillwater and got a degree in Agriculture Conservation. He was working in Western Oklahoma when he met and married La Donna Bailey on July 4, 1965. They have a home in Woodward, Oklahoma and have three girls. Kathryn Luann was born on January 27, 1968, Julie was born June 11, 1970 and Laura was born May 18, 1972. La Donna has a degree in elementary education. She taught school the first two years and is a substitute teacher now. The government sent them to Pakistan for a few months in the summer of 1982.

Harry Allan was born June 14, 1940, on the farm. He went to Oklahoma A & M Technical Training School at Okmulgee, Oklahoma on refrigeration. He is employed at the Stillwater Boomer Lake Power station. Harry bought and lives on a farm northeast of Perkins, Oklahoma.

He married Delores Smith, August 29, 1970, at Orlando, Oklahoma. They have two children a boy and a girl. Chris Allan was born December 21, 1971, at Perry Memorial Hospital. Susan was born on March 25, 1974 at Perry Memorial Hospital.

Ernest and Kathryn still live on the farm. They have rebuilt the house. Dad has retired from farming because of ill health. He still makes a small garden and does all his lawn mowing. The oldest son, Bud, is planting the wheat and harvesting it. The second and youngest brothers are cutting the hay and putting it up. The farm has been in three generations of the Petermann's. Mom and Dad celebrated their 60th Wedding Anniversary on August 5, 1985.

Christian Pfeiffer

By Kathrine Linn

Christian and Margaret Pfeiffer were both immigrants of Germany. Christian was the son of Mr. and Mrs. John David Pfeiffer. Margaret was the daughter of Fred and Rosa Kisner. Rosa passed away September 9, 1885, at the age of 45 years. Fred passed away September 1, 1907, at the age of 70 years.

Christian and Margaret settled on a farm on the Noble-Logan County Line, part of the farm was in each county. Margaret purchased 46.5 acres which was called a fraction in Noble County. She sold eggs to pay for this land.

The Pfeiffers had four sons: William, born in 1892, John born on September 15, 1894, and twins, Otto and Fred, born on February 10, 1898. They all attended Star School just 1½ miles from their house which enabled them to walk to and from. The family attended a small country church called Zion Church. Most of it's members were German immigrants. They made their living by farming, milking cows, raising chickens, raising big gardens and growing fruit from their many fruit trees.

All the farm work was done with horses. Milk, cream and eggs were kept in the cellar in a tub of water to keep them from spoiling. Sometimes they were put in a bucket with a long rope and lowered into the cistern just about the water level. You had to be careful not to spill the milk and cream into your drinking water.

The entire family worked in the field so Margaret would take a pot of coffee and add whole eggs to the coffee. As the coffee cooked, so did the eggs. They took this along to the field many days.

Margaret bought oatmeal by the 100 pound bags. She fed this to her baby chickens. The eggs and cream were taken to Orlando in a wagon by Margaret. She used only this money to buy her groceries.

William, the oldest, served in World War I, Barracks 15. After his duty in the service, he married and worked for Swift and Co. out of Fort Worth, Texas. Later, he purchased a farm at Keller,

Sons of Christian and Margaret Pfeiffer (L to R): William, John, Otto, and Fred on the old homestead.

Texas, and farmed for a number of years until his health made him stop. He passed away May 6, 1972, at Fort Worth, Texas.

John married a neighbor girl Elizabeth Le-Brond-Bulling (see John F. Pfeiffer). Christian Pfeiffer had a stroke and passed away on March 2, 1927, at his home. He was laid to rest in Zion Cemetery, a mile south of the family home. Otto and Fred both lived at home with their mother. At this time neither was married.

In the 1930s, the big Oil Boom hit Orlando. Oil was discovered on their land. Two wells were drilled on the fraction which Margaret had bought. The discovery of oil seemed to cause her more trouble than help her life. She felt the wells ruined the land.

Otto and Fred both had oil wells on their land, so they lost a lot of farm land to this. Fred bought a ranch at Fredonia, Kansas and moved there. It was there he met and married Ruth Angus of Arlington, Nebraska on April 24, 1940. Otto continued to farm at home until he was forced to quit due to poor health. Fred and Ruth then returned to Orlando to help care for the farm.

Margaret moved to the home of her son, John and his wife, Elizabeth. She lived with them a number of years until her peaceful death on August 1, 1958. She was 94 years old at her death.

Otto and Fred were large contributors to their community. They gave generous contributions to the church, church parsonage and cemetery of Orlando. Otto spent a good part of his last years in and out of the hospitals. He passed away on April 10, 1967, at Oklahoma City in the Presbyterian Hospital. Things seemed to double up on Fred with the loss of his twin brother, Otto, then his wife within a year's time. Ruth had gone to visit her folks at Arlington, Nebraska, on May 10, 1968, for Mother's Day. She passed away suddenly at the home of her mother on May 16, 1968.

Fred was very lonely but continued to use his good fortune to help others. Most of his contributions now were in

Wedding picture of Christian and Margaret Pfeiffer in the early 1890s.

memory of his wife and brother. He built an addition to the Old Carnegie Library at Guthrie in 1970, which is a modern structure called "Pfeiffer Memorial Building". He also purchased the land across the street from the library to use as a parking lot. Fred also installed new entry gates on the Summit View Cemetery in Guthrie where he and his wife are buried. He also donated generously to civic and religious organizations in his home town, and provided funds to make improvements on the Orlando Methodist Church. The donation of a 2-ton fire truck to the town of Orlando was a real boost to the community. He also paid for building a permanent structure to house the fire-truck. Fred gave a large donation toward a new ambulance at Arlington, Nebraska, in memory of his wife. The year 1976, found Fred giving a donation of $152,400.00 to the Stillwater hospital. Dr. Tim Smalley attended Fred and he wanted Smalley to have what he needed in the hospital to help people.

Fred donated all his antique machinery to Payne County in 1977. He had offered the machinery to Perry, but they couldn't get land to build a building for it. Stillwater managed to build a new metal building at the fair grounds where the machinery is on permanent display.

Much of Fred's time was taken up driving around and checking on his farms and visiting with friend. The Pfeiffers were a hard working German family that didn't take time to go on vacations.

Fred had a stroke on April 5, 1976. After his recovery, he lived alone at his home until he was robbed, beaten and left tied up on June 25, 1979. After this ordeal, he moved a house to Red Rock near the home of a niece, Kathrine Linn, and her husband. He lived alone in his home, but took his meals at his nieces'. On April 30, 1981, he fell and broke his hip. He was in and out of the hospital until his death on July 15, 1981.

John F. Pfeiffer
By Kathrine Linn

John F. Pfeiffer was born of pioneer parents, Mr. and Mrs. Chris Pfeiffer who came to Oklahoma in 1889. John was born September 15, 1894, on a farm west of Orlando.

Elizabeth (LeBrond) Bulling was born on June 23, 1898, in Missouri. Her mother died at the time of her birth, so she was taken in and raised by an aunt and uncle, Mr. and Mrs. Chris Bulling who also lived west of Orlando.

Both John and Elizabeth attended Star School, a one-room school with about 40 to 60 pupils who attended. One teacher taught all 8 grades. They had known each other for years before deciding to marry on March 29, 1917. They moved to a farm they had purchased.

John's father, Christian, had Angus cattle, so he too began raising Angus. In 1920, he bought his first registered Angus. He was one of the oldest and largest Angus Breeders in the state of Oklahoma at one time. This is the beginning of the fifth generation of his family to breed Angus cattle. John's father, John, himself, all of his four children, his grandchildren and now his great-grandchildren have shown and raised Angus cattle. John's children were not allowed to show anything but Angus steers and heifers when they were in 4-H Club work.

John and Elizabeth attended a rural German Church they called the Zion Church. Their parents helped establish the church shortly after the run. John was very active in his community as he held positions on the church board, school board, and the fair board. He helped many other farm programs. He was a Fifty-year Mason of the Mulhall lodge. Elizabeth was active in home demonstration work, served on Red Cross Drive, and church and school committees. She was a 4-H leader in her community and a member of Mulhall Eastern Star. John and Elizabeth were honored in 1962, when they were chosen as "WKY Farmer-Rancher of the Year."

John and Elizabeth had four children. A daughter, Margie Mae, was born December 26, 1918. She married Bill Jeans of Orlando in Noble County. They had two children: Donald Jeans, (the first grandchild), was delivered at Margie's home and Elizabeth helped deliver him. Lois Ann Jeans was born after Margie and Bill moved to a farm west of Ponca City. Margie died January 15, 1966.

The second child, another daughter,

Wedding picture of John and Elizabeth Pfeiffer - March 29, 1917.

Jean Marie was born September 24, 1920. She married Delbert Jelsma of Guthrie. They also moved on a farm west of Ponca City. They have two sons, Johnnie and Darrell.

On March 8, 1922, another daughter, Kathrine Elizabeth, was born. I married H. A. Linn of Verden. We live on a farm at Red Rock and have a son, John Aaron, and a daughter, Patty Jo.

The fourth child, John Henry, was born on November 25, 1927. He married the former Alline Henke of Orlando. They live on a farm near Orlando and have six children: John Jr., Jolene Ruth, JoVona Ruth, James Frederick, Jerry Lee, Jackie Sue and Jay David. Jolene died shortly after her birth.

John and Elizabeth and their children worked hard milking cows, farming and raising a big garden. They canned all their winter food supplies and traded wheat for flour. (They never knew what it was to BUY a loaf of bread.) They did all their own butchering, and froze it by hanging it in a tree in winter. The intestines were scraped on one side, then the other and the tube was stuffed with head cheese by using a lard press. The meat was cut into two inch squares, browned on all sides and canned. Lard was rendered and stored for the year's supply.

John and his family farmed their land, (much of which is in Noble County), raised cattle, hogs, and chickens. Large gardens and an orchard were part of the work and they used horses and mules for transportation and farm work. The crops were cut with binders, then shocked and thrashed. Neighbors all worked together, but it still lasted for weeks. Young boys liked to tie bundles to the wagon, but still found time to do mischievous things over the noon hour.

Jean and I carried water to cattle on a bundle wagon from a pond a mile from home. Jean was driving the mules one day when she turned too short and turned the wagon over. All the water spilled, the mules got scared and ran

Family of John and Elizabeth Pfeiffer. Seated (L to R): Elizabeth, John Henry, John. Standing (L to R): Katherine (Pfeiffer) Linn, Jean (Pfeiffer) Jelsma, Margie (Pfeiffer) Jeans.

off and the wagon was torn up.

We dipped water from the pond in buckets and filled all the barrels. We had to put the water in the center of the wagon or it would turn the wagon over in the pond. Sometimes we got the wagon stuck in the pond and had to unload all the water to get it out, then drive the wagon back in a new place and refill the barrels.

I shocked wheat, oats and feed and helped the hired man. I also gathered all the scattered bundles and worked in the field helping my father every day when not in school.

All of the children worked hard helping build the family farm. Each of them won many honors in showing Angus cattle at various local, state, and national stock shows. The grandchildren and great-grandchildren are continuing the tradition.

All of John and Elizabeth's grandchildren were promised $50.00 if they did not smoke by their 21st birthday. To my knowledge, all 12 have collected their money and none are smokers today. (That $50.00 was big money 45 years ago!)

John at the age of 83, did his chores night and morning, rain or shine. On July 8, 1978, he was entered in the hospital and on September 10, 1978, he passed away. Elizabeth at the age of 87 still lives alone on the family farm.

Our parents worked hard and so did all of their children. As the old saying goes, "Work never hurt anyone." They always tried to leave Sunday free and never planned to work that day. There were always lots of young folks around and we had lots of fun. With God's help our needs were always met. Today, we all live on farms and all raise Angus cattle. (For Katherine and her family see H. A. (Cotton) Linn).

(L to R): George Pfrimmer holding Ethel, Earl Pfrimmer. Painting by James Skluzacek from a faded photograph.

George Pfrimmer
By Ethel Shoop

George Pfrimmer was born near Corydon, Indiana, April 10, 1856. George was the oldest child of Charles and Martha Cline Pfrimmer. Charles was born October 30, 1829, in Alsace-Lorraine, which was a part of Germany. When he was 14 years old, he didn't want to join the army so he stowed away on a large vessel with his parent's consent. The officers on the vessel found him after a day or so and couldn't bring him back so made him work on the vessel to pay his way. He stayed in the East for some time and worked at whatever he could get to do to make his living and finally worked his way to Indiana and that is where he met and married his wife. They were farmers and lived there until their deaths.

George Pfrimmer and Ella Swan were married at Corydon, Indiana, February 19, 1887. Ella was the daughter of Dudley H. Swan and Ruth Cunningham Swan. After George and Ella's marriage they went to western Kansas, near Colby, where he owned some land. The land was in an arid region so crops were not very good. Being a carpenter by trade, George worked at this, digging wells, and any other available work. For this reason they sold their land and came to Oklahoma, near Crescent where a younger brother lived. This brother got a farm of 160 acres in the 1889 opening in Old Oklahoma.

A son, Earl, was born June 10, 1889, while in Kansas. They brought what few things they had with them. The cow was tied to the back of the wagon and had to walk all the way. This made them go very slow. Other things such as clothing, bedding, a bed, stove, etc., were put in the covered wagon. While living at Crescent he rented some land for farming and did carpentry work until the opening of the Cherokee Strip. George trained a pony to ride in the race.

George made the run on horseback from the line just north of Orlando. He went as far as Red Rock Creek just south of where Billings is now. The farm he wanted, just across the creek on the west side, had someone already there. He didn't know if it was a "Sooner" or not. He didn't know just what to do but decided he couldn't risk a contest, so he started back south. He staked the northwest quarter of section 18 in Oakdale township.

There were three brothers and a brother-in-law in the race and all were fortunate and each filed on a farm of 160 acres. All lived on their farms long enough for the farms to belong to them.

George Pfrimmer had built a small house of one room, 14 feet by 16 feet, near Crescent with the siding being 1x2s running up and down. After filing on the land, he went back to Crescent. He tore the house down and moved it to the farm.

The closest place to get mail, groceries, and kerosene was a small store at a place called Polo. Polo was 4½ miles from that farm. The means of travel was a big lumber wagon, walking, or horseback.

Heat was supplied by wood or coal in a four hole iron cook stove. The coal was purchased in Perry which was 16½ miles from the farm. Later the towns of Billings and Garber were located about 10½ miles from the farm.

Being a carpenter, he built and helped build a great many of the first houses in that area. He got $1.00 per day for carpenter work. A day was considered from sunup to sundown.

A daughter, Ethel, was born the following year after the opening. Three other children were born as time went by: Paul, Pearl, and Raymond.

The first crops raised on the sod ground was kaffir corn and castor beans. Kaffir corn seed was ground in the coffee grinder and made into bread as flour was not always available.

George Pfrimmer was bitten by a rattlesnake while putting hay into the wagon. He killed the snake, got the rattles off, (there were six rattles and a button), then went into the house. His wife sent his older son who was 6½

Back Row (L to R): John Pfrimmer, Marion Pfrimmer Charles Pfrimmer. Second Row: Louis Mossler, Emma Pfrimmer Mossler holding Grace Mossler, Lydia (Hickman) Pfrimmer, Jesse, Charlotte, Elias, Ella (Swan) Pfrimmer, George, Roscoe, Martha, Charles. Front Row: Flora Mossler, Clarence Mossler, Sadie Mossler, Grace Pfrimmer, Pearl Pfrimmer, Frank Pfrimmer, Earl Pfrimmer, Ethel Pfrimmer.

years old on a horse to get some whiskey from a neighbor. She had heard of getting a live chicken, killing it but not letting it bleed, splitting it down the back and immediately putting it on the bite. So she did this, put his foot inside and wrapped a tea towel around it to hold it in place. It was left on until after the neighbor came with the whiskey. He made him take some liquor but really had to pour it down. When the chicken was taken off his foot, the inside of the chicken was green as it had absorbed the poison.

At that time people had to load their own gun shells. The shells were brass. The caps were put in first, then the powder, then a thing called a wad, then the shot and another wad. He was putting in the caps and for some unknown reason it fired right over the open powder and exploded! His face, neck, chest, and arms were badly burned. The explosion made it burn deeper. In taking his clothes off it pulled the skin right off with it. The Doctor had trouble in getting the burns to heal. Finally, he got a new prepared gauze called Iodaform and put it on all the burned parts of his body. This helped and after a long time it healed, but it was aways very tender and scarred and it always bothered him. He couldn't shave so he had to wear whiskers and have them trimmed.

Ella Pfrimmer did the plowing, sowing the wheat, oats, and corn while her husband worked. In 1902, he started a new house and moved into it in the spring of 1904. The house is still in the family. George Pfrimmer died April 19, 1915. Ella Pfrimmer died February 7, 1936. They are buried in the Polo cemetery.

Corinne Pierce-Riney
By Kathy Bradford

Corinne Irene Pierce was born on a farm in Whitewater, Kansas near the Whitewater River, northeast of Wichita on January 29, 1890. When Corinne was three her parents went to the opening of the Cherokee Strip and filed claim for 160 acres in Noble county, Oklahoma. Her father's brother, Charles filed on the homestead NW of George's and his sister, Gertrude Beach and her husband filed across the road north of George's. Bunch Creek runs across the three farms which are located 2 miles east and 2 miles south of Billings, Oklahoma and are still owned by relatives of Corinne.

Their home was a big 4-bedroom house, there was a big barn, a large granary and several hog sheds. With the homestead came tornadoes, drought and grasshopper invasions. In later years, Corinne said the family knew nothing but hard work. When Corinne was 16 her mother died of Tuberculosis. When she was 19, her father died of heart trouble. Corinne had an older brother and sister, but the responsibility for the four younger sisters seems to have fallen on her. Corinne farmed the girls out to relatives whenever she could find a paying job.

She went with the Threashing Crew to Pratt, Kansas, when she was 20. They hired out on the farm of James and Sarah Riney. It was there she met John Beed Riney, the 16 year old son of James and Sarah. He was a handsome young man, a bit shy, which he tried to hide with a gruff exterior. He worked for his father on the Pratt farm. John and Corinne married January 2, 1912. They lived with his parents on the farm and Corinne worked morning to night for her new husband's parents. She insisted her sister Alice, stay with them.

On October 4, 1917, Anthol Wayne was born on the farm at Pratt. Anthol's father "created" Anthol's name from the names of two family friends, Ansel and Lenthol.

Corinne disliked living with John's parents, but John was reluctant to go out on his own. In 1921, John's parents decided to lease the Kansas farm and move to Oregon. Alice and a nephew of James came along. Two other married sisters of Corinne's came to Oregon about the same time. They were Ora Pierce and Ethel May Pierce.

A sister, Eunice (Una), was born October 22, 1898 in Billings, Oklahoma. She married Grant Washburn Varner May 16, 1917 in Enid, Oklahoma. Mr. Varner was born November 14, 1893 in Towanda, Kansas. He passed away November 25, 1979 in El Dorado, Kansas and was buried in Towanda cemetery. They are the parents of six children: Milburn Pierce who died March 15, 1934, Lela Maxine was born February 8, 1921 in Towanda, Kansas. She married Marshall E. Henry December 13, 1940 in Wichita, Kansass. Ivan (Delbert) was born July 29, 1927 in Towanda, Kansas. He married Esther Marie McDowell July 24, 1959 in West Chester, Iowa. Raymond Varner was born November 16, 1929 in Towanda. He married Mary E. Van Arsdale February 12, 1983 in Towanda. Wilma Marie Varner was born December 4, 1934 in Towanda. She married Joseph Tucker Lill August 4, 1955 in Towanda. Donald Lee Varner, Sr., was born August 14, 1939 in El Dorado. He married Lynda Jean Faulkner September 16, 1962 in El Dorado.

Ethel May Pierce was born September 25, 1901 in Billings, Oklahoma. She married William Orval (Wik) Wikstrom. Orval was born October 4, 1898 in Columbia county, Oregon. He died 31 May 1968 in Winslow, Arizona and is buried in Yakima, Washington. Both Ethel and her husband were pilots.

Alice Pierce was born September 28, 1904 in Billings, Oklahoma. She married Loren Wilson December 1, 1922 in The Dalles, Polk county, Oregon. They moved from the Dalles to Vancouver, Washington in 1943. Loren Wilson was born May 24, 1905 in Dallas, Oregon. He passed away in 1982 in Vancouver, Washington. They had two sons: Lorence R. born August 31, 1924 in Dalles, Oregon. He married Myrtle Knudson. Rex R. Wilson was born December 5, 1928 in Dalles, Oregon. He married Virginia Hart January 2, 1952

John Riney and Corinne Pierce on their wedding day July 2, 1912 in Pratt, Kansas.

Children of Charles Pierce (back): Lulu Maude, (front): left, Millard Monroe; right, Edgar Crawford.

Clarence Emery Pierce (1891 - 1953).

in Stevenson, Washington.

The Rineys purchased a farm a mile north of Monmouth, Oregon. It had a large two-story house, a barn and amazingly fertile soil. The family was astonished as the abundance of fruits and vegetables produced in the lush Willamette Valley.

Corinne was still not happy sharing a house with her in-laws. She often begged John to strike out on his own, but he hesitated. Finally, when it was obvious that Corinne was on the verge of a nervous breakdown, John got a job at the Teacher's College in Monmouth doing campus chores. They moved to a rented house in town. Albert George was born April 15, 1925 and that completed the family. During the next 13 years, John was to have several jobs, then when his parents died he was left half of the Monmouth farm. Corinne helped the boys in their never-ending chores and in 4-H work in the few spare hours. There was never enough money and Anthol's sheep project was sold by his father for needed cash. Corinne and John died within a year of one another in their mid 70's and are buried near Salem, Ore.

Charles E. Pierce
By Kathy Bradford

Charles Edgar Pierce was the fourth son born to Martin M. Pierce and Lydia Ann Joshlin. He was born 2 February 1870 in Bushnell, Fulton Co., Ill.

Charles Pierce married Katie Crawford on 24 December 1893 near El Dorado, Kansas. They made their home for a short time near El Dorado, and on 1 February 1894 they moved to their homestead near old White Rock, Noble Co. Oklahoma. They lived in White Rock until 1910 when they moved to Billings, OK. The homestead was located in the northwest quarter of section 3 in White Rock township.

Charles Pierce died 28 December 1962 in Enid, OK. He was buried 31 December 1962 in the Union cemetery, Billings, OK. Catherine (Kate) Crawford was born 26 April 1872 in Greencastle, IN. She was an active member of the First Christian church in Billings. She died 29 June 1936 in Billings, OK. Charles then married Mrs. O.O. Jenkins in Ponca City, OK.

From their life together, Charles and Katie Pierce had three children. They are: Lulu Maude Pierce, born 28 October 1894. She was born at the homestead of her parents, two miles east one half mile south of Billings. On 24 March 1912, Lulu died from consumption.

Edgar Crawford Pierce was born 14 December 1899 in Oklahoma. He married Edith Murray in Billings, OK. Their children: Edgar Charles born 5 January 1923 and Mary Ellen Pierce born 1 January 1930.

Millard Monroe Pierce was born 11 May 1901. He was married 3 April 1923 at Enid, OK to Minnie Novotny (b-17 September 1898). He managed oil well supply stores in Texas and Oklahoma. He died 10 March 1977. He is buried in the Mt. Vernon cemetery, north of Billings, OK. Their child: Donald Eugene Pierce was born 10 January 1929.

Clarence L. Pierce
By Kathy Bradford

Clarence L. Pierce was the third son born to Martin Monroe Pierce and Lydia Ann Joshlin. He was born 9 March 1864 in Fulton Co, Ill. Four of the ten children to Martin Monroe Pierce obtained homesteads in Noble county, although the parents stayed in Towanda, Kansas. Martin Monroe Pierce was born 8 March 1827 in New York State. He was married between 1845 and 1850 possibly in New York to Lydia Ann Joshlin. Both of his parents were born in Massachussetts. Lydia was born 14 August 1827 in Rochester, Monroe Co., NY. Her father was born in New York and her mother in Rhode Island. Mr. and Mrs. Pierce moved from Illinois to Butler Co, Kansas in 1870. They homesteaded near El Dorado and lived there until their deaths, Mr. Pierce 17 March 1880 and Mrs. Pierce 20 August 1905. They are buried in Towanda, KS.

In 1893, Clarence married Emma McFarland in Noble Co, Ok. He made the run for a claim at the opening of Noble Co. Oklahoma and located on what is known as the Captain Wallace farm near Billings. This farm is the northeast quarter of section 10 in White Rock township. To avoid contest litigation on the same land, he sold his interest in the claim to Mr. Wallace. His brothers, George and Charley, were old residents of Noble county, as was also his sister, Mrs. Nick Beach.

Clarence L. Pierce died 12 March 1901. His remains were brought for interment in the White Rock cemetery (now Union) and a funeral service was conducted at the home of his brother, Charley. His death resulted from consumption.

They were the parents of four children. Two known are: Tessie Pierce, born 2 December 1889, married Ike Sparks and George Stewart; and Clarence Emery Pierce, Jr. born 26 May 1891 died 21 April 1953 and is buried in Towanda cemetery, Towanda, KS.

George G. Pierce
By Kathy Bradford

George Gilbert Pierce was the first son born to Martin M. and Lydia Ann Joshlin Pierce. He was born 19 September 1854 in Bushnell, Illinois. He was the oldest of a family of ten

George Pierce family in 1904. Back Row (L to R): Corinne, Bonnie, Fred. Second Row (L to R): Eunice, Cora, Ora, George. Front Row (L to R): Ethel, Alice sitting on George's lap.

children, seven boys and three girls. He was a tall, big-boned man with black hair and a dark moustache and beard. He was also a very hard worker.

At the age of 16, he moved from Illinois to El Dorado, Butler County, Kansas with his parents. He was a farmer in Kansas and Oklahoma. George Pierce had six brothers. They were James A., Clarence L., Charles Edgar, William Cameron, Frank and Herbert. He had three sisters, Gertrude, Emma G., and Dollie A. Pierce.

On July 4, 1886 in El Dorado, Kansas, George married Cora Bell Valentine. Cora was born November 16, 1866 in Elmira, Chemung County, New York. She was a medium-boned woman with long dark hair that was worn twisted on the top of her head. She was the daughter of Frederick Valentine and Amelia Branch.

During George and Cora's life together, they had eight children. They were Bonnie, Blanche, Frederick William, Corinne Irene, Ora Eva, George Gilbert Jr., Eunice Viola (Una), Ethel May and Alice Agnes Pierce. They lived in Kansas for nine years.

In 1891, George and his family moved to Oklahoma, two years before the opening of the Cherokee Strip and lived in Orlando, Oklahoma. When the opening day came, he made the race and secured a fine claim on which he lived until his death.

On July 20, 1903 George filed his United State Patent Homestead Cert. #2957, Application #824 in Noble county, Perry, Oklahoma. He purchased the sw quarter of section 3 in White Rock township, containing 160 acres.

On his homestead he raised cattle, horses, hogs and chickens. He grew corn, wheat, alfalfa, oats and had a large vegetable garden which gave them their supply of food for the winter. He also raised feed for his animals.

On the farm was a big barn, machinery shed, cow barns, horses and a hayfork and hay loft. The machinery he had consisted of binders, corn planters, harrows, drills and a wheat binder.

Although their hours were filled with hard work, they did find time to socialize. Their family social functions included visiting relatives and neighbors and picnics and dances. Holidays were spent at home with the family or at a relative's home. Some of their neighbors were the Yosts, Chestnuts and Armstrong families.

On November 18, 1906, George lost his beloved wife. Cora passed away of Tuberculous at her home in Billings, Oklahoma. She was buried in the White Rock cemetery (now Union) Billings, Oklahoma.

On the 20th day of May 1909 George Pierce had made his final will and testament. His Executor was Emanual Smith, a personal friend. He willed his home and land to his son, Frederick, with the provision that he take care of his three youngest daughters, Alice, Ethel and Una, until each of them became years of age or got married. He gave to his son, Frederick, one third of all his personal property after debts were paid. His daughters received the remainder and residue of his personal property to share and share alike.

George and Cora worked and farmed their land until their death. On October 23, 1909 at 5 pm at his home four miles SE of Billings, George Pierce passed away. He was 55 years old. The doctor in attendance was Dr. Bradford of Billings, Oklahoma. Mr. Pierce died of heart trouble and was laid to rest in the White Rock cemetery (now Union) beside his wife Cora.

Bonnie Blanche Pierce was born April 12, 1887 in Towanda, Butler county, Kansas. She married Thomas Hobbs in Missouri. Bonnie died October 14, 1921 in Missouri. They had no children.

Frederick William Pierce was born October 4, 1888 in Towanda, Kansas. He was a farmer. He moved to Oklahoma in 1892 and returned to Kansas in 1927. He married Florence Varner on March 28, 1917 in her parent's home in Fairview Township. Florence was born February 9, 1892 between El Dorado and Towanda, Kansas. She was the daughter of Miltom Emery Varner and Cora Frances Washburn. He died November 1979 in El Dorado, Kansas. They had two children: Cora Vivian Pierce and Mariner Pierce.

George Gilbert Pierce Jr. was born September 6, 1895 in Billings, Oklahoma. He died at the age of three, December 3, 1898 in Billings. He is buried in the Union cemetery.

Ora Pierce-Hixon
By Kathy Bradford

Ora Eva Pierce was born September

Clarence Hixon and Ora Pierce on their wedding day July 19, 1916 in Cullison, Kansas.

27, 1893 in Billings, Noble county, Oklahoma. As a young girl she attended Frog Holler school, which was approximately ¼ mile away from their home. The teacher taught children from the first to the eighth grade. Ora completed schooling up to the eighth grade. She played with neighborhood children and her school friends. Two of her friends were Anna Chestnut and Nellie Lohman. Some of the games she played were ball, hide and seek, and tag. Her favorite pastime was staying over night with a girlfriend. For entertainment, when she became of age, she was allowed to attend the dance socials.

Ora lived on the homestead with her parents. With 160 acres of land, there were many chores to be done. She picked corn cobs, milked the cows, fed the animals, chopped wood, worked in the corn fields cutting out the weeds that the cultivator missed and shocked wheat. Her two older sisters, Blanche and Corinne, helped her mother clean house, cook, can, and take care of the other children. Everyone was expected to do their part, as with eight children in the family, there was plenty of chores for all.

When Ora was 13, her mother died. Three years later her father died. Her brother, Fred, was now in charge of the family. He lived on the homestead and had a woman come in and take care of his younger sisters and clean the house while he worked on the farm. When Ora's sister, Corinne, married, Ora moved to Pratt, Kansas with Corinne and her husband, John Riney.

Ora worked for a family in Pratt, Kansas. On April 1, 1916, she met her future husband, Clarence Ernest Hixon. Mr. Hixon was invited over for Sunday dinner. After the meal was over and Mr. Hixon had gone home, the woman she worked for asked her how she liked Mr. Hixon. She said, "He's mine if I never get him." After three months of courting, they married July

19, 1916 in Cullison, Pratt county, Kansas at the County Judge's Office.

Clarence Hixon was born 31 July 1890 in Englevale, Crawford county, Kansas. He was the son of Cyrus L. Hixon born June 7, 1857 in Wabash, Indiana. Cyrus died March 4, 1894 in Englevale, Kansas. Clarence's mother was Emma B. Dosser, born January 31, 1865 in Ft. Scott, Kansas. She died April 1, 1934 in Liberal, Kansas. Clarence was a farmer by trade. He had three sisters, Florence, Alva and Nellie Hixon.

Ora and Clarence spent their first night of married life at the Riney home. Twenty years later, Mr. Hixon took his wife back to Kansas for the honeymoon they never had.

As Corinne and her family had already moved to Oregon, Clarence and Ora decided to follow. In 1934, Ora, Clarence and their three children came west and drove to Oregon in a Ford automobile. They settled in Salem and later moved to Grants Pass, Oregon.

Mr. Hixon worked various jobs while they lived in Oregon. He worked in the hop fields, the bulb farms, and then the wood and pulp mills in Oregon. Ora also worked. She was employed by the Redwood Hotel, Henry Turks Bulb Farm and worked at a hospital.

On February 25, 1974, Clarence died in Grants Pass, Oregon. At 91 years of age, Ora Eva Pierce Hixon is still living on Fourth Street in Grants Pass, Oregon. She still enjoys crocheting, knitting, gardening, crossword puzzles, growing flowers and just plain "Digging in the Dirt". She has crocheted her great-grandchildren beautiful afghans to remember her by in the years to come. She has nine grandchildren, 19 great-grandchildren and and one great-great grandson.

During Clarence and Ora's marriage they had three children. Marvin Dee was born September 24, 1917 in Cullison, Kansas and married Ruth M. Holyman April 19, 1937, in Grants Pass, Oregon. Orpha Mae was born July 26, 1919 in Cullison and married Dale Marsland June 30, 1937. Verla Allene was born September 23, 1921 in Cullison and married Ira Truman Bradford November 20, 1939 in Medford, Oregon.

Napoleon Poland
By Mrs. E. M. (Edna) Barnes

Napoleon and Jeanette (LePlant) Poland were born and grew to maturity in New York State. Napoleon was born February 10, 1854. Jeanette was born January 3, 1852. Napoleon's family for three generations before him, lived near Cooperville, New York. Jeanette's family home was near Plattsburg, New York.

Napoleon's great-grandfather was Captain Antoine Pauline who served in the Canadian Army before coming to Cooperville and later, in the Revolutionary War, serving as interpretter for General LaFayette. Antoine was born in September 1737 in Grenoble, France. His parents were Antoin Paulint and Dominique Valsise. His wife, Theodistes Cottard was born in 1750. She was the daughter of Pierre Cottard and Agness Burgloise in Canada. They were married January 2, 1767 in the Parish of St. Antoine de Chambly, Canada.

The Poland Catholic church still stands near Cooperville, New York, all the colored glass windows in honor of someone in the Poland family. The Poland Cemetery is nearby where a number of the family are buried.

Napoleon and Jeanette were married January 19, 1875, in Plattsburg, New York. It is believed they, along with Napoleon's sister, Mary and Jeanette's brother, Jacob, who were also married, came to Kansas together on the train in 1877.

Napoleon made the Old Oklahoma run and the Cherokee Strip run. Napoleon played his violin for many dances and parties. He was accompanied by a cousin, Tom Page, who organized the first band in Perry.

Napoleon drilled water wells. They milked cows and sold milk and butter. Jeanette did sewing for people, especially wedding dresses. She could also write and draw beautifully.

They were still in Kingman, Kansas, when Napoleon and his brother, Samuel, made the run into Old Oklahoma on horseback. Napoleon got a place in Guthrie — Third street and College Avenue. Samuel got a place in Reno (now El Reno). Napoleon's family lived at that address in Guthrie for four years. Their home was on the west bank of Cottonwood Creek which often flooded.

Because of the depression and drought, Napoleon decided to try for a farm in the Cherokee Strip. He rode to the Orlando starting point on a mule, violin under his arm and made ready for the run along with probably 100,000 others. Napoleon ran north of Perry and staked 160 acres on the east side of what is now Highway 77, about two miles north of Ceres (nw section 2 in Red Rock township). The family came to the farm soon and built a sod house in which to live.

In the fall of 1899, Lawrence Poland, Napoleon's father, came to visit from Northern New York. While here he became ill and died of a ruptured gall bladder. The body was shipped from Red Rock to Wichita, Kansas and buried in the Calvary Cemetery, where Jacob LePlant, Jeanette's brother and his wife, Mary Poland LePlant are also buried. Later, Clarissa, Napoleon's mother, came to visit and decided to stay. Naploeon built a room on the south of the house for her. There she put her bed, a cook stove, her rocking chair and other things. She lived there until her death, January 27, 1918, of what was thought to be a stomach cancer. She could understand some English but couldn't speak much of it. She kept an immaculate house but she was a difficult person with whom to live. She caused Jeanette a lot of trouble and unhappiness.

Jeanette had had a stroke a few years earlier and was practically an invalid. Napoleon stopped farming, rented out his land and stayed home to care for Jeanette and to protect her from the disagreeableness of his mother.

Jeanette died, suddenly, of another stroke, only four days after Clarissa's death. Both are buried in the Catholic Cemetery in Perry. Napoleon later bought a house in Wichita, Kansas, where he lived until his death caused by a heart attack, November 4, 1933. He is buried in the Catholic Cemetery, between his wife and mother. His children were: William Napoleon, Calrissa H., Julius J., Edith Adeline, and Oralyne Mary.

George Stuart Prather
By Thelma Holmes

The first Prather to come to America was from the ancestral home called Latton on Eton waters in Wiltshire, England in 1622 on the ship Marie Providence to Newport, Virginia.

Eight generations later, in 1883, Stuart Prather was born to Nannie Isabell (Brown) and John Wesley Prather near Cedar Bluff, Tazewell County, Virginia. John Wesley was born in Bath County, Kentucky, January 2, 1844 and died March 11, 1906 at Billings, Oklahoma. He is buried in the Riverview Cemetery. He married Isabell Brown March 25, 1869 in Virginia.

When Stuart was about two years of age, he moved with his parents to Barber County, Kansas and later to Hunnewell, Kansas where he with his brothers C. William, Thomas W., Edwin and sister Anna (Mrs. Jens Breinholt) watched from the roof of a cowshed, the start of the race for land into the Cherokee Strip on Stepember 16, 1893. His father took land five and one-half miles north of Billings, Oklahoma - just north of the Noble-Kay County line. This is where Stuart was reared.

On the homestead farm, his father ran a blacksmith shop, store and Owens post office. The Prather brothers and sister Anna sang and played music at church, community gatherings, schools and funerals as this new country was being developed.

As a young man Stuart played baseball with the Owens team from Billings. Quite often they played with the zeal of professional ball of today but with no money involved.

After the death of his father, Stuart lived on at the family home, caring for his mother until her death in 1941. He then retired and moved to Billings. In 1964 he moved to Garber, Oklahoma to be near his niece, Mrs. Quincy (Thelma) Holmes.

"Uncle Stuart", as he was fondly called by his younger friends, passed away at the age of 83 years. He will long be remembered for his love and kindness to all whose lives he touched.

Albert L. Pricer
By Harold A. Pricer

Albert Leo Pricer was born March 13, 1888, in Kingman County, Kansas. His parents were Austin and Mary Delcenia (Elwood) Pricer. He lived in Kingman and Reno Counties until 1902 when his parents migrated to Ford County, near Wright, Kansas. As a teenager he worked for Mr. Collingwood in Reno County. They moved from Ford County, Kansas in 1905 to Perry, Oklahoma Territory.

In Perry, he worked for his father and uncle in the livery stable business. Later he was employed in construction work and as a tank builder. On November 15, 1917, he was married to Martha Elizabeth Schomaker in Perry, by A. Duff Tillery, the County Judge. Soon after he entered the United States Army and served until the finish of World War I.

After returning to Perry he built his home at 710 Maple Street and here all of their children were born. On August 7, 1920, the first child, Harold Albert was born. Exactly one year later, Paul Henry arrived on August 7, 1921; Dorothy Louise, the only daughter, was born April 15, 1924. The last child was Robert Leo and he was born January 12, 1926. Robert Leo died six months later on July 11, in the hospital at Guthrie, Oklahoma. Paul Henry lost his life during World War II as a flight engineer on a B-24 type aircraft.

In 1934, Albert changed his profession and went to work in the oil fields in Kansas. In 1952, he went into the motel business and continued this work until he retired to his home in Hutchinson, Kansas. He died at St. Elizabeth Hospital in Hutchinson on November 26, 1964, and was buried at Grace Hill Cemetery in Perry.

Austin Pricer
By Hellen Neuerburg

Austin Pricer was born September 8, 1852, in Ross county, Ohio, to David Pricer Jr. and Malinda Edmiston Pricer. As a young child he started moving west with his parents. They settled in Des Moines, Iowa. At the age of 19 years old, he met Mary Delcenia Elwood, age 17 years old (birthdate: August 30, 1854) at a party of young folks. They fell in love and were married December 14, 1871 in the home of her parents, John Sinclair and Eliza (Hodson) Elwood. For more adventure of the west, they traveled by oxen and covered wagon to Brown county, Kansas, in 1872, where they endured all the hardships of the early settlers of Kansas. In 1873, they moved to Reno County, Kansas, near Hiawatha.

To this union eleven children were born. Their first child, a daughter, Eliza Emma, on August 2, 1873. Their second child, Columbus Edwin was born July 11, 1875; during this year they farmed 25 acres of corn, 20 acres of wheat and 5 acres of oats. He had $25.00 worth of machinery, owned $640.00 real estate and $160.00 personal property. Their third child, William David, was born March 2, 1877. The following children are as follows: Cynthia Ellen on April 13, 1879,

Austin and Mary Pricer on their golden wedding anniversary, December 14, 1921 in Perry.

Charles S. on December 2, 1880, Infant daughter, April 26, 1883, died the same day, Henry Oswell on July 14, 1886, Albert Leo, March 13, 1888, John Jay on October 13, 1889, Malinda Jane on March 22, 1892, and infant son on December 8, 1896, died the same day.

Austin Pricer was blind in his early 30s for 7 years. His eye sight was restored by an Indian using very strong medicine (medicine was rust color). When on a handkerchief, the color stain was impossible to wash out. He used this medicine the remainder of his life.

While living in Kansas, they gathered cow chips for fuel, and also gathered chips and Buffalo bones and hauled them 40 and 50 miles to a trading post to sell them in exchange for their necessities of life.

Austin learned to talk with the Indians in their language and learned their customs and ways of life. By understanding the Indians he got a job in a lumber mill at Hutchinson, Kansas to help the Indians in their buying. In 1902, Mary and Austin moved to Ford county, Kansas, near Dodge City. He met Jesse Chisholm and rode as a cowboy with the Long Horn cattle herds to the markets. Riding over the trails, he came as far as the Indian Territory north of Perry. When he returned home he found they had been wiped out by the grasshoppers and locusts. While he was riding the prairie gathering cow chips and bones and riding the trails, Mary was home guarding their belongings and home from the marauding Indians.

So in 1905, he and Mary were discouraged and decided to move again. After seeing the new county of the Indian Territory and the loss of their farming, he decided to join his brother-in-law, Jim Elwood in Perry.

So in 1905, he and his wife, Mary, and three children, Albert, John and Malinda, moved to Perry. Jim and Austin were in partnership from 1905 in the

(Standing) (L to R): Columbus Edwin, William, Charles, Henry, Albert, and John; (Seated) (L to R): Ellen, Austin, Mary Delcenia and Lyda.

livery stable business until 1909. Austin Pricer was appointed Sexton of Grace Hill cemetery and remained so for 25 years until his death in September 10, 1923 at the age of 80 years and 2 days. He and Mary were married for 58 years and 2 months.

Austin and his wife raised two granddaughters, Hellen (Neuerburg) and Martha (Hogan) from infancy after the death of their mother, Emma, son Edwin's wife, on Septemebr 20, 1908. The Pricers bought a home at 102 E Cedar street around 1909 and lived there until February 20, 1929. Mary his wife proceeded him in death on February 20, 1929. Austin lived with his son, Henry until he passed away in 1932. There have been 65 grandchildren born to this couple.

John P. Pritchett

By Callie Anthis DeVilbiss

John Phelps Pritchett (March 29, 1851 - February 22, 1920) was born on a plantation near Frankfort, Kentucky. His mother was Serepta Carolina Pritchett. J. P. left home at age 14, and made his own way. The family searched but could not locate him. These were Civil War years, and people were shifting! The Civil War closed in 1865, that was the year J. P. Pritchett left his Kentucky home. Serepta Pritchett and family moved north out of Kentucky. Her other known children were: Will Pritchett who settled on a farm near Terra Haute, Indiana; Jimmie Pritchett, lost in Civil War and never heard from again; Mary Pritchett Bows around Crissman, Illinois; and Lou Pritchett Day who moved to Girard, Kansas where she died.

Minnie Elizabeth (Jones) Pritchett (July 22, 1862 - March 26, 1936) was from Danville, Illinois. She had a brother James Eddie Jones and a sister, Bell Jones Smith. Minnie was visiting her relatives in Terre Haute, Indiana when she met J. P. Pritchett, who had finally made contact with the rest of his family. They were married July 22, 1881 at Danville, Illinois.

John Phelps and Minnie Elizabeth Pritchett made their first home at Pittsburg, Kansas. Their first child, Erma, was born there September 10, 1883. The second child, Hattie, my mother, was born September 10, 1884 on Erma's birthday at Girard, Kansas. The family then moved out on Plains about 18 miles south of Garden City, Kansas. In the winter of 1886, Minnie and Hattie (Erma had died) made a train trip to Danville, Illinois, where Edward Bernard was born January 31, 1886. Callie Serepta was born October 31, 1887 near Garden City, Kansas.

The family came in covered wagon to Old Oklahoma in 1889 when it opened for settlement. Streams had to be forded. On one occasion a horse balked in midstream, John waded and led the horse across. About a dozen hens drowned. Minnie had begged to have the chickens placed higher for the crossing but was assured they would be alright. On the bank of the stream, water was heated, the chickens dressed, and the surplus given to others on the trail. Then at the end of the long trek they stopped in West Guthrie, and lived in wagon under cottonwood trees for two weeks.

John and Minnie had eight children: Erma Pritchett (September 10, 1883 died at age 16 months); Hattie May Pritchett (September 10, 1884 - July 18, 1972); Edward (Edd) Pritchett (January 31, 1886 - August 23, 1978); Callie Serepta Pritchett (October 31, 1887 - August 13, 1904 buried at Mulhall); William Oswald Pritchett (stillborn September 1889 buried at Clarkson cemetery grave unmarked); Kenneth Sylvester Pritchett (February 13, 1891 - February 18, 1978); Elsie Bell Pritchett (1894 - December 23, 1927); and Seth Barrett Pritchett (September 27, 1889 - February 13, 1985).

Hattie married Howard Judson Anthis. They were the parents of six daughters: Etta, Iva, Callie Mae, Dorothy, Elsie, and Ina. See Howard J. Anthis story.

Edward married Lulu Ethel Anthis. She was the daughter of Charles and Mary (Bowman) Anthis, born on homestead southeast of Mulhall August 8, 1890 and still living in 1986. They had one child, Eddie Lou born February 11, 1925.

Kenneth Sylvester Pritchett married Pearl Florance Lyter. They had seven sons: Paul (September 29, 1911) married Lila Loula; Ervin Pritchett (1912) married Ruth Quhn; Alva Lyle Pritchett (May 31, 1914 - October 27, 1979) married Dorothy Bietler; Doyle Eugene Pritchett, his wife is Sylvia; Jack Willard Pritchett, wife Mildred; John Edd Pritchett, wife Marie; and Marvin Pritchett, married Leann Pyeatt. Kenneth and Pearl Pritchett are buried at Roselawn Cemetery Mulhall, Oklahoma.

Elsie Pritchett married Joseph R. Fitzpatrick September 1912. They moved to Los Angeles, California in 1914. They had two children Robert Eugene Fitzpatrick (September 25, 1913 - November 4, 1979) and Elizabeth Mary Fitzpatrick (November 19, 1918 - January 1, 1937).

Seth Pritchett married Vada Bell Carpenter February 26, 1921. They had four daughters: Betty Bell (Bourdette); Barbara Jean Pritchett; Beth Marie (Judkins); and Beverly June (Maple).

When J. P. Pritchett left the Kentucky home in 1865, he went down into Texas; mingled with the Indians, learned their language and fathered two sons and a daughter. The marriage was dissolved and these children were lost to the rest of the family.

Lila Loula Pritchett

By Lila Loula Pritchett

I, Lila Loula, was born July 1, 1918, at my maternal grandparent's home at 431 Elm Street in Perry. My father was Frank R. Loula; my mother was Tillie Nemec. I attended Perry High School, graduating in 1936. On June 1, 1937, I married Paul G. Pritchett, son of Kenneth and Pearl Pritchett, from north of Guthrie. He was assistant manager of the Perry Safeway store. We lived in Kansas and Texas for a short time while Paul worked in the oilfields. In 1939, we moved to the farm, where we lived and farmed until buying a home in Perry at 703 Fourteenth Street in 1952.

After moving to town, Paul worked at Oklahoma Tire and Supply as assis-

Pritchett Family about 1890 (L to R): Bell Jones Smith, Nettie Jones, Edd Jones, John P. Pritchett, Minnie E. Jones Pritchett.

312 / History of Noble County

Front Row (L to R): Hal D. Pritchett, Kenneth F. Pritchett. Back Row (L to R): Frank R. Loula, Paula Kaye Pritchett, Paul G. Pritchett - April 1952.

tant manager until March, 1955, at which time he joined the Perry Police force. He served as Night Chief, working with Police Chiefs: C.O. "Pete" Devilbiss, Gene Wood, and Orlin Johnson, until his retirement in September, 1975. He continued to raise cattle, and collect and sell antiques from our shop "Paul's Antiques." This shop was located in our present home at 1102 Fir Avenue, where we have lived since 1963. It was built in about 1928 by Fred Yahn.

In 1982, Paul was appointed Perry Police Chief to finish out the unexpired term of Mike Wolfe. At the completion of this term, he filed for and was elected Police Chief, a position he now holds.

We have three children: Kenneth Frank, born October 5, 1940; Hal Duane, born March 9, 1943; and Paula Kaye, born April 11, 1951. Kenneth is the mechanic for the City of Perry vehicles and has two children: Vickie Jean Petermann, Oklahoma City, and Kenny Dean, of Stillwater.

Hal is bookkeeper and accountant for Oklahoma Natural Gas Company here in Perry. He also farms and raises cattle on the family farms. He and Carol, daughter of Ray and Cecilia Nagel, west of Perry, have three children: Theresa Marie, a student at Central State University; Mary Catherine, a student at Perry High School; and Paul Raymond (P.R.) a student at Perry Elementary School.

Our daughter, Paula Kaye, was the first baby born in the new Perry Memorial Hospital two days after it opened. She is married to Dean Thompson, grandson of Rex and Alta Thompson, Perry, and resides in Fort Worth. She is Special Education supervisor for the Everman Independent School District.

Tharon H. Province
By John H. Province

At high noon on Saturday, September 16, 1893, my grandfather, Tharon H. Province, mounted upon a thoroughbred Morgan racehorse which he had bred and brought from Wetzel county, West Virginia, started on an historic land run near Orlando, known as the Cherokee Strip Outlet. He staked a claim on a piece of land known as SE ¼ of 34-23N-1W which is eight miles due north of Perry in Red Rock Township.

It is known that Tharon brought at least two or three Morgan horses to Oklahoma and it is believed that his oldest son, Benjamin Franklin, who was nineteen years old at the time, also made the "run" and staked a piece of land known as the NW ¼ of 2-22N-1W in Black Bear Township. Since he was not yet twenty-one years old and eligible to file for a claim, his grandmother, Elizabeth Brown (Province) Moore filed and was granted a land patent signed by Theodore Roosevelt on May 11, 1905. This was later deeded to my father, Joseph Spencer Province, and his brother, Jasper Ellsworth.

The earliest known vital records of the Province family (1767) are found in Frederick county, Virginia near the small community of Berryville, now Clarke County, Virginia. Other printed historical records place my fifth great grandfather, Thomas Province, (1757) on a Tommyhawk Claim near Redstone "Old Fort", later named Fort Burd, now Brownsville, Fayette County, Pennsylvania.

Tharon H. Province, the youngest of five children born to Benjamin Franklin Province (1819-1859) and Elizabeth Brown (1824-1908), was born March 2, 1852, near Masontown, Fayette County, Pennsylvania. He married Casandra "Cassie" Ann Rose on November 25, 1873. Later they lived in Washington and Greene Counties, Pennsylvania, and in Monogalia and Wetzel counties, West Virginia, before migrating to Oklahoma. By today's standards, Tharon would probably be known as an entrepreneur, having spent a short time living and purchasing property in Broken Arrow, Tulsa County, Indian Territory, before making the "run" in 1893. He sold the Noble County farm about 1915 and returned to Broken Arrow. There, he acquired more property, then traded it all for land in Ripley County, Missouri, with the idea of giving each of his three youngest children a homestead of their own. Now you know the rest of the story. Not one responded. It was in the height of the 1930 Depression. Grandpa died in 1932 and was buried in a small Methodist Church cemetery located on one of the pieces of land he had purchased near Gatewood, Missouri.

Attesting to being an entrepreneur, he once told me that he hired Henry S. Johnston as his lawyer for fifty dollars

Province Homestead about 1898. (L to R): Joseph Benjamin, Harriette, Jasper. Seated: Tharon and Cassie Ann.

per year. The governor later told me this was probably the worst business deal that he had ever made.

Tharon and Cassie had five children, all born in West Virginia: 1) Elizabeth Ann, born September 12, 1874, married Meade Jones. They remained in West Virginia. She died in 1951. 2) Benjamin Franklin, born September 6, 1876, married Margaret Nicewander, a Perry girl, and they lived all their lives just north of Ceres, Oklahoma. He died January 11, 1952. 3) Harriette Francis, born December 6, 1881, married (1st) John H. Dunlap in Pennsylvania. He was killed in a train accident. She married (2nd) Samuel Sanderson and lived in Kansas. She died January 1, 1961. 4) Jasper Ellsworth, born May 3, 1883, never married. He died May 7, 1965. 5) Joseph Spencer, my father, born July 8, 1884, married Willa Lenora Bagby on December 25, 1906. He died May 15, 1964, and she died November 9, 1954. Both are buried in Grace Hill cemetery, Perry, Oklahoma. To this union seven children were born: 1) John H., born October 8, 1907, married Helen D. Green of Magnolia, Arkansas. We have one daughter, Marilyn Ann, who married Hugh Douglas Braymer of Oklahoma City. 2) Hattie Lucille, born January 6, 1909, married Earl Nolen Gaines of Crossville, Alabama. They had two children, Earlene, who married Edward Chatham, and Earl Nolen, Jr. Lucille married (2nd) John L. Clements. All live near Renton, Washington. 3) Helen Josephine born October 5, 1911, married Chester L. Burke, a Perry boy, and they had two children, Wilma Lee who married Torsten Arthur Burgerson, Jr. and Billy Joe. Helen died March 21, 1980, and is buried in Grace Hill. All lived in California or Arizona. 4) Hazel, born September 12, 1911, and died December 18, 1926, by asphyxiation in a tragic bathroom heater accident. She was attending Perry High School at the time. 5) Maxine Olive, born November 21, 1914, married

Cassie Ann and Tharon H. Province 1912.

Willa Lenora (Bagby) and Joseph Spencer Province wedding December 25, 1906.

William Caney "Bill" Hartman and they have two sons, Billy Mac, who married Joan Powell of Perry and Joe, who married Lindsey "Lindy" Merrill of Bartlesville. Maxine and Bill are the only ones who have remained "loyal" and lived in Noble County and Perry all their lives. 6) Nellie Mae, born November 22, 1916, married (1st) Maurice Erwin and (2nd) Murl D. Brown. Nellie died January 12, 1974. They had no children and lived in California. 7) Raymond Spencer, born August 6, 1927, married Cora Belle Junkins of Lucien and they have three children: Raymond Spencer, Jr., who married Patricia Diane Sanborn, Steven, who is single and a large oil tanker captain, and Timothy, who is a student at the University of California at Los Angeles. All live in California and Washington State.

Elizabeth Province Moore, my great-grandmother, deeded "her" farm to my father, Joseph Spencer, and my uncle, Jasper Ellsworth. She then returned to Washington County, Pennsylvania. I was born on this farm, which was later known as the old Voss place. The family doctor was Dr. Keeler of Perry. Our immediate neighbors were the Undernehr, Prentice and Schlitz families.

We then seemed to start moving eastward in one-mile increments. First, to the old Mossman place where my sisters, Lucille and Helen, were born. Dr. Coldiron of Red Rock was the family doctor. I can remember when my sister Helen was born. My father saddled the pony about midnight, went to Red Rock, and returned about four o'clock in the morning with Dr. Coldiron, who drove a buggy with two horses. Could you imagine that now! Our neighbors were Anton and Joe Prusa and the Graham and Hynek families.

We then moved another mile east to the Minor farm where my sister Hazel was born. Again, Dr. Coldiron. Our neighbors were the Cermacks.

Our next, and last, move in this area was another mile east into the Otoe Indian Reservation on a place owned by George Hoogadora. It seemed that land was easier to lease there, but there were also no fences. So part of the deal usually meant building three-barb-wire fences. And you can't imagine how many post holes that meant digging, and wire stretching. No winter rest, for sure.

My sisters, Maxine and Nellie, were born there. Again, Dr. Coldiron. Our neighbors were the Dicksons, Kellys and Bowmans, along with our landlords, the Hoogadoras, Raymond and Robert Gawhega, and our other Indian friends, Eva Wildbird, Sussie Redeagle, Jim Arkekehta and the Truman Dailys.

The family was fairly successful in this area, both in cattle and farming. We had one of the first gasoline-kerosene-engine farm tractors and threshing machines. (The Dicksons much earlier had steam engines and threshing equipment.)

I can remember one year about 1916 that the drought was so bad and the pond water so low that my dad sold most all of his cattle to a Perry cattle buyer by the name of Whitney. And that very night we had the biggest rain of the year.

I also remember that in 1918 (the end of World War I) wheat was three dollars a bushel. Instead of hauling the new grain crop to the elevator in Red Rock and selling, my dad put in another crop. By the time he got around to hauling and selling, the price was down to a dollar and ten cents a bushel and he had about 8,000 bushels in storage.

He then bought the old Huntzinger farm ten miles southwest of Perry and remained there until about 1960.

The Economic Depression of the 1920s and 1930s never let the farmers fully recover. Wheat was selling for $.90 a bushel and oats for $.15 a bushel, and you couldn't go far on that. My high school allowance was $1.00 per week above room and board.

I am not sure how we would have made it without our many Perry friends and merchants, namely, Hershel Stroud (always a friend of the poor); Emmett Delaney, a U.S. Marshal; Crowder and Johnson, our grocers; Jones Produce, where we sold our cream and eggs; the Malzahn Blacksmith Shop (Gus) who sharpened the plow shares; and, of course, the bankers where you borrow $25.50 for a buck a month.

We wouldn't have had it any other way and will always be eternally grateful to our pioneer ancestors.

Leopold Radgowsky

By Millie Highfill

Leopold Radgowsky was a member of a royal Russian family which made its home at Odessa before World War I and the Russian revolution. He spent six years in the Odessa conservatory and as a graduation test, when he was only 18 years old, he led a symphony of 125 pieces.

The following year, Radgowsky was made leader of the Imperial Russian band, similar to our Marine band. He played for the former Czar four times, and received his compliments. He would smile wistfully as he talked of how the small czarevitch loved music so much that he'd stand breathless while the band played, and then would ask a hundred questions and try to blow the French horn.

The war came on and Radgowsky joined the artillery, taking his band with him to the front for four years. During

(L to R): Raymond, Nellie, Maxine, Helen, Lucille, John, Willa Lenore and Joseph S. Province.

Professor Radgowsky.

the war, his entire family was killed. In lulls he and his musicians would travel up and down the line, playing to keep up the army's courage. The revolution started and Radgowsky fled. The rest is in darkness as he couldn't talk about it, except he found himself in Prague, Czechoslovakia, leading the life of an ex-Russian with plenty of money. Suddenly, the ruble was nearly worthless and he had pockets full of paper money that wouldn't buy a cup of coffee, but he had his music. He went to Paris and started all over, with a Russian band he collected there. They went to London for a winter's season and there the Miller brothers of the 101 Ranch hired them.

Radgowsky stayed two years and Bert Shaw, a barber and musician convinced him that Perry was a good place to live. Shaw took him one afternoon and they trotted from house to house in Perry asking for music pupils. They obtained eight and Radgowsky stayed. Soon pupils drove in from all the counties around and Radgowsky taught from breakfast until bedtime, conducted the high school band, a drum corps and the Perry Symphony.

He started with one English word "Howdy-do", but Bert Shaw knew enough French to get through to the Russian and Radgowsky at the end "had a fasicinating accent and a mere shortage of vocabulary." He always had trouble with his English. Instead of saying uppity, he said his students were "high in the head." His students could always please him by asking for vanilla ice cream, which he thoroughly loved. Radgowsky died April 19, 1938 in Perry, Oklahoma and is buried in the Grace Hill cemetery.

Albert C. Ratliff

By Jessie Lee Ratliff

Albert Carr Ratliff was born in Annapolis, Missouri, March 5, 1885. His parents were Carrol Walter and Lucinda Meade Ratliff. He had an older sister Mary (Sullins) and three younger brothers: Walter, Mose and Hansel.

In 1893, the family left Missouri in a covered wagon and made the tiring trip to Oklahoma. At the opening of the strip, Carrol Ratliff made the run and filed a claim at what became Ceres, Oklahoma. The Ceres Baptist Church still stands on the north west corner of their place. The farm is now owned by Dr. Laverne Ratliff and is farmed by his brother, Orla.

Albert grew up helping his father on the farm. His education was limited to the first six grades. He attended Longview rural school when he was not needed to help on the farm.

On July 16, 1905, Albert and Bessie Rose Jones were married at Ceres by Rev. James Eldridge, the pastor of Ceres Baptist Church. Bessie was the daughter of pioneers, Jay and Nancy L. Jones, who had come from Kansas and filed their claim east of Billings on the quarter where the Glenrose school was built. Prior to her marriage, Bessie had taught for two terms in a rural school west of Perry.

The young couple lived west of Red Rock until buying a quarter section of land located six miles north east of Red Rock. They moved there in 1922, with their two sons: Jay Carol, and Erwin Earl. In November, 1922, another son, Alfred Keith was born.

After a lingering illness, Bessie died on July 7, 1935. She is buried in the Ceres Cemetery. On July 30, 1938, Albert married Hazel Nash, a family friend from Topeka, Kansas. They continued to live on the farm until his health failed. On January 5, 1957, they moved into Red Rock where they lived until Albert passed away on December 2, 1958. He, too, is buried in the Ceres Cemetery.

Albert Ratliff and family were faithful members of the Baptist Church. Albert served his community in many ways. He was serving as board member of the Red Rock Farmers Co-op when he gave up farming due to failing health. He also served as a school board member in his rural school district. In his younger days he was very active in the Odd Fellows Lodge.

His family consisted of three sons. Jay Carol was born in 1907, Erwin Earl was born in 1911, and Alfred Keith was born in 1922. Jay and Earl became farmers in the Red Rock area. Keith was employed by Continental Oil Company at Ponca City. He is retired and lives at Heavner, Oklahoma. Jay and Earl remained in the Red Rock area.

Jay married Jessie Lee Worley of Sallisaw in 1936. They had three children, Nancy Carol (Robertson), Mickey Jay, and Margaret Ann (Buntt).

Earl married Helen Domeny of Red

Albert and Bessie Jones Ratliff - 1905.

Rock in 1937. They had two children: Bobby Gene, and Carolyn Sue (Davis).

Keith married Lorraine Copeland of Mineral Springs, Arkansas, in 1945. They had two sons, Donald Ray, and Rickey Neal.

All of Albert's grandchildren are married and so far there is a total of fifteen great-grandchildren and one great-great-grandchild. Hazel Nash Ratliff, age 96, is a resident of the Ponca City Nursing Home.

Carrol Ratliff

By Linda Ratliff

The feeling of being caught in a hopeless situation led to the decision that helped determine the destiny of the Ratliff families that now live in Noble County. Carrol Walter Ratliff and Lucinda Meade were married June 15, 1875, in Iron County, Missouri. Times were difficult for everybody but they had the spirit we've come to admire in the early pioneers.

When the logging company where he worked started paying for work done by script to their company store that wasn't good anywhere else, they began to look for a way out. Carrol began to farm and raise some hogs, and after a while had saved enough money to feel they could strike out on their own.

By March 1893, their family had grown to include one daughter, Mary Jane, now 12, and four sons, Albert Carr, age 7, Walter Lemroe age 5, Mose Aaron age 2, and Hansel Engledove, six months. The birth of Hansel left Lucinda very weak and a near bed patient the remainder of her life.

With many hopes and dreams for his family, they started for a new life with all they owned in a logging wagon loaded with salt pork, a few pieces of furniture and a cot for Lucinda.

Carrol Ratliff family - Front Row (L to R): Mose Aaron, Lucinda, Carrol, Hansel Engledove. Back Row (L to R): Albert Carr, Walter Lemroe, and Mary Jane.

Most of the responsibilities usually handled by the wife and mother fell to Mary. The boys were expected to do their share of chores as they traveled too.

The logging wagon soon proved to be too cumbersome for the rough prairie. The family met a young man returning to Missouri from the wilderness of Indian Territory with a lighter wagon. By mutual agreement, they transferred all belongings from one wagon to the other and continued on their separate ways.

They also encountered two very young teenage boys trying to make their way back to their family in Texas. The boys were glad to have the companionship of a family and stayed with them until they reached the Walnut River. The boys were a real blessing as they would help provide food by hunting rabbits or catching a mess of fish for supper.

When they reached the Walnut River, near Arkansas City, the made camp and stayed there a week doing laundry and resting for the remainder of their trip. It was while they rested that the young men traveled on their way.

They came into Oklahoma from the southern part of Kansas. When they reached Red Rock Creek, the Indians had set up a toll bridge. With very little money, they elected to find another way to cross the creek. After they crossed up stream, they continued south toward Perry and camped on the Black Bear Creek.

As they traveled south they hoped to find a way of earning some money. The hope soon faded as they found no place to work in Oklahoma City, which was only about four years old at that time. The journey that started in March ended in May near Purcell where Carrol bought a plow and broke sod for $1 an acre to have a little income for his family.

Lucinda's health didn't improve. The family survived by doing without so she could have needed medical care.

In September, as they camped near Guthrie, Carrol left his family in the young hands of Mary and Albert. He borrowed a horse and rode from Mulhall to Ceres trying to decide where to stake his claim. As he rode north of Red Rock Creek, he could see a cloud of dust in the sky from riders riding from the northern border. Knowing he needed to make a decision soon, he staked his claim where the Ceres Baptist Church now stands (NW ¼ 14-23N-1W).

The family lived in a borrowed dugout along Red Rock creek near the homestead after the run. Lucinda had to be treated by a doctor that would visit from Red Rock. He told them she could not survive if she didn't get better medical care.

A neighbor, who had lived in Guthrie before the run, let the family rent one of his houses there for $2 a month so Lucinda could regain part of her failing health.

For the next two years, the family lived in Guthrie. Carrol earned money by hauling water at 10ᶜ a barrel. The family saved until they had enough to buy a cow and twelve hens for when they moved back to the farm.

Each summer Carrol went to the farm to plant pumpkins, watermelons and corn which was sold.

In September 1895, he moved his family back to the property where he staked his claim. They lived in a dugout until a one-room house could by built.

The fruits of this family continue today in Noble County and across the United States. Carrol lived until July 6, 1923, dying at the age of 67 from lock jaw. Lucinda survived him by six years. She died August 3, 1929, at the age of 74. Thank God for the courage and fortitude of these people to whom so many owe their lives!

Erwin Earl Ratliff
By Helen Ratliff

Erwin Earl Ratliff was born March 18, 1911, three miles west of Red Rock, Oklahoma, Noble County, the son of Albert Carr Ratliff and Bessie Rose Jones Ratliff. He was married May 16, 1937, to Helen Josephine Domeny, born May 16, 1918, daughter of Harry Owens Domeny and Bessie May Fowler Domeny. This marriage took place in the couple's little farm home. This home was a small frame house bought for $125.00 from the old Three Sands oil field and moved to Earl's father's farm.

Earl raised wheat, oats and cotton. He had several blacks hired to work and pick the cotton. The threshing machine did the threshing of grains. Earl would help Helen peel potatoes late at night after the supper crew had been fed, to feed the sixteen crew members that would be setting at the breakfast table early the next morning. Having no refrigerator nor one modern convience made feeding the hired hands quite a struggle.

We started milking a few cows in early marriage. Ran the milk through the hand-crank cream seperator. When we got a five gallon can of cream, Earl would take it to the train in Red Rock and ship it to Blue Valley Creamery Co. in Wichita, Kansas. One of the cream cans sits in the home today (forty eight years later). The mail carrier was watched for each morning to see if that cream check for less than $2.00 would be in the mail. That check would buy a lot of groceries, probably a pair of needed shoes or we would put some of it in the bank.

Earl's father, Albert, was a widower. He married a year after we did in June, 1938, to a lovely school teacher, Hazel E. Nash, of Topeka, Kansas.

October 15, 1941, Bobby Gene Ratliff, our first child, was born in Ponca City, Oklahoma. It had been raining several days and was still raining when Bobby decided he wanted to enter the world. It was 11:00 pm; Earl's dad got on the tractor and followed us to the highway that is now 177. It was a mud and sand road with many mud holes along the way. North of the Salt Fork river bridge our car drowned out. Earl went to a house near by and almost couldn't convince the people he needed a pull "real bad" and that his wife was in the car and was on the way to the hospital to have a baby. The man was finally convinced and gave us a pull.

Carolyn Sue Ratliff, our second child, was born October 9, 1943, in Ponca City, Oklahoma. October 1948, a 320 acre farm was for sale. We bought this farm

(L to R): Helen Ratliff, Carolyn (Ratliff) Davis, Earl Ratliff, and Bobby Ratliff Sr. - January 1986.

three miles north and ¼ west of Red Rock, S½ of 34 24N 1E and moved on it November, 1948. We were in the Marland school district. Bobby and Carolyn both graduated from Marland in 1959 and 1961 respectively. Earl and Helen attended both Red Rock and Marland schools. About 1952, we bought eighty acres of farm land E½ of SE¼ Sec 12 23N 1E.

Many busy years were spent with the children and their activities such as school sports, 4-H and FFA. We were never too busy to attend the weekly church services at Ceres Baptist church 13 miles north of Perry, Oklahoma on US 77. Earl attended this church from an infant going in a wagon until 74 past years now. Earl is a former member of the Northern Oklahoma Hereford Breeders Association and the Red Rock Sportsman Club. Helen is a member of the Red Rock Eastern Star and was an adult 4-H leader for 25 years.

Bobby attended college at Northern Oklahoma. He married October 21, 1961, Bessie Marie Cales born October 13, 1941. They lived east of Ponca City eleven miles for a few years on a piece of land they bought. Two children were born: Jan Marie, November 11, 1962, and Bobby Gene Jr. December 31, 1963. After buying 120 acres NW of Red Rock, Bobby moved a house on the land and moved his family to this location. Their third child, a daughter, Cindy Sue, was born January 27, 1968. Jan attended American beauty college and worked as a beautician, she is now working at Anthonys. Bobby Gene Jr. attended Ponca Vo-Tech and is a brick mason. He is now working on the new Wal-Mart store being built in Ponca City. Cindy will be a senior in Red Rock school, graduating spring 1986; she plans to attend college. Jan Marie Ratliff married November, 1984, to Ricky Lee Burk; they live west of Marland, Oklahoma on a farm. Both work in Ponca city and also farm.

After attending college at N.O.C. Carolyn Sue married September 22, 1962, Floyd Thomas (Tom) Davis born August 1, 1942. Tom worked at Ditch Witch. Two children were born: Russell Lee (Rusty) Davis May 26, 1963, and Randel Wayne (Randy) born May 6, 1966. Carolyn, Tom and sons moved to Leesburg, Florida, October 1968, to work for Ditch Witch, living there seven years. They moved back to Perry, November 1975. Tom formed the "Big D Construction Co." Russell attended Oklahoma State University and N.O.C., he is in business with his father. Russell married May 4, 1984, Cecilia Ann Schiltz, born August 26, 1963. Cecilia graduated from OSU May 1985 with a bachelors degree in business administration and is working as a marketing representative at Tabor's Inc. in Perry. Randel graduated from Perry High School May 1985 and will attend N.O.C. 1985-86.

Hansel Ratliff
Mrs. Maurine Sheets

Hansel Engledove Ratliff and Liza Mae Stockton were married August 9, 1923, in Perry, Oklahoma. Both Liza and Hansel's parents had claimed homesteads in the "Cherokee Strip Land Run".

When Hansel was born in Iron County, Missouri, on October 13, 1892, plans were being made by his parents Lucinda (Cindy) Meade Ratliff and Carol Ratliff to come to Oklahoma. In March of 1893, the Ratliff family with baby Hansel and four other children left on their journey. Carol Ratliff made "the run" and staked a claim 13 miles north of Perry in the Ceres Community where Hansel grew to manhood.

Hansel attended Longview school for six terms but refused to continue his formal education because brother "Mose" had completed the eighth grade and was finished. Hansel couldn't bear going to school with brother Mose out hunting, fishing and trapping. In the early years school attendance was not compulsory and Hansel was an outdoor sportsman. His mother, Cindy was an invalid (bedfast) from the time of his birth so after sister Mary left the home, a lot of Hansels' time was spent caring for his mother and helping with household chores. Of course he helped his father with the farm work and he learned some blacksmithing and how to repair harness, all the trades necessary for survival in the newly established land. In 1918, the clouds of the first World War were hanging over the land and Hansel received the call to the army. At this time he was 24 and single living with his mother and father on the farm.

Liza Ratliff.

He worked hard to get the wheat ground ready and part of it sowed before he had to leave. On October 3, 1917, he boarded the train in Perry for San Antonio, Texas and was attached to Company D. First Battalion, 357th Regiment, 90th Division. He was in Camp Travis Texas until leaving for New York June 10th, 1918. Arriving on the shores of France July 18, he remained in France until the end of WW I. After armistice he was stationed with the army of occupation in Germany for a period of six months arriving home in Ceres the spring of 1919. Hansel came back to live with his parents and pick up where he left off farming. In the fall of 1921, he started courting a neighbor girl, Liza Mae Stockton. Liza was the daughter of Luther (Lute) T. Stockton and Mary Bell (Nin) Mangus Stockton, who had also come to Oklahoma in the Cherokee Strip land run and had claimed land three miles west and ½ south of Ceres. Liza was born November 20, 1899, on the Stockton homestead. She attended school at Pleasant Valley for 8 years then boarded in Perry in order to further her education to train to teach school. Liza took a teaching position at I X L in the "Three Sands" oil field the fall of 1918, and taught there for one year. The following year she taught at Pleasant Valley. Much of Liza and Hansel's courting consisted of going to neighbor's homes and playing party games. Party games were played with several couples and was much like square dancing except they used no musical instruments and no caller. The music or rythym was from the group singing such songs as "Skip to my Lou", etc. Sometimes Hansel and Liza along with Liza's sister Erma and her beau Martin Diehm (the two couples

Hansel Ratliff in 1917.

double dated a lot) would go to a movie at Perry.

In the Spring of 1923, Hansel asked Liza to marry him. In August of 1923, they married and came to the old Ratliff homestead to live. Hansel's father had died in July before he and Liza were married in August so Hansel's mother lived with them until shortly before her death in 1929. When the estate was settled Hansel and Liza took the money left them and their share of the farm and bought out the other heirs so they were the second owners of the original claim.

At the time of their marriage "old Highway 77" that passed through Ceres was under construction. The building of "77" highway was quite an event. Hansel got a lot of work from the highway construction in his well equipped blacksmith shop. Mules were used on the construction for pulling all the road equipment — road graders, etc. Also in 1923, the Three Sands oil field was just beginning and horses were used there to pull wagons — there were no trucks. This also provided extra work for Hansel after farmwork and wheat sowing.

Liza and Hansel were always active in the Ceres Baptist Church. The church being located on the Ratliff farm made it handy for ministers to drop in or come for dinner after church. Liza cooked many meals for the ministers and their families.

Four children were born into the family. Maurine the oldest arrived in 1926 and three years later Orla came into the family, Glen was born in 1931, during the dark days of the depression at an estimated weight of 4 lbs. He was premature and they kept him alive by keeping him close to the kitchen stove (wood fire). Lavern the youngest joined the family in 1937. All of the children were born at home with a doctor coming from Perry or Billings.

Hansel always provided a good living for his family. Sometimes there wasn't much cash but always a place to live with plenty of wood to cook and heat the home, and plenty of food from the garden, livestock and wild game. Hansel mended the family shoes with a sewing awl and shoe last. Liza kept busy sewing, canning and cooking for threshers in addition to her regular household duties. She always took an active part in community activities and was a member of the Ceres Community Club. She helped raise the money for the Ceres Community Center.

Liza and Hansel were wonderful parents and an inspiration for their children to achieve their goals. Lavern is a family doctor at Pawnee, Oklahoma. Glen is employed by the government in Fresno, California, as the manager of a cotton classing office. Maurine is employed as a secretary in Blackwell, Oklahoma City Schools and is also a wife and mother. Orla has always been active in farming and is still engaged in farming in the Red Rock Community.

Hansel was stricken with rheumatoid arthritis in his later life and suffered severely with the disease for several years. Due to his crippled condition it was necessary for him to spend his last few months in the Perry nursing home and on August 13, 1972, he passed from this life. The day before Hansel's death his youngest grandchild, Kyle, succumbed to cancer and the family laid both to rest on the same day.

Liza moved to Perry shortly after Hansel entered the nursing home and lived at 1008 Cedar until her death April 13, 1980.

The lives of Hansel and Liza were the continuation of the dream of their parents (Lute and Nin - Carol and Cindy) had when they came to this new land. They helped enact the laws, build the roads and schools and improve the farms that helped make our state and nation what it is today.

Jay Carol Ratliff
By Jessie Lee Ratliff

Jay Carol Ratliff was born to Albert Carr and Bessie Jones Ratliff, January 13, 1907, the same year Oklahoma became a state. He received his education in the Red Rock School until his twelfth year, and due to a tutition problem between the rural school and Red Rock School, he graduated from Marland High School in 1926.

He has farmed all his life. He has been a registered Hereford breeder for over half a century. He is a charter member of the Northern Oklahoma Hereford Breeders Association.

In 1936, he and Jessie Lee Worley of Sallisaw were married in Oklahoma City by the Rev. James R. Eldridge, the same minister who married his parents in 1905. Rev. Eldridge waited with them until after midnight on April 11, so they could be married on April 12, Jessie Lee's twenty-fourth birthday. It was also a rare Easter Sunday. Easter had not fallen on that date since 1936.

Jessie Lee had attended Oklahoma A. & M. College for three years and taught

J.C. and Jessie Ratliff April 1981. Back Row (L to R): Todd and Melissa Roberson, J.C. Ratliff, Kim and Mike Ratliff. Front Row (L to R): Kelly Roberson, Jessica Buntt, Jessie Ratliff, Patricia Buntt. In Front: David Buntt.

at the Long Branch School for two terms.

They had three children. Nancy Carol was born at Stillwater, March 13, 1938; Michael (Mickey) Jay was born at Stillwater April 6, 1940; and Margaret Ann was born in Ponca City June 17, 1946.

Nancy and Mickey finished college at Oklahoma State University. Nancy married Edward Roberson, son of Earl and Ellen Roberson, of Red Rock. They have three children: Kelly Dana, Todd Michael, and Melissa Jaye-Ann. Kelly attended Miami Jr. College two years, married Beatrice Blanchard of Disney, Oklahoma, and they have a daughter, Natasha. Both work in Ponca City. Todd attended Northern Oklahoma College at Tonkawa and is employed at Ponca City. Melissa is enrolled at Oklahoma State University.

Mickey married Linda Mae Love of Red Rock, daughter of Ophie and Pauline Love. They have two children: Kimberly Beth and Michael Jay Jr. Kim has finished two years at Oklahoma State University. She is married to Ron Little of Sulphur, and they make their home in Vinita, Oklahoma. Mike is a student at Red Rock High School.

Ann attended Oklahoma State and Ponca City Business College. She married James W. Buntt of Red Rock, son of J.B. and Ruth Mary Buntt. They have three children: Jessica Ann, David James and Patricia Suzanne. All are students in the Shidler School. Ann and Jim are both employees of Phillips Oil Company. The other two families have remained with farming in the Red Rock community.

Jay remains busy with farming, but has turned the management to his son, Mickey. They live northeast of Red Rock where Jay shares his love for his Hereford cattle with his hobby of raising geese, unusual ducks and pigeons. They both enjoy their flowers, garden and lawn care.

Mickey Ratliff
By Linda Ratliff

Michael Jay Ratliff (Mickey) and Linda Mae Love were married at the First Baptist Church of Ponca City on June 2, 1962, after a long courtship of seven years.

The all important first date was a class party on March 25, 1955, when Mickey was a high school freshman and Linda a seventh grader at Red Rock. The party was a trip to Ponca City for skating and a movie. Not surprising, because of the young beginning, there was only one date that first year.

Mickey graduated from high school in 1958 and from Oklahoma State University with a degree in Agriculture Economics in May 1962. Linda

Mickey Ratliff family (L to R): Mike, Mickey, Linda and Kim in November, 1984.

graduated from high school in 1960 and from Ponca City Business College in November, 1961.

The first year and a half after marriage they lived in Ponca City, where Linda worked for a heating and air conditioning firm and Mickey commuted daily to Red Rock, where he farmed with his dad.

In August 1964, the time seemed right to move to Red Rock. A house owned by Mary Chaplin which was located just about one block south of the water tower was rented and for almost eleven years that was home. During that time two children were born. Kimberly Beth was born November 14, 1964, and Michael Jay, Jr. (Mike) was born February 10, 1970.

Although the miles weren't as long, Mickey continued to commute to the country to do his farming. They hoped to have a home in the country and bought a farm from the Morris Brown family with that hope in mind. However, Oklahoma Gas and Electric Company deemed it more important that they have the property and acquired it through condemnation in 1973. The farm is now at the bottom of Sooner Lake, located about one fourth of a mile west of the dam.

The years have been filled with work and activities for the children. Kim, for many years, was a real tomboy who really would rather have been born a boy rather than a girl. She was interested in the livestock and 4-H events from the time she was old enough to get involved. Her main interests were "boy" type projects, but with some encouragement, she also learned to sew and do some cooking. She graduated from Red Rock High School in 1983 and attended Oklahoma State University for two years. It was while a student at OSU she met Ron Little from Sulphur. Ron and Kim were married June 1, 1985, at the First Baptist Church in Ponca City.

Mike is also involved in the 4-H program and has followed his granddad's and dad's leading and developed an interest in Hereford cattle. Basketball is his first love and he lives for ball season. He has been hampered some what since a baby with asthma but has learned to make the most of it. Like many farm boys of the past, he is his dad's right hand man during the summer months helping with wheat harvest, hay, and field work.

The family is active in the activities of the First Baptist Church in Red Rock. Mickey serves as a deacon and teaches the adult men's Sunday School class and Linda teaches a children's Sunday School class.

Mickey and Linda both enjoy working with the 4-H program as adult volunteers. Mickey is a member of the Red Rock Lions Club, serves as fire chief and civil defense director for the Town of Red Rock. In 1976, Linda was appointed as Clerk and Treasurer for the Town of Red Rock and in December 1983, was employed in the office of the Red Rock Farmers Co-op.

Mickey has been a member of both the Northern Oklahoma Hereford Breeders and the American Hereford Breeders all of his adult life. He has followed his father's occupation of farmer-rancher. When time permits, Mickey enjoys hunting and fishing and Linda enjoys needle craft and sewing. As time allows, travel has become a favorite pasttime.

Orla Ratliff
By Orla Ratliff

Orla D'Wayne Ratliff was born on September 18, 1929, at Ceres, Oklahoma. He was the second child of Hansel and Liza Ratliff. Orla had the privilege of growing up on the location where his grandfather, Carrol Ratliff, staked a claim during the Cherokee Strip Run.

In March of 1951, Harry Cassell, an oil well pumper, moved his family to Red Rock from Rayville, Louisiana. This was significant for Orla because during a revival meeting at the Ceres Baptist Church, he noticed one of Harry's daughters. Orla and Betty Fay Cassell started dating and were married on November 17, 1951.

Betty was a Junior in high school when they married, but she promised her father that she would complete her education. Two months after their wedding, Orla, was inducted into the service. Betty was glad she had high school to help fill her time. It was during the spring semester of the Junior year that she found she was expecting their first child.

Betty had to drop out the first semester of her Senior year because Sheri Lynn was born on October 5, 1952. Betty kept her promise to her father and attained her high school diploma. She even had her own cheer-

Betty and Orla Ratliff in 1951.

ing section when her daughter shouted out, "That's my mommy," during the graduation ceremonies.

Orla and Betty are Baptists, and have been faithful in attending church and loving and worshipping God. Betty has been the pianist and taught a Sunday School class most of their married life, so it has been up to Orla to see that their children behaved in church. Orla serves as a deacon in the First Baptist Church of Red Rock.

Orla served two year in the United States Army. Fourteen months of this was in Korea, Headquarters Company 79th Engineer Construction Battalion 8th Army.

When he came home, they moved east of Red Rock. The location of their home was on the east edge of Noble County where Oklahoma Gas and Electric Company put their plant.

When their daughter was five years old, they moved west of Red Rock. During the nine years they lived at this location, four more children were born. Rhonda Gail born May 8, 1957; Marla Dawn born December 19, 1961; Rod Allen born September 19, 1963; and Rex Wade born January 20, 1965.

When their youngest child was a year old, they moved to their present residence which is northeast of Red Rock. April 2, 1986 will mark 20 years of living at their present home.

Orla and Betty are active in the American Agriculture Movement. In December of 1977, to draw attention to the plight of the family farm and because of low prices, farmers started tractor cades. Through the tractor cades a national organization came about called A.A.M. to lobby for better prices and try to save the family farm. In January 1979, three tractors from Noble County joined the national tractorcade to Washington, D.C. Their son, Rod, age 15, went with Orla on the tractorcade that took three weeks to get to Washington, D.C. Orla is serving as a National Delegate and also a director of the A.M.M. Political Action Committee.

Sheri married Trent Martens on December 29, 1973. They have two children, Adam Walter and Andrea Cassell. Sheri has her masters degree in Speech Pathology. The Martens' family live at Fairview, Oklahoma, where Trent is a farmer-rancher, and Sheri teaches.

Rhonda married Patrick Kelly on May 16, 1981. They have a son, Michael Brian. Rhonda is a registered nurse and works at the O'Donoghue Rehabilitation Institute in Oklahoma City. Pat works in customer relations for Oklahoma Gas and Electric Company. The Kellys live in Edmond, Oklahoma.

Rod graduated from Oklahoma State Tech, Okmulgee, and is locally employed. Marla and Rex are working toward their college degrees.

Dale B. Ream
By June Ream

Dale Birdell Ream was one of seven sons born to Henry Ream and Anna Jane Leverton in Huntington, Indiana on June 23, 1906. The family moved to Blackwell, Oklahoma when Dale was seven years old.

Widower Henry, a Dunkard, had a son and three daughters by a previous marriage. A steam engineer, he died in Blackwell as the result of a refinery accident on September 6, 1917, when Dale was eleven years old.

After the death of his father, Dale found employment with John Palm at Palm's Shoe Store where he worked until he went into his own business, opening a shoe department in Locke's Ready-To-Wear.

He later moved to McAlester and then to Ponca City where he married on September 8, 1937, Doris June DeSpain, the daughter of William Edward DeSpain and Edyth Louisa Cooke (b. June 19, 1919, in Pratt, Kansas). They became the parents of two daughters, Charlotte Ann, born January 25, 1939, and Karen Dale, born February 14, 1940.

Dale first came to Perry from Blackwell when he was 16 years old. It was at the height of the Three Sands Oil Boom. He found a summer job driving a truck, despite his mother's objections that he was too young and too small to work in the oil fields. He survived the

Home of Dale Ream - 1945.

Dale and June Ream - 1953.

first month on the generosity of a fellow worker, Faye Foster who let him share his bed & the owner of the Palace Cafe, who extended him credit for one meal a day (he chose a sack lunch) until he received his first pay check. He remained until school started and proved his point to his mother.

In September, 1941, he returned permanently with his wife and daughters as bulk agent for Continental Oil Company which was the supplier for the Beckham and Cockrum Conoco Station at the southwest corner of the square. This station had always been open 24 hours per day, but with the coming of gasoline rationing, the Federal Government also restricted the hours a station could stay open. Nothing at that station had ever been locked and when it was discovered that it would take nearly 100 locks to "close up", and those locks were not available, an appeal was sent to Washington, D.C. Permission was granted for it to stay open, making it the only "All-Night" station between Wichita, Kansas and Oklahoma City.

June learned the operation of the bulk plant in anticipation of her husband's possible departure for armed services, but due to his health and age, he was never called to arms so instead he put his energy into civic and church work. The war effort consumed a great deal of his time as the onset of World War II increased demands on individuals willing to participate in these activities at the same time that there was a constant decrease in manpower as Noble countyans went elsewhere for defense work and to serve in the armed forces. Dale was the Chairman of the Noble County War Bond sales and participated in the aluminum drives. As a bulk agent he was also involved in gasoline and tire rationing in addition to the separate financial drives involving such organizations as the Boy Scouts, Camp Fire Girls (which he later served as Council President). Red Cross and other organizations now represented by the United Fund.

June's interests were directed on a Red Cross Home Nursing Course, folding bandages and helping tend the family "Victory Garden" located south of C Street in the vicinity of the old light plant. The girls did their part by pulling their red wagon around the neighborhood with the assistance of their friend Jean Ann Lemler, collecting waste grease to be used in the manufacture of munitions. June's other activities included being a Blue Bird Leader, taking charge of the Junior Missionary Society of the Methodist Church, a member of the Marigold Garden Club, a Homeroom Mother each year and being active in the Parent Teacher's Association. The Ream family were active in the First Methodist Church, Dale and June singing in the chancel choir and the girls singing in the Juionr Choir. Dale served as President of the Board of Stewards in the 1940's and June is presently serving on the Board of Trustees. The Reams joined other interested Perryans in bringing quality musical presentations to the area, through the Colombia Concert Series. Names known later throughout the music world such as George London (later Director of the Kennedy Center for the Performing Arts), Midred Dilling (who throughout her lifetime was America's premier harpist) and Susan Reed, folk singer and zither player (later seen on the Today Show with frequency) were but a few of the artists that area audiences were privileged to enjoy as a result of these efforts.

Dale, a member of the Blackwell Masonic Lodge and President of the Lions Club was a member of the committee that during the acute physician shortage during the war, recruited Dr. J. E. Beech to Perry. Dale was also a Rotarian, a member of the Perry Golf and Country Club as well as member of the Chamber of Commerce.

Dale became the Manager of the Perry Chamber of Commerce from 1952-54 and again from 1959-65, before starting his own insurance and real estate agency. In the interim he owned and operated a shoe store on the south side of the square as well as being Executive Director for the Oklahoma Polled Hereford Breeder's Association.

His death in 1980 brought to an end a fierce commitment and loyalty to Perry and the Noble County area. He could tell you who lived on every section, North, South, East, and West, what crops they grew and how many head of cattle they ran. He understood most of the familiar connection and relationships and defended county family customs however unique. He had a rule that his family should not shop outside of Perry and that only Perry establishments be frequented. A transplanted Perryan, he had a pride in the area that he expounded to visitors. Although he paid for his girls to travel, he seldom traveled outside the state of Oklahoma preferring to experience the locally available activities.

Dorothy Swanson Reilly
By Dorothy Swanon Reilly

As the second daughter of Victor and Tony Swanson, I remember being told that on the wedding day of my mother and father, my mother's family were giving a wedding party with dancing, etc. My father left and didn't return until the next morning. He didn't believe in dancing.

Since my father had no sons, his three daughters had to help with jobs ordinarily done by boys. He loved to tinker with old cars and machinery. We always had an old car, generally a Model T Ford. He would take it apart, grind valves, scrape off the carbon that had accumulated on the head plus other things necessary to have a good running car. He also did all the mechanical work on his tractor. My brother-in-law, Walter Sparks, was amazed at all the levers that had to be pulled, pushed and what have you to get started.

My father had a tractor and threshing machine that he hired himself and a daughter out to thresh the grain of neighbors. The tractor pulled the threshing machine to the farm where the grain was to be threshed. When it was set up the tractor ran the thresher by a long belt. It was the job of the daughter to sit on the tractor and watch to see that no belts came off. If they did, she shut down the machine immediately. It was also her job to watch to see that straw was coming out of the blower. It could get clogged easily if a belt was loose or came off. As far as I know his interest in machinery was what started him threshing.

He also had a well driller and drilled many water wells. To find a good vein of water, he would "witch". He would take a forked stick, hold one fork in one hand, and the other fork in the other hand, walk around, and where the end of the stick turned down there was a vein of water. He swore by his success in using this method. My sister, Agnes, helped him when he drilled wells.

He was noted for the good watermelons he raised. He seemed to know when they were ready to be picked. He had many faithful customers in town that bought melons from him year after year. Many times people from Perry would come out to the farm and eat melons fresh from the field. One year he was able to buy a new Ford car from the melons he raised and sold.

He also did blacksmithing. He had an

Victor Swanson tinkering with one of his cars.

anvil, forge and bellow. It was my job to turn the handle on the bellow to make a hot fire. He would sharpen plow shears, etc. The iron would be red hot and he would pound it into whatever shape he needed. The blacksmith shop was just west of the cellar he built.

My sister, Thelma, remembers him building the cellar. The rocks were placed together in the shape of an arch. It still stands. I have restored it to some extent.

John J. Reilly
By Leo Reilly

John James (Jack) Reilly was born March 25, 1863, in Ireland. When his father brought he and other family members to America they settled in Pennsylvania, in the area around Centralia, which has received so much publicity the last few years because of the underground coal mine fire slowly undermining the whole community. I have been told by family members that when my father participated in "the Run" he started from Mulhall. He staked out a claim for the southeast ¼ of section 7 of Oakdale Township. This is ½ mile east of the Garfield county line. Oakdale Township was named after Mr. Dale and Mr. Oakley. The present Enid Cutoff from I-35 runs along the north boundary, with the Billings Road as the east boundary.

Government regulations required that a habitation be built and occupied six months out of the year and a furrow be ploughed around the perimeter. He constructed a sod house which was replaced by some frame buildings around the turn of the century. He married Agnes Sommars, one of four daughters of Mr. and Mrs. Fred Sommars, who lived about five or six miles northeast of Perry. She was born December 2, 1875. The other daughters were Clara, Annie (Mrs. Max Schaffer) and Julia (Mrs. John Metz). There were five sons. Albert settled just south of Chanute, Kansas. He died about 20 years ago. The four other sons did not live in this area.

Left to Right: Agnes (Sommars), Leo in crib, Fred and John J. Reilly. (courtesty of Cherokee Strip Museum - Perry)

We four Reilly boys: Fred, Leo, Owen, and Hubert, went to the Antelope Valley grade school. The building is no longer there. I still remember the longest mile in the world — or so it seemed — on a cold morning. The teachers I can recall were Earl Disney, Ernest Shoop, Mrs. Bittman, Hazel Scott, Edna Back and Hulda Fredekind. When we boys reached high school age we bought another farm, just west of Perry, in 1922, and lived on it until selling it in 1927. This the site of the Ditch Witch factory. While living on this farm our neighbors and good friend, John Mount, continued operating the first farm and lived on it until he retired. Our mother remarried in 1927 and we relocated on our step-father's farm at Westphalia, Kansas. She died in January, 1964. Our oldest brother, Fred, died in September, 1983. I retired in 1973. My wife died in January, 1978. Four of my children live in this area. A daughter, husband and family live in St. Joseph, Missouri. Owen and his wife Leeta, live in the Rio Grande Valley, Edinburg, Texas. Their children also reside in Texas. Herbert and his wife, Ruby, live in Denver, where he settled after World War II, where he served in 39th Engr. Comb Btn in Africa, Anzio Beachhead, Sicily and Italy. I remember some of the old timers discussing "how it was." A shopping trip to Perry could mean loading a wagon the day before to set out at 4:30 the next morning with a group of neighbors. To ford the Black Bear all of the horses in the caravan had to be hitched together to pull each of the wagons in turn to the other side of the stream. The routine was reversed when making the return trip with loads of lumber, etc., arriving after dark. Health care was something else. I remember when my brother, Herbert, was born about 3:30 in the morning when it was 13 below zero outside. Dr. Renfrow drove a horse and buggy 9 miles on a dark country road. On another occasion they were taking me to the doctor to treat a badly swollen jaw. We met Dr. Renfrow coming from the other direction and waved him to stop. He sat me down on the running board of a Model T on a dusty road and extracted the molar, then went on to his original call. On another occasion when my dad had returned from Kansas City from treatment after a horse fell on him the doctors decided he should have a blood transfusion, but the procedure was not yet common practice. Dr. Kreueger sent him direction by mail on how to handle it. Another exciting day was when a steam engine blew up while threshing on an adjoining farm, killing two men. In the early twenties, I was unexpectedly on the scene in Three Sands when "Hookie" Miller and "Two Gun" John Middleton were gunned down by Jackson Burns, standing less than ten feet away. Why was I so close?? I was too scared to run.

Ellen T. Renfrow
By Dr. W. Frank Renfrow

My mother, Ellen Titsworth, was born February 27, 1875 to John and Mary Titsworth near Rushville, Indiana. When she was five years old her parents moved to a farm near Sedalia, Missouri. She was married to Thomas Franklin Renfrow March 11, 1894. They moved to Oklahoma in 1894 and to White Rock in 1896 and to Billings in 1899.

My mother married when she was 18 years old. She came from Missouri in a covered wagon and moved into a 10' x 14' sod house. She lived outdoors most of the time except for cold weather and when it rained, which was all too infrequent during their first year on the homestead. Mother cooked outdoors for four or five people, most of the time.

Mother was a small person, five feet two inches in height and she weighed 108 pounds. She had asthma and was allergic to numerous foods, but she managed to live with her allergies and never complained. Her health did improve and she apparently thrived on living more or less outdoors. After leaving the claim and moving to White Rock, my sister, Irlene was born August 19, 1896. In 1899, when the Renfrow family moved to Billings, I was born May 5, 1901. I unfortunately inherited asthma and was allergic to many foods. The worst offender was milk in any form. Cow's milk, goat's milk and several forms of milk formulas caused me to have colic. They finally had to use Eagle Brand Condensed Milk to avoid adverse conditions. Irlene was blessed with very good health and did not have asthma or food allergies.

My mother soon became involved in Christian Church work and W.C.T.U. She was also active in the Lady's Aid Society. After the first Christian Church was built, mother played the organ and was president of the Sunday School and also taught a Sunday School class.

Mother raised chickens and canned lots of fruits and vegetables and kept a large cellar filled with supplies. She made hominy, shelling white corn and boiling it with wood ashes. The kernels needed lye to dissolve the hard outer coat on the corn kernels. Then she would bake the corn cobs and boil them and made syrup.

Mother was also quite active in the Lady's Auxillary of the county and State Medical Society. She was a charter member of the Oklahoma State Medical Society Lady's Auxillary.

After Dad volunteered for service in the Medical Corps of the Army in 1917, Mother and I moved to a ranch we owned in Osage County, Oklahoma. We moved into a small log cabin with no conveniences and lived there for a few months until a larger house was built. We had 880 acres of timberland and about 100 acres of farm land. We had 60 head of cattle, 50 head of sheep, 150 chickens and 30 pigs and there were also horses to care for. We also had one hired hand to help with the work.

Mother worked in the field gathering crops with us at harvest time and she also helped with the plowing. Because a large percentage of our land was rocks, it was difficult for one person to handle the plow. Mother started to raise chickens again, work in a large garden, help milk seven or eight milk cows and seperate the cream and make butter. We sold eggs, vegetables, fruit and butter to a small store in Osage. Osage was the railroad division point for the main freight line on the railroad and none of the people in Osage had gardens, cows or chickens so any fresh produce was most welcome. Mother and I were called by the "natives", "the widow and her son up on the hill." We had no source of water on the hill. We had drilled a well 350 feet deep and got no water. We got our drinking water from an Artesian well about a half mile from the house. The well was an abandoned test for oil wells. Our other water came from a small stream fed by springs. Our only transportation was by farm wagon, horseback or by walking. I walked to school at Cleveland High School which was three and a half miles on the other side of the Arkansas River.

During the winter of 1917-1918 we had a very cold spell with 18 inches of snow and sleet which stayed on the ground for six weeks. The Arkansas River froze over and we drove a team and wagon across to Cleveland instead of crossing the bridge. The ice on the little creek where we watered our stock got to be 14 inches thick. I had to go down every morning and chop out the ice to get to the water. Our hired hand had gone to Billings to bring back a freight car load of oat straw for cattle feed. He was stranded in Billings because of 24 inches of snow and could not get back from Billings.

We ran out of wood for our stoves which all burned wood. Fortunately a neighbor came up to see about us and he stayed two days. He cut up enough wood to last us three or four weeks. I had to cut hay out of the barn where it had been stored for three years, a fork full at a time. We survived and so did all of our stock.

After Dad returned from France, he decided to move to South Texas and not practice medicine. After losing all of his savings trying to make it as a farmer, Mother and Dad moved back to Billings. Mother's health began to fail because of her high blood pressure. Mother had a stroke and had some physical and mental residual damage. She was unable to be active and her general health deteriorated. On August 12, 1945, Mother complained of a severe headache and died a few hours later from a cerebral hemorrage. She was 68 years old.

Thomas Franklin Renfrow
By Dr. W. Frank Renfrow

My father, Thomas Franklin Renfrow, was born December 17, 1891 on a farm near Knob Noster in Pettis County, Missouri. He stayed at home and went to a country school until he was 13 years of age. His mother died after his 13th birthday. He left home and worked as a farm hand for neighboring farmers to make enough money to enable him to continue his education. He was rather large for his age, heavily built and quite strong. One older brother did give him some money but dad still had to drop out of school for several months so he would have enough money to study medicine at the St. Louis School of Medicine and Surgery - later the Washington School of Medicine and Surgery.

In 1893, Dad decided to make the run into the Cherokee Strip. Before leaving for Oklahoma he married my mother, Ellen Titsworth. Riding his trusty mule, he made the race and staked a claim near the present site of Covington, Oklahoma. The next morning a big rough looking claim jumper came over and told him that he had already staked that claim. Dad went into his little tent where he had a long barreled pistol, which he put inside his belt. He told the jumper to get off his claim. The man left and there was no further confrontation.

Dad sent for his wife and younger brother W. R. (Toad) Renfrow and a cousin Mark Renfrow. They came by covered wagon from Missouri bringing some furniture, farm machinery and four horses. Dad bought two oxen and with the help of his brother and cousin he built a sod house that was 10 x 14 feet. They broke land and planted wheat for the winter. It was a dry fall and winter and the wheat did very poorly. Life in the small sod house was quite crowded. Mother did all the cooking outside in a sort of lean-to porch except for rain and extremely cold weather. Dad's brother and cousin slept in a tent under the stars, weather permitting.

Dad decided to return to St. Louis in the fall of 1894 to finish his last year of school and get his degree, which he got in 1895. He and mother moved back to the claim that fall. Due to the continued poor crop prospects, they moved to White Rock and built a house and barn there. The house served as both office and home. Mother served meals to travelers and had one or two rooms to rent. The barn served as livery stable. Together they managed to make a living. My sister, Irlene, was born in White Rock in 1896. When White Rock was moved to Billings at the coming of the railroad in 1899, the Renfrows decided to move there in the same year. They hitched 12 horses to the building at White Rock and moved it to the new town about four miles from White Rock. Dad constructed stone buildings in Billings. The first was a stone two-story office building which he completed in 1900. His office was on the second floor and a bank occupied the ground floor. He built two more stone buildings on Main Street.

I was born on May 5, 1901, in the white house Dad had moved to Billings. We moved into the first rock house in 1904.

My father made many calls in the county for as many as 14 miles in all directions. In the horse and buggy days that would take about three and a half to four hours. Dad delivered lots of babies at home as there was no hospital in Billings. He would frequently spend the night at the farmer's house until the baby arrived. In the winter at night, Mother who was a poor sleeper when Dad was not home, would hear the team and buggy come home. She would get up and see that Dad was asleep and she would cover him up with a large buffalo skin lap robe. She would unhitch and unharness the horses and put them in the barn. She would led Dad sleep until he awakened the next morning.

At times in the winter the east and west roads would be closed by deep snow drifts and Dad would go on calls by horseback with his medicine bags behind the saddle. He had a heavy bear skin coat which he wore. In 1907, he purchased his first automobile, a Ford Model T. He had to do all the upkeep and needed repairs as there were no garages in the county.

Dad liked to fish and hunt. He liked good music and had a player piano and rolls of opera. He had many classical records for his Victrola. He would attend as many meetings as possible of the County and State Medical Society.

During World War I, Dad volunteered at age 48 and reported for duty at Fort Bliss, Texas in 1917. He was sent to France and Field Hospital 39 and stayed there until 1919. He was quite disturbed when he got home and no longer wanted to practice medicine. After two years in the Rio Grande Valley near Brownsville, Texas, they returned to Billings and fixed up the rock house. Dad had his office there as well as their living quarters. They converted the rock barn into apartments and for a while used them as a hospital. Mother fed the patients and served as nurse.

Mother's health was failing in the late 1930s. She had high blood pressure. She died August 12, 1945. Dad was not quite the same after her death. Although he kept working he also had health problems. He had an attack of undulant fever and he suffered a stroke in 1948. He was forced to quit medicine after 50 years of practicing in Billings. Dad was a patient in Veteran's Hospital in Little Rock, Arkansas for four years and died on July 8, 1954. My parents are buried in the Union cemetery in Billings, Oklahoma.

John Elmer Rhea
By Dorothy Durkee

John Elmer Rhea was born October 13, 1896 to Jennie Mae (Mathews) and Frank Rhea in Denton, Texas.

At fourteen his grandmother he was living with died. Her church inherited her home, so out of a home, he was out of school and on his own.

He got a job as a cowhand on the cattle drives from Texas north to market. He wasn't long discovering there were men who hitched rides on trains and had camps a short distance from the tracks. He said, "One evening I saw a chicken and thought if I can catch it I'll eat good tonight!" So I started chasing it thru the brush, suddenly looked up and there was a woman! I said, my chicken got away and darned if she didn't help me catch it."

He started working in the oilfields at Burkburnet, Texas when it was a boom town. All types of humanity were there to make money or take it away from someone who had. Late one night he took his usual route to his room. It was through a sleazy part of town. A guy with a knife said, "Give me your

Gladys Mae (Austin) and John Elmer Rhea - October 4, 1920.

money." John said he thought the man was unsure of himself and money was too hard to get to give up so easy. So John said, "This side of the street is mine, I work it! You can work the other side if you want to! To his surprise the guy said, "Yeh-Yeh-I don't want no trouble", and took off.

Don't lose your temper, and if there is a commotion and people running toward it, run the other way, were two things he impressed on we kids that he said he learned there. Losing his temper he had almost killed a man, and where a mob is there is probably violence and police. So you may get hurt or arrested.

I'm not really sure why he came to the Billings area in 1917. He started work on the Hayton farm just west of the Austin farm and was soon courting my mother Gladys Austin, in spite of her father's objections.

World War I put the romance on hold. He enlisted in the navy at Kansas City, Missouri June 4, 1918 and was on active duty until May 22, 1919. He enlisted as a Fireman 3rd Class and was a Machinist Mate 2nd Class when he was released from active duty at his request. He stayed in the Naval Reserve until September 30, 1921. He was stationed in Seattle, Washington where he was an automobile driver and mechanic in charge of repair work on motor trucks and marine gas engines.

He returned to Billings and Gladys. Charles A. Austin (born August 2, 1875 in Fayette County, Iowa) still objected, even if Gladys (born May 22, 1899) was 21. Her mother, Lillie Dott Bennett (born August 21, 1877 in Randalia, Iowa) was for them. The battle ended when Charles died September 22, 1920. John and Gladys married October 4, 1920. Their first child Dorothy Dott, was born in Billings, October 10, 1921. She married Charles Durkee and they live south of Billings. Their son Robert Elmer Rhea was born November 11, 1929, in Blackwell. His first marriage was to Ruby Maxine Abel. Three of their children live in Kay County. Robert and his wife, Mickey, and their children live in Wisconsin.

John and Gladys lived in Billings until 1926. There was a fire in their home and John was badly burned. While unable to work he got a job with Continental Oil Company so the family moved to Ponca City. He took advantage of educational opportunities offered by the company, taking such courses in Advanced Math and Language.

The company transferred them to the Unbbard lease near Blackwell. He had to give up playing on the Co. Baseball team, but his other sport swimming could be enjoyed by the family at the company pool. He taught Dorothy to swim but Gladys was content to just enjoy the water. Deciding the hours were too long, work too hard for the salary he quit and came back to Billings.

He ran a pipe line gang, then worked for Hayton and Son until WW II. They moved to Vancouver, Washington, where he worked as a pipefitter on Liberty Ships and Gladys as a cook in the shipyards cafeteria.

The war ended and back to Billings they came. He went back to work for Hayton and Son. Recreation facilities were few in Billings but he often played dominoes and checkers at the Pool Hall and was an active, loyal member of the American Legion. They both enjoyed square dancing. Gladys was again active in the Billings Christian Church and the Rebecca Lodge.

They were divorced in 1946 and Gladys married W. V. Montgomery, whom she had fell in love with and went to live in Ponca City.

John married Elva Lanham. She was a young widow the age of his daughter with five children, Donald, Bonnie, Jerry, Ruth and Linda.

He enjoyed the children and I believe they loved him as they still remember him on Memorial Day.

I can only guess why they divorced, I don't think they even knew for sure. I believe she really loved him but he couldn't believe she was satisfied with an old man.

John was working at Haytons when he became ill. He worked until July 7 and died of lymphatic cancer July 22, 1961. He is buried at Perry's Grace Hill cemetery.

Gladys worked in cafes and owned ones in Tonkawa and Ponca City as long as she was physically able.

She was injured in a car wreck in 1973 and never really recovered. She suffered a number of strokes and she died July 28, 1974 from a stroke. She had joined her husband Monty in the Catholic Church.

It had been agreed that she would be buried by John and Monty by his first wife. One can only guess why she is buried at the Union cemetery at Billings beside her father.

Bartholomew Ringler
By George W. Hall

Bartholomew Ringler, a name little known to the people of Perry was the formal christening given by the parents of a baby born at Rockport, Indiana, January 4, 1858, and thus dignified, he started his journey in life. However, he was too intensely human for form and ceremony even in name and soon adopted the flexible derivative of "Barney". Thus, it was as Barney Ringler the people of Perry knew and loved and honored him.

Barney and Miss Lena Fest were married January 9, 1886, and in that year established a home in the historic village of Medicine Lodge, in Barbour County, Kansas.

Barney was a natural pioneer and he soon passed on to Las Vegas, New Mexico, and from thence to Trinidad, Colorado, but all of the time was interested in the development of the new Oklahoma Territory and joined the home seekers at the opening of the Cherokee Strip and settled in Perry. Barney discovered that the lot he staked on during the run was an alley, so after all his efforts of going through the run, he ended up having to buy the lot next to the alley at Fifth and Fir.

Barney built his home on Fifth and Fir, and opened his shop on the south side of the square. In business, Barney was an artisan of high order in the making of men's and women's boots and shoes and he was also a skilled taxidermist and was blessed with mechanical ingenuity in numerous and varied lines.

Barney and Lena prospered, and had six children and it should be noted that the members of the family spent most of their entire lives in Perry.

Benjamin better known as "Benny" was the eldest son and was a cobbler in his father's Leather Shop. Benny loved to fish and hunt, and if he wasnt' at the shop, you could usually find him at his favorite fishing place.

Matilda Victoria (Tillie) was the next child. She worked a good many years as Chief Telephone Operator. In 1919, she married Ora Hall, a Banker in Perry. They had five children. The youngest, Barney Jackson, died at an early age. The other four graduated from the University of Oklahoma. Ora R. Jr., received his Law degree. Willa June received her degree in Fine Arts and Music. Betty Ruth received her degree in Education, and George Washington received his BS degree, majoring in Finance.

Barney Ringler's Shoemaker and Taxidermist Store. (left) Barney Ringler — (right) Benny Ringler.

Albert, the third child, became a pharmacist and had the Ringler Drug Store on the west side of the square. He served in World War I, at which time he was exposed to poison gas and died shortly after he returned from the war.

Bill, the fourth child, went into business with his father, and the shop expanded to include many other types of leather goods. He married Dolly Wadsworth, and had a daughter, Willa Lou. Bill was known for his gardening and the beautiful roses he grew, and he also enjoyed boating, hunting and fishing.

Mabel Lena, the fifth child, attended Teachers College in Oklahoma City, and after receiving her degree, taught for several years in Perry's Grade School. She married Irvin Krisher a veteran from World War I, who after the war, served as a policeman in Perry. They had three children, who were named Doris Mae, Yvonne, and Bill. Yvonne died at an early age. Bill graduated from the University of Oklahoma, where he was an All American football player; he now lives in Dallas, Texas. Doris married Leslie Poke, had two sons, and is now living in Oklahoma City.

Ruth, the sixth child, was a Beauty Queen in her senior year at Perry High school in 1921. She attended Teachers College in Oklahoma City, and after receiving her degree, taught eight years in Blackwell, Oklahoma, before marrying Loran Laughlin in 1935. They had a son, Jack, who was born in 1937. Jack was in law school in Wyoming, when his father called him back to Utah, to help in the family's Gas Distribution Business. Jack was killed in an air crash that same year.

Looking back one can see the many ways the Ringler family enjoyed the people and life in Perry. Barney played the fiddle, and was one of the best callers at square dances in Noble County. Mabel and Ruth played the piano during the Silent Movie Era. Mabel taught Rhythm Band to the little ones; Tillie was active through the years in Study Club and Garden Club. All of the Ringlers and their various families were long time members of the First Baptist Church and helped in the growth of the Church. Yes, the Ringlers and their descendants received much and contributed much to the early days of Perry, in Business, Education, Music, and most of all their ability to bring their love of life to the community.

Elmer E. Ripley
By Betty L. Ripley

Elmer Ellsworth Ripley was the son of Lewie Scott Ripley and Cordelia Jane Carrinder. His father homesteaded land near Lela. A family by the name of Schanzenbach homesteaded on the first place east of the Ripley's and their daughter, Ida, had caught the eye of the oldest son, Elmer E. They were married in 1910, and made a home NW of Lela five miles. He farmed and herded cattle on the plains in his early years. The family consisted of Lewie Scott, Elmer, Eugene, Louesa, died in infancy, Walter, Mary F., Joseph E., and Robert L.

Times were hard and their greatest loss came when Ida M. died at the early age of thirty seven on May 28, 1927. Not only was the wife and mother of the home gone, but Elmer's health had become a serious problem, as he was having great difficulty in walking. Though their future looked bleak, Elmer refused to give up any of his children for others to raise. He reared his through sheer determination, and taught them the right values, by logic and talking to them. His communication with his children was an art in itself, he had a story to tell with a moral and usually humor, for all the situations that arose, to give his position extra clout. He raised them under very difficult conditions, so talking to them was an absolute, yet he earned their respect and obedience. The children had to learn responsibility before their childhood had hardly

Barney Ringler's Shoe Shop. (left) Barney Ringler — (right) Lena Ringler.

(L to R): Lewie S. Ripley, Eugene Ripley, Mary F. Ripley, Robert L. Ripley, Joseph E. Ripley, Elmer E. Ripley Jr. - children of Elmer E. Ripley, Sr. - September, 1941.

Lewie S. Ripley
By Betty L. Ripley

Like most Americans, we trace our heritage back to the Old Country, but starting with the fifth generation born in America — Lewie Scott Ripley was born in Logan County, Illinois, on August 20, 1858, to George Washington Ripley and Martha Jane Downing Ripley. His father was "bound out" to Col. Isaac R. Braucher, after the death of his mother, to learn the milling trade, at the age of eight. He was raised as a member of the family.

Lewie Scott was only three years old and sister, Florence, was one year old, when their father, George W. Ripley enlisted as a private in Co. B 32nd, Illinois Volunteer Infantry. George became a First Lieutenant, attached to the Army of General Tecumseh Sherman, under General U.S. Grant, and was wounded at the Battle of Shiloh. He was at Vicksburg, battled through Tennessee, and at the seige of Atlanta, and was present at it's surrender on September 2, 1864.

After the war, George returned to Illinois until he homesteaded in Barton County, Missouri, in 1867. He sold it to new settlers and moved further west into Kansas in 1870, and bought a farm in Montgomery County, Kansas. When they settled there, the prairie grass was tall enough to cover a wagon. With his ability as a blacksmith, carpenter and engineer, the place began to show improvements, such as a new well, the home, plus other structures. Martha was a good helpmate and mother, she made soap and candles, sewed clothes, quilts and most of the household items, as well as taught her girls. They had thirteen children, losing four as infants, leaving nine, of which two were twins. Six children lived in Pawnee County for different periods of time and four were buried at Pawnee, those being: Florence E. Ripley (Burch), Almira Ripley (Babb), Ruth Ripley (Platz), John Marcus Ripley; and their mother.

Lewie Scott had received what schooling was available, and then went back to Illinois, where he was born and worked two years. On returning to Kansas he worked on the farm of the first sheriff on Montgomery County. At twenty two, he asked his childhood sweetheart, Cordelia Jane Carrinder of Caney, Kansas, for her hand in marriage, and they were wed in 1880.

By the fall of 1888, Lewie and Cordelia had three children, Belle, Elmer Ellsworth, and George G. Though he was settled and had responsibility, Lewie had not forgotten the Oklahoma Territory to the south, and the opportunities it provided. So that winter, Lewie, his brother, Elmer, his brother-

begun. Mary, at nine became the woman of the house, the boys became the providers, by raising crops and cattle, and working in the neighbors' fields. Elmer was always very proud of his family, their accomplishments, and his heritage as "Settler Stock". Though his body became paralyzed and he was a total invalid for twenty nine years, his faculties were as keen and sharp as a needle. His spirit was always positive even though he was in pain most of the time. He treasured his children and grandchildren, family and friends. He shared his pioneer wisdom with his family in such a way, that made them proud of their heritage.

As the Depression came bringing real financial problems to all, it too was lived through and the real worth of people was shown. As though this was not enough of a test to meet, on it's heels came the "Dust Bowl". Many words were written, by many writers, mostly those that had not lived through it, so lots of times a slanted viewpoint was given. The courageous people that existed through those awful days would tell you, they still felt the land would again, give them their dreams. They had to abide by their faith and the words, "this too shall pass...". Many were unable to do this, and packed up and moved away, while the others coped with their situation, and held on, like that preverbal bulldog, to what they had sacrificed for. Even though the "Dust Bowl" days required survival, it coined the word "Okies" meant to be degrading, by some. But the true "Okies" proved it was a name to be proud of, by remaining in the state, and fighting for independence, by being dependent on the God given land.

Elmer and his family moved a few miles north into the Otoe Country in 1930 — here the "kids" attended the one room school called "Lone Star" — just a short distance from home. Again sadness came to Ripley's in the death of Walter, on September 9, 1941.

Then came World War II to shatter many future plans or at least, set them aside. It touched everyone, in some fashion, and the Ripley's were no different. Their patriotic heritage found all five of Elmer's sons joining in Uncle Sam's service, and this left a daughter and two daughters-in-law to care for Elmer and the home front. Lewie and Eugene joined the Navy C-Bees, Elmer and Robert went into the Army, and Joseph into the Air Corp. The words Admiralty, Aleutians, Okinawa, Iwo Jima, N. Guinea, Rhineland, Germany, Italy and Yugoslavia became very familar to Elmer, as he closely followed the news daily.

With prayers answered, all five sons returned safely, to pick up their lives again, in thanks and peace. Lewie went back to his career as a welder, he and his wife Grace lived in Liberal, Kansas, until they retired and moved to Perry. He still owns the place next to the home place on the west, having lived there until a fire took their home. Eugene bought the home place from his sister, Mary, when she moved to Arizona with her husband, William C. Eakin. Eugene married his brother-in-law's sister, Stella, and they still own and reside on the homeplace. Elmer and his wife Georgia, lived south of Lela on a farm in Pawnee County and in Wichita, Kansas until he retired in Perry, Oklahoma. Joe has been in the selling business in Perry, he and his wife Betty, lived there 38 years. Robert owns the homestead and half section that his grandfather, Lewie S. Ripley had. Elmer E. Ripley passed from this life on February 15, 1960, and is buried in the Lela Cemetery, by his wife and two children. He leaves a legacy of his proudest possessions — one daughter, five sons, ten grandchildren, twenty one great-grandchildren, and three great-great-grandchildren.

Back Row (L to R): Lewie S. Ripley, his father Elmer E. Ripley Sr., George G. Ripley and India Ripley. Front Row: William Ripley, Robert Ripley, Homer R. Ripley, Lewie S. Ripley Jr., John L. Ripley, Lewie S. Ripley Sr., Cordelia J. Ripley and Cordelia Ripley - 1908.

in-law, and his uncle went into this land to hunt furs, but mostly to examine the land. They travelled by covered wagon, loaded with supplies to get through the winter. They forded the Arkansas River, where Ralston, Oklahoma is now, and went south until they came to the Pawnee Indian Agency. By following the Black Bear Creek west about 10 miles, they set up camp along the Bear, and were now two miles south of Otoe land, and three miles west of the Pawnee reservation. Lots of wild game, furs, plenty of grass, and water available, and with the Indians peaceful and friendly, it surely would be a great place to make a home. In the very early spring they headed home, sold their furs on the way at Arkansas City, Kansas, and were feeling excited about this enticing land. They had made friends with the Indians and other families scattered in the area, but summer was needed at home, to prepare for the return journey with their families.

Lewie later helped survey the land for the Cherokee Strip opening, by measuring 160 acres buried a large marked rock at each corner to designate the allowed acreage. Returning to the spot they hunted in, Lewie, his brother, Elmer, his sister Florence's husband, Charlie Burch, and their families were among eight white families that lived in the area, later known as Lela, south of the Black Bear Creek. Feeling that before long this land would be opened up too, a dugout was called home, until they were able to help each other build log cabins. The US soldiers stationed at Fort Reno burned the settler's cabins, after setting out their belongings, but not to be driven away, they settled again in dugouts.

When the required time to leave the Indian Territory was drawing near, Lewie made arrangements to rent land from an Indian friend, William Morgan. For a space on the Indian allotment, Lewie built a one room log cabin, storage area, and dug a well. He felt his family was safe on Morgan's land since he was a friend and he had been the first Indian to take up the white man's dress and ways. Other Indians, in the area he had made friends with, were members of the Chou-Wee Band of the Pawnee tribe. War Chief, at that time, was their chief. Lewie had learned to speak their language well enough to communicate very well, and spent time with the Jake's. His friend Jake called Lewie by his second name, Scott. When Jake heard about the Run, he wanted to help his friend "Scott", to be sure he was able to settle near by, he wanted to meet Ripley halfway with a fresh horse and trade horses, but when Lewie told Jake he couldn't do that, that was against the rules, Jake could not understand, "why, you couldn't trade horses whenever you wanted to?"

In making preparations for the Run, Ripley traded his team of horses for a thoroughbred stallion, he called "Fred". The horse was trained like a race horse, by being run for long distances to improve his speed and strength. The day came and Ripley was ready, he and "Fred" headed for the location he had in mind to homestead, and did. It was three miles south of Lela, it had a natural spring on it, and would make a good place for his family. He filed his claim in Perry, county seat of Noble County. Lewie did not want on the Black Bear because of the danger of flooding; his family had already escaped this threat while Ripley was gone. A Texas outlaw, by the name of "Three Finger Jake", was camping in the vicinity, when the Bear flooded, he remembered passing the dugout and rode back to awake Cordelia and her four children. Though he was an outlaw, he had compassion for a woman and children.

The Dalton Gang camped and rode through that area as well. One morning when Ripley was up early looking for a milk cow that had strayed, he came upon the Camp of the Dalton's. Leader Bob Dalton said, "You're up kinda early aren't you, Lew?", "Well, I'm not up any earlier than you are, and I'm a lot closer to home!"

At last Lewie Scott Ripley and family was settled into a permanent home. The family grew, eleven in all, a house had been built, and improvements made a fine homestead. Later he bought the half section north, paying 20 percent interest rate. This homestead and half section is still owned and lived on by a grandson, Robert L. Ripley.

A. L. Ritthaler
By Kathryn Ritthaler

Ludwig and Elizabeth (Schweitzer) Ritthaler, together with seven children, immigrated to America from the province of Galicia in Austria-Hungary in 1885. They settled near Halstead, Kansas, where four more children were born.

Eight years later, the Cherokee Outlet in Oklahoma was opened to white settlement and three members of this family entered the race for land on September 16, 1893: Ludwig, his eldest son, Jacob; and his future son-in-law, Peter J. Schmidt. Peter married Margaret, the eldest Ritthaler daughter, in 1896.

Peter sought employment on a cattle ranch owned by the Goering brothers — my father, John C., and his brother, Joe C. Goering. The young couple moved into the upper rooms of our home at Moundridge, Kansas. My mother, Marie, and Margaret, became bosom friends and shared the work.

The Schmidt's first child, a son, was born June 19, 1897. He was named John in honor of my father. My mother, Marie, was expecting her child in the fall, and Margaret sewed baby clothes for that child. I, Kathryn Frances (Goering) Ritthaler, was that child. I

Al and Kate Ritthaler.

was born October 31, 1897, and inherited those clothes. We couldn't have known we would become future sisters-in-law.

The Ritthaler families left Kansas in 1897, traveling in covered wagons, crossing creeks and rivers minus bridges, fearing reprisals in the Indian territory, where homes were dugouts and log cabins. The three claims were located east of Perry. Elizabeth was a strong fearless character despite her small stature, and swift, airy butterfly movements. Although communication with her family continued she did not see them again after immigrating to the United States. The Ludwig Ritthalers donated the southwest corner of their claims to the Zion Lutheran congregation, for a church and so the first Lutheran church in Noble county was born. It still carries the name of Zion Lutheran to this day.

A widow and her son, Bill, named Dalton, were neighbors of the Ritthalers. Bill would suddenly disappear and be gone for weeks and would return at night. Reaching Mule Creek, Bill would give a loud weird cry, and one of the Ritthaler brothers would say, "Old Bill is back home." Bill was a pro with guns, he was swift and sure handling fire-arms, and never missed a target. He and the brothers would race the horse, shoot at cans placed on fence posts and Bill never missed.

August Ludwig Ritthaler, youngest member of Ludwig's family, is known as Al Ritthaler, in Noble county. Al was on his own at 12 years of age. Ludwig, his father, was deceased, March 7, 1909. He lived about sixteen years after Al was born, October 10, 1893, and most of his childhood was spent in Noble county. At a very young age, he was hired as driver for Dr. Will Brengle, whose patients were scattered throughout the county. During the severe diptheria epidemic, Dr. Will and Al were out day and night trying to save the children. Many deaths occured because anti-toxins were unavailable.

Al's summers were spent in Kansas harvesting wheat. We met in Moundridge, Kansas, and were married April 29, 1917, in my home. My father, Rev. John C. Goering, was officiant. Our daughter, Lucille Kathryn, was born in Castleton, Kansas, July 11, 1918. No matter where we were, the Oklahoma hills always called us back. In 1923, Al bought two trucks and initiated the first transfer line in Perry, hauling freight for the businessmen. Freight was brought in by the Santa Fe train. Later, when it was brought in by huge overland trucks, directly from the factories, Al sold his trucks.

We also managed a small grocery store for a time. We were members of the Presbyterian church, where we were actively involved. He held the office of Elder and Deacon, and served on many committees while I served in the music department of the church.

Al commenced working as a volunteer at the Perry fire station, February 1, 1931, and was appointed as Assistant Fire Chief, September 1, 1931, by mayor, Fred Kretch. He served until February 23, 1946. Later we moved to Stillwater, to be near our daughter, Lucille Graham. After a severe seige of illness, Al was deceased March 23, 1964. He is interred in Grace Hill cemetery at Perry, Oklahoma. I am still living at age 88, in Stillwater, Oklahoma.

Residing in Perry was a happy time for us. We are grateful for the privilege of being a part of the activities there. In fact we deserted the Kansas Jay Hawks and joined the Oklahoma Sooners.

Frank F. Ritthaler

By Mary Ellen Ritthaler Smelser

Frank F. Ritthaler was born April 6, 1886, in Halstead, Kansas. His father was Ludwig Ritthaler and his mother was Elizabeth (Schweitzer) Ritthaler. He moved with his family to Oklahoma in September 1893, when he was seven years old. He was not old enough to participate in the Cherokee Strip opening, but he did watch it from a hillside, he said.

Soon after moving to Noble County, the whole family fell ill, possibly with influenza. Mr. Orlando Walkling lived near the family at that time. He stayed with them until they were well and saved their lives. Mr. Walkling was a very remarkable man and was still earning his own living at the age of 106.

My father engaged in farming when he became of age. He had a farm about six miles east of Perry. Everytime he passed the place, when I was a child, I remember he referred to the farm as "Poverty Knob."

Frank Ritthaler was married to Alice Barnes, daughter of Dick and Emma Jane Barnes, in the Barnes home, two miles east of Perry. The date of the marriage was February 17, 1909. Alice was born May 24, 1885, and died January 20, 1919, after giving birth to three children, Emma Marie on December 6, 1909, Richard William on February 11, 1916, and Retta on June 19, 1917.

Frank Ritthaler worked as a deputy County Assessor for some time in Noble County. In 1920, he was appointed County Tax Assessor when the incumbent County Assessor died. He retired from the position of County Tax Assessor in December, 1948, after having campaigned for the job every two years and winning against some tough opponents. I remember his political speech consisted of "I would appreciate it if you would vote for me." That was all. My father was a Republican and there has always been a majority of Democrats in Noble County, so he proved to be a popular County Tax Assessor, to his credit. After he retired as Tax Assessor, he went to work for the Perry Daily Journal as the farming correspondent. He enjoyed this job very much and his only complaint was that people wouldn't let him go. They kept visiting with him long after his business with them was over.

Emma Marie Ritthaler and Raymond Gatewood were married on May 10, 1931. They had seven children. Tommy was born August 21, 1934, Alice on November 11, 1935, Bob on December 19, 1937, Jim on March 21, 1941, Larry on April 21, 1946, Billy on December 19, 1947 and Linda on June 8, 1949. They now reside in Wyandotte, Oklahoma, where they have a large farm with Champion Limousin cattle. Their children have distinguished themselves as farmers, bankers, engineers and Mary Kay champion salespersons.

Richard William Ritthaler married Carol Bobbitt on November 17, 1942. Carol's father was a grocer in Perry for many years. His grocery store was on Sixth Street. Richard and Carol had two children. Rickie was born on April 6, 1946, on her Grandfather Ritthaler's birthday. Grandpa Ritthaler was very fond of Rickie and enjoyed playing with her immensely. Richard and Carol's son, Chris, was born June 25, 1949, in his Grandmother Ritthaler's kitchen. Richard Ritthaler retired from Shell Oil Company after working for Shell almost thirty years. Chris is now a speech pathologist in public schools in Jefferson Parrish, Louisiana. Rickie is a computer operator for an insurance company in Oklahoma City and a Mary Kay salesperson.

Retta Ritthaler married Otto Marshall on March 14, 1937. Retta worked hard to help her husband become a minister. They had one son, David Marshall, who was born January 6, 1938. David is now a Professor in a Christian Church College in Grand Forks, North Dakota. He has a Ph.D. in Linguistics. Retta died in childbirth in Temple, Texas on October 19, 1940.

After the death of Alice Barnes Ritthaler, my father stayed single till November 23, 1921, when he married Elizabeth Richardson, who had come to Noble County as an ex-school teacher and was working as the County Home Demonstration Agent. Mary Ellen Ritthaler was born on November 3, 1922, and Frank Ritthaler, Jr. was born on December 25, 1925 in Perry.

Mary Ellen Ritthaler married Irwin Neil Smelser on April 10, 1948, in Enid, Oklahoma. They had five children, but only three lived. Mary Jo was born January 19, 1956, Karen Sue was born May 19, 1958, and Edwin Keith was born September 27, 1961. Mary Jo works as a real estate salesperson/secretary. Karen works as a bookkeeper and secretary. Edwin works as a farrier, after learning the profession at Alpine, Texas at Sul Ross University.

Frank Ritthaler died at the age of 62 on January 15, 1949, in Oklahoma City. Elizabeth Ritthaler died at the age of 88 in Riverside, California on September 10, 1975.

Frank Ritthaler, Jr. died on December 24, 1944, at the age of 19. He was on a troopship going from England to France. The ship was torpedoed just off the coast of France. My parents were informed that he was missing in action at first, but they finally received word that he had been killed, after many weeks of thinking he was missing. Aunt Kate Ritthaler composed a poem about my brother's death and dedicated this poem to him:

Sleep on, Brave Lad

*You who died in vain, and faced
the sorrow and the pain,
Of bloody war machines that
main and kill
Now we will never know
your skill,
to make this world a better
place to live,
With everything you had to give.
So now, brave lad, sleep on,
and rest in peace.
For you, this is an end of pain,
an endless sweet release.
You did not fail, brave lad,
You did your very best
Your fruitless efforts are
forever blest.*

- Kathryn F. Ritthaler 1981

I would also like to mention that my cousin, Franklin Ritthaler, son of Henry Ritthaler, was killed on the Island of Leyte in the Phillipines during World War II. Also, his brother, Paul Ritthaler, was captured on the Island of Guam by the Japanese in 1942. Paul was a Marine and worked as a baker, which helped him to survive imprisonment. He was released in 1945, after the war ended.

My father was very fond of family gatherings. He and his brother, Jake, were born on the same day, April 6. They got together every year on their birthday and had a party. Everyone brought homemade cake and ice cream. There were card games and dances, with our own family band playing. The band consisted mostly of Aunt Maggie Smith's boys, Paul, Art and Bill. The highlight for me was when I got to dance with my Uncle John, when I was about ten years old. The family continued to gather together every year on Decoration Day in May, for many years. There were many joyous family reunions, which I remember, with gratitude.

Jacob Ritthaler
By Doris Bronner

In 1893, when the Cherokee Run was opened to settlers, Jacob Ritthaler came to Oklahoma for the run with his father, Ludwig Ritthaler. Jake was only twenty-one years old and the oldest son of Ludwig and Elizabeth Ritthaler.

Jake was born Jacob Ritthaler in Falkenstien, Salicia, Austria-Hungary on April 6, 1872. He migrated to the United States with his mother, Elizabeth and father, Ludwig, and seven brothers and sisters. They landed in New York in April of 1884. They settled near Halsted, Kansas in Harvey County where four more children were born.

When the run was started with a gun shot at 12 o'clock noon on September 16, 1893, Jake and his father each rode a horse to stake their claims. Jake staked his 160 acre claim five miles east of Perry, Oklahoma.

Jake stayed all night on his claim because if it was left unattended someone else could "jump" your claim and claim it for themselves. The first thing he had to do was make a home so he made a dug-out, his grandmother lived with him until he was married. He cleared his land for farming and built a house.

Jake married Hulda Schulze on April 23, 1899 at a little country church between Stillwater and Mulhall, Oklahoma. Hulda was born October 12, 1880 at Peoria, Illinois. Their first son died at childbirth, they later had four daughters and three sons. They were Marie, Ludwig, Anna, Kathryn, Jake, Martha and William.

When Marie was a baby, Jake traded his farm for a farm eight miles east of Perry. Ludwig was born here and later Jake traded for a farm two and a half miles south. They built a house down in the southeast corner of the section because of a pretty low place and a creek. This was where Anna, Kathryn, Jake and Martha were born.

Jake moved his family to Colorado for six months and then came back to Noble County, Oklahoma and lived west of the Old Lutheran church for six months. This was where William was born. They moved back to the house on the home place and lived there several years before building a new three bedroom house upon the hill. Jake built a one room house about twenty-five feet from his back door for his mother so she wouldn't have to share their home. She lived in this house for thirty years.

William "Bill" took over the farming at an early age and stayed with his folks until married. Martha came home and took care of the folks then, until

Jake Ritthaler Family about 1936. (L to R): Martha, Anna, Marie, Kathryn, Hulda, Jake, Luie, Jake and William.

Elizabeth Ritthaler - 1934.

they sold the farm and moved to Morrison, Oklahoma. They celebrated their Golden Wedding anniversary April 23, 1950 on the farm. Hulda died March 27, 1952 and Jake, January 28, 1956.

Marie Ritthaler was born July 3, 1901. She married James Alva Duncan, March 3, 1925. Their children are James, Hulda (Henry), Shirley (Moody) and Lois Marie (Moore).

Ludwig "Luie" Ritthaler was born June 30, 1903. He married Pearl Hoggett in the fall of 1927. Their children are Eva (Graham), Louise, Wayne, Martha (Kerns) and Charles.

Anna Augusta Ritthaler was born August 12, 1905. She married Ernest "Babe" Edwards June 18, 1932. They had two boys, Robert "Bob" Ernest Edwards and James "Jim" Allen Edwards.

Kathryn Emma Ritthaler was born April 13, 1908. She married Ernest Alfred Petterman, August 5, 1925. They had six children: Albert, Alfred, Doris Ann (Bronner), Walter, William and Harry.

Jake Julius Ritthaler was born February 27, 1910. He married Annabell Eckhoff, November 22, 1933. They had four children: Phyllis Joy, Rodney Ray, Leo Richard and Lenna Mae.

Martha Elizabeth Ritthaler was born August 4, 1912. She married Clarence McCurry, July 10, 1953 and they had one daughter, Sandra (Hamann).

William "Bill" George Ritthaler was born March 30, 1915. Bill married Esther Zemp, September 20, 1941. Their children are Sharon Kay (Wheatley) and Randy Ray.

John Ritthaler
By Laura H. Ritthaler

John, second son of Ludwig and Elizabeth (Schweitzer) Ritthaler, was born May 14, 1874, in Lehmberg, Austria. At the age of 12, he came with his parents and his brothers and sisters. Their boat docked in New York in April, 1885. From there, the family traveled by rail to Halstead, Kansas, where they settled. During his teen years in Kansas, John worked as a farm hand for neighbors and friends.

When the Cherokee Outlet, Indian Territory was opened to settlement in September, 1893, John's father, Ludwig; his older brother, Jacob, and a friend, Peter Schmidt, made the run into the outlet and staked claims east and south of what would become Perry. The Ritthaler family and John moved south to settle in the new land.

John had developed an interest in cooking and worked as a chef for Harvey House restaurants in Newton, Kansas and Rogers, Arkansas, and at Lee Huckins Hotel in Oklahoma City, as well as several other areas. At one time, President Theodore (Teddy) Roosevelt was visiting Col. Zack Mulhall near Orlando, Oklahoma. They dined at a restaurant where John was working as chef and John made coffee for the president and his Rough Riders. The community of Mulhall was named for Col. Zack Mulhall.

In his book, "Hunting the Grizzly Bear", Roosevelt tells of his love for hunting. It is here that the toy teddy bear originated.

During his chef days in Oklahoma City, John met Ida Thiele and after several months of courtship they were married May 14, 1899 in Marina, Oklahoma, also the date of John's birthday. Their wedding celebration lasted three days.

This seems like a long time but we must remember those were horse and buggy days and people who came quite a distance stayed over in order to renew friendships and visit with relatives.

Five daughters and three sons were born to this union: Elizabeth on March 17, 1900; Otto Walter on November 22, 1901; Bertha Rose on August 25, 1903; Ernest F. Frederick on October 9, 1904; Laura Hulda on October 12, 1906; Walda Gertrude on June 16, 1909; Albert Edward on September 15, 1919. Bertha Rose survived only three months, Ernest Fredrick died at age 19, Walda Gertrude Scroggs died at age 36, and Otto Walter died in 1968 at age 67. Elizabeth, Rudulph, Laura and Albert all reside in Wichita, Kansas. Alma Esther Kangas lives in Phoenix, Arizona.

John and Ida returned to Perry where John and his brother, Jacob, opened a restaurant. After a while, John decided to go back to the land and moved to the farm six and one half miles east and south of Perry. He lived there and farmed the land until 1947,

John Ritthaler (right) during his 'chefing' days. The man on the left is unidentified.

when he bought a house in the 400 block of Grove Street in Perry and moved into it. He lived there until his death in 1952. John was a charter member of Christ Lutheran Church in Perry.

Lucille Ritthaler-Graham
By Lucille Graham

I would like to express my sincere gratitude and appreciation to the citizens of Noble county, who stimulated and influenced my interest in the Fine Arts, throughout the school systems, and at the community level. Perry is a pleasant reminder of friendships, and of people who I shared in my involvement. I want to take this time and space to recognize them:

First is the Sisters of Divine Providence at St. Josephs Academy, Sister Charles and especially Sister Romwald, violin teachers, who taught me the meaning of discipline — and whose kind interest and dedicated teaching skills provided me with violin instruction through personal supervision that enabled me to be placed in the string section of the Perry High School Orchestra. In 1929, I remember Sister Romwald saying, "Don't let the double stops discourage you. If you don't succeed the first one hundred times, just keep practicing," (in reference to supervised practice period). In 1933, through the influence of Sistern Romwald, I was accepted as a violin student by Dr. Erich Sorantin of Our Lady of the Lake College, San Antonio, Texas.

Second is Noble county's International Treasure: Professor Leopold Radgowsky, Conductor of the Band and Orchestra, of Perry Schools, whose loyalty and dedication to the community was reflected in the fine achievements of his students. I remember the rhythm and wave of his baton for which I had a healthy respect — being positioned inches away from it. His love for vanilla ice cream was well known to many members of the or-

Lucille Graham in the Studio Gallery in August, 1968. The painting is entitled "Red Sails in the Sunset".

chestra. His contribution to Noble County's heritage will be remembered currently and long into the future. He said to me, "Keep you head high, but don't be high in the head," (in reference to being accepted as violin student of Dr. Erich Sorantin).

I remember the parade held for Mrs. Eleanor Roosevelt on March 11, 1937. Following the parade she said, "One of the best High School bands I've ever heard." Mrs. Roosevelt, wife of President Franklin Roosevelt, made a detraining stop at Perry and was taken by auto to Alva, where she dedicated the Jesse Dunn building.

Next is LeOla Dotts, dancing instructor who established the LeOla Dotts School of Dance circa 1932-33, in residence at 735 Kaw Street. She taught me the meaning of beauty and grace in character and classic ballet, tap and adagio dancing. Her recitals in the High School auditorium testified to the measure of her great energy and talent. Later, as LeOla Stone, she established a ballet school in the San Fernando Valley in California. Her recitals were choreographed by the famous George Balanchine, and accompained by the San Fernando Valley Symphony. She said, "Use all of your expression. Put all you have into it — its going to be worth it to you," (in reference to dancing).

Lastly is Ina (Heaton) Ingersol, English teacher and drama coach who taught me the importance of elocution, good dialogue and diction, and the entire Perry Public School System for a learning experience and allowing my participation in operaettas, glee clubs, the High School Quartet, plays and all activities I was priviledged to be a part of.

I was born July 11, 1918, at Castleton, Kansas, the daugher of August Ludwig Ritthaler and Kathryn Frances (Goering) Ritthaler. I attended Perry schools and was a member of the graduating class of 1936. I married William Clarence Graham of Stillwater on July 11, 1939, in the home at 609 Ivanhoe Street, Perry, Oklahoma. Vows were read by Rev. David Thomas, minister of the Presbyterian church. We settled in Stillwater, which became our permanent home. On November 5, 1943, Michael Allen Graham, was born in Stillwater, Oklahoma. Mr. Graham was a WW II veteran. He attended Oklahoma A. & M. College. Prior to his retirement in 1978, he was employed by the Married Student Housing Division at Oklahoma State University.

Our son, Dr. Michael Graham, lives in Petaluma, California with his wife, Sidney, and their three children, Deirdre, Leslie, and Christopher. He is a political science instructor at San Francisco State University, San Francisco, California.

All my previous training in the Arts further influenced me to become a serious painter. With the support of my family and by request of noted landscape artist Jacques Hans Gallrein, on May 5, 1968, the Studio Gallery was established and I became his artist assistant and custodian of the art collection. On September 28, 1973, I received a certificate of merit from Mr. Gallrein. This academic recognition influenced me to continue my pursuit as an artist and teacher. All the fine art training which I received in Noble county made this plateau in my career possible. I wish to take this time to say thank you to Perry — my home town.

Ludwig Ritthaler
By Darlene Roads

Ludwig and Elizabeth (Schweitzer) Ritthaler were both born in Galicia, Austria-Hungary — Ludwig in Brickendau and Elizabeth in Falkenstein. They immigrated to America in 1884. Ludwig was 36 years of age and Elizabeth was 34.

Although Ludwig's mother was of the House of Sennker, the family fortunes had waned. Elizabeth, born daughter of Roesch from Zehaus, Switzerland, and her family had maintained their financial and social status through the generations. She was a distant cousin of the famous Dr. Albert Schwitzer, physician, musician and philosopher.

Elizabeth's marriage to a skilled furniture maker had been arranged; however, she and Ludwig fell in love and were married in 1871. She was 20; he was 22. This disregard of family wishes did not set well with her family even after the birth of seven children — Jacob in April, 1872; John in May, 1874; Leopold in March, 1876; Margareth in March, 1878; Kate in March, 1880; Philip in January, 1882; and Henry in February, 1884.

Shortly after Henry's birth, Ludwig, Elizabeth and their seven children together with Ludwig's brothers, Philip and Henry and two sisters embarked on the long and tedious journey to the New World. They brought nothing except necessities with them and traveled steerage on the boat as they had no money. Their boat docked in New York in April, 1885, and they traveled by train to Halstead, Kansas, where Frank was born in April, 1886. Frank was followed by Rose in May, 1888; Rudolph in December, 1890; and August in October, 1893, completing the Ritthaler family of eleven children. Elizabeth bore four more children, two boys and one girl were born prematurely and one girl, Elizabeth, lived only three months, from March 1,

The Ritthaler family — this photo was taken October 22, 1906 on the occasion of the marriage of Rose Ritthaler to John Monroe Sinn. Rose still has her wedding flowers in her hair. Seated (L to R): Rudolph, John, August, and parents, Elizabth and Ludwig. Standing (L to R): Kate (Weid), Lee, Philip, Margaret (Schmidt), Frank, Jacob, Henry and Rose (Sinn).

to June 1, 1897. She is buried in Zion Lutheran cemetery.

Ludwig became a farmer and his family settled peacefully in Kansas. In 1891, Philip returned to Europe and brought their mother back to the United States. Barbara Ritthaler, or "Grandma Muny" as she was called, could neither read, write nor speak English. She was completely bald and always wore a "granny cap". After the marriage of her eldest granddaughter, Margareth, Grandma Muny made her home with "Maggie" and her husband until sometime after 1900. Philip and Henry left Kansas and settled in Michigan and Mother Ritthaler apparently went with them as records show that she died October 9, 1908 and is buried in Alpena county, Michigan.

In 1893, word was spreading that the last unsettled portion of Oklahoma Territory, the Cherokee Outlet, was to be opened for settlement. The new territory and the pioneer spirit once again called to Ludwig. Jacob had turned 21 in April, 1893, and Margareth had become acquainted with a young man named Peter Schmidt who had also immigrated from Austria-Hungary. And so it was that Ludwig, Jacob and 24-year-old Peter Schmidt were on the starting line at 12 noon, September 16, 1893.

The three men traveled at a rapid pace and staked their claims on land located six miles east and two miles south of Perry. During the next few weeks, the men worked feverishly to build shelters for their families so they could join them in Oklahoma Territory as soon as possible. Ludwig was granted a Homestead Patent on March 7, 1903 for the SW¼ of Section 26 in Noble township containing 160 acres.

Once again, Ludwig and his sons turned to farming — tilling the soil, planting the crops and asking the Lord's blessings on their efforts. They were not alone in their prayer requests and soon many others of a Lutheran background were gathering for prayer meetings and church services. It soon became clear that home services would not be enough and about 1898, Ludwig and Elizabeth donated the southwestern corner of their claim for a church building. The Ritthalers also provided meals for the workmen — carpenters, rock haulers and others — who donated their time and labor during the building process. The church is still located at the original site.

The first of the eleven children to leave home was Margareth, the eldest daughter, who married Peter J. Schmidt on December 26, 1896 in Guthrie, Oklahoma. In 1899, the three oldest boys all married. Jacob and John remained in Noble county, however Leopold eventually settled in Colorado. Frank, Rudolph and August all married eventually and settled in Noble county while the other children settled in Kansas or Colorado.

Ludwig died in March, 1909 at 60 years of age and is buried at Grace Hill cemetery. Jacob built a small house on his farm and there Elizabeth lived independently, visiting her other children for brief periods. As her health began to fail, she moved in with Margareth and Peter who had by then left the farm. Elizabeth died October 13, 1940, five days short of her 89th birthday. She had at that time, 49 grandchildren, 43 great-grandchildren, and one great-great-grandchild. She is buried next to her husband at Grace Hill cemetery.

Rest of the Ritthalers
By Darlene Roads

Fifteen children were born to Ludwig and Elizabeth (Schweitzer) Ritthaler. Two boys and one girl were born prematurely and did not survive. One girl was born March 1, 1897 and died in June of the same year. Both of the girls were named Elizabeth and family tradition indicates that two of the premature babies were twins. Of the remaining eleven children, five sons and one daugher remained in Noble County. Three sons and two daughters went back north to settle.

Leopold, third son of Ludwig and Elizabeth, was born in Austria-Hungary, nine years before the family immigrated to America. He was 17 years old when his father and eldest brother, Jacob, made the run into the Cherokee Outlet. Lee worked the land with his father and brothers. On October 3, 1899, he married Josie Slama in Perry, Oklahoma. Sometime during the ensuing five years, Lee and Josie traveled north and west and finally settled in Rocky Ford, Colorado. Their two sons were born there — Eddie in 1904 and Walter in 1905. Lee worked for American Crystal Sugar Co. for 39 years and was vice president of the company when he retired. Josie died in 1948 and Lee passed way in 1958 on what would have been the couple's 59th wedding anniversary.

Kate was only five years old when Ludwig and Elizabeth embarked on their journey to America. She might have celebrated her fifth birthday on March 17, 1885, aboard the ship. In 1899, at age 19, Kate met and married Karl Weid, who had immigrated from Bavaria, Germany. Kate and three of her brothers, Jacob, John and Leopold, were all married during 1899. Kate and Karl also settled in Rocky Ford, Colorado. To them were born one son and three daughters. Margareth was born on the last day of July 1901. Their son, Paul, was born April 10, 1902 and died February 12, 1904, at one year and ten months of age. Lucille was born August 1, 1905, but tragedy struck again when she died three years and four months later. Edna, who was always called "Mike", was born in 1906. Karl operated a bakery and restaurant business for 35 years. He died in 1947 and Kate followed him on December 23, 1956. Both are buried in Rocky Ford, Colorado.

Philip spent the longest time looking for the right girl to be his wife. He finally found Rose Kathryn Morlock and they were married February 3, 1912, three weeks after Philip's 30th birthday. Philip and Rose settled in Moundridge, Kansas, where they raised two sons and two daughters. Karl Phillip was born in December, 1913; Wilburn James in March, 1915; Kathryn Louise in February, 1924; and Ruby Rose in October, 1926. Rose died in March, 1955, and Philip in February, 1970. Both are buried in Moundridge, Kansas. Of the eleven children of Ludwig and Elizabeth, Philip survived the longest, being 88 years, one month old at the time of his death.

Henry was the last of the Ritthaler children born in Austria-Hungary. He was about 14 months old when their boat docked in New York in April, 1885. Henry married Emma Elizabeth Ewy early in 1911 and they moved to Swink, Colorado, where John Henry was born late that same year. Margaret Emma arrived in June, 1913. The family then moved to Rocky Ford, Colorado, where Vernon Harold was born September 1, 1915. Another move was made to La Junta, Colorado, where Paul Richard arrived December 3, 1917. Lucille Irene made her appearance November 27, 1919, and the youngest, Franklin Donald was born September 16, 1925. On December 25 of the same year, another Frank Ritthaler was born in Perry, Oklahoma. When the cousins reached their 18th birthdays, each in turn entered military service. And in 1944, tragedy struck twice. Franklin Donald was killed in February and Frank was lost at sea in the English Channel on December 24, one day before his 19th birthday. Henry operated a bakery in Rocky Ford until he retired. He died in 1955, and Emma died in 1967. Both are buried in Rocky Ford.

Rose, the youngest daughter, was born May 19, 1888, after Ludwig and Elizabeth had settled in Halstead, Kansas. She was six years of age when the family moved south into Oklahoma Territory. In 1906, she met John Sinn and on October 22, of that year, they were married. John and Rose moved around quite a bit during the early years of their marriage. Their eldest daughter,

Gladys, was born May 5, 1908, at Cherokee, Oklahoma: Arthur was born June 10, 1920 at Garber, Oklahoma; Victor was born July 7, 1912 at Covington, Oklahoma; Harold, January 25, 1914; Helena, August 10, 1916; and Dorothy, October 15, 1918, all at Fairland, Oklahoma. The Sinn family then moved north to Pittsburg, Kansas, where Walter was born March 25, 1922, and Elmer Lee arrived January 21, 1926. Rose was the last of the Ritthaler children when she passed away May 9, 1976 - 10 days short of her 88th birthday.

The sons and daughters of Ludwig and Elizabeth have all departed this life as have their spouses with the exception of Kathryn Francis Goering Ritthaler, widow of the youngest son, August. Kathryn resides in Stillwater, Oklahoma, and has generously shared her memories to make these writings possible.

John Robedeaux
By Perry Daily Journal

John Robedeaux, one of the oldest and best known members of the Otoe Indian Tribe, and who lived ten miles east of Red Rock, lies dead at his home Monday and his tribesmen and fellow Indians are preparing and gathering to pay their last respects to him.

Robedeaux died at 6:30 Saturday afternoon when he stepped on a running automobile and accidently fell, striking the ground and breaking his neck.

In company with his two daughters, his son-in-law and a small child, he was returning from Pawnee. During the trip home he had frequently opened the door to dispose of some tobacco which he was chewing. On opening the door he stepped out on the running board, missed his step and fell, striking the ground and breaking his neck almost instantly.

Fred A. Davis and Son of Perry were called and the body was removed to the home.

Robedeaux was 80 years old at the time of his death and had been a resident of this particular section of Oklahoma for many years, having come to the state before the opening and at that time several other members and leaders of this tribe came to Oklahoma.

He was well known not only among the white race of the state but among many of the Indian tribes of the state. He was a popular member of his tribe and considered by the younger Indians as one of their leaders. He also was held in high esteem by his pale face friends and was declared by some of his neighbors as being one of the best friends and neighbors they ever had.

Although no date for the funeral had been set on Monday the Indians were gathered for the Otoe feast and the give away which usually follows the Indian ceremonies.

As a rule the ceremonies at an Indian funeral continue through most of a day with the various Indian leaders talking before the services by the white man are offered. The outstanding members of a tribe usually pay their respects to a dead leader in their own language and the sacredness of the occasion is brought to the white listener by the tone of the voice because he does not understand the language of the Indian.

It is expected that not only will the members of the Otoe tribe gather for the funeral but many members of the Ponca tribe will be in attendance as well as many, many white people.

Burial will be made in the Otoe Cemetery. Dated February 27, 1928.

Ray Robinson
By Frances Robinson Lynn

Ray Paul Robinson was born February 25, 1905 in Payne County. He came to Morrison, Oklahoma in 1928 to work for his brother-in-law in his hardware store. He worked there until he was called into service of his country March 10, 1942. He was on active duty in 357th Infantry until November 27, 1944. When it was decided all men 38 years old be released to do defense work, he went to work at Douglas Aircraft Company in Tulsa, Oklahoma. There he met me (Francis Neal Bush born June 15, 1916 in Lafayette, Tennessee) and after the end of the war with Germany he came back and bought half interest in the Houser Hardware Store in Morrison. We were married August 11, 1945 at Bowden, Creek County, Oklahoma. We bought a little house on 4th Street in Morrison, Oklahoma. We were active in the United Methodist Church and American Legion. Ray was a charter member of the Lions Club.

We had three children, Paula Rae born April 22, 1946, Joe Neal born December 28, 1947 at the hospital in Stillwater, Oklahoma and Mary Eva born October 28, 1952 at the hospital in Perry, Oklahoma.

All of our children were good students and active in sports. Paula and Joe graduated from Oklahoma State University. Mary had two years at Oklahoma State University, then married Richard J. Christensen from Grove, Oklahoma and moved to Tulsa, Oklahoma where she graduated from Tulsa University.

Joe worked with his dad in the hardware store for three years before his dad retired. He then attended Seminery at Southern Methodist University. He is now pastor of Goodrich United Methodist at Norman, Oklahoma. Paula married Kenneth King and they have two children Steven Kenneth and Scott Daniel. They live five miles from Morrison, Oklahoma.

Ray died September 3, 1983. I still live in our little house on 4th Street, that we added to as our family grew. I still garden and care for my flowers and shrubs. On August 25, 1985 Elbert F. Lynn from Livingston, New Mexico and I were married.

Henry Jacob Rupp
By Rena Rupp Carrier

Henry Jacob Rupp, born January 6, 1897, near Rembo, Oklahoma in Pawnee County, moved to Noble County in 1900 with his parents, Jacob and Luise Rupp, an older brother, Rudolf Adolf and a sister, Emma Louise, from southwest of Pawnee, Oklahoma to a farm on the same section as the town of Lucien. At Lucien they lived for a cou-

25th Anniversary August 11, 1970. (L to R): Mary (Christensen), Frances, Paula (King), Ray and Joe Robinson.

Rock house - 1960 farm of Henry and Marie Rupp.

ple of years in a two room rock house dug half its height into the ground with Henry's grandmother Rupp. Later, a totally above ground house was built. There Henry grew up and gained two more brothers, Arthur Meno and Adolph Daniel, and three more sisters, Anna Matilda, Marie Elizabeth, and Elizabeth Wilhelmina. As his father was ill much of the time, the job of farming fell largely on him and his older brother. Because of this, he was unable to attend school regularly and was 18 years of age when he completed the eighth grade. Also, in 1915, his father died and he assumed much of the responsibility of the farm and assisting his mother to rear the two brothers and four sisters younger than him. In 1917, his youngest sister died.

World War I came along and he was drafted into the army. He was in training as a medic at Galveston, Texas, when the war ended. After being discharged, he returned and became active in the family farm again.

In 1926, he and two friends went to California to work. Henry worked in a raisin factory for six months, decided farming in Oklahoma was more to his desire, and returned to the family farm.

About 1920, he visited his cousins near Halstead Kansas, where at a birthday party, he met Marie Emelia Rilling, daughter of Samuel and Emelia Rilling of Hesston, Kansas. From this meeting a romance developed. They married on Marie's twenty-eighth birthday, March 11, 1928, in Garden Mennonite Church north of Halstead, Kansas. Their first residence was on a farm 2 ½ miles south of Lucien on the Garfield County side of the Noble County border. They lived there for five years where their first two children, Melvern Samuel and Delmer Noel, were born. In 1933, they moved to a farm 9¾ miles east of Perry where their daughter, Rena Fern, was born. They moved to the farm across the highway in 1935, where their last child, Larry Alden, was born.

In 1941, Henry and Marie bought the farm across the road east of the one where they were living. In 1942, this became the third farm the family lived on which cornered on the intersection that once was called "Pete's Corner", (two miles west of Bill's Corner). The walls of this house are 18 inches thick and built entirely of local sand rock in 1900-1902. Henry and Marie lived there until 1971 when they moved to Perry.

After returning from California, Henry became a partner with Jake Frank in the operation of a steam engine powered threshing machine. He and Jake threshed grain for farmers from Lucien to Covington for several years until Henry moved east of Perry. An enclosed wagon (cook shack) was taken along with the threshers in which meals for the crew were prepared and eaten. The first summer after marriage, Marie was the cook for the threshing crew. A few years around 1940, he operated a threshing machine for his brother. Combines were beginning to be used, so the threshing business declined and commercial threshers ceased operation during World War II.

During the 1930s and into World War II, Henry also owned one of the early engine powered hay balers with which he did much custom baling. Then after World War II he bought another baler with which he and his sons did custom baling for a few years.

In 1969, Marie suffered a massive stroke which left her an invalid. Henry devoted all his time caring for her until her death in 1972. He lived alone in Perry for six years until his death in 1978.

Henry and Marie were active in church and community affairs. He served on the Sumner Public School Board and later was a school bus driver for several years. Henry reduced his farming activities in 1962, when Larry took over farming the crop land. A few years later he sold his chickens after selling eggs to Stillwater Hatchery for over twenty-five years. Then in 1970 he completely quit any farming operation with an auction of his livestock and machinery.

One son, Delmar, died in 1966 after a lengthly illness leaving a wife and two children.

Although the farm Henry and Marie owned still remains with their children, none of their children live in Noble County. However, they live in the adjoining counties of Payne and Kay. Also, Delmar, at the time of his death lived in Payne County.

Cupid did not shoot his arrows very far for their children as all four children married Noble County residents, Melvern (Sam) married Norma Jean VanBebber, Delmar married Doris Brand, Rena married Burl Carrier and Larry married Judy Tautfest.

There are thirteen grandchildren and as of Summer 1986 there are seven great-grandchildren of Henry and Marie. The grandchildren are not remaining as nearby as their parents. In 1986, one grandchild is living in Edmond, Oklahoma, one in Tulsa, Oklahoma, one in Minnesota, one in Colorado, one in New Mexico, one in Texas and one in Nebraska. The others are in Payne or Kay counties with the exception of one living in Noble county.

Jacob Rupp
By Rena Rupp Carrier

Jacob Rupp, born September 29, 1859, near Einsiedel, Galicia, Austria-Hungary (now in U.S.S.R.) came to the United States in 1882 after serving four years in the Austria-Hungarian army. He migrated with his mother, two brothers and two sisters. A brother and a married sister preceded him to the U.S.A.

He first settled on a farm near Halstead, Kansas. With a fast saddle horse he bought for the purpose, he made the Cherokee Strip Run September 16, 1893. After a hard ride from Caldwell, Kansas, he staked a claim along the Salt Fork River near Deer Creek. However, since he delayed filing for his claim, someone else filed before he did. He then continued to Pawnee County and claimed a farm southwest of Pawnee near the former town of Rembo.

Daniel Rupp, one of Jacob's brothers, also made the run and staked a claim south of Lucien. Later he moved to Arkansas where he lived until his death in 1937.

Jacob returned to Kansas were he married Luise Just September 13, 1894, at Newton, Kansas. Luise was born near Kiev, Ukraine, U.S.S.R., January 27, 1877. She came to the U.S.A. with her parents, brother and three sisters in 1892. Her family first settled in Halstead, Kansas. Her father also made the run into the Cherokee Strip and homesteaded northeast of Morrison in Noble County. However, she remained in Newton, Kansas, where she worked as housekeeper until her marriage.

After marriage, they lived in a one-room house on Jacob's farm until 1900. Three of their children, Rudolf Adolf, Henry Jacob and Emma Louise were born there. In 1900, they sold their farm in Pawnee County and purchased the southwest quarter of the same section as the Lucien townsite from Jacob's mother. Their first house was a two-room dug-out rock house. One child, Arthur Meno, was born in this house. Before long, one wall of the semi-dugout collapsed, so a new above ground frame house was built. In this

Children of Jacob and Luise Rupp about 1914. Front Row (L to R): Elizabeth, Henry, Rudolf and Marie. Back Row: Anna, Arthur, Emma and Adolph.

house the last four children, Anna Matilda, Adolph Daniel, Marie Elizabeth and Elizabeth Wilhelmina were born. This house began with two rooms and a shed kitchen but has been added to several times and is presently occupied by a grandson, Dennis Rupp.

Jacob was always in poor health and died in 1915. His wife continued farming with the help of the children. Then their youngest child, Elizabeth, died at the age of seven. During World War I, she found it difficult to continue farming as her two oldest sons, Rudolf and Henry, were drafted into the Army. After the war, with her sons back, things improved so she continued farming until her youngest son, Adolph, married. Adolph took over operation of the farm when he married and later purchased it from Luise.

All of their children, except Arthur, (he has spent most of his adult life in Edmond and Oklahoma City) have lived all or most of their lives in Noble County or in the east edge of Garfield County.

There were twenty-three grandchildren. As of 1986, six live in Noble County, five live in adjoining counties, five have died and only four live outside of Oklahoma. There are fifty-five great-grandchildren and several great-great-grandchildren.

Frank M. Sanders
By Lucille Sanders Payne

Frank Martin Sanders was born at Rothville, Missouri, to James M. Sanders and his wife, Sarah, on December 10, 1866 and died on December 14, 1950. His wife, Ollie Pore Sanders was a native of Rothville, Missouri. She was born on March 27, 1877, and died on March 4, 1963. A few years after husband Frank's death, she moved to Perry, Oklahoma where she lived until her death in 1963.

Shortly after the opening of the Cherokee Strip on September 16, 1893, Sanders having recently graduated from Chillicothe Business College in Chillicothe, Missouri, came to Perry looking for land to buy. He purchased 160 acres of land, six miles west of Red Rock, Oklahoma or twelve and a half miles north of Perry, built a house and returned to Rothville, Missouri, to marry his boyhood sweetheart, Ollie Pore of Rothville. Together, they returned to their new farm home near Red Rock.

Frank and Ollie were parents of three children. The first child, a boy, died at birth on December 31, 1905. Two years later, a daughter Lucille, and on October 15, 1909, another son, Ray, who died on June 11, 1975 age 66 years.

As time went on Frank and Ollie built a new, larger home on their farm, to accommodate their growing family. Frank did custom threshing with an early day threshing machine to help finance the farming operations. Wife Ollie cooked for the threshing crew as they harvested wheat for the neighboring farmers. Many times during the harvest season, Frank and crew worked up to the wee hours of the morning, repairing machinery.

In later years, Frank and Ollie attended the World's Fair in Chicago, Illinois. The Model T Ford had just been put on the market. Frank was so impressed with it, that he bought a new one for $1,000 and had it shipped to Red Rock by railray flat car.

He drove this new car throughout the country side and later, opened a Ford Agency in Red Rock. Many times, neighbors would have to get out of their carriages and hold onto the horses to prevent a run away, as they were frighened by the Model T Ford.

Neighbors were upset and hostile towards Sanders, because of this, but later became reconciled, as one by one began buying Fords from Frank.

One of his first sales was to Dr. Coldiron of Perry. After paying off his note for the Model T, Coldiron found and displayed his proof of purchase in his office.

Sanders was always ready to help a friend or neighbor whether it was a stalled car on the road, or someone who had suffered a loss.

In later years, he built a building in the small town of Ceres, ½ mile north of this homestead on Highway 77. He sold gasoline, repairs, tractors, Ford Cars, and groceries. This was during the oil boom days, when the Three Sands oil field was at its peak. This brought a booming business to Sanders Station, known as Minute Oil Station, located 13 miles north of Perry on busy Highway 77.

As Sanders added more land to his farming operation, and as his Service Station kept him occupied, the farming operation was taken over by his son, Roy and wife, Marjorie, and wife Ollie. Frank was an early riser, going to work at his filling station at daylight, return home for a noon meal, a quick nap, and return to work till late night hours.

Frank and Ollie were aggressive pioneers, always ready to try new things as they were put on the market for sale. He was one of the first in the community to install a Delco light system, for electricity. Also, butane gas for heating and cooking. He made an effort to be first in the neighborhood to utilize new things.

When the first farmers Co-op elevator was started in Red Rock, Sanders took an active part in helping raise money by selling stock. He was President of the Co-op for some 20 years. Later years, a new, larger elevator was built, and still operates today.

Frank and Ollie were loyal charter members of the Christian Church in

Frank Sander's farm near Red Rock, Oklahoma during Three Sands oil boom.

Frank M. Sanders and wife Ollie - 1906.

Ceres, Oklahoma. Many times, Frank and Ollie would invite the congregation to their home for a Sunday basket dinner. As many as 75 to 100 people would attend. One Sunday, after dinner, Frank decided to show off his new motorcycle. As the guests gathered in the yard to watch, he circled around in the pasture for all to see, but when he decided to stop, he discovered he didn't know how to stop the cycle, so had to continue riding till he ran out of gas. Needless to say the motorcycle was soon sold, at Ollie's request.

During the time that Frank was Chairman of the Christian Church board, a tornado leveled the church building. But with the help of the congregation, both labor and finances, a new building was built on a new buiding site in Ceres, donated by Frank and Ollie Sanders. The church still stands today with some of its faithful members coming from Perry.

Frank and Ollie also gave the building site for the Ceres Community building, owned by Members of Ceres Community Club, and is used today as a meeting place for the members.

Lucille and Ray both attended grade school at Bowden Country school, three miles from their home. They drove a Shetland pony hitched to a two wheel cart to school. As Oklahoma is noted for its hail storms, Ray and Lucille were caught up in one, returning home from school. The pony stopped in the middle of the road and refused to move until the storm passed. Needless to say, they remembered the incident. Both Lucille and Ray graduated from high school, in Perry, Oklahoma.

The picture of Frank and a neighbor, standing in front of the oil derrick, was taken on one of Frank's farms, west of Red Rock, during the oil boom in Noble County. It was the second highest paid lease at that time in Noble County. Also on this farm Sanders built the second largest barn in Noble County at that time. A tornado leveled the barn several years ago. The land is now owned by daughter, Lucille Payne, who resides in Tampa, Florida.

Joseph M. Sanders
by Dorothy Tipps

I was born June 23, 1858, at Belmont, Iowa. I moved with my parents to Mahasha County in 1861, and moved again to Washington County, Kansas, in 1871.

I was married to Malinda Johnson February 23, 1879, and lived in Kansas until the year of 1890. Then I moved to Payne County, which was six miles west of Perkins, I moved my family with me.

We were on the road thirteen and one half days. This same route can now be traveled in less than one day by car. We came in a covered wagon drawn by two horses and led an extra horse. We lived there till the spring of 1894.

I was then a young man of high ambition with a family of six children and knew the only hopes of making them a living was to get me a piece of land.

I registered at Stillwater several days before the opening. I stood in line two days among thousands of others, and was afraid to step out of line for fear someone would get my place. At that, others pushed in ahead of me who arrived much later than I.

On the fifteenth day of September in the fall of 1893, I went to Orlando. I started from four miles south of the Cherokee Strip line. The government soldiers were there to see that everything was started fair. At that, many did go ahead and stake claims before the time to go. These were called "Sooners".

At the sound of the gun, at twelve o'clock high noon, we started. I was among those on horseback, on a horse I called "Mug", while others were in wagons, carts and rigs of all descriptions. Those on horseback were in the lead and looking back the rest appeared like cattle or animals.

I was two hours and ten minutes from the time I started until I staked the place I now own. I lived there twenty-six years.

When I made the race I had a family of six children. Times were hard and there was no money. I was in debt one hundred dollars when I made the race. In those days one hundred dollars looked like a thousand now. Sometimes we could not find enough money to mail a letter. There was plenty of work to be done but no one was doing any hiring.

I and my family endured many hardships. There were no schools and no churches. At times many families, together with my own, only had molasses and cornbread to eat. To be able to buy a sack of flour was a luxury.

All kinds of diseases were prevalent and a doctor was twenty six miles away. Later, Doctor Brafford and Doctor Renfrow came to White Rock, later to Billings.

In the early days as many others did, I had to leave my family and go to Kansas where the country was more settled to find work. I worked for one and one-half dollars a day and have worked for seventy-five cents a day and taking my own dinner. We had it to do, or starve.

My house had no windows, no floor and no door. It had only one room. I built the house out of cotton wood, native lumber. I cut the trees myself from my grove west of Perkins, hauled them to this small town on the Cimmaron River, then hauled them to my farm and built the greater part of the house myself.

I finally saved enough money to buy a window glass, so I went to Perry to get one and broke it before I got home.

This room still remains in my house although altered in appearance, the structure is the same. As the years passed by and my family increased, I added more rooms.

Our implements were a walking plow, a harrow, and a walking cultivator. A drill was a scarce implement and if there happened to be one, it was borrowed for miles around. Everyone possessed a hoe which was bright from use, not like the present hoes which are hung up and only used a few times a season.

Joseph M. Sanders and Malinda Johnson Sanders.

In the fall of 1899, I discovered I had a voice for auctioneering and took this up for a vocation until 1918. I do not know if I could ever raised my family if it had not been for this outside money. When I started I was getting one percent when I gave up my work I was getting two.

I am now a retired farmer living in the town of Billings. Many of the old settlers have died, many are too old to work. A few have prospered and retired. Automobiles and airplanes have taken the place of wagons and buggies. I wonder if the people of today enjoy themselves any better riding in their automobiles than we did behind our horses. The life of My Grandpa Joseph Sanders — Dean Taggart, 1929 continued by the family.

Many sorrows attended our way. Of the six coming to Oklahoma all preceded him in death except one. He was the father of 14 children. His wife and eight children preceded him in death. The children who survive him are Mrs. Lewis Rinn of Ninnekah, Charles Sanders of Harrah, Mrs. Frank Taggart, Mrs. Paul Welk, Mrs. John Casey and Loren Sanders, all of Billings; 14 grandchildren, and 10 great-grandchildren. Also two sisters, Mrs. Elizabeth Canfill of Sweetwater, Texas, and Mrs. Jane Chappel of Haddam, Kansas.

Malinda Johnson Sanders, daughter of Elipalet and Laura Johnson was born in Marion County, Iowa, on January 27, 1859, near Charton. At the age of seven she moved with her parents to Washington County, Kansas, where she grew to womanhood. On February 23, 1879, she and Joseph M. Sanders were married. They lived in Kansas until 1890, when they moved to Payne County, Oklahoma, near Perkins. From there they moved to the town of Billings, where they resided until their deaths. Before her death, March 3, 1939, the Sanders celebrated their 60th Wedding Anniversary on Februay 23.

Maximillian Schaffer
By Catherine Schaffer Menke

Maximillian Schaffer was born October 7, 1861 in Zwiefel, Germany, son of John and Annie Schaffer. They came to America about 1875, to Carrol, Iowa. He married Annie Sommars in 1892, at Stanton, Texas. Annie was born June 21, 1871, in Lacona, Iowa, the daughter of Mr. and Mr. Fred Sommars.

Max, as know by his friends, left his wife, Annie, and three-weeks-old daughter at Stanton, Texas and traveled to Orlando, Oklahoma to join in the race for a homestead in the Cherokee Outlet. He rode horseback and filed on a claim thirteen miles northwest of Perry

Maximillian and Annie Schaffer and family — 1898.

in the Polo community (Oakdale township). After the proper paper work was done so he could hold his claim, he returned to Stanton, Texas to secure what implements he had and returned in two covered wagons, accompanied by his brother-in-law, John Sommars. They lived in the covered wagons until a sod house was constructed. A little later, they were joined by Annie and baby who traveled by railroad to Perry and was met by Max and a lumber wagon. It was a long weary ride for all of them following the trails, since there were no roads or bridges.

Food for the family was a serious problem, however, a cow was purchased and wheat was raised. Max loaded a wagon bed with wheat and traveled to Enid to have flour made so Annie could bake bread. Since Enid was 26 miles west of their farm, it took two days to make the trip. Their water supply came from a shallow well which was dug as soon as possible.

In the late 1890's a frame house was built and at last the home became more livable. The house is still being occupied at the present time.

Their second daughter was born July 1, 1896, died October 21, 1897 and is buried in the Polo cemetery.

Annie's parents, the Fred Sommars, also came from Stanton, Texas in the late 1890's and settled on a farm about five miles northwest of Perry.

Max and Annie were the parents of eight children: Annie Marie, born August 9, 1893 died March 7, 1964; Clara; Twins, born December 2, 1897 - Clarence died November 27, 1913 and Clara (Cannon); John; Catherine (Menke) and Helen (McNeil).

Max died September 14, 1920 at the age of 59 years of cancer. Annie lived to be 90 years of age and passed away August 3, 1961, in Coffeyville, Kansas, where she was living with her son, Henry and daughter, Anna. They are buried in the Catholic cemetery at Perry beside their two sons and one daughter.

Christ Schieffer
By Marie Ewy

Christ Schieffer was born in Germany September 17, 1863. He passed away at Perry, Oklahoma December 15, 1939. He was the son of Joseph (1834) and Catherina Schieffer. The family along with Christs' three half-sisters came to America in 1865. It is not known where they first settled but they lived in Grant County near Cassville, Wisconsin in November 1874. In March, 1879, Joseph mortgaged all crops on 120 acres of land in Shelby County, Iowa to buy the farm.

Christ married Anna Catherina Lausen in Council Bluffs, Iowa on September 14, 1887. Anna was born in Germany May 9, 1865 and passed away August 8, 1944 at Perry, Oklahoma.

Christ and Anna had the following children: Catherine (June 14, 1888 — August 9, 1919); Joseph (April 15, 1890 — January 8, 1892); Lillbe baby (died at birth November 1891); Margaretha (February 12, 1893 — March 1, 1893); John Christina (February 11, 1894 — February 17, 1920); Marea Margaret (December 29, 1895 — March 1909); Christina Joseph (May 25, 1897 — September 6, 1974); Ernest Joseph (April 11, 1899 — April 19, 1899); Frank Joseph (June 25, 1900 — September 21, 1980); Carl Peter (January 28, 1903 — February 18, 1920) and Henry Martin (November 21, 1905 — January 15, 1985).

Both Christ and his father, Joseph, moved their families to Muenster, Texas where Catherina passed away in December 1896.

Christ farmed and Anna raised chickens and churned butter, selling butter and eggs to buy groceries. In 1904, they moved their family to Noble County, Oklahoma, settling on a farm two miles north of Perry where they lived until their deaths. Their children attended school at St. Josephs' Academy and Pleasant Hill School District #33.

Joseph lived with his sister Margaritha Fischer in Muenster, Texas after the death of his wife. He came to Perry to live with his son in later years where he died April 1, 1918. He is buried in the family plot at Mt. Calvary Cemetery.

Christ Schieffer home, two miles north of Perry, Oklahoma. (L to R): Anna holding Henry, Christ holding Carl, Joseph, Frank, John, Mary, Katie and Christ J. — 1906.

Christ and Anna (Lausen) Schieffer on Wedding Day — September 14, 1887 at Council Bluffs, Iowa.

Catherina married John Bengforts. They had five children: Christin died in infancy; Margaret, Florenz, Joe and Marie. All lived in Texas.

Christian Joseph married Anna Marea Neuerburg May 1, 1918 at Perry. They had eight children: Josephine Marie (Soulek); Paul Joseph; Walter Matthew; Eda Lee Frances (Cruse); Christina Anastacia (Schneider); Teresa Ann (Rogers); Lillie Alice (Kukuk) and Audrey Elizabeth (Kukuk).

Frank married Rose Ableidinger. They had four children: Catherine (Johnson); Philomeme (Saha); Joan (Schultz) and John Joseph who died at birth. Joan and John were twins.

Henry married Alice Quick. They had one daughter, Ruth Ann (Hunt).

During the 1920 influenza the entire Christ Schieffer family came down with influenza. Noble County neighbors came in to care for the family. Carl and John died one day apart and were buried in a double funeral in the family plot at Mt. Calvary Catholic Cemetery.

Christian Joseph Schieffer

By Marie Ewy

Christian Joseph Schieffer was born May 25, 1897 at Muenster, Texas, the son of Christ (September 17, 1863-December 15, 1939) and Anna Lausen Schieffer (May 9, 1865 - August 8, 1944).

In 1899, his parents, his sisters, Katie and Mary, his brother, John, and he, moved to Oklahoma and settled on a farm two miles north of Perry. Chris was 2 years old. He and his sisters and brother drove a horse and buggy to school at St. Joseph's Academy. Also he attended Pleasant Hill School.

He farmed for his father, and helped the neighbors when they had extra work. Later, he worked for the Wells-Fargo Express Company. Chris and Anna Mae Neuerburg (December 5, 1895 - December 13, 1979) were married on May 1, 1918, at Perry, Oklahoma. Their attendants were John Schieffer and Josie Neuerburg.

He registered for army duty on June 5, 1918, and was called to duty on September 5. He left Perry with a group of Noble County boys going to Camp Logan at Houston, Texas. He served in the medical detachment as a mounted orderly. He was discharged in February, 1919. His detachment was ready to go overseas, but the Armistice was signed on November 11, 1918.

The house they had prepared to live in, along with some of their furniture, burned to the ground, so when he came home from camp they had to find a new place. All they could find was an old house west of Perry. On August 1, 1919, they moved northwest of Perry to a farm belonging to Bill Mason.

That winter was the flu epidemic. His brothers, John and Carl, died and were buried with a double funeral on February 20, 1920. The neighbors came in and helped care for the family, since they were all ill.

Their first child, Josephine Marie was born February 22, 1920. By that time the house on his uncle John Lausen's place had been rebuilt. Marie was 6 weeks old when they moved into it. It was northeast of Perry.

On July 5, 1921, their oldest son Paul Joseph was born, and on March 28, 1923, their second son Walter Matthew was born. In the meantime the congregation had started building a new Catholic Church in Perry. Chris put in many hours working on it, both alone and with his team of horses and wagon.

In 1924, the family moved six miles west of Perry to the Weeder farm. They needed more land for farming, and the Sams oilfield was coming into production. They paid $4.00 for nine hours labor, and more for a man and team.

An interesting incident happened on the move to the Weeder place, that could have been serious, but was very funny to the children watching. Uncle Henry was driving two horses hitched to a hayrack wagon piled high with loose hay. (Hay was stacked in big piles in the fields those days.) Henry was sitting on top, singing and being funny, when he came to the driveway of the place. It had a sharp turn in it. The horses were going too fast for the turn, and as they went around the turn, the wagon turned over and dumped Uncle Henry and the hay into the Tamarak bush. He came clawing his way out of the hay like a clown, since he wasn't hurt. The horses were just standing there, like it was all in the day's work. It was an incident long remembered.

On February 11, 1925, their second daughter, Eda Lee Frances was born and on January 22, 1927 the third daughter, Christina Anastacia was born. It was two and a half miles to school, because one mile road was closed, and since the children had to walk they moved again. This time to the Grundeman farm, north of the Gansel elevators, five miles west of Perry, next to her father's farm. It was just three-fourths of a mile to White School, District #15.

Teresa Ann was born October 28, 1931, and Lillie Alice on April 11, 1936. Audrey Elizabeth was born May 24, 1937. During those years the family endured the depression and the dust bowl, seeing the chickens go to roost in midday and getting out of school early to beat the dust storm home.

Chris continued farming and working in the Sams Field. At one time, the crew would leave before 7 a.m. and drive to Watchhorn, close to Morrison, Oklahoma, to work and then driving home, putting in over 12 hours a day for several weeks. This was before paved roads or heated cars. Chris was milking two to three cows before and

Schieffer Family in 1972. (Front Row, L to R): Marie (Soulek) (Ewy), Chris Schieffer, Anna Mae Schieffer, Audrey (Kukuk). (Back Row, L to R): Paul J. Schieffer, Walter M. Schieffer, Eda Lee (Cruse), Christina (Schneider), Teresa Ann (Rogers), Lillie Alice (Kukuk).

Wedding of Chris and Anna Mae Schieffer. Attendants in back: Josie (Timmons) Mae's sister and John Schieffer, Chris' brother.

after work at that time, also.

On August 28, 1937, they moved to the old home place two miles north of Perry to take care of his parents until they passed away. Chris continued working in the oil field until May 1941 and he continued to farm. He passed away September 6, 1974. Anna Mae moved into Perry and enjoyed playing dominoes with her neighbors and quilting at the St. Ann's sewing club at church. She belonged to the Noble County Homemakers Club. She also loved to make quilts. She passed away December 13, 1979. There are 143 living descendants.

Ludwig Schiewe

By Hattie Shiever and Rose Stengle

Ludwig Schiewe was born in Germany, February 13, 1849 and grew to manhood there, making his living as a farmer.

In August 1872, he married Friedrika Nitz in Paulinofke Russia, state of Kiev. Friedrika was born in Poland in 1854 and grew to womanhood there.

Later in 1874, they moved to Rockvitch Russia. Life was hard there. The government had promised them land, in exchange for clearing and improving it. However, years later this arrangement was considered non-legal and the land taken away from them. The years by, and a family of seven sons and one daughter were born to them. Micheal born 1874, Stephen 1876, Julius 1878, Emil 1882, Louis 1885, Edward 1887, Amelia 1891, Rheinhold 1894, and Adolph who was born in America in 1896. Three additional sons had died in infancy.

A better way of life was on the minds of many in the old country. They had heard and dreamed of opportunities being available in America. The government had changed in many European Areas, and certainly not in favor of the people's welfare. Life was becoming more difficult. This subject no doubt, was also discussed in the home of Ludwig Schiewe. They too, decided to take this matter seriously. It was a difficult decision to make for the problems would be many. The language barrier most of all would be difficult to overcome. However, their decision had been made. It was arranged that their son, Stephen, who was then 17 years of age, would go to America to see what opportunities were there, and other better ways of life. Stephen left Berlin, Germany for America in 1893. Landing in New York, staying with friends in other parts of the country, he observed and was delighted, America was very favorable. This information was passed on to his family. So in 1894, the rest of the family came to America. They made the voyage by ship, with a net of 4000 people on board. The voyage took 3 weeks, air travel was many years away. When they reached America they stayed with friends by the name of Mittelstat. Later, they resided, for eight years at Worthington, Minnesota. The winters were extremely cold there. So having opportunities to settle in a warmer area, they came to Oklahoma in 1902. First living 12 miles east of Perry which is known as Bill's Corner, on from there 1 mile north and ½ miles east. Later they moved and purchased a farm, two miles north and one mile east of Morrison. Later, also purchasing the one quarter, south of them. Here they made their homes until their deaths.

At the immigration office, being one by one registered, some of the family members last name was misspelled. However, they decided to leave it, since it would have involved some problems, they decided to leave it that

Seated (L to R): Fredrika (Frieda) Schiewe, Ludwig Schiewe. Standing: Adolph Schiewe.

way. Therefore brothers, their last name is not spelled the same. Sons Michael, Emil, Edward, Amelia and Rheinhold last name was Schiewe, and Stephen, Julius and Louis was spelled Shiever.

Their youngest son, Adolph, served in World War I and reached the rank of Corporal. He was wounded in the service. T.B. set in resulting in the loss of one leg. This ailment also led to his death, October 26, 1921. He is buried in the Morrison cemetery.

Ludwig died in 1911 at age 61 years of age. The cause of his death was due to an accident with horses. He was pinned beneath the overturned wagon, severly injuring his liver, where he later contracted cancer. He is buried in the Morrison Cemetery. Friedrika, his wife, lived on their farm, near Morrison, until her death in 1931 at the age of 77. She is buried beside her husband in the Morrison Cemetery.

So for another family America was indeed a land of liberty and opportunities. With many struggles, trials, and tribulations, they had found a better way of life.

Charles Schlehuber

By Norma Snell

Gottlieb and Christina Dean Schlehuber came over from Germany and settled in the Cincinnati, Ohio area. With them came their two children, Elizabeth and Charles.

Gottlieb became a citizen in 1844. He worked at farming and as a dairy man. They had three more children, George, Charlotte and John Henry.

Their son, George, married Mary C. James in 1865. George worked as a carpenter in Cincinnati, Ohio. George and Mary had eight children, Elizabeth, Soffie, Charles L., Emma, John, William, Louie and Albert. Charles worked in a buggy factory when he was only nine. Charles was my grandfather.

In 1882, Mary C. died leaving George with eight young children to care for. Elizabeth had married Perry Hayes but helped her father as much as she could.

Charles' grandparents, Gottlieb and Christina, left Ohio for Nebraska, taking young Charles with them. George went to North Platte, Nebraska, in 1884, with the rest of the family where he homesteaded too.

Gottlieb died about the first of April, 1889, in Custer County, Nebraska. His widow, Christina, farmed the land until 1891. At such time, Christina went with George and the other children and grandchildren to Oklahoma.

Young Charles had worked for area farmers and ranchers, including being

Charles Lewis and Margaret J. Kent Schlehuber about 1910.

a stable boy for Buffalo Bill on his ranch. He soon left and followed his family to Oklahoma.

Christina died October 3, 1893, at Pawnee, Oklahoma. A few years later her family had her moved to Stillwater, for burial, to be with her children.

Charles was going to ride when they opened the strip, but fell sick and was unable to go. He was staying at Boomertown, where he met Margret Kent, who with her family had come from Missouri.

Charles and Margret were married in Stillwater on June 3, 1896. Since Charles was unable to make the run he bought the farm that his father-in-law, Jacob S. Kent, had got in the run.

George lived with his son Charles and helped build his home. Soon after, George remarried Aldulah J. Fulp, on September 21, 1896. After their marriage, they moved to Stillwater and owned land in the college addition and south of town also. George died September 18, 1899, married Maud Hetherington; George, born August 30, 1901, married Cleo Gilbert; Joseph, born June 21, 1904, married Stella Bilyeu; Jacob, born May 25, 1910; married Pearl Webl; Paul, born May 3, 1912, married Elnora Clark; Charles, born April 14, 1914, married Jackie Bell; Richard, born July 4, 1917, married Imogene Seba; Duane, born January 24, 1920, married Ada Long. It has been said Margret lost at birth or stillborn births as many as lived.

Charles raised cattle, horses and mules for the army. When they dropped the calvary and didn't need horses anymore, Charles raised cattle and farmed. They made many cattle drives to Wichita, Kansas. They both liked music and dancing. Charles was on the school board and on the co-op board in Morrison, Oklahoma.

Charles Louis died in April, 1954, after a long illness in his home with his wife and children with him. He is buried in Perry, Oklahoma.

Margret stayed a couple of years on the farm, then selling out, lived with her son, Frank, and visiting once in a while with the other boys. Later she went to a home. Margret stayed in fairly good health and could get around by herself. She was always bright and cheerful. Margret Jhrusha died in October, 1974, and was buried at Perry, Oklahoma.

George William Schlehuber
By Frankia Story

George William Schlehuber was born in Cincinnati, Ohio to Gottlieb and Christina (Deane) Schlehuber (immigrants from Germany) in 1844. July 23, 1864, George Schlehuber married Mary James (immigrant from England) in Cumminsville now a part of Cincinnati, Ohio. To this union eight children were born: Elizabeth Christian (Hayes), Charlotte Henrietta died in infancy, Charles Louis, Emma Viola (Shaw), George William, John R., Louis H., and Albert Charles. Wife Mary died of cancer October 25, 1882.

In 1884, George and his family along with his parents and his brother John and his family came by wagon to Custer county, Nebraska. They settled in the Milldale area near what is now Callaway, Nebraska.

In 1893, George and sons: Charles, William, John, Louis and Albert, George's married daughter, Elizabeth (Lizzie), her husband Perry Hayes and their family, George's mother, Christina, George's brother and sister and their families: John and Henrietta (Pandorf) Schlehuber and their children Charlotte and John, Andrew and Charlotte (Schlehuber) Beiser and daughter, Charlotte moved to Morrison, Oklahoma. Gottlieb Schlehuber had died in Custer county, Nebraska in March, 1889.

Christina Schlehuber died October 5, 1893 and is buried in Fairlawn cemetery in Stillwater, Oklahoma.

George was a carpenter by trade. He lived in Noble county several years but later moved to Stillwater, Oklahoma, where he died September 18, 1899.

Charles married Maggie Kent and lived in the Morrison area until his death in 1954.

William left Oklahoma after 1900 and went to New York. He died February 16, 1950 in Interlaken, New York.

John R. was a barber. He was in partnership with E. M. Blancett in Stillwater Oklahoma. John died October 28, 1904.

Louis H. was a barber. He died in Tulsa, Oklahoma in January 23, 1936.

Albert married Bernice E. Primmer May 3, 1899. She was the daughter of Henry Primmer in Auburn township in Noble county, Oklahoma. Albert and Bernice lived in that area for several years before moving to Colorado Springs, Colorado.

The Perry Hayes family moved to Stillwater, Oklahoma in 1895 where they lived until their deaths. Perry died in 1934 and Lizzie died in 1947.

Henry Schomaker
By Harold A. Pricer

My grandfather, Henry Schomaker, was born January 22, 1860, in Augustendorf, Hanover, Germany. He was the son of Johann and Meta (Prigge) Schomaker. An older brother, Claus, preceded him to the United States and assisted in earning passage for Henry to come to this country. Henry left Gnarrenburg, Bremervorde, his home in Germany on January 13, 1883, and arrived in America in 1885, joining his brother, Claus, in McPherson County, Kansas.

They worked until they had passage for one sister, Meta Katharina, who came to America and joined them in McPherson, County, Kansas. All three later lived in Noble County, Oklahoma.

On September, 11, 1890, Henry was

The Schlehuber family about 1945. Charles Louis and Margaret - sitting (L to R): Duane, Richard, Charles, Paul, Jacob, Joseph, George, Frank and Gladys.

married to Caroline Auguste Seehaver at the Lutheran Church in Spring Valley Township of McPherson County, Kansas. She was born December 1, 1863 in Perth County, Ontario, Canada, the daughter of Michael and Eva Rosine (Scheerbart) Seehaver. Her parents were both born in Germany. Their first son, John Fred, was born November 8, 1891. The second son, William Henry, was born October 16, 1893. The third son, Carl Edwin, was born May 3, 1896. These three sons were all born near Canton, Kansas.

In 1897, Henry and his existing family moved to Oklahoma Territory and settled on a farm two miles north of Lucien. Here their four daughters were born. The first was my mother, Martha Elizabeth (Pricer) who was born August 11, 1898, in a corn crib as their home had not been completed. The next daughter was Clara Louise (McGuire) who was born December 18, 1900. Anna Pauline (Moelling) was born October 3, 1902, and Dora Helena (Ayres) was born February 13, 1907.

In 1919, they moved to Perry and lived on the southwest corner of 7th and Noble streets. Henry was a lifelong member of the Lutheran Church and was an active member of the church council while he lived in Perry.

On March 23, 1923, he died in his sleep on his farm near Lucien, Oklahoma. My grandmother, Caroline, continued to live at their home in Perry until March 6, 1941 when she died following an extended illness.

My great aunt, Meta Katharina (Schomaker) Metcher, lived just east of a small park on Locust street in Perry, during my childhood. She and her husband, John Dietrick Metcher, later moved to Ponca City. My great uncle, Claus, farmed a couple of miles south of Perry. One of my memories of him was the wonderful watermelons that he grew on his farm.

Anton Schwartz
By Maxine Endicott

Anton Martin Daniel Schwartz was born in Holstead, Denmark, on December 15, 1856. He was sponsored to the United States by a family in Kansas. He arrived in Marion, Kansas, on May 19, 1883. Anton Schwartz and Else Margrethe Andersen were married at Morganville, Kansas, in 1888. Mrs. Schwartz had made the journey from Hygum, Denmark, her birthplace, alone.

To this union were born three children: Carrie Schwartz, John Andersen Schwartz, and Mary Schwartz Bridal. They lived in Clyde, Kansas, where Mr. Schwartz farmed until 1905 when they made the trip by train to Perry, Oklahoma, and bought their 160 acre farm northwest of Perry (Section 10, of Warren Valley Township). The farm is still owned by descendants of Anton and Else Margrethe Schwartz.

Anton was a successful farmer, and the family was well thought of in the community. They were one of the first families in the community to have natural gas for heat and lights from a huge City Service gas line that crossed their property.

Because of the language barrier, Mrs. Schwartz did not enter into many community affairs. But there were a few Danish families in Perry and around Sumner who met for coffee on Sunday afternoons. Some of the names were Hvolboll, Hendrickson, Larson, Neilsen, and Mason. The Hansens from Ponca City were frequent visitors.

Anton and Else Margrethe Schwartz were members of Christ Lutheran Church. They became naturalized American citizens on February 21, 1921. On June 1, 1933, Anton was working in his garden when he passed away suddenly. Else Margrethe died April 30, 1936.

A check for taxes on a 1921 Model T Touring car was found among receipts and records. The amount was $25.

A granddaughter, Maxine Schwartz Enidcott, visited the birthplace of her paternal grandmother, Else Margrethe Andersen Schwartz, in Hygum, Denmark, in the summer of 1952. She visited the cousins and saw places her grandmother had seen and even walked down the well-worn aisle of the little Lutheran Church her grandmother attended.

In 1984, Mrs. Endicott's granddaughter, Laura Jane Bigbee, made the trip to Denmark and saw the same places and visited some of the same people.

Karen (Carrie) Kathrine Schwartz, eldest child of Anton and Else Schwartz, was born August 23, 1889, in Concordia, Kansas. She moved to Oklahoma in 1905 with her family to the farm in Warren Valley Township. She attended Lone Star School. She never married and spent a lot of her time gardening, raising chickens, canning and helping her parents. She also did sewing for her nieces and nephews.

She was a charter member of the Whipple Ladies Aid which first met in each hostess' home in the community. Later they carried on meetings in the school house. This Aid still meets there today.

At the death of her parents the farm was divided, and she moved to Perry. Her residence was 1011 Kaw Street. She owned the entire block. She sold lots intermittently for residences. She continued to raise chickens, which she dressed for sale. She had her own milking cow, which she pastured in the block north of her property. She always had lovely flowers.

She was a member of Christ Lutheran Church in Perry. In March, 1971, she entered the Perry Nursing Home. She died at the age of 84. She was buried in Grace Hill Cemetery.

John Andersen Schwartz, the only son of Anton and Else Margrethe Schwartz, was born on October 10, 1890, in Clyde, Kansas. John attended Lone Star School and graduated from the eighth grade, having taken many subjects that are now taught in high school. He loved music, and he and his wife-to-be (Cecil Exie Yowell) took in many evenings in the Opera House that was in Perry at the time. His favorite comedian was Buster Keaton, who of course, was from Perry and become quite famous.

On November 22, 1914, he married Cecil Exie Yowell. The wedding took place at the Yowell home. To this union were born four children: John Bernard -1915, Carlin A. - 1917, Cecil Elaine -1918 and Elsie Maxine - 1920. The family lived on the Debord farm a mile west of Whipple school on Warren Creek.

In 1936, they moved to the farm inherited from Anton Schwartz and lived there until 1968 when they moved to 719 Grove Street in Perry. John was in ill health, and he passed away June 18, 1969. He was buried in Grace Hill cemetery.

The third and youngest child of Anton and Else Schwartz was Mary Katrina, born December 24, 1892, at Louisburg, Kansas. She came to Oklahoma with her family in 1905. She attended Lone Star School.

On May 26, 1921, she graduated from Nurses training at Phillips University Hospital in Enid and worked there as an X-ray technician until her marriage. She was married to John Henry Bridal of Marshall, Oklahoma, on January 4, 1928. They lived on a farm five miles east of Enid. Their only child, John Howard Bridal, was born there on October 11, 1930.

Mary was a member of Christ Lutheran Church in Perry. She was confirmed on February 13, 1944. A. J. Brase was pastor at that time. In 1941, Mary and her son John moved to Perry and lived at 1025 12th Street. John attended Christ Lutheran School, and Mary was employed at Perry Memorial Hospital until 1967. She passed away February 6, 1972 in the Perry Nursing Home. She was buried in Grace Hill cemetery.

John Scott
By Mary Louise Allen

John Henry Scott was born May 27, 1862, at Center Point, Iowa, the eldest of twelve children. Catherine Agusta Richardson was born August 28, 1866, at Cedar Rapids, Iowa. Her mother died when she was small and she was raised by her sister Clara Tripplett in Moline, Illinois. They were married May 3, 1884, at Emmettsburg, Iowa. John Scott owned teams of draft horses and made a living with various work using them, such as building grades for the expanding railroads of the 1880's.

While living at Lincoln, Nebraska, a son David William was born October 19, 1885, but only lived nine months. Their second son Elmer Grant was born on June 7, 1887. Their first daughter Iva Bell was born June 28, 1889, in Eureka, Kansas, from where the family moved on to Oklahoma City.

John Scott made the run to Perry on horseback, while Catherine followed, driving the team that pulled the covered wagon, in which rode their children, Elmer and Iva and their friend, Mrs. A.I. Acres and her children, Addie and Allen. Iva's memory of the day was that it was hot, windy, dusty and the children had fun chasing tomato can wrappers.

The Scott family made their home in a tent on the banks of Cow Creek for a few days. Then they obtained a lot which became their permanent home. When a man tried to jump their claim, Catherine took the shotgun and ran him off.

The Scotts, with Catherine driving one of the teams, hauled lumber from Orlando, to build their house, and A.I. Acres' Big Horn butcher shop, located on the north side of the square. Mrs. Scott recalled spending the night on the prairie. With the fear that they would be robbed, they slept a distance away from the wagons.

By October they had succeeded in building a one room frame house, working at night, using a wagon and boxes instead of a ladder. Catherine held the lantern for John while he worked.

Thru the years the Scotts added to the house until it had six rooms, with the original room serving as the dining room. Two of their children were born in this house, Hazel Anna, July 14, 1899, and Ettie Adella, October 16, 1902.

John Scott was house mover and builder. A granddaughter recalls being told that he helped moved the houses from White Rock to a new site, along the Rock Island railroad, called Billings.

Catherine Scott did beautiful handwork; her children and grandchildren were the lucky recipients of her embroidery, crochet and quilts. She could tan a hide for a rug, make a cheese and carefully preserved the food John annually raised in one of the most

John and Catherine Scott the day of their 50th wedding anniversary, May 3, 1934.

beautiful gardens in their neighborhood. He was well known in Perry for his successful gardening.

Important to John and Catherine Scott was their active participation in the life and worship of the First Baptist Church having been baptized January 30, 1896, into the membership of the congregation.

On February 11, 1938, John Scott met his wish to "die with his boots on," dying of a heart attack as he closed the backyard gate on his way to work. Still living in the house they built, Catherine died December 16, 1955.

The Scott children attended and graduated from the Perry schools. Graduating in 1908, Elmer left Perry to become an electrician and installed telephone switchboards in such places as Roundup, Montana, and Mexico. He married Della Barnett and they lived in Mitchell, South Dakota, where he ran a car body and paint shop. He accepted a job with Bell Telephone and later Western Electric as a radar specialist. He installed the radar equipment in the battleship U.S.S. Oklahoma. Elmer died December 26, 1949, at Springdale, Arkansas.

Iva graduated in 1907 and that fall taught at Antelope Valley. Her teachers contract called for "a term of six months commencing on the 7th day of October, 1907, for the sum of 37 and 50/100 dollars per month." said contract signed by Geo. Pfrimmer and W.C. Cook. An accompanying letter stipulated that "You do or pay for your own janitor service." Iva also had to furnish her own school bell and dictionary. She later taught at Lone Star, Perry and Stillwater.

On October 19, 1919, Iva married Harry V. Shoop at the Grant Shoop home, in Oakdale township. They lived for 46 years on the Shoop homestead. Harry died August 5, 1965, with Iva passing away February 18, 1978.

Ettie graduated in 1921 and followed in her sisters footsteps, teaching. While teaching at Whipple she met Erle Hughes. They married May 18, 1924, at the Scott home and started farming in the Whipple area. Later Erle was manager of the Perry Mill and then became manager of the Farmers Co-op at Marshall. They were living in Enid when Erle died on July 20, 1958. Ettie married Ed Brand on June 27, 1964, and they lived in Woodward until Ed's untimely death in 1969. Etta now lives at Madill, Oklahoma.

Hazel finished Perry High School in 1918. She taught at Antelope Valley and in the Red Rock area, where she met Charles Postelwait, a prosperous young rancher. They were married at the home of the bride, September 23, 1919, the twenty-first birthday of the groom. At one time they lived in Painesville, Ohio, where Charles drove a freight truck to New York City. They moved back to Perry and raised their family. Charles now lives in Enid. Hazel died August 2, 1975, having been born, married and dying in the house her parents built at 422 Ivanhoe Street.

John W. Sears
By Charles Sears

John William Sears was born in February 1873 at Fall River, Kansas. He was the son of Mary Mollie (Ridgeway) and Daniel Washington Sears. He married Hattie May Martin, January 28, 1892 at Severy, Kansas. Hattie was born in October 1874 in Kansas. When they came to Noble County they had one son Floyd A., who was born in March of 1893 in Kansas. They came by wagon and made the Cherokee Strip run. They homesteaded the northwest quarter of section 35 in Autry township.

Seven more children were born on their homestead north of Glencoe, Oklahoma. They were: Jesse (Jay) W. born in November 1894; Charles F. born November 1896, an infant that died at birth in 1901; Viva Pearl born in 1902; Harold William born in 1907, Alma born in 1910 and Mary Wilma born in 1912.

John played the violin and in addition to farming he claimed he "witched" for water. With the ends of a forked branch from a tree he walked over the land. When he felt the stick turn in his hands he knew there was water underground. Many water wells were located in this way. He was also a handyman and made his first tractor from an old Model T Ford by adding heavy iron wheels.

His son Charles, now 90 years of age, and his wife Grace (Kinamer) purchased the homestead in the early 1930s and still live on it. Charles and Grace's only child, Jimmie Lee, lives with his second wife (Rosalie) on the farm. Also Jimmie's first wife, Maryln and daughter live on the farm in mobile homes.

Dr. Seid's dentist office. This chair is in the Cherokee Strip Museum - Perry. (courtesy Cherokee Strip Museum - Perry).

Frederick C. Seids

By Mildred Highfill

Dr. Frederick Charles Seids was born January 2, 1874, in Bryan, Ohio and first came to Oklahoma in 1889, to work in a general store owned by his brother-in-law, J. J. Cummings in Mulhall. Later, he was manager of a similar business at Stillwater, but he soon returned to Ohio to study pharmacy. Later, he changed to dentistry and in 1896, earned a degree from Western Dental College, now part of the University of Missouri, at Kansas City, Missouri. In April 1896, Fred C. Seids returned to Mulhall, Oklahoma. Here he borrowed a barber chair and put it in his room in the hotel. He pulled teeth for 50¢ and cleaned them for $1.00 while waiting to take the Dental Board examination. He passed the board and was the 43rd dentist registered in Oklahoma Territory. He came to Perry in 1896 to begin his practice and opened his office in the Globe building on the west side of the square.

Extracted from his unpublished "Memoirs": "When I came to Perry, the streets were maintained as the country roads were, with a team of horses and a road scraper. The gutters around the square, when it rained, were flushed of accumulated trash. The electric light provided by the water and light plant came on according to the sunlight about four or five o'clock in the evening and continued until 10 o'clock in the morning, there was no day current. However, many times it didn't come on at all for days at a time. The water was provided by a gentleman named Bill Case and his horse drawn wagon. It was customary for each building to have a barrel at the front entrance on the sidewalk. This was filled daily and used for drinking, all culinary purposes and baths. Each barrel was provided with an iron cover which fitted over the top and this was a favorite seat for town loafers. The water in the barrels which Bill Case delivered was brought from a huge spring in southeast Perry. For fire protection and household, garden and lawn use, a charter had been granted for a water system. A dam had been erected on Cow Creek which was suppose to furnish an ample supply of water for fire protection and other uses. The water always had a mud content, however, which was colored red from the clay on the water shed. We talked of our baths as the famous red baths.

In November of 1898, I took down with typhoid fever. At the time I was living at the Agricola Hotel, which was conducted by Mrs. M. B. Tally. It was a small hotel across the alley and near the corner of Fifth and "D" Streets. Mrs. Talley was a good hotel manager, and her food was excellent. The hotel was not an ideal place for one suffering from typhoid fever, however, Mrs. Fred Farrar, who lived in the house on the corner across west from the Presbyterian church offered a room in her house. Six of my friends came with a stretcher and carried me all of those blocks to the Farrar home. I was so ill that I do not remember who they were. There was an epidemic of typhoid fever in Perry about this time and among the numerous cases was that of my friend, Henry S. Johnston."

Dr. Seids was an avid hunter and he continued: "At that time, it required no skill and little effort to drive out in a team and buggy along the main road and kill fifteen or twenty quail. There were many times, too, when there were plover, ducks and geese and now and then a prairie chicken. In May and June there was a terrific crop of young fox squirrels. Rueb Brothers Cafe was a real mecca for good food. They understood the preparation of any kind of game. They would dress and prepare whatever we brought in. Many times when we had a good bag of game, we would divide it with our friends. Fishing, too, was as interesting as hunting. Along Red Rock Creek there were overflow channels which grew wonderful lilies, and the lily pads would be literally covered with bull frogs and the water underneath swimming with the finest bass. Also I want to tell of the slough that runs across the Trumbla farm and the Brisco place and Dr. Southard's homestead not far north of Perry. During the fall rains and colder weather, this was always a resting place for geese and ducks in their southern flights and I have seen this area covered with geese and ducks of every description. It was a hunters paradise."

In 1898, he served on the city council. In the same year be became a Mason. On June 24, 1909, Dr. Seids married Faye Hughes of Perry. She was the daughter of A. A. Hughes, photographer. There was one child, Lysbeth (Fritzie) who later married W. D. Keith. During the mid 1930s Fritzie toured the states with the Horace Heidt orchestra as harpist and soloist on his radio program. Faye Seids died in 1913, and is buried in Grace Hill Cemetery, Perry. Dr. Seids married Leonora Miller of Chattanooga, Tennessee on July 21, 1927 at Ponca City, Oklahoma. He represented Noble County in the 22nd legislature of Oklahoma in 1947.

For a number of years before his death, he was interested in growing fruit trees and flowers especially iris.

Dr. Frederick C. Seids, pioneer dentist.

He was interested in growing and grafting pecan trees. He was active in the Perry Chamber of Commerce and the Presbyterian Church. He retired in 1963 after 67 years of practicing dentistry in Perry. He died January 21, 1967 and is buried beside his first wife.

Edward Benjamin Shaw
By Frankia Story

Edward Benjamin Shaw was born in Harper County, Nebraska to Orrin F. Shaw and Elizabeth (Jaquis) Shaw on July 23, 1873.

In 1884 Edward's parents Orrin and Elizabeth Shaw moved to Custer County, Nebraska. It was in this county that Edward met and married Emma Viola Schlehuber in December 1891. Emma was the daughter of George and Mary (James) Schlehuber. Emma was born in Cincinnati, Ohio.

Their first son, Edward William Shaw, was born in Custer County, Nebraska on August 8, 1892, their second son Robert Earl was born in Harper County, Kansas on October 1, 1894 and their third son, Don Orrin was born in Lincoln County, Oklahoma on September 23, 1897.

The Shaws arrived in Morrison, Oklahoma the first part of April in 1895. Emma's brother Charles Schlehuber had homesteaded in the Morrison area in 1893. The Shaws lived in the Morrison area for a year, leaving Morrison they settled near what is now Meeker, Oklahoma and lived there until their deaths. Edward B. died October 17, 1949 and Emma died July 18, 1959. Their sons: Edward W. died December 22, 1937, Robert E. died March 23, 1973 and Don O. died May 7, 1973.

Orrin F. Shaw
By Frankia Story

Orrin Ferris Shaw was born in Greenfield, New York, to Edward M. (immigrant from Ireland) and Elizabeth (Whitford) Shaw, on June 4, 1839. In 1856, he, along with his parents, several aunts and uncles and his 79 year old grandmother (Betsy Whitford), came by wagon to Butler county, Iowa and settled in New Hartford. Orrin was a blacksmith by trade. He married Elizabeth Jaquis shortly after he came to Iowa. In approximately 1873, he and his family moved to Nebraska, settling in Harlan county, near Alma.

In 1884, Orrin accompanied by his son, Robert William, and Robert's brother-in-law, Benjamin McArthur, came to Custer county, Nebraska. They first went to the Goosecreek area, near Milburn, but decided to settle in the lower end of Lower Powell Canyon, just north of what was to be the Finchville townsite. All three took out preemptions (A Pre-emption was 160 acres you could own by living on the land one and a half to two years and paying a price of $1.25 per acre.) They returned to Harlan county and brought their families with them the same year.

Orrin and Elizabeth had six daughters, and a son, Edd, besides son, Robert. Edd was not old enough to file a claim, but did so when he reached the required age.

The six daughters were: Cora (Morrell), Harriet (Mylar), Sarah (Robison), Minnie (Griffith), Olive (Lisle) and Abbie (Koehler).

After several years, they heard of the land opening up in Oklahoma, so Orrin, his wife, son, Edd, and daughters Olive and Abbie left for Oklahoma the year was 1894. They spent the winter of 1894 in Harper county, Kansas and left for Oklahoma early spring of 1895. They arrived at Morrison, Oklahoma the first part of April.

They lived in Morrison for a year, where Orrin was a blacksmith and farmer. Leaving Morrison, they settled near what is now Meeker, Oklahoma and lived there till their deaths, Elizabeth passed away in 1916 and Orrin in 1921. Many of the Shaw are still living in and near Meeker.

James H. Shehi
By Helen Gardner Gottschalk

James Harvey Shehi was born July 7, 1832 in Monmouth, Ill., the second son of Mary McDonald LaRue and John M. Shehi. He had asthma as a child, which interfered with his schooling and as a result, he searched for a climate that might improve his health. He traveled overland with an ox team to Willamette Valley, Lyon county, Oregon, in 1850, and took claim under the first Homestead Act. Making bucks and wood-chopping during the first fall, his health did improve. He went to Northern California in 1851 and tried prospecting and mined for a while in southern Oregon. In 1855, he sold out and taking passage on the steamer "John L. Stevens" in San Francisco, California to Panama, crossed the Isthmus on a mule; boarded the "Central America" for his Atlantic passage to New York City, then back home to Illinois.

Military service included: an enlistment in the Army against the Rouge River Indians in the spring of 1851 in Northern California. In 1862, he enlisted in the 83rd Illinois Infantry but was refused due to his health.

As a citizen of Kansas, he became active in public affairs, serving his township as Trustee, Treasurer, School Board member and State Representative in 1874 and '75. He was

Ethelda and James Shehi about 1860.

elected County Sheriff for a four year term in 1875.

The major crime committed during his tenure as Sheriff was the murder of Rev. Samuel Woolpert, who lived in Wakefield, Clay county, Kansas, and was taking a load of apples from his home to Topeka, when he was killed by J.B. True.

Newspaper stories relate the events surrounding the murder and confession of J.B. True, when the jail was encircled with a "Lynch Mob" which dissolved when Sheriff Shehi informed them that True had confessed and told him where to find the body. The trial, the removal of True to a Lawrence jail for protection, his escape from the jail, the recapture and the sentence are all related in the Louisville and Wamego newspapers of that time period. One story tells: "The sheriff had no problem handcuffing his prisoners, handcuffs not being an item of his equipment. He just cut the buttons off the criminal's trousers, thus eliminating handcuffs, as both hands were required to hold up his trousers."

His first marriage was to Ethelda Melvin Shute. She was born March 28, 1837 in Clinton county, New York. She died April 9, 1883 in Fostoria, Kansas. She was the daughter of William and Betsey Shute. They were married October 11, 1858 at Galesburg, Illinois.

His second marriage was to Mrs. Theresa Price 23 December 1884. She was born September 22, 1845 in Alsace, France. She died July 14, 1932 in Perry, Oklahoma. She was the daughter of Mary Walcor and Michael Kathofer and a widow of Lot Price. She is buried beside her first husband at Wamego, Kansas city cemetery.

James Harvey was accidently shot September 22, 1877 by the District Clerk, the bullet passing through his lungs and entering the right breast, where it lodged. He recovered from this injury but his obituary suggests this might have hastened his death. He died December 31, 1906, in Fostoria, Kansas. He went back to Kansas to die so he would save the expense of shipping the body back to be buried beside his first wife. He homesteaded in Walnut township (nw ¼ of section 18).

James Harvey and Ethelda had ten children: George Washington, Martha, Henry Clay, Winfield Scott, James S., Frances E., John, William, Merritt, and Cecila. Cecila was born October 10, 1881 in Fostoria, Kansas and died December 5, 1944 in Perry, Oklahoma. She married James Gardner June 8, 1905 at Perry, Oklahoma. When her father died, she inherited his homestead in Walnut township. She lived on this farm and raised her two children: James Harvey Gardner and Helen Gardner Gottschalk.

D. Theodore Sherrard

By Marceil S. Phillips

My father, the late David Theodore (Ted) Sherrard was born February 25, 1887, in Winfield, Kansas to David Sylvester & Anna G. Sherrard and was one of 13 children.

He spent his childhood days in Winfield, Kansas and attended Kansas State University where he received an engineering degree in 1910. He then took an apprentice course with Westinghouse Electric Company in Pittsburgh, Pennsylvania. The first of June, 1912, he made application for a job to work on the Panama Canal. Later that month, he received a telegram from the Isthmian Canal Commission in Washington, D.C. telling him of his appointment. The position open then was assistant switchboard operator and the "General Conditions of Employment" included free rent in the Canal Zone, transportation to and from the Isthmus, six weeks annual vacation and in case of illness or injury, "free medical care and attendance at the hospitals." He was to be paid $112.50 per month which was based on an eight-hour day with time and a half for overtime. His foreman at the Westinghouse plant said it was the best thing in the world for him to go.

The trip to Panama was on the ship Alliance and left New York City July 9, 1912, with about 100 passengers aboard. On arriving in the Canal Zone, he was assigned to the Power Plant at the Miraflores Generating Station in the Pacific Division. The Canal Lock closest to the Pacific Ocean was the Miraflores Locks located about 200

Electric locomotive which towed boats through the Canal at Gatun. Ted Sherrard is shown in the middle.

yards from the Power House. The other two sets of locks were located at Pedro Migual only several miles northwest and the Gatun Locks on the Caribbean Ocean entrance into the Canal. The Power Plant supplied electrical power to three or four surrounding villages as well as construction equipment like cement mixers and pump motors.

The actual work he did in the power plant was relatively clean. His job was to see that the machinery was running all right. He also made a record of the amount of electricity being used every half hour and the amount used each day. After a week on the day shift, he was moved to nights since he was the last man on the job. A few months later, he was transferred to the Caribbean end of the Canal Zone to do test work on the Gatun Locks. There were about 500 motors on the Gatun set of locks alone. His specific job in the beginning was to test the Emergency dams at the Gatun Locks.

As a result of this transfer to Gatun, Mr. Sherrard was right in the middle of many events leading to the opening of the canal. In October and November of 1913 various dignitaries began to come to the canal to see how things were going. The last of December, testing of the spillway gates at Gatun Dam were made for the first time. After the spillway the "test gang" was busy testing the working of the lock apparatus. Mr. Sherrard was working at times nine to eleven hours. On Sunday, January 11, 1914, a tug was put through the locks on its way to Colon for repairs, making the complete trip from the Pacific Ocean to the Atlantic Ocean. However, he noted that no boat had yet made the entire trip through the canal in one journey. He also put the tug, Reliance, through the locks. Two years before it had made the trip around Cape Horn and was considered the first boat to entirely circumnavigate South America.

The first towing locomotives arrived on the Isthumus the first of February. Located on each side of the locks, the job of these locomotives was to pull the ship through. They worked on electricity like the locks. By March, 1914, Mr. Sherrard was ready to take a vacation and go home. He left Gatun on April 1 to look for a job in the States; even though he stated that he enjoyed the work and life there!

After coming back to the States he enlisted in the National Guard in the State of Kansas August 6, 1914, and was honorably discharged on April 23, 1917. He married Angeline M. Allen in Sumner, Oklahoma on April 11, 1917, and they lived on a farm east of Perry for a few years; traveling to the farm from Sumner by horse and wagon. They became parents of three children: Marceil Edith born August 1, 1918, twins, Marian Elizabeth and Maxine Theodora, June 3, 1920. After the twins were born the family soon left the farm and moved to Perry where Mr. Sherrard became a letter carrier from 1924 until his retirement in 1949. After enjoying several years of retirement traveling and visiting his children and grandchildren, he was stricken with cancer and after a lengthy illness passed from this life November 11, 1973 at the age of 86. My mother passed away December 9, 1940, and they are buried in the Sumner Cemetery 12 miles east of Perry.

Mr. and Mrs. Ted Sherrard taken in April, 1917, traveling to their farm east of Perry from Sumner.

Virginia, David and Grant by car they drove to school.

Mary Ann (Hensley) and David Sherrard May 5, 1944.

David Sherrard
By Mary Ann Sherrard

David Sylvester Sherrard was born October 18, 1920, on the farm six miles south and three east of Perry, Oklahoma, that his parents, Martha Almira (Aten) and Ralph Edwin Sherrard bought in 1910.

He attended New Hope rural school, one mile south and ½ mile east of this home, through grade school. He walked or rode their horse, "Mollie", to school. They had a shed at the school to keep and feed the horses through the day. His brother and sister, Grant and Virginia, had also ridden Mollie to New Hope. When the north wind and snow blew, he bundled up and Mollie brought him home after school.

He drove a Model A Ford to Perry High school graduating in 1938. They got up early, milked the cows, separated the cream from the milk, ate breakfast and then he took the cream into town on the way to school.

During the dry year of 1936, they had a sale, rented out the farm and moved to Stillwater and back to Perry, where he graduated. He worked at the Phillips Station on 7th.

In 1938, they moved back to the farm. On March 13, 1942, he enlisted in the United States Coast Guard, during World War II. He attended "boot camp" at New Orleans, Louisiana. After spending some time at Norfolk, Virginia, attending an engine and police school, he returned to New Orleans and served aboard a Coast Guard Patrol Boat at the mouth of the Mississippi River.

His best friend, Lowell Highfill, got his 16 year old sister-in-law, Mary Ann Hensley, to write to him. They began corresponding and on May 5, 1944, they were married at Edmond, Oklahoma.

Mary Ann is the daughter of Lilly Cleo (George) and Marion Stuart Hensley. She was born August 7, 1926, at Slick, Oklahoma.

In June, 1944, Mary Ann went to New Orleans to be near David. Their son, Larry David, was born there, February 26, 1945. After Germany surrendered, David was on a train in Texas on the way to go to Japan. When Japan surrendered on August 14, 1945, he went to Alameda, California, then returned to New Orleans and received his discharge, September 13, 1945.

In 1948, they rented a farm eight miles south of Perry, where their son, Ralph Marion, was born March 17, 1949.

In 1950, they moved to the Gardner place which is in the northwest quarter of the same section of the Sherrard place.

When his parents moved to Perry, six months later, August 28, 1958, they moved to the home place where they still live.

For 20 years, David and his brother, Grant, farmed together almost 1,000 acres of wheat, from Lake McMurtry area almost to Billings. Larry and Ralph helped with the farming as well as cattle and alfalfa when they were out of school.

David retired in 1982. They have remodeled the house but they still live in the house where he was born.

They are active members of the First Baptist Church which he has attended all his life, except for the time they were in Stillwater.

Larry David Sherrard
By Sue Sherrard

One of the third generations of the Sherrards to live in Noble County was Larry David Sherrard. Larry was born on February 26, 1945 in New Orleans, Louisiana to David Sylvester Sherrard and Mary Ann Hensley Sherrard. When David got out of the Coast Guard, the three of them returned to the family farm in March, 1946.

In September of 1950, Larry started to school in the country southeast of Perry at Lone Elm. In the years attended there, he had three teachers. They were Mrs. Buzz Clark, Mrs. Gertrude Norman, and Mrs. Edith Zondler.

In July 1956, Larry attended 4-H camp in Ponca City. They were learn-

Grant and Virginia on "Mollie" - David Sherrard on steps of their house.

ing how to make rope halters when he stuck his pocket knife thru his eyeball. He spent two weeks in Oklahoma City in St. Anthony's Hospital receiving, at least three shots a day.

In 1957, Lone Elm School was closed due to low attendance. He then transferred to Fairview School which was five miles away from Lone Elm. His teacher was Mrs. Gertrude Dunivan. Both Lone Elm and Fairview were one room schools, with one teacher for all eight grades.

In August of 1958, Larry entered Perry High School as a freshman. He was involved in FFA his last four years, raising show calves, pigs and helping his dad with the family farming operation.

In May 1962, Larry graduated from Perry High School. He received a BA degree from Tonkawa in 1964. Then he attended OSU for one year and the Oklahoma School of Business and Banking in Oklahoma City for one year.

On April 2, 1966, Larry and Sue Davis were married at the First Baptist Church in Perry, Oklahoma. He enlisted in the US Navy in Oklahoma City and left for San Diego and bootcamp on August 11, 1966. He was in training schools in the Great Lakes for about six weeks, in Washington D. C. for 3½ months. He served on two new ships during his four years of active duty. He was a plank owner on the USS Niagara Falls AFS-3 and also on the USS White Palins AFS-4 when each was commissioned. They were supply ships. They put supplies on ships while on the move. He served in the Pacific. Larry received his final discharge in June 1972.

His first son, William David, was born December 8, 1967 in Perry. His second son, Brian Linza, was born January 26, 1969 in Perry. On February 13, 1976, his only daughter was born in Enid. Her name is Bobbette Janelle.

Since receiving his discharge Larry has gone back to Oklahoma State for one year and worked mainly in the oilfield. He has worked for Sun Exploration and Production since September 21, 1980. On March 1, 1985, he was promoted to Operator and transferred to Desdemona, Texas from Snyder, Texas where his employment with them began.

As of this writing, he and his family are living in De Leon, Texas, since there were no schools in Desdemona.

Ralph E. Sherrard
By Mary Ann Sherrard

Ralph Edward Sherrard was born in Winfield, Kansas, April 2, 1885, the son of Anna Gazelle (Lippincott) and David

L-R Front: Grant, Ralph and Martha Sherrard. Back Row: Virginia (Goss) and David Sherrard.

Sylvester Sherrard. He was raised on a farm southeast of Winfield, with eight brothers and two sisters. He attended a rural school there. They attended the First Baptist Church in Winfield. One time something scared the horses and they ran away. They were found at the hitching post in front of the church.

He attended a Telegraphers School at Winfield and then Wichita, washing dishes for his room and board. When he graduated he landed a job as a telegrapher for the Santa Fe Railroad at Sutton, Kansas. He persuaded Martha Almira Aten, a girl he met in church at Winfield, to come to Garden City to marry him. They were married March 16, 1907. She was born December 4, 1884, at Gypsum, Kansas, the daughter of Elizabeth A. (Pooler) and Benjamin Stewart Aten. She worked as a seamstress at Brady Brothers Store in Winfield.

He taught her telegraphy and they worked all over western Kansas, southeast Colorado and Newkirk, Oklahoma. They boarded the other operator, lived on that money and saved their salaries.

Ralph had two cousins in Payne County, Elmer Rollen (John) Sherrard at Yates, Camp Redlands now, and Ella (Sherrard) Robison in Stillwater. Henry Robison had this farm six miles south and three miles east of Perry for sale. Ralph and Martha bought it February 13, 1909. They continued working five more years before moving down. On November 10, 1913, Ralph Grant joined the family. They were working at Newkirk at the time and in 1914, they moved to a two story frame house east of now Camp Redlands and waited for the farm to be vacated. It was there, Virginia Elizabeth was born August 30, 1914.

In the fall of 1914, they moved to the farm with two babies, a cow and lots of determination.

They joined the First Baptist Church February 3, 1918, after they got their new car in 1917. They were active in organizing Rural Sunday School in three school houses. He was elected a deacon of the First Baptist Church October 5, 1919 and was active as long as able.

The freight line between Stillwater and Perry went through the farm and the prints of the trail are still visible. They traded at the store at Yates run by the John Sherrards. Martha took the two babies and the eggs to the store in the buggy. Something frightened the horses, a wheel hit a rock, broke the tongue and the horses ran away. Grant fell out, a wheel passed over him, hurt him but he was OK. Martha was sitting on Virginia's blanket so she didn't fall. She walked to a house, called John and he came after

Martha and Ralph Sherrard at Sutton, Kansas.

Sherrard home - 1944 in Walnut township.

her. John's wife, Stella, helped her clean the eggs that weren't broken.

On October 18, 1920, David Sylvester, was born on the farm. In 1922, the house sat up on the hill north of the barn. They hired movers, horses and logs, and took the house west, south and back east where it now sits. One man and the team moved the house. The south bedroom, and large screened in porch was added after it was moved.

They worked together, raised a big garden, canning, milking cows and raising feed for the stock. They were active in the community, she helped anytime there was illness in the community and helped deliver lots of babies in the area. She belonged to the Willing Workers and Ladies of '76 Home Demonstration Club.

On March 16, 1957, they celebrated their 50th Wedding Anniversary with a reception. The last of 1957, they bought a new house and moved to Perry. They saw the days of the horse and buggies, cars and jet airplanes. They flew by jet to California.

Their children gave another reception on their 60th Wedding Anniversary, March 16, 1967. They lived to observe their 65th Anniversary in 1972, before he passed away June 20, 1972. She lived until November 19, 1974, just short of her 90th birthday.

Stephen Shiever
By Rosie Shiever Stengle

Ludwig and Frieda Nutz Schiewe were married in 1872, in Poland. They moved to Russia. Their family consisted of nine children: Michael, Stephen, Julius, Emil, Louis, Edward, Amelia, Reinhold and Adolph.

In June 1894, they came to the United States where the attendant in immigrations spelled their name Schiewe. Though they came from Russia, they were German ancestry.

Stephen Shiever, (Steve) left the colony of Rockavitch, Kief, Russia on August 1, 1893, at 17 years of age, as his father asked him to go check out the new country. Steve was adventuresome, ambitious and his goals set high for the new country and new future.

There were 4000 people on his ship and it took 33 days to cross the Atlantic Ocean. He landed in New York, New York on September 11, 1893. At the immigration office, they spelled his name Shiever. He was determined to learn the language and educate himself. He migrated to Wisconsin and finally to Worthington, Minnesota. He worked for Mrs. Harline, saved his money and became better acquainted. In November 1898, he came to the vicinity of Morrison, Oklahoma.

He met and married Emma Just who resided with her parents, Christ and Wilhelmena Just who lived on the farm northeast of Morrison, SE ¼ Sec 4-21N-3E.

Steve purchased equity in a quarter NE¼ Sec 4-21N-3E, started farming with horses and the hoe was used fluently. He also accumulated a few head of cattle and chickens. Mama would make butter to sell along with the eggs. Often she would walk to Old Lela which was located one-half mile north of the famous swinging bridge located three miles east of Morrison and is still in use. She would do her shopping and carry groceries home, usually just flour, sugar and bare necessities.

Mr. Davis lives on the NW¼ Sec 4–11N-3E. His teenage daughter was practicing on her bicycle when she was stricken with a heart attack and passed away. They buried her on that land near the track. Mr. Davis no longer wanted to live on the place and sold it to papa.

Papa worked very hard but was determined. He worked for Mr. Sayre who lived near Lela. He grubbed trees and stumps, clearing the ground for farming. The days were long and he would walk to and from work after working from daylight until dark. His pay was $9.00 a month. Along with this work they did their own farming.

Steve one day thought there must be a much easier way so he bought a house and some vacant business lots in Morrison where he again worked hard. He hauled all of the rock for the building on the north side of Woolsey Ave. across the street from the Citizens State Bank. This building is still standing and is known as the S Shiever 1903 Building. The building had a full basement and a dumb waiter at the end.

It didn't take long and papa knew the city life wasn't for him. He moved back to the country and bought the 160 acres from Mr. Lawson NW¼, Sec 3-21N-3E. They built a two story house, which we always knew as our "home place". My, the love and joy we did share there.

Our home was open house for all. They took families in who were poverty stricken and helped them until they could find work. Weekends and holidays were most memorable.

Despite the large family, World War I, hail storms, droughts, grasshoppers, and all the adversities, papa and mama kept their strong faith and worked on. Many times I know they had to have worked with a very heavy heart, but we didn't sense it.

Papa bought a 160 acre farm in Pawnee County and another 160 acre in Noble County. Their family wasn't small and through the years were many heart aches, but also through the years, we spent many happy evenings singing. While in Europe, papa sang in the choir so he and mama would lead our singing and we all enjoyed the evenings.

They lost their first baby boy with crib death in 1899, and he was buried on the farm where they lived.

Edward L. was born June 21, 1901. He attended Enid Business College and married Olga Beier. They had four children: Edwin Fred, Leslie Adolph, Gaylene Olga and Janice Elaine. Edward L. was co-owner with his father and operated the Shiever General Store for twenty eight years. He also bought a section of land, raised cattle and rented the cultivated ground out. He couldn't get the farm out of his system. Edward L. left this life December 6, 1952, along with his son Edwin and wife, due to an accident.

Anna L. was born March 25, 1903, and married Fred Wegner. They owned and operated a grocery store in Inglewood, California, had one son, Edward Eugene. Anna passed away February 14, 1980, with cancer.

Theodore R. was born January 13, 1905. He contracted diptheria which settled in his eye. He passed away with cancer of the eye December 6, 1907.

Fay Emma was born June 28, 1907. She attended Enid Business College and worked for the City of Ponca City several years. She then chose California for her home. She left this life April 1, 1980, after a battle with cancer and a heart attack.

Wanda Matae was born June 30, 1909. She married Lee Bamberger. They farmed and lived in and near Perry, Oklahoma. They later moved to Santa Fe, New Mexico where she passed away February 27, 1971, after a lengthy illness with cancer. They had three children, Lee Stephen, Buddy (W.D.) and Wanda Jean. Lee Stephen lost his young life in an accident December 6, 1959.

Evert Stephen was born May 9, 1911. He married Hattie Helene Widiger April 24, 1938. He, like his father, loved farming and ranching. He bought farms here as well as at Winfield, Kansas. They had three children, Marvin Evert, Dennis Stephen, and Annetta Gayle. Evert lost his life February 23, 1973, in a tractor accident.

Stephen Shiever family 1921. Front Row (L to R): Stephen R., Frieda W. and Rosie C. Second Row (L to R): Evert S., Wanda M., Fay E. Back Row (L to R): Stephen, Emma, Edward L. and Anna L.

Frieda Wilhelmina was born July 10, 1912. She married Clark V. Field. He owned and operated grain elevators, farmed and ranched and operated the Perry Livestock Exchange. They had two daughters, Janet Roselee and Nancy Denise. Frieda entered her eternal rest after a lengthy fight with cancer July 23, 1974.

Rosie Christine was born September 30, 1915. She married Howard Stengle. He served in the Air Force and later owned and operated the Red Front Garage in Morrison for twenty eight years. Rosie was employed in the Citizens State Bank for 26 years. They still have their home in Morrison.

Stephen Reinhold (Steve) was born September 29, 1917. He married Ethel Deloris Cowell. Steve was engaged in farming and ranching. He also was a Rural Letter Carrier. He served in the Air Force in the Control Tower and after his term in the service, he returned to farming, ranching and carrying the mail. He retired after thirty-five years of service on the mail route. They still reside at the old home place. We still gather there and have lovely times, the old joyous memories return, but what a grand life for all. Steve and Ethel have three sons, Stephen Craig, Randy Lynn, and Vance Lee.

Papa had many friends, many influential. He retired and moved to Morrison but toyed with politics. I must say he was not radical. He always appreciated a country that was free as he had a taste of the other kind. One of the things he was instrumental in was getting the pavement to go through Morrison. He loved everyone and most of all he loved his country as he had love, faith and trust in his God.

Emma or mama had a very busy life, loved her family and worked very hard for her family. Her childhood was very lonely. She, too, crossed the ocean at the early age of eleven with her parents. There were no children for her to play with, and she would often say, "I can recall the prairie, and its loneliness and peace, and a vast hawk hanging motionless in the sky." She recalled how beautiful nature was as she clung to God. She had great faith and trust and love for her God. As for me, I can only be grateful for having Christian parents who were honest, worked hard and with God's help, papa accomplished his goals.

Mama passed away quietly after a bout with kidney cancer on August 24, 1963. Papa was bed ridden for three years, suffered cancer and passed away quietly December 30, 1957. He was always a God fearing, law-abiding citizen.

I am so proud of my nephews and nieces and their families. I think I still have a great family. Prejudice? Maybe, but much love.

May Belle Shinn
By Marjorie Bowles

May Belle Shinn, daughter of John Bush Shinn (1830-__) and Charlotte Fielding (1836-1890) was born May 13, 1871 in Griggsville, Illinois.

The date of the earliest entry in the Shinn family history is the year 1066, when the Shinn and Lippincott families, who intermarried for at least two generations, were listed as owners of land estates in the Doomesday Taxation Book of William the Conqueror. Then, some six hundred years later, we find that three Shinn brothers emigrated to America from Hartford, England, arriving on the ship "Kent" in 1677. One of the brothers, John Shinn, settled in Burlington, New Jersey, and became a prominent overseer of the provincial capitol there. Little is known about his wife, except that her name was Jane. It is from this John Shinn and Jane, that May B. Shinn is descended.

John and Jane's son was John Shinn, Jr. who married Ellen Stacy. They, in turn, were the parents of George Shinn, who married Elizabeth Lippincott of the Lippincott publishing family of Philadelphia. George and Elizabeth's son was John Shinn II, who married Lydia Carter. And from this union, three generations of ministers were descended.

John and Lydia's son, the Reverend John S. Shinn, was a Quaker minister and teacher. His wife was Martha Parker. To them was born the very prominent minister, Rev. John Shinn IV, who moved from New Jersey to Ohio in 1822. The farmland which he acquired there lies under what is now Cincinnati. In 1830, he moved to Pike County, Illinois, and was a close friend of Peter Cartwright, who "converted" him to Methodism that same year. This conversion set a precedent for his descendants, who, to this day are all Methodists, except May. In 1831, John and his wife, Hannah Redrow (1788) settled one mile east of Griggsville, a small community of Pike County, where he procured land for all his sons. The couple's family was large — in fact, so numerous were all the Shinn's, that the locality was called "Shinntown". In 1834, he built the first "Meeting House" on his land. After the death of Hannah, he married Rebecca Lippincott, of the same family lineage as Elizabeth Lippincott.

John and Hannah contributed another minister to the Shinn family line, the Rev. James Shinn, who was born in 1806, while the family was still living in Salem County, New Jersey. He moved to Ohio in 1824, and three years later met and married Mary Smith (1807) whose parents had come to America from Holland.

Now we come to the times of May Shinn, for the Rev. James Shinn and Mary Smith were her grandparents — for her father, John Bush Shinn (1830) was their son, born to them in Hamilton County, Ohio. He became a school teacher and was married at the age of 23 to Charlotte Fielding

(1836-1890) who was the daughter of David Fielding and Mary Moore Smalley (1836-1886). They are buried in Bethel Methodist cemetery which surrounds the picturesque steepled white, frame, Victorian country church. The large family plot, beneath the shade of a huge, spreading cypress, on the sloping banks of a quiet stream, holds generations of the Shinn and Fielding families. John and Charlotte had moved to Griggsville, Illinois, where May Shinn was born.

In her youth, May was "old for her age", and was married when she was but eighteen to Samuel Elmer Laird (1867-1944), a young farmer from nearby New Salemm, Pike County, Illinois. The couple set up housekeeping in New Salem, where Laird continued to manage his father's farms. To this union, six children were born, three of whom were born in Illinois: LeOla May Laird (1890-1971); Shirley Carl Laird (1892-1970); and Helen Beatrice Laird (1898-1946). In 1899, the family moved to Oklahoma, where their last three children were born on the family farm just north of Perry: Samuel Paul Laird (1901-1959); Willa Kathryn Laird (1909-1970); and Marjorie Belle Laird (1911).

In 1912, Mr. Laird was appointed the first County Agent of Noble County, and was responsible for the County's agricultural exhibits at the State Fair in Oklahoma City. In this, Mrs. Laird was extremely helpful because of her artistic abilities. She helped to design and construct exhibits which consistently won top prizes.

She served as president of the Perry Parent-Teacher Association during Max Chamber's term as superintendent of schools. Her most important accomplishment during her tenure was the organization and management of a health clinic for underprivileged children. For one day, the basement of the Presbyterian Church was transformed into a hospital, with local doctors, assisted by local nurses, performing minor surgeries for whatever the families could afford to pay. Scores of operations were performed without even one casualty.

For several years she was Mother Advisor to the Rainbow Girls — a daughter organization of the Masonic Lodge and Eastern Star.

She was modest, quiet, spiritual and steadfast. She dedicated her life to being a helpmate and loving companion to her husband, and to being a wise, loving and tolerant mother.

She died of a massive paralytic stroke on July 4, 1952, surrounded by her four remaining children: LeOla, Carl, Kathryn, and Marjorie. She is buried beside her husband in Grace Hill Cemetery, Perry, where all of her deceased children, except Paul, are also buried.

Lincoln Grant Shoop
By Mary Louise Allen

County pioneer Lincoln Grant Shoop was born in Kittanning, Pennsylvania, October 14, 1864, to Jacob and Martha Shoop.

His father served as a Captain in the calvary during the Civil War. After the war, in 1867, the Shoop family moved to Camden county, Missouri, to a farm near Linn Creek. As a boy Grant farmed with his father, cut timber and hewed railroad ties. He attended the country schools then sparsely scattered throughout the Ozark hills. At the age of sixteen he began his apprenticeship as a printer in the office of **The Reveille** at Linn Creek.

Grant met Nancy Emily Miller at a party celebrating his fourteenth birthday and they became fast friends and afterwards schoolmates. Seven years later, on April 22, 1886, at her home in Sedalia, Missouri, she became his wife. Nancy, known to all as Nannie, was born March 10, 1864, at Louisville, Kentucky.

Following their marriage Grant and Nannie moved to Syracuse, Kansas, where he was employed as assistant foreman and editor of the newspaper. It was here that their son Harry Vincent was born March 6, 1887.

On April 22, 1889, Grant rode the first southbound train into the new Oklahoma Territory. Failing to stake a claim for farmland, he walked into Guthrie on the morrow. There he secured a lot and found work setting type on the first newspaper actually printed in Guthrie, Will T. Little's **Guthrie Get-up**. Shortly afterward he organized the Guthrie Typographical Union and was its first president. It was the first printers' union in Oklahoma.

In August Mrs. Shoop joined her husband after the birth of their daughter Martha Elizabeth (Bess) on

Harry and Iva Shoop with Mary Louise in front of farm home, 1922.

Nannie and Grant Shoop at the farm, on a 1930s Sunday.

July 22, 1889, in Garden City, Kansas. Their second daughter Mame Foster was born June 6, 1891, in Guthrie.

When the gun fired on September 16, 1893, Grant Shoop made the run from a point just west of Orlando, on his well-trained horse Polly. Grant and Wilson Shoop, Carrol Stovall and Fred Gang raced together and staked claims on adjoining land.

Following in a wagon driven by Will Shoop, were Nannie, son Harry, Wilson Shoop's wife Ellen and her son Ernest. They came to Black Bear creek where they spent the first night on what became known as the Howard farm, ten miles northwest of Perry. The next morning, at sunrise, they moved to the adjacent quarter east of that, a better farm and less likely to be contested. This they won and it was their home from that day on.

Wilson Shoop secured the quarter just north of his brother Grant's claim. After chasing cattle in the rain, Wilson contracted pneumonia and died in March, 1894. He was buried in the German Evangelical Cemetery at Orlando. Ellen Shoop proved up their claim and then moved back to Missouri. Being ill with consumption she soon died leaving their children, Ernest and Blanche to be raised by their father's mother and brothers, including Grant.

In 1899, during the "Seal Session" of the territorial legislature, Grant served as a journal clerk in the upper house of that legislature. In the county election of 1900 he was elected Register of Deeds for Noble County and re-elected in 1902.

An ardent Republican, in 1910 he was chairman of his party's campaign committee followed by an appointment as a member of the county election board. In 1922 he was appointed postmaster at Perry which office he held until 1934.

Nannie kept things going on the farm when Grant was so busy. Although they had a house on Grove Street and lived in Perry during his years as Register of Deeds, and while the children attained their education, they continued to maintain their farm home. Nannie passed away on January 12, 1935, after a brief illness.

After leaving the post office Grant spent most of his time farming. He had well bred stock and chickens on his Sunny Brook farm. For many years he had the best rose-comb Rhode Island Red hen.

A member of the Presbyterian church since boyhood he was active in all church affairs and was an elder in the local church. He was also an active member of the Masonic and Knight Templar lodges.

Grant was interested in the '89ers organization attending every April meeting and served as its president in 1938.

On December 18, 1939, while returning from a business trip to Tulsa, his car was wrecked and Mr. Shoop sustained injuries which resulted in his death on March 16, 1940.

Harry Shoop received his education in the Polo and Perry schools. Following which he spent some years in Colorado working in the gold mines at Victor and Cripple Creek and using his spare time to prospect on his own. He returned to Noble County and farmed until World War One when he spent some months in the army at Camp Pike, Arkansas.

On October 19, 1919, he married Iva Scott, the girl whose pigtails he dipped in the inkwell during the eighth grade. Rev. M. M. Munger performed the ceremony at the Shoop's country home. Harry died at age 78 and Iva lived to be 88.

Bess Shoop graduated from Perry High School in 1908. She taught school in Noble County and worked in the Register of Deeds office. On May 31, 1914, she married Thomas Orrin Munger at her parents' home, with the groom's father, M. M. Munger officiating. Bess and Tom's first home was in Waukomis where he taught school. Tom entered business for himself in 1916, and in 1918, with R. W. Treeman, began operating Treeman and Munger Seed and Feed Store in Perry.

Elected to the state House of Representatives in 1933, Tom served Noble County well for two terms.

Bess and Tom were living in Enid at the time of his death on May 12, 1966, and Bess' death on November 23, 1981.

Mame Shoop attended Polo and Perry schools. Mame and Allen Merriman were united in marriage October 15, 1911, in the Shoop's rural home. They immediately left for Allen's ranch in Montana, where they lived until 1914. Moving back to Noble County they farmed until January 16, 1923, when Allen became a rural mail carrier, the position he held until his retirement in 1949. Allen died March 15, 1963, and Mame passed away on April 26, 1969.

Ernest Shoop, born October 27, 1887, in Linn Creek, Missouri, lived with his Uncle Grant while he attended Perry High School, graduating in 1909. Ernest married Ethel Pfrimmer on June 29, 1913.

He started teaching in rural schools in 1911 and taught 14 years in Noble County, plus one year in Garfield County. Ernest and Ethel, also a teacher, spent 18 years employed by the Federal government in Indian schools in New Mexico and Arizona. Moving back to Perry, Ernest served Noble County as County Superintendent for fifteen years. Ernest passed away August 27, 1977. Ethel still resides in Perry.

Three generations have tilled the soil of Grant Shoop's homestead and have found that he did indeed claim a fair piece of land.

Peter Smith
By Darlene Roads

When Ludwig and Elizabeth Ritthaler left Austria-Hungary, seven of their children had been born. Margareth, the eldest daughter, was seven years of age at the time of the voyage. There were no entertainments on the boat and many times, Margareth danced the polka with her nine-year-old brother, Leopold, for the enjoyment of the captain and other passengers.

A year after Margareth and her family arrived in America and made their way to Kansas, where they settled, a young man named Peter J. Schmidt also made his way to America. Peter was born July 14, 1869 at Kirnica, Galacia, Austrai-Hungary. He was 16 years old when he left his homeland — possibly to avoid conscription into the military.

Peter also traveled to Kansas to join his brother, John, who had arrived a year earlier. They lived in a "soddy", a cave dug into the side of a hill with a wooden front door. Sometime during the next few years, their mother joined John and Peter in Kansas, and then tragedy struck. While the young men were away from home one day, heavy rains fell saturating the ground over the soddy. There was a cave-in and their mother was unable to escape.

Peter and John traveled back to Halstead, Kansas, where they became acquainted with the Ritthaler family. When Ludwig Ritthaler and his son, Jacob, decided to make the run into the Cherokee Outlet, Peter decided to go with them.

Two years after the run, Peter and

Peter and Margareth at the back door of their home at 608 Maple Street, Perry, Oklahoma.

Margareth were married on December 26, 1895 at Guthrie. They went to Moundridge, Kansas, where they began their family.

John Ludwig was born June 19, 1897, followed by Anna on March 30, 1899. At this time, Pete and Maggie returned to the homestead east and south of Perry. Their second son, Frank, was born in 1900, but did not survive. Emma Elizabeth was born October 23, 1901, Carl Edward on December 23, 1903, Rose Olga on December 9, 1905, Arthur Leopold on July 10, 1910, Minnie August on October 5, 1912, Paul Walter on October 24, 1914 and William August on July 14, 1917. Minnie became ill with croup and choked to death in her father's arms when she was 3½ years old.

After Pete and Maggie returned to Perry, Maggie's grandmother, Barbara Ritthaler, "Grandma Muny", lived with them and helped take care of the children.

Pete and Maggie lived near Zion Lutheran church and during the winter, Pete went to the church on Sunday mornings to fire up the wood stove. He would then return home, gather the family and go back for the worship services.

Trips to town were infrequent and many times, only Peter went to town with a list of purchases to be made. He also took items to be sold or traded for goods that were needed by the family.

On one occasion, during the war, soliders were in Perry looking for horses to buy for the cavalry. Peter had a fine team which he had drove in that day. Maggie began looking for him to come home at the usual time, but he did not appear. The time grew later and later. Finally, as she was preparing to send the older boys looking for him, Peter came trudging up the drive. He had sold one of the horses to the cavalry and, since the other horse was hitched to a double-tree, the only way to get home was for Peter to carry the load of the second horse.

Around 1920, the family name of Schmidt was changed to Smith.

In the 1920s or 30s, Pete and Maggie moved into Perry. They moved into a house at 608 Maple Street and were living there when Pete died May 21, 1940. He was buried at Zion Lutheran cemetery by little Minnie.

Maggie continued living there for many years. John and Emma had neither one married, and they lived with their mother, caring for her. Around 1950, Maggie, John and Emma moved into a house on Elm Steet, only one block from the square. Since Emma had never learned to drive, she could then walk to work at the courthouse and did not have to depend on John to take her. She was also closer to her church, St. Rose of Lima Catholic church.

John operated the Perry Saw Shop for many years and it was somewhat of a landmark in the 500 block of Delaware.

Maggie died September 15, 1964, at the age of 86. She, too, is buried at Zion Lutheran cemetery with Pete and little Minnie.

Loren J. Snodgrass
By Loren Snodgrass

Loren Joseph Snodgrass was born June 28, 1924 in Elkland, Missouri, the son of Orville E. Snodgrass and Inez (Callian) Snodgrass. They moved to Seminole County where Loren attended Mountain View High School and after graduation he went to O.S.U. He was in the Navy from 1943 to 1946.

On June 5, 1948 he married Reva Rae Simmons in Seminole, Oklahoma. Reva was born May 14, 1926 at Healdton, Oklahoma, the daughter of Milton D. Simmons and Doris (Tannehill) Simmons.

He went to work for Atlantic Richfield Company (ARCO) at Covington, Oklahoma and moved to Perry in 1951.

His art training includes study with Jacque Hans Gallrein for years and art classes at Oklahoma State University. The subject matter of his paintings has been varied, but he prefers "Western and Historical" themes which he researched extensively before beginning a painting. He formerly taught adult painting classes in Perry. His paintings are owned by individual collectors in several states.

Loren and Reva had two children they are: Lorita Rae born May 8, 1949 at Seminole, Oklahoma. Lorita married Jack Cline of Covington, Oklahoma. They have three children: Rangar, Tiffany (died at 3 years of age) and Jackie.

Reva and Loren Snodgrass.

Debra Ann was born July 1, 1953 at Stillwater, Oklahoma. Debra married Kenneth Charles II (Chuck) Cheney of Perry. Their children are Chad, Robin and Joey.

Josef Sokol
By Clarence M. Koch Jr.

Josef and Anna Sokol came to the United States from (Bohemia) Czechoslovakia in 1881 by boat. Anna's mother, Anna Elizabeth (Hylak) Vavara, and two brothers, Stephen and Jesse Vavara and Josef and Anna's children, George, Mary and Anna came on the boat with them. They left Bohemia because of religious persecution, they were being forced into a certain religion that was not acceptable to them. Anna's father stayed behind as well as Josef's father, Venal Sokol and his mother, Terase (Myshek) Sokol.

At the time of their entry to this country Josef was about 31 years of age and Anna was about 25. George was 4 years of age and Mary and Anna were both younger. According to the 13th United States census of 1910 for the Black Bear township of Noble County, Oklahoma, Josef and George had evidently learned to read and write English well enough to become naturalized citizens of this country.

After immigration, they moved to Iowa where their daughter, Frances Jane (Jennie) Sokol was born on August 18, 1888, at Oxford Junction, Iowa. Mary and Anna died at the ages of 5 and 6 from diptheria that took many lives. Jennie was a tiny baby who survived the diptheria that also left George crippled. While in Iowa Josef worked for the railroad, he spoke broken English and was rather hard to talk with, he had a full beard. One day he was digging a snow drift out for the railroad and found a gold watch, years later he gave it to his grandson, Larkin J. Kirtley, who in turn gave it to his son, Clane and Clane still has it. Anna was less than 5 feet tall and loved to raise flowers. She was a good cook and a hard worker. George was known to be a wanderer. He was a bachelor and went off on fruit harvest a lot. Stephen and Jesse (Anna Sokol's brothers) went to Alaska to the gold rush and came back pretty well off. The small pieces of gold that Jennie Kirtley gave her grandchildren were pieces of this gold!! Stephen and Jesse took some dry good materials with them to Alaska and went by boat part of the way. They were not far from shore when the boat tipped and when they recovered their belongings the dye in the materials had all run together, but it didn't seem to matter for the natives bought it anyway.

In 1893, Josef and Anna's family boarded a train in Iowa to come to the Oklahoma Territory for the opening of the Cherokee Strip land run. Their daughter, my grandmother, Jennie remembered her parents telling about boarding the train in Iowa. As they were boarding the train Josef was approached by an unknown person wanting his sheep lined clothing and boots. The man told Josef that he wouldn't be needing them in Oklahoma Territory as it was warm weather down there. Josef did give them to him and needless to say he certainly wished more than once that he had kept them. They made the run and staked a claim on a ¼ section of land just northwest of the present location of I-35 and US64, Cimarron turnpike in Noble County, Oklahoma.

They lived in a dugout for a time not too far from where the Sokol house still stands. The opportunity arose that they were able to buy the ¼ section of land directly south of them for $25.00 and a hot meal. Today US64 runs through the south ⅓ of this ¼ section of land. These farms are still owned by their grandchildren and heirs. The two brothers Jesse and Stephen came to Oklahoma after the run and located a farm 15 miles north and west of Perry for the Sokol's to buy. They brought their cows, horses, wagon and farm equipment, and household goods by train.

They came in the fall of 1893, and there were only wagon trails to follow and some were not well marked. The day after they arrived a northerner blew in and a heavy snow followed. They were snow bound for weeks out on the prairie.

Anna's brothers Jesse and Stephen later sold their farm moving west. Josef and Anna planted a garden, orchard and feed for their livestock. They also had a smoke house and cured all their meats there. They also kept pigeons and bees. Josef was known by many to be the "Keeper of the Bees". He had several hives and real good

Anna (Vavara or Vavra) Sokol.

honey that the family and friends alike shared.

Their daughter Jennie learned the English language and communicated for them and took care of business. Anna Sokol's mother homesteaded a 40 acre farm next to them to the north. Josef and Anna Sokol's land is still owned by their grandchildrena and heirs. Since Jennies family came from Czechoslovakia they weren't able to speak much English. It was difficult to attend school but Jennie was a good student and was the top student when she graduated from the 8th grade and was the top student in 1907, when she graduated from Perry High School. Jennie took teachers training and taught schools at Fairview and Sunnyslope. She was a good seamstress and accomplished pianist, loved poetry and was a wonderful mother to her 10 children. She was a good cook and enjoyed church work and quilted with the ladies group for years. The Sokols moved to Perry around 1920 and resided on Cedar Street (across from East Park) until their deaths. Anna died May, 1930 and Josef lived until December 1942. George Sokol died in 1940. On June 12, 1910, Jennie married Charles T. Kirtley, also a son of pioneer Noble countyans and they had ten children. Charles T. and his father, William H. Kirtley's history also appear in this book. Josef and Anna Sokol and her mother, Anna Vavara and George Sokol, Charles T. and Jennie Kirtley are all buried at the Mount Carmel cemetery north of Perry.

Joe John Soulek
By Marie Ewy

Joe John Soulek, son of John L. (1877-1948) and Antonia Sedivy Soulek (1877-1968) was born March 31, 1915, at Munden, Republic County, Kansas. His mother said it was during a blizzard, and the doctor had to drive his horse and buggy down the railroad tracks to get to the house, because the roads were snowbound. The family lived on a farm, between Tabor and Munden. The family returned to Perry, Noble County in 1922. Joe was 7 years old. He had started school at Euria school in Republic County, Kansas. He attended school in Noble County at Willow Creek. It was a one room school, as were most rural schools in those days. All 8 grades were taught in one room.

Joe Soulek Family 1968. Front (L to R): Joe, J.D., Marie. Back Row (L to R): Patricia, Alfred, Jim, Mary Jo.

Joe married Marie Schieffer May 6, 1941, at Perry. They lived with his folks northwest of Red Rock, Oklahoma, the first year, farming together. After the attack on Pearl Harbor, he enlisted in the Army Air Force in September 1942. He trained at Dalhart and Amarillo, Texas and Sioux City, Iowa, and left the states from Mitchell, South Dakota for duty as an air force mechanic in England. He spent many nights in the subways of London during the "Blitz of Britian." He returned home in September 1945. While Joe was overseas, Marie worked at Douglas aircraft in Oklahoma City.

They bought a farm northeast of Perry and farmed, raising everything usually found on a farm, including wheat, oats, barley, cows, sheep, hogs, chickens, a big garden, and two daughters and three sons. Mary Jo was born May 7, 1946 (married Dennis Stanley). Patricia Ruth was born August 1, 1947 (married Ken Novy). Alfred William was born November 27, 1949 (married Joy Schmidbauer/Jean Lyon). James Joseph was born July 2, 1951 (married Sandra Anderson). J.D. (Joseph Donald) was born January 20, 1957 (married Jaylene Ferda).

Joe did carpentry work along with farming, while Marie raised a big garden and chickens and delivered quarts of cream and dozens of eggs to customers in Perry. She also worked at Perry Memorial Hospital from 1954 to 1970.

Joe was diagnosed as having cancer in August, 1960. He continued to work and do his farming until December 1968. He passed away March 10, 1969. There are eight grandchildren.

Marie attended Blackwell General Hospital School of Practical Nursing, graduating in 1971. She worked there as a licensed practical nurse, retiring in 1982. Mary Jo's children: Robert Deloraine Stanley (October 6, 1965 in Perry, Oklahoma). Keri Denice Stanley (May 1, 1968 in Perry, Oklahoma). Patricia's daughter: Anitra Nicole Novy (September 9, 1977 in Oklahoma City, Oklahoma). Alfred's children: Shannon Marie Soulek (November 28, 1972 in Perry, Oklahoma), and Jeremy Joseph Soulek (April 1, 1975 in Perry, Oklahoma). James's children: Brent Joseph Soulek (September 8, 1976 in Oklahoma City, Oklahoma) and Amy Colene Soulek (April 25, 1979 in Wichita, Kansas). J.D.'s son: Jay Truman Soulek (April 23, 1984 in Tulsa, Oklahoma).

John L. Soulek
By Marie Ewy

John L. Soulek was born March 4, 1877, at Steiten, Czechoslovakia, the son of Rosalie Marie (Cejka) and Joseph Frank Soulek. Both of his parents were born in Vratkov, Czechoslovakia, his father in 1843, and his mother, October 10, 1855. In 1879, the family, consisting of parents, John and little brother, Joe, came to America. The journey to America on the ship was a great hardship with two young children. They had to use ocean water to wash their clothes. The children broke out with a

Front (L to R): John, Antonia and Ted. Back Row (L to R): Helen (Nemec), Joe, Mary (Zavodny), Josie (Zavodny), Bess (Tearney), Minnie (Curran) - about 1937.

rash, and they discovered the sea water was very salty, causing the problem. They settled in Republic county, Kansas, in the Munden area where they farmed.

They came to Oklahoma in 1894, and Joseph bought a claim 5 miles east and 2 miles north of Perry. He received the patent on the farm in 1904, patent number 3272 for the southwest quarter of section 3 in Noble township. Joseph and Rosalie's children were: John L., Joseph born April 21, 1879; Frank born 1882 died 1957; and Elmer born 1885 died 1961, they were bachelor farmers; Mary born December 15, 1891 died December 20, 1975. She married Joe Sterba. The son, Joseph, was a policeman in Oklahoma City. He died March 20, 1909, of typhoid fever, he is buried in a little cemetery, seven miles east and one mile north of Perry. On the same stone is Mary Cejka died November 23, 1895, age 73 and John Cejka 1857-1927.

John L. Soulek, at the age of 17, came to Noble county with his family in 1894. He told of a big Indian chief coming to their house the day after they got there and wanted him to work for him on a big cattle ranch in Indian Territory. William (Bill) Sparrow was the ranch foreman. John worked for them for several years.

John L. Soulek and Antonia Sedivy were married at Perry, Oklahoma, October 9, 1900. Antonia was born April 17, 1877 and came to America from Czechoslovakia in 1898, at the age of 21. She and a friend made it to Appalchia, close to Pittsburg, Pennsylvania, when their money ran out. They worked for families there to get enough money to continue their way to Oklahoma. Her sister Lizzie (Mrs. Frank Sekora), other sisters who came later were: Mary (Mrs. Joe Kopp) and Anna Kodesh.

John and Antonia lived on a farm east of Perry, where their son, Ted, was born February 19, 1902. Ted ran a creamery, egg station and feed store on east Cedar Street, after working for Paul Jones for a time, in the same kind of business. He married Ethel Strickland. They had no children. He died in 1948.

John's daughter, Minnie, was born June 6, 1905. She married John Curran. They had seven children. The family moved to Oklahoma City, where John L. worked in a packing plant, trimming hams. Their daughter, Bess, was born there July 30, 1906. She married Bock Tearney. They had twins, Bill and Carolyn.

The Soulek's daughter, Josie was born April 19, 1909, after the family had moved back to a farm east of Perry. In those days babies were born at home with a relative or friend in attendance with (or without, in some cases), the doctor. Seems like grandmother Rosalie had a lot of baby chickens to take care of, so the mother-to-be had to go to grandmother's house to await the stork. She had left a pan of bread started at home and the cow ate it. How that came about the story didn't say. Josie married Edward Zavodny. They had two daughters.

The family returned to Republic county, Kansas about 1914. Joe John was born March 31, 1915 and died March 10, 1969. He married Marie Schieffer. They had five children. Helen was also born in Kansas on April 15, 1918. She married Stanley Nemec. They had two children.

The family returned to Noble County in 1922, living on farms east and north of Perry. In 1943, they bought a house at 1321 Cedar Street across from Lions West Park, where they lived out their lives. Grandma had her flowers and a small garden. She liked to crochet and visit. Grandpa just visited and watched the children playing in the park. John L. died in 1948 and Antonia in 1968. They were true pioneers.

Clarence C. Space
By Lois Strickland

Clarence Clemont Space was born September 18, 1885, in Cambridge, Illinois, the son of Jonathan Space and Nellie Bowling. Jonathan's ancestry can be traced to Edward Dothy who came to the American continent on the Mayflower. Clarence married Lillie Jane Ools on November 7, 1905. She was born January 25, 1888, the daughter of Lem Ools. Clarence freighted with a team of horses and a wagon between Higgins, Texas, and Ivanhoe, Oklahoma. He would go to Higgins, get a load of groceries and then deliver them to Ivanhoe and all the stores between the two towns. He homesteaded a farm in Ivanhoe, but then after a while, he traded it for a homestead in Kingfisher, Oklahoma

Later, he traded the Kingfisher homestead for a piece of unimproved land in Victoria, Texas. In Victoria, he worked for a Japanese farmer, planting fig trees. He traded his farm in Victoria to the Japanese farmer for a new wagon and a team of horses and returned to Oklahoma in 1914. He moved first to Yukon, Oklahoma, and then to Valley, Oklahoma.

From Valley, he moved to Cleveland, Oklahoma, where he worked for the Ranch Creek Oil field. From there, he moved to Perry, Oklahoma. He lived there until he moved to Chelsea, Oklahoma, where he bought forty acres of land. This was about 1941. He lived there until the house burned in 1953. He sold the farm and moved to Oklahoma City, where he lived with his son, Edgar, until Edgar built him a house on his (Edgar's) land. He died December 2, 1957, and was buried at Hayward, Oklahoma. His wife followed him in death on December 27, 1969, and was buried beside her husband at Hayward.

Clarence and Lillie had eleven children. They were:

1. Emmitt Lloyd (Red), born June 21, 1908, at Ivanhoe. He married Edith Mary George at Cleveland, Oklahoma, on July 7, 1931. He lived in Perry about 6 years. He worked for Forney's Dairy

Antonia and John Soulek - November 26, 1942.

and for Bud Warren at the casine plant. He died September 27, 1984, and is buried at Chelsea, beside his wife who preceded him in death on November 3, 1962.

2. Francis Clemont was born April 5, 1910, at Ivanhoe, and married the first time to Estella Thornbrue on May 26, 1931, at Perry, Oklahoma. Estella died March 21, 1975. Then he married Bertha Marie Tasier. They live at Wannette, Oklahoma.

3. Violet Verona was born November 16, 1911, at Dover, Oklahoma. She married Harley Enoch George on August 24, 1929. She died March 1, 1977, at Oklahoma City and is buried there.

4. Anna Lee was born September 14, 1913. She married Ted George. Ted was a brother to Edith and Harley George. She died November 14, 1932, and was buried at Hayward. Ted died on July 8, 1976.

5. Lucy May was born June 26, 1915. She married Sam Thornbrue. Sam died on November 4, 1974.

6. Hettie Leona was born March 25, 1917. She married first, Claude Alexander on October 2, 1932; and the second time to Wilson Caedmon Tyler on September 28, 1959.

7. Hazel Irene was born March 26, 1919. She died June 26, 1922, and is buried at Valley, Oklahoma.

8. Gracey Beatrice was born between 1919 and 1923. She died March 13, 1931, and is buried at Valley, Oklahoma.

9. Everett Edgar was born December 28, 1923. He married Ada Taylor.

10. Nellie Coreine was born June 16, 1925, and died December 15, 1927, and is buried at Valley, Oklahoma.

11. Faye Doriene was born April 14, 1927. She married Sam Francis Newsom on June 21, 1951. Sam died October 29, 1983. He is buried at Edmond, Oklahoma.

Ellen V. Speer
By Gertrude Speer Dunivan

George Turner and Mary (Hill) Turner, and children moved from Half Rock, Missouri in 1873, to a homestead west of Wellington, Kansas, one mile west of Milan, near Sakaskia River. With a yoke of oxen, he broke the native sod with a heavy plow so corn and an orchard could be planted.

Ellen Vashti Turner was the 6th child born to George and Mary Ann Turner on September 12, 1877. The older sisters were: Sarah, Lavina, Nancy, Theresa, and Ira. Later children were: Isabel, Judith, William and Fultz.

The Turner family in Sumner county, Kansas worked a sheep ranch with several hundred sheep. The 5 younger children were born in a dugout with attic near the river west of Milan. The

Ellen Vashti (Turner) Speer.

children herded sheep and helped with feeding and shearing the wool. During the winters, snow storms and blizzards often kept the children indoors for days. Their principal food in the winter was cornmeal mush, syrup and mutton. George Turner had a good education for his time and taught his children to read, write and some arithmetic. In 1889, a disease spread through the sheep which caused an entire loss of the herd and the Turners gave up their farm there near Milan and moved to Central Oklahoma with 4 yoke of oxen to break the native sod for planting crops near Purcell, Oklahoma.

It was in March 1889, the Turner family left their home with 3 covered wagons and their entire amount of clothing, bedding and pots and pans. The youngest son, Fultz died of pneumonia near Purcell, at the age of four years.

Ellen V. Turner, 13 years old, was sent by train to Half Rock, Missouri to help care for her Grandmother Hill, who was an invalid. Ellen remained in Missouri for 16 months where she met her cousins, aunts and uncles besides her grandparents. She attended better schools there and received more clothing than ever, but missed her brother and sisters, so homesick at times because letters often took more than 4 weeks from Oklahoma City to Kansas City and beyond.

In late 1893, Ellen Turner returned to her parents near Tryon, Oklahoma. Her married sister, Sadie (Sarah) Tracy lived near. Ellen lived with her and attended a rural school with Ida Tracy.

In the spring of 1894, Ellen (16 years old) helped her parents move with teams of oxen to their 160 acre farm 11 miles east of Perry, Oklahoma. She and her sisters had learned to drive oxen teams to wagons and plows. Her father had traded a grey mare and $50.00 to Ben Smith for 160 acres of native land east of Perry (Auburn Township). Their father built a house of native sawmill lumber and covered it with shingles. The Turner family of 6 members and a married daughter, Nancy, and her 3 children lived in the 1 room house.

Ellen and her sisters helped their father plant cedars, walnut and fruit trees on their new land. The girls attended Windy Center school during 6 winter months. The Turner girls often worked for neighbor families at cooking for threshers or to care for illness in pioneer families. They received $2.50 for 6 days work. They were able to buy their shoes and material for dresses and coats. All clothing was made by hand. Later, a sewing machine was purchased.

On February 26, 1901, Ellen married a farmer, Lawrence Speer, who lived on a near-by farm. They farmed 160 acres and leased 160 acres of school land adjoining for cattle. In 1903, Ellen and Lawrence Speer built a 2 room house with plastered walls, where they raised three children: Gertrude, Chester and Wayne. Ellen Speer helped work with Red Cross in 1918 and with patriotic programs after World War I. She enjoyed poetry, reading and fancy work of crocheting. Also she made tables, chests and chicken houses for poultry. She raised geese and plucked the feathers for filling pillows and feather beds. Later, they were able to purchase a mattress.

Her hobby of taking camera pictures and enlarging them was enjoyed by family and friends. She canned and preserved summer fruit and vegetables to provide food for winter months. She made quilts and comforts for the cold season. On April 2, 1931, Ellen Speer passed away after a week's illness at age 53. She is buried by the side of her husband in Pleasant Valley cemetery.

Lawrence Speer
Chester Speer

In the spring of 1893, three covered wagons left a farm in Winterset, Iowa and started southward. Two horseback riders accompanied these covered wagons. One of the horseback riders was Lawrence Speer, my father. It was his duty to ride on ahead of the wagons to find a suitable campsite with water for the night.

Coming through Kansas, they camped for the night and after having breakfast started on their way again. It was a cloudy day and the sun could not be seen. There were no roads, only rolling prairie. When noon came they discovered they had traveled in a circle and were back where they had eaten breakfast. This must have been very

Lawrence Speer's "Batchelor Shack" with Lawrence, his cousins John Smith, Mrs. Banks and her husband; others unkown, about 1900.

discouraging since they were only able to travel about 25 miles in a full day.

The Speer family had come to Iowa from Indiana in the 1850's. Jesse Speer, Lawrence's father obtained 120 acres of fine rich land in Iowa. He was self-educated by reading many books and taught schol in the community. One of his students was Eliza Ellen Osburn, whom he later married. Lawrence was born to this union October 4, 1871. He had three brothers, Lafayette, Warren, and Thurman. He had a sister, Myrtle, a cousin's child, whom his parents took as part of their family when Myrtle's mother died when Myrtle was one week old.

Lawrence grew up on the Iowa farm. He was a character in a local talent play in which he played the part of "Sut Lovemgood." The nickname, "Sut", followed him the rest of his life.

It took 21 days for the covered wagons to arrive at Perkins, Oklahoma, where Jesse Speer bought a 160 acre farm two miles south and one mile east of Perkins. Since Jesse had four sons approaching manhood, they had come to stake land in the Cherokee Strip. Lawrence made the run riding a mule named Mike. He staked his claim by tying his red bandana hankerchief to a pole, nine miles north of his starting position. He slept on his new land that night using his saddle for a pillow. Next day, he located the cornerstone (nw 22 in Auburn township). He built a "batchelor shack" out of native sawed lumber.

He broke the sod by plowing it with a walking plow which could cover about an acre and half a day and was a tiring job. When the mule named Mike became old, he was put on a "pension" for the rest of his life with free grass in the summer and oats and hay in winter.

Lawrence worked on the construction of the new railroad near his farm in 1901 with two horses and a scraper to haul dirt to make the grade for the railroad. He received $1.50 for a day's work.

The farm he staked was upland and not suited for growing corn. In 1907, he bought 80 acres adjoining his farm on the west. Spring Creek flowed through this 80 acres and provided bottom land to be farmed. He paid $30 per acre for the 80 acres.

Lawrence served on the school board, township board, election board and cemetery board for the new Pleasant Valley cemetery.

Lawrence "batched" on his homestead for eight years and then married Ellen Vashti Turner, a neighbor girl whom he had first seen while she was driving a team of oxen for her father. She was known as "Ti" from the last part of her middle name. Their children are: Gertrude (Dunivan) born in Dec 1903, Chester, born in 1910 and Wayne, born in 1922.

In 1917, Lawrence purchased one of the first automobiles in the community, a new Model T Ford Touring car.

Ti died April 2, 1931 of a stroke. The son, Wayne, was only 8 years of age, so Gertrude and her family moved into the home to help provide for the needs of her father and brother.

On February 1, 1939, Lawrence had a heart attack while attending to business in the court house in Perry and died about 4 hours later. He is buried beside his wife in the Pleasant Valley cemetery.

Joe Spillman

By Hazel Chessmore

Joe, born Joseph Amos Spillman, November 29, 1863, in Yadkins County, North Carolina, was the second son of Pleasant Henderson and Nancy Miriam Patterson Spillman. The family moved from North Carolina, in the early 1870s, to Gernell, Iowa, where other family members were living. They went by train, a new experience for Joe, and arrived in weather that was much cooler than North Carolina. Joe said he thought he was going to freeze. They lived in Iowa, until the death of his mother in 1886. Shortly after her death, they moved to Blue Mound, Kansas. It was there Joe met and married LaRena Florence White in 1889.

LaRena, who was called Rena, was the oldest child of John Silas and Sarah Elizabeth Davidson White. She was born in Washington County, Iowa, June 11, 1867. She and her family had moved from Iowa to Galletin, Missouri. There she had qualified for and received her teaching certificate. But the climate was damp and two members of the family had consumption, she was advised to go to a dryer climate. She went to Blue Mound to live with friends and secure work. She and some other girls went down to hear a group of young men playing and singing. As young ladies did and still do, she said, "Well, I like the one playing the violin" (Joe).

Joe and Rena farmed in Bourbon County, Kansas. During this time, two children were born: Ernest and Josephine. The young family decided the promise of free land in Oklahoma was one that could not be passed up. They packed their belongings in a covered wagon. They took a good supply of staples and water, but left their farm machinery in Kansas. They traveled to Old Oklahoma, to the home of friends, Edgar and Lou Rogers, in Sac and Fox country near Chandler, Oklahoma. There they farmed one year but because the weather was hot and dry their crops were not good. The summer of the opening of the Cherokee Strip, the family worked for a farmer by the name of John Payne. The Paynes lived in what is now the Lake McMurtry area. Mr. Spillman helped with the farm work while Mrs. Spillman helped Mrs. Payne with the housework.

When the day of the opening came, Joe left his wife and children and got a place in line. He stood in line for several hours. A drink of water cost 10¢. It was hot and dusty and he had a sick headache, but he didn't dare leave his place in the line. When the shot was fired, he rode across into the Strip. He rode hard about 17 miles north and east, and just south of Long Branch, staked his claim. Shortly after he drove his stake, a man rode out from the creek, his horse was fresh. As Joe used to tell his grandchildren, "I pulled my gun out and told him to move on. Probably couldn't have hit him, I was so nervous." But the man moved on.

For the run, Joe rode a little bay mare called Molly, a good little horse. They kept her shoes and hung them over the door of their home.

The first home was a log cabin. They bought the cabin from the Paynes - traded a shotgun for it. They tore it down, marking the logs and moved it.

Front Row (L to R): Josephine, Rena, Faye, Joe, Opal. Back Row: Seth, Lois, Elizabeth, Alta, Ernest. Spillman Family 1919.

They spent the first winter in the log house without much chinking between the logs. They did finish it, making a loft for sleeping and a lean-to kitchen. They dug a cellar, and since it was a dry year, they went to Long Branch and dug a well.

Joe went back to Blue Mound, to get his farm machinery. Rena was left alone with the two children and the livestock. Food was not plentiful but she was capable and resourceful. One of the fond memories is of the wild grape jelly and wild grape pudding she made.

Joe cleared the land and planted corn, kaffir, wheat and oats. When he plowed the first strip around the field, Rena and the children planted peach seeds brought from Kansas. There are still sprouts from those trees.

As the years passed, five more children were born: Seth, Lois, Elizabeth, Opal, and Alta. Then in 1902, they bought the 80 acres adjoining them on the west. It was closer to school. There was a small house on the land but Mr. White, Rena's father, built a nice house. The log cabin was moved and the barn was built around it. They drilled two wells and got plenty of water. One more child, Faye, was born. Besides the crops, Joe raised cattle and horses and mules and hogs. The family bought another 80 acres to the west and 160 acres of pasture land one mile south. He often shipped cattle to St. Jo and Kansas City. On one of the trips, he had sold his cattle and been paid in cash. He was walking up town when a fellow came toward him. The fellow pulled a gun and demanded his money. Joe said, "You #?©#, get over on the other side of the street, I'm working this side." It worked.

Three men got together and established a school. The first school was in a house that belonged to Mr. Barrett. The school board members were Joe Spillman, Shadrick Beasley and John Biggs. Mr. Barrett gave them a corner of his land and a school building was built. All of the children attended school at Barrett, District #81. The first teacher was Homer Cox in 1895.

The Spillmans had many pleasant evenings. Joe played the violin. Of course, having six girls they bought an organ. They owned a banjo, madolin and guitar. They could all play (by ear), so would sing and have a good time. This all took place after the cows were milked, hogs fed, milk separated, calves fed, wood carried in, supper over and dishes washed. They enjoyed the many old hymns as well as the popular songs of the time.

Joe and Rena never turned anyone away that needed help. They had a good fruit orchard and it was not unusual to share with families that had none. They always had a large garden — lots of good food was preserved and stored in the cellar. They cured the pork in the smoke house built back of the house. There were also turkeys, geese, guineas and chickens. One of Joe's favorite foods was pie, but he also loved hot biscuits with a liberal amount of homemade molasses.

They were real pioneers. Hard working, good managers, always striving to better themselves and guide their children to be self-supporting. Rena would keep material on hand so the six girls would have garments when needed. She made nice shirts for the boys until they were young men.

They bought a new Chevrolet in 1915. It was a joy to all of the family. All eight children were old enough to drive and always wanted to do the driving.

The Spillmans were active members of the community. Joe loved his coyote dogs. He was never too tired to listen to the hounds. Rena was a charter member of the Oak Hill Home Demonstration Club. She loved flowers and always had lovely roses.

In his later years, Joe was affectionately known as Uncle Joe to most of his friends. Rena passed away in October, 1937. Joe lived another 22 years. He died March 10, 1959, at the age of 95. The homestead and other land holdings remain in the family.

Samuel St. Clair
By John St. Clair

Samuel St. Clair was born in Westmoreland County, Pennsylvania, November 20, 1829 and grew to manhood near the scene of his birth. After 1850 he moved to Titusville in that state and was married to Rachel Morrow March 15, 1855 at Titusville. Rachel was born in October of 1834 in Indiana County, Pennsylvania where she spent her early life.

On August 29, 1859, Samuel St. Clair was at Titusville, when Colonel Drake struck oil there. He met two men, James Parker and William Barnsdall who were anxious to drill on land near by, owned by Parker. When they found that Samuel's father had drilled for salt or salt water forty years before, they hired Samuel to drill their well if his father would help. They agreed to pay $1.50 per day and a $50 bonus if oil was struck. Samuel hired his cousin, Hugh Jamison, to help. An old man by the name of Winans, in the employ of Barnsdall accompanied them to the oil regions. Winans had a spade, saw and hatchet. They selected a hole in the ground 3 feet deep and 5 feet square, 150 yards from the creek. Winans cleaned out the leaves with his spade and the oil came up in the water in small dark lumps like buckshot and spread on the water. Soon the oil was a quarter of an inch thick.

The question was how to start drilling as no tools could be bought. Drake would not let them see his tools and no blacksmith knew how to make tools for the purpose. Samuel's father made a pattern for a drill and a blacksmith made a tool for a four inch hole. Casing was brought 45 miles from Erie. They had no money to buy an engine so they decided to try drilling with a spring pole. In this way they drilled from 5 to 6 feet per day, using only a center bit and no reamer. They had oil all the way from the surface and at a depth of 76 feet they struck the flow, gas throwing the oil 30 feet high to the top of the derrick. They turned it into a 700 barrel tank which it soon filled to overflowing and ran to the creek, flowing away all winter. It was the best of oil but of no value then as there was little use for it. Thus Samuel St. Clair is credited with drilling the first flowing oil and gas well or gusher. Samuel continued in the oil business for several years before and after the Civil War.

In 1862, he enlisted in Company D 18

Pennsylvania Cavalry at Titusville and served through out the war in this company. Soon after the close of the war in 1865 he moved to Vinton, Iowa where he purchased a farm and resided until he retired from farming and moved to Spirit Lake, engaging in the mercantile business. In 1902 they moved to Oklahoma where Samuel purchased land adjoining Billings on the east. He built a fine house which was the family home for several years. They moved to Enid for awhile and when his health failed they moved back to Billings.

Samuel and Rachel were the parents of 7 children, the oldest two died in infancy. The others were: Mrs. Robert Moncrieff, Mrs. J. F. Farris, John F., Mrs. M. F. Beerman and Hugh Edwin.

Samuel died March 9, 1917 and was buried in the Union Cemetery at Billings, Oklahoma. Grandsons acted as pallbearers. Rachel died November 2, 1927 at the age of 93 years. Six grandsons as pallbearers carried her to her last resting place beside her husband.

Azor J. Stackhouse
By Henry Stackhouse Jr.

My great-grandfather, Henry Stackhouse, moved his family from Kentucky to Indiana and finally pioneered a homestead in Kansas. My grandfather, Azor J. was the fifth child out of six, four boys and two girls. Azor J. was born in Vincennes, Indiana. My great-grandfather's homestead was on the Soloman River in northern Kansas near Beloit. An Indian raid in the 1880s burned my great-grandfather's house and most of his belongings. All of the family escaped. Henry went to work on the railroad that was being built west of Kansas City. He saved up enough money to go back and buy another farm near the Beloit, Kansas area. Henry farmed, ran a general store, and raised mules. During the Civil War, Henry, having a large family, paid a man $500 to serve in his place in the Northern Army.

My grandfather Azor J. (commonly called A. J.) attended country schools, and spent much of his youth farming and herding cattle. He attended a business school and also learned telegraphy. He had to make a decision between being a farmer or a telegrapher and chose farming.

A. J. met my grandmother, Alice, while she was teaching school near where A. J. lived. Alice's father, John Wines, was in the Civil War as a drummer boy (incidently my brother Bill has his drum sticks). John Wines was a cooper by trade, that is, he made wooden barrels and wooden tubs. In his latter years he moved to Blackwell, Oklahoma, and he is buried in the Blackwell Cemetery.

A. J. and Alice had the pioneer spirit. They went to Steamboat Springs, Colorado, and staked a claim. While there, grandmother taught school. She became pregnant with my father, Henry A. Stackhouse, and went back to Fairbeau, Minnesota, where her parents lived, for my father's birth. A. J. finished teaching the school term in her absence.

My father, Henry, was born February 3, 1890. He was a premature baby and was placed on a blanket behind the stove and was not expected to live. He is ninety-five years old as of this writing.

A. J. made the Cherokee Strip race on September 16, 1893. That year was very dry and the Salt Fork River was easy to cross. He did not get a claim. A. J. and Alice, lived on a farm called the Friday place, which is just south of the Three Sands oilfield for two years. While they lived there, one of the first deaths occurred. Alice was often called upon to care for the sick in the community. When this lady died, Alice groomed her for the burial. A. J. took a team of horses and a wagon and went to Cross (now a part of Ponca City) to get a coffin for this lady's burial.

A. J. heard of a claim that was being contested at Ceres, thirteen miles north of Perry. He paid each of the contestants one hundred dollars and proved up on the farm. The first home they lived in was a sod dugout with a frame lean-to. Spiders, centepedes, and an occasional snake were common problems. Water wells had to be dug with a pick and shovel. The land was broken for planting with a walking plow. Corn was the first crop planted, however the dry weather soon convinced the farmers that wheat was a better crop for this area.

In 1901, A. J. had a large wheat crop with a good price (about $1.00 per bushel). He would take a load of wheat, ford the Salt Fork River, and sell it to the elevator in Tonkawa. He then would buy a load of lumber and haul it back to the farm. Thus the two story house was built which still stands today. My father, Henry, has lived in this house most of the time until the present.

Alice taught rural schools in Noble County. One school she taught was named Pleasant Valley. Years later, my mother, Lillian, taught the same school. Alice would ride from the farm to the school she taught in a two wheeled buggy. On one occassion when it had rained hard and the creeks were up she swam a horse across to get to school. She was advised by the school board not to do that again.

A. J. was an early day Justice of the Peace and many of the men in the community called him Judge. My father remembers grandmother cleaning the house, setting chairs, getting the children quiet and ready to hold court. A. J. was able to get the contestants to settle their disputes amicably. He also married a few couples.

A. J. and Alice moved to Perry when my parents married. A. J. continued to work on the farm and he was also engaged in other enterprises. Alice was a very social person so she became a clerk for Wackers Variety Store and later, worked in the J. C. Pennys store when it was located on the north side of the square. The management of the Pennys store at the time was a Mr. and Mrs. Hart who were relatives of the founder Mr. Penny. After A. J. died in 1937, Alice taught a women's Bible class in the First Baptist Church for many years. In the 1950s, Alice was named sweetheart of Oklahoma on the old channel 4 Danny Thomas Show. She died in 1960 at the age of ninety-two.

Henry A. Stackhouse
By Henry Stackhouse Jr.

Henry A. Stackhouse was born February 3, 1890 in Fairbeau, Minnesota at the home of John Wines, father of Henry's mother. Henry's father, Azor J. Stackhouse made the run for a claim in the Cherokee Strip but did not get land. He paid each of two contestants $100 for the land. In 1901, he built a two story house where Henry has lived most of his life.

Henry attended Longview rural school which was one mile north and one mile east of Ceres. His parents bought a small house in Red Rock so Henry and his younger sister, Murriel, could get more schooling. Red Rock had a school that included a ninth grade. Henry then went to the Normal College at Edmond, Oklahoma. There was just one building at that time. While he was attending school he saw the moving of the capital from Guthrie to Oklahoma City. The procession came through Edmond led by a white Stanley Steamer automobile. It was quite impressive.

Henry saw his first car when he was about 8 years old (1898). It scared him so that he ran to a neighbor's house as fast as he could go for protection. These cars would also scare the horses pulling buggies. A man would have to hold the bridle on the horse until the car passed with its exhaust fumes and dust cloud.

Henry was seventeen (1907) when the Indian Nation and the territorial nation were wedded into the state of Oklahoma. He met Lillian Whistler when her father, Charles Whistler, moved his family to Oklahoma around 1906. Charles farmed a year or two in the Ceres community and then moved to Perry and operated a business. He was not a Catholic but he thought the Sisters ran a better school, so Lillian attended the Catholic parochial school in Perry. Charles was not too happy with Oklahoma and moved back to Warrensburg, Missouri.

After a few years of correspondence Henry and Lillian were married in 1917. They celebrated their 60th Anniversary before she passed away. Lillian taught school at Pleasant Valley, Sunny Slope, Red Rock and Bowden. She took college courses at Northern Oklahoma College at Tonkawa and also Central State Teacher's College in Edmond.

When Henry and Lillian were married they moved to the farm at Ceres. His parents, A. J. and Alice, moved to Perry. Henry and Lillian had two sons: Henry A. and William Charles.

Henry has been very active in community and church affairs. Besides farming he operated a county road grader. He worked on the construction of Highway 77 in 1928, especially the bridges over and near Red Rock Creek. For several years he was a member of the board for the Farmer Cooperative Grain Elevator located at Red Rock. He was also a board member for over 30 years for the Kay Rural Electric Cooperative which serves the northern half of Noble County as well as all of Kay County. He also taught the Adult Bible Class for the Ceres Baptist Church for over 50 years. He still serves as a Deacon.

Jessie T. Stanley
By Thelma Bittman

Jessie Townsend Stanley was born in Mercer county in Missouri to John J. Stanley and Frances Clark Stanley on October 10, 1843. He was married to Francis Holland on September 8, 1862 in Coffey county, Kansas. They were parents of four daughters, Addie, Clara, Bell and Cordelia. Frances passed away in Mondeville, Missouri in 1874.

Jessie volunteered in the Army on the 7th day of August 1863. At the time of his enlistment, he was 5 foot 8¼ inches tall, light complected, blue eyes and light hair, his occupation at that time was farming.

He was a private in Company C - 9th regiment of the Kansas Calvary, he served three years before being honorably discharged the 29th of June 1865.

He was married to Elizabeth Hunt February 9th 1880, in Burlington, Coffey county, Kansas. To this union one son was born, Alfred Jessie Stanley. Jessie came to Oklahoma during the land rush and settled close to Pleasant Valley, which was called Cowboy Flats,

Jessie T. Stanley home near Morrison - on the far left is Alfred Stanley, next is Elizabeth and Jessie Stanley, all others unidentified.

where he was a rider with the mail from Guthrie to Pleasant Valley.

He moved to Morrison, Oklahoma in 1911, where he worked as a handy man and later, he worked laying rails for the railroad.

He registered to vote in Morrison, May 2, 1916, as a Republican and refused to cross his ballet at any election.

Elizabeth Stanley died December 15, 1919, after suffering several years with cancer. Jessie received a pension from the government in 1913. It was $21.50 a month in 1918, it was raised to $27.00 a month, and in 1925, an increase was granted to veterans so on May 9th, 1925, he started receiving seventy two dollars a month.

Jessie moved to Perry in 1929, to be near his daughter, Mrs. Pete (Delia) Cordes. He danced a jig at the 16th celebration in 1933 at the age of 90 years.

He walked to town daily and scorned men of 60 and 70 that were stooped with age. He was 92 years, 6 months old when he passed away at Cook's Perry Hospital on north 6th street. He had fallen at his home on Elm street and fractured his hip. He died April 15, 1938 and was buried in Morrison cemetery by his wife, Elizabeth.

Luther T. Stockton
By Erma Stockton Diehm

Luther Thomas Stockton was born February 22, 1871, in Clark, Missouri, the son of Joe and Liza Stockton. He met Mary Belle Mangus in 1890 or 1891, when she went to visit her brothers, Charles and William Mangus Jr. in Clark, Missouri. Mary Belle Mangus was the daughter of Susan and William Franklin Mangus, Sr. who had a family of ten children. She spent her childhood in Sedelia, Missouri, where she was born on March 20, 1871. Mary Belle, nicknamed Nin, had a fair education and was able to help her children in school.

When she met Luther Stockton, she didn't want to marry a farmer in Missouri and move in with his family as so many young couples did. Mary Belle did promise to marry him. Luther told her he was going to Oklahoma and get a farm in the opening of the Cherokee Strip. Luther bid Mary Belle goodbye and boarded the train with his good riding horse for Perry, Oklahoma Territory. His uncle, Thomas Stockton, came with him.

They were fortunate and each got a

Jessie Townsend Stanley with his military award.

Stockton family at the 60th Wedding Anniversary, November 24, 1953. Seated (L to R): Blanche (Bruton), Luther, Mary Belle, Liza (Ratliff); Standing (L to R): Roy, Erma (Diehm), Wayne.

farm, joining each other. Luther staked his land, then rode to Perry to file his claim. It was hot and dusty and he had to stand in line. He also had to lead his horse along. When he got up within third in line, a man scared his horse. By the time he quieted his horse, he was seventy-third in line.

Luther was twenty three years old and he had for his own some horses and a span of mules. His father shipped him his horses and also some machinery. Sleeping on the ground and eating dry bread and fat bacon, caused him to lose his voice with a bad case of tonsillitis, but Mary Belle's brother, Willie Mangus, was a doctor. He saved the day by burning out Luther's tonsils with caustic Balsom and Luther and Mary Belle were married November 24, 1893. After a brief honeymoon, Luther went back to Oklahoma alone, to live on his farm and hold his claim. SE ¼ of section 18 in Red Rock Township.

He made a dugout to live in and also dug a well, which is still pumping plenty of water (1985). Mary Belle decided to come to Oklahoma on her husband's birthday, February 22, 1894. She baked the cake and boarded the train for Oklahoma, but by the time she got to Kansas City, she got real sick. Then she discovered she was going to have a baby. When she arrived in Perry, she was sick, tired and homesick and didn't want to stay but she did stay and didn't go back to Missouri until four of her children were born.

Luther sold his span of mules to his father, Joe Stockton, for six hundred dollars and as there were no banks in Perry at this time, his father sent them twenty five dollars a month to live on.

There were no fences so they had to stake the horses out on a fifty foot rope. Their first wheat crop averaged eighteen bushels per acre for which they received seventy-five cents a bushel. He had to mortgage his horses to buy a wagon to haul the wheat to market. After paying off the mortgage on the horses he put the rest of the money in the bank which was now established. On August 24, 1894, a son was born, Roy Taylor. They didn't have much money so Luther carried the mail from Ceres to Whiterock on horseback everyday. On March 21, 1896, a daughter, Blanche Edna, was born. Soon after that they built a one room house, then later built on five more rooms. On December 18, 1897, Luther Wayne was born.

Mary Belle had a good education and was quite a doctor. On November 20, 1898, a daughter, Liza Mae, was born, and on November 17, 1903, a daughter, Erma. Erma didn't have a middle name but used the initial S. for Stockton. The children were educated in the Pleasant Valley school and usually drove a horse and buggy the two and a half miles.

Mary Belle died at the age of 85 on May 3, 1956. Luther died on April 1956. They are buried in Grace Hill cemetery, Perry. They lived to see all of their 17 grandchildren grown and married.

John A. Streller

By John A. Streller

During the Bicentennial year of our Nation's founding, the John A. Strellers' were selected as Farm Bureau's Family representative from Noble County. John was born in Willowdale, Kansas on January 26, 1910. His father, John A. Streller, was an immigrant from Hungary, and herded cattle on the Kansas prairie.

A major turning point in John's life was to return home in 1929 from Oklahoma A and M College, where he had been an honor student in the School of Business. His father needed his help to support five younger children. Wheat was 26¢ per bushel, and cattle were 5¢ a pound. Despite adverse conditions, John began to become more interested in farming as a career. He saw a demonstration to prevent the soil erosion by terraces built with a terracer, powered by six horses.

Another major decision was made when John married Dorothy Halsig on October 14, 1936, in Mt. Vernon, Kansas. Dorothy was born January 25, 1914, the daughter of Dr. and Mrs. Peter Halsig, a Veterinarian. They started housekeeping in a two-story native stone house on a 160 acre rented farm, four miles north of Perry. Their assets consisted of $300. in cash, 280 bushels of wheat, 13 head of cattle and a Model "A" Ford. The land was barren, since this was during the dust bowl era. Their first wheat crop made four to ten bushels per acre, due to the drought.

With REC coming in 1938, the Strellers were able to start modernizing their home, and purchased their first electric refrigerator. They later became minute men of the Blackwell REC. They bought the first share of the Farmers Co-Op, and served on the educational committee for many years.

Several years after the addition of three sons, Eugene, Johnny, Gerald and one daughte, Mariann, to the family, the Strellers added two rooms to their home, which was a family project in decorating the new rooms.

With the progress of farming techniques, due to modern machinery, terracing and fertilization, their farm grew from 160 acres to over 1500 acres of crops and pasture. The Strellers had their share of crop failures, partly due to hail and drought. They were especially plagued by flooding in their fields, and livestock operations during heavy rains,

WKY Farm Family of the Month 1947 - John and Dorothy Streller.

Wedding of John and Dorothy Streller, October 14, 1936 — on Dorothy's right are her parents Mr. and Mrs. Peter Halsig — on John's left are his parents John and Anna Streller.

as their home farm was located on the Black Bear Creek bottom. They cooperated with the Soil Conservation Service which built upstream flood control lakes on Black Bear Creek, and there has been no more flooding on their farm.

When their children became school age, the Strellers became involved in school activities. John was a member of the Rose Hill School Board. He was instrumental in preserving the Rose Hill school building for future generations, and assisted in its removal to the Cherokee Strip Museum grounds west of Perry. Dorothy helped organize the Rose Hill 4-H Club, and was the first president of the Noble County 4-H Leaders Association. The Strellers both served as 4-H adult leaders, and Dorothy received the 4-H Leaders meritorious award. Another highlight of her 4-H leadership, was to accompany the Noble County poultry judging team to Chicago, where they won third in the Nation. She was an active member in Black Bear Homemakers Group, and held offices in her local club, as well as the County council.

The Strellers are charter members of the Noble County Farm Bureau. Dorothy was Chairman of the Farm Bureau Auxiliary for six years. John was an insurance agent for ten years. In 1965, they received the conservation farmers award from the Indian Soil Conservation Association.

Church activities have always been at the hub of the Streller family. They are members of the Catholic Church. Dorothy has been Secretary of the Altar Society, and a Sunday School teacher for many years. She helped organize the St. Joseph's School's Mothers Club. John has served on the church committee under four pastors. He has been Grand Knight of the Knights of Columbus, and Secretary for the St. Rose Perpetual Cemetery. He is a director of Rotary Club, and is on the agricultural committee. Dorothy is a precinct election board official. John also was a precinct official for forty-six years, fifteen of which he served as Chairman of the Noble County Election Board.

Their children are all making it on their own now. Eugene is a graduate of Oklahoma State University, in mechanical engineering, and is a program analyst and director of material management of Oklahoma City Air Logistics Center. He is married and has two children. He was a junior master Farmer in FFA and president of his church youth group. Johnny is a graduate of Oklahoma State University, in industrial engineering. He also works for the Oklahoma City Air Logistics Center, as an industrial engineer. He is married and has two children. He was president of the Rose Hill 4-H Club, and Noble County 4-H Club, a member of the Perry High School student council, and president of his youth group. Gerald has a BS degree in electrical engineering, and a BA degree in Scholastic Philosophy from Conception Seminary. He served four years in Army Security Administration. He is a computer analyst for Block and Veach Consulting Engineering Company, Kansas City, Missouri. He was president of the Rose Hill 4-H Club, and the Noble County 4-H Club. Mariann is a graduate of Oklahoma State University, with a BA degree in education. She is now Mrs. Dick McPherson, and is an administrative assistant in the New York Metropolitan Regional Medical Program. She was on a state 4-H meats judging team, reserve champion in Noble County 4-H dress revue, and also president of Rose Hill 4-H Club and secretary for her church youth group. All the children are active in their church and community.

Abraham Stotts
By Lawrence LaVerne Emmons

Abraham (A.B.) Stotts family came into Oklahoma with the Land Opening of 1893, took a homestead of 160 acres several miles southeast of Perry, Oklahoma; it was southeast ¼ of section 19, T 20N R 1E, in Noble County. No information on Great-grandpa Stotts, but great-grandma Stotts immigrated from Germany. Grandpa A.B. Stotts was born in Illinois on September 28, 1849 and died in Oklahoma of cancer on July 24, 1912. He was buried at Fairview cemetery near his homestead. A brother, Ebenezer Stotts moved to Stillwater in the early 1900s, and later bought a farm northwest of there. Somewhere along the line, he and his wife Sarrah adopted two children: Vern Dee and Marie Barr. A Riley Stotts of Kansas visited in Oklahoma. He was Eb Stotts son.

The Stotts brothers had an uncle Herman Santsenberg (unsure of name spelling) who moved to Washington State about 1870. His wife's name was Sarrah. They had a dry land wheat farm in Horse Heaven District of southeast Washington before moving to Yakima.

Grandma Mahala Lucretie (Powers) Stotts was born in Kansas, October 26, 1861. She came into Oklahoma in 1893 with her husband, A.B. Stotts and older children. More children were born in Oklahoma on the homestead. Only "family names" are known of Powers great-grandparents and Buckles great-great-grandparents on this line.

As the A.B. and Mahala Stotts children grew to adulthood they moved to Washington State to Uncle Herman and Aunt Sarrah's place; became established mostly in Yakima. After the death of A.B. Stotts in 1912, Mahala and two younger children, Goldie and Edward followed the rest of the family to Yakima. On February 14, 1937, Mahala died of cerebral stroke in Nampa, Idaho. She was buried in Tahoma Cemetery, Yakima, Washington. There were eight children.

Dora Maude (Stotts) Emmons (November 2, 1886-January 2, 1965)

House of A. B. Stotts homestead. Back Row (L to R): Edyth, Mahala, next one maybe Goldie, Dora and Evert.

married Arthur C. Emmons, a neighbor in Oklahoma. There were three children: Hazel Maude Emmons born December 11, 1912; Lawrence LaVerne Emmons, January 15, 1916, and Cecil Clifford Emmons, June 19, 1918. All lived at Yakima.

Everett Stotts (January 31, 1888-1972) married Dell C. Phillips from Oklahoma. They had three children: Anna Lucille Stotts, April 26, 1913; Frank Loudon Stotts, January 28, 1918, died age four, 1922; Goldie Ruth Stotts, March 17, 1920. Marriage dissolved, second wife, Catherine Blouin, friend from past in Oklahoma. Later years, moved to Florida, both died and buried there.

Nora May (Stotts) DeVilbiss (March 9, 1889-November 10, 1973) married Ray DeVilbiss in Oklahoma February 22, 1909. They had four children: Wiley Wayne DeVilbiss March 20, 1910; Leslie Raymond DeVilbiss June 30, 1913; Ralph Paul DeVilbiss June 12, 1916; Velma Faye DeVilbiss May 27, 1918. More on this line in the Ray DeVilbiss History.

Ora V. Stotts (1891-1901) age ten; was buried by his father, A.B. Stotts, in Fairview cemetery.

Edith (Stotts) Kerns (July 8, 1893-September 2, 1963) was born in Oklahoma and married Howard Kerns from Oklahoma. She died in Yakima, Washington. They were the parents of two children: Charles Lloyd Kerns born December 12, 1912 and Faye Maxine Kerns, November 19, 1917. Edith is buried in Tahoma Cemetery, Yakima.

Harold Stotts (August 5, 1895-November 6, 1969) born in Oklahoma. He moved to Yakima in 1915, met Delores Ballinger, and married in 1917. Delores died in 1977. They had one son, Lyle Stotts March 21, 1924. He was an Army Pilot during World War II, later became a medical doctor. He married Irene Lund; practiced medicine in Seattle, Washington, later move to, and practiced medicine in Bridgeport, Connecticut. They had three children: John Marshall Stotts February 14, 1947; Donald Holden Stotts February 15, 1950; and Rebecca Ann Stotts May 22, 1956. Lyle still lives in Connecticut but the marriage is dissolved.

Goldie (Stotts) Chittenden (September 16, 1898-May 20, 1973) moved to Yakima in 1915. She met Elmer J. Chittenden, and married 1920. They lived in Yakima and Aberdeen, Washington and later moved to Nampa, Idaho where he died in 1940. She died in Emmett, Idaho and is buried there. They had four children: Clarence Elmer Chittenden October 27, 1921; Ruth Esther Chittenden September 1, 1924; Kenneth Alfred Chittenden July 3, 1926; and Lela Carol Chittenden June 10, 1930.

Edward T. Stotts (February 6, 1903-February 11, 1982) moved from Oklahoma homestead to Yakima, Washington in 1915. He married Audrey Rose, who was from a small town near Oklahoma City. He worked for Cascade Lumber Co. in Yakima almost all his adult life; retired in 1968. They were the parents of two daughters; Mahala Jean Stotts born November 15, 1937; and Mary Anne Stotts born June 2, 1950.

The only living child left in Oklahoma in 1915 of A.B. Stotts and Mahala (Powers) Stotts was Nora May. She and husband, Ray DeVilbiss bought Emmons homestead (1 mile south of Edson DeVilbiss west place) where they raised their family.

Alfred L. Strickland
By Ethel Malget

Alfred L. Strickland was born in Susquehanna County, Pennsylvania in 1824. He married Harriett Jayne in 1848 and they had eight children: Sarah born December 17, 1848; John, 1850; Carria, Ada, Emma, Charles, Archie, Alfred born May 22, 1862. With the winters being so cold and the snow so deep, they started for Burden Kansas in a covered wagon. The oldest girl, Sarah, stayed in Pennsylvania with her grandfather, Sylvester Strickland (August 7, 1791 - October 1876). He is buried in Strickland Hill cemetery. Sarah then married William Brooks and they had two girls, Hattie and Lila Brooks. Hattie had no children, Lila married William Edward Lott and they had one boy, Audley Lott born in 1908 and still living in South Montrose, Pennsylvania.

Alfred L. Strickland stayed in Kansas and worked until the opening of Old Oklahoma where his son, Alfred N. Strickland, got a claim in Orlando, Oklahoma. So the family lived in a dugout and cleared the land and raised cattle.

My mother's folks, Edwin Vile and his wife, Fannie and four children: Alice born December 17, 1874 died 1957; Ella Vile Murphy, born 1887, died 1969; Edwin Jr.; and Mable born 1890, died 1977 were also living in the Orlando area. Edward Vile was born in Brussell, England in 1842. He came across from England at the age of 21. His wife, Fannie Shaw Vile was born in Fort Scott, Kansas in 1854 and died in 1927. They came to Orlando, Oklahoma from St. Joseph, Missouri and lived on Alfred's farm until 1893 when the Strip was opened. Mr. Parson came from Burden, Kansas and married Ada Strickland. He got a farm in Old Oklahoma on what is now highway 86 just across the Stillwater Creek. A girl, Iva was born there.

All the Vile and Strickland children went to school to Mrs. Archie Strickland who later married Mr. George Rule and taught school in Sumner after the Stillwater Dam took her farm. Alice Vile went to school in Orlando which was taught by Miss Hitman Ogle, later she lived in Perry and was County Superintendent as Mrs. E. J. Miller.

In 1893, when they opened the Strip for the run, my grandfather, Alfred L. Strickland, made the run. His farm was two miles east on Highway 64 (East ½ NW ¼ of Section 19 in Rock Township). He and his children lived in a dugout until Alfred N. helped him build a little house. He deeded his farm to his children and went back to Kansas where he died in 1899, his wife had died in 1879. They are buried in Burden, Kansas.

Grandfather Vile's claim is two miles north and 2½ miles east of the Strickland claim (Section 6 of Rock Township). When he staked his claim he found he had a Sooner and just got 80 acres. They had a long lawsuit but Grandfather didn't win.

While the Viles and Stricklands were living in Orlando, my father, Alfred N. Strickland and Alice Vile were married in Mulhull, Oklahoma in 1893 and lived and built up his claim. Two girls were born here, Hattie Burrough Strickland, May 14, 1895 and Edna Welch Strickland, October 1, 1896. Then after his father's death, he sold his farm to Dr. Sharp and he and Alice and the two girls moved to Pawnee, Oklahoma where a boy, John was born January 4, 1900. Then they started to Burden, Kansas in a covered wagon and on to Florence, Colorado. They stopped in Burden, Kansas and visited his sister, Carria Bolack, then on across the prairies of Kansas and the three Strickland children had the small pox. My mother thought they would die and be buried on the prairie of Kansas, but they made it to Florence, Colorado and the law quarantined them. The law made them live in what they called a pest house, across the Arkansas River out on a hill away from everyone. After a month or two they let my father Alfred go to work as a carpenter on a Hotel that was being built in the town of Florence. Then three more children were born: Ralph Strickland, January 23, 1902; Charles, October 17, 1905 and Ethel, November 24, 1908. Ralph died in 1983, Charles in 1986. Ethel married Ted Soulek, he died in 1947 and she then married Joe Malget, April 19, 1951.

Alfred N. Strickland died in Florence, Colorado in June 16, 1938 and is buried in Burden, Kansas in the Strickland family plot. Alice Strickland died April 7, 1957 in Perry, Oklahoma and is buried in Grace Hill cemetery.

Lazarus P. Stumpff

By Marjorie Brier Cramer

My grandfather, Lazarus Powell Stumpff (nickname Ladd) was born in Pottsville, Kentucky, in Washington County, on the 16th day of January in 1852. He was born to Johnston C. Stumpff and Rachael Burns Stumpff. When he was 2 years old he came with his parents to St. Joseph, Missouri in 1854. Making the trip by steamboat down the Ohio River and up the Mississippi River to St. Louis and on to St. Joseph. They had 5 children.

James H. Stumpff, an older brother of L. P. Stumpff came to Guthrie in 1889 before the Cherokee Strip Opening. He had a hardware store in Guthrie and one of the first automobiles. He married Florence Maxwell in St. Joseph before he came to Guthrie. My grandmother, Mary Ida Maxwell, married Lazarus Stumpff in St. Joseph, Missouri, in 1878. Mary's mother was Christine Epperson, whose family came over from England and settled in Albermarle County, Virginia. There is the Epperson Mountain in the Big Blue Mountains named after them. Christine Epperson married Joseph Reeves Maxwell and they settled in Kansas on a farm where they raised their 4 children: Florence, Frank, Mary Cora, Ota, and Tobias.

Christine Epperson Maxwell is buried in the Grace Hill Cemetery in Perry. She passed away in 1910, at the home of her daughter Mrs. Ota (Elmer) Rice. Mrs. Ota Rice and her husband, Elmer, are buried in Enid, Oklahoma, where they made their home.

Mr. and Mrs. James H. Stumpff moved from Guthrie to Oklahoma City and from there to Beverly Hills, California, where they both passed away and are buried in Forest Lawn Cemtery in Los Angeles.

My grandfather came from Wichita, Kansas to the opening of the strip and rode an old Bay Mare to stake a claim 4½ miles northwest of Orlando on Cow Creek. He brought his family soon after from Wichita. They came by train and lived in a dugout until they built them a home. There were four children: Maxwell Powell, 14 years old; Guy Johnston, 12 years old; Edith Mary, 9 years old; and Christine, 6 years old.

The next year after the opening of the strip they had a school and a church called the Lawnview. They lived on the farm with Mrs. Stumpff and the boys helping with the farm work and Mr. Stumpff keeping up with his work. He was a stonemason and worked in many places like Tonkawa, Ardmore, Guthrie, etc.

Front Row (L to R): Ota Rice holding cornstalks, Ray Rice in wagon, Christine Stumpff, Mary Ida Stumpff, Edith Stumpff. Back Row: Guy Stumpff, James H. Stumpff, Ladd Stumpff, Elmer Rice, Max Stumpff about 1895.

In 1911, they moved to Perry from their farm which they still kept and rented. Their children had married. Guy J. Stumpff married Mary Adcock of Orlando. Edith married James Elba Brier. Christine married a Methodist minister, Vernon Ludlow.

Mr. Stumpff established the Perry Marble and Granite Works in 1912. He dealt in Foreign and Domestic Granite Monuments, Statuary and Lawn fencing. Many of the monuments in the Grace Hill Cemetery were carved by Mr. Stumpff.

They lived for many years at 806 Cedar street and they both were active in the Christian Science church and helped to build the little church on Delaware St. at the south corner of 8th Street. Mrs. Stumpff and her two sisters, Florence and Ota, became Christian Science practioners.

After Mr. Stumpff passed away, Mrs. Stumpff lived in Arizona for three years with her daughter, Christine and then moving back to Perry lived with her daughter, Edith, until her death three years later. She passed away in 1950, at the age of 88. The Stumpffs and their children are all gone leaving 7 grandchildren still living.

Max Stumpff and his daughter, Maxine, are deceased leaving a son, Jack Stumpff in La Mesa, California. He has a son, Mark.

Guy Stumpff had a daughter, Thelma Wetzel, deceased leaving a son, Leonard in Pryor, and a daughter, Mary Jo Smith in Denver, Colorado.

Edith Stumpff Brier (born October 6, 1884 in St. Joseph, Missouri) and a daughter, Maxine Douglass, and her son, Tatum, are deceased. Leaving a grandson, James Brier Douglass in Kennewick, Washington, and daughter Marjorie Brier Cramer, living in Perry. Marjorie has a daughter, Virginia St. Pierre, Tulsa, Oklahoma and a son, Gerry Cramer in Houston, Texas and a daughter, Sally Russell, in Ardmore, Oklahoma.

Christine Ludlow and her husband Vernon lived in Arondale, Arizona for many years. They helped to establish the Methodist Church there. They lived in Arondale until their deaths. They had four children which are still living: Tom, Mary Elma, and Ellen Burton, and Paul, who lives in California. Numerous grandchildren and great-grandchildren survive.

John Pinkney Sullins
By Darrell Sullins

Born in Missouri, February 10, 1850, John Pinkney Sullins was the youngest of 14 children born to John and Malinda Thompson Sullens, (some spelled name with ins, others ens) who came to Missouri from Kentucky. John Pinkney married Mary Jane Denton, who was born April 23, 1853, and they had four sons: Arthur Denton, (June 11, 1873 - April 9, 1943); Walter Deward; and Oscar Leo, born December 6, 1881, who were born in Missouri and Oliver Clarence, (1884 - 1924), who may have been born in Oklahoma. Having operated a store in Missouri, they moved to a farm near Moore, in Old Oklahoma Territory.

John P. went to Orlando, Oklahoma, for the September 16, 1893 run into the Cherokee Strip. He wanted to get on a train going north, but it was overcrowded and he was not able to get on, so just before the train pulled out he crawled beneath a car and onto the truss rods. He lost his hat crawling onto the rods and the man who found it took to John P.'s wife and told her he had been killed by a train and his hat was all that was left, which she believed until

John Pinkney Sullins and son Oliver.

Sullins Brothers store, Red Rock, Oklahoma before 1912.

John P. returned home a month or so later. John P. rode the rods from Orlando to Red Rock, where he got off at the Depot, crossed Red Rock Creek and walked northwest the four miles across the Otoe Indian Reservation to the Indian Meridian. He arrived at the southeast quarter of section 12 and the man that staked that quarter told him the northwest quarter wasn't staked, so he walked on over and staked a claim on the northwest quarter of section 12-23N-1W of the Indian Meridian, just moments before others arrived, and the land in that area was all taken.

After registering his claim at the land office in Perry, he went back home at Moore. In April 1894, he moved his wife and sons, Oscar L., who was 12 years and Oliver C. to the new homestead. Arthur and Walter were going to school at Norman and came up later. They moved in a wagon pulled by oxen and drove their cows to the farm one mile north and one mile east of what was to become Ceres. They broke the sod that Spring with oxen and a sod plow. They lived in a dugout for a few years until they could build a 28 foot square house with the roof running up from the four walls to a square flat center with the chimney in the center.

One time in the dugout Mrs. Sullins looked up and an Indian was standing in the doorway. He would look at her, then at a knife laying on a table and then at a watermelon on the floor, until Mrs. Sullins cut the melon and gave him a piece. After he ate the whole melon, he went on his way.

The homesteaders were required to live on the place 5 years to "Prove up" before they got title, but some were not able to do so. Such was the case on the SE quarter of section 2, diagonally northwest to the Sullins' and J.P. paid the man a small sum for the rights and his sister, Martha, came down from Missouri and lived with Oscar on the place the remainder of the 5 years. Oscar was probably around 14 years old. Then the fellow east of the homestead pulled out and J.P. bought it for Ollie, but I think it was already proved up. Walt got a farm one half mile east of Ceres and Arthur got his farm one east and one half south of Ceres. I do not know when or how they obtained theirs.

Sometime in the early 1900's the Sullins Brothers opened a General Store in Red Rock. I believe all the boys lived in Red Rock at this time, though this may not be correct. They sold groceries, clothes, shoes, hats, bolts of cloth, etc. This was when Red Rock was in its growth stage. It grew from the influx of settlers, and dwindled after the automobile became popular as people were able to drive to Perry and Ponca City to shop.

Mary Jane died on March 12, 1916, and John Pinkney on February 13, 1929. Oscar moved his family back to the farm around 1918, later he moved to the original homestead where he farmed for the rest of his life. He died on November 3, 1953. Oscar married Flova Delphas Tipton September 28, 1910 at El Dorado, Kansas. She was born January 19, 1887 and died January 15, 1975.

Oscar and Flova were parents of: Katherin Clare, born April 6, 1912, married Marion Veach; John Keith, born December 21, 1914, died November 22, 1964; Oscar Kenneth, born January 19, 1917, lives in Red Rock; Debert Leo, born August 31, 1921; Billie Darrell, born July 15, 1929, who with his family lives on the old homestead.

Oscar L. Sullins
By Darrell Sullins

Oscar Leo Sullins came to Noble County with his parents, John F. and Mary D. Sullins, in April, 1894 to their homestead a mile north and a mile east of what was to become Ceres, Oklahoma.

Oscar was born December 6, 1881 in the Spring Garden, Missouri area of Cole County, southwest of Jefferson City. His family moved to Moore, Oklahoma, where they farmed, before his dad staked a claim in the Cherokee Strip.

After moving to their claim, he helped his father with the farm where they used oxen for pulling. Oscar's Aunt Martha Hindes had sent food from Missouri to them the first year to help them make it till they got a crop harvested. This helped considerably as food and money were scarce the first year. The spring planted crops like corn would not be harvested until fall and wheat planted in the fall would not be harvested until the next spring.

When the man who homesteaded the place diagonally northwest of Sullins' farm wanted to leave, J.P. bought it for Oscar for just a few dollars, but it still had to be proved up the remainder of the required five years of living on it, before Oscar could get a patent. His Aunt Martha came down from Missouri to live with Oscar on the claim the required time left and he then received title to the SE ¼ of section 2-23N-1W of the Indian Meridian.

In the early 1900's Oscar joined his brothers, Walter, Arthur, and Oliver in the Sullins Brothers General Store in Red Rock. The store was the second

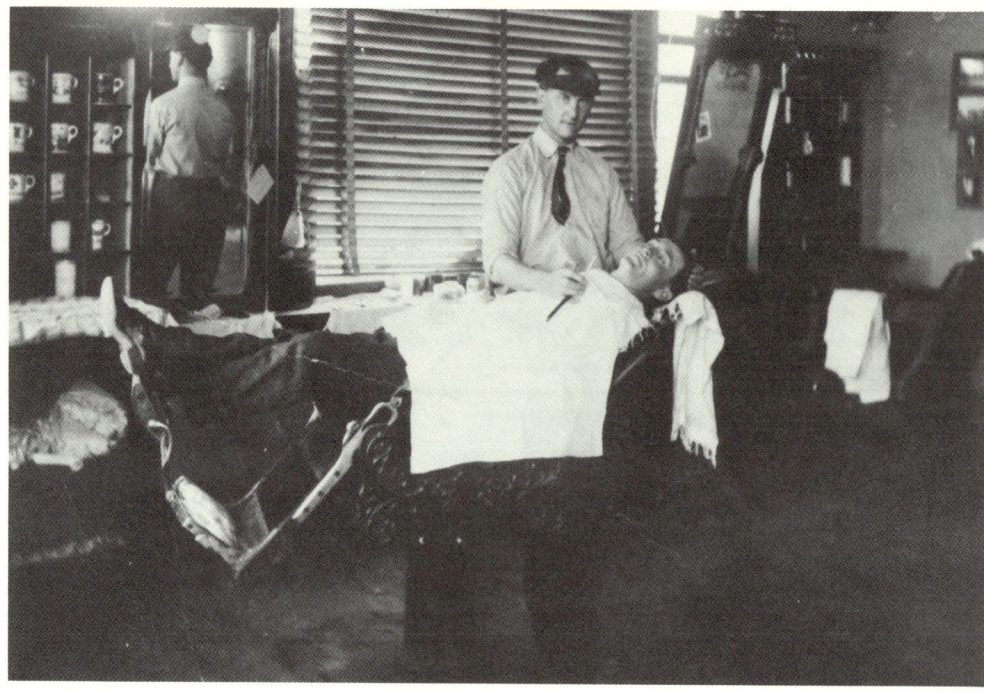

Oscar Sullins in barber chair in Red Rock early 1900's. Personal shaving mugs in left background.

building from the west in the second block from the east, on the south side of Main street. The building is no longer standing.

Oscar and Flova Delphas Tipton, (January 19, 1887 - January 15, 1975), were married September 28, 1910 in El Dorado, Kansas. Flova originally came to Red Rock to visit her brother, Will, who was the depot agent. He later was at the Perry depot for a while. Flova later taught school at Red Rock. A while after she married Oscar, Flova began working in the Sullins Brothers store. She told about, when working in the store, the older Indian women would come in and look at things and say "Tahana?", which was asking "How much?", so between the store, and teaching in the Red Rock School before they were married, she was able to understand a small bit of the Otoe language. Oscar and Flova moved from Red Rock back to the farm around 1918, and then later to his dad's homestead where he lived and farmed the rest of his life. Oscar died November 3, 1953.

Oscar had a steam engine and threshing machine and later tractors and pull combines. He had farmed with oxen, horses and mules, steam engines and tractors. From walking, to horses, to Model T and new cars, he was real thrilled when he got to fly in an airplane.

Oscar had a sorrel horse, that had been a wild Mustang, that he called Seagle, that he would ride driving cattle to a pasture east of Red Rock about ten miles from home, then he would pull the bridle off and the horse would come home on his own. Oscar would come back in a car. One time, he loaned the horse to a fellow to ride home several miles. When the fellow got home, he tied a note to the saddlehorn, saying to "let this horse pass, he is going home." In due time, Seagle arrived home.

In early days, Oscar was on the Red Rock township board, as the township was the local Government for fixing roads and bridges at that time. They maintained the roads with a team of horses and a drag and later a horse-

Oscar Sullins, left, other man unidentified. In background Red Rock School prior to 1911.

Oscar Sullins' steam engine on thrashing machine - water wagon on left.

Oscar Sullins' thrashing machine.

Oscar Sullins, wife Flova, daughter Katherine and sons Keith, Kenneth, Delbert and Darrell - about 1945.

Mark, wife Kathryn, Daniel, Jean, Valinda, and Darrell - 1980.

drawn grader.

Oscar and Flova had five children: Katherine Clare, John Keith, Oscar Kenneth, Delbert Leo, and Billie Darrell.

Katherine married Marion Veach and had two daughters: Joyce Kay and June Ann; Keith married Charlotte Bruner and had two sons: John Keith and David Bruce; Kenneth married Evelyn Raff, and had two sons: Harold Kenneth and Douglas Brent; Delbert married Joyce Clark and had a daughter: Marilyn Elaine and a son: Clark Leo; Darrell married Norma Jean Foreman, and had two sons: Daniel Ernest (February 10, 1956 - August 29, 1985), and Mark Wayne, and a daughter: Valinda Jean. Darrell, Jean and Valinda live on his granddad's old homestead. Mark married Kathryn Henderson.

William M. Sullins
By Forrest Sullins

William Marion Sullins was born March 30, 1878, on a farm near Eldon, Missouri. At the age of twenty-one, being a member of a large family of twelve children, unemployed and hungry, he walked out of Missouri to Oklahoma. He settled near what is now Ceres in Noble County. He met and later married Mary Jane Ratliff April 2, 1902.

Mary was born February 8, 1880, in a one-room log cabin at Annapolis, Missouri about one hundred miles south of St. Louis. She started school when she was eight years old and went three terms of nine months. She finished the fifth grade.

Her father lost the farm where they lived and the family came to Purcell, Oklahoma, where he "broke sod" for $1.00 an acre to support the family. The family later moved in a covered wagon to a site near Mulhall where he borrowed a saddlehorse to make the Cherokee Strip run on September 16, 1893. He started near Mulhull and rode to Ceres. He looked up and saw runners coming from the north so he staked out his farm. It is located across from present-day Ceres. The Ceres Baptist church now stands on the northwest corner of the original homestead.

Soon after staking the claim, it was necessary to move near Guthrie to obtain medical care because the mother was ill. They remained there for two years. While in Guthrie, Mary's father hauled and sold barrels of water at 10¢ a barrel. They saved their dimes until they had a cigar box full. Then they bought a cow and 12 hens to take back to the farm.

In September of 1895 they went back to the homestead and built a dugout to cook in and a large sod room to sleep in. The Father went to Red Rock Creek to

William Sullins family in 1916 (L to R): Loyd Leonavis, William Marion, William Alvin, Mary Jane, Paul Hansel, Forrest Jasper (small blonde in front).

get timber to make clap boards to cover the sod house. Mary and her father plastered the sod house inside. It was comfortable but not very pretty.

Mary did not get to go back to school until she was eighteen years old.

After Will and Mary were married they traded 80 acres of wheat for 80 acres of blackjack land in Woods County, Oklahoma. The place had a good well, one room, a shed, kitchen, log barn, log chicken house, brush fence and a corn crop on it. Will had to work in the wheat harvest in Kansas to earn money. He returned home with smallpox and Mary got the disease and lost the baby she was carrying. She later gave birth in Woods County to William Alvin on July 1, 1903, and Paul Hansel on August 21, 1904.

It was difficult to make a living on land covered with blackjacks and sand, so they sold the place for $350.00. They came back to a place eight miles east of Red Rock where their third child, Loyd Leonavis, was born on June 4, 1906. After several years they moved back near Ceres where Forrest Jasper was born on September 4, 1912. The day Forrest was born, Will got in a buggy to go to Red Rock for a doctor. Consequently, the baby arrived before Will and the doctor got back.

Mary's father sold Will and Mary the east one-half of the homestead so that they could be near in case her parents needed them. In 1918 they built a house on their land. They raised their sons and continued to live in this home until their deaths. Will passed away on March 21, 1954 and Mary died on February 24, 1966. Forrest is their only son now living.

Will and Mary never had much in a material way, but they always were there to help anyone who was in need. They cared for, loved, and had compassion for those who were helpless, hopeless, sick, or in trouble.

Victor Albert Swanson

By Dorothy Swanson Reilly

Victor Albert Swanson was born April 27, 1875 at Woodhull, Illinois, the son of Karl August Svensson and Anna Hansdotter. Karl Svensson was born March, 18, 1822 in the parish of Krakhult, Sweden, the son of Sven Davidson and Anna Catharina Johansdotter. Karl married Anna Maja Pettersdotter, December 28, 1845 in Svallarp, a small village in Sweden where they both lived. Their children were Anna Christina, Sven Petter, Clara Mathilda, Carl Johan, Johanna, Gustave Alfred, Frans August and Otto Emil. They emigrated to America in 1869. Anna died soon after they reached America. Sometime between 1870 and 1875 Karl married Anna Hansdotter at either Andover or Woodhull, Illinois. Anna was born July 21, 1840 at Jarbo, Sweden. Anna had a daughter, Tilly Christine, born May 21, 1870. Neither the name of Anna's father or husband is known. She had come to America in 1870.

Victor Swanson was the oldest of the children born to Karl and his second wife, Victor had a brother, Anton William, born July 11, 1877, at Woodhull Illinois, who died at the age of 5 years of the coup, and a sister, Ida, born June 14, 1897 at Florence, Kansas. Ida married Rev. Hiram Ruby in 1902, at Perry, Oklahoma Territory. Their children were: Sheridan, Ernest, Naomi, Chester and Fred. On June 12, 1921 she married Rubin Ross at Perry, Oklahoma.

Too young to make the run, Victor Swanson came to Oklahoma in 1901 and bought a claimants rights to the south half of the northeast ¼ of section 15 in Walnut township. His half-brother, Frank, had the north half of the same quarter section. Frank had changed his name from Frans August Svensson to Frank August Palm. Frank and his wife, Julie E. Flora, had three daughters who died in infancy, Henrietta, May 30, 1897; Ester, September 8, 1900, and an unnamed girl, November 10, 1897. They also had three sons, Walter Frank born March 10, 1892 at Moline, Illinois; Melvin, born January 12, 1902 at Perry, Oklahoma Territory and Clifford Lawrence, born April 23, 1905. Frank and his wife got discouraged in a few years after proving up and getting a government patent no. 2407. They left the farm, which they sold to Victor for $2,000 and returned to Woodhull, Illinois.

In his testimony for final proof of his homestead entry, Victor A. Swanson, on October 17, 1906, gave his age as 31, stated he was unmarried and had made these improvements on the farm: 2 room house, stable, blacksmith shop, orchard with 50 trees, all fenced, one well, total value $500.00.

Victor Swanson married Antoinette Zmotony, April 20, 1908 at Stillwater, Oklahoma. Their children are: Thelma, born March 26, 1909. She married George Ennis at Stillwater, Oklahoma, May 27, 1931. George was born August 3, 1909 and died March 7, 1975. They had one child, Kathleen, born January 28, 1942, who married Dr. Walter Flores, February 22, 1975. Dr. Flores is from Bolivia, South American.

Dorothy, the second child of Victor and Tony Swanson was born December 15, 1915. She married Thomas Reilly at Chicago, Illinois, June 29, 1963.

Agnes, the third daughter, was born March 17, 1921. She married Donald Sparks, February 26, 1943, at Muskogee, Oklahoma. Their children are Lois Carol, born February 26, 1944

Tony and Victor Swanson at their wedding April 20, 1908.

at Bloomington, Illinois; Robert born 1945, died in infancy and Donald Dell, born March 14, 1957 at Dallas, Texas.

The parents of Victor, Carl A. Swanson died September 30, 1911 and his wife, Anna L. Swanson died January 29, 1936. They are buried in Shelton cemetery in Walnut township. Victor A. Swanson died February 6, 1951 at Perry, Oklahoma. Tony Swanson died January 1973. They are buried in Grace Hill cemetery.

Charles Swearingen
By Gladys Swearingen

"We're off for our race", Charlie said proudly as he and five others: S. L. Swearingen, a single brother; A. W. Greenleaf, a brother-in-law, who with his father made the race without filing; Frank Shaddy, a hired hand of a year; and Ed and Ott Hamilton, both unmarried neighbors — all from Independence, Kansas, started lumbering down the dirt road in a covered wagon from his well-established home, leading six horses which they hoped would carry them to victory in the richer land.

Fortified with boxes of fried chicken, smoked meat, homemade bread, coffee and other necessities for hungry men which his wife had packed for them, they were ready to batch with their tin dishes, iron skillets, and two-gallon coffee pot, during the week journey.

The Swearingens were leaving 160 acres of prairie land four miles west of Independence, bought for them with money from their father's Indiana estate. They went around the Cherokee Strip lands to avoid being Sooners, and traveled through Cherokee, Osage and Creek nations, coming into Old Oklahoma. When they came to the Arkansas River the Indians had charge of the toll crossing, a make-shift ferry of logs on which the wagons were floated across. They drove to a few miles southeast of Stillwater where Charlie's mother had a place, 160 acres of leased school land, where they left the horses. They went to the line north of Stillwater to register to make the race. There was such a crowd at the registration booth they had to stand in line for three days. They ate standing up and drank what water was brought to them. Eva, his wife, worked in a food booth, so they ate although the food was mainly black-eyed peas.

Charlie staked a claim with a make shift flag made of his handerchief and a shoot. It was near Black Bear Creek on the southwest corner of section 9 in Autry township. He had run ten miles in thirty minutes. He built a claim house, a box-like affairs of twelve inch pine lumber 14 ft. x 20 ft., boarded up and down with slats over the cracks, two rooms below, with three windows and an attic above with one window. Two doors, both in the kitchen, were directly

Swearingen house in 1985.

opposite each other. They hauled all materials from Wharton.

Eva had returned to Kansas while Charlie built the house. When, on January 15, 1894, she with her sister Flora and Eva's two little girls arrived in Wharton at two o'clock in the afternoon no one was there to meet them. Eva told about it later "We sat in the dismal depot and ate our shoe-box lunch. The rows of wooden benches around the walls, the rough, dirty floors, and the pot-bellied coal burning stove didn't lessen the tiring wait. We talked little except for repeated comments "wonder when Charlie'll get here?" We paced from bench to door for sight of him. About four he came, an eternity of waiting but still he had the shopping to do. When we got started to the claim I don't remember but I can never forget the end of the trip. We bundled the two girls up, making it as comfortable as possible for the ride to the claim near Autry in our fringed-top open surrey. We jostled along seemingly without end and finally about eleven o'clock we stopped in front at a small house. Outside the shack was unpainted and univiting, inside, barren and cold, no fire and the stove flat on the floor minus its legs. Only one bed up, a featherbed flattened where Charlie had slept, piles of everything on the floor, boxes of bedding and clothes, dishes and cooking utensils, canned fruit — a hundred gallons of it — packed in oats, a small sewing rocker, a half dozen wooden bottom, round top backed chairs. Nothing that looked like home."

They soon had beds up and in the next three weeks had put up shelves to hold the dishes, pounded nails in the walls to hold their clothes. They nailed rag carpets over the north door and side wall to keep out the wintry blasts, leaving one way in and out.

In 1896, Charles and a Mr. Holstein with the help of five hired men — John Jajek; John Frame; Jesse James, son of a settler to the west of them; a Mr. Olsen and Bert Hetherington, Whispering Charlie's son, made bricks from the sand and clay on the claim. The materials were throughly ground and mixed with a certain proportion of water in a mechanical grinder powered by one horse. The pulverized mixture was poured into wooden molds large enough for four bricks which, when firm, were laid in the sun to dry before being burned in the home-made arched kilns with three sections for wood fires, kept burning day and night. For two years the brick were kept in the kilns, located in the space that was later the front yard, waiting the accumulation of money for the house building.

When the house was completed, it was a two-story red brick, consisting of downstairs - kitchen, dining and front rooms, with one bedroom and two full length porches across both the front and back; upstairs were two enclosed bedrooms on the east and two on the west, separated only by a wall to chimney closet. An open doorway extended to the outer front wall near which a door opened onto an upper porch, the size of the lower one. A railing enclosed it, making overflow or hot night sleeping quarters.

Charles W. Swearingen was born January 1865 in Indiana. His father was born in Pennsylvania, and his mother in Ohio. His wife's name was Eva. She was born in February 1871, in Kansas, her father was born in New York, her mother in Ohio. Their children: Goldie O. born July 1891, in Kansas; Orpha Gladys born in November 1893, in Kansas; Jewel T. born May 1896 in Oklahoma, infant daughter died October 30, 1898, Charles Dennis born March 14, 1901 died January 29, 1903, twins Melvin and Merlin born 1910 in Oklahoma. In 1920, the family moved to California near Exeter. Charlie died in 1935 — Eva in 1959. They are buried in California.

O.T. Swearingen
By Dean Gilbert

Obed T. Swearingen Jr. (or O.T. as he was better known) was born October 4, 1883 in Gentry county, Missouri, the son of Obed T. and Elizabeth (Kent) Swearingen. His parents were farmers near Stansberry, Missouri. He attended school in Stansberry and later assisted his father in farming.

On October 2, 1905, he and Nellie L. David were married at Ravenwood, Missouri. Nellie was born on April 26, 1888, the daughter of William and Liza (Campbell) David.

They moved to Morrison, Oklahoma in 1907. O.T.'s two brothers, Jake and Joe, had moved here previously and told O.T. there were opportunities here. O.T. and Nellie located two miles north and east of Morrison, on what was known as the

O.T. and Nellie Swearingen.

Kent farm, living with his mother and sister Flossie, until later they moved to a rock house on the northwest corner of the Kent farm. It was the first time for them to be away from home. Living in this new country was lonesome for Nellie and many times she desired to move back to Missouri.

O.T. and Nellie purchased eighty acres in Otoe township, Pawnee county in about 1912. He leased additional land from the Red Rock and Otoe Indians. O.T. with the assistance of neighbors moved a two room house on a pole wagon for their home. Later, additional rooms were built on to the house as the size of their family increased.

He farmed and raised cattle. Also for many years he worked for Pawnee County as Road Maintance operator. He started with a horse drawn grader, then later using a tractor and last the motor patrol.

O.T. was always interested in new things. They owned one of the first automobiles, Maxwell, icey ball refrigerator, carbide lighting and cooking system, radio and gravity water system.

O.T. was an avid hunter. He spent most of his spare time hunting wild game and trained bird dogs. He was proud of his marksmanship, entering shooting matches.

Nellie always had a large garden and a hen house full of chickens. Living several miles from town she was often called upon to assist in delivery of babies, until the doctor could get there, some babies arrived before the doctor did.

Many of the teachers of Lone Star school roomed and boarded in their home. Due to Nellie's health in 1958, they sold their farm and moved to Pawnee so she could be close to her doctor.

O.T. and Nellie had five children: Locie Marie was born in Missouri, October 1, 1906. She married B.H. Fairchild. They live in Liberal, Kansas. Vinna Leota was born September 4, 1911. She married James V. Adams. She died in July 1985. Dorrel Irene was born August 4, 1914. She married Wayne Coffman. They live in Oklahoma City, Oklahoma. William T. was born April 26, 1919. He married Bettie Jones. They live in Fairfax, Oklahoma. Eva Waldine (Dean) was born June 25, 1921. She married Richard M. Gilbert. They live north of Morrison, Oklahoma.

Nellie died January 25, 1964. O.T. died October 11, 1967. They are buried in Pawnee cemetery.

Clem T. Talliaferro
By Mildred Highfill

Clem Tasmania Talliaferro, better known as "Tally" was born September 25, 1872, at Brownsville, Tennessee. Tally entered the Roger Williams University in Nashville, Tennessee, at the age of 16. He graduated four years later in 1892, with a bachelors degree. He taught school in Arkansas during the summer. There he contracted malaria fever and went back to his old home in Hayward county, Tennessee, because he thought he was going to die. Later, he went to Minnesota, but took a doctor's advice to "come west." On the train, he heard of the land opening and thought a farm might help him get rid of the disease. Tally left the train in Fort Worth and came north again. He started from the southern line near Orlando on foot and staked a claim on a farm north of Perry. It seems he was in a corner of the plot and that another man was in the other corner. Tally gave way and was reimbursed for doing so. Returning to Perry, he borrowed 50¢ worth of peanuts, roasted them and sold them. With the money he bought some fruit, sold it and invested again until he had money to set up a store. He bought a lot where the Post Office now stands. There he set up his first store, some gunny sacks strung over some poles. This was government property and Tally had to move. In 1915, he built a general store, just off the northeast corner of the square and continued in business until his death.

He married in 1895 in the territory. His wife, Lillie, was from the delta country near Natchez, Mississippi. She was born in October, 1871, and died in 1942. He remarried September 20, 1948, to a school teacher from Los Angeles.

Tally was the first man voted a lifetime member in the Perry Chamber of Commerce. He was also a member of the Price Hall lodge and the African Methodist Episcopal Church.

He learned to speak nine languages in his lifetime, several of these from his customers during his 60 years in business. He could speak some Dutch, English, Otoe Indian, Spanish, German, Latin, Greek and French.

No one but Tally knew how many philanthropies he had, but wouldn't tell much about them. It is known that he helped his school financially and that he was more or less responsible for the building occupied by his church.

Monroe Tsa Toke
By Sharon Courtright

A. Monroe Tsa Toke was named for his great uncle Monroe Tsa Toke, who was one of the Kiowa Five tutored by Professor Oscar B. Jacobson, then head of the school of art of O.U. Some of the work of the first Monroe Tsa Toke is featured at the Oklahoma Historical building in Oklahoma City. The Kiowa Five had a great impact on the Indian art movement of the 1930s.

The "original" Monroe Tsa Toke died at a fairly young age and Monroe Tsa Toke of Red Rock, Oklahoma, never knew his namesake. Tsa Toke said he believes his art is most influenced by Lee Monnet Tsa Toke, son of the Kiowa Five Monroe Tsa Toke and a Cheyenne Indian artist, Archie Blackowl.

Although he began drawing cartoon characters in third grade, Tsa Toke said he had no formal education until he entered college. Basic art techniques and art terms which were commonly known to others in his college art classes were foreign to Tsa Toke. Becaused of his interest in Indian art styles, Tsa Toke did much research on his own. His works include a variety of authentic Indian symbols. Tsa Toke says he feels compelled at times, to paint certain things. He has completed countless hours of research on the Kiowa history, myths, customs and costumes so his paintings will be as authentic as possible. Many of the paintings done by Tsa Toke depict family history. He sometimes paints from old family photographs.

Tsa Toke's ancestry has been traced back to Hunting Horse, a Kiowa chief who served as an Indian scout under General Custer. Hunting Horse, as was the Indian custom, had two wives. They were sisters, Peat-Mah and Peat-O-Mah. Tsa Toke is descended from Peat-O-Mah's family which adopted the Kiowa name of Tsa Toke, meaning Hunting Horse. Peat-Mah's descendents adopted the surname of Horse.

A native of the Anadarko, Oklahoma area Tsa Toke attended Carnegie public schools and is a graduate of Riverside Indian School. He received his bachelor of arts degree in art education from Southwestern Oklahoma State University in December 1975.

He assumed his first teaching position as art instructor at Red Rock school in January 1976. Tsa Toke said he believes art is just as important as English, Math or other subject areas in secondary schools. He said his class is one where his students can come to relax and enjoy themselves while using their minds, hands and imaginations. He teaches the students the basic art techniques while allowing them to develop their own art styles.

Some of Tsa Toke's artwork, along with that of some of his art students, appears on the teepee at the Cherokee Strip Museum, Perry. He has for a number of years, entered the art competition at the Noble County free fair. Tsa Toke completed a painting which was used on the cover of the 1977-78 Red Rock school yearbook. That cover was selected as one of the 10 best in the nation by Josten's American Yearbook Company.

Johanna, Tsa Toke's wife is a former Kiowa Indian princess of the tribe. She is a receptionist at Red Rock school. Their daughter, Fawn, is a kindergarten student at Red Rock. Another daughter, Dawn was born in September 1986. The Tsa Toke family, during the summer months, travels throughout the state with the Oklahoma department of tourism, performing authentic Indian dancing.

Tsa Toke is a member and past president of the Red Rock Lions Club and soon will represent the Lions organization as deputy district governor. He is a member of the Red Rock Sportsman's Club, has been named as honorary chapter farmer by the Red Rock Future Farmers of America by the United States Jaycees.

He was co-chairman of Minority Involvement Programs with the Oklahoma State committee on human and civil rights in 1983-84; served as co-chairman of the Oklahoma Indian Caucus of Teachers of 1983-84; is a former member of the Stillwater Arts Council; and was a member of the Red Rock staff development committee in 1982. He took part in a state summer leadership conference in 1983-84; a national American Indian/Alaska Native conference in 1984; a state Indian Caucus.

Andrew Jackson Testerman
By Bessie (Testerman) Hopkins

Andrew Jackson Testerman was born at Pineville, Missouri, November 9, 1843. At the beginning of the Civil War he enlisted in the 8th Missouri Calvary and was discharged before the expiration of his term of enlistment on account of disability. Later he volunteered in the 46th Missouri Infantry for one year and at the expiraton of that period he enlisted in the 57th Missouri Infantry. This was in the Union Army.

On July 19, 1866, he married Mary E. Lauderdale. She was born Mary E. Shields in Aley Culesy Valley, Georgia on November 28, 1842. She came with her parents to southwest Missouri when a child. She united with the Baptist church at the age of 14. In 1860, she married Dempsey Lauderdale. They had one son, W. J. Lauderdale. Dempsey had four children by a previous marriage, two boys and two girls, and when he died Mary was left with five children to raise.

Mary and "Uncle Jack" as he was called had eight children: Eli Thomas born August 2, 1867; Smith Andrew, Joshua H. born 1871; Annie Bell (Powell) born June 1876; a daughter who married Mr. Libbey; Laura Jane (McClure) born September 1881; Lucy M. (Freeman) born September 1883; and John R. who died in infancy.

In 1881, the family moved from Pineville, Missouri to the Cherokee Reservation in old Indian Territory and located near where the town of Grove is now situated. They moved to Cushing, Oklahoma in the spring of 1893 and on September 16 of that year Mr. Testerman was among the number who made the run into the Cherokee Strip.

Uncle Jack possessed a forceful character and had the courage of his convictions in all matters. About 1907, Mr. and Mrs. Testerman moved to Morrison where she died May 7, 1915. He died March 31, 1923. His funeral services were held at the Baptist church conducted by Christian Science ladies from Ponca City. They are buried in the Morrison cemetery.

Their children are: Tom, Smith and Josh, all took part in the "run" as well as a son-in-law, Lyman McClure. For information on Tom and Josh see their family stories. Smith married Nannie. They had no children of their own but adopted four: Russell, Clara Mae, Raymond, and Rachael. Smith continued to farm his homestead and gradually built up a poultry farm and shipped many eggs and fryers to the Tulsa, Oklahoma market. The Tulsa Chamber of Commerce, needing a reliable source of poultry induced Smith to move his poultry business to Tulsa. Smith sold his farm and moved his family to Tulsa, where they lived until their deaths.

Eli Thomas Testerman
By Millie Highfill

On July 28, 1940, Mr. and Mrs. Tom Testerman celebrated their golden wedding anniversary on the farm they homesteaded in the run at the opening of the Cherokee Strip in 1893.

Eli Thomas Testerman was born August 2, 1867 in Missouri, the son of Mary E. (Shields) and Andrew Jackson Testerman. He married Rebecca Jane Edwards July 28, 1890. Rebecca was born November 10, 1867 in Austin, Texas. She was of an old New England family, Scotch Calvinist of Colonial times. There were several ministers in her family, the most famous was Jonathan Edwards.

To this union was born eight children: Ray H. born June 1890; Jackson born July 1892; Juanita (Allen) born April 1894; Reed born June 1895; McKinley born June 1895; Flynn born May 1899; Wayne and Theodore.

Tom died July 22, 1941 and Rebecca February 17, 1942. They are buried in the Morrison cemetery.

Tom Testerman was active in Oklahoma politics, a strong republican. The first election in the new state he ran for sheriff and was defeated in the primary. The next election he was elected as State Representative to the State Legislature. He served several terms in the State House of Representatives and then was elected to the State Senate representing Noble and Pawnee counties. He was a member of the State Representatives when the capitol was moved from Guthrie to Oklahoma City.

In the House and in the Senate Tom was a strong champion for the preservation of the state's natural resources, especially the native timber land. He was strong for Woman's Suffrage amendement to the U.S. Constitution.

Tom was a great friend to the Otoe Indians. They trusted him and his judgment. Many mornings Indian men would come out of the barn, where they had slept the night before, ready for breakfast. After breakfast they would talk over their problems with Tom and return to their reservation.

Tom's last active years were spent in the oil business as an independent operator in the Burkburnette, Texas area and the Red River between Oklahoma and Texas. Tom and Rebecca Jane spent their last years in retirement on the homestead south of Morrison, Oklahoma.

Josh H. Testerman
By Bessie (Testerman) Hopkins

Joshua Hugh Testerman was born December 21, 1871 in Pineville, Missouri, the son of Mary E. (Shields)

(L to R): Flavilla Davis, Hattie and Josh Testerman.

and Andrew Jackson Testerman. He came with his father and brothers and made the run in 1893.

Josh married Hattie Gertrude Davis, March 16, 1898. Hattie was born December 2, 1877 at Boonville, Indiana, the daughter of Flavilla (Ryman) and George Berry Davis. She came with her parents to Dunlap, Kansas and about the year 1889 came to Stillwater, Oklahoma where she attended A & M College. At the opening of the Cherokee Strip, she resided on her father's homestead near Morrison, Oklahoma.

To this union eight children were born: Laura Blanche (January 3, 1899 - January 19, 1899); Florence Leona (March 29, 1900 - April 14, 1926); Beulah (Knorr) November 22, 1901; Bessie (Hopkins) (September 15, 1903); J. Paul (January 31, 1906); Eveylyn (Tate) (October 11, 1907 - July 12, 1982); Letha (Tate) (December 3, 1912); and Willa (October 1914 - August 3, 1985). They attended Jefferson rural school south of Morrison, Oklahoma.

Poem by J. H. Testerman written in 1945:

HERE'S TO ALL THE OLD TIMERS

You are looking on some old has-beens
  Relic of the early days,
Sooners, once they said we were,
  But we don't care for praise,
For our hearts are with the dear old pals
  That now no more we see,
Who by our side made the ride,
  Of eighteen ninety-three.
We made a vow we'd win that race
  To be the first was our aim.
We rode a steed that took the lead
  And held it to our claim.
Our abode, we built of sod
  And covered it with clay,
And in sod houses worshipped God,
  Just as we do today.
Fifty-two years since then has passed,
  The future we proudly face.
And say to our pals who have rode on
  "Ride on and win the race."
When you've put stakes on your claim
  And a furrow on your line,
Prepare to welcome your buddies
  You long ago left behind,
For when we get the signal
  Coming from the other side
We will climb into the saddle
  And take that long last ride,
While we are here our greatest pride
  Will be these words "We made the ride
The ride that filled weak hearts with fear,
  The ride that tamed the last frontier."

Hattie united with the Methodist Episcopal church in early girlhood and with her husband was baptised at Morrison, Oklahoma about 1914. Hattie died March 17, 1936 and was buried in the Morrison cemetery.

Josh married Ida Bales, a widowed sister to Rebecca Jane Edwards September 19, 1939. She died in August of 1942 and was buried in Salem, Oregon. Josh died in 1953 and his buried beside his first wife.

Herman Thiele

By Joan Miller and Peggy Gottschalk

Herman Thiele, born September 14, 1853, in Saxony, Germany, to Johann G. T. Thiele (January 17, 1817 - November 11, 1896) and Sophia Phillips (1823-1906), was a carpenter by trade. His wife, Fredericka (Ricka), was born either in Russia or Poland. Two children, Albert and Elfrieda were born in Germany. Herman and Fredricka were living on a farm in Russia cleared out by hand with axes. They were living in Russia when their second daughter, Lavertha, was born. In the rich soil they grew flax, and lots of potatoes which they ate and fed to their milk cows. Winters were horrible. During their frequent blizzards, they had to tie a rope between them and the house in order to find their way back from the barn after choring. There were acres of woods nearby and the family members had to be extremely careful of the packs of wolves that lived within those boundaries.

The Russian government never made their promise good to give the German people a clear title to their land if they would clear it. This was during the time the Russian persecution was starting. Although Fredricka's parents were living in Russia and were probably Russian citizens, Herman and Fredricka were German citizens. They knew their only hope for survival was to flee to the New World.

Herman and Fredricka left Russia to come to America in 1893. They came through New York on a passenger/freighter ship. Three children, Albrecht (Albert), Elfrieda, and Lavertha, came with them on their journey. The trip was long and tiring. There was little food, medical supplies, or living quarters. At one time, Albert stole some food from the ship's officers to give to his family. It took six weeks to get to America. Thiele's had another child, Wilhelm, who died in Russia as they were waiting on their papers to come to America. When it was time to leave, they took Fredricka's sister's child in his place. Her name was similar to Wilhelm's and they were about the same age. Wilhemine (Minnie Widiger) accompanied the others on the trip. There was quite a scene when they arrived in New York and officials discovered the switch in children. They were going to send Minnie back, but thanks to God's grace, the officials had a change of heart and allowed the child to stay. Herman's parents, Johann and Sophia came with the group, along with his brother and his wife, Reinhold and Katharina.

From New York, they came by train to Moundridge, Kansas. Louis Thiele, another brother to Herman, was living there with his family. While in Kansas, the Thiele's were blessed with their fifth child, Friedrich.

When the Cherokee Strip was opened into Oklahoma, Herman made the run

Herman Thiele Family circa 1909. Front Row (L to R): Otto, Gustav, Mr. & Mrs. Herman, Ida, Carl. Back Row (L to R): Fred, Albert, Elfrieda, Lavertha.

Alfred Thiele at the original Thiele homesite.

Otto and Nena Thiele.

for the free land. They came through the Blackwell area. Gus Widiger, Fredricka's brother-in-law, made the run with him. They came as far as what is now known as Perry, but no land was available. Everything had been claimed. Gus was able to obtain a piece of land near Perry, but Herman could not. Herman and Gus returned to Kansas so that they could work together in the corn fields and gain enough money to return to Oklahoma. On September 1, 1893, Herman signed his first naturalization paper in McPherson county, Kansas. He was 39 years old at this time.

The families returned to Oklahoma in 1894, and settled in Noble county. They came by a covered wagon, two horses pulling them and a cow tied on behind. Albert, 12; Elfrieda, 6; Lavertha, 2; and Fred was just a baby. The trip was long and hard. There were many barriers in their path. One of the hardest was crossing the swollen rivers. Once they got their families settled on the Widiger farm, the men returned to Kansas to work in the fields. They worked for 50¢ a day. They saved as much money as possible and sent it home to the women and children. Fredricka had a few chickens which layed eggs for them to use.

Their first home was a soddy. Grandpa plowed the soil and Grandma built the sod house. Then as time went on, they built another home which had a dirt floor. The cattle were kept in one portion of this home.

On November 5, 1900, Herman signed his citizenship papers filed in Noble county, Territory of Oklahoma. On October 5, 1910, he contracted the purchase of school and public lands of the state of Oklahoma in Noble county. The description: NE ¼, 33-21N-2E (160 acres). The purchase price was $4,000.00. The mortgage was paid off 15 years later. Four children were born here: Gustav Herman (January 12, 1897), Ida Mae (March 11, 1900), Carl Gerhardt (September 8, 1902), and Otto Reihold (August 28, 1904). The house which Mrs. Otto (Nena) Thiele lives in today was built in the early 1900s by Herman and Fredricka.

Fredricka and Herman are buried in the Richburg cemetery just east of the original Thiele homestead. Johann G. T. Thiele is buried just south of the homestead in a private cemetery (Ewy). Sophia is buried in the Zion Lutheran cemetery just east of the farm.

Otto Thiele
By Joan Thiele Miller

Nena, born December 11, 1907, at Ringwood, Oklahoma, was the youngest of the Baetz family, her husband, Otto Thiele, who was born at Perry, August 28, 1904, was the youngest member of his family. Otto attended Pioneer rural school (District #40) through the eighth grade. Nena attended rural Fremont and Willow Creek school through the eighth grade and one semester in the Perry public schools. Otto and Nena met in a restaurant, but he had been acquainted with her brother. In those days neighbors got together for school programs, pie and box suppers, weiner roasts and even butchered hogs together. Many times there were problems of getting places over the muddy roads and sometimes the wagon was used to get to various places.

On October 5, 1927, Otto and Nena were married at Perry and moved to his parents' farm, five miles east and two south of Perry. To this union was born three children, Paul Otto (April 28, 1930), Joan Esther (May 14, 1935), and Peggy Marie (March 20, 1937). All live in the Perry area, within a 2 mile radius of the Perry farm.

Otto and Nena spent all their life on the farm. Otto worked as a farmer-rancher and worked at various other jobs during his lifetime. He hauled rock for the country for many years and then took a job with Loyd Jones Well Service where he worked until his death. For many years he did custom thrashing for the neighrbors.

Thrashing was a lot of work both for the men and women. The women were busy cooking breakfast, dinner, a lunch for the men in the afternoon and usually several men stayed for supper and even spent the night. They had teams of horses to pull the bundle and grain wagons, so they too had to be fed and kept all night. The crew usually had about eighteen men as they moved from farm to farm.

Nena kept busy on the family farm and with her hobbies. She milked cows and did the chores while Otto was working off the farm. She raised her own garden and canned and froze fruits and vegetables for the family. She has many hobbies which include candle-making, plaster craft and crocheting.

Paul, Joan and Peggy attended Pioneer country school, the same school their father attended as a child. Peggy started school a year early, permissable then, and took two grades together, thus making her in the same grade as Joan. We kids walked the mile and one-half each day to and from school, and only on rare occassions were we given a ride. Then we attended the Lutheran parochial school and later Junior and Senior High school in Perry. Because of the early start in school, Peggy graduated the youngest member of her class, turning sixteen two months before graduation. Following graduation, Joan and Peggy both were employed at the Perry Daily Journal.

Paul Thiele graduated from Perry High school in 1948. He farmed in Perry until 1956, when he and his family moved to Batavia, Illinois. Cindy Thiele, born January 20, 1951, married

December 10, 1977, to Kirk Fure, resides in St. Charles, Illinois, with her husband and family of two children, Candi and Daniel. She works full time for AT&T telephone company. Richard Thiele, born June 20, 1952, and married to Gwen Lanzer on May 3, 1980, resides in Iron Mountain, Michigan, with his wife and two children, Lauren and Adam. He is a construction engineer for Blundt Construction Co. Joyce Thiele born December 15, 1954 and married October 14, 1978, to John David, has two children, Johnathan and Alicia. She is head dietician at Delnor Hospital in St. Charles, Illinois.

In 1967, Paul remarried in Ilinois to Elizabeth Jane Millett. In 1968, they moved back to Perry, Oklahoma, to farm and sell MoorMan Feeds. Kern Thiele, (November 5, 1964) who is planning on entering the military service, Jennifer, (March 26, 1969) who is a junior at Perry High School and Shannon, (August 11, 1971) a Freshman at Perry Junior High School, are their children.

Joan married Ray Gottschalk, May 29, 1954, and Peggy married James Gottschalk, brothers, on June 25, 1955. The Gottschalk family lived about five miles from the Thiele family and the fathers had worked together on the threshing crews when their children were growing up. We also attended high school together, and rode the same school bus. Debra Kay and Diane Lanee Gottschalk were born to Ray and Joan Gottschalk. Debra was born in Lawton, Oklahoma, May 10, 1955, while Ray was serving with the US Army at Fort Sill. Diane Lanee was born in Perry, Oklahoma, May 17, 1958, while the family lived at 807 Maple.

Joan married Dr. Starling Miller January 21, 1977. He had a veterinry practice at this time. He later sold the practice and went into the real estate and auction business, which they are still active in. In 1979, a home was built on the family homestead, across the yard from "Grandma Thiele" (Nena is lovingly called Grandma by many). We also farm and raise cattle. Debra Kay married Tim Hooper, June 12, 1977. They have one daughter, Leslie Brooke. Debra works at the County Clerk's Office and assists Tim at their greenhouse and nursery, "Four Seasons". Their home and business is in Perry. Diane Lanee married Eric Hines January 20, 1983. One son, Derek Jonathan, was born to this marriage. Diane is employed at Charles Machine Works in Perry and Eric is employed at Oklahoma General Electric Plant at Red Rock. They live on an acreage about 6 miles from the Thiele homestead.

James and Peggy had four children: Teri Gail born May 5, 1957, Douglas

Otto Thiele's threshing machine, and a bundle wagon with a cousin, Eleanor Meyer and her friend, Gertie Thiele (no relation), shown pitching bundles with our neighbor, Joe Vaverka.

Lee born February 20, 1960, Gregory Otto born May 21, 1965, and Gayla Beth was born June 30, 1967. They reside on a farm, located five miles east of Perry, which they purchased 2 years after their marriage. James farms and works in the Research and Development Department at Charles Machine Works, where he has been employed for nearly 30 years. Teri married Stephen Thomas Houska, April 26, 1980. They have three sons, Ryan Douglas, Matthew Thomas, and Brady James. Teri is a substitute rural mail carrier and Steve is employed by Charles Machine Works, on the farm working with Mary Malzahn's cattle operation. Douglas married Paula June Longan, January 3, 1981. Doug is currently a Game Ranger at Mangum, Oklahoma in Greer county and Paula is attending college. Greg is a college student in Automobile Restoration in McPherson, Kansas and Gayla graduated from high school in 1985, and plans to enroll in Northeastern College at Miami, Oklahoma.

Charles S. Thomason
Helen Marie Lewellen

Charles S. (Charlie) Thomason was born May 29, 1872, at Bethany, Illinois. Mr. Thomason spent his early boyhood in Moultrie County, Illinois around Sullivan, where he attended school with his seven brothers and two sisters. His mother died when he was in his early teens. When about 18, Charles moved with his father, a few of his brothers and two sisters to Emporia, Kansas, where he attended Kansas State Normal School.

He came to Oklahoma and his brother, Robert, during the opening of the Sac and Fox country but was not old enough to make the run, until the opening of the Cherokee Strip. Mr. Thomason made the run and filed upon a claim 8 miles north of Perry and 1 mile east.

He was a pioneer teacher in several districts in Noble County for 6 years and taught the first school ever held in his home district of Sunny Slope. It was held in an old dwelling house — almost a shack.

On November 24, 1898, he was married to Emma Smith of Perry, to this union were born two children, Nina Ellen and Carl D.

In 1909, he moved with his family from the farm to Perry in order to have better school opportunities for his children. He accepted the position of Deputy County Clerk at this time. He served in the County Court House in several capacities for a number of years. He was County Clerk in 1930-31.

He served as a Rural Mail Carrier when the first motor routes were in-

Charles S. Thomason famly 1986. L-R: Charles, Nina Ellen, Emma S. and Carl David in front.

stalled in Noble County. After serving in his various public capacities for many years, Mr. Thomason was an employee of the Farmers and Merchants Bank of Perry until the "Bank Holiday" forced the bank to close it's door.

He was a Past Master of the Masonic Lodge; a Past Emminent Commander of The Knights Templar and also a memberof the original Advisary Council when the charter was secured for the Perry Chapter of the Order of DeMolay.

Mr. Thomason was converted and baptized in the Christian Church when very young and was an active member in all departments of the Church until ill health forced him to be semi-invalid and he and his wife retired to their farm home.

Mr. Thomason died July 15, 1939, at his farm 8 miles north and 1 mile east of Perry at the age of 67 years. This was the very same farm he claimed in the Cherokee Strip Land Run.

He was survived by his wife, Emma Smith Thomason, one son Carl D. (Buzz), one daughter Nina Neal, and one granddaughter, Helen Marie Neal; all lived in Perry at the time of his death.

S. Emma Thomason
By Helen Marie Lewellen

Sarah Emily Smith was born in Chanute, Kansas, December 5, 1875. Her parents, Mr. and Mrs. David Richard (Dick) Smith, her sister, Lottie, and she moved to Stillwater in 1892, and it was there that she attended A. & M. College as it was called in those days. She made a lot of friends in college. There were only six boys and two girls in the graduating class of 1896. But due to the severe illness of her mother, she had to drop out of college to take care of her. Therefore, she didn't become one of the first graduating students of A. & M. College.

When the opening of the Cherokee Strip Land Run happened on September 16, 1893, her father made the run on horseback into the new country, hoping to stake a claim. "Emma", as she changed her name in college, her sister, Lottie, and mother followed behind with their wagon holding their belongings. They were prepared to move there and live on that claim.

As Emma's father, Dick Smith, was staking his claim 5 miles north of Perry, along the Black Bear Creek, he came upon a "Sooner" with gun in hand who informed Emma's father that the land belonged to him. Much to the disappointment of the family, there was nothing to do but move back to Stillwater.

Emma Smith Thomason - 1937.

Several years later the family moved to Perry and bought property on "F" street, and Emma met Charles (Charlie) S. Thomason. Charlie was fortunate to get a farm in the Cherokee Strip Land Run 8 miles north and 1 mile east of Perry, Oklahoma Territory. After a period of courting Emma and "Charl" (as she called him) were married on Thanksgiving Day, November 24, 1898.

They farmed the land and Charlie taught school on the side. There were two children born to them on the farm, Nina Ellen in 1900, and Carlton David in 1904. In 1909, the family moved to town and bought a home at 611 N. 7th Street. Emma joined several of the Ladies Societies and was Recorder of the Royal Neighbors of America for almost fifty years.

She was a member of the First Christian Church for over sixty-five years, where she was active in all the departments of the church.

Family of Emma Smith - 1895. (In back) Lottie Smith, D. R. Smith, Kizziah Jane Smith. (In front) Emma Smith.

Emma outlived all her immediate family. She passed away July 22, 1975, at the age of 99 years and 6 months. She passed along a great heritage to her only granddaughter, Helen Marie Neal Lewellen (Mrs. Jack D.) of Perry, three great-grandchildren, Sandra Lewellen Davison (Mrs. Sam S.) of Stillwater, Colin D. Lewellen and Kelly Neal Lewellen of Perry, and six great-great-grandchildren, Sindy, Suzanne and Samuel Davison of Stillwater; Carey, Tiffany, and Jason Lewellen of Perry.

Addie May Thompson-Burns
By Addie May Burns

I, Addie May Thompson, was born January 29, 1917, at Perry, Oklahoma, the daughter of John and Lillian Thompson. I attended high school at Blaine school where I took cooking and sewing. I was good in spelling and arithmetic. I also played basketball. I never liked to miss a day or to be tardy. In those days the teacher or principal was allowed to whip the children if they got out of line, so I tried to avoid anything at home or school that might cause me to get a whipping. I had a certain time to go to bed and, as I got older, a time I had to be in at night. I started to go to dances in and around Perry. My brother, James, and I won dancing contests.

On Saturday, the farmers would come to town and do their weekly shopping. I would meet my girl friends in the courthouse park. My father and brother took care of the park and kept it beautiful with flowers, trees and green grass. There was a fish pond full of goldfish. My father would pick a bouquet of flowers and I would take them over to the theater, then I could go in free.

Sometimes I walked 6 or 7 miles to Sunday School and even walked back sometimes, which was fun to do.

I went to Guthrie and lived with my sister, Rena, for two years. I worked at the Beatty Drug and Lunch store as an assistant in the lunch department for a year. I left there and went to Enid, Oklahoma, where I worked as a housekeeper, until I married Bennie Nathaniel Burns in 1939 in Enid. Bennie was born September 2, 1910. Soon after our marriage Bennie entered military service. I moved to Vancouver, Washington, with my two children in 1945 to join my recently discharged husband.

I was co-founder of the Oklahoma Club for the Portland-Vancouver area. I encouraged my daughter and son to deliver the "Black Dispatch," an Oklahoma based black newspaper. I was employed by Sears, Roebuck and Co. and then started my own janitorial service. I have been involved in many community activities either as sponsor or volunteer. I am a former member of the

Addie May Thompson Burns.

P.T.A. with my two sisters, Rena, and Mary Ann. I live in a beautiful home overlooking the Columbia Rier and Portland, Oregon, with my husband, a recently retired *Washington State employee.

I am a member of the Methodist church, the VFW, and St. Joseph Hospital Women's Auxiliary. I love to fish, play bingo, do ceramics and keeping my yard pretty with lots of flowers. I am also a dog racing enthusiast.

I have four children, Delores J. Hayes, Benford T. Burns, Gerald E. Burns and Eloise J. Thompson. I have 13 grandchildren and 2 great-grandchildren.

In 1977, I hosted the Thompson family reunion attended by 200 relatives.

Aurelia Thompson-Hamilton
By Aurelia Hamilton

I, Aurelia Loretha Hamilton was born January 8, 1904, in Beaumont, Texas. I am the 4th child of John Arthur and Lillian Daisy Thompson. When I was a small girl, our family moved 12 miles east of Perry, where I attended Noble county grade school in District #74 (Oak Grove #2). We were transported to school by covered wagon approximately 12 miles southeast of Perry. I was the youngest child attending the school, at the age of 5 years old.

When I was 7 years old, our family moved to a log cabin, then I attended school in a room of one of the family's homes near by. During that time, we only had 6 months of school each year.

When I was a teenager, our family moved closer to Perry and I attended Blaine Elementary school where I completed the 8th grade. From there, I went to Booker T. Washington Consolidated High school in Luther, Oklahoma and graduated there. After high school, I attended Langston University in Langston, Oklahoma. There I majored in Elementary Education and Home Economics. I received a BS degree from there. Post Graduate

Aurelia Thompson Hamilton in front of the Blaine school in Perry.

work was done at Colorado State College in Greeley, Colorado.

In 1924, I began teaching in Noble county in a one room school, the Bar L in the Bressie Flats, which was a part of the 101 Ranch. I taught in school district #74, (Oak Grove #2), where I attended as a child. I also taught in school district #46 (Star). These schools all had grades through 8. In 1938, I started teaching in the Blaine High school in Perry.

During my teaching career, I was active in 4-H clubs, and all other school activities, I never taught outside the county I was reared in (Noble County).

In 1927, I married Benjamin Hamilton, who was also a graduate from Langston University. We had no children. In 1945, I retired from teaching and moved to Chicago, Illinois. There I went into business as Aurelia's Kitchen. Aurelia's Kitchen was a variety grocery store and a Tastee Freeze. I took a course in Small Business Management, then my brother, Ed and I opened up Ed's Bar-b-Q next door to Aurelia's Kitchen. We stayed in business until 1976 at which time I moved to Wichita, Kansas.

After settling in Wichita, I joined the "Foster Grandparents" program and I worked 3 years with Head Start at Little School. I worked 2 years with Youth Development tutoring students. I presently work for the Kansas Elk Training Center for the Handicapped. I am a member of the Baptist church where I taught Sunday School and sang in the choir.

Editor's note: Mrs. Hamilton died March 1, 1985 at the home of her sister, Bertha Roseborough, in Perry. She was buried in the Grace Hill cemetery.

Bertha Thompson-Roseborough
By Bertha Roseborough

I, Bertha Thompson Roseborough, was born April 23, 1921 at 911 South Boundary street in Perry, Oklahoma, the 13th child of John Arthur Thompson and Lillian Daisy Thompson. I started to school at the Blaine school in Perry, where I played the triangle in the Rhythm Band. I began to take private music lessons for twenty five cents a lesson. The lesson lasted one hour. For the next eighteen years, I continued to take lessons, meanwhile playing the piano for Sunday school, and the BYPW in the evening.

While in grade school, I won the leading role of Cinderella, later in our senior class play, "Close Lip", I was the lead, Mrs. Radcliff. I played the piano in recitals given at the high school and assisted in high school music class, playing the piano for the teacher as a helper.

I was Secretary of the Senior Class, sang in the Glee Club. The Glee Club sang at Oklahoma City and Tulsa for the Teacher Association meetings. I graduated from Blaine high school in 1941.

I married Carl Sango Roseborough on June 1, 1942. He was born May 16, 1918 at Wahola, Oklahoma. He belong to the St. Monical Catholic church in Tulsa, where he was an altar boy. He came to Perry in 1939, with W. G. Parker to play ball (basketball, football, and baseball). He was a graduate of Blaine High school. He then became a member of the AME church, a mason, and a member of the Heralds of Jericho. He served as a scout master and for a number of years sponsored an Easter egg hunt in Perry. He was assistant basketball coach to W. G. Parker and managed both boys and girls softball teams.

Bertha and her dog Chamey in 1924.

He was employed as a cook and at the Borden Milk plant before becoming the first black employee of division four of the state highway department. He retired October 1, 1982. Carl and I took a Food Production and Conservation Class at the Blaine High school in 1943 which my sister, Aurelia Hamilton, taught.

Meanwhile, I taught private piano lessons in the home. Later, I became a member of the Eastern Star and held all positions. In 1954, I became owner and operator of a night club, the Sing-a-Pore Play House at 1003 South Boundary. I played center field on a Perry softball team, The Drifter.

In 1945, I joined the Mount Olive AME Methodist church. In 1962, I worked at the Cherokee Strip for 10 years as a head cook and overseer of the kitchen, serving the first buffet dinner to the stock holders.

Each year for several years, the Perry Garden Clubs held a Christmas lighting contest and I, won prizes each year, two years, back to back, winning the Grand Prize.

I began taking organ lessons in 1973 from Doris Rudolph. On December 4, 1983, as a student of Dr. Joann Curmutt, I was a participant in the yule recital at the First United Methodist Church in Stillwater. I played an organ solo. For the Fall term, beginning August 23, 1984, I enrolled at the Keyboard Art Studio at 702 North Driden Circle, Stillwater. In September, I became a member of the Cimarron Chapter of the American Guild of Organists.

Carl died August 13, 1982 and is buried in Grace Hill cemetery at Perry. I still live in the house my parents bought when they came to Perry.

John A. Thompson
By Bertha Roseborough

John Arthur Thompson was born in Little Rock, Arkansas, March 16, 1874. He changed his name from Thomas to Thompson since there was difficulty with the mail service. After living in Atlantia, Texas for several years, he married Lillian Daisy Davis in Atlantia, Texas. They lived in Beaumont, Texas, where Hattie, Rena, Eria, and Aurelia Loretha were born. Eria died July 20, 1903 at the age of four months.

They came to Oklahoma in 1910 and settled 12 miles east of Perry. The children attended Noble county grade school in district #74 (Oak Grove #2). The children were transported to the school by a covered wagon. Alma Edith and Homer were born here.

In 1912, they moved to a farm near Hayward in Garfield county, Oklahoma. They lived in a log cabin on the claim where John farmed. The children

John A. Thompson with one of his floral wreaths.

attended a one room school near by. John brought horses and cattle to Perry for sales while living here. Mary Ann, Peotra, James Monroe, and Dolly Mae were born here.

The family then moved to a farm ½ mile east of Grace Hill cemetery. While here, the first World War started, John was denied from serving in the army because there were too many in the family. He was called on to break horses for the Army. He herded them from Mulhall to the farm to be broken.

After the war, the family moved to Perry and bought four lots at 911 South Boundary Street, which are still in the family. When he came to Perry, he worked in the courthouse as a landscaper as well as farming in Noble county. He also did landscape work for other people in Perry. His yard was noted for flowers and its fish pond. He made wreaths for funerals. Addie Mae, Edward, and Bertha, were born here.

Lillian Thompson.

The children attended the Blaine school in Perry.

In 1922, the family made a float that won first place in the Cherokee Strip celebration parade from flowers in the yard.

John also enjoyed hunting and

John A. Thompson family in 1927. Seated on ground (L to R): Bertha, Edward. Seated on chairs (L to R): Addie Mae, Peotra, Lillian, John, Hattie, and Dollie Mae. Standing (L to R): Homer, Mary Ann, Rena, Aurelia, Alma, and James.

fishing. He kept squirrel, rabbit and opposum on the table, which the family enjoyed. Lillian was a great cook and taught this to all of her children. John died in 1932. Lillian died in 1962. They are buried in Grace Hill cemetery.

The 50th reunion of the descendants of the late John and Lillian Thompson, was held August 21, 1977, at the home of Mr. and Mrs. Bennie Burns, Vancouver, Washington. Over 200 attended the event.

James M. Thompson
By James Monroe Thompson

I, James Monroe Thompson, was born in Noble county, 12 miles southeast of Perry, Oklahoma, on March 23, 1913 in a log cabin. There were 13 children (9 girls and 4 boys). I was the 9th child and the 3rd son of John Arthur Thompson and Lillian Daisy Davis Thompson.

From the log cabin, the family moved to a farm near Perry, Oklahoma, ½ mile east of Grace Hill cemetery. Shortly after World War I, our family moved to Perry, Oklahoma and I enrolled in Blaine High school. While in school, I played the trumpet in the band. I also played basketball and was a scout leader and Scoutmaster.

At the age of 14, I was in a serious auto accident. Doctors announced it was a fatal accident and said I would not make it. My dad would not accept that, so he sent me to Guthrie, Oklahoma, where I layed up for 3 days. So they sent a hearse to pick up my body. The nurse was messing around, went to the refrigerator, got a cold mirror and put it over my face. She saw vapor on the mirror and told the doctors I was alive!

In coming up, I helped my dad with the keep of the courthouse yards. We did this until his death in 1932. After that, I was a dishwasher and cook for Gay D. Marcy under the supervision of my brother, the Chief Cook, Homer Thompson, for two years. Then I worked for Gay D. Marcy's Furniture as a delivery boy and serviceman for 12 years.

On June 4, 1938, I married Virgil Crowl. Virgil and I had 4 children: James Monroe Thompson Jr. - born December 2, 1938; Thelma Arlene Thompson born in 1939 and died at 6 months old with pneumonia; Patricia Ann - born August 13, 1940; and Sandra Mamie - born January 26, 1943.

In 1942, after Pearl Harbor, I came to Wichita, Kansas and went to work for Basham's Appliance Service as a Service Technician. There, I worked for 23 years. After which, in 1970, I went into business for myself as Thompson's Repair Shop.

In 1943, after getting established in Wichita, I bought a home in Wichita and moved my family. Shortly after the move, Virgil and I divorced. I was left with the 3 children to rear.

In 1947, I met Armine J. Gadlin. We were married March 13, 1948. Armine then became the sweetest mother and wife one could ask for. She helped in raising and educating my three children.

On March 5, 1952, Armine and I had a son, Winifred A. Thompson. We now have 10 grandchildren and 6 great-grandchildren. In 1967, we bought our present home, in Wichita, Kansas, where we are both active in the Fred Douglas Masonic Lodge No. 99.

Edward L. Thompson
By Bertha Roseborough

Edward L. Thompson was born June 11, 1919 in Perry, Oklahoma, the youngest son of four brothers to John Arthur and Lillian Thompson. Edward attended Blaine High school in Perry. He played the drum in the school band, was a boy scout and later became a scout master.

His first job, at the age of 12, was dishwashing for the Marcy family at their place of business, The Gem Cafe. Later, he became a cook, taught by his older brother, Homer.

James Monroe Thompson about 1927.

Edward Thompson in his naval uniform.

In 1938, Edward married Arlene Breckenridge, the daughter of Mr. and Mrs. Joe Breckenridge of Hennessey, Oklahoma. While working for the Cass Construction Company, that was building the airport north of Perry, the couple had their first child, a son, Edward Joseph, born Pearl Harbor Day, December 7, 1941.

In 1942, Ed and his family moved to Los Angeles, California, where he then went to welding school, while working at the Cal Shipyards. In 1945, he joined the US Navy and was a Seaman First Class. After leaving the Navy, the family then moved in 1948 to Chicago, Illinois, where Edward worked for several companies, the Pullman Car Company, General Motors and International Harvester.

In April 1949, the couple had their second child, a girl, Theresa Anne. In 1950, he started working for the Crown Welding Company, where he soon became the head welder and later, promoted to Foreman.

In 1955, the family then moved to Gary, Indiana, where the couple had their third child, another baby girl, Kathe Marie, born January 1957.

In 1965, the family then moved back to Chicago where they have been residing ever since. Edward has since retired from Crown Welding after 34 years of service. His wife is still working for the Board of Education in Chicago. Ed relaxes now by doing what he likes best, cooking and preparing his famous Bar-B-Que sauce.

The Thompson children are: Edward Thompson, sometimes called Joey or Ed, who completed his general studies and went on to graduate from college, received his masters and other various awards, scholarships and certificates, which add to the many credits of his educational background. Having married and divorced he is now working and living in Auroa, Colorado, with his son, Michael.

Theresa Thompson Ford completed her general studies and also attended college, but not before marrying and having two sons, Shannon and Daren. Her major in Early Childhood Development, enabled her to become the Director/Parent Coordinator of a Head Start Pre-School Program in Chicago. She later divorced.

Kathe Thompson graduated from High school and went on to receive her nursing degree as a Registered Nurse. She then joined the US Navy where she is continuing her nursing career while seeing the world.

Homer Thompson
By Bertha Roseborough

Homer Thompson was born August 11, 1908 at Berwin, Oklahoma near Ardmore. He came to Noble County in 1916 with his parents Lillian (Davis) and John Arthur Thompson. He was a 7-month premature baby and had to be fed with an eye dropper. He had trouble with breathing and his parents would take him down into the cellar where it was cooler. He grew up to be the strongest and biggest one of the family.

He attended Blaine School in Perry. He helped his father, John Thompson, when he was a custodian at the courthouse park.

He was married February 1, 1934 in Perry to Edna Mayberry and they lived at 719 Ash Street. They had one son, Donald. Homer was a veteran of W.W. II and a member of the New Prospect Baptist Church. He also belonged to the Cherokee Lodge No. 18 of Masons, was a member of the Independent Order of Odd Fellow Lodge No. 3984 and the Chamber of Commerce.

Homer worked in Marcy Cafe for 20 years and became chief cook in 1932. In 1949 he went into the Bar-B-Q business for himself. The first location of Thompson's Golden Bar-B-Q was at 717 Ash Street. The business grew and was moved to the corner of 11th and Perry Avenue (site of Taber's Octoplex

(L to R): Edward and Homer Thompson - 1934.

in 1986). One time the Thompson Bar-B-Q was listed among the top ten restaurants in the United States.

His hobby was buying, rebuilding and racing Go-Karts. Over a period of 16 months, as his son's mechanic, The Homer Thompson Kart Brigade racked up a tally of 373 trophies.

No other traits stood out as well as his care and concern for his fellowman. He never turned a hungry person away or let him leave without some financial aid. His restaurant was a favorite eating place with the white people of Perry as well as the Blacks.

On Christmas eve in 1961 he was giving a party for the employees of his cafe when a car with several men came down the highway. This was the main road in Perry at that time. Seeing the activity around the cafe, they decided to join the fun. When Homer tried to force them to leave, one of the men pulled a gun and shot him. He died on Christmas Day, 1961 and is buried in Grace Hill.

J. A. Thompson - Children
By Bertha Roseborough

This is the rest of the children of Lillian (Davis) and John Arthur Thompson whose story has not already been written.

Rena was born October 16, 1901 in Texas and came with her parents to Noble County. She attended the Blaine school in Perry. She married Charles McDowell April 19, 1924. They had three children: Geradine, James and Charles. She died March 17, 1984 and is buried in Forest Lawn, Hollywood Hills, Los Angeles, California.

Erie was born July 20, 1903. She died at the age of four months and is buried in Grace Hill cemetery at Perry, Oklahoma.

Alma Edith was born March 10, 1906. She married Edward Bragg.

Rena Thompson McDowell.

They had five children: Ivy, Louise (Cook) George, Edward and Ethel. She loved to sing and was a good worker in her church. She died November 17, 1948 and is buried in Enid.

Mary Ann was born August 25, 1909

Mary Ann (Thompson) Billingslea.

Alma Thompson Bragg.

Peotra Thompson.

at Atlanta, Texas and moved to Oklahoma as a young girl. She attended Blaine High School in Perry, Oklahoma. She moved to Ponca City, Oklahoma in 1941. Later, she moved to Portland, Oregon. She was a member of the CME Methodist Church and once was honored for being the youngest grandmother present with the largest number of grandchildren. She married Bill Phillip. She died November 15, 1961. Bill celebrated his 100th birthday in August. He lives with his six children dividing his time between them: Loretha in Berkley, California; Willie (Sonny Boy) in Chicago, Illinois; Alice, Johnny, Marie and Genieva in Portland, Oregon.

Dollie Mae was born February 25, 1915. She attended school at Blaine High in Perry and at Enid High school in Enid. She could play the piano by note but could also play anything she heard. She played for the Holiness church and the organ at the CME Methodist church. She played the leading role in the senior play although she was sick with pneumonia at the time and died a few days later.

Peotra played the E flat alto horn in the Perry High School band. He took manual training and was a member of the Future Farmers of America. He married Rosetta Brown and they had one daughter, Aurelia Helen (Bolton). They lived near Pawnee, Oklahoma on a farm in 1931 where he was engaged in farming. They moved back to Perry in 1933 where he worked for E. E. Nelson. He died March 12, 1939 and is buried in Grace Hill cemetery at Perry, Oklahoma.

Hattie married Woodly Patton and had six children: Woodly Jr., Joann, Mary, Matthew, Joseph and Rachael. She did farm work with her father. She trained horses. She is buried in the Grace Hill cemetery at Perry, Oklahoma. She belonged to the Church of God in Christ.

Estell Thompson
By Alice Ruge

Estell was a pioneer child of pioneer parents. Her father, Curtis, was the first child of Byrnes Harlan and America Harlan, the parents of eight children. After America passed away, Byrnes remarried and had nine more children. He lived in Washington, D.C. where he died in early 1900s. A veteran of the Mexican War, he had lost a leg near Corpus Christi, Texas. He was buried in the National Cemetery, Washington, D.C.

Estell's father, Curtis Harlan, and her mother, Martha Eliza Harner Harlan, were married in Clark County, Illinois, May 16, 1867. Both Curtis and Martha were born in 1846. Martha lost her parents quite young and was reared by a family named Mundy. There were other children in her family.

The first two children born to Curtis and Martha died in infancy. Estell was the third child, born, March 20, 1870, in Bates County, Missouri. They had twelve children, four sons and eight daughters. Three daughters lived to marry. Two sons lived past twenty but did not marry. They had eleven grandchildren.

When Estell was eight years of age, her parents moved by covered wagon to Boliver, Denton County, Texas. Her father was advised not to go further West due to Indians. They remained there for several years, but were back in Missouri in 1884. By 1887, they were living ten miles west of Savannah, Indian Territory. Estell was living in Savannah with a lady, a milliner, and going to school. Both Curtis and Martha had good educations and saw that their children also had the best education available.

Stories Estell told her children of their travels by covered wagon included their camping at night where other travellers were also camping for protection from the Indians. The only incident with Indians was the time when they were trying to steal the horses; however, they were unsuccessful.

She related another incident which occurred while the family was crossing a deep stream. A little brother was sitting on a trunk in the back of the wagon. The trunk floated out and when they reached the other shore, the little boy and trunk were missing. They soon discovered he had held onto the back of the wagon and was safe.

The year, 1888, finds the Harlan family living near Wagoner, Indian Territory, where the Harlan and Thompson families met. John Thompson, a son, and Estell were married October 24, 1889. (see family of John Newton Thompson).

Shortly after, the Harlan family moved again and bought a farm three miles west of Shawnee, Indian Territory, where they built a two story home of oak, which is today lived in and in good repair. It has been visited recently

Hattie Thompson Patton.

Home of Martha and Curtis Harlan, three miles west of Shawnee, Oklahoma. It is occupied today.

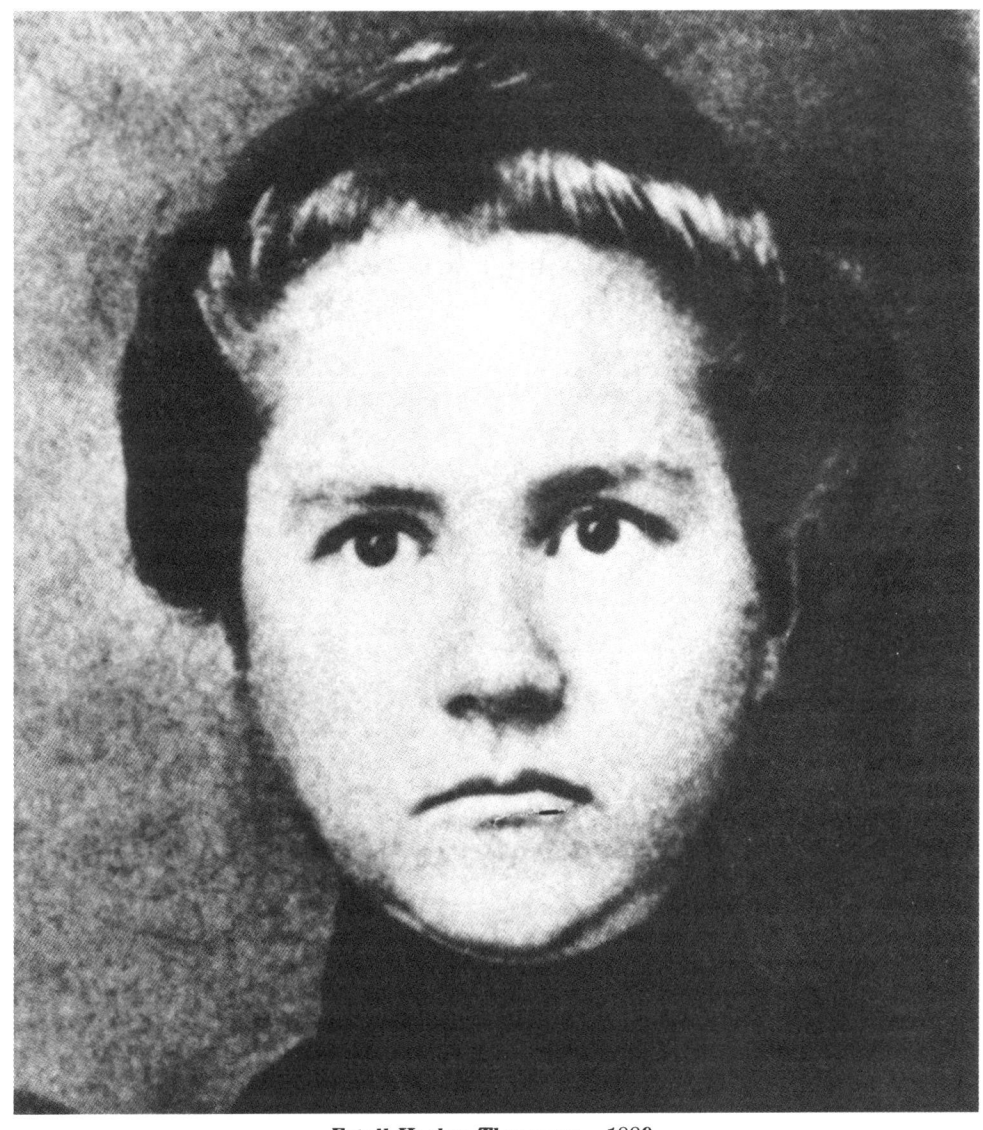

Estell Harlan Thompson - 1889.

(1984) by some of Estell's children, who remember having spent happy days with Grandma and Grandpa.

While living on this farm one daughter married, but the Harlan family lost five other children who are buried in the old Shawnee Town Cemetery in Tecumseh. Curtis was buried there in the family lot in 1918, Martha in 1923.

John and Estell moved from Wagoner to Stillwater, Oklahoma, where their first son, Allen Coe, was born. It was there that John decided to run in the Cherokee Strip in 1893.

Estell loved the farm and was a good homemaker who worked hard especially at harvest time. She made the clothing for her children and was never idle. When it came time to sell and move to Oklahoma City, she did not want to leave but, a good wife, she went along with John's wishes as she always did throughout their life together.

An industrious person, she could do all kinds of handwork. As a very young girl, she carded wool, spun the yarn and knit herself a pair of stockings. She was also very artistic. During the years, especially after John's death, while living with her children, she made a hobby of piecing quilts. Each child and grandchild received a quilt from her.

The last nine years of her life she lived with her daughter, Alice, in Bandera, Texas. In 1982, Alice donated a "Crazy Quilt" Estell had made while living on the farm near Morrison, to the museum in Perry, Noble County, Oklahoma. It was worn and made of many fabrics, but did show the many embroidery stitches she had done.

Until the end of her life, Estell was interested in current events. For example: Would man finally get on the moon? She was mentally alert, had good eye sight and, besides her handwork, did quite a bit of reading. She was a good Christian and strong in her faith. She was much loved by her children and grandchildren, in fact, all who knew her. She was the last survivor of the Curtis Harlan family, passing on April 15, 1958.

John N. Thompson
By Zethyl LeStourgeon

John Newton Thompson was born at Washington, Indiana, on January 4, 1856, the eldest of four brothers and three sisters. After he was grown, his father purchased a houseboat and, with his wife and children, travelled down the Mississippi and Arkansas Rivers. After spending some time at Fort Smith, Arkansas, they settled in the Indian Territory, near Wagoner, sometime in the 1890s.

Estell Harlan was born in Jamestown, Bates County Missouri, on March 20, 1870. Sometime between July 4, 1887, and March 6, 1889, her parents, along with several children, moved to Wagoner, Indian Territory, where the Thompson and Harlan families met. The families were both active in the Methodist Church, John's father farming and preaching as a missionary to the Indians, Estell's father farming.

John and Estell were married October 24, 1889, in the Cooweescoowee District, Cherokee Nation, Indian Territory. On a honeymoon trip to Fort Smith, John bought his bride a side saddle.

Sometime later they moved to Stillwater, Payne County, Indian Territory. There a son, Allen Coe, was born February 15, 1892.

John, by then familiar with the area, had selected a piece of bottom land for which he would make the run when the "Cherokee Strip" was opened in 1893. He had acquired a horse of race breeding which he put through a training regimen for a time prior to the run. His preparation bore fruit. On the day of the run, he made it to the location from the starting line in 38 minutes, successfully staking his claim on the southeast ¼; section 11; Township 21 north; Range 2 east of Indian Meridian. Estell followed in a buckboard with her baby, along with a friend, Mrs. J.D.E. Owen, who was following her husband in a covered wagon, along with an infant. Estell was confident she would find John, recognizing him as far as the eye could see because he wore a shirt she had made for him especially for the occasion. The Thompson and Owen families spent their first night, September 16, 1893, on adjoining claims after the land had been burned off to discourage "Sooners" presence. The families were to remain friends and correspond through the years after the

New home in Oklahoma City circa 1907.

Thompson family taken about 1913. Front row: (l to r) John Newton, Erma Belle, Estell (holding Winnie Zethyl), Inez Onieta. Back row (l to r): Alice Elizabeth, Martha Estell, Allen Coe, C. Harlan.

Thompsons moved on to Texas. Their descendants are in contact even to this day, nearly a century later.

On his claim about 3 miles north of Morrison, near Black Bear Creek, John built a small house, planted an orchard, and built a broom factory. His principal crop was broom corn which, after harvesting, he made into brooms, thus being remembered in the area as "Broomcorn" Thompson. The raising of broom corn and broom manufacturing was to continue as one of his economic mainstays throughout John's life.

Four more children, one son and three daughters, were born to John and Estell while living on their claim. All were attended at birth by Dr. Whittenburg. They were: Martha Estell-August 27, 1885; C. Harlan-August 11, 1898; Alice Elizabeth-March 25, 1902; and Inez Oneita-June 12, 1904. All were baptized in the Methodist Episcopal Church South were John was a deacon at the church in Morrison.

In 1906, they sold the farm and moved to Oklahoma City where John bought 25 acres just outside the city. He built a large brick home, barn, and a number of chicken houses of a type very modern for that time, where he continued raising fancy and show poultry, a pursuit he had begun on the farm. Another daughter was born while the family lived in Oklahoma City; Emma Belle-April 7, 1907.

In 1908, John sold the Oklahoma City property and bought land in Texas. In early 1909, the family moved to Corpus Christi, Texas, where John continued in the broom business. In 1911, John again moved his family, this time not so far, to Beeville, Texas, where he was associated with the Fortuna Broom Company. It was there that John and Estell had their last child, a girl; Winnie Zethyl, born December 6, 1912.

They both lived out their lives in Texas, together until John's sudden death in a highway accident December 8, 1937, at age 82. Estell lived on with her children until a natural death April 15, 1958, at age 88. They were both laid to rest in Pearsall, Texas, where they have since been joined by the three eldest of their children.

First home on the Thompson claim (l to r): Allen Coe, C. Harlan, Estell Harlan Thompson, Martha Estell, John Newton Thompson, girl on the gate post is Ellen Turner Speer.

Poultry houses and prize chickens located in and near the fruit orchard, on homestead farm, Morrison, Oklahoma, 1905.

They are survived by four daughters, 15 grandchildren, and numerous great-grandchildren.

Their time spent as young pioneer settlers on the American Frontier which was to become Noble County, State of Oklahoma, undoubtedly strengthened them for long and productive lives and is held as a matter of considerable pride by their descendents.

Claude O. Travis
By Claude O. Travis

Claude O. and Mildred R. Travis came to Noble County in October, 1936, renting a farm southeast of Red Rock from Richard Schultz. Mildred was teaching the rural school in Claude's home district when they were married. In the spring of 1936, they moved to a farm in Kay County. The 1930s were noted for being "hard" years. Three crops put out that spring failed. Hail ruined one crop, excessive rain ruined another, and exceedingly dry weather ruined the third. So Claude rented the Red Rock place which was mostly grass and stocked it with cattle.

Claude's parents were James E. and Bertha Travis. They lived on a farm south of Hunter in Garfield County. A soldier had homesteaded on the quarter section but didn't want to prove up on it. He traded it to Claude's father, who wasn't old enough to file on a claim. Travis traded a team of ponies, harnesses and a light wagon and received the deed signed by Theodore Roosevelt. Claude grew up on that place, enjoying hunting, fishing, and doing the farm chores and work.

Mildred's parents were Aminadab and Laura Ann Conklin. They were farming in Osage County raising corn and hogs and in Garfield County, raising wheat and cattle. In the spring at the farm in Osage County near Foracre, they would plant and tend the corn crop. When the corn was 'laid by' they would move, in covered wagons, to the farm in Garfield County, near Garber to get ready to harvest the wheat. After the harvest, plowing and seeding the wheat, the family returned to Osage County to harvest the corn. Mildred was born in Osage County, the third child in the family. That was too much moving for a family with three small children, so the Osage farm was closed down, and the folks stayed on the Garber farm. Mildred grew up there.

Mildred's father had made "the run" on a mule to get a homestead, but didn't get one. Later he traded a team and a spring wagon for a claim, much as Claude's father had done.

While Claude and Mildred lived on the Red Rock farm, three children were born: Benjamin Claude, David

Orion, and Laura Ann.

When Claude's father passed away in 1943, Claude and his family returned to his mother's farm to care for things. The next year they moved to a ranch east of Winfield, Kansas. There, the family participated in church, school, 4-H and other social activities of the Tisdale community. But when Ben was ready for high school, the three children drove the eleven and a half miles into Winfield and attended the Winfield schools. There was no rural bus service.

During the war years, Claude drove fifty some miles to Wichita where he helped build Boeing B-47 bomber planes. The family built a Grade-A dairy barn and sold milk to the Preston Dairy in Winfield. Mildred taught a rural school north of Winfield at Rock.

The next move was to Coal County, Oklahoma, north of Coalgate. The children attended a consolidated school seven miles east of the farm, and Mildred taught school there. As the children graduated from high school they went to colleges of their choice. Ben, and later Laura Ann graduated from Southeastern college at Ada, both receiving Bachelors degrees in Education. David chose Murray Agricultural College at Tishimingo. He graduated from this junior college valedictorian of his class. Mildred was then teaching in Boise City, Cimmaron County, and both David and Laura Ann went to the Agricultural College at Goodwell. The next year David went to Kansas State College at Manhattan, and Laura returned to Ada. David continued in school, and earned bachelors degree, Masters degree and Doctors degree.

After graduation from college in 1960, Ben taught school in Crown Point, New Mexico. After one year there, he married Brenda Nuner, whom he had known at Ada. They lived in Crown Point and three children were born: Annette, Steven, and Barbara. Later, they moved to Albuquerque and Ben taught there until 1967 when they moved to Del City, Oklahoma. Ben has taught every year since graduation, earning his Masters degree during summers.

David worked a year in western Kansas at an agricultural experiment station in Garden City. There he met and married Glenda Cleveland in 1966. They went to Kirksville, Missouri where he taught in the University there and she taught math in a high school. In 1976, their son, Glenn was born.

After Laura graduated from Ada, she accepted a school in Amarillo, Texas, where she taught two years. Then she resigned and went to Alburquerque where Ben lived and taught several years. There she met and married Melvyn Joe Weiss who was working in the federal forest service. After some years there, he was transferred first to Louisiana, then Georgia, and finally to New Hamphire where they now live.

David and Glenda, always active in church, applied for foreign mission service and were accepted and sent to Brazil for one year in June 1973. Then they were sent to Bangalore, India for a four year term, leaving the States in 1980. In September their second son, John David was born. In June of 1984 they returned for a year furlough. While back, they lived in Enid and Shawnee. David taught a course in missions at O.B.U. the spring semester.

On June 16, 1985, the three Travis children held a reception in honor of their parents Golden Wedding anniversary. It was held early in order that David and his family could be present. They were to leave for India for another four years the 21st of June. The detaining of a plane load of people in Beirut by Lebonese terrorists made everyone very anxious until word was received that the family had arrived safely in Bangalore. Soon after arriving, the family attended the Bangalore Statewide Annual Mission Meeting. At this meeting, David was chosen to serve as Mission administrator for the area. David teaches agriculture at the University there and is instrumental in sponsoring improved agricultural precepts to the men in the rural areas, and mother-child health and sanitation to the women.

Though their children are scattered from Noble County to half way around the world, all are doing what they feel the Lord wishes them to do, and Claude and Mildred are quite content. They are retired and are living in Red Rock.

Marquis D. Tucker
By Mrs. Donald H. Hooper

At the time of the Opening of the Cherokee Strip, my grandparents, Marquis D. and Jane J. Tucker, along with their two sons, Edwin A. and Victor D., made the run in one wagon, and another son of my grandmother, Austin C. and his wife, Louise Nicewander, made the Run in another wagon. My grandfather was a carriage maker, and Uncle Austin later became sheriff, and served two terms until he had to hang a man in the court house square, after which, he would not run for that office again.

My grandparents settled at the corner of Tenth and Division streets, where they lived for many years. My Dad and Uncle Vic joined the Army at the time of the Spanish-American War. It was over so quickly that my Dad was soon discharged, but Uncle Vic was sent to the Philippines, where he served for a couple of years. My Dad moved to Memphis, Tennessee, where he met my mother, Mrs. Ida May Zellers-Landsberger, who was a widow with two young sons, Earl G. and Charles G. They were married in 1908, and to them were born Sylvia M., and Bernice J. in Memphis, and later, Louise E. and Edwin M., in Cushing, Oklahoma. We lost our mother in 1920, and later, we moved to Perry, in 1923. My father worked for a while in the oil fields, and later on became a roofing contractor. He also worked for Donaldson and Yahn for a few years. He died in 1958.

After my school years were over, I married Barney Enright, Photographer and owner of the Enright Studio, and to us was born our daughter, Judith Ann in 1940. We lost him in 1941 from a heart attack, when Judy was a year old. I took over the Studio and operated it all through the War. In 1947, I closed the Studio, and went to work for Hal Owen in Oklahoma City. Later on, I met Donald H. Hooper and we were married in 1951. We moved to California, and some years later, moved to Rochester, New York, where he worked for Kodak for a number of years. Then we went to Rhode Island, where he taught in a School of Photography for ten years, and then we came here to Chittenango, to be near Judy.

Judy met Richard L. Beals in one of the Youth Groups at our Presbyterian Church in Rochester and found they were both attending RIT in Rochester. They were married in September after graduation, and have two sons, John S. and Mathew T. John is studying Real Estate, and Mathew is studying Journalism and Law at Brockport, New York.

Bernice married Cecil L. Daniels, and to them were born Stephen T. and Phillip C. Both attended the Perry schools. Phillip joined the Army and later was killed in an auto accident, in 1964, not far from his base in Crete, Nebraska. Steve became a florist and operated a shop in Perry for several years, later moving to Oklahoma City, where he now owns an Interior Decorating Shop. Bernice was a nurse in Perry for many years, and Cecil had charge of the school bus garage, also for many years. Bernice died in 1973, and Cecil preceded her in death, the year before in 1972.

Louise married Harold A. Moore, of Blackwell, in 1939, and they settled in the state of Washington. Harold died in 1963. Louise is now retired and lives in Tumwater, Washington. She worked as accountant in the state capitol offices for quite a few years before her retirement.

Ed went into the Navy in 1939, and served through most of the War, until he was sent back to California in 1944 from Australia, due to having cantracted tuberculosis along with nearly a dozen other of his shipmates. He was hospitalized for some time and finally recovered to a certain extent. He married Frances Huddleston in 1946, and they had one daughter a year later, Sylva Jane. Frances also had a daughter, Susan Anita, by a former marriage. Ed died in 1963, and Frances worked in the library, until a little while ago, when she retired, and moved to Oklahoma City. Sylvia Jane is married and has one daughter, Polly, and Sue lives with her mother.

One final note of interest that I would like to include, is that out in Grace Hill cemetery, in the Soldier's Circle, are buried my grandfather, M.D. Tucker, who served in the Civil War, for the north side, then next to him is my Uncle Vic, who served in the Spanish-American War, then my nephew, Phil, of the Army Air Force and finally, my brother, Ed, who served in World War II.

Walter F. Turner

By Mrs. Elton (Elizabeth) Turner

Walter Forest Turner was born August 7, 1865, at Wellsville, Missouri. His father's name was William, but it is not known when he died as Walter was very young. His mother remarried and was affectionately called Grandma Cottle.

Looking for adventure, at the age of 17, he left Wellsville and eventually came to Oklahoma, as he heard of the opening of the Cherokee Strip in 1893. He set stakes on a piece of land, and one who was not playing fair, tried to beat him to it. He challenged him to a fist fight but he was a coward and got on his horse and rode away, however, he returned later and shot Walter's horse. The land on which he had staking rights was 160 acres located in the northwest ¼ of section 25 Township 21 North, Range 3 East of Indian Meridian. This is in Noble County, three miles north of Glencoe on Highway 108.

During pioneer days he had many experiences, living in a dugout, where he had several times taken a snake out of his bed, one time selling it to a circus at Perry.

Being one who enjoyed trains, he would go to Tampico, Mexico, after crops were in and return in time to harvest the crop. He was a Fireman on the Mexican Central Railway.

Down the road a mile, which is now called Walts Corner, and which was then called Orinsville, there was a General Store run by Walter Cassiday. A young lady, Jennie Dorothy McKinley worked there as a clerk and made hats for ladies and girls. Walter met this lady and courted her. On February 8, 1899, they were married at Perry, Oklahoma. To this union one son, Elton McKinley, was born on August 24, 1901. They continued to live on the farm till 1910, when they moved to Oklahoma City, where Walter worked for the Morris Packing Plant. In 1912, the cable broke on the freight elevator he was operating causing it to fall three floors and he was hurt internally. He died September 30th at the age of 47. Jennie passed away in October of 1952.

Being without a father, Elton felt he should earn his living, so at the age of 17, after attending Chillicothe Business College, taking Business Course and Telegraphy, he started as a Station Helper at Unionville, Missouri, for the CB and Q Railroad, working a short time then transferring to the Rock Island Railroad as Agent Operator in parts of Iowa, his last job being 25 years at Shell Rock, Iowa, thus ending 47 years of service. When 21, he purchased the farm from his mother and it remained very dear to him all through his life, coming to Oklahoma every year to keep the building in repair.

On August 7, 1936, he was united in marriage to Elizabeth Moser, at Unionville, Missouri, by his grandfather, Elijah McKinley. To this union four children were born namely: Juanita Ruth Dippert, Richland, Missouri, who has two children — Janice and Barbara Homan; Arlyce Shroeder of Denver, Iowa, who has three children — Angela, Andrew and Amy; Forest Elton who died November 8, 1951, at the age of 5, and Stephen Mark.

In August 1966, Elton, Elizabeth and Stephen moved to Glencoe to the farm.

Front Row (L to R): Ervin, Krista, Andra, and Matthew. 2nd Row: Andrew Schroeder, Barbara Homan, Amy Schroeder, Angela Schroeder, Janice Dippert. Back Row: Juanita, Jim Dippert, Elizabeth, Janet, Stephen, Arlyce and Al.

Walter F. Turner shortly after Land Run.

Elizabeth (Moser) and Elton Turner.

Jennie and Walter Turner 1899.

On May 30th 1971, Stephen married Janet May Porter of Stillwater, Oklahoma. To this union four children were born namely: Krista, Audra, Erin and Matthew. They are living in the house Elton and Elizabeth built the first year they lived here on the farm. Elizabeth lives in a mobile home on the place too. Stephen farms some of the land and the rest is rented for pasture. He works for Moore Forms Inc. in the Maintenance Department in Stillwater, Oklahoma.

Elton passed away December 15, 1980, at the age of 79. This farm is still dear to the heirs and Stephen hopes to keep it up through the years as the Turner homestead.

William M. Turner
By Neva Turner Artall

William Miller Turner, better known as Bill Turner, was born near Milan, KS, on October 31, 1884. He came to Oklahoma in 1893, at the age of 9 years with his parents, George and Mary Turner and five of his sisters. His father worked some land but mostly he raised cattle.

Bill's schooling was short, only through the 3rd grade. When he was about 20, he went to Lincoln Co. OK, to break new ground and clean the land of stumps and large boulders. He worked oxen, two to eight head. The oxen were better than horses because they were stronger and moved at a slower, more even pace.

In Lincoln Co. he met and married Sara Evelyn (Sadie) King on May 14, 1913. Sadie was born July 9, 1894. They moved back to Noble Co. and lived on several rented farms east of Perry.

Bill bought a quarter section 12 miles east of Perry where he built a two story house on the northeast corner of the farm and called it "Bill's Corner." The family moved there in the spring of 1923. He started a filling station on that corner with three 50 gallon drums. One for gasoline, one for kerosene, and one for motor oil. He used a glass canning jar to measure the motor oil, and one and two gallon cans to measure the gasoline. The customers usually brought their own containers for the kerosene.

There were more covered wagons than cars on the highway which was just plain dirt roads. Sadie served "lemonade" from a pitcher on the kitchen table and charged by the glass or pitcher full. She stocked dry beans, vinegar and sugar in the bulk. She sacked beans and sugar in brown paper bags in 5 and 10 pounds. The customers brought their own jugs for vinegar. Flour came in 25 or 100 pound sacks. People used the flour sacks to make underwear or tea towels. A popular brand "Pride of Perry" was often seen on the clothes line across the seat of some underwear.

Bill built an ice-box 3' x 6' in the corner of the store. It held three 125 pound blocks of ice in the bottom and the top was used for food and cold drinks. He sold ice mostly to neighbors to make ice cream. Very few had an ice box. They would use a wash tub and wrap the ice in newspapers to keep it until they were ready to use it. Twelve cents bought 25 pounds.

Later on, Bill went modern and got a gasoline pump. You had to pump the gasoline by hand up to a clear glass bowl with the gallons marked on the side. He installed an electric system. It was 32 volts and made enough electricity to light the store and living quarters which were above the store, also two large signs each side of the store. Sadie got her first electric iron. Bill built an extra small station about 1924 with gas and oil only, to hold the rights of all the land.

One day, Sadie had gone to Perry and Bill was running both stations. He always went in a run. He was filling a Nitro truck with gasoline at the center station. As he stepped from behind the truck, a car from the west hit him broadside. He jumped, went over the hood and grabbed the running board and was dragged 25 feet and then run over by a back wheel. He had no broken bones but was badly brusied and hide was scraped from his back. Two weeks later, another driver asked Bill if the man was killed that had been hit. Bill told him, "No, I was just too tough for a little old Ford." The Ford had to have its radiator straightened before it could travel.

Bill and Sadie had three children: Neva Theresa, born November 21, 1914, married Carlie Malzahn; Lavina Elizabeth, called Dutch, was born April 30, 1920, and married Harold Helm. Delilah Fay, nicknamed "Shorty" was born September 27, 1923. Delilah married Gilbert Pinkerton.

Bill leased Bill's Corner in 1926 and moved to the Covington-Garber oil field, because of Sadie's bad health. He needed extra money and wanted to be near her at Enid, OK. They moved back to Bill's Corner in 1933. Neva, who was then 19, took over the cream station in the room back of the store. They bought cream and eggs. Eggs were 12 cents a dozen. Bill Turner died July 6, 1960. He is buried in the Pleasant Valley cemetery at Sumner, OK.

Charles Van Arsdell
By Nina Ball

My parents, Charles A. and Nellie L. Van Arsdell, along with their sons, Bruce Lee, 16, and William Joseph, 12, and myself at age 6, moved to Noble County in 1936, from the Lake Carl Blackwell area west of Stillwater, where Charles was born May 13, 1897, to Geanetta and Henry Van Arsdell.

Charles' father, Henry S. Van Arsdell, was born in Sharpsburg (Bath County) Kentucky, and moved with his parents, John and Minerva, to Augusta, Kansas, at the close of the Civil War. Henry and his father made the run of April 22, 1889, into Oklahoma Territory and settled with their families. While felling trees and carving out farm land, they also were leaders in organizing the first church and building a community building. Minerva died January 8, 1900, and John died October 4, 1914, and are buried in the Shelton cemetery in the southeast corner of Noble County.

About 1917, Charles and Nellie Hoggatt, along with friends, Russell Highfill and Edna Coate, went to the Oklahoma State Fair at Oklahoma City. They boarded the train at Perry and

Bill and Sadie Turner in 1913.

then took the streetcar out to the fair. Charlie, as he was called, wore a new pair of shoes, and along toward evening his feet began to hurt. He sat down, took his shoes off to rest his feet but when he tried to put his shoes back on his feet were so swollen it was impossible. He went home carrying his shoes which didn't bother Charlie but Nellie was so embarassed she was glad to get back in the buggy at Perry to go home.

Charlie and Nellie were married in 1918, and their friendship with Russell and Edna Highfill lasted until their deaths. Charlie served in the army in WW I and then farmed his father's homestead until the lake was built and the farm sold.

When Charlie and Nellie moved to Noble County, there was no electricity available at their Black Bear bottom farm located 12 miles east and 2 north of Perry in the Oak Grove School District of the Morrison community. Charlie was one of the first to join the Rural Electric Cooperative and helped subscribe other members to bring electricity to the area. There was a two-story house on the place on Black Bear. Charlie had propane gas piped to the house. Nellie decided to clean the oil cook stove before storing it and somehow the oil she was using caught fire. Nellie went to the telephone and gave the emergency ring. When someone answered she said, "My house is on fire" and hung up. It took some time before the people on the line could locate the fire and call the fire department. By the time the fire department came the 14 miles the house could not be saved but they did save the other buildings. They sprayed water on the propane tank to keep it from exploding. Sometime after the fire the tank was still so hot that they couldn't put their hands on it. When others in the neighborhood installed propane the tanks were placed farther from the buildings. Charlie and Nellie built a new house and later built a larger one a mile north and a mile east on land they bought.

Charlie served on the Board of Directors of the Noble County Soil Conservation District. He also was Vice-President of the National Farm Loan Association, served on the Federal Land Bank Board of Directors and was a member of the Perry Chamber of Commerce, the American Legion, and Morrison Lions Club. He served on the Noble County Free Fair Board for many years, part of the time as president. Charlie and Nellie were both active members of the Morrison Methodist Church where Nellie taught Sunday School and was a leader in the women's group for many years. She was active in the Oak Grove Home Demonstration Club and County Extension work.

(L to R) standing: Charles Van Arsdell, Russel Highfill; seated: Nellie Hoggatt and Edna Coate about 1917 at the fair.

Besides wheat, alfalfa and small crop farming, Charlie was a breeder of registered Herefords. He was the first president of the Northern Oklahoma Hereford Breeders Association, formed in 1944. Charlie's brother, W. E. "Jake" Van Arsdell, lived nearby and was also known for his fine Herefords. Charles died on February 9, 1954, while his cattle were in the show ring of the 19th Annual NOHB show and sale. Nellie, after Charlie's death, served as house mother at one of the dorms at Northern Oklahoma College at Tonkawa and later at OSU. Nellie was born September 14, 1896, at Orlando, Oklahoma Territory, the daughter of Christina (Emmons) and George Ludwig Hoggatt. She died in California in 1973. Charlie and Nellie are buried in the Fairlawn Cemetery, Stillwater, Oklahoma.

Bruce Van Arsdell served in WW II, and became a custom combine harvester based in Perry, and made the run from Texas to Canada each season. He died of a heart attack July, 1967.

Bill Van Arsdell received his doctorate from OSU, served in WW II and became a professor of animal science at the University of Arizona. He was voted professor of the year in 1963, and that summer while on vacation, had a fatal heart attack.

I left Noble County after graduation in 1948, from Perry High School, married Dean Ball (class of   ) and moved to California in 1963. Our family of four are grown and married. I have written books entitled *Through It All*, and *Jo Jo Starbuck*. Since 1965, I have written for many Christian periodicals. I am now editor of *Cattle 'N Saddle*, which covers all the 4-H and FFA events.

F.M. VanBebber Children
By Jack F. VanBebber

Roy Jerome, the eldest child of Francis and Ila Vanbebber, was born February 27, 1897; died January 9, 1972. He married Viola Evelyn Franklin of Buffalo, Oklahoma, November 10, 1934. They were parents of two sons, Charles Marion and Verne Lewis. Roy was a farmer, a veteran of World War I, and a member of the First Christian Church of Orlando.

Bessie Mable was born May 22, 1898. She remained single and contributed much to the success of the family and to the nieces and nephews with her care and advice. She is a member of the First Baptist Church of Perry, the Dorcas Sunday School Class and the Missionary Prayer Group.

Harriet Mildred was born October 19, 1899; died December 7, 1974. She married Horace Tefteller of Tyler, Texas, on September 10, 1924. They had one daughter, June (Tefteller) Wurtz. Harriet was graduated from Perry High in 1921. Later, she was a professional nurse and a devoted member of the First Baptist Church.

Ralph Lapier was born May 28, 1901, and married Helen Faye Gardner, April 15, 1930. They had two daughters, Joan Faye (VanBebber) Bamberger, and Norma Jean (VanBebber) Rupp. Later Ralph married Grace (Hageman) Washabaugh. Ralph's occupations included farming and oil field work, chiefly with the Magnolia Co. He was a former member of the Odd Fellows Lodge. Ralph and Grace are members of the First Baptist Church in the Claude Community of Stevens County, Oklahoma.

Raymond "Ray" was born January 12, 1903, and died May 15, 1951. On August 17, 1930, he married Hazel Mary Winsworth of Tulsa. They had three daughters: Ramona Clementine, a victim of polio, who died in the summer of 1946; Wymoma Ila (VanBebber) Passow and Karen Sue (VanBebber) Bode. Ray was active in Perry Masonic Lodge #78 and a member of Perry First Baptist Church. He was employed for 21 years by Magnolia Oil Co., and also engaged in farming.

Bertha Esther VanBebber was born August 31, 1905, and died June 19, 1963. On November 2, 1936, she married Joseph Stone, who was killed by an explosion nine days after marriage. Later, Bertha married Albin Schallenberg of Guthrie. To that union two sons, Earl Francis and Van Henry, were born. After graduation from Perry High, she majored in home economics, in Oklahoma A & M (now OSU). She was graduated from the Baptist college of Nursing in St. Louis,

Missouri, and worked as a nurse until the illness preceding her death.

Mary L. VanBebber was born April 27, 1908. She remained single and devoted her life to professional service. In 1927, she was graduated from Perry High. In Oklahoma A & M, Mary earned a Bachelor of Science degree in home economics; in Central State College, a Bachelor of Science degree in education; in Maryland University, a Masters Degree in speech and hearing. In the early 1940s she taught speech to the hard of hearing in the old Borden General Hospital in Chickasha. From 1946 until 1974, Mary L. lived in Silver Springs, Maryland and was a speech therapist in Walter Reed Army Medical Center. She is a life member of the Speech and Hearing Association. After retirement, she moved to Axtell, Kansas. She is working there with the Senior Citizens Program.

Glenn Herbert was born December 10, 1910, and died May 8, 1961. After completing study at Whipple School, he attended Perry High. In the late 1930s he married Shirley Winefred Wood of Perry. To this union was born Gene Warren and Doris Christine (VanBebber) Whitchurch. Glenn worked for Oklahoma oil companies, purchased the land shares of the majority of the family members and farmed the home place up until his death. He attended Perry First Christian Church.

Dorothy Jane VanBebber was born January 19, 1914; died February 24, 1972. In November, 1948, she married Earl F. Ritterbusch of Guthrie. She was a Perry High School graduate and completed nurse training in Enid with honors. During World War II, she was a Lieutenant in the Army Nurses Corps in England. Dorothy was employed as a nurse in various places. Her last employment was in Medford, Oregon, where she and her husband were living at the time of her death.

Earl Martin VanBebber was born May 10, 1918. On September 19, 1943, he married Mildred Louise (Simpson) Coleman in California. To this union two sons, Richard Earl and Jack Jeffrey, were born. He attended Perry High, wrestled on the Maroon team, and was graduated in 1938. He continued his studies in OSU. There he wrestled on the Cowboy team, coached by Art Griffith. In Bethlehem, Pennsylvania, in March 1951, wrestling at 155 lb., Earl won the NCAA title. Later in 1941, he moved to California. During World War II, Earl was in the service for Uncle Sam. He and his wife remained in California and for a number of years have lived in Tracy. They are members of Tracy First Baptist Church and Earl is a member of the Elks Lodge. Dealing in real estate and the hardware business have been Earl's chief business occupations.

Francis M. VanBebber
By Jack F. VanBebber

Francis Marion VanBebber, son of George Noah VanBebber and Mary (Jackson) VanBebber, was born January 18, 1863, in Macoupin County, Illinois, near Scottsville. In 1894, one year after the race for land into the Cherokee Strip, F.M. VanBebber left Illinois to seek a place in the new frontier. On arriving, he went to the home of a distant relative, Rev. Morrow, who lived west of Edmond.

John and Jane (Tribby) Jeffrey and their children lived near Rev. Morrow. The Jeffreys had a daughter, Ila, born June 20, 1874, in Greene County, Indiana, near Solisberry. VanBebber fell in love with her, but to his dismay the Jeffreys moved to Cowley County, Kansas.

VanBebber went to Perry, bought out a squatter's rights on a farm, (ne 12) in Warren Valley township, five miles west and one-half mile north of Perry. He built a two-room house on the farm in the area now known as the Whipple community. After making some additional improvements, he hurried to Kansas.

On May 10, 1895, he and Ila Jeffrey married in Atlanta, Kansas, and returned to what is known as the VanBebber homeplace. After the family began to increase, the two-room house was built into a two-story white structure. In a few years, Mr. VanBebber was able to buy more land to the north on the east side of the section line. Black Bear Creek bordered the land on the north.

The VanBebbers were parents of six boys and five girls. Women in the community often took turns acting as midwives at the times child birth were due. On a number of occassions, Mrs. VanBebber picked up her basket containing items needed to aid in a delivery. She would step up into the buggy that had her horse Daisy hitched up for the trip. She then headed to the Huffington's, hoping to be there on time for the delivery. On a number of occasions, Mrs. Huffington returned the favor.

For livelihood the garden provided a variety of vegetables. The wheat and corn, ground in the Perry mill, and stored at home in 50-gallon cans in the smoke house or upstairs, helped to provide bread for the family. The hogs, sheep, turkey, guineas, and chickens, supplemented by wild geese and quail, provided the meat.

The numerous gallons of molasses prepared on the home cane press appeased the desire for sweets. The orchard supplied the fruit. During the summers, hundreds of jars of farm products were canned and stored in the cellar.

All the children attended the Whipple School, and Mr. VanBebber served at one period on the Whipple School Board. He was also active in the Perry Odd Fellows lodge.

When church services were held in the Whipple School, Dad VanBebber hitched the horses to the wagon and Mother Ila saw that the children were ready to go.

The children spent happy days playing in the barn loft and hiding in the hay. Cow chip throwing provided an economical sport. A minimum of time was devoted to play and a maximum for work. The farm years produced many happy memories for the family,

Francis M. VanBebber family around 1927. Front Row (L to R): Glenn Herbert, Earl Martin, Francis Marion, Ila (Jeffery) VanBebber, Mary L., Bessie Mable, Bertha Esther, Harriet (Hattie) Mildred (VanBebber) Tefteller, and Horace Tefteller. Back Row (L to R): Jack Francis, Raymond (Ray), Roy Jerome, and Ralph Lapier.

composed of the parents, six sons, and five daughters. The children were: Roy Jerome, Bessie Mable, Harriet Mildred, Ralph Lapier, Raymond, Bertha Esther, Jack Francis, Mary L., Glenn Herbert, Dorothy Jane, and Earl Martin. Dad (F.M.) VanBebber's desire was to have a dozen children, but Mother Ila halted the stork at eleven. F.M. died June 6, 1930, Ila died September 25, 1966, they are buried in Grace Hill Cemetery.

Jack F. VanBebber
By Jack F. VanBebber

Jack Francis, the seventh child of Francis Marion and Ila (Jeffrey) VanBebber, was born July 27, 1907. He attended Whipple Grade School and Perry High School. In high school, Frank Briscoe, who started the wrestling program in Perry in 1922, was Jack's coach. And it was Coach Briscoe who stirred Jack's desire to be a winning wrestler. Wrestling honors netted Jack one bronze medal, one silver and two gold. For wrestling ability and sportsmanship, he won the F.Z. Beanblossom gold medal.

Jack also played football two years in Perry High and was graduated in 1927, with a desire to go to Oklahoma A & M to study for a Masters Degree. Knowing that Jack was eager to attend college, the Briscoes offered him a room and breakfast for the first semester. Jack accepted the offer. And to help pay his way, he worked at twenty-five cents an hour on three jobs: dish washing in Lynn's Beanery, delivering milk for the college dairy and sweeping in Whitehurst Hall.

In the fall of 1927, Jack made the freshman wrestling team. And in the Olympic tryouts in the summer of 1928, in Grand Rapids, Michigan, he won a bronze medal in the welter-weight class (158 lbs.).

On the Oklahoma A & M Cowboy team from 1929-31, Jack was coached by the legendary Edward Clark Gallagher. In collegiate competition, he was undefeated, winning three consecutive NCAA titles and four AUU medals. The Oklahoma A & M annual, **The Redskin**, of 1931 says, "The most polished amateur wrestler in the United States is the title conferred on Jack VanBebber, Captain of the 1931 all-victorious championship team."

Wrestling and work were not Jack's only interest in college. He was a member of the Acacia Fraternity and the Ag-He-Ruf-Nex club. He served one year as Junior Senator.

In January of 1932, Jack and his wrestling buddy, Conrad Caldwell, dropped out of college. Hitchhiking, they headed for Los Angeles, California, to train for the Olympics. After ar-

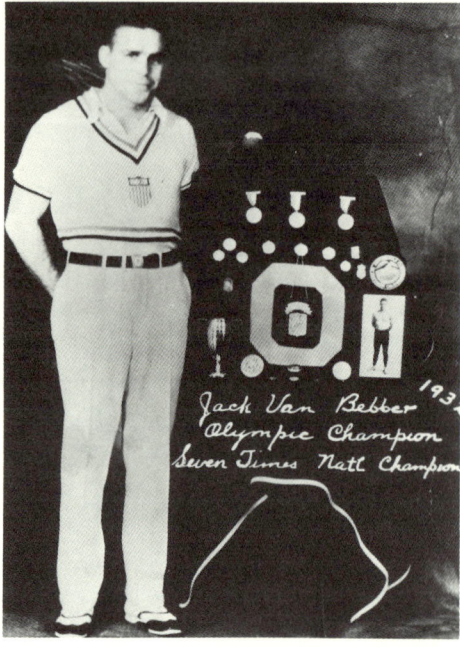

Jack VanBebber, in late 1932, displays wrestling medals and awards featured in the big "O" is the gold medal in the Los Angeles Olympics.

riving in Los Angeles, they found work in Safeway warehouse and trained in the Los Angeles Athletic Club, which sponsored them.

Jack won the Pacific Coast title in the welterweight class in the wrestling tournament in Los Angeles in the summer of 1932. Conrad won in the light heavy-weight (191 lb.) class.

The LAAC paid the tournament expenses and a member donated an old model T Ford to Jack and Conrad for transportation. With high hopes, they left Los Angeles in late June for the AAU tournament in New York City. To keep in training, they alternated on driving and jogging all the way into the city. In the matches there, Jack accomplished the outstanding feat of being the only tournament competitor to pin all of his opponents, a total of eight. He earned an AAU title, bringing his total AAU titles to three.

Strained by wrestling in the early morning hours, Jack became paralyzed. Luckily, his condition improved enough for him to travel on to Columbus, Ohio, where the final Olympic tryouts were scheduled for that week. After he reached Columbus, his weakened condition caused his kidneys to block. Stress followed. Then fortunately, a bait of watermelon made his kidneys function. And when the tournament opened, Jack suited out for the round.

When the Olympic Games opened in late July, in Los Angele, Jack defeated his preliminary opponents from Mexico, Denmark and Canada. A disheartening situation followed the day of the final match. A messenger brought a note to Olympic Village saying that Jack's match had been moved up an hour and no transportation was available to send for him. That forced Jack to have to weigh-in by three o'clock, less than two hours from that time. The heat was fiery and the Olympic Auditorium lay about six miles beyond the Olympic Village.

Hoping to hitch a ride, Jack dressed, and running, he left the village. Cars and cars passed him. He tried to ignore the heat and the pain by praying and jogging on down the avenue. A Los Angeles Club member recognized him, picked him up and he signed in on time.

In the Olympic auditorium that August day, Jack met the feared Eino Leino of Finland for the final free-style welter weight match. Winning by decision after a hard-fought battle, Jack triumphed — triumped to earn the gold medal for God and country.

In the fall of 1932, Jack returned to Oklahoma A & M, and in May, 1933, he was graduated with a Bachelor of Science degree in agriculture. He coached wrestling and served as assistant economics instructor at Texas Tech in Lubbock. Later, he resigned to go to work for Phillips Petroleum Company.

He was working in the Texas panhandle when he met Julia Eleanor Slough of Wellington, Texas. They married May 25, 1939. Three years later, during World War II, Jack was called to serve and was gone for four years. That time was spent chiefly in the Pacific area. After returning from the service, Jack resumed employment with Phillips. In 1971, he retired, credited with 39 years with the company.

Through the years, Jack indulged in reminiscences pertaining to wrestling. And he was surprised and pleased with three special laurels he received long after his days on the mat. A laurel in the 1950s was to be named as one of the top ten athletes in America during the first half of the twentieth century by the Helms Hall of Fame of Los Angeles. Frank Godsoe, sports writer in Amarillo, Texas, said that was a monumental honor that placed Jack in the select company with Jesse Owens

Jack and Julia VanBebber shortly after their marriage in 1939.

Jack VanBebber, gold medal winner of the 158 pound free style wrestling. Eino Leino, of Finland, second place winner, stands below.

and Jim Thorpe. In 1972, recognition for outstanding achievements as a competitor, Jack was honored as a distinguished member with induction into the National Wrestling Hall of Fame in Stillwater. Later in January of 1979, he was inducted into the Jim Thorpe Hall of Fame in a Tulsa ceremony.

During his working years, Jack was active in each community where he lived. He was a Worthy Patron of the Eastern Star in Dumas, Texas, and a Rainbow dad. He is a 50-year member of the Masonic Lodge, a member of Guthrie Scottish Rite of Freemasonary, and of First Baptist Church of Perry. Jack yearned for the scenes of his youth, so he and his wife settled down in Perry in 1978. Jack died April 13, 1986 and is buried in Grace Hill Cemetery, Perry.

Russell E. VanBuskirk
By Cheryl (VanBuskirk) Kerr

Russell Eugene Van Buskirk was born August 14, 1909, on a farm near Avard, Oklahoma. His parents, Charles and Cora Van Buskirk came to Avard from Iowa. They raised six children.

Russell attended school in Avard and Alva. After graduation from high school, in 1928, he began teaching at Mount Vernon, west of Alva and went to Chicago as part of the National 4-H Judging Team of Woods County.

The following year, he attended Oklahoma A&M College in Stillwater and married Viola May Egan, August 2, 1930. Viola's parents, James and Lelah, bought a farm one mile north of the Van Buskirk farm after James' retirement from the Frisco railroad.

In 1937, after alternately teaching in rural schools and attending college, Russell received his degree in education from Northwestern State Teachers College in Alva. Viola also taught and attended college during those years. Their first child was born August 5, 1937, a daughter named Lois Jean.

In the fall of 1937, Russell was the high school principal and football coach at Boise City and went to Tyrone the following year to be superintendent of schools. Their second daughter, Rosalie Sue, was born March 26, 1939.

For the next twelve years, Russell was Superintendent of Deer Creek Schools in Grant County. Because of a shortage of teachers caused by the war, Russell assumed the coaching responsibilities in addition to the duties of superintendent.

During their years at Deer Creek, three children were born: Darlene, March 5, 1941; Joy Cheryl, January 23, 1944 and Jerry Russell, June 13, 1947. Viola taught elementary.

The Van Buskirk family spent many summers in Boulder, Colorado while Russell worked on his degree. He received his Masters Degree in History in 1948 from the University of Colorado.

From 1951 to 1957, the Van Buskirks lived in Hominy, Oklahoma where Russell was superintendent of schools and Viola taught first grade. An English teacher at Hominy, Mrs. Minnie Canada, praised him highly. She thought he was the best superintendent she had worked for.

Their final move was to Morrison, Oklahoma July of 1957, where Russell was Superintendent of Morrison Schools for the following twenty-three years. Viola taught second grade at Morrison for twenty-four years. Russell and Viola soon became known as Mr. and Mrs. Van to the community. They were quite active in school, church and community activities.

Band, wrestling, football and six new classrooms were added under Mr. Van's leadership. The school grew to be one of the best schools in the area. Because of his foresight, along with the school board's, land was purchased to be used at a later date for a new football and tract complex.

Many teachers began their teaching careers with Mr. Van. It was said that, even though his training would be rough, when you had finished teaching under him for one year, you could teach anywhere. He expected his teachers to be dedicated and professional. In return, he backed his faculty one hundred percent.

Parents, students and teachers knew they could rely on him for a fair decision, reflecting a combination of experience, wisdom and objectivity. He treated everyone with equal consideration. His leadership earned him the respect of teachers, parents, students and caused him to be recognized as an outstanding educator by people in surrounding communities.

He served on the Tri-Country O.E.O. board, was on the advisory board to organize the Indian-Meridian Vo-Tech School, received recognition for thirty years of dedication work as adult 4-H leader, received the Honorary Chapter Farmer Degree from the Morrison F.F.A., and was asked to serve as ac-

Viola and Russell E. Van Buskirk - 1980.

Russell E. and Viola Van Buskirk at his retirement party - May 10, 1980.

Mr. Van at his desk in Superintendent's office at Morrison School.

ting County Superintendent of Schools for two years.

Upon retirement in 1980, Governor Nigh proclaimed May 10, 1980 as "R.E. Van Buskirk Day" in recognition of his dedicated service to education and the honor of being the only person who had taught fifty years in Oklahoma before retiring. He was presented this proclamation at the retirement party which was held at the Calvin Pauley Ranch near Morrison. Leslie Fisher, State Superintendent of Schools, presented a citation honoring him for his gift of fifty years of service in Woods County, Cimarron County, Texas County, Grant County, Osage County and Noble County. Senator Dahl and Representative Johnson presented to him documents of resolutions passed by the Senate and the House of Representatives honoring him for his outstanding contributions to the betterment of education in Oklahoma. The city of Morrison, in appreciation of his contributions to the community, dedicated the city ball park in his name. A large sign "R. E. Van Buskirk Field" was presented to him that night and later placed at the entrance of the park. There were many other gifts presented and a big feast was enjoyed by everyone. The following year, Viola retired after having taught forty-four years.

Russell is a charter member of the Morrison Lion's Club, Chairman of the Noble County Democratic Party, has served in the church as song leader, deacon, elder and chairman of the board. Both Russell and Viola continue to support school functions, sports events and community activities. They are active members of the Morrison Christian Church and belong to the choir. In their spare time they farm and raise cattle. They are very proud that all five Van Buskirk children were able to receive their degrees from college and are now teaching. Lois Jean, who married John Hellstern is in Fort Worth, Texas. They have three children: Joyce, Janice and James. Sue Criner is in Phoenix, Arizona with her son Eric. Darlene Ponder is in Garland, Texas. Her three daughters are Sherri, Vicki, and Lori. Cheryl, Mrs. Mike Kerr, has two children: John and Angela. They live in Morrison. Jerry Van Buskirk lives in Ponca City. He and his wife, Jan (Harris) have two sons: David and Danny.

Anton Vasek
By Dorothy Vasek

Anton Vasek was born March 3, 1855, and his wife, Victoria Josephine (Jak) was born August 27, 1852 in Bohemia, Czechoslovakia. In 1882, they and their three year old daughter came to the

Victoria and Anton Vasek.

United States. They homesteaded land near Hutchinson, Minnesota. Anton had a brother, John, who came to Minnesota and another brother who went to Italy.

They moved farther west in Minnesota and built a sod house. They were in Indian Territory. The Indians would enter their house without knocking, help themselves to food and then quietly leave. Later, the railroad was built three miles from their home at the town of Olivia. Anton received his Naturalization Papers and became a US citizen February 6, 1897, in Redwood County, Minnesota.

They had nine children-five sons and four daughters: Anton Jr., Joseph, William, James, Louis, Louise (Vasek) Dale, Rose (Vasek) Benesh, Bessie (Vasek) Calhoun, Emma (Vasek) Stengle.

In 1901, Anton and one of his sons went to Oklahoma with a team of horses and a wagon. They bought a farm three miles west of Morrison. They moved the family to Oklahoma by train and shipped the cattle and machinery by freight train. Daughter Louise got married the day the family left and she stayed in Minnesota. Later, James and Joseph moved to Oregon. Anton Jr. and William moved to Canada. Rose (Vasek) Benesh and Bessie (Vasek) Calhoun moved to Oklahoma City. Emma (Vasek) Stengle stayed in Morrison.

Louis married Sophia Frank in 1923. They lived on the home place with the parents and farmed the place. They had two sons: Louis Anton and Theodore (Ted) Julius.

Victoria Josephine (Jak) passed away January 2, 1929. Anton passed away December 25, 1939.

After the parents death, Louis and Sophia purchased the farm. Louis passed away in 1944. Sophia, in 1946, married J.D.E. Owen and they farmed the place until 1953 when the farm was sold.

Orlando Walkling
By Mildred Highfill

Orlando Walkling was born January 2, 1868, in Kansas. His father was Orlando Walkling, an Englishman, born in New York. His mother was a Shawnee Indian, born in Ohio. He learned to tan hides, make ropes and leathercraft from his Indian mother.

He worked with the surveyors who located the Rock Island railroad between McAlister and Oklahoma City.

Walkling was in Coffee county, Kansas, working for one of the largest cattle feeders in Kansas, when he heard of the Cherokee Strip opening. He had little idea of where it was or how it laid, although he had crossed the western part of it hunting for stray horses. Five other young men were going so Walkling decided to join them. He had three horses and a wagon with sheet and bows, so they rigged the wagon up with a camping outfit, feed and grub. The others just had saddle horses.

The covered wagons commenced to pass the ranch a month before the run, some with signs painted on the covers such as "Oklahoma or Bust" or "In Cleveland we trusted. In Nebraska we busted. But let her rip. We will make it in the Strip." They started about August 20. They just fell in line, for by that time the roads were full of travelers, all headed south. They were about eight days on the road. The last few days, it was a steady stream of wagons, buggies, carts and horsebackers. It was something like an army on the march. They helped themselves to all the corn in the fields along the road, and stacks of feed that were near the roads were simply foraged. Rail fences were all used for campfires. If chickens from the farm houses got in the road or close to it, they seldom got back.

Walkling had come without much money, but managed to make enough to buy food for himself and feed for his horses while waiting, by selling his place in the line at the registration booth, hauling hay for horses and water from a small hole dug in a creek bank. He rode a fast pony to make the run and staked a claim just south of Honeywell, Kansas.

When he got to Perry, he found that someone had already filed on it. He began hauling lumber and corrugated iron and working on Perry streets. He and his team may have turned the first furrows that was done toward grading the streets. Walkling later got a job working on the Wolleson building, digging the foundation and hauling rock. He plowed the ground in the courthouse park to plant alfalfa and then to plant grass and trees. Later, he took his team of oxen to Guthrie, on the Cimmarron River, and dug up little cedar trees to plant in the Catholic cemetery. Several pine trees were purchased and Walkling set them and more cedars out at Grace Hill cemetery.

Walkling traded an extra horse for the relinquishment of some land east of Perry. He homesteaded 160 acres, the SE quarter of section 23 in Noble township. He married Lavinia, maiden name unknown, in 1896. She was born in November of 1872.

Walkling began clearing the land and set out 110 acres of fruit trees. He hauled posts and firewood to Perry, as he cleared his land. He had three quarter sections and a 40-acre plot at the peak of his fruit-farming career.

He put in a cannery and in one year canned 85,000 three-pound cans of peaches besides shipping 50 carloads of fresh peaches to Chicago.

One day as he stood on the railroad landing in Perry, a Salvation Army woman got off the train and handed him a bundle. Wrapped neatly inside were twins — a boy and a girl.

After 30 years on the farm, the Walklings moved into Perry, to send the twins to school. They started a grocery store and meat market which they ran for nearly 20 years.

The Walklings moved from Perry, to California, in 1942, after losing their holdings during the dust bowl and the depression.

He went to work in a slaughterhouse. He bought land on Oregon Drive in Modesto, California, and put in a poultry-slaughter business. He kept goats and raised calves on goat's milk for the market. He made and sold rope and under his house he raised hot-bed mushrooms. Lavinia died in California, in 1951, and Walkling remarried.

Orlando Walkling was self-supporting until his death, he was making moccasins, tomahawks, headbands, lariat ropes and walking canes. He died February 9, 1974, at the age of 106 years, the last of the homesteaders of Noble county.

Robert H. Wall

By Mrs. James D. Elder

Robert Hicks Wall (September 17, 1878) escaped the cotton-growing, plantation life of his family in Lilesville, North Carolina, by going west in 1905, where his asthma problems became intolerable. For two years he worked at odd jobs where he could live and work. This brought him to Noble County in 1907, where he found the climate more healthful.

Zillah May McDaniel (November 1, 1889) was helping the neighbors with the harvest cooking when they met. They married on Christmas day, 1910, and moved south of Billings, where he owned and worked mule teams in the MidCo Oilfield. Their first child, a daughter, was stillborn in 1912; Robert Lee was born December 15, 1914.

Six years of the rugged oil-field life were enough, and they moved to a farm southeast of Billings. Virginia May was born there August 13, 1918, and McDaniel on October 22, 1922. The mule teams came in handy for doing road work as well as farming; poll taxes for males over 21 were $5.00 and could be paid by working two days on the roads or hiring someone in their place if they had no time.

Robert H. was a member of the Billings Masonic Lodge and eventually became a 32 degree Mason. Zillah belonged to the Eastern Star and the Community Women's Club. They attended the Methodist Church in Bill-

Robert H. Wall with his mule team at the MidCo Oilfield southeast of Billings, Oklahoma - 1912.

ings. Robert H. was a member of the Township Commission and the Indianola school board. Their home was large enough to accommodate the "School Marm" and many a morning saw them "breaking the road" to the schoolhouse at dawn to start the fire, clean and pump water.

In 1924, they moved to the Renfrow farm and raised wheat, cattle and sheep. During this period they exchanged mules for a team of Percherons and bought their first car — a model T Ford with isinglass curtains. The team still came in handy when there was deep ruts in a muddy road.

The house was close by Red Rock Creek that overflowed. Robert H. would wade the small swag to the barn, a bucket in each hand in water up to his armpits, to do the chores, but the land raised good crops. Much of the work was shared with neighbors. Butchering was a big day — the women canned and prepared the sausages, lard and meat, and it also was doughnut and crackling time — making use of the hot lard. And of course the harvests could never be done alone. This created a close-knit community and made for life-long friends.

1930 was a bad year. Zillah fell ill about the same time the wheat ripened and harvest arrived. Ten men were brought out from Billings to help cut, stack and run the threshing machine and wagons, and were still there ten days later, billeted about the house, porches and barn, waiting for the sun to shine. All that summer relatives and friends rushed in to help where needed, it also convinced Robert H. that one of the new combine machines might be a good investment.

In 1935, they moved to a farm near Tonkawa where Virginia would attend the University Preparatory Junior College and McDaniel would go to highschool. Robert Lee would continue at A & M College at Stillwater. Zillah became active in the Round Grove Club, the Tonkawa Garden Club, the Methodist Women's Guild, and the Eastern Star. Robert H. farmed until he retired in 1946, and moved to 404

North 6th Street in Tonkawa. He remained active, working part-time for the Coop Elevator, raising a huge garden, and keeping a beautiful yard. At age 91, he passed away November 20, 1969. Zillah lived alone for the next ten years, continuing her fine needle work and crocheting that won many blue ribbons at the Kay County Fairs. She was 89 when she died on February 2, 1979. Zillah and Robert H. are both buried in the family plot in the Billings Cemetery, Billings, Oklahoma.

The children are: Robert Lee Wall (December 15, 1914) married Anita Merlee Seeger (December 17, 1915) on June 20, 1936. They have a daughter Sherrie Lee Wall (September 9, 1948). Virginia May Wall (August 13, 1918) married James David Elder (September 4, 1917) on July 3, 1939. They have two children, Virginia Sue (December 13, 1940), and James Robert (January 17, 1943). Virginia Sue Elder married William Ross Hensley (November 21, 1938) on August 29, 1959. Their children are: Kyle Ross (November 17, 1971), Karri Jane (August 20, 1980, lived one hour), and James Everette (April 1, 1984). James Robert Elder married Susan Lee Green (January 15, 1945). Their children are: Deborah Lynn (March 17, 1968), and Michelle Susan (August 24, 1969). They divorced and he married Dona Avan Amos (July 31, 1954) on January 23, 1981. They have a daughter, Jennifer Yvonne (April 7, 1982). McDaniel Wall (October 22, 1922) married Maxine Evelyn Gibson (October 33, 1924) on January 31, 1948. Their children are: Labrenda Jean (November 7, 1952), and Terry Don (January 31, 1963). Labrenda Jean Wall married Steven Martin Swain (June 12, 1956) on August 2, 1975. Their children are: Jason Allen (October 18, 1978), and Justin Bradley (October 18, 1978). Terry Don Wall married Patricia Thomas (March 19, 1965) on May 18, 1984.

William A. Warner
By Lucile W. Plumer

The opening of the Cherokee Strip to settlement was exciting news to young men in northeastern Kansas. Ever since his older brother had participated in "The Run", Will Warner had the urge to go to the new territory. He had a high school education; had worked as a family member of a well-to-do farmer in Brown County for several years and had saved money to buy his own farm. This he did in 1898, at age 25.

The "claim" (SW¼-Sec22-Twp21-1E-IM) was five miles east and one-half mile south of Perry, O.T., the county seat of Noble County. On it was a bachelor's shanty put up by the previous owner, Jacob Ritthaler, and a drilled well on a strong vein of water which never failed. There was also a small but constant spring in the pasture area. Later a stock well was dug and walled with sandstone. This was topped with a chain-cup pump.

After sowing a field of wheat that first fall, he went back to Brown County to shuck corn and earn ready cash, as he had paid for his farm and would need more for improvements. He became champion corn shucker for the county that fall, then returned to his bachelor quarters. The seasons passed, wheat was again planted, and he went back to Fairview to marry Edith E. Carrier on 25 October, 1899.

They came to OK Territory by train and were soon settled. The shanty was a far cry from the large homes both had been accustomed to. Especially they missed the large shade trees. They set about improving their home. They set out several cotton-wood trees for quick shade. During the winter Will enlarged the little dug-out root cellar into a real stone-walled cave with arch roof of stone quarried on the farm. He was an accomplished stone mason and built many arch bridges in the county. In later years, he and two younger men built a number of concrete bridges in Seminole County.

Time passed. Women raised gardens, saved and traded seeds, raised chickens and did all the work without modern-day appliances. Men exchanged work on large projects, and families spent Sundays visiting in each other's homes, playing games and relaxing. Pitching horseshoes was a favorite with the men. At times Saturday dances were held in their homes. At the smaller houses the men set the

Wedding Picture - Will and Edith Warner - October 1899.

furniture outside to make room for dancing, and replaced it at the end of the evening. Will usually played his harmonica.

During these years two children were born: Lucile in October, 1900, and Ray in August, 1902.

Will was a gifted person, intellectual as well as adept at manual tasks. He was a splendid carpenter, having worked with a master builder in Kansas. A new house was planned, he sold a span of mules for $300, and bought sufficient lumber to build a six-room two-story house similar to his boyhood home in Kansas.

In 1906-1907, they and a neighbor couple made a trip to California in covered wagons, the men working at various projects along the way as each had a good team of mules. On this trip a third child, Edgar, was born in Albuquerque in October, 1906. They covered the California coast from San Diego to San Francisco before returning home.

Soon all was back to normal on the farm; fields prepared, crops planted, fences mended, and repairs done to buildings and machinery. Edith picked up her butter and egg customers, delivering by means of her little buggy and a fast, little driving horse.

Will was involved in helping organize a mutual farm insurance group. All were local farmers and dues were assessed whenever a member had a loss. It covered fire and possibly tornado damage to buildings. They were also subscribers to the first party-line telephone running east from town. There were about twelve members, each with a code ring. Later Will installed carbide lights, possibly the first in the neighborhood. The plant was

The five Warner children circa 1920: Ray, Edgar, Lucile, Mabel and Jennie.

situated in the cement block house which had replaced the little frame "wash house".

In the meantime, two more children had arrived: Jennie Ellen, October 1909, and Mabel Opal, October 1912, making the family complete.

Will was always interested in civic affairs and involved in whatever was current and needed. He served as chairman of Pioneer School board several years while his children were in school there; was inspector of the township election board a number of years, and also chairman of the Board of Noble Township, responsible for upkeep of roads in the township. At that time men worked out their "poll tax" on road maintenance. Years later while living in Perry he became a Councilman, and worked on the cemetery and sanitation committees.

"Vacations" consisted of Fourth-of-July celebrations with the usual picnic fare, firecrackers and fireworks, and a speaker — always a politician in election years. Many years these picnics were held in the Smoot grove just east of Sumner. Then there was the "16th Celebration", commemorating the opening of the Cherokee Strip, complete with elaborately decorated buggies, carriages and other vehicles. Picnic dinners were spread on the grass in the Court House park, under the many trees set out by Will Little.

A carriage and pair of trotting horses furnished family transportation. About 1915 a Ford touring car replaced them; then came a Fordson tractor to speed up farm work. Ray was of a mechanical bent and kept the machines in good running order.

Will and Edith were both in touch with progressive movements in farming and home improvements. They worked with the County Farm Agent and the Home Demonstration Agent, as they were called. The family was County Fair conscious and won many prizes. Will served on the Fair Board, and was superintendent of the farm products division for many years.

They were determined their children should be well educated. After sending two through high school from the farm, it was decided to move to Perry so a house was planned and built at 807 Kaw Street. Will was a capable and reliable carpenter. Besides building several houses on his own, he worked with the Marshbanks brothers doing finish and cabinet work.

The children were all through school and on their own. The Great Depression had struck and building slowed down, so in 1931 Will and Edith returned to the farm where they could raise much of their food and have an income from rental of the town property.

Back on the farm he remodeled the house and started raising sheep with the help of son Ed, who was a sheep specialist with A & M College (Oklahoma State Univ.), Stillwater. During this time Will was serving as a member of the Farm Security Administration promoting soil conservation through terracing and crop rotation. He was also chairman of Noble County "AAA", a Federal agricultural program, and represented the county at a meeting in Washington, D.C. in May 1935, called to discuss farmers' problems.

After Will's death in 1943, Edith went back to the house in town which she kept until her death in 1969, at age 93, living with daughter Mabel the last years.

By 1985 there were four living children (Ray died in 1977), seven grandchildren, thirteen great-grandchildren, and three gr-gr-grandchildren.

Will and Edith really helped to tame the wild, rugged land they loved and gave their family sterling examples of vision and perseverance that are an inspiration to their progeny.

Milo W. Watson

By Milo W. Watson

Mr. and Mrs. Milo W. Watson, who have been associated with the Perry Daily Journal since 1943, originated at Savonburg, Kansas, where they attended high school together and were married June 14, 1936, in Chanute, Kansas. Mrs. Watson was the former Anne Dicus.

Watson began a career in newspapering as a printer's apprentice on

Milo and Ann Watson - 1986.

the weekly Moran (Kansas) Herald in June, 1934, and joined the daily Chanute Tribune, September 10, 1934, as a member of the news staff.

October 1, 1936, they moved to Buffalo, Oklahoma, where Watson was in charge of both news and advertising on the weekly Harper County Journal until February 1, 1943, at which time they moved to Perry.

Their daughter, Carolyn Anne, was born in Buffalo, May 3, 1938. Their second daughter Mary Lee, was born in Perry, September 19, 1943.

Watson was named advertising manager upon joining the Daily Journal. On January 1, 1945, he became part owner of the newspaper in association with W. K. Leatherock, editor and publisher.

He was named publisher upon the death of Mr. Leatherock, February 10, 1949, and continued in that capacity with Mrs. Leatherock retaining her interest in the paper. In 1972, the Watsons purchased Mrs. Leatherock's interest.

Their daughter, Carolyn, was married to Richard M. Adkins of Muskogee in 1959. They now live at Fort Gibson where Richard is counselor in the school system and Carolyn is a vice president of Phoenix Federal Savings & Loan.

They are parents of three. The eldest, Greg, is married to Pam Cooley of Frederick, Maryland, and they live in Walkersville, Maryland. They have one daughter, Melissa, and a son, Justin.

Their son, David, is married to Kim Moydell of Fort Gibson, and they live in Muskogee where David is director of office services, at Phoenix Federal Savings & Loan, and Kim is employed by the First National Bank in Muskogee.

Their daughter, Patty Anne, is a second year student at Oklahoma State University in Stillwater.

The Watsons' daughter, Mary Lee, was married to John A. Streller of Perry in 1961. They live in rural eastern Oklahoma county near Newalla. John is an industrial engineer with Tinker Air Force base and Mary Lee is an industrial engineer technician, also at Tinker.

Their eldest son, Jeff, holds a degree in oil field geology from the University of Oklahoma. He is married to Charlene McCright of Norman who is also a graduate of OU in languages. They have one son, Jarrod.

The Strellers' youngest son is Brett, a senior student at Harrah high school in the class of 1986.

The Watsons have been active in the Oklahoma Press Association since 1936. Watson has served on most OPA committees at one time and was a member of the board of directors eight years. He served as president of the state association in 1967-68. Mrs. Watson simultaneously served as presidents of the women's group of the press association.

In 1984, he was presented the Milt Phillips Award for outstanding contribution to community journalism at the summer convention in June at Texhoma.

In Perry, Mrs. Watson was active in Band Boosters, Camp Fire, Order of Rainbow for Girls and the PTA. She is a past president of the Perry Study Club and has spent 15 years as a volunteer for Red Cross at the two local nursing homes. She has been an avid golfer for 35 years.

Watson is past president of the Chamber of Commerce, Perry Rotary club, United Fund of Perry, chairman of Board of Stewards of First United Methodist church, lay leader and the Watsons shared work as directors of Senior MYF at the church for many years.

The 42 years the Watsons have been with The Journal, have been accented by dedication to promoting Perry and Noble county in all aspects.

Perry is the smallest town in Oklahoma to have a six-day daily publication, a distinction made possible because of unrestrained support of the community.

The transition was made from hot-type printing to offset and later to computerized typesetting to keep abreast of the most modern developments in this profession. Credit for these strides is given to the dedicated staff of this community newspaper who have shared their skills and dedication to continue to operate a daily newspaper for this wonderful area.

Eugene C. Webb
By Ladene Webb

Eugene Clifford "Gene" Webb was a life long resident of the Morrison community. His roots here began with his

Eugene Webb.

great-grandfather, Daniel T. Hileman, homesteading the se¼ of section 5, range 21 north, 3 east (Autry township) Noble county, Oklahoma Territory, about 1½ miles north of Morrison.

Daniel T. Hileman was born in June 1842, in Pennsylvania as were his parents. He married Margaret Ann Perdue. She was born in August 1856 and her parents were born in Virginia. The 5 children of this marriage, all born in Missouri, were Lillie R. (Willis), Allison A., Carl L., Roy E., and Robert D. Daniel T. served during the Civil War in Co. C 35 Mo. Inf. His musket and a cast iron bed brought to Oklahoma territory in a wagon still remains in Gene's family. The original homestead stayed in the Hileman family until around 1960, when it was sold to E.W. Morrison. Daniel and Margaret are buried in Morrison cemetery.

Allison Andrew Hileman, born October 2, 1877, was Gene's grandfather. He married Hattie F. Miles, born in South Dakota, August 19, 1878. They had 4 children: Charles Dell, Stella M. (Webb), Nellie Fay (Marion) and Raymond Allison. Allison and Hattie are also buried in the Morrison cemetery. Hattie's father, Charles Miles dug a well by hand on a farm about 2 miles east of Morrison which is still in use in 1986. Allison either bought or inherited the original homestead as it remained in his possession until his death. Gene helped farm the original homestead for many years as he grew up on a farm called the Kent place across the road south which his father's family owned.

Stella May (Hileman) Webb, born December 2, 1904, was Gene's mother and she married Irvin Lewis Webb, born June 2, 1905. They had 4 children: Eugene C., born May 5, 1926, Elma May (Masters) December 12, 1927, Allen Lewis, November 12, 1929 and Carl Raymond, December 19, 1931.

Stella was born in a dug out on her grandparent Miles farm about 2 miles south of Morrison, which Gene could remember seeing as a child. Irvin and Stella were childhood friends and lived most of their married life on the Kent place on Black Bear Creek. Black Bear Creek was a source of income and recreation for the entire community. There was an enormous native pecan grove on the Kent place and the creek banks served as a picnic, play, fishing area for the neighborhood of Prairie Center.

Eugene C. Webb married Laden (Crockett) Marshall, born July 24, 1930 and they had 3 daughters, Karen Luann (Jones) born August 20, 1954, Robin Jean, March 16, 1956 and Laurie Ladene (Coleman) November 12, 1959. Ladene had 2 children by a previous marriage, Linda Kaye (Watkins) May 9, 1947 and Johnnie Delbert Marshall, October 29, 1948.

Gene attended Prairie Center grade school as did his mother and all his brothers and sister. His mother; Gene, and all of Gene's children graduated from Morrison High School. Gene also taught business and was principal at Morrison High School from 1955-1959. Gene graduated from Oklahoma A&M College in 1953 and obtained his MA Degree in 1959.

Adalaska Perdue, a deaf-mute who was Stella's uncle, taught all the Webb children to communicate with him by means of "talking on their hands." They in turn, taught several of the students at Prairie Center. Gene retained this ability after he was grown and one time stopped to help an elderly couple who had a flat tire. They were both deaf-mutes who were delighted to find he could communicate with them.

The early settlers were not always wise in their farming practices. Much of the topsoil eroded and washed down Black Bear during the floods. In 1950, Gene purchased a bulldozer and devoted his life to the restoration and conservation of the land. Gene built many of the terraces and ponds in the area around Morrison and in Noble, Pawnee and Payne counties.

Gene was always interested and involved in community and church affairs. With his bulldozer, he helped build the present day ball diamond west of Morrison school and leveled lots for the show site for the F.F.A.

Gene served in World War II in Germany and was a charter member and past commander of the Christie-Jones American Legion Post in Morrison. He was serving as treasurer at the time of his death. He had formerly served as chairman of the Noble County Republican Central committee and was a former member and chairman of the Noble County Election Board.

Gene was a member of the Christ Lutheran Church in Perry, Oklahoma and served as chairman of the congregation, taught Sunday School for 15 years and was on the board of elders.

In 1956, Gene and Ladene purchased the se ¼ of section 9, range 21 north, 3 east; making this home for the 30 years they were married before Gene's death February 11, 1984. Ladene still resides on the "Old Dollarhide place." Gene is buried in the Morrison cemetery where his great-grandfather, grandfather and mother are buried.

Gene gew up, raised his family and lived his entire life less than 2 miles from his great-grandfather's claim.

Julian E. Wells
By Howard Wells

My paternal grandparents, the Orsmus Wells, came from Vermont state, shipping their possessions by rail to Hutchison, Kansas. They settled in Ness County, Kansas, where they lived in a sod house. They experienced prairie fires and severe Kansas blizzards. In the early 1890s, they moved to Oklahoma near Crescent but later moved near Covington. They are buried near Fairmont, Oklahoma. Their children were: Warren, Julia, Eli, Julian, and Fannie.

My maternal grandparents were Emery Osborn and Elizabeth Elliott. Grandfather was a Civil War veteran. He brought his family from Indiana to a claim he had staked near Crescent. They remained in Oklahoma the remainder of their lives and are buried near Crescent. Their children were: Andy, Jane, Susanna, Mary, Ella, Della, and Alice. Aunt Ella never married and is living today in a home in Enid at the age of 102.

My father, Julian Elroy Wells, made the "run" in the Oklahoma Cherokee Strip on September 16, 1893, settling near Covington. Mother and Father, Julian E. Wells and Susanna Elliott, were married in 1898, in a log cabin near Crescent. They began their new home near Covington, in a two-room frame house, on the claim that Father had staked. Seven of their eleven children were born in this small house. Their children and birth dates are: Lillie Sisson (1899) Ponca City; Merrill (1901) deceased 1973; Orvile (1902) Katy, Texas; Raymond (1903) Ratliff City, Oklahoma; Howard (1905) Anthony, Kansas; Lizzie North (1907) and Leona Trenton (1909) both of Perry; Eli (1911) Cushing, Oklahoma; Julian (1912), Emery (1919), and Lorene Hasenfratz (1921) all of Ponca City. Howard, Julian, and Emery served in the US Army. Julian's term of duty was in the European Combat during WW II.

Julian E. Wells family about 1924. Front Row (L to R): Julian, Lorene, Susanna, Julian E., Emery, Eli. Second Row (L to R): Raymond, Leona, Merril, Lillie, Orville, Lizzie, Howard.

Lillie recalls her first train ride, an eighteen mile trip with her daddy from Covington to Perry in 1910. Later that year the family loaded their belongings on a wagon and moved to Perry. Father built a house in Perry for his family and the house is standing today.

I, Howard, remember Father for his musical talents, playing the piano and a violin that he purchased in 1920. I inherited the instrument and I fiddle it some every day. All we children had some musical abilities. Orville, Julian, Emery, and I have played for many social gatherings and church services. Father was always generous in sharing our home to any who needed a meal or a bed. He was a good story teller and entertained the children often with rousing tales, especially ghost stories. I respect my father for his Christian life and spiritual inheritance that he left to us.

I remember Mother as a very special person, full of love, patience, and a never-complaining attitude. Even during the hard times and drought years, Mother, somehow, always had food on the table for her brood. She taught us to love and respect all people, no matter what they had or didn't have.

Some things we remember as we were growing up were: walking to school carrying a cold, skimpy lunch (no fruits like oranges, apples, or bananas as they were luxuries); sleeping on straw ticks in cold, very crowded quarters; clothes and bedding made from feed, flour, and salt slat sacks; and working at odd jobs for very meager wages. We were happy because we hadn't kown any other way of life.

Entertainment was family oriented. The girls had rag and paper dolls that were homemade, the boys did boxing and wrestling, and with neighbor kids we played blackman and ball. No playing cards were allowed in our house, if the folks knew about them. We did play Rook and Flince with cards as the quiet games. We cherish the "fun" times we had neighboring with the good people of the Polo and Whipple communities.

Some rural schoolmate families that I remember fondly are the Lovells, Mickishs, Crosses, Gangs, Farrises, Kukuks, Swartzs, Taylors, Hughes, and Kirks. We all had a jolly time at the Whipple and Pike's Peak Schools. Teachers I remember are Minnie Bowright, Letha Davis, Maude Yost, Edith Goe, and Etta Hughes Scott.

I feel privileged to have lived during the time of so much progress in our country. We have seen drastic changes in technology, a man on the moon, Civil Rights Movement, retirement benefits, Social Security, refrigeration and cooling, and all the comforts of home and travel that we enjoy today.

We, the eleven children of Julian and Susanna Wells, lived in Garfield and Noble Counties during all of our growing-up years. We have known hardships and sadness but the good times and a strong faith in God have over-shadowed all else. Father died in 1933, of leukemia. Mother, then, lived in Perry until her health failed. She died in Ponca City in 1942, at the home of her daughter, Leona. Our parents are buried, near the friendly communities of fond memories, in the Polo Cemetery. All the Wells clan gather in Perry once a year for an all family reunion. This 1985 gathering will be our 47th reunion.

Roy H. West
By Minnie West Worrell

My father rode a horse 42 miles from Caldwell, Kansas, to stake a claim in the Cherokee Strip. He "proved up" his claim, living in a sod house that he built, until he and my mother were married at Wellington, Kansas, August 19, 1896. They lived the first year in the sod house. My father hauled lumber from Caldwell, built a house and barn. For water, they dug a well not far from the house. The first barn was of straw and poles.

Trading posts began to spring up all over the Strip. Nardin in Kay County, was the closest for a time — 17 miles north of the farm. Red Rock later was established. Either town was a day's drive there and back for supplies.

I remember my father telling about hauling wheat to Ponca City. A group of neighbors — to name a few that I remember — Betty, Hurst, Kettenring, Weaver and Holmes — sometimes as many as 12 or 15 farmers would form a wagon train and take wheat to Ponca City. They had to go when the Salt Fork River was low as there were no bridges. This was a two day venture. They all camped together at a wagon camp.

The next morning they would load up with coal and supplies such as flour, sugar, coffee, etc. and start for home.

Coyotes and Bobcats were common. Mother told of seeing a herd of antelope each morning about a half mile from the house.

White Rock was a trading post about 7 miles from the farm that they traded at until Rock Island built the railroad out from Enid, and Billings was started near the turn of the century.

With the exception of about two years my father lived on and farmed his claim (southwest ¼ of section 17 in Bunch Creek Township) until his death in 1929.

The farm was held by the family until 1975 when it was sold at auction to the great-grandson of a man that my father hunted coyotes with years before.

Roy Henry West (my father) was born at New Boston, Illinois March 25, 1871. He lived in his home state until manhood when he moved to Iowa and then to Kansas, remaining there until the opening of the strip. He married Madoria Vandelm at Wellington, Kansas, August 19, 1896. She was born February 26, 1873 in Kansas. Their children were: Roy, Edgar, Vernon and a daughter, Minnie (Worrell). Roy died May 2, 1929. Medora moved into Billings in 1943 where she lived until she died June 17, 1955. They are buried in the Union Cemetery at Billings, Oklahoma.

Emery E. Westervelt
By Mildred Highfill

Emery Emmanuel Westervelt was born in Allegheny City, now a part of Pittsburg, Pennsylvania, December 11, 1863, the son of Emery and Caroline H. (Connelly) Westervelt. Emery was a descendant of Lubbertsen Van Westervelt, who with his wife and four children sailed to America from Amsterdam, Holland, and arrived at New Amsterdam, Province of New York, May 23, 1662. Lubert's grandson, Kasparus, moved his family to Dutchess County, New York, in 1744. Emery's grandfather, Matthew Westervelt, moved from Poughkeepsie, New York, to a farm about ten or eleven miles northeast of Columbus, Ohio, in 1818. Emery's father, Emery Westervelt, was born there in 1824. Caroline Rebecca Connelly was born in 1829, a few miles from the Westervelt farm in Ohio. Caroline's father, Edward Connelly, was born in Ireland and came to America in 1797. Edward's wife, Mary Baker Graham, arrived in America in 1789, at the age of 12. Mary's father, Rev. William Graham, was born in Paisley, Scotland, and served as a minister and missionary in Scotland and Ireland under Rev. John Wesley who arranged for him to come to America with his family, but he became ill and died during the voyage and was buried at sea. William's wife, Catherine Baker, lived only three weeks after landing with her children at Christain, Maryland. The children were taken by Methodist families and were widely scattered, Mary being taken by a family who lived in Lancaster County, Pennsylvania. She and Edward Connelly were married in 1807, in Strasburg, Pennsylvania. He was a shoemaker at that time. Several years afterward they moved by wagon to a farm northeast of Columbus, Ohio, where Caroline Rebecca was born in 1829.

Caroline Connelly and Emery Westervelt were married in 1850. He was a contractor and builder in Columbus, Ohio. A few years later, they moved to Pittsburg, Pennsylvania, where he was a professor in Duff's College. They moved from there to Philadelphia, then to New York. In 1870, they went to Colorado with their two young children, Emery E. age 7 and Carrie age 4. Deciding to return to Pittsburg, the family stopped at Fairbury, Illinois, at the home of James Westervelt, brother of Emery, whose wife was Caroline's sister. They spent five years in Pittsburg and returned to Fairbury, where they built a home where Emery died in November, 1898.

Emery Emmanuel Westervelt received his education in Allegheny City, Pennsylvania, and Fairbury, Illinois. Then he studied telegraphy and worked at Monticello and at Forest, Illinois until 1887. In 1888, he located on a claim in eastern Colorado, and the year following returned to telegraphy in Arkansas City, Kansas. In 1889, he was stationed at Guthrie as telegrapher manager and ticket agent for Western Union Telegraph Co. In 1892, he was sent to Perry where he remained until 1901.

Emery married Harriet M. Ingram, daughter of Kate J. Ingram. Hattie was born in October, 1873, in Kansas. They were the parents of one daughter, Lucile, born May 21, 1894, in Oklahoma.

Mr. Westervelt wrote in his unpublished autobiography: "Before the opening prairie chickens were quite plentiful and were shipped out by express, also some deer. Men came in the country and baled hay and shipped it out. A stock car arrived containing a large pile of wooden stakes for marking of townsites and I was asked if I knew where the townsite was to be located. I knew where as well as the location of mile stones around there so I was instructed to have them unloaded, which I did.

The railroad had made no preparations at Wharton for this great influx of people. The depot was small, side tracks would hold but 30 or 40 cars. I requested an officer in charge of soldiers to place a guard at the water tank as water was being carried away and being wasted. This was done and a limited amount of water was carried away. The freight depot had been emptied of freight and I had it filled with express piled high.

The side tracks were full and there were about 1000 carloads of lumber waiting to come into the yards. We arranged to unload two trainloads a day. The lumber was unloaded at Perry from a train on the main track. We arranged with lumber dealers to have 4 men for each car and as soon as the train stopped the unloading began. It took about 3 hours to unload the entire train."

George P. Westervelt
By Mildred Highfill

George Pitcairn Westervelt was born September 1, 1870 in Fairbury, Livingston county, Illinois. George was the son of Emery Westervelt and Caroline Rebecca Connelly. He had a brother Emery and a sister Carrie. George attended grade school and high school at Fairbury but had to leave because of lack of money. He entered railroad service in December, 1886 at $20 a month with the prospect of learning telegraphy. In 1889, he left the railroad and took a job and bookkeeper and yard helper at a lumber yard, but due to illness he lost that job. He went back to the railroad as a day operator. He was active in the Presbyterian church and sang in choir and also in a double mixed quartette.

In February 1893, his sister died after a long illness and his mother became ill. He took a leave of absence from the railroad and helped to take care of his mother.

In September 1893, he went to Perry to make the "run" and obtained a leave of absence from the railroad for 2 month. He and his brother obtained a handcar and hid it in a strawpile but the day of the opening the trains were running and no handcars were permitted, so he rode in on the train.

He got a lot across the street from the west side of the square. He had a tent, 14' x 17' with two tent poles sent up from Guthrie. He left a friend to hold his lot while he walked to Wharton (a mile) to get his tent. After he found a man with a wagon and hauled the tent to Perry, a man with four friends had jumped his lot when he returned. The lot jumpers and friends refused to let George put up his tent because this was regarded as legitimate settlement. That night after the others were asleep, George and his friend put up the tent. He decided to put up a fence around his lot and again let the lot jumper and his friends back in and they put up a tent in front of George's. George and his brother decided to put up a permanent building and after a fight in which the Deputy Marshall appeared and told them the case had to be settled by the Townsite board, the other men took their tent and left without saying anything, but he paid $300 to the man on the next lot who claimed his tent was on George's lot first.

The man who had bought several lots just south had erected several one room houses on them to rent. He wanted to nail a house to the building the Westervelt brothers were building and when refused, caused trouble by claiming their building extended onto his lots. When the lots were surveyed it was found the building extended 2" on his lot, so they had to move it with jacks. In 1907, George and his mother went to Oklahoma City, where she died in 1921. George went to work for Pioneer Telephone and Telegraph Co.

Leo M. Wetzel
By Nona Wetzel

Leo M. Wetzel was born September 22, 1897 in Perry, Oklahoma, the son of Thomas M. and Annie Wetzel. He attended school in Perry and went into service when he was a junior in high school. He served with the United States Navy in World War I. After returning from service he finished high

Leo Wetzel and two daughters - (Left): Bonnie, (Right): Dorcas.

school, graduating about 1920. He attended Oklahoma A & M College at Stillwater now O.S.U. He married Bonnie Zoe Waltermire December 18, 1921. Bonnie was born at Perry, Oklahoma on January 13, 1902, the daughter of Ellwood James and Mattie Elleanore Waltermire. She taught school for a short time at Frederick in Tillman County, Oklahoma. She belonged to the Oak Grove Extension Club and the First Christian Church of Morrison, Oklahoma. She enjoyed cooking, canning and taking care of her family. They had five children, Bonnie, James, Dorcas Lee, Leota Jane, and Shirley Lou.

Bonnie born June 22, 1923 at Stillwater, Oklahoma lives in Oklahoma City, is single and does child care.

James was born September 21, 1924 at Medford, Oklahoma. James flies with American Airlines. He has two daughters Lisa and Annette. He married Freda.

Dorcas Lee, born December 4, 1925 at Medford, Oklahoma is a nurse. She married Orlan Mercer and they have four children, David, Donald, Denny and Charlotte.

Leota Jane was born September 21, 1929 in Guthrie, Oklahoma. She died November 2, 1946 when a horse fell on her. She was a senior in Morrison High School.

Shirley Lou was born March 27, 1933 at Perry, Oklahoma. She married Omer Vermillion and they have three children, Dale Wayne, Doyle and Judy. Shirley died October 10, 1976 from an accident when she fell down a flight of stairs.

After the death of his first wife Leo married Nona Muriel Laughlin on April 28, 1942 in Enid, Oklahoma. Nona was born in Glencoe, Oklahoma February 17, 1912, the daughter of Ray and Lora L. Laughlin. Nona taught school at the following rural schools in Noble County, Pikes Peak, Highland, Prairie Center, White Hall and at the

Nona and Leo Wetzel.

Morrison school. She also taught the I.X.L. school in Payne County, Oklahoma. She is a member of the White Hall Home Demonstration Club, American Legion Auxilliary and the Christian Church.

Leo was a farmer and rancher. Leo and Nona farmed with horses until 1949 when they traded the horses for a small Ford tractor at Pawnee, Oklahoma. This made the farming easier and soon they were farming more acres. They grew oats, corn, cotton, wheat and alfalfa. They also put up prairie hay. Leo enjoyed making gardens and growing flowers. He also liked to travel.

Leo and Nona had one child, Charlene, born August 23, 1948 in Stillwater, Oklahoma. Charlene married Jan Wells. They have two children, Janette L. and Charlie E. Charlene teaches 7th grade Math in Bartlesville, Oklahoma. Her husband, Jan, works for Niper (National Institute of Petroleum and Energy Research).

Tom Wetzel
By Nell Coldiron

Tom Wetzel (1875-1958) was christened Thomas Maxium Wetzel after his garndfather. Tom was born in Paris, Illinois. His grandparents came over from Germany in the early 1800s. Tom's father, Nicholas Maxium Wetzel was born on the ship coming to America. The family lived on a farm so Tom learned farming and liked it very much. He volunteered for the Spanish-American War in 1898. He was in the Fourth Illinois Division. After the war he came to Oklahoma and settled in Noble County on a farm southwest of Perry. (His family in Illinois had moved to Loxley, Alabama.) This was in 1900. In 1902, he met Anna Huffington at a country

Back Row: Leo Wetzel and Luticia Wetzel. Front Row: Nell, Tom, Nick, Wilma, Anna Wetzel.

dance. They were married that same year.

Anna Huffington was born in St. Joseph, Missouri, in 1881. She moved to Oklahoma in 1894 to a farm north of Perry that her older brothers, Frank and Jim, got in the run for the Cherokee Strip. Anna finished the eighth grade at the Whipple School, which was just across the road from their farm. When she married Tom she had a baby son, Leo, by a former marriage but he was adopted by Tom who always loved him and thought of him as his own.

The Wetzels moved to Perry in 1910, so the two children of school age, Leo and Luticia, could go to a better school. Shortly after coming to Perry, Tom got into police work. He was Chief of Police for several years as well as Deputy Sheriff and Sheriff for six years. He owned the Elite Cafe and Rooms. All of his friends, many of which were farmers, urged him to run for Sheriff of Noble County. He did and was elected in 1914. He was proud of his office and the new Courthouse. He was sheriff until 1920. He worked for the State in Granite, Oklahoma at the detention home for boys. He also worked for the Highway Department.

Tom and Anna had five children: Luticia (1903-1985), Nick Wetzel (1905-1967), Edwin Wetzel (1906-1907), Nell Wetzel (1908), Wilma Wetzel (1915-1966).

Luticia married Heston Cathey. They had two boys, Tom and Dan, and five grandchildren. She had her degree from Oklahoma University and taught school for twenty years. She was a graduate of Perry High School and member of the Christian Church.

Nick, also a graduate of Perry High and a member of the Christian Church, got his degree from A. and M. (now Oklahoma State University) in Horticulture. He and his wife, Marie Wolfe Wetzel, owned the Perry Greenhouse.

Nell graduated from Perry High and was a member of the Christian Church. She went to college in Enid at Phillips University and at Edmond State Teachers College. She taught school three years. In 1930, she married Victor Coldiron. They moved to California in 1931, and lived there until Victor's death in 1980. They had three children: Daisy Ann Coldiron, was born in April of 1934, and died at the age of twelve of infantile paralysis. She is buried at Grace Hill Cemetery. Vicki who lives in Maui, Hawaii is a graduate of the University of Southern California and also a former school teacher. Her mother, Nell, lives with her since her father's death. Terry who lives in Southern California is married to Patricia Mayfield. They have one son, Christopher. Terry is an administrative vice-president at a California savings and loan.

Wilma married Bill Lynch. Both graduated from Perry High and were members of the Christian Church. While living in Perry, they owned a nursery and greenhouse. They moved to California and settled in Yacaipa where they owned and operated Lynch Flower Shop. Wilma loved music and was very active in the Unity Church.

Leo Wetzel (1898-1983) graduated from Perry High but before his senior year he joined the Navy to fight in World War I. He was in the Navy four years then came back to Perry and finished high school. A star football player and editor of the yearbook, Peroma, he married his high school sweetheart, Bonnie Waltermire. They had five children. After Bonnie's death at a young age he married Nona Laughlin. They had a daughter. Nona raised the Wetzel children and helped on the farm out north of Morrison.

Tom Wetzel lived in Perry from 1910 until his death in 1958. He and his family lived at 620 Holly for almost 13 years. After his wife Anna died in 1929, he later married Anis Johnston. Tom was always a good friend to all that knew him.

Washington Whitlow
By Jannis Culver

Washington Whitlow's parents and family came to Caddo County, Oklahoma from Osceola, Missouri in 1896, when Washington Whitlow was fourteen years of age. His parents, Bud and Ann (Bledsoe) Whitlow, with their five children, including Washington, his brother, Elmer, and three sisters, Olive, Kate, and Elizabeth, settled near Minco, Oklahoma.

Washington was born July 23, 1882, in Osceola, Missouri, the son of a farming family whose main crops were corn and cotton. Upon moving to Oklahoma, the family continued their farming operations with the help of Washington, as he grew to adulthood. In addition to farming, during those early years, his father became the manager of a cotton gin, operated in conjunction with a grain elevator for corn.

Washington and Viola Enyart, both residents of the Minco community, were married in 1902. His wife, Viola, was born September 27, 1887, in Macon County, Missouri, the daughter of Abraham, "Abe" and Minnie Enyart, and she came with her family from Macon County, Missouri, to the Minco community in 1901. Her family consisted of her parents, one brother, Leonard, and three sisters, Elsie, Lora and Pearl.

Washington and Viola Whitlow became the parents of two daughters, Thelma May, born 1903, and Viola Minnie born 1907, while living in the Minco community. They moved from the Minco community during the years when oil discoveries in Oklahoma created boomtowns over-night, and construction employment was at an all time high; especially, the construction of wooden oil derricks. Washington worked in the oil fields constructing these wooden oil derricks, also building pipelines for gas and crude oil.

During this period, Washington and Viola became the parents of a son, William Abram, born 1909, at Uncas, Kay County, Oklahoma, and another son, James Leonard born 1914, in Garber, Garfield County, Oklahoma. They were, now, the parents of four children, two daughters and two sons.

In later years, as a pipelane contractor, Washington was responsible for the gas lines laid in the towns of Crescent, Garber, and Billings, Oklahoma. The

Viola and Washington Whitlow and grandchildren Jannis and Billy Hayton.

Richburg Brass Band seated L to R: Gus Widiger, Pete Smith, Fred Reck and Adolph Froelich. Back row: Julius Widiger, Charles Hirschman, Julius Froelich, Rudolph Zifsman, Gus Fredekind and Ted Widiger.

family lived in Garber, Oklahoma six years before moving to Billings, Oklahoma in the 1920s.

The Depression of the 1930s forced a halt to most of the construction business and the family, once again returned to their earlier occupation of farming in the Billings and Marland areas.

Viola (Enyart) Whitlow died October 23, 1943, and Washington Whitlow died January 31, 1960. Burial for both is in the Billings Union cemetery.

At the time of Washington's death, he had six grandchildren and seven great-grandchildren. The only one of Washington and Viola's children, now living is William "Bill" Abram, who resides in Billings, Oklahoma. James died in 1973 in Long Beach, California. Viola M. (Whitlow) Hayton died in October, 1983, in Stillwater, Oklahoma, and Thelma M. (Whitlow) Haga died July 1985, in Fort Worth, Texas.

Julius Widiger

By Hattie (Widiger) Shiever

Julius Widiger was born October 13, 1861, in Heinsthat, Valynier, Russia. His ancestors were Swedes. He came to America with his parents, Wilhelm and Alwine Widiger in 1875. The family consisted of the parents, and four sons: Ernst, Julius, Gustav, and Henry. Their destination was Moundridge, Kansas, where the father, Wilhelm, had a teaching position promised. He was to teach the children of the Mennonites, who had arranged for his passport earlier. The Wilhelm Widigers resided in Moundridge, Kansas, where he taught school and also took a course in weaving rugs. Julius worked at various jobs, mostly for farmers, since this type of work was the easiest to obtain, as Moundridge was still a small town. He later worked as a tenant farmer and quickly learned the ways of farming. Learning from the more well established and experienced farmers in the area.

Since their father was a school teacher, Julius and his brothers received first hand educations. On November 10, 1889, Julius as married to Emilie Anklam in Moundridge, Kansas. While living in Kansas two sons were born to them — Theodore and Arthur.

When the Cherokee Strip was opened, a group of families and acquaintances, among them Julius Widiger, decided to make the run. Julius made the run with a wagon drawn by two horses, and staked a claim southeast of Perry. After he had filed, he returned to Kansas for family and possessions. The Kansans traveled in a group, mostly in covered wagons, with milk cows tied to the back of the wagons, and extra horses and maybe a coop of chickens.

When Julius reached his claim, "a claim jumper" had taken over the claim and filed on the same piece of land. Julius' only witness did not want to get

L to R: Wilhelm Widiger, seated friends, names unknown, who had been converted to the Christian faith by Wilhelm. Back row: Alvena Widiger, Henry Widiger, Julius Widiger and Emilie Widiger.

involved, as there would have to be a lawsuit filed. The "claim jumper" was a woman and they were favored, so Widiger realized it was not feasible to sue and so lost his claim. He learned later the lady did not "prove up" but traded the right for a team of horses. He also learned her witnesses were hired.

Widiger did lease a quarter of school land from the State, eight miles east and two south of Perry, as he had decided to remain in Oklahoma. The land had to be cleared of timber, before he could build a house. A one room building was first built with only a dirt floor. As soon as possible a rug made with strong fiber, that could be swept clean, was added. Water was hauled from a spring — until a well was dug. In about 1913-15, some of this land was offered for sale by the state. Julius Widiger, as well as others, purchased the land they were living on. After making Oklahoma their home, eight children were born here: Lydia, Sophia, Karl, Herbert, Mathilda, Alvena, Maria, and Hedwig (Hattie).

The Kansas group had staked claim or settled in the area southeast of Perry. They brought their religion with them. At first reading services were held in homes. Julius served many times as the substitute pastor. He had a fine voice and led the group in singing hymns.

The first Zion Lutheran Church was built about 1897, five miles east and two south of Perry. Built with volunteer labor, Widiger being one of the volunteers.

A brass band was organized with Julius as director. This band consisted of a group of ten or twelve, all male. The members changed as new ones joined and others moved away. This band played in church services, anniversaries, birthday parties, marriages and funerals. One evening the band was to play at a surprise birthday party for one of the neighbors. It was a cold winter night, as they waited outside to commence their music, moisture in some of the valves in their instrument stuck, only a number of squeaks and whistles were heard, to spoil their fun.

The first fireflies that the group of homesteaders from Kansas saw, caused a panic. They thought that someone was trying to set their crops on fire. They had never encountered these insects before.

Julius's son Arthur, worked in Perry as a typesetter — for a man by the name of Pietrusky, who published then a weekly newspaper, The Perry Neuigkeiten. Arthur had paid a friendly visit to a family who was ill. He drank some of their water and also became ill with dreaded typhoid. Mr. Pietrusky at first thought it was a boyish prank, to get out of work and Arthur became quite ill before his parents were notified. They came to take Arthur home, on the way he lost consciousness, and it was two weeks later when he regained his senses.

As the years passed improvements were steadily made. A nice large house was built. Julius and Emilie lived on this homestead until his death, October 21, 1935. Emilie died February 17, 1961. Both are buried in Grace Hill cemetery.

Eldon Will
By Eldon Will

Eldon Will was born September 24, 1939 on the home farm. He is the son of Adella (Owen) and George C Will. Eldon grew to manhood on the farm his grandfather homesteaded. He married Nedra Overholt October 22, 1960 at the Lost Creek Evangelical United Brethern Church south of Stillwater. Nedra was born February 14, 1939, daughter of Wilfred and Alice Overholt of Stillwater. Rev. Thomas Kirby, a cousin of Nedra and former pastor of the United Methodist church of Perry, officiated.

During the first year of their marriage, the Wills lived in Oklahoma City where Nedra was employed by the state welfare department at the capitol and Eldon was an oilfield worker.

In 1961, they moved west of Morrison where they constructed an all new home on a parcel of land homesteaded in 1893 by Eldon's grandparents. The Wills have continued on the farmstead since that time. Nedra worked two more years transferring to the Payne county office of public welfare.

Eldon and Nedra are active members of the Morrison Christian church. Nedra is treasurer of the women's group of the church and Eldon is a member of the board of elders.

Nedra is a five-year charter member of the Morrison Young Homemakers Organization, 23 year member of the Oak Grove extension homemaker group and a member of the Morrison United Fund committee. She has held offices in and worked on a number of projects of these organizations.

Eldon participates in local and county activities in addition to operating a grade A dairy. He was a three year member of the Noble County Farm Home Administration, a seven year member of the board of directors of the Farmers Exchange Cooperative and a 17 year member of the Morrison board of education.

Eldon and Nedra have three children: Brenda Kay was born March 22, 1962 and graduated from Oklahoma State University. She is an accountant for Conoco in Ponca City.

Nedra and Eldon Will - 1985.

Randall Wayne was born February 28, 1964. He has 2½ years of college. He farms and works at Ditch Witch in Perry.

Bryon Jay was born October 18, 1976. He is a third grader in the Morrison school.

William Karl Fredrick Will
By Adella Owen Will

William Karl Fredrick Will was born in Central Wisconsin, near the small village of Almond on October 25, 1971. His full name was William Karl Fredrick Will, but he always used the signature William Will. His parents had come to the United States as young adults from Northern Germany, near the Baltic Sea.

At age 16, his mother died and William left home to make his own living. He worked in the timberlands of Northern Wisconsin some years, then moved into Northwestern Iowa where he worked as a farm hand. In 1898, he and Rosa Johanna Karly were married at the German Lutheran Church in Remsen, Iowa. They then moved to a farm near Akron, Iowa.

About 1900, they moved to a farm in Jackson County, Minnesota. The land was flat and swampy and during the five years they were there they were unable to harvest a crop due to wet seasons. They returned to Iowa and in 1909 moved to Noble County, Oklahoma, on the recommendation of friends that had come to Oklahoma earlier. They bought the east half of section 20 of 22 North 1 West (Black Bear Township): six miles north and 2 miles west of Perry, where they lived until retiring in 1947 when they moved to 821 Delaware in Perry.

William Will died June 28, 1952. Rosa Will was born December 25, 1879 and died February 24, 1958. Both died of diabetes.

Their family consisted of: George C.

Will born May 11, 1903. He died October 19, 1976. He married Adella Owen on August 20, 1929. She was born April 4, 1906. He was a farmer.

Laurence A. Will was born May 8, 1905. He married Mildred Klingenburg October 28, 1936. She was born March 23, 1913. He was an employee at the Oklahoma Highway Department.

Ethel M. Will was born February 9, 1908. She married Eugene A. Crane May 11, 1931. He was born December 9, 1904. They are medical missionaries.

Alice F. Will was born March 25, 1910. She married Arthur S. Lutz July 20, 1941. He was born August 11, 1905. She is a teacher.

Arthur J. Will was born January 24, 1912. He died February 5, 1975. He married Clara Klingenberg September 25, 1939. She was born February 16, 1920. He was a farmer.

Walter T. Will was born February 21, 1915. He married Gladys Cross August 26, 1943. She was born September 27, 1916. He is a teacher.

Stanley S. Will was born June 16, 1917. He married Bennie Taylor June 6, 1944. She was born September 2, 1919. He is a minister.

Lennice A. Will was born December 22, 1919. She married George Scott. She is a nurse.

Frank W. Will was born February 27, 1925. He married Madoline Bauman June 4, 1948. She was born October 21, 1928. He is an engineer.

Nathaniel H. Wilson

By Anita Ann Brown

Nathaniel Henderson Wilson was the son of Samuel D. Wilson and Matilda Malinda (Henderson). He was the namesake of Matilda's father; Nathaniel Henderson and was born February 13, 1846 in Tennessee.

Nathaniel came to Texas with his family prior to the Civil War. The Wilsons farmed their land in Buena Vista, Shelby County, Texas.

In May of 1864, at the age of 18, Nathaniel followed his father's footsteps to Camp Wigfall and volunteered himself for the Confederate States Army. During this tour of duty he served in Company F, Borders Texas Regiment, under Col. John Border and Captain D. F. Smith. He was honorably discharged and released at Buena Vista, Texas in July 1865.

On November 13, 1867, Nathaniel married the love of his life, Elizabeth Sweazea, (born December 2, 1851). She was the daughter of his father's friend and neighbor, Matthais Sweazea and Hannah (McFadden). Nathaniel and Elizabeth remained married til their deaths.

To this union was born eight

Nathaniel and Elizabeth (Sweazea) Wilson.

children: Martha Lucinda (December 21, 1868) married Ambrose Stanton; several children. Benson Bellzora (September 20, 1871) married Mack Bingham, they had 12 children. Bell had coal black hair in her 80s. Henderson Herington (September 16, 1873) never married, died October 10, 1922. Helen Hestella (September 12, 1876) married Thomas Benton Buckbee, they had six children. Emily Elizabeth (April 2, 1878) married Harv Dillard, they had seven children, she died in 1953. Jessie Denson (February 9, 1883) married Della Rebecca Tummell, they had three children, he died February 19, 1959. Eula August (January 21, 1888) married Wesley Kelly, they had no children, she died August 8, 1960. Samuel Sweazea (May 1, 1889) married Maude Ann Wilson (no relation) they had eight children, she died October 19, 1959.

About four years after the death of Elizabeth's murdered father, it is believed they left Buena Vista with the rest of the Sweazea family. They traveled to and fro within the state of Texas, giving birth to children along the way. It must have been a weary road for them to travel for it is believed they were in hiding and feared for their lives as they wandered.

By 1880, Nathaniel and Elizabeth were located in Jack County, Texas near the Oklahoma border. Nathaniel was a quiet and gentle man. He never complained about rough times he had encountered. It is said Nathaniel owned a grocery store in Texas. Perhaps it was in Jack County. He gave credit to the local customers. A drought came and the customers were unable to pay their debts to Nathaniel and his store folded. Flour was sold by the barrel then.

It must have been about 1892, that Nathaniel moved his family into Oklahoma. They first lived at Midlothian, Lincoln County on 160 acres of farm land. They lived in an antique two story house. Their lots were numbered 16 and 17. Their main cash crop was cotton. They also grew corn for the horses and mules.

Nathaniel's son, Samuel Sweazea Wilson (my great-grandfather) raised his family on this land. Samuel's son, Lloyd Elmer Wilson (my grandfather and favorite "story-teller") still owns a portion of that land to this day. He is 78 years old now and resides in Shawnee.

In addition to farming Nathaniel also earned money by working for the railroad. The Santa Fe Railroad ran north into Lincoln County, through Meeker, Payson and Sparks. He also helped to build the Fort Smith and Western Railroad that ran into Fort Smith, Arkansas.

Nathaniel and Elizabeth must have loved children. "Pa", as he was called, was always agreeable when asked by his children if they could have a party. Many parties were given at their home with lots of music. Good times were enjoyed by all.

As Nathaniel became a grandfather he spend many evenings with Lloyd Elmer while Elizabeth and the rest of the family were in church. They would lay in the yard and Nathaniel would teach his grandson to read to stars. He would point out the stars and the dippers and the moon. He told Lloyd he would never get lost in the night if he would watch the stars. As they lay there star-gazing and probably dreaming, they would fall asleep, spending the rest of the night, together, there in the yard. In the morning Nathaniel would have warm water at breakfast as he did not care for coffee. My grandfather still recalls the advice Nathaniel gave him as a young boy, "Take care of your business. Let the other man's business alone."

Nathaniel and Elizabeth Wilson removed to Perry, Noble County, Oklahoma in what year I am not certain. They lived there until the Lord was ready for Elizabeth. Their address was 6th Street.

Elizabeth joined the South Methodist Church at the age of thirty-two. She was a good christian wife and mother. She was in poor health for quite some time.

Nathaniel would awaken in the middle of the night to the sound of Elizabeth rattling dishes and such in the kitchen. Pretending as if he thought it was a cat in the kitchen, he would come in saying, "Scat, Scat, Cat" and then would laugh. Perhaps Pa was trying to ease Elizabeth's pain by making her laugh with him. He would find her taking soda for her ongoing stomach trouble. She bore her suffering well, but it caused her death on October 26, 1919 at the age of 67 years, 10 months, and 23 days.

After Elizabeth's death, Nathaniel helped care for their son, Henderson. Henderson loved music and was a well practiced violinist. He never married. On October 10, 1922, he died in Perry of creeping paralysis. Most likely this was polio or possibly arthritis. There were no medications for his ailments in those days. He was a laborer and once lived on South Seventh Street, Perry. After Henderson's death, Nathaniel went back to Lincoln County to the home of his son, Samuel.

Nathaniel applied for his pension from the Civil War in Perry, Oklahoma in May of 1922, somehow I wonder if he ever received a penny from his pension as he died three days after a stroke on December 14, 1922 in Meeker, Oklahoma, just three years later than his wife. He must have missed his beloved Elizabeth by his side. He worked up until the day of his stroke. He never regained consciousness.

His body was taken to Chandler, Oklahoma. Jessie D., another son, of Perry drove his rag-top Model T automobile to Chandler to pick up his father. The casket was attached to the rag-top and was transported to Grace Hill cemetery in Perry were he was laid to rest with his beloved Elizabeth. His son, Henderson and Jessie D. and his family are also there.

Margaret E. Winkler
By Dorotha J. Winkler

Margaret E. Casebier Winkler homesteaded land in Rock township, 8 miles south of Perry. She was born October 26, 1847. She married Joseph Winkler on November 14, 1865. They had four children, all born in Xenia, Dallas county, Iowa: John Leroy (Roy) born January 26, 1869; Jennie born November 30, 1872; Sadie, and Marie born August 17, 1880.

Joseph Winkler was a farmer in Iowa, and died of pneumonia after getting wet swimming cattle across a flooding creek. Roy was twelve years old when his father died. Margaret

Roy and Mable Winkler - 1906.

Margaret Winkler in front yard, Marie Winkler holding horse, Roy Winkler with team. The bicycle man and mounted horseman were with the traveling photographer. Homestead soon after run in 1893.

moved her family to Kansas, by covered wagon, where her parents, John and Sarah Casebier, lived.

When the Cherokee Strip Run was to be held on September 16, 1893, Roy was there on horseback. When he got off to stake a claim, something scared his horse and it ran away. He ran after the horse but couldn't catch it. By then, someone else had staked his claim, so he lost his horse and saddle and had no claim. Later, Margaret purchased the northeast quarter of section 27 in Rock township. They built a house and started farming. Margaret proved up on the claim and received patent number 6161.

Margaret's parents, John Casebier, born March 25, 1912, died April 18, 1902, and Sarah Casebier, born January 20, 1819, died December 10, 1908, later moved to Orlando, Oklahoma. When John Casebier died, Sarah Casebier came to live with Margaret on her farm. Margaret's daughters married and Roy continued to care for his mother and grandmother on the farm. The Casebiers are buried in the Fairview cemetery near the farm. Margaret died May 21, 1912, and is buried at the Fairview cemetery.

Jennie, Margaret's oldest daughter, married Harley Swisher. They had two sons: Vinton (Tony) and Armond L. ((Bill). They moved to Twin Falls, Idaho, in the early 1920s, where they farmed. Both boys are also farmers. Rita, Tony's wife, is a school teacher. They have an adopted daughter. Tony had a cherry orchard in Greenacres, Washington. Bill's wife is also a school teacher. They have no children. Tony and Bill both died of a heart condition.

Sadie Winkler, the second daughter, married Garl Maupin, who died at an early age. They did not have children.

Marie Winkler married Wirt Maupin. They had one daughter, Isla, and another daughter who died in infancy. Isla Maupin married Clyde Traywick. They have a son, Donald, and a daughter, Delores. Donald married Dorothy Frazier. They have a son and daughter. Delores married James Harvey. They have two daughters, DeLesa and Rene' and two sons, Scott and Shawn. The girls are married and the boys are attending school.

John Leroy (Roy) Winkler, son of Joseph and Margaret, married Mabel A. Bourdette September 19, 1906, at her parents' home, a log cabin, in Payne county, approximately 30 miles south of Perry. Mabel was born September 28, 1882, at Winfield, Kansas, the daughter of Joseph Rutan and Callie Bell Bourdette. Their children: Joseph Farrel, born November 21, 1909; twins: Charles Marden and Helen Maxine, born September 23, 1911, and Dorotha J., born November 19, 1913. The children attended the Fairview school. Roy died January 1, 1928, and is buried in the Fairview cemetery beside his mother. Mabel died December 17, 1959, and is buried in the Fairlawn cemetery in Stillwater.

Farrel, oldest of Roy and Mabel Winkler's children, married Addie Hickman. They had no children. He died of a heart attack on July 12, 1959.

Dorotha J. Winkler is the youngest child of Roy and Mabel Winkler. She

Front Row L-R: Roy Winkler, Margaret Winkler, Harley Swisher. Back Row L-R: Sadie Winkler (Maupin), Marie Winkler (Maupin), Jennie Winkler (Swisher) before 1900.

lives on the original homestead south of Perry, Oklahoma. She graduated from Oklahoma State University and taught school several years. She stayed home and cared for her mother. In later years, she worked for War Price and Rationing Board in Perry, and the State Highway Department, Perry. The last 15 years before retirement in 1975, she was Deputy County Assessor for Noble county. She has been a faithful worker in the Presbyterian church.

Maxine Winkler-Parks
By Dorotha J. Winkler

Helen Maxine Winkler was born September 23, 1911, on her grandmother's homestead in Rock township. She was the daughter of John Leroy (Roy) Winkler and Mabel A. Bourdette Winkler. She had a twin brother, Charles Marden Winkler. Maxine taught school in Noble county for several years. Among the rural schools were Echo, and Pioneer. She met Moody Ray Parks while he was teaching at Fairview school. She married him on August 19, 1933. He also taught school in the Birds Nest school near Marland, Oklahoma. Later, they moved to Ponca City and he worked at Continental Oil company until his retirement. Maxine died June 3, 1982, after open heart surgery. Moody died June 2, 1983, of cancer. They had four children: Martha, born October 3, 1934; Lucerne, born December 10, 1936; Charles Moody, born September 26, 1943; and Dennis Allen, born November 11, 1944.

Martha Parks married Bill Harrisberger. She teaches school in Tulsa, Oklahoma, and has a masters degree in Education. Bill has an Engineering Degree and worked at Continental Oil company in Ponca City and for Dowell Inc. in Tulsa. They live in Tulsa. They have two children: Charles Allen, born January 20, 1962; and Alison, born September 26, 1963. Charles graduated in 1983 from Oklahoma Baptist University. He is Youth Director at a Baptist church in Claremore, Oklahoma. When Alison graduates from Oklahoma Baptist University in 1985, she plans to teach religion in college.

Lucerne Parks married Victor Weber at Ponca City. They both graduated from Oklahoma State University. They live in Chicago, Illinois; where they both teach school. Both have MS degrees. They have five children: Natalie, born January 3, 1959; Angela, born March 7, 1961; Stephanie, born March 15, 1963; Kent, born February 2, 1965; and Aaron, born November 6, 1967. Natalie Weber married Peter Lira, who is a football coach in Illinois. Natalie is working on her Masters degree and plans to teach Home Economics. Angela Weber graduated from college and works as a Recreational Therapist at a hospital in New Orleans, Louisiana. Stephanie Weber is in college in Chicago, Illinois, majoring in Biology. She plans to teach. Kent Weber is working on an Engineering Degree at Oklahoma University. Aaron Weber is attending high school in Chicago.

Charles M. Parks married Gayla Connor. They have two children: William C., born February 10, 1982, and Elizabeth L., born May 5, 1984. Charles has a Doctorate Degree from Oklahoma State University in Industrial Engineering. He was Vice-President of the Bank of Co-op at New Orleans, Louisiana. Recently, he moved to Baton Rogue, La.; where he is an Engineering Professor at Louisiana University.

Dennis A. Parks is single. He lacks a very few hours having a Masters degree in Business from Oklahoma State University. He is a computer Analyst for Aminoil Oil Co. at Houston, Texas.

Gus C. Wollard
By Mary Lee Campbell

It was in 1901, eight years after the opening of the Cherokee Strip to settlement, six years before Oklahoma statehood, that Gustavus Clements Wollard came to Perry.

He was always known as Gus. He was born July 3, 1867, on a farm near Richmond, Missouri, the son of Mr. and Mrs. John Wollard. The grandparents of Gus C. Wollard had migrated from North Carolina in 1820 and settled in that Missouri region. As people moved to the frontier, settlements were established and the first John Wollards had donated the land for the town of Richmond.

Gus C. Wollard grew up in that area and helped on the farm before seeking work in other areas. Before going to Perry he had sought to stake a claim in the opening of the Pottawatomie, Sac and Fox Indian lands in 1891, but the land on which he claimed was part of the land designated as a street in Tecumseh, Oklahoma, so he went on to Perry.

He had been a traveling salesman in the Territories selling cigars and candy for a St. Louis firm. He continued in that work after moving to Perry but soon opened a grocery store with his brother, Swain Wollard.

Economic conditions that made it impossible to collect the credit accounts on the store's books caused the two brothers to close the firm.

Gus C. Wollard — 1867 - 1931.

Some time later he became a mail carrier on a route that extended in the direction of Sumner. He gave up this work when the government doubled the size of the routes but kept the pay at the same figure.

It was then that he became a real estate agent selling mainly farm properties. His office was located in the front of the Walter Powers Abstract Company on the north side of the Perry square. In those days the phone number was 68.

He branched out into the field of handling right-of-way acquisitions for oil company pipelines. And as the oil business grew he became active in oil leasing.

Gus C. Wollard was a member of the Masonic lodge in Perry but he was particularly active in the Knights of Pythias. In 1923 he was elected Grand Chancellor (state president) of this body.

He developed a keen interest in politics and was elected a state delegate to the Democratic National Convention at New York City in 1924.

When his long-time friend, Henry S. Johnston, became a candidate for governor, Wollard served as his state campaign manager, and after Johnston's election he became chairman of the State Board of Affairs. He resigned the chairmanship after two years but remained on the board for a time before returning to Perry.

He was an avid hunter and fisherman and taught numerous young men in Perry many points about these sports. One of his hobbies was gardening.

He was an excellent cook and often prepared foods for men's get togethers. He died December 30, 1931 a little more than 30 years after his marriage at Lawson, Missouri, to Mary Miller Smith, of that town, and to whom three daughters were born.

Mary Miller Smith Wollard.

Mary Wollard
By Mary Lee Campbell

It was on April 16, 1902, that Mary Miller Smith, a member of a pioneer Missouri family, and Gus C. Wollard were married at Lawson, Missouri.

He took his bride to Perry, Oklahoma, which was to be their home for the rest of their lives. Both were active in various phases of life in the community for the many years that followed.

Mrs. Wollard's grandparents had settled in Ray County, Missouri, in 1840, moving there from Greensboro, North Carolina. Her parents, James Addison Smith, and Catherine Miller Smith, lived on a farm near Lawson but he was also a banker, heading up the local Lawson bank.

She had attended Elizabeth Aull College, Lexington, Missouri, before working in a millinery store in Kansas City, Missouri, and later starting her own millinery shop at nearby Gallatin, Missouri.

The Smith family was a religious one, proud of the fact that there had been a Presbyterian elder in the family dating back to the Revolutionary War period.

Their first home in Perry was at the corner of Jackson and Eighth but in 1916, they moved into their last home located at 1013 Elm Street.

Mrs. Wollard was a charter member of the Tuesday Afternoon Club. She taught a Sunday School class of junior boys in the Presbyterian church for many years.

The Wollards lived briefly in Oklahoma City while two of their girls were in college and he was employed by the state.

Three daughters were born to them: Lucinda Catherine, June 26, 1905; Mary Lee, November 5, 1906; and Blanche Victoria Jo, January 12, 1914.

Lucinda Wollard received a BA degree from Phillips University, Enid, in 1927, and taught mathematics at Central State College and at Capitol Hill Junior High, Oklahoma City, before her marriage in 1929, to Vernon Thornton. Most of their life was spent in Bartlesville, where he was in the research department of Phillips Petroleum Company. Later, they retired to an acreage east of Stillwater, which he developed.

Three sons were born to them: Dr. Gus Thornton, now chief of staff on Angels Memorial (Veterinary) Hospital, Boston, Massachusetts; Dr. John William Thornton, professor of biology at Oklahoma State University, Stillwater; and Dr. Vernon Thornton, veterinarian at Norwell, Massachusetts. They are all married and have children.

Mary Lee Wollard graduated with Bachelor of Oratory and BA degrees from Phillips University in 1928 and taught in the Perry elementary grades for four years before her marriage in 1932 to O. B. Campbell, who was then managing editor of the Perry Daily Journal.

They moved that year to Medford where they remained until 1935, at which time they moved to Vinita, Oklahoma, where they have since lived and where Campbell was owner and publisher of the Vinita Daily Journal for 30 years.

Two children were born to them: John C. Campbell, owner of a public relations firm, Rockville, Maryland, and Mrs. Patti (Don) Hoover, Tacoma, Washington. Two daughters and a step-son of the John Campbells, and two sons of Patti and Don form these families.

Jo Wollard attended the College of Emporia, at Emporia, Kansas for two years and then received a BA degree from the University of Oklahoma in 1936. Prior to her marriage she did social work at Guthrie and Miami.

She married Roy Garten, Jr. in 1938 and they have spent most of their married life in Ponca City, Oklahoma, where he was employed as a geophysicist with Continental Oil Comany, until his retirement. Two children were born to them: Dr. Ted Garten, a professor at Missouri Central College, Warrensburg, Missouri, and Mrs. Nancy Kevin, Huntsville, Alabama. Ted and his wife have three children and the Kevins two.

Mrs. Wollard died June 18, 1959.

James L. Wood
By Mrs. Ted Newton

James L. Wood (born January 30, 1833) and Elizabeth Lytle (born April 29, 1840) were married in Louisville, Kentucky. They moved to Osage county, Kansas. When the Cherokee Strip was opened, sons, Robert and James (Jake) made the run and staked claims next to each other, about eight miles south of Perry, just south of what is now the Fairview school house.

Father and mother and sisters and brothers came later: Sally who married and moved to California, Mattie who later married R. Swart, whose family had a farm close by, they too moved to California. While in Oklahoma, they had a grocery store in the front room of their house. Margaret stayed home. Jasper later joined his sisters in California.

George (Pony) who married Leota Woods, stayed in Oklahoma and Perry with their children: Edna, Jap, Elizabeth (Newton), Georgia and Jane. He sold mules and horses to the Army during World War One. Later Pony was in the cattle and horse business

George (Pony) Wood, Leota Wood and children Edna, Jap and Elizabeth - taken 1907.

Edna, Jap and Elizabeth Wood taken about 1910.

Early Cherokee Strip celebration parade on north side of the square in Perry, prior to statehood. Notice the Woodruff sign on the building.

with W. P. Elliott. George and Leota Wood are buried in Grace Hill cemetery in Perry.

When the Lottery for land in what is now Lawton, Oklahoma was held, Jake Wood sold his farm and won land there, where he lived the rest of his life.

Robert farmed his claim until a harvesting accident crippled him. He sold his farm and with his sister, Margaret moved to California.

James L. Wood died December 15, 1912. Elizabeth Lytle Wood died December 21, 1916 in California. Her body was shipped back to Noble county and she was buried south of Perry in the Fairview cemetery.

Bradford J. Woodruff

By Dorothy Ebersole

A thirst for adventure led Bradford Joseph Woodruff in the late 1800s from his home in Ashford, New York, to the excitement and freshness of a new life in what was the frontier in the Midwest part of America. He eventually settled in Colby, Kansas, opening a department store there and becoming active in community affairs and in the Masonic Lodge. He married a young Colby lady and they became the parents of two boys, Marsh Bradford and Raymond Michael.

He had heard of, and became interested in a thriving little city in the Cherokee Outlet of Oklahoma — Perry, Oklahoma Territory. After the early death of his wife, he and his sons moved in 1900 to Perry, where he established the Woodruff Mercantile Company on the north side of the city's downtown square. The store occupied all of two store buildings, and offered everything from notions and household necessities to a men's clothing department, shoe department, a complete grocery store, and ladies' ready-to-wear and millinery on the second floor. A mezzanine was the center of bookkeeping and cashier services.

B.J., as he was called by almost everyone, bought the quarter block at the corner of Eighth and "H" streets, rebuilding the home on the premises by adding two stories and remodeling the interior.

Meanwhile, Effa Lee Carlock had come to Perry shortly after the opening of the Cherokee Strip to live with her sister and brother-in-law, Samuel H. Harris, Noble County's first county attorney. She left after a short time to enroll in the first class of the University of Oklahoma in Norman, returning in a few years to stay with the Harrises, working as a secretary in her brother-in-law's law office.

In 1900, when the Woodruff store was opened, she took over the bookkeeping and secretarial work for B.J. A romance developed, and she and B.J. were mar-

The Woodruff family house, 721 8th Street in Perry, B. J. and Effa standing in the yard. The house is still in the family as Sam Ebersole, grandson of B. J. and Effa, lives there today.

ried in 1901, Effa Lee then becoming the "mother" of the two little boys. In 1905, a daughter, Maxine, was born to them, and in 1915, another daughter, Dorothy arrived on the scene.

B.J. Woodruff was involved in many community activities, including the presidency of the board of education, the Masonic Lodge (in which he rose to become state commander of the Knights Templar), and was a trustee of the First Presbyterian church. In another capacity, during the governorship of Henry S. Johnston, he made many trips to Oklahoma City to serve with the Board of Affairs in buying clothing and other materials and necessities for the resident of the state's institutions — orphanages, hospitals, etc.

A series of strokes and the beginning of a long bout with cancer forced him to close the store in the late 1920s, and his life on earth ended May 12, 1931.

His wife, too was involved in many affairs of the city, serving as president of the Parent-Teacher Association, president of the Ladies' Aid Society of the Presbyterian church, (also later a trustee), president of the Ladies Tuesday Afternoon club, a member of the Pioneer Ladies' bridge club, and often volunteering her aid in community and political projects. She died in 1971 at the age of 94.

Many coats of paint have been applied through the years to the side of the Woodruff Mercantile store next to the westernmost alley on the square's north side, but the name of B.J. Woodruff still seeps through and is visible to all who look for it.

Marsh B. Woodruff

By Marcia W. Dunn

From the time of his birth on June 14, 1894, Marsh Bradford Woodruff

Marsh Woodruff at home after his return from WW I.

seemed destined to be one of those "people who love people", for his gregarious and affable nature was evident throughout his entire life.

Marsh was born in Colby, Kansas, the older son of Bradford Joseph and Elizabeth Marsh Woodruff. His brother, Raymond Michael, appeared on the scene a year later. The boys' mother died when they were quite young, and their father. B.J. (as he was known by almost everyone) brought them with him in 1900, to Perry, Oklahoma Territory, a buoyant little town that showed potential as a growing, friendly community.

About a year after B.J. opened a department store on the north side of the downtown square, Marsh and Raymond had a new "mother" — Effa Lee Carlock, who had returned to Perry after attending the University of Oklahoma, and became the secretary and bookkeeper for B.J. They were married in 1901, and both became active in community affairs.

Life in Oklahoma Territory was full of interesting experiences for Marsh and Raymond. They learned to fish and hunt at an early age. When their father took them to the lake by Grace Hill cemetery to learn to swim, they amazed him by jumping in and paddling away.

At age ten, Marsh met his future bride, Winifred Brengle. He and neighborhood buddies were frightening horses by throwing paper in their faces. One of these horses pulled the buggy drive by Winifred's mother.

During his high school years, Marsh participated in sports, drama and almost any extra-curricular activity the school had to offer. After high school graduation, he enrolled in classes at the University of Michigan, Ann Arbor, joining his two cousins from New York (the birth state of his father). He received a Bachelor of Arts degree in 1917. It was just in time to join the Army during World War I. He served in the signal corps. After the war, he did graduate work at Maryland and Yale Universities.

On April 25, 1925, at Perry, Marsh and Winifred were married. She had been a school teacher and at the time of their marriage Winifred was manager of the Southwestern Bell Telephone Co. in Perry. They have one daughter, Marcia Woodruff Dunn, who lives in Woodward.

The business career of Marsh Woodruff was varied. He worked in his father's dry goods store, taught school, coached football, sold life insurance, and was chief warden of the state fish and game department. He found his favorite job in managing Chamber of Commerce organizations in Perry, Blackwell and Woodward.

While in the Perry Chamber of Commerce, Marsh was highly instrumental in organizing an association of Hereford breeders which later developed in to the Northern Oklahoma Hereford Breeders Association.

Marsh was one of those who organized a weekly community auction sale which was operated by the Chamber of Commerce and manned by volunteers from among the town's businessmen. The sale later was sold to private enterprise.

He is credited with finding the site and helping to develop the airport north of the city of Perry. During the war, he served as a member of the Noble County Draft Board.

In 1944, Marsh left Perry to become manager of the Blackwell Chamber and from there went to Woodward to fill a similar position.

Reading was a hobby of Marsh's and the Woodward library contains 233 books from his collection. His interest in stamps caused him to correspond with people all over the world through the philatelic association. The Boy Scouts of America received his help. He tested boys for merit badges.

Marsh was an accomplished speaker and made many talks before civic clubs across the state. For three years, he was a guest lecturer at the University of Oklahoma.

While serving as president of the state association of Chamber of Commerce secretaries, Marsh advised so many young managers that he became known as the "Dad" of Oklahoma Chamber of Commerce.

His ability to be friends with the people in all walks of life was one of his outstanding characteristics. He dedicated his life to his community. His happy, generous heart, together with a cheerful and tolerant outlook on life was contagious. He inspired others to dedication.

Marsh's death followed a heart attack in Woodward in 1959. He was brought for burial back to Perry, the town which he always loved and which in his heart was really "home". Winifred, his wife, died in 1964, and her internment also was in Perry.

Calvin L. Young
By Velda Young Zimmerman

Calvin Luther Young, his father, James Young, his brother-in-law, Jim McFarland, his cousins, Armour and Oscar Henderson, his mother's cousin, George McFarland, and his future wife's distant cousin, Matthew Chestnut made the Run into the Cherokee Strip from one mile west of Orlando to stake claims, September 16, 1893. Keeping their horses out of sight of the crowd calmed them so they made better time. Calvin rode his cow pony, black Topsy and led another horse to ride turn about to rest them. They loaned their best riding horse to Mr. Chestnut for he was an older man with several children so needed a farm.

James Young drove a rig with a breaking plow in it and flying their church banner "For Christ's Crown and Covenant." They had scouted the land and hoped to settle near White Rock Creek for wood and water. Hendersons staked along the creek and Mr. Chestnut between the creeks, but the next day they found Calvin's stake was a few feet on Oscar's claim.

A stranger came from the creek and said he had staked Mr. Chestnut's first but when he saw Chestnut's friends and Calvin started plowing his claim for him which established his possession, the man left. They found ashes of several campfires at the creek so the man had come before the race which made him ineligible to take a claim. Youngest son, Arthur Chestnut, has lived and retired on his father's claim on which Union Cemetery stands.

Calvin and his father and Jim and George came back on the upland for their claims with a common corner for Calvin, James and Jim. George's touched another corner of Calvin's. Jim had a baby daughter, Carrie, but the other young men were bachelors. Calvin stayed to guard against claim jumpers while the rest returned to west of Edmond. Later, he walked to Enid to take the train, meeting an otter which he shot but having no knife had to carry the heavy creature until a man with a team and wagon gave him a lift. He always carried a pocket knife after that.

In the spring, they returned and built a soddy on Calvin's claim where they all lived until Jim hauled lumber from Perry and built his house.

Mrs. Holmes was the only woman

Farm team of Calvin L. Young.

who spent the winter on their claim. Grandma Young, driving across the prairire to invite her to church services was the first woman she saw. The men had cut poles and brush from Red Rock Creek to make a brush arbor for church services as the Indians did.

Watching the arrival of newcomers — their neighbors-to-be — was fascinating.

As Calvin drove the breaking plow, his father walked ahead, barefooted, through pools to learn if they were shallow enough to plow through. Sharp pain in his heel caused him to turn and be bitten again, on the great toe, by a rattler. Calvin sucked out the poison as best he could, and went to Weavers, the nearest house. Mr. Weaver rode two miles west and north to Dr. Brafford's while Mrs. Weaver helped Grandma Young all night. Ben Mendenhall was only eight years old but always remembered Grandpa's black, swollen foot, but Grandpa survived fourteen years.

Calvin and Jim were partners, Calvin working the fields and Jim caring for their livestock. Winters, Calvin and help herded cattle on wheat pasture before there were fences. They all ate at Jim's table but seven warmer months they each slept on their own claim as required to prove up.

Instead of breaking the sod with slow oxen, Calvin increased his horse team to move more quickly. He kept increasing his team until it was regularly 18 or 19 horses hitched abreast in one long line, and later even as many as 24, for a short time.

Calvin had been a first day student at what is now Central State University at Edmond, two years before homesteading, and later returned for three winters to be graduated valedictorian of his class in 1899. That summer he met Mother, Margaret Black. His doctor said if he would live three years he must live in the open air, the Rock Island built a spur to the southwest corner of Weaver's claim, and now Billings, north and west of the water tower, is on grandfather's claim.

George sold Father his claim before my parents were married on November 9, 1904. Father pulled his five roomed house a mile by road and joined it to George's three roomed house where I was born November 22, 1905. I am typing in this house 79 2/3 years after M.B. Shultz, later long time Noble County Treasurer was first to announce my birth. Everyone else was busy so he answered the phone when Mother's sister, Mrs. Armour Henderson called and he told her a baby girl had arrived. He was building cabinets in the kitchen — they are still in use.

In 1907, greenbugs ate all the oats and all the wheat. There was no harvest so Calvin fitted a shack like a camper and took his wife and daughter during week days to churches and schools in six counties, giving chalk talks campaigning for Oklahoma to become a constitutionally dry state, which it became, November 16.

When his wife's health required, he studied many therapies and treated her and became a licensed Chiropractor in Oklahoma and Kansas. He was licensed and ordained to the Cumberland Presbyterian ministry and was pastor of Liberty Church in Alfalfa County for a year but transferred to the United Presbyterian Church, farming for a living but preaching for the good he could do. He would preach anywhere they wanted services but could not afford a pastor, fifteen places within fifteen miles of home, a wonderful way to meet fine Christians. How I enjoy hearing, "I remember when your father preached at . . ."

My daughter Eileen and her husband Wesley Learned farm the place and added the Faris house for rooms for their six children. Calvin has three grandchildren, two girls and a boy, and sixteen great-grandchildren, eight boys and eight girls.

Charles A. Young
By Charlene Young Hechler

Charles Allen Young was born September 1, 1899, in Medford, Oklahoma, the first of three children to Cord A. and Julia (Beckham) Young. His early childhood was rather traumatic as he was shuffled about among relatives due to economic and domestic stresses. The family moved to Helena when he about 10 years old. His father was an independent carpenter, working when work was available, and his mother took in laundry (washing on a washboard) to keep the family together during the lean times. Dad still remembers his job as "pick-up and delivery" boy, pulling his "Little Red Wagon" full of clothes all around Helena. He attended school in Helena until he was about 16 years old and in 10th grade, then he decided that he had enough education and needed to be out in the world working and earning.

On November 10, 1918, following a severe bout with the "flu", he reported to Cherokee, Oklahoma, for induction into the Army. However, the group was told to go home and report in the morning. The next morning the world awoke to find that Armistice was declared — so he missed WW I by a hair!!

Freda Louise was born April 23, 1899, in Hamel, Madison County, Illinois, the third of seven children to Edward and Minnie (Kase) Henke. The family moved to Oklahoma in 1905 to live on a farm near Kremlin. Her father died in November 1910 as the result of Typhoid Fever, leaving her mother with a farm and seven children to care for. The children attended a rural school (Pleasant Valley) near Kremlin, then entered Kremlin High, where mother completed 11th grade, finishing her High School education in Enid where she graduated in 1920. She and her two sisters, Nora and Edna, roomed together in Enid, where she began work as a sales clerk for Kress' 5¢ & 10¢ Store. It was while working there that she met Dad who was also working in Enid for Swift & Co.

They were married on January 14, 1923, in Pond Creek, Oklahoma, and lived in Enid over a year when they bought and moved onto a farm near Hunter. A year or so later, upon realizing that a baby was on the way, they sold the farm and moved to Helena where Dad bought the Dray Line. He says, "I had a team of horses and a wagon and I hauled anything anyone wanted hauled." At that time heating was done mostly with coal, so the bulk of his work was loading, hauling, and unloading coal for home use. The baby (Me!!) was born February 24, 1926, in the hospital in Enid.

When we became residents of Noble County in 1929, we moved into a farm house on "The Beech Place", located 1½ miles south, 2 miles east of Billings. I was, of course, too young to remember much about it, but I do clearly recall the big porch on the east and south side of the house. My first brother, Charles Wesley was born on December 2, 1929, and I vividly recall seeing him asleep in my doll buggy on

Charlie and Freda Young Autumn of 1966.

that porch on the warm spring days.

In August, 1930, we moved a little further southeast to "The Howe Place", 3½ miles south and 4½ miles east of Billings. The house was a typical frame farmhouse with several large Maple trees in front bordering the roadside. There was the usual large kitchen with room for hanging all the outdoor garments needed in winter; the wash-stand with water bucket and wash basin; the kitchen table and chairs; the big wood-burning stove for cooking and heating; and the cansole radio with Dad's rocking chair and smoking stand beside it. The kitchen was "the living area" in those days — especially in winter. At bedtime in winter, we'd each take our turn getting our P.J.'s on behind the stove where it was warm, then mother would hand each of us a little warm "package" (a hot flat iron wrapped in newspaper and towel) and we'd scamper off to bed with our "bed-warmer."

I remember several springs when our baby chicks arrived (300 or so) and the weather was so cold that my parents feared for their survival if they were put in the brooder house, so we'd cover the southeast corner of the kitchen floor with newspapers (including the area under the stove), put a couple of boards to "pen them in their corner", and turn loose all those "peeping little balls of yellow fluff" until they were a bit stronger or the weather a bit warmer. On occasion, there was also a baby piglet kept in a cardboard box on the oven door to keep warm and grow a little stronger after being trampled or lain on by "Mama Pig" — or just because it was the "runt of the litter" and unable to fend for itself! This stove incidentally, was my mother's pride and joy! — "A Kalamazoo — Direct to You" — in a beautiful soft green and ivory color combination.

Dad was primarily a wheat farmer, doing the farming with horse-drawn equipment at first, then as time passed, buying his first Allis-Charmers tractor. At varying times, however, he also raised hogs, sheep, beef cattle, and had a herd of "milk cows". Often in the spring when we'd have heavy rains, Red Rock Creek would flood and back up in the low areas. We had a slough between our house and barn which became waist deep (on Dad) with churning, muddy water and a strong current, and Dad waded through it both night and morning to "do the milking, separating, and take care of the livestock."

I remember the hot summer nights when we'd move our old iron bedstead out in the front yard under the big Maples where Mom and Dad would sleep while we three kids slept on our mattresses laid on the front porch. Some evenings Mom and we kids would sit on the porch and sing the old hymns.

On May 25, 1933, my second brother, Ray Allen, was born at home. Since I was 7 years old then, I remember Dad telling me to take my brother Charles and "Go outside and play because Mama isn't feeling very well".

In 1944, our parents bought and moved to "The McCoy Place", 2½ miles south and 7 miles east of Billings, where they lived until 1964, when they bought a house in Billings, retired and "moved to town" where they now reside.

Charles A. Young Children
By Charlene Young Hechler

I, Charlene Young Hechler, was born February 24, 1926, in the hospital in Enid, Oklahoma to Charles Allen Young and Freda Louise (Henke) Young. We moved to Noble County in 1929, to the "Beech Place", located 1½ miles south, 2 miles east of Billings, where my first brother, Charles Wesley, was born December 2, 1929. Later we moved to the "Howe Place", 3½ miles south and 4½ miles east of Billings. It was here my second brother, Ray Allen, was born onn May 25, 1933.

I started and ended my school days while living there. I entered first grade at Indianola School, a mile north of us. Dad bought a Shetland pony for me to ride to school. She was all white; her name was Midget; and she didn't really care to go to school!! On several occasions she just reared up, dumped me off, and went back home while I walked on to school. My first teacher was Miss Foreman; my second was Phillip Merriman; and there were 12 or 13 students in the eight grades at that time.

In 1934, three school districts, including Indianola, were consolidated into Valley Center School, which I attended through 8th grade, graduating in 1939. Charles received his entire elementary education there, and Ray attended 5½ years there, transferring to Banner School in 1944, when our parents bought and moved to the "McCoy Place", 2½ miles south and 7 miles east of Billings, where they lived until 1964.

The three of us attended and graduated from Billings High School. Charles left the area in 1948, to join the Marine Corps. He served in Korea, and following his discharge in September 1953, he married Kaye Liberty from Kirkwood, Missouri, and entered college at Stillwater, Oklahoma. He continued his education in Raleigh, North Carolina and upon completion there, they journeyed to St. Paul Minnesota, where he is now a Professor of Animal Sciences with the University of Minnesota. They have three children: a son, Michael, who is married and two daughters, Sharon and Janet. Mike is an Assistant Professor in Natural Sciences and working on his PhD in Geology at Westfield State Collge in Springfield, Massachusetts, Sharon is working on her PhD at Duke University in Durham, North Carolina, and Janet is a Science teacher for grades 1 through 6 at St. Pascal's in St. Paul, Minnesota.

Ray Allen entered the Air Force shortly after graduation in 1950, and served in Germany where he met and married Ingelore Heese of Fromberg Bei Shwandorf. They returned to the US in the Autumn of 1954, he was discharged from service, and they returned to Billings where he accepted employment with William Hayton & Son. He also began gradually assuming much of the responsibility for our father's rather extensive farming ventures. On May 2, 1965, he was accidentally drowned and is interred in the Union Cemetery southeast of Billings, Ray and Inge have one daughter, Lore Rae, born August 17, 1957, who is a Speech Therapist in private practice residing in San Diego, California.

I have lived in Florida for nearly thirty years, finally becoming an R.N. in 1969. I was widowed in 1977, remarried in 1981, have one daughter, Norine Williams Turner, who teaches Math and Computer Science to 11th and 12th grades in Salt Lake City, Utah. She has two teenage daughters, Robin, 16 years old, and Terry, who is 13.

I look back at those "good old days" (??!!) when Mom and Dad got up at 5:00 am so Dad could milk several cows, separate and care for the milk and cream, eat breakfast, and harness several horses or mules and get to the field to plow, drill, or whatever, for a full day in the heat and dust, only to come in and do it all over again before bedtime. And, Mom, meanwhile, washing (on a washboard in the early years — then a gasoline-powered Maytag), ironing with flat irons (no wash-n-wear then!), raising and caring for a big garden, canning everything beyond the immediate needs, raising and caring for a flock of chickens, besides doing the routine daily chores of cooking, cleaning, sewing and mending.

We heated with wood; there was always a wood pile to replenish each fall, and a wood-box to keep filled. We pumped and carried our water from a well — for drinking, cooking, washing, and for watering the garden and the chickens. We used kerosene lamps (one Aladdin) and a battery-operated radio until I was in 8th grade when REA got that far out into the country and we became "electrified". On the rare occasions that we "went visiting" relatives or friends the visits were usually of short duration because we had to get home to "feed the chickens, gather the eggs, and do the milking".

Eliza Jack Young
By Velda Y. Zimmerman

My paternal grandmother, Eliza Jack, was born in County Antrim, Northern Ireland, February 15, 1834, third child and first daughter of John and Margaret McFarland Jack. Her name was really Elizabeth, but her mother died before Eliza was a year old and her grandmother Elizabeth Knox McFarland, for whom she was named, reared her, so, to avoid confusion, she was always called Eliza. Her mother was the oldest child and only daughter of her Grandmother. Her father kept his four year old son but he felt two year old Armour would be better cared for by his grandmother, and of course baby Eliza, also.

Grandma McFarland was living in Ireland when rain rotted the potato crop and there was real hunger. The rain that rotted the potatoes grew fine cabbage. They sold their sow and butchered the pigs and put them down in brine, but when hungry people came begging, she would give them an apron filled with cabbage and a piece of pork. From that time, she kept no stone unturned to move her family to America, and succeeded, before the great potato famine struck Ireland. They were safely in Coshocton County, Ohio, near the town of Keene before the great potato famine.

Eliza gew up with a houseful of uncles. One shot a wild turkey and sent her to pick it up. She grabbed its legs but it lifted her from the ground with its wings so she had to let it go.

They were a station on the Underground Railroad. Once a handsome young black man was found hiding in his barn by one of their neighbors who brought him to them. He had crossed the Ohio River to the home of Quakers who helped him, but his master and another man found him there. The Quaker man engaged the men in conversation after putting much wood in the stove and when the room grew hot, opened a window for ventilation and one of the girls stood in front of the window and the other one motioned him toward it so he climbed out of the window and ran, but was shot in the leg as he fled. The uncles had a fine horse and buggy and dessed the black man well and drove through the town with him while brothers mingled with the men who decided he must be a free negro. The brothers wanted them to try to capture just to have the laugh on them. Of course they took him on to another station that night.

Another close call was when a black mother with several children were being hauled in daylight to another station and were passing a school where the children were playing and a little black runaway lifted the quilt a bit to see the children who set up a big outcry that slaves were escaping. The boys drove into the woods and told the mother and children to hide and return to a certain tree after dark when they would pick them up. Then they drove along and men came to them looking for the runaway slaves the children reported. The brothers excused the children for thinking they saw something and were convincing. That night the mother was at the right tree with every child, so they delivered them safely.

Eliza was sent to Academy which was an unusual privilege. When her grandfather died, he included her in his will in place of her mother. After his death, she went to Indiana with her grandmother and taught school until her marriage to James Young. (See James Young).

As a child living with her Irish grandmother, she was teased for her strange speech and ways until she went with her grandmother to a women's work meeting where she carded wool so skillfully one mother went home and told her daughter never to tease Eliza Jack again as she had shown herself so capable. This girl quit teasing her and since she was a leader, the others quit, too.

Grandmother taught her children, "Just do your work well and you will be accepted". When their children said they didn't know how to do something, their father would say,"Just do the best you can, You'll never learn younger".

Eliza's home was always open to those in need of care — especially the aged. She would care for them in her home when their family wouldn't, or if they had no family, as with John Cannon, aged 90, whose stone they erected in Union Cemetery.

She had a topless buggy to which she drove her faithful bay pony, Queen, to visit her children. After Queen died, when Eliza was past 80, her great-granddaughter, Mava Young, was so excited seeing her walking up the road to visit them on her farm, one and one-quarter miles from where she lived with her daughter, Nancy McFarland, that Mava told her mother "Great-grandmother is coming!" She had walked a mile to our house and then after visiting awhile, had walked on.

When they moved to Kansas from Indiana, and she saw the neighbors could not afford woolen dresses for church, she sent Mary's and Nancy's woolen dresses back to Indiana for relatives there to wear and dressed her daughter in cottons like the neighbor girls could afford.

If she saw a woman who was a good seamstress but had a large family, she might quietly buy a bolt of muslin for making underclothing for the daughters.

Her Christmas gifts to granddaughters included a child's rocker, doll's trunk, set of china dishes, dolls, gold lockets, an Indian paper Bible with leather cover.

When she was 86, her daughter, Nancy from whom she had never been separated, moved to Florida with her family. Her oldest son, John, built a room for her like the one she had at Nancy's, onto his house for her, and welcomed her into their home where she saw her oldest granddaughter married. She lived to be 88, but gradually failed in health. Her sons, John and Calvin, sat up with her nights, and her daughter, Nancy, returned to help for some time. She died June 7, 1922. The Rev. George R. McBurney of Sterling, Kansas, preached her funeral sermon based on Ecclesiastes 7:1b "the day of death (is better) than the day of one's birth", explaining that we rejoice at the birth of a baby into this world of trial, pain and woe, and how much more we should rejoice in the birth of a saved soul into eternity with the Lord. What a comforting thought!

Forty-three years later, his grandson preached from the same text at the funeral of Mother's youngest sister.

James Young
By Velda Y. Zimmerman

My grandfather, James Young, was born May 6, 1829, in Beaver County, Pennsylvania, the fourth child and first son of John and Mary Ann Clyde Young. When James was two, they moved to Logan County, Ohio, and were charter members of the Reformed Presbyterian Church. Mary Ann died at the birth of their seventh child. Later, John re-married.

When James and his brother John

James and Eliza (Jack) Young about 1903.

heard of a charivari, they wondered what it was like, and knowing their parents would not permit them to go, went to bed as usual but slipped out the window and went. Real damage was done but the perpetrators ran, and James and John who were "innocent bystanders" were recognized and sued for damages. Their father's lawyer told him to have the boys leave the state immediately and stay away while their parents testified in court to what they knew — that the boys went to bed as usual — the rest was hearsay and not admissible as evidence by the parents. The boys fled to Indiana.

In the Lake Eliza congregation, Lake County, farthest northwest county of Indiana, James met a young school teacher, Eliza Jack, whom he married November 30, 1853. Three of their seven children born in Indiana ultimately came to Noble County, second child and first son, John W. Young, sixth child and fourth son, Calvin L. Young, and seventh child and third daughter, Nancy, Mrs. J.C. McFarland.

They sold their first farm to move closer to church and school, its payments to pay for the farm they bought, but the buyer never made a payment. Fortunately, a railroad was being built to Chicago so the men got jobs building and Calvin who was only twelve was water boy, Eliza rented their upstairs bedrooms to the building crew and provided their meals, so they managed to pay for the new farm and had two farms to sell when two bouts of pneumonia suffered by their oldest boy, John, reputed to cause tuberculosis if he suffered a third attack, caused them to decide to move to the high, dry prairies of Kansas, settling near Zenda, in Kingman County, in 1883.

When Old Oklahoma was opened to settlement, April 22, 1889, three sons and a daughter were old enough to take claims, and did, twelve miles west of Edmond. The family lived with the second daughter on her claim, but she and her brother contracted measles in their late 20s and died, John's wife died at the birth of their seventh child, second son died of tuberculosis, and Harvey, first son of J.C. and Nancy Young McFarland, died at the age of two.

When the Cherokee Strip opened, James had not used his homestead right so joined his son, Calvin, son-in-law, Jim McFarland, nephews Armour and Oscar Henderson, Eliza's cousin, George McFarland, and Matthew Chestnut in making the Run and staking claims. His claim is from the water tower of Billings north a half mile and west a half mile. A granddaughter, Viola Wylie of Hays, Kansas, owns the part of his claim adjacent to her father's claim which she also owns.

James and Eliza slept in their house the warmer months each year until they had proved up on their claim, just as Calvin did, but they all ate together at McFarland's where they celebrated their 50th wedding anniversary, November 30, 1903. On that occasion, they each received a new rocker so Nancy cared for the new baby, Grandma Young the one next older, and Grandpa Young, the one older than that. With five boys and three girls, the rockers had much use.

Jim took care of the livestock, Calvin worked the fields, James helped wherever needed, whether fencing or grandchildren. Grandma Eliza helped daughter, Nancy, in the house and with her children and gardened diligently. When she was a girl, tomatoes were called "Love Apples" and grown in the flower gardens for their beauty but supposed to be deadly poison so Grandmother never tasted one in her life, but grew them faithfully.

James and Eliza were Covenanters, Reformed Presbyterians who were determined to read the Bible for themselves and worship as they believed it taught. When Scotland had Catholic rulers determind to make Catholicism the religion of Scotland, they burned every Bible they could find. One woman saved theirs by baking it in a loaf of bread where they did not find it. Men often had to hide in caves in the hills while their wives kept the home farm producing enough to care for the children and the father in hiding. Women grew strong with the responsibility. Men often escaped to Ireland where their families joined them and ultimately came to America and religious freedon.

James Young's parents were born in Pennsylvania which had been settled by Quakers who do not kill. Indians killed settlers so Quakers soon offered western Pennsylvania land to Scotch-Irishmen who would defend them from the Indians. James Young's parents were charter members of their congregation in Logan County, Ohio, near Bellegontaine. His mother died there at the birth of their seventh child. His father later remarried and his second wife died at the birth of their seventh child. Eight years later, his father died, but a sister, Agnes mothered the children who migrated to Eskridge in Wabaunsee County, Kansas. Aunt Agnes lived to be 93, cherished by the younger boys as if she had been their mother.

As a young man, James had such good balance that he danced a jig on the ridgepole of a barn when just the frame was up. He was inventive enough to design a plow and have it patented. Although he was a farmer with three young sons, he was an Indiana volunteer the last year of the Civil War. Eliza treasured his letters home and kept them the rest of her life. None of her letters reached him so she took the three little boys by train to his camp but had to change trains on the way. The depot agent would not tell her how to go to the next train because it was not on their line. She found the way but always told her children to be thankful modern competitors are more accommodating.

They kept the Sabbath as a day of worship and rest, wherever they went, and had services in homes or schools, inviting the neighbors. When Billings was settled, they built a church where the funeral home now stands, and were buried from it. James died March 25, 1909. Eliza died June 7, 1922, at the age of 88, in the home of her son, John.

Margaret Black Young
By Velda Y. Zimmerman

Margaret S. Black, my mother, born April 12, 1876, in Clay County, Kansas, third child and second daughter of John and Margaret Chestnut Black who were charter members of the Republican City

Margaret S. Young and Calvin L. Young.

Reformed Presbyterian Church, and whose grandparents were members of the Hebron Reformed Presbyterian Church which did not vote, grew up among many cousins as her father had two sisters and her mother had four brothers nearby with families. She was christened Margaret S. — her father wanted her named Susan for his little sister but her mother disliked the name "Susan" so he just said "S". When my father asked what "S" Stood for, he called her "Sadie" as his special love name for her.

Her seatmate for seven years and roomate for two years moved to Colorado so Margaret was saving her money to go visit her when her sister, Anna, and her fiance Armour Henderson, persuaded her to accompany them on the train to Oklahoma so Anna wouldn't be disappointed in her future home and would know what to prepare for it. Margaret thought that would be her only chance to see a "new country" so she went. Calvin Young and his sister Nancy's husband, Jim McFarland, came to meet their cousin's fiancee. Mother did not know which one was married but she thought the tall one was the most interesting man she had ever met. He suggested Armour take the girls to the dedication of Freedom Church but Armour lost the way, and never got there, so Calvin rode the pony home dejected.

His sister invited her to her home, and he asked her to accompany him in his topless buggy to the far pasture to check on the cattle. As they passed the present site of the town of Billings, he told her there was where the new town would be. He suggested that instead of taking the train to visit their uncle and aunt who had introduced Armour and Anna, that Armour would drive his topless buggy, and he would drive his topless buggy to Guthrie where the girls had friends to visit over night, and then on to Edmond the next day.

Armour's buggy did tip over at a slanting place, but no one was hurt. Conversations of each couple was private, unheard by anyone else, yet they were traveling together. Each couple's ideas were so congenial, they could never be interested in anyone else. The girls returned home from Edmond by train. Calvin and Armour rode in one buggy and led the other to return home, together.

Margaret wrote Calvin a postcard telling of her safe journey home, mailing it to Kingman County, where the cattle were, but he left with a carload of cattle to sell at Kansas City without riding out to the post office to call for his mail. He went home by Clay Center to visit Margaret. He and her father were instant friends, but her brother asked him to explain the difference between their two churches and her mother came into the room and said shortly that they wouldn't discuss religion, not knowing her son had asked. Calvin was supersensitive and felt cut to the quick. Then as he sat between the two sisters in the back seat of the spring wagon, after Young Peoples Meeting at Hebron, a young man, assuming Calvin to be Anna's fiance, stepped up and tried to make a date with Margaret, who he occasionally escorted home from parties she'd gone to with her brother. Calvin felt devastated. He felt he had made a fool of himself. He did ask Margaret to send him a piece of the wedding cake, but he did not write back to her, and her mother and Anna sent him the cake without giving her a chance. Her mother invited the young man to dinner when Armour was there. He had objected to Margaret going to Oklahoma, saying she'd marry some Indian, there. Calvin had dressed as an Indian in the Fourth of July parade, and how Margaret wished they had a picture of him to show!

Calvin asked Armour to intercede for him but she thought he was asking her to be interested in him which made her furious for she knew how much her sister loved him. He felt her fury but didn't know why, so told calvin he could do nothing...had to look out for himself. Father sent her a beautiful valentine but the postmark was completely oblitereated so she had no idea it came from him. She made a lot of pies--she could cry while she made the pastry. About a year passed. Calvin received an anonymous note saying that Margaret was seeing no one any more. He thought her father sent it, but she was sure only her mother would do it, finally convinced Margaret's heart was with Calvin.

Calvin returned to see her and they became engaged. He helped her go to school a year in Salina and two years at Tonkawa. His mother wanted them to be married on their 50th wedding anniversary, November 30, 1903, wearing her black silk wedding dress which fit Margaret perfectly, but Margaret was a skilled seamstress who wanted to make her own wedding dress of cream mohair and lace. Calvin wanted to be married on November 9, birthday of William, his favorite brother, who had died December 30, 1899. The first day of school at the first institution of higher learning in Oklahoma, where he had been a first day student, now Central State University at Edmond, and from which he was graduated valedictorian of his Class of 1899, had been November 9, also, so they waited until November 9, 1904, to be married by Margaret's uncle Robert Chesnut, a minister as her sisters, Mary and Amelda were in Clay Center in high school and her father had gone to the World's Fair at St. Louis and to his birthplace nearby.

The wedding was at noon, followed by a wedding dinner. Then it snowed. Guests missed their train and had to spend the night in the high school girls' room in town.

Calvin had planned a fabulous honeymoon, first visiting relatives at Eskridge, then spending a month viewing the Louisiana Exposition at St. Louis, and another month Calvin helped tear down Fair structures. The Mississippi River froze over so he walked across it on the ice. They visited Uncle Robert, the minister who performed the marriage ceremony. They visited Calvin's birthplace in Indiana and the relative there, the city of Chicago, and took the train to Galveston, Texas, for a week by the Gulf, collecting seashells, before returning to Oklahoma in March.

The right two people were together, wonderful parents, whose lives were shared until Father's death at 78, May 29, 1947, and Mother's death at 78, January 4, 1955.

Anna Honegger Zimmerman

By Velda Young Zimmerman

Anna Honegger Zimmerman was born September 19, 1866 in Canton Zurich, Switzerland, fifteenth child of one set of parents. She was only five when her father died.

Her mother moved from Thalwil, west of Lake Zurich, to Wald, a factory town east of Lake Zurich where she and the children fifteen years old, or older, worked in the mill. They lived in a highrise apartment house, near the mill. When Anna was fifteen, she had to quit school and work in the mill, but she had studied diligently in school.

Lutheranism was the state religion but Anna's mother had been converted

Seated: Charles Zimmerman and grandchild Eiken. Standing (L to R): Anna Honegger Zimmerman, Rev. Calvin L. Young and Margaret S. Young.

to Methodism in which Anna and her sisters joind her, and to which she was a faithful follower all her life.

The older children married in Switzerland and remained there, but younger brothers came to America and wrote back for their mother and sisters still at home, to come also.

When Anna was twenty-one, she and her mother and two sisters came to America and took jobs near the coast to pay for their passage, but one sister, Babraba, met a young man near her brothers' in Illinois, and they were married. When their first child was expected, Barbara wrote back for the older of her two sisters to come to help her when the baby arrived. This sister had met a young man she did not want to leave so Anna asked her mother if she could not go to Barbara. She did go and helped Barbara, Mrs. Will Combrink, when the first of her eight children, Henry, was born.

Anna stayed in Illinois and worked in the homes of English speaking people so she learned English well. There she met Charles B. Zimmerman who spoke French in his home in Alsace, German in school after Germany conquered Alsasce, Latin, his six years as an altar boy in the Catholic Church which enabled him to understand the meaning of the Scriptures so he joined Anna in the Farman Methodist Church in which their eight children were christened and confirmed.

Eight children, four sons and four daughters: Will, Emil, Arthur, Louise, Ester, Emma, Helen and John were born to them.

In January, 1910, the Zimmermans and Combrinks came together by train to Billings, in Noble County, where Combrinks and Zimmermans had bought farms. The Methodist Sunday School enrolled 19 new members the day the two families first came to church.

When drouth destroyed a fine looking corn crop their first two years, Mr. Zimmerman was ready to give up, but Anna sent the older children out to work and saved their earnings in a sock and they paid their interest when it was due.

She martialed their forces to grow a garden, poultry, their own meat, milk and butter, and they prospered. Of course the men changed from corn to wheat which could be grown.

She did not complain at living in a smaller house than they had in Illinois. The girls had the upstrairs bedroom under the eaves and the boys' beds were on each side of the stairway, under the sloping roof of the story and a half house.

Compton School was only a mile away where the girls and John walked. Emma started to Billings High School and then became a trained nurse for life in Enid Memorial Hospital. Helen and John finished Billings High School, Helen in 1923 and John in 1924. Helen taught school until her marriage to Alva Holley. Louise married Reinhold Barkett and lived on their Noble County farm the rest of her life. Arthur married Beth Caskey and lived in Billings until retirement. Will married Iva Spencer whose father had the Billings Telephone company and they served Red Rock until they took over a company at Syracuse, Kansas. John married Margaret Byers and they lived on the Zimmerman farm until they went into the hatchery business in Nicoma Park. Esther married Robert Pursifull who was in Midco and Three Sands oil fields before Seminole and Elk City but they have retired to Tonkawa and are the only survivors of those mentioned above. They will soon celebrate their 62nd Wedding anniversary and Robert has celebrated his 91st birthday. They have three sons, a daughter, many grandchildren and great-grandchildren.

Charles and Anna Honegger Zimmerman retired to Billings when John married and lived there the rest of their lives. She walked to church as long as she was able and Emil would bring her home after church. Her Bible was her constant companion and her faith never wavered. Truly she could say, "I have kept the faith. Henceforth there is laid up for me a crown of rightiousness, which the Lord, the righteous judge, shall give me at that day: and not to me only, but unto all them also that love his appearing." 2 Timothy 4: 7,8.

Charles B. Zimmerman
By Velda Y. Zimmerman

Charles B. Zimmerman was born in French Alsace, June 15, 1859. When he was a schoolboy, Germany attacked Alsace and he and his mother fled to the snowy woods with the other mothers and children. One mother screamed, "We'll all die! We'll all die!". He was proud of his mother's courage when she replied, philosophically, "We'll all die sometime."

When the battle was over and they returned to their village, blood had literally run into the well in the center of town where they all got their water. After that, he had to go to school in German, but his mother permitted only French to be spoken at home. As an altar boy, he studied six years of Latin so when he took his military training in the German army, they had him help the medics because of his knowledge of Latin. After he was home from military training, he was notified he was to return for more training. Rather than do that, he slipped into Switzerland and came to America. After he was here, he was notified it was another Charles Zimmerman who was to serve, but he could not afford to return. In his job in brick construction work, he interpreted French, German, Italian and some Spanish for his employer until a load of bricks fell on his head. When he had recovered sufficiently, he went to work on a farm in Illinois. There he met a Swiss girl, Anna Honegger, born September 19, 1866, in Canton, Zurich, fifteenth child of one set of parents. She was only five when her father died so when she was fifteen, she had to quit school to work in the mills. The two brothers came to America and wrote back for their mother and sisters at home to come over so they did, when Anna was 21. The older sister, Barbara, met and within three weeks, married Will Combrink. When their first son, Henry, was to be born, she wrote asking her next sister to come to take care of them but the next sister did not want to leave her boy friend, so Anna, the youngest, asked her mother if she could go. She did go and that is how she met Charles Zimmerman in Illinois. They both spoke German. He was writing her a letter when his employer asked him to drive a young team to the mower. The team ran away and he was thrown on a post the mower struck, crippling his leg, but they married October 1, 1889, and he farmed for one landlord whose sons took over the farming after ten years and then ten years for another landlord whose sons were ready to take over just when his brother-in-law, Will Combrink, was planning to come to Oklahoma to buy a farm so he came along and also bought a farm, the west half of Section 19, Township 23 North, Range 2 West in White Rock Township.

In January, 1910, the Zimmermans and their eight children and the Combrinks and seven of their eight children

Front Row (L to R): Charles B. Zimmerman, Helen Holley, John Zimmerman, Anna Zimmerman. Back Row: Louise Barkett, Emil Zimmerman, Emma Zimmerman, Arthur Zimmerman, Will Zimmerman and Esther Pursifull.

came by train to Billings. The Zimmermans lived five miles south and a mile west of Billings and the Combrinks two miles north of town. The day the two families went to church they increased Methodists by nineteen people.

They planted corn which looked fine until hot winds blew and burned it up. The seller was sure he would get his farm back but Mrs. Zimmerman had the older children work out and bring her their money which she put in a sock. When the farm payment came due, there was money to pay it. The second year the corn again looked fine before scorching in the hot wind, but again the contents of the sock saved them. Then they wised up and planted wheat which grew in the cool months and was harvested before the hot winds.

In 1917, Will and Arthur were conscripted in the first draft and sent to France. Will had been born July 14, 1890, married Iva Spencer, and died January 3, 1955. Emil was born December 17, 1891, married Velda Young, and died September 8, 1952. Arthur was born July 12, 1893, married Beth Caskey, and died September 17, 1969. Louise was born October 21, 1895, married Reinhold Barkett, and died November 2, 1968. Esther was born April 1, 1898, married Robert Pursifull, and they have celebrated their 61st wedding anniversary. Robert will be 91 on September 12, 1985. Emma was born November 3, 1900, nursed until retirement, and died November 23, 1979. Helen was born August 7, 1904, married Alva Holley who died in 1953, married Paul Sparks, June 17, 1969, and died July 12, 1967. John married Margaret Byers, and died October 27, 1967.

Charles Benjamin Zimmerman had a strong set of values. As a renter, he scrupulously paid his rent, making sure his landlord received every penny due him.

When the children ate some apples from a neighbor's tree limbs hanging over the fence as they walked home from school, he took them to the neighbors to apologize. The neighbor assured him they were welcome to the apples, but he wanted his children to respect the property of others.

The children and grandchildren helped the Zimmermans celebrate their 50th wedding anniversary, October 1, 1939. Charles B. Zimmerman died October 6, 1940, and Anna Zimmerman died April 15, 1945.

Emil H. Zimmerman
By Velda Y. Zimmerman

Emil Henry Zimmerman, second son of Charles B. and Anna Honegger Zimmerman, was born December 17, 1891, on a farm near Straun, Illinois. One day before he was old enough to move about, he disappeared from the bed where his mother left him. She found him under the bed, happily playing with his hands, and decided toddler Will had pulled him off the bed and shoved him under. Tall corn grew all about and when he was older he went out to the field with his father but tired and started back to the house. When he did not appear, his mother hunted through the tall corn for him and fortunately found him fast asleep, between the rows. He drove a team behind his father and his brother, Will, when he was only five. He was the "horse boy" of the family. Horses sense a driver who understands them.

When Arthur, Louise, Ester, Emma, Helen and John were babies, their mother often had to stay home with them but his father would take the older boys to church.

Emil always worked. Since German was the one language his parents shared, they spoke German at home and belonged to the German Methodist Church. Emil had to learn English at school, but he was a good listener, learned to speak English quickly, and spoke better English than many college graduates. He could always outrun his schoolmates.

When he was just eighteen, the family moved to a farm five miles south and a mile west of Billings, in January, 1910. His mother's sister Barbara, Mrs. Will Combrink, who also had eight children, moved to a farm two miles north of Billings, coming by train at the same time. The day the two families went to the Methodist Church, they added 19 to the Sunday School Roll. Afterwards, both families would go to one home to dinner. The Zimmermans rode by my home in an open surrey with the parents and John in front and the four girls in the back seat. Behind them came the three big boys in a top buggy. I always admired the tallest one, Emil, built so like my father, but I never dreamed he would be available when I grew up for he was a six-foot three-inch eighteen year old while I

Emil and Velda Zimmerman and children Eileen, Loyalea and Ywain.

was a pre-school four. When I was eight, I looked at him and thought, "I'll notice him particularly for he's the kind of man I'll marry when I grow up." I was always looking for a man like him in my generation but never found one. He was an expert corn shucker and shucked Iowa and Illinois corn.

Will and Arthur were taken in the first draft in World War I. Emil was called in the second draft but excused by the county since he was the only able-bodied man on the farm. He was called again on the third draft but excused by the state for the same reason. He was called again on the fourth draft but there was no place to go for deferment so he packed his bag to take the next troop train, when the armistice was signed.

He continued farming until John married and their parents moved to town. He stayed a year to help John get started farming before taking an oil field job at Seminole, where he lived with the Pursifalls. John soon left the farm to run a hatchery in Nicoma Park so Emil returned to the farm and batched. He and his brother-in-law, Reinhold Barkett, each farmed a half section and rented another quarter they farmed together.

The summer of 1936, Emil read in the Billings News that Velda Young and Mildred Baker had toured Texas and visited Texas Centennial. He wished he had been with them. A year from then, he and Velda Young were on their honeymoon. On July 31, 1937, he and Velda Sadie Elizabeth Young were married in her home by her father, The Rev. Calvin L. Young, witnessed by their mothers, Mrs. Anna Zimmerman and Mrs. Margaret Young. The bride was attended by the groom'a sister, Emma Zimmerman as bridesmaid, and the groom was attended by John Black, cousin of the bride, as best man.

The high point of their honeymoon was Pike's Peak, as Emil had never seen a mountain, before, although his mother had grown up in the Swiss Alps.

Two daughters and a son were born: Eileen Fern, July 5, 1938; Loyalea Velda, April 26, 1941; and (Emil) Ywain on August 20, 1943.

In 1944, they moved to their farm near Sterling, Kansas, where Emil succumbed to internal cancer, September 8, 1952, when he was sixty, leaving daughter Eileen, 14; Loyalea, 11; and Ywain, barely 9.

On August 13, 1957, Eileen married Wesley William Learned, son of Wilmer and Vivian Hendeshot Learned. On May 20, 1963, Loyalea married Charles Eugene Carraher, son of Charles E. Sr. and Addie Curless Carraher. On August 10, 1964, Ywain married Donna Mae Kessler, daughter of Jack and Elaine Kessler.

There are now sixteen grandchildren, eight boys and eight girls. They are: Learneds: (Wesley) Lewain, June 30, 1958; Alan Emil, February 24, 1960; Laren Layle, April 27, 1962; Sherilyn Eileen, June 11, 1964; Merryle Layne, October 12, 1967; and Lovella Louise, June 5, 1970. Carrahers: Charles Emil, February 28, 1964; Shawn Michael, November 9, 1966; Michelle Loyalea, October 3, 1968; Erin Yale, February 10, 1970; Heather Renae, August 15, 1971; Colleen Yvette, September 1, 1976; Shannon Sharee, April 20, 1978; and Cara Lea, February 11, 1983. Zimmermans: Donald Ywain, January 9, 1969 and Renk Elaine, August 15, 1973.

Alan Learned married Sandra Parnell, December 18, 1982. She was the fifth generation of friends of our family but they met at college and became interested in one another without knowing of the long family friendships. The first place her great-grandfather, Jasper Milligan, farmer near Billings from 1912-1925, was taken calling on a neighbor by his mother when he was an infant was the home of my great-grandmother. My grandmother, a girl of 14, carried the baby around in her arms. The families moved to Kansas and Jasper married my mother's first school teacher. She and my mother always loved each other dearly. Mother was the only one besides their family present at her death from cancer, early Christmas morning, 1924. Alan is going for his Doctorate in Chemistry at the University of Utah. Sandra is Executive Secretary for a Doctor.

Zimmerman family 1950. Emil and Velda and children Eileen (standing). Seated Ywain and Loyalea.

Velda Young Zimmerman
By Velda Young Zimmerman

I, Velda Sadie Elizabeth Young Zimmerman, am writing this in the house where I was born, November 22, 1905, near Billings, in Oklahoma Territory, 79 ²/₃ years after.

July 31, 1937, I married Emil Henry Zimmerman in this room. This summer, five of our grandchildren are home, here, but this fall, three of them will be in college in West Virginia, Texas and Kansas, and only one yet in high school.

I had wonderful parents, loving, understanding, wise. We were all creative people. My first August, Bunch Creek flooded and was going to wash out the dam father had made for a stock pond. He called mother and her visiting sister, Amelda, upstairs to watch it. When I complained, downstairs, he held me and walked me up, step by step. Another day I disappeared. Mother and Amelda looked everywhere. Where could a crawling baby go? Then a bell tinkled — father's school bell, sitting on the hall floor upstairs. I had crawled upstairs which was pitch dark with all the doors closed.

When I tramped on the strawberries my second summer, Mother set me down and put some berries in my lap and told me about God who made the berries for us to eat, not to tramp on. That night when they said their prayers, I wanted to say one too, so she taught me "Now I Lay Me" without the reference to death.

My third August they got me a puppy named Tom Brown for the man who sold him, and he was my constant companion outdoors. They thought if anything happened to me, Tom Brown would come home, but we came home together for fourteen years and two months and I've placed a little concrete memorial stone in his memory at the foot of Father's memorial stone in Union cemetery.

Father was always studying something by shaded kerosene lamp on the dining table long winter evenings. Before I could read, Mother brought out her geography and showed me the maps and explained the directions, mountains and rivers running to the seas so I have a geographic memory and like to travel to see other places. She took me to visit first grade and asked Mrs. Long and Mrs. Ponton if I could visit their daughters when my parents had an errand for groceries. They and my mother and Mrs. Hayton and Mrs. Reed visited with our wonderful first grade teacher, Miss Hattie Pruitt, first day of school.

The door of our new brick school room was locked and could not be opened but the janitor helped some of us through the open window while he unscrewed the hinges and took off the door to let the rest enter. Miss Pruitt held up a shiny red apple and asked us what it was. When we said "apple" she chalked an apple outlne on the board and told us that was a picture of an apple. Then she printed APPLE on the board and told us that was another picture of an apple. Then she printed "apple" on the board and told us that was another picture of an apple. Then she wrote in script "apple" and said that was still another. I was fascinated. I didn't want to go home. I wanted to stay and learn more! After school was out in May, Miss Pruitt married Fay McMullen, twin brother of our Principal Ray McMullen, and moved to Iowa.

In April of second grade, Mother and I spent ten days visiting my father in

Oklahoma City where he was taking treatment for a growth on his lower eyelid and studying Chiropractic. We visited a zoo, a circus monkey escaped into trees across the street until drowned down by the fire department, so Mother had me write about it to her sister teaching school who had her five 4th grade girls answer, which started me on my favorite activity, writing letters, as Uncle Sam's mail finds our friends wherever they are.

During the "flu" epidemic of 1918, my parents kept me home from school, herding horses along the roadside, studying my lessons, but when I returned to school in February, I took old-fashioned diptheria with after-paralysis. Mother took it from me, much more severely, but she saved me from choking to death. By September, I was able to walk to school, embarrassed to repeat 8th grade, but soon known as a brilliant student who knew all the answers. People are uncomfortable until they know something about us, but rarely look farther than the one thing they learn. My new class had not had our good start with the wonderful Miss Pruitt, so I was graduated valedictorian of the Class of '24. In 1929, I took my B.A. from Sterling College in Kansas, "cum laude".

That summer, Sterling was flooded, Mother and I visited Colorado until it snowed, Sterling until it snowed, Billings until it snowed (Father put in the crop after his renter died in August), visited Mother's sister in Arkansas until it snowed, joined Father in Ausin, Texas for Seminary, until it snowed (snows there about every ten years).

We remained on the Billings farm during the Depression. Realizing other farm children were "depressed on farms, I started a Circle Letter among readers of Cousins League of Farm and Ranch, mailing it the day of the 101 Ranch Sale, still circulating fifty + years.

When I had saved $43 egg money, I visited friends in Kansas, Nebraska and Iowa, on my way toward the Chicago Fair until Mother's lifelong friend asked me to return to Colorado with her and her sister-in-law for $4. I did. To get a job, I became a student at Greeley, Colorado, taking two terms of typing and living in the home of Professor Finley who had taught Mother at Tonkawa and whose wife had taught her Sunday School class.

Friends brought me home via Galveston and the Billigs of Sealy, Texas. In 1936, Mildred Baker and I visited Texas friends and attended Texas Centennial. Emil Zimmerman read about our trip in Billings News and wished he had been with us. A year later, we were on our honeymoon. I had admired him from the first time I saw him, a 6 ft. 3 in. 18 year old when I was a pre-school 4. When I was 8, I looked at him and thought, "I'll notice him particulary for he's the kind of man I'll marry when I grow up." never dreaming he was the man, but I never found anyone like him in my generation. We lived on the Zimmerman farm 5 miles south and 1 mile west of Billings until Eileen was ready for school. Loyalea and Ywain were younger. Wesley and Eileen Learned and Lewain, Alan, Laren, Sherily, Merryl and Lovella live on the Young farm one-half mile north of Billings. Emil succumbed to internal cancer in five locations, September 8, 1952, but his wonderful disposition is still with us in his three children and sixteen grandchildren.

Noble County Normal Institute June 22, 1911 - Perry, Oklahoma on steps of "Old Central" 9th and Fir Streets.

Appendix A
HOMESTEADERS

Auburn Township
21 North Range 2 East

Homesteader	Patent #	Section #
Adams Sarilda J.	4199	21
All Lois M.	3246	23
Altizer George H.	1452	29
Antle William G.	6099	9
Baker William L.	273	18
Barrows Vernon W.	3141	22
Bateman Alexander	3191	12
Blackburn William G.	4234	31
Bogle Estella T.	803	6
Bowers Willard C.	4226	19
Brandon William N.	6162	10
Brewer Eli	2799	30
Brown George W.	719	4
Buckingham John F.	6707	17
Budworth William W.	2295	10
Buffington Lewis L.	7575	17
Burger Christian S.	5733	4
Buzzo George H.	788	26
Carney Theophilous C.	4027	32
Carter Mack C.	716	4
Clancy Bridget C.	2484	24
Clark Albert P.	5613	12
Clifton Susie	3683	12
Combs Alonzo F.	662	35
Conley John D.	4064	2
Covey Stephen H.	1903	5
Crane Jackson W.	2634	2
Daily Patrick	4290	9
Dawson Thomas H.	7173	4
DeBolt Amos	1293	15
Diebold Matthew	755	31
Dotts John	1246	30
Eckroat Peter F.	1351	15
Edwards William A.	6188	34
Evans Henry J.	6255	3
Eyler William O.	10155	10
Fehring Paul	6473	18
Fields James	1276	26
Flin John M.	5734	24
Frank Christ	4268	29
Frank John	2012	26
Gillmore Abednego	574	29
Graves Edward C.	2595	1
Gray Elizabeth I	4118	31
Hardesty John O.	657	7
Harding Albert	4438	14
Harrington Richard	2725	31
Harvey Hiram H.	5555	17
Hellberg Frederick	2703	27
Hess William A.	4437	21
Hopkins Isaac	6207	30
Hornberger Flora	4200	28
Hughes Henry C.	2969	10
Hull John C.	4196	1
Johnson Julia A.	914	27
Johnson Melvin	1366	30
Jones Andrew J.	9905	35
Jones Eli	3291	8
Jones Frank	656	7
Jones Pleasant A.	4096	25
Kafka John Sr.	4320	32
Kennicutt William H.	1711	21
Kerns George W.	5844	20
Kilso David L.	1495	3
Kime Isaac	2693	9
Kircher Charles F.	8294	15
Knowles George F.	1256	11
Koch Christopher	5873	28
Kopp Alois	4189	20
Lacy Charles H.	94	8
Lauderdale Marcus L.	4491	12
Lauener Fred	968	25
Lesh John	1485	19
Linden David J.	2449	14
Linden John	1314	14
Lunger Joseph L.	2970	3
McBride Carrie	1277	4
McCracken Thomas W.	2281	7
McCracken Thomas W.	3221	19
McCray Arthur	6737	34
McCurry James A.	2759	25
McDole Jacob B.	9988	25
McGeorge Thomas L.	2761	12
Millikan William F.	2662	3
Mitchell Robert J.	420	2
Mitchell Winford N.	976	11
Moberly Benjamin F.	2786	26
Moberly John B.	4186	35
Moore William N.	4436	23
Nichols Mial P.	973	19
Nichols Nettie Mae	787	12
Nichols William B.	4201	23
Nixon Daniel C.	6380	32
Notley Robert	6261	2
Olson Lewis H.	3266	1
Osborn Fred	4097	24
Osten Louis	6461	27
Owen James D.E.	2606	11
Palmer Thomas R.	1792	5
Poole William B.	373	8
Primmer William H.	1600	10
Randall George W.	2291	18
Riehemann Herman H.	2280	6
Riehemann John Henry	3251	6
Schlehuber Charles L.	1279	1
Schutz Charles	1702	24
Seals Alexander	1261	26
Shepherd Edmond	417	22
Shepherd Miram K.	4302	6
Smith George V.	4026	32
Smith Joel L.	5577	20
Smoot Mary I.	1957	5
Speer John W.	4439	15
Speer Lawrence	4207	22
Stegelmann Ernest	972	28
Thompson John N.	3966	11
Thurlo Charles H.	6256	7
Treat John S.	6340	31
Turner George W.	4017	21
Tyer Robert	592	22
Unland Edward A.	5551	20
VanAuken Frederick W.	5910	29
VanAuken James H.	572	29
Vandeventer James	1263	35
Vasek Anton	10156	14
Vollmer John	1203	17
Waller Benjamin F.	4046	27
Wallingford Charles W.	790	8
Wallis John H.	4355	34
Warnholz Marcus	419	28
West William H.	1699	25
White Charles R.	2574	23
Woods Louis O.	2640	28
Woolsey James P.	1030	5
Youree Alexander	7471	18
Zemp Joseph	1432	34

Autry Township
21 North Range 3 East

Homesteader	Patent #	Section #
Adams James F.	2378	3
Adams William	845	29
Akers Charles E.	6693	12
Allen Ethan	6852	10
Allen William E.	280	21
Anderson Hiram	1416	26
Ashlock John W.	9778	2
Baggett James N.	5659	26
Bates Lydia J.	2508	26
Bilyeu Simon N.	4069	34
Blasier Earl	481	19
Branson Clarence E.	3145	23
Campbell Mitchell	2599	11
Canaday Albert C.	2378	14
Canavan William E.	983	8
Caples Almon	6465	7
Caples Orrin	6466	7
Casity Andrew J.	1394	22
Charley John E.	889	25
Clark Henry F.	1415	23
Coe Loyd	4105	24
Collins Martin L.	980	1
Connely James W.	5675	32
Cook Allen	7	10
Cox James F.	1431	25
Crays Thomas A.	190999	21
Crites James E.	1428	24
Crockett David F.	3159	28
Cunningham Alfred	6156	9
Custer Dorothy	5546	27
Dale James R.	680	6
Daniels Allen	4451	15
Davis George B.	715	6
Davis John L.	4454	4
Day William B.	2465	30
Dever Alfred M.	7459	12
Dever Dewitt L.	4299	11
Dever Olive C.	6223	12
Dollarhide Charles S.	3528	9
Downey William F.	10566	28
Dravneok Andrew H.	5851	22
Drennen Thomas E.	566	3
Dunn Samuel M.	3190	11
Edmonson Columbus L.	358	1
Edmonson Voorhees S.	558	1
Eidson John R.	6665	34
Eisfeldt Albert	5563	17
Ellis John F.	4007	25
Elwood Harley H.	2644	18
Elwood James	1701	17
Emick Lucy C.	5741	22
Emmerson David	2458	31
Enloe Frances M.	1395	27
Frame John S.	5715	5
Frederickson Ole	2600	1
Griffith George W.	556	29
Hall Charles R.	7210	9
Hall Ethan A.	3134	34
Hall Henry W.	1393	35
Hall Latin J.	457	11
Hamm Levi	4450	14
Harting Rudolph	4315	27
Hastings Frank M.	679	6
Hetherington Charles N.	6436	10
Hibbs George J.	6262	31
Hickman Sarah E.	6226	26
Hileman Allison A.	7422	32
Hileman Daniel T.	4154	5
Hines Joseph	1392	19
Hirschler Veronika	2403	3
Hoggatt William	767	27
Hull George	819	5
Hull John	295	8
Hull Miran	433	6
Hull Thomas W.	6148	5
James Henry	1486	18
James William J.	583	2
Johnston J. Henry	2647	20
Jones Benjamin F.	4244	14
Just Christ	2598	4
Kent Abraham L.	3210	17
Kent Jacob	958	8
Kent Samuel J.	107	8
Kerr Elias	6263	31
Kindt John	500	19
Kniseley William T.	3125	35
Lane Daniel T.	3975	17
Larrison John H.	5587	4
Lauderdale William J.	2455	32
Libby Ivory H.	4432	21
Long Fielding H.	978	2
Loper Charles	1430	20
Masoner Morgan	6049	20
McAdow James F.	7145	21
McClellan Charles M.	50	11
McClure William L.	5842	21
McCurry William A.	2760	30
McKinnon Uriah B.	582	14
Miller Abraham	3146	23
Monforte Joseph C.	600	10
Monhollon Isaiah	1070	18
Moore James W.	2459	30
Morgan Patrick M.	5966	15
Morrison Roselda	5679	17
Norris Charles I.	7209	4
Perryman James T.	144	8
Platz Charles S.	1414	24
Pooler William E.	1235	29
Potts Alexander	6033	28
Prather Charles N.	955	18
Prather James W.	2256	28
Ramsey John	3157	22
Rentfro Belle	4074	12
Robbins Daniel	3053	32
Robinson George	741	7
Sabrovskie Ludwig	2045	34
Sadler Madison H.	3951	15
Sanders David	833	7
Sayre Wesley A.	4446	12
Sears John W.	1396	35
Shiever Stephen	6753	4
Slack William K.	3158	27
Sprague John R. Jr.	2992	32
Stafford Nellie	1017	30
Swearingen Charles W.	3211	9
Taulbee Green M.	4103	24
Testerman Andrew J.	681	20
Testerman Eli T.	2460	19
Teter Samuel	274	7
Thompson George E.	2457	31
Turner Walter	1413	25
Underwood Joseph	5559	2
Webb Horace M.	4486	15
Webb Lou	6149	9
Webb Sanford	5560	2
Wells Eliga	4104	23
Wheeler Holland	308	29
Williams Edward W.	1310	25
Williams Swain O.	2784	35
Wright Jacob E.	4266	9

Black Bear Township
22 North Range 1 West

Homesteader	Patent #	Section #
Acres Allen I.	3133	34
Arnold Clinton L.	2620	14
Baker Samuel	6398	17
Barnes George A.	1626	20
Barnes Leonard	1518	22
Barnes Marion L.	7558	17
Beale Charles M.	242	10
Belcha Frank	6022	8
Bowman Mary E.	812	12
Briscoe Andrew	2827	35
Briscoe Harry	2702	35
Brokaw John P.	6143	10
Brown William H.	1072	27
Carter William M.	109	17
Casey Daniel	467	3

Homesteader	Patent #	Section #
Chisam William B.	124	28
Chrz Anton	2169	32
Civish Anton	589	25
Cizek Joseph	4005	12
Conaster Jospeh L.	998	25
Cook Michael	454	1
Coyle Ed J.	345	21
Darmer John R.	98282	5
Datel James	952	7
Davidson Henry S.	761	21
Dolezol Ella	6551	6
Dykes May	3062	20
Eret Anna	4165	4
Everett Turner C.	910	18
Fairbanks Levi W.	2694	29
Field Mary P.	786	11
Firestone Sarah E.	6093	27
Gengler Peter	990	5
George Thomas J.	484	15
Grant Thomas W.	707	22
Gravin Carrie E.	02444	23
Guthrey Maude	416	21
Harrah William C.	465	31
Harrison Hubert	4117	32
Hausam Andrew	2855	24
Henriksen Niels P.	691	14
Holcomb Charles L.	2420	15
Holmes James E.	749	18
Hostetter Francis H.	2585	19
Howard Joseph W.	71	32
Hubbartt Mary E.	2646	20
Humphrey Christoher C.	2022	9
Hynek Fanny	376	2
Hynek Joseph H.	3979	11
Janousek Joseph	2509	31
Jedlicka Albert J.	529	26
Johnson Davis M.	1764	6
Jones Charles H.	3131	2
Jones Fred F.	1318	2
Jones Negley H.	356	3
Jones William W.	4188	28
Kasl Barbara	6554	8
Kasl Joseph J.	2573	17
Keith Alonza G.	717	1
Kenton Orville M.	6192	34
Kerns Tina M.	5586	28
Kirchner Peter L.	5960	30
Kirchner William H.	453	26
Kirtley Hattie	1045	29
Kirtley William M.	214	29
Kostecka Joseph	2635	25
Kostecka Thomas	4155	24
Lausen Christan	4179	22
Lester Melvin J.	337	15
Little William Thomas	3815	30
Lovenburg Jerome J.	2841	6
Maupin Charles S.	4219	35
McCarthy Phillip	2619	23
McLimans John R.	7231	8
McMullen William	1543	6
Minor Charles S.	5564	12
Minor James W.	4279	1
Minor John L.	1411	1
Minor Lucy A.	276	19
Monnett Norman N.	5840	27
Monnett Rachel	890	15
Moore Elizabeth	1068	2
Moore Thomas H. Jr.	827	26
Morgan Robert W.	5554	7
Mouser George H.	959	32
Nemec Albert	1061	9
Nemec Annie L.	1062	10
Newton John	5735	9
Nicewander Austin C.	530	31
Novak Frank R.	2443	7
Palecek Vincent	3318	24
Palmer Fred A.	1035	3
Parker Charles H.	573	34
Parker Walter A.	2395	34
Pattison Willis W.	144	28
Pease Sarah L.	664	19
Pomeroy Charles I.	28	31
Prochazka Wencel	1005	25
Prokop Frank	597	10
Prucha Vaclav	3169	22
Queen John B.	30	23
Quinton John J.	2016	28
Rasmussen Rasmus	5935	30
Rendla Charles	590	26
Risdon Clarence P.	2967	18
Romine George G.	4185	18
Rothgeb Daniel D.	1262	11
Routh John	684	29
Schmutzer Henry J.	2787	4
Seton Clark	3160	14
Silver Jacob R.	608	8
Skalenda Frank	4443	19
Smith George A.	1063	21
Smith Sylvia	5665	21
Sokol Joseph	4272	7
Stroud Ephraim J.	1034	9
Swarens Barton L.	6008	30
Swartz Frank	3977	4
Sykora Frank	717	24
Taylor Newton E.	2021	8
Taylor William J.	1372	35
Thomason Charles S.	5572	12
Thompson Ai	1312	23
Thompson E. D.	515	4
Thompson Robert L.	989	5
Vavra Anna	4062	6
Waltermire Elwood J.	72	14
Warren Andrew E.	212	11
Wilcoxen Albert F.	2778	27
Willbarger Harvey H.	1935	5
Wilson Elba N.	8360	8
Young James K. O.	518	3

Bunch Creek Township
24 North Range 2 West

Homesteader	Patent #	Section #
Akins Joseph N.	130	10
Armstrong James S.	1252	35
Arney David L.	6503	20
Back Georgia A.	3707	22
Back Phillip G.	3640	22
Ball James E.	562	26
Bankston Ed	4131	8
Beach Nicholas J.	2071	34
Beaudoin Frank H.	1721	3
Bell Leonard	1000	25
Betty Robert C.	2179	20
Bollinger John F.	217	14
Borland Louis	5725	2
Brewer Parmelia	5902	6
Brown John F.	947	21
Brown Larren A.	906	27
Brown Vance	6950	21
Bryant Metellus	1755	15
Buzzard Paul	200	5
Chiles Archibald H.	1854	8
Clavin James	4081	2
Compton Robert M.	3099	12
Coomes James E.	429	4
Cooper Sarah A.	4121	24
Curby William	5809	23
Davis James M.	95	17
Dixon Frank	720	15
Dufek Frank	1447	9
Edgerly Charles C.	5566	24
Edgerly Truman A.	982	24
Einwachter John	6314	25
Elliott Elisha V.	1053	32
Elliott Perry S.	1253	32
Fehrenback Philip	3744	2
Foster Amos M.	2178	7
Fraizer David C.	2377	8
French Charles E.	6479	9
Fuls Wilbur	325	6
Glines James E.	903	10
Gottlieb Kletke	1862	2
Grimes William	392	6
Haile Thomas A.	3549	27
Hair Eugene	5900	3
Hansen Hans B.	1023	1
Harrison Rebecca	2020	22
Harrison Walter S.	3960	23
Hedgecock Barney J.	1855	9
Heimback George	2057	5
Henderson Armour J.	2819	34
Henderson Oscar W.	2981	34
Henry Barbara A.	5565	4
Hickl Frank	6874	1
High Clark E.	983	4
High Frank P.	2042	3
Hoge Edward O.	904	12
Hoge Zimri W.	907	1
Holmes John L.	905	18
Huckelberry Charles F.	435	12
Huddleston David F.	3317	34
Hudson Alfred L.	4405	31
Hurst James P.	1897	20
Imhof Samuel	2982	15
Jenkins George W.	1356	1
Kern William J.	7012	28
Kettenring Martin S.	203	29
Kratzer Adolf	2753	14
Lalicker Charlie S.	965	18
Lawson John	5905	23
Lawson Reuben G. B.	7170	35
Lemmon Bertie O.	1057	32
Lemmon William P.	1693	32
Logan Maurice S.	1788	1
Lowry James A.	437	35
Lundbeing Charles T.	2171	14
Lusk Selah	1908	26
Macy Claude	981	11
Major Joseph E.	2980	31
Maltby George K.	6058	24
Maltby William H.	1488	25
Martin Robert	1255	6
Matthiesen Andrew	3641	23
McCluskey James	6865	17
McFarland George	3031	19
McFarland James C.	3616	30
McGaha Marion W.	2752	11
McKeown Frank S.	1966	28
McKeown Peter H.	1967	28
McKeown Thomas	1968	29
Menihan William H.	6059	29
Moore Richard	5825	17
More Anson B.	2422	8
Murray Addison	4453	25
Murray George	7493	26
Myers Merit C.	4469	27
Nelson John A. D.	964	19
Noonan James C.	3348	20
Odenwald Joseph Christopher	3734	11
Olmstead Eugene	4120	7
Opdylke Levi	5817	19
Pitts Stephen A.	5943	31
Ponton Louis	6288	12
Renfrow Lee Ann	2019	22
Riley Abraham	2060	5
Riley Andrew J.	2054	4
Riley Elmer	2053	5
Rout Virgil	2755	35
Sanders Joseph	2979	21
Schwaba William E.	1052	30
Seegers George	3745	11
Seitz Adam	35	18
Seitz Charles S.	2176	7
Seitz James B.	2177	7
Sell David M.	967	10
Sheldon Fannie K.	4214	21
Smith Charles H. L.	1027	29
Strobel Albert G.	197	10
Tribbey G. William	1141	24
Waggoner McClellan	6929	26
Walsh Walter	6101	18
Ward Camille	7216	14
Weaver Leonard	200	29
West Roy W.	3201	17
Wilkins Frederick	1319	15
Wilkins Magdalena	6861	31
Wilson Margaret J.	202	30
Winter Frank	2448	28
Wolf Adam	81	3
Yeoman Joseph W.	664	9
Young Calvin L.	3617	19
Young James	201	30

Glenrose Township
24 North Range 1 West

Homesteader	Patent #	Section #
Baggs Alexander	531	26
Barrett Myrtle	1983	19
Barrett William	387	19
Beeks Frank	2263	12
Bellmon George D.	5971	29
Billups Oliver C.	6084	6
Birkes Frank M.	1818	34
Blair Deziel	5860	19
Blubaugh Cletus	1199	27
Brookhart Catharine M.	2094	4
Buck Stephen R.	1791	5
Burch Joel M.	297	30
Campbell James A.	6319	1
Cannon David C.	1382	34
Carpenter Andrew R.	2008	30
Carpenter William D.	5604	31
Carter William	697	20
Case Franklin M.	1930	29
Chambers Fred S.	262	28
Chapman Ernest B.	634	21
Chubb Otis T.	1802	19
Cobb Louis M.	2343	28
Collier Martha J.	5951	24
Collier Thomas H.	5953	25
Collier William L.	5952	24
Cook George W.	5775	2
Corley William J.	3532	18
Eastman Leburtis D.	2104	14
Eastman Reuben	2103	14
Emmons Whitter R.	637	21
Evans David E.	1709	10
Folk Frank P.	3136	12
Folk Joseph Jr.	587	22
Folk Mary I.	1790	23
Fountain Shermain	592	29
Frailey Thomas A.	2621	7
Frailey William T.	2136	18
Frederick John D.	1295	4
Freiday Frederick A.	1722	9
Garrett Hugh	5584	28
Gasaway Emily	1355	6
Graber Joseph H.	606	14
Hays George G.	1398	11
Hays Granvil A.	605	3
Holeman Pinkie B.	4294	17
Hook William C.	1018	32
Hubka Anne	10822	10
Huff Willis E.	2872	17
Johnson Harvey H. J.	2262	12
Jones Frank H.	6057	6
Jones Jay	1201	28
Justra Frank	1562	3
Kirk Robert	3212	4
Kirkpatrick Roeland F.	941	20
Kite Emmet B.	1165	27
Kite George W.	289	22
Kopecky Joseph	7828	24
Logan James	1055	6
Long Peter	205	14
Lusk Susan	2791	32
Manny Francis	7217	8
Manny Henry	7215	8
Mayhew James D.	2007	31
McCutchen William F.	5977	11
McGowan Frank F.	3580	7
Moore James	151	2
Moore Reuben L.	2064	11
Morris Jacob	607	15
Murray Fred	5767	17
Murray William H.	5751	30
Norman Caleb F.	1054	22
Norman John A.	399	26
Novacek Joseph	1453	26
O'Neill Peter W.	648	20
Osborn William N.	1784	27
Osborne Rachael	5704	21
Owens John R.	2792	32
Parker William S.	6330	23
Pearcy Benjamin B.	3896	9
Pearcy Milly E.	3897	9
Pettit Thomas	636	20
Pettit William	4073	30

Homesteader	Patent #	Section #
Phelps Elmer B.	128	10
Pilkington Andrew A.	1982	35
Pilkington Thomas F.	2678	35
Plumb Emma	5826	15
Postelwait Samuel	251	31
Ranes James	1228	34
Read Henry A.	635	29
Reed Andrew J.	2790	32
Regnier Louis J.	2264	1
Rence David H.	1710	11
Robb Mary A.	1047	27
Rosecrans Burd P.	2953	18
Ruzek Anne	6805	3
Ruzek Rudolph	829	3
Saper Mary A.	429	8
Sauer Joseph	1723	7
Seymour George H.	1929	19
Shawver Lee	1668	2
Siler Addison W.	2279	24
Siler Green B.	6329	23
Siler John W.	4133	23
Sipe Phillip	4142	1
Sokol Frank	1987	18
Southard Joseph	2277	5
Southworth Charles H.	589	1
Stanek Joseph	2062	26
Stransky Joseph	4311	35
Stransky William	4312	35
Sumner Jeff D.	604	10
Talbott Charles D.	6251	22
Turner James	1470	5
Vanek Albert	1986	2
Wallace William P.	793	12
Welch William R.	207	8
Wells Edward R.	1365	15
West Willis A.	1698	9
White Walter H.	6	25
Wieland Frank G.	404	17
Wilkins Frank B.	6353	34
Wilkins Fred J.	5724	31
Wintermute William H.	6792	4
Writt James E.	7983	7
Writt Joseph	3958	5
Wyckoff Edward C.	4191	25
Wyckoff Seth W.	5700	15
Yates John N.	5702	25

Lowe Township
20 North Range 2 West

Homesteader	Patent #	Section #
Adcock John L.	3290	23
Albin Ellsworth L.	6441	1
Albin William L.	6052	1
Allen John L.	957	4
Anthis Georgia Ann	5457	24
Axhelm Otto	254	8
Bailey Ernest T.	6439	1
Baltimore Charles	1406	4
Beadles James B.	18	10
Bolay Joseph	4478	21
Brauning William	7264	30
Brier John T.	7274	14
Chadwell Thomas	6051	5
Cooley Frances M.	1268	3
Cowan Charles R.	3267	32
Cox Jasper N.	2135	9
Cox Wade	6775	6
Ditto Lewis N.	376	2
Donahoe Andrew J.	6931	8
Donahoe Edward L.	369	11
Dorland Emma A.	909	19
Dowell Frank D.	1979	31
Dunn Robert F.	9454	24
Ellison Ellert	4434	31
Ellison Emma	751	31
Evans George W.	5886	22
Farr Mary F.	6813	19
Foot Frank S.	7266	23
Fowler George W.	7265	26
Fredericks Fred	1202	28
Guthrie George W.	6544	6
Haines David M.	1521	12
Hamblin Calvin M.	4467	8
Harleman Gabriel	3289	26
Harman Simeon A.	4065	2
Hay Reinhold	3963	17
Henn Frederick	5535	29
Henn William Jr.	5536	32
Hines Shedrick M.	7352	14
Hitsman Alanson E.	4300	35
Hoffsommer Adam	3965	9
Huff Lysander	6592	26
Huntzinger John M.	753	4
Isenberg Hermann	9506	25
James Alice E.	4150	27
Jerome Mansfield	4468	15
Johnson Emma	4324	35
Johnson James H.	2079	15
Johnson Richard M.	2076	10
Johnson Robert C.	2080	3
Jones Louis B.	7355	12
Ketch Alva W.	4056	24
Ketch Amos R.	2821	23
Ketch George J.	4057	25
Kirk Joseph G.	5936	3
Kolb William J.	1936	28
Koseba Charles	585	18
Kuhlman John A.	2382	23
Linden Harry	2738	30
Lippincott James	737	5
Long John H.	5537	28
Mauthe Joseph	578	20
Mayer Christian	1780	6
Mayer Frederick	1606	30
McKeown John L.	4022	5
Miller Ludwig	6202	18
Mills Duke	480	4
Minugh Charles A.	853	12
Moelling Fredrick	6283	18
Moelling John	6284	19
Morton Robert L.	6278	26
Mosely Mark A.	145	10
Moutray George M.	1947	1
Moutray James G.	1946	12
Mugler Fred	1200	28
Nauerth Jacob	4395	7
Neiman Fred H.	7269	35
Noonan Fred	2272	6
Palmer Richard S.	161696	11
Pfeiffer Gottlob J.	4194	30
Pfrimmer Elias E.	4224	7
Pratt Frank W.	2077	10
Pratt Harry V.	7407	11
Pratt Morton R.	1080	7
Pratz George	3818	18
Rice Elmer T.	4265	11
Rotterman Adam A.	597	15
Rucker Philip S.	534	20
Sampson Charles L.	4466	9
Schafer Henry	6619	27
Schnurr Anthony	6617	25
Sharp Eckley G.	16	34
Shelton Margaret C.	1367	14
Shoemaker Anna L.	3987	34
Simkins John	7267	27
Sisk Margaret C.	54292	2
Smith Daniel D.	6956	29
Smith George A.	1130	4
Smith Presley	2674	24
Snodgrass William S.	7234	7
Snyder Alexander	3964	8
Snyder Martin	1697	8
Snyder Ray	4276	14
Sprong David M.	1059	21
Staig Samuel	5538	1
Stanford John P.	1126	2
Starkey Arthur	591	27
Steinner Mathias	2623	21
Strode William W.	6446	5
Stumpff Lazarus P.	4284	15
Sult Peter	540	17
Tate Samuel S.	4368	15
Tubbs Hiram	6832	23
Urban Carl	5716	19
Vanbebber Napoleon	6618	24
Wagner Abraham	7268	34
Weber Charles	3252	20
Weber Wilhelm	1105	21
Weber Wilhelm Jr.	191	20
Weid Margaretha	1315	17
Whitmore James R.	2078	9
Wolff George	4059	22
Wolff Martin	6127	17
Wustenhofer Leo	1772	22
Young Simon W.	148	29
Young William T.	2669	25

Noble Township
21 North Range 1 East

Homesteader	Patent #	Section #
Aigner Sebestian	3997	31
Albertin William G.	8170	35
Allen Francis M.	6071	1
Allen Robert	2654	24
Arnett Everett	4157	1
Baker William H.	6048	5
Barkley Hattie	2463	31
Barrett Joseph W.	5631	32
Barrett Sara C.	5632	32
Benke Charles	6041	15
Bommer Washington G.	7260	34
Bowdon Thomas L.	409	6
Bowlby Frank S.	852	22
Boyle John S.	962	23
Brasch William F.	6800	29
Brennan Joseph M.	9805	12
Broome John F.	4470	7
Brown William	1050	28
Browning Charles W.	802	1
Brubaker Katharine	4350	11
Butterfield John L.	1797	8
Caldwell John	851	19
Campbell Jesse	2063	6
Carpenter Ira B.	6610	30
Cejka Jan	2157	14
Christner Christian H.	1077	30
Clark Raymond W.	2593	10
Cleland William A.	811	21
Clifton Charles A.	6220	1
Crain Salena	4192	4
Dalton William T.	177	12
Davis Robert	2737	10
Dempsey Mary J.	590	7
Diller George D.	3974	21
Dotts Jesse W.	1334	27
Douglass John H.	613	29
Douglass Joseph A.	612	21
Durkee Rodney H.	2658	20
Eisfeldt Albert	5563	17
Ellis John F.	4007	25
Ely Sallie M.	1218	6
Enfield Emily	6664	18
Evans James C.	2117	9
Ewart Thomas P.	4140	17
Ewart William	2255	20
Ewy Edward	5713	27
Fetter Philip	1759	24
Field Thomas D.	4060	15
Finlayson Ella J.	37	30
Flower Warren A.	1583	11
Friedekind Gustav	5908	14
Gorath John J.	8096	29
Hall Dora K.	3280	11
Hansen Mattie E.	1448	23
Hargrove Alice	6514	4
Hemstreet Albert N.	2673	24
Hendricks Aleck	20	7
Hendricks Charles	21	5
Hendricks Levi	22	7
Hendricks Martha	19	7
Herrick John	2414	32
Horn John	4267	10
Hurley David A.	3999	8
Ireland Judson F.	6509	8
Jacobs Joseph T.	6266	20
Johnson Petty	4445	35
Keele Samuel M.	2416	34
Keeler John F.	108909	22
Koelzer Anna	6389	19
Koelzer Henry	6388	30
Kraemer Adolph	3265	18
Kral Vencel	4209	5
Lambert Edker H.	4068	8
Lambert Marion	5562	9
Lancaster Thomas L.	4269	2
Latimer William T.	1298	29
Lattin Hall G.	9338	12
Lawing John R.	832	26
Layman Daniel	1129	23
Lennon Alice	1043	29
Linville Henry C.	468	26
Malcolm William H.	1086	4
Manzilla Wayne	6169	31
Mark Moab	470	25
Masek John	6438	2
Mathis Joseph C.	1969	20
McGrath John	3973	5
McKay Henry M.	2594	9
Metz John J.	8244	10
Moore Isaac A.	924	25
Moore Theresa	2059	34
Neel William	7294	3
Nemecek Josef	2584	3
Newcomb Louisa	1708	5
Nicholson Henry C.	452	18
Omelia Martin	4079	11
Omelia William	4286	11
Osborn John G.	2586	3
Osborn William S.	3192	3
Piatt Joel F.	2603	7
Pickering Asbery S.	1073	1
Piterka John	4377	27
Ramey Thomas	2033	7
Rathburn Columbus C.	7241	28
Reed Robert E.	2675	15
Renfro Ethel L.	4415	1
Rice Eugene J.	6309	18
Ritthaler Jacob	1566	15
Ritthaler Ludwig	225	26
Rousavell Lincoln J.	1104	14
Rowland Junat M.	959	6
Rupp William	4353	21
Russell Thomas	5850	32
Serles James M.	2284	4
Singleton Charles F.	5788	7
Slama Joseph	4376	27
Sneed Edward C.	4111	22
Sommars Fredrick	6508	9
Soulek Josef	3272	3
Soward Tom H.	1785	31
Stahl John	6249	17
Steadman Benjamin T.	739	2
Stevens Osrow	2653	19
Stickel Emanuel	5558	35
Stiver Mathias	6023	34
Straub Joseph	1118	14
Strickland Alfred L.	762	19
Sullivan Lewis J.	745	2
Swanson Marie L.	6165	28
Swope James H.	427	12
Sylvester Jennie	2421	28
Tobin John W.	898	26
Triggs William M.	1118	23
Viets Henry	7149	6
Viles Edwin	7437	6
Walkling Orlando	2355	23
Warner William A.	7464	22
Webster William T.	2641	24
Widiger Gustav A.	5552	32
Wilbur Leon	5502	6
Wilkinson Margaret E.	7446	35
Williams Henry A.	9923	17
Williams Thomas H.	6960	8
Willis George W.	6682	18
Wood John C.	7340	19
Ziesch John	4404	35
Ziesch Sigmund	6694	35

Oakdale Township
22 North Range 2 West

Homesteader	Patent #	Section #
Anderson Andreas C.	1561	28
Austin Joseph K.	5923	2
Ballinger Eastham L.	773	5
Barnes Richard P.	5561	26
Barnes Wesley	4375	20
Barrett James P.	2415	23
Barrett Thomas	876	15
Besco James E.	2777	1
Bilderback Jeremiah A.	3968	6
Billings Abraham O.	4282	8

Homesteader	Patent #	Section #
Birnel Lyman M.	4281	19
Blakeslie Delbert D.	819	29
Boardman Edward	6164	31
Bond James	828	28
Brink Robert J.	2961	18
Brock Clifford	764	23
Brown Joel	1607	5
Brown John C.	1633	9
Burke Harvey H.	6905	4
Chaddock Henry C.	2677	23
Churchill Clemma	2027	1
Cleveland Edward W.	947	35
Cole Dow L.	4113	29
Cowell Andrew D.	588	12
Cowell Jay J.	6996	26
Creighton Alexander A.	5789	12
Creighton John M.	2740	24
Cross Orlan E.	4479	8
Dale Anderson	5576	18
Daylor Bernard D.	1758	12
Dennis Laughlin	328	7
Detweiler Oliver B.	4464	11
Earl Fremont R.	6395	28
Eaton Alexander	763	6
Fairchild John	4301	7
Gage Walter R.	2779	2
Gallant Doc	5961	25
Gang Fred W.	2266	35
Gill William H.	5990	34
Glendening Emma	4019	3
Glendening Harper	954	3
Glendening John	565	11
Goff George F.	2748	9
Gooch Charles M.	893	17
Good Ella N.	2250	19
Gumm Newton J.	1472	24
Hackett Emry	7049	30
Hager Adolf	5967	25
Hamilton Ruben	1081	28
Hannah Robert M.	1213	22
Hardwick James C.	3992	19
Harrow Emma	4098	7
Henry Roy E.	7015	4
Hester Eber	6039	30
Hickman George V.	3135	22
Hicks Millard F.	3171	2
Hoglen Thomas	2887	1
Hollingsworth Nero D.	312	20
Hollingsworth William J.	1340	19
Holmes Jessie	5629	14
Honeywell John	2417	5
Hoover George H.	709	4
Hoover William C.	707	3
Hoppe Arthur	4001	23
Hughes Benjamin	2265	26
Jeans John Henry	4465	11
Jobe John W.	6047	15
Ketch George W.	6553	12
Ketch Thomas H.	5456	12
King Henry W.	5962	24
Kline Sylvester	785	8
Kruse Seut	4224	5
Largent William H.	6383	10
Lee Ezra J.	1888	21
Lumber Winnie	5975	25
Mayers Redmond J.	423	26
McInturff Isaac H.	6219	29
Mitchell William E.	5526	32
Monnington John	4208	4
Morrison James S.	6793	22
Morse Arthur W.	1131	17
Murphy Charles	1912	17
Murray Joseph Jr.	6663	22
Murry William L.	6352	35
Nichol Archie B.	7576	3
Nixon James H.	2854	14
Oakley John W.	5614	17
Olson Andrew C.	305	24
Padgett William E.	6170	21
Parker Joel D.	1771	21
Payne Francis M.	234	25
Peden Hiram	4442	1
Pennington Elizabeth	4134	27
Pennington Thomas	4455	9
Peters Moses M.	919	10
Pfrimmer George	4380	18
Pfrimmer John W.	240	30
Pursley Ernest E.	523	34
Pursley John	263	30
Riley John J.	3923	7
Rogers Docia A. C.	4000	14
Routh William	1033	10
Schafer Gottlob	383	6
Schaffer Max	6098	20
Shay John C.	5760	21
Shoop Lincoln G.	2783	24
Shoop William E.	6010	27
Shortridge William L. D.	895	34
Simpson Edward W.	26	31
Smelser John S.	4317	15
Smelser William O.	3065	27
Snyder Marcus J.	5578	10
Sommars Julia	925	20
Stout Charles E.	4283	9
Stovall Carroll D.	4115	35
Sullivan Marion F.	849	29
Swartz Joseph	4203	14
Thompson David	6035	31
Tontz Maggie	2648	2
Tucker William F.	2529	8
Turner Henry C.	2962	15
Underwood Charles A.	437	18
Ussery Bedford	282	11
Watts James A.	1988	32
Way William N.	816	27
Weeks James S.	485	8
Wilkinson Oliver C.	6147	32
Wiseman Mary J.	1337	31
Wolf John W.	6906	6
Wright William H.	3998	32

Red Rock Township
23 North Range 1 West

Homesteader	Patent #	Section #
Adkinson Euphrasia J.	87	17
Allen David	7484	18
Ashton Lena	1230	12
Atchison Andrew J.	1757	3
Atherton Henry Lincoln	1624	26
Barrodale Isaac	6732	29
Beaty William A.	4322	25
Blair Stephen	5798	9
Bostian Peter A.	2485	28
Bowden Rolandus A.	775	23
Brighton Nute	1403	15
Brock Edward S.	5832	29
Brock Finess	238	24
Burns Louise E.	410	19
Burnside John	971	26
Butler Frederick W.	2048	30
Byrn Riley P.	1571	30
Cable Isaac N.	38	17
Cagle Byron E.	6042	22
Carpenter Samuel D.	402	8
Casey Thomas D.	293	34
Caywood Alfred C.	394	32
Cermak Florin	5695	25
Chessher Wesley A.	1781	11
Christensen Niels C.	774	5
Cobb William F.	1042	8
Coe Benjamin	229	27
Condie John	1763	14
Cooper James	4274	3
Covey Byron	644	15
Covey Cornelius E.	3180	10
Covey Edwin F.	4035	10
Crane John F.	5556	31
Crane Miner L.	370	31
Crane Robert R.	5861	17
Crane Stephen S.	3139	31
Crow Charles A.	776	22
Darroch Abraham	294	28
Davis William S.	3796	18
Dillaplain William H.	2197	35
Donnelly Laura	6876	22
Dougan W. McKay	261	24
Dunham Harry S.	64	26
Dunham James J.	293	27
Dunham Peyton R.	4309	23
Dunham Ralph P.	2582	27
Durell John M.	5494	7
Fannin Alfred V.	1313	29
Faulkner Charles	5945	1
Foreman John H.	5783	21
Foreman John P.	7467	21
Foster Charley	1113	21
Foster George A.	2596	18
Foster Joseph T.	1114	20
Foster Robert	348	21
Gale Charles E.	1229	3
Gale Jonathan H.	1227	4
Garrett Sephus A.	1560	30
Gibson Cordelia	489	8
Gilpin William E.	970	6
Gladson Oscar W.	1569	30
Greer Francis D.	6792	24
Hamlin Hiram D.	1981	12
Hamlin William B.	1980	1
Hartert Charles J.	890	5
Hicks Edwin S.	4323	30
Hicks Howard	5557	31
Hopkins Oren	1061	20
Horn Jane	4202	20
Howe Arthur M.	1789	7
James Ira	6978	12
Johnson Bede	190	20
Jones William T.	97	6
Kelly Francis M.	502	7
Kinney Andrew J.	4235	9
Kinney Margaret T.	1625	4
Kirk Silvester	2156	5
Kirwin Albert W.	428	21
Krchov John	52380	32
Kuballa Frank	3288	2
Lang Kate V.	4401	26
Lowe Eli B.	1769	9
Lyhane Daniel T.	5944	19
Lysinger Henry P.	2764	34
Main Davis	2793	6
McClain Jacob S.	2035	2
McCormisk James S.	330	1
McCubbins Churchill H.	892	23
Mornhinweg Allen P.	1570	23
Morris John W.	686	32
Mounts John D.	4211	6
Murray Azilda	6569	4
Nagels Maurice	8203	32
Nuser William E.	1767	10
Poland Napoleon	6006	2
Potts Thomas P.	3995	3
Powell Troy	365	21
Prentice William	2655	34
Province Tharon	225	34
Prusa Anton	3273	35
Ratliff Carrol W.	4371	14
Reed Isreal H.	7014	19
Richardson James T.	1038	30
Riggs Silas S.	554	25
Roberts Robert L.	105	17
Robinson George E.	2659	8
Robinson Thomas G.	2138	29
Sailer John	533	5
Sanders Frank M.	6442	14
Siler William B.	5914	15
Smith David F.	1765	9
Smith Joseph C.	2315	28
Speer John T.	974	11
Speer Robert C.	899	10
Stackhouse Azor J.	5527	11
Stanley Jasper N.	5684	8
Stewart Joseph M.	850	1
Stockton Mollie	70	18
Stollenwerk Joseph W.	426	35
Stoner William M.	1223	35
Sullins Arthur D.	3986	14
Sullins John F.	3270	12
Sullins Oscar L.	98278	2
Sullins Walter D.	5862	11
Sutton Thomas F.	1623	4
Swacker John W.	1404	15
Tearney Henry	52	19
Tearney Joseph M.	40	19
Vance Newel W.	1076	28
VanSlyke Everett E.	2029	1
Walker William W.	4045	27
Waltermire Mattie E.	4138	22
Wells Charles E.	1405	28
Wenger David	1042	8
Witherspoon John F.	154	25

Rock Township
20 North Range 1 West

Homesteader	Patent #	Section #
Abraham Alonzo G.	2354	34
Adams Samuel A.	2781	9
Albers John B.		3
Allman Clarinda Jane	1281	4
Ames Wilson D.	4213	2
Baird Harry	209	35
Baker Marion B.	7020	10
Banta Allen M.	5726	18
Barton Charles	2273	10
Bartow Barneybus	542	14
Beach Robert E.	3219	35
Bender Oscar H.	2661	4
Billinski Joseph	682	17
Bonebrake Golias	5570	21
Booton Martin E.	561	9
Brand Philip	6697	6
Brown Francis A.	2787	4
Brown Samuel A.	1451	23
Burnison James S.	478	23
Burton George W.	512	22
Calori Flavio	1454	21
Campbell Alexander T.	1294	27
Campbell Thomas A.	82	15
Capers Ambrose M.	2991	19
Chmielecki John	687	17
Chmielecki Joseph	702	18
Clark Samuel	5784	28
Crockett Daniel J.	6228	23
Cross Solomon	6955	29
Crow Harry T.	148	35
Crowell John H.	5906	29
Daumon George	1036	7
Dennis George F.	1071	11
Dickinson Albert S.	1768	22
Easlick Henry	2121	1
Eldred Louis H.	1084	18
Ezzard Abraham H.	6265	4
Fehring Louis	8660	8
Fisher Milton A.	6362	12
Floyd John W.	840	29
Francis James H.	401	15
Fredericks Henry	1060	11
Froman Marion	1927	12
Galbreath Francis M.	4049	3
Gammon Silas	512	31
Garbe Herman	5758	7
Gish William D.	7008	34
Glasglow Maize R.	488	1
Glien Mathias F.	6570	3
Graham Farris	6136	27
Grant Robert	6381	25
Green Jesse F.	4369	28
Greening Thomas S.	10699	5
Groom Edward F.	7151	10
Hackenberg James M.	1096	34
Haman David	298	32
Hanon Andrew J.	8015	28
Hastings Sarah	1390	25
Haynes William	2591	15
Hazen Louisa	6545	3
Horn Henry	1381	20
Hubbartt Charles P.	9086	17
Hudson Anna	6467	14
Hunt John	1694	26
Hunter Alexander	430	5
Jackson Levi	1945	8
Jandera Frank	3161	20
Johnechick Frank F.	438	6
Johnson Andrew	498	15
Johnson August	7421	31
Kelly Leonard E.	6040	35
Kennedy Elias M.	6997	12
Kennedy Martha J.	1522	27
Kidd Minerva	7097	32
Kling Jacob	1753	12
Knori Samuel	9823	7
Launer Edward	1978	5
Lenz Ludwig	1712	20
Linville James L.	1674	34

Homesteader	Patent #	Section #
Lumpkin Lucius O.	5949	34
Lute George A.	2409	32
Marchbanks Jesse E.	6240	34
Martin Mary Ellen	527	15
Mason Thomas B.	178	31
Maupin Cornelius	601	26
McCauley Edward	503	29
McCoy John M.	1641	3
McDowell Richard	581	32
McDowell Thomas	192	29
McGuire Joseph	2590	30
Mikes Frank	2471	10
Mitchell Jesse A.	4072	2
Modrell George W.	1335	10
Morton Laura S.	6780	8
Nielsen Niels	4025	8
Nightingale Taylor	4374	30
Norris Isham F.	736	20
Nugent Mary A.	486	14
Palovcik Stefan	1883	24
Pecore Levi	489	19
Pohlman Charley	9906	20
Powers John A.	4099	6
Randolph Lowell W.	1766	30
Robinson Matt	4370	19
Robinson Thomas	5799	11
Roeser Peter H.	6342	22
Ross James M.	6853	2
Russ George	242	19
Rypinski Max	709	2
Sargent Samuel	1590	18
Schurkens John P.	6399	5
Shoaf John	03530	6
Short Riley	1083	25
Simpson Henry M.	42	35
Skalenda John	8230	24
Speakman David F.	2688	18
Spicer Ida M.	1485	35
Stewart Peter Y.	5640	5
Stoltenberg Laura L.	2379	2
Strom Alfred	6957	21
Svelan Stephen	4114	24
Swhindig John	5573	26
TenCate John	1348	1
Terrill Monroe	316	15
Tetik Thomas	6546	25
Tetyak Paul	2908	24
Thurston Harry R.	317	8
Trussel Edward M.	2927	22
Trussel Marcus O.	3024	22
Trussel Samuel	6312	23
Vecera Josef	3168	17
Vogel Max	2762	1
Wagner John G.	3279	25
Walton William	4480	32
West Harry F.	8817	15
White John P.	79	30
White Robert	5895	32
Wilder Charles R.	1762	20
Wills George G.	10088	11
Winkler Margaret	6161	27
Winsett Marier	3198	27
Wise John F.	5389	31
Wood Robert A.	2586	26

Walnut Township
20 North Range 1 East

Homesteader	Patent #	Section #
Allen Betsy	3993	29
Ater Henry M.	2125	28
Baker Calvin M.	7021	4
Barrett Cassius C.	10754	6
Barrett Edwin	2380	2
Barrett James D.	2602	3
Bartlett Joseph E.	725	1
Beasley Shadrick	2032	11
Benton Opal	675	3
Berger Enos	1212	1
Biggs Hiram	6009	32
Biggs Rowena	6213	11
Biggs Taylor	663	9
Bilyeu Wilber	1770	2
Bock William	5763	35
Buchanan Nancy	4067	35
Buchwald Ferdinand	4204	19
Busse Albert	3988	21
Callark Henry	5594	22
Campbell Samuel	2641	31
Carbet William H.	6734	26
Chadwick Joseph H.	5759	6
Clary Charles S.	10420	26
Clary Harrison S.	963	25
Clinger Milton B.	2747	17
Coate Thomas J.	6118	30
Coate Walter J.	5484	32
Corbett Celestain C.	8838	25
Courtright Sherman	8328	30
Courtright Stephen D.	6117	31
Cox Thomas M.	2965	18
Dent Sherman W.	3835	27
DeVilbiss Edson	8062	31
Dexter Daniel E.	4261	14
Dittman Benjamin G.	326	17
Donnelly Frank	1931	20
Dotts David M.	5974	20
Doxey Mary	6166	22
Dvorak Franz	1450	5
Elgin Alex	5719	29
Elgin Monroe	6053	19
Elliot Lewis J.	5567	14
Emerson James R.	1494	29
Ewy Peter	6016	4
Fillmore Benjamin R.	2500	35
Fillmore David H.	4447	34
Finnell Dovie	63	22
Francis Grant	581	17
Frymire Phoebe J.	70044	23
Getchell Albert A.	975	18
Goley Alfred M.	1015	31
Gottschalk Ernest	4139	20
Gowty Thomas J.	856	7
Graham Farris	6136	27
Gwinn Harvey S.	7050	10
Hamp Nellie	5697	24
Hanson Christopher	1096	14
Hanyka Vaclav	2486	25
Hartzell William C.	2046	8
Hasenfratz Ignatz	53855	5
Hasenfratz Joseph	6037	4
Henson Frank J.	1336	30
Hladik Frantisek	2726	20
Hodge Julia	6995	27
Hodge Robert	10775	10
Hoggatt George L.	608	34
Holly Coe	563	18
Howell John F.	6338	2
Hughes Theodore	2217	3
Hughes Thomas	7420	12
Jett William D.	2031	14
Johnson Daniel W.	2034	12
Johnson James H.	6655	34
Johnson Robert	2874	23
Jones George A.	9309	9
Kelly Hester	3220	32
Kinnan John S.	6260	12
Kinnan Philip	6259	12
Kirchner Frank	894	3
Kirchner Jermiah F.	2251	9
Koller Henry	5869	4
Lane Edwin C.	1172	27
Leekley Mary A.	6214	7
Livengood Israel S.	6212	9
Long Charles	1525	25
Manlove Lucy J.	5759	6
Manlove Ray H.	1209	6
Martin Lizzie	5591	17
Mathews Benjamin F.	4457	9
Mayfield Stephen	4123	34
McKee James R.	7011	26
McQuain Daniel V.	2511	23
McQuain Grant	5521	23
Mielke Carl F.	6542	1
Moore John H.	1808	21
Morris Orsemus	4024	8
Neil Charles W.	6721	11
Norman Moses R.	5871	7
O'Larey Timothy	4013	29
Olmstead Leonard	4431	31
Page Hattie	10309	4
Page John A.	6962	8
Palm Frank A.	2407	15
Palmer William F.	1568	10
Parker John F.	1568	10
Parker John F.	8552	24
Payne James H.	2899	35
Payne John L.	2896	34
Petterson Johanna	6632	15
Pinkerton David F.	7364	30
Poles Carter	6138	26
Possee Benjamin F.	4289	12
Powers Minerva	2736	14
Randolph Milton	6183	25
Raynor James W.	4278	24
Reynolds Henry	6379	15
Rupp Peter	6428	10
Ruth John W.	7166	10
Sandy James	4028	7
Shehi James H.	6486	18
Shelton James P.	1383	32
Shockey Elmer	5619	24
Silvey John H.	2365	35
Sneed Thomas	1567	28
Spillman Joseph	2379	1
Steadman Isaac	5499	22
Steadman Mary	8292	24
Stotts Abraham	4116	19
Straub Lawson	1519	1
Suttle George	6158	26
Swanson Victor A.	8681	15
Swart Reinhart	4392	30
Tapp Walter	4365	5
Taylor Alvertus	3887	24
Tesh Alexander	2049	27
Tesh James H.	2126	28
Tesh Nellie A.	6153	28
Thompson Darby H.	2633	22
Thompson William S.	6384	29
Volz Friederike	6334	30
Vosburg Henry	8175	15
Watson Lillie B.	1786	6
Watson William S.	1449	5
Weaver Michael W.	2394	12
Webb John	685	21
West Alanson	6829	27
Willets Henry W.	6724	11
Williams Sallie	4293	8
Wilson Robert J.	6423	19
Wise Lida A.	4485	15
Woods Sidney C.	1526	25
Woodson Jack W.	2122	23
Wretling Charles	67289	21
Yoakum Newton H.	2030	11
Zimmerman Garrett		21
Zisman Rudolph	1221	2

Warren Valley Township
21 North Range 2 West

Homesteader	Patent #	Section #
Ableidinger Ambrose	6174	22
Anson Jasper	596	32
Baker Nathan A.	224	32
Bales Nathan W.	1357	5
Ballard Earnest	1166	10
Ballard Eugene	1222	15
Ballard Frank	517	15
Barnes Henry C.	4010	7
Barrett James P.	2415	23
Beatty James	2383	7
Bechtel Mary E.	227	24
Beitman Frances M.	2798	12
Belwood Charles M.	683	26
Bryan James S.	78	12
Bryant Henry C.	8330	1
Burke Edward	3820	5
Burke Lizzie A.	3972	4
Burke Richard	4393	9
Burke William J.	7129	4
Cady Wallace T.	2701	9
Carrier Frank J.	6088	25
Clark George W.	8774	20
Cockrum James E.	2643	10
Colvert Elias A.	4020	6
Compton Margaret	7790	24
Compton Thomas	4078	26
Cooper George W.	570	27
Corbett John	6109	5
Cox Eliza A.	6014	6
Craig Asa M.	948	23
Curtis William	5615	4
Davis Albert L.	693	14
Dayton Annie E.	1984	2
Dayton Herbert J.	3170	3
Dennis Batson J.	1115	19
Dorsey Joseph	4440	21
Dowell John M.	1338	2
Dowell Regina	2587	9
Doyle Anastatia	7462	5
Driskill Elbert M.	2797	28
Dunlap John	2128	27
Ely Richard M.	1219	12
Flushe August	365	26
Ford Walter	1373	11
Friend Albion R.	5915	3
Gage Walter R.	2779	2
Gaston Anna	4061	28
Gillespie John T.	162	31
Glofelty Samuel S.	2339	9
Godsey George T.	133	4
Goodwill Ernest W.	1302	14
Graham William J.	1056	27
Grimes James	50747	24
Groetken Herman J.	2342	23
Guthrie Samuel	896	34
Guthrie William	6403	31
Haley Ellis	4009	25
Haynes Charles M.	2353	18
Highsmith John O.	5913	34
Holsinger Martin L.	1933	26
Hoover Hernando C.	83	3
Howe Nelson A.	3181	10
Huffington Clinton S.	2597	1
Hughes John M.	4243	25
Jenkins William M.	1487	35
Johnson Charles A.	7327	8
Johnston William E.	1885	18
Kindt Henry	5947	6
Kinnaman Willis L.	2061	11
Kiser Thomas A.	4077	2
Kunz Emma	4428	21
Lewis James L.	41	29
Lichti John	6662	29
Lord George W.	174	31
Macy Frank	5703	17
Madden James A.	1572	35
Maloch William A.	253	15
Markwell William	4275	17
Martin James P.	1490	21
Mason John W.	2727	1
Mason Richard C.	2728	1
Mateer John K.	1033	29
McGuire Oswell	5581	20
McGuire William	4291	17
McKee James E.	961	27
McNeal Harriet E.	891	31
Miller Delos	2356	27
Mills Alice	4071	18
Mills George W.	4239	7
Moore William	6056	9
Mosier Barney	2368	8
Mossler Louis	4477	6
Myers Calvin	1535	19
Myers Lee	1280	18
Neuerburg Frank	7235	21
Neuerburg John	6116	23
Nieswander Lee D.	2351	25
Nipher Fred D.	6747	1
Painter William	4008	10
Patterson James W.	7051	28
Patterson John D.	165	14
Powell James M.	747	35
Price Henry	24	24
Primrose William H.	1642	30
Pugh Edith	462	34
Pugh Laura B.	6332	22
Rice Christian H.	1290	17
Richart James W.	152	19
Rist John	4039	30
Rosa Loren C.	6794	2
Rupp Elizabeth	7154	30
Sams Nathan Leroy	4156	15
Sattler Charles F.	1913	4
Schuler William	5647	29
Scrivner Charles B.	9742	20

Homesteaders / 419

Homesteader	Patent #	Section #
Shields Isaac	4023	18
Smelser Athton P.	1016	9
Smith Horace A.	3018	35
Smith James W.	6425	19
Stahl Florence V.	1297	30
Swank Charles F.	1210	32
Ticer Robert L.	744	32
Tobin Charles E.	2405	2
Tobin John	1637	11
Troub Jacob F.	45	7
VanBebber Everett	210222	1
VanBebber Francis M.	4141	12
Warner George W.	1071	11
Weeder Adolf	6175	22
White George E.	4292	24
Whittaker John	4321	34
Wolfinger Peter B.	2645	14
Wolleson Adolph Jr.	6189	28
Young Joseph	4277	22
Zink William H.	7124	23

Watkins Township
21 North Range 1 West

Homesteader	Patent #	Section #
Albright Ann J.	8613	19
Anthony Robert S.	3305	27
Augustine Jennie	5668	20
Augustine Tobias	5664	15
Baker Thomas J.	6589	4
Barnard James M.	6382	1
Barnard Montie M.	4137	24
Bean William G.	2406	29
Beard Jacob	2976	10
Bonfils Thomas L.	137	28
Boyes Hiram L.	135	20
Boylan Charles A.	5736	18
Briggs Tamma H.	4210	29
Brockman Dora M.	5856	35
Brockman Frederick F.	6178	26
Brockman Henry G.	5660	26
Brown Alvira	599	12
Brown James F.	1704	7
Brown Lena	4066	2
Bryan George T.	518	10
Bryant John W.	425	21
Burke Joseph Y.	3	7
Cassidy Peter J.	1004	30
Chaney David	387	6
Chenoweth Bob C.	6068	12
Clark Edgar M.	1687	27
Clark John T.	461	15
Cook Thomas A.	7	22
Cook William B.	4396	9
Crawford Lewis A.	2407	28
Crist Daniel H.	6385	30
Crosby George W.	219	28
Cummings James J.	6985	23
Delaney Charity S.	5466	32
Delaney Joseph M.	6587	31
Donoho James O.	716	25
Doyle Joseph H.	2622	26
Duncan Thomas D.	275	14
Easton Charles W.	5658	12
Edington Rosie A.	3010	5
Endres Margaret	9100	26
Fitzpatrick Mary A.	8866	19
Folan Edward	2326	5
Folan Nellie	2370	18
Foreman Hugh H.	377	24
Fuller John E.	225	24
Gage William D.	865	14
Goley Theodore C.	5998	24
Gordon Jane E.	2360	5
Gray Florida	4148	29
Grimsley Joseph R.	439	32
Guthrey Maude	416	21
Hall Willie H.	471	6
Hamaker Nettie	1934	12
Hart George Y.	6264	34
Harvey J. Nolen	5796	4
Hellwig Charles W.	534	2
Hellwig Ernest W.	954	1
Hempling George	6130	32
Henderson William	464	6
Hendley John	786	11
Hendrick Laura	1354	34
Henry William T.	2592	31
Hinchey Florence	427	27
Hock John R.	446	20
Hummel Otto	5661	35
Humphrey William H.	4100	8
Hutchison Humphrey L.	5853	1
Huyck Charles M.	236	21
Jackson William J.	4048	1
Jones James E.	569	12
Jordan Emeline	13	27
Jordan Sallie	14	22
Keyser James P.	466	5
Laird Joseph M.	8039	10
Lavington Robert A. N.	1224	19
Ludwig Henry	6370	30
Maddox Cates A.	706	14
McDaniel Charles	1333	11
McGrath Timothy	1	22
McKee Alice J.	571	12
Meyer Dora	4456	4
Millard Jane	1349	28
Miller Oscar F.	7071	9
Moir Alexander	3569	18
Moore Martin	226	20
Moore Samuel A.	7125	23
Morgan John M.	52406	3
Morris Collar	139	20
Myers Simon P.	714	34
Nelson Jacob H.	4083	11
Nims Eugene D.	544	25
Pancoast J. L.	1032	22
Phenis Austin S.	4316	1
Ragan Jermiah	2968	29
Rathburn Edwin F.	1502	2
Ray Edward S.	10700	35
Ray Philip H.	4273	25
Reed Charles E.	722	22
Reed Theodore	1807	7
Richardson Stephen E.	441	21
Ringeisen Edward J.	198	25
Robinson Edward	2441	19
Roy Thomas A.	2862	18
Scheffer Christ	8415	3
Schurkens John G.	4018	17
Schurkens William	4372	28
Scoresby Carrie	163	8
Shirley Joseph S.	504	17
Short Milo B.	7360	17
Shrader Charles D.	1311	17
Smith James O.	2354	25
Smith Lemuel Theodore	6738	14
Smith Noah L.	291	2
Smith Ralph W.	290	2
Snyder John H.	564	4
Sorensen Catherine	5598	3
Southard Robert W.	6142	3
Spurlock Millie	460	9
Stephenson Robert	469	8
Stoltenberg Earnest G.	1127	31
Strebel Carl	4178	25
Streby John L.	4205	30
Studebaker Benjamin F.	2679	34
Sunfield Philip	445	35
Taylor James M.	287	9
Treadway James A.	4313	21
Troutman John A.	51	20
Trumbla John Sr.	2782	2
Van Cleef Rhesa G.	84	10
Vann George G.	5676	32
Verhoeff Ira	6129	31
Walker Charles P.	5808	23
Wilkinson Arthur	991	8
Williams Jordan R.	90	11
Williams Judith P.	9337	7
Wills Austin D.	02419	23
Wirt Edward L.	97	27
Wright Nathan	7331	8
Young Clarence R.	463	24

White Rock Township
23 North Range 2 West

Homesteader	Patent #	Section #
Abbott Joseph H.	1911	35
Abshear Alexander	3983	8
Adams Jap	288	20
Alsop Basil B.	7005	32
Arnett Lina	2642	31
Arnold John D.	570	11
Back Joseph W.	4357	6
Banta Abe L.	1056	5
Beasley Harry E.	1282	24
Beasley William L.	1283	25
Bliss Ursula	5633	22
Boulton Charles L.	2252	12
Bowling Elva Kate	6528	26
Brant Charles A.	969	24
Brown James M.	708	3
Burt Joseph	646	29
Chaney Walter D.	2055	9
Chestnut Matthew	3030	4
Christopher John	1278	25
Clark Forrest C.	3178	35
Collins Banajy C.	1000	7
Compton Miller L.	3377	30
Compton Thomas J.	4435	21
Conway Michael R.	3922	7
Craft Thomas N.	5972	20
Crosby Samuel D.	6946	30
Davis Samuel E.	3382	19
Dawson Lincoln E.	185	19
Deal Barbra	2488	23
Derr Jacob	3985	9
Detwiler Daniel J.	766	29
Doyle Patrick J.	3247	15
Dronberger John E.	6232	26
Dunbar Thomas L.	7013	32
Dunn Archibald	1484	30
Durkee George D.	3376	27
English George R.	5920	26
Faucett William N.	1760	22
Fry George	6998	23
Fuller Charles	5922	34
Funk Eldy	2445	23
Gladson George V.	1489	25
Gleason John F.	711	20
Goff Lydia S.	6279	21
Goff William E.	85	17
Goff William H. H.	6937	31
Graves Francis N.	6515	15
Graves Horatio S.	221	28
Graves William C.	568	10
Greenler Mattannah	1492	25
Grubbs John C.	1121	23
Harbison Martha J.	1004	22
Hare Samuel	953	29
Harlow Samuel T.	3924	7
Henry John W.	888	11
Hicks Benjamin F.	3172	35
Hines Dan	4082	5
Holroyd Edwin	5805	17
Hoover William T.	2105	22
Howe Alfred	5509	26
Howe Ransom F.	2972	12
Humphries Frank	3029	2
Hunt Benjamin F.	519	31
Irwin Hardin M.	411	23
James Charles E.	645	21
James Robert F.	3921	18
Jones Charles E.	645	21
Kammerdiener Frank	6903	14
Kearns Lillie	4167	35
Kirk Coleman B.	3984	17
Kirk Robert	3149	24
Love Howard W.	415	2
Love Mary J.	1397	1
Lowan Benjamin	6904	9
Mason John	6517	10
McCammon Franklin P.	1049	11
McCaslin Clarence H.	5866	29
McCaughtry James H.	887	4
McCoy Daniel L.	5921	27
McDaniel Clinton S.	2134	15
McDaniel William A.	6557	15
McIntyre Allen D.	3746	7
McKay Robert J.	4084	2
McQuiston David C.	1500	14
Milbourn Richard	295	32
Miller Louis	712	6
Moore George F.	6060	32
Moore William D.	1254	30
Newsom Charles H.	440	34
Nichols John B.	765	11
Noyes Paul	12	3
O'Connor William	1245	2
Pearcy Henry A.	4452	8
Phrendable Margaret	2403	28
Pierce Charles	2998	3
Pierce George	2957	3
Potter Andrew J.	5978	5
Renfro Charity J.	1226	6
Renfrow Earl S.	992	1
Robb John W.	5892	12
Rowland Sobeska E.	780	28
Shoup Cyrus L.	2541	27
Smith Charles F.	364	14
Snyder William	6250	14
Spratt William M.	976	21
Staley John F.	7577	4
Starkey Charles K.	3165	31
Swingle Henry C.	2540	9
Tapp Elizah	431	20
Tate Oscar F.	2487	24
Trehey Thomas	228	18
Trehey William	49	18
Tucker Allen W.	951	28
Uhrig Peter Paul	2539	10
Veach Jesse	4180	27
Wagoner Hannah	5486	6
Wallace James R.	1001	10
White Cynthia	914	19
White Richard M.	598	2
Whittaker Reuben M.	3898	8
Williams Thomas	5693	34
Williams Willis A.	2866	18
Williamson M. Baxter	321	12
Williamson Peter N.	6628	12
Wilson Patrick	230	17
Wilson Virgil A.	950	19
Wise John S.	999	8
Wood Alfred T.	299	5
Wright Belle	6253	1
Wright Frank	4423	1
Younger Alexander L.	1170	4
Younger Joseph T. Sr.	5744	34

Cooper's store, Billings, Oklahoma about 1905.

Old bandstand — courthouse park — Perry about 1918.

Badge worn by William Tighlman as City Marshall (Chief of Police) at Perry, Oklahoma Territory — 1893.

Tractor demonstration Perry, Oklahoma — March 27, 1920.
Plowed one acre in 45 minutes.

Cost of plowing:		
Tractor operator @ 40¢ per hr.		$0.30
1¾ gal. of kerosene @ 12¢ per gal.		0.21
.7 of gal oil @ 80¢ per gal		0.07
Total cost of plowing 1 acre		$0.58

INDEX

The page number(s) following the surname listed in this index, is the page on which the story containing this name begins.

—A—
Abbott, 56, 85, 108
Abel, 88, 322
Abledinger, 93
Acers, 119, 248, 249, 287, 341
Adamson, 225
Adcock, 142, 362
Adkins, 282, 391
Adler, 132
Ainsworth, 27
Akers, 106, 112, 120, 148, 161, 162, 250, 294
Albers, 135, 136
Alexander, 302, 353
Allen, 27, 36, 77, 120, 270, 297, 344
Altman, 135
Amend, 98
Ammerman, 27
Andersen, 340
Anderson, 56, 67, 148, 197, 244, 256, 299, 352
Andrew, 197
Andrews, 56
Angus, 303
Ankelm, 397
Anson, 79
Anthis, 121, 122, 170, 172, 311
Appleman, 90
Arkeketa, 12, 250
Arkush, 27
Armstrong, 85, 168, 169
Arnold, 233
Arterburn, 106
Asp, 73
Atchison, 71
Aten, 345, 346
Atherton, 36
Austin, 180, 322
Ayers, 339

—B—
Babb, 270, 325
Back, 134, 320
Baetz, 123, 146, 370
Bagby, 88, 89, 108, 115, 312
Bailey, 37, 87, 268, 302
Bain, 104
Baker, 36, 394
Balduff, 124
Bales, 269
Ball, 290, 383
Ballinger, 359
Bamberger, 98, 223, 347, 384
Banke, 248
Banks, 11, 27, 98
Banta, 124
Barkett, 409, 410
Barnes, 220, 327
Barrett, 77
Bartlett, 127
Bartow, 125
Bass, 222
Bauman, 398
Bay, 126, 127, 161
Bazzell, 154, 237
Beach 128
Beaghler, 248
Beal, 244
Beals, 381
Bean, 128
Beard, 112, 160
Beathers, 233
Bebee, 186

Beck, 56, 111, 129, 229, 273
Beers, 96, 130, 227
Beier, 127, 131, 132, 228, 347
Beiser, 339
Bell, 338
Bellmon, 27, 103, 133, 134, 139, 262
Benefield, 199
Benes, 135
Benesh, 388
Bengforts, 336
Benke, 135, 136
Bennett, 129, 262, 322
Bereihan, 36
Berger, 73
Berkey, 240
Bethan, 97
Bevis, 26
Beymer, 271
Bieberdorf, 130
Biederman, 223
Bietler, 311
Bigbee, 340
Biggs, 127, 205
Bilbrey, 184
Billings, 104
Bilyeu, 172, 338
Bingham, 399
Bird, 282
Bishop, 161
Bittman, 100, 153, 320
Black, 253, 404, 408
Blair, 145, 226
Blakey, 133
Blackenship, 268
Blecha, 49
Bledsoe, 396
Bloom, 133
Blouin, 359
Blue, 225
Bobbitt, 327
Bodkins, 299
Bolay, 136, 191
Boles, 88, 162
Bolinger, 179
Bolton, 377
Bolzinger, 283
Bond, 280
Bonds, 96
Bonfy, 127
Boone, 100, 203, 258
Boright, 248
Bostick, 26
Boulton, 174
Bourland, 98
Bourdette, 400
Bowden, 71
Bowen, 241
Bowers, 104, 189
Bowlen, 170
Bowles, 27, 89, 137, 138
Bowman, 36, 90
Box, 36
Boyce, 96
Boydston, 209
Boyer, 96, 100, 106
Boyston, 233
Brafford, 240
Bragg, 377
Braly, 33
Brand, 135, 332, 341
Brandenburg, 149
Brandon, 91
Branham, 172

Branson, 139, 186, 276
Brant, 195
Brasch, 94
Brase, 94
Brasier, 56
Braymer, 312
Breckenridge, 376
Breinholt, 140, 225, 309
Brengle, 140, 141, 326, 403
Bressie, 56
Brewer, 223
Bridal, 340
Brier, 142, 362
Briftol, 173
Brinker, 105
Briscoe, 26, 386
Brock, 71
Brodie, 190
Brogan, 27
Brokop, 98
Brook, 97
Brookhart, 104, 106
Brooks, 31, 361
Brorsen, 36
Browen, 108
Brown, 104, 166, 229, 271, 272, 273, 287, 296, 309, 312
Brubacher, 187, 189
Bruner, 241, 364
Bruton, 268
Bryan, 27
Bryant, 143
Buckbee, 399
Bucklin, 130
Buffington, 256
Bullen, 97, 101
Bulling, 303, 304
Bullock, 235
Buntin, 270
Buntt, 314, 317
Burba, 237
Burch, 270, 325
Burdue, 96
Burgerson, 312
Burk, 161, 162, 315
Burke, 271,

—C—
Clarke, 12
Cleghorn, 12
Clemmons, 276
Clendenin, 240, 241
Cline, 241, 351
Coate, 77, 154, 155, 221, 222, 284, 285, 383
Cochrane, 226
Cockrum, 156, 157, 205
Coffee, 297
Coffelt, 36
Coffman, 158, 367
Colcord, 27
Coldiron, 55, 77, 116, 158, 159, 160, 395
Cole, 124
Coleman, 177, 206, 384, 392
Collings, 28
Collins, 100, 160, 161, 162, 219, 294
Colton, 23
Colvin, 107, 158, 233
Combrink, 36, 271, 409, 410
Combs, 87
Conard, 228

Conarro, 220, 222
Condit, 191
Conklin, 380
Connelly, 394
Connor, 226
Conover, 27
Consort, 147
Conway, 105
Cook, 67, 94, 196, 341, 377
Cooley, 391
Coombs, 161, 162
Cooper, 91, 104, 115, 165, 186, 191
Copeland, 133, 314
Copenhaver, 239
Corall, 216
Cordell, 162
Cordes, 36, 163, 358
Cornell, 171
Cottingham, 201
Couch, 27
Courtright, 154
Covey, 71, 163, 164
Cowan, 294
Cowell, 240, 347
Cox, 104, 164, 165, 177, 232
Coyle, 93, 97, 100, 165
Crabtree, 111
Craft, 263
Craig, 166, 220, 258
Craighead, 191
Cramer, 142, 179
Crampton, 182
Crane, 34, 280, 398
Cranford, 201
Crawford, 167, 246, 307
Crazy Bear, 83
Creel, 181
Cress, 103
Criner, 387
Crocker, 209
Crockett, 73, 108, 392
Cromwell, 128, 302
Crosby, 85
Cross, 199, 206, 284, 398
Crossman, 269
Crouch, 191
Crow, 71
Crowder, 167, 235, 248
Crowe, 185
Crowl, 376
Cruickshank, 89
Crumley, 104
Cruse, 336
Cruts, 36, 109
Culp, 179
Culver, 214
Cummings, 161, 342
Cunningham, 31, 115, 305
Curd, 233
Curle, 107
Curran, 352
Currell, 36
Currier, 29
Curtis, 79, 148, 241
Cutler, 27

—D—
Dailey, 168
Daily, 288
Dale, 67, 68, 320, 388
Dalton, 15, 154
Danford, 140, 225, 226
Daniels, 99, 115, 229, 240, 293, 297, 381

Darmer, 169
Daughtery, 27
David, 371
Davidson, 189
Davis, 98, 100, 104, 106, 156, 157, 186, 190, 265, 314, 315, 345, 375, 376, 377
Davison, 262, 373
Dawson, 77, 110, 172
Day, 181, 182, 291
Deals, 175
Dean, 298, 338
Deigal, 229
Delaney, 89, 91, 93
Delaute, 106
DeLodge, 83
Dennerd, 201
Denney, 127
Dennis, 111, 276
Denslow, 170
Denton, 363
Deppen, 192
Deroin, 12, 69, 168, 250
Derr, 109, 134, 160, 170
DeSpain, 319
Dever, 107
DeVilbiss, 170, 171, 172, 312, 359
Devine, 87, 291
Devore, 36, 157
Dick, 161
Dicus, 391
Diebold, 127
Diehm, 173
Dierlem, 140
Dierolf, 197
Diggs, 27
Dillard, 399
Dilliplain, 71
Dippert, 382
Disney, 105, 186, 320
Divine, 26, 188
Dixon, 174, 209
Dodson, 184
Dolezal, 36, 169
Domeny, 111, 174, 315
Donahue, 103
Donaldson, 107, 219
Donart, 233
Donegan, 93
Donley, 36, 258
Donnelly, 73
Donovan, 178
Doolin, 15
Dormire, 296, 218
Dothy, 353
Dotts, 36, 271
Doughty, 27
Douglas, 142
Dover, 233
Dowdy, 249
Dowell, 197
Downey, 174, 193, 194, 270, 276
Doyle, 27, 36, 87, 100, 175, 248, 263
Drace, 23, 75
Drager, 283
Drake, 27
Drawberg, 161
Driesel, 276
Dronberger, 175
Drum, 104
Dubois, 106
Dufek, 127, 270, 272
Duis, 98
Dulaney, 27
Dunagan, 177
Dunaway, 104
Dunbar, 183
Duncan, 97, 232, 329
Dundas, 177, 284
Dunham, 71, 90
Dunivan, 160, 178, 345, 354
Dunkin, 97
Dunlap, 312
Dunn, 111, 115, 223, 403
Dunnum, 71

Dupy, 134, 175
Durbin, 179, 235
Durkee, 36, 147, 179, 180, 181, 182, 183, 322
Dwyer, 89

—E—
Eakin, 324
Ebert, 299
Ebey, 140
Eby, 36, 90, 96, 183, 244, 248, 271
Eccles, 232
Eckhoff, 223, 328
Eckley, 298
Edgar, 236, 284
Edgington, 233
Edmondson, 96
Edmonson, 107
Edson, 90
Edwards, 164, 201, 233, 328, 369
Egan, 387
Ehler, 256
Eikleberry, 158
Ekhoff, 283
Elder, 389
Eldridge, 71, 177, 184, 314
Elgin, 77, 185
Elk, 83
Elliot, 103, 393
Ellis, 96, 104, 223
Elmore, 173
Elwood, 310
Emick, 139, 186, 195, 233
Emmons, 359
Endicott, 340
Engler, 186
English, 28, 104
Ennis, 366
Enright, 90, 381
Enyart, 214, 396
Erwin, 312
Essary, 31
Evans, 36, 286
Eveland, 133
Evers, 154
Ewing, 127
Ewy, 65, 77, 93, 149, 187, 188, 189, 233, 331
Eyler, 166

—F—
Faber, 200, 201
Fairchild, 189, 367
Fairman, 217
Fannin, 145
Faragher, 104, 190
Farr, 148
Farrar, 27, 342
Fawcett, 106
Faw Faw, 12, 179
Feken, 240
Fells, 168
Felt, 97
Fent, 235
Fenwick, 150
Ferda, 196, 352
Ferguson, 197
Fest, 323
Field, 347
Fielding, 348
Fields, 112
Fillmore, 190
Fish, 297
Fisher, 67, 133, 189, 336
Fitchett, 34, 106
Fitts, 87
Fitzpatrick, 311
Flanigan, 254
Flock, 27
Flora, 366
Flynn, 27
Foch, 161
Folger, 106
Foltz, 191
Foote, 121
Ford, 376

Foreman, 191, 214, 364
Forney, 36
Forshee, 166
Forshu, 156
Foster, 90, 100, 192, 240, 248
Foucart, 192
Fowler, 174, 315
Fox, 154
Frailey, 96
Frazier, 400
Frank, 34, 132, 174, 186, 193, 194, 195, 233, 332, 388
Franklin, 195, 267, 384
Fredekind, 320
Freeman, 248, 270, 369
Freeze, 299
Freland, 220
French, 233
Freuh, 236
Freymann, 201
Frick, 198
Friend, 27
Fritsche, 94, 123
Frueh, 36
Fruits, 175
Fry, 100, 106, 175, 208, 223, 240, 255
Fuller, 201, 276
Fulp, 338
Fuxa, 131

—G—
Gaines, 79, 111, 312
Gaiser, 88
Galbreeath, 27, 88
Gallin, 376
Gallagher, 299
Gallant, 280
Gallrein, 102, 329, 351
Galoway, 127
Gang, 240, 241, 349
Gardner, 343, 384
Garn, 27
Garnett, 104
Garrett, 104, 105
Garten, 402
Garvey, 99
Garvie, 89, 199, 263
Garvin, 89
Gatewood, 327
Gemmell, 173
Gengler, 200, 201, 256
George, 221, 345, 353
Gerke, 256
Gerken, 94
Geronimo, 28
Gibble, 276
Gibson, 389
Gideon, 275
Gieschen, 94, 98
Giger, 154
Gilbert, 27, 201, 202, 278, 338, 367
Gilchrist, 133, 198
Gillen, 273
Gillespie, 11
Gipe, 203
Glenn, 177
Glentzer, 248
Gloeckler, 184
Gockley, 218
Godbey, 253, 254
Godown, 230
Goe, 203
Goering, 326
Goff, 85
Goley, 204
Golliver, 146, 157, 205, 244
Goodwell, 127
Goodwin, 149
Gorath, 94
Gordon, 291
Gottlieb, 90, 100
Gottschalk 343, 371
Gould, 183
Gowty, 243, 244

Graham, 97, 102, 326, 328, 329, 394
Grammer, 232
Grange, 205
Grant, 36, 104, 206, 218
Graves, 104
Gray, 106, 160, 290
Green, 12, 88, 209, 312
Greenleaf, 367
Greer, 71
Gregory, 233
Grey, 55
Griffeth, 106, 107, 343
Grimes, 27, 36
Groom, 187
Grother, 156
Grubbs, 194
Gum, 1156
Guthrey, 27, 88
Guthrie, 33, 266

—H—
Haak, 239
Haber, 136
Hackinson, 36
Haga, 396
Haile, 96
Hale, 295
Haley, 71
Hall, 56, 90, 107, 115, 116, 207, 208, 286, 323
Halsey, 209
Halsig, 360
Hamann, 131, 328
Hamblin, 79, 111
Hamilton, 367, 374
Hamm, 36
Hamous, 90
Hampton, 34
Hangartner, 186
Hanna, 272
Hannah, 67, 143
Hannon, 234
Hansbrough, 273
Hansen, 115, 188
Harding, 100, 233, 276, 285
Hardy, 206
Harlan, 378, 379
Harleman, 61
Harlow, 40, 209, 210, 211, 212
Harmer, 233
Harnden, 166
Harper, 273
Harrington, 203
Harris, 27, 108, 244, 387, 403
Harrison, 104, 219
Hart, 223
Hartman, 36, 312
Harting, 245
Hartung, 209, 210, 211, 212
Harvell, 179
Harvey, 277
Hasenfratz, 189, 393
Haskell, 270
Hasting, 168, 283
Hatchitt, 12
Hauer, 94
Hay, 213
Hayes, 276, 338
Hayne, 34, 214
Haynes, 73
Hays, 133
Hayton, 103, 214, 215, 396
Hayward, 216
Heath, 287
Heatherington, 115
Hediger, 98
Heese, 406
Hejduk, 149
Hejtmanek, 34
Helcher, 406
Heldt, 94
Hellstern, 387
Helm, 383
Helton, 276
Hembree, 143

Kempfling, 137, 263
Kenderson, 297, 364, 404, 407, 408
Kendren, 90, 91
Kendrick, 217
Kenke, 304, 305
Kenry, 104, 137, 320
Kensley, 221, 222, 345
Kenson, 190
Kentges, 205
Kerber, 207
Kerbert, 206, 218
Kermann, 94
Kerndon, 300
Kerrick, 219, 287
Kess, 93, 111, 145, 248
Ketherington, 171, 283, 367
Hickl, 105
Hicks, 34, 166, 220
Higgins, 209
Highfill, 34, 105, 154, 220, 221, 222, 345, 383
Hildebrand, 127, 197, 276
Hileman, 392
Hill, 27, 267, 354
Hillman, 265
Hinde, 272
Hines, 105, 223, 371
Hirschman, 223, 299
Hise, 36, 136
Hitsman, 281
Hixon, 308
Hobbs, 307
Hockenberry, 236
Hodge, 26, 91, 223
Hodges, 224
Hoff, 128
Hoffman, 285
Hofman, 213
Hogan, 310
Hoggatt, 27, 233, 328, 383
Hoisington, 209
Holley, 409, 410
Hollingworth, 96, 297
Holloway, 199
Holmes, 104, 140, 225, 226, 309, 404
Holt, 152, 179, 180, 181, 209
Homan, 270
Homer, 247
Honegger, 409, 410
Honeyman, 191
Hook, 149, 152, 226
Hooper, 371
Hopkins, 278, 369
Hoppe, 240
Hopper, 90, 191, 214
Horn, 36, 171, 172
Horse Chief Eagle, 83
Horton, 33, 34, 149
Hoskins, 71
Hosteller, 36
Hostutler, 211
Hotson, 253
Houska, 371
Houston, 231
Hovey, 2278
Howard, 100, 131, 144, 228, 230
Howe, 268, 278
Howendobler, 130
Hoyt, 27
Hubbartt, 49
Hubbell, 222
Huchthausen, 94
Huddleston, 104, 381
Hudson, 101, 250
Huene, 56, 229
Huffington, 229, 241, 385, 395
Huffman, 90
Huggins, 154, 286
Hughes, 67, 160, 240, 241, 242, 341, 342
Hulbert, 256
Huyll, 106, 108, 209
Humphrey, 88, 228, 230, 231
Humphries, 191
Hunt, 92, 358

Hunter, 73, 96, 232
Hurley, 240
Hurt, 107, 144, 149
Husband, 186
Husselton, 128
Huston, 36, 37
Hutchison, 183
Hylak, 351
Hynek, 148

—I—

Imel, 292
Ingmire, 223
Ingram, 394
Inscho, 128
Irion, 226
Iske, 242
Ittner, 174
Ivers, 232, 269

—J—

Jack, 407
Jackson, 128
Jacobs, 27
Jacques, 192
Jak, 288
James, 34, 115, 158, 186, 187, 193, 233, 295, 338, 339, 343
Jaquis, 343
Jarrett, 79
Jayne, 361
Jeans, 304
Jeffrey, 385
Jehlicka, 270
Jelinek, 233, 299
Jelsma, 304
Jenkins, 98, 289
Jensen, 223, 288
Jerome, 234, 244
Jhrusa, 338,
Jirous, 127
Johannes, 132
Johnson, 23, 77, 98, 100, 153, 166, 179, 183, 191, 197, 233, 235, 236, 248, 267, 281, 335, 342
Johnston, 27, 37, 38, 89, 98, 100, 102, 103, 104, 174, 237, 300, 312 395
Jones, 12, 21, 26, 49, 87, 126, 128, 131, 145, 156, 201, 227 238, 239, 240, 273, 280, 311, 312, 314, 315, 317, 368, 392
Joshlin, 307
Junkin, 312
Just, 94, 132, 239, 333, 347

—K—

Kahn, 161
Kappas, 128
Karcher, 131, 132
Karly, 398
Kearns, 175, 191, 359
Keaton, 89, 240
Keddington, 127
Keehn, 239
Keele, 240, 241
Kehres, 289
Keith, 127, 342
Kelley, 135
Kelly, 106, 161, 318, 399
Kemnitz, 98, 236, 242, 282
Kennedy, 36, 100, 157, 167, 183, 243, 244
Kennemer, 245
Kent, 158, 244, 338, 367
Kepley, 284
Kerns, 220, 282, 328
Kerr, 103, 199, 245, 246, 387
Kessler, 411
Kettenring, 104
Keturakat, 94
Keyser, 119, 248, 249, 287
Kidder, 247
Kihega, 103, 250
Kinamer, 341
Kindt, 220

King, 23, 27, 138, 207, 268, 332, 383
Kingery, 36
Kinnerman, 104
Kinney, 225, 226, 289
Kirby, 27
Kirchner, 33, 255
Kirk, 56
Kirkendall, 250, 294
Kirkhart, 79, 236
Kirtley, 67, 251, 252, 254, 351
Kiser, 185
Kisner, 303
Kistler, 206
Klaus, 94
Klein, 268
Klingbeil, 131
Klingenburg, 398
Knight, 131, 153
Knopfel, 188
Knorr, 369
Koch, 251, 253, 254, 255
Kodesh, 352
Koehler, 343
Koelzer, 200, 256
Kolb, 197
Koller, 65, 135
Kopp, 148, 235, 352
Kraemer, 167, 276
Krauleidis, 98
Krebbs, 267
Kreig, 179
Kreigh, 106
Kretch, 90
Kriegar, 131
Krisher, 323
Krug, 187
Kryder, 248
Kukuk, 127, 181, 256, 281, 292
Kuntz, 94, 248

—L—

Lacy, 37
LaDue, 168
Lady, 241
LaGrone, 96
Laird, 33, 36, 137, 257, 258, 259, 278, 283, 348
Lamb, 100
Lamberts, 276
Lampe, 127, 214
Landress, 205
Lane, 107, 259
Lange, 94
Lanham, 322
Lankford, 252
Lanzer, 371
Latta, 97
Lau, 90, 94
Lauderdale, 107, 115, 178, 369
Laughlin, 174, 260, 323, 395
Lausen, 336, 337
Lawhon, 170
Lawson, 262
Learned, 260, 404, 411
Leatherock, 391
LeBus, 261
Ledin, 98
Lee, 195, 267
Lehmkuhl, 200
Leland, 154, 155, 285
Lemler, 294, 319
Lemmon, 104, 143, 159, 160
Lenski, 163
Leonard, 256
LePlant, 309
Lesh, 65, 262
Lewellen, 266, 290, 373
Lewis, 107, 126, 133, 190
Ley, 36
Liberty, 406
Liddle, 141
Liebrand, 191, 272
Liggett, 115
Lindeman, 36, 93, 263, 281
Linn, 87, 263, 303, 304

Lippincott, 61, 346
Lisle, 343
Little, 21, 36, 98, 207, 318, 349, 390
Little Bear, 232
Littleton, 237
Livingston, 27
Lobsitz, 36
Lockett, 211
Lodge, 237
Loewen, 139
Logan, 106, 265
Logue, 156
Lohman, 308
Long, 89, 104, 105, 171, 245, 266, 274, 338
Longan, 371
Loula, 267, 311
Love, 195, 267, 317, 318
Lovekamp, 223
Lovelady, 71
Loveless, 131
Lovell, 142
Lowe, 104
Loyd, 179
Ludlow, 362
Ludwig, 129
Luter, 263
Lutz, 398
Lydick, 186
Lynch, 27, 36, 395
Lynn, 332
Lyon, 352
Lytle, 402

—M—

Mack, 127, 188
Mackey, 280
Madsen, 75
Maehr, 94
Magness, 96
Mahan, 251, 252
Mahlo, 245, 246
Main, 268, 298
Maine, 187
Mair, 161
Maletare, 291
Malget, 361
Maloch, 100
Malone, 23, 87, 291
Maltz, 94
Malzahn, 37, 94, 114, 163, 383
Mangus, 358
Manning, 128
Marak, 232
Marchbanks, 258
Marcy, 90, 376
Marion, 392
Marks, 111
Marland, 31, 109
Marlow, 233
Marshall, 232, 263, 269, 327
Martens, 318
Martin, 36, 79, 209, 270
Masat, 34
Masheter, 174, 270
Mason, 270, 271, 272, 273, 337
Masters, 272, 392
Mateer, 79, 111
Matthiesen, 36, 273
Mauney, 179
Maupin, 400
Maxwell, 36, 281, 362
Mayberry, 377
Mayfield, 98, 395
McAlister, 109
McArthur, 343
McCade, 65
McCafferty, 33, 34
McCandless, 116
McCart, 223
McClellan, 90, 112, 115
McClintic, 26
McClintie, 87
McClung, 177
McClure, 199, 233, 274, 369

McCluskey, 105, 266, 273, 274
McCollough, 85
McCormick, 85, 93, 146, 263, 275
McCosh, 165
McCoy, 26, 87, 108, 175
McCray, 247
McCright, 391
McCroskey, 276
McCubbins, 276
McCullough, 104
McCune, 248
McCurry, 106, 276, 328
McDaniel, 94, 116, 214, 389
McDaniels, 248
McDowell, 377
McEachern, 245
McFall, 208
McFarland, 277, 307, 407
McFerron, 133
McGehee, 106
McGlintie, 115
McGraw, 254
McGuire, 339
McIntire, 26
McKee, 79, 156
McKeever, 235
McKinley, 382
McKinney, 71, 125, 257, 258, 259, 278
McKinnis, 27
McKinstry, 158
McMahoon, 65
McMeekin, 201, 202, 278
McMichael, 27
McMillen, 223, 275, 276
McNeal, 36, 79
McNeil, 336
McPheeters, 143
McQuiston, 258
McSwain, 115
McWilliams, 143
Meade, 314
Megenity, 191, 214
Mehr, 201
Meier, 149
Melaugh, 289
Mendenhall, 404
Menihan, 105
Menke, 336
Mentz, 27
Mercer, 395
Mercing, 223
Merkel, 94
Merrill, 88
Merriman, 67, 85, 279, 280, 349
Metcalf, 283
Metcher, 339
Metz, 320
Meyer, 94, 291
Meyers, 26, 79
Michael, 203
Micken, 156
Mielke, 65, 167, 281
Migler, 193, 194
Mildfelt, 36, 289
Miles, 392
Miller, 27, 28, 31, 38, 55, 104, 109, 184, 196, 263, 281, 291, 342, 349, 371
Millett, 371
Milligan, 34, 282, 411
Mills, 282, 297, 299
Milner, 185
Minor, 71
Miries, 130
Mitchell, 150, 168, 184, 220, 283
Mock, 136
Mockley, 93
Moelling, 79, 283, 299, 339
Monhollon, 108
Montgomery, 90, 150, 160, 322
Monticello, 150
Moody, 328
Moore, 34, 49, 77, 81, 91, 96, 100, 111, 115, 149, 155, 162, 177, 206, 222, 284, 285, 286, 289, 328, 381

Mora, 23
Moran, 156, 274
Morgan, 23, 27, 97, 208, 219, 248, 287, 291
Morlock, 331
Morrell, 343
Morris, 23
Morrison, 106, 108, 287
Morrow, 96, 153, 356
Mosena, 288, 299
Moser, 382
Mossman, 299
Mouser, 36, 289
Moydell, 391
Mugler, 96
Muir, 140
Mulhall, 28
Muller, 131
Murray, 280, 307
Murry, 240
Musick, 98, 131
Myers, 21, 97
Mylar, 343

—N—
Nagel, 100, 311
Nash, 314
Neal, 103, 139, 262, 290, 372
Nebergall, 289
Nedbalck, 161
Nelson, 33, 36, 96, 156
Nemec, 191, 267, 311
Neuerburg, 291, 292, 310, 336, 337
Neumeyer, 270
Newell, 106, 108
Newman, 67, 198
Newsom, 353
Newton, 49, 98, 151, 271, 293, 294
Nicewander, 36, 312
Nichols, 71, 106, 161, 193, 233, 250, 293
Nicholson, 36
Nicol, 280
Nichols, 71, 106, 193, 233, 250, 294, 295
Nicholson, 36
Nida, 254
Nielsen, 65
Nitz, 338
Nix, 119
Noonan, 104
Norman, 211, 345
North, 393
Norton, 149
Notley, 34, 107
Novotny, 307
Nummy, 130

—O—
Oakley, 67, 296, 320
Odenwald, 105
O'Donnell, 105, 233
Oestereich, 94
Oetting, 94
Ogden, 254
O'Grady, 201, 223
Oliver, 184
Oltmanns, 131
O'Neil, 175
Ools, 353
Orchard, 299
O'Roke, 253, 254, 255
Orr, 71, 272
Osborn, 65, 133, 181
Osborne, 239
Osten, 302
Otto, 282
Overbey, 297
Overholt, 138, 398
Owen, 34, 100, 108, 115, 193, 216, 261, 298, 379, 381, 398
Owens, 225, 268, 298

—P—
Palm, 366
Palovik, 291
Pancoast, 286

Pankratz, 93
Pansegrau, 131
Paris, 191
Parke, 27
Parker, 90, 103
Parks, 61, 401
Parnell, 260, 411
Par-thap-inga, 12
Partsch, 105
Passow, 223, 282, 283, 299, 384
Patterson, 177, 270, 272, 355
Patton, 377
Pauley, 199, 299
Paulsen, 233, 288, 299
Payne, 259, 334
Peabody, 172
Pearson, 98, 215
Peebler, 67
Pell, 226
Pender, 300
Pendley, 174
Pennco, 248
Pennington, 279, 280, 301
Penny, 260
Perdue, 392
Perry, 21
Perryman, 108, 115
Peter, 223
Peterman, 142, 302, 328
Peters, 245
Petersen, 282
Peterson, 190
Pett, 98
Pfeiffer, 263, 303, 304
Pfrimmer, 129, 305, 341, 349
Pharr, 268
Phillip, 377
Phillips, 128, 247, 301, 359, 370
Picket, 83
Piel, 94, 256
Pierce, 128, 306, 307, 308
Pietrusky, 94
Pike, 142,
Pinkerton, 383
Pitts, 143
Platz, 325
Plumer, 100, 111
Plumley, 55
Pogue, 283
Pohlman, 73
Poland, 309
Pollman, 94
Ponder, 387
Pooler, 346
Pore, 334
Porter, 152, 161, 294, 382
Posey, 299
Postelwait, 230, 341
Powell, 369
Powers, 100, 172, 359
Prather, 106, 140, 309
Pressler, 89
Price, 156, 205, 343
Pricer, 132, 292, 299, 310, 339
Primeaux, 83
Primmer 339
Primrose, 79
Pritchett, 311
Prokop, 49
Prouty, 88
Province, 312
Pruca, 49
Pryor, 156
Pug, 209
Pursifull, 181, 409, 410
Purvis, 36
Pusch, 201
Puttenat, 299
Pyeatt, 311
Pyland, 186

—Q—
Qualls, 34
Queen, 179
Quhn, 311
Quick, 283
Quinton, 93

—R—
Radgowski, 137, 313, 329
Raff, 364
Rankin, 107
Ransom, 229
Rasmussen, 152
Ratliff, 71, 174, 263, 267, 314, 315, 316, 317, 318, 365
Raum, 27
Ray, 124, 229
Raymond, 97
Ream, 100, 319
Reckert, 100
Rector, 107
Redding, 36
Red Leaf, 83
Redman, 214
Reed, 87, 98, 103, 115, 139, 170, 184, 276, 298
Regnier, 133
Reid, 106, 145
Reilly, 320
Reininga, 94
Render, 36
Renfro, 204
Renfrow, 104, 321, 322
Renshaw, 199
Reschke, 152
Reub, 291
Reynolds, 129, 193
Rhea, 180, 322
Rheam, 170
Rhoades, 149
Rice, 61, 79, 156, 362
Richards, 187
Richardson, 21, 27, 34, 269, 327, 341
Richmond, 161
Rickert, 90
Rieker, 166, 193, 290
Riley, 137
Rilling, 332
Rinehart, 129
Riney, 306, 308
Ringler, 36, 208, 248, 323
Rinn, 335
Ripley, 324, 325
Ripperberger, 136
Ritthaler, 34, 94, 98, 102, 187, 262, 302, 326, 327, 328, 329, 330, 331, 350, 390
Roach, 270
Roads, 106
Robbins, 104, 219
Robedeaux, 332
Roberson, 317
Roberts, 186, 226
Robertson, 314
Robinson, 97, 106, 144, 245, 332
Robison, 343, 346
Rockford, 141
Rockwell, 297
Rodda, 188
Rode, 94
Rodolph, 100
Rosesler, 191
Rogers, 23, 71, 73, 152, 241
Rolling, 61
Romero, 179
Rosa, 240
Rose, 312, 359
Roseborough, 374
Ross, 196, 209
Rough Face, 83
Roush, 189
Royse, 235
Rupp, 36, 127, 132, 179, 187, 203, 239, 332, 333, 384
Rust, 219
Rutschinski, 131
Ruzicka, 262
Ryman, 369
Rymer, 115

— S —

Sachs, 171
Sahland, 232
Sale, 163
Sales, 233
Sanders, 71, 93, 108, 129, 334, 335
Sanderson, 312
Santsenberg, 359
Sapp, 88, 96
Sappington, 154, 210
Sargent, 276
Sater, 115
Saunders, 150
Savage, 105
Saylers, 104
Sayre, 198
Schafer, 61
Schaffer, 147, 320, 336
Schallenberg, 384
Schanzenbach, 324
Schevold, 262
Schieffer, 291, 336, 337, 352
Schiever, 132, 299
Schiewe, 338
Schiltz, 315
Schimek, 302
Schlehuber, 244, 338, 339, 343
Schmaltz, 34
Schmidbauer, 352
Schmidt, 326, 330, 350
Schnaitman, 67
Schnieder, 161, 200, 256
Schnore, 71
Schomaker, 310, 339
Schoonover, 206
Schott, 270
Schroeder, 269
Schultz, 36, 240, 380
Schulz, 94
Schulze, 328
Schwartz, 340
Schweitzer, 326, 327, 330
Scoles, 230, 231
Scott, 132, 320, 341, 349, 398
Scruggs, 23
Sears, 341
Seba, 338
Secrest, 291
Sedivy, 352
Seeger, 389
Seehaver, 339
Seeliger, 103
Seelingar, 194
Seids, 342
Sekora, 352
Sell, 67
Seltzer, 294, 295
Senter, 209
Serby, 181, 182
Settle, 127
Sevey, 55
Sexton, 283
Shaddy, 367
Shanafelt, 92, 175
Sharp, 253, 280, 288
Shaw, 90, 175, 264, 313, 343
Shay, 240
Sheets, 100
Shehi, 343
Sheilds, 369
Sheldon, 226
Shellady, 207
Shelton, 77, 149, 169, 256
Shepherd, 182
Sherrard, 344, 345, 346
Shiever, 94, 233, 239, 265, 347
Shiflet, 240, 241
Shingleton, 174
Shinn, 257, 277, 348
Shirly, 240
Shirman, 188
Shoop, 240, 320, 341, 349
Short, 233,
Shorter, 223
Shoupe, 248
Shrader, 27, 137, 138
Shroeder, 382
Shultz, 214, 404
Shute, 343
Sigler, 245
Silver, 71, 230
Simmons, 106, 351
Sims, 34, 96
Sinn, 331
Sisk, 214
Sisson, 393
Skalenda, 291
Slama, 331
Sloan, 34
Slough, 386
Smalley, 348
Smelser, 280, 327
Smeltzer, 205
Smith, 36, 40, 67, 91, 96, 98, 142, 146, 157, 189, 225, 226, 248, 256, 274, 282, 299, 302, 350, 362, 372, 373, 401, 402
Snodgrass, 351
Snyder, 179
Sokol, 251, 254, 351
Sommars, 136, 320, 336
Sommerhauser, 240
Soulek, 65, 336, 352, 361
Sowers, 100
Space, 353
Spahr, 193, 194
Sparks, 307, 320, 366, 410
Sparrow, 165, 248, 352
Speake, 267
Speakman, 267
Speer, 276, 354
Speir, 160
Spencer, 179, 189, 409, 410
Spillman, 355
Spradberry, 96
Springs, 77
St. Clair, 356
Statts, 36
Stackhouse, 71, 357
Stacy, 348
Stafford, 96
Stahl, 97, 135
Staley, 245, 276
Stanley, 97, 352, 358
Stanton, 399
Starkey, 152
Starr, 274
Start, 294
Steadman, 77
Steen, 292
Steichen, 34, 169
Steinson, 98
Stem, 282
Stengle, 388
Stephens, 293, 294
Stevens, 96, 174, 201, 292
Stewart, 26, 96, 106, 307
Stieferman, 132
Stikey, 302
Stines, 67
Stockdale, 109
Stockton, 173, 316, 358
Stoltenberg, 94
Stone, 250, 384
Stoneburner, 162
Stotler, 150
Stotts, 170, 171, 172, 359
Stout, 127, 267, 280
Stovall, 240, 349
Strahan, 190
Streller, 360, 391
Strickland, 361
Strothman, 127
Stufflebean, 153
Stumbaugh, 88
Stumpff, 20, 142, 362
Sturgeon, 93
Stute, 283
Sullins, 36, 71, 164, 191, 214, 314, 363, 364, 365
Sutherland, 286
Sveland, 103, 270
Svenson, 235
Swain, 389
Swan, 305
Swank, 281
Swanson, 320, 366
Swart, 77, 169, 179
Swearingen, 233, 367
Sweazea, 399
Sweger, 169
Swelander, 126, 127
Swendig, 73
Swiger, 301
Swineford, 23, 115
Swingle, 104, 271
Swisher, 400

— T —

Tabor, 198
Taggart, 124, 335
Talbot, 146, 244
Talley, 85, 342
Talliaferro, 98, 368
Tannehill, 351
Tate, 89, 90, 152, 233, 276, 369
Tautfest, 332
Taylor, 27, 37, 89, 103, 109, 188, 353, 398
Tearney, 352
Teel, 106
Tefteller, 384
Terry, 89
Testerman, 115, 186, 276, 369
Thiele, 131, 281, 329, 370, 371
Thomas, 27, 97, 130, 267, 389
Thomason, 290, 372, 373
Thompson, 56, 104, 108, 127, 129, 130, 131, 201, 297, 311, 373, 374, 375, 376, 377, 378, 379
Thornbrue, 353
Thornhill, 27
Thornton, 402
Thorpe, 143
Thralls, 67
Thrash, 34
Thurman, 77, 237
Tibbs, 261
Tidwell, 111
Tighlman, 15, 27
Tillery, 27
Timmons, 291
Tinnen, 149
Tipton, 363, 364
Titsworth, 321, 322
Tobin, 291, 292
Todd, 97
Tolsdorf, 132
Tontz, 156, 157
Towery, 208
Tracy, 354
Travis, 380
Traywick, 400
Treadway, 294
Treiner, 254
Trenton, 393
Trexler, 126
Trimble, 67
Triplett, 341
Trout, 120
Trowbridge, 283
Trumbla, 90
Trumbo, 234
Tsa Toke, 368
Tucker, 36, 276, 381
Tuetken, 132
Tull, 140
Tummell, 399
Turner, 162, 285, 345, 382, 383
Turvey, 200
Tyler, 353
Tyre, 31, 276

— U —

Umwake, 34
Undernear, 34
Underwoods, 67
Unzicker, 165

— V —

Valentine, 307
VanArsdell, 34, 383
VanBebber, 26, 332, 384, 385, 386
VanBuskirk, 245, 387
Vandelm, 394
Vandeventer, 67, 154
Vanhoy, 26
Van Trump, 278
Van Tuyl, 195
Varner, 306, 307
Vasek, 193, 299, 388
Vavara, 251, 351
Veach, 36, 36
Veirs, 96
Vermillion, 395
Viering, 124
Viet, 148
Viets, 94, 197
Vile, 361
Vinson, 127
Vivian, 97, 165
Voight, 36, 94, 281
Voise, 132, 189, 223
Volz, 15
VonTorne, 245
Vonderheiden, 27
Voogden, 93, 263
Voris, 100
Voss, 91, 94

— W —

Wade, 130
Wagner, 161, 201
Waldrop, 268
Walker, 115
Walkling, 90, 327, 388
Wall, 389
Wallerstedt, 27, 34
Walsh, 105
Walston, 280
Waltermire, 179, 395
Walters, 132
Ware, 198
Warner, 161, 223, 256, 390
Warren, 209
Wasabaugh, 71, 384
Washington, 98
Watchorn, 31
Waters, 83
Watkins, 88, 150, 392
Watson, 36, 90, 103, 106, 302, 391
Watters, 96
Watts, 40
Wayne, 26
Weathers, 241
Weaver, 104, 404
Webb, 115, 186, 197, 235, 299, 392
Webl, 338
Webster, 166
Wechel, 208
Wegner, 347
Wehmeier, 94
Weid, 331
Weidemen, 27
Weiss, 380
Welch, 88
Welk, 335
Welker, 226
Wells, 152, 157, 171, 226, 241, 280, 393, 395
Wenner, 97
West, 36, 149, 394
Wester, 150
Westervelt, 11, 23, 394
Wetzel, 36, 158, 362, 395
Whaley, 106
Wharton, 88
Wheatley, 328
Wheeler, 291
Wheelock, 200
Whelan, 166
Whistler, 357
Whitaker, 177
Whitchurch, 384
White, 85, 104, 180, 218, 240, 355

White Eagle, 83
White Horse, 12
White Mule, 12
Whitewater, 12
Whitford, 343
Whitlow, 206, 214, 396
Whitney, 34, 229
Whitten, 205
Whittenberg, 108
Whorton, 27
Widiger, 347, 370, 397
Wiebe, 299
Wiehe, 90
Wilde, 94, 131
Wilford, 276
Wilkerson, 107, 271
Wilkes, 96
Wilkey, 264
Wilkins, 147, 190

Will, 298, 398
Willett, 116
Wiley, 209
Williams, 104, 107, 124, 239
Willis, 392
Wills, 34
Wilson, 36, 71, 104, 147, 272, 306, 399
Wines, 357
Winger, 171
Wink, 256
Winkler, 400, 401
Winters, 91, 100, 199, 253
Wire, 161
Witters, 125
Wolcott, 96
Wolf, 210
Wolfe, 183, 395
Wolff, 233

Wollard, 401, 402
Wolleson, 90
Wonda, 267
Wood, 26, 261, 269, 270, 294, 311, 384, 402
Woodruff, 204, 403
Woodside, 106
Woolsey, 115
Wooten, 164
Worley, 314, 317
Worrell, 394
Wright, 124, 147, 208
Wurtz, 384
Wyatt, 75, 106
Wylie, 396

—Y—

Yahn, 103
Yeary, 191

Yoce, 96, 248
Yost, 175
Young, 36, 67, 97, 104, 404, 405, 406, 407, 410, 411, 412
Younger, 104
Youree, 110
Yowell, 340

—Z—

Zavodny, 177, 352
Zelllers-Landsberger, 381
Zemp, 328
Zers, 200
Zickefoose, 283
Ziesch, 98
Zimmerman, 77, 260, 409, 410, 411, 412
Zmotony, 366
Zondler, 345
Zorba, 90

Threshing wheat near Perry 1920s.

Polo Christian Sunday School - 1895.

Perry water and light plant 1930's. (L to R): James Gardner, Herbert (Bert) Gardner and S. A. Timmons.

Erecting a windmill near Billings, Oklahoma about 1915.

Three Sands oil field late 1920s. The derrick in foreground is the drilling rig operated by Boone Drilling Company.

Drilling floor on rotary rig. (L to R): Arthur Berry, Albert Ashbrier, Harvey Diehm, "Chief" in rear unidentified, Charles Kemnitz, Lynn Stewart.

Back of Coyle Cotton gin, 1903.

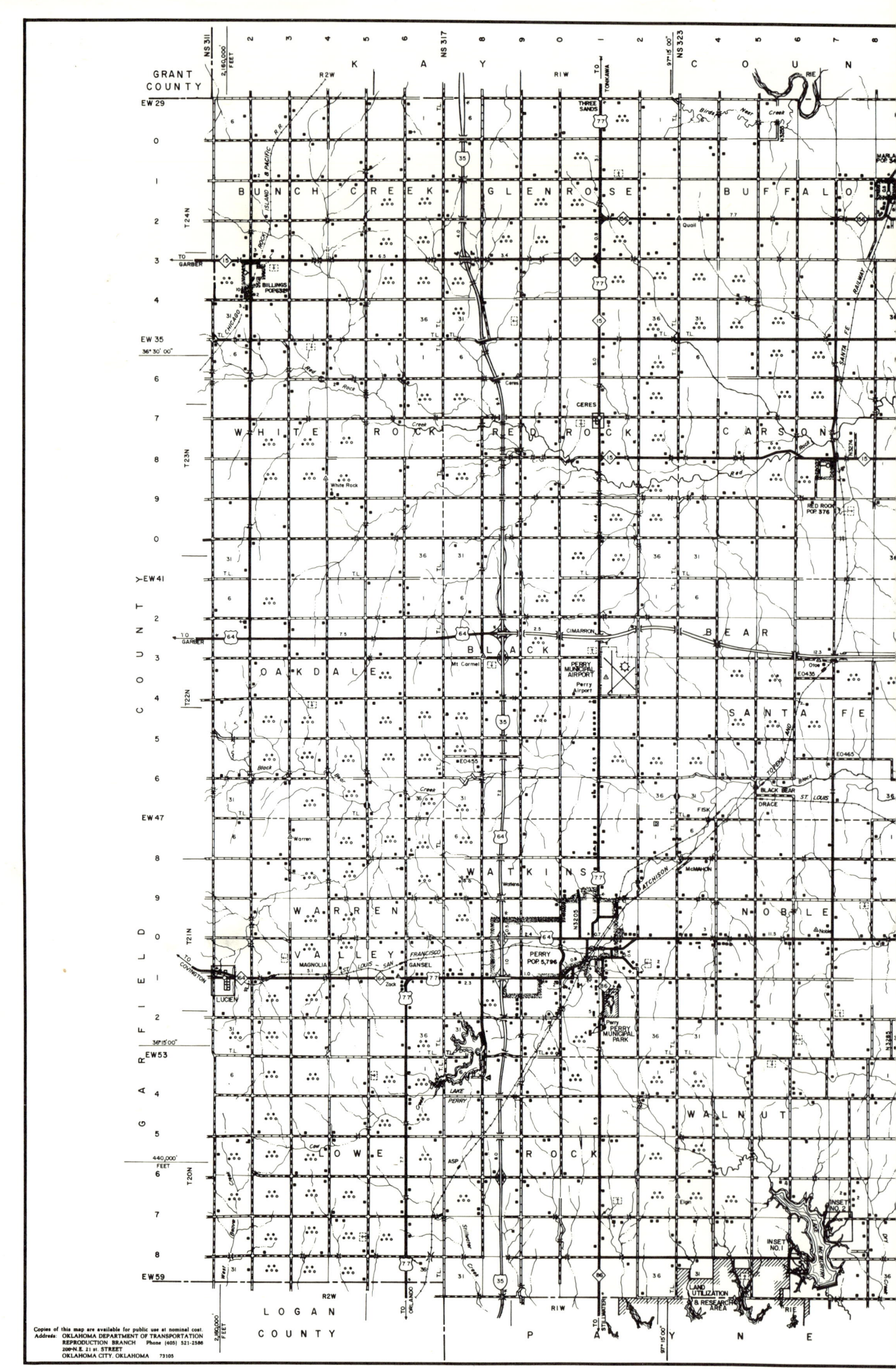